Strategic Management
Text and Cases

Peter Wright
Memphis State University

Charles D. Pringle
James Madison University

Mark J. Kroll
University of Texas at Tyler

ALLYN AND BACON
Boston • London • Toronto • Sydney • Tokyo • Singapore

Editor-in-Chief: Bill Barke
Senior Executive Editor: Rich Wohl
Series Editor: Susan Nelle Barcomb
Developmental Editor: Janis Jackson Hill
Series Editorial Assistant: Sarah Carter
Assistant Developmental Editor: Carol Alper
Cover Administrator: Linda Dickinson
Composition and Manufacturing Buyer: Louise Richardson
Editorial-Production Service: Woodstock Publishers' Services
Copy Editor: Carol Beal
Text Designer: Nancy McJennett

Library of Congress Cataloging-in-Publication Data

Wright, Peter.
  Strategic management: text and cases / Peter Wright. Charles D. Pringle, Mark J. Kroll.
    p.   cm.
  Includes bibliographical references and index.
  ISBN 0-205-13421-1
    1. Strategic planning.   I. Pringle, Charles D.   II. Kroll, Mark J.   III. Title
HD30.28.W75   1992
658.4'012-dc20   91-33034
                                                                                CIP

Printed in the United States of America

10 9 8 7 6 5 4 3 2 1   96 95 94 93 92 91

Contents

iii

CHAPTER
3

Organizational Direction: Mission and Goals   45

CHAPTER
4

Corporate-Level Strategies   69

CHAPTER
5

Business Unit Strategies   95

CHAPTER
6

Functional Strategies   121

CHAPTER
11

Strategic Management in Not-for-Profit Organizations   245

PART
II

Cases in Strategic Management

Strategic Management Case Analysis   265

SECTION
A

Formulation and Implementation: Single-Product or Single-Service Businesses

SECTION
B

Formulation and Implementation: Multiproduct Firms

SECTION
C

Formulation and Implementation: International Firms

Preface

Our purpose in writing a new strategic management text was twofold: to provide students with the most current, comprehensive, state-of-the-art analysis of the field of strategic management, and to promote student understanding of the material with highly applied, innovative learning features.

To accomplish our first goal, we have incorporated the most up-to-date coverage of the strategic management literature into this text in a clear, easy-to-read style. This coverage includes the most relevant and exciting multidisciplinary contributions to the field. Strategic management is a relatively young discipline, which has borrowed from, built upon, and contributed to such business fields as economics, management, marketing, finance, operations management, and accounting, among others. In recent years, however, exciting developments from such diverse fields as psychology, sociology, and anthropology have also broadened and enriched the knowledge base of strategic management. Students will gain new insights from these cutting-edge, integrative developments.

The strategic management and business policy course is designed to help students integrate and apply what they have learned in their separate functional business courses, as well as to gain experience in using the tools of strategic analysis. To help facilitate this process and promote student learning—the second major goal of our text—we have built-in a number of innovative learning tools. You will find this book rich with applied material—realistic business examples carefully woven throughout the text, provocative discussions of strategic management conducted by well-known companies, and experiential exercises to help students think strategically. And, since the core of the strategic management and business policy course is case analysis, our text provides an excellent, diverse collection of up-to-date cases containing meaningful decision situations.

Our book is comprised of two major parts. Part I, "The Concepts and Techniques of Strategic Management," consists of 11 chapters, carefully integrated from a conceptual perspective and by a consistent writing style, which introduce the major concepts and methodologies of strategic management. Part II,

"Cases in Strategic Management," provides a broad selection of 38 cases that allows students to apply and integrate their knowledge of the strategic management process.

STATE-OF-THE-ART COVERAGE

Along with traditional coverage, this text incorporates a number of innovative topics and provides several unique chapters that give it a distinct competitive advantage over other textbooks in strategic management. This state-of-the-art coverage includes the following material:

- The differences between intended and realized strategies are carefully explained in Chapter 1.
- In Chapter 3, the concept of stakeholder goals is used to integrate relevant literature from economics, finance, and management. In addition, this chapter explores how movement toward conglomerate diversification may be influenced by the desire of top managers to preserve their positions and to enhance their compensation. Several different perspectives are considered in viewing managerial ethics in Chapter 3.
- New research-based literature on corporate diversification in unrelated industries is presented in Chapter 4.
- Chapter 5, a unique chapter on business unit strategies, shows the relationship of those strategies to such concepts as quality, product/process/system innovations, leverage through distinctive competence, market share, profitability, risk, value analysis, and strategic groups.
- Chapter 6 offers unique coverage of how integration of functional activities can help a business attain superior product design, customer service, speed, and product/service guarantees.
- A framework is presented in Chapter 7 for helping top management assess the effectiveness of its organization's structure.
- Chapter 8 offers innovative discussion of how strategy is implemented through managerial leadership, the appropriate use of power, and the molding of organizational culture.
- A unique approach to strategic control in Chapter 9 presents multiple types of control standards and several different and useful ways of exerting strategic control.
- Global issues are not only integrated throughout the text but are comprehensively covered in Chapter 10, "Strategic Management and the World Marketplace." This unique chapter revists all strategic management processes covered in Chapters 2 through 9 in the context of the world marketplace.
- Chapter 11 is devoted exclusively to strategic management in not-for-profit organizations. This chapter revisits all strategic management processes covered in Chapters 2 through 9 in the context of not-for-profit organizations.
- Differences in strategic mangement processes in large and small companies are examined in separate sections throughout the chapter portion of the text.

CASES

Part II, "Cases in Strategic Management," includes a rich, wide-ranging collection of cases. A special introductory section preceding the cases, "Strategic Management Case Analysis," is designed to help students prepare written case analyses by offering specific guidelines and methodologies. Concluding the case analysis section are several suggestions for enhancing student performance in the strategic management course and for working within a group.

We have selected 38 cases, which students and instructors should find interesting and thought-provoking to read. Cases range from some of the largest, best-known businesses in the world, to small, developing organizations. Company operations range from those of large, multidivisional enterprises to smaller, single businesses. The collection includes a broad cross section of industries and organizations—domestic, foreign and multinational—with operational settings ranging from the United States to China, South America, Europe, and Canada. Students will read about enterprises as familiar as a neighborhood video rental store and as exotic as a new joint venture in China. The case selection also reflects a conscious effort to expose students not only to the diversity of enterprise but also to the diversity of the individuals who manage those enterprises. The following are key features of case selection:

- In keeping with the increasing globalization of business and AACSB's concern for the internationalization of the business curriculum, we have selected cases that provide a more global perspective of business. Included are cases involving enterprises based in a foreign country, such as "KNP Paper N.V." and "Club Med Inc.," U.S. companies with multinational operations, such as "Caterpillar Inc. in Latin America"and "Citicorp," foreign firms with extensive U.S. operations, such as "Northern Telecom, Inc." and "Cineplex Odeon," and even foreign small business, such as "Spottiswoode & Spottiswoode Ltd."

- Students are exposed to enterprises owned and managed by women and minorities such as "Spec's Music, Inc. A & B," "Hands Around Our Jobs," and "Shades of Black, Inc."

- A concerted effort was made to include the cases that not only relate the history and present condition of an enterprise, but also present real issues the organization must face if it is to survive and prosper. While these issues may range from exploiting new opportunities to taking steps needed to survive, the student will be required to make critical decisions regarding the future of the organization when analyzing the case.

- The case selection provides students with an opportunity to practice both their corporate-level and business-level strategic management skills.

- Several small business cases have been included, which address such issues as small business startup, growth, and survival.

- Not-for-profit cases are as varied as a major tourist attraction, such as "Mud Island," and a large healthcare facility, such as "Lakeshore, Incorporated."

- Two excellent business ethics cases highlight events that made headline news around the world. In "Union Carbide of India: The Bhopal Gas Incident" students are provided with a very complete account not only of the events leading up to the tragedy, but also of the manner in which the parent firm reacted to it. In "The Tragic Crash of Flight 191," students are exposed to the seamier side of business, as various parties who are potentially liable seek to extricate themselves from any responsibility.

Perhaps more important than any other feature of our case selection is the quality of the writing. Special attention was given to finding cases that are well written, interesting to read, and include ample information for analysis.

SPECIAL LEARNING FEATURES OF THIS TEXT

We have consistently integrated theory with practice throughout the chapter portion of the book. You will find that strategic management concepts are liberally illustrated with examples from actual, well-known organizations.

To further promote student learning, we have built into this text a number of special features to help students understand and apply the concepts presented. Each chapter of the text provides the following learning features:

- A **strategic management model** helps to visually illustrate the important stages in the strategic management process. This model is introduced and explained in Chaper 1, then reappears at the beginning of each chapter, with the portion to be discussed in a given chapter highlighted. The strategic management model serves as a student's roadmap throughout each chapter of Part I.
- **Key concepts** are boldfaced in the text when first introduced and are immediately defined. A list of key concepts with definitions appears at the end of each chapter.
- **Strategic Insight boxes** throughout the chapter portion of the book show successful and unsuccessful applications of strategic management concepts in companies such as Timberland, Southwest Airlines, Sears, Roebuck and Company, Knight-Ridder, and Coca-Cola. Each of the 40 Strategic Insight boxes appearing throughout the chapters is carefully integrated into the content of each chapter and serves to reinforce key concepts.
- A detailed **chapter summary** helps reinforce the major concepts that the student has learned in the chapter.
- End of chapter **discussion questions** test the student's retention and understanding of important chapter material and can be used as a tool for review and classroom discussion.
- **Strategic Management Exercises**—unique to this text—appear at the end of each chapter. These experiential exercises offer students the opportunity to apply their knowledge of the chapter material to realistic strategic business situations.

SUPPLEMENTS

Details of the comprehensive supplement package that accompanies the text can be found in the Instructor's Annotated Edition. The package includes:

- An Instructor's Annotated Edition
- An Instructor's Manual with test items and transparency masters
- Allyn & Bacon Test Manager, a computerized test bank
- CASE ANALYST, spreadsheet templates for case analysis
- *The Microcomputer Version of the Business Strategy and Policy Game* by David L. Eldredge and James R. Marshall, which works on all IBM PC-compatible computers
- Integrated CNN video programs including videos tied to the "Strategic Insight" boxes in the chapter portion of the text and CNN Video Industry Notes tied to specific cases
- A unique Just-in-Time Publishing Program

We are deeply indebted to many individuals for their assistance and support in this project. We especially wish to thank our manuscript reviewers. These colleagues were particularly able and deserve considerable credit for their helpful and extensive suggestions. They include:

William P. Anthony, *Florida State University*
B. R. Baliga, *Wake Forest University*
Robert B. Brown, *University of Virginia*
Peng Chan, *California State University, Fullerton*
George B. Davis, *Cleveland State University*
Louis R. Desfosses, *State University of New York, Brockport*
Pierre E. Du Jardin, *Bentley College*
Philip C. Fisher, *University of South Dakota*
Manolete V. Gonzalez, *Oregon State University*
Stevan R. Holmberg, *The American University*
Michael J. Keeffe, *Southwest Texas State University*
Daniel G. Kopp, *Southwest Missouri State University*

William Litzinger, *University of Texas, San Antonio*
James Logan, *University of New Orleans*
Michael Lubatkin, *University of Connecticut*
Daniel A. Sauers, *Louisiana Tech University*
Charles W. Schilling, *University of Wisconsin, Platteville*
Jeffrey C. Shuman, *Bentley College*
Carl L. Swanson, *University of North Texas*
James B. Thurman, *George Washington University*
Robert P. Vichas, *Florida Atlantic University*
Richard J. Ward, *Bowling Green State University*
Carolyn Y. Woo, *Purdue University*

We are deeply indebted to our colleagues who have so generously permitted us to use their excellent cases in this text. The selection process was lengthy and rigorous, and we take considerable pride in presenting the cases that this text contains. The author(s) of each case is identified on the first page of the case. A list of case contributors appears below.

Robert Anderson, *College of Charleston*
David Atchison, *University of Utah*
Alan Bauerschmidt, *University of South Carolina, Columbia*
Lew G. Brown, *University of North Carolina*
James A. Brunner, *University of Toledo*
Mei-Lung Chen, *North Carolina Central University*
Youngil Cho, *North Carolina Central University*
James J. Chrisman, *Louisiana State University*
H. Allan Conway, *University of Calgary*
R.L. Driggans, *University of Tennessee*
John Dunkelberg, *Wake Forest University*
Jim Frierson, *University of Texas, Tyler*
Ken Gardner, *University of South Carolina*
Juan J. Gonzalez, *University of Texas, San Antonio*
Ernst P. Goss, *Salisbury State University*
M. Ray Grubbs, *Millsaps College*
C. Ray Gullett, *University of Texas, Tyler*
Cecelia L. Harper, *University of Texas, Tyler*
Marilyn M. Helms, *University of Tennessee*
Fred Jacobson, *University of Texas, Tyler*
Mark J. Kroll, *University of Texas, Tyler*

Hooshang Kuklan, *North Carolina Central University*
Frank Leibold, *University of South Carolina*
John Leslie, *University of South Carolina*
John P. McCray, *University of Texas, San Antonio*
Robert McGlashan, *University of Houston, Clear Lake*
Robert McNamara, *University of South Carolina*
Timothy S. Mescon, *Salisbury State University*
Tomasz Mroczkowski, *American University*
Thad Munnerlyn, *University of South Carolina*
Lester A. Neidell, *University of Tulsa*
John E. Oliver, *Valdosta State University*
Robert A. Orwig, *Mississippi State University*
John Ozmun, *Northern Arizona University*
Carol A. Reeves, *University of Miami*
Thomas M. Rieff, Owner, *Crystal Lawn Service*
Lisa K. Rowe, *Mississippi State University*
JoAnn K.L. Schwinghammer, *Mankato State University*
Richard Sharpe, *University of North Carolina*
Susan M. Sharpe, *Millsaps College*

Arthur Sharplin, *McNeese State University*
John W. Simmons, *University of Texas, Tyler*
Marian P. Simmons, *Millsaps College*
Timothy Singleton, *North Georgia College*
Barbara A. Spencer, *Mississippi State University*
Daniel Sullivan, *University of South Carolina, Columbia*
Marilyn L. Taylor, *University of Kansas*

Natalie T. Taylor, *Babson College*
Raphael Thompson, *North Carolina Central University*
Robert P. Vichas, *Florida Atlantic University*
George S. Vozikis, *The Citadel*
Randall K. White, *Auburn University, Montgomery*
Joseph Wolfe, *University of Tulsa*
Marilyn Young, *University of Texas, Tyler*

We extend our sincere thanks to Dennis Patzig, James Madison University, for his outstanding contributions in preparing annotations for the Instructor's Annotated Edition, and to John Parnell, Memphis State University, for his excellent work on the Instructor's Manual. In addition, we gratefully thank Marshall Schminke and James Anderson of Creighton University for developing the superior CASE ANALYST software package to accompany this text. The guidance and assistance of the staff at Allyn & Bacon have been superb. We particularly wish to thank Jack Peters, who was responsible for initiating this project, and Janis Jackson Hill, senior developmental editor, who so capably brought it to fruition.

Administrators at each of our universities have been most supportive of our work. We particularly wish to thank Dean Otis W. Baskin and Management Chairman Thomas R. Miller of Memphis State University; Dean Robert E. Holmes of James Madison University; and President George F. Hamm, Vice President of Academic Affairs Thomas L. Fernandez, and Dean Robert T. Partain of the University of Texas at Tyler.

Finally, but certainly not least, the support, patience, and understanding of special family members—William, Mahin, and Teresa Wright; Anne Marie and Erin Pringle; and Nghi Kroll—were not only helpful but essential in making this book a reality.

The Concepts and Techniques of Strategic Management

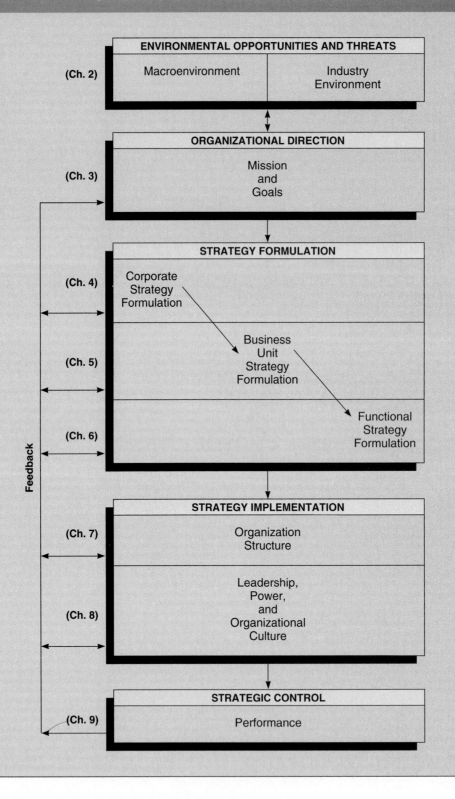

STRATEGIC MANAGEMENT MODEL

ENVIRONMENTAL OPPORTUNITIES AND THREATS

(Ch. 2)

| Macroenvironment | Industry Environment |

ORGANIZATIONAL DIRECTION

(Ch. 3)

Mission
and
Goals

STRATEGY FORMULATION

(Ch. 4)

Corporate
Strategy
Formulation

(Ch. 5)

Business
Unit
Strategy
Formulation

(Ch. 6)

Functional
Strategy
Formulation

STRATEGY IMPLEMENTATION

(Ch. 7)

Organization
Structure

(Ch. 8)

Leadership,
Power,
and
Organizational
Culture

STRATEGIC CONTROL

(Ch. 9)

Performance

Feedback

1

CHAPTER

Introduction to Strategic Management

Managers face no greater challenge than that of strategic management. Guiding a complex organization through a dynamic, rapidly changing environment requires the best of judgment. Strategic management issues are invariably ambiguous and unstructured, and the way in which management responds to them determines whether an organization will succeed or fail.

Strategic management is challenging because it is far more than simply setting goals and then ordering organization members to attain those goals. An organization's strategic direction depends upon a variety of considerations. Among them are top management's assessment of the external environment's opportunities and threats or constraints, and management's analysis of the firm's internal strengths and weaknesses. Simultaneously, the top management team must take into account the competing desires and needs of the organization's various stakeholders (or interested parties), because their support is essential to successful strategy implementation. Stakeholders include not only the organization's managers and employees but also the firm's owners (i.e., stockholders), suppliers, customers, creditors, and community members.

This text focuses on strategic management. The issues and processes discussed are real ones that are directly relevant to all types of organizations— large or small, international or domestic, diversified or single-product, and profit or nonprofit. The material contained herein should provide keen insight into strategic management and an appreciation of its vital role in enhancing organizational effectiveness.

WHAT IS STRATEGIC MANAGEMENT?

■ Strategic Management Defined

Since the word *strategy* or some variation of it is used throughout the text, its definition should be clear. **Strategy** refers to top management's plans to attain outcomes consistent with the organization's mission and goals. One can look at strategy from three vantage points: (1) strategy formulation (i.e., developing the strategy), (2) strategy implementation (i.e., putting the strategy into action), and (3) strategic control (i.e., modifying either the strategy or its implementation to ensure that the desired outcomes are attained).

Strategic management is a broader term that encompasses managing not only the stages identified above but also the earlier stages of determining the mission and goals of an organization within the context of its external environment. Hence, strategic management can be viewed as a series of steps in which top management should accomplish the following tasks:

1. Analyze the opportunities and threats or constraints that exist in the external environment.
2. Analyze the organization's internal strengths and weaknesses.
3. Establish the organization's mission and develop its goals.
4. Formulate strategies (i.e., corporate-level, business unit–level, and functional-level) that will match the organization's strengths and weaknesses with the environment's opportunities and threats.
5. Implement the strategies.
6. Engage in strategic control activities to ensure that the organization's goals are attained.

Although the various steps in this process are discussed sequentially in this book, in reality they are highly related. Any single stage in the strategic management process must be considered in conjunction with the other stages, because a change at any given point will affect other stages in the process. These stages are discussed sequentially throughout the text only to make them more understandable.

In its broadest sense, strategic management consists of managerial decisions and actions that help to ensure that the organization formulates and maintains a beneficial fit with its environment. Thus, strategic managers evaluate their company's evolving strengths and weaknesses in the context of changing opportunities and threats in the external environment. Maintaining a compatible fit between the business and its environment is necessary for competitive viability. Since both the environment and the organization change with the passage of time, this process is an ongoing concern for management.

■ Model of Strategic Management

As an aid in envisioning the strategic management process, a schematic model of this process is presented in Figure 1.1. At the top, the model begins with an analysis of environmental opportunities and threats. In the next stage, the organization's mission and goals are linked to the environment by a dual arrow. This arrow means that the mission and goals are set in the context of environmental opportunities and threats. The organization, in other words, is affected by environmental forces. But the organization can also have an impact upon its environment.[1]

Federal legislation, for instance, can be influenced by lobbying activities; the ecological environment can be improved through corporate social responsibility actions; customer behavior can be swayed through advertising and sales promotion; large, economically powerful retailers can affect the actions of suppliers; and pricing strategy and product improvements certainly influence the activities of competitors.[2]

Strategic Management Model   Figure 1.1

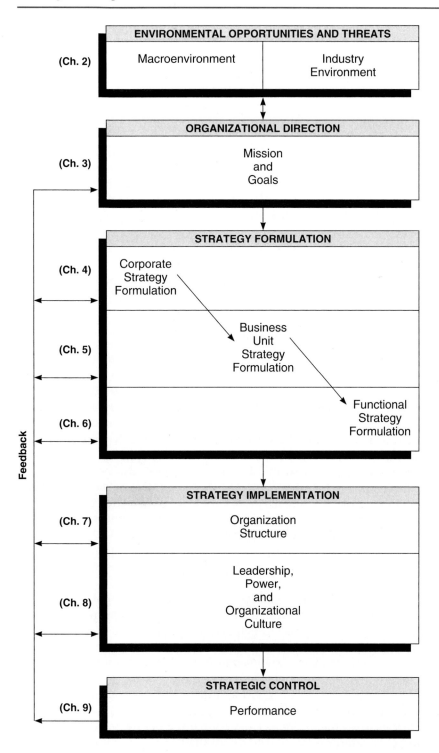

The mission and goals of the organization drive strategy formulation at the corporate, business unit, and functional levels, as demonstrated by the one-way arrow. At the corporate level, the decision makers are the chief executive officer (CEO), other top managers, and the board of directors. Most of the strategic decisions at the business unit level are made by the top manager of the business unit and his or her key executives, and the decision makers at the functional level are the heads of the functional areas (i.e., the managers of such departments as production, finance, marketing, and research and development).

The next arrow depicts the idea that strategy formulation sets strategy implementation in motion. Specifically, strategy is implemented through the organization's structure, its leadership, its distribution of power, and its culture. Then, the final downward arrow indicates that the actual strategic performance of the organization is evaluated. To the extent that performance fails to meet the organization's goals, strategic control is exerted to modify some or all of the stages in the model in order to improve performance. The control stage is demonstrated by the feedback line that connects strategic control to the other parts of the model.

More details on the strategic management model are provided in the next eight chapters. At the beginning of each chapter, the part of the model that is to be featured is highlighted. In Chapters 10 and 11, the entire model is revisited through a focus, respectively, on international and not-for-profit organizations.

■ Importance of Strategic Management

Most of the significant current events covered in such business publications as *Fortune, Business Week,* and *The Wall Street Journal* involve strategic management concepts. Hence, an understanding of the business world requires familiarity with the strategic management process. As domestic and foreign competition intensifies, and during those periods when government's influence on business operations expands, an understanding of strategic management becomes even more essential.

Employees, supervisors, and middle managers must also be familiar with strategic management. An appreciation of their organization's strategy helps them relate their work assignments more closely to the direction of the organization, thereby enhancing their job performance and opportunity for promotion and making their organization more effective.

■ Evolving Study of Strategic Management

During the 1950s, the Ford Foundation and the Carnegie Corporation funded an analysis of business school curricula and teaching. From this research came the Gordon-Howell report, which concluded that formal business education at universities should be broadened and should conclude with a capstone course that would integrate students' knowledge from such courses as accounting, finance, marketing, management, and economics.[3] Most business schools accepted the conclusions of this report and developed a capstone course that became known as "Business Policy."

The initial thrust of the business policy course was to integrate the functional areas within an enterprise so that it could attain a consistent direction. The direction would be one that capitalized upon its strengths while de-emphasizing its weaknesses, relative to the opportunities and threats presented by the organization's external environment.

Over time, the parameters of this capstone course expanded to include more formal analyses of the organization's macroenvironment, industry environment, mission and goals, strategy formulation, strategy implementation, and strategic control. This expanded conception of the field began to be referred to as *strategic management,* as opposed to the more narrow term *business policy.*[4]

STRATEGIC DECISIONS

■ Who Makes the Decisions?

The chief executive officer (CEO) is the individual ultimately responsible for the organization's strategic management. But except in the smallest companies, the CEO relies on a host of other individuals, including members of the board of directors, vice presidents, and various line and staff managers. Precisely who these individuals are depends upon the type of organization. For instance, businesses with centralized decision-making processes generally have fewer managers involved in strategic decisions than do companies that are decentralized. Businesses that are organized around functions (i.e., production, marketing, finance, personnel, etc.) generally involve the vice presidents of the functional departments in strategic decisions. Firms with product divisional structures (e.g., the home appliance division, the lawn mower division, the hand tool division, etc.) usually include the product division managers along with the CEO. Very large organizations often employ corporate-level strategic-planning staffs to assist the CEO and other top managers in making strategic management decisions.

Inputs to strategic decisions can be generated in a number of different ways. For example, an employee in a company's research and development department may attend a conference. At the conference, a new product or production process idea that seems relevant to the company may be discussed. Upon returning from the conference, the employee may relate the idea to his supervisor, who, in turn, may pass it along to her boss. Eventually, the idea may be discussed with the organization's marketing and production managers. As it moves from one area to another, the idea becomes increasingly clear and specific. Ultimately, it may be presented to top management in a formal report. The CEO will eventually decide to adopt or reject the idea. But can we actually say that this strategic decision was made solely by the CEO? In a sense, the answer is "yes," because it is the CEO's responsibility to decide which alternative the company will adopt. But from a broader perspective, the answer is "no," because most strategic decisions result from the streams of inputs, decisions, and actions of many people. Top management is ultimately responsible for the final decision, but its decision is the culmination of the ideas, creativity, information, and analyses of others.

As another example, sales representatives often inform the sales manager that a certain customer or group of customers could be better served by some modification to one of the company's products. The sales manager may communicate this information to the engineering department, which may, in

The Human Side of Strategy at TCBY, Commodore International Ltd. and Jeffries Group

To any employee, whether manager or operative worker, salary is important in two ways: its absolute amount and its size in comparison with the salaries of other employees. In the United States, the difference between the compensation of the chief executive officer (CEO) and that of the average manufacturing employee has steadily widened. While CEOs earned 34 times as much as their employees in the 1970s, the gap between the two had grown to 130 times by 1990. Some CEOs even earned more than 1000 times their employees' pay. (By comparison, the ratio in Europe is 20 to 1, and in Japan, 15 to 1.)

The potential problems with this tremendous gap are numerous: increased worker alienation and lack of commitment, greater difficulty in motivating employees, reduced productivity at a time when U.S. business can least afford it, the threat of more unionization, and the possibility of stockholder involvement in setting executive pay levels. On top of these issues is the perception in some companies that when the company is not performing well, workers and middle managers are either laid off or forced to take pay cuts, while top managers continue to receive very large salaries.

Take the case of TCBY, the nation's largest frozen-yogurt franchise. Between 1985 and 1989, as the company's profits steadily climbed, franchise holders did not object to CEO Frank Hicking-botham's $1.7 million salary nor to his business purchases of a corporate jet and a Rolls-Royce. But when earnings tumbled in 1990, the situation changed dramatically. Angry franchise holders formed an association, complaining that the CEO was living too luxuriously compared with the franchise owners.

Or consider Commodore International Ltd., a personal-computer manufacturer. When its 1990 profits declined by 97 percent, its CEO received a 40 percent pay raise. In fact, his $1.75 million cash salary exceeded the company's net income of $1.5 million.

The lesson from these incidents—and similar ones in companies from a variety of industries—is that all employees should share in prosperity as well as in decline. Enlightened CEOs not only are aware of compensation gaps but also have symbolically removed other sources of potential dissatisfaction. These moves have included closing private executive dining rooms, eliminating reserved parking spaces, and doing away with private exercise rooms reserved only for top management.

A more drastic measure is that taken by Frank Baxter, CEO of Jefferies Group, a brokerage firm. When his company's earnings fell, he took a 30 percent pay cut, from over $900,000 in 1988 to about $630,000 in 1989. His theory? "We feel we have to perform if we are going to get paid. We don't want to get paid for showing up."

SOURCES: C. Hymowitz, "More Employees, Shareholders Demand That Sacrifices in Pay Begin at the Top," *The Wall Street Journal*, 8 November 1990; K. Ballen, "Let Them Eat Bread," *Fortune*, 24 September 1990, p. 9; W. Zellner, "Flaring Tempers at the Frozen-Yogurt King," *Business Week*, 10 September 1990, pp. 88–90; J. Nelson-Horchler, "What's Your Boss Worth?" *The Washington Post*, 5 August 1990; K. M. Kristof, "The Pay-for-Performance Myth," *The Washington Post*, 22 July 1990 (source of quotation).

response, develop a prototype model of the revised product. Other inputs are usually sought from various departments regarding the strengths and weaknesses of the revised product. Finally, all of these ideas are communicated to top management, which must base its "go" or "no-go" decision on the managed streams of external and internal inputs, decisions, and actions of other individuals. Note that the key input for the decision came from outside the organization, via customers who provided the initial idea.

▪ Characteristics of Strategic Decisions

As noted in the preceding section, strategic decisions usually involve several parts of an organization or, perhaps, even all of its components. Only top management has the appropriate broad perspective and the authority needed to make these strategic decisions.

In addition to involving more than one area of an organization, strategic decisions usually require obtaining and allocating sizable resources (i.e., human, financial, informational, and physical resources). Finally, strategic decisions involve a lengthy time period, anywhere from several years to more than a decade. Consequently, strategic decisions are future-oriented with long-term ramifications.

STRATEGIC MANAGEMENT: A CONTINUOUS PROCESS

Once a planned strategy is implemented, it often requires modification as environmental and/or organizational conditions change. These changes are often difficult or even impossible to forecast. Not even the Central Intelligence Agency (CIA), for example, was able to predict such a major event as Iraq's 1990 invasion of Kuwait, so it is not surprising that management is often unable to foretell the future. In fact, it is a rare situation indeed in which top management is able to develop a long-range strategic plan and implement it over several years without any need for modification.

Hence, an **intended strategy** (i.e., what management originally planned) may be realized in its original form, in a modified form, or even in an entirely different form. Occasionally, of course, the strategy that management intends is actually realized, but usually, the intended strategy and **realized strategy** (what management actually implements) differ.[5] The reason is that unforeseen environmental and/or organizational events occur that necessitate changes in the intended strategy. The full range of possibilities is illustrated in Table 1.1.

Intended Strategy, Realized Strategy, and Results: Range of Possibilities   **Table 1.1**

1. What is intended as a strategy is realized with desirable results.

2. What is intended as a strategy is realized, but with less than desirable results.

3. What is intended as a strategy is realized in some modified version because of an unanticipated environmental and/or internal requirement or change. The results are desirable.

4. What is intended as a strategy is realized in some modified version because of an unanticipated environmental and/or internal requirement or change. The results are less than desirable.

5. What is intended as a strategy is not realized. Instead, an unanticipated environmental and/or internal change requires an entirely different strategy. The different strategy is realized with desirable results.

6. What is intended as a strategy is not realized. Instead, an unanticipated environmental and/or internal change requires an entirely different strategy. The different strategy is realized with less than desirable results.

STRATEGIC INSIGHT

Strategy in the Automobile Industry: Japanese Inroads

Contrary to popular belief, the world's first workable cars were not manufactured in the United States but in France and Germany. In fact, automakers in those two countries dominated car manufacturing until Henry Ford began producing cars through assembly line techniques. By 1920, Ford alone produced almost half of the cars in the world. This U.S. leadership in car production continued for the next several decades.

By the 1950s, however, U.S. carmakers were becoming complacent. They routinely produced large, heavy cars with powerful engines. Following their policy of "planned obsolescence," U.S. manufacturers gave these cars annual cosmetic changes, designed to make it clear which consumers were driving the latest models. While U.S. car companies were concentrating on styling and sales, European producers were developing an impressive array of technological improvements, including disc brakes, rack-and-pinion steering, front-wheel drive, unitized bodies, and fuel injection systems. By 1970, European automobile exports were twenty-five times those of the United States.

When the first oil price shock hit the United States in 1974, American carmakers were virtually unprepared. American consumers began to turn to the more fuel-efficient European models and, increasingly, to Japan's small economical vehicles. Detroit's carmakers grudgingly began to manufacture smaller cars. But their attitude was best summed up by the comment of Henry Ford II: "Minicars mean miniprofits."

By the late 1970s, American consumers were turning to Japanese cars in record numbers. Not only were the cars more economical, but most buyers felt that they were of higher quality than American-made cars. Frightened, U.S. automakers sought government protection. At the behest of the U.S. government, the Japanese "voluntarily" agreed to import restrictions in the early 1980s.

Ironically, however, these restrictions provided Japanese automakers with the impetus to construct plants in the United States to avoid the restrictions. Although they originally only assembled cars in America, today Honda, Toyota, and Nissan have established research and development, engineering, and design centers in the United States. In fact, by 1990, Honda was producing cars that were totally planned and built in America—mostly by Americans. Honda's top management believed that having all of the functions required to design and build cars in one place was more efficient. That way, everyone who was involved in the cars' production could communicate easily.

By 1990, the Japanese could build cars in the United States more cheaply than American manufacturers could, even when they spent more to import parts from Japan. Estimates were that the Japanese could make a compact car in the United States for about $800 less than their U.S. competitors. Not surprisingly, the Japanese share of the U.S. auto market was between 28 and 30 percent, and the Honda Accord became the best-selling car in the United States. Over a million Japanese cars were produced in the United States by 1990, compared with about a thousand just eight years earlier.

Japan's auto companies, however, were not content to dominate the small-car segments of the U.S. market. By the early 1990s, they had introduced luxury cars selling for about $40,000 to compete with Cadillac, Lincoln, and such European makes as Mercedes and BMW. Honda even introduced a Ferrari look-alike sports car, the Acura NSX, which sold for over $60,000.

By 1992, Japan's automakers were turning their attention even further westward as the European Economic Community began to tear down its trade barriers. That large and lucrative market held the appeal for Japanese car companies that the U.S. market had in 1970.

SOURCES: D. Woodruff, K. L. Miller, L. Armstrong, and T. Peterson, "A New Era for Auto Quality," *Business Week*, 22 October 1990, pp. 84–96; A. Taylor III, "Japan's New U.S. Car Strategy," *Fortune*, 10 September 1990, pp. 65–80; A. Miller and F. Washington, "Japanese Cars: Born in the USA," *Newsweek*, 9 April 1990, pp. 36–37; D. Cordtz, "The First Hundred Years: How the U.S. Auto Companies Blew Their Stranglehold on the Industry," *Financial World*, 22 August 1989, pp. 54–56.

As an example of the difference between intended strategy and realized strategy, consider Honda's entry into the U.S. motorcycle market.[6] When Honda established an American subsidiary in Los Angeles in 1959, its intended strategy was to emphasize the sale of motorcycles with 250-cc and 305-cc engines despite the fact that its smaller 50-cc model was a big seller in Japan. Honda's top managers believed that American consumers would prefer larger models. But Honda's 250-cc and 305-cc bikes met a disappointing response from U.S. motorcyclists. The intended strategy failed.

During this time, Honda's executives were using their own 50-cc motorcycles to commute in traffic-congested Los Angeles. The convenience and appearance of the motorcycles began to be noticed by automobile drivers, pedestrians, and retailers. Orders for the 50-cc model began to come in from some motorcycle retailers, but Honda was reluctant to fill them because management did not wish to be associated with a no-frills motorcycle. When the huge retailer Sears, Roebuck expressed an interest in selling the 50-cc model, however, Honda executives changed their minds. The intended strategy of selling 250-cc and 305-cc motorcycles was modified to emphasize sales of the 50-cc machine. This modified strategy was realized with desirable results (i.e., alternative 3 in Table 1.1).

Honda's overwhelming success in selling its 50-cc motorcycle gradually convinced its executives to build upon that base by expanding into the larger-bike categories. This intended strategy was realized with desirable results (i.e., alternative 1 in Table 1.1) from the late 1960s through the mid-1980s.[7]

Honda's success during this time was partially based on its reliable, sturdy products. But Honda was also successful because of weak competition. With the exception of a lethargic Harley-Davidson, Honda did not face any competitive threat from American companies, and European and Japanese competitors had not matched Honda's investment in the U.S. market. This scenario began to change during the mid-1980s, however.

Foreign competitors became more assertive in the American market, particularly in the small and midsized lines. And following a management-led leveraged buyout in 1981, Harley-Davidson began to reassert its dominance in the large-motorcycle market. While Honda was busy battling competitors with product offerings in all sizes of bikes, Harley-Davidson increased its market share for the largest motorcycles from 23 percent in 1983 to 60 percent in 1990.[8] Honda's sales, meanwhile, dropped from $1.1 billion in 1985 to $230 million in 1990, and its share of the U.S. motorcycle market plunged from 58 to 28 percent during that period.[9] Hence, as the competitive situation changed rapidly after 1984, Honda's results deteriorated. The years from 1985 through 1990, therefore, may be characterized as an intended strategy that was realized with less than desirable results (i.e., alternative 2 in Table 1.1).

This text assumes that strategies need to be examined continuously in light of changing situations. Table 1.1 presents the range of outcomes that are possible as an organization implements its strategy. Therefore, whenever reference is made to plans for strategic formulation and implementation in the text, recall that management's intended strategy is rarely realized in its original, unchanged form.

OVERVIEW OF THE TEXTBOOK

This presentation of the strategic management process begins with an analysis of the environment in which a company operates. All businesses are concerned with two levels of environments. The broader of these is the macroenvironment, which is comprised of political-legal, economic, technological, and social trends that have an effect on all organizations. But each organization also has a more specific environment, known as an industry, in which it operates. The industry defines the company's unique set of customers and competitors. The first step in strategic management is analysis of these two levels of environments. Chapter 2 provides a framework for understanding and analyzing the macroenvironment and industry.

Since strategic management consists of structuring a compatible fit between the organization and its environment, the reason for the existence of the business (i.e., its mission) must be defined within its environmental context. Once the company's identity is clearly understood, top management must formulate goals to give the organization direction within the opportunities, threats, and constraints of its environment. Establishing the organization's mission and goals is the subject of Chapter 3.

After its mission and goals are established, the organization's strategy must be addressed. Strategy formulation occurs at three organizational levels: corporate, business unit, and functional. Chapter 4 focuses on corporate-level strategy formulation. At this level, the essential question is: "In what businesses or industries should we be operating?" The chapter presents the strategic alternatives that are available to management along with appropriate analytical frameworks.

At the business unit level, the question that must be answered is: "How should we compete in each of the businesses or industries in which we have chosen to operate?" (The difference between corporate-level and business unit strategies is illustrated in Figure 1.2.) Chapter 5 identifies the alternative, generic business unit strategies that are available to management and explains under what circumstances each is appropriate.

Chapter 6 analyzes the formulation of functional strategies (i.e., strategies in production, marketing, research and development, finance, etc.). It emphasizes the interdependence of an organization's functional strategies and their relationship to the company's business unit strategies.

Figure 1.2   **Corporate- and Business Unit–Level Strategic Questions**

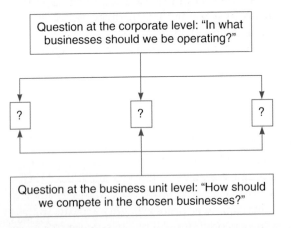

After the examination of strategy formulation at these three levels, the discussion turns to how these strategies can be implemented. The organizational structure adopted by a company plays a key role in strategy implementation. Chapter 7 identifies the structures available to management and discusses the circumstances under which each is likely to lead to effective implementation of the organization's strategies.

Other essential aspects of strategy implementation are presented in Chapter 8. How the CEO and the top management team secure the cooperation of the organization's members by exercising leadership and informal power is discussed in some detail. Then, the key role played by organizational culture in implementing strategy is analyzed.

As strategies are implemented, the process of strategic control begins. Strategic control consists of determining the extent to which the organization's goals are being attained. This process often requires management to modify its strategies and/or implementation in some fashion so that the company's ability to reach its goals will be improved. Strategic control is the subject of Chapter 9.

Strategic management is discussed in the context of the world marketplace in Chapter 10. Here, the contents of Chapters 2 through 9 are revisited through a distinctly international perspective.

The process of strategic management is applied to not-for-profit organizations in Chapter 11. Although the basic principles of strategic management apply equally to profit and not-for-profit organizations, there are some differences that require examination. A diagrammatic overview of Chapters 2 through 11 is shown in Figure 1.3.

Finally, the second section of the text begins by presenting an overview of strategic management case analysis. The methodology discussed will help in analyzing the cases contained in the latter part of the text.

Cases, which present the strategies and operations of real companies, provide the opportunity to apply the knowledge gleaned from Chapters 1 through 11 to analyses of real situations. Case analysis encourages active, involved learning rather than passive recall of the book's contents.

Some of the cases are narrow, primarily involving single issues. These cases provide opportunities to apply knowledge to a specific issue, problem, or situation. Most, however, are broad, encompassing many different aspects of an organization and its environment. The advantages of such cases are several. First, they encourage the application and integration of what has been learned in this text with knowledge gained from other courses and even from one's work experience. Second, they provide a vehicle for analyzing a total organization versus one narrow aspect or functional area of that company. Third, they promote the awareness that varied aspects of the organization and its environment, and their interrelationships, must be examined to formulate and implement strategies effectively.

S U M M A R Y

Strategic management refers to the process that begins with determining the mission and goals of an organization within the context of its external environment. Appropriate strategies are then formulated and implemented. Finally, strategic control is exerted to ensure that the organization's strategies are successful in attaining its goals.

Figure 1.3   **Overview of the Book**

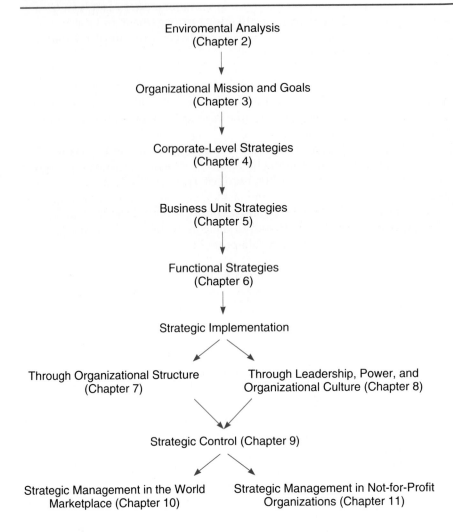

Determining organizational strategy is the direct responsibility of the chief executive officer (CEO), but he or she relies on a host of other individuals, including the board of directors, vice presidents, and various line and staff managers. In its final form, a strategic decision is molded from the streams of inputs, decisions, and actions of many people.

Strategic management is a continuous process. Once a strategy is implemented, it often requires modification as environmental and/or organizational conditions change. Because these changes are often difficult or even impossible to predict, a strategy may, over time, be modified so that it bears only a slight resemblance to the organization's intended strategy. This realized strategy is the result of unforeseen external and/or internal events that require changes in the organization's intended strategy. Thus, strategies need to be examined continuously in the light of changing situations.

KEY CONCEPTS

Intended strategy The original strategy that management plans and intends to implement.

Realized strategy The actual and eventual strategy that management implements. The realized strategy often differs from the intended strategy because unforeseen environmental and/or organizational events occur that necessitate modifications in the intended strategy.

Strategic management The continuous process of determining the mission and goals of an organization within the context of its external environment, formulating appropriate strategies, implementing those strategies, and exerting strategic control to ensure that the organization's strategies are successful in attaining its goals.

Strategy Top management's plans to attain outcomes consistent with the organization's mission and goals.

DISCUSSION QUESTIONS

1. In what sense does the CEO alone make the company's strategic decisions? In what sense does the CEO *not* make the company's strategic decisions alone?

2. Explain the difference between an intended strategy and a realized strategy. Relate an example of a company whose ultimate realized strategy differed from its original intended strategy.

3. How can an understanding of strategic management be beneficial to your career?

REFERENCES

1. See J. B. Barney, "Types of Competition and the Theory of Strategy: Toward an Integrative Framework," *Academy of Management Review* 11 (1986): 791–800; J. Child, "Organizational Structure, Environment, and Performance: The Role of Strategic Choice," *Sociology* 6 (1972): 1–22; and J. A. Schumpeter, *The Theory of Economic Development* (New York: Oxford University Press, 1934).

2. J. G. Longenecker and C. D. Pringle, "The Illusion of Contingency Theory as a General Theory," *Academy of Management Review* 3 (1978): 682.

3. R. A. Gordon and J. E. Howell, *Higher Education for Business* (New York: Columbia University Press, 1959).

4. M. Leontiades, "The Confusing Words of Business Policy," *Academy of Management Review* 7 (1982): 46.

5. H. Mintzberg, "Opening Up the Definition of Strategy," in J. B. Quinn, H. Mintzberg, and R. M. James, eds., *The Strategy Process* (Englewood Cliffs, N.J.: Prentice-Hall, 1988), pp. 14–15.

6. R. T. Pascale, "Perspectives on Strategy: The Real Story Behind Honda's Success," *California Management Review* 26 (1984): 47–72.

7. S. Phillips, "That 'Vroom!' You Hear Is Honda Motorcycles," *Business Week*, 3 September 1990, pp. 74–75.

8. R. Rose, "Vrooming Back," *The Wall Street Journal*, 31 August 1990.

9. Phillips, "That 'Vroom!' You Hear."

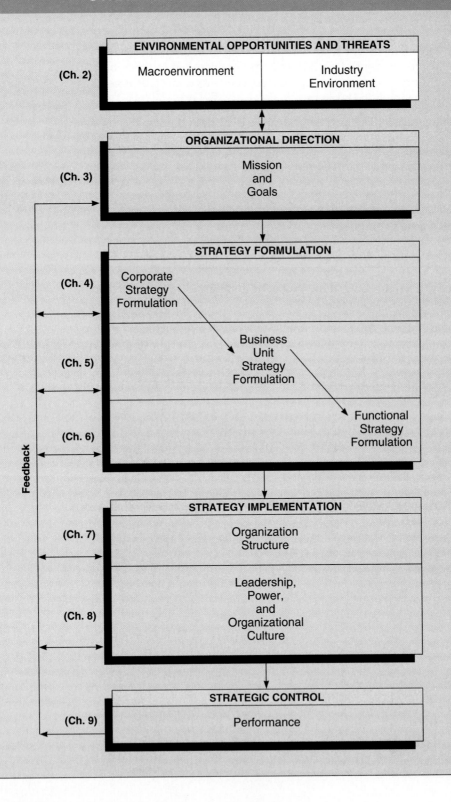

STRATEGIC MANAGEMENT MODEL

ENVIRONMENTAL OPPORTUNITIES AND THREATS

(Ch. 2)

Macroenvironment	Industry Environment

ORGANIZATIONAL DIRECTION

(Ch. 3)

Mission
and
Goals

STRATEGY FORMULATION

(Ch. 4)

Corporate
Strategy
Formulation

(Ch. 5)

Business
Unit
Strategy
Formulation

(Ch. 6)

Functional
Strategy
Formulation

STRATEGY IMPLEMENTATION

(Ch. 7)

Organization
Structure

(Ch. 8)

Leadership,
Power,
and
Organizational
Culture

STRATEGIC CONTROL

(Ch. 9)

Performance

Feedback

Environmental Opportunities and Threats

Strategic management involves three levels of analysis: the organization's macroenvironment, the industry in which the organization operates, and the organization itself. These levels are portrayed in Figure 2.1. This chapter focuses upon the first two levels—the macroenvironment and industry. Then, Chapter 3 begins our analysis of the firm.

Every organization exists within a complex network of environmental forces. All firms are affected by political-legal, economic, technological, and social systems and trends. Together, these elements comprise the **macroenvironment** of business firms. Because these forces are so dynamic, their constant change presents a myriad of opportunities and threats or constraints to strategic managers.

Each business also operates within a more specific environment termed an **industry:** a group of companies that produces competing products or services. The structure of an industry influences the intensity of competition among the firms in the industry by placing certain restrictions upon their operations and by providing various opportunities for well-managed firms to seize the advantage over their competitors. As we shall see in this chapter, successful management depends upon forging a link between business and its environment through the activities of environmental analysis.

ANALYSIS OF THE MACROENVIRONMENT

All organizations are affected by four macroenvironmental forces: political-legal, economic, technological, and social. Although very large organizations (or several firms in association with one another) will occasionally attempt to influence legislation or, through research and development, will pioneer technological or social changes, these macroenvironmental forces are generally not under the direct control of business organizations. Hence, the purpose of strategic management is to enable the firm to operate effectively within environ-

Figure 2.1   **Three Levels of Analysis**

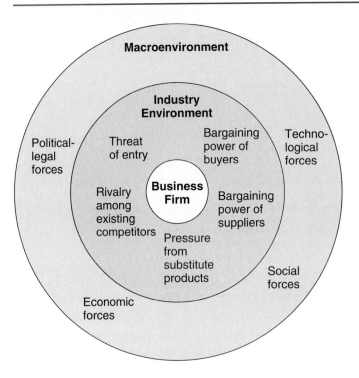

mental threats or constraints and to capitalize on the opportunities provided by the environment. To accomplish this purpose, strategic managers must identify and analyze these national and global macroenvironmental forces, which are described in the following sections.

■ Political-Legal Forces

Political-legal forces include the outcomes of elections, legislation, and court judgments, as well as the decisions rendered by various commissions and agencies at every level of government. As an example of the impact of these forces, consider the automobile industry. The U.S. government's insistence on having cars meet gradually increasing fuel economy standards has affected the size and design of cars, their engine size, and their horsepower. Although American automakers have viewed these regulations as a constraint upon the types of models that they can make and sell, Japanese car manufacturers have perceived it as an opportunity to make inroads into the prosperous American market.

On the other hand, the U.S. government's imposition of import fees on automobiles and its success in convincing Japanese manufacturers to restrict "voluntarily" their exports to the United States have provided opportunities for American firms to increase their car sales. Unfortunately, the U.S. car producers did not take advantage of all of these opportunities to increase their market share. But some Japanese carmakers have successfully adapted to these constraints by building manufacturing plants in the United States.

Finally, the American government led a coalition of European, Canadian, and Japanese governments to reduce the value of the U.S. dollar relative to the currencies of major trading partners. The strengthened foreign currencies and weakened U.S. dollar translated into lower prices for American cars versus those of their overseas rivals. We can see, then, that the U.S. political-legal system has had a major impact on the automobile industry.

On a more global scale, the 1985 decision by the Commission of the European Community to form a single European market for the twelve-nation European community by the end of 1992 presents both opportunities and threats to U.S.-based firms. One of the major opportunities is the attractive nature of this large, affluent market, which some U.S. firms may have avoided up until now because they considered the market too fragmented and its trade regulations overly complicated. However, a possible threat is that a consolidated market may allow European firms to build a solid base upon which they can develop into much stronger world competitors.

A nation's political-legal system greatly influences its business operations and the standard of living of its citizens. Historically, higher standards of living have been associated with nations whose economic systems are probusiness. In the United States, capitalism has contributed significantly over the past two centuries to America's unparalleled economic growth. But even free enterprise has its weaknesses. By the beginning of the twentieth century, such undesirable social consequences as unsafe working conditions, child labor, low wages, monopolistic competition, deceptive advertising, and unsafe products made it clear that some degree of governmental regulation was necessary. Examples of some of the more significant regulations are shown in Table 2.1.

Not all of the legislative and judicial movement in American society, however, has been in the direction of greater regulation of business. In the late 1970s and the 1980s, a major shift in national policy occurred, which reversed this trend in several industries. This "deregulation" movement eliminated a number of legal constraints in such industries as airlines, trucking, and banking. This reversal of historic trends presented both new opportunities and threats to organizations in the affected industries.

Airline deregulation, for instance, offered opportunities to entrepreneurs to start companies such as Southwest Airlines and People Express. For established firms, though, like TWA, Eastern, and United, the reduction of regulation posed a threat by creating intense cost and price competition. In banking, deregulation presented vast opportunities for expansion in services and geographic scope. Banks began offering brokerage services, for example, and mergers across state lines became common. On the other hand, deregulation intensified competition for banks, because nonbanking firms, such as money market funds and brokerage houses, began competing directly with banks for consumers' savings.

▪ Economic Forces

Like political-legal systems, economic forces also have a significant impact on business operations. As prime examples, we will consider the impact of growth or decline in gross national product and increases or decreases in interest rates, inflation, and the value of the dollar. These changes present both opportunities and threats or constraints to strategic managers.

Table 2.1   **Examples of Government Regulation of Business**

Legislation	Purpose
Sherman Antitrust Act (1890)	Prohibit monopoly or conspiracy in restraint of trade
Pure Food and Drug Act (1906)	Outlaw production of unsanitary foods and drugs
Clayton Act (1914)	Forbid tying contracts, which tie the sale of some products to the sale of others
Federal Trade Commission Act (1914)	Stop unfair methods of competition, such as deceptive advertising, selling practices, and pricing
Fair Labor Standards Act (1938)	Set minimum-wage rates, regulations for overtime pay, and child labor standards
Wheeler-Lea Amendment (1938)	Outlaw deceptive packaging and advertising
Antimerger Act (1950)	Make the buying of competitors illegal when it lessens competition
Equal Pay Act (1963)	Prohibit discrimination in wages on the basis of sex when males and females are performing jobs requiring equal skill, effort, and responsibility under similar working conditions
Occupational Safety and Health Act (1970)	Require employer to provide a working environment free from hazards to health
Consumer Product Safety Act (1972)	Set standards on selected products, require warning labels, and order product recalls
Equal Employment Opportunity Act (1972)	Forbid discrimination in all areas of employer-employee relations
Magnuson-Moss Act (1975)	Require accuracy in product warranties

Gross National Product

Gross national product (GNP) refers to the value of a nation's annual total production of goods and services and serves as a major indicator of economic growth. Moderate, consistent growth in GNP generally produces a healthy economy in which businesses find increasing demand for their outputs because of rising consumer expenditures. Opportunities abound for both established and new businesses during such prosperous times.

On the other hand, a decline in GNP normally reflects reduced consumer expenditures and lower demand for business outputs. When GNP declines for two consecutive quarters, the national economy is considered to be in a recession. During such times, competitive pressures on businesses increase dramatically; profitability suffers and business failure rates increase. However, even recessions provide opportunities for some firms. Movie theaters are normally strong performers during hard economic times, providing escape from financial worries for their patrons. Likewise, trade school enrollments often increase as unskilled laborers attempt to learn trades to improve their job marketability.

Interest Rates

Short- and long-term interest rates significantly affect the demand for products and services. Low short-term interest rates, for instance, are particularly beneficial for retailers such as Sears and Kmart because such rates encourage consumer spending. For other businesses, such as construction companies and automobile manufacturers, low longer-term rates are especially beneficial because they result in increased spending by consumers for durable goods.

Interest rate levels greatly affect strategic decisions. High rates, for instance, normally dampen business plans to raise funds to expand or to replace aging facilities. Lower rates, by contrast, are more conducive to capital expenditures and to mergers and acquisitions. But some businesses may buck these trends. For example, firms that own apartment buildings usually benefit when long-term interest rates rise, because potential home buyers find that they cannot qualify for mortgage loans and are forced to rent until rates decline significantly.

Inflation Rates

High inflation rates generally result in constraints on business organizations. They boost various costs of doing business such as the purchases of raw materials and parts and the wages and salaries of employees. Consistent increases in inflation rates will constrict the expansion plans of businesses and cause the government to take action that slows the growth of the economy. The combination of government and business restraints can create an economic recession.

Of course, inflation can present opportunities for some firms. For instance, oil companies may benefit during inflationary times if the prices of oil and gas rise faster than the costs of exploration, refining, and transporting. Likewise, companies that mine or sell precious metals benefit since such metals serve as inflation hedges for consumers.

Value of the Dollar

As we have seen, the value of the dollar relative to other major world currencies can be affected by international agreements and the coordinated economic policies of governments. Currency exchange rates, however, can also be affected by international economic conditions. When economic conditions boost the value of the dollar, U.S. firms find themselves at a competitive disadvantage internationally. Foreign customers are less inclined to buy American-made goods because they are too expensive relative to goods produced in their own home markets. Likewise, U.S. consumers find that their strong dollars can be stretched by buying foreign-made products, which are less expensive than goods produced domestically.

For example, in 1990, Caterpillar was in the midst of a major cost-cutting program designed to maintain its position as the world leader in heavy machinery. Yet even as it reduced its cost structure, its efforts were being undermined by the rise in the value of the dollar vis-à-vis the Japanese yen. In a sixteen-month period alone, the dollar climbed 30 percent against the yen. The resultant difference in exchange rates gave Caterpillar's chief Japanese competitor, Komatsu, such a substantial price advantage in the U.S. market that it completely negated Caterpillar's extensive cost-cutting program.[1]

The dollar's value affects the strategic decisions of managers. When it is strong, American manufacturers tend to locate more of their plants abroad, make purchases from foreign sources, and enter into joint ventures with firms in other countries. However, when the dollar is relatively weak, less financial incentive exists for American companies to purchase from foreign sources or build new plants overseas.

■ Technological Forces

Technological forces include scientific improvements and innovations that provide opportunities and constraints or threats for businesses. The rate of technological change varies considerably from one industry to another. In electronics, for example, change is rapid and constant; but in furniture manufacturing, change is slower and more gradual.

Changes in technology can affect a firm's operations as well as its products and services. Recent technological advances in computers, robotics, lasers, satellite networks, fiber optics, and other related areas have provided significant opportunities for operational improvements. Manufacturers, banks, and retailers, for example, have used advances in computer technology to perform their traditional tasks at lower costs and higher levels of customer satisfaction.

From another perspective, however, technological change can decimate existing businesses and even entire industries, since it shifts demand from one product to another. Examples of such change include the shifts from vacuum tubes to transistors, from steam locomotives to diesel and electric engines, from fountain pens to ballpoints, from propeller airplanes to jets, and from mechanical typewriters to electronic ones and then to computer-based word processors.

Interestingly enough, these new technologies are often invented outside of the traditional industries that they eventually affect. In the early 1970s, for example, traditional watchmaking companies failed to monitor and understand the impact of seemingly unrelated developments in the semiconductor industry. Yet these technological advances provided the opportunity to manufacture low-cost but highly accurate digital watches. While such old-line companies as Timex ignored these developments, high-tech firms in Japan and the United States revolutionized the watch industry. Traditional watchmakers missed the substantial profits that were made on the millions of digital watches sold during the latter half of the 1970s.

■ Social Forces

Social forces include traditions, values, societal trends, consumer psychology, and a society's expectations of business. Traditions, for instance, define societal practices that have lasted for decades or even centuries. For example, the celebration of Christmas in many countries in the Western Hemisphere provides significant financial opportunities for card companies, toy retailers, turkey processors, tree growers, mail-order catalog firms, and other related businesses.

Values refer to concepts that are held in high esteem by a society. In the United States, for example, major values include individual freedom and equality of opportunity. In a business sense, these values translate into an emphasis on entrepreneurship and the belief that one's success is only limited by one's ambition, energy, and ability. These values, over the past century, have attracted millions of immigrants to the United States in search of economic and political freedom. And these values are consistent with the trend toward business deregulation discussed earlier. We can expect, therefore, to find a more vibrant and dynamic business environment in the United States than in countries that place less value on the freedom of the individual and equality of opportunity.

Societal trends present various opportunities and threats or constraints to businesses. For example, the health-and-fitness trend that began several years ago has led to financial success for such companies as Nike (sport shoes) and Nautilus (exercise equipment) and the makers of diet soft drinks, light beer, and bottled water. This trend, however, has financially harmed businesses in other industries such as cattle raising, meat and dairy processing, tobacco, and liquor.

For example, over the past ten years, the consumption of beer and hard liquor by the 18-to-34-year-old segment of the U.S. population fell significantly. This trend is of considerable concern to brewers and distillers because that age group comprises 40 percent of the U.S. population and has traditionally accounted for 50 percent of the beer consumption. The reasons include not only the health-and-fitness trend but also a growing nationwide revulsion toward drunk driving, the increased legal liability of hosts who serve alcohol to their guests, and a general increase in "sin taxes" (i.e., taxes on alcohol and tobacco products) at the federal and state levels. As a result, many alcohol makers are diversifying into nonalcoholic drinks.[2]

Societal trends also include demographic changes. Fast-food chains, for instance, are currently wrestling with a pressing problem. Teenagers, who comprise 85 percent of the fast-food work force, are declining in number by 5 million between 1981 and 1995, while the number of preteen children (primary customers for fast food) is increasing by 4 million. The result is more customers for fast-food restaurants with fewer people to serve them. These pressures are resulting in increased hiring of the elderly, attempts to reduce turnover among teenage employees, and improvements in productivity.[3]

Demographic trends can dramatically affect business opportunities. The baby boom, which lasted from 1945 through the mid-1960s, initially provided opportunities for such businesses as clothing and baby apparel manufacturers, private schools, record companies, candy and snack makers, and so on. Later, as the baby boomers entered the job market, businesses were blessed with a tremendous pool of job applicants. As they continue to age, the baby boomers will spend vast sums of money for health care needs, leisure activities, and vacation alternatives.

Consumer psychology also presents its own opportunities and constraints. For instance, the attempt by Coca-Cola in the mid-1980s to change the taste of its flagship soft drink was thwarted when consumers refused to switch to the new taste. The soft-drink giant was forced to bring back its traditional drink and rename it "Classic Coke." In this area, it is consumer perceptions that count, not reality. When red dye #2, for example, was found to be dangerous for human consumption, Mars eliminated the red M&M candies from its packages for several years, even though the dye used by Mars was not the dangerous red dye #2.

Finally, a society's expectations of business present other opportunities and constraints. These expectations emanate from diverse groups referred to as **stakeholders.** These groups affect and, in turn, are affected by the activities of companies. Stakeholders include a firm's owners (stockholders), members of the board of directors, managers and operating employees, suppliers, creditors, distributors, customers, and other interest groups.

Capitalizing on Technological and Social Forces at Knight-Ridder

Environmental analysis helps a company take advantage of changing technological and social forces. One such example is Miami-based Knight-Ridder, a firm that has achieved annual sales of $2.3 billion in the information industry.

Founded in 1903, Knight-Ridder was originally a newspaper company. Its first major newspapers were the *Miami Herald* and *Akron Beacon Journal*. Since that time, it has purchased numerous newspapers and today owns such well-known publications as the *Detroit Free Press, Philadelphia Inquirer,* and *San Jose Mercury News.* Its newspaper business, which includes a news syndication service, a newsprint mill, and newspaper printing plants in twenty-nine cities, provides 88 percent of its sales revenue.

Increasingly, however, Knight-Ridder is taking advantage of technological innovations to expand its information network. Along with its television and radio stations, the company owns an on-line newswire service for financial markets, a cable/pay television channel, and an electronic information retrieval service. Its various information services reach more than 100 million people in 129 countries.

The company has also been cognizant of changing social forces. According to its CEO, James Batten, the firm successfully capitalized upon an opportunity provided by demographic changes in Miami several years ago. Observing that the Miami area was becoming home to over two hundred fifty thousand residents of Cuban origin, management believed that the time was right to introduce a Spanish-language daily newspaper. The paper, *El Nuevo Herald,* became an instant success and is now the largest of its kind in the United States.

At the broadest level, stakeholders include the general public. Increasingly, in recent decades, the general public has expected socially responsible behavior from business firms. Although social responsibility will be discussed in the following chapter, consider just one element of social responsibility—pollution. The public's concern about pollution has resulted in various forms of legislation that have constrained the operations of firms in such industries as automobiles, energy, and mining. On the other hand, this legislation has provided an opportunity for firms such as Waste Management to sell its services in reducing pollution.

In a more limited sense, stakeholder groups may hold conflicting expectations of business performance. For example, stockholders and unionized employees may have financial goals that clash. Chapter 3 will elaborate further on this topic.

■ Environmental Scanning

The preceding sections were able to examine only a few of the important macroenvironmental forces that affect organizations. Examples of other significant forces are identified in Table 2.2.

How do managers recognize the various opportunities or constraints and threats that arise from changes in the political-legal, economic, technological, and social arenas? They engage in **environmental scanning**—the gathering and

Examples of Additional Macroenvironmental Forces   Table 2.2

Political-Legal Forces	Social Forces	Economic Forces	Technological Forces
Tax laws	Attitudes toward product innovations, lifestyles, careers, and consumer activism	Money supply	Expenditures on research and development (government and industry)
International trade regulations		Monetary policy	
Consumer lending regulations	Concern with quality of life	Unemployment rate	Focus of R&D expenditures
Environmental protection laws	Expectations from the workplace	Energy costs	Rate of new-product introductions
Enforcement of antitrust regulations	Shifts in the presence of women in the work force	Disposable personal income	Automation
Laws on hiring, firing, promotion, and pay		Stage of economic cycle	Robotics
Wage/price controls	Birth rates		
	Population shifts		
	Life expectancies		

analysis of information about relevant environmental trends. Evidence indicates that environmental analysis that leads to appropriate strategic management decisions contributes to organizational success.

For instance, one study of sixty-eight major corporations that had experienced four years of decline concluded that an inadequate response to environmental change contributed to their downhill slide.[4] Another study compared firms that ranked in the top quarter of the food-processing industry with those in the bottom quarter and found that the annual reports of the more successful companies were replete with environmental analysis. Those of the less successful firms reported little, if any, evidence of environmental-scanning activities.[5]

Responses to a survey of Fortune 500 firms that were asked to identify the major payoffs of their environmental-scanning activities included an increased general awareness of environmental changes, better strategic planning and decision making, greater effectiveness in governmental matters, better industry and market analysis, and sound diversification and resource allocation decisions. However, the respondents also indicated that the results of their environmental analyses were often too general or uncertain for specific interpretation.[6]

Although macroenvironmental forces influence the operations of all firms in a general fashion, a more specific set of forces within an industry directly and powerfully affects the strategic-planning activities of the firms within that industry. Figure 2.2 presents a diagrammatic representation of the impact of macroenvironmental and industry forces. These industry forces are discussed in the following section.

ANALYSIS OF THE INDUSTRY

Professor Michael E. Porter of Harvard University is the nation's leading authority on industry analysis, and the following overview of industry forces is based on his work.[7] Porter contends that an industry's profit potential (i.e., the

Figure 2.2   **Macroenvironmental and Industry Forces That Present Opportunities and Threats to Firms**

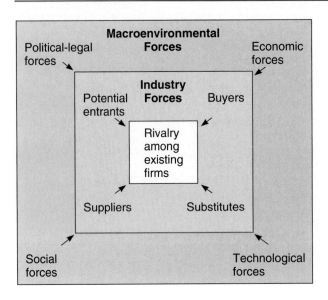

long-run return on invested capital) depends on five basic competitive forces within the industry:

1. The threat of new competitors entering the industry.
2. The intensity of rivalry among existing competitors.
3. The threat of substitute products or services.
4. The bargaining power of buyers.
5. The bargaining power of suppliers.

These forces can be quite intense in industries such as tires or steel, where returns are generally low, but may be relatively mild in such industries as cosmetics and toiletries, where returns are often high.

The key to competing effectively is for the company to find a position in the industry where it can influence these five forces in its favor or can effectively defend itself against them. Such a strategy requires an understanding of these competitive forces, which are described in the following sections.

■ Threat of Entry

As new competitors enter an industry, the industry's productive capacity expands. Unless the market is growing rapidly, a new entry intensifies the fight for market share, thereby bidding prices down and lowering industry profitability. The likelihood that new firms will enter an industry rests on two factors: barriers to entry and the expected retaliation from existing competitors. Each factor is discussed in the sections that follow.

Barriers to Entry

High barriers and/or expectations of sharp retaliation reduce the threat of entry. There are seven major **barriers to entry,** that is, obstacles to entering an industry. Each barrier is described below.

Economies of Scale.   **Economies of scale** refer to the decline in unit costs of a product or service (or an operation, or a function that goes into producing a product or service) that occurs as the absolute volume of production per period of time increases. Substantial economies of scale deter new entrants by forcing them either to come in at a large scale, thereby risking a strong reaction from existing firms, or to come in at a small scale, with its accompanying cost disadvantages. For example, Xerox and General Electric failed in their attempts to enter the mainframe computer industry some years back, probably because of scale economies in production, research, marketing, and service.

Product Differentiation.   Established firms may enjoy strong brand identification and customer loyalties that are based on actual or perceived product differences, customer service, or advertising. New entrants must spend a great deal of money and time to overcome this barrier. Product differentiation is particularly important in baby care products, over-the-counter drugs, cosmetics, and public accounting. Large brewers, such as Anheuser-Busch, have gone even further by coupling their product differentiation with economies of scale in production, marketing, and distribution.

Capital Requirements.   The need to invest large financial resources to compete creates a third type of entry barrier. Large amounts of capital may be necessary for production facility construction, research and development, advertising, customer credit, and inventories. Some years ago, Xerox cleverly created a capital barrier by renting its copiers rather than only selling them. This move increased the capital needs for new entrants.

Switching Costs.   **Switching costs** refer to the one-time costs that buyers of the industry's outputs incur if they switch from one company's products to another's. Changing from an established supplier to a new supplier may require the buyer to retrain employees, purchase new ancillary equipment, and/or hire technical help. Most customers are reluctant to switch unless the new supplier offers a major improvement in cost or performance. For example, nurses in hospitals may resist buying from a new supplier of intravenous (IV) solutions and kits since the procedures for attaching solutions to patients and the hardware for hanging the IV bottles differ from one supplier to another.

Access to Distribution Channels.   To enter the distribution channels already being used by established firms, a new firm must often entice distributors through price breaks, cooperative advertising allowances, or sales promotions. Each of these, of course, reduces profits. Existing competitors often have distribution channel ties based on long-standing, or even exclusive, relationships, meaning that the new entrant must create a new channel of distribution. Timex was forced to do exactly that decades ago to circumvent the channels dominated by the Swiss watchmakers.

STRATEGIC INSIGHT

Enormous Barriers to Entry in the Airline Industry

One of the major purposes of deregulating the airline industry in 1978 was to encourage new start-up ventures, thereby increasing the amount of competition in the industry. For a while, it worked; new companies such as Southwest Airlines, Midway Airlines, and People Express helped to lower ticket prices significantly.

But over time, the major airlines have succeeded in erecting enormous barriers to entry. Consider the following obstacles:

• Major carriers hold twenty- to forty-year leases on almost all of the passenger-loading gates at big airports.

• They have 95 percent of the landing rights (i.e., permission to take off and land in certain time slots) at four key airports.

• They own the computer reservation systems, pay travel agents extra commissions for bringing business to them, and charge small carriers hefty fees for tickets sold through those systems.

• They operate frequent-flier programs that are far too costly for a new airline to offer and that encourage passengers to avoid switching airlines.

• Their computer-pricing systems enable them to selectively offer low fares on certain seats and to certain destinations, thereby wiping out a start-up airline's pricing edge.

• Most have a large number of U.S. hub airports, a feeder system to those hubs, and international routes that tie into the hubs. Such systems take decades and hundreds of millions of dollars to acquire.

• The purchase of used airliners, a traditional means of entering the industry, has been partially closed owing to new, more stringent noise control requirements. The major airlines already have a significant number of new aircraft—either in their fleet or on order—that meet those requirements.

As a result of these obstacles, less than fifteen years after deregulation, the airline industry's best routes and markets were concentrated in the hands of a few huge carriers.

SOURCES: M. M. Hamilton, "Airline Industry Faces Major Shakeout," *The Washington Post,* 25 October 1990; R. L. Rose and J. Dahl, "Skies Are Deregulated, But Just Try Starting a Sizable New Airline," *The Wall Street Journal,* 19 July 1989.

Cost Disadvantages Independent of Scale.   Established firms may possess cost advantages that cannot be replicated by new entrants regardless of their size or economies of scale. These advantages include proprietary product technology (e.g., Polaroid's monopoly on instant photography), favorable access to raw materials (e.g., Texas Gulf Sulphur's control of large salt dome sulphur deposits), favorable locations (e.g., McDonald's locations at interstate highway exits), and the learning or experience curve (i.e., the tendency for unit costs to decline as a firm gains experience producing a product or service; an example is Federal Express's efficient operations or Toyota's production process).

Government Policy.   Governments can control entry to certain industries with licensing requirements or other regulations. For instance, entry into the taxicab business in most large cities is controlled by licensing, and entry into the liquor retail business is heavily regulated by states. Even pollution control requirements can serve as an entry barrier because of the need for a certain level of technological sophistication and cost.

Expected Retaliation

Entry may well be deterred if the potential entering firm expects existing competitors to respond forcefully. These expectations are reasonable if the industry has a history of vigorous retaliation to new entrants or if the industry is growing slowly. Retaliation may also be expected if the established firms are committed to the industry and have specialized fixed assets that are not transferable to other industries, or if the firms have sufficient cash and productive capacity to meet customer needs in the future.

■ Intensity of Rivalry Among Existing Competitors

Competition intensifies when one—or more—of the firms in an industry sees the opportunity to improve its position or feels competitive pressure from others. It manifests itself in the form of price cutting, advertising battles, new-product introductions or modifications, and increased customer service or warranties. The intensity of competition depends on a number of interacting factors, which are discussed in the sections below.

Numerous or Equally Balanced Competitors

One factor is how many companies are in the industry and how equally balanced they are in terms of size and power. Industries that are dominated by one or a few firms are less competitive, because the dominant firm often acts as the price leader. But industries that contain only a few firms that are roughly equivalent in size and power are more likely to be highly competitive, since each firm will fight for dominance. Competition is also likely to be intense in industries with large numbers of firms, since some of those companies believe that they can make competitive moves without being noticed.

Slow Industry Growth

Firms in industries that grow slowly are more likely to be highly competitive than companies in fast-growing industries. In slow-growth industries, one firm's increase in market share must come at the expense of other firms' shares.

High Fixed or Storage Costs

Companies with high fixed costs are under pressure to operate at near-capacity levels to spread their overhead expenses over more units of production. This pressure often leads to price cutting, thereby intensifying competition. The U.S. airline industry has experienced this problem over the past several years. The same is true of firms that have high storage costs. For that reason, profits tend to be low in industries such as lobster fishing and hazardous-chemical manufacturing.

Lack of Differentiation or Switching Costs

When products are differentiated, competition is less intense because buyers have preferences and loyalties to particular sellers. Switching costs have the

Two Equally Balanced Competitors: PepsiCo and Coca-Cola

Consolidated industries that contain only a few companies can be highly competitive. One of the best examples is the soft-drink industry, where Coca-Cola and PepsiCo have been fighting for dominance for many years. Although most consumers probably consider these two fierce competitors to be similar types of firms, they are actually quite different.

PepsiCo, for instance, is considerably larger than Coca-Cola. The Purchase, New York, corporation's $17.8 billion in sales (placing it 23rd on the 1990 Fortune 500) and 266,000 employees considerably overshadow Atlanta-based Coca-Cola's $10.4 billion in sales (47th on the 1990 Fortune 500) and 21,000 employees. A second distinction is that most of Coca-Cola's sales come from the soft-drink market, but PepsiCo is more diversified. Over the past twenty years, Coca-Cola made several attempts at diversification (e.g., motion pictures, coffee, tea, and wine), but none was particularly successful. PepsiCo, on the other hand, consists of three major product divisions: soft drinks, snack foods (e.g., Frito-Lay), and fast-food restaurants (Pizza Hut, KFC, and Taco Bell).

Analysts consider both firms to be extremely well managed. For example, PepsiCo was ranked fifth on Fortune's 1990 "Most Admired Corpora-

tions" list, with Coca-Cola following closely in sixth place.

The battle arena for the two firms is the soft-drink market. Most of their competition has taken the form of advertising, customer service through attempts to maximize shelf space in retail outlets, and new-product introductions. Although the two are fairly evenly matched in the U.S. market (i.e., Coke has a small lead in grocery shelf sales and a larger one in fast-food and fountain sales), Coca-Cola clearly dominates markets outside the United States by a four-to-one margin, accounting for 47 percent of the world's soda sales.

Their competitive moves occasionally backfire. Virtually everyone is familiar with Coca-Cola's debacle in attempting to replace its original formula with New Coke. PepsiCo, too, has experienced misfortune. When it purchased Pizza Hut, Kentucky Fried Chicken (now KFC), and Taco Bell, it prohibited these restaurants from serving Coke, Sprite, or any of the other Coca-Cola products. Although this move increased its soft-drink sales substantially, one of PepsiCo's largest customers, Burger King, switched from selling PepsiCo's products to Coca-Cola's soft drinks because it did not want to enrich the owner of three of its major competitors.

SOURCES: *Moody's Handbook of Common Stocks* (New York: Moody's Investors Service, Spring 1991); "The Fortune 500 Largest U.S. Industrial Corporations," *Fortune,* 22 April 1991, p. 286; A. L. Sprout, "America's Most Admired Corporations," *Fortune,* 11 February 1991, p. 53; W. Konrad, "The Real Thing Is Getting Real Aggressive," *Business Week,* 26 November 1990, pp. 94–104; "The 'Stateless' World of Manufacturing," *Business Week,* 14 May 1990, p. 103; M. J. McCarthy, "As a Global Marketer, Coke Excels by Being Tough and Consistent," *The Wall Street Journal,* 19 December 1989.

same effect. But when products or services are less differentiated, purchase decisions are based on price and service considerations, resulting in greater competition.

Capacity Augmented in Large Increments

If economies of scale dictate that productive capacity must be added only in large increments, then capacity additions will lead to temporary overcapacity in the industry and resultant price cutting. This problem characterizes the manufacture of chlorine, vinyl chloride, and ammonium fertilizer.

Diverse Competitors

Companies that are diverse in their origins, cultures, and strategies will often have differing goals and differing ways of competing. These differences mean that competitors will have a difficult time agreeing on a set of "rules for the game." Industries with foreign competitors and industries with entrepreneurial owner-operators may, therefore, be particularly competitive.

High Strategic Stakes

Rivalry will be quite volatile if firms have high stakes in achieving success in a particular industry. For instance, Sony or Toyota may have perceived a strong need to establish a solid position in the U.S. market to enhance its global prestige or technological credibility. These desires can even involve the willingness to sacrifice profitability.

High Exit Barriers

Exit barriers can be economic, strategic, or emotional factors that keep companies from leaving an industry even though they are earning a low—or possibly negative—return on their investment. Examples of exit barriers are fixed assets that have no alternative uses, labor agreements, strategic interrelationships between that business unit and other business units within the same company, management's unwillingness to leave an industry because of pride, and governmental pressure to continue operations to avoid adverse economic effects in a geographic region.

■ Pressure from Substitute Products

Firms in one industry may be competing with firms in other industries that produce **substitute products,** which are alternative products that satisfy similar consumer needs but differ in specific characteristics. Substitutes place a ceiling on the prices that firms can charge. For instance, the producers of fiberglass insulation were unable to raise their prices despite unprecedented demand during a severe winter because of the availability of insulation substitutes such as cellulose, rock wool, and Styrofoam. In contrast, firms that produce products that have no substitutes are likely to be highly profitable.

■ Bargaining Power of Buyers

The buyers of an industry's outputs can lower that industry's profitability by bargaining for higher quality or more services and playing one firm against another. Buyers are powerful under the following circumstances:

• Buyers are concentrated or purchase large volumes relative to total industry sales. If a few buyers purchase a substantial proportion of an industry's sales, then they will wield considerable power over prices.

• The products that the buyers purchase represent a significant percentage of the buyers' costs. If the products account for a large portion of the buyers' costs, then price is an important issue for the buyers. Hence, they will shop for a favorable price and will purchase selectively.

STRATEGIC INSIGHT

Wal-Mart's Buyer Power

Different buyers possess varying degrees of leverage that they use to bargain with suppliers. For instance, large automobile dealers and national car rental companies normally have strong bargaining power (compared with smaller buyers) with the carmakers. Similarly, McDonald's and Burger King are powerful bargainers with the soft-drink producers.

As an extreme example of buyer power, consider Wal-Mart, America's largest retailer. Founded by Sam Walton in 1969 in Bentonville, Arkansas, this firm expanded by exploiting a marketing niche: southern towns that were too small to attract a major discount department store. By 1991, Wal-Mart had 1600 stores with sales of over $32 billion. Its growth was so extraordinary that on the last day of its 1990 fiscal year, Wal-Mart opened 36 stores simultaneously. By 1991, Wal-Marts were beginning to appear in major cities, going head to head with competitors such as Kmart and Target. Few, if any, analysts believed that Wal-Mart was likely to lose that competition.

Wal-Mart's particular strength is its strong sales per square foot. While a typical Kmart generates sales of about $150 per square foot, the average Wal-Mart generates $250 per square foot. Higher sales per square foot cause operating costs, as a percentage of sales, to decline. This decline allows the store to lower its prices, which, in turn, increases sales even more, and the cycle repeats itself. As Wal-Mart pulls customers from its competitors' stores, the competitors find their sales per square foot declining, meaning that operating costs as a percentage of sales rise, thereby shrinking the store's profit margin.

The resultant power that Wal-Mart gains from its huge annual sales increases gives it a considerable advantage in dealing with suppliers. In some cases, Wal-Mart buys all of a supplier's annual production, giving it almost total control over the suppliers' prices and delivery schedules. For instance, Wal-Mart purchases all of the television sets made by the Sanyo plant in Arkansas. In other cases, Wal-Mart has literally purchased its supplier. For example, the retailer bought McLane Company in 1990. McLane is a $2.9 billion specialty distributor of cigarettes, candy, and perishable goods. In still other cases, Wal-Mart works with suppliers to help them lower their distribution costs through computer-to-computer ordering. Finally, it requires some suppliers to be responsible for storing, delivering, and setting up the inventory for a specified amount of space in the store. Few suppliers, of course, are likely to balk at Wal-Mart's requirements.

SOURCES: B. Saporito, "Is Wal-Mart Unstoppable?" *Fortune,* 6 May 1991, pp. 50–59; *Moody's Industrial Manual,* Vol. 2 (New York: Moody's Investors Service, 1990); S. Caminiti, "The New Champs of Retailing," *Fortune,* 24 September 1990, p. 85.

• The products that the buyers purchase are standard or undifferentiated. In such cases, buyers are prone to play one seller against another.

• The buyers face few switching costs. Switching costs, of course, lock buyers to particular sellers.

• The buyers earn low profits. Low profits create pressure for the buyers to reduce their purchasing costs.

• Buyers can engage in **backward integration** (i.e., become their own suppliers). General Motors and Ford, for example, use the threat of self-manufacture as a powerful bargaining lever.

• The industry's product is relatively unimportant to the quality of the buyers' products or services. When the quality of the buyers' products is greatly affected by what they purchase from the industry, the buyers are less likely to have significant power over the suppliers.

• The buyer has full information. The more information the buyer has regarding demand, actual market prices, and supplier costs, the greater the bargaining power of the buyer is.

■ Bargaining Power of Suppliers

Suppliers can squeeze the profitability out of an industry that is unable to recover cost increases in its own prices. The conditions that make suppliers powerful basically mirror those that make buyers powerful. Hence, suppliers are powerful under the following circumstances:

• The supplying industry is dominated by a few companies and is more concentrated than the industry to which it sells. Selling to fragmented buyers means that concentrated suppliers will be able to exert considerable control over prices, quality, and selling terms.

• There are no substitute products. If buyers have no alternative sources of supply, then they are weak in relation to the suppliers that exist.

• The buying industry is not an important customer of the suppliers. If a particular industry does not represent a significant percentage of the suppliers' sales, then the suppliers have considerable power. If the industry is an important customer, however, suppliers' fortunes will be closely tied to that industry and they will find that reasonable pricing and assistance in such areas as research and development are in their best interests.

• The suppliers' product is an important input of the buyers' business. If the product is a key element in the buyers' manufacturing process or product quality, the suppliers possess significant power.

• The suppliers' products are differentiated or they have built-in switching costs. Product differentiation or switching costs reduce the buyers' ability to play one supplier against another.

• The suppliers pose a credible threat of **forward integration** (i.e., can become their own customers). If suppliers have the ability and resources to operate their own manufacturing facilities, distribution channels, or retail outlets, they will possess considerable power over buyers.

We can see, then, that—at one extreme—a company could operate quite profitably in an industry with high entry barriers, low intensity of competition among member firms, no substitute products, weak buyers, and weak suppliers. On the other hand, a company doing business in an industry with low entry barriers, intense competition, many substitute products, and strong buyers and/or suppliers would be hard-pressed to generate an adequate profit. The key, of course, is for management to scan and understand the industry in which it operates and to position its company as favorably as possible within that industry. In fact, the next few chapters are devoted to an examination of this key issue in strategic management.

FORECASTING THE ENVIRONMENT

Environmental and industry scanning and analyses are only marginally useful if all they do is reveal current conditions. To be truly meaningful, such analyses must forecast future trends and changes. Although no form of forecasting is foolproof, several techniques can be helpful: time series analysis, judgmental forecasting, multiple scenarios, and the Delphi technique. Each method is described in the following sections.

■ Time Series Analysis

Time series analysis attempts to examine the effects of selected trends (such as population growth, technological innovations, changes in disposable personal income, or number of suppliers) on such variables as a firm's costs, sales, profitability, and market share over a number of years. This methodology also enables management to relate such factors as seasonal fluctuations, weather conditions, and holidays to the firm's performance. Likewise, time series analysis can reveal the effect of economic cycles on the organization's sales and profits. The purpose is to make a prediction about these variables in the future.

Because time series analysis projects historical trends into the future, its validity depends upon the similarity between past trends and future conditions. Any significant departure from historical trends will weaken the forecast dramatically. Unfortunately, departures from historical trends seem to be occurring with increasing frequency.

A second potential weakness in time series analysis is that it provides quantitative answers. Managers must take care that they do not place too much confidence in these results. The use of numbers and equations often gives a misleading appearance of scientific accuracy.

■ Judgmental Forecasting

When the relationships between variables are less clear than they are in time series analysis or when they cannot be adequately quantified, judgmental forecasting may be used. In **judgmental forecasting,** an organization may use its own employees, customers, suppliers, or trade association as sources of qualitative information about future trends. For instance, sales representatives may be asked to forecast sales growth in various product categories from their knowledge of customers' expansion plans. Survey instruments may be mailed to customers, suppliers, or trade associations to obtain their judgments on specific trends.

For example, Allied Corporate Investments, a Los Angeles broker for buyers and sellers of businesses, originally specialized in relatively low-priced small businesses. In 1980, however, it conducted a judgmental forecast, asking its research staff, sales force, and outsiders (such as banks, customers, and the Chamber of Commerce) to forecast what business opportunities might be available in the future. The consensus of the forecast was that the Los Angeles economy would expand and the value of businesses would be substantially bid up. In response, Allied opened several more offices, contacted commercial sections of foreign embassies to inform them of business opportunities, and brokered more expensive businesses. As a result of its judgmental forecast, its volume of business has increased by ten times.

■ **Multiple Scenarios**

The increasing unpredictability of environmental change makes it incredibly difficult to formulate dependable assumptions upon which forecasts can be based. One means of circumventing this troublesome state is to develop multiple scenarios about the future. In **multiple scenarios,** the manager formulates several alternative descriptions of future events and trends.[8]

One scenario, for example, may specify the economic conditions thought most likely to occur at some future point. Alternative scenarios may use a more optimistic assumption and a more pessimistic assumption. The same process can just as easily be used to express differing assumptions about technology, political elections, environmental regulation, oil prices, strikes, and other events. Three scenarios will be sufficient in most cases.[9]

In formulating scenarios, strategic managers must identify the key forces in the macroenvironment and industry, assess their likely interrelationships, and estimate their influence upon future events. Contingency plans can then be prepared to cover the various conditions specified in the multiple scenarios. These plans may be general statements of action to be taken, without completely specifying the intended operational details. Contingency plans usually specify trigger points—events that call for implementing particular aspects of a plan.[10]

■ **Delphi Technique**

In certain cases, the **Delphi technique**[11] may be used to forecast the future: If the trend to be forecasted lies within a particular field of study, then experts in that field can be identified and questioned about the probability of the trend's occurring. For instance, if a home building firm would like to know when it will become feasible to build entire housing developments with solar energy as the sole source of electricity, heating, and cooling, the firm would compile a list of experts in the field of solar energy. Each expert would then be mailed a questionnaire asking for his or her judgments as to when knowledge of solar energy will be sufficiently advanced to rely solely on it for home energy needs. The respondents will fill out the questionnaires, without communicating with each other, and return them to the home building company.

The company will compile the results and send a summary of the results to each respondent along with a second questionnaire. After reviewing the summary and observing the other experts' judgments, each respondent will then fill out and mail in the second questionnaire. Some respondents may alter their judgments on this questionnaire as a result of reviewing the judgments of the other members. This process of responding–receiving–feedback–responding continues until consensus is reached. The home builder will then rely, at least partially, on this consensus in formulating the firm's plans for the future.

In the previous paragraphs, several forecasting techniques were presented. Examples of others are shown in Table 2.3.

SUMMARY

Each organization exists within a complex network of environmental forces comprised of (1) the national and global macroenvironment and (2) the industry in which the organization competes. Because these forces are dynamic, their

Table 2.3   **Other Forecasting Techniques**

Technique	Description	Weakness
Econometric forecast	Simultaneous multiple regression systems	Assumes past relationships will continue into the future
Sales force forecast (judgmental)	Aggregate sales force estimate	Potential bias in opinions
Managerial forecast (judgmental)	Aggregation of estimates made by R&D, production, finance, and marketing managers	Potential bias in opinions
Consumer survey (judgmental)	Aggregate preferences of consumers	Potential bias in opinions
Brainstorming (judgmental)	Idea generation in supportive group interaction	Potential bias in opinions

constant change presents numerous opportunities and threats or constraints to strategic managers.

Four macroenvironmental forces affect business strategy. Political-legal forces, in the broadest sense, include a government's basic stance toward business operations and, more narrowly, the outcomes of elections, legislation, and court judgments, as well as the decisions of various commissions and agencies at all levels of government. Economic forces comprise elements such as the impact of growth or decline in gross national product and increases or decreases in interest rates, inflation, and the value of the dollar. Technological forces include scientific improvements and innovations that affect a firm's operations and/or its products and services. Social forces include traditions, values, societal trends, consumer psychology, and a society's expectations of business. To identify and understand changes and trends in these forces, managers engage in environmental scanning.

A more specific set of forces within a firm's industry directly and powerfully affects management's strategic planning. Professor Michael Porter of Harvard University has identified five basic competitive industry forces: the threat of new entrants in the industry, the intensity of rivalry among existing competitors in the industry, the pressure from producers of substitute products or services, the bargaining power of buyers of the industry's outputs, and the bargaining power of suppliers to the industry's companies. The goal of a competitive strategy for a firm is to find a position in the industry where it can best defend itself against these competitive forces or can influence them in its favor.

Strategic planners must not only understand the current state of the macroenvironment and their industry but also be able to forecast its future states. Although forecasting is an inexact science, four techniques can be particularly helpful: time series analysis, judgmental forecasting, multiple scenarios, and the Delphi technique.

KEY CONCEPTS

Backward integration   A process in which a firm becomes its own supplier by acquiring a current supplier or creating a new company to produce its supplies.

Barriers to entry   Obstacles to entering an industry. The major barriers to entry are economies of scale, product differentiation, capital requirements, switching costs, access to distribution channels, cost disadvantages independent of scale, and government policy.

Delphi technique   A forecasting procedure in which experts in the appropriate field of study are independently questioned about the probability of some event's occurrence. The responses of all the experts are compiled, and a summary is sent to each expert, who, on the basis of this new information, responds again. Those responses are then compiled and a summary is again sent to each expert, with the cycle continuing until consensus is reached regarding the particular forecasted event.

Economies of scale   The decline in unit costs of a product, an operation, or a function that goes into producing a product, which occurs as the absolute volume of production per period of time increases.

Environmental scanning   The gathering and analysis of information about relevant environmental trends.

Exit barriers   Obstacles to leaving an industry. Exit barriers can be economic, strategic, or emotional.

Forward integration   A process in which a firm becomes its own customer by acquiring a current customer or creating a new company to purchase its outputs.

Industry   A group of companies that produces products or services that are in competition.

Judgmental forecasting   A forecasting procedure in which employees, customers, suppliers, and/or trade associations serve as sources of qualitative information regarding future trends.

Macroenvironment   The general environment that affects all business firms. Its principal components are political-legal, economic, technological, and social systems and trends.

Multiple scenarios   A forecasting procedure in which management formulates several plausible hypothetical descriptions of sequences of future events and trends.

Stakeholder   An individual or group who is affected by—or can influence—an organization's operations.

Substitute products   Alternative products that may satisfy similar consumer needs and wants but that differ somewhat in specific characteristics.

Switching costs   One-time costs that buyers of an industry's outputs incur if they switch from one company's products to another's.

Time series analysis   An empirical forecasting procedure in which certain historical trends are used to predict such variables as a firm's sales or market share.

DISCUSSION QUESTIONS

1. Give an example, other than those in the text, of how political-legal forces have presented an opportunity and a constraint to a particular industry or business organization.

2. Explain how changes in the value of the dollar affect the domestic and international sales of U.S.-based companies.

3. Give an example, other than those in the text, of how technological forces have presented an opportunity and a constraint to a particular industry or business organization.

4. Select a specific business organization and identify the stakeholders of that particular firm.

5. Using your university as an example, explain how political-legal, economic, technological, and social forces have affected its operations over the past decade.

6. Identify an industry that has low barriers to entry and one that has high barriers. Explain how these differences in barriers to entry affect the intensity and form of competition in those two industries.

7. Give some specific examples of exit barriers. How do they affect competition in those industries?

8. Aside from the examples given in the text, identify some products whose sales have been adversely affected by substitute products.

9. Identify an industry in which the suppliers have strong bargaining power and another industry where the buyers have most of the bargaining power.

10. What are the strengths and weaknesses of time series analysis as a forecasting technique?

STRATEGIC MANAGEMENT EXERCISES

1. Select a specific company with which you are somewhat familiar. From your recollection of current events (i.e., what you may have read in newspapers or magazines or what you may have heard on television or radio), identify some of the important macroenvironmental opportunities and constraints or threats for this company.

2. From your recollection of current events (i.e., what you may have read in newspapers or magazines or what you may have heard on television or radio), identify and analyze the industry forces for an automobile company of your choice.

3. Select a major company for which there is considerable information available in your university library. Conduct a macroenvironmental

analysis for that company. Your analysis should contain four sections: political-legal forces, economic forces, technological forces, and social forces. (See Appendix 2A for help in locating sources of macroenvironmental information.) Worksheet 1 (below) may help to structure your analysis.

You need not limit yourself to the items listed under "Important Information." In some cases, other items that you discover in your research will be of equal or greater importance.

Once you have identified the important components of each macroenvironmental force, you should determine whether each presents an opportunity or a threat to your company. You might assign a " + " to opportunities and a " − " to threats, or you might list each item under the subheadings "Opportunities" and "Threats." (You can refer to the beginning of the case section, "Strategic Management Case Analysis," for further details.)

4. Conduct an industry analysis for the company that you selected in Exercise 3. Your analysis should contain information in five areas: threat of entry, intensity of rivalry among existing competitors, pressure from substitute products, bargaining power of buyers, and bargaining power of suppliers. (See Appendix 2A for help in locating sources of industry information.) The worksheet on the following page should help you organize your work.

Now, determine whether each component that you have identified constitutes a potential opportunity or threat to your company.

5. Assume that you have been asked to develop an environmental forecast for the bookstore at your university, using the judgmental forecasting technique. Attempt to forecast the environment of the bookstore by writing a summary report based on questions that you ask several employees of the bookstore and several customers of the bookstore. Since you may not have access to suppliers or trade associations, include your own judgment of what opportunities and threats the environment holds for the bookstore.

Macroenvironmental Analysis   **Worksheet 1**

Macroenvironmental Force	Important Information
Political-legal	Outcomes of elections, legislation, court judgments, and decisions rendered by various federal, state, and local agencies
Economic	GNP, short- and long-term interest rates, inflation, and value of the dollar
Technological	Scientific improvements, inventions, and the rate of technological change in the industry
Social	Traditions, values, societal trends, consumer psychology, and the public's expectations of business

Worksheet 2

Industry Analysis

Industry Sector	Important Information
Threat of entry	Extent to which the following factors prevent new companies from entering the industry: economies of scale, product differentiation, capital requirements, switching costs, access to distribution channels, cost disadvantages independent of scale, government policy, and expected retaliation
Intensity of rivalry among existing competitors	Number and relative balance of competitors, rate of industry growth, extent of fixed or storage costs, degree of product differentiation and switching costs, size of capacity augmentation, diversity of competitors, extent of strategic stakes, and height of exit barriers
Pressure from substitute products	Identification of substitute products, and analysis of the relative price and quality of those products
Bargaining power of buyers	Concentration of buyers, their purchase volume relative to industry sales and to the buyer's costs, product differentiation, buyers' switching costs, buyers' profits, possibility of buyers integrating backward, importance of the product to the quality of the buyer's product, and amount of information possessed by the buyer
Bargaining power of suppliers	Number and concentration of suppliers, availability of substitute products, importance of the buying industry to the suppliers, importance of the suppliers' product to the buyer's business, differentiation and switching costs associated with the suppliers' product, and possibility of suppliers integrating forward

REFERENCES

1. R. L. Rose, "Caterpillar Sees Gains in Efficiency Imperiled by Strength of Dollar," *The Wall Street Journal*, 6 April 1990.

2. T. Y. Wiltz, "It's Enough to Drive the Distillers to Drink," *Business Week*, 25 June 1990, pp. 98–99; M. Charlier, "Youthful Sobriety Tests Liquor Firms," *The Wall Street Journal*, 14 June 1990.

3. A. Miller, "Burgers: The Heat Is On," *Newsweek*, 16 June 1986, p. 53.

4. D. Schendel, G. R. Patton, and J. Riggs, "Corporate Turnaround Strategies: A Study of Profit Decline and Recovery," *Journal of General Management* 3 (Spring 1976): 10–11.

5. E. H. Bowman, "Strategy and the Weather," *Sloan Management Review* 17 (Winter 1976): 56.

6. J. Diffenbach, "Corporate Environmental Analysis in Large U.S. Corporations," *Long Range Planning* 16, no. 3 (June 1983): 109, 112–113.

7. M. E. Porter, *Competitive Strategy* (New York: Free Press, 1980), pp. 3–4, 7–14, 17–21, 23–28. Reprinted with permission of The Free Press, a Division of Macmillan, Inc., from *Competitive Strategy: Techniques for Analyzing Industries and Competitors*, by Michael E. Porter. Copyright © 1980 by The Free Press.

8. L. Fahey and V. K. Narayanan, *Macroenvironmental Analysis for Strategic Management* (St. Paul, Minn.: West, 1986), p. 215.

9. R. D. Zentner, "Scenarios in Forecasting," in J. K. Ryans, Jr., and W. L. Shanklin, *Strategic Planning: Concepts and Implementation* (New York: Random House Business Division, 1985), p. 44.

10. C. D. Pringle, D. F. Jennings, and J. G. Longenecker, *Managing Organizations: Functions and Behaviors* (Columbus, Ohio: Merrill, 1988), p. 114.

11. N.C. Dalkey, *The Delphi Method: An Experimental Study of Group Opinion* (Santa Monica, Calif.: Rand Corporation, 1969).

APPENDIX 2A: SOURCES OF ENVIRONMENTAL AND INDUSTRY INFORMATION

■ ──────────────────────────────── ■

Much valuable information on environmental and industry conditions and trends is available from published or other secondary sources. Managers should consult these sources prior to gathering expensive primary data.

Local libraries, for instance, contain introductory information on the political-legal, economic, technological, and social components of the macroenvironment in almanacs and encyclopedias. University libraries provide government publications that are rich with political-legal and economic data. Additional information can be obtained from business literature indexes, business periodicals, and reference services. Regularly published periodicals and newspapers such as *Business Week, The Wall Street Journal,* and *Fortune* provide excellent, timely macroenvironmental and industry information. More specific sources of information that may be found in many libraries are listed in Table 2A.1.

Other highly specific information may be obtained from the annual reports of companies, reports of major brokerage firms (such as Merrill Lynch), and trade publications (examples include *American Paints and Coatings Journal, Modern Brewery Age, Quick Frozen Foods,* and *The Retail Grocer*).

Information on the macroenvironment and industries may also be assimilated from radio business news, television shows (such as "Wall Street Week" and "Money Line"), suppliers, customers, and employees within the industry. And a visit to a branch office of the U.S. Commerce Department can be helpful. The Commerce Department has an extensive bibliography of its own publications, which is available at the branch offices.

Managers can use these sources of information along with assistance from consultants to forecast changes so that the firm can modify its strategy appropriately. Professional consulting firms are available in all major cities and many midsize locales. University professors in all areas of business administration and other disciplines such as sociology, psychology, engineering, and the sciences can also provide expert consulting in relevant areas.

Name of Index	Breadth of Information	Description
Business Periodicals Index	Political-legal Economic Technological Social Industry	Identifies periodicals in all aspects of business and industries. Its "Book Reviews" covers publications on a variety of topics.
Funk & Scott Index of Corporations & Industries	Industry Economic Suppliers Competitors	Identifies periodicals and brokerage reports on all SIC (Standard Industrial Classification) industries. Its yellow pages provide weekly updates, its green pages provide lists of articles and dates, and its white pages list information on articles about specific companies.
New York Times Index	Political-legal Economic Technological Social Industry	Provides an index of articles published in the New York Times.
Public Affairs Information Service Bulletin	Social Economic Political-legal	Provides a subject listing on national and international journals, books, pamphlets, government publications, and reports of private and public agencies.
Reader's Guide to Periodical Literature	Political-legal Economic Technological Social Industry	Provides an author and subject index on periodicals and books.
Social Science Index	Political-legal Economic Social	Provides an author and subject index on periodicals and books.
Wall Street Journal/ Barron's Index	Political-legal Economic Technological Social Industry	Provides an index of articles published in The Wall Street Journal and Barron's. Also includes a list of book reviews.
U.S. Industrial Outlook	Political-legal Economic Technological Social Industry	Gives the U.S. Department of Commerce's annual forecasts for over 350 industries.
Predicasts Forecasts	Political-legal Economic Technological Social Industry	Provides forecasts (as a quarterly service) of products, markets, and industry and economic aggregates for the United States and North America. Forecasts are grouped by SIC numbers and many go into the 21st century.
Standard and Poor's Industry Surveys	Political-legal Economic Technological Social Industry	Profiles and analyzes 33 basic industry groups. Trends and projections are detailed. Also contains analyses of each industry's leading performers.
Corporate & Industry Research Reports	Political-legal Economic Technological Social Industry	Provides analyses and forecasts of 8000 U.S. companies and 600 industries from analytical research reports of 68 securities and institutional investment firms.

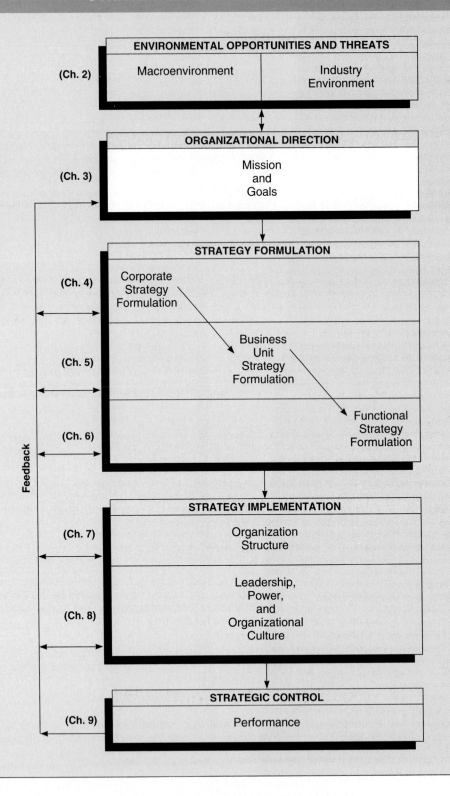

STRATEGIC MANAGEMENT MODEL

ENVIRONMENTAL OPPORTUNITIES AND THREATS

(Ch. 2)

| Macroenvironment | Industry Environment |

ORGANIZATIONAL DIRECTION

(Ch. 3)

Mission
and
Goals

STRATEGY FORMULATION

(Ch. 4)

Corporate
Strategy
Formulation

(Ch. 5)

Business
Unit
Strategy
Formulation

(Ch. 6)

Functional
Strategy
Formulation

STRATEGY IMPLEMENTATION

(Ch. 7)

Organization
Structure

(Ch. 8)

Leadership,
Power,
and
Organizational
Culture

STRATEGIC CONTROL

(Ch. 9)

Performance

Feedback

3
CHAPTER

Organizational Direction: Mission and Goals

As we saw in the preceding chapter, an assessment of the opportunities and constraints in the organization's environment is the first step in formulating strategy. In this chapter, we turn from the environment to take an inward look at the firm. This second step in the strategy process—establishing the organization's mission and goals—requires management to determine the direction in which the organization is to move within its environment.

Organizational direction is difficult to determine unless management has clearly delineated the firm's purpose. Hence, this chapter begins with a discussion of the organization's *raison d'être*, its reason for existing.

THE ORGANIZATION'S MISSION

Organizations are founded for a purpose. Although this purpose may change over time, it is essential that employees understand the reason for the organization's existence, that is, the organization's **mission.** Often, the organization's mission is defined in a formal, written **mission statement**—a broadly defined but enduring statement of purpose that identifies the scope of an organization's operations in product and market terms.[1]

This section examines the organization's mission at the corporate level and the business unit level. Changes in the organization's mission over time are then discussed, followed by an overview of the relationship between the organization's mission and its strategy.

■ Mission and Organizational Level

The mission of an organization, at the corporate level, is stated in fairly broad terms. For instance, the management of General Motors (GM) has stated the firm's overall mission as follows:

> The fundamental purpose of General Motors is to provide products and services of such quality that our customers will receive superior value, our employees and business partners will share in our success, and our stockholders will receive a sustained, superior return on their investment.[2]

Certainly, a large number of activities can be covered by such a broad statement. Such disparate GM undertakings as manufacturing vehicles, producing electronics and defense products, and providing information systems and technology can all be included in this mission statement. However, in each of these cases, the statement indicates that GM intends to furnish superior value to customers, to have employees and business partners share in the firm's success, and to provide a sustained, superior return to stockholders on their investment. So even though very broad, this corporate-level statement does provide direction to the company.

At the business unit level, the mission becomes narrower in scope and more clearly defined. For example, the mission of the Chevrolet business unit would include manufacturing safe and reliable economy cars, sports cars, sedans, and trucks. The Hughes Aircraft subsidiary's mission would be to produce electronic components and systems for defense and industrial customers. And the mission of the Electronic Data Systems business unit would encompass designing and operating information systems for both public and private organizations (including General Motors itself).

■ Mission and Change

Corporate and strategic business-level missions will generally change over time. In many cases, the change will be slow and gradual, but in some instances, the change may take place very rapidly. As an example of a firm whose mission changed gradually, consider Primerica. At one time, Primerica was known as American Can Company and was engaged in the container manufacturing and packaging businesses. Over the years, the company diversified into financial services and specialty retailing. When it finally sold its can and packaging operations, its name no longer fit its businesses, and it was renamed Primerica. Obviously, its mission had also gradually changed from manufacturing to services. Now its mission is to provide life insurance to individual consumers, originate home mortgages, provide mutual and pension fund management, and offer retail services for recorded music and audio/video products.

UAL, Inc. (United Airlines), serves as an example of a firm whose mission changed quickly. In 1987, UAL's chief executive officer, Richard Ferris, decided to broaden the company's mission. Rather than only provide air travel, UAL would become an integrated travel service company with operations encompassing the total service requirements of travelers. The firm would expand into rental cars (to provide customers transportation to and from airports) and hotels (where customers could stay while on trips). To reflect this broadened mission, the firm's name was changed from United Airlines to Allegis. The new mission

STRATEGIC INSIGHT

A Blurred Mission at Sears

Prior to 1975, Sears, Roebuck was the dominant national force in U.S. retailing. As a full-line general merchandiser with 850 stores, Sears was a regular shopping stop for most of America's families. That dominance ended abruptly, however, as the retail industry experienced rapid and dramatic changes. Sears' private-label business was eroded by the growing popularity of specialty retailers, such as Circuit City and The Limited, and its cost structure was successfully challenged by such low-overhead discounters as Wal-Mart and Kmart.

Initially, Sears reacted by attempting to emphasize fashion with such labels as Cheryl Tiegs sportswear. But high-fashion models did not mesh well with Sears' middle-America image. In fact, Sears allowed the key post of women's fashion director to remain vacant from 1980 until 1989. Turning next to diversification, Sears tried to convert its dowdy image into a "financial supermarket" by purchasing Dean Witter Financial Services and Coldwell Banker Real Estate. But in-store kiosks never caught on with customers, and the expected synergy between these two subsidiaries and Sears' Allstate Insurance business unit and its Discover Card failed to materialize.

Next, management modified the store's image to one that sold nationally branded merchandise along with private-label brands at "everyday low prices." The idea was to create individual "superstores" within each of the Sears outlets to compete more effectively with powerful niche competitors. Sears' original intent, which was widely publicized, was to depart from its traditional practice of holding weekly sales to save on advertising expenses and inventory handling while offering stable, everyday low prices. But the "everyday low prices" turned out to be, in some cases, higher than Sears' old sale prices, advertising expenses climbed rather than declined, and Sears continued to run special sales. By this time, customers were totally confused. Sears' response was to announce that, once again, it was going to emphasize women's fashions and would advertise them in such magazines as *Vogue* and *Mademoiselle.*

As of 1990, Sears' operating costs were 30 percent of revenues (versus 18 percent at competitor Wal-Mart), putting it at a severe competitive disadvantage in pricing. And its inability to define a mission for itself and to establish a clear image in the customer's mind made it improbable that the store would ever again dominate the U.S. retailing landscape.

SOURCES: K. Kelly, "At Sears, the More Things Change . . . ," *Business Week*, 12 November 1990, pp. 66–68; M. Oneal, "Shaking Sears Right Down to Its Work Boots," *Business Week,* 17 October 1990, pp. 84–87; B. Saporito, "Markdowns at Sears Roebuck," *Fortune,* 10 September 1990, p. 16; A. Miller and P. King, "Retailing Perestroika," *Newsweek,* 3 September 1990, p. 52; D. Warsh, "Outflanked and Undercut, Sears Seeks the Path to Its Former Glory," *The Washington Post,* 22 August 1990; and F. Schwadel, "Sears' Glitzy Ads Target Affluent Fashion Market," *The Wall Street Journal,* 15 August 1990.

was quite controversial, and various groups that had vested interests in the company believed that those interests would be better served by the firm's original mission—passenger and cargo air transportation. Within four months, Mr. Ferris was fired and the company's name and mission reverted to their previous forms.

■ Mission and Strategy

An organization with a keen sense of its own identity is far more likely to be successful than one that has no clear understanding of its reason for existence. For example, Armco diversified widely a decade ago in an attempt to shelter

Figure 3.1   **The Role of the Organization's Mission**

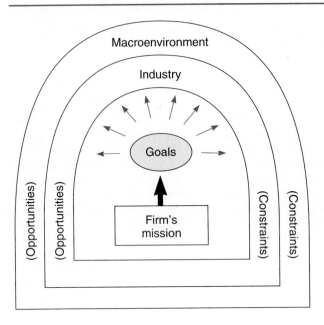

itself from fluctuations in the steel industry. But it found itself in alien territory when it moved into financial services and insurance. After acquiring an insurance holding company, Armco's managers discovered that they "had very few people in [their] management group who could ask the right questions and trouble shoot in that part of [their] operations."[3] They determined to limit future diversification to markets with which they were familiar.

By contrast, Kmart Corporation identifies itself as a general merchandise retailer that distributes a wide range of merchandise through a chain of discount department stores. To satisfy its broad array of customers, the company sells staple merchandise at low prices, as well as a selective mix of national brands. This clear sense of mission has undoubtedly been influential in Kmart's success since the early 1960s.

Hence, effective management requires not only an understanding of the environment but also an awareness of the organization's mission. Successful companies are those that are able to mesh their particular strengths and weaknesses with the environment's opportunities and constraints. A clear sense of purpose is necessary before an organization can move to the next step in formulating strategy—establishing its goals—because it is difficult to know where one is going if one does not first know who one is. Figure 3.1 summarizes the discussion up to this point.

THE ORGANIZATION'S GOALS AND OBJECTIVES

This section focuses on organizational goals and objectives. On the surface, it appears that establishing organizational goals is a fairly straightforward process. As will become evident, however, this process is actually quite complex.

Various stakeholder groups have different goals for the firm. The organizational goals that eventually emerge must balance the pressures from the different stakeholder groups so that the continuing participation of each is assured.

■ Goals and Objectives Defined

Whereas the mission is the reason for the existence of the firm, the organization's **goals** represent the desired general ends toward which efforts are directed. **Objectives** are specific, and often quantified, versions of goals. For example, management may establish a goal "to expand the size of the firm through internal growth." From this goal, a number of specific objectives may be derived, such as "to increase sales by 10 percent each year for the next eight years." As another example, management's goal may be "to become the innovative leader in the industry." On the basis of this goal, one of the specific objectives will be "to have 25 percent of sales each year come from new products developed during the preceding three years."

As you can see, objectives are verifiable. That is, with the objectives in the preceding paragraph, management will be able to answer the question: "Has this objective been attained?" Without verifiability, objectives will not provide a clear direction for managerial decision making, nor will they permit an assessment of organizational performance. Examples of verifiable objectives are shown in Table 3.1. Note that at the end of 1989, Hanna's management was able to determine whether each of those objectives had been attained.

Objectives of M. A. Hanna Company　　　　　　　　　　　　　　　　　　**Table 3.1**

Strategic Objectives for 1989	Financial Objectives for 1989
Add sales of at least $100 million on an annualized basis from acquisitions in the polymers/specialty chemicals industry.	Increase net sales and operating revenues from the formulated polymers segment by 15% through internal growth and strategic acquisitions.
Generate proceeds of at least $25 million from divestitures of unproductive assets and other non-operating items.	Increase fully diluted earnings per share from operations by at least 20%.
Double small-investor ownership in the common stockholder base by improving communications with individual investors and the retail investment community.	Generate sufficient income from operations to yield at least a 16.5% return on beginning common stockholders' equity.
Improve employee evaluation and compensation systems and expand the pay-for-performance concept with the objective of having all employees on performance incentive programs by December 31, 1990.	Review the common stock dividend pursuant to Hanna's policy of maintaining a sustainable dividend that recognizes earnings growth as well as the capital needs of the business units.

Source: M. A. Hanna Company Quarterly Report, First Three Months of 1989.

Note: M. A. Hanna is the world's leading custom compounder of plastics and was the fastest-growing company in the Fortune 500 in 1988.

Table 3.2	**General Goals of Kellogg's Stakeholders**

Stakeholders	*Goals*
Customers	Customers would likely want Kellogg's goals to include providing healthy, quality foods at reasonable prices.
General public	The general public would likely want Kellogg's goals to include providing goods and services with minimum costs (i.e., pollution), increasing employment opportunities, and contributing to charitable causes.
Suppliers	Suppliers would likely want Kellogg's goals to include remaining with them for the long term and purchasing from them at prices that allow the suppliers reasonable profit margins.
Employees	Employees would likely want Kellogg's goals to include providing good working conditions, equitable compensation, and promotion opportunities.
Creditors	Creditors would likely want Kellogg's goals to include maintaining a healthy financial posture and a policy of on-time payment of debt.
Distributors	Wholesalers and retailers would likely want Kellogg's goals to include remaining with them for the long term and selling to them at prices that allow for reasonable profit margins.
Stockholders	Stockholders would likely want Kellogg's goal to be the maximization of returns on their equity.
Board of directors	Directors would likely want Kellogg's goals to be to keep them as directors and to satisfy the demands of the other stakeholders so that the directors would not be liable to lawsuits.
Managers	Managers would likely want to benefit personally from Kellogg. Other management goals are to expand Kellogg's market share in the cereal business, to make compatible growth-oriented acquisitions, to boost capacity, to improve productivity, and to launch new cereals worldwide.

■ Goals and Stakeholders

Various stakeholders will have different goals for the firm. Each stakeholder group—owners (stockholders), members of the board of directors, managers, employees, suppliers, creditors, distributors, and customers—views the firm from a different perspective. To illustrate this point, Table 3.2 delineates the goals of selected stakeholders for Kellogg Company.

Rationality suggests that stakeholders establish goals from the perspective of their own interests. Because of the diversity of these interests, top management faces the difficult task of attempting to reconcile and satisfy each of the stakeholder groups while pursuing its own set of goals. Since the interests of various stakeholder groups are quite different, a close examination of some of their interests can be enlightening.

■ Goals of Top Management

Ideally, the goals of top management should be to attempt to enhance the return to stockholders on their investment while simultaneously attempting to satisfy the interests of other stakeholders. In reality, however, the first of these goals has received more emphasis because, at least in theory, the ultimate control of the firm lies in the stockholders' hands. Stockholders (i.e., the firm's owners) appear to be primarily interested in the extent to which top management is able to maximize profits in order to pay them dividends and increase the market value of their stock.

However, the motivation of top management to maximize profits has been questioned for many years. In fact, for as long as absentee owners (i.e., stockholders) have been hiring professional managers to operate their companies, questions have been raised concerning the extent to which these hired managers actually attempt to increase the wealth of the absentee owners. During this century, as larger and larger firms with ever more diffuse ownerships have emerged, the issue of whose interests the hired top executives actually serve has been widely examined.

Although researchers have studied this issue from a number of different angles, underlying many of the studies is one common philosophical premise: Top managers act primarily in their own interests. What remains to be resolved is whether top managers, by furthering their own self-interests, are also acting in the best interests of the firm's shareholders. From this research, three schools of thought have emerged, which are described in the sections that follow.

Management Attempts to Increase Its Own Rewards

The argument of researchers adhering to the first school of thought is that hired top managers tend to pursue strategies that ultimately increase their own rewards.[4] In particular, top executives are likely to increase the size of their firms since larger rewards usually accompany larger organizational size and its greater responsibilities.

Perhaps the major work in this area can be traced to Herbert A. Simon,[5] who won the 1978 Nobel Prize in economics for his research on managerial decision-making behavior. Building on Roberts's[6] study of executive compensation, Simon suggests that a reward differential exists at each managerial level in an organizational hierarchy. That is, first-level supervisors receive the lowest managerial salaries, but salaries increase with each succeeding level in the organization up through the chief executive officer's (CEO's) salary. The larger the organization and the greater the number of levels in its hierarchy, the greater the rewards will be for top-level executives. Hence, top managers have a powerful incentive to increase the size of their firms.

This interest in organizational growth does not necessarily mean that top management is unconcerned with the firm's profitability or market value, but it does suggest to researchers that top managers are likely to emphasize business performance only to the extent that it discourages shareholder revolts and hostile takeovers. Simon suggests, for instance, that the difference between what a firm's profits can be and what its profits actually are represents "organizational slack," which will only be reduced if outside pressure is applied.[7]

Other researchers also conclude that it is unrealistic to assume that managers will automatically make decisions that are in the best interests of stockholders.[8] They reason that rarely do the interests of managers and shareholders coincide. Consequently, they conclude, top managers will attempt to ensure that their organization meets average performance expectations while behaving in ways that will maximize their own financial and nonfinancial benefits. Two empirical studies support this view by concluding that top executives only attempt to meet acceptable performance goals. When acceptable goals are not met, then

Maximizing Personal Benefits at Cen Trust Bank and Lone Star Industries

The early 1990s provided numerous examples of top managers enriching themselves while their organizations were failing. Consider the following two examples.

Florida's largest savings and loan institution, Cen Trust Bank, was taken over by federal regulators in February 1990, after it incurred a $245 million loss and continued to face a rapidly deteriorating financial position. Investigations indicated that despite its weak financial stance, some of Cen Trust's top managers were spending company funds on museum-quality art, a business yacht, a business jet, limousines, and high salaries for themselves.

Cen Trust's chairman was ousted from his position amid allegations that he had received $4.8 million in compensation during 1989, while the thrift lost almost $120 million. Furthermore, other accusations included allegations that much of the firm's museum-quality art hung in his own house

(where it was guarded by security personnel at a cost to the thrift of more than $300,000) and that his 95-foot yacht (studded with gold nails) was staffed by a crew paid by Cen Trust.

Meanwhile, in another industry, the nation's largest cement company, Lone Star Industries, faced bankruptcy proceedings, while its chairman/CEO continued to live a flamboyant life-style. For instance, although the company was headquartered in Stamford, Connecticut, the chairman/CEO lived in Florida. When visiting headquarters, he would stay in New York City's expensive Plaza Hotel, about fifty miles away. A *Business Week* investigation showed that Lone Star Industries paid $148,329 during 1989 for his bills at the Plaza, while the company was incurring a $271 million loss. He also maintained a helicopter and plane at a cost of $2.3 million to the company, while ordering his managers to fly coach and limit their restaurant expenses to $45 per day.

SOURCES: L. Driscoll, "For James E. Stewart, It Was a Wonderful Life," *Business Week,* 20 May 1991, pp. 40–41; "Taking an S&L Bath," *Newsweek,* 14 January 1991, p. 26; L. Driscoll, "As His Company Struggles, A CEO Digs In—At the Plaza, The Ritz . . . ," *Business Week,* 5 November 1990, pp. 134–136; J. Fierman, "The People Who Set the CEO's Pay," *Fortune,* 12 March 1990, pp. 58–59; D. Skidmore, "U.S. Takes Over Huge Miami Thrift After Reports of Lavish Spending," *The Memphis Commercial Appeal,* 3 February 1990.

top managers will undertake cost-cutting measures and forgo financial and nonfinancial benefits until acceptable performance levels are restored.[9]

Management Responds to Pressure from Significant Stockholders

A second school of thought maintains that the degree to which top managers will implement strategies that benefit stockholders depends on the extent to which ownership of the firm is concentrated.[10] Significant stockholders (i.e., those holding 5 percent or more of a firm's stock) can force managers to act responsibly by demanding information from management, using their voting power, or threatening to sell their stock to permit a takeover.[11]

Evidence indicates that the top managers of corporations that have at least one significant stockholder have less managerial discretion than managers of firms with more diffuse ownership.[12] The top executives of companies with a significant stockholder, then, are likely to be rewarded on the basis of the firm's performance (i.e., profitability); top managers of firms without a single major stockholder are more likely to be rewarded on the basis of nonperformance criteria, such as an increase in the size of the firm.[13]

It is interesting to note that firms managed by an individual who is also a significant stockholder reward that individual in the same way as firms that have diffuse ownership. In such cases, there is little association between the firm's financial performance and the top manager's rewards. Presumably, owner-managers believe that they will benefit more by pursuing strategies that will justify increasing their financial and nonfinancial rewards than they will by boosting profitability, which would benefit them as stockholders.[14]

Management Shares the Same Interests as Stockholders

A third school of thought contradicts both of the preceding schools by proposing that the interests of top management are the same as those of the stockholders. Indeed, some studies do reveal positive associations between business performance and managerial rewards. One study, for example, found that profits, not the size of firms, determine top management rewards.[15] Another points to the existence of a significant relationship between common stock earnings and the rewards of top executives.[16]

In a widely cited theoretical work, Eugene F. Fama argues that the self-interests of hired top managers require that they behave in ways that benefit the stockholders.[17] His argument is based on the premise that the market for managerial talent provides an effective disciplining force. If top managers do not promote the interests of stockholders, this information will result in a lowering of their value in the managerial labor market. This lowered value will adversely affect the managers' alternative employment opportunities.[18] Managerial performance may also be indirectly evaluated by the stock market, because it implicitly judges top management's performance by bidding the firm's stock price either up or down.[19]

From a different perspective, John Child proposes that stock option plans and high salaries bring the interests of top management and stockholders closer together.[20] According to his reasoning, top executives wish to protect their salaries and option plans and can only accomplish that by striving for higher business performance.

This concept of congruent interests has gained support from other scholars, but for different reasons.[21] They suggest that managerial jobs contain "structural imperatives" that force managers to attempt to maximize profits.

> Before the rise of the large stock corporation, individuals who filled the roles of entrepreneur were probably motivated to realize profits. If they did not act as if they were so motivated, however, the failure of their firms would eventually remove them from their positions. . . . The behavior exhibited by entrepreneurs was a structural requirement of the position of entrepreneur itself rather than merely a function of the motivation of individuals who became entrepreneurs.[22]

Similarly, managers would be removed from their positions if they failed to maximize profits. Therefore, these scholars reason that top managers will be motivated to enhance profitability, and "even if they are not so motivated, they must act as if they are if they wish to remain in their positions of authority."[23]

As we can see from the preceding discussion, the issue of whether top managers will attempt to maximize their firms' profits or whether they will pursue a more narrow goal of self-enrichment has not been satisfactorily resolved. Compelling evidence and logic exist on both sides of the controversy. Also unresolved is how motivated top managers are to satisfy the interests of stakeholders beyond the owners of the firm. We turn now to another controversial area—the goals of the board of directors and stockholders.

■ Goals of the Board of Directors and Stockholders

Legally, boards of directors are responsible for such aspects of corporate leadership as selecting and replacing the chief executive officer, representing the interests of the firm's shareholders, advising top management, and monitoring managerial and company performance.[24] There is evidence, however, that board members have in many cases failed to fulfill their legal roles.[25] A common explanation for this failure is that boards have long been considered "creatures of the CEO."[26] Often, board members are nominated by the chief executive officer, who, in return, expects the directors to support his or her strategic decisions. For their support, the directors receive generous compensation. One British member of several corporate boards once described board membership as follows:

> No effort of any kind is called for. You go to a meeting once a month in a car supplied by the company. You look both grave and sage, and on two occasions say "I agree," say "I don't think so" once, and if all goes well, you get 500 [pounds] a year. If you have five of them, it is total heaven, like having a permanent hot bath.[27]

Directors sometimes behave in this fashion, not only because they wish to show their loyalty to the chief executive officer, who appoints and compensates them (average annual compensation is over $50,000 for serving on the board of a major corporation), but also because they often make decisions based primarily on information provided by the CEO.[28] As one CEO put it: "[My board members] often have to have blind faith in management. It would take them a month to really understand some of the decisions they make."[29]

In theory, the primary goal of the board is to safeguard the interests of the stockholders. Technically speaking, board members are elected by the stockholders. In reality, however, stockholders are limited to casting a "yes" or "no" vote for each individual nominated to the board by top management. Each nominee's credentials are briefly stated in management's mailed "notice of annual meeting of shareholders," and few stockholders will have much knowledge regarding the nominees beyond these basic facts. Hence, most stockholders will simply follow the recommendations of top management.

Therefore, it is not surprising to find that board members are often beholden to top management for their positions. In such cases, the directors' basic loyalties lie with the CEO rather than with the stockholders. Frequently, this loyalty takes the form of approval of lavish compensation packages for top management. In some cases, these packages may even conceal the actual amounts that top managers receive. For example, stockholders did not know that F. Ross Johnson was granted 40,000 shares of stock before RJR Nabisco was acquired by Kohlberg Kravis Roberts. One account described it as follows:

> Johnson received around $20 million, most of which the shareholders didn't know he had coming until the takeover. . . . Shareholders may not always have a legal right to override the decisions of their own board of directors. But they surely have a right to know what their boards have decided.[30]

Ignoring the stockholders' interests has begun to diminish in recent years, however. The turning point was the 1985 decision by the Delaware Supreme Court that Trans Union Corporation's directors had accepted a takeover bid too quickly. They were accused of failing to read the sales contract before approving it, not soliciting an independent, outside opinion on the fairness of the sales price, and approving the sale of the company in a hasty, two-hour meeting dominated by the CEO. They were held personally liable for the difference between the offer they accepted and the price the company might have received in an open sale. The directors had to pay $13.5 million of the $23.5 million settlement—the excess over their liability insurance coverage.[31]

The pressure on directors to acknowledge stockholder wishes continues to increase. For instance, stockholder suits against directors rose by almost 70 percent over the past ten years.[32] But the major source of pressure in recent years has been from institutional investors. These stockholders—chiefly pension funds, mutual funds, and insurance companies—own $1 trillion of stock in U.S. corporations. By virtue of the size of their investments, they wield considerable power and are becoming more active in using it. For example, the California Public Employees' Retirement System and Pennsylvania Public School Employees' Retirement System recently launched a proxy battle that led Honeywell's management to restructure the company. Considering that institutional investors own large chunks of many major companies (i.e., 89 percent of Capital Cities/ABC, 82 percent of Lotus Development, 81 percent of Southwest Airlines, and 80 percent of Whirlpool), their potential power is quite impressive.[33]

On the other side, however, it should be emphasized that some board members have played effective stewardship roles. Many directors promote strongly the best interests of the firm's shareholders and various other stakeholder groups as well. Research indicates, for instance, that board members are invaluable sources of environmental information.[34] By conscientiously carrying out their duties, directors can ensure that management does not solely pursue its own interests by focusing management's attention on company performance.[35]

Society is increasingly expecting higher standards of conduct from corporate boards of directors. Directors are coming under greater pressure to make comprehensive disclosures on firm activities and financial data, to ensure that the company complies with environmental laws and regulations, to make certain that the provisions of the Foreign Corrupt Practices Act are upheld, and so on. Legally, board members are held responsible for these activities regardless of whether top management is supportive of these measures. Directors do exist who believe that their job is to represent shareholders. For example, the chairman of the board of Compaq Computer states that "the owners of the company should be represented by the directors. That has ceased to happen at lots of companies where management dominates the board."[36] Murray Weidenbaum, an economist who serves on three corporate boards, does not "view the director's role as helping the CEO. The role of the director, the legal obligation, is to represent the shareholders."[37]

■ Goals of Creditors

Creditors of a corporation include bondholders, banks, and other financial institutions. Their primary goal is to influence the firm to maintain a healthy financial posture in order to safeguard both the principal and interest on their loaned funds. Recent trends toward acquisitions and mergers that involve financial leverage have given creditors increasingly powerful roles in corporate America. In fact, should the trend toward heavy debt financing continue, an increasing number of business decisions may be transferred to creditors. Such decisions could include choices as crucial as the selection of top management, the identification of acquisition targets, and the determination of which products to produce and where and how to produce them. Furthermore, as mergers and acquisitions continue, fewer competitors will remain in the marketplace, and many of those who do remain will be heavily financed by creditors.

The increased power of creditors can result in market distortions. For example, unprofitable Pan Am Corporation, which operated one of the oldest fleets of airplanes in the airline industry, was on the brink of bankruptcy for years. Yet in 1989, after losing $2.5 billion over the preceding decade, it tried (but failed) to buy Northwest Airlines—a much larger and more profitable competitor. It could only attempt this through the strong support of a group of creditors—such as Bankers Trust, Morgan Guaranty, Citicorp, and Prudential-Bache—which was willing to provide financing of $2.7 billion.

■ Conflicting Goals

It is evident from the preceding discussion that the goals of top managers, boards of directors, and creditors are not always congruent with the goals of the firm's shareholders or other stakeholder groups. Broadly speaking, of course, the goals of all stakeholders are best served when the firm functions as a viable entity. It is then able to supply goods to customers, contribute to society's standard of living, provide employment, and channel financial benefits to all stakeholders.

We must realize, however, that a viable firm has the power to benefit each stakeholder group differentially. For instance, tough bargaining with suppliers will transfer benefits from suppliers to stockholders, managers, and customers. Being less responsible in controlling environmental pollution transfers benefits from society (because the general public bears the costs of pollution) to a number of stakeholders who benefit from the financial savings. Bestowing extremely generous compensation on top management transfers benefits from stockholders, employees, and customers to upper-level managers. In fact, a recent survey by a New York consulting firm reveals that 66 percent of employees and 73 percent of stockholders believe that senior managers receive too much compensation at the expense of other stakeholders.[38]

Perhaps the most common suggestion for making the goals of top management and stockholders more congruent is to award shares of stock or stock options to top management. The rationale is that significant stock ownership would align the interests of top management with the interests of shareholders. Attempts to align the interests of upper-level management with those of other stakeholder groups have also been negatively imposed through lawsuits—that is, fines imposed on the firm by various public agencies and court decisions.

SOCIAL RESPONSIBILITY AND ETHICS

One of an organization's primary goals is its obligation to operate in a socially responsible manner. This section examines corporate social responsibility and the related area of managerial ethics.

■ Corporate Social Responsibility

Our society grants considerable freedom to business organizations. In return, businesses are expected to operate in a manner consistent with society's interests. **Social responsibility** refers to the expectation that business firms should act in the public interest. Certainly, businesses have always been expected to provide employment for individuals and to provide goods and services for customers. But social responsibility implies more than that. Today, society expects business to help preserve the environment, to sell safe products, to treat its employees equitably, to be truthful with its customers, and, in some cases, to go even further by training the hard-core unemployed, contributing to education and the arts, and helping revitalize urban slum areas.

Some observers, ranging from Adam Smith to Milton Friedman, have argued that social responsibility should not be part of management's decision-making process.[39] Friedman has maintained that business functions best when it sticks to its primary mission—producing goods and services within society's legal restrictions. In other words, its sole responsibility is to attempt to maximize profits. When it goes further than that by tackling social problems, business is spending money that should more properly be returned to its stockholders. The stockholders, who have rightfully earned the money, should be able to spend that money as they see fit, and their spending priorities may differ from those of business.

In reality, however, business is part of society, and its actions have both economic and social ramifications. It would be practically impossible to isolate the business decisions of corporations from their economic and social consequences.

In fact, top managers may find a number of areas where their interests, various stakeholders' interests, and society's interests are mutually compatible. For example, a firm that pollutes the atmosphere because it fails to purchase costly antipollution equipment is harming not only society but also, ultimately, its own stakeholders. With a polluted environment, the quality of life of the firm's stockholders, directors, managers, employees, suppliers, customers, and creditors suffers. As another example, if businesses do not contribute to the education of young people, their recruitment efforts will suffer and they will eventually experience a decline in the quality of their work force. This result benefits no group of stakeholders.

Many government regulations over business operations came into being because some firms refused to be socially responsible. Had organizations not damaged the environment, sold unsafe products, discriminated against some employees, and engaged in untruthful advertising, laws in these areas would not have been necessary. The threat of ever more government regulation exists unless companies operate in a manner consistent with society's well-being.

Ideally, then, firms that are socially responsible are those that are able to operate profitably while simultaneously benefiting society. But realistically, it is not always clear exactly what is good for society. For example, society's needs for high employment and the production of desired goods and services must be balanced against the pollution and industrial wastes that are generated by these operations. Despite these difficulties, however, many firms in their annual reports express, at least in general terms, how they are socially responsible. General Motors, for instance, has published an annual *Public Interest Report* for over twenty years. A recent issue described GM's efforts in such areas as clean air,

STRATEGIC INSIGHT

Social Responsibility at GM

Each year, General Motors publishes a *Public Interest Report* detailing its corporate activities in the area of social responsibility. Although describing all of these activities would require several pages, a few of the areas in which GM is involved are listed below.

- A corporationwide UAW–GM education program publishes *Straight Talk*, a magazine intended to educate teenagers about AIDS and HIV infection.
- GM offers hourly and salaried employees a Tuition Assistance Plan for improving specific skills or even for pursuing studies not related to their jobs.
- GM has presented a program called "Skilled Trades and Engineering: Explore the Possibilities" to over two hundred thousand junior and senior high school students, especially minorities and young women. The program attempts to enhance understanding of the rewards and opportunities in engineering and skilled trades.
- GM donates an average of $35 million annually in cash grants, scholarship assistance, and equipment to colleges and universities.
- Since 1978, the General Motors Cancer Research Foundation has recognized scientists throughout the world for their achievements in the detection, prevention, and treatment of cancer.
- GM was the sole sponsor of "The Civil War," a widely acclaimed (and widely watched) ten-hour special that appeared on PBS television stations in 1990 and 1991.
- Since 1970, GM has used its Motor Enterprises, Inc., subsidiary to provide start-up capital for new minority businesses.
- GM's Minority Supplier Development Program has been, since 1968, the largest of its kind in the nation. In 1989, for example, GM purchased $1.15 billion in materials and services from minority suppliers. As part of this program, GM provides consulting and training programs to aid potential minority suppliers in receiving GM's business.

SOURCE: *General Motors Public Interest Report 1990* (Detroit: General Motors Corporation, 1990).

ozone depletion, global warming, waste management, automotive safety, minority programs, philanthropic activities, higher-quality products, and greater operating efficiency.

■ Managerial Ethics

Closely related to issues of corporate social responsibility are the ethics of individual managers. **Ethics** refers to standards of conduct and moral judgment—that is, whether managers' decisions and behaviors are right or wrong. (Table 3.3 presents one company's view of ethical behavior.) What is morally right or wrong, of course, has been argued since the beginning of civilization, and as we might expect, there are few generally accepted global standards of ethical behavior. Even in the same nation, various people may look at ethical issues from different perspectives. Over the past several years, for example, many American corporations have "restructured" to become more competitive. Part of the restructuring process inevitably involves mass layoffs of employees. Is it right to lay off employees so that a company can compete more effectively with foreign firms and—in essence—assure its survival, or is it wrong to put people with family and financial responsibilities and obligations out of work?

Ethical behavior can be viewed in several different ways. First, it may be considered from the perspective of self-interest. Adam Smith proposed that if

---

Excerpts from Electronic Data Systems' (EDS) Code of Conduct **Table 3.3**

We conduct EDS' business in accordance with both the letter and spirit of the applicable laws of the United States and of those foreign countries in which EDS does business. We will conduct our business in the center of the field of ethical behavior—not along the sidelines, skirting the boundaries. . . . We must be honest in all our relationships and must avoid even the appearance of illegal or unethical conduct. For example, no employee of EDS will give or receive bribes or kick-backs; make improper political contributions; abuse proprietary or trade secret information, whether EDS' or our suppliers', business partners' or customers'; or misuse the company's funds and assets. . . .

The success of EDS rests directly on the quality of our people and our services. The integrity of all our people is an essential part of this quality that we offer to our customers. If our integrity ever became suspect, the future of EDS would be in jeopardy. . . .

When in doubt, measure your conduct against this Golden Rule of Business Ethics: Could you do business in complete trust with someone who acts the way you do? The answer must be YES.

Source: Excerpted from *EDS Code of Conduct,* copyright © 1990, EDS, Dallas, Texas. Reprinted with permission.

---

each individual pursued his or her own economic self-interests, society as a whole would benefit. Milton Friedman, as mentioned earlier, believed that firms that attempt to maximize their profits within the legal regulations of society behave ethically.

Smith and Friedman viewed ethics economically, but Charles Darwin approached the issue from a biological perspective. In this sense, ethics can be explained implicitly in terms of survival of the fittest. Some species survive at the expense of other species. The survivors are those who are either instinctively or deterministically able to structure compatible fits with their environments. Ethical behavior, in a Darwinian sense, then, encompasses survival of one at the expense of the destruction of another. Hence, self-interest is at the heart of the approaches of Darwin, Smith, and Friedman. It is ethical to take care of oneself.

A second way of viewing ethics also involves the concept of self-interest, but in a broader sense. From this perspective, if an individual always promotes his or her interests at the expense of others, eventually the individual will be isolated by others. Selfish children find themselves without playmates, just as selfish managers are unable to secure the cooperation of their peers or supervisor. Hence, individuals should be concerned with the welfare of others because it serves their own interests in the long run.

A third common perspective of ethics bases the concepts of right and wrong on religious beliefs. In the United States, the strongest religious tradition is the Judeo-Christian heritage, although other religious viewpoints also prevail. From this perspective, it is "God's will" for individuals to behave in ways that benefit others. Behaving in a correct manner involves treating other people as one would wish to be treated. The concept of selfishness is frowned upon, and individuals are cautioned against ignoring the plight of others who are less fortunate.

Another view of ethics differs from all of the preceding by holding that human beings are inherently concerned with others. This concern is not based on either selfish or religious reasons but is simply a natural condition of human-kind. In wars, soldiers help the wounded at the expense of their own lives. In natural disasters, individuals sacrifice their own lives in attempts to save others. Such naturally unselfish behavior is not without precedent, for it also occurs outside the domain of human beings. Certain species of animals, such as ele-phants, dolphins, and bison, routinely show great concern for the welfare of their family members, even to the point of protecting them with their own lives.

However ethical behavior is viewed, evidence exists that ethical operations may be related to organizational success. For instance, in certain parts of the country, Quaker or Mennonite entrepreneurs are often successful because of their reputations for being conscientious, reliable, trustworthy, and willing to stand behind their firm's products or services. Some research also reveals that enterprises with high ethical and social standards tend to be more profitable than companies lacking in those areas.[40] Other evidence even suggests that investors shun companies that are not socially and ethically responsible because they consider them to be risky investments.[41] And some institutional investors (i.e., mutual funds, universities, states, cities, and churches) only invest in stocks that represent firms known for their high social and ethical standards.

In summary, behavior that is ethically considerate of other stakeholders and socially responsible makes good business sense. "Your satisfaction guaranteed or your money back" is a statement made by many businesses that consider their own success dependent upon the satisfaction of their customers. And when products or packages are labeled "biodegradable" or "recyclable," they reflect their manufacturers' convictions that their social responsibility will ben-efit society as a whole as well as their own image in the marketplace.

STAKEHOLDERS AND TAKEOVERS

An ever-present threat to many organizations is a takeover by another firm, group, or individual. This section presents an overview of takeovers and exam-ines their advantages and disadvantages from various perspectives.

■ An Overview

Any firm whose stock is publicly traded constantly faces the possibility of a takeover. Depending upon the form in which a takeover occurs, different groups of stakeholders will be affected in various ways.

A **takeover** refers to the purchase of a significant number of shares of a firm by an individual, a group of investors, or another organization. Takeovers may be attempted by outsiders or insiders.

Attempts to take over a company by an individual, group, or organization that is outside the organization may be friendly or unfriendly. A friendly take-over is one in which both the buyer and seller desire the transaction. In recent years, General Electric's takeover of RCA, Capital Cities' takeover of ABC, and Greyhound's takeover of Trailways illustrate friendly takeovers. An unfriendly takeover is one in which the target firm resists the sale. Recent examples of unfriendly takeovers include Carl Icahn's successful bid for TWA and Sir James Goldsmith's unsuccessful bid for Goodyear.

Unfriendly takeovers are sometimes precipitated by **raiders**—individuals

STRATEGIC INSIGHT

The Risk of LBOs for Campeau and First Brands

Leveraged buyouts (LBOs) carry significant risks because of the heavy debt that accompanies them. Certainly, one of the most dramatic examples was Campeau Corporation's purchase of Federated Department Stores—owner of such well-known stores as Filene's, Foley's, Bloomingdale's, Lazarus, and Rich's. Although Campeau was able to sell some of the stores to help pay the $7.5 billion debt it incurred in the purchase, it was not able to cover its interest payments from the operations of the remaining stores, even though those stores operated profitably! As a result, the entire company filed for Chapter 11 bankruptcy protection in 1990. Analysts concluded that Campeau paid too much for Federated on the basis of unduly optimistic assumptions about retail sales growth and the market value of the stores.

But some LBOs have been quite successful. First Brands (producer of Prestone Antifreeze,

Glad Bags, and Simoniz Car Wax) was once a business unit of Union Carbide. Alfred E. Dudley, a Union Carbide manager, persuaded other managers and various investors, such as First Boston, to take First Brands private for $674 million in debt financing. The result, in 1986, was a new company with a debt burden of 8.8 times its equity capital. Management immediately cut its labor force by almost 10 percent, reduced costs, and increased quality. The production equipment for Glad Bags was sold and leased back, which raised $168 million, and European subsidiaries were sold for $27 million. The cash resulting from these transactions was channeled into capital spending, research and development, and a small acquisition. Since the LBO, the company has introduced thirty-four new products or product modifications. Operations in 1989 showed a profit of $60.9 million on sales of $1.2 billion.

SOURCES: L. Reibstein and C. Friday, "Seven Deadly Sins of Debt," *Newsweek,* 29 January 1990, p. 53; "Bankruptcy Petition Brings Fresh Risks for Allied, Federated," *The Wall Street Journal,* 16 January 1990; J. A. Trachtenberg, R. Melnbardis, and D. B. Hilder, "An Extra $500 Million Paid for Federated Got Campeau in Trouble," *The Wall Street Journal,* 11 January 1990; T. Vogel and L. J. Nathans, "First Brands: Anatomy of an LBO That Worked," *Business Week,* 4 December 1989, p. 104.

who believe that the way a company is being managed can be significantly improved. Raiders purchase a large number of shares in the target firm either to force a change in top management personnel or to manage the firm themselves.

Other reasons for takeovers by outsiders include acquisitions by investors or creditors for financial purposes or acquisitions by another firm for strategic reasons. For example, Chrysler's takeover of American Motors several years ago provided Chrysler with immediate expansion of product lines, production capacity, and market share.

Transfer of ownership to organizational insiders, such as employees or top managers, may occur gradually through special types of takeovers known as **employee stock ownership plans (ESOPs).** Since the enactment of a tax law in 1974 that encouraged ESOPs, many closely held firms (i.e., those with only a few stockholders) have been partially turned over to their managers and employees. This process usually begins when the principal owner of the closely held firm retires, or when an ESOP plan is developed as a benefit or motivational incentive for the firm's employees. As the employees receive more and more shares of stock over a period of time, the ownership of the firm is gradually turned over to them.

The transfer of ownership to insiders may also occur suddenly through a takeover by the firm's employees or top managers. In one of the most publicized takeover attempts in American business, F. Ross Johnson, the CEO of RJR Nabisco, and his top management group attempted to take the firm private (i.e., concentrate its ownership in their hands). However, their bids were topped by the investment firm of Kohlberg Kravis Roberts & Company, which paid about $25 billion for the firm.

Sudden takeover attempts often (but not always) rely heavily on borrowed funds to finance the acquisition. Borrowing funds to purchase a firm is referred to as a **leveraged buyout (LBO).** When a takeover is financed in this fashion, the company is burdened with heavy debt, which must be paid back either by funds generated from operations or by the sale of company assets, such as subsidiaries or product divisions.

■ Pros and Cons

Takeovers have been both defended and criticized. Their defense generally consists of pointing out the useful role that takeovers play in replacing ineffective management. For instance, T. Boone Pickens, Jr., a renowned corporate raider, has argued:

> After decades of sovereign autonomy, the professional managers of many large, publicly held corporations are finding themselves on the firing line. They are being asked to justify lackluster performance and questionable strategies. They are being called on to address the chronic undervaluation of their securities.[42]

Takeovers have been criticized from several perspectives. One argument is that the primary goal of some takeover attempts is for the raider to make short-term profits. Even the bidder who ultimately loses out to a higher bidder usually pockets a considerable profit because of the increase in the stock's price brought about by the bidding. Such a losing bidder is said to have engaged in "greenmail." In some cases, management will attempt to take the firm private, usually through a leveraged buyout, to prevent the unfriendly takeover. This action will limit the firm's future strategic options because it must make heavy interest payments on its newly acquired debt for many years. These payments make it difficult for the firm to finance research and development activities, to explore new markets, and to promote and advertise its goods and services.

Bondholders, too, suffer from LBOs. As company debt increases following an LBO, the firm's bonds become more risky to purchase since their ultimate redemption is less certain. This increase in risk results in a deterioration of the credit rating of the firm's bonds and a loss of value to the bondholders.

Finally, most takeovers are followed by layoffs of employees and managers. But more than those employees and their families are affected. For example, when Gulf Oil was taken over by Chevron, Gulf's Pittsburgh headquarters was closed. Nearly six thousand employees either were transferred from Pittsburgh or were fired. This move had a significant negative impact on the many Pittsburgh-area firms that supplied various products and services to Gulf. Additionally, the city suffered because of lower tax revenues, and the price of real estate throughout the city declined.

For these reasons, some states have passed laws that protect their firms from takeovers. For example, Boeing is the largest employer in the state of Washington. When T. Boone Pickens attempted an unfriendly takeover of Boeing in 1987, a bill was passed by state legislators that put a five-year ban on the sale of Boeing's assets to pay off creditors. This act effectively nullified Pickens's bid, because his only way to repay the debt he would incur in buying the company was to sell off some of its assets.

SUMMARY

Organizations are founded for a particular purpose, known as the organization's mission. The mission, at the corporate level, is stated in fairly broad terms but is sufficiently precise to give direction to the organization. At the business unit level, the mission is narrower in scope and more clearly defined. It is essential that an organization carefully understand its mission, because a clear sense of purpose is necessary for an organization to establish appropriate goals.

Goals represent the desired general ends toward which organizational efforts are directed. From the organization's goals, management formulates objectives—specific, verifiable versions of goals. However, various stakeholder groups, because of their own interests, will desire different goals for the firm. Because of the diversity of these interests, top management faces the difficult task of attempting to reconcile and satisfy the interests of each of the stakeholder groups while pursuing its own set of goals.

Controversy exists over the extent to which top management actually attempts to maximize return on the stockholders' investment. One school of thought argues that top managers pursue strategies, such as increasing the size of their firm, that ultimately increase their own rewards. Another proposes that top managers in firms in which ownership of the corporation is concentrated will attempt to maximize profits. A third school theorizes that top management's interests coincide with those of the firm's stockholders for various reasons.

Controversy also exists over the extent to which boards of directors serve as "creatures of the CEO" versus the degree to which they represent the interests of the stockholders. Certainly, recent legal trends have emphasized the boards' stewardship of the stockholders' interests.

Of considerable concern in the strategic decision-making process are the concepts of corporate social responsibility and managerial ethics. Social responsibility refers to the extent to which business firms should act in the public interest while conducting their operations. Ethical considerations involve questions of moral judgment in managerial decision making and behavior. Society today demands that companies operate in a socially responsible manner and that managers exhibit high ethical behavior in their conduct.

Finally, stakeholder groups are affected by corporate takeovers. The impact differs, depending upon whether the takeover is friendly or unfriendly and whether it is engineered by outsiders or insiders. Takeovers, from a societal viewpoint, have both defenders and critics.

KEY CONCEPTS

Employee stock ownership plan (ESOP)   A formal program, administered by a trust, that transfers ownership of a corporation—through shares of stock—to its employees. The program is usually initiated by the organization's owners for financial, tax, and/or motivational reasons.

Ethics   Standards of conduct and moral judgment.

Goals   Desired general ends toward which efforts are directed.

Leveraged buyout (LBO)   A takeover in which the acquiring party borrows funds to purchase the firm. The resulting interest payments and principal are paid back by funds generated from operations and/or the sale of company assets.

Mission   The reason for an organization's existence.

Mission statement   A broadly defined but enduring statement of purpose that identifies the scope of an organization's operations in product and market terms.

Objective   A specific, verifiable, and often quantified version of a goal.

Raider   An individual who attempts to take over a company because he or she believes that its management can be significantly improved. Raiders purchase a large number of shares in the target firm either to force a change in top management personnel or to manage the firm themselves.

Social responsibility   The expectation that business firms should act in the public interest.

Takeover   The purchase of a significant number of shares in a firm by an individual, a group of investors, or another organization. Takeovers may be friendly—in which both the buyer and seller desire the transaction—or unfriendly—in which the target firm resists the sale.

DISCUSSION QUESTIONS

1. Do corporate-level missions and business unit missions usually change over time? Why or why not?

2. Explain the relationship between an organization's mission and its strategy.

3. Explain the difference between a goal and an objective. Give an example of each, different from those given in the text.

4. Why is it essential that objectives be verifiable?

5. Why do various groups that are stakeholders in the same organization have different goals? Should they not all be pulling together in the same direction?

6. How might the goals of top management differ from those of the firm's board of directors? How might they be similar?

7. Explain the relationship between corporate strategy and social responsibility.

8. Explain the relationship between corporate strategy and managerial ethics.

9. What might be the impact of a takeover on such stakeholder groups as the acquired company's stockholders, top management, and operating employees?

10. What are the risks for the acquiring party in a leveraged buyout?

STRATEGIC MANAGEMENT EXERCISES

1. Select a particular type of business that you may wish to start.

   a. Develop a written mission statement for that business.
   b. Construct a set of goals for the business.
   c. From the set of goals developed in part b, formulate specific, verifiable objectives.
   d. Devise a statement of social responsibility for the business.

2. Select a company that has a written mission statement. Evaluate its mission statement along each of the following criteria:

   a. Is the mission statement all-encompassing yet relatively brief?
   b. Does the mission statement delineate, in broad terms, what products/services the firm is to offer?
   c. Does the mission statement define the company's geographical operating parameters (i.e., whether it will conduct business locally, regionally, nationally, or internationally)?
   d. Is the mission statement consistent as it moves from the corporate level to the business unit level?
   e. Is the mission statement consistent with the company's actual activities and competitive prospects at the corporate level? (For instance, Chrysler's mission of using its technology to operate both in the automobile industry and in the defense industry failed to match its competitive stance. Facing powerful international competition in the automobile industry required Chrysler to concentrate totally on that industry. As a result, it was forced to sell its nonvehicle businesses.)
   f. Is the mission statement consistent with the company's actual activities and competitive prospects at the business unit level? (For instance, General Motors' mission of providing quality outputs matches the operation of its Electronic Data Systems business unit, but the quality of its vehicle products has been questioned by many industry observers and customers.)

REFERENCES

1. J. A. Pearce II, "The Company Mission as a Strategic Tool," *Sloan Management Review* 23 (Spring 1982): 15.

2. J. K. Clemens, "A Lesson from 431 B.C.," *Fortune*, 13 October 1986, p. 164.

3. G. Brooks, "Some Concerns Find That the Push to Diversify Was a Costly Mistake," *The Wall Street Journal*, 2 October 1984.

4. M. Aoki, *The Co-Operative Game Theory of the Firm* (Oxford, England: Clarendon Press, 1984); W. Baumol, *Business Behavior, Value and Growth* (New York: Macmillan, 1967); J. K. Galbraith, *Economics and the Public Purpose* (Boston: Houghton Mifflin, 1973); H. A. Simon, "Theories of Decision Making in Economics and Behavioral Science," *American Economic Review* 49 (1959): 253–283; O. E. Williamson, "Dynamic Stochastic Theory of Managerial Behavior," in A. Phillips and O. E. Williams, eds., *Prices: Issues in Theory, Practice and Public Policy* (Philadelphia: University of Pennsylvania Press, 1967).

5. H. A. Simon, "The Compensation of Executives," *Sociometry* 20 (1957): 32–35.

6. D. R. Roberts, "A General Theory of Executive Compensation Based on Statistically Tested Propositions," *Quarterly Journal of Economics* 20 (1956): 270–294.

7. H. A. Simon, *Administrative Behavior* (New York: Macmillan, 1957).

8. Aoki, *Co-Operative Game Theory*; A. A. Berle and G. C. Means, *The Modern Corporation and Private Property,* rev. ed. (New York: Harcourt, Brace & World, 1968).

9. M. Kroll, P. Wright, and P. Theerathorn, "Whose Interests Do Hired Top Managers Pursue? An Examination of Select Mutual and Stock Life Insurers," *Journal of Business Research* (in press); and O. E. Williamson, *Economic Organization: Firms, Markets and Policy Control* (New York: New York University Press, 1986), pp. 6–27.

10. L. Gomez-Mejia, H. Tosi, and T. Hinkin, "Managerial Control, Performance, and Executive Compensation," *Academy of Management Journal* 30 (1987): 51–70; M. C. Jensen and W. H. Meckling, "Theory of the Firm: Managerial Behavior, Agency Costs and Ownership Structure," *Journal of Financial Economics* 3 (1976): 305–360; D. Leech, "Ownership Concentration and the Theory of the Firm: A Sample Game Theoretical Approach," *Journal of Industrial Economics* 35 (1987): 225–240; W. A. McEachern, *Managerial Control and Performance* (Lexington, Mass.: Lexington Books, 1975); G. R. Salancik and J. Pfeffer, "The Effects of Ownership and Performance on Executive Tenure in U.S. Corporations," *Academy of Management Journal* 23 (1980): 653–664.

11. C. W. Hill and S. A. Snell, "Effects of Ownership Structure and Control on Corporate Productivity," *Academy of Management Journal* 32 (1989): 25–46; Leech, "Ownership Concentration"; Salancik and Pfeffer, "Effects of Ownership and Performance."

12. Williamson, *Economic Organization.*

13. Gomez-Mejia, Tosi, and Hinkin, "Managerial Control, Performance"; McEachern, *Managerial Control and Performance.*

14. Jensen and Meckling, "Theory of the Firm"; McEachern, *Managerial Control and Performance.*

15. W. G. Lewellen and B. Huntsman, "Managerial Pay and Corporate Performance," *American Economic Review* 60 (1970): 710–720.

16. R. T. Masson, "Executive Motivations, Earnings, and Consequent Equity Performance," *Journal of Political Economy* 79 (1971): 1278–1292.

17. E. F. Fama, "Agency Problems and the Theory of the Firm," *Journal of Political Economy* 88 (1980): 288–307.

18. Y. Amihud, J. Y. Kamin, and J. Romen, "Managerialism, Ownerism, and Risk," *Journal of Banking and Finance* 7 (1983): 189–196.

19. Fama, "Agency Problems."

20. J. Child, *The Business Enterprise in Modern Industrial Society* (London: Collier-Macmillan, 1969).

21. D. R. James and M. Soref, "Profit Constraints on Managerial Autonomy: Managerial Theory and the Unmaking of the Corporation President," *American Sociological Review* 46 (1981): 1–18.

22. James and Soref, "Profit Constraints," p. 3.

23. James and Soref, "Profit Constraints," p. 3.

24. S. A. Zahra and J. A. Pearce II, "Boards of Directors and Corporate Financial Performance: A Review and Integrative Model," *Journal of Management* 15 (1989): 292.

25. J. Bacon, *Corporate Directorship Practices: Membership and Committees of the Board* (New York: The Conference Board, 1973); J. C. Baker, *Directors and Their Functions* (Boston: Harvard University Press, 1945); Berle and Means, *Modern Corporation;* C. C. Brown and E. E. Smith, *The Director Looks at His Job* (New York: Columbia University Press, 1957); M. T. Copeland and A. R. Towl, *The Board of Directors and Business Management* (Boston: Harvard University Press, 1947); E. J. Epstein, *Who Owns the Corporation? Management vs. Shareholders* (New York: Priority Press, 1986); J. M. Juran and J. K. Louden, *The Corporate Director* (New York: American Management Association, 1966); H. Koontz, *The Board of Directors and Effective Management* (New York: McGraw-Hill, 1967); J. K. Louden, *The Director: A Professional's Guide to Effective Board Work* (New York: Amacom, 1982); M. L. Mace, *Directors: Myth and Reality* (Boston: Harvard University Press, 1971); O. E. Williamson, *The Economics of Discretionary Behavior: Managerial Objectives in a Theory of the Firm* (Englewood Cliffs, N.J.: Prentice-Hall, 1964); S. G. Winter, "Economic Natural Selection and the Theory of the Firm," *Yale Economic Essays* 4 (1964): 225–231.

26. A. Patton and J. C. Baker, "Why Won't Directors Rock the Boat?" *Harvard Business Review* 65, no. 6 (1987): 10–18.

27. L. Herzel, R. W. Shepro, and L. Katz, "Next-to-the-Last Word on Endangered Directors," *Harvard Business Review* 65, no. 1 (1987): 38.

28. Zahra and Pearce, "Boards of Directors," p. 295.

29. S. P. Sherman, "Pushing Corporate Boards to Be Better," *Fortune,* 18 July 1988, p. 60.

30. G. S. Crystal and F. T. Vincent, Jr., "Take the Mystery Out of CEO Pay," *Fortune,* 24 April 1989, p. 220.

31. M. Galen, "A Seat on the Board Is Getting Hotter," *Business Week,* 3 July 1989, p. 72; Sherman, "Pushing Corporate Boards," p. 62.

32. W. E. Green, "Directors' Insurance: How Good a Shield?" *The Wall Street Journal,* 14 August 1989.

33. B. D. Fromson, "The Big Owners Roar," *Fortune,* 30 July 1990, pp. 66–78.

34. J. Pfeffer, "Size, Composition, and Function of Hospital Boards of Directors: A Study of Organization-Environment Linkage," *Administrative Science Quarterly* 18 (1973): 349–364; J. Pfeffer and G. R. Salancik, *The External Control of Organizations: A Resource-Dependence Perspective* (New York: Harper & Row, 1978); and K. G. Provan, "Board Power and Organizational Effectiveness Among Human Service Agencies," *Academy of Management Journal* 23 (1980): 221–236.

35. M. S. Mizruchi, "Who Controls Whom? An Examination of the Relation Between Management and Board of Directors in Large American Corporations," *Academy of Management Review* 8 (1983): 426–435.

36. Sherman, "Pushing Corporate Boards," p. 58.

37. Sherman, "Pushing Corporate Boards," p. 60.

38. T. D. Schellhardt, "Managing," *The Wall Street Journal,* 19 October 1989.

39. A. Smith, *An Inquiry into the Nature and Causes of the Wealth of Nations* (Chicago: Encyclopaedia Britannica, 1952); M. Friedman, "The Social Responsibility of Business Is to Increase Its Profits," *New York Times Magazine,* 13 September 1970, pp. 33, 122–125.

40. E. H. Bowman and M. Haire, "Strategic Posture Towards Corporate Social Responsibility," *California Management Review* 18 (Winter 1975): 49–58.

41. E. H. Bowman, "Corporate Social Responsibility and the Investor," *Journal of Contemporary Business* 2 (1973): 21–43.

42. T. B. Pickens, Jr., "Professions of a Short-termer," *Harvard Business Review* 64, no. 3 (1986): 75.

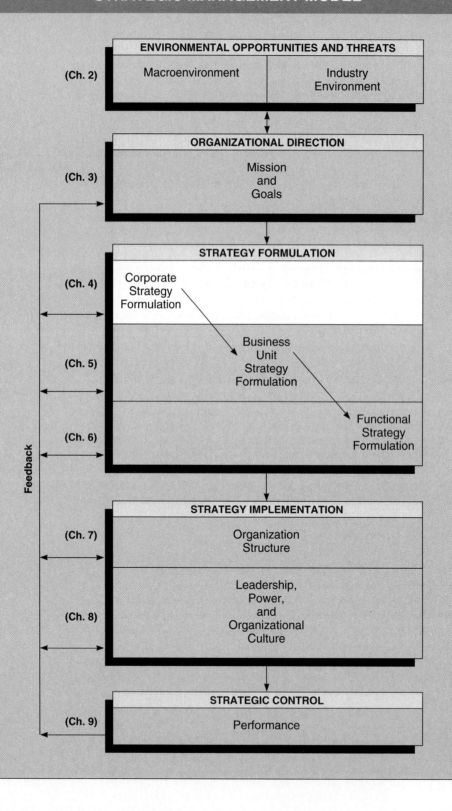

STRATEGIC MANAGEMENT MODEL

ENVIRONMENTAL OPPORTUNITIES AND THREATS

(Ch. 2)

| Macroenvironment | Industry Environment |

ORGANIZATIONAL DIRECTION

(Ch. 3)

Mission
and
Goals

STRATEGY FORMULATION

(Ch. 4) Corporate Strategy Formulation

(Ch. 5) Business Unit Strategy Formulation

(Ch. 6) Functional Strategy Formulation

STRATEGY IMPLEMENTATION

(Ch. 7) Organization Structure

(Ch. 8) Leadership, Power, and Organizational Culture

STRATEGIC CONTROL

(Ch. 9) Performance

Feedback

Corporate-Level Strategies

Once the organization's mission, goals, and objectives are delineated, as was discussed in the preceding chapter, top management can formulate the firm's strategy. Strategies exist at three levels: the corporate level, the business unit level, and the functional level. The focus of this chapter is **corporate-level strategy**—the strategy top management formulates for the overall company. The following two chapters discuss business unit and functional strategies.

At the corporate level, the basic strategic question facing top management is: "In what particular businesses or industries should we be operating?" After answering this question, management must then develop a strategy that will guide the firm's operations in each of these businesses or industries. This chapter explores the strategic alternatives that are available to corporate-level managers.

STRATEGIC ALTERNATIVES

Before selecting a specific corporate-level strategy, top management must conduct an explicit analysis of its firm's internal strengths and weaknesses and the environmental opportunities and threats that face the firm. This analysis helps management adopt a particular corporate profile (i.e., in which businesses and industries to operate). Once a profile is chosen, management must decide whether the firm should pursue a strategy of growth, stability, retrenchment, or some combination of those alternatives. This section explores these vital issues.

■ S.W.O.T. Analysis

Underlying any successful selection of strategies is an analysis of the firm's internal strengths and weaknesses and the opportunities and threats that are posed by the external environment. This process of examining the firm and its environment is termed **S.W.O.T. analysis** (i.e., strengths, weaknesses, oppor-

Table 4.1	**Framework for S.W.O.T. Analysis**		
Sources of Possible Environmental Opportunities and Threats			
Economic forces	Political-legal forces	Social forces	Technological forces
Industry forces			
Possible Organizational Strengths and Weaknesses			
Advertising	Distribution	Leadership	Product/service quality
Brand names	Economies of scale	Location	Promotion
Channel management	Environmental scanning	Management	Public relations
Company reputation	Financial resources	Manufacturing and	Purchasing
Computer information system	Forecasting	operations	Quality control
Control systems	Government lobbying	Market share	Research & development
Costs	Human resources	Organizational structure	Selling
Customer loyalty	Inventory management	Physical facilities/equipment	Technology
Decision making	Labor relations	Product/service differentiation	

tunities, and threats). The framework presented in Table 4.1 identifies many of the variables that management should analyze.

The point of the analysis is to enable the firm to position itself to take advantage of particular opportunities in the environment and to avoid or minimize environmental threats. In doing so, the organization attempts to emphasize its strengths and moderate the impact of its weaknesses. The analysis is also useful for uncovering strengths that have not yet been fully utilized and in identifying weaknesses that can be corrected. Matching information about the environment with a knowledge of the organization's capabilities enables management to formulate realistic strategies for attaining its goals.

For example, Genentech, the largest biotechnology drug company in the United States, found in 1990 that in spite of being highly profitable, it simply did not have sufficient financial resources to continue to compete effectively. The costs and risks of the biotechnology field are astronomical. To raise the capital necessary to continue to be a major force in the industry, Genentech's owners sold 60 percent of the firm to Switzerland-based Roche Holding. The deal was structured so that Genentech could retain its autonomy while gaining the resources to accomplish its goals.[1] Hence, Genentech attempted to correct one of its weaknesses so that it could continue to pursue environmental opportunities.

■ Corporate Profiles

S.W.O.T. analysis can help management determine in which business or businesses the firm should be operating. Broadly speaking, a firm may adopt any one of three corporate profiles: It can compete in one business or industry, in several related businesses or industries, or in several unrelated businesses or industries. Each profile has certain advantages and disadvantages.

By competing in only one industry, a firm benefits from the specialized knowledge that it derives from concentrating on a limited business arena. This knowledge can help firms offer better products or services and become more efficient in their operations. McDonald's, for instance, has been able to develop a steadily improved product line and maintain low per-unit cost of operations over the years by concentrating exclusively on the fast-food business. Wal-Mart has also benefited from operating only in the retailing industry. And Anheuser-Busch has limited its scope of operations largely to the brewing industry, from which it derives more than 80 percent of its sales and 90 percent of its profits.

Operating primarily in one industry, however, increases a firm's vulnerability to business cycles. Should industry attractiveness decline—through a decrease in consumer demand for the industry's products or an onslaught of severe competition from existing or new competitors—the firm's performance is likely to suffer.

Companies that compete in related businesses also face certain advantages and disadvantages. The primary advantage is that improvements in outputs and efficiencies in operations may be transferred from one business to another. For example, a number of operational and marketing strengths of Coca-Cola's soft-drink business have been applied to its Minute Maid fruit juice business. But firms operating in related areas also face the same threat that single-business firms do. A shrinkage in consumer demand or a rise in price competition can adversely affect all of the firm's businesses.

This disadvantage can be overcome by operating in unrelated businesses. Rather than put all of its eggs in one basket or a few closely related baskets, the firm scatters its eggs around. So if one of the industries in which the company operates suffers a downturn, this decline in performance can be offset by increasing sales in the other unrelated industries in which the firm operates.

But operating in several unrelated industries is no panacea. Managing any large enterprise is a complicated endeavor, and that process becomes even more complex when it involves unrelated businesses. Well-known firms such as ITT, for example, have experienced performance problems in attempting to manage diverse and unrelated business units. In fact, ITT divested itself of a number of its unrelated business units to try to improve its performance.

As we have seen, each of the corporate profiles has its advantages and disadvantages. Deciding which profile is best suited for a particular company involves S.W.O.T. analysis. That is, comparing a company with its competitors by using the factors identified in Table 4.1 helps management select the most appropriate profile. Note, however, that S.W.O.T. analysis is not a one-time occurrence. Systematic scanning of the environment and of the firm's strengths and weaknesses, vis-à-vis those of its competitors, helps management know when it is time to modify its corporate profile.

Once a particular profile has been adopted, over time it can be maintained or changed. In this context, top managers have four corporate-level strategies available to them. They may elect to pursue a strategy of growth, stability, retrenchment, or a combination of those. The available strategies are listed in Table 4.2.

S.W.O.T. analysis helps in determining which of these corporate strategies is most appropriate for a particular firm. In a broad sense, the firm's critical weaknesses or valuable strengths may be analyzed in the context of the abundant opportunities or critical threats posed by the macroenvironment and industry. This analysis is illustrated in Figure 4.1.

Table 4.2   **Corporate-Level Strategies**

1. Growth strategies
   a. Internal growth
   b. Mergers
   c. Horizontal integration
   d. Conglomerate diversification
   e. Vertical integration
   f. Joint ventures

2. Stability strategy
3. Retrenchment strategies
   a. Turnaround
   b. Divestment
   c. Liquidation
4. Combination strategies

As shown in Figure 4.1, when a firm possesses valuable strengths and operates in an environment of abundant opportunities, a corporate growth strategy is appropriate. On the other hand, the corporate stability strategy is more suited for a firm that possesses moderate strengths in an environment of moderate opportunities. And a firm with critical weaknesses operating in a threatening environment will find a corporate retrenchment strategy most appropriate. Finally, a firm that operates several different businesses may require a combination of these strategies. One of its businesses, for instance, may need a growth strategy, another may be more suited for the stability strategy, and still another may require a retrenchment strategy. Each of these strategic alternatives is discussed in the following sections.

■ Growth Strategies

Firms may select a **growth strategy** to increase their profits, sales, and/or market share. Growth may also be pursued to lower per-unit costs or to satisfy managerial motivations, as discussed later in this chapter. Regardless of the reason, growth may be attained in a variety of ways. The following subsections describe the six key growth strategies firms can use.

Figure 4.1   **S.W.O.T. Analysis**

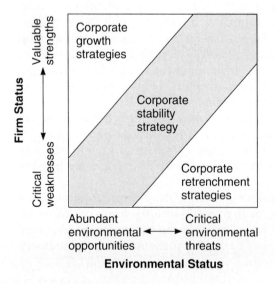

Internal Growth

Internal growth is achieved through increasing a firm's sales, production capacity, and work force. Some companies consciously pursue this route to growth rather than the alternative route of acquiring other firms. Their belief is that internal growth better preserves their efficiency, quality, and image. McDonald's, for instance, has never purchased other fast-food restaurant chains. To maintain its high standards for cleanliness, service, and product consistency, it has grown by granting franchises only to people who are willing to be trained in the McDonald's way.

Likewise, American Airlines prefers to grow internally. American was the only U.S.-based airline to expand its services to three continents (Europe, Asia, and South America) at once, and its chairman, Robert L. Crandall, was asked why American did not buy ailing Pan Am or TWA as a quick way to enter these overseas markets. He responded:

> We've always said we don't want to buy another airline. We don't want to acquire another airline's airplanes. We don't want another airline's people. . . .[2]

Mergers

Many firms elect to grow through mergers. In a **merger,** two or more firms combine into one through an exchange of stock. Normally, mergers involve firms of roughly similar sizes. They are undertaken to share resources and gain market power. For example, Sperry and Burroughs merged to form Unisys several years ago in an attempt to compete more effectively against giant IBM in the computer industry. In another industry, the merger between Wells Fargo and Crocker National Bank in California enhanced the revenue growth of both organizations.

Horizontal Integration

Many firms expand by acquiring or creating other companies in their same line of business. There are several reasons for engaging in this process of **horizontal integration**. One of the primary reasons is to increase market share. This increase should lower the firm's costs through scale economies. The increase in market share also provides the company with greater leverage to deal with its suppliers and customers. In addition, greater size enables the firm to promote its products and services more efficiently to a larger audience and may permit greater access to channels of distribution. Finally, horizontal integration can result in increased operational flexibility. For instance, when Texas Air Corporation acquired Continental Airlines, Eastern Airlines, and People Express, it attempted to gain flexibility through increased access to more airport hubs, air routes, and resources.

The overall reason for engaging in horizontal integration, then, is to take advantage of the benefits of synergy. When the combination of two or more business units results in greater effectiveness and efficiency than the total yielded by those businesses when they were operated separately, then **synergy** has been attained. An example of synergy is Chrysler's purchase of American Motors. The combination of these two firms is a greater competitive threat to

Horizontal Integration in the Paper Industry: Union Camp and Georgia-Pacific

The horizontal growth of one major firm in an industry is likely to affect all of its competitors. Consider the U.S. paper industry. For decades, this industry was characterized by nonantagonistic competition. Even when mergers occurred, they were considered friendly. Because competition was not cutthroat, firms like the $2.75 billion Union Camp Corporation were able to survive even during severe economic downturns.

Then in 1990, Union Camp's largest competitor, Georgia-Pacific, changed the rules of the game by acquiring Great Northern Nekoosa in a hostile takeover. The purchase gave Georgia-Pacific annual sales of more than $10 billion, placing it 34th on the 1990 Fortune 500. Overnight, Georgia-Pacific became the world's largest paper products producer. Its new size and synergistic fit with Great Northern Nekoosa gave it such economies of scale that Georgia-Pacific became the lowest-cost producer of several major lines of paper products.

Georgia-Pacific's low-cost position, combined with an economic recession, placed significant pressure on Union Camp and other companies in the industry to reduce their costs dramatically. As price pressures and discounting increased, these firms faced the unpleasant prospect of being underbid in the industry's price competition.

Union Camp, however, did enjoy some advantages. Its strong balance sheet enabled it to continue expanding aggressively, primarily through internal growth. Georgia-Pacific, on the other hand, found that its acquisition of Great Northern Nekoosa increased its annual interest expense from $63 million in 1989 to $163 million in 1990. To reduce its debt, it was forced to keep capital spending low and sell $1 billion in assets.

other automobile manufacturers than were the two firms when they were owned and operated separately.

Antitrust legislation, of course, restricts some forms of horizontal integration. The Chrysler purchase of American Motors was approved because Chrysler was far smaller than either General Motors or Ford, and American Motors was close to being forced out of business. But many mergers that would substantially lessen competition in an industry—such as a hypothetical one between GM and Ford—are usually prohibited by the U.S. Justice Department.

Conglomerate Diversification

Horizontal integration provides an example of related diversification, that is, diversification that occurs when a firm acquires or creates other businesses in the same industry. But firms may also expand through unrelated or **conglomerate diversification,** in which a firm acquires or starts businesses in industries that are unrelated to its original business. For example, ITT Corporation owns such diverse entities as the Hartford Insurance Group and Sheraton Corporation and also operates in such varied industries as automobile parts, defense, and pulp and timber.

As we pointed out earlier, the primary benefit of conglomerate diversification is risk reduction. This benefit is especially important for businesses that operate in industries subject to rapid technological change. Even if a technological breakthrough by a competitor renders the operations and products of one

STRATEGIC INSIGHT

The Complexity of Conglomerate Diversification for Carlson Companies

Until the late 1960s, Carlson Companies operated in a single business, trading stamps, as the Gold Bond Stamp Company. However, it followed the path of many other enterprises in the 1970s, diversifying into unrelated businesses. By the end of that decade, Carlson Companies had become a conglomerate involved in eleven different business lines. Carlson soon learned the lesson, however, that many other conglomerates did: It is difficult to manage divergent businesses profitably. Consequently, Carlson Companies sold most of its businesses to concentrate in only three areas—travel, hospitality, and marketing services.

Today, Carlson is a privately owned firm with $6.2 billion in annual sales and 63,000 employees. Curtis L. Carlson serves as chairman of the board and his son-in-law, Edwin C. "Skip" Gage, is CEO.

Management describes the firm as "synergistically diversified." Its individual business units complement, support, and create business for each other. For instance, its travel agents and tour companies book reservations in its hotels, resorts, motels, and inns. One of its hotel chains is Radisson Hotels. Radisson Hotels host conventions and meetings often arranged by one of Carlson's marketing services, such as the company that provides employee and sales motivation programs.

Next door to the Radisson may be a TGI Fridays or Dalts, two of the restaurant chains owned by Carlson. Even more synergy should flow from Carlson's superluxury cruise ship, SSC *Radisson Diamond,* which was recently launched. Designed to serve the most upscale segment of the market, the huge ship has fully equipped meeting facilities.

Carlson Companies is extremely aggressive, expanding its operations almost constantly. To take advantage of the falling trade barriers in Europe in 1992, the firm bought a London-based marketing group in 1990. Carlson already provides twenty-eight different marketing services to businesses in the United States, Australia, and Japan. It is now expanding those services into France, Germany, Italy, and Spain.

The Radisson Hotel chain operates in the United States, Russia, Australia, India, Mexico, Switzerland, Spain, Thailand, Canada, and the Caribbean. It plans to add a new hotel every ten days through the end of this century. Currently, almost forty countries tie into Radisson's 800 number telephone line, and 45,000 travel agents worldwide access its reservation system. A recent advertising campaign claimed that "If there's not a Radisson Hotel where you're going, give us a few days."

of the corporation's business units obsolete, its other business units can continue to operate effectively in unrelated industries.

Earlier, we referred to the problems involved in managing unrelated businesses. Some conglomerates, however, are managed quite effectively. TRW, for instance, has generally demonstrated successful financial performance. This firm, which began in Ohio as The Steel Products Company in 1916, now produces such diverse products and services as spacecraft, software and systems engineering support services, electronic systems, automotive original and replacement equipment, consumer and business credit information services, computer maintenance, pumps, valves, and energy services.

Vertical Integration

Another growth strategy is **vertical integration,** in which a firm acquires or creates other companies in the firm's distribution channel. Backward vertical integration occurs when the companies acquired or created supply the firm with products or components. An example of backward vertical integration is Du Pont's purchase several years ago of Conoco. Conoco, an oil company, supplies petroleum products that Du Pont uses in manufacturing its chemicals. By buying its suppliers, a firm assures itself of a steady source of supply at a predictable price.

A firm engages in forward vertical integration when it acquires or creates companies that purchase its products. The acquired companies are closer to the end user and in some cases are retail organizations. When Exxon buys service stations from independent dealers, when Van Heusen opens its own retail outlets, or when Tandy operates its own Radio Shack stores, these firms are engaging in forward vertical integration. These actions enable a firm to gain greater control over the distribution, display, sale, and service of their products.

Joint Ventures

Joint ventures are partnerships in which two or more firms carry out a specific project or cooperate in a selected area of business. Joint ventures can be temporary, disbanding after the project is finished, or long-term. Ownership of the firms, of course, remains unchanged.

Joint ventures may be undertaken for a variety of reasons—political, economic, or technological. In certain countries, for instance, a foreign firm may only be permitted to operate if it enters into a joint venture with a local partner. In other cases, a particular project may be so large that it strains a single company's resources. So that company may enter into a joint venture with another firm to gain the resources to accomplish the job. Other projects may require multidimensional technology that no one firm possesses. Hence, firms with different, but compatible, technologies may join together. Or in other cases, one firm may contribute its technological expertise while another contributes its managerial talent.

■ Stability Strategy

Rather than use a growth strategy, some firms adopt a **stability strategy,** in which they attempt to maintain their size and current lines of business. These firms, then, do not attempt to grow either through increased sales or through the development of new products or markets.

Why might a firm adopt this strategy? In some cases, it may be forced to do so if it operates in a low-growth or no-growth industry. Second, it may find that the costs of expanding its market share or of entering new-product or new-market areas is higher than the benefits that are projected to come with that growth. Third, a firm that dominates its industry through its superior size and competitive advantage may pursue stability to reduce its chances of being prosecuted for engaging in monopolistic practices. And finally, smaller enterprises that concentrate on specialized products or services may choose stability because of their concern that growth will result in reduced quality and customer service.

As an example of the last reason, consider Peet's Coffee and Tea, a group of eight coffeehouses that employs 170 employees in the San Francisco Bay area. These establishments serve only the finest freshly roasted coffee to the accompaniment of piped-in classical music. Although the owner of Peet's, Gerald Baldwin, has received numerous lucrative offers to franchise his business

STRATEGIC INSIGHT

International Joint Ventures in the Food, Camera, and Auto Industries

Joint ventures between firms headquartered in different countries have become increasingly popular in recent years. Consider the following examples:

Nestlé and General Mills

• Nestlé, which is the world's largest food company and is headquartered in Switzerland, has joined with U.S.-based General Mills to penetrate the European market with products such as Wheaties and Cheerios. These strong U.S. brands are able to use Nestlé's powerful channels of distribution.

Polaroid and Minolta

• Polaroid, headquartered in Massachusetts, has entered into a venture with Japan's Minolta to sell Polaroid's most expensive consumer instant camera. With sales of instant cameras stagnating, Polaroid wants to find ways of selling more cameras so that it can also sell more film, its most profitable product. Minolta, which does not have an instant-camera product, believes that the Polaroid, sold as the Minolta Instant Pro, will open new markets for the company.

General Motors and Raba

• In the auto industry, General Motors entered a joint venture with Raba, a Hungarian truckmaker, to build engines and trucks for the newly opened East European market. Through the venture, GM gains quick access to the Hungarian market, and Raba acquires superior technology and management.

Ford and Mazda

• Likewise, Ford and Japanese-based Mazda jointly designed a 1991 automobile, with Ford styling the outside of the car and Mazda engineering the inside. The result was the Ford Escort/Mercury Tracer/Mazda Protege. Designed to be a "global car," it is assembled in twelve locations and sold in ninety markets. Both automakers indicate that they gained considerable knowledge from working with each other, and Ford estimates that it may have saved $1 billion by developing the car with Mazda rather than by doing it alone.

SOURCES: "Nestlé to Help General Mills Sell Cereals in Europe," *The Wall Street Journal,* 1 December 1989; R. Suskind, "Minolta Puts Name on Polaroid," *The Wall Street Journal,* 23 June 1990; J. S. Lublin, "GM Pioneers Eastern Europe for Venture," *The Wall Street Journal,* 11 January 1990; J. B. Treece and A. Borrus, "How Ford and Mazda Shared the Driver's Seat," *Business Week,* 26 March 1990, pp. 94–95; W. Brown, "Annual Auto Guide: The Wheels of 1991," *The Washington Post Magazine,* 21 October 1990, p. 32.

nationwide, he has always refused. His concern is that with growth, quality may suffer. He fears, for instance, that some franchisees might serve coffee that was not freshly roasted to cut their costs and increase their profits.

■ Retrenchment Strategies

Growth strategies and the stability strategy are normally adopted by firms that are in satisfactory competitive positions. But when a firm's performance is disappointing or, at the extreme, when its survival is at stake, then **retrenchment strategies** may be appropriate. Retrenchment may take one of three forms: turnaround, divestment, or liquidation. Each strategy is described below.

Turnaround

The intent of a **turnaround** is to transform the organization into a leaner and more effective business. It includes such actions as eliminating unprofitable outputs, pruning assets, reducing the size of the work force, cutting costs of distribution, and rethinking the firm's product lines and target markets.

Take, as an example, what may be the most famous turnaround in American business history. Chrysler Corporation, by the late 1970s, was on the verge of bankruptcy. Its newly hired CEO, Lee Iacocca, implemented a dramatic turnaround strategy. Large numbers of blue- and white-collar employees were laid off, the remaining workers agreed to forgo part of their salaries and benefits, and twenty plants were either closed or consolidated. Iacocca also implemented a divestment strategy (discussed in the following section) by selling Chrysler's marine outboard motor division, its defense business, its air-conditioning division, and all of its automobile manufacturing plants located outside of the United States. These actions lowered the firm's break-even point from an annual sales level of 2.4 million cars and trucks to about 1.2 million. By 1982, Chrysler began to show a profit, after having lost $3.5 billion in the preceding four years.

The years from 1982 until 1987 were particularly good ones for Chrysler, with record sales and profits. But as international competitors from Japan, South Korea, and various European countries exerted increasing competitive pressures, Chrysler's profits were dramatically reduced. As a result, Chrysler again had to adopt a turnaround strategy by closing one-third of its assembly plants. It also attempted to divest its aerospace and defense electronics businesses in order to channel all of its resources into vehicle production.

Divestment

When a corporation sells or "spins off" one of its business units, as Chrysler did, it is engaging in **divestment.** Divestment usually occurs when the business unit is performing poorly or when it no longer fits the corporation's strategic profile. The business unit may be sold to another company, to its managers and employees, or to an individual or group of investors. As companies reposition themselves in certain markets or product lines, such sales are fairly common. For instance, General Electric, Westinghouse, and Singer have all sold their computer businesses. Singer also sold its original core business unit that produced sewing machines and began to concentrate on high-technology electronics.

Divestment can also occur through a spin-off. In this case, shares of stock in the business unit that is to be spun off are distributed. The stock of the parent corporation and the spun-off business unit then begin to trade separately.

Liquidation

A strategy of last resort is liquidation. When neither a turnaround nor a divestment seems feasible, **liquidation** occurs through termination of the business unit's existence by sale of its assets. Most stakeholder groups suffer in liquidations. Stockholders and creditors often lose some or all of their funds, managers and employees lose their jobs, suppliers lose a customer, and the community suffers an increase in unemployment and a decrease in tax revenues.

■ Combination Strategies

In some cases, particularly in periods of rapid environmental change, **combination strategies,** utilizing two or more of the strategies discussed above, may be required. As an example, consider Emerson Electric's competitive situation in the mid-1980s. For years, this firm maintained a reliable, high-quality image in its electric motor division. This division produced motors for power tools, industrial uses, and appliances. Emerson's strengths were not only reliability and quality but also continuous product improvements through research and development. Its weakness was high labor costs, since all of its operations were in the United States. The environmental opportunity for Emerson was the long economic recovery that started in the mid-1980s. This recovery provided increased demand for Emerson's products. Threats, however, appeared in the form of Japanese and Taiwanese firms with lower labor costs.

As the foreign firms began to invade the U.S. market with prices as much as 30 percent below Emerson's, Emerson was able to meet the threat effectively because of its understanding of its own strengths and weaknesses and of its environment. To reduce its costs, Emerson adopted a turnaround strategy by closing 49 of its 250 manufacturing plants and eliminating 3000 high-cost jobs. Simultaneously, it integrated horizontally by acquiring overseas operations in such low-cost countries as Mexico and quickly expanded those operations through internal growth. Because of its careful analysis and implementation, Emerson was able to meet this new competitive threat through a combination of strategies.

Companies that operate multiple business units often adopt a combination of strategies simultaneously. One business unit, for example, may grow internally while another grows by acquiring an independent firm and another is retrenching. These differences occur because the business units operate in varying markets, facing differing degrees of competition and dissimilar rates of environmental change.

Firms with a number of business units are said to manage a *portfolio* of businesses. The following section discusses some of the major analytical frameworks that are used by portfolio managers.

PORTFOLIO FRAMEWORKS

Perhaps the most recognized of all portfolio frameworks is the one developed in 1967 by the Boston Consulting Group (BCG), a firm that specializes in strategic planning. The framework, originated by Alan J. Zakon of BCG and William W. Wommack of Mead Corporation, has since been elaborated upon by Barry Hedley, a director of BCG. The following sections describe the BCG framework, as well as another strategy, the GE framework, in detail.

■ Original BCG Framework

The **original BCG portfolio framework** is illustrated by the matrix shown in Figure 4.2. The market's rate of growth is indicated on the vertical axis, and the firm's share of the market is indicated on the horizontal axis. Each of the circles represents a business unit. The size of the circle reflects the business unit's annual sales, the horizontal position of the circle indicates its market share, and

Figure 4.2   **The Original BCG Framework**

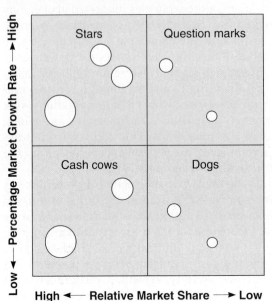

Source: Reprinted with permission from *Long Range Planning*, vol. 10, B. Hedley, "Strategy and the 'Business Portfolio,' " © 1977, Pergamon Press, plc.

its vertical position depicts the growth rate of the market in which it competes. For instance, the circle in the lower left corner of the matrix symbolizes a business unit with relatively large sales and a very high share of its market. Its market, however, is stagnant, exhibiting little growth. Using this framework, management can categorize each of its different businesses as stars, question marks, cash cows, or dogs, depending upon each business unit's relative market share and the growth rate of its market.[3]

A star is a business unit that has a large share of a high-growth market (i.e., one with an annual growth rate of 10 percent or more). Although stars are profitable businesses, they usually must consume considerable cash to continue their growth and fight off the numerous competitors that are attracted to fast-growing markets. Question marks are business units with low shares of rapidly growing markets. Many question marks are new businesses just entering the market. If they are able to grow and become market leaders, they evolve into stars; but if they are unable eventually to command a significant market share despite heavy financial support from corporate headquarters, they will usually be divested or liquidated.

Turning to the lower half of the matrix, a cash cow is a business unit that has a large share of a slow-growth market (i.e., one growing at an annual rate of less than 10 percent). Cash cows are highly profitable because they dominate a market that does not attract many new entrants. Because they are so well established, they need not spend vast resources for advertising, product promotions, or consumer rebates. The excess cash that they generate can be used by the corporation to support its stars and question marks. Finally, dogs are business units

Neglecting a Cash Cow at Diamond International

From the perspective of the original BCG portfolio framework, U.S. Playing Card was a cash cow for its parent company, Diamond International. Although cash cows do not require vast expenditures for advertising or product promotions, they must still be managed carefully so that they will generate as much excess cash as possible to invest in stars and promising question marks. But Diamond International neglected its U.S. Playing Card subsidiary by allowing the number of highly paid unionized employees to grow without corresponding increases in productivity and by failing to maintain and replace aging machinery and equipment.

Over time, the cash cow became a dog and was divested by Diamond International. The business, however, continued to perform poorly until it was purchased in 1986 by Ronald Rule. Rule engaged in a successful turnaround through such actions as cutting labor costs by one-third, replacing the company's union labor with nonunion employees, and purchasing state-of-the-art machinery and equipment. Today, U.S. Playing Card produces 220,000 decks of cards daily and holds a 70 percent share of the U.S. market and a worldwide market share of 45 percent. Its annual sales amount to $83 million.

U.S. Playing Card is now owned by the Jesup Group of Stamford, Connecticut. It accounts for over a quarter of Jesup's annual revenues and serves as a cash cow for some of Jesup's other product lines: laminated plastics, plastic materials and resins, adhesives and sealants, and synthetic rubber.

that have small market shares in slow-growth (or even declining) industries. Dogs are generally marginal businesses that incur either losses or small profits.

Ideally, a corporate portfolio should have mostly stars and cash cows, some question marks (because they represent the future of the corporation), and few, if any, dogs. To attain this ideal, corporate-level managers can use any of the four alternative strategies described in the following sections.

Build Market Share

One of the portfolio strategies is to build market share. To accomplish this end, managers must identify promising business units that currently fall into the question mark category. Management then attempts to transform these businesses into stars. This process of increasing market share may involve significant price reductions, even if that means incurring losses or marginal profitability in the short run. The underlying assumption of this strategy is that once market share leadership is attained, profitability will follow.

Hold Market Share

Another strategy is to hold market share. In this situation, cash cows are managed so as to maintain their market shares, rather than to increase them. Holding a large market share generates more cash than building market share does. Hence, the cash contributed by the cash cows can be used to support stars and selected question marks.

Harvest

Harvesting means milking as much short-term cash from a business as possible, usually while allowing its market share to decline. The cash gained from this strategy is also used to support stars and selected question marks. The businesses harvested are usually dogs, question marks that show little promise of growth, and perhaps some weak cash cows.

Divest

Divesting refers to selling or liquidating a business unit. It usually provides some cash to the corporation (from the sale) and stems the cash outflow that would have been spent on the business in the future. As dogs and less promising question marks are divested, the cash provided is reallocated to stars and question marks with the potential to become stars.

For example, one of Miller Brewing Company's few new-product failures was Matilda Bay wine coolers. Spending about $30 million to enter the market in 1987, Miller made Matilda Bay the number-four-selling wine cooler in the country by the end of 1988. However, its sales plunged 50 percent the next year, and it lost money for seven straight quarters. Discounts to retailers failed to revitalize the product. Miller attempted to sell Matilda Bay but was unable to find a buyer. So it liquidated its wine cooler business. Some analysts credited Miller with cutting its losses quickly. The funds that had been targeted for Matilda Bay were instead channeled into promising new products such as Miller's Genuine Draft beer.[4]

As is evident, the BCG portfolio framework heavily emphasizes the importance of market share leadership. Cash cows and stars are market share leaders. Some question marks are cultivated to become leaders as well, but less promising question marks and dogs are usually targeted either for harvesting or divestiture. This emphasis on market share has been heavily criticized, leading the Boston Consulting Group to reformulate its portfolio framework.

■ Revised BCG Framework

The **revised BCG framework** is illustrated in Figure 4.3. In place of the star, question mark, cash cow, and dog categories are volume, specialization, fragmented, and stalemate business units. Only the volume business is targeted for market share leadership. The volume business generates high profitability through large market share and its accompanying economies of scale. Business units denoted by specialization, however, are those able to yield high profits even though they have a low market share. Because they have selected a market niche in which to operate, they are able to distinguish themselves from their competitors in the market. The appropriate strategies for these two types of business units, according to BCG, are for the volume business unit to attempt to gain even greater market share and for the specialization unit to maintain its low market share.

The next category is fragmented businesses. This term refers to business units operating in fragmented industries. A fragmented industry is one in which numerous firms, perhaps even thousands, exist. Examples include the motel, restaurant, and retail clothing industries. Fragmented industries are characterized by low barriers to entry. (By contrast, a consolidated industry, such as the

The Revised BCG Framework

Figure 4.3

Maintain and Support	Divest
Volume (emphasize market share leadership)	Stalemate (regardless of relative market share)
Specialization (emphasize maintenance of low market share)	Unprofitable fragmented (regardless of relative market share)
Profitable fragmented (do not emphasize market share)	

U.S. automobile manufacturing industry, has high barriers to entry and, there-fore, contains only a few very large competitors.) Businesses in this category can be highly profitable—or unprofitable—regardless of their market share. A local motel or restaurant, for example, can be quite successful, as can Holiday Inn or McDonald's. So fragmented business units should be cultivated for profitability while the importance of market share is de-emphasized. The BCG recommends that profitable fragmented business units be maintained and supported and that unprofitable units be divested.

In the final category, a stalemate business is one that has low, or no, profit-ability because its industry offers poor prospects. Again, market share is not a consideration in this category. The recommendation for stalemate businesses is that they be divested.

These strategic recommendations are reflected in Figure 4.3. Business units shown on the left side of the figure should be maintained and supported, but those on the right side should be divested.

■ GE Framework

Another well-known portfolio framework was developed by General Electric (GE) with the help of McKinsey and Company, a consulting firm. As shown in Figure 4.4, the **GE framework** categorizes business units according to industry attractiveness (low, medium, or high) and business unit strength (weak, aver-age, or strong). The ideal business unit is one that is strong relative to its com-petitors and operates in an industry that is attractive. Some of the criteria used to determine industry attractiveness and business strength are shown in Table 4.3.

As shown in Figure 4.4, a corporation's most successful business units fall in the top left section of the diagram, and its least successful ones are in the bottom right section. Average business units fall in between. Strategically, the corpora-tion should divest itself of the business units in the bottom right section while supporting those in the top left area. The average business units will receive less support than those in the upper left unless they are perceived as candidates that have the potential for highly profitable operations.

Both the GE and BCG portfolio frameworks may be used by corporate-level management to evaluate each of their business units, to make strategic deci-

Figure 4.4   **The GE Framework**

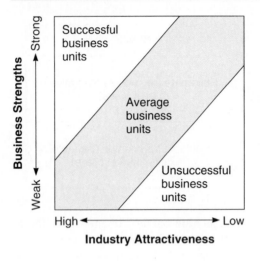

Table 4.3   Criteria for Determining Industry Attractiveness and Business Unit Strengths

Industry Attractiveness Criteria	*Business Unit Strength Criteria*
Annual industry growth rate	Market share
Cyclicality of the industry	Firm profitability
Historical profitability of the industry	Per-unit cost of operation
Macroenvironmental opportunities and constraints particularly relevant to the industry	Process R&D performance
Overall industry size	Product quality
Seasonality of the industry	Managerial and personnel talent
Intensity of competition	Market share growth
Industry predisposition to unionization	Operation capacity
Rate of innovation in the industry	Technological know-how
	Product R&D performance
	Brand reputation

sions, and to reallocate resources. Although our discussion has focused on large firms with multiple business units, some small, privately held companies are also active in a number of businesses. These frameworks may be used by their top managers to evaluate the strategies used by each of their businesses.

ISSUES IN STRATEGY FORMULATION

Several issues in strategy formulation are examined in this section. The first is whether diversification reduces or increases a firm's competitive risk. A related issue is the impact of diversification on a corporation's financial performance. Finally, the relationship of diversification and corporate-level involvement in business unit operations is analyzed.

■ Diversification and Risk

As we have seen, diversification is common among corporations. It occurs for several reasons. First, when firms face declining prospects in their industry, they often diversify into other, more vibrant industries.[5] An example is USX, once the nation's largest steel producer. Under its former name, U.S. Steel, this company diversified into oil and gas businesses some years ago as the attractiveness of the steel industry declined in the face of strong foreign competition.

A second reason for diversification is to avoid committing all of the firm's resources to one industry. Any industry, no matter how profitable at certain times, will experience economic downturns.[6] The company that operates only in one industry, then, ties its financial success to the particular cycles of that industry. Acclaim Entertainment, Inc., serves as an example. It became profitable by creating video games for Nintendo Company. However, its president, Gregory Fischbach, was aware that Acclaim needed to diversify beyond Nintendo games. He knew all too well the vulnerability of being a one-product company, because he had previously served as vice president of Activision, Inc. Activision produced software for Atari Corporation's video games, which were hot-selling items in the early 1980s. When the video game craze fizzled a few years later, both Atari and Activision suffered huge losses.

So firms often diversify to reduce their risk. But they may also diversify if they have excess resources (i.e., more money than they need to reinvest in their current businesses).[7] An example from several years ago is ITT under the leadership of CEO Harold Geneen. The company, which was in international telecommunications, was transformed by Geneen into a conglomerate with over a hundred business units.

Viewed from another perspective, diversification may increase corporate risk.[8] Observing the wave of diversification that began in the 1960s and continues to this time, one can draw two conclusions: (1) Mergers and acquisitions have subjected many firms to high debt risk because management has financed the acquisitions with borrowed funds; and (2) many diversifications have resulted in firms leaving their areas of expertise, thereby increasing their competitive risk.[9] These two factors resulted in drastic declines in profits and stock prices of conglomerates in the later 1960s and early 1970s and again in the early 1980s. In fact, by 1990, many firms that had financed their acquisitions primarily through debt were beginning to default on their interest payments even though the economy was healthy. In 1989 alone, bond defaults and debt moratoriums totaled more than $4 billion.[10] The more successful conglomerates tend to be those that balance their risks by not assuming excessive debt.

■ Diversification and Performance

Beyond the relationship between diversification and risk looms another question: Is diversification more profitable than operating in a single industry, and if so, what type of diversification is most profitable? In an attempt to answer this question, Rumelt compared the performance of three types of corporations: those that operated in a single industry, those that diversified into related areas, and those that diversified into unrelated businesses.[11] His results suggest that corporations in single businesses or related diversified businesses outperform conglomerates. A number of subsequent studies have reached the same general conclusion.

In a related study, Lichtenberg examined the productivity of 17,000 manufacturing plants and concluded that the greater the number of industries in which a plant's parent firm operates, the lower the productivity of that plant is. As a result of this adverse impact of diversification, the proportion of companies that operated in more than twenty industries declined 37 percent between 1985 and 1989. His conclusion is that this reversal of the conglomerate diversification trend should have a favorable impact on productivity.[12]

Perhaps corporations in single or related diversified businesses perform well because they are able to capitalize on expertise developed around common skills, resources, technology, and markets. By contrast, conglomerates may find it more difficult to develop these types of synergy. Of course, this is not to say that conglomerates cannot perform well. Certainly, exceptions exist, such as Paramount Entertainment, Inc., which is successful in such unrelated industries as films, apparel, cigars, zinc, books, and automotive parts. But on the average, corporations that diversify into unrelated industries trail their counterparts that operate in single or related diversified businesses.

Another set of studies indicates that diversifying into unrelated businesses rarely benefits shareholders financially.[13] We wish to emphasize that not all studies are in agreement in this area; in fact, one shows that unrelated diversification results in higher financial performance than related diversification.[14] But the evidence against conglomerate diversification is quite impressive. Then, why do corporations continue to diversify into unrelated industries? There are probably three reasons: position preservation, wealth preservation, and compensation enhancement. Each reason is explained below.

Position Preservation

By not putting all of their eggs into one basket, top executives attempt to reduce risk. This risk reduction can benefit both the company and the executives. When organizations falter, their top managers often lose their jobs.[15] Unrelated diversification should reduce this risk and help upper-level managers preserve their professional positions. Even if the corporation is not as profitable as it might be otherwise, its risk of dissolution is lower.

Wealth Preservation

Top corporate executives ordinarily have a significant portion of their personal wealth invested in their firm's stock.[16] To diversify their investments, they may be inclined to involve their corporation in unrelated businesses. Hence, conglomerate diversification can preserve the personal wealth of top management.

Compensation Enhancement

A number of studies show that as organizations grow in size, their top managers receive greater compensation.[17] A common expectation is that increasing organizational size makes the task of management more difficult. This greater level of difficulty should be rewarded through higher compensation. Hence, top managers have an incentive to increase the size of their firms. The fastest way to grow is through acquisitions of other businesses.

■ Corporate Involvement in Business Unit Operations

We have seen that corporations may have multiple business units in the same industry, in related industries, or in unrelated industries. How closely corporate-level managers become involved in the strategy formulation and operation of those business units varies from one firm to another. Historically, corporations that have diversified into unrelated businesses operate in a relatively decentralized fashion.[18] In **decentralization,** firms tend to employ small corporate staffs and allow the business unit managers to make most strategic and operating decisions. These decisions involve functional areas such as purchasing, inventory management, production, finance, research and development, and marketing. Examples of decentralized corporations are Paramount, Litton Industries, and Textron.

Alternatively, corporations whose business units are in the same industry or in related industries usually operate in a centralized fashion. Under **centralization,** most major decisions affecting the business units are made at corporate headquarters, so these companies have large corporate staffs. Examples include Chrysler, Coca-Cola, and Sears, Roebuck.

Corporate involvement in business unit operations can be conceptualized as shown on the continuum below. Involvement can range from being highly centralized to being almost completely decentralized.

Centralized corporations  Decentralized corporations

Corporations, of course, may be found at literally any point on this continuum. Decisions regarding centralization and decentralization are not of the either-or variety. Instead, a firm's decision-making processes are termed *relatively centralized* or *relatively decentralized.* Most companies, therefore, are not located at either of the extreme ends on the continuum.

Companies that are relatively centralized make many functional decisions—such as those in purchasing, marketing, finance, and production—at the corporate level. The more commonality in those functional activities across the firm's business units, the greater the tendency is to coordinate those activities at the corporate level. Such centralized decisions can result in efficiencies and consistencies across all business units.

For instance, quantity discounts are larger if the same products are purchased at the corporate level for all business units than if each business unit purchases them separately. As another example, a corporation can borrow more funds at a lower interest rate than separate business units can. And central coordination can encourage business units to buy components, if possible and economically feasible, from other business units within the same corporation instead of buying them from outside the company.

Centralization, however, also incurs costs. As the organization grows, larger and larger corporate staffs are required. As the staff increases, so does the distance between top corporate management and the business units. Top managers are forced to rely increasingly on their staff for information, and they communicate downward to the business units through their staff. These processes result in obvious problems in communication and in the proliferation of bureaucratic procedures.

Decentralized corporations are able to eliminate these problems since highly decentralized firms maintain only skeletal corporate staffs. But they are seldom able to benefit from coordinated activities across their business units, since each operates as at least a semi-independent entity. Therefore, synergy may be less in a decentralized organization.

SUMMARY

Prior to selecting a corporate-level strategy, top managers engage in S.W.O.T. analysis. By matching the organization's strengths and weaknesses with the environment's opportunities and threats, management is better able to formulate successful strategies for attaining its goals. In choosing a strategy, top management may adopt any one of three general corporate profiles: They may compete in a single business, in several related businesses, or in several unrelated businesses. Once this decision has been made, a corporate-level strategy must be chosen to guide the firm's operations in its selected business or businesses.

A growth strategy is designed to increase a firm's profits, sales, and/or market share. Growth may be attained in any of several ways: internal growth, mergers, horizontal integration, conglomerate diversification, vertical integration, or joint ventures. A second strategy, stability, is one in which a firm attempts to maintain its size and current lines of business. Firms having performance problems may adopt one of three retrenchment strategies: turnaround, divestment, or liquidation. Finally, a combination of the above strategies may be appropriate.

Corporations with multiple business units often adopt a combination of strategies simultaneously. Because managing several businesses at once is quite complex, a number of portfolio frameworks are available to assist managers. The best-known frameworks are those developed by the Boston Consulting Group (BCG) and General Electric (GE). They allow corporate-level managers to evaluate the performance of each of their business units, to make strategic decisions for each unit, and to reallocate resources from one unit to another.

Diversification is a common strategic direction for many businesses. Most firms diversify to reduce risk or to reinvest excess resources. However, diversification may, in some instances, increase risk—particularly if diversification is heavily financed with debt. Studies generally show that organizations that operate in single businesses or in related businesses outperform those that diversify into unrelated businesses. But top managers have other reasons, aside from the firm's financial performance, for engaging in conglomerate diversification, such as preserving their position or their wealth or enhancing their compensation.

Corporate-level managers must decide on the extent to which they will be involved in strategic and operational decision making at the business unit level. Usually, corporations that have diversified into related businesses remain fairly centralized, and conglomerates operate in a relatively decentralized fashion.

KEY CONCEPTS

BCG portfolio framework (original) A strategic-planning framework developed by the Boston Consulting Group that categorizes a firm's business units by the market share that they hold and the growth rate of their market. Using these two variables, one can classify each business unit as a star (high share of a fast-growing market), cash cow (high share of a low-growth market), question mark (low share of a fast-growing market), or dog (low share of a low-growth market).

BCG portfolio framework (revised) The more recent framework developed by the Boston Consulting Group that categorizes a firm's business units as volume (generates high profitability through large market share), specialization (yields high profits by operating in a market niche), fragmented (operates in a fragmented industry in which market share is unrelated to profitability), and stalemate (incurs low or no profits because its industry offers poor prospects).

Centralization An organizational decision-making process in which most strategic and operating decisions are made by managers at the top of the organization structure (i.e., corporate headquarters).

Combination strategies A corporate-level strategy involving some combination of the following strategies: internal growth, merger, horizontal integration, conglomerate diversification, vertical integration, joint venture, stability, turnaround, divestment, and/or liquidation.

Conglomerate diversification A corporate-level growth strategy in which a firm expands by acquiring businesses in industries that are unrelated to the corporation's original business.

Corporate-level strategy The strategy that top management formulates for the overall company.

Decentralization An organizational decision-making process in which most strategic and operating decisions are made by managers at the business unit level.

Divestment A corporate-level retrenchment strategy in which a firm sells one or more of its business units.

GE framework A strategic-planning framework developed by General Electric Company that categorizes a corporation's business units according to industry attractiveness and business unit strength.

Growth strategy   A corporate-level strategy intended to increase profits, sales, and/or market share. Firms that adopt this strategy may grow internally or may grow externally through merger, horizontal integration, conglomerate diversification, vertical integration, and/or joint venture.

Horizontal integration   A corporate-level growth strategy in which a firm expands by acquiring or creating other companies in its same line of business.

Internal growth   A corporate-level growth strategy in which a firm expands by increasing its sales rather than by acquiring other companies.

Joint venture   A corporate-level growth strategy in which a firm expands by entering into either a temporary or a long-term partnership with another firm to carry out a specific project or cooperate in a selected area of business.

Liquidation   A corporate-level retrenchment strategy in which a firm terminates one or more of its business units.

Merger   A corporate-level growth strategy in which a firm combines with another firm through an exchange of stock.

Retrenchment strategy   A corporate-level strategy undertaken by a firm when its performance is disappointing or when its survival is at stake.

Stability strategy   A corporate-level strategy intended to maintain a firm's present size and current lines of business.

S.W.O.T. analysis   A corporate-level analysis intended to match the firm's strengths and weaknesses (the S. and W. in the name) with the opportunities and threats (the Q. and T.) posed by the environment.

Synergy   A situation in which the combination of two or more business units results in greater effectiveness and efficiency than the total yielded by those businesses when they were operated separately.

Turnaround   A corporate-level retrenchment strategy intended to transform the firm into a leaner and more effective business by reducing costs and rethinking the firm's product lines and target markets.

Vertical integration   A corporate-level growth strategy in which the firm acquires or creates other companies in the firm's distribution channel.

DISCUSSION QUESTIONS

1. Explain the purpose of S.W.O.T. analysis. Why should it precede strategy selection?

2. What do you feel are the advantages that internal growth has over growth through mergers and acquisitions? What particular advantages might mergers and acquisitions have over internal growth?

3. Explain the distinction between horizontal and vertical integration, and the distinction between horizontal integration and conglomerate diversification.

4. Why would a firm prefer to engage in a joint venture over a more permanent arrangement?

5. Why would management adopt a stability strategy? Do you feel that such a strategy is viable over a lengthy period of time? Why or why not?

6. When is a retrenchment strategy appropriate? Identify some criteria that will help determine what particular retrenchment strategy should be used.

7. Explain the purpose of portfolio framework analysis.

8. What are the differences and similarities between the original and revised BCG frameworks, and between the original BCG framework and the GE framework?

9. Why do firms engage in conglomerate diversification? What are the dangers of this form of diversification?

10. What types of organizations are likely to operate in a relatively centralized (versus a relatively decentralized) fashion? Why?

STRATEGIC MANAGEMENT EXERCISES

1. Identify a particular type of business that you might wish to start, assuming that you have the necessary financial resources. Furthermore, assume that after some period of time during which the business is successful, you wish to adopt the growth strategy for your company. Explain how your firm might expand through each of the following strategies: internal growth, merger, horizontal integration, conglomerate diversification, vertical integration, and joint venture.

2. Select a well-known company for which there is a considerable amount of published information. Using Table 4.1 as your outline, conduct a S.W.O.T. analysis for this firm. You may be unable to address all of the factors listed in Table 4.1 owing to a lack of information, and as you conduct your research, you may be able to identify factors not shown in Table 4.1.

   Now, using your S.W.O.T. analysis, recommend a specific corporate-level strategy for this firm to adopt. Explain your rationale.

3. Using information in your library, identify three firms: one that is in a single business, one that is in several related businesses, and one that is in unrelated businesses. Now, insofar as information permits, explain the advantages and disadvantages of the corporate profile that each company has selected.

4. Choose a corporation that has multiple business units (either related or unrelated). Attempt to place each business unit in one of the categories of the original BCG portfolio framework (i.e., star, cash cow, question mark, and dog). Now categorize each along the lines of the revised BCG

> portfolio framework (i.e., volume, specialization, fragmented, stale-
> mate). Finally, attempt to place each business unit into one of the cate-
> gories in the GE framework (i.e., successful, average, unsuccessful).

REFERENCES

1. J. Schwartz and D. Glick, "Deep Pockets for Biotech," *Business Week,* 19 February 1990, p. 54.

2. B. O'Brian, "American Air Expands into Three Continents, Flexing Its U.S. Muscle," *The Wall Street Journal,* 8 June 1990.

3. B. Hedley, "Strategy and the Business Portfolio," *Long Range Planning* 10, no. 2 (February 1977): 9–14.

4. J. F. Siler, "How Miller Got Dunked in Matilda Bay," *Business Week,* 25 September 1989, p. 54.

5. R. P. Rumelt, *Strategy, Structure, and Economic Performance* (Boston: Division of Research, Graduate School of Business Administration, Harvard University Press, 1974).

6. C. A. Montgomery, "The Measurement of Firm Diversification: Some Empirical Evidence," *Academy of Management Journal* 25 (1982): 299–307; R. A. Bettis, "Performance Differences in Related and Unrelated Diversified Firms," *Strategic Management Journal* 2 (1981): 379–393.

7. N. Capon, J. M. Hulbert, J. U. Farley, and E. L. Martin, "Corporate Diversity and Economic Performance: The Impact of Market Specialization," *Strategic Management Journal* 9 (1988): 61–74.

8. D. H. Ciscel and T. M. Carroll, "The Determinants of Executive Salaries: An Economic Survey," *Review of Economics and Statistics* 62 (1980): 7–13; C. Galbraith, B. Samuelson, C. Stiles, and G. Merrill, "Diversification, Industry Research and Development, and Market Performance," *Academy of Management Proceedings, '86* (1986): 17–20.

9. D. L. Beattie, "Conglomerate Diversification and Performance: A Survey and Time Series Analysis," *Applied Economics* 12 (1980): 251–273; J. R. Carter, "In Search of Synergy: A Structure-Performance Test," *Review of Economics and Statistics* 59 (1977): 279–289; A. Michel and I. Shaked, "Does Business Diversification Affect Performance?" *Financial Management* 13 (1984): 18–25; Capon et al., "Corporate Diversity," pp. 61–74.

10. C. Farrell with L. J. Nathans, "The Bills Are Coming Due," *Business Week,* 11 September 1989, p. 84.

11. Rumelt, *Strategy, Structure, and Economic Performance.*

12. F. R. Lichtenberg, "Want More Productivity? Kill That Conglomerate," *The Wall Street Journal,* 16 January 1990.

13. Montgomery, "The Measurement of Firm Diversification," pp. 299–307; Bettis, "Performance Differences," pp. 379–393.

14. Michel and Shaked, "Does Business Diversification Affect Performance?" pp. 18–25.

15. Y. Amihud and B. Lev, "Risk Reduction as a Managerial Motive for Conglomerate Mergers," *Bell Journal of Economics* 7 (Autumn 1981): 605–617.

16. Ciscel and Carroll, "The Determinants of Executive Salaries," pp. 7–13.

17. M. Firth, "Takeover, Shareholder Returns, and the Theory of the Firm," *Quarterly Journal of Economics* 94 (1980): 235–260; W. A. McEachern, *Managerial Control and Performance* (Lexington, Mass.: Lexington Books, 1975).

18. D. K. Datta and J. H. Grant, "Relationships Between Type of Acquisition, the Autonomy Given to the Acquired Firm, and Acquisition Success: An Empirical Analysis," *Journal of Management* 16 (1990): 29–44.

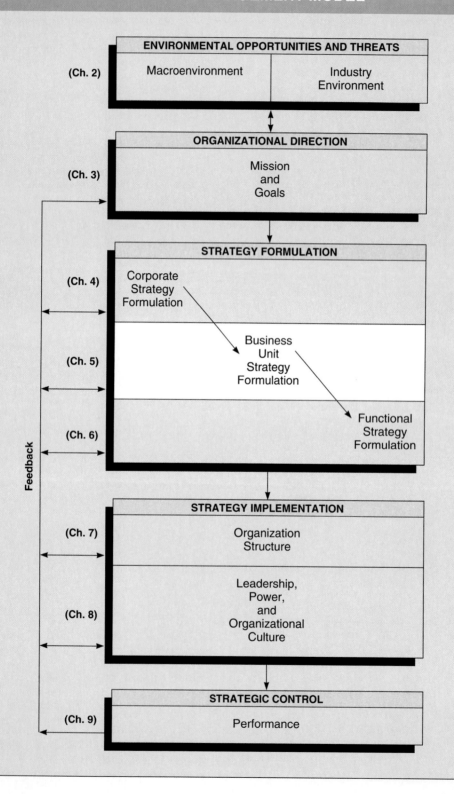

STRATEGIC MANAGEMENT MODEL

ENVIRONMENTAL OPPORTUNITIES AND THREATS

(Ch. 2)

Macroenvironment | Industry Environment

ORGANIZATIONAL DIRECTION

(Ch. 3)

Mission and Goals

STRATEGY FORMULATION

(Ch. 4)

Corporate Strategy Formulation

(Ch. 5)

Business Unit Strategy Formulation

(Ch. 6)

Functional Strategy Formulation

STRATEGY IMPLEMENTATION

(Ch. 7)

Organization Structure

(Ch. 8)

Leadership, Power, and Organizational Culture

STRATEGIC CONTROL

(Ch. 9)

Performance

Feedback

5

CHAPTER

Business Unit Strategies

Once top management has formulated the organization's corporate-level strategy, the managers of the firm's business units must adopt a strategy to guide their operations. A **business unit** is an organizational subsystem that has a market, a set of competitors, and a mission distinct from those of the other subsystems in the firm. The concept of the strategic business unit was pioneered by General Electric Company. At GE, for example, one business unit manufactures and markets major appliances such as ranges, refrigerators, dishwashers, and clothes washers and dryers. Another business unit is responsible for producing and selling jet engines to airplane manufacturers. In total, GE contains over two hundred strategic business units. Each of these business units adopts its own strategy consistent with the organization's corporate-level strategy. Because each business unit serves a different market and competes with different companies than the firm's other business units, it must operate with its own mission, objectives, and strategy.

A single company that operates within only one industry is also considered a business unit. For instance, an independent company that builds and sells swimming pools is considered a business unit. In such an organization, corporate-level strategy and business unit strategy are the same. Hence, the focus of this chapter is on organizational entities that contain their own functional departments, such as production and sales, and operate within a single industry.

Managers of these business units can choose from a number of **generic strategies** to guide their organizations. These strategic alternatives are termed *generic* because they can be adopted by any type of business unit, whether it be a traditional manufacturing company, a high-technology firm, or a service organization. Of the seven strategies available and discussed in this chapter, three are most appropriate for small business units; the remaining four are used by large business units.

GENERIC STRATEGIES FOR SMALL BUSINESS UNITS

This section presents the generic strategies that are most appropriate for small business units. These are the niche–low cost, niche-differentiation, and niche–low-cost/differentiation strategies.

■ Niche–Low-Cost Strategy

The **niche–low-cost strategy** emphasizes keeping overall costs low while serving a narrow segment of the market. Business units that adopt this strategy produce no-frills products or services for price-sensitive customers in a market niche. The no-frills outputs of one business differ little from those of competing businesses, and market demand for these outputs is elastic.

Depending upon the prevailing industry forces, customers are generally only willing to pay low to average prices for no-frills products or services. Hence, it is essential that businesses using this strategy keep their overall costs as low as possible. Therefore, they emphasize keeping their initial investment low and holding operating costs down. For instance, these organizations will purchase from suppliers who offer the lowest prices, and they will emphasize the function of financial control. Research and development efforts will be directed at improving operational efficiency, and attempts will be made to enhance logistical and distribution efficiencies. Such businesses will de-emphasize the development of new or improved products or services that might raise costs, and advertising and promotional expenditures will be minimized. Figure 5.1 portrays the strategic position of a business unit (Southwest Airlines) that competes with the niche–low-cost strategy. Its location on the chart reflects its strategy of low costs and minimal product/service differentiation.

Ideally, the small business unit that adopts the niche–low-cost strategy com-

Figure 5.1   **A Business Competing with the Niche–Low-Cost Strategy**

Cost

Southwest

Differentiation

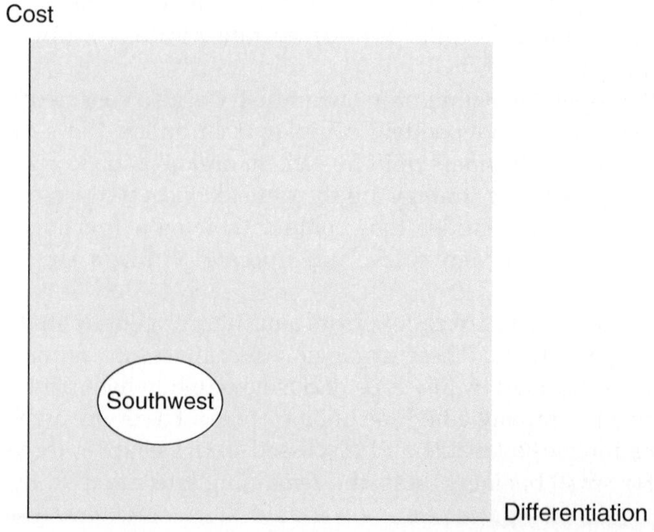

Southwest Airlines' Niche–Low-Cost Strategy

Southwest Airlines, a Texas-based carrier with $1.2 billion in annual revenue, has used its niche–low-cost strategy so successfully that it has become one of the most profitable airlines in the United States. Beginning as a short-haul airline between the older in-town airports of Dallas and Houston in 1967, its no-frills, frequent-departure flights were instantly popular with price-sensitive and time-conscious travelers.

Even as it has expanded, the airline has maintained its policy of no assigned seating or first-class seats, it still serves no meals, and it has never belonged to a computer reservation system (which, in itself, saves the company $25 million annually). Its boarding passes are made of sturdy plastic so that they can be reused.

Yet even with its lack of frills, Southwest has a reputation for quality, as demonstrated by its youthful and fuel-efficient fleet of airplanes, excellent record for on-time flights, and few passenger complaints. Its secret of success in an industry where successes are few is its solid management. Southwest has been able to keep its operating costs low while maintaining an ample supply of cash and a healthy balance sheet. Management places a heavy emphasis on high aircraft utilization and high employee productivity. And the airline only flies routes where it is the dominant carrier, so it is able to set passenger ticket prices.

By keeping its costs low, Southwest is price-competitive not only with other airlines but also with such alternative modes of transportation as personal automobiles and rental cars. For instance, at one time, competing airlines charged $62 for the flight from Dallas to San Antonio. Southwest charged $15 for the same flight. Obviously, this low price even beat the cost of making the 270-mile drive between the two cities.

petes only where it enjoys a cost advantage relative to large, low-cost competitors. For example, small local businesses in industries with high transportation costs—such as cement, tiles, and asphalt—can underbid their big rivals because of their lower delivery costs.

Businesses that compete with the niche–low-cost strategy will deliberately avoid responding to new product and market opportunities for fear of increasing their costs. Such businesses value technological stability in their organizations. Stable technologies enable them to produce no-frills outputs at low costs.

An important vulnerability of the niche–low-cost strategy is that intense price competition periodically occurs in markets with no-frills outputs. For instance, several years ago, Laker Airways used the niche–low-cost strategy very successfully by providing a first in the airline industry—no-frills, low-priced trans-Atlantic passenger service. However, the major airlines eventually responded by offering virtually identical service. The resulting price war drove Laker Airways out of business. The large competitors, because of their greater financial resources, were able to survive the shakeout even though many of them incurred financial losses.

Another important vulnerability of this strategy is technological obsolescence. Businesses that value technological stability, and consequently avoid responding to new product and market opportunities, may eventually find that their products have become obsolete and are no longer desired by their customers.

■ Niche-Differentiation Strategy

The **niche-differentiation strategy** is appropriate for business units that produce highly differentiated, need-fulfilling products or services for the specialized needs of a narrow range of customers or a market niche. Because these outputs are intended to fulfill a deeper set of customer needs than either no-frills goods or differentiated goods (discussed later under the differentiation strategy), and because the market demand for these outputs tends to be inelastic, these goods or services can command high prices. Hence, cost reduction efforts are not emphasized by businesses competing with the niche-differentiation strategy.

In fact, these businesses tend to be deliberately inefficient. The reason is that they continuously attempt to create new product and market opportunities or respond to them. Both actions are costly. Therefore, they highly value technological fluidity in their organizations to create and/or keep pace with state-of-the-art developments in their industries.

Broadly speaking, high prices are acceptable to certain customers who need product performance, prestige, safety, or security. For instance, some customers may be willing to pay high prices for state-of-the-art stereo component systems that perform at wide-range frequencies and low sound distortions (i.e., performance needs). Another cluster of customers will pay very high prices for designer clothes (i.e., prestige needs). Yet another group of industrial buyers will pay significantly more to suppliers who continuously improve the reliability of the nuts and bolts they produce to fasten the wings of an airplane to its body (i.e., safety or security needs). Figure 5.2 shows the strategic position of a business unit (Bijan) which serves the specialized needs of select customers. Note that high costs and high product/service differentiation characterize the niche-differentiation strategy.

The exclusive Beverly Hills retailer Bijan demonstrates this strategy. Bijan buys specialized, quality products only for customized needs that tend to

Figure 5.2   **A Business Competing with the Niche-Differentiation Strategy**

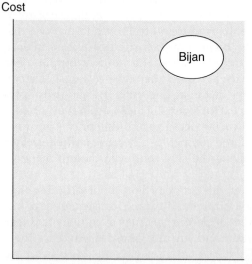

A Business (Porsche) Competing with the Niche–Low-Cost/Differentiation Strategy and Another Business (Rolls-Royce) Competing with the Niche-Differentiation Strategy

Figure 5.3

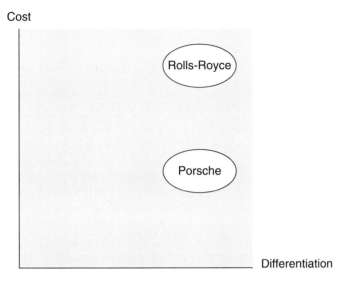

change frequently and carries one-of-a-kind costly merchandise. Shopping at Bijan is done only through personal appointment.

The chief vulnerability of this strategy is that competitors who emphasize cost control may be able to offer similar products at predatory prices. In fact, using niche-differentiation in conjunction with lower costs can be a particularly effective strategy for a number of small business units in select industries.

■ Niche–Low-Cost/Differentiation Strategy

Business units that compete with the **niche–low-cost/differentiation strategy** produce highly differentiated, need-fulfilling products or services for the specialized needs of a select group of customers or a market niche while keeping their costs low. Figure 5.3 reflects the strategic position of a business unit (Porsche) that has adopted this strategy. Note that this business has low costs relative to Rolls-Royce, for instance, while offering a high degree of output differentiation.

How can a business simultaneously differentiate its products or services and lower its costs? The following discussion presents several ways these dual objectives can be attained. These methods are listed in Table 5.1. (Note that although these routes are discussed in the context of small business units, they also pertain to large business units that adopt the low-cost–differentiation strategy, which is discussed later in this chapter.)

Dedication to Quality

A consistent, continual dedication to quality throughout the business not only improves outputs but also reduces costs involved in scrap, warranty, and service after the sale. **Quality** is defined as "the totality of features and character-

Table 5.1   **Ways Organizations Can Simultaneously Differentiate Their Products/
Services and Lower Their Costs**

1. Dedication to quality
2. Process innovations
3. Product innovations
4. Systems innovations
5. Leverage through distinctive competence

istics of a product or service that bear on its ability to satisfy stated or implied needs."[1] Hence, a high-quality product or service conforms to a predetermined set of specifications and satisfies the needs of its users. In this sense, quality is a measure of customer satisfaction with a product over its lifetime, relative to customer satisfaction with competitors' product offerings.[2]

Quality consultant Philip B. Crosby states that building quality into a product does not cost a company more because the costs of rework, scrap, and servicing the product after the sale are reduced, and the business benefits from increased customer satisfaction and repeat sales. If features are added to improve the product's fitness for use, fewer repairs are necessary, and the customer is pleased. Even though adding a feature may require a manufacturer to charge a premium price, the cost of the product to the customer over the product's lifetime may actually be lower.[3]

Process Innovations

Activities that increase the efficiency of operations and distribution are termed **process innovations.** Although these improvements are normally thought of as lowering costs, they can also enhance product or service differentiation.

> Recently, a computer manufacturer invested $20 million in a flexible assembly system. The investment made good operational sense because it paid for itself in less than a year. Strategically, the investment was even more attractive. Production time was cut by 80%, and product quality improved tenfold.[4]

In this case, costs were lowered, and the significant increase in product quality helped differentiate the product from those of the organization's competitors.

Product Innovations

Although it is common to think of **product innovations** in the context of enhancing differentiation, such improvements can also lower costs. For instance, over the years, Philip Morris developed a filter cigarette and then, later, cigarettes with low tar and nicotine levels. Although these innovations differentiated its product, they also helped lower its costs. The techniques used to produce these cigarettes (i.e., freeze drying and reconstituted tobacco sheets) allowed the company to use less tobacco per cigarette and a lower-quality tobacco to produce a higher-quality product at a dramatic reduction in per-unit costs.[5]

Systems Innovations

Some of the most rewarding strategic advantages hinge not on new products or services but on a change in conventional systems for getting existing products or services to the market. As an example, Savin Business Machines employed **systems innovations** to differentiate its product and lower its costs through innovations at virtually every link of the business system. Savin purchased its components from outside suppliers that offered low prices. It developed a more efficient method of producing its office products systems. Then, it entered into contracts with office products dealers rather than hiring a costly sales force to parallel that of its rivals. The result was a higher-quality product that was produced at a lower cost.[6]

Leverage Through Distinctive Competence

There are other innovative ways to lower costs and heighten differentiation. For instance, small manufacturers normally suffer from a disadvantage in purchasing relative to their larger competitors, since big firms can obtain quantity discounts and often receive substantial engineering support from their suppliers. However, Porsche, a relatively small manufacturer of sports cars, has overcome this problem by using leverage through distinctive competence.

> Even though Porsche purchases small quantities of goods for its operations, it gets competitive prices and significant technical support from its suppliers. The reason is that Porsche does quite a bit of outside engineering for giants such as General Motors, Ford, Volkswagen, etc. Suppliers wish to be a part of Porsche's outside engineering developments in order to have the inside track for future orders forthcoming from those larger companies. Hence, it is to the benefit of suppliers to keep Porsche a very satisfied customer.[7]

Porsche, then, is able to use its **distinctive competence**—a business's ability to do something particularly well in comparison with its competitors—in engineering to persuade its suppliers to discount their prices, which lowers Porsche's costs. At the same time, Porsche has obtained high-quality supplier support.

Porsche has also creatively lowered its costs and heightened its differentiation in the area of promotion. Rather than spend substantial sums on mass advertising, Porsche has concentrated its efforts on public relations. Knowing that automobile enthusiasts perceive a certain "mystique" associated with Porsche cars, the company has used this leverage to cultivate a close relationship with such magazines as *Road and Track*, *Motor Trend*, and *Car and Driver*. These magazines report extensively on Porsche cars, at no cost to Porsche.

GENERIC STRATEGIES FOR LARGE BUSINESS UNITS

This section presents the generic strategies that are most appropriate for large business units. These are the low-cost, differentiation, and low-cost/differentiation strategies. Finally, in some instances, large business units may employ some combination of generic strategies. This approach is termed multiple strategies.

■ Low-Cost Strategy

Large businesses that compete with a **low-cost strategy** produce no-frills products and services industrywide. That is, they address a mass market comprised of price-sensitive customers. The outputs of one business differ little from those of other businesses, and the market demand for the outputs is elastic. Consequently, companies using this strategy attempt to lower their costs in their functional areas. For instance, purchases are made from suppliers that offer quantity discounts and the lowest prices. Mass production is pursued whenever possible to lower production costs per unit. Finance plays an influential role since cost control is a high priority. Research and development efforts are directed at improving operational efficiency, and attempts are made to improve logistical and distribution efficiencies. Such businesses de-emphasize the development of new or improved products or services that may raise costs, and advertising and promotional costs are minimized. Figure 5.4 portrays the strategic position of a large business unit (Wal-Mart) that competes with the low-cost strategy. As may be seen, Wal-Mart offers low-differentiated services at low costs relative to Neiman-Marcus, for instance. Its purchasing costs are generally the lowest in the industry, and as in other discount department stores, its services are minimal.

Pursuing a low-cost strategy is consistent with acquiring a large share of the market. A large market share allows scale economies in such areas as purchasing (quantity discounts), manufacturing (mass production), financing (lower interest rates are usually available to large firms), and distribution (mass wholesaling and merchandising).

Small business units competing with the niche–low-cost strategy keep their costs down through a low initial investment and low operating expenses, but large business units that pursue a low-cost strategy rely on large market shares and scale economies. For example, a small bank offering no-frills services benefits from operating in a small, unpretentious building (low initial investment).

Figure 5.4   A Business (Wal-Mart) Competing with the Low-Cost Strategy and Another Business (Neiman-Marcus) Competing with the Differentiation Strategy

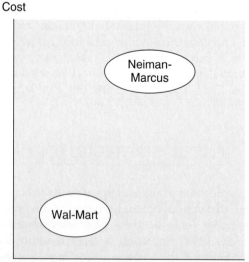

Its fixed and variable costs are relatively low because it operates with few employees and limited assets relative to large banks with head offices, bank branches, and many employees. By contrast, a large bank offering no-frills services benefits from the economies of scale that can be gained through large-volume operations. So even though both the niche–low-cost strategy and the low-cost strategy rely on keeping costs down, the means of attaining this goal are different.

Examples of companies that compete with the low-cost strategy can be found in the commodities industries, which produce and sell no-frills products. A well-known historical example in the manufacturing arena is the Ford Motor Company, which used to compete with the low-cost strategy. The Model T, a no-frills automobile, was mass-produced and sold at a low price to a large and growing market.

Manufacturers that choose to use a low-cost strategy today, however, are particularly vulnerable to intense price competition, which drives profit margins down.[8] Under these circumstances, their ability to improve outputs, augment their products with superior services, or spend more on advertising and promotion is severely limited.[9] As they begin to lose customers to competitors with superior products, they will, in response, lower their prices, which puts even more pressure on their profit margins. The prospect of being caught in this vicious cycle keeps most manufacturers from adopting the low-cost strategy. For example, Foster Grant Corporation, the sunglass manufacturer, filed for Chapter 11 bankruptcy in 1990, when it could no longer maintain its profit margins against a flood of inexpensive sunglasses imported from Taiwan and China.[10]

Another important vulnerability of this strategy is technological obsolescence. Manufacturers that value technological stability, and consequently avoid responding to new product and market opportunities, may eventually find that their products have become obsolete and are no longer desired by their customers.

Outside of manufacturing, however, there are successful businesses that compete through lower costs. Wal-Mart, for instance, purchases at rock-bottom prices because of its enormous volume and its well-known expertise and toughness in negotiations. Furthermore, it keeps inventory and transportation costs low through its well-designed, regionally located distribution centers. Nevertheless, Wal-Mart is potentially vulnerable to a repositioned Sears, Roebuck and other low-cost discounters.

■ Differentiation Strategy

Businesses that employ the *differentiation strategy* produce unique products or services industrywide. That is, they address large markets with a relatively inelastic demand. Their customers are generally willing to pay average to high prices for unique outputs. Because customers are relatively price-insensitive, businesses emphasize quality in each of their functional areas. For instance, purchases are made from suppliers that offer high-quality raw materials, parts, and components, even if the cost is relatively high. The production department emphasizes quality over cost considerations. Research and development activities focus on developing new or improved products and services, and the company's sales efforts are generously supported with advertising and promotion. Although the finance function is important, it does not dominate organizational

Figure 5.5   **A Business Competing with the Differentiation Strategy**

Cost

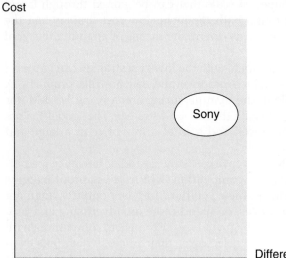

Differentiation

decision making. If a business suddenly finds itself faced with a competitor's superior products, it may well borrow money immediately to improve its products, even if the prevailing interest rate is high.

Businesses that compete with the differentiation strategy attempt to create new product and market opportunities or respond to them. These actions, of course, are costly. Therefore, such organizations value technological fluidity so that they may create or keep pace with new developments in their industries.[11]

Figure 5.5 portrays the strategic portion of a business unit (Sony Engineering and Manufacturing, maker of televisions and video and audio hardware) that uses the differentiation strategy; note its high costs and high differentiation. Such a company requires a large market share so that it may establish a unique image throughout the industry.[12] To attain this end, the business may either acquire patent protection or develop strong brands that create consumer loyalty. Sony is an example of a successful differentiator.

Others have not been as fortunate and have had to change their strategy. Xerox is an example of such a business. For years, Xerox copiers were made with costly, internally produced components, and they were heavily advertised and promoted. And for years, the company was able to pass along its high costs to its customers in the form of high prices.[13] However, Xerox, like other businesses using a differentiation strategy, found itself vulnerable to new competitors with similar products at lower costs and prices.[14] As Japanese competitors began to offer high-quality copiers that were produced more efficiently and priced significantly lower than Xerox products, Xerox was forced to restructure its operations dramatically to reduce its costs. It now follows the generic strategy discussed below.

■ Low-Cost–Differentiation Strategy

Organizations that compete with a **low-cost–differentiation strategy** serve, for the most part, the same large, relatively price-insensitive markets for unique products or services that were discussed above. This strategy is illustrated in Figure 5.6. The business (Anheuser-Busch) shown in the figure maintains low costs while offering differentiation.

This particular strategy is relatively controversial. Some theorists believe that competing simultaneously with low costs and differentiation is inconsistent. That is, a business that emphasizes differentiation cannot also maintain low costs, and a business that keeps costs low cannot produce differentiated outputs.[15] However, a growing volume of theoretical and empirical work demonstrates that a dual emphasis on low costs and differentiation can result in high performance.

We believe that the low-cost–differentiation strategy is possible to attain and can be quite effective. This strategy begins with an organizational commitment to quality products or services. Thus, the organization is active technologically in order to improve output quality. By providing high-quality outputs, the business differentiates itself from its competitors. Because customers for particular products or services are drawn to high quality, the business unit that offers such quality will experience an increasing demand for its outputs. This increasing demand results in a larger market share, providing economies of scale that permit lower per-unit costs in purchasing, manufacturing, financing, research and development, and marketing. Such businesses as Anheuser-Busch and Coca-Cola and many of the large business units of General Electric and IBM differentiate their outputs through high quality while they simultaneously maintain low-per-unit-cost operations.

For instance, Anheuser-Busch is the largest producer of beer in the United States, with a market share of 42 percent. Because of its size, the company benefits from quantity discounts in purchasing and from other scale economies in its processing operations, its research and development activities, and its marketing functions. Even with its low costs, however, Anheuser-Busch differentiates itself through its taste and its advertising (e.g., "This Bud's for you" and "The night belongs to Michelob") and by emphasizing its high-quality raw

---

A Business Competing with the Low-Cost–Differentiation Strategy **Figure 5.6**

Cost

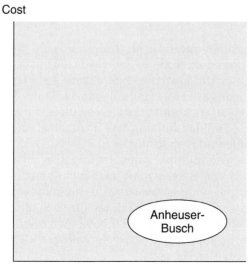

Differentiation

STRATEGIC INSIGHT

The Low-Cost–Differentiation Strategy: A Giant Success at Giant Food

Perhaps no business has used the low-cost–differentiation strategy with any more success than the $3.2 billion Giant Food supermarket chain that dominates the Washington, D.C., area and is destined to grow nationally. The store has differentiated its services by being among the first to offer gourmet meals to go, fresh pizza made in-house, a half-price salad bar during the summer, and a "frequent-buyer" program that rewards customer loyalty with credits toward future shopping trips. Even further differentiation has taken the form of offering more Asian goods in areas with substantial Vietnamese and Thai populations and extensive lines of vegetarian foods in neighborhoods with large groups of Seventh-Day Adventists.

Yet at the same time, it has managed to keep its costs at rock bottom through such innovative ideas as manufacturing its own house brands, milk, soda, ice cream, ice cubes, and plastic packagings; building many of the shopping centers in which its stores are located; producing its own television ads; and even doing its own exterminating.

The chain, whose after-tax profit margins are triple the industry average, is highly competitive. When Safeway's restructuring raised its costs, Giant exploited that weakness by cutting its own prices further and increasing its coupon offerings. When threatened by no-frills stores, it has responded by offering its customers substantial coupon discounts.

No cost-savings potential is overlooked. When its shopping center construction crews are not building the chain's own centers, they are earning over $20 million annually from outside contracts.

SOURCES: D. Foust, "Why Giant Foods Is a Gargantuan Success," *Business Week*, 4 December 1989, p. 80; K. Swisher, "In Southern California, 'Ethnic Supermarkets' Spice Up Profits," *The Washington Post*, 16 September 1990.

materials (e.g., "choicest hops, rice and best barley") and its production process (e.g., "brewed by our original process"). Additionally, this business keeps pace with market developments and introduces new products periodically, with Bud Dry being a recent example.

■ Multiple Strategies

In some cases, large business units employ **multiple strategies,** or more than one of the strategies identified in the preceding sections. For instance, a business that uses the differentiation strategy or the low-cost–differentiation strategy may also adopt one of the niche strategies used by small companies. Figure 5.7 portrays the strategies of two hotels: Hyatt uses both the differentiation strategy and the niche-differentiation strategy; Holiday Inn employs a combination of low-cost–differentiation and niche-differentiation strategies.

Large business units may compete with multiple strategies for either proactive reasons (i.e., attempting to modify some segment of their environment to enhance their effectiveness) or reactive reasons (reacting to environmental change to maintain their effectiveness). For example, Holiday Inn, one of the largest companies in the hotel/motel industry with 1600 hotels worldwide, maintains its preeminent position by competing proactively with both low-cost–differentiation and niche-differentiation strategies.

Businesses Competing with Multiple Strategies: Hyatt Competes with Differentiation and Niche-Differentiation; Holiday Inn Competes with Low-Cost–Differentiation and Niche-Differentiation

Figure 5.7

Cost

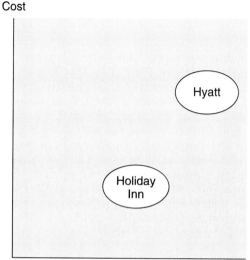

Differentiation

Its low-cost–differentiation strategy is revealed through its use of scale economies in purchasing and financing and its nationwide reservation system, which keeps costs low, and its differentiation through its quality rooms and services. Additionally, the company heavily advertises and promotes its quality accommodations. But to appeal to more than one customer group, this business reserves a small section of some of its inns for the more discriminating customer. In these sections, spacious suites with plush furnishings, wet bars, refrigerators, and hair dryers are provided, along with complimentary food, newspapers, and beverages. As might be expected, the price that Holiday Inn charges for these suites is significantly higher than its price for ordinary rooms. This niche-differentiation strategy requires a higher initial investment per suite and higher operating costs. By using multiple strategies, Holiday Inn appeals to different groups of customers.

Likewise, Hyatt offers special suites in each of its hotels to elite customers. However, even its regular rooms are advertised to discriminating customers who are willing to pay higher-than-average prices for a hotel room.

R. J. Reynolds provides an example of a large business that reactively competes with multiple strategies. For years, Reynolds employed a low-cost–differentiation strategy for its cigarette brands. But as the Liggett Group and other smaller firms began to produce generic (i.e., no-brand) cigarettes in the early 1980s, Reynolds responded by also adopting a niche–low-cost strategy. The company positioned its otherwise lackluster-performing brand, Doral, against generic cigarettes by reducing its costs of production and its price.[16]

It is important to note several exceptions to the above discussion. First, a large business unit that uses a low-cost strategy is unlikely to employ multiple strategies. A combination of the low-cost strategy with a niche–low-cost strategy is redundant, since both strategies concentrate on no-frills outputs at low costs. Combining the low-cost strategy with either of the other niche strategies

STRATEGIC INSIGHT

AT&T's Multiple Strategies

The most familiar side of AT&T's business to the consumer, of course, is its telephone division. This business unit pursues a low-cost–differentiation strategy in attempting to control costs while at the same time offering long-distance service and a number of related unique services to a huge market.

Less well known is AT&T's Data Systems Group. For seven years, this business unit also used a low-cost–differentiation strategy to compete head to head with IBM, Digital Equipment, and Hewlett-Packard for the computer business of corporate customers. From 1983 through 1989, that business lost almost $3 billion. By 1990, however, AT&T modified this division's approach to a niche-differentiation strategy.

It now aims its sales efforts at a narrow segment of the corporate market. Particularly appealing are such businesses as airlines and brokerage houses that account for an enormous volume of daily transactions. These customers, as well as such federal government divisions as the Air Force and Federal Aviation Administration, have responded favorably to AT&T's ability to tailor computer networks to their specialized needs.

As a result of this change in strategy, AT&T's computer business is beginning to turn around. And the potential for growth is great. Presently, computers represent less than 6 percent of the firm's annual revenue, and AT&T's share of the U.S. computer market amounts to only about 2 percent, compared with IBM's nearly 30 percent.

SOURCE: Data from J. J. Keller, "In Computer Industry, No One Is Laughing at AT&T's Effort Now," *The Wall Street Journal*, 12 January 1990.

is probably unworkable because it is difficult for an organization to operate primarily on the foundation of a no-frills philosophy (and all that it implies) while simultaneously producing highly differentiated products.[17]

Second, a large business unit that competes with the differentiation strategy is unlikely to employ a niche–low-cost strategy or a niche–low-cost/differentiation strategy because low costs are not emphasized by its managers.

Third, large business units will not adopt as their sole strategy any of the three niche strategies identified earlier as being appropriate for small business units. A small market share with relatively low sales figures cannot justify sizable expenditures on research and development, operations, and marketing.[18] Of course, enlightened managers of small business units and entrepreneurs are well aware of these restrictions on the operations of large business units. Hence, small enterprises are often strategically buffered from head-to-head competition with large firms. The market that small companies have carefully chosen is simply too small to attract large organizations as major competitors.

The seven generic strategies that have been discussed in this chapter are summarized in Table 5.2. The emphasis of each strategy, its market coverage, the characteristics of its products and services, its market demand, and its pricing are all identified.

Generic Business Unit Strategies and Their Ramifications   **Table 5.2**

Generic Business Unit Strategy	Emphasis of Business Unit	Market Coverage	Characteristics of Products and Services	Market Demand	Pricing
Niche–low-cost	Lower overall costs	Niche	No-frills	Elastic	Depending on industry forces, low to average
Niche-differentiation	Specialized quality	Niche	Highly differentiated	Inelastic	High
Niche–low-cost/ differentiation	Specialized quality and low costs	Niche	Highly differentiated	Inelastic	High
Low-cost	Lower overall costs	Industrywide	No-frills	Elastic	Depending on industry forces, low to average
Differentiation	Quality	Industrywide	Differentiated	Relatively inelastic	Depending on industry forces, average to high
Low-cost–differentiation	Quality and low cost	Industrywide	Differentiated	Relatively inelastic	Depending on industry forces, average to high
Multiple strategies	Mixed	Mixed	Mixed	Mixed	Mixed

RELATIONSHIPS AMONG GENERIC STRATEGIES, BUSINESS UNIT SIZE, MARKET SHARE, AND PROFITABILITY

This section examines the relationship between generic strategy and business unit size, with a particular emphasis on midsized business units. That relationship will then be expanded to show how generic strategy selection relates to market share and profitability.

■ Generic Strategies and Business Unit Size

The preceding sections identified generic strategies appropriate for small and large business units. Midsized business units were not discussed because these organizations normally perform poorly in comparison with small or large competitors.[19] The reason is that midsized businesses do not possess the advantages of their smaller or larger counterparts. Whether the business unit is considered small, midsized, or large, of course, depends upon its size relative to the size of its competitors in the industry.

The competitive superiority that small businesses enjoy over midsized business units includes their flexibility in meeting specific market demands and their quicker reaction to environmental changes. Additionally, because of their lower investments, they can pursue small orders that would be unprofitable for midsized businesses. Finally, they can capitalize on their small market shares by creating an image of exclusivity. Customers who buy products for prestige purposes do so only if the market has relatively few of those products.[20] For instance, consumers who purchase Rolls-Royce automobiles would be alienated if they began to see a Rolls-Royce on every block, because the prestige of exclusivity is the primary reason for their purchase. Management at Rolls-Royce is quite aware of this situation; the company limited its sales in the United States in 1988 to fewer than thirteen hundred cars.

The crucial advantage that a large business has over the midsized company lies in its ability to translate its economies of scale into lower costs per unit.

Therefore, since midsized business units do not have the advantages of either small or large firms, they have two strategic options to increase their effectiveness. First, they may, over time, expand their operations to take advantage of scale economies. Second, they may retrench in order to avail themselves of the advantages possessed by small companies. The feasibility of expansion or retrenchment depends upon various competitive and industry forces.

■ Generic Strategies, Market Share, and Profitability

The discussion thus far suggests certain relationships among generic business strategies, market share, and profitability. Some of these possible relationships are shown in Figure 5.8. The vertical axis represents business unit profitability, and the horizontal axis reflects market share. The two U-shaped curves represent proposed relationships between market share and profitability.

Part A of curve 1 represents business units that compete with the niche–low-cost/differentiation strategy. These are small businesses with small market shares, yet they are quite profitable because of their flexibility and their ability

---

Figure 5.8   Generic Strategies, Market Share, and Profitability

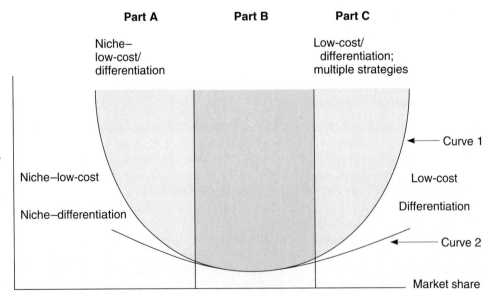

to produce outputs that fulfill customers' particular needs for prestige, performance, or safety.

Part C of curve 1 shows large business units that compete with the low-cost/differentiation strategy and those that compete with multiple strategies. These businesses have large market shares and are very profitable because of their scale economies and the unique nature of their outputs.

Part B of curve 1 portrays businesses with midsized market shares. Their profitability is lower than that of either of the other sets of business units because they do not have the flexibility of smaller businesses or their ability to produce outputs that fulfill customers' particular needs for prestige, performance, or safety. Nor can they achieve the scale economies of larger business units. To increase their profitability, these businesses must either retrench (and move up toward part A) or expand (to move up to part C).

On curve 2, part A shows business units that compete with the niche–low-cost strategy or the niche-differentiation strategy. These small businesses with small market shares are less profitable than those that adopt the niche–low-cost/differentiation strategy (on part A of curve 1).

Part C of curve 2 represents large business units competing with either the low-cost strategy or the differentiation strategy. Although they have large market shares, their profitability is less than that of businesses using the low-cost/differentiation strategy or multiple strategies (on part C of curve 1). Finally, part B of curve 2 converges into part B of curve 1 to portray midsized businesses with low profitability.

It is important to realize that these U-shaped relationships may not hold in all industries. For example, in retailing, recall that Wal-Mart has high profitability even though it employs the low-cost strategy. Also, the relationships will be distorted in fragmented industries containing numerous small companies of similar size. Examples are industries that produce adhesives and sealants, fasteners, and apparel. Alternatively, in consolidated industries with only a few businesses, the relationships may also not hold. For example, the aircraft manufacturing industry is comprised chiefly of Boeing, McDonnell Douglas, and Airbus. Since Airbus is owned by a consortium of European governments, Boeing devotes most of its resources to manufacturing commercial aircraft, and McDonnell Douglas places its emphasis on government contracts for military aircraft, this industry would not be accurately represented by the U-shaped curves.

Recall that when we refer to *large* or *small*, these terms are industry-specific. A large firm in a fragmented industry would be considered quite tiny in a consolidated industry.

We have seen that small business units that compete with the niche–low-cost/differentiation strategy may outperform small business units that employ a niche–low-cost strategy or a niche-differentiation strategy. Similarly, large business units that use either the low-cost–differentiation strategy or multiple strategies can often outperform those large business units that compete with a low-cost strategy or a differentiation strategy.

The major reason for these performance differences has already been discussed. Small businesses using a niche–low-cost strategy or large business units with a low-cost strategy are particularly vulnerable to intense price competition. Similarly, small companies that use the niche-differentiation strategy and large enterprises competing with a differentiation strategy eventually find themselves in competition with new entrants that are able to offer alternative products at lower prices. As we pointed out, however, we cannot conclude that these particular strategies are never effective. In fact, as we have seen, some businesses employ them most profitably. But the probability may be low that these strategies will be as effective as the niche–low-cost/differentiation, low-cost–differentiation, or multiple strategies.

RISK, VALUE ANALYSIS, AND STRATEGIC GROUPS

This concluding section of the chapter analyzes how generic strategies are related to risk, value, and strategic groups. First, those conditions under which business unit managers may select more risky generic strategies are identified. Then the generic strategies that are most likely to provide market value to consumers are discussed. Finally, the way in which a business unit can gain an advantage over competitors that are in the same industry and have adopted the same generic strategy is examined.

■ Generic Strategies and Risk

Although managers vary significantly in their propensities for taking **risks**— that is, for pursuing a strategy with some possibility of suffering a loss—sufficient evidence exists for us to generalize about the conditions under which executives are more or less likely to choose risky strategies. For instance, managers are likely to be more risk-averse when their business is performing at or slightly above its target level or when it is in a "marginal win" situation.[21] However, managers may be more prone to take risks when (1) the performance of their business unit is below its target level or it is in a loss situation, or (2) their organization's performance is much above its target level or it is in a "big win" situation.[22]

Examples of these tendencies may be witnessed at football games. The team that is ahead by slightly more than one touchdown is likely to take few chances and will concentrate on running out the clock by calling conservative plays. However, the team that is behind is likely to select relatively risky plays in its attempt to catch up. And a team that leads an opponent by a wide margin will also take risks, not only in its play calling but also in its use of second- and third-stringers.

Extending this analogy to the top managers of strategic business units, we would expect that businesses that are less profitable or are losing money and businesses that are extremely profitable will take larger risks than will business units that are somewhat above average in profitability.[23] Why might managers behave in this manner? The rationale is that managers of organizations that are highly successful feel safe in taking risks because of their history of success, and they can afford to absorb the losses that may accompany risk taking. In losing businesses, managers feel pressured to take high risks because catching up frequently requires a "bold stroke." Managing conservatively is unlikely to result in the large gains that a losing business must obtain. Therefore, it is only those managers who run businesses that perform marginally above the average who seek to avoid risks.

■ Generic Strategies and Value Analysis

The marketplace rewards business units that are able to offer better **value,** which is the worth of a good or service in terms of its perceived usefulness or importance to consumers. Those businesses that compete with differentiation while maintaining low costs (i.e., niche–low-cost/differentiation, low-cost–differentiation, and multiple strategies) are usually better positioned to offer value than are business units that emphasize only differentiation (i.e., the strategies of niche-differentiation and differentiation) or low costs (i.e., the niche–low-cost and low-cost strategies).

The ultimate judge of value is the consumer. Consumers compare the price and quality of any one business unit's outputs with the price and quality of competitors' outputs. Business units that offer poor value to their customers in the form of relatively high prices and relatively low quality face negative prospects. If they hold to their price level, they will lose market share and profitability. Likewise, if they maintain their market share by discounting their prices, they will also suffer lower profits. In either case, they will be hard-pressed to generate the necessary funds to increase their product quality so that their higher prices can be justified.

On the other hand, business units that offer good value (i.e., competitive prices and high quality) to their customers face bright prospects. If they increase their prices, they may be able to maintain their market share if consumers perceive that the new price-quality relationship is still fair relative to competitors' outputs. The worst that can happen is that they will lose market share but will be able to maintain or even increase their overall profits on the reduced sales through their higher prices. Alternatively, these businesses may reduce their prices, which will increase their market share and allow them to lower their costs through economies of scale. The result will be increased profitability.

Our discussion suggests that business units that compete with the niche–low-cost/differentiation strategy, the low-cost–differentiation strategy, or multiple strategies are usually better positioned to offer superior value to customers. Of course, better value is not confined to these strategies. Wal-Mart, for instance, offers superior value to its customers through its low-cost strategy. But the ability to offer high value is often enhanced by adopting one of these three strategies.

■ Generic Strategies and Strategic Groups

Most industries are comprised of a number of business units that compete more directly with certain businesses in the industry than with others. Groups of direct competitors are identified by the similarity of their strategic profiles, and each collection of direct competitors is termed a **strategic group.** As an example, assume that an industry contains many businesses, each of which employs one of the seven generic strategies that has been discussed. Such an industry can be portrayed as shown in Figure 5.9.

All twenty business units in this industry compete with one another. But business units within each strategic group engage in more direct and intense competition with each other. Since the businesses within a single strategic group use the same generic strategy, how can one of the businesses in the group gain a competitive advantage over the others?

Figure 5.9   **Groups of Business Units in an Industry Competing with Different Generic Strategies**

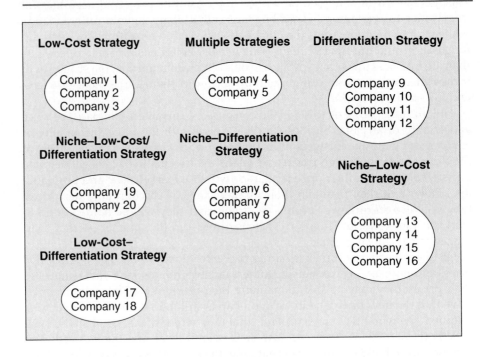

In most cases, each business unit attempts to develop a distinctive competence (a concept introduced earlier in this chapter) relative to its competitors in the same strategic group. This distinctive competence can come from an organization's particular strengths in any functional area, such as purchasing, inventory management, manufacturing, finance, research and development, marketing, information gathering and analysis, or human resource management. However, the strongest distinctive competencies result from the synergistic combination of strengths in several of these areas. McDonald's, for instance, uses its distinctive competence in the following areas to outperform its rivals:

- Purchasing in large quantities at significant discounts.
- Fast service inside the restaurant and at the drive-in window.
- Consistent quality control in products, service, and cleanliness.
- Systematic development of new products.
- Solid financial management that allows steady expansion.
- Site analysis and real estate expertise that result in profitable locations.
- Advertising and promotion that inculcate powerful brand recognition and customer loyalty.

This discussion indicates that business units position themselves competitively on two levels. At the industry level, they select a particular generic strategy that places them in a specific strategic group. McDonald's, for instance, competes in the fast-food restaurant industry by using a low-cost–differentiation strategy. This generic-strategy selection places McDonald's in the strategic group occupied by such businesses as Burger King, Wendy's, and Hardee's.

Within this strategic group, McDonald's uses its distinctive competence to enable it to compete favorably with its direct rivals. Although the businesses in this strategic group also compete with other fast-food restaurants, ranging from Krystal's (a niche–low-cost chain that offers only one variety of hamburger) to gourmet take-out delicatessens (which compete on a niche-differentiation basis), the competition with businesses in these other strategic groups in the fast-food industry is less direct than with those competitors who are members of the same strategic group.

The purposes, therefore, of strategic management of a business unit are, first, to adopt a generic strategy that enables the business to capitalize upon the opportunities in the broad industry environment and, second, to match the distinctive competence of the business unit with the more specific opportunities in its strategic group environment.

Businesses normally experience difficulty in moving from one strategic group to another. In fact, strategic groups are quite stable and remain distinct from one another because of this relative immobility. Group-specific mobility barriers arise because the businesses in each group make strategic decisions that cannot easily be duplicated by enterprises outside the group. Such decisions require "outsiders" to incur significant costs, elapsed time, and/or uncertainty about the outcome of their decisions.[24] Thus, businesses in a lower-performing strategic group find it difficult and costly to switch to a higher-performing strategic group.

SUMMARY

Once top management has formulated an organization's corporate-level strategy, the managers of the firm's business units must adopt a generic strategy to guide their operations. Three generic strategies are available for small business units: the niche–low-cost strategy, the niche-differentiation strategy, and the niche–low-cost/differentiation strategy. Large business units may choose from among the low-cost strategy, differentiation strategy, low-cost–differentiation strategy, or multiple strategies.

Analysis of these strategies leads to the conclusion that either small or large business units are likely to be more effective than midsized business units. Small businesses have the advantages of flexibility and/or the ability to produce outputs that fulfill customers' particular needs for prestige, performance, or safety; and large companies possess the advantage of economies of scale. The evidence further suggests that for small businesses, the niche–low-cost/differentiation strategy is more likely to be successful in the long run than either of the other two strategies. For large business units, a choice of either the low-cost–differentiation strategy or multiple strategies is more likely to result in success than is the choice of either the low-cost or the differentiation strategy.

The choice of a generic strategy is an attempt to capitalize upon the opportunities in a broad industry environment. This choice places a business unit into a particular strategic group within the industry. The members of each strategic group compete directly and intensely with each other by trying to match their distinctive competence with the more specific opportunities in the strategic group environment.

KEY CONCEPTS

Business unit   An organizational subsystem that has a market, a set of competitors, and a mission distinct from those of the other subsystems in the firm.

Differentiation strategy   A generic business unit strategy in which a business produces unique products or services industrywide for large markets with a relatively inelastic demand.

Distinctive competence   An organization's ability to do something particularly well in comparison with its competitors.

Generic strategy   A strategy that can be adopted by any type of business unit, regardless of its industry or product/service line.

Low-cost–differentiation strategy   A generic business unit strategy in which a business maintains low costs while producing unique products or services industrywide for large markets with a relatively inelastic demand.

Low-cost strategy   A generic business unit strategy in which a business produces, at the lowest cost possible, no-frills products and services industrywide for large markets with a relatively elastic demand.

Multiple strategies   A strategic alternative for a business unit in which the organization simultaneously employs more than one of the generic business strategies.

Niche-differentiation strategy   A generic business unit strategy in which a business produces highly differentiated, need-fulfilling products or services for the specialized needs of a narrow range of customers or a market niche. Since the business's outputs are intended to fulfill a deep set of customer needs, prices are high and demand for the outputs is relatively inelastic.

Niche–low-cost/differentiation strategy   A generic business unit strategy in which a business produces highly differentiated, need-fulfilling products or services for the specialized needs of a select group of customers or a market niche while keeping its costs low.

Niche–low-cost strategy   A generic business unit strategy in which a business keeps overall costs low while producing no-frills products or services for a market niche with elastic demand.

Process innovations   A business unit's activities that increase the efficiency of operations and distribution.

Product innovations   A business unit's activities that enhance the differentiation of its products or services.

Quality   The totality of features and characteristics of a product or service that bear on its ability to satisfy stated or implied needs.

Risk   The possibility of suffering loss.

Strategic group   Within an industry, a select group of direct competitors who have similar strategic profiles.

Systems innovations   A business unit's activities that increase the efficiency of any of its functional systems (e.g., purchasing, finance, marketing).

Value   The worth of a good or service in terms of its perceived usefulness or importance to a consumer. Value is usually judged by comparing the price and quality of one business's outputs with those of its competitors.

DISCUSSION QUESTIONS

1. How does a business unit strategy differ from a corporate-level strategy?

2. Small business units have a choice of three generic strategies. Explain each of these strategies, and give an example of a business unit that competes with each strategy.

3. Large business units have a choice of four generic strategies. Explain each of these strategies, and give an example of a business unit that competes with each strategy.

4. Explain the difference between a niche–low-cost/differentiation strategy and a low-cost–differentiation strategy.

5. How is it possible for a business to differentiate its outputs and, simultaneously, lower its costs?

6. Explain *distinctive competence*, and give examples of three businesses that have attained distinctive competence in one or more functional areas.

7. Why might we expect the performance level of midsized business units to be lower than the performance level of either small or large business units?

8. Explain the relationship that we would expect to find between the generic strategy selected by a business unit and its market share and profitability.

9. Why might we hypothesize that business units that compete with the niche–low-cost/differentiation strategy, the low-cost–differentiation strategy, or multiple strategies are better positioned to offer superior value to customers than are business units that use other strategies?

10. What is a strategic group? Select an industry and identify, by name, some of the business units that comprise two of the strategic groups within that industry.

STRATEGIC MANAGEMENT EXERCISES

1. Assume that you have conducted market research that indicates the need for a bookstore close to your campus. Further assume that you believe that either of two generic strategies could be successful for the bookstore: the niche–low-cost strategy or the niche-differentiation strategy. Respond to the following questions for *each* of these two strategies. Note that your responses for the two strategies will be quite different.

   • What type of physical store should you create?
   • What kinds of books would you carry in your inventory?

- What in-store services would you provide?
- Would you generally charge low, average, or high prices?

Now, answer these same questions for a small business and a generic strategy of your own choosing.

2. Assume that you have the financial resources to own a national chain of video stores. Further assume that you believe that either of two generic strategies could be successful for this chain: the low-cost strategy or the low-cost–differentiation strategy. Describe the physical aspects of your stores, their services, their advertising programs, and so on, for *each* of these two strategies.

   Now, describe these same characteristics for a large business and a generic strategy of your own choosing.

3. Select an actual business and analyze its strategic profile (i.e., which generic strategy has it adopted?). What improvements might you suggest for this business?

REFERENCES

1. ANSI/ASQC, *Quality Systems Terminology, American National Standard* (1987), A3-1987.

2. D. A. Garvin, *Managing Quality* (New York: Free Press, 1988).

3. P. Crosby, *Quality Is Free* (New York: McGraw-Hill, 1979).

4. E. A. Haas, "Breakthrough Manufacturing," *Harvard Business Review* 65, no. 2 (1987): 76.

5. R. H. Miles, *Coffin Nails and Corporate Strategies* (Englewood Cliffs, N.J.: Prentice-Hall, 1982).

6. F. W. Gluck, "Strategic Choice and Resource Allocation," *The McKinsey Quarterly* 1 (1980): 22–23.

7. P. Wright, "Winning Strategies for Small Manufacturers," *Planning Review* 14 (1986): 20.

8. W. J. Abernathy and K. Wayne, "Limits of Learning Curve," in Harvard Business School, eds., *Survival Strategies for American Industry* (New York: Wiley, 1983), pp. 114–131; R. Luchs, "Successful Businesses Compete on Quality—Not Costs," *Long Range Planning* 19, no. 1 (1986): 12–17.

9. R. D. Buzzell and B. T. Gale, *The PIMS Principles* (New York: Free Press, 1987).

10. K. H. Hammonds, "Foster Grant Runs for the Shade of Chapter 11," *Business Week*, 3 September 1990, p. 44.

11. P. Wright, M. J. Kroll, C. D. Pringle, and J. A. Johnson, "Organization Types, Conduct, Profitability, and Risk in the Semiconductor Industry," *Journal of Management Systems* 2 (1990): 33–48.

12. P. Wright, "A Refinement of Porter's Strategies," *Strategic Management Journal* 8 (1987): 93–101.

13. R. Buaron, "New Game Strategies," *The McKinsey Quarterly* 3 (1981): 24–40.

14. W. D. Vinson and D. F. Heany, "Is Quality Out of Control?" *Harvard Business Review* 55, no. 6 (1977): 114–122.

15. M. E. Porter, *Competitive Advantage: Creating and Sustaining Superior Performance* (New York: Free Press, 1985).

16. Wright, "Refinement of Porter's Strategies."

17. P. Wright, "The Strategic Options of Least Cost, Differentiation and Niche," *Business Horizons* 22 (1986): 21–26.

18. Wright, "Refinement of Porter's Strategies."

19. S. Schoeffler, R. Buzzell, and D. Heany, "Impact of Strategic Planning on Profit Performance," *Harvard Business Review* 52 (1974): 137–145; M. E. Porter, *Competitive Strategy* (New York: Free Press, 1980); Wright, "Refinement of Porter's Strategies"; L. Feldman and J. Stephenson, "Stay Small or Get Huge—Lessons from Securities Trading," *Harvard Business Review* 66, no. 3 (1988): 116–123; M. T. Hannan and J. Freeman, "The Population Ecology of Organizations," *American Journal of Sociology* 82 (1977): 946–947.

20. P. Wright, "Systematic Approach in Finding Export Opportunities," in Harvard Business School, eds., *Managing Effectively in the World Marketplace* (New York: Wiley, 1983), pp. 331–342.

21. D. Kahneman and A. Tversky, "Prospect Theory: An Analysis of Decision Under Risk," *Econometrica* 47 (1979): 263.

22. W. Chang and H. Thomas, "The Impact of Diversification Strategy on Risk-Return Performance," *Strategic Management Journal* 10 (1989): 271–284; E. H. Bowman, "Risk Seeking by Troubled Firms," *Sloan Management Review* 23 (1982): 33–42.

23. Chang and Thomas, "Impact of Diversification Strategy"; Bowman, "Risk Seeking by Troubled Firms."

24. J. McGee and H. Thomas, "Strategic Groups: Theory, Research and Taxonomy," *Strategic Management Journal* 7 (1986): 141–160.

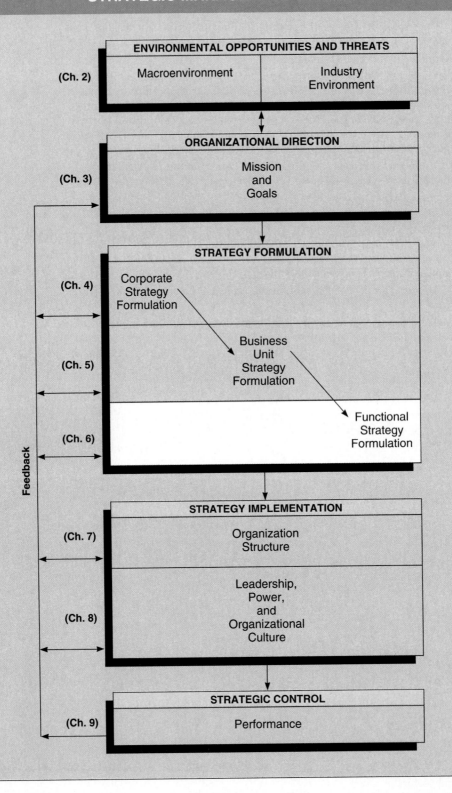

STRATEGIC MANAGEMENT MODEL

ENVIRONMENTAL OPPORTUNITIES AND THREATS

(Ch. 2)

| Macroenvironment | Industry Environment |

ORGANIZATIONAL DIRECTION

(Ch. 3)

Mission
and
Goals

STRATEGY FORMULATION

(Ch. 4)

Corporate
Strategy
Formulation

(Ch. 5)

Business
Unit
Strategy
Formulation

(Ch. 6)

Functional
Strategy
Formulation

STRATEGY IMPLEMENTATION

(Ch. 7)

Organization
Structure

(Ch. 8)

Leadership,
Power,
and
Organizational
Culture

STRATEGIC CONTROL

(Ch. 9)

Performance

Feedback

6
CHAPTER

Functional Strategies

We have seen in the preceding chapters that the corporation's mission, goals, and objectives establish the parameters within which the firm's individual business units operate. Each business unit, of course, develops its own goals and objectives within these parameters and then pursues those ends by implementing the generic strategy or strategies that appear most appropriate. Proper implementation of generic strategies requires that considerable attention be given to the business unit's functional areas. All organizations, regardless of their size, must perform certain functions—production, marketing, finance, research and development, and so on. No strategy can be successfully carried out without careful planning, execution, and coordination of these functional tasks.

In formulating **functional strategies**—the strategies pursued by the functional areas of a business unit—managers must be aware that these functions are interrelated. Each functional area, in attaining its purpose, must mesh its activities with the activities of the other functional departments, as shown in Figure 6.1. And a change in one department will invariably affect the way other departments operate. Hence, the strategy of one functional area cannot be viewed in isolation; rather, the extent to which all of the business unit's functional tasks mesh smoothly determines the effectiveness of the unit's generic strategy.

Many companies are learning this lesson. Boeing's unsettling experience, for instance, with discontinuities among its production, human resource, and marketing functions in the manufacture and delivery of its 747-400 airliner has resulted in significant changes. Its new 777 airplane will be designed and built by teams of marketing, engineering, manufacturing, finance, and service representatives so that each functional area will always know what the other is doing.[1]

This chapter examines functional strategies in the areas of purchasing, production/operations, finance, research and development, marketing, human

Figure 6.1   **Interrelationships Among Functional Departments**

ENVIRONMENT

Finance

Production/operations management

Human resource management

Environmental inputs

Environmental outputs

Purchasing and materials management

Marketing

Management information systems

Research and development

ENVIRONMENT

resources, and information systems. Then the ways in which these functional strategies can be integrated to achieve certain competitive advantages are analyzed.

PURCHASING AND MATERIALS MANAGEMENT

All organizations have a purchasing function. For example, in manufacturing companies, the purchasing department buys raw materials and/or parts so that the production department may process them into a finished product for the marketing department to sell. In retailing organizations, individual buyers purchase clothing, toys, furniture, and other items from manufacturers for resale to the ultimate consumer.

Purchasing interacts extensively with the organization's environment, as illustrated in Figure 6.1. Its tasks are to identify potential suppliers, evaluate them, invite bids and price quotations, negotiate prices and terms of payment, place orders, follow up on those orders, inspect incoming shipments, and pay suppliers.

A business unit's purchasing strategy will differ, depending upon which generic strategy it adopts. Companies that use either the niche–low-cost strategy or the low-cost strategy emphasize purchasing at the lowest costs possible. Large organizations are able to purchase at low costs through their ability to demand quantity discounts. [The terms *large* and *small* are relative ones referring to an organization's size (usually measured in annual sales or total assets) in relation to the size of its competitors in the industry.] And buyers that are larger than their suppliers and whose purchases represent a significant percentage of their suppliers' sales also possess considerable negotiating clout.

Small companies, however, must attain low-cost purchasing in other ways. A recent purchasing trend for small businesses is to form industry networks—that is, band together with other small businesses in the same industry—to pool their purchasing requirements. Such a network is able to wield as much power as a single large business in demanding quantity discounts and exerting negotiating clout. Other small businesses may attempt to develop contacts with domestic and foreign suppliers that are able to offer limited supplies at low prices. In many cases, an extensive search can locate such suppliers.

We wish to emphasize that low costs are not the only consideration in purchasing activities. It is more accurate to state that businesses using niche–low-cost or low-cost generic strategies should seek out the "best cost." The best cost is as low as possible consistent with the quality of the purchased good or service. A low price is useless if the item breaks in the production process or fails to perform for the customer. On the other hand, excessive quality unnecessarily raises costs and prices.[2]

Organizations that use the generic strategy of niche-differentiation or differentiation emphasize the procurement of high-quality inputs, even if they cost more than alternative offerings. In these cases, the quality of the parts or products takes precedence over cost considerations.

When management pursues a niche–low-cost/differentiation or low-cost–differentiation generic strategy, however, emphasis is placed on buying high-quality inputs at low costs. As pointed out in the preceding chapter, even small businesses that adopt niche–low-cost/differentiation may be able to attain this purchasing goal through the development of distinctive competence, as Porsche has done.

Using multiple strategies, of course, requires a mixture of purchasing plans. At Holiday Inn, for instance, cost is a consideration in purchasing furnishings and accessories for the Inn's regular rooms. But the company buys higher-quality items—at higher costs—for its top-of-the-line suites. These suites feature more expensive linens, towels, soaps, shampoos, and beverages.

The purchasing function is the first step in the materials management process. From the materials management perspective, purchasing, the operation of storage and warehouse facilities, and the control of inventory are interrelated functions;[3] consequently, they can only be efficiently and effectively conducted if they are viewed as parts of a single task.[4]

As an example of how these functions are interrelated, consider the **just-in-time inventory system.** This system of inventory management was popularized by Japanese manufacturers to reduce materials management costs. Using this technique, the purchasing manager asks suppliers to ship parts just at the time they are needed by the company to use in its production process. Such a system, of course, holds inventory, storage, and warehousing costs to a minimum.

Although American manufacturers are turning to this system in growing numbers, it is important to realize that just-in-time deliveries work particularly well in Japan because large Japanese manufacturers buy many of their inputs from small local companies. Hence, the giant buyers have considerable bargaining power over their much smaller suppliers. (In fact, some Japanese manufacturers own controlling interests in their suppliers, giving them even more power to control deliveries.) Such a system is likely to work well in the United States when the manufacturer has greater bargaining power than its suppliers.

However, in the reverse situation, a just-in-time system is unlikely to evolve. Another hindrance to its use is that some suppliers, owing to the high demand for their products, are occasionally late in their deliveries by weeks or even months. However, most American-based suppliers are small concerns, with under $5 million in annual sales and fewer than thirty employees.[5] Hence, the just-in-time system may be applied for the majority of suppliers.

Most large U.S. manufacturers are currently reducing the number of suppliers that they use from a dozen or more to two or three to control delivery times and quality.[6] These companies then attempt to build strong and enduring relationships with their suppliers and provide them with detailed knowledge of their requirements and specifications. Buyer and supplier work together to improve the quality and lower the costs of the purchased items.

> This involves taking a *long* term view of the buyer/supplier relationship and also involves commitment to building an enduring cooperative relationship with individual suppliers where information is readily shared and both organizations work to meet shared goals.[7]

PRODUCTION/OPERATIONS MANAGEMENT

Production/operations management (POM) involves the process of transforming inputs, such as raw materials and parts, into outputs. Its basic objective is to ensure that the outputs produced have a value that exceeds the combined costs of the required inputs and the transformation process. Transformation process costs include labor, supplies, and physical plant and equipment.

Although POM is most often associated with manufacturing processes, managing operations is crucial to all types of organizations. Credit card companies, for instance, must satisfy customers' desires for timeliness, accuracy, and company responsiveness. Hospitals must diagnose medical problems and attempt to heal patients. Prisons must house prisoners and try to rehabilitate them. Insurance companies must meet their clients' demands for fast, responsible, thorough coverage. Each of these POM examples from service organizations requires a careful analysis of those organizations' operations. Hence, the transformation of inputs into outputs is not limited to manufacturers. The service organizations just described must transform a customer's credit purchase into a cash payment to the retailer, help sick patients become well, attempt to convert criminals into responsible citizens, and pay for restoring a damaged automobile or house to its original condition.

The following sections describe POM strategies for small and large business units and discuss the quality considerations emerging currently in POM.

■ POM Strategies for Small Business Units

POM strategies differ, of course, depending upon which generic strategy the business unit adopts. Small business units that compete with the niche–low-cost strategy emphasize low initial investments in their plants, equipment, and outlets to hold their fixed costs down, and they attempt to keep their variable operations costs as low as possible. Because of new technological innovations, some industries, such as steel manufacturing and film developing, can create small physical plants that are cost-competitive with much larger companies.

The experience curve concept is based on three underlying variables: learning, economies of scale, and capital-labor substitution possibilities. Learning refers to the idea that the more an employee performs a task, the more efficient he or she should become at the job. Increases in volume, therefore, permit the employee to perform the task more often, resulting in greater expertise. This reasoning holds for all jobs—line and staff, managerial and nonmanagerial—and at all levels—corporate, business unit, and functional. Learning does not occur automatically, however. For instance, as experience is gained with a particular product, production managers, operative employees, and design engineers have the opportunity to learn more about how to redesign the product for manufacturing and assembly. By taking advantage of this opportunity, a business is able to conserve material, gain greater efficiencies in the manufacturing process, and substitute less costly materials, while simultaneously improving the product's performance. Such techniques, for instance, allowed Ford Motor Company's business units to trim their manufacturing costs by more than $1.2 billion in 1989—and Ford thereby was able to replace General Motors as America's most profitable automobile maker.[10]

Economies of scale at the business unit level refer to reductions in per-unit costs as volume increases. Capital-labor substitution means that as volume increases, an organization may be able to substitute labor for capital, or capital for labor, depending upon which combination produces lower costs and/or greater effectiveness. For example, a car manufacturer may operate highly automated factories in economically advanced nations because of the high cost of labor. But the same manufacturer may employ more labor and less automation in its factories located in developing nations, to take advantage of the lower cost of labor in those areas.

Putting all three of these variables together, Figure 6.3 portrays how the overall experience curve promotes lower unit costs as volume increases. Hence, as a business gains greater market share, its per-unit costs can decrease as it takes advantage of the experience curve. However, investing in greater plant capacity is not necessarily an automatic route to lower unit costs. As can be seen from the curve in Figure 6.3, the experience curve flattens at point A on the graph. Production beyond that point will not lower unit costs any further.

Although large business units benefit from the experience curve, the particular generic strategy adopted by a given business unit will have different ramifications for success. For instance, many (but not all) businesses that compete with the low-cost strategy tend to buy their way to lower costs. In other words, they sell their products or services at low prices, even if those prices are initially below their costs. The low prices increase their volume, thereby permitting them to lower their costs through use of the experience curve. These businesses, however, are particularly vulnerable to business units that are also able to attain low costs but offer better-quality products and services.[11]

A different approach is taken by business units that compete with the differentiation and low-cost–differentiation generic strategies. Instead of charging average or low prices, they charge average to high prices, seeking to gain market share by offering higher-quality outputs. The increase in sales also allows them to lower their costs. But the managers of the business units that adopt differentiation as their strategy do not actively capitalize on the opportunities presented by lower costs, whereas managers of businesses that compete with low-cost–differentiation do.[12] Hence, adopters of differentiation as a generic strategy are vulnerable to competitors that offer alternative products, but at

Figure 6.3   **Experience Curve**

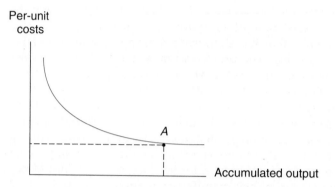

lower, or even predatory, prices. The low-cost–differentiation adopter is less vulnerable than businesses using either of the preceding strategies, however, because this strategy emphasizes lower costs (as protection against low-cost companies) and high-quality outputs (to protect against differentiated businesses).

Regardless of the generic strategy adopted, large business units that use the experience curve take a significant risk. Increases in volume often involve substantial investments in plant and equipment and a commitment to the prevailing technology. The risk is that if technological innovations should make the plant's production processes obsolete, millions of dollars in capital equipment may have to be written off. How may this need to invest in plant and equipment be balanced against the risk that technology will change? History provides a partial answer.

Virtually any technology is improved upon over time. But at some point, further improvements become prohibitively expensive. At such times, emphasis should be placed on developing innovations, even at the risk of rendering obsolete the company's prevailing technology. A major vulnerability in using the experience curve is that managers become psychologically dependent upon the organization's technology both because they are familiar with it and because they have committed so many resources to it. Consequently, when a competitor develops a new technology, the company can quickly become technologically obsolete.

As an example, consider NCR, a business that once had the lowest costs (through the experience curve) in the mechanical cash register industry. When Burroughs and other competitors developed a fully integrated electronic cash register that was superior in performance, the market demand quickly shifted from the technologically obsolete mechanical cash register to the new product. As a result, NCR lost its competitive edge.

■ Quality Considerations

An issue of increasing importance in production/operations management in recent years is quality. This concept, introduced in Chapter 5, refers to the totality of features and characteristics of a product or service that bear on its ability to satisfy stated or implied needs. Historically, quality has been viewed largely as a controlling activity that takes place somewhere near the end of the production process, an after-the-fact measurement of production success. As such, efforts to ensure quality increased the costs associated with making that good or service available. For this reason, quality and productivity have been viewed as conflicting; one was increased at the expense of the other. This fallacious orientation has clearly hindered quality improvement in many companies.

Over the years, however, more and more managers have come to realize that quality is not something that is measured at, or near, the end of the production process but, rather, is an essential ingredient of the product or service being provided. Consequently, quality is part of the overall approach to doing business and becomes the concern of all members of the organization. When quality comes to be viewed in this way, the following conditions prevail:

- Making a quality product decreases the quantity of defects, which causes yield to increase.
- Making a product right the first time reduces the number of rejects and time spent on rework.
- Making the operative employees responsible for quality eliminates the need for inspection.

These conditions also apply to service quality, whether the service is performed for the customer or for some other department in the same organization. The ultimate result is that quality is viewed as reducing, rather than increasing, costs.[13] As quality consultant Philip B. Crosby points out:

> Every penny you don't spend on doing things wrong, over, or instead of, becomes half a penny right on the bottom line. . . . If you concentrate on making quality certain, you can probably increase your profit by an amount equal to 5% to 10% of your sales.[14]

W. Edwards Deming, the world-renowned consultant, concurs by stating that improvement of quality converts the waste of employee hours and machine time into the manufacture of good product and better service. Management in some Japanese companies observed as early as the late 1940s that improvement of quality naturally and inevitably begets improvement of productivity.[15] This process is illustrated in Figure 6.4. As you can see, such a process is essential to businesses competing with the niche–low-cost/differentiation or low-cost–differentiation generic strategies. If below-average industry prices are charged, the business benefits because it may increase its market share and, subsequently, reduce its costs. If average or above-average industry prices are charged, the business benefits from greater profit margins. Even companies that adopt differentiation as their strategy can develop a distinct competitive advantage by focusing on the quality of their products and services.

Consider the case of Xerox, which uses the low-cost–differentiation strategy. It is fighting heavy competition from Japanese copiers by improving its quality and that of its suppliers. In 1982, prior to its quality drive, only 92 percent of the parts that suppliers shipped to Xerox were defect-free; and when a customer pushed the "copy" button on a Xerox machine, he or she had only a 90 percent chance of getting a good copy. By 1988, however, the ratio of defect-free parts supplied to Xerox had climbed to 99.97 percent. Today, the quality of Xerox copiers has so improved that a customer's chance of getting a good copy is 98 percent. Xerox's ultimate goal is zero defects.[16]

Figure 6.4   **The Deming Chain Reaction**

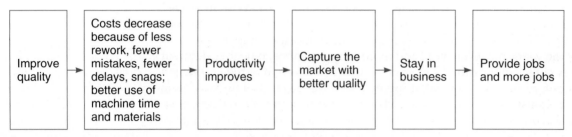

Source: Reprinted from *Out of the Crisis* by W. Edwards Deming by permission of MIT and W. Edwards Deming. Published by MIT, Center for Advanced Engineering Study, Cambridge, Mass. 02139. Copyright 1986 by W. Edwards Deming.

FINANCE

The finance function encompasses not only cash management but also the use of credit and decisions regarding capital investments. Ideally, each business would like to have a surplus of internally generated cash, beyond what is needed for expenditures, to allow it to reinvest the cash back into the business. In this way, the future viability of the enterprise is assured. However, a company resorts to borrowing funds when strategic decisions require cash beyond what can be generated from operations. Long-term capital investment decisions focus on the allocation of resources and, hence, are linked to corporate and business unit strategies in an obvious fashion.

Business units that compete with the niche–low-cost or low-cost generic strategies pursue financial strategies that are intended to lower their financial costs. Insofar as possible, they attempt to keep their costs within the limits of the funds they are able to generate from operations. If borrowing becomes necessary, they try to borrow during times when credit costs are relatively low. If they sell common stock to generate additional funds, they time the sale carefully to coincide with a bull market (i.e., a market in which stock prices, on the average, are rising). Their capital investment decisions center on plant and equipment, technology, and research and development efforts that can lower their cost positions even more. Furthermore, they attempt to time major equipment purchases from foreign producers when the dollar is strong relative to the foreign currency.

Business units that adopt the niche-differentiation or differentiation generic strategies pursue financial strategies that fund quality enhancements. To stay in step with their competitors' product improvements or innovations, they direct their financial efforts toward upgrading their present and future outputs. If internal funds are insufficient, then they will attempt to raise money either through selling common stock or borrowing funds. Stock may be sold even though stock prices in general are relatively low, and funds may be borrowed even if interests costs are relatively high. In other words, these business units place the highest strategic priority on quality maintenance and enhancement rather than on financial considerations.

Finally, those business units that compete with the niche–low-cost/differentiation, low-cost–differentiation, or multiple strategies use their financial function, on the one hand, to lower costs and, on the other hand, to promote quality enhancements. Because, as we saw earlier, such business units ordinarily perform well, they tend to have stronger financial positions than other business units, which allow them greater flexibility. These business units often have cash surpluses, can borrow funds at competitive rates, and are able to command high prices for new stock offerings. Hence, their investment strategies revolve around financial considerations that attempt to lower costs and heighten differentiation simultaneously. Further specifics on financial considerations are offered in Exhibit 1 of "Strategic Management Case Analysis."

RESEARCH AND DEVELOPMENT

Research and development (R&D) has two basic components: product/service R&D and process R&D. **Product/service R&D** refers to efforts that ultimately lead to improvements or innovations in the company's outputs. **Process R&D** aims at reducing the costs of operations and making them more efficient. The more dynamic the industry environment, the more important R&D efforts of both kinds become.

Business units that compete with the niche–low-cost and low-cost strategies emphasize process R&D to reduce their operations costs. However, those business units that use the niche-differentiation and differentiation strategies place more importance on product/service R&D to produce improved and new innovative outputs. Finally, adopters of the niche–low-cost/differentiation, low-cost–differentiation, and multiple strategies simultaneously stress both product/service R&D and process R&D efforts.

Organizations with effective R&D departments are, in essence, lowering their risks by making themselves more competitive. Product/service R&D focuses on market competitiveness, and process R&D emphasizes cost competitiveness. But R&D efforts also involve risks of another kind.

Process innovations, for instance, may be too technologically sophisticated to be implemented effectively. As an example, consider General Motors's Saturn project. The original concept was to develop a new technology—through robotics, just-in-time inventory practices, close supplier relationships, and more flexible work rules—to manufacture automobiles that would involve only one-third the labor hours that the Japanese expend on car production. But after investing about $5 billion on the project, GM is disappointed in Saturn. The process innovations have had numerous equipment failures, and GM has been unable to achieve the production cost cuts that it had predicted.

Likewise, product/service innovations also involve risks. Once they are introduced, new products or services may find little market demand. RJR Nabisco, for example, spent millions of dollars to develop and produce its "smokeless" cigarette, Premier. Although introduced to the market with considerable fanfare, smokers refused to switch to the new product, and it was canceled within a few weeks of its introduction.

This example illustrates the problems inherent in **technology transfer,** the process whereby a company transforms its scientific discoveries into marketable products. Some companies accomplish this transfer exceedingly well. Hewlett-Packard, for example, estimates that about 60 percent of its research results in product applications. In fact, over 50 percent of its sales come from products developed within the past three years. This remarkable record results from a two-tier arrangement in which corporate R&D operations work on projects with three-to-seven-year time horizons, while each business unit has its own R&D function that concentrates on shorter-range product applications.[17] But no one method is best. General Electric, another highly innovative firm, operates through a corporate-level R&D department that then demonstrates its inventions to each of GE's business units. This system has resulted in some unexpected applications; for instance, a device that was invented to protect coal-spraying nozzles in a locomotive was subsequently used to create a new generation of energy-saving light bulbs. Likewise, a medical diagnostic instrument invented for human body imaging is now also used as a cost-saving tool for inspecting jet engines.[18]

MARKETING

Marketing consists of four strategic considerations: products/services, pricing, channels of distribution/location of outlets, and promotion. The particular generic strategy adopted by the business unit influences how these various marketing strategies are planned and executed.

As we saw in the preceding chapter, business units that compete with the niche–low-cost and low-cost generic strategies produce no-frills products/services. Although these outputs are undifferentiated or minimally differentiated with respect to those of their competitors, they are by no means unreliable or shoddy. For example, Motel 6 Inc. offers no-frills rooms. They are clean and contain comfortable, but low-priced, furniture and beds. Motel 6 offers few services; for instance, it has no restaurants, or conference rooms. Its simple brand name, Motel 6, is intended to convey the impression of economy services.

Consistent with its no-frills outputs, Motel 6 normally charges low prices. In particular circumstances, it may be able to charge average prices, but this is possible only where its competitors are either few or far removed. Because it is a service company, channels of distribution are not relevant, but geographic location is. Motel 6 has been successful in choosing locations, primarily near interstate highway exit ramps. Promotion efforts are undertaken at low costs and attempt to convey to the traveling public that Motel 6 offers satisfactory economy lodging.

Different marketing strategies are pursued by businesses that use the generic strategies of differentiation and low-cost–differentiation. Marketing unique, quality products and services that are distinguishable from the outputs of rivals requires approaches considerably at variance from those described in the preceding two paragraphs. For example, Holiday Inn offers larger rooms with better-quality furnishings than Motel 6. Holiday Inns also contain such features as restaurants, shops, swimming pools, and conference rooms. The brand name Holiday Inn is intended to give the impression of quality. Average to high prices are charged for Holiday Inn rooms, depending upon the competitive situation; and promotional efforts convey a unique, quality image.

STRATEGIC INSIGHT

The Importance of Distribution and Production Capacity at Colgate-Palmolive and Coors

The role of distribution is often overlooked amid the more glamorous marketing functions of advertising, selling, and designing products and packages. Although less visible, distribution is certainly as important as these other aspects of marketing.

Consider a company that has used distribution to its distinct advantage: Colgate-Palmolive. This multiunit company's most profitable business is not toothpaste or soap; it is, surprisingly, pet food. Part of the secret to the success of its Hill's Pet Products division is distribution. Unlike better-known and much larger competitors such as Ralston Purina, Hill's sells its pet food almost exclusively through veterinarians. Its premium-priced product (i.e., a single can of dog food costs about $2) comes in several formulations, ranging from diet food for overweight pets to low-sodium meals for animals with heart conditions. Although Ral-

ston Purina and Iams have similar products, they face considerable difficulty breaking into Hill's long-established distribution channel.

On the other hand, a good product can be ruined by a lack of production capacity, so that the product cannot even reach the market. Coors was the first brewer to hit the market with a premium bottled draft beer, Coors Extra Gold. It was an instant success—in fact, far more successful than Coors had anticipated. The company quickly ran out of supplies, while distributors begged for more. While Coors struggled with its distribution difficulties, Miller introduced its Genuine Draft. Even as Coors was forced to drop all mass media advertising for Extra Gold because it could not meet market demand, consumers turned to Miller's new beer and quickly made it one of the top-ten-selling brands in the United States.

SOURCES: B. Hager, "The Pet Food That's Fattening Colgate's Kitty," *Business Week*, 7 May 1990, p. 116; M. Charlier, "Bottled Draft Beers Head for Collision as Anheuser Readies Challenge to Miller," *The Wall Street Journal*, 1 May 1990.

Still other marketing strategies are followed by business units that adopt the niche-differentiation and niche–low-cost/differentiation generic strategies. These businesses tend to offer specialized, high-quality to highest-quality products and services to meet the particular needs of a relatively small market. Holiday Inn Suites, featured in some Holiday Inns, offer spacious rooms, wet bars, hair dryers, and complimentary food, beverages, and newspapers. The brand name attempts to convey the impression that in addition to having access to Holiday Inns' restaurants, shops, swimming pools, and conference rooms, customers will be further pampered by these extra features. High prices are charged for these suites, and promotional campaigns address the relatively few potential customers who desire the suites' extra features.

HUMAN RESOURCE MANAGEMENT

The human resource management function includes such major activities as planning for future human resource needs, recruiting personnel, placing people in new jobs, compensating them, evaluating their performance, training them and developing them into more effective employees, and enhancing their work

Timberland Leaves the Competition Behind

For years, the Abington Shoe Company produced shoes for other firms. Its marketing strategy primarily revolved around the issues of price competition and distribution. But over time, competition became extremely intense, as rival companies imported shoes from the Far East, where labor costs were quite low.

Perceiving that continued price competition was a losing game, Abington began to refocus its strategy. The company had designed a rugged, waterproof insulated boot under the brand name Timberland in the early 1970s. By 1978, the boot accounted for over 80 percent of the company's output. So the family-owned company decided to quit manufacturing for others and concentrate on producing rugged boots and shoes under its own name. The company's name was changed to Timberland and the New Hampshire–based operation is today managed by the son and grandson of the founder.

Timberland's annual sales of $156 million come from the sale of its shoes, apparel, and accessories such as backpacks to a worldwide market. In fact, Timberland bucks the trend toward foreign imports by actually exporting 30 percent of its annual output to Hong Kong, Taiwan, Japan, and Western Europe.

Using a niche-differentiation strategy, Timberland stresses the quality of its products, not their price, to discriminating customers. The ruggedness of Timberland shoes is exemplified by the company's equipping the contestants in the annual 1000-mile Iditarod winter dogsled race in Alaska with a pair of Timberland snow boots. Each pair of those boots costs $500 to manufacture.

The Swartz family, which controls Timberland's stock, believes that family ownership has two major advantages: It prevents outside takeovers, and it allows the company to concentrate on long-run strategies without being distracted by Wall Street pressure for quarterly financial results.

environment. These activities have become increasingly important in our society. The average employee, for instance, will spend more of his or her adult life at work, traveling to and from work, preparing for work, poring over work at home, and engaging in social activities related to work than he or she will spend with the family, in leisure pursuits, or in sleep.

Because work is important to society, organizations that wish to have a strong, competitive work force must create certain working conditions for their employees. Progressive organizations consider human resources their most precious asset. Consequently, personnel needs for customized fringe benefits, child day care, and flexible working hours are given equal consideration with such traditional needs as training and development, job enrichment, and promotional opportunities.

The wave of mergers and acquisitions in the 1980s, inevitably followed by organizational restructuring and massive layoffs, disillusioned formerly loyal employees. Prior to this time, many workers assumed that as long as they performed well, they would have a job with their company for as many years as they wished. The 1980s not only ended that dream for those who were laid off but also created anxiety among those who survived the cutbacks. It is difficult for a company to eliminate as much as 20 percent of its work force and still retain a commitment among those who remain.

Hence, a priority in the 1990s for business units, regardless of their particular generic strategy, is to develop commitment among their employees to the organization and to the job. Such an ambitious human resource strategy, according to Andrall E. Pearson, former CEO of PepsiCo, requires top-level management to become actively involved in the strategy.[19]

The first step is to set high performance standards. According to Pearson, one top manager shocked his employees by rejecting a seemingly demanding and competitive plan that projected profits on a good sales gain for the third year in a row. Instead, he required his managers to return with a plan that kept the projected volumes but cut cost levels 5 percent below the preceding year's costs.[20]

Aside from setting challenging goals, how do top managers get high performance standards to permeate the organization? Pearson suggests that when faced with problems or opportunities, successful companies rely on their human resources rather than on particular concepts or principles.

> When [organizations] have a strategy or business problem or a big opportunity, they turn to the individual who has the right skills and style for that job. Then, having made the match, they delegate responsibility without hemming the person in with a tight job description or organizational constraints. Then managers feel more responsible for results simply because they are more responsible.[21]

Of overwhelming importance to maintaining high performance is the design of appropriate reward systems. Rewards, in the usual sense of recognition, pay raises, and promotions, must be tied to high performance and must encourage behavior that promotes the necessary teamwork and cooperation among employees. Organizations are increasingly linking performance to pay and other incentive systems such as profit sharing and stock options. One of the most ambitious programs in this regard is that of PepsiCo. In 1989, this cola, snack-food, and restaurant giant created a stock option plan for all 100,000 employees who average at least thirty hours of weekly work. (Traditional stock option plans usually include only top-level executives.) As D. Wayne Calloway, PepsiCo's chairman and CEO, put it: "It's been part of our whole culture to say 'you are important' to every employee."[22] The intent of this SharePower program is to "make employees identify more with the company and their work, encourage them to stay longer, and increase productivity."[23] With this sort of innovative management, it is no accident that PepsiCo is widely recognized as one of the world's premier consumer products companies.

Human resource policies that encourage and reward teamwork have progressively become more necessary, because the successful planning and execution of diverse functional strategies depend upon the cooperation of people within and across departments and functional areas. For example, such concepts as quality circles, team product development, and just-in-time inventory assume and encourage a cooperative spirit among the individuals and groups involved.

INFORMATION SYSTEMS MANAGEMENT

A well-designed information system can benefit all of a business unit's functional areas. A computer-based decision support system that contains a central

Goal Congruence at Carlson Companies

Edwin Gage, CEO of Carlson Companies, considers motivating employees to be a key part of his organization's culture. As he puts it:

> Employees do things for their reasons—not [top management's]. Now if you put together programs including compensation, incentives, recognition that matches up the corporation's [benefits] with the employees' [benefits] . . . so you are going [to] the same place, have the same goals, that really is what turns people on.

This matching of interests is referred to as creating "goal congruence." The more congruent the goals of a company are with those of its employees, the more effective and efficient the organization will be. Common examples of goal congruence include commission payments for sales representatives (i.e., the more they sell, the more both they and the company make) and financial incentives for improving quality (i.e., the higher the quality, the greater the company's sales revenues will be and the higher the take-home pay of its employees will be).

Other examples include the following:

• Fair treatment for female and minority employees. As these individuals, who have generally been excluded from top management ranks, find that performance is rewarded regardless of gender or race, they become more committed to the organization, and the company's performance reflects the increased effort that results from this commitment.

• Enhanced training and development programs. In the long run, investments in training and development programs more than pay for themselves. Employees have more satisfying careers and become more effective job performers, thereby making their organizations more efficient and more effective competitors in the marketplace.

• Provision of child care, whether through on-site locations or community networks. Employee turnover and absenteeism are likely to decline, making the organization more productive; and employees experience fewer of the hassles often associated with having to make their own child-care arrangements.

data base permits each functional area to access the information it needs and to communicate electronically with the other functional departments as necessary. In this way, each department can keep abreast of what other departments are doing and coordinate its efforts appropriately. Some organizations store their data in a mainframe computer that is linked to personal computers in functional departments. Others use more decentralized networked systems in which smaller "server" computers share their data with personal computers or workstations in various functional areas.

This advantage is not the only benefit of an efficient information system, however. Such systems can cut internal costs while they promote differentiation and quality through a faster response to the market's needs. In fact, some businesses owe their high performance to their information systems. It is important to realize that the system need not be particularly complicated or sophisticated. For instance, Domino's Pizza has grown to become a leading pizza chain through a simple information system. Its kitchens, delivery vehicles, and telephone lines form coordinated information hubs in each location, so that usually within thirty minutes of the time a customer places a telephone order, the pizza is delivered to the customer's home.

On the other hand, some companies' information systems are quite elaborate. In the financial services area, Merrill Lynch uses a complex technology interface of communications and data processing between its brokerage offices and its bank. Because of this system, Merrill Lynch was able to develop its Cash Management Account, which helped to eliminate traditional boundaries between the banking and securities industries. Consequently, Merrill Lynch has gained about 450,000 new accounts and $60 million in annual fees.[24] In the retail industry, The Limited designed a sophisticated global information system that links its hundreds of stores to its Columbus, Ohio, headquarters and to its textile mills that are owned and operated by The Limited in Hong Kong. Sales information from each of its stores is gathered and analyzed in Columbus. Within less than a week, the Hong Kong textile mills are already producing more of what is selling well and less of those items that are experiencing slow turnover.[25]

Most organizations' information systems evolve through four stages of growth. Initially, companies use electronic data processing for cost reduction accounting applications, such as billing and payroll. In the second stage, computer applications spread into all functional areas. Such applications include forecasting, inventory control, cash flow, personnel records, and sales analyses. The next stage focuses on certain control activities, such as in purchasing and scheduling. The final stage is the most sophisticated, involving decision support applications such as planning models, simulations, and on-line uses in human resources, cost analyses, and order entries.[26]

The fourth stage permits management to develop competitive advantages that would not otherwise be possible. The Dutch paint manufacturer Akzo Coatings gained a decided advantage over its competitors by using its information system to reduce the anxiety of body shop customers (who worry about the cost of repairing their damaged cars) and body shop owners (who fear they will underestimate the costs of repairs). Akzo's computerized system gives body shops instant access to spare-parts costs, repair procedures, and labor cost guidelines for 2000 car models. Shop employees simply enter a description of the car to be repaired, the repairs required, and the parts needed into a personal computer. They instantly receive a repair cost calculation. This use of information technology gave Akzo a two-year lead over its competition.[27]

INTEGRATING THE FUNCTIONS

For a business unit's generic strategy to be successful, each functional area must do more than simply operate efficiently. Overall strategic success requires that all functional activities be tightly integrated so that their operations mesh smoothly with one another. Those businesses that are best able to achieve functional integration are those most likely to attain the competitive advantages detailed in the following paragraphs.

■ Superior Product Design

Although product design has been recognized as an important competitive dimension for years, it is receiving increased attention in the 1990s. Until recently, design was primarily associated with product appearance. But now, the concept is being broadened to include such features as designing a product for easy manufacturability so that fewer parts have to be purchased. Additionally, increased emphasis is being put on improving the product's functionality (i.e., ability to perform its purpose) and quality.

Gaining a competitive advantage through superior product design involves all functional areas. Even in those companies where production/operations management has been the dominant function, the revised emphasis is on the interrelationships of all functional areas. For instance, when Caterpillar reorganized so that it could compete more effectively with heavy-equipment manufacturers from Japan, it first "intended to move only its design engineers to the plants to work more closely with the production people. . . . [Then the question became] why just the manufacturing and the engineering people . . . so marketing and pricing folks [also moved] into the plants."[28]

A well-designed product is attractive and easy to build, market, use, and maintain. Simplicity drives the best-designed products. But superior product design alone is not sufficient to gain a substantial competitive edge; design must be combined with superior service.

■ Superior Customer Service

Developing and maintaining the quality of customer service is often more challenging than improving product quality. The reason is that the consumer perceives service value primarily at the time the service is either rendered or not rendered. As one manager put it:

> You can tell me how awful someone's behavior was, but there is nothing for me to go back and look at. There aren't any artifacts, like broken gizmos I can go back and test.[29]

All functional areas must work together to provide the customer with product and service value. For example, a supermarket must fulfill several customer needs. First, it must offer value to customers in their shopping. Carrying the products that customers desire, at competitive prices, means that the purchasing, inventory, information systems, finance, and human resource management functions must communicate with one another and cooperate closely. Next, the store must make certain that its employees are able to respond to customer inquiries. This objective requires effective human resource management practices in hiring and training. Then, the supermarket must ensure that it stocks sufficient quantities of the items that it advertises. Meeting this objective requires interaction among the purchasing, inventory, information systems, and marketing functions. Finally, the store must provide the means for customers to check out their purchases accurately and quickly, requiring the close cooperation of information systems and human resource management.

The importance of service cannot be overemphasized. In a recent survey, over one-third of the respondents indicated that they choose businesses that charge high prices but provide excellent service over companies that offer low prices but mediocre service.[30] As one observer points out:

> Despite all the talk these days about quality and customer satisfaction, most companies provide more lip service than customer service. Companies that really do provide service can command premium prices for their products. . . . [For example,] at Premier's [a business that provides hard-to-find fasteners and other related

items] . . . charges are typically between 10% and 15% more than competitors' prices—and sometimes as much as 200% higher.[31]

Personal attention is an important way that some businesses provide superior service. Personal attention involves paying heed to details, addressing customers' concerns, answering technical questions, and providing service after the sale. Such attention often plays an important psychological role as well. For example, the top managers of one industrial products supplier routinely visit plants to which the company has sold its products. In speaking of the psychological aspect of those visits, one manager indicated:

> We know our machine products are reliable and do not require visits. But when our clients see us physically inspecting their machines, sometimes merely dusting them off, they derive a sense of security and comfort that our products are in their plants, albeit at higher costs to them. When they are asked for a reference on suppliers, they usually suggest our firm.[32]

■ Superior Speed

Speed in developing, making, and distributing products and services can give a business a significant competitive advantage. In fact, a recent survey of fifty major U.S.-based companies revealed that speed (alternatively referred to as "time-based strategy") was a top priority.[33] To illustrate the point, consider the comments of two managers:

> We can design, produce, and deliver before our big competitors get the paperwork done.
>
> We have a lock on our customers. . . . You see, it may take some of our big buyers several weeks [to complete a purchase order], during which time their engineers request an order, their purchasing department receives the request and communicates it to the suppliers. We are in constant touch with the plant engineers, and normally we know what their next purchases are before their own purchasing departments. Consequently, we can normally deliver their needs overnight or within a few days.[34]

Some companies have taken these lessons to heart. General Electric, for instance, used to spend three weeks on an order for its custom-made circuit breaker boxes. It now spends three days. AT&T can design a new telephone today in one-half of the time it took a few years ago. And Motorola, which used to produce electronic pagers three weeks after receiving an order, can now do it in two hours.[35]

The importance of superior speed in serving customers should not be overlooked. For example, Premier, the fastener company mentioned above, received a call one day from one of its customers, Caterpillar. A $10 electrical relay had malfunctioned, bringing one of Caterpillar's assembly lines to a halt. A Premier representative located a replacement part in a Los Angeles warehouse and had it placed immediately on a plane bound for St. Louis. When it arrived, a Premier employee picked the part up and delivered it to Caterpillar. As might be expected, Caterpillar and other firms are willing to pay significantly higher prices for Premier's products because of the superior service they receive.[36]

■ Superior Guarantee

Even in the best-managed businesses, problems occasionally arise that result in less-than-acceptable product or service quality. Hence, companies must take steps to guarantee an acceptable level of quality. Highly successful companies often go to great lengths to back their guarantees. For example, the famous retailer and mail-order house L. L. Bean accepts customer returns of its products for any reason, even after several years. A pair of hunting boots that was returned after ten years would be immediately replaced by a new pair with no questions asked.[37]

Many companies, however, ignore this competitive advantage. Often, guarantees lapse after a very short time period or contain too many exceptional conditions to be effective competitive weapons. For instance, some companies guarantee their electronic products for only ninety days; others are sufficiently confident of their product quality to offer one-year guarantees. Some airlines guarantee that their passengers will make connecting flights on time if no delays are caused by air traffic control problems or poor weather conditions. Unfortunately for the passengers, the majority of flight delays are due to these two factors.

Because of its intangible nature, a service guarantee is even more challenging to provide than a product guarantee. Christopher W. L. Hart, a business researcher and consultant, suggests that the following five desirable characteristics be included in service guarantees:[38]

- The guarantee should be unconditional, with no exceptions.
- It should be easily understood and written in simple language.
- The guarantee should be meaningful by guaranteeing what is important to the customer and making it worth the customer's time and effort to invoke the guarantee, should he or she be dissatisfied.
- The guarantee should be convenient to invoke and not require the customer to appeal to several layers of bureaucracy.
- The customer should be satisfied promptly, without a lengthy waiting period.

These characteristics, of course, should also be included in product guarantees.

SUMMARY

Once corporate-level and business unit generic strategies are developed, management must turn its attention to formulating and implementing strategies for each business unit's functional areas. Here, the manager should not view the strategy of one functional area in isolation, because it is the extent to which all of the functional tasks mesh smoothly that determines the effectiveness of the unit's generic strategy.

A business unit's purchasing strategy will differ depending upon which generic strategy it adopts. Companies that use the niche–low-cost strategy or the low-cost strategy emphasize purchasing at the lowest costs possible. Those that use niche-differentiation or differentiation stress the procurement of high-quality inputs, even if they cost more than alternative offerings. Organizations that pursue niche–low-cost/differentiation or low-cost–differentiation attempt to buy high-quality inputs at low costs, and those that employ multiple strategies use a mixture of purchasing plans. Purchasing is the first step in the materials management process, followed by storage and warehousing functions and inventory control. The latest trend in materials management, the just-in-time inventory system, ties these functions together.

The next functional strategic area is production/operations management (POM). Small business units that compete with the niche–low-cost strategy emphasize low initial investments in their plants, equipment, and outlets to hold their fixed costs down, and they attempt to keep their variable operations costs as low as possible. Small businesses competing with niche-differentiation stress POM strategies that yield superior quality, and those that use niche–low-cost/differentiation emphasize POM activities that simultaneously lower costs and heighten differentiation. Large business units, on the other hand, are able to take advantage of the experience curve by using learning, economies of scale, and capital-labor substitution possibilities to their advantage. To gain market share so that they may enjoy the experience curve, large business units that compete with the low-cost strategy may sell at low prices to increase volume. Large enterprises that use differentiation or low-cost–differentiation may attempt to gain market share by offering higher-quality outputs. But using the experience curve entails risks, such as becoming wed over time to an obsolete technology.

One of the primary considerations in any POM strategy is product or service quality. Businesses that build quality in, rather than attempt to inspect for quality after production has occurred, are able to enhance both productivity and profitability.

In the finance function, business units that compete with the niche–low-cost and low-cost strategies pursue financial strategies intended to lower their financial costs. Companies that adopt niche-differentiation and differentiation strategies develop financial strategies that fund quality enhancements. And those that use niche–low-cost/differentiation, low-cost–differentiation, and multiple strategies use their financial function both to lower costs and to promote quality enhancements.

Research and development (R&D) has two basic components: product/service R&D and process R&D. Business units competing with the niche–low-cost and low-cost strategies emphasize process R&D to reduce their operations costs; those that use niche-differentiation or differentiation place greater importance on product/service R&D; and adopters of niche–low-cost/differentiation, low-cost–differentiation, and multiple strategies simultaneously stress both types of R&D.

In marketing, the particular generic strategy adopted by a business unit influences the types of products or services the business offers, its prices for those products or services, the channels of distribution it uses, the location of its outlets, and its advertising and promotional policies. The key is to strive for consistency among these elements.

In the 1990s, effective organizations will manage their human resource function so as to maintain a strong, competitive work force. This goal requires attention to personnel needs and the development of strategies that strengthen organizational and job performance commitment and teamwork across functional areas.

Tying all of these functions together is the organization's information system. Well-designed information systems are capable of cutting internal costs while they promote differentiation and quality through faster responses to the market's needs.

Finally, it is essential that the business's functional activities be tightly integrated. An organization that is able to mesh its functional strategies smoothly is more likely to gain a competitive advantage based on superior product design, customer service, speed, and/or guarantee.

KEY CONCEPTS

Experience curve   The reduction in per-unit costs that occurs as an organization gains experience producing a product or service. The experience curve concept is based on three underlying variables: learning (i.e., the more an employee performs a task, the more efficient he or she should become at the job), economies of scale (i.e., the decline in per-unit costs of a product or service as the absolute volume of production increases per period of time), and capital-labor substitution possibilities (i.e., as volume increases, the organization may be able to substitute labor for capital, or capital for labor, depending upon which combination produces lower costs and/or greater effectiveness).

Functional strategy   The strategy pursued by each functional area of a business unit. Functional areas are usually referred to as "departments" and include purchasing/materials management, production/operations, finance, research and development, marketing, human resources, and information systems. Their strategies may take various forms, depending upon which generic strategy the business unit adopts.

Just-in-time inventory system   An inventory system, popularized by the Japanese, in which suppliers deliver parts just at the time they are needed by the buying organization to use in its production process. Used properly, such a system holds inventory, storage, and warehousing costs to a minimum.

Process R&D   Research and development activities that concentrate upon reducing the costs of operations and making them more efficient.

Product/service R&D   Research and development activities that are intended to lead to improvements or innovations in the firm's products or services.

Technology transfer   The process whereby a company transforms its scientific discoveries into marketable products.

DISCUSSION QUESTIONS

1. What is the relationship among corporate-level strategy, business unit strategies, and functional strategies?

2. Explain the linkage that a just-in-time inventory system provides between the purchasing and production functions. What are the implications for quality?

3. POM concepts are equally applicable to manufacturing and service organizations. Explain the POM process at a university.

4. What are some of the more important relationships among the POM, finance, and R&D functions?

5. What sorts of POM strategies might a small business unit adopt to compete effectively with a large business unit?

6. Relate the concept of the experience curve to the production operations of an automobile assembly plant.

7. Explain the relationship between quality and productivity.

8. What is the linkage between long-term capital investment decisions and the organization's corporate and business unit strategies?

9. Give, and explain, an example of (1) a business that emphasizes product/service R&D, and (2) another business that emphasizes process R&D.

10. What are some of the major relationships among marketing, information systems, and human resources management?

STRATEGIC MANAGEMENT EXERCISES

1. Assume that two groups of investors are each planning to start a restaurant in the same city. The first group wishes to appeal to family meal needs, and the second wants to appeal to the needs of people who prefer gourmet food in particularly nice surroundings on special occasions. As is evident, different functional strategies will need to be adopted by the two restaurants. How would you suggest that each restaurant plan and implement its functional strategies? Be specific in your suggestions. If you need further information, either conduct relevant research or make reasonable assumptions.

2. Assume that you are asked to consult for a top-of-the-line restaurant in New York City that competes with the niche-differentiation strategy. While attending management's strategic-planning session, you learn that the managers would like to broaden their appeal in the New York City market. One way of doing that, they believe, is to reduce their prices. In order to attain that end, they must cut costs. Therefore, one manager suggests that in order to reduce costs, they should make some of their purchases locally instead of purchasing from the highest-quality suppliers worldwide. (Currently, the restaurant flies in certain foods from foreign countries at considerable cost.) Another manager believes that the restaurant should use less expensive tablecloths and napkins. Finally, another wishes to cancel the restaurant's live musical entertainment to save money. Through these cost-cutting measures, the managers believe that they can reduce their prices and become more competitive.

   What advice would you give these managers regarding their functional strategies?

3. Contrast the functional strategies that are followed by two automobile manufacturers: (1) Ford, which, as one of the world's largest producers, competes with the low-cost–differentiation strategy; and (2) Rolls-Royce, a relatively small company, which uses the niche-differentiation strategy. Specifically, how might you expect these two companies to differ in carrying out each of the following functional strategies: purchasing/materials management, production/operations, finance, research and development, marketing, human resources, and information systems?

4. Select a specific company on which you will be able to obtain information.

   a. Determine which generic business unit strategy this company has adopted.
   b. Analyze the company's functional strategies in purchasing/materials management, production/operations, finance, research and development, marketing, human resources, and information systems.
   c. Analyze the extent to which these functional strategies mesh smoothly with one another and with the business's generic strategy.
   d. Make suggestions for improvements in the company's functional strategies.

REFERENCES

1. D. J. Yang, M. Oneal, S. Toy, M. Maremont, and R. Neff, "How Boeing Does It," *Business Week*, 9 July 1990, pp. 46–50.

2. E. E. Scheuing, *Purchasing Management* (Englewood Cliffs, N.J.: Prentice-Hall, 1989), p. 4.

3. T. H. Hendrick and F. G. Moore, *Production/Operations Management*, 9th ed. (Homewood, Ill.: Irwin, 1985), p. 336.

4. J. G. Miller and P. Gilmour, "Materials Managers: Who Needs Them?" *Harvard Business Review* 57, no. 4 (1979): 145.

5. S. P. Galante, "Distributors Bow to Demands of 'Just-in-Time' Delivery," *The Wall Street Journal*, 30 June 1986.

6. J. Dreyfuss, "Shaping Up Your Suppliers," *Fortune*, 10 April 1989, p. 116.

7. J. Browne, J. Harhen, and J. Shivnan, *Production Management Systems: A CIM Perspective* (Workingham, England: Addison-Wesley, 1988), pp. 158–159.

8. E. A. Haas, "Breakthrough Manufacturing," *Harvard Business Review* 65, no. 2 (1987): 75–81.

9. See Boston Consulting Group, *Perspectives on Experience* (Boston: The Boston Consulting Group, 1976); G. Hall and S. Howell, "The Experience Curve from an Economist's Perspective," *Strategic Management Journal* 6 (1985): 197–212.

10. O. Port and W. Zellner, "Pssst! Want a Secret for Making Superproducts?" *Business Week*, 2 October 1989, p. 106.

11. T. Peters and N. Austin, *A Passion for Excellence* (New York: Random House, 1985), p. 53.

12. R. D. Buzzell and B. T. Gale, *The PIMS Principles* (New York: Free Press, 1987), Chap. 6.

13. R. Johnson, W. O. Winchell, and P. B. DuBose, *Strategy and Quality* (Milwaukee: American Society for Quality Control, 1989).

14. P. Crosby, *Quality Is Free* (New York: McGraw-Hill, 1979), p. 1.

15. W. E. Deming, *Out of the Crisis* (Cambridge, Mass.: Massachusetts Institute of Technology, Center for Advanced Engineering Study, 1986).

16. J. Main, "How to Win the Baldrige Award," *Fortune,* 23 April 1990, p. 104.

17. G. Bylinsky, "Turning R&D into Real Products," *Fortune,* 2 July 1990, pp. 72–73.

18. A. K. Naj, "GE's Latest Invention: A Way to Move Ideas from Lab to Market," *The Wall Street Journal,* 14 June 1990.

19. A. E. Pearson, "Six Basics for General Managers," *Harvard Business Review* 67, no. 4 (1989): 94–101.

20. Pearson, "Six Basics," p. 95.

21. Pearson, "Six Basics," p. 99. Reprinted by permission of the *Harvard Business Review.* Excerpt from "Six Basics for General Managers" by Andrall E. Pearson (July-August 1989). Copyright © 1989 by the President and Fellows of Harvard College; all rights reserved.

22. J. Solomon, "Pepsi Offers Stock Options to All, Not Just Honchos," *The Wall Street Journal,* 28 June 1989.

23. J. Solomon, "Pepsi Offers Stock Options."

24. H. C. Lucas, "Utilizing Information Technology: Guidelines for Managers," *Sloan Management Review* 28 (Fall 1986): 40; R. I. Benjamin, J. F. Rockart, M. S. S. Morton, and J. Wyman, "Information Technology: A Strategic Opportunity," *Sloan Management Review* 25 (Spring 1984): 6.

25. R. B. Chase and D. A. Garvin, "The Service Factory," *Harvard Business Review* 67, no. 4 (1989): 67.

26. C. F. Gibson and R. L. Nolan, "Managing the Four Stages of EDP Growth," in L. M. Salerno, ed., *Catching Up with the Computer Revolution* (New York: Wiley, 1983), pp. 25–43.

27. "Information Power," *Business Week,* 14 October 1985, p. 111.

28. J. Main, "Manufacturing the Right Way," *Fortune,* 21 May 1990, p. 54.

29. A. Bennett, "Making the Grade with the Customer," *The Wall Street Journal,* 12 November 1990.

30. A. Bennett, "Many Consumers Expect Better Service and Say They Are Willing to Pay for It," *The Wall Street Journal,* 12 November 1990.

31. D. Milbank, "Service Enables Nuts-and-Bolts Supplier to Be More Than Sum of Its Parts," *The Wall Street Journal,* 16 November 1990.

32. P. Wright, "Competitive Strategies for Small Businesses," in A. A. Thompson, Jr., A. J. Strickland III, and W. E. Fulmer, eds., *Readings in Strategic Management* (Plano, Tex.: Business Publications, 1984), p. 90.

33. B. Dumaine, "How Managers Can Succeed Through Speed," *Fortune,* 13 February 1989, p. 54.

34. Wright, "Competitive Strategies," p. 89.

35. Dumaine, "How Managers Can Succeed," p. 54.

36. S. Phillips, A. Dunkin, J. Treece, and K. Hammonds, "King Customer," *Business Week,* 12 March 1990, p. 88.

37. B. Uttal, "Companies That Serve You Best," *Fortune,* 7 December 1987, p. 98.

38. C. W. L. Hart, "The Power of Unconditional Service Guarantees," *The McKinsey Quarterly,* Summer 1989, pp. 75–76.

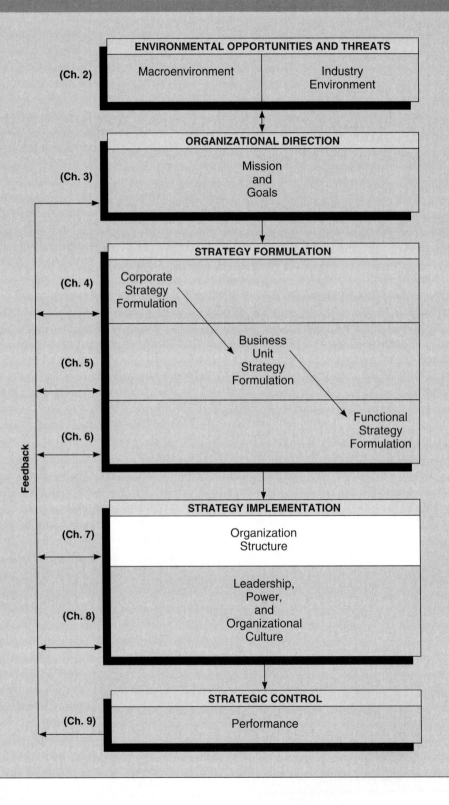

STRATEGIC MANAGEMENT MODEL

ENVIRONMENTAL OPPORTUNITIES AND THREATS

(Ch. 2)

| Macroenvironment | Industry Environment |

ORGANIZATIONAL DIRECTION

(Ch. 3)

Mission
and
Goals

STRATEGY FORMULATION

(Ch. 4)

Corporate
Strategy
Formulation

(Ch. 5)

Business
Unit
Strategy
Formulation

(Ch. 6)

Functional
Strategy
Formulation

STRATEGY IMPLEMENTATION

(Ch. 7)

Organization
Structure

(Ch. 8)

Leadership,
Power,
and
Organizational
Culture

STRATEGIC CONTROL

(Ch. 9)

Performance

Feedback

7
CHAPTER

Strategy Implementation: Organizational Structure

The three preceding chapters dealt with strategy formulation at the corporate, business unit, and functional levels. This chapter and the following one address the implementation of these strategies. Successful strategies must not only be well formulated to match environmental opportunities and constraints or threats but also be carried out effectively.

Effective strategy implementation requires managers to consider a number of key issues. Chief among them are how the organization should be structured to put its strategy into effect and how such variables as leadership, power, and organizational culture should be managed to enable the organization's employees to work together in carrying out the firm's strategic plans. This chapter deals with the first of these key issues—structuring the organization. Leadership, power, and organizational culture will be addressed in the following chapter.

ORGANIZATIONAL GROWTH

Organizational structure refers to the ways that tasks and responsibilities are allocated to individuals and the ways that individuals are grouped together into offices, departments, and divisions. The structure, which is reflected in an organization chart, designates formal reporting relationships and defines the number of levels in the hierarchy.[1]

Normally, when small businesses are started, they consist of an owner-manager and a few employees. Neither an organization chart nor formal assignment of responsibilities is necessary at this stage. Structure is fluid, with each employee often knowing how to perform more than one task and with the owner-manager involved in all aspects of the business. If the organization survives those crucial first years and becomes successful, it is because of the increased demand that it has created for its products or services. To meet this

Figure 7.1   **Organization of the Enterprise at Start-up and with Growth**

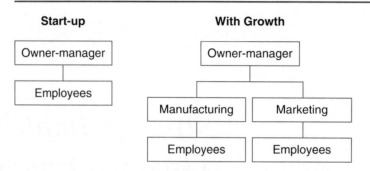

increased demand, the business must grow. With growth, the organization of the business begins to evolve from fluidity to a status of more permanent division of labor. The owner-manager, who once was involved in all functions of the enterprise on a hands-on basis, now finds that his or her role is becoming more managerial and less operational. As new employees are recruited, each is assigned to perform a specialized function.

As Figure 7.1 illustrates, growth expands the organization's structure, both vertically and horizontally. In this figure, the owner-manager's hands-on activities have been taken over by managers who specialize, respectively, in manufacturing and marketing. Each of them manages employees who work only in one specialized functional area. The organization has now added one vertical level—a managerial one—and has expanded horizontally into two separate departments. The following sections discuss these two types of organizational growth.

■ Vertical Growth

Vertical growth refers to an increase in the length of the organization's hierarchical chain of command. The **hierarchical chain of command** represents the company's authority-accountability relationships between superiors and subordinates. Authority flows down the hierarchy from the highest levels in the organization to those at the bottom, and accountability flows upward from bottom to top. In Figure 7.1, the organization on the right has three levels in its hierarchy. Employees at each level report to the manager who is in charge of their specific operations. The number of employees reporting to each manager represents that manager's **span of control.**

Figure 7.2 illustrates two extremes in organizational configuration. At the left is a **tall organization,** comprised of many hierarchical levels and narrow spans of control. The other structure is a **flat organization,** which has few levels in its hierarchy and a wide span of control from top to bottom. It is important to note that each of these configurations represents an extreme. Rather than being at either extreme, many organizations fall somewhere in between. Hence, we speak of organizations as being "relatively tall" or "relatively flat."

According to John Child, a management researcher, the average number of hierarchical levels for an organization with 3000 employees is seven.[2] Consequently, we might consider an organization with about 3000 employees and

Tall and Flat Organizational Structures

Figure 7.2

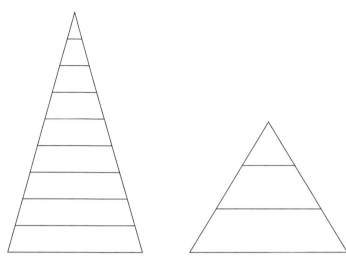

Tall organization, with 9 levels   Flat organization, with 3 levels

four hierarchical levels to be relatively flat, but another of similar size with nine levels would be considered relatively tall.

Because relatively tall organizations have a narrow span of control, the managers in such organizations have a relatively high degree of control over their subordinates. The opposite, of course, is true in relatively flat structures. Both managers and operative employees in tall organizations also tend to have jobs that are more narrowly specialized than those in relatively flat structures. Because managers in tall organizations have more control readily available to them and because almost everyone in the company is a specialist, authority in tall organizations is usually centralized at the top of the hierarchy. Only at that level are there individuals who deal with and understand all parts of the organization's operations.

Conversely, authority is more decentralized in relatively flat structures, because a manager with a broad span of control must grant more authority to his or her employees; the manager is unable to keep up sufficiently with all developments to make the best decisions. Decisions are more likely to be made by the employee who is on the scene and is most familiar with the situation. As might be expected, employees in flat organizations are less specialized than those in taller ones.

Strategically speaking, both organizational types have certain advantages.[3] The relatively tall, centralized organization allows for better communication of the business's mission, goals, and objectives to all employees. It also enhances coordination of functional areas to ensure that each area works closely with the other functions and that all work together to attain the business's goals and objectives. Finally, in these organizations, planning and its execution are relatively easy to accomplish since all employees are centrally directed. Tall organizational structures are well suited for environments that are relatively stable and predictable.

Relatively flat structures also have their advantages. Administrative costs are usually less than those in taller organizations, because fewer hierarchical levels require fewer managers, which, in turn, means fewer secretaries, offices, and fringe benefits. A second advantage is that decentralized decision making allows managers at various levels to have more authority, which may increase their motivation to assume responsibility for their areas's performance. Third, because of the greater freedom in decision making, innovations are encouraged. Flat structures, therefore, are appropriate for more dynamic environments.

The automobile industry provides an illustration of the advantages of flat structures in a changing environment. Prior to the 1970s, the U.S. car industry was relatively stable. Foreign competition, with the possible exception of Volkswagen, was fairly insignificant, and companies such as General Motors, Ford, Chrysler, and American Motors introduced new models annually every September. By the early 1970s, however, Japanese manufacturers began making steady inroads in the U.S. market; and by the latter part of the decade, the industry's competitive environment was becoming considerably more dynamic. U.S. carmakers in the 1980s became increasingly aware that their tall organizational structures were less effective than they had once been. But despite massive cutbacks, their structures remain relatively tall. Ford, for example, has seventeen layers of organization, from the worker on the assembly line to the CEO's office. General Motors has twenty-one or twenty-two, depending on the particular plant. Toyota, by contrast, has only seven layers. At the plant level, a Toyota foreman reports directly to a plant manager, but a Ford foreman has to go through three levels of management to reach the plant manager.[4] Toyota's superior flexibility, speed of decision making, and lower administrative costs give it a significant advantage over its American competitors. Ford and the other U.S. carmakers are now flattening their structures.

The same movements are apparent in other industries. General Electric, in an attempt to increase its flexibility and reaction time and lower its costs, reduced the number of its management layers between the factory floor and the executive suite from nine to as few as four in some of its divisions.[5]

■ Horizontal Growth

Returning to our earlier illustration of a small business with an owner-manager, recall that success necessitates growth. This growth is not only vertical, as just discussed, but also horizontal. **Horizontal growth** refers to an increase in the breadth of an organization's structure. In Figure 7.1, the small business segmented itself horizontally into two departments—manufacturing and marketing. If the company continues to grow, it will eventually need specialists in such areas as personnel, accounting, and finance. Right now, the owner-manager is carrying out those functions; but with growth, his or her expertise will be increasingly needed for strategic management. Individuals will need to be hired to manage the personnel, accounting, and finance activities. Thus, with growth, the structure of an organization is broadened to accommodate the development of more specialized functions.

As an example, consider the comments of T. J. Rodgers, founder of Cypress Semiconductor Corporation. Using a niche-differentiation strategy, this enterprise grew to a $135 million company in five years by developing superfast memory chips. With such rapid growth, however, Rodgers quickly found himself overextended.

STRATEGIC INSIGHT

Flattening the Structure at Goodyear

As the decade of the 1980s drew to a close, competition in the worldwide tire industry intensified significantly. France's Michelin became the largest tire company in the world through its acquisition of U.S.-based Uniroyal-Goodrich, surpassing longtime world sales leader Goodyear. Following closely was Japan's Bridgestone, which purchased American tiremaker Firestone. Rounding out this new oligopoly was fourth-place Pirelli of Italy, which also acquired an American company, Armstrong Tire & Rubber.

These mergers were not well timed, since they coincided with a major slump in the U.S. automobile industry. Michelin, for instance, incurred a loss of approximately $460 million as it found car markets weakening, the dollar declining against the French franc, and its debt increasing to record levels from its expensive acquisition. To offset its losses, it reduced its capital spending by 60 percent, proceeded with layoffs, and cut its prices aggressively.

Meanwhile, Bridgestone announced that it intended to become the world's number-one tiremaker. It committed from $1.5 to $2.5 billion to upgrade and expand Firestone's operations, but it continued to experience major difficulties in integrating the operations of the two companies.

Goodyear responded by flattening its organizational structure in 1990. Prior to its restructuring, Goodyear had 43 district offices reporting to 5 regional divisions, which, in turn, reported to corporate headquarters in Akron, Ohio. Its new structure, by contrast, contains only 28 regional offices that report directly to headquarters, thereby eliminating one hierarchical level. Goodyear believes that the move will help the company achieve "a flatter, more efficient and responsive organization."

SOURCES: S. Solo, "Flat Tiremakers," *Fortune,* 3 December 1990, pp. 14–15; S. Toy and Z. Schiller, "Michelin: The High Cost of Being a Big Wheel," *Business Week,* 5 November 1990, p. 66; "Goodyear Plans to Restructure," *Harrisonburg (Va.) Daily News-Record,* 21 June 1990; G. Stricharchuk, "Goodyear Squares Off to Protect Its Turf from Foreign Rivals," *The Wall Street Journal,* 29 December 1989; Z. Schiller, "Can Bridgestone Make the Climb?" *Business Week,* 27 February 1989, pp. 78–79.

At about $50 million in revenues, I felt I could run it. . . . I could name everybody in the company. But as it grew larger, I found myself stretched. One Friday night at 11 P.M., I realized that if there wasn't a change, I'd have to stop sleeping within six months to keep up the pace.[6]

In other words, a new business may originally have its owner-manager and its few employees performing multiple functions on a daily basis. With growth, however, each function expands so that ultimately no one individual can be intimately involved—either physically or intellectually—in all of the company's functions. This is the point at which various key functional areas are formally set apart as departments and existing employees and new hires are each assigned to one of these newly formed functional units.

This functional structure, elaborated upon in the following section, is the way small businesses typically organize as they experience growth. This structure, of course, is not the only form available to management. After the functional structure is discussed, other forms are also presented. But in all cases, growth involves both vertical and horizontal elaboration. It is the strategic direction of the firm that determines the specific type of structure that is most appropriate.

ORGANIZATIONAL STRUCTURE

As an enterprise grows to become an established business, it will adopt one of a number of different organizational structures to implement its strategy. Over time, as the size and direction of the enterprise change, it may shift to another structure. Many large, well-known companies change structures every decade or so in order to carry out their strategy more effectively. This section discusses the six types of structures that are available to organizations: functional, product divisional, geographic divisional, multidivisional, strategic business unit, and matrix.

▪ Functional Structure

As suggested in the preceding section, the initial growth of an enterprise often requires it to organize by functional areas. The **functional structure** is characterized by the simultaneous combination of similar activities and the separation of dissimilar activities on the basis of function. This structure is by no means limited to small businesses. Companies of any size that have a single product line or a few similar product lines are well suited to the functional organizational structure. Small businesses, however, are likely to have only a few functional departments; larger organizations may be quite differentiated, both horizontally and vertically. Figure 7.3 shows a large business that has experienced both vertical and horizontal growth.

Comparing this business with the one shown in Figure 7.1, we can see that growth brings about more extensive horizontal expansion. Rather than simply dividing its employees into manufacturing and marketing functions, this organization has grown so that it also needs specialists in purchasing, finance, and research and development. Furthermore, its growth has also resulted in vertical extensions. Manufacturing has become so complex that it has had to segment itself into the functions of production, engineering, and quality control. Engineering contains two additional levels—laboratory research and new-product development. Likewise, marketing has been divided into market research, distribution, and promotion functions.

A functional structure has certain strategic advantages and disadvantages. On the plus side, this structure emphasizes the functions that the organization must carry out. Specialization by function is encouraged, with the resulting benefits that specialization brings. For instance, when functional specialists interact frequently, they may realize synergies that increase their department's efficiency and effectiveness. Furthermore, their interaction can result in improvements and innovations for their functional area that may not have occurred if there had not been a critical mass of specialists organized within the same unit. On the psychological side, working closely on a daily basis with others who share one's functional interests is likely to increase job satisfaction and, hence, contribute to lower turnover.

In addition, the functional organization facilitates the processes of planning, organizing, motivating, and controlling groups of personnel. Translating the organization's mission, goals, and objectives into action is easier when each functional area is activated to plan, organize, motivate, and control within its own boundaries. Finally, the training and development of personnel is often

A Functional Structure with Vertical and Horizontal Growth **Figure 7.3**

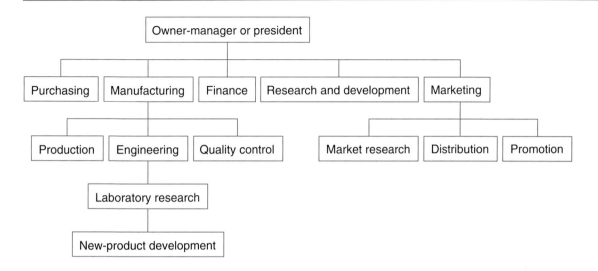

more efficient than in other structures because the training centers on standard types of functional skills.

This structure, however, is accompanied by some disadvantages. Because the business is organized around functions, rather than around products or geographic regions, it is difficult to pinpoint the responsibility for profits or losses. If an organization's sales have declined, is the problem due to purchasing, research and development, manufacturing, or marketing? In a functional structure, such problem analysis can be quite ambiguous.

Along these same lines, a functional structure often creates a narrow perspective of the organization among its members. Marketing personnel, for instance, are likely to view the organization totally from a marketing perspective, because they have little experience with other functional areas. The same is true for employees in manufacturing, finance, and other functions. Problems and opportunities are perceived more in terms of the interests of each functional area rather than in the way that they affect the overall organization. Consequently, different solutions to the same problem or different strategies to take advantage of an environmental opportunity are advanced as desirable by the various functional departments.

Finally, communication and coordination across functional areas are often difficult. For instance, employees in manufacturing view their function as being central to organizational success, and operational problems are attributed to other functional areas. Marketing, meanwhile, views increased sales as primarily attributable to its efforts, but slow sales are manufacturing's fault. It should be clear that as functional departments begin to proliferate, coordination becomes increasingly difficult. Functional differentiation presents management with the challenging task of coordinating disparate activities so that a unified, logical whole may be attained.

Whenever an organization begins to expand its product lines significantly or grows geographically, the functional structure begins to lose its strategic usefulness. Management then faces the issue of changing its organization's structure to one more appropriate to its strategy.

STRATEGIC INSIGHT

Removing the Blinders at Ford

One of the potential weaknesses in a functional structure is that it can encourage employees to take a narrow perspective of their organization. It is easy for functional managers and operative employees to look at problems from the standpoint of marketing or production or some other functional specialty rather than see them from the viewpoint of the company as a whole.

Ford Motor Company, America's third-largest corporation with over $98 billion in 1990 sales, has devised a program to reduce this problem. In a $5\frac{1}{2}$-day session for middle managers, the managers are first grouped by their functional specialties. Then they are asked to "think about how their function works within the company, how others perceive it, and how it ought to work."

As they discuss their thoughts with managers from other functional areas, they begin to realize how narrow their perspective is. That is, they tend to view Ford primarily as a manufacturing company or a finance company or a company that specializes in personnel. As a result of the session, they learn to take a broader view of the organization, realizing that their particular function is only one of many interrelated activities that must be accomplished for Ford to attain its goals. Ford terms this process "chimney-breaking."

In a broader sense, Ford's joint venture with Mazda to develop the 1991 Escort helped Ford engineers expand their perspective. Traditionally, Ford-made fenders contained slots rather than bolt holes so that an assembly line worker could pull a fender into place when it did not line up accurately. (One Ford engineer termed this process "quality through adjustment.") Mazda's fenders were made to more exacting specifications, and Mazda's engineers scoffed at Ford's inexact tolerances. In fact, they issued a challenge to Ford's engineers. They would take a Mazda 323 apart and reassemble it five times while the Ford team did the same with a Ford Tempo. The Ford engineers accepted the challenge. After the fifth reassembly, 90 percent of the Mazda's parts still fit together satisfactorily, but only 48 percent of the Ford's did.

The Ford engineers were convinced. They decided that parts for the 1991 Escort had to meet 40,000 specific tolerances, which was eight times the number for other Ford automobiles.

SOURCES: "The Fortune 500 Largest U.S. Industrial Corporations," *Fortune,* 22 April 1991, p. 286; J. B. Treece, "How Ford and Mazda Shared the Driver's Seat," *Business Week,* 26 March 1990, pp. 94–95 (source of second quotation); W. Kiechel III, "The Organization That Learns," *Fortune,* 12 March 1990, pp. 133–136 (source of first quotation).

■ Product Divisional Structure

The product divisional structure is well suited for businesses with several product lines. Rather than organizing the firm around functions, the **product divisional structure** focuses on the company's product categories. Figure 7.4 illustrates this structure for a firm that manufactures and sells home appliances. Its activities and personnel are grouped into three product divisions: refrigerators and ranges, washers and dryers, and small appliances. Each product division will contain its own functional areas. The small appliances division, for instance, may have its own manufacturing and marketing departments, because the products that it makes and sells may require different manufacturing methods and channels of distribution than those of the other two divisions. Other functions, however, such as finance, may be centralized at the top of the organization, because they benefit the organization as a whole and because

Product Divisional Structure   **Figure 7.4**

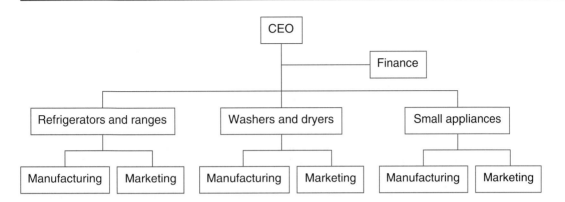

economies of scale can be realized. For example, the corporation as a whole can obtain more favorable interest rates when borrowing money than could the small-appliances division alone.

This structure is also widely used in nonmanufacturing organizations. For instance, supermarkets typically have a number of product managers (e.g., produce manager, meat manager, dairy manager, and bakery manager) who report to the store manager; and department stores are divided into product areas such as women's sportswear, men's shoes, children's wear, furniture, and appliances. Universities, being service organizations, are also usually organized by "product" divisions: history, mathematics, computer sciences, marketing, art, and so on.

The advantages of the product divisional structure are several. Rather than emphasizing the functions that the organization performs, the structure puts an emphasis on product lines. The result is a clear focus upon each individual product category and a greater orientation toward customer service. Also, the ability to pinpoint the responsibility for profits or losses is greatly enhanced, since each product division becomes a profit center to which profits or losses may be directly attributed. A **profit center** is an organizational unit charged with a well-defined mission and is headed by a manager accountable for the center's revenues and expenditures. So it is clear to upper management which divisions are operating profitably and which are incurring losses. Furthermore, the product divisional structure is ideal for training and developing managers, since each product manager is, in effect, running his or her "own business." Hence, product managers develop general management skills—an end that can be accomplished in a functional structure only by rotating managers from one functional area to another.

As an example of a company that adopted a product divisional structure, consider Eastman Kodak Company. By the early 1980s, Kodak's emphasis on the mature photography business had caused it to miss a number of environmental opportunities, such as the burgeoning popularity of the 35-mm camera and the introduction of the video recorder. So that it might focus its environmental-scanning efforts more directly, Kodak restructured into seventeen product divisions, including photographic development, graphics, chemicals, cattle feed nutrients, and electronic publishing. Management believed that the switch would increase the firm's ability to make quick decisions and to take advantage of opportunities in different product areas as they arose.[7]

Of course, the product divisional structure also has its disadvantages. In some ways, it can be more expensive to operate than a functional structure, because more functional personnel may be required. In Figure 7.4, for example, because the firm has three manufacturing departments rather than only one, the total personnel expense for manufacturing is likely to be higher than if only one department were necessary. Such extra expenses raise the firm's break-even point. Obviously, this disadvantage is offset to some extent by the ability of each manufacturing department to focus upon producing only one product line. Second, the coordination of activities at headquarters becomes more difficult. Top management finds it harder to ensure that all of the firm's marketing personnel, for instance, are following the same policies and procedures when serving customers. This problem can become fairly significant when an organization has forty or fifty product divisions, which is fairly common among large firms. In addition, the customer can be confused by being called on by different sales representatives from the same firm. Third, since each product manager emphasizes his or her own product area, what may be in the best interests of the firm may be overlooked as product managers compete for resources such as money, physical space, and personnel.

In fact, disadvantages like these led Nestlé's U.S.-based subsidiary to convert its product divisional structure to a functional structure in 1991. By consolidating such product lines as Carnation, Stouffer Foods, Quik, and Taster's Choice under one manager, Nestlé saved at least $30 million in overhead and administrative expenses. It also allowed the business unit to benefit from increased economies of scale and coordination.[8]

■ Geographic Divisional Structure

When a firm operates in various geographical areas, an appropriate structure may be the **geographic divisional structure,** in which activities and personnel are grouped by specific geographic locations. This structure may be used on a local basis (e.g., a city may be divided into sales regions), on a national basis (e.g., northeast region, mid-Atlantic region, southeast region, midwest region) or on an international basis (e.g., North American region, Latin American region, Western European region, Middle Eastern region). Figure 7.5 illustrates a national company (at the top) and an international company (at the bottom) organized by geographic divisions.

There are a number of advantages to organizing geographically. First, products and services may be better tailored to the climatic needs of specific areas. For example, retailers may stock heavier clothing for their outlets in northern states and lighter clothes in southern stores. Second, a geographic divisional structure allows a firm to respond to the technical needs of different international areas. For instance, in many parts of the world, the electrical system is different from that in the United States; the geographic structure allows firms to accommodate these geographic differences. Third, producing or distributing products in different national or global locations may give the organization a competitive advantage. Many firms, for example, produce components in countries that either have a labor cost advantage or are located close to essential raw materials. The final product may then be assembled in still another location that is more appropriate for the advanced technology required or that is closer to the final consumer. Fourth, a geographic organization may better serve the consumer needs of various nations. For instance, the need for hair-grooming prod-

Geographic Divisional Structures   **Figure 7.5**

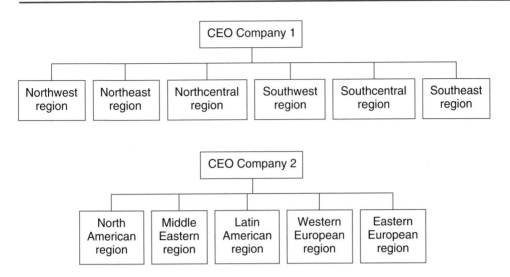

ucts differs from one society to another, and the geographic structure allows firms to respond to these differing needs. Fifth, organizing along geographic lines enables a company to adapt to varying legal systems. Automobile insurance companies within the United States, for example, often have a geographic division for each state, because no two states have the same insurance regulations. Finally, geographic divisions allow firms to pinpoint the responsibility for profits or losses, because each division is a profit center.

The disadvantages of a geographic divisional structure are similar to those identified earlier for the product divisional structure. Often, more functional personnel are required than would be the case for a functional structure, because each region has its own functional departments. Coordination of companywide functions is more difficult than in a strictly functional organization, and regional managers may emphasize their own geographic areas to the exclusion of a companywide viewpoint.

■ Multidivisional Structure

As a firm continues to expand by adding more and more product lines, it may outgrow all of the preceding structures. At this stage, firms with multiple product lines may adopt the **multidivisional structure,** in which the company is partitioned into several divisions, with each division responsible for one or more product lines.

Consider Maytag as an example. At one time in its history, this appliance firm had a fairly simple structure with three product divisions—gas range products, laundry products, and electric range products. But it continued to diversify its product lines by acquiring Magic Chef (a producer of air conditioners, refrigerators, and furnaces), Toastmaster (a manufacturer of small appliances), and Hoover (a maker of vacuum cleaners and European major appliances). Maytag's current structure is depicted in Figure 7.6. As you can see, the multidivisional structure encompasses several divisions, with each division comprised of one or more product lines.

Figure 7.6   **Multidivisional Structure of Maytag**

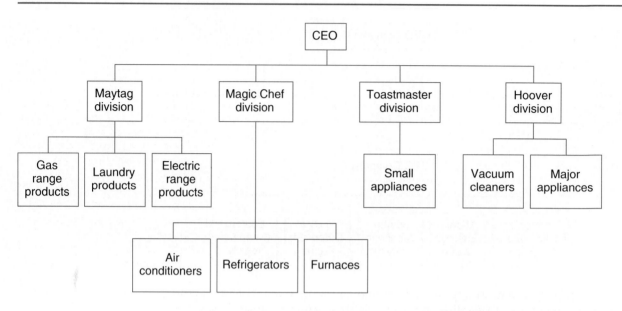

The multidivisional structure has several advantages. First, continued growth is facilitated. As new product lines are created or acquired, those lines may be integrated into an existing division or may serve as the foundation for a newly developed division. Second, since each division has its own top-level strategic managers, the work load of the CEO's headquarters staff is lightened. This gives the CEO more time to analyze each division's operations and to decide on resource allocations on the basis of the portfolio analysis techniques discussed in Chapter 4. Third, authority is delegated downward to each division and, within each division, to each product line. This decentralization allows for a better alignment of each division and product line with its unique external environment. Fourth, accountability for performance can be logically evaluated at the product line level as well as at the divisional level.

As is true with each structure discussed, however, the multidivisional structure has certain disadvantages. First, the distribution of corporate overhead costs across the divisions is difficult and relatively subjective. Inevitably, the distribution results in some divisional managers feeling that their divisions have received too heavy an allocation. Second, dysfunctional divisional rivalries often emerge as each division attempts to secure a greater share of the firm's resources. Third, when one division makes components or products that another division needs, conflicts can arise in setting transfer prices. *Transfer pricing* refers to the price that one division charges another division for its products or parts. The selling division normally prefers to charge a relatively high transfer price to increase its profits, but the purchasing division prefers to pay a relatively low transfer price to lower its costs.

■ Strategic Business Unit Structure

Organizational growth may ultimately require that related product lines be grouped into divisions and that the divisions themselves then be grouped into

STRATEGIC INSIGHT

 ITW's Multidivisional Structure

Illinois Tool Works (ITW), headquartered in a Chicago suburb, is a low-profile manufacturer of nails, screws, bolts, strapping, wrapping, valves, capacitors, filters, adhesives, tools and machines, plastic buckles, plastic loops that hold six-packs together, Zip-Pak resealable food packages, and Kiwi-Lok nylon fasteners. ITW ranked 176th on *Fortune*'s 1990 list of the 500 largest industrial corporations in the United States, with sales of $2.6 billion and 15,700 employees. Its primary markets are the construction, automotive/truck, electronics, agricultural, and telecommunications industries.

The company searches for market niches and often dominates those in which it operates. At the corporate level, the firm follows a growth strategy, with most of its business units pursuing a niche–low-cost or niche–low-cost/differentiation strategy.

In addition to focusing on internal growth, ITW pursues a strategy of horizontal integration by regularly acquiring smaller firms that complement ITW's core businesses. Its ninety product lines are grouped into nine divisions. Most of the product lines are relatively small, with about $30 million in annual revenue. Each product line manager controls manufacturing, marketing, and research and development. When a new product with commercial possibilities is developed, it is often split off to form a new business unit.

ITW seeks to keep costs as low as possible. Its largest division, the construction products group, generates $420 million a year but has only three headquarters employees: a president, a controller, and a shared secretary.

Its carefully formulated strategy and appropriate structure have helped ITW to rank consistently as the number-one firm in the metal products industry in *Fortune*'s annual survey of "Most Admired Corporations."

SOURCES: "The Fortune 500 Largest U.S. Industrial Corporations," *Fortune*, 22 April, 1991, p. 292; "How Companies Rank in 32 Industries," *Fortune*, 11 February, 1991, p. 72; *Moody's Handbook of Common Stocks* (New York: Moody's Investors Service, Spring, 1991); *Wards' Business Directory of U.S. Private and Public Companies*, Vol. 1 (Detroit: Gale Research, 1991); R. Henkoff, "The Ultimate Nuts & Bolts Co.," *Fortune*, 16 July 1990, pp. 70–73.

strategic business units. This **strategic business unit structure** is particularly well suited to very large, diversified firms. An example of such a firm is illustrated in Figure 7.7.

The major advantage of the strategic business unit structure is that it reduces corporate headquarters' span of control. Rather than managers at the corporate level having to control many divisions, they need control only relatively few strategic business units. This reduction in span of control also lessens the chance that headquarters will experience information overload as the various organizational units report on their operations. A final advantage is that this structure permits better coordination between divisions with similar missions, products, markets, or technologies.

The strategic business unit structure, however, has a number of disadvantages. First, corporate headquarters becomes more distant from the division and product levels with the addition of another vertical layer of management. Second, rivalry between the strategic business unit managers for greater shares of corporate resources can become dysfunctional and can negatively affect the corporation's overall performance. Third, this structure complicates portfolio anal-

Figure 7.7   **Strategic Business Unit Structure**

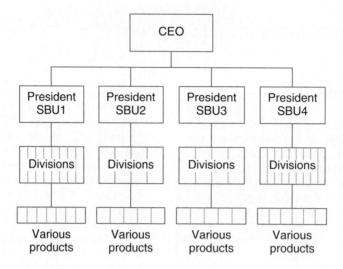

ysis. For instance, a strategic business unit may be considered a poor performer overall, but some of its divisions may be stars.

Note that it is important not to confuse the concept *strategic business unit* with that of *strategic business unit structure*. When we are discussing strategy formulation, the term *strategic business unit* may be used in more than one way.[9] A single company that operates within a single industry (e.g., a business that builds swimming pools) is a strategic business unit. But a product division or geographic division of a large multidivisional firm is also a strategic business unit. *Strategic business unit* may even be used to refer to the large firm's multidivisional level that combines several related product divisions or geographic divisions. More specifically, a strategic business unit is an organization or a division, product line, or profit center of an organization that produces a set of related products/services for well-defined markets or customers in competition with identifiable competitors.

When our reference point is strategy implementation, however, the term *strategic business unit structure* is used to identify the organizational structure type discussed in this section of the chapter. That is, a strategic business unit structure is one in which related product lines are grouped into divisions and those divisions are then grouped into larger entities referred to as strategic business units, as shown in Figure 7.7.[10]

■ Matrix Structure

Up until this point, each of the organizational structures discussed has possessed a single chain of command. That is, each employee in those structures reports to only one manager. The structure discussed in this section, however, is unique in that it possesses a dual chain of command. The **matrix structure** is one in which both functional and project managers exercise authority over orga-

Matrix Structure **Figure 7.8**

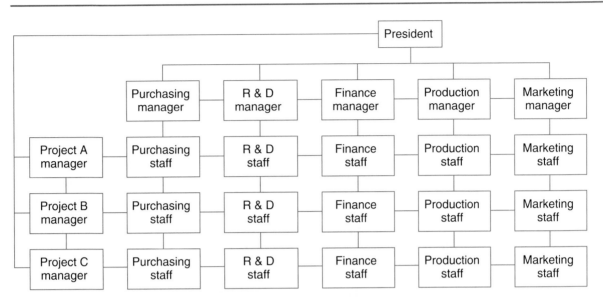

nizational activities. Hence, personnel within the matrix have two superiors—a project manager and the manager of their functional department.

The matrix structure is most commonly used in organizations that operate in industries where the rate of technological change is very fast. For example, firms such as Digital Equipment, Apple, TRW, Lockheed, and Boeing all use a matrix structure. As shown in Figure 7.8, a matrix structure contains literally two organizations—a functional organization (shown horizontally across the top) and a project organization (shown vertically at the left of the chart). In project A, for example, the project manager has brought together some members of the organization's functional departments to work on a specific project. In a construction company, for instance, that project might be the building of a refinery in Thailand. When it is completed, the personnel in project A will return to their functional departments. As another example, in the computer industry, project A might be the development of a new, more powerful personal computer. During the time they are assigned to the project, the employees are accountable not only to the project manager but also to the manager of the functional department from which they came.

Some companies use a matrix even though the rate of technological change in their industry is not particularly fast. For example, Toyota used the matrix structure to develop the Lexus, its entry into the top-of-the-line luxury-car market. A number of engineering, marketing, R&D, and finance personnel were brought together to work on developing an automobile that would compare favorably with the best offered by the West German, British, and U.S. automakers.[11]

A variation to the traditional project form of the matrix structure is reflected in Procter & Gamble's (P&G) use of this system. Although many people associate the matrix structure most closely with high-technology enterprises, P&G actually pioneered this form of organization in 1927. At P&G, rather than a project manager being in charge of a temporary project, each of P&G's individual products has a brand manager. The brand manager pulls various specialists, as they are needed, from their functional departments. For instance, if a detergent, such as Tide, is experiencing slowing sales, the brand manager for Tide might call together members of the R&D department to develop a new additive, members of the advertising staff to create ads for "new, improved Tide," members of the packaging department to design a new container for the detergent, and so on. Each brand manager reports to one of twenty-six category managers, an individual who is in charge of all related products in a single category (e.g., detergents such as Tide, Cheer, and Ivory Flakes). It is this manager's responsibility to coordinate the advertising and sales of related products so that competition among the products is minimized.[12] As we can see, then, P&G uses a mixture of a matrix structure and a multidivisional (i.e., category) structure.

In whatever form it is used, the matrix structure offers certain advantages. First, by combining both the functional structure and the project (or product) structure, a firm can enjoy the advantages of both forms. Second, the matrix is a cost-efficient structure because project managers pay only for the services of functional personnel when they need them. The remainder of the time, these functional employees are working in their own departments and are not on the payroll of any particular project. By contrast, in a strictly project form of organization, the functional employees are employed full-time within a single project or product division.

Third, a matrix organization has considerable flexibility. Employees may be transferred with ease between projects, a flexibility that is greatly reduced in a more permanent form of structure. Fourth, a matrix permits lower-level functional employees to become intimately involved in a project. They are responsible for making and implementing many of the decisions at the project level. Hence, their motivation may be enhanced, and their job satisfaction is also likely to be relatively high.

Fifth, the matrix structure is an excellent vehicle for training and developing general managers. Each project manager, in a sense, is running his or her "own business." The skills developed at this level are essential skills for higher-level positions in the organization. Finally, top management in a matrix is freed from day-to-day involvement in the operations of the enterprise and is, therefore, able to concentrate on strategic problems and opportunities.

Although the matrix has numerous advantages, it is also accompanied by some significant disadvantages. First is the greater administrative cost associated with its operation. Because coordination across functional areas and across projects is so important, matrix personnel spend considerable time in meetings exchanging information. Although this communication is essential, it consumes valuable time that could otherwise be spent on actual project implementation. Second, matrix structures are characterized by considerable conflict, which takes two forms. One is conflict between project and functional managers over budgets and personnel. The other is conflict among the project managers themselves over similar resource allocation issues.

Finally, working in a matrix can be a source of considerable stress for some functional employees. Reporting to two bosses can create significant amounts of role ambiguity and role conflict for an individual. As might be expected, some organizations have found managing a matrix to be so complicated that they have reverted to more traditional types of structure such as the product divisional form.

EVOLUTION OF ORGANIZATIONAL STRUCTURE

In a pioneering work, Alfred D. Chandler, a management researcher, investigated the evolution of the organizational structures of seventy leading firms.[13] His findings indicated that structure follows strategy. That is, when a firm adopts a new strategy, its organizational structure does not change immediately; rather, the structure generally endures until administrative problems arise and the firm's performance declines, events that usually occur within a few years of the new strategy's adoption. As a response, management then aligns the firm's structure to its new strategy. Improvements in financial performance usually follow this alignment.

The major reason that structure does not change simultaneously with strategy is resistance by the organization's managerial and operative personnel. Changes in organizational structure involve shifts in formal authority-accountability relationships and modifications in comfortable informal relationships. Some individuals will find their power base eroded, while others will find theirs enhanced; likewise, the status of some employees declines, while that of others increases.

In spite of resistance, however, eventually the firm's structure is changed to reflect its new strategy. According to research, the strategy-structure evolution generally follows several stages.[14] In the first stage, the enterprise is an extension of the entrepreneur who is involved in all of its activities. Daily problems and operating issues usually require the entrepreneur to maintain organizational flexibility. Short-term thinking normally characterizes this stage. The failure or success of the enterprise can be directly linked to the entrepreneur's abilities, skills, and personality characteristics.

In the second stage, the entrepreneur serves as captain of a team of key players. The team members are recruited in order to form a division of labor along functional lines. At this point, the business's structure inevitably changes from a simple, fluid form to a more enduring functional structure.

The third stage finds the organization growing from a single-product company to one of many products (either related or unrelated) for different markets. The structure during this stage changes from functional to either product, geographic, multidivisional, or matrix. At headquarters, the performance of the various units of the firm is evaluated and rewarded according to criteria established by top management.

In the fourth stage of development, numerous related and unrelated products/markets characterize the scope of the firm. Here, the firm's structure changes from product, geographic, multidivisional, or matrix to the strategic business unit structure.

Obviously, not all businesses proceed through all four stages of this evolutionary development. Some remain at the first, second, or third stages of development for decades or for their entire existence. But large, mature firms often exhibit this evolutionary pattern.

There is some evidence, however, that structure does not always neatly follow strategy. Sometimes, in fact, an organization's structure may influence its strategy. For instance, there is some evidence that firms with product divisional structures have a propensity to diversify even further because a divisional structure lends itself to diversification.[15] In such a case, the firm's structure may actually be influencing its strategy.

ASSESSMENT OF ORGANIZATIONAL STRUCTURE

The key issue in this chapter is how an organization can implement its strategy by designing its structure appropriately. In this section, we wish to examine how managers can assess the effectiveness of their organization's current structure in that regard. There are, unfortunately, no hard-and-fast rules for evaluating the appropriateness of an organization's structure. However, the extent to which a structure is—and will continue to be—effective in helping the organization implement its strategy can be at least partially assessed by answering the following questions. These questions are highlighted in Table 7.1.

• *Is the structure compatible with the corporate profile and the corporate strategy?* Recall that at the corporate level, a firm may be in one business, several related businesses, or several unrelated businesses. Although the one-business company may effectively adopt the functional structure, that option is less viable for organizations that are in several related or unrelated businesses. The reason is that the functional structure promotes specialization of functional activities. This form of specialization is beneficial for a business that primarily produces and markets a single-product line such as home furniture or semiconductors, but it is inappropriate for one in multiple businesses. In such cases, a product divisional or multidivisional structure can more appropriately emphasize the company's products and services rather than its functions. Hence, an organization's structure should be compatible with its corporate profile.

Its structure should also be compatible with its corporate-level strategy. For instance, if the corporation intends to grow continuously through diversification, it may find its growth eventually stymied by a product divisional or geographic divisional structure. The reason is that horizontal expansion places an ever-increasing burden on corporate-level management owing to the widening span of control. At some point, it is not humanly possible to keep up with the activities of all of the firm's product or geographic divisions. Hence, continued diversification may eventually require adopting the multidivisional or strategic business unit structure.

• *At the corporate level, is the structure compatible with the firm's business units?* A product divisional structure, for instance, may be more appropriate than a geographic divisional structure for a corporation with business units that produce fasteners, cutting tools, and hand tools. The reason is that the demand for these products is based on their technical specifications and perceived quality. Each product division can, therefore, concentrate on producing and marketing its own product line. However, a geographic divisional structure may be better suited to a corporation with business units that sell retail clothing and shoes. These items are sold together, and demand for them will differ from one geographic region to another depending on climate, culture, and tradition. Hence, they can be marketed more effectively through specialization based on geographic location.

• *Are there too few or too many hierarchical levels at either the corporate or business unit level of analysis?* It is important that an organization's structure match the nature of the environment in which it operates. Flat organizations, with relatively few hierarchical levels and wide spans of control, are better

Checklist for Determining the Appropriateness of Organizational Structure	Table 7.1

1. Is the structure compatible with the corporate profile and the corporate strategy?

2. At the corporate level, is the structure compatible with the firm's business units?

3. Are there too few or too many hierarchical levels at either the corporate or business unit level of analysis?

4. Does the structure promote coordination among its parts?

5. Does the structure allow for appropriate centralization or decentralization of authority?

6. Does the structure permit the appropriate grouping of activities?

suited for dynamic, fast-changing environments than tall structures are. Conversely, tall organizations, with relatively numerous hierarchical levels and narrow spans of control, operate more effectively in stable, predictable environments than flat ones do.

Corporate-level managers must also realize that the firm's business units need not necessarily have the same structures. Some business units may operate in relatively dynamic environments, and others may compete in relatively stable environments, necessitating differences in their structures.

Overall, in answering this particular question, a manager may find it helpful to compare the configuration of his or her organization with those of its competitors.

• *Does the structure promote coordination among its parts?* Varying degrees of coordination among an organization's parts may be necessary, depending upon the particular situation. For instance, firms with multiple unrelated business units that operate fairly autonomously may find that relatively little coordination among the business units' operations is required. However, within each business unit, management may find it essential to coordinate closely the activities of functional departments. Firms with multiple related businesses usually require greater coordination of their business units' activities, and companies that operate in only one business generally concentrate on coordinating their functional processes.

As a rule, the more complex an organization, the more difficult coordination is to achieve. So relatively simple organizations can attain coordination through their management hierarchy, but somewhat less simple organizations coordinate through cross-functional committees and task forces. Very complex businesses may have to establish special, permanent coordinating units that integrate, for example, the activities of R&D, production, and sales.

• *Does the structure allow for appropriate centralization or decentralization of authority?* The extent to which decision making should be systematically delegated downward in an organization depends upon a number of factors. One, obviously, is organizational size. In general, very large organizations tend to be more decentralized than very small ones, simply because it is difficult for the CEO of a very large company to keep up with all of the organization's operations.

Another factor is the number and type of businesses a firm is in. Firms with large numbers of unrelated businesses tend to be relatively decentralized, allowing the heads of the diverse business units to make most of the decisions affecting those units. In such cases, corporate-level management's primary responsibility is to determine the overall corporation's mission, goals, and strategy and leave the actual operating decisions to those on the scene. By contrast, organizations in only one business can more easily be managed in a centralized fashion.

The type of environment affects the need for decentralization. Organizations in rapidly changing environments must be relatively decentralized so that decisions can be made quickly by those who are closest to the situation. At the other end of the spectrum, organizations in relatively stable environments can be managed effectively through centralized decision making, since change is relatively slow and fairly predictable. In such cases, the majority of decisions follow a routine pattern, and procedures can be established in advance for many decision-making situations.

Finally, the degree of decentralization must be compatible with the organization's structure. Decentralization is far easier to attain in product divisional, geographic divisional, multidivisional, strategic business unit, and matrix structures, because each division, strategic business unit, or project can be operated as a relatively autonomous profit center. Functional structures, however, do not easily lend themselves to decentralization. It is difficult for an organization to be effective when personnel, finance, production, marketing, and R&D operate independently of one another.

• *Does the structure permit the appropriate grouping of activities?* The extent to which organizational activities are appropriately grouped affects how well strategy is implemented. For instance, related product lines should be grouped together. Customers are confused when they are called on by one sales representative for personal computers but have to contact another sales representative from the same company to purchase a printer for the computer. Likewise, some department stores insist on selling men's suits in one department, but ties and dress shirts are in another department down the aisle. As another type of example, it is difficult to hold a product divisional manager fully responsible for sales of a product when he or she had no control over either the development or the production of the product. A true profit center concept requires that one individual be in charge of all of the functions affecting a product's sale.

SUMMARY

Implementing strategy requires management to consider how the organization should be structured. In new, small companies, structure is fluid, with each employee often knowing how to perform more than one task and the owner-manager being involved in all aspects of the business. Success leads to growth, however—both vertical and horizontal. With growth comes a more permanent division of labor.

Vertical growth refers to an increase in the length of the organization's hierarchical chain of command. Organizations in stable, predictable environments often become relatively tall, with many hierarchical levels and narrow spans of control. Conversely, companies in dynamic, rapidly changing environments usually adopt flat structures, with few hierarchical levels and wide spans of control.

Horizontal growth refers to the segmentation of the organization into departments or divisions. The first formal structure usually adopted by a growing business is the functional structure, an organizational type that forms departments along functional lines—manufacturing, marketing, finance, research and development, personnel, and so on. Its strengths are that it emphasizes the functions that the organization must carry out, which results in a number of advantages; it facilitates the processes of planning, organizing, motivating, and controlling; and it is an efficient structure for the training and development of personnel. Its weaknesses, however, are that it makes pinpointing the responsibility for profits or losses difficult, it creates a narrow perspective of the organization among its members, and it inhibits communication across functional areas and coordination of their disparate activities. Whenever an organization begins to expand its product lines significantly or grow geographically, the functional structure begins to lose its strategic usefulness.

The product divisional structure is well suited for businesses with several product lines because the firm is structured around its product categories. This structure's strengths are that it emphasizes the firm's product lines, it makes coordination of functions easier because each product division has its own functions, it allows responsibility for profits or losses to be pinpointed since each product division is a responsibility center, and it encourages development of general managers. Its weaknesses are that it may be more expensive to operate than a functional structure because more functional personnel are required, it inhibits coordination of functions at the corporate level, and it creates dysfunctional competition among division managers for corporate resources.

The geographic divisional structure is used by firms that operate in various geographic areas. Structuring around location provides such advantages as tailoring products/services to climatic needs of specific areas, responding to the technical needs of different international locations, gaining a competitive advantage by producing or distributing products in different locations, serving the consumer needs of various nations better, adapting to varying legal systems, and pinpointing the responsibility for profits or losses. The disadvantages of this structure are the same as those for the product divisional structure.

As a firm adds more product lines, it may eventually adopt the multidivisional structure, in which similar product lines are organized into divisions. This structure facilitates continued growth, frees corporate management for strategic planning, decentralizes authority to individual divisions and product lines so that decision making is quicker, and enables management to pinpoint responsibility for profits and losses. Its unique weaknesses are that the distribution of corporate overhead costs is subjective and difficult to make, dysfunctional divisional rivalries often occur, and transfer pricing from one division to another can become a source of contention.

Further growth may lead an organization to adopt the strategic business unit structure. In this case, divisions with similar missions, products, markets, or technologies are combined under a strategic business unit. This further reduces corporate headquarters' span of control and permits better coordination. However, it also distances corporate headquarters from the product level, can create dysfunctional rivalries between strategic business units, and complicates portfolio analysis.

A final organizational form is the matrix structure, which is a combination of the functional structure and the product/project structure. The matrix enjoys the advantages of both structural types, it is cost-efficient for each individual project or product, it is flexible, it permits lower-level employees to become highly involved in projects, it helps train and develop general managers, and it frees top-level management for planning. But the matrix also is associated with greater administrative costs, greater conflict, and higher stress.

Research indicates that, usually, a change in organizational strategy precedes a change in the firm's structure. That is, structure follows strategy. However, in some cases, an organization's structure may influence the strategic decisions that it makes.

To determine whether an organization's structure is appropriate for implementing the organization's strategy, a manager must analyze how compatible the structure is with such features as the organization's corporate profile, corporate strategy, business unit strategy, need for coordination, number of hierarchical levels, degree of decentralization, and grouping of activities.

KEY CONCEPTS

Flat organization   An organization characterized by relatively few hierarchical levels and a wide span of control.

Functional structure   A form of organizational structure in which jobs and activities are grouped on the basis of function—for example, sales, manufacturing, and finance.

Geographic divisional structure   A form of organizational structure in which jobs and activities are grouped on the basis of geographic location—for example, northeast region, midwest region, and far west region.

Hierarchical chain of command   The authority and accountability chain that links superiors and subordinates in an organization.

Horizontal growth   An increase in the breadth of an organization's structure.

Matrix structure   A form of organizational structure that combines a functional structure with some form of divisional structure (usually product or project divisions). It contains a dual chain of command in which the functional manager and the project/product manager exercise authority over the same employees.

Multidivisional structure   A form of organizational structure that contains several divisions, with each division comprised of one or more product lines.

Organizational structure   The formal ways that tasks and responsibilities are allocated to individuals and the ways that individuals are formally grouped together into offices, departments, and divisions.

Product divisional structure   A form of organizational structure whereby jobs and activities are grouped on the basis of types of products or services—for example, automobiles, computer services, and electronics.

Profit center   An organizational unit charged with a well-defined mission and headed by a manager who is accountable for the unit's revenues and expenditures.

Span of control   The number of employees reporting directly to a given manager.

Strategic business unit structure   A form of organizational structure in which related product lines are grouped into divisions and those divisions are then grouped into larger entities referred to as strategic business units.

Tall organization   An organization characterized by relatively many hierarchical levels and a narrow span of control.

Vertical growth   An increase in the length of the organization's hierarchical chain of command.

DISCUSSION QUESTIONS

1. Why does organizational growth require greater formalization of roles within the organization?

2. Why does organizational growth require both vertical and horizontal expansion?

3. Explain why a relatively tall organizational structure is not appropriate for a dynamic, rapidly changing environment.

4. Why is a functional structure often appropriate for small businesses?

5. As an organization that is structured functionally begins to add new products to its original product offerings, it often changes its structure to a product divisional form. Explain why.

6. What is the rationale underlying the geographic divisional structure?

7. Explain the difference between a multidivisional structure and a strategic business unit structure.

8. A matrix structure is a combination of which two forms of organizational structure? Explain.

9. Of all of the forms of organizational structure discussed—functional, product divisional, geographic divisional, multidivisional, strategic business unit, and matrix—which is the most flexible? Explain why.

10. Why does "structure follow strategy"? Are there any exceptions to this general rule?

STRATEGIC MANAGEMENT EXERCISES

1. Assume that you have started a pizza restaurant in your town. Furthermore, assume that your restaurant has become very successful and that you eventually expand on a national basis. Draw an organization chart that portrays your business at the very beginning. Then, draw two more organization charts that show the vertical growth and the horizontal growth of your company as it grows to become a nationwide business.

2. Assume that you own a business that produces casual furniture. Draw a functional organization chart for your business. Now, assume that your business expands into furniture retailing. Draw a product divisional structure that encompasses your manufacturing and retailing operations.

3. Choose a company and examine its latest annual report. Sometimes, an explicit organization chart is contained in the report. Other times, a summary chart is provided. In still other cases, there may be no structure depicted, but there is sufficient information for you to draw a rough sketch of the structure. Once you have determined the organization's structure, identify what type it is (i.e., functional, product divisional, geographic divisional, multidivisional, strategic business unit, matrix, or a combination of two or more of these). Explain your reasoning.

4. Select a business that has existed for at least ten years. Detail how its organizational structure has evolved over time. Explain why it changed from one structure to another at certain junctures. Or if it has maintained the same structure during its life, explain why. Can you offer suggestions for improving its present structure?

5. From library research, identify an organization that is using a corporate growth strategy (discussed in Chapter 4). Analyze how this organization's strategy has influenced its structure. Is its current structure the optimal structure for this enterprise? If not, what structure might be more appropriate?

6. From library research, identify an organization that is using a corporate retrenchment strategy (Chapter 4). Analyze how this organization's strategy has influenced its structure. Is its current structure the optimal structure for this enterprise? If not, what structure might be more appropriate?

REFERENCES

1. J. Child, *Organization: A Guide for Managers and Administrators* (New York: Harper & Row, 1977), p. 10.

2. Child, *Organization*, pp. 50–70.

3. P. R. Lawrence and J. W. Lorsch, *Organization and Environment: Managing Differentiation and Integration* (Homewood, Ill.: Irwin, 1969); R. Duncan, "What Is the Right Organizational Structure?" *Organizational Dynamics* 7 (Winter 1979): 59–80.

4. J. B. Treece, "Will GM Learn from Its Own Role Models?" *Business Week*, 9 April 1990, p. 62; "Japan's Edge in Auto Costs," *Business Week*, 14 September 1981, p. 97; "Ford's Financial Hurdle," *Business Week*, 2 February 1981, p. 62.

5. J. A. Byrne, "Is Your Company Too Big?" *Business Week*, 27 March 1989, p. 88.

6. Byrne, "Is Your Company Too Big?" p. 90.

7. L. Helm and J. Hurlock, "Kicking the Single-Product Habit at Kodak," *Business Week*, 1 December 1986, pp. 36–37; "Kodak Is Trying to Break Out of Its Shell," *Business Week*, 10 June 1985, p. 92.

8. Z. Schiller and L. Therrien, "Nestlé's Crunch in the U.S.," *Business Week*, 24 December 1990, pp. 24–25.

9. See C. W. Hoffer, "Toward a Contingency Theory of Business Strategy," *Academy of Management Journal* 18 (1975): 784–810.

10. R. P. Rumelt, *Strategy, Structure, and Economic Performance* (Boston: Harvard University Press, 1974).

11. A. Taylor, "Here Comes Japan's New Luxury Cars," *Fortune*, 14 August 1989, pp. 62–66.

12. B. Dumaine, "P&G Rewrites the Marketing Rules," *Fortune*, 6 November 1989, pp. 34–48; A. Swasy, "In a Fast-Paced World, Procter & Gamble Sets Its Store in Old Values," *The Wall Street Journal*, 21 September 1989.

13. A. D. Chandler, *Strategy and Structure* (Cambridge, Mass.: MIT Press, 1962).

14. See M. Salter, "Stages of Corporate Development," *Journal of Business Policy* 1 (1970): 23–37; D. H. Thain, "Stages of Corporate Development," *Business Quarterly*, Winter 1969, p. 34; L. E. Greiner, "Evolution and Revolution as Organizations Grow," *Harvard Business Review* 50, no. 4 (1972): 37–46.

15. Rumelt, *Strategy, Structure*, pp. 76–77; L. E. Fouraker and J. M. Stopford, "Organizational Structure and Multinational Strategy," *Administrative Science Quarterly* 13 (1968): 47–64.

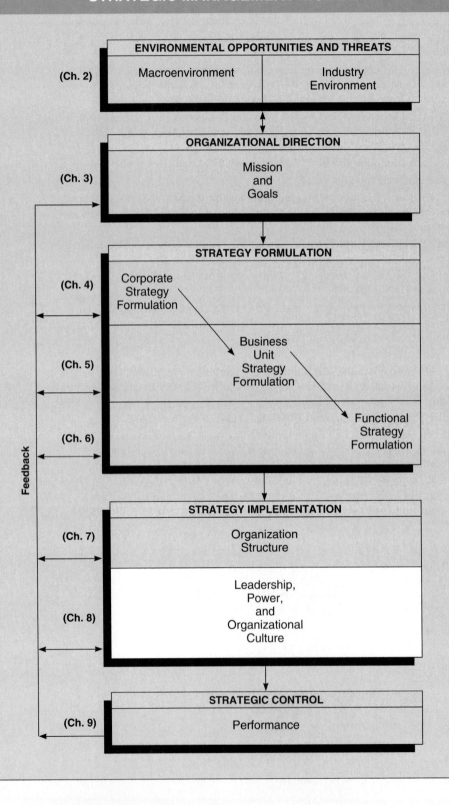

Strategy Implementation: Leadership, Power, and Organizational Culture

Any strategy, no matter how well-conceived, is doomed to failure unless it is effectively implemented. The preceding chapter examined how an organization should be structured to carry out its strategy. This chapter analyzes implementation from another perspective. Our interest here is in how an organization's chief executive officer (CEO) as well as other top managers can use their office and influence to ensure that the organization's members are implementing strategies effectively.

The top management team has at least two means at its disposal to encourage managers and other employees to put their full efforts into strategy implementation. The first resource is leadership. The CEO is recognized as the organization's principal leader, one who sets the tone for the members of the firm. By influencing the behavior of others through formal and informal means, the CEO and other top managers attempt to ensure that organizational members channel their efforts into appropriate directions. The second resource is organizational culture. All organizations have a culture; the key for the CEO and other top managers is to understand and manage the culture in such a way that it facilitates—rather than hinders—the firm's strategic actions.

LEADERSHIP

Although some people equate *leadership* with *management*, the two concepts are not synonymous. For example, over time, a manager plays many roles. Several of them are not directly related to leadership. For instance, as a *resource allocator*, the manager determines the distribution of organizational resources such as money, time, and equipment. As a *monitor*, he or she receives information and analyses related to internal operations and external events. And as a *dissemina-*

tor, the manager transmits information received from the external environment to members of the organization. All of these roles are part of the manager's job. Another role is that of *leader*.[1] A manager exhibits **leadership** when he or she secures the cooperation of others in accomplishing an objective. Hence, it is evident that the term *manager* is considerably broader than the term *leader*.

Although this chapter emphasizes the role of the CEO as the organization's leader, it is important not to overlook the fact that leadership is required at all organizational levels and in all functional areas. Strategies cannot be implemented through the CEO's efforts alone.

The need for organizational leadership has never been more important. As John P. Kotter, a management researcher, points out, in the relatively stable and prosperous 1950s and 1960s, the saying "If it ain't broke, don't fix it" prevailed. Under this axiom, it was clear that too much leadership "could actually create problems by disrupting efficient routines."[2] But as has been emphasized throughout this book, today's world is too dynamic and turbulent for an organization to compete effectively by simply continuing—no matter how efficiently—to do what it did in past years.

Remaining competitive requires an organization to design strategies appropriate to the environment and its changes and to implement those strategies effectively. These activities require competent leadership in the person of the CEO. It is the CEO who must articulate the organization's mission and objectives and then offer inspiration, motivation, and support to the organization's members as they work together to implement the firm's strategies. As Warren G. Bennis, a management researcher, has stated: "Leadership can be felt throughout an organization. It gives pace and energy to the work and empowers the work force."[3] Furthermore, a recent review of leadership research concludes that top-level managers have a substantial impact on organizational performance.[4] For example, when CEO Sam Walton visited his Wal-Mart stores each year, he demonstrated to all managers and employees that he worked hard and was concerned with the well-being of each store in the far-flung chain.

Just as organizational leadership is more important now than in past decades, it most surely will become even more essential in the coming years. Frequent environmental change and the growing complexity of organizations are trends that are likely to accelerate. Figure 8.1 portrays how external environmental changes and internal organizational complexity increase the importance of competent leadership.

It is important to remember throughout this chapter that good leadership is a necessary, but not sufficient, condition for organizational effectiveness. Although research demonstrates that leadership is an important determinant of organizational performance, it is clear that organizational effectiveness also depends on factors beyond the leader's control.[5] As we saw in Chapter 2, such factors as economic conditions, industry structure, international developments, governmental policies, and technological innovations influence organizational results.

This section examines the concept of leadership. First, the formal role, or office, of the leader is explored. Then the focus turns to the leader's style of leadership—the way the leader behaves in exercising authority and making decisions. Finally, how the leader works with other managers as a member of the top management team is analyzed.

The Changing Business Scene and Its Consequences for the Leadership Factor

Figure 8.1

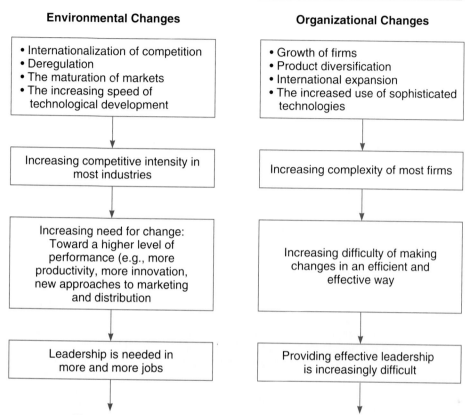

Environmental Changes

- Internationalization of competition
- Deregulation
- The maturation of markets
- The increasing speed of technological development

↓

Increasing competitive intensity in most industries

↓

Increasing need for change: Toward a higher level of performance (e.g., more productivity, more innovation, new approaches to marketing and distribution)

↓

Leadership is needed in more and more jobs

↓

Organizational Changes

- Growth of firms
- Product diversification
- International expansion
- The increased use of sophisticated technologies

↓

Increasing complexity of most firms

↓

Increasing difficulty of making changes in an efficient and effective way

↓

Providing effective leadership is increasingly difficult

↓

The leadership factor has become significantly more important

Source: Reprinted with permission of The Free Press, a Division of Macmillan, Inc., from *The Leadership Factor* by John P. Kotter. Copyright © 1988 by John P. Kotter, Inc.

■ The Office of the Leader

Anyone who occupies the office of chief executive officer has the right to influence the behavior of the organization's members. In the case of a corporation, the CEO has been granted **formal authority** by the board of directors to influence specific aspects of employees' behavior. In a small entrepreneurial company, the CEO's authority may stem from ownership of the firm.

Why do employees follow the direction of the CEO? Their motivation may be "an internalized value, such as obedience to authority figures, loyalty to the organization, respect for law, reverence for tradition, or merely the recognition that submission to authority is a necessary condition for membership in the organization."[6]

In any case, the chief mechanism for wielding formal authority is through the CEO's control over resources and rewards. These can cover a broad spectrum, including pay and bonuses, career progress, budgets, delegation of authority and responsibility, formal recognition of accomplishments, and status symbols.[7]

A Lack of Leadership at Exxon?

Exxon, the second largest corporation in the United States (by sales revenue), experienced a series of disasters in 1989 and 1990. During the spring of 1989, its oil tanker *Exxon Valdez* spilled 11 million gallons of crude oil into Alaska's Prince William Sound; on Christmas Eve, 1989, its refinery in Baton Rouge, Louisiana, exploded; and on New Year's Day, 1990, a broken pipeline leaked 567,000 gallons of Exxon heating oil into the water near New York harbor. But other companies have managed to weather disasters and crises. Why then, by early 1990, was morale at Exxon reported to be so low? It was not because of the disasters per se but because of a perceived lack of leadership at the top of the corporation.

During the turbulent 1970s, American CEOs learned how to react to a disaster—become highly visible on the scene, apologize to the people affected, and give assurances that steps are being taken to insure that it can never happen again. But when the *Valdez* disaster occurred, Exxon CEO Lawrence Rawl remained in New York City and refused to comment publicly on the oil spill for a week. When he finally did talk, he mostly blamed the spill on others. He indicated that he didn't go to Alaska immediately because he had other things to do.

This incident is indicative of what many observers of Exxon believe is a lack of leadership. During the falling–oil price days of the mid-1980s, Exxon reacted much as most other oil companies did by laying off workers and cutting costs. By 1990, however, when most of its competitors began increasing their oil exploration and acquisition activities, Exxon continued to make cuts in such areas as R&D and overseas exploration. As competitors expanded their efforts to build relationships with the major producing countries, such as Saudi Arabia, that dominate world oil production, Exxon's top management made little attempt to cultivate those relationships.

Industry analysts indicated that Rawl was failing to articulate a long-term strategy for the changing environment. Observers termed Exxon's strategic direction "vague." Even *Business Week*, in an editorial, called for Exxon to abandon its "parochial, short-term corporate strategy" and "take the long-term view."

SOURCES: P. Nulty, "Exxon's Problem: Not What You Think," *Fortune*, 23 April 1990, pp. 202–204; C. Welles, "Exxon's Future: What Has Larry Rawl Wrought?" *Business Week*, 2 April 1990, pp. 72–76; "Exxon Should Live Up to Its World Stature," *Business Week*, 2 April 1990, p. 128 (source of quotations).

The effective leader ensures that the organization's reward systems are consistent with its strategic direction. For instance, a company that wants to emphasize product innovation must allocate sufficient budget resources to R&D personnel, reward risk-taking behaviors, and not reward actions that are designed to maintain the status quo. For example, at 3M, pay raises and promotions are tied to innovative results. Managers and employees are simply not rewarded for standing still.

■ The Style of the Leader

Every leader has a distinctive **leadership style**—the characteristic pattern of behavior that a leader exhibits in the process of exercising authority and making decisions. Some leaders are flamboyant; others are quiet and contemplative. Some seek broad-based participation when making decisions; others arrive at decisions primarily on their own with little input from others. Whatever the style, an organization's leader sets the tone for the firm's members. His or her style is a matter of considerable interest to employees at virtually all levels, and it is an important variable in determining how committed the employees are to the firm's mission and objectives and how much effort they will put into implementing the company's strategies.

The most appropriate leadership style is a matter of considerable controversy. Much of the current research indicates that **contingency-based leadership** is the most effective—meaning that leaders are advised to adopt a style that is best for the particular situation that they are facing.[8] The usefulness of this research for our purposes, however, is limited, because most of this literature focuses upon the styles of leaders of relatively small groups or even leaders as they interact with individual subordinates. Here, our concern is with leaders of entire organizations or business units. Upper-level leadership is qualitatively different from leadership at lower levels.[9] From this perspective, the most pertinent body of knowledge available is the recent work on transformational and transactional leadership styles.[10] These styles and how they are used in practice are discussed in the paragraphs that follow.

Transformational and Transactional Leadership Styles

With **transactional leadership,** managers use the authority of their office, much as we just described, to exchange rewards such as pay and status for employees' work efforts. By contrast, with **transformational leadership,** managers inspire involvement in a mission, giving followers a "dream" or "vision" of a higher order than the followers' present reality. In effect, the transformational leader motivates followers to do more than they originally expected to do by stretching their abilities and increasing their self-confidence. Organizational members are "transformed" by becoming more aware of the importance of their tasks and by being helped to transcend their own self-interest for the sake of the organization's mission.[11]

Steven Jobs, the founder of Apple Computer, serves as an example of a transformational leader. In the company's early days, he was able to inspire his employees with his vision of making computing power accessible to a wide range of customers. Without his employees' willingness, and even enthusiasm, to put in long hours of work and to generate innovative ideas, Apple would never have been able to revolutionize the computer industry. By contrast, transactional leaders are less interested in inspiring followers than in ensuring that their organizations operate effectively and efficiently. The typical transactional leader is often concerned with increasing sales, market share, and profits incrementally rather than with "transforming" the organization.

Management researcher, Bernard M. Bass proposes that most leaders exhibit both transactional and transformational styles, although they do so in different amounts.[12] Ultimately, the distinction between the two leadership styles is that leaders who are largely transactional continue to move their organizations in line with historical tradition, resulting in incremental improvements. Transformational leaders, however, lead their organization toward a future that may result in significantly different processes and levels of performance.[13] These proposed differences are illustrated in Figures 8.2 and 8.3.

Note that transactional leadership is tied to the past and is hypothesized to enhance an organization's performance steadily, but not dramatically. The pro-

STRATEGIC INSIGHT

Leadership Style at Southwest Airlines

Herb Kelleher has built Southwest Airlines into one of the most profitable and fast-growing airlines in the country through fastidious implementation of a niche–low-cost strategy. In doing so, he has managed to win the trust and respect of his employees.

Now the nation's ninth-largest airline, Southwest has grown from a local carrier in Texas that specialized in no-frills flights between Dallas and Houston to one that offers service to both the Midwest and the West Coast. As it continues to grow, Southwest's strategy will evolve from niche–low-cost to low-cost. It has expanded profitably even though it offers no on-board meals, no assigned seating, no interairline baggage transfers, and no listings on computer reservation systems. In some areas, standby tickets can be purchased through automated teller machines in convenience stores.

The market for this bare-bones service is short-haul passengers who value price and frequent departures. To serve these passengers efficiently, Southwest's planes are able to arrive at an airport gate, unload baggage and passengers, load new baggage and passengers, and leave within ten minutes. How? By having employees who are considerably more productive than those in the rest of the airline industry. As one ramp supervisor put it: "When that plane comes in at 1:50 and you take off 200 bags and put on 200 more, and it takes off at 2:00, nobody needs to tell you you did good." This employee has missed work once in seven years. "If I'm a little sick, if it's sleeting, I can come to work."

Why are employees this dedicated? One pilot says that "it's not a Mary Kay-type atmosphere

where we're all starry-eyed. It's mutual respect." This respect starts at the top with CEO Kelleher. He has established excellent rapport with his employees and seems to be able to work out amenable agreements with which both sides are happy, unlike the bitter negotiations that have characterized labor contracts at several other airlines. Through profit-sharing plans, cross-utilization of workers, and Kelleher's concern for employees, the company has managed to forge an atmosphere of trust and loyalty.

Kelleher, for instance, is highly visible. He often takes Southwest flights and frequently visits the service areas where the planes are maintained. The visits are invariably upbeat and optimistic, with Kelleher dressing in a casual fashion (often in a Southwest Airlines shirt) and kidding with the crew. He knows individuals' names and sends birthday and Valentine's Day cards to each employee.

Most of all, though, he seems to care. He and all the other top managers of Southwest Airlines work at least once every three months as baggage handlers, ticket agents, and flight attendants. The point is to create an understanding of what each employee encounters on his or her job. As Kelleher explains, "When you're actually dealing with customers, and you've done the job yourself, you're in a better position to appraise the effect of some new program or policy."

His actions support his words. When the airline experienced hard times in 1987, Kelleher reduced his salary, cut all the company officers' bonuses by 10 percent, and reduced his own bonus by 20 percent.

SOURCES: A. Farnham, "The Trust Gap," *Fortune*, 4 December 1989, pp. 56–78 (source of first quotation, p. 74, and third quotation, p. 78); S. Loeffelholz, "The Love Line," *Financial World*, 21 March 1989, pp. 26–28; "Patchy Applause for Cash Machines," *Fortune*, 5 December 1988, p. 16; J. H. Taylor, "Risk Taker," *Forbes*, 14 November 1988, p. 108; F. Gibney, Jr., "Southwest's Friendly Skies," *Newsweek*, 30 May 1988, p. 49 (source of second quotation); J. E. Ellis, "These Two Airlines Are Doing It Their Way," *Business Week*, 21 September 1987, pp. 58–62.

ponents of transformational leadership, on the other hand, suggest that because it is linked to the future, it can make significant changes in organizational performance. Also note that we propose that an organization's performance

The Perceptual Difference Between Transactional and Transformational Leadership

Figure 8.2

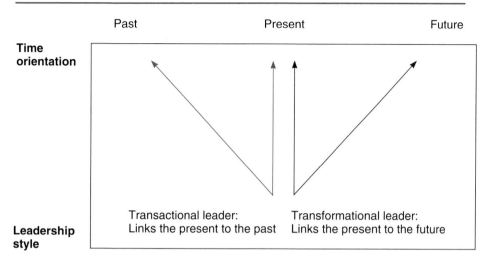

declines somewhat shortly after the transformational leadership process begins. Dramatic changes in the way an organization operates often result in short-term declines in performance, because organizational members may initially resist changing from the status quo and may experience difficulty in rising to the new expectations.

Both transactional and transformational leaders can exhibit all of the leadership styles identified in the well-known leadership theories. These include such commonly studied styles as task-oriented leadership (i.e., emphasizing task effectiveness) or relationship-oriented leadership (i.e., emphasizing the building of relationships with employees), as well as those styles that emphasize directing employees, encouraging employee participation in decision making,

Hypothesized Results of Transactional and Transformational Leadership Styles

Figure 8.3

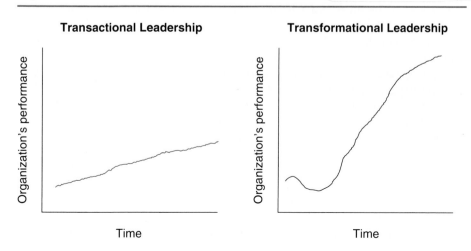

or setting goals. But even as these two types of leaders engage in the same style, their intent may be quite different. For instance, the transactional leader may delegate responsibility to an employee as a reward for fulfilling an agreement, but a transformational leader may delegate for the purpose of developing employee skills.[14]

Leadership Style in Practice

When is a transactional style needed and when might a transformational style be required? As we have seen above, most leaders will exhibit both behaviors, although one may predominate. In general, we can propose that organizations that are meeting or exceeding their objectives and that do not foresee significant changes in their environment can be well led through a transactional style. Increasingly, however, because of the intensity of domestic and foreign competition and dramatic environmental changes, many organizations require transformational leadership. Even casual perusal of such publications as *The Wall Street Journal, Business Week,* and *Fortune* will illustrate the strategic difficulties that many firms are facing.

Consider, for instance, the different strategic directions taken by IBM and Canon when they entered the copier business in the 1970s. Pursuing a transactional style, IBM's top management concentrated on developing products that were similar to that of the market leader—Xerox—and they imitated Xerox's service, pricing, and distribution. IBM's efforts were such a failure that it withdrew from the copier market. By contrast, Canon's top management used a transformational approach. Rather than duplicating Xerox's strategy, Canon concentrated on smaller copiers and taught its sales force to make presentations directly to department managers and secretaries who desired decentralized copying facilities, rather than a centralized copy center. This approach contrasted dramatically with the traditional route of selling to the head of the duplicating department. Today, Canon is a major player in the copier industry.

Because transformational leadership is of considerable importance and is likely to take on even more significance, we will examine that process in detail at this point. Researchers Tichy and Devanna, who studied twelve CEOs, propose a three-stage process of transformational leadership.[15] Each stage is described below.

Recognize the Need for Change.   First, the transformational leader must recognize the need for change and be able to persuade key managers in the organization of that need. This task may be difficult when changes in the environment are gradual and the organization is still meeting its objectives. As Peter F. Drucker, a management theorist and consultant, emphasizes, the best time to cast off the past is when the organization is successful—not when it is in trouble. When an organization is successful, its resources are allocated "to the things that *did* produce, to the goals that *did* challenge, to the needs that *were* unfulfilled."[16]

To overcome this tendency, Tichy and Devanna suggest that leaders measure the performance of their organizations against that of their competitors and not just against last year's performance. Additionally, measures of organizational performance must include more than the typical economic indicators, such as earnings per share, market share, and return on investment or assets. They should also include such measures as customer satisfaction, product quality as

STRATEGIC INSIGHT

Henry Ford: Transactional and Transformational Leadership

Henry Ford (1863–1947) illustrates a leader who combined both transactional and transformational leadership styles:

> In 1914, he made a deal that workers found hard to resist. He offered them the unusually high wage for that time of $5 a day in exchange for their accepting rigid control of their behavior both inside and outside the plant. No idle time was to be tolerated. Internal spies were employed to enforce disciplinary rules. Yet, it was this same Henry Ford who revolutionized the automobile industry, making possible the mass production of the cheap, affordable automobile for the mass market.

How did Henry Ford transform the automobile industry? The transformation began with an argument between Ford and his partner Alexander Y. Malcolmson in 1905. Ford wanted to produce a simple, inexpensive car, but Malcolmson favored a more expensive and exclusive line. Malcolmson lost the argument and subsequently sold his interest in the company, leaving Ford to concentrate on the Model T—a sturdy, black automobile with a four-cylinder, 20-horsepower engine. Introduced in 1908, the car sold for $825.

The Model T clearly met the needs and the financial resources of American consumers. Over ten thousand cars were sold the first year. Within five years, annual unit sales reached about a half-million. When production of the car ceased in 1927, 15 million Model Ts had been sold by Ford Motor Company.

By concentrating on one type of affordable automobile, Henry Ford created a mass market for the Model T. In turn, the huge demand for the car gave rise to the use of assembly line production with standardized parts. The volume enabled Ford to reduce the price of the car without decreasing profits. By 1913, the car's selling price had dropped to $500. It fell to $390 two years later and sold for $260 in 1925. Meanwhile, the time required to produce the car declined from $12\frac{1}{2}$ worker-hours in 1912 to $1\frac{1}{2}$ worker-hours in 1914.

This single car literally transformed not only the automobile industry but also the life-style and work habits of an entire nation. The impact of Henry Ford's transformational leadership continues to this day.

SOURCES: Arthur M. Johnson, "Henry Ford," in *The Encyclopedia Americana, International Edition*, Vol. 11 (Danbury, Conn.: Grolier, 1990), pp. 566–567; Robert Sobel, "Henry Ford," in *The World Book Encyclopedia*, Vol. 7 (Chicago: World Book, 1990), p. 380; B. M. Bass, *Leadership and Performance Beyond Expectations* (New York: Free Press, 1985), p. 27 (source of quotation).

compared with competitors', new-product innovations, and other similar indicators.

Create a Shared Vision.   Once the need for change is recognized, the leader must inspire organizational members with a "vision" of what the organization can become. In entrepreneurial ventures, this vision may be developed by the leader; but in large corporations, the vision is more likely to evolve through a participative process involving the CEO and key managers in the firm.[17] But Andrall E. Pearson, former CEO of PepsiCo, makes it clear that it is the leader's role to "spearhead" this effort, not just preside over it.[18] He also emphasizes that no strategic vision is permanent: "Lasting competitive edges are hard to generate."[19] Therefore, the transformational process is ongoing and not a one-time event.

An important part of the vision is high performance standards. From observation, it is clear that transformational leaders "stretch" their followers' abilities. High-performing organizations rarely pursue moderate goals or performance standards. Pearson observes: "This doesn't mean arbitrary, unrealistic goals that are bound to be missed and motivate no one, but rather goals that won't allow anyone to forget how tough the competitive arena is."[20] In such cases, the CEO must provide a role model for the organization's members. Transformational CEOs must "set a personal example in terms of the long hours they work, their obvious commitment to success, and the consistent quality of their efforts."[21] Consider, for instance, the behavior of a transformational CEO whose car is always among the first in the parking lot in the morning, one of the last to leave in the evening, and one of the most consistently present on the weekends. Contrast this example with that of CEOs who boast frequently of their golf handicaps and who usually arrive at work late and leave early.

Besides serving as role models, transformational leaders must communicate their vision clearly and completely to all of the members of the organization. Management researchers, Warren G. Bennis and Burt Nanus, reinforce the importance of this suggestion by stating that the lack of a clear vision is a major reason for the declining effectiveness of many organizations in recent years. Clear communication of a vision creates a focus for the employees' efforts, and it is important that this vision be repeated over and over and not be allowed to fade away.[22] Few suggestions are more timely. The consulting firm Booz, Allen & Hamilton reported in 1990 that only 37 percent of senior managers think that other key managers completely understand new organizational goals, and only 4 percent of the senior managers believe that middle managers totally understand those goals.[23]

The common conception of the transformational leader as a dynamic, charismatic personality is only occasionally true. Many CEOs have effectively led their organizations through major transformations without being charismatic figures. Undoubtedly, charisma helps a leader influence others, but it is hardly a requirement for a transformational leader.

Institutionalize the Change. Finally, the transformational leader must institutionalize the changes that have been created. The CEO must first ensure that the change is proceeding as planned. As David A. Nadler, a management researcher, points out, all too many CEOs have learned, to their chagrin, that the changes they ordered never occurred. The reason is usually a lack of feedback mechanisms. Those mechanisms that were effective during stable periods often break down during turbulent-change periods. In such situations, top management must develop multiple and highly sensitive feedback devices.[24] Feedback through multiple channels is essential, because change programs, even though successful, often have side effects such as the creation of new problems.

The CEO must also realize that the institutionalization of significant change (i.e., making the new ways of behaving a regular and normal part of organizational life) takes time. Encouraging organizational members to work and interact in different ways requires a new reward system. Since people are likely to behave in ways that lead to the rewards they desire, rewards such as pay increases and promotions should be linked to the types of behavior that are required to make the organization change effective. Management researcher, Aaron J. Nurick recommends that if the organization benefits financially from the change program, then its members should share in the gains. The connection between organizational improvement and the employees' well-being thus becomes clear. Without such rewards, employees are unlikely to see involvement as worthy of their efforts.[25]

At all three of these stages identified by Tichy and Devanna, it is essential that the CEO have clear, accurate, and timely information. Bennis makes a number of suggestions, based on his own experience and research, for ensuring that such information reaches the CEO.[26] These suggestions include that the CEO not rely exclusively on his or her assistants and intimate associates for information. Thus, the CEO should be accessible to the members of the organization and to its customers and should read more than staff summaries for information on the environment. Second, he proposes that CEOs rotate their key assistants every two years to ensure continuing openness. He also recommends that these assistants be in contact with the organization's constituent groups so that they will understand their obligations and the limits of their power. Finally, he believes that CEOs should actively encourage their advisors to act as devil's advocates so that "groupthink" (i.e., the situation that results when group members emphasize the importance of solidarity over critical thinking) does not prevail.

■ The Leadership Team

Although this chapter focuses primarily upon the CEO, no single individual can possibly lead a complex organization alone. Therefore, most CEOs spend considerable amounts of time and effort developing a team of top-level managers. Typically, the **top management team** is headed by the CEO and is comprised of executives immediately below the CEO's level on the organization chart. However, such teams may also include middle managers, depending upon the desires of the CEO and the situation facing the particular company. A group of compatible managers who work well together and complement each other's abilities can provide a very powerful sense of direction for a company.

Why are many organizations today emphasizing team building at the top management level? There are a number of excellent reasons:[27]

- The CEO has a complex integrative task and cannot possibly be effective at that task without working closely with the individuals who are in charge of the organization's major activities (functions, products, regions, etc.).
- Subordinate managers usually possess greater expertise about the operating components of the organization and their own fields than the CEO does.
- The outcomes of a team's deliberations—versus the decisions of a single manager—are more likely to be innovative, because they come from a group of individuals possessing different skills, perspectives, and information.
- Team members, and their divisions or departments, should be more understanding and supportive of organizational decisions because they have a voice in shaping those decisions.
- Communication among top managers is enhanced because of their regular, frequent meetings.
- The lower-level managers on the team receive valuable developmental experience.

A benefit of the team approach can be seen in the following example. When Richard Miller became CEO of Wang Laboratories in 1989, the company was experiencing serious financial difficulties. He immediately put together a "turn-around team" comprised of about seventy middle managers from all parts of the company. One of their tasks was to identify assets that could be sold to raise cash. In little over a month, the team found assets with a value of about $800 million that could be sold. Miller's role was to motivate the team and ensure that none of the asset sales would weaken the company in the long run.[28]

The ideal team is one in which the members exhibit loyalty to, and trust in, one another. Managers learn to have confidence that the other members will carry out their various functions in an effective and timely manner. Above all, team members show a willingness to help and support each other. Such teams are open to change and innovation and reflect a sense of excitement about the team's mission.[29]

Top management teams must not overlook the importance of symbolism. Leaders must be aware that through their behaviors, they are communicating messages to their employees. When James A. Unruh became CEO of Unisys in 1990, one of his first moves was to have the office wall that separated him from other top executives torn down. This action not only brought him into closer contact with his team members but also expressed to individuals throughout the organization that he wanted openness to characterize the operations of Unisys.[30]

POWER

To influence the behavior of others, a leader must possess power. This section examines the need to acquire power and then explores the ways a leader can use power to implement strategy.

■ The Role of Power

Although the popular conception of a CEO is of an individual who wields great amounts of power, this perception is far from correct. In fact, each time a manager climbs to a higher rung on the hierarchical ladder within an organization, he or she becomes more, not less, dependent upon other people.[31] In some sense, the CEO is the most dependent of the managers in an organization, because how well or how poorly the CEO (and, consequently, the organization) performs depends upon the performance of all of the organization's members. This is not to say that a CEO does not have formal authority to influence the behavior of employees, because he or she does. But we do wish to emphasize that trying to control the behavior of others solely through formal authority has its limitations.

The first of these limitations is that CEOs soon find out that not everyone in today's organizations passively accepts and enthusiastically carries out a constant stream of orders from above. Subordinates may resist orders, subtly ignore them, blatantly question them, or even quit. As Robert H. Miles, a management researcher, points out: "The raw use of power doesn't have the acceptance it did 25 years ago. People aren't willing to put up with it."[32]

Techniques of Using Power

Figure 8.4

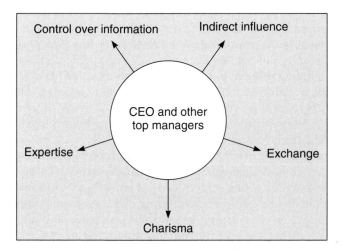

Second, CEOs are always dependent upon some individuals over whom they have no formal authority.[33] Common examples include members of the board of directors, customers, and influential members of government regulatory agencies.

Hence, effective implementation of strategy requires the CEO to influence the behavior of others in ways that rely upon formal authority but also in ways that do not. In the latter sense, the CEO must acquire power over those individuals upon whom he or she is dependent. By **power,** we refer to the ability—apart from formal authority or control over resources and rewards—to influence the behavior of other people. The following section explains how top managers can use power to implement strategies.

■ Techniques of Using Power

Top managers can wield power in a number of ways, as illustrated in Figure 8.4. This section discusses these common techniques that CEOs and other top-level managers employ to implement organizational strategies.

Expertise

A major source of power for many top managers is expertise.[34] Managers generally establish this power base through visible achievement. The greater the achievement, the more power the manager is able to accumulate.[35]

Expertise refers to a manager's ability to influence the behavior of others because these individuals believe that their manager is more knowledgeable about a problem, an opportunity, or an issue than they are. Managers who reach the CEO's office by rising through the firm's ranks will often be viewed as experts because it is clear to the organization's members that their CEO mastered a variety of jobs on the way to the top and, hence, is familiar with the employees' tasks. An executive who is hired from outside the firm to become its

CEO may or may not enter that job with expert power, however. If the individual is from a company in the same industry, though, he or she is more likely to be viewed as an expert.

For example, Lee Iacocca was probably perceived as an expert by Chrysler's employees when he was hired as that firm's CEO because he had spent most of his career prior to that time at Ford, where he had successfully held a variety of jobs. On the other hand, when John Sculley became CEO of Apple Computer, his expertise was as a marketing whiz at PepsiCo. Although much of his marketing experience could be transferred to the personal-computer business, one could have predicted that his expert power would be constrained by his limited knowledge of computers. To overcome this constraint, Sculley attempted to learn all that he could about computers after being hired at Apple.

Management researcher Gary A. Yukl suggests that leaders who possess expert power must take care in how they communicate that expertise to others. He cautions such leaders to avoid acting superior to others who possess less expertise and not to speak in an arrogant, condescending manner. As he points out, sometimes expert leaders who are trying to sell their proposals to others "fire a steady stream of arguments, rudely interrupt any attempted replies, and dismiss any objections or concerns without serious consideration."[36]

Control over Information

Control over information refers to a manager's access to important information and control over its distribution to others.[37] Henry Mintzberg's research indicates that the CEO is normally the single best-informed member of an organization. He or she is formally linked to all of the organization's key managers. Since each of these managers is a specialist relative to the CEO, the CEO is the person who best sees the totality of the organization and is most knowledgeable about its internal activities. He or she also has a number of external contacts—in other companies, in regulatory agencies, and so on—which provide excellent sources of information. Although the CEO may not know everything, he or she usually knows more than anyone else.[38]

Since the CEO has more information than anyone else, he or she is able to interpret information in order to influence the perceptions and attitudes of others.[39] If the leader's information is more complete than that of any other individual, no one will be able to question his or her decisions effectively. Even the board of directors may prove impotent, because its power based on legal standing can be overcome by the CEO's power of information and knowledge.[40]

Exchange

The use of exchange as a power base is very common. In **exchange,** a leader does something for someone else and can then expect that person to feel a sense of obligation toward the leader. Hence, when the leader makes a special request of that person later, the person will usually feel obligated to carry out that request. CEOs may even develop friendships with others in terms of exchange, knowing that friendship carries with it certain obligations.

In the following description of a manager by one of his subordinates, Kotter illustrates that successful managers may go out of their way to do favors for people:

> Most of the people here would walk over hot coals in their bare feet if my boss asked them to. He has an incredible capacity to do little things that mean a lot to people. Today, for example, in his junk mail he came across an advertisement for something that one of my subordinates had in passing once mentioned that he was shopping for. So my boss routed it to him. That probably took 15 seconds of his time, and yet my subordinate really appreciated it. To give you another example, two weeks ago he somehow learned that the purchasing manager's mother had died. On his way home that night, he stopped off at the funeral parlor. Our purchasing manager was, of course, there at the time. I bet he'll remember that brief visit for quite a while.[41]

Exchange power becomes more potent with time. As managers consistently illustrate that they are friendly and considerate, are concerned with the needs of others, and grant fair treatment, they are likely to develop considerable exchange power. Such power, however, can dwindle quickly if managers act in a hostile or arrogant manner toward those they are attempting to influence.

Indirect Influence

Top managers can often get others to implement the organization's strategies through **indirect influence**—that is, by modifying the situation in which individuals work. One variation of this technique involves making permanent changes in the organization's formal reward systems. In such cases, only those individuals who correctly carry out the organization's strategy will receive bonuses, pay raises, or promotions. Carrying this concept further, a manager can modify the organization's structure or even the physical layout of offices and departments to weaken groups or individuals who oppose certain aspects of the strategy.

Opposition to an organization's strategy is not unusual. Strategic change often reduces the status and power of some individuals while enhancing that of others. Those who believe that their status will be diminished often oppose the new strategy, if not openly, then through delaying tactics and other quiet forms of noncompliance.

In another type of indirect influence, the CEO may place only those individuals who are supporters in responsible positions. A loyal supporter, for instance, can be placed in charge of an important task force or committee to ensure that the group's recommendation coincides with the strategic direction set by the manager. Obviously, this technique must be used with care. If the CEO is surrounded only by loyal supporters, strategic decisions can become characterized by groupthink, and questions and objections that should be voiced may never arise.

Charisma

Another highly effective power base for influencing the behavior of others is charisma. **Charisma** refers to a leader's ability to influence others through his or her personal magnetism, enthusiasm, and strongly held convictions. Often, leaders are able to communicate these convictions and their vision for the future through a dramatic, persuasive manner of speaking.[42] As Yukl points out, charismatic leaders attempt to create an image of competence and success. Their aura of success and personal magnetism make them role models for their employees. The more that followers admire their leaders and identify with them, the more likely they are to accept the leaders' values and beliefs. This acceptance enables charismatic leaders to exert considerable influence over their followers' behaviors.[43]

The more success the charismatic leader has, the more powerful he or she becomes. This combination of charisma and expertise can be extremely potent in influencing the behavior of others. Hence, charismatic leaders who set high standards of performance that are realistic are likely to have highly motivated and committed organization members.

As some researchers have pointed out, charismatic leaders are most likely to be effective during periods of organizational crisis or transition.[44] Times of stress are more likely to encourage employees to respond to a leader who appears to have the answer to the problems that the organization is facing. If the leader's strategy results in early successes and if organizational performance begins to improve, the leader's power base will increase dramatically.

ORGANIZATIONAL CULTURE

Organizational culture refers to the values and patterns of belief and behavior that are accepted and practiced by the members of a particular organization.[45] Because each organization develops its own unique culture, even organizations within the same industry and city will exhibit distinctly different ways of operating. The following sections discuss the evolution of organizational culture, the impact of culture on an organization's strategy, and the methods leaders use to shape organizational culture.

■ The Evolution of Culture

The purpose of organizational culture is to enable a firm to adapt to environmental changes and to coordinate and integrate its internal operations.[46] But how do appropriate values, behaviors, and beliefs develop to enable the organization to accomplish these ends?

For many organizations, the first—and major—influence upon their culture is their founder. His or her assumptions about success form the foundation of the firm's culture.[47] For instance, the primary influence upon McDonald's culture was the fast-food company's founder, Ray A. Kroc, who died in 1984. His philosophy of fast service, assembly line food preparation, wholesome image, and devotion to the hamburger are still reflected in McDonald's operations today. Kroc's influence is the primary reason why McDonald's did not diversify outside the fast-food industry, did not specialize in made-to-order hamburgers, prohibited franchisees from being absentee owners, encouraged franchisees to experiment with new products, targeted advertisements and sales promotions to both adults and children, and opened Ronald McDonald Houses near major medical centers to provide low-cost housing to families of sick children.

As Yukl points out, the set of beliefs about the distinctive competence of the organization (i.e., what differentiates it from other organizations) is one of the most important elements of culture in new organizations. These beliefs directly affect organizational strategies and operations. For example, a company that owes its success to developing innovative products is likely to respond to a decline in sales with new-product introductions; a company that offers a common product at a low price would respond with attempts to lower costs even further.[48]

However, as time passes, Yukl notes, "segments of the culture that were initially functional may become dysfunctional, preventing the organization from adapting successfully to a changing environment."[49] McDonald's, for instance, has departed from some of Kroc's precepts in order to continue its success under changing conditions. As customers have become more interested in a diversified menu, McDonald's has expanded from hamburgers to fish and chicken sandwiches and even pizza. Increasing societal emphasis on healthy diets has led to new products such as salads, cereal, and low-fat hamburgers and yogurt, as well as to modifications in the food preparation process. The company even made its first departure from fast food to take advantage of its strong brand name by licensing Sears, Roebuck & Company to sell children's clothing with the McDonald's name emblazoned on it.[50]

So, in general, we can say that the foundation of an organization's culture reflects the values and beliefs of its founder. But the culture is modified over time as the environment changes. Environmental change renders some of the firm's culture obsolete and even dysfunctional. New elements of the culture must be added as the old are discarded in order for the organization to maintain its success. But as Figure 8.5 illustrates, a given organization's culture may also change to reflect the powerful influence of a transformational leader other than the founder.

For example, although Alexander Graham Bell founded Bell Telephone Company, the major influence upon its culture was Theodore N. Vail, who became its CEO thirty years later. Vail's slogan of "one policy, one system, universal service" led him to seek government regulation for the company. He envisioned the firm, which became known as American Telephone & Telegraph (AT&T), as a natural monopoly that had to put the public interest ahead of profits.[51] This vision resulted in such cultural elements as stability, predictability, lifetime employment, and secure managerial career planning never envisioned by Bell, the founder.

As another example, in recent years, the culture of Walt Disney Company has changed significantly. The founder's influence on the conservative family entertainment company was such that for years after his death, executives would wonder "What would Walt have done?" before making decisions. As the company lost ground to its competitors by releasing an outdated line of family movies, its newly hired CEO, Michael Eisner, brought in a new team of managers who had never known Disney. By freeing its top management of the elements of the past, which had become dysfunctional, Eisner was able to begin producing the types of movies that are popular with today's moviegoers.[52]

■ Impact of Culture on Strategy

Organizational culture can facilitate or hinder the firm's strategic actions. Because culture reflects the past, periods of environmental change often require significant modification of the organization's culture. It is essential that changes

Figure 8.5   **Evolution of Organizational Culture**

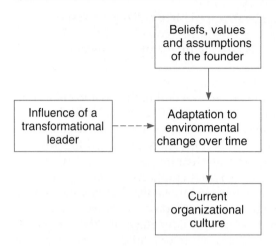

in strategy be accompanied by corresponding alterations in organizational culture; otherwise, the strategy is likely to fail. Conservative organizations do not become aggressive, entrepreneurial firms simply because they have formulated new goals and plans.[53]

Management researcher Edgar H. Schein points out that a firm caught in changing environmental conditions may devise a new strategy that will make sense from a financial, product, or marketing point of view. Yet the strategy will not be implemented because it requires "assumptions, values, and ways of working" that are at variance with the organization's culture.[54] An organization can change its strategy and its structure and yet will find its employees reverting to their prior ways of operating if it does not confront the assumptions underlying its culture.[55]

Strategies involving mergers and acquisitions are particularly vulnerable to cultural problems. Mergers between two organizations often are easier to accomplish on paper than in reality. Reality may reveal that the cultures of the organizations and the personalities of their top executives fail to mesh as easily as corporate assets. Perhaps no case more dramatically illustrates this issue than the acquisition of Electronic Data Systems (EDS) by General Motors (GM) in the mid-1980s.

This merger brought together two disparate cultures. Bureaucratic, tradition-bound, by-the-book GM found itself attempting to absorb a far smaller firm best characterized as possessing a "can-do, anything-is-possible" entrepreneurial spirit that mirrored the values of its founder and CEO, H. Ross Perot.

Dallas-based EDS, a nonunion firm, had an extremely stringent hiring and selection process followed by a grueling trial and training period that could last as long as two years. Those who survived displayed unusually high morale and a devotion for doing whatever was required to accomplish the task.

By contrast, GM's white-collar workers, accustomed to automatic pay raises and cost-of-living adjustments, felt threatened by the EDS practice of rewarding only job performance. GM employees were taken aback by the hard-driving competitiveness of the EDS workers, with their unquestioning adherence to rigid dress and personal-grooming codes. As one observer commented, "EDS merging with GM is like a Green Beret outfit joining up with the Social Security Administration."[56]

Frustrated by GM's lack of flexibility and slowness to change, top-level EDS executives, particularly Perot, began to criticize GM publicly, behavior that antagonized GM's management and board of directors. At the end of 1986, Perot was planning to chastise the GM board for considering paying end-of-the-year bonuses to senior management following a $338.5 million operating loss in the preceding quarter and a decision to lay off 29,000 workers. To forestall the criticism, the board voted unanimously to pay Perot about $700 million to leave EDS and an additional $50 million to buy out three other EDS executives.[57]

Since Perot's departure, the merger has proceeded at a faster and smoother pace. EDS, however, has managed to retain some of its founder's values. Its *1989 Annual Report*, for instance, states:

> Our training and human development programs, which rank among the finest in the industry, are absolutely essential to the vitality of EDS. As we grow in numbers, we will ensure that the principles and values which have made EDS successful do not become lost or diluted. We take great pride in these values, which can only be taught and handed down by our own individual examples.[58]

Perhaps because managers become so accustomed to their organization's culture, they fail to consider it explicitly prior to merging with another firm. It is often only after a merger has occurred and problems of meshing operations have arisen that managers understand the difficulties of blending two different cultures.

■ How Leaders Shape Culture

CEOs, other than the founder, can be influential in shaping the organization's culture so that it becomes more appropriate for its present or anticipated environment. Transactional leaders are less likely to modify the firm's culture than transformational leaders. As Bass points out: "The transactional leader works within the organizational culture as it exists; the transformational leader changes the organizational culture."[59]

How can a leader change the organization's culture? Schein advocates five "primary embedding mechanisms" for altering culture.[60] The first mechanism is systematically paying attention to certain areas of the business. This objective may be accomplished through formally measuring and controlling the activities of those areas or, less formally, through the CEO's comments or questions at meetings. For instance, a top manager can direct the attention of organizational members to controlling costs or to serving customers effectively. By contrast, those areas that the leader does not react to will be considered less important by employees.

The second mechanism involves the leader's reactions to critical incidents and organizational crises. The way a CEO deals with a crisis—such as declining sales, new governmental regulation, or technological obsolescence—can emphasize norms, values, and working procedures—or even create new ones. For instance, some companies have reacted to declining profits by cutting compensation across the board; all employees, including top management, take the pay cut. This action emphasizes a belief that "we are a family who will take care of each other." Other firms, by contrast, lay off operative employees and middle

PepsiCo's Distinctive Culture

Surely one of the most distinctive U.S. corporate cultures is PepsiCo's. New managers are put through a rigorous training program likened to Marine Corps boot camp, with those who can't meet the standards washing out. Once through the program, each manager is given considerable freedom. Risk taking is encouraged and second guessing is rare.

An important value is winning. New managers quickly learn that the fastest path to success lies in beating their competition—both inside and outside the company. A "creative tension" is fostered among departments, and "careers ride on tenths of a market share point." Furthermore, "consistent runners-up find their jobs gone. Employees know they must win merely to stay in place—and must devastate the competition to get ahead." Not surprisingly, the typical managerial work week is sixty hours.

PepsiCo may take management development more seriously than almost any other corporation. CEO Wayne Calloway spends up to two months a year personally reviewing the performance of the firm's top 550 managers. He expects those below him to spend about 40 percent of their time on personnel development and performance evaluation.

The managers who survive the intense atmosphere are rewarded with first-class air travel, stock options, bonuses that can reach 90 percent of salary, fast promotions, and fully loaded company cars. Those who don't meet the firm's expectations are out.

These values are consistent with PepsiCo's strategic direction. Managers are given considerable autonomy and are encouraged to "love change" and move quickly to take advantage of opportunities. These quick reflexes are of paramount importance in marketing consumer products and have made PepsiCo one of the premier marketing firms in the world.

SOURCES: "Corporate Culture: The Hard-to-Change Values That Spell Success or Failure," *Business Week*, 27 October 1980, pp. 148–154 (source of quotations, pp. 151, 148); T. Hall, "Demanding PepsiCo Is Attempting to Make Work Nicer for Managers," *The Wall Street Journal*, 23 October 1984; A. Dunkin, "Pepsi's Marketing Magic: Why Nobody Does It Better," *Business Week*, 10 February 1986, pp. 52–57; B. Dumaine, "Those High-flying PepsiCo Managers," *Fortune*, 10 April 1989, pp. 78–86; P. Sellers, "Pepsi Keeps on Going After No. 1," *Fortune*, 11 March 1991, pp. 62–70.

managers, while maintaining (or even increasing) the salaries of top management.

The third mechanism is to serve as a deliberate role model, teacher, or coach. As we have seen earlier in the chapter, the visible behavior of the leader communicates assumptions and values to subordinates.

The way top management allocates rewards and status is a fourth mechanism for influencing culture. Leaders can quickly communicate their priorities by consistently linking pay raises, promotions, and the lack of pay increases and promotions to particular behaviors. For instance, General Foods found that the changing environment of the 1980s rendered its historical emphasis on cost control and earnings less effective. To redirect the efforts of managers to diversification and sales growth, top management revised the compensation system to link bonuses to sales volume rather than only to increased earnings and began rewarding new-product development more generously.[61]

The fifth mechanism identified by Schein involves the procedures through which an organization recruits, selects, and promotes employees and the ways it dismisses them. An organization's culture can be perpetuated by hiring and promoting individuals whose values are similar to the firm's. By contrast, an organization attempting to alter its culture can accelerate that change by hiring employees whose beliefs and behaviors more closely fit the organization's changing value system.

In addition to these five primary embedding mechanisms, Schein also identifies several "secondary reinforcement mechanisms."[62] These include the organization's structure, its operating systems and procedures, the design of its physical space, various stories or legends that are perpetuated about important events and people, and formal statements of organizational philosophy. These mechanisms are labeled *secondary* because they work only if they are consistent with the five primary mechanisms. The primary embedding mechanisms and secondary reinforcement mechanisms are summarized in Table 8.1.

As an example of the secondary mechanisms, the belief that open communication and close working relationships are important is reflected in the open designs of the headquarters of companies such as Levi Strauss in California and Corning, Inc. in New York.[63] As another example, Food Lion—a rapidly growing supermarket chain in the southeastern United States that emphasizes low prices in no-frills stores and a constant awareness of costs—illustrates the use of stories about important people. One tale reveals how obsessed with numbers the chain's founder, Ralph Ketner, is. While waiting for freight trains at railroad crossings, he even adds the numbers on the cars, delivering the total as the caboose passes by. His numerical obsession is conveyed to Food Lion employees, who quickly learn to focus their attention on figures such as individual product prices, costs, sales volume, and linear shelf space.[64]

Schein emphasizes the critical linkage between leadership and organizational culture by stating that "the unique and essential function of leadership is the manipulation of culture."[65] Culture is created by the actions of leaders; it is institutionalized by leaders; and when it becomes dysfunctional, leadership is required to change it. What a CEO needs most, according to Schein, is an understanding of how culture can help or hinder the organization in attaining its mission and the skills to make the appropriate changes.[66]

Mechanisms for Embedding and Reinforcing Organizational Culture **Table 8.1**

Primary Embedding Mechanisms

1. What leaders pay attention to, measure, and control
2. Leader reactions to critical incidents and organizational crises
3. Deliberate role modeling, teaching, and coaching
4. Criteria for allocation of rewards and status
5. Criteria for recruitment, selection, promotion, retirement, and excommunication

Secondary Articulation and Reinforcement Mechanisms

1. Organization design and structure
2. Organizational systems and procedures
3. Design of physical space, facades, buildings
4. Stories about important events and people
5. Formal statements of organizational philosophy, creeds, charters

---

Source: E. H. Schein, *Organizational Culture and Leadership* (San Francisco: Jossey-Bass, 1985), Chap. 10.

SUMMARY

Top-level managers have two tools to encourage organizational members to put their full efforts into strategy implementation: leadership and organizational culture. In today's dynamic and turbulent world, the importance of leadership cannot be overemphasized. The firm's leaders must articulate the organization's mission and objectives and then inspire, motivate, and support the firm's members as they work together to implement the organization's strategies.

The CEO, simply by virtue of the office, possesses the potential to influence the behavior of the organization's employees. This source of influence is termed *formal authority*. Through it, the CEO can control resources and rewards. Additionally, each CEO has a distinctive leadership style that sets the tone for the firm's members. Some leaders use a transactional style, exchanging rewards for employees' work efforts. This style can be effective in firms that are already performing well and do not anticipate significant environmental change, because it encourages employees to continue to engage in high performance.

In companies that are experiencing competitive difficulties or are undergoing environmental change, a transformational leadership style is preferable. A transformational leader inspires involvement in a mission, giving followers a "vision" of a higher order and motivating them to stretch their abilities. Such leadership is thought to make significant changes in organizational performance.

Because no single CEO, regardless of how talented he or she may be, can lead a complex organization single-handedly, most companies emphasize top management teams. Led by the CEO, such teams of executives are able to enhance the organization's coordinative activities, creativity, information flows, and strategy implementation.

In influencing the behavior of others, CEOs and other top managers have available, in addition to their formal authority and leadership style, various other techniques for wielding power. For instance, managers who are perceived as experts in their field often have significant influence over the behavior of others. They can also use their access to important information and control over its distribution to affect behavior. Leaders often use exchange as a power base, doing something for others to create a sense of obligation. Also, a manager can indirectly influence others by modifying the organization's structure, physical layout, or reward system. Finally, a manager who possesses charisma can have a powerful impact upon followers.

Organizational culture refers to the values and patterns of belief and behavior that are accepted and practiced by the members of an organization. A given organization's culture reflects the influence of its founder, its experiences after the departure of its founder, and, at times, the powerful influence of a transformational leader other than the founder.

An organization's culture can facilitate or hinder the firm's strategic actions. The firm's values and beliefs directly affect organizational strategies and operations. This influence can help the organization operate effectively, but it can also prevent the organization from adapting successfully to a changing environment. It is essential that changes in strategy be accompanied by corresponding alterations in organizational culture.

A leader can change the organization's culture through such mechanisms as paying systematic attention to certain areas of the business, serving as a deliberate role model, and allocating rewards and status. Leaders can also set an example for the firm's members through the way in which they react to organizational crises and through the processes the organization uses to attract, hire, and promote employees.

KEY CONCEPTS

Charisma   A leader's ability to influence the behavior of others through his or her personal magnetism, enthusiasm, strongly held beliefs, and charm.

Contingency-based leadership   The concept that the most effective style of leadership depends upon the particular situation.

Control over information   A situation in which a manager has access to important information and controls its distribution to others to influence their behavior.

Exchange   A situation in which a leader does a favor for someone so that he or she will feel a sense of obligation toward the leader.

Expertise   A manager's ability to influence the behavior of others because they believe that the manager possesses greater expertise or is more knowledgeable about a situation than they are.

Formal authority   The official, institutionalized right of a manager to make decisions affecting the behavior of subordinates.

Indirect influence   The influence on the behavior of others brought about by modifying the situation in which they work.

Leadership   The capacity to secure the cooperation of others in accomplishing an objective.

Leadership style   The characteristic pattern of behavior that a leader exhibits in the process of exercising authority and making decisions.

Organizational culture   The values and patterns of belief and behavior that are accepted and practiced by the members of a particular organization.

Power   The ability, apart from functional authority or control over resources or rewards, to influence the behavior of others.

Top management team   A team of top-level executives, headed by the CEO.

Transactional leadership   The capacity to motivate followers by exchanging rewards for performance.

Transformational leadership   The capacity to motivate followers by inspiring involvement and participation in a mission.

DISCUSSION QUESTIONS

1. Explain the difference between leadership and management. Give examples of each concept.

2. Delineate the relationship between an organization's reward system and its strategic decisions.

3. Explain transactional leadership, and give examples. Identify the conditions under which it is likely to be effective.

4. Explain transformational leadership, and give examples. Identify the conditions under which it is likely to be effective.

5. What is the role of clear, accurate, and timely information in each of the three stages of the transformational process?

6. Explain the concept of managerial dependency and why it requires the CEO to develop sources of power other than formal authority.

7. Give examples of leaders you have known who wielded power through expertise; through control over information; through exchange; through indirect influence; and through charisma.

8. Think of an organization with which you are quite familiar. Describe its culture. Explain how its culture may have evolved.

9. Give an example of an organization whose culture is appropriate for its strategy. Now, give an example of a firm whose culture has hindered its strategy.

10. Relate a story about an important event or a person that reflects elements of a particular organization's culture.

STRATEGIC MANAGEMENT EXERCISES

1. Assume that you are the CEO of a commercial airline that competes with the low-cost strategy. Describe an appropriate organizational culture for your company.

2. Assume that your airline (Exercise 1) has now changed its strategy from low-cost to low-cost–differentiation. As CEO, what changes might you consider implementing in style of leadership, exercise of power, and organizational culture?

3. Find, in your library, an example of transformational leadership. Explain the situation fully: Who is the leader? What is the organization? Why was transformational leadership necessary? What characteristics and/or behaviors made the manager a transformational leader? What were the results of his or her attempts to transform the organization? (Particularly good sources for this exercise are *The Wall Street Journal, Business Week,* and *Fortune.*)

4. From library research, identify two companies that are currently merging or have engaged in a merger within the past few years. Learn as much as you can about each company's organizational culture. What problems are the two businesses having in combining their cultures? From your research, what other problems can you predict will occur in the future?

REFERENCES

1. H. Mintzberg, *The Nature of Managerial Work* (New York: Harper & Row, 1973), Chap. 4.

2. J. P. Kotter, *The Leadership Factor* (New York: Free Press, 1988), p. 11.

3. W. Bennis, *Why Leaders Can't Lead: The Unconscious Conspiracy Continues* (San Francisco: Jossey-Bass, 1989), p. 22.

4. D. V. Day and R. G. Lord, "Executive Leadership and Organizational Performance: Suggestions for a New Theory and Methodology," *Journal of Management* 14 (1988): 453–464.

5. G. A. Yukl, *Leadership in Organizations,* 2nd ed. (Englewood Cliffs, N.J.: Prentice-Hall, 1989), pp. 263–266; J. Pfeffer, "The Ambiguity of Leadership," *Academy of Management Review* 2 (1977): 104–112.

6. Yukl, *Leadership in Organizations,* p. 15.

7. Yukl, *Leadership in Organizations,* pp. 17–18.

8. As examples, see F. E. Fiedler, *A Theory of Leadership Effectiveness* (New York: McGraw-Hill, 1967); R. J. House, "A Path-Goal Theory of Leadership Effectiveness," *Administrative Science Quarterly* 16 (1971): 321–338; G. Graen and J. F. Cashman, "A Role Making Model of Leadership in Formal Organizations: A Developmental Approach," in J. G. Hunt and L. L. Larson, eds., *Leadership Frontiers* (Kent, Ohio: Kent State University Press, 1975); P. Hersey and K. H. Blanchard, *Management of Organizational Behavior: Utilizing Human Resources,* 4th ed. (Englewood Cliffs, N.J.: Prentice-Hall, 1982), pp. 150–175; V. H. Vroom and A. G. Jago, *The New Leadership: Managing Participation in Organizations* (Englewood Cliffs, N.J.: Prentice-Hall, 1988).

9. Day and Lord, "Executive Leadership," p. 459.

10. This distinction was first made by J. M. Burns, *Leadership* (New York: Harper & Row, 1978).

11. B. M. Bass, *Leadership and Performance Beyond Expectations* (New York: Free Press, 1985).

12. Bass, *Leadership and Performance,* p. 22.

13. B. M. Bass, "Leadership: Good, Better, Best," *Organizational Dynamics* 13 (Winter 1985): 26–40; N. M. Tichy and D. O. Ulrich, "SMR Forum: The Leadership Challenge—A Call for the Transformational Leader," *Sloan Management Review* 26 (Fall 1984): 59–68.

14. Bass, *Leadership and Performance,* p. 29.

15. N. M. Tichy and M. A. Devanna, *The Transformational Leader* (New York: Wiley, 1986).

16. P. F. Drucker, *Managing in Turbulent Times* (New York: Harper & Row, 1980), p. 44.

17. Tichy and Devanna, *Transformational Leader.*

18. A. E. Pearson, "Six Basics for General Managers," *Harvard Business Review* 67, no. 4 (July-August 1989): 96.

19. Pearson, "Six Basics," p. 97. Reprinted by permission of the *Harvard Business Review.* Excerpt from "Six Basics for General Managers" by Andrall E. Pearson (July-August 1989). Copyright © 1989 by the President and Fellows of Harvard College; all rights reserved.

20. Pearson, "Six Basics," p. 95. Reprinted by permission of the *Harvard Business Review.* Excerpt from "Six Basics for General Managers" by Andrall E. Pearson (July-August 1989). Copyright © 1989 by the President and Fellows of Harvard College; all rights reserved.

21. Pearson, "Six Basics," p. 95. Reprinted by permission of the *Harvard Business Review.* Excerpt from "Six Basics for General Managers" by Andrall E. Pearson (July-August 1989). Copyright © 1989 by the President and Fellows of Harvard College; all rights reserved.

22. W. Bennis and B. Nanus, *Leaders: The Strategies for Taking Charge* (New York: Harper & Row, 1985), pp. 27–33, 87–109.

23. S. Feinstein, "Labor Letter," *The Wall Street Journal*, 1 May 1990.

24. D. A. Nadler, "Managing Organizational Change: An Integrative Perspective," *Journal of Applied Behavioral Science* 17 (1981): 294.

25. A. J. Nurick, "The Paradox of Participation: Lessons from the Tennessee Valley Authority," *Human Resource Management* 24 (Fall 1985): 354–355.

26. Bennis, *Why Leaders Can't Lead*, pp. 140–141.

27. The first two reasons are based on D. C. Hambrick, "Guest Editor's Introduction: Putting Top Managers Back in the Strategy Picture," *Strategic Management Journal* 10 (1989): 6. The remaining reasons are based on R. A. Eisenstat and S. G. Cohen, "Summary: Top Management Groups," in J. R. Hackman, ed., *Groups That Work (and Those That Don't): Creating Conditions for Effective Teamwork* (San Francisco: Jossey-Bass, 1990), pp. 78–79.

28. B. Dumaine, "The New Turnaround Champs," *Fortune*, 16 July 1990, p. 38.

29. G. H. Varney, *Building Productive Teams: An Action Guide and Resource Book* (San Francisco: Jossey-Bass, 1989), p. 133.

30. J. Weber, "Can James Unruh Recharge Unisys?" *Business Week*, 30 July 1990, p. 72.

31. J. P. Kotter, "Power, Dependence, and Effective Management," *Harvard Business Review* 55, no. 4 (July-August 1977): 125–136.

32. T. A. Stewart, "New Ways to Exercise Power," *Fortune*, 6 November 1989, p. 53.

33. Kotter, "Power, Dependence," p. 128.

34. J. R. P. French, Jr., and B. Raven, "The Bases of Social Power," in D. Cartwright, ed., *Studies in Social Power* (Ann Arbor, Mich.: University of Michigan Press, 1959), pp. 150–167.

35. Kotter, "Power, Dependence," p. 130.

36. Yukl, *Leadership in Organizations*, p. 47.

37. A. Pettigrew, "Information Control as a Power Resource," *Sociology* 6 (1972): 187–204.

38. H. Mintzberg, *Power in and Around Organizations* (Englewood Cliffs, N.J.: Prentice-Hall, 1983), pp. 121–122.

39. A. Kuhn, *The Study of Society: A Unified Approach* (Homewood, Ill.: Irwin, 1963).

40. Mintzberg, *Power in and Around*, p. 122.

41. Kotter, "Power, Dependence," p. 130. Reprinted by permission of the *Harvard Business Review*. Excerpt from "Power, Dependence, and Effective Management" by John P. Kotter (July-August 1977). Copyright © 1977 by the President and Fellows of Harvard College; all rights reserved.

42. D. E. Berlew, "Leadership and Organizational Excitement," in D. A. Kolb, I. M. Rubin, and J. M. McIntyre, eds., *Organizational Psychology: A Book of Readings*, 2nd ed., (Englewood Cliffs, N.J.: Prentice-Hall, 1974); R. J. House, "A 1976 Theory of Charismatic Leadership," in J. G. Hunt and L. L. Larson, eds., *Leadership: The Cutting Edge* (Carbondale, Ill.: Southern Illinois Press, 1977).

43. Yukl, *Leadership in Organizations*, p. 206.

44. Bass, *Leadership and Performance*, pp. 37–39; J. A. Conger and R. Kanungo, "Toward a Behavioral Theory of Charismatic Leadership in Organizational Settings," *Academy of Management Review* 12 (1987): 637–647.

45. C. D. Pringle, D. F. Jennings, and J. G. Longenecker, *Managing Organizations: Functions and Behaviors* (Columbus, Ohio: Merrill, 1988), p. 594.

46. E. H. Schein, *Organizational Culture and Leadership* (San Francisco: Jossey-Bass, 1985), p. 9.

47. E. H. Schein, "The Role of the Founder in Creating Organizational Culture," *Organizational Dynamics* 12 (Summer 1983): 14.

48. Yukl, *Leadership in Organizations*, pp. 215–216.

49. Yukl, *Leadership in Organizations*, p. 216.

50. For recent articles on McDonald's culture, see R. Henkoff, "Big Mac Attacks with Pizza," *Fortune*, 26 February 1990, pp. 87–89; R. Gibson and R. Johnson, "Big Mac, Cooling Off, Loses Its Sizzle," *The Wall Street Journal*, 29 September 1989; P. Moser, "The McDonald's Mystique," *Fortune*, 4 July 1988, pp. 112–116.

51. Bass, *Leadership and Performance*, p. 25.

52. K. Kerwin and A. N. Fins, "Disney Is Looking Just a Little Fragilistic," *Business Week*, 25 June 1990, pp. 52–54; B. Dumaine, "Creating a New Company Culture," *Fortune*, 15 January 1990, p. 128.

53. Pringle et al., *Managing Organizations*, p. 309.

54. Schein, *Organizational Culture*, p. 30.

55. Schein, *Organizational Culture*, p. 33.

56. L. P. Cohen and C. F. McCoy, "Perot's Singular Style Raises Issue of How He'll Fit at GM," *The Wall Street Journal*, 2 July 1984.

57. Cohen and McCoy, "Perot's Singular Style"; D. Darlin and M. G. Guiles, "Some GM People Feel Auto Firm, Not EDS, Was the One Acquired," *The Wall Street Journal*, 19 December 1984; "How Ross Perot's Shock Troops Ran into Flak at GM," *Business Week*, 11 February 1985, pp. 118–122; "GM Boots Perot" and "Perot to Smith: GM Must Change," *Newsweek*, 15 December 1986, pp. 56–62; "GM Hasn't Bought Much Peace" and "The Risks of Running EDS Without Perot," *Business Week*, 15 December 1986, pp. 24–27; T. Moore, "Make-or-Break Time for General Motors," *Fortune*, 15 February 1988, pp. 32–42. Pringle et al., *Managing Organizations*, p. 310.

58. EDS, *1989 Annual Report*, p. 3.

59. Bass, *Leadership and Performance*, p. 24.

60. This discussion is based on Schein, *Organizational Culture*, pp. 224–237.

61. "Changing the Culture at General Foods," *Business Week*, 10 February 1986, pp. 52–57.

62. Schein, *Organizational Culture*, pp. 237–242.

63. T. R. V. Davis, "The Influence of the Physical Environment in Offices," *Academy of Management Review* 9 (1984): 273.

64. W. E. Sheeline, "Making Them Rich Down Home," *Fortune*, 15 August 1988, pp. 50–55.

65. Schein, *Organizational Culture*, p. 317.

66. Schein, *Organizational Culture*, pp. 316–317 and 320.

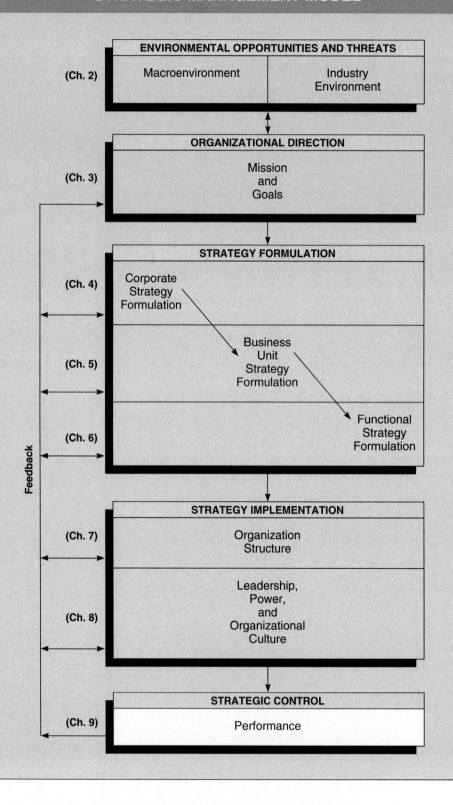

STRATEGIC MANAGEMENT MODEL

ENVIRONMENTAL OPPORTUNITIES AND THREATS

(Ch. 2)

Macroenvironment | Industry Environment

ORGANIZATIONAL DIRECTION

(Ch. 3)

Mission
and
Goals

STRATEGY FORMULATION

(Ch. 4)

Corporate
Strategy
Formulation

(Ch. 5)

Business
Unit
Strategy
Formulation

(Ch. 6)

Functional
Strategy
Formulation

STRATEGY IMPLEMENTATION

(Ch. 7)

Organization
Structure

(Ch. 8)

Leadership,
Power,
and
Organizational
Culture

STRATEGIC CONTROL

(Ch. 9)

Performance

Feedback

9

CHAPTER

Strategic Control

The activities of planning, implementing, and controlling are closely linked. Chapters 3, 4, 5, and 6 focused on planning—establishing the organization's mission and goals and developing its corporate-level, business unit, and functional strategies. Then, implementing those strategies was discussed in Chapters 7 and 8. We now turn to the task of control.

Strategic control consists of determining the extent to which the organization's strategies are successful in attaining its goals and objectives. If the goals and objectives are not being reached as planned, then the intent of control is to modify the organization's strategies and/or implementation so that the organization's ability to accomplish its goals will be improved.

Control, in the business administration sense, is most often discussed in the context of budgeting. It is important to understand that strategic control is much broader than this traditional usage of the term. In the control of budgeted expenditures, the focus is usually for a time span of a year or less; quantitative measurements are used to determine whether actual expenditures are exceeding planned spending; the emphasis is on internal operations; and corrective action is often taken after the budget period has elapsed. But in strategic control, the focal time period usually ranges anywhere from a few years to over a decade; qualitative and quantitative measurements are taken; management assesses both internal operations and the external environment; and the process is ongoing, because top management cannot wait for several years to evaluate results. By then, it will be too late. These differences are summarized in Table 9.1.

OVERVIEW OF THE STRATEGIC CONTROL PROCESS

The strategic control process consists of several steps. First, top management must decide what elements of the environment and of the organization need to be monitored, evaluated, and controlled. Then, standards must be established

Table 9.1   **Differences Between Strategic Control and Budgetary Control**

Strategic Control	*Budgetary Control*
Time period is lengthy—ranging from a few years to over ten years.	Time period is usually one year or less.
Measurements are quantitative and qualitative.	Measurements are quantitative.
Concentration is internal and external.	Concentration is internal.
Corrective action is ongoing.	Corrective action may be taken after budget period has elapsed.

with which the actual performance of the organization can be compared. These first two steps will be strongly influenced by the organization's mission, goals, and objectives, which direct management's attention to certain organizational and environmental elements and to the relative importance of particular standards.

Next, management must measure the company's actual performance. These measurements will generally be both quantitative and qualitative. The performance measurements will then be compared with the previously established standards. If performance is in line with the standards or exceeds them, then no corrective action is necessary. (When performance exceeds standards, management should consider whether the standards are appropriate and whether they should be raised.) However, if performance falls below the standards, then management must take remedial action. These steps are delineated in Figure 9.1.

Figure 9.1   **Steps Involved in Strategic Control**

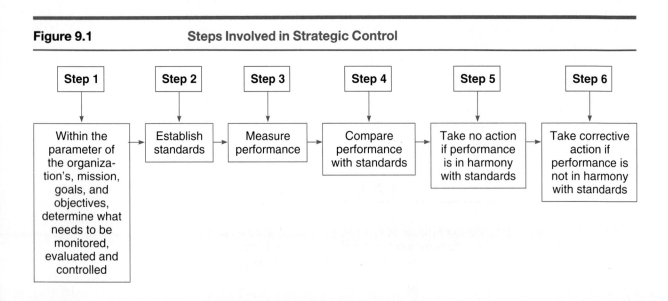

FOCUS OF STRATEGIC CONTROL

The focus of strategic control is both internal and external. Neither element can be examined in isolation, because it is top management's role to align advantageously the internal operations of the enterprise with its external environment. In fact, strategic control can be visualized as "mediating" the ongoing interactions between environmental variables and the company's internal dimensions. Relying upon quantitative and qualitative performance measures, top management uses strategic control to keep the firm's internal dimensions aligned with its external environment. The role of strategic control as a mediator is portrayed diagrammatically in Figure 9.2.

The following sections discuss three key areas that must be monitored and evaluated in the process of strategic control: the macroenvironment, the industry environment, and internal operations.

■ Macroenvironment

The first focus of the strategic control process is usually the organization's macroenvironment. Although individual businesses normally exert little, if any, influence over the forces in the macroenvironment, these forces must be continuously monitored. Changes or shifts in the macroenvironment have strategic ramifications for the company. Consequently, strategic control involves continuously examining the fit between the company and its changing external environment.

In this context, strategic control consists of modifying the company's operations to defend itself better against external threats that may arise and to capi-

---

Strategic Control as a Mediator   **Figure 9.2**

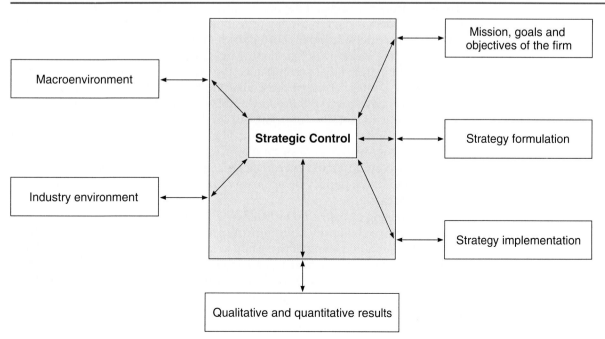

talize on new external opportunities. For example, among the massive changes in federal income tax regulations in 1986 was a phasing out of the tax deductibility of consumer interest payments (excluding mortgage interest). One insurance company monitoring this change responded quickly by producing thousands of individually tailored reports explaining in a few pages how the tax changes would affect its policyholders.[1] The firm's intent was to persuade its customers to repay loans they had taken out against their whole-life policies, since the interest on those loans was no longer tax-deductible and the cash value buildup on a policy would now receive favorable tax treatment. For years, policyholders had been accustomed to borrowing against the cash value of their policies at low interest rates and deducting the interest payments. These actions represented a huge drain on company funds.

According to one report, the insurance company has been successful "in convincing customers to repay millions of dollars on their loans and is at the same time generating massive new sales of single-premium life insurance, which is both liquid and nontaxable under the new law. The ability to respond to environmental change is paying a handsome dividend."[2]

■ Industry Environment

Strategic control also involves monitoring the industry environment. Again, the purpose is to modify the company's operations so that it can better defend itself against threats and better capitalize on opportunities. It is important to remember in this regard that environmental analysis—both at the macroenvironment and at the industry levels—is not confined to the past or present; top management also needs to estimate future environmental trends.

Take, for instance, the response of companies in two different industries to changing energy costs. Because gasoline prices were relatively low during the 1980s, American automobile manufacturers reduced their emphasis on producing small economy cars and devoted more attention to larger automobiles. Consumers responded well to the bigger cars since their interest in fuel economy waned as gas prices dropped. Both parties, then, were relatively pleased: Consumers got the larger cars that they wanted, and manufacturers received the higher profit margins that accompanied the sale of larger, more expensive cars.

However, strategic control must take the future into account. Historically, energy prices have been volatile. Any number of world developments can cause prices to shoot up literally overnight. But smaller, more fuel-efficient cars cannot be produced and distributed overnight. Hence, potential skyrocketing gasoline prices posed a threat. American car manufacturers had not given enough attention to this possibility, and hence, their strategic control was shortsighted in that respect. (Recall that rapidly rising energy prices in 1979 severely dampened the sale of large cars.)

In the housing industry, home builders also responded to lower energy costs and competitive rivalry by building larger and larger homes in upper-middle-class neighborhoods. Many of these houses contained massive foyers and large lofts, requiring significant heating and cooling energy. As energy prices jumped, the utility expenses for owners of these houses became exorbitant. Although the home builders did not have to pay for the increased cost of utilities, surely their reputations suffered.

STRATEGIC INSIGHT

Misalignment in Japan

By failing to adapt to the changing values of their society, some Japanese businesses are losing their best and brightest young scientists. One thirty-four-year-old molecular biologist, who had been with a laboratory for four years, asked to be allowed to conduct independent research on human genes. He was refused because he was too young. Only after many years of accumulating seniority would he be able to conduct the research in which he was most interested.

Today, he is employed in Philadelphia researching human chromosomes. He has published the results of his work in prestigious scientific journals and supervises five other researchers.

Well-known scientists claim that the practice of pure science in Japan is inferior to that of other developed countries. The reasons are such deeply ingrained traditions as strict seniority, acquies-

cence to authority, and a stable—but not very mobile—work force. Obviously, Japanese organizations require changes in their value and reward systems if they are to be competitive in this particular area. The internal dimensions of their scientific research organizations are not aligned properly with the changing external macroenvironment.

Japanese scientists are the edge of a growing trend. By the late 1980s, almost 5 percent of the Japanese work force was annually leaving one employer for another. That figure represented an 80 percent increase in job-hopping in just five years. Among the hiring companies were U.S.-based Lotus Development and Germany's Daimler Benz and BMW. Even Japan's Sony joined the trend, hiring about seventy mid-career job switchers in one year.

SOURCES: S. K. Yoder, "Japan's Scientists Find Pure Research Suffers Under Rigid Life Style," *The Wall Street Journal,* 31 October 1988; Masayoshi Kanabayashi, "In Japan, Employees Are Switching Firms for Better Work, Pay," *The Wall Street Journal,* 11 October 1988.

■ Internal Operations

Strategic control also involves the internal operations of the business through monitoring and evaluating its strategy formulation and implementation. Corrective action may then be necessary. Monitoring and evaluating the company's operations involve viewing its present and future strategic posture relative to its past posture. The bases for monitoring and evaluating are the qualitative and quantitative standards established by top management.

Qualitatively, the broad question asked is: "How effective is our strategy in accomplishing our mission and goals?" Consider the goal of product leadership, for instance. In evaluating its product leadership, an organization compares its products with those of competitors and determines the extent to which it pioneers in the introduction of basic products and product improvements.

But pioneering is not enough. A company must also follow through. Xerox, for instance, introduced the first commercial fax machine in 1964, but today, its machines account for only 7 percent of U.S. fax sales. Likewise, Raytheon was the first company to market a microwave oven—in 1947—but today, 75 percent of all microwave ovens in U.S. homes are made in the Far East.[3]

In the broad quantitative sense, management will ask: "How effective is our strategy in attaining our objectives?" (Recall that objectives are specific, quantifiable versions of goals, which, in turn, are desired general ends toward which organizational efforts are directed.) For instance, management can compare the firm's 11.2 percent rate of return on investment over the past year with its stated objective of 10 percent and conclude that its strategy has been effective in that particular respect.

Whether evaluating a strategy's effectiveness is undertaken relative to the company's rivals or relative only to itself, the point of strategic control is to take corrective action if negative gaps exist between intended and actual strategic results. Viewed in this fashion, strategic control has provided the impetus for the development of portfolio frameworks, presented in Chapter 4, and it underlies the Profit Impact of Marketing Strategy (PIMS) program discussed in the following section.

STRATEGIC CONTROL STANDARDS

Evaluating an enterprise's performance may be accomplished in a number of ways. Management, for instance, often compares current operating results with those from the preceding year. A qualitative judgment may be made about whether the business's products or services are superior to, inferior to, or about the same as last year's. Several quantitative measures may also be used, including return on investment (ROI), return on assets (ROA), return on sales (ROS), and return on equity (ROE).

Confining control standards only to comparisons of current performance versus past performance, however, can be myopic, because it ignores important external variables. For example, assume that a business's ROI has increased from 8 to 10 percent over the past year. Management might consider that a significant improvement. But the meaning of this measure depends upon the industry in which the company operates. In a depressed industry, an ROI of 10 percent may be outstanding, but that same return in a growth industry will be disappointing, since the leading firms may earn 15 to 20 percent. An improvement in a company's ROI is less encouraging, then, if its past performance has been significantly behind that of its major competitors.

A second weakness in comparing a business's current results with those of the past is that such comparisons can distort managerial rewards. For instance, a decline in profitability from one year to the next can negatively affect managerial bonuses. However, if the drop was industrywide, the lower performance may actually be due to unfavorable external variables and not to poorer performance by management.

This section examines a variety of standards that can be used for strategic control. These standards can be based on data derived from the PIMS program, published information that is publicly available, ratings of product/service quality, innovation rates, and relative market share standings. Viewed broadly, these standards include both quantitative and qualitative information.

■ PIMS Program

Clearly, then, a thorough evaluation of a business's performance must take into account the performance of its competitors. For that reason, the PIMS program

STRATEGIC INSIGHT

Broadening a Myopic Perspective at GM

Three decades ago, General Motors (GM) developed a quantitative standard for measuring the quality of the automobiles it was manufacturing. On its scale, a score of 100 was perfect; each defect a new car contained lowered its score by one point. So a car with a score of 80 contained 20 defects. GM's management established a score of 60 as "passing."

But when too many cars failed to attain a passing grade, rather than take corrective action and improve the quality of its outputs, management decided to modify the standard. The new standard for perfection was raised from 100 to 145. As a result, a car with 41 defects that would have "failed" under the old standard now had a passing score of 104.

GM and the other U.S. automakers, however, became increasingly serious about product quality as pressure from foreign competition steadily increased during the 1970s. But even by 1980, the quality of American-made cars was still suspect. A Detroit consulting firm, Harbour & Associates,

reported that GM's 1980 cars averaged 7.4 defects per car, Chrysler's averaged 8.1, and Ford's averaged 6.7. Meanwhile, Japanese-made autos averaged only 2.0 defects.

American manufacturers continued to stress quality improvements throughout the 1980s, however. By 1990, GM had cut its defects per car to 1.7, Chrysler to 1.8, and Ford to 1.5. Japanese carmakers, however, maintained their lead by reducing their defect rate to 1.2 per car. (The most common auto defects involve electrical accessories, paint and trim, engines, and squeaks and rattles.)

GM increasingly began to realize the role that customer service played in quality considerations. When 1100 of its new Saturn sedans were recalled because they left the factory with improperly mixed antifreeze that would create holes in the cooling systems, GM took a large step forward in customer service. Rather than recall the cars for free repairs, the usual approach of automakers, GM offered to exchange each car with the defective coolant for a new Saturn.

SOURCES: J. Burgess, "GM to Replace 1,100 Saturn Sedans," *The Washington Post,* 11 May 1991; P. Ingrassia, "Auto Industry in U.S. Is Sliding Relentlessly into Japanese Hands," *The Wall Street Journal,* 16 February 1990; A. Taylor III, "Why U.S. Carmakers Are Losing Ground," *Fortune,* 23 October 1989, p. 100; M. Keller, *Rude Awakening: The Rise, Fall, and Struggle for Recovery of General Motors* (New York: Morrow, 1989), pp. 29–30.

was developed; the **PIMS program** is a data base that contains quantitative and qualitative information on the performance of more than three thousand business units. It helps management of participating companies evaluate the performance of their companies relative to the average performance of other businesses in the same industry. When a company's results compare unfavorably with others in the same industry, strategic control is required.

PIMS was developed as a result of General Electric's (GE) efforts to evaluate systematically the performance of its business units in the 1960s.[4] Using a program developed by Professor Sidney Schoeffler of Harvard University, GE's top managers and corporate staff began to assess business unit performance in a formal, systematic fashion. Subsequently, other companies were invited to join the project, and in 1975, Professor Schoeffler founded the Strategic Planning Institute to conduct PIMS research. The program now consists of more than three thousand business organizations.

Each of the participating businesses provides quantitative and qualitative information to the program. Included are data on variables such as relative market share, product/service quality (relative to leading competitors), new products and services introduced as a percentage of sales, relative prices of products and services, marketing expenses as a percentage of sales, value of plant and equipment relative to sales, and research and development expenses as a percentage of sales. Two profitability measures are used: net operating profit before taxes as a percentage of sales (ROS), and net income before taxes as a percentage of total investment (ROI) or of total assets (ROA).

Each of these variables may be used for strategic control purposes. For instance, if a business's product quality is consistently judged to be below average in its industry, then this information can be used to improve quality. Below-average profitability signals management that changes in strategy formulation and/or implementation may be necessary.

To take full advantage of PIMS, a business needs to be a participating member of the PIMS program. However, all businesses may improve their strategic control by comparing their situations with some of the PIMS principles.[5] PIMS, of course, is not the only source of strategic control data. A number of other information bases are discussed below.

■ Published Information for Strategic Control

Fortune annually publishes the most and least admired U.S. corporations with annual sales of at least $500 million in such diverse industries as electronics, pharmaceuticals, retailing, transportation, banking, insurance, metals, food, motor vehicles, and utilities. Company performance is evaluated along the following eight lines:

- Quality of products/services
- Quality of management
- Innovativeness
- Long-term investment value
- Financial soundness
- Community and environmental responsibility
- Use of corporate assets
- Ability to attract, develop, and keep talented people

The most admired companies are those that rank high on these variables, and interestingly enough, they are also businesses that exhibit relatively high profitability.

Although *Fortune*'s list consists of very large, publicly traded companies, the information in the listing may nevertheless provide valuable guidelines for the strategic control of smaller businesses in similar industries. In addition to *Fortune*, publications such as *Forbes, Industry Week, Business Week,* and *Dun's Business Month* also evaluate the performance of companies in various industries.

Which particular measures of comparison to use, of course, must be determined by top management. But a number of variables are considered important for strategic control because they significantly affect performance. They are discussed in the following sections.

■ Product/Service Quality

Interestingly, over the years, there has been a positive relationship between the quality of products and services that companies produce and the profitability of those firms. This relationship is illustrated by the *Fortune* listing described above. Recall that quality has two key aspects—the conformance of a product or service to the internal standards of the firm, and the ultimate consumer's perception of the quality of that product or service. It is important to distinguish between these two aspects of quality, because a number of products that have conformed to internal standards have not sold well. So although conformance to standards is a necessary condition for a product's or service's success, it is not sufficient. Ultimately, a firm's outputs must be perceived as superior by the marketplace.[6]

To evaluate product quality, *Fortune* asks some eight thousand executives, outside directors, and financial analysts to judge the outputs of the largest firms in the United States. About four thousand responses are usually received.[7] According to the results, those firms whose outputs are perceived to possess high quality are also the higher-performing companies.

Taking a different approach, the PIMS program assesses quality through judgments made by both managers and customers.[8] A meeting is held by a team of managers in each of the PIMS participating businesses. These managers identify product/service attributes that they believe influence customer purchases. They then assign a weight to each attribute. Finally, they rate the quality of each attribute of their company's outputs relative to those of the products/services produced by the leading competitors in their industry. These ratings are augmented by survey results from customers who also rate the quality of the products produced by businesses in the industry. The results of the PIMS program suggest a strong positive correlation between product quality and business performance.

One publication, *Consumer Reports,* may be used by executives as a means for strategic control of output quality. Literally hundreds of products are evaluated by this publication annually. Since the evaluation by *Consumer Reports* is unbiased (i.e., it does not accept advertising), it is an excellent source of product quality information for competing businesses. Even if the products of a particular business are not evaluated by this publication, that company can still gain insight on how its competitors' product quality is measured.

Certainly, it is imperative that an enterprise, regardless of its size, engage in some means of assessing the relative quality of its products and services. If the quality of its outputs compares favorably with that of the competition, then no direct action may be necessary, although emphasizing high quality in future advertising might prove to be advantageous. If the company's outputs do not compare favorably with the competition's, then corrective action is essential.

■ Innovation

Innovation may be conceptualized, measured, and controlled in different ways. Many researchers have approached this subject by focusing on expenditures for product research and development (R&D) and process R&D.[9] These studies conclude that the more money spent on developing new or improved products and processes, the higher the level of innovation is likely to be. This same approach is taken in the PIMS program.

Some firms plan and control their programs for innovation very carefully. 3M, for instance, has established a standard that 25 percent of each business unit's sales should come from products introduced to the market within the past five years. The standard is taken quite seriously by 3M managers, since "meeting the 25% test is a crucial yardstick at bonus time."[10] Currently, about a third of 3M's sales come from products introduced within a five-year period.[11]

Some observers have suggested that the strategic control of innovation must emphasize incremental improvements in products and services rather than sweeping, fundamental innovations. Several attribute the Japanese superiority over U.S. business performance in some industries to the Japanese emphasis on incremental innovations. A continuous series of incremental innovations means that each year, the company's outputs improve as a result of small, but numerous and cumulative, innovations.[12]

■ Relative Market Share

A business's size and market share, relative to its largest rivals in the industry, are important in formulating and implementing strategy and in controlling the company's strategic direction. Recall from Chapter 5 that both small and large market shares can lead to high performance. In large, leading companies, relative market share and growth in relative market share play important roles in managerial performance evaluations.[13] Managers at all levels in the organization are partially evaluated on their contributions to the company's gains in relative market share. Such gains, of course, also depend upon other strategic variables, such as product quality, innovation, pricing, and industry forces. Thus, changes in relative market share may serve as a strategic control gauge for both internal and external variables.

For instance, several years ago, Johnson & Johnson chose to extend its product line of baby shampoo, baby powder, and baby oil to mail-order educational toys. But after a decade, its annual toy sales had still not exceeded $25 million, a very small share of the gigantic toy market. In 1989, newly appointed chairman and CEO Ralph S. Larsen made the strategic decision to divest the toy business. As he stated, "If a business doesn't have a reasonable prospect of achieving leadership, we have a responsibility to exit it."[14]

For successful smaller businesses, relative market share serves as a strategic control barometer in another way. The discussion in Chapter 5 suggested that some businesses may strategically plan to maintain a low market share. In this event, the strategic control of market share may emphasize variables that do not promote market share growth. Such variables may include policies that encourage high prices and discourage sales events and price discounts. Empirical research has concluded that for certain companies in particular industries, emphasizing increases in relative market share is counterproductive.[15]

Strategic control actions for maintaining a small market share may include limiting the number of product/markets in which the company will compete. A small market share combined with operations in limited product/markets "enables a company to compete in ways that are unavailable to its larger rivals."[16]

IBM Finds It's Tough to Stay on Top

Even the world's premier corporations must continually monitor their environment and modify their operations if they are to stay in their enviable positions. One such company that took its eye off the ball during the late 1980s was IBM.

Long the world's dominant computer company, IBM virtually owned the large mainframe market and set the standards for personal computers during the 1980s. By the end of the decade, however, it was slipping rapidly. Although it still controlled 80 percent of the mainframe market, business customers were increasingly switching to the lower-cost, but equally sophisticated, workstations of Digital Equipment, Hewlett-Packard, and Sun Microsystems. (In fact, between 1975 and 1988, industrywide mainframe sales in dollars fell from 78 to 35 percent of total U.S. computer sales.) In the personal-computer industry, IBM was still the leader but was losing ground rapidly to such aggressive competitors as Compaq Computer. And in early 1990, it still had no laptop computer products.

Dramatic corrective action was instituted in late 1989: IBM phased out ten thousand jobs (through attrition and incentives), began cutting its prices by as much as 25 percent, slashed $2.3 billion from its earnings as a restructuring charge, and streamlined its decision-making processes. Many industry observers, however, felt that these actions were insufficient. Some criticized IBM for maintaining its no-layoff policy and recommended that up to fifty thousand employees be terminated. As one observer pointed out, IBM's ratio of overhead costs to revenues was over 30 percent, compared with the 15-to-17 percent range of such competitors as Fujitsu and Amdahl.

SOURCES: R. J. Samuelson, "The Future of Big Blue," *Newsweek,* 22 January 1990, p. 49; "IBM at $97: A Screaming Buy or a Sucker's Bet?" *Fortune,* 1 January 1990, pp. 26–27; J. Hammer and L. Rosado, "Big Blue Bites the Bullet," *Newsweek,* 18 December 1989, p. 48; J. W. Verity, "What's Ailing IBM? More Than This Year's Earnings," *Business Week,* 16 October 1989, pp. 75–86; P. B. Carroll, "Hurt by a Pricing War, IBM Plans a Writeoff and Cut of 10,000 Jobs," *The Wall Street Journal,* 6 December 1989.

EXERTING STRATEGIC CONTROL

Strategic control may be exerted in a number of different ways to ensure that the organization is performing in accordance with its mission, goals, and objectives. Some of the more important ways are presented in this section.

■ Control Through Multilevel Performance Criteria

Strategic control through **multilevel performance criteria** involves setting performance standards for individuals, functions, products, divisions, and strategic business units. In the first instance, controlling individual performance depends upon what the individual employee does. An office worker's performance might be monitored by measuring the number of orders processed per day; a factory worker's daily production could be evaluated; and a sales representative's monthly sales figures could be appraised. Some jobs, of course, are less subject to quantitative measurement. Examples include a research and development scientist, whose work might not show results for months or years; a corporate planner; and individuals who work in teams.

Control at the functional level may include controlling for the volume of production and defect rates incurred in the manufacturing function. In marketing, performance control might include evaluating sales volume and measuring the level of customer satisfaction through interviews or questionnaire surveys.

At the product, divisional, and strategic business unit levels, strategic control of performance may include evaluating productivity improvements, sales growth, and changes in market share. In a qualitative sense, performance control can also include judging how product, divisional, and strategic business unit executives cooperate with one another to attain synergy for the overall organization.

At all levels, from the individual to the strategic business unit, corrective action should be taken if actual performance is less than the standard that has been established. On the other hand, should performance in some area—such as a function, division, or strategic business unit—be far above the standard, management should attempt to ascertain the reasons for the excellent performance. In some cases, the methods that one unit is using to achieve above-standard performance can be transferred to other organizational units, thereby improving their performance as well.

■ Control Through Marketplace Performance

Control through marketplace performance can take place by monitoring the company's return on investment (ROI), return on equity (ROE), or other measures of profitability that were mentioned earlier. These evaluations take the form of comparisons vis-à-vis the performance of competitors in the marketplace. The PIMS program, of course, evaluates profitability in this manner. Growth in relative market share may also be evaluated for strategic control.

In addition to monitoring and evaluating the key areas discussed earlier in the chapter, top management monitors the price of the company's stock. Price fluctuations suggest how investors value the performance of the firm. Management is always very concerned over sharp price changes in the firm's stock. A sudden drop in price will make the firm a more attractive takeover target. Sharp increases often mean that an investor or group of investors is accumulating large blocks of stock to engineer a takeover or a change in top management. Hence, managers continuously monitor price changes in their firm's stock.

■ Control Through Organizational Variables

A final way that strategic control can be exerted is through organizational variables. Control can be effected directly through the formal organization or indirectly through the informal organization.

The Formal Organization

The **formal organization**—the management-specified structure of relationships and procedures used to manage organizational activity—can facilitate or impede the accomplishment of the enterprise's mission, goals, and objectives. As we have already seen, the formal organization determines who reports to whom, how jobs are grouped, and what rules and policies will guide the actions and decisions of employees. Chapter 7 illustrated, for instance, how an organization's structure can become outmoded and no longer appropriate for its mission. At such times, strategic control will dictate a change from, say, a functional structure to a product divisional structure. That change will have to be accompanied by appropriate modifications in organizational reward systems so that the new forms of required behavior will be rewarded and older, less appropriate behaviors will not be.

For example, some organizations that have changed from functional or product divisional structures to matrix structures have experienced considerable difficulty. Such a dramatic change cannot be accomplished overnight, yet some top managers have evidently believed that by drawing a new organization chart and explaining it to their employees, new appropriate behaviors would naturally follow. But they do not. Employees must understand the compelling reasons underlying the change to a matrix structure to divorce them from their old ways of behaving, and they must then be trained extensively in the new types of behaviors that will be required. After this groundwork is laid, the change to the matrix structure must be accompanied by a new organizational reward system that encourages teamwork, frequent reassignment of personnel, greater participation, and open communication. Concomitantly, it should discourage loyalty to a functional area and to one boss.

The importance of clearly communicating the organization's values to all employees and establishing a reward system that reinforces those values cannot be overemphasized. When management overlooks the key role that values and rewards play, or when the relationship among values, communication, and rewards is inconsistent, then informal organizational patterns develop to counterbalance the flaws and inconsistencies.

The Informal Organization

The **informal organization** refers to the interpersonal interactions that naturally evolve when individuals and groups come into contact with one another. These informal relationships can play destructive or constructive roles in helping the organization pursue its mission, goals, and objectives.

When it is obvious to everyone that what is valued by the organization is also what is actually rewarded, then the informal organization tends to promote the attainment of the organization's desired purposes. But when the organization's value system is ambiguous, or when inconsistencies exist between what is valued and what is rewarded, then the informal organization develops its own set of consistent values and rewards. For example, most organizations claim to reward high job performance. If, in fact, employees discern that most of the major promotions and pay raises actually go to individuals who have the greatest seniority, regardless of their level of performance, then this "informal value" is communicated throughout the organization. Managers' exhortations to perform better will be largely ignored by employees, because they realize that the formally touted value of high performance is vacuous.

The informal organization cannot be directly controlled by management. It can, however, be influenced indirectly by ensuring that the formal organization is consistent in the sense that it clearly communicates its values and then rewards behaviors that are compatible with those values. It may also be influenced through the informal behavior of managers.

STRATEGIC INSIGHT

Values Versus Rewards

Most businesses state publicly that high job performance is the basis for determining merit pay raises for their employees. This expectation for employee performance is often communicated throughout the organization. However, this stated value is at variance with reality in some companies. And the informal organization quickly realizes this discrepancy and discounts the importance of high job performance.

For instance, in 1989, the Hay Group, a consulting firm, reported that "outstanding workers" in 459 U.S. industrial firms received an average 7.7 percent pay increase, and "satisfactory performers" got 4.7 percent. A computer programmer making about $40,000 a year who was rated "outstanding" would, therefore, receive only about $17 to $20 a week (after taxes) more than an "average" programmer. It is unlikely that this amount would serve to reinforce high job performance.

Ira Kay, a managing director of compensation consulting for the Hay Group, recommends reducing or replacing the traditional fixed salary increase with performance-based rewards. He emphasizes that "rewards must be constructed to pay out significantly more than the typical merit increase if performance is high, and less than the typical merit increase if performance lags."

It is clear that many businesses are beginning to adopt such plans. Some firms no longer attempt to keep their employees even with inflation, preferring to base pay on actual performance. A Conference Board survey of 537 companies found that 82 percent of the businesses responding had at least some element of pay for performance. As a spokesperson for AT&T commented: "The days of incremental, plodding salary increases based on tenure, not talent, are gone."

Meaningful distinctions in pay increases between high job performers and those whose performance is low or merely average are likely to close the perceived gap between stated values and actual rewards.

SOURCES: M. Roman and W. Konrad, "You'll Probably Get a Raise—If You Keep Your Job," *Business Week*, 19 November 1990, p. 54 (source of second quotation); I. Kay, "Do Your Workers Really Merit a Raise?" *The Wall Street Journal*, 26 March 1990 (source of first quotation); S. Feinstein, "Labor Letter," *The Wall Street Journal*, 6 March 1990; A. R. Karr, "Labor Letter," *The Wall Street Journal*, 21 November 1989; N. J. Perry, "Here Comes Richer, Riskier Pay Plans," *Fortune*, 19 December 1988, pp. 50–58.

For instance, when managers interact with employees during the workday or off-hours, employees learn quickly if their ideas are solicited, respected, and taken seriously. Informal bonds of mutual trust and respect are translated into loyalty to the organization and to the supervisor.

Managers may also communicate informally simply through their behavior. One manager commented on his CEO's work schedule as follows:

> He was the first one in the office. His car was in the lot by 7:00 every morning, and he never left before 6 p.m. That told people a lot about what he expected from us.[17]

In another case, the owner-manager of an amusement park asks different employees to walk with him through the park during their breaks. As they walk, the manager smiles and greets customers. If there is litter on the grounds, he picks the trash up and deposits it into receptacles. If customers ask questions or appear to need directions, he assists them. The message is very clear: The owner-manager values a clean amusement park and a friendly, courteous, customer-oriented staff.

SUMMARY

Strategic control consists of determining the extent to which the company's strategies are successful in attaining its goals and objectives. If the goals and objectives are not being reached as planned, then the intent of control is to modify the enterprise's strategies and/or implementation so that the organization's ability to accomplish its goals will be improved. In strategic control, the focal time period usually ranges from a few years to over a decade; qualitative and quantitative measurements are taken; management assesses both internal operations and the external environment; and the process is continuous and ongoing.

On the basis of the organization's mission, goals, and objectives, top management selects what elements of the environment and of the organization need to be monitored, evaluated, and controlled. Then, standards are established to which the actual performance of the business will be compared. Next, management measures the company's actual performance—both quantitatively and qualitatively. If performance is in line with the standards or exceeds them, then no corrective action is necessary. However, if performance falls below the standards, then management must take remedial action.

The focus of strategic control is both internal and external. Top management's role is to align advantageously the internal operations of the business with its external environment. Hence, strategic control can be visualized as "mediating" the interactions between environmental variables (in both the macroenvironment and the industry environment) and the organization's internal operations.

Evaluating a company's performance may be accomplished in a number of ways. For instance, current operating results can be compared with results from the prior year, both quantitatively and qualitatively. However, management must also evaluate important external variables such as the performance of competitors. Several external comparison bases can be used, but chief among them are the focal company's relative product/service quality, its innovative ability to develop new products and services and improve its production and customer service delivery processes relative to those of its competitors, and its relative market share.

Strategic control can be exerted by top management in a number of different ways. First, management can control performance at several different levels—individual, functional, product, divisional, and strategic business unit. Control can also focus on marketplace performance through monitoring key financial ratios and changes in the firm's stock price. Finally, strategic control can be exerted directly through the formal organization by clear communication of the organization's values and a determination that the company's reward system is consistent with those values; and it can be exerted indirectly through the informal organization by appropriate managerial behavior.

KEY CONCEPTS

Formal organization   The management-specified structure of relationships and procedures used to manage organizational activity.

Informal organization   Interpersonal relationships and interactions that naturally evolve when individuals and groups come into contact with one another.

Multilevel performance criteria   Performance standards that are established for each of the following levels: individual employee, function, product line, division, strategic business unit, and organization.

PIMS program   A data base, termed the Profit Impact of Marketing Strategy (PIMS), that contains quantitative and qualitative information on the performance of more than three thousand business units.

Strategic control   Determining the extent to which an organization's strategies are successful in attaining its goals and objectives.

DISCUSSION QUESTIONS

1. Although strategic control and control in the more traditional budgetary sense are similar in some respects, they also differ significantly. Explain their similarities and differences.

2. What roles do the organization's mission, goals, and objectives play in strategic control?

3. Explain how strategic control mediates the interactions between the business's internal dimensions and its external environment.

4. In strategic control, management might compare the organization's performance this year with its performance in previous years. What are the strengths and weaknesses of this one comparison?

5. What is the PIMS program? How can it aid in strategic control?

6. "If a business unit's performance is below standard, corrective action should be taken. If its performance is above standard, no managerial action is necessary." True or false? Why?

7. What is the relationship between strategic control and changes in the firm's stock price?

8. How are organizational values and rewards related to strategic control?

9. Give an example from your own experience of a manager who communicated organizational values through his or her informal behavior.

STRATEGIC MANAGEMENT
EXERCISES

1. On the basis of your own perceptions as a consumer, compare the relative quality of two competing products (other than automobiles) or services that you have purchased. How might your perceptions be used by the manufacturers or sellers of these products/services in strategic control?

2. Over the past decade, the U.S.-based automobile companies have attempted to improve the quality of their cars relative to those of Japanese manufacturers. One way U.S. executives can exert strategic control is through comparing the quality of their cars with the quality of Japanese automobiles. Assume that you are a top-level manager with one of the U.S.-based car companies. Refer to a recent *Consumer Reports* issue that evaluates cars. Determine how the quality of the American company's car(s) compares with that of its Japanese rival(s). From your strategic control assessment, would you say that the American car company should take corrective action? Justify your answer.

3. Select a company of your choice. From library research, what source or sources of information can you obtain that may assist the management of that company in making strategic control decisions? Describe the source(s), the information contained, and how the information might be used by management for strategic control.

4. Select an airline company. Conduct library research on your chosen company so that you can elaborate on how strategic control has affected the direction of the company. Recall that strategic control consists of modifying a company's operations to maintain a compatible fit between the company and the changing environment.

REFERENCES

1. W. J. Bruns, Jr., and F. W. McFarlan, "Information Technology Puts Power in Control Systems," *Harvard Business Review* 65, no. 5 (September-October 1987): 89–94.

2. Bruns and McFarland, "Information Technology," p. 92.

3. T. A. Stewart, "Lessons from U.S. Business Blunders," *Fortune,* 23 April 1990, p. 128.

4. C. H. Springer, "Strategic Management in General Electric," *Operations Research* 21 (1973): 1177–1182.

5. R. D. Buzzell and B. T. Gale, *The PIMS Principles* (New York: Free Press, 1987).

6. J. M. Groocock, *The Chain of Quality* (New York: Wiley, 1986).

7. P. Wright, D. Hotard, J. Tanner, and M. Kroll, "Relationships of Select Variables with Business Performance of Diversified Corporations," *American Business Review* 6, no. 1 (January 1988): 71–77.

8. Buzzell and Gale, *The PIMS Principles,* Chap. 6.

9. Buzzell and Gale, *The PIMS Principles*, Chap. 6; P. Wright, M. Kroll, C. Pringle, and J. Johnson, "Organization Types, Conduct, Profitability, and Risk in the Semiconductor Industry," *Journal of Management Systems* 2, No. 2 (1990): 33–48.

10. R. Mitchell, "Masters of Innovation: How 3M Keeps Its New Products Coming," *Business Week*, 10 April 1989, p. 61.

11. R. Mitchell, "Masters of Innovation," pp. 58–63.

12. O. Port, "Back to Basics," *Business Week*, Special 1989 Bonus Issue, pp. 14–18.

13. Buzzell and Gale, *The PIMS Principles*, Chap. 5.

14. J. Weber and J. Carey, "No Band-Aids for Ralph Larsen," *Business Week*, 28 May 1990, p. 86.

15. W. E. Fruhan, Jr., "Pyrrhic Victories in Fights for Market Share," and R. G. Hamermesh, M. J. Anderson, and J. E. Harris, "Strategies for Low Market-share Businesses," in R. G. Hamermesh, ed., *Strategic Management* (New York: Wiley, 1983), pp. 112–125; 126–138.

16. Hamermesh, Anderson, and Harris, "Strategies for Low Market-share Businesses," p. 135.

17. J. Gabarro, "Socialization at the Top—How CEOs and Subordinates Evolve Interpersonal Contracts," *Organizational Dynamics* 7 (Winter 1979): 14.

STRATEGIC MANAGEMENT MODEL

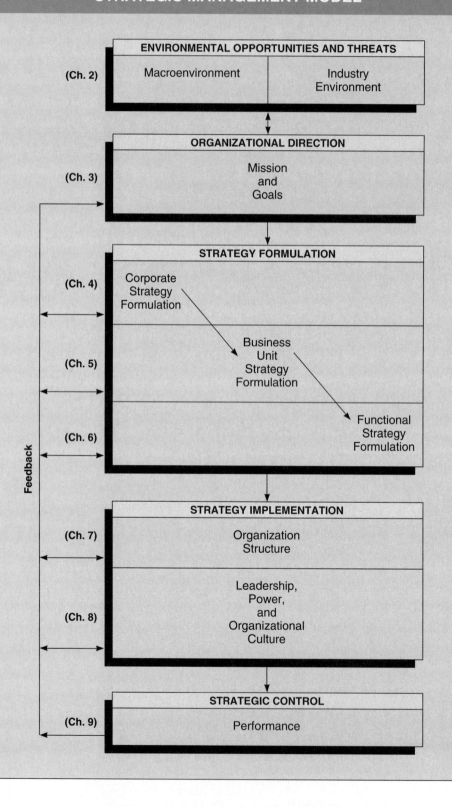

ENVIRONMENTAL OPPORTUNITIES AND THREATS

(Ch. 2)

| Macroenvironment | Industry Environment |

ORGANIZATIONAL DIRECTION

(Ch. 3)

Mission
and
Goals

STRATEGY FORMULATION

(Ch. 4) Corporate Strategy Formulation

(Ch. 5) Business Unit Strategy Formulation

(Ch. 6) Functional Strategy Formulation

STRATEGY IMPLEMENTATION

(Ch. 7) Organization Structure

(Ch. 8) Leadership, Power, and Organizational Culture

STRATEGIC CONTROL

(Ch. 9) Performance

Feedback

10

CHAPTER

Strategic Management and the World Marketplace

Few businesses based in the United States can escape the impact of foreign competition. Besides widely publicized international competition in such industries as automobiles, motorcycles, steel, tires, and watches, American-made goods also compete head to head in their home markets with foreign firms in product lines such as fans, luggage, outerwear, jewelry, musical instruments, dolls, hand tools, consumer electronics, sporting goods, zinc, blouses, suits, semiconductors, and shoes. Among the home bases of the 500 largest industrial corporations in the world, 32 countries are represented, including Zambia and Panama. U.S.-based corporations still dominate the list with 164 companies, followed by Japan with 111 and Britain with 43.[1] In select areas, the United States is no longer at the top. In banking, for instance, the United States places only 2 banks in the world's top 50; Japan accounts for 20, Germany has 8, and 6 are based in France.[2]

Even though a company may choose to operate only within a confined local area, that choice does not exempt the business from foreign competition. Foreign firms conduct business in virtually every industry represented in the United States. Some American-based businesses, of course, choose to operate in other countries through one or more of the ways that this chapter discusses. But in any case, virtually every top manager must have an understanding of the issues involved in international strategic management.

OVERVIEW OF INTERNATIONAL OPERATIONS

This chapter focuses primarily on businesses that choose to operate internationally. This involvement may range from limited activities such as purchasing from foreign sources or exporting to a foreign market to operating throughout the world as if there were no national boundaries. To give you some idea of the

Table 10.1	Selected Statistics on U.S. Exports and Imports (in millions of dollars)				
Category	1970	1975	1980	1985	1988
Exports of U.S. merchandise	42,590	106,561	216,668	206,925	308,014
Imports of U.S. merchandise	39,952	96,573	244,871	345,276	441,282
Selected Products					
U.S. food exports	4,356	15,484	27,744	19,268	26,415
U.S. imports	5,375	8,503	15,766	18,649	20,107
U.S. petroleum exports	488	908	2,833	4,707	3,679
U.S. imports	2,764	24,814	77,637	49,607	38,175
U.S. pharmaceutical product exports	420	866	1,932	2,708	3,941
U.S. imports	87	235	509	1,084	1,859
U.S. aircraft and parts exports	2,656	6,136	12,816	14,373	20,004
U.S. imports	274	519	1,885	3,578	5,168
U.S. tire exports	186	544	511	343	772
U.S. imports	205	475	1,143	1,923	2,448
U.S. iron and steel exports	1,185	2,382	2,998	1,152	2,017
U.S. imports	1,952	4,037	6,692	10,226	10,274
U.S. automobile exports	822	2,852	3,919	6,020	8,312
U.S. imports	3,722	7,124	16,776	36,475	47,005
U.S. clothing exports	198	403	832	754	1,556
U.S. imports	1,269	2,562	6,430	14,949	21,518
U.S. professional, scientific, and controlling instruments exports	857	1,792	5,256	6,505	8,889
U.S. imports	356	726	2,654	3,211	5,174

Source: *Statistical Abstract of the United States, 1990* (U.S. Department of Commerce, Bureau of the Census), pp. 811–814.

magnitude of international trade, we list some selected statistics on U.S. exports and imports in Table 10.1.

Ordinarily, international operations evolve gradually. Most enterprises begin their involvement with foreign countries through importing or exporting products. If particular sites overseas possess attractive resources or markets, a business may become further involved through licensing select organizations in those countries to use its technology, production processes, or brand name. Alternatively, the enterprise may enter into partnerships or joint ventures with foreign companies as a means of penetrating certain markets. Gradually, the company may become more deeply involved by initiating direct investments in select countries. Such investments may include the company's starting its own operations abroad or buying portions or all of the ownership of foreign-based organizations. U.S. and foreign direct investments are shown in Table 10.2.

In this chapter, business operations will be considered on three levels: international, multinational, and global. **International businesses** are those that are minimally or moderately involved in foreign operations. They may purchase from foreign companies, export to other nations, enter into licensing agreements with foreign-based organizations, or conduct joint ventures with foreign firms. **Multinational organizations** are companies that are heavily involved in over-

U.S. and Foreign Direct Investment (in millions of dollars)   **Table 10.2**

Year	U.S. Direct Investment Abroad	Foreign Direct Investment in the United States	Largest Targets of U.S. Direct Investments		Largest Foreign Direct Investors in the United States	
1960	31.9	6.9	1. Canada	61.2	1. United Kingdom	101.9
1965	49.5	8.8	2. United Kingdom	48.0	2. Japan	53.4
1970	75.5	13.3	3. West Germany	21.7	3. Netherlands	49.0
1975	124.1	27.7	4. Bermuda	19.9	4. Canada	27.4
1980	215.4	83.0	5. Bahrain	18.9	5. West Germany	23.8
1985	230.3	184.6				
1988	326.9	328.9				

Source: *Statistical Abstract of the United States, 1990* (U.S. Department of Commerce, Bureau of the Census), pp. 794–797; *Statistical Abstract of the United States, 1981*, p. 834.

Direct investment refers to investors in one country owning at least 10 percent of a private enterprise in another country.

seas operations through direct investments abroad. They function on a country-by-country basis, with their subsidiaries operating independently of each other. **Global firms** are also heavily involved in foreign business and have made direct investments overseas, but their subsidiaries operate interdependently. These distinctions are summarized in Table 10.3. Further elaborations on these differing levels of involvement are made in many of the following sections of this chapter. We begin with an examination of the international macroenvironment.

Varying Levels of International Operations   **Table 10.3**

Organization	Level of International Involvement
Domestic organization	Chooses to operate totally within the confines of the United States.
International organization	Elects minimal or moderate international involvement. May purchase from foreign sources, export to other countries, license operations to foreign firms, or enter into joint ventures with foreign-based companies.
Multinational organization	Chooses heavy international involvement. Makes direct investments abroad through starting its own operations in other countries or buying part or all of the ownership of foreign-based firms. Subsidiaries operate independently of one another on a country-by-country basis.
Global organization	Elects heavy international involvement. Makes direct investments abroad through starting its own operations in other countries or buying part or all of the ownership of foreign-based firms. Subsidiaries operate interdependently as a single, coordinated system.

MACROENVIRONMENT

As an organization's environment expands from domestic to international, management faces not only a larger number of environmental elements but also far greater environmental complexity. Chapter 2 suggested how certain macroenvironmental forces have strategic implications for top management. This section follows that same format but concentrates upon international forces in the macroenvironment: political-legal forces, economic forces, technological forces, and social forces.

■ Political-Legal Forces

All nations have their own particular laws and regulations that affect business activities. Some countries, for example, have rigid guidelines for hiring and firing employees; some require that a certain percentage of those employed by a foreign-owned business be citizens of the country in which the business operates; and some require that a portion of what is produced within their boundaries be exported in order to earn foreign exchange. These laws and regulations that are particular to each nation offer opportunities or pose threats to the business interested in operating across national boundaries. At times, the degree of opportunity or threat is influenced by major world political-legal trends, as discussed in the following subsections.

Trends from World War II to the Early 1980s

The years between the end of World War II and the early 1980s can be characterized as a period during which the predominant political-legal trend was for the governments of industrialized countries to exert more influence over business operations. This trend was exhibited by governments in such countries as Great Britain, France, West Germany, Italy, Canada, and Japan. In some cases, governments even owned major manufacturers. For instance, Great Britain owned Jaguar and British Leyland, and West Germany owned Lufthansa. In France, the socialist government of Prime Minister François Mitterand nationalized some major firms such as ITT-France and Honeywell-Bull in 1981. And Canadian legislation was passed requiring that energy companies operating within the borders of Canada be owned by Canadians.

This same trend also characterized the operations of businesses in less industrialized parts of the world. Communist governments, of course, permitted little, if any, free enterprise, preferring to run their economies through centralized state planning. In developing nations, key industries such as utilities, communications, steel, and raw materials extraction were generally owned by the government.

A second political-legal trend during this time period involved increased trade protection. Many countries increased the protection of their domestic industries through tariffs, import duties, and import restrictions. For example, in Latin American countries, import duties on a variety of products ranged from under 40 percent to more than 100 percent.[3] European and Southeast Asian nations also imposed heavy duties on imports. Even the United States imposed import fees on a variety of products, including food, steel, and cars. Furthermore, the United States convinced Japanese manufacturers to restrict "voluntar-

STRATEGIC INSIGHT

Entering the Japanese Auto Market

Much has been made of the barriers erected by the Japanese government to prevent foreign-made automobiles from being sold in Japan. And, in truth, many barriers exist. But aggressive automakers seem to find ways to compete on Japanese soil.

BMW, for example, viewed Japan as a growth market as early as a decade ago. It was able to penetrate the market by adapting its models to Japanese regulations and consumer needs, offering extended warranties, investing heavily in service facilities and parts inventories, conducting its own training for Japanese mechanics, and supervising its operations closely. Its commitment was unwavering; analysts estimated that BMW paid almost half a billion dollars alone for choice real estate on which to build showrooms in Tokyo. By 1990, BMW had 120 outlets in Japan and sold over 33,000 cars there.

Other German companies, such as Volkswagen, Mercedes, and Audi, were following suit. The result? In 1990, about two-thirds of the foreign cars registered in Japan were made in Germany. Other European countries—particularly Range Rover, Peugeot, and Volvo—accounted for another 20 percent of the Japanese import market. By contrast, American automobile makers held only about 10 percent of the market, and that figure included 5000 Hondas manufactured in the United States and shipped to Japan for sale.

The Germans' aggressive move into Japan could pay off for years to come. Japan is the world's second-largest automobile market, and Japanese car buyers have exhibited extreme brand loyalty. In fact, some analysts estimate that almost 70 percent of them buy from the same company—and often even from the same salesperson—every time they purchase a new car.

SOURCES: T. R. Reid, "U.S. Automakers Grind Gears in Japan," *The Washington Post,* 23 September 1990; "Roger Smith Reflects on Role at GM," *The Wall Street Journal,* 31 July 1990; B. Powell, "Saying 'Sayonara' to Japan," *Newsweek,* 26 March 1990, p. 37; C. Rapoport, "You Can Make Money in Japan," *Fortune,* 12 February 1990, p. 92; B. Yates, "The Road to Mediocrity," *The Washington Post Magazine,* 17 December 1989, p. 35; M. Berger, "How Germany Sells Cars Where Detroit Can't," *Business Week,* 9 September 1985, p. 45.

ily" their exporting of cars to the United States. Likewise, European countries instituted import quotas on selected products such as Japanese stereos and watches.

Protectionist measures did not only involve the protection of home industries from foreign imports. Restrictions were also placed on exporting advanced technology to other countries. The United States, for instance, banned the export of certain electronic, nuclear, and defense-related products to many nations.

There were, of course, countervailing trends. To offset the impact of some of the protectionist measures, twenty-three countries entered into the cooperative General Agreement on Tariffs and Trade (GATT) in 1947. GATT has assisted in eradicating or relaxing quota and import license requirements, introducing fairer customs evaluation methods, opposing discriminatory internal taxes, and serving as a mediator between governments on trade issues. GATT membership has now reached ninety-five nations.

Another move in lessening trade restrictions was the European Economic Community. Beginning in 1992, all trade restrictions were abolished among the twelve-member Western European nations.

Trends Since the Early 1980s

By the middle to late 1980s, however, trends toward the reversal of trade protectionism and strong governmental influence in business operations were becoming evident. In the United States, the economic policies of the Reagan administration reduced, on the whole, governmental influence in business operations by deregulating certain industries, lowering corporate taxes, granting more generous depreciation allowances, and relaxing rules against mergers and acquisitions. A similar trend was evident in Prime Minister Margaret Thatcher's government in Great Britain. Jaguar, for instance, was sold to individual investors (and later purchased by Ford Motor Company), as was British Telecom. As the trend spread, France's insurance industry and previously nationalized banks and manufacturing businesses were sold to investors.

The trend even extended to communist countries. Many of the countries of Eastern Europe overturned their governments and began to permit free-enterprise operations and to invite foreign investment in their economies. Even the Soviet Union rejected communism and derailed a coup in August 1991 that sought to replace the progressive leaders, Gorbachev and Yeltsin, with hard core communist leaders. As a result of these developments, numerous firms, including those based in the United States, have found a more receptive political-legal climate throughout much of the world.

■ Economic Forces

Common economic indicators such as gross national product (GNP) can suggest opportunities for businesses when an economy is expanding or, conversely, can warn of threats when the economy is contracting. But the most challenging international economic variables for strategic planners are interest rates, inflation rates, and currency exchange rates.

For example, the cost of borrowing is very high in a number of Latin American countries. Annual interest rates can exceed 100 percent. High interest rates are often accompanied by excessive rates of inflation. In small nations, like Bolivia, annual inflation has been as high as 26,000 percent![4] But even larger and more industrialized countries, like Brazil, have experienced annual inflation rates of 2700 percent.[5] Such common decisions as pricing products or estimating costs become almost impossible to make under such conditions. Furthermore, high inflation rates cause the prices of goods and services to rise and, hence, become less competitive in international trade.

Currency exchange rates present challenges because of their dramatic changes over time. For instance, the Mexican peso was devalued by about 75 percent relative to the world's major currencies during the 1980s. Since U.S. firms operating in Mexico received pesos for their products and services, their pesos would buy far fewer dollars than before the devaluation. The devaluation, therefore, reduced their profits considerably.

■ Technological Forces

Technology has a major impact on international business operations. For years, manufacturing firms in technologically advanced societies have sought plant location sites in countries with low labor or raw materials costs. Developing nations have generally welcomed such entrants. With them come an influx of financial resources, the opportunity for work force training, and the chance to acquire new technologies. In many cases, this interaction has benefited the developing country. Furthermore, some observers have even predicted that production technologies will be transferred from more advanced countries to such newly industrializing nations as Mexico, Brazil, Spain, Taiwan, Hong Kong, Singapore, and South Korea.[6] (In this chapter, the term **technologically advanced nations** is used to refer to the United States, Canada, Japan, Australia, New Zealand, and the major industrial powers of Europe. The term **newly industrializing nations** refers to developing nations that have experienced rapid industrial growth over the past two decades. They are identified in the above paragraph. **Developing nations** is the term employed to refer to countries that have not yet experienced significant industrial development and includes any country not grouped under the two other categories.)

However, the experiences of other developing nations have been quite disappointing. Although the firm's decision to operate in a foreign country is made for economic reasons, the host country often expects—but does not necessarily get—specific economic and social help in the form of assistance to local entrepreneurs, the establishment of research and development facilities, and the introduction of products relevant to its home market.[7] Such relationships do provide on-the-job training and improve the local economy, but the overall long-term contribution to the host country is questionable in the minds of some leaders of developing nations.[8]

Among the disappointments have been the results of technology transfer from the foreign firm to the host country:

> For example, firms such as Leyland Motors, General Electric, and Daimler Benz have structured plants in various [developing nations]. The basic problem has continued to be the almost total dependence of the host countries on the multinationals for the provision of parts, motors, and product innovations.[9]

However, technology transfer is not the only source of disappointment for host countries. Their leaders also point to discontent with extractive industries:

> Whatever the raw material, it is argued, the nature of extractive industry constitutes a systematic depletion of the valuable national assets of the host country, while leaving little of enduring value. . . . All the training and technological transfer of this kind are highly specific to the nature of the industry. When bauxite, coal, and other ores are exhausted, the local people's gained knowledge can rarely be transferred to other national undertakings.[10]

Within this context, some of the leaders of developing nations have acquired negative attitudes toward foreign firms. Nevertheless, these countries will continue to need the expertise of the technologically advanced nations. The key is for each party—the company and the host country—to develop an understanding of the wants and needs of the other. In an economic and technological sense, both parties need each other, and both can benefit significantly from a successful relationship.

■ Social Forces

Each of the world's countries has its own distinctive **culture**—that is, its generally accepted values, traditions, and patterns of behavior. Not surprisingly, these cultural differences interfere with the efforts of managers to understand

and communicate with those in other societies. The unconscious reference to one's own cultural values—the **self-reference criterion**—has been suggested as the cause of most international business problems. Individuals become so accustomed to their own ways of looking at the world that they believe that any deviation from their perspective is not only wrong but also, perhaps, incomprehensible. But companies that can adjust to the culture of a host country will usually have the competitive edge. For instance, by adapting to local tastes rather than rigidly adhering to those of its U.S. customers, Domino's has found profitable business overseas through selling tuna and sweet corn pizzas in Japan and prawn and pineapple pizzas to Australians.[11]

Culture strongly influences the values that individuals hold. In turn, values influence the goals that individuals and organizations in a particular society set for themselves. The goals of managers in firms from technologically advanced countries, therefore, are likely to clash with the goals of the leaders of developing nations:

> On a macro-level, incongruencies in values have resulted in a major controversy over whether business unit goals should be influenced by market forces or by political priorities. The leaders of the multinationals have argued for market conditions influencing business decisions, whereas the developing nations have primarily sought corporate undertakings which benefit long-term social programs as well as business decisions which boost local employment.[12]

As an example, consider the differences in goals between the French automobile manufacturer, Peugeot, and the government of Nigeria. Peugeot operated a large automobile assembly plant in Nigeria. Because the port of Lagos was not being utilized as fully as the Nigerian government wanted, it required Peugeot to import all needed components and supplies for its Nigerian assembly plant through that port. Under this shipping plan, the parts and supplies had to be trucked across 500 miles of bad road to reach the plant. Not only was this requirement time-consuming and unreliable, it was also more expensive than the previously employed daily cargo flights from France direct to the plant.[13]

On a micro level, managers of firms from technologically advanced nations often hold goals that are based on valuing mass production and efficient operations. However, mass production assumes certain worker-machine ratios, and efficient operations require particular worker-machine interfaces. Thus, these managers may demand behavior from local personnel that gives priority to productivity. The local employees, however, may resist these demands because they believe, on the basis of their own values, that business decisions should be secondary to social and religious norms. For instance, in some countries, it is customary to take a nap after lunch. In others, religious requirements call for taking several breaks during the workday to pray.[14]

It is clear that cross-cultural differences in norms and values require modifications in managerial behaviors:

> Doing business abroad often requires a great deal of patience and perseverance. In America, "getting down to business" and being efficient in pursuing and attempting to close sales agreements are considered desirable. . . . The U.S. businessperson is seen as displaying perseverance by quickly moving on to the next potential customer rather than by patiently pursuing an uninterested prospect. . . . Perseverance takes on a different connotation overseas. Whereas the American persists in

certain large markets to make sales, successful foreign businesspersons are tenacious with select customers within those markets.[15]

In some countries, making the first business deal may take months or even years. The reason is that until personal friendships and trust develop between the potential buyer and seller, the people of those countries are unwilling to commit themselves to major business transactions.[16] After the first breakthrough, however, business transactions may become routine.

Differences in social norms and languages can present opportunities or pose constraints. For instance, Mr. Donut shops are well accepted in Japan, even though the concept of "coffee and doughnuts" is not a Japanese custom. Perceived mainly as a fast-food breakfast outlet in the United States, Mr. Donut is viewed by the Japanese as a snack-food stop. Hence, the differences in norms, rather than posing a constraint to Mr. Donut, have served as an opportunity.

Social norms that are not well understood by outsiders often constrain business transactions. For instance, Japanese business executives expect their clients or suppliers to interact socially with them after working hours. These interactions can consume up to three or four hours an evening, several times a week. Westerners who decline to attend such social gatherings regularly are seriously handicapped in transacting business, because these social settings are requirements for serious business relationships.

STRATEGIC INSIGHT

 Tips for Doing Business in Asia

- Dress appropriately—men in traditional business suits and women in plain dresses or conservative suits.
- Realize that the Japanese rarely express negative emotions to foreigners. Hence, you can misread their intentions because they may smile even when angry.
- Exchange business cards with your hosts. Bilingual cards are especially appreciated. Show respect by carefully reading each card you receive.
- Control your physical gestures: Don't backslap, pat heads, or cross your legs. Even using your hands may make Japanese executives uncomfortable.
- Avoid jokes and conversation about politics.

- Always eat a bit of whatever food is offered; but never completely clean your plate, or you will be perceived as still being hungry.
- Avoid giving flowers, since the wrong color or type can insult the recipient.
- Do not call on a company without an introduction. In Japan, particularly, meetings are taken very seriously.
- Bring an interpreter to a meeting.
- Never bring your company's lawyer to a meeting before a deal is closed. Business relationships should be built on trust.
- Never brag—not even about your family. The Japanese, for instance, tend to be humble, even about their children's accomplishments.

SOURCES: A. B. Stoddard, "Learning the Cultural Tricks of Foreign Trade," *Washington Business*, 18 June 1990, p. 11; F. H. Katayama, "How to Act Once You Get There," *Fortune, Special Issue: Asia in the 1990s*, Fall 1989, pp. 87–88; T. Holden and S. Woolley, "The Delicate Art of Doing Business in Japan," *Business Week*, 2 October 1989, p. 120.

Of course, differences in language can also present challenges. Sometimes, seemingly unimportant variations lead to major blunders in international business.[17] For instance, Pepsi's "Come Alive" advertisement, effective in the United States, translated into the German language as "coming alive after death." General Motors, attempting to sell its Chevrolet Nova in Mexico, realized too late that "Nova" conveyed the meaning in Spanish that "it does not go."

INDUSTRY ENVIRONMENT

The nature of industry competition in the international arena differs from one country to the next. In some nations, competing successfully may not necessarily depend on such familiar American concepts as pricing, bargaining power, the threat of new entrants, or substitute products. Rather, engaging in competition may only be possible if the company is willing to barter by trading the firm's products and services for goods from the host country. A number of Japanese companies, as an example, trade their products for oil in some markets of the Organization of Petroleum Exporting Countries (OPEC).

The industry environment is complicated by the potential for linkages between domestic and international competitive forces. For instance, when a strong overseas competitor enters the domestic market of a firm, the firm's most effective response may be to counter its foreign competitor's move by entering its domestic market:

> Effective counter-competition has a destabilizing impact on the foreign company's cash flows, product-related competitiveness, and decision making about integration. Direct market penetration can drain vital cash flows from the foreign company's domestic operations. This drain can result in lost opportunities, reduced income, and limited production, impairing the competitor's ability to make overseas thrusts.[18]

From a global perspective, industry analysis can be quite challenging. A firm, for instance, may produce its parts in one nation, assemble them in other countries, and sell the final product to another group of nations. As an example, RCA has located its business units in such diverse countries as Taiwan, Japan, Mexico, and Canada. The operations of these business units are coordinated with those of other RCA units located in the United States. Each business unit performs complementary manufacturing or support functions. Hence, one unit may manufacture components; others may perform subassembly work, warehousing, or distribution. Each business unit is an integral link in the overall strategy of RCA's world operations.[19] As might be expected, such industry forces as market position, bargaining power of suppliers and customers, and the threat of new entrants or substitute products have different ramifications for each of RCA's business units, even though, in unison, these units produce television sets.

MISSION, GOALS, AND OBJECTIVES

An organization's mission, the reason for its existence, may be closely intertwined with international operations in several ways. For instance, a firm may have the need for inputs from abroad. Wrigley, the chewing gum manufacturer, would be unable to produce its products without the gum base derived from trees in Southeast Asia. Virtually all of Japan's industries would come to a standstill if imports of raw materials from other nations were halted, since Japan's natural resources are quite limited.

Organizational mission and international involvement are also connected through the economic concept of **comparative advantage.** This concept refers to the idea that certain parts and products may be produced more cheaply or with higher quality in particular countries owing to advantages in labor costs or technology. Also, certain raw materials and natural resources may be extracted more economically in particular locales. For instance, the cost of drilling for oil is significantly lower and its availability is significantly greater in Saudi Arabia than in Europe. Since oil is the basic raw material for producing many chemical products, European chemical firms have sought joint ventures with oil companies in Saudi Arabia. For this reason, Japanese chemical companies are not major world competitors. Japan has no oil, and Japanese chemical firms have, to date, been unsuccessful in arranging joint ventures with firms in oil-producing countries.

Finally, some firms' missions require international connections for prestige reasons. The attempt to surround a perfume product, for instance, with a certain "mystique" seems to necessitate New York, London, and Paris connections. You may have noticed that the more prestigious brands of cosmetics and perfumes often have "New York, London, and Paris" conspicuously inscribed on their packages.

A firm's goals and objectives may also require global involvement. To reduce costs, for example, a firm may seek production sites in foreign countries. Or for political-legal reasons, organizations may need to locate manufacturing facilities abroad. For instance, the Japanese carmakers established goals and objectives requiring significant increases in sales volumes in the United States. When the U.S. government encouraged these firms "voluntarily" to restrict their exports to the U.S. market, they reacted by building plants in America. In this way, they were able to attain their goals and objectives relating to increased U.S. sales. By 1990, over a million Japanese cars were produced in the United States, compared with about one thousand in 1982.[20]

CORPORATE-LEVEL STRATEGIES

In Chapter 4, we saw that firms have available to them several corporate-level strategies: growth, stability, retrenchment, or a combination of these. Using growth strategies, many firms attempt to gain market share to reduce their unit costs of operations. Large increases in sales are sometimes only available through global expansion. Coca-Cola and PepsiCo realized many years ago that significant increases in sales were more likely to be achieved overseas rather than in the already saturated U.S. marketplace.

Likewise, Caterpillar has become the world's leading construction equipment maker because of its global involvement.[21]

> Two-thirds of the total product cost of construction equipment is in heavy components—engines, axles, transmissions, and hydraulics—whose manufacturing costs are capital intensive and highly sensitive to economies of scale. Caterpillar turned its network of sales in different countries into a cost advantage by designing product lines that use identical components and investing heavily in a few large-scale, state-of-the-art component manufacturing facilities to fill worldwide demand.[22]

Joint Ventures: A Popular Way to Enter Foreign Markets

Increasingly, American companies are looking to joint ventures as efficient ways to enter foreign markets. In the decade of the 1980s, for instance, U.S.-based firms formed over 2000 joint ventures with European companies and 365 with firms in the Soviet Union alone. Additionally, such companies as Occidental Petroleum, Atlantic Richfield, Texaco, Xerox, and Coca-Cola have engaged in joint ventures with firms in China since the mid-1980s.

Why the popularity of joint ventures? Both partners often hope to achieve several ends: lowering the costs (and the risks) of high-technology product development, increasing sales so that greater economies of scale may be attained, broadening a firm's product line by joining with a company that makes complementary products, and gaining a lookout post so that other competitors' moves may be more easily tracked.

Louis Kraar describes a joint venture as "a marriage." The relationship thrives on compatibility and trust; jealousy can damage it (many partners are polygamous, that is, have several partners); and the divorce rate is high.

Texas Instruments' Ventures with Hitachi and Kobe Steel

Some start in odd ways. Texas Instruments sued Hitachi for patent infringement in 1986. In the course of the legal proceedings, the two firms came to have a better understanding of each other's technology—and a growing respect for the other's capability. The result was a joint venture between the two to develop a 16-megabit DRAM (dynamic random access memory) chip. Texas Instruments then formed another joint venture with Japan's Kobe Steel to build a world-class factory to produce the chips.

Chrysler's AMC Venture with Beijing Automotive Works

Of course, some joint ventures end in failure. After four years of on-again and off-again negotiations, American Motors Corporation (AMC), now a subsidiary of Chrysler, and the Chinese-owned Beijing Automotive Works jointly agreed to produce Jeeps. China offered not only a huge market but also low labor costs and an excellent location for exporting to all of Asia. AMC investors responded to news of the joint venture by pushing AMC's stock price up by 40 percent in two weeks.

But problems arose quickly. Most fundamentally, the two partners could never agree on the nature of the Jeep to be produced. And AMC learned too late that it did not have the right to convert its Chinese earnings into dollars—meaning that the venture often did not have enough hard currency to buy parts from Detroit, because most of its output was sold inside China. As the shaky partnership continued, American managers learned that Beijing Automotive Works was hoarding proceeds from Chinese sales at about the same time that China announced a hefty increase in duties on parts kits imported from Detroit. Shortly thereafter, in June 1989, the Chinese government's repression of the Tiananmen Square demonstrators convinced AMC officials to depart from the country, leaving the Chinese to run the assembly line on their own.

SOURCES: P. A. Langan, "The New Look of Globalization," *Fortune,* 23 April 1990, p. 18; O. Port, "Why Texas Instruments and Kobe Make a Nice Couple," *Business Week,* 2 April 1990, p. 87; P. Galuszka and R. Brady, "The Chill Is Gone, and U.S. Companies Are Moscow-Bound," *Business Week,* 5 June 1989, p. 64; "Top American Joint Venture Investments in China," *The Washington Post,* 28 May 1989; L. Kraar, "Your Rivals Can Be Your Allies," *Fortune,* 27 March 1989, pp. 66–76; J. Mann, *Beijing Jeep* (New York: Simon & Schuster, 1990).

Corporate growth strategies may include joint ventures, license agreements, or direct investments. **International joint ventures** are partnerships of two or more firms from different nations who join together to accomplish specific projects or to cooperate in select areas of business. One of the best-known examples of an international joint venture is the automobile production facility in California that is owned jointly by General Motors and Toyota.

An **international license agreement** is the granting of permission by a firm in one country to a company in another nation to use its technology, brand name, production processes, or other operations. A fee is paid to the granting firm by the company being licensed. For example, pharmaceutical firms such as Merck and Upjohn have licensed organizations in other parts of the world to produce and sell their brands of drugs.

Direct investments may take place in one of two ways. A firm may engage in internal growth by establishing physical facilities and operations in another country. Many well-known companies, such as IBM and Citicorp, pursue this route. Alternatively, a company may grow externally by purchasing all or part of the ownership of a foreign firm. For example, Electrolux of Sweden purchased U.S.-based Poulan/Weedeater. The motivation for purchasing a foreign company may include integrating vertically or horizontally or becoming more diversified.

Stability is a corporate strategy that a firm adopts when its goal is to maintain its current size and scope of operations in the world. Such a strategy obviously would not include engaging in new joint ventures, license agreements, or direct investments.

When a firm's performance is disappointing, a corporate retrenchment strategy may be necessary. Retrenchment may involve revising products/markets in particular nations, pruning assets and work forces in other locations, selling or spinning off parts of world operations, selling the entire business, or—in the worst-case scenario—liquidating the whole corporation. Firestone, for instance, attempted to reverse its poor performance in the early 1980s by selling its operations in five foreign countries and reducing its ownership to a minority position in other foreign subsidiaries. Eventually, however, Firestone was sold to Bridgestone, a Japanese-based competitor.[23]

The following subsection examines how management can analyze the organization's strengths and weaknesses and the environment's opportunities and threats on an international scale. Then we look at the extent to which individual organizations can become involved in overseas business.

■ International S.W.O.T. Analysis

In determining corporate-level strategies, top management must evaluate the firm's strengths and weaknesses and the international environment's opportunities and threats. In the first part of the S.W.O.T. analysis (i.e., strengths, weaknesses, opportunities, and threats), management can use the following questions as guidelines in evaluating the company's strengths and weaknesses:

- Does the firm have a strong market position in the countries in which it operates?
- Does the firm's product/service quality compare favorably with that of its world competitors?
- Does the firm have a technological advantage in the world regions where it operates its major businesses?
- Does the firm have a strong brand reputation in the countries in which it sells its products/services?
- Are the firm's managers and employees more talented than those of its major world competitors?

- Does the firm's financial profile compare favorably with the industry's?
- Is the firm consistently more profitable than its world rivals?
- Are the firm's product and process R&D efforts likely to produce better results than its competitors'?
- Are the firm's various world operations subject to unionization?

Answers to these questions may serve as a basis for evaluating the firm's strengths and weaknesses relative to those of its competitors.

The following questions can guide management's thinking about the opportunities and threats that exist in the firm's external environment:

- What threats and opportunities do political-legal forces present?
- What threats and opportunities are presented by economic forces?
- What threats and opportunities do technological forces present?
- What threats and opportunities are presented by social forces?
- What is the size of the industry?
- What are the growth rate and growth potential of the industry?
- Is the industry cyclical? If so, can the cyclicality be smoothed out across different world markets?
- Is the industry subject to fluctuations in demand because of seasonal factors? If so, can these seasonal factors be smoothed out across different world markets?
- How intense is world competition in the industry?
- What is the median industry profitability? What is its potential profitability?
- Is the industry susceptible to unionization?
- What is the rate of innovation in the industry?

■ Level of Operations and Market Share

As we saw earlier in this chapter, a business may be involved only in its domestic market or it may compete overseas at one of three levels: international, multinational, or global. Within the domestic, international, or multinational context, an enterprise may compete successfully with a high or low market share. However, firms that choose to compete at the global level usually operate effectively only through maintaining a high market share. The relationship between level of operations and market share is illustrated in Figure 10.1.

Some businesses may be involved only in their domestic market. In certain cases, they may not yet be subject to foreign competitive pressures. Some realty companies that compete only in local towns serve as examples. On a national basis, these companies operate with very small market shares. Other competitors, such as Century 21, sell real estate nationwide and have large market shares.

Moving outside the domestic market, some companies choose to be involved on an international basis. They operate in various countries but limit their involvement to importing, exporting, licensing, or joint ventures. For example, Rolls-Royce exports its automobiles from England to other countries, and it has a small worldwide market share.

Still other companies are involved multinationally. They have direct investments in other countries, and their subsidiaries operate independently of one another. As an example, Colgate-Palmolive has attained a large worldwide mar-

Competing Domestically, Internationally, Multinationally, Globally, and Market Share Goals

Figure 10.1

LEVEL OF OPERATIONS

		Domestic Organizations	International Organizations	Multinational Organizations	Global Organizations
MARKET SHARE GOALS	High	Domestic, high share	International, high share	Multinational, high share	Global, high share
	Low	Domestic, low share	International, low share	Multinational, low share	

ket share through its decentralized operations in a number of foreign markets.

Finally, some firms are globally involved. They have direct investments abroad and operate their subsidiaries interdependently. Caterpillar is an example of such a firm. Some of its various world subsidiaries produce components in different countries, other subsidiaries assemble these components, and still other units sell the finished products. Caterpillar has achieved its low-cost position by producing its own heavy components for its large global market. If its various subsidiaries operated independently and only produced for their individual regional markets, Caterpillar would be unable to realize economies of scale.

Global firms must attempt to gain a high market share. Coordinating an interdependent global system is extremely complex, and this complexity—and expense—can only be justified when a high market share is attainable and it is feasible to coordinate the operations of multiple subsidiaries.

BUSINESS UNIT AND FUNCTIONAL STRATEGIES

Business units may adopt any one of a number of generic strategies, as discussed in Chapter 5. If low market share is the business unit's goal, then management may choose from among the strategies of niche–low-cost, niche–differentiation, or niche–low-cost/differentiation. These strategies are appropriate for domestic, international, and multinational enterprises. For instance, Rolls-Royce, an international company, uses the niche-differentiation strategy. It maintains a small market share internationally by selling its cars only to very wealthy buyers in particular nations.

On the other hand, if the goal of a business unit is to attain a large market share, it has available the low-cost, differentiation, low-cost–differentiation, or multiple strategies. These strategies may be adopted by domestic, international,

Coca-Cola: A Multinational Firm

Almost half of all the soft drinks consumed in the world are made by Coca-Cola. (Its nearest competitor, PepsiCo, has less than one-fourth of the world market.) And its overseas business is quite profitable. In 1989, for instance, 80 percent of Coke's operating earnings came from overseas sales.

What's the secret behind Coke's international success? There may be several.

First, the firm's brand name has been well known across the globe since World War II. Second, Coke's management is patient. It spent several million dollars in China and waited fifteen years to make a profit. Third, it pays attention to the details. Coke considers no retail outlet too small to sell its products. In Japan, for instance, Coca-Cola has held seminars for owners of mom-and-pop stores on how to compete with larger outlets.

Fourth, it is consistent, unless the situation requires flexibility. In much of the world, Coke's package, logo, taste, and advertising are the same. But in countries that are unfamiliar with soft drinks, Coke has modified the flavor of its products to conform more closely to local tastes.

Fifth, it enters new markets intelligently. For instance, to cut through red tape and speed up the entry process, Coke often offers bottling franchises to the nation's most powerful companies. Then to control the bottlers, it sometimes buys part of the firm. In the 1980s alone, Coke invested more than $1 billion in bottling joint ventures.

And the future looks bright indeed. Although annual sales growth in the United States averages only 2 or 3 percent, sales increases in Mexico and Brazil, Coke's next largest markets, were 27 and 24 percent, respectively, in 1989. And the best news is that people outside the United States currently consume only 14 percent as much soda as Americans. The company predicts that its sales in the year 2000 will be double those of 1990. Its biggest challenge during this decade, says Chairman Roberto Guizueta, will be keeping up with demand.

SOURCES: W. Konrad, "The Real Thing Is Getting Real Aggressive," *Business Week,* 26 November 1990, pp. 94–104; P. Sellers, "Coke Gets Off Its Can in Europe," *Fortune,* 13 August 1990, pp. 68–73; M. J. McCarthy, "As a Global Marketer, Coke Excels by Being Tough and Consistent," *The Wall Street Journal,* 19 December 1989.

multinational, and global companies. An example of a domestic business that uses the low-cost strategy successfully is Wal-Mart. McDonald's is an international company that has experienced success with the low-cost–differentiation strategy. Colgate-Palmolive serves as an illustration of a multinational firm that has successfully employed the low-cost–differentiation strategy. And Caterpillar operates with success as a global firm using low-cost–differentiation.

No generic strategy can be successfully implemented without careful planning, execution, and coordination of each business unit's functional departments. In formulating functional strategies, managers must be aware that functions are interrelated. Each functional area, in attaining its purpose, must mesh its activities with the activities of the other functional departments. The extent to which all of the business unit's functional tasks mesh smoothly determines the effectiveness of the unit's generic strategy.

For domestic, international, and multinational companies, the coordination of functional strategies is undertaken independently within each business unit.

Hence, international and multinational companies generally coordinate functional strategies on a country-by-country basis. Global firms, however, coordinate functional strategies across the firm's business units located in various countries, since their units' actions are interdependent.

STRATEGY IMPLEMENTATION

Earlier, in Chapters 7 and 8, we learned that structure and behavior are key aspects of strategy implementation. Whatever organizational structure is adopted by a business that operates in two or more countries, the relationship between its headquarters and its subsidiaries may be either bilateral or multilateral.[24] International and multinational firms generally have bilateral, independent relationships between their headquarters and subsidiaries. This type of relationship, in which the headquarters interacts independently with each subsidiary, is depicted in Figure 10.2. Global firms, on the other hand, usually maintain multilateral, interdependent relationships between their headquarters and subsidiaries. Figure 10.3 portrays this situation in which the operations of the subsidiaries are interdependent.

Certainly, operating outside one's own country offers special challenges in areas such as leadership and maintaining a strong organizational culture. Some countries, for instance, resist innovation and radical new approaches to conducting business. Others, however, welcome such change. In Sweden, for instance, Volvo's team approach to producing cars, first implemented in 1974, was so well received by its work force that its latest plant, opened in 1989, has gone even further, employing autonomous work groups that manage themselves.[25]

Recall the dangers of the self-reference criterion. All too often managers believe that the leadership styles and organizational culture that worked in their home country should work elsewhere. But as we have seen, each nation has its own unique culture, norms, traditions, values, and beliefs. Hence, it should be

---

Bilateral Relationships Between Headquarters and Subsidiaries of International or Multinational Organizations

Figure 10.2

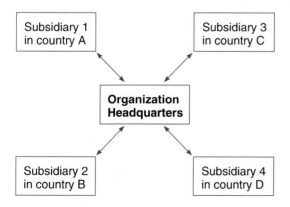

Figure 10.3   **Multilateral Relationships Between Headquarters and Subsidiaries of a Global Organization**

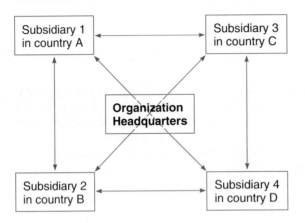

obvious—but often is not—that leadership styles, motivation programs, and organizational values and norms must be tailored to fit the unique culture of each country in which the organization operates.

SUMMARY

This chapter focuses on businesses that choose to operate internationally. Ordinarily, international operations evolve gradually. Most companies begin their involvement with foreign countries through importing or exporting products. They may become further involved through licensing select organizations in other countries to use their technology, production processes, or brand names. Or they may enter into partnerships or joint ventures with foreign companies as a means of penetrating certain markets. Still deeper involvement may be achieved by initiating direct investments in particular countries.

There are three levels of foreign business operations: international, in which a domestic company is minimally or moderately involved in foreign operations through importing, exporting, licensing, or conducting joint ventures; multinational, in which the enterprise makes direct investments abroad and operates each of its foreign subsidiaries independently on a country-by-country basis; and global, in which the firm also makes direct investments abroad but operates its subsidiaries in an interdependent fashion.

Much as a domestic company does, the organization that chooses to engage in international commerce must analyze its macroenvironment and industry environment. The difference, of course, is that as an organization's environment expands from domestic to international, management faces not only a larger number of environmental elements but also far greater environmental complexity.

Within the organization, mission, goals, and objectives may be closely intertwined with international operations in several ways. Likewise, corporate-level strategies must take into account unique international considerations.

Enterprises that operate at the international or multinational level may compete successfully with either a high or a low market share, depending upon their particular mission and goals. Global firms, however, must usually maintain a high market share for effective operations.

At the business unit level, the generic strategies of niche–low-cost, niche-differentiation, and niche–low-cost/differentiation are appropriate for international and multinational businesses that desire to maintain a low market share. On the other hand, if the business unit's goal is to attain a high market share, it has available the low-cost, differentiation, low-cost–differentiation, and multiple strategies. These strategies may be adopted by international, multinational, and global companies.

In determining functional strategies, international and multinational businesses coordinate their functional activities on a country-by-country basis. Global firms, however, coordinate functional strategies across the firm's business units located in various countries, since their units' actions are interdependent.

As management implements its strategies, it must take into account the unique culture of each country in which its business operates. The leadership styles, motivation programs, and organization culture that worked in the United States may need to be tailored to each individual international setting.

KEY CONCEPTS

Comparative advantage   The concept that products or parts can be produced less expensively or with higher quality or that natural resources can be extracted more economically in particular geographic locations owing to advantages in labor costs, technology, or availability of such natural resources as minerals and timber.

Culture   The generally accepted values, traditions, and patterns of behavior of a societal group.

Developing nation   A country that has not yet experienced significant industrial development.

Direct investment   When investors in one country own at least 10 percent of a private enterprise in another country.

Global organization   A firm, heavily involved in foreign trade through direct investments, that operates its subsidiaries in an interdependent fashion.

International organization   A business that is minimally or moderately involved in foreign operations. It may import or export goods, enter into licensing agreements with foreign-based organizations, or conduct joint ventures with foreign companies.

International joint venture   A partnership of two or more organizations from different nations who join together to accomplish specific projects or to cooperate in selected areas of business.

International license agreement   The granting of permission by an organization in one country to a company in another nation to use its technology, brand name, production processes, or other operations. A fee is paid to the granting organization by the company being licensed.

Multinational organization   An organization, heavily involved in overseas operations through direct investments, that functions on a country-by-country basis, with its subsidiaries operating independently of one another.

Newly industrializing nation   A developing nation that has experienced rapid industrial growth over the past two decades. This category includes Mexico, Brazil, Spain, Taiwan, Hong Kong, Singapore, and South Korea.

Self-reference criterion   The unconscious reference to one's own cultural values.

Technologically advanced nation   A nation that is grouped among the major industrial powers of the world. This category includes the United States, Canada, Japan, Australia, New Zealand, and the industrialized nations of Europe.

DISCUSSION QUESTIONS

1. Identify as many types of businesses as you can that are not directly affected by foreign competition.

2. Get the latest listing of the world's largest industrial corporations. How many U.S.-based firms are on the list? How does this figure compare with a listing from 1960 or 1970?

3. Explain how a domestic company, over time, expands to become a global firm. What are the normal stages in this process?

4. Discuss fully the differences between a multinational enterprise and a global firm.

5. What is the major distinction between an international enterprise and a multinational organization?

6. Forecast what future world political-legal trends might affect international business.

7. How do the objectives of a multinational or global organization differ from those of the host country? Why do they differ?

8. Explain how the self-reference criterion can lead to problems for U.S. managers operating abroad.

9. Why might an organization's mission influence management to engage in international operations?

10. Explain the relationship between a business's level of operations and its market share goals.

STRATEGIC MANAGEMENT
EXERCISES

1. Select a well-known energy company. From your recollection of current events, what global opportunities and threats does the macroenvironment pose for this company? Identify several specific opportunities and threats for each of the following forces: political-legal, economic, technological, and social.

2. Identify a particular company in a well-defined industry, such as automobiles or computers. From your recollection of current events, analyze that company's industry environment from an international perspective. You may wish to use relevant sections of the "Industry Analysis Worksheet" from Exercise 2 in Chapter 2 to guide your analysis.

3. Acquire the annual report of a business that operates in more than two countries. Does its annual report specifically identify its mission and goals in international terms? What suggestions would you make to improve this company's mission and goal statements?

4. Using a global firm of your choice, determine what corporate-level and business unit–level strategies it has adopted. Give evidence to support your answers.

5. Assume that you are a member of the top management team of a food-processing company that follows a corporate growth strategy. Your company has decided to expand into both the western and eastern regions of the European continent. Specifically, which countries would you suggest as appropriate for joint ventures? Why? Which are more appropriate for licensing agreements? Why? In which would you prefer to make direct investments? Why?

REFERENCES

1. "The Global 500: The World's Biggest Industrial Corporations," *Fortune*, 29 July 1991, pp. 238–280.

2. "The Global Service 500: The 100 Largest Commercial Banking Companies," *Fortune*, 26 August 1991, p. 174.

3. *International Financial Statistics Yearbook* (Washington, D.C.: International Monetary Fund, 1989).

4. *International Financial Statistics Yearbook*.

5. C. S. Manegold and M. Kepp, "Elegant Armed Robbery," *Newsweek*, 2 April 1990, p. 30.

6. R. B. Reich, *The Next American Frontier* (New York: Times Books, 1983).

7. A. R. Negandhi, "Multinational Corporations and Host Governments' Relationships: Comparative Study of Conflict and Conflicting Issues," *Human Relations* 33 (1980): 534–535.

8. P. Wright, D. Townsend, J. Kinard, and J. Iverstine, "The Developing World to 1990: Trends and Implications for Multinational Business," *Long Range Planning* 15, no. 4 (July-August 1982): 116–125.

9. Wright et al., "Developing World," p. 119. Reprinted with permission from *Long Range Planning,* 15, P. Wright et al., "The Developing World to 1990: Trends and Implications for Multinational Business," © 1982, Pergamon Press plc.

10. Wright et al., "Developing Worlds," p. 119. Reprinted with permission from *Long Range Planning,* 15, P. Wright et al., "The Developing World to 1990: Trends and Implications for Multinational Business," © 1982, Pergamon Press plc.

11. M. J. Williams, "Rewriting the Export Rules," *Fortune,* 23 April 1990, p. 89.

12. P. Wright, "MNC—Third World Business Unit Performance: Application of Strategic Elements," *Strategic Management Journal* 5 (1984): 232.

13. Y. L. Doz, C. A. Bartlett, and C. K. Prahalad, "Global Competitive Pressures and Host Country Demands: Managing Tensions in MNCs," *California Management Review* 23 (Spring 1981): 63.

14. P. Wright, "Doing Business in Islamic Markets," *Harvard Business Review* 59, no. 1 (January-February 1981): 34–40.

15. P. Wright, "Systematic Approach to Finding Export Opportunities," in D. N. Dickson, ed., *Managing Effectively in the World Marketplace* (New York: Wiley, 1983), pp. 338–339.

16. P. Wright, "Organizational Behavior in Islamic Firms," *Management International Review* 21, no. 2 (1981): 86–94.

17. D. Ricks, M. Y. C. Fu, and J. S. Arpan, *International Business Blunders* (Columbus, Ohio: Grid, 1974).

18. C. M. Watson, "Counter-Competition Abroad to Protect Home Markets," in D. N. Dickson, ed., *Managing Effectively in the World Marketplace* (New York: Wiley, 1983), p. 359.

19. P. Wright, "The Strategic Options of Least-Cost, Differentiation, and Niche," *Business Horizons* 29, no. 2 (March–April 1986): 22.

20. A. Miller and F. Washington, "Japanese Cars: Born in the USA," *Newsweek,* 9 April 1990, p. 36.

21. T. Hout, M. Porter, and E. Rudder, "How Global Companies Win Out," in D. N. Dickson, ed., *Managing Effectively in the World Marketplace* (New York: Wiley, 1983), pp. 188–191.

22. Hout, Porter, and Rudder, "How Global Companies Win Out," p. 189.

23. Z. Schiller, "Can Bridgestone Make the Climb?" *Business Week,* 27 February 1989, pp. 78–79; "Survival in the Basic Industries: How Four Companies Hope to Avoid Disaster," *Business Week,* 26 April 1982, pp. 74–76.

24. Wright, "MNC—Third World Business Unit Performance," pp. 231–240.

25. J. Kapstein and J. Hoerr, "Volvo's Radical New Plant: 'The Death of the Assembly Line'?" *Business Week,* 28 August 1989, pp. 92–93.

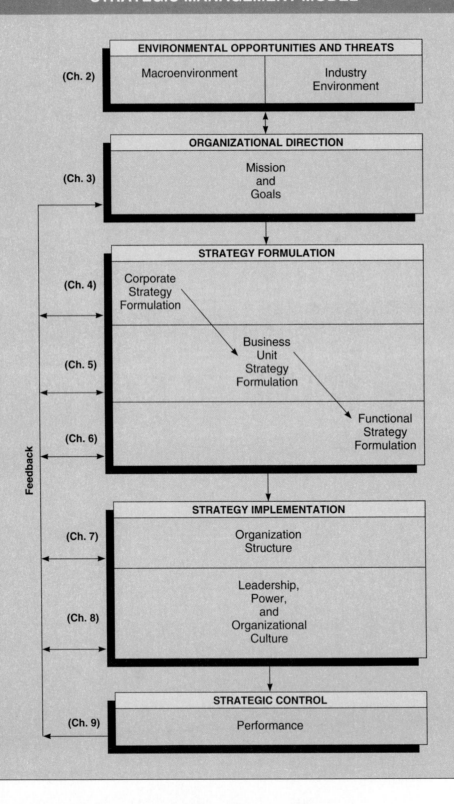

STRATEGIC MANAGEMENT MODEL

ENVIRONMENTAL OPPORTUNITIES AND THREATS

(Ch. 2)

| Macroenvironment | Industry Environment |

ORGANIZATIONAL DIRECTION

(Ch. 3)

Mission
and
Goals

STRATEGY FORMULATION

(Ch. 4)

Corporate
Strategy
Formulation

(Ch. 5)

Business
Unit
Strategy
Formulation

(Ch. 6)

Functional
Strategy
Formulation

STRATEGY IMPLEMENTATION

(Ch. 7)

Organization
Structure

(Ch. 8)

Leadership,
Power,
and
Organizational
Culture

STRATEGIC CONTROL

(Ch. 9)

Performance

Feedback

Strategic Management in Not-for-Profit Organizations

The basic principles of strategic management presented in this book are equally applicable to profit and not-for-profit organizations. It is important, for instance, that all organizations analyze their environment; formulate a mission, goals, and objectives; develop appropriate strategies; implement those strategies; and control their strategic direction. However, in a more specific sense, there are some distinct differences between profit and not-for-profit organizations that have significant strategic implications. This chapter examines those differences.

TYPES OF NOT-FOR-PROFIT ORGANIZATIONS

Although not-for-profit organizations can be categorized in a number of different ways, a basic classification consists of two groups: private not-for-profit organizations (which we will refer to as nonprofit organizations) and public not-for-profit organizations (which we will term public organizations). Some significant differences between business organizations and these two types of not-for-profit organizations are illustrated in Table 11.1.

Nonprofit organizations are entities that attempt to contribute to the good of society and are supported by private funds. Examples of such organizations include the following:

- Private educational institutions (e.g., Harvard University, the University of Chicago).
- Charities (e.g., Easter Seal Society, March of Dimes).
- Social service organizations (e.g., Alcoholics Anonymous, Girl Scouts of the U.S.A.).
- Health service organizations (e.g., Houston's Methodist Hospital, Johns Hopkins Health System).

Table 11.1

Some Differences Between Profit and Not-for-Profit Organizations

	Business Organization	*Nonprofit Organization*	*Public Organization*
Ownership	Private	Private	Public
Funding	Sale of products and services	Membership dues, contributions from private and/or public sources, sale of products and services	Taxes and user fees
Types	Single proprietorship, partnership, corporation	Educational, charitable, social service, health service, foundation, cultural, religious	Federal government, state government, local government

- Foundations (e.g., Ford Foundation, Rockefeller Foundation).
- Cultural organizations (e.g., Los Angeles Philharmonic Orchestra, Chicago's Field Museum of Natural History).
- Religious institutions (e.g., St. Patrick's Cathedral, Memphis's Bellevue Baptist Church).

Public organizations are those created, funded, and regulated by the public sector. They are largely synonymous with what we commonly term *government* and include agencies at all levels of government, such as the following:

- Federal government agencies (e.g., Internal Revenue Service, United States Navy, Environmental Protection Agency).
- State government agencies (e.g., University of Kentucky, Texas Department of Corrections, Pennsylvania Turnpike Authority).
- Local government agencies (e.g., Dallas Public Library, Dade County Sheriff's Department, New York City Transit Authority).

Both nonprofit and public organizations are indispensable to maintaining a civilized society. Many of society's essential needs cannot be provided by for-profit organizations. For instance, most individuals could not afford to pay for private police protection; and each major city has one or more "charity" hospitals where the indigent can receive medical care.

The products and services of businesses can be obtained only by those who pay for them, but the outputs of public organizations and those of many nonprofit organizations are available to virtually all members of society. For instance, anyone—even a tourist—can receive the protection of a city's police force; anyone can travel along a toll-free interstate highway; and any child with birth defects is eligible for help from the March of Dimes. Some nonprofit organizations, of course, restrict their goods or services only to those who pay for the cost of providing the outputs. Examples are private universities (which exist to provide the public an alternative to secular or mass education) and some cultural organizations (which must sell tickets to cover their costs but also usually offer some special annual events that are free to the public at large).

STRATEGIC ISSUES FOR NONPROFIT AND PUBLIC
ORGANIZATIONS

This section examines some key strategic management issues in nonprofit and public organizations. First, we look at how environmental analysis is conducted by these organizations. Then, we determine how they develop their mission, goals, and objectives. We analyze next how they formulate, implement, and control their strategies. Finally, we suggest some ways that not-for-profit organizations can increase their strategic management effectiveness.

■ Environmental Analysis

As the environment of not-for-profit organizations becomes increasingly dynamic, strategic management becomes more and more important. For example, nonprofit organizations have recently experienced reductions in federal aid and changes in tax laws that have reduced the incentive for corporations and individuals to make contributions. Simultaneously, competition for financial donations among nonprofits has increased with the rise of organizations dedicated to combatting AIDS, Alzheimer's disease, child abuse, and drunk driving.[1]

Likewise, organizations that once had a near monopoly in certain services, such as the U.S. Postal Service, are experiencing rapid change. Over the past few years, the Postal Service has felt increasing competitive pressure in express mail and the parcel business from such rivals as United Parcel Service and Federal Express. Additionally, in first-class mail, the Postal Service is losing business to a product substitute—the business-owned facsimile (fax) machine. Under such conditions, the necessity of planning well and operating effectively and efficiently becomes clear.

Two of the primary ways in which the environment of not-for-profit organizations differs from the environment of business organizations are in their sources of revenue and in the composition and concerns of their stakeholder groups. The following subsections explore these differences.

Sources of Revenue

Although there are a number of differences between businesses and not-for-profit organizations, perhaps the chief distinction is the source of the organization's revenues. Business income is derived almost exclusively from a single source—the sale of its products and services to individuals or organizations. Not-for-profit organizations, however, may receive revenue from a number of sources: taxes, dues, contributions, and in some instances, sale of their products or services. These differences are illustrated in Figure 11.1.

Some of the contributors of revenue to certain organizations may never use, at least in a direct sense, the organizations' outputs. For instance, consider a family violence center. The center's purpose is to provide a haven for women and their children from abusive spouses, but the center must rely on others, who may never use the center, for financial support. Another example is the local public school system. Public schools have been asked to shoulder increasing responsibilities as society has changed. They are being looked to as sources of prevention training for drug abuse and teenage pregnancy, as locations for

Figure 11.1   **Sources of Income for Profit and Not-for-Profit Organizations**

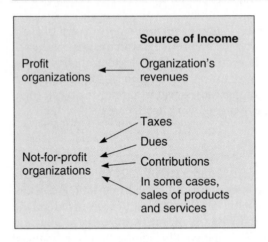

after-school care for latchkey children, and as institutions that must increase the quality of education for their children. The financial support for pursuing these goals must come from all of the school district's taxpayers—not just the parents of the students who attend the schools. Consequently, some taxpayers may be reluctant to support higher taxes for the public schools.[2]

Successful businesses know their customers and their needs. They recognize that satisfying their customers' needs is the sole reason for their existence. But not-for-profit organizations have a less direct relationship with their "customers." Those they serve are not necessarily those who contribute financially to their operations. Hence, their strategic planning must be twofold: planning for serving their clients or customers, and planning for securing the financial funding to provide those services.

The first type of planning—to serve customers—may sometimes have to be done with little or no input from the customers. For instance, agencies that handle the problems of the mentally ill or those that safeguard children can hardly survey their clients to ascertain their needs. In such cases, agencies often plan their services on the basis of discussions with professionals who have expertise in that particular field and what similar agencies in other locales have done. The second type of planning—to acquire financial funding—may become quite political. A government agency, for instance, must compete against other agencies for the limited funds available; and those that are most successful are often the ones that acquiesce to demands made of them by those who control the funds. Defense Department appropriations, for instance, often depend upon the department's compliance with congressional wishes.

External Constituencies and Stakeholders

Strategic planning in business, as we have seen, involves taking into account the varying goals of the organization's stakeholders (e.g., its owners, employees, customers, creditors). The same is true for not-for-profit organizations, but the stakeholder groups and concerns are significantly different. This difference can best be seen in public organizations.

Although the managers of a government entity may engage in rational strategic planning, these plans may be ignored by political leaders who must respond to public pressure to win reelection. What may be rational in an economic sense may be politically unwise.

> Political leaders have learned that government often works only when a consensus forms to deal with a perceived crisis. The solutions may not conform with any plan, and governmental actions may be taken without regard to rational priorities. Nevertheless, the most important consideration may be that the actions are acceptable to the various constituency groups that are able to affect the decision. Since this occurs at all levels of government on a regular basis, it will be frustrating to managers who want government to function in an orderly manner. Government is not an orderly procedure because there are too many people with a variety of perspectives who are involved in reaching decisions.[3]

This greater number and diversity of stakeholders may result in less managerial autonomy for public agency managers than for managers in business. Because government agencies are "owned" by all citizens, their activities may often be more closely monitored by their constituents. This greater visibility means that mangers' decisions are more public.

For instance, numerous volunteer groups serve as watchdogs over various aspects of federal government operations. During the 1990 debate over ways of reducing the federal deficit, it became apparent that a significant number of congressional votes could be mustered for various types of tax increases. In response to that movement, two groups—Citizens Against Government Waste and Action Group to Save America's Economy—placed large advertisements in newspapers such as *The Washington Post*, lobbying for a reduction in government waste rather than a tax increase. The groups charged, for instance, that the IRS had failed to collect $87 billion in delinquent taxes; the Defense Department had an inventory of $29 billion in unneeded spare parts; and $22 billion could be attributed to losses from poor financial management in various federal agencies. Overall, they claimed, over $280 billion of waste (and of the federal deficit) could be eliminated in five years without raising taxes.[4]

In addition to being subject to public visibility, managerial actions are also scrutinized carefully by oversight agencies such as legislative bodies, courts, and executive groups. Hence, although managers of public organizations may not need to concern themselves with such business threats as hostile takeovers, foreign competition, or bankruptcy, they have a complicated environment in which to operate. They must serve customers or clients who may be separate from the organization's sources of funding. But the organization's operations must satisfy both the customers and the funding sources, as well as a number of other constituents and oversight agencies. This complexity is illustrated in Figure 11.2.

■ Mission, Goals, and Objectives

Not-for-profit organizations need clearly-defined missions, goals, and objectives. This section explores this need and examines some reasons why clarity in organizational direction is often lacking.

Figure 11.2   **Stakeholder Constraints on Public Organizations**

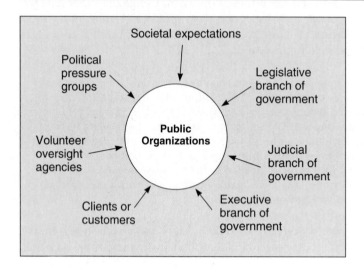

Mission

Certainly, having a well-focused mission and clear goals and objectives is as important to not-for-profit organizations as it is to businesses. Management researcher and consultant, Peter F. Drucker points out that "the best nonprofits devote a great deal of thought to defining their organizations' missions."[5]

As an example, consider the Girl Scouts of the U.S.A.[6] In 1976, Frances Hesselbein became national executive director of the organization, which was experiencing several problems. In a diverse society, it was comprised mostly of white, middle-class girls; Scout leaders were becoming increasingly difficult to recruit as women entered the work force in growing numbers; the Boy Scouts of America were considering extending membership to girls; and membership in the Girl Scouts had declined steadily for eight years.

Hesselbein's first step was to examine the mission of the Girl Scouts. The organization's management considered these questions: "What is our business?" "Who is the customer?" "What does the customer consider as value?" They decided that the Scouts existed for one major reason: to help girls reach their highest potential. As Hesselbein explained:

> More than any one thing, that made the difference. Because when you are clear about your mission, corporate goals and operating objectives flow from it.[7]

This strong self-identity helped the Scouts reject pressures from women's rights activists to support their causes and from charities to act as door-to-door canvassers. Today, although Hesselbein is no longer president, the organization numbers 2.3 million girls (15 percent of them are from racial minorities); conducts market research to determine the needs of modern girls; awards the most popular proficiency badges for math and computer expertise instead of for good grooming and hosting a party; sports uniforms designed by Halston and Bill Blass; and publishes monographs on such issues as teen pregnancy, drug use, and child abuse.

STRATEGIC INSIGHT

A Nonprofit Organization's Mission: Howard Hughes Medical Institute

An important—but little known—nonprofit organization is the Howard Hughes Medical Institute. Founded in 1953 by billionaire aviator-industrialist Howard R. Hughes, the Institute states its mission as follows:

> The primary purpose and objective of the Howard Hughes Medical Institute shall be the promotion of human knowledge within the field of the basic sciences (principally the field of medical research and medical education) and the effective application thereof for the benefit of mankind.

The institute is a scientific and philanthropic organization with the principal purpose of conducting biomedical research. It accomplishes its scientific mission by funding research through laboratories located in some of the most prestigious academic medical centers, hospitals, universities, and other research institutions in the United States. Its philanthropic goals are attained by financially supporting various aspects of science education, from elementary school through postgraduate training.

At the beginning of 1990, the institute had total assets of about $6.4 billion, including $5.8 billion invested in equities, private partnerships, and nonequity securities. Earnings from this investment portfolio support the institute's operations. In 1989, the institute funded almost $200 million in medical research and support services and spent an additional $42 million on science education.

How effective are these expenditures? In 1989, a Hughes investigator at the University of Michigan and his collaborators discovered the gene for cystic fibrosis. A few weeks later, another Hughes investigator at the University of Colorado shared the Nobel Prize in chemistry with a researcher at Yale University. The two scientists independently discovered that RNA can act as an enzyme in addition to its established role as a carrier of genetic messages. And these are only two of the more visible discoveries made by scientists whose research is funded by the Howard Hughes Medical Institute.

SOURCE: *The Annual Report of The Howard Hughes Medical Institute 1989* (Bethesda, Md.: Howard Hughes Medical Institute).

Goals and Objectives

Although having clearly a defined mission and goals is essential to an organization's success, many not-for-profit organizations fail in this regard. Businesses, for instance, can easily measure sales, market share, profits, return on investment, and so on. But not-for-profit organizations do not usually have such clear goals.

One of the reasons for this lack of clarity is that many of the goals are value-laden. Some states, for example, held fierce debates over mandatory seat belt laws. Was the goal to protect the lives of automobile drivers and passengers, or was it to protect the rights of those individuals to choose—or not to choose—to buckle up? Is the goal of a prison system rehabilitation of prisoners or punishment?

Second, not-for-profit goals often involve important trade-offs. This situation can be illustrated by the debate surrounding the potential closing of any military base. Its closing will reduce the federal deficit, but it will also harm the economy of the local area. Which is the more important consideration?

Growth Strategies for Churches

One of the nation's largest churches is Willowcreek Community Church in South Barrington, Illinois, a Chicago suburb. Although the church was founded only in 1974, it now has over thirteen thousand parishioners. Its founder and pastor, Bill Hybels, adopted the growth strategy, based on business fundamentals. He originally went door to door asking people why they did not attend church. From this market research, he began to offer services that catered to the needs of his "customers." For instance, he holds full services on Wednesday evenings because some working parents prefer to spend Sundays with their children. And for those unable to attend any of the services, he provides his sermons on cassette tapes.

Another huge religious institution following a growth strategy is Houston's Second Baptist Church. With a Sunday morning attendance of twelve thousand, the church complex covers 32 acres. In 1984, however, the church was simply a conventional church on a large plot of land. Its incoming pastor, H. Edwin Young, was familiar with the demographics of the area: thousands of young families and single people new to Houston. He sold his vision of a growing church to his congregation and persuaded them to pledge over $17 million needed for new physical facilities while the church borrowed over $26 million for additional construction costs.

Pastor Young dispatched church members to study office management techniques at Xerox and IBM and parking and people skills at Disney World. He varied religious services to fit particular needs. In addition to the traditional Sunday morning service, there is a Sunday evening service that caters to a mostly singles crowd; and on Wednesday nights, separate services are offered, one traditional and one with religious rock music.

Today, computers regulate mood lighting during church services; shuttle buses bring latecomers in from outlying parking decks; parking attendants empty the church's numerous parking lots every Sunday in half an hour; billboards and television ads invite people to visit this "Fellowship of Excitement"; an information desk is staffed with cheerful attendants; aerobics classes are held daily beginning at 6:00 A.M.; and a restaurant offers two types of menus: "saints" for those who prefer a low-calorie meal and "sinners" for those who desire richer food.

SOURCES: R. G. Niebuhr, "Megachurches Strive to Be All Things to All Parishioners," *The Wall Street Journal*, 13 May 1991; P. F. Drucker, "What Business Can Learn from Nonprofits," *Harvard Business Review* 67, no. 4 (1989): 89.

Third, goals may often be deliberately vague, broad, and general, such as "protect our environment" or "help the homeless." Broad, general goals are more likely to secure the support of diverse stakeholders and provide inspiration for organization members. Also, vague goals are less likely to invite close scrutiny and debate than specific goals are and, hence, may avoid alienating potential supporters. Universities, for instance, often publicize their goal of offering a high-quality education. Few could argue with such a goal, and it helps skirt such issues as whether research or teaching is more important, how selective the university's admissions policies should be, and how much emphasis will be given to sports programs. Debates on any of these issues are almost certain to alienate some stakeholders, thereby reducing the flow of funds to the university.

Goals in public organizations are often vague because leadership is subject to frequent turnover. Changes in direction, for instance, can occur in a state where a Democrat replaces a Republican governor. Four years later, election results can alter the state's direction yet again. Vague goals, such as "operate the state for the benefit of all of its citizens," therefore, are likely to have more permanency and lend more of an aura of stability than very specific goals will.

Goals may sometimes not reflect the needs of the organization's "customers" as much as they reflect the wishes of the organization's financial donors. Church-affiliated universities, for instance, may make decisions that anger their students but conform to the wishes of the denomination that accounts for much of their financial backing. Some nonprofit organizations, in fact, may be reluctant to turn down substantial funding, even if the donor insists that the funds be used for a purpose outside the basic mission of the organization. Again, vague goals may appear more appropriate in such situations.

The question, of course, is whether these reasons for establishing vague goals are valid. We do not believe they are. Although formulating goals and objectives is more challenging in not-for-profit organizations than in businesses, having clarity in direction is essential if organizations are to operate effectively. Perhaps the major reason for our belief is that without clear goals, an organization has no way to measure its progress or its effectiveness.

Both nonprofit and public organizations must bring together their various stakeholders to hammer out a set of specific, measurable goals. The process will often not be smooth, since each stakeholder group may have its own agenda. Even so, without this process, these organizations will be unable to measure their performance.

Virtually every organization can define specific, if not quantifiable, objectives. Ways of determining cost-benefit ratios and standards are essential. For instance, the family violence center mentioned earlier could formulate a means of measuring how effectively it is able to prevent its clients from suffering further abuse and how well it enhances its clients' self-esteem. However, it also needs to define such performance ratios as expenditures per client per day. Since such organizations typically cannot begin to help all of those who need their help, the more tightly they can control their costs, the more clients they can serve. Broad measures of costs per month or per year cannot help control costs as effectively as more specific ratios. Such standards act as a surrogate performance measure when profit figures are not applicable.[8]

■ Strategy Formulation, Implementation, and Control

The processes of implementing and controlling strategy are often more complicated in not-for-profit organizations than in businesses. This section examines some of those complications.

Strategy Formulation and Implementation

Corporate and business unit strategies are usually the same ones used in not-for-profit organizations. In general, we can say that most of these organizations attempt to satisfy specific societal needs. For instance, the American Red Cross rushes to aid individuals who are victims of natural disasters; the Salvation Army ministers to the physical and religious needs of homeless persons. The U.S. Navy keeps the sea lanes of the world open; the Army concentrates on ground defense. Within a state, some universities serve as major research and graduate institutions; others concentrate on teaching undergraduates.

Often, one of the features that distinguishes not-for-profit organizations from businesses is the presence of greater political constraints upon their strategic choices. In public organizations, for instance, many decisions are subject to the approval of oversight agencies and the legislative and executive branches of government. These strategic decisions become even more politicized by their public visibility in the press. In a 1986 report, for example, the National Academy of Public Administration complained about the complexity of the controls and rules over managerial decisions in the federal government.[9]

Even if strategy could be formulated unfettered by political considerations, implementation of the strategy can be a problem. Public managers have weaker authority over their subordinates than business managers do. Such decisions as pay, promotion, termination, and disciplinary action are often subject to rules rather than to managerial discretion. And employees who enthusiastically carry out the strategy of the organization may receive the same rewards as those who ignore the strategy to pursue their own ends. Also, many functional strategies are greatly constrained by rules governing such areas as purchasing and personnel. For instance, a recent General Accounting Office survey of federal government employees revealed that 5.7 percent of those surveyed were "poor performers." Although some of these employees improved their performance, voluntarily quit, or were removed from their jobs, almost 40 percent never improved and were not asked to leave. That group received over $1 billion in annual salaries.[10] Finally, the frequent turnover of leadership, discussed earlier, may discourage employees from channeling much effort into strategy implementation, since they know that the current strategy may be short-lived.

Because our political system is designed to ensure frequent turnover through regularly scheduled elections and through limitations on how long individuals can hold some offices, government leaders are encouraged to take a short-range approach to strategic management. Voters in the next election may be more likely to reelect officials who have benefited them during the past several months than those who have an excellent long-range plan but have demonstrated little in the way of immediate results.

Although nonprofit organizations may operate under fewer constraints than public organizations, implementation of strategy can be constrained by those who oppose the strategy. For instance, public abortion clinics may be picketed by right-to-life advocates. More important, however, may be the constraints imposed by the nature of the work force in many nonprofit organizations. Often, the bulk of the workers are volunteers who receive no pay for their services. As long as the direction of the organization is consistent with their values and beliefs, they will cooperate in implementing strategic decisions. But should the agency's direction deviate from their values, they may quit the organization and even actively oppose its operations.

In fact, many nonprofit organizations develop their organizational culture around a cause. Often, the founder of the organization and the members exhibit the attitudes and behaviors of "true believers" who are willing to work long hours at little or no pay to further their particular beliefs and values. Many environmental groups as well as pro- and antiabortion organizations possess such powerful cultures. Few businesses are able to develop their culture around such powerful and emotional goals.

Another consideration is that businesses often have more attractive financial compensation packages than not-for-profit organizations do. Individuals who are motivated by such considerations, therefore, will often seek employment in

STRATEGIC INSIGHT

Implementing Strategy on the New York City Subway

When Robert R. Kiley became chairman of New York's Metropolitan Transportation Authority in 1983, he faced problems of mammoth proportions. New Yorkers were losing confidence in their huge mass transit system. (New York's bus and rail system transports 5.2 million passengers each weekday; its subways have 6200 rail cars operating on 705 miles of track through 463 stations.) Take one example: Riders were avoiding the New York City subway in increasing numbers because of frequent delays, out-of-service trains, door malfunctions, dirt, and spray can graffiti. At the huge subway car repair shop at 207th Street, employees were accustomed to working about four hours a day and spending the rest of their time playing cards, reading the newspaper, working crossword puzzles, and drinking beer.

Kiley set about rejuvenating a capital improvement program and repairing the decayed miles of subway lines. Simultaneously, he began trying to reform the management system. Middle managers belonged to a union and were promoted on the basis of seniority and test scores rather than on job performance. Any action to discipline workers was likely to be challenged by the workers' unions, and the disciplinary action was often not supported by headquarters. When Kiley attempted to get legislation passed to remove the managers from the union, political opposition arose to block his efforts. So he turned to negotiation and finally freed one-fourth of the middle managers (about 1200 individuals) from the union and civil service control by contributing $1.8 million to the health and welfare funds of the unions that were involved.

Change was gradual but impressive. With managers' pay now based on performance, they began to suspend workers who committed infractions and dismissed others for more serious violations of the rules. By 1988, the repair work force had dropped from over 1,000 to 680, and productivity had increased by 35 percent. The breakdown rate for trains, from 1983 to 1988, fell by 50 percent; derailments decreased significantly; arrival times became increasingly reliable; and by 1990, spray can graffiti virtually disappeared as trains were washed after every circuit of their route.

SOURCES: D. Machalaba, "Transit Manager Shows New York Subway Isn't Beyond Redemption," *The Wall Street Journal*, 14 October 1988; S. C. Fehr, "Metro Eyes Ex-N.Y. Transit Chief," *The Washington Post*, 13 February 1991; S. C. Fehr, "Views on New Metro Chief Take Divergent Routes," *The Washington Post*, 4 March 1991.

business organizations. This choice reduces the pool of talented workers from which public and nonprofit organizations can choose. In addition, the trend toward two-income families has certainly diminished the number of volunteers available to nonprofit organizations.

Not-for-profit organizations may also implement their strategies in a more centralized fashion than businesses.[11] As we saw in an earlier chapter, many businesses have responded to increasing environmental change by decentralizing their decision making. Although environments in many cases are equally dynamic for public and nonprofit agencies, the same trend has not occurred there. Because so many differing stakeholder groups must be considered when management implements strategy, often only the top managers are fully aware of how stakeholders' attitudes are changing.[12] For this reason, implementation decisions are made at the top levels of the organization. In addition, under the civil service system in public organizations, which primarily rewards seniority rather than merit, few employees are able to perceive a connection between their job performance and their compensation. Since incentives are not used to channel their behavior into the appropriate areas of strategy implementation, their behavior is instead controlled through an extensive network of rules and procedures, resulting in a bureaucratic configuration in which decision-making authority is centralized.

A further difficulty with implementation of strategy in some not-for-profit organizations is that these institutions are staffed largely by professional people who see themselves as committed to the profession rather than to the particular organization for which they currently work. For instance, physicians are said to be engaged in the practice of medicine (a profession) rather than working for a particular hospital. College professors are often referred to (and view themselves) as professors of physics or history rather than as employees of a specific university. In such cases, they "will probably publish more, spend less time on college committees, devote less time to teaching and students, attend more professional meetings, and be more willing to leave the college"[13] than the individual who identifies more with the organization than the profession. The problem that this perspective poses from the organization's viewpoint is that such persons may have primary loyalty to their profession rather than to the organization that employs them.[14] Therefore, strategic managers may need to persuade middle- and lower-level managers to emphasize their responsibilities to the organization as well as those to their profession.

Strategic Control

Without clearly stated goals and objectives, strategic control becomes very difficult to achieve. For instance, the quality of education in public schools might be measured in several ways. One way is to determine how well students can solve problems and communicate those solutions, with the measurement taken once at the beginning of a period of time and again at the end of that time period. If the results are less than the school district has set as its goal, then corrective action must be taken. Likewise, a church that did not increase its membership as much as it desired during a particular year would have to take some corrective action, as would a police department that failed to meet its goal of solving 80 percent of the crimes committed during a twelve-month period.

Control is more difficult, obviously, when goals are not clear or when an organization has conflicting goals. Recall the example of the family violence center used earlier. The particular community in which it operates feels that it has been successful because its services are well publicized and fully used. However, it has very nearly gone bankrupt trying to help all who need its services, and its director feels that the center has just begun to scratch the surface!

In some cases, nonprofit organizations have literally had no goals in certain key areas. The prestigious University of Chicago hospital, for instance, had no budgeting system to track its costs until 1989.[15] Without standards, the hospital's management could not determine the cost of a procedure, such as an appendectomy. Lack of both cost goals and cost information made the control of costs virtually impossible.

Even under conditions in which the corrective actions that should be taken are clear, control may still not occur. For instance, in business, when a project or program is no longer contributing to a firm's profits, decisions are made either to rejuvenate the program, if appropriate and possible, or to terminate it. Hence, profit serves as a readily acceptable yardstick to help management determine the amount of resources that various programs should receive.[16]

This means of control is not available to not-for-profit organizations. In fact, only rarely are programs terminated, particularly in government. This fact can quickly be demonstrated by virtually any debate on how to reduce the federal deficit. Few individuals want their taxes raised, but any proposal to terminate a program (and, hence, lower expenditures) quickly brings an outcry from those stakeholders who will be adversely affected by the program's demise. As a result, governments at all levels continue to add programs that are needed but rarely end any of their ongoing programs. But strategic control requires that a manager make choices, because it is simply not possible to do everything well.[17] Even when a lack of funding makes it imperative to cut programs, the programs cut are not necessarily the ones least needed; often, the programs eliminated are the ones that are less likely to create a highly vocal protest from their constituents.

Even charitable, nonprofit organizations may behave in similar ways. For instance, sometimes, the mission of an agency is actually accomplished or its environment changes so that its mission becomes unnecessary. As an example, consider the Mothers' March of Dimes organization, which was originally established to support research that would lead to a cure for polio. With the widespread distribution of the Salk vaccine in the 1950s, polio ceased to be the threat it once was. But the March of Dimes did not go out of existence. Instead, it adopted a new cause—birth defects—in order to sustain itself.

■ Improving Strategic Management

Although some of the difficulties in implementing strategic management concepts in not-for-profit organizations are unlikely to disappear (e.g., the desire of elected officials to be reelected minimizes an emphasis on long-range planning), other problems can be overcome. The concepts of effective strategic management presented in this book are not limited to business institutions. Both nonprofit and public organizations can benefit significantly by analyzing their environmental opportunities and constraints and by formulating a mission and goals that allow them to fulfill the needs of some segment of society. They must then develop a strategy that relates their strengths and weaknesses appropriately to their environment and allows them to create a distinctive competence in their operating arena. An organization structure must be fashioned that enables the agency to deal effectively with its environmental demands; and a culture should be established that enhances—rather than interferes with—its operational effectiveness.

Some not-for-profit organizations are highly effective, of course. But for those that are not, these basic principles of strategic management can be most useful in increasing their ability to carry out their mission. In some of these situations, the culture may be such that improvement is virtually impossible without a major change. Strong transformational leadership may be required, along with a significant modification in policies, so that employees' attitudes and practices can be unfrozen and changed. Top management's commitment to the concept of change must be complete and highly visible. Concurrently, reward systems must be altered to encourage creativity, new ways of doing old things, and service to the agency's clients or customers.

STRATEGIC INSIGHT

The "If-Onlys" and "Them" Culture

Although we often view organizational culture as a positive force, a culture that is inappropriate for its environment can have negative ramifications. At the extreme, culture can even provide an excuse for inaction. Two researchers suggest that the culture of public organizations is sometimes comprised of "if-onlys" and "thems." These terms may be offered as excuses for nonperformance or as explanations of failure. Such excuses and explanations reflect the numerous constraints under which managers in government operate. "If-onlys" are illustrated by the following statements:

- If only I could fire Jones, then we could get this department in shape (reflects civil service constraints).
- If only the budget division would stop setting expenditure ceilings (reflects legislative constraints).

"Thems" refer to the "adversaries" of public organization managers—that is, the groups that influence or set the constraints. These groups include politicians, the press, consumer groups, and so on.

[If-onlys and thems] foster an elaborate myth that insulates the organization from its environment by creating the expectancy that performance will always be something less than it could be.

When fully institutionalized as part of the culture, if-onlys and thems can produce a wholly negative focus and become defense mechanisms for resisting change and denying the possibility that new technologies might improve organizational performance.

SOURCE: J. W. Whorton and J. A. Worthley, "A Perspective on the Challenge of Public Management: Environmental Paradox and Organizational Culture," *Academy of Management Review* 6 (July 1981): 359–360.

Certainly, such change cannot occur overnight. One authority suggests that top management start gradually to chip away at detrimental cultural aspects and look for special opportunities to implement strategic management principles in narrow, well-defined areas. In this way, management can devote the resources and time that are required for success.[18]

Finally, we would be negligent if we did not emphasize the need for managerial training. In some nonprofit organizations, the top-level managers may be individuals who were sensitive to a particular need in our society and created an organization to serve that need. But even the best of intentions cannot serve society as effectively as good intentions combined with managerial skills. The most socially oriented of programs must, in the long run, use each of its dollars and the time of its employees as effectively and efficiently as it possibly can. Otherwise, all of those who are in need of its services may never receive them or may receive only partial care.

SUMMARY

Strategic management principles apply equally to businesses and not-for-profit organizations. But these two types of institutions differ in some important ways that have strategic implications.

Perhaps the chief distinction is their source of revenue. Businesses generate income in the form of sales revenue; not-for-profit firms may receive revenue from such diverse sources as taxes, dues, contributions, or even sales. But a business's revenue is derived directly from its customers—those who purchase its products or services. However, a not-for-profit's revenue often comes from individuals who may never even use the outputs of that organization. For instance, a public organization may provide welfare payments to families below the poverty level. However, the sources of those funds are taxes paid by income earners with relatively higher salaries. Similarly, a nonprofit organization such as a privately owned museum may allow the public to view its exhibits for no admission fee. But its revenues may be generated by the interest from an endowment created by a family many decades ago. Therefore, not-for-profit organizations must engage in two types of strategic planning—how to serve their clients or customers, and how to secure the necessary financial funding to provide those services.

A second distinction between businesses and nonprofits is that planning in some not-for-profit firms, particularly public organizations, may be complicated by political considerations, which are not relevant to businesses. The large number and diversity of stakeholders in a government agency means that its managers' decisions are more public than they are in other types of organizations. These decisions must be responsive to the wishes of varying constituencies, requiring management to engage in a difficult balancing act.

Although having a clear mission and goals is essential to an organization's success, many not-for-profit organizations fail in this area. Several reasons account for this shortcoming: Goals tend to be value-laden; they often involve important trade-offs; they may be deliberately vague, broad, and general; leadership is subject to frequent turnover, particularly in public organizations; and the goals may not reflect the needs of the organization's customers as much as they reflect the wishes of the organization's financial supporters. The problem, of course, is that vague goals cannot help management measure an organization's progress or its effectiveness.

Strategy implementation in not-for-profit organizations, particularly public agencies, is often highly visible and political. But even if strategies could be implemented in a rational fashion, public managers would still operate under another unique constraint. They have weaker authority in such areas as pay, promotion, termination, and disciplinary action than business managers have. By the same token, managers in private nonprofit firms must often supervise a work force comprised largely of volunteers, which poses a different set of constraints. Other distinctions exist as well. For instance, research shows that not-for-profit organizations implement their strategies in a more centralized fashion than businesses do, and they are sometimes staffed by professional people who may be more committed to their profession than to the organization for which they currently work.

Strategic control, of course, is difficult to achieve when goals are not clearly defined and measurable. It is made even more difficult by the fact that not-for-profit organizations, unlike businesses, cannot usually terminate programs even if they have outlived their usefulness. Just the threat of program termination quickly brings an outcry from those stakeholders who will be adversely affected by the program's demise, and they often wield sufficient political power to forestall termination indefinitely.

However, both nonprofit and public organizations can benefit significantly by following the principles presented in this book. They, as well as businesses, should analyze their environmental opportunities and constraints and formulate mission and goals that allow them to fulfill the needs of some segment of society. They should then develop a strategy that relates their strengths and weaknesses appropriately to their environment and allows them to create a distinctive competence in their operating arena. To implement their strategy, they must fashion an organization structure that enables them to deal with their environmental demands and a culture that enhances their organizational effectiveness. Cultures and reward systems that are too constraining must be altered to improve the organizations' operating efficiency and their long-term effectiveness.

KEY CONCEPTS

Nonprofit organization   A form of not-for-profit organization that is supported by private funds and exists to contribute to the good of society.

Public organization   A form of not-for-profit organization that is created, funded, and regulated by the public sector.

DISCUSSION QUESTIONS

1. Your text states that "nonprofit and public organizations are indispensable to maintaining a civilized society." Explain why.

2. Explain how not-for-profit organizations differ from businesses in the way that they derive their revenue. What are the implications of these differences for strategic management?

3. We have seen that the top managers of public organizations probably have less autonomy than business CEOs because of the greater number and diversity of stakeholders in public organizations. Explain how multiple stakeholder interests can reduce managerial autonomy.

4. Why do not-for-profit organizations often have vague, general goals rather than clear, specific ones?

5. What are the disadvantages of vague, general goals?

6. Select a not-for-profit organization and describe the specific societal needs that it attempts to satisfy. Does it have any competitors? If so, who are they?

7. How does the implementation of strategy in not-for-profit organizations differ from that in businesses?

8. Why is strategy implementation more centralized in not-for-profit organizations than in businesses?

9. From a strategic perspective, what are the difficulties of managing professional employees? Volunteer employees?

10. Why do public organizations have more difficulty terminating programs than businesses have?

STRATEGIC MANAGEMENT EXERCISES

1. Assume that you have the resources and backing to found a university. Formulate a mission statement for your university. Now, develop a set of goals for the university. How would you ensure that the needs of your university's "customers" are met through the goals that you have devised? (Note that customers would include employers of the university's graduates, graduate schools that accept your graduates, students, parents who pay tuition, etc.)

2. Use your own university to answer the following questions: What is your university's mission? What are its major goals? Base your answers on written documents, if they exist; otherwise, you will need to derive your answers from interviews and observation.

   Now, determine what your university's distinctive competence is. (See Chapter 5 for a review of this concept.) What strategies must your university pursue to maintain this distinctive competence? If your university has no particular distinctive competence, what might it do to attain a distinctive competence that would be consistent with its mission and goals?

3. Select a nearby public library as the focal point for this exercise. After gathering information on the library, determine how it might formulate and implement appropriate strategies to serve its constituents and stakeholders better. Give specific examples.

4. The Department of Housing and Urban Development (HUD) is supposed to provide housing for low-income citizens. But in the late 1980s, it became evident that much abuse and fraud had taken place in this organization. From library research of this scandal, suggest how the use of strategic control techniques might have prevented these problems at HUD from ever occurring.

REFERENCES

1. J. A. Byrne, "Profiting from the Nonprofits," *Business Week,* 26 March 1990, p. 67.

2. W. H. Newman and H. W. Wallender, "Managing Not-for-Profit Enterprises," *Academy of Management Review* 3 (1978): 24–31.

3. Reprinted from W. H. Eldridge, "Why Angels Fear to Tread: A Practitioner's Observations and Solutions on Introducing Strategic Management to a Government Culture," in J. Rabin, G. J. Miller, and W. B. Hildreth, eds., *Handbook of Strategic Management* (New York: Dekker, 1989), p. 329, by courtesy of Marcel Dekker Inc.

4. "An Open Letter to the President and the Congress," *The Washington Post,* 13 May 1990.

5. P. F. Drucker, "What Business Can Learn from Nonprofits," *Harvard Business Review* 67, no. 4 (1989): 89.

6. Bryne, "Profiting from the Nonprofits," pp. 67, 70–74.

7. Bryne, "Profiting from the Nonprofits," p. 72.

8. P. D. Harvey and J. D. Snyder, "Charities Need a Bottom Line Too," *Harvard Business Review* 65, no. 1 (1987): 14–22.

9. National Academy of Public Administration, *Revitalizing Federal Management* (Washington, D.C.: National Academy of Public Administration, 1986).

10. D. Priest, "Study Ties Job Success to Bosses," *The Washington Post*, 9 October 1990.

11. P. C. Nutt, "A Strategic Planning Network for Non-profit Organizations," *Strategic Management Journal* 5 (1984): 58.

12. J. Ruffat, "Strategic Management of Public and Non-Market Corporations," *Long Range Planning* 16, no. 4 (1983): 75.

13. W. G. Bennis, N. Berkowitz, M. Affinito, and M. Malone, "Reference Groups and Loyalties in the Out-Patient Department," *Administrative Science Quarterly* 2 (1958): 484.

14. Newman and Wallender, "Managing Not-for-Profit Enterprises," pp. 24–31.

15. J. F. Siler and T. Peterson, "Hospital, Heal Thyself," *Business Week*, 27 August 1990, p. 68.

16. Eldridge, "Why Angels Fear to Tread, p. 329.

17. Eldridge, "Why Angels Fear to Tread, p. 330.

18. Eldridge, "Why Angels Fear to Tread, p. 335.

Cases in Strategic Management

Strategic Management Case Analysis

Most of you are majoring in some aspect of business administration and are already familiar with case analysis. A case portrays a real organizational situation and requires you to analyze that situation and then develop recommendations for future action. The difference between the cases in strategic management and those in previous courses is that the cases here assume a broader perspective. Cases in finance have a financial orientation, and those in organizational behavior usually focus on individual or group behavior; but the cases in this book reflect a broad, companywide perspective. Each case presents a real business organization, and businesses in a wide variety of industries and operating situations are represented.

You have probably already taken a series of courses that specialize in various functional areas, such as marketing, accounting, finance, and production/operations management. This knowledge can prove very useful to you when you begin working as a functional specialist (e.g., accountant, financial analyst, or sales representative). However, most successful business executives eventually move above the functional level into general management positions. As this upward movement occurs, they typically encounter a very different set of problems from those that they dealt with as functional specialists. Unfortunately, their functional expertise is of limited assistance to them in either diagnosing or resolving these general management problems. Success in such activities requires the integration of knowledge in a wide variety of areas, both theoretical and functional. Hence, the objective of this textbook—and the course it accompanies—is to help you develop a general management capability by exposing you to a number of situations that require the integration of knowledge from different functional areas. The contents of this book provide the fundamental framework needed to bring together and integrate what you have learned in other courses so that you will be able to analyze these cases from a companywide perspective.

This introduction should help you analyze the cases contained in this book and assist you in organizing and presenting your thoughts in written form.

READING THE CASE

Case analysis requires you to read the case carefully and to read it more than once. Some students read the case quickly to get an overview of the situation presented and then reread it slowly, taking notes on the important issues and problems. Subsequently, they begin to organize and analyze the case information. However, each person must develop his or her own approach to case analysis. No single technique works well for everyone.

Since cases reflect reality, it should not be surprising that some of the information is not well organized, that irrelevant information is presented, and that relevant information may be dispersed throughout the case. Information rarely comes to us in neatly tied packages. One of your first tasks, therefore, is to organize the information in the case. An outline that can help you organize the material is discussed in the following section, or your professor may provide you with his or her own guidelines for organizing the issues in the case.

Students often have questions about the time frame of a particular case. We have found it most efficient to assume that you are analyzing the case in the year(s) that the case covers. For instance, if the last year covered in the case is 1989, then you should not ordinarily analyze the case with information gathered since that date. In some instances, however, your professor may ask you to update the case, particularly if, at the case's end, significant pending problems and issues are still unresolved.

WRITING THE CASE ANALYSIS

The guidelines presented in the following subsections for the written analysis of cases are offered to help you organize and present your thoughts. (If your professor gives you a set of guidelines, by all means, use those.) As you read the case carefully, you may organize and analyze the information in the case under each of the headings used for the following subsections.

■ Macroenvironment

The macroenvironment, the broadest of all of the sections in your analysis, is intended to help you decipher the macroenvironmental information you extract from the case and organize it selectively under such headings as "Political-Legal," "Economic," "Technological," and "Social." You should read the case for both explicit and implicit information in these categories. Outside research may be necessary to increase the information available in one or more of these areas. Then within each category, your task is to determine what opportunities and threats are presented to the firm featured in the case by that macroenvironmental force.

One way of accomplishing this end is to use headings and, under each heading, discuss how the external forces may act as opportunities or threats to management. Another way is to use brief, descriptive sentences for each heading's topic. For example, if the case is on General Motors, the following "Economic" heading may be used with a brief sentence:

Economic

(Opportunity)   The relatively low recent value of the dollar (compared with its value in the early 1980s) versus foreign currencies has helped GM become more price-competitive.

A threat or constraint may be noted as shown below:

Political-Legal

(Threat)   The U.S. government is demanding higher and higher fuel efficiency standards from U.S. automakers.

A number of different factors may be listed under each of the macroenvironmental headings, depending upon the range of information provided in the case and the extent of your research outside what's given in the case. Some cases may have many relevant factors under, for instance, the heading "Political-Legal" but few under "Technological."

■ Industry Environment

The industry environment section requires you to extract information from the case and from any other available source through your own research and then organize and analyze it under the five industry forces discussed in Chapter 2: "Threat of Entry," "Intensity of Rivalry Among Existing Competitors," "Pressure from Substitute Products," "Bargaining Power of Buyers," and "Bargaining Power of Suppliers." You should use these headings to help you organize your analysis.

For example, assume that the case you are analyzing is General Motors. Under the heading "Threat of Entry," you might mention that economies of scale act as a barrier to domestic companies that may seek to enter the U.S. automobile industry. However, more and more vehicle producers from abroad have entered the American market over the past several years. Thus, although the threat of new entry from U.S. sources is limited, the threat of foreign automakers' exporting their products to America and even building manufacturing facilities in the United States is certainly present.

Under "Bargaining Power of Suppliers," you might mention that most suppliers of automobile parts do not have strong positions relative to GM. For instance, the major U.S. steel companies are not working at full capacity and, hence, would be anxious to sell to GM.

This is not to say that suppliers generally have weak bargaining power. In certain industries, some suppliers possess relatively strong bargaining power relative to buyers. For instance, Monsanto's NutraSweet unit had a strong bargaining position as a supplier to the soft-drink producers until its patent for aspartame expired in 1992.

The point of analyzing the macroenvironment and industry environment, of course, is to relate the opportunities and threats in these two areas to the firm featured in the case. A review of Chapter 2 should help you in this analysis.

■ Mission, Goals, Objectives, Social Responsibility, and Ethics

Parts or all of the heading "Mission, Goals, Objectives, Social Responsibility, and Ethics" may be used for your analysis. Sometimes, information is explicitly provided on these topics; other times, it is implicit, forcing you to read between the lines. One question that you might consider posing and analyzing is the following:

1. Is there an explicit or implicit statement of the firm's mission? Does it accurately portray the direction in which the firm is going, or are the firm's operations incompatible with its mission?

You may recall that in Chapter 3, the mission of General Motors (to continue our example) was stated in the following way:

> The fundamental purpose of General Motors is to provide products and services of such quality that our customers will receive superior value, our employees and business partners will share in our success, and our stockholders will receive a sustained, superior return on their investment.

Unfortunately for GM, there has been a gap between its mission and its actual operating results. Surveys of car owners indicate that GM is not perceived as offering superior value to its customers.[1] In fact, a car produced by Toyota and sold under the GM brand (Geo Prism) has sales far below those of its "twin" product, Corolla, which is produced and marketed by Toyota.[2] Furthermore, GM has laid off large numbers of employees, and its stock has not been a top performer.

Another question you might consider is posed below.

2. Are the expressed or implied goals and objectives of the firm consistent with one another? Is there evidence that these goals and objectives are being attained?

In Chapter 3, we indicated that the goals of various stakeholders often differ. And Chapter 8 pointed out that compromise may be important in helping resolve these differences. Sometimes, however, compromise is not attainable, and the effectiveness of the firm suffers as a result. For example, in the middle to late 1980s, H. Ross Perot—head of Electronic Data Systems, a subsidiary of GM; a member of the GM board of directors; and a major stockholder in GM—desired a course of action for GM that differed significantly from the course favored by GM's top management. Because compromise was unattainable, GM's management purchased Perot's stock holdings for about $750 million, at a time when GM had just incurred a large quarterly loss.

Here is another question you might consider for your analysis.

3. Is the firm operating in a socially responsible manner? Are the decisions and actions of its managers ethical?

As we emphasized in Chapter 3, analysis in the areas of social responsibility and ethics can be difficult, because the guidelines are not always clear-cut. If the case contains these issues, you may have to formulate your own answer to dilemmas such as whether it is socially responsible to lay off employees to enhance a firm's competitiveness or whether social responsibility can be better served by keeping the employees on the payroll, even at the expense of the firm's profits and, perhaps, survival.

■ Corporate Strategies

In analyzing the corporate strategies of the firm, you might consider the following questions:

1. How appropriate are the firm's corporate strategies for its macroenvironment and industry environment?
2. Which specific strategies has the firm adopted—growth, stability, retrenchment, or a combination of these? How effective have these strategies been?

Some corporations have effectively adopted growth strategies, but others have been less successful. Firms that have grown through unrelated acquisitions have, in many cases, found that they do not have the managerial knowledge to conduct all of their businesses in a competitive manner. In a few cases, however, unrelated diversification has been an effective strategy.

Some companies have grown successfully by developing or acquiring businesses with a common core. General Electric, for example, has attained success through involvement in businesses that share a common technological core. In another industry, Philip Morris has been one of the world's most successful consumer products firms, particularly with its tobacco and food businesses. However, Philip Morris was unable to transfer its expertise in consumer products to its marketing of 7-Up, which it eventually divested.

A strategy of retrenchment may be appropriate in certain situations. For instance, Tambrands diversified in the 1980s from a single-product company into such unrelated businesses as home diagnostics and cosmetics. These acquisitions, however, provided "little more than a stream of operating losses and management distraction that has hurt its basic tampon business."[3] In its retrenchment strategy, Tambrands sold both the diagnostics and cosmetics businesses at a loss. However, since pruning those operations, it has performed well by concentrating solely on its tampon business.

■ S.W.O.T. and Portfolio Analyses

You have already analyzed the opportunities and threats in the firm's environment; now, it is time to relate that analysis to the firm's strengths and weaknesses. In this examination of strengths, weaknesses, opportunities, and threats (i.e., S.W.O.T. analysis), of particular concern is an evaluation of the firm's strengths and weaknesses relative to its competitors.

Sometimes, for instance, the business units of a corporation are pitted against strong competitors that concentrate primarily in one line of business. For example, Grand Metropolitan PLC's Burger King business unit has consistently been outperformed by McDonald's. Perhaps the fact that McDonald's concentrates its efforts solely in the fast-food restaurant business works in favor of McDonald's and against Burger King. Besides Burger King, Grand Metropolitan owns several diverse businesses: wine and spirits (J&B, Black Velvet, Gilbey's, Baileys, Smirnoff, Inglenook, Lancer, Almaden), pet food (Alpo, Tabby), yogurt, dairy products, and other foods.

As another example, Anheuser-Busch has consistently performed better than Philip Morris's Miller beer. Again, Anheuser-Busch focuses primarily on the beer business, but Philip Morris's major interests are in tobacco and food products.

However, business units can also benefit significantly from a corporation's core specialties. For example, Pizza Hut, a unit of PepsiCo, is quite competitive within an industry that includes many companies that concentrate only on the pizza business. Its success is largely due to its corporate owner's financial support and expertise in marketing consumer products.

If the company that you are analyzing has multiple business units, you will wish to examine those individual units within the context of the original or revised BCG framework or the GE framework. Portfolio analysis can provide you with further insights regarding the issues in the case. These issues can easily be overlooked when you examine only the corporate "forest" and largely ignore the business unit "trees." Chapter 4 can be of assistance in this analysis.

■ Business Unit Strategies and Functional Strategies

If the case is about a corporation with individual business units, then the units may have adopted different generic business unit strategies. If the firm is in a single business, such as McDonald's or Tambrands, then its business unit and corporate-level strategies are the same. In either case, your task is to identify which business unit strategies the firm has adopted and to evaluate how appropriate those strategies are. Are they compatible with the firm's product/markets and with its objectives for market share? Do they enable it to compete effectively? Here you will wish to refer to Chapter 5 and review the seven generic strategies available to business units.

As discussed in Chapter 6, business unit strategies strongly influence functional strategies; and conversely, the extent to which functional strategies are effectively implemented helps determine the success of the business strategies. In this section of your analysis, you will want to explore the consistency of the business unit strategies and the supporting functional strategies.

For example, if the business unit has adopted a niche–low-cost or low-cost strategy, then it would be inconsistent for it to formulate a marketing strategy with costly advertising and promotion. However, expensive promotional campaigns would be consistent with the niche-differentiation or differentiation strategies.

Your analysis may extend to other considerations as well. For instance, a firm that produces a high-priced luxury product with the niche-differentiation strategy should not pursue a goal of substantially increasing its production/operations capacity and market share. Consumers who purchase luxury products or services do so only as long as the items are relatively unique.

■ Strategy Implementation

The actual implementation of corporate, business unit, and functional strategies is considered in this part of your analysis. Reference to Chapter 7 will help you in evaluating the relationship of the firm's structure to its strategies. Is this structure suitable for a firm with these strategies? Or has the firm outgrown the need for this structure?

Chapter 8 should assist you in determining whether the CEO's leadership style and use of power are appropriate for the firm's strategies. Also consider whether the organization's culture is supportive of the strategies that it is attempting to implement.

Note that some cases will give you considerable information on strategy implementation, organizational charts, organizational culture, and the CEO. Others will provide little data on these matters. If your professor encourages outside research, you can usually collect at least some information on these issues if the firm is a large, publicly held corporation.

■ Strategic Control

Although strategic control was discussed in Chapter 9, the actual process involves every aspect of strategic management. That is, strategic control is a process that must occur in the analysis of the following aspects of the firm:

- Macroenvironment
- Industry environment
- Mission, goals, and objectives
- Strategy formulation
- Strategy implementation

In this section of your analysis, you will want to determine which aspects of the case are in particular need of strategic control scrutiny and, if possible, attempt to bring them together to draw overall conclusions. It is helpful, as Chapter 9 points out, to compare this year's results with those of the firm in previous years. Alternatively, strategic control may be examined by comparing the firm's qualitative and quantitative results with those of its rivals. If you have access to the PIMS program, you may wish to use it for these comparisons.

Besides PIMS, there are other sources of data available for assessing strategic control. They include Dun & Bradstreet's *Industry Norms and Key Business Ratios* and various publications by Value Line, Standard and Poor's, Moody's, and Robert Morris Associates. Additional information can be gleaned from annual reports and 10-K reports of the firm's chief competitors. Recall that strategic control involves not only quantitative data but also qualitative information. Annual reports and industry analyses, such as those by Standard and Poor's and Moody's, are particularly rich in qualitative information.

Financial ratios are central to your quantitative analysis. The idea is to calculate certain key ratios and then compare them with (1) the median ratios in the industry; (2) the ratios of the firm's major competitors; and (3) the firm's ratios in prior years in order to discern trends. Exhibit 1 lists many of the most important ratios, shows how to calculate them, and indicates what they mean.

A less common ratio, market to book value, should also be calculated. Simply divide the firm's latest stock price by its book value per share; the result helps indicate whether investors view the firm's future positively. If the ratio is greater than 1, then investors forecast that the company's return on equity is expected to be greater than its required rate of return. If it is less than 1, then the firm's forecasted return on equity is less than its required rate of return. This ratio allows you to assess how favorably the stock market views the strategic direction of the firm.

■ Your Recommendations for Future Action

In the preceding sections of your analysis, you have probably identified issues, problems, and inconsistencies that need to be addressed. At this point, you should make recommendations in those areas. That is, what should the company do next? In some cases, modifications may need to be made in the firm's corporate-level strategies; in others, only one or several of the functional strategies (e.g., financial strategy or marketing strategy) may need improvement.

The recommendations should be addressed to the firm's top management and should be well organized and well thought through. Also, they should be feasible in terms of financial, human, and physical resources. Here, your ability

Exhibit 1   **Financial Ratios**

Ratio	Formula	What the Ratios Represent
Liquidity Ratios		
Current ratios	$\dfrac{\text{Current assets}}{\text{Current liabilities}}$	Indicates how much of the current liabilities the current assets can cover; ordinarily, a ratio of 2 to 1 or better is desirable
Quick ratio or acid-test ratio	$\dfrac{\text{Current assets } - \text{ inventory}}{\text{Current liabilities}}$	Indicates how much of the current liabilities the current assets can immediately cover, excluding the inventory (since inventories may not be subject to immediate sale or may have a lower market value than book value)
Inventory–to–net working capital ratio	$\dfrac{\text{Inventory}}{\text{Current assets } - \text{ current liabilities}}$	Indicates to what extent net working capital may be threatened by inventory buildup
Activity Ratios		
Inventory turnover	$\dfrac{\text{Net sales}}{\text{Inventory}}$	Indicates how many times average inventory of finished goods is sold per year
Days of inventory	$\dfrac{\text{Inventory}}{\text{Cost of goods sold } \div 365}$	Indicates the number of one day's inventory the firm has at a given time
Net working capital	$\dfrac{\text{Net sales}}{\text{Net working capital}}$	Measures how efficiently net working capital is used to produce net sales
Asset turnover	$\dfrac{\text{Sales}}{\text{Total assets}}$	Measures how efficiently the company's total assets are used to produce sales
Fixed-asset turnover	$\dfrac{\text{Sales}}{\text{Fixed assets}}$	Measures how efficiently fixed assets (plant, equipment, buildings, etc.) produce sales
Average collection period	$\dfrac{\text{Accounts receivable}}{\text{Sales for year } \div 365}$	Measures the number of days it takes to convert accounts receivable into cash
Accounts receivable turnover	$\dfrac{\text{Annual credit sales}}{\text{Accounts receivable}}$	Measures the number of times accounts receivable is turned over in a year
Accounts payable period	$\dfrac{\text{Accounts payable}}{\text{Purchases for year } \div 365}$	Indicates the number of times accounts payable is turned over in a year
Days of cash	$\dfrac{\text{Cash}}{\text{Net sales for year } \div 365}$	Measures the number of days of cash on hand within the context of recent revenue levels
Leverage Ratios		
Debt-to-asset ratio	$\dfrac{\text{Total debt}}{\text{Total assets}}$	Indicates the percentage that borrowed funds are utilized to finance the assets of the firm
Debt-to-equity ratio	$\dfrac{\text{Total debt}}{\text{Stockholders' equity}}$	Indicates the percentage of funds provided by creditors as compared with owners

Ratio	Formula	What the Ratios Represent
Leverage Ratios		
Long-term debt–to–equity ratio	$$\frac{\text{Long-term debt}}{\text{Stockholders' equity}}$$	Indicates the percentage of funds provided by long-term creditors as compared with owners
Times interest earned	$$\frac{\text{Profit before taxes} + \text{interest charges}}{\text{Interest charges}}$$	Measures the capability of the firm to make good on its yearly interest costs
Profitability Ratios		
Return on investment	$$\frac{\text{Net income before taxes}}{\text{Total assets}}$$	Measures rate of return on total assets employed
Return on equity	$$\frac{\text{Net profit after taxes}}{\text{Stockholders' equity}}$$	Measures the rate of return on the book value of total stockholders' equity
Return on sales	$$\frac{\text{Net operating profit before taxes}}{\text{Net sales}}$$	Indicates ratio of return on net sales

to convince your instructor and classmates of the accuracy of your analysis and the power of your recommendations is of utmost importance.

In the final part of this section, you may want to deal with a synthesis of your proposals as they affect the entire organization. Remember that a change that you recommend in one aspect of the organization's strategies or operations may affect several other parts of the company.

We must emphasize that not all cases provide comprehensive information on all of the topics discussed in this chapter. Some may focus only on specific areas, such as ethics or new-product development. The framework presented here encompasses the total organization within its environment. Consequently, you may or may not be able to use this entire set of topics in analyzing any particular case. However, in any case analysis, you may find the information in Exhibit 2 useful. This table relates each section of your analysis to the corresponding chapter in this textbook. Prior to beginning your analysis, it may help you to scan or reread the discussion in the text regarding a particular issue.

COURSEWORK SUGGESTIONS

We would like to conclude by offering you some suggestions on how to perform well in the strategic management course.

1. Be actively involved in the course. At a minimum, you should attend all classes and participate fully in the class discussions. Participation involves asking questions, expressing your views, providing relevant examples from your own experience or outside reading, and helping extend the discussion to other related issues. Of course, case discussions can only be exciting when you have prepared for each class by knowing the facts and understanding the issues in the case. Thorough preparation will enable you to convey your knowledge and

Exhibit 2   **Cross-Reference Information for Case Analyses**

Section of Analysis	Textbook Chapter
Macroenvironment	Chapter 2, "Environmental Opportunities and Threats"
Industry environment	Chapter 2, "Environmental Opportunities and Threats"
Mission, goals, objectives, social responsibility, and ethics	Chapter 3, "Organizational Direction: Mission and Goals"
Corporate strategies	Chapter 4, "Corporate-Level Strategies"
S.W.O.T. and portfolio analyses	Chapter 4, "Corporate-Level Strategies"
Business unit strategies and functional strategies	Chapter 5, "Business Unit Strategies"; Chapter 6, "Functional Strategies"
Strategy implementation	Chapter 7, "Strategic Implementation: Organizational Structure"; Chapter 8, "Strategy Implementation: Leadership, Power, and Organizational Culture"
Strategic control	Chapter 9, "Strategic Control"

understanding to others clearly and persuasively. These skills are of considerable importance to a practicing manager.

2.   As you participate, remember that this is a broad-based course in strategic management. Regardless of your particular academic major, attempt to view the issues in the case more broadly than you ordinarily might from the more limited perspective of a marketing major or a finance major, for instance. Remember that the goal is an integrated set of recommendations to top management.

3.   Do not approach class discussions with a closed mind. A good discussion can bring out many different facets in a case—probably more than you can generate through an individual analysis. Listen to the other members of the class and evaluate their contributions carefully.

4.   Do not let yourself be intimidated by a bad experience. Eventually, everyone in class may make an inane comment, may panic and lose the train of thought in midsentence, or may realize as he or she is speaking that what is being said is incorrect. Do not let these experiences affect your willingness to participate in the future. Participation in case analysis is an excellent training ground for future business presentations and committee meetings.

5.   Do not suggest the use of a consultant. You are the consultant and should have specific, detailed recommendations for top management.

6.   Learn to work well within a group. Many professors form teams of students in the strategic management course. Teamwork adds realism to the study of the cases since, in reality, groups of key executives deal with strategic plan-

ning in business organizations. Working in a group, however, presents a particular set of challenges. Hence, we offer these suggestions:

- If you are allowed to select your group members, ensure that they have similar objectives for their grade in the course (i.e., if you are aiming for an A, do not join a group comprised of students who wish to just squeak by, even if they are your best friends) and that you all have compatible schedules that permit you to meet outside of class.

- Try to form a group that is made up of individuals with different academic majors. Synergy is more likely to occur when the group has students who are majoring in different fields, such as finance, accounting, information systems, human resource management, and production/operations management.

- Do not divide the case into parts and assign an individual to each part. This technique will result in a fragmented, piecemeal, and disjointed analysis. Even if the primary responsibility for various parts of the case is assigned to specific individuals, every member of the group should be involved in all parts of the case analysis.

- Cooperate closely with one another. Through cooperation and a free exchange of ideas, the team should be able to devise innovative solutions to case problems. But the only way to accomplish this is for every member to participate fully during the team meetings. Ideally, only one person should talk at a time, while the others listen. One member should record all of the ideas expressed. If one person is particularly shy, others should encourage that person to talk by using such techniques as asking "What is your opinion on that issue?"

- Divide the work equitably. If one member is not doing his or her fair share, you must diplomatically, but quickly, inform that person that more is expected.

- Prepare thoroughly for the oral presentation. It is essential that you rehearse, as a group, several times. Ensure that each member knows his or her cue for speaking. Do not bring extensive notes and read from them. On the other hand, do not memorize your part word for word. Rather, prepare an outline of your part, and then let the key points on the outline guide your presentation.

- Get accustomed to speaking before people. Such presentations are routine in most aspects of the business world, so this course gives you an excellent opportunity to overcome your hesitancy to talk before a large group. If you have prepared well and have rehearsed several times, your presentation will be well received by your audience, even though you personally may feel a bit uncomfortable.

SUMMARY

The remainder of this textbook contains cases. A case portrays a real organizational situation and requires you to analyze that situation and then develop recommendations for future action. To accomplish these ends, you will need to take a broad, companywide perspective.

After reading the case carefully several times, you will want to take notes to organize your analysis and presentation. We suggest that you analyze the case by using the following outline:

- Macroenvironment
- Industry environment
- Mission, goals, objectives, social responsibility, and ethics
- Corporate strategies
- S.W.O.T. and portfolio analyses
- Business unit strategies and functional strategies
- Strategy implementation
- Strategic control
- Your recommendations for future action

Finally, we offer several suggestions for enhancing your performance in the strategic management course and for working within a group.

REFERENCES

1. P. Ingrassia and J. B. White, "With Its Market Share Sliding, GM Scrambles to Avoid a Calamity," *The Wall Street Journal*, 14 December 1989.

2. J. B. Treece, "Will Detroit Cut Itself Loose from Captive Imports?" *Business Week*, 4 September 1989, p. 34.

3. A. Dunkin, "They're More Single-Minded at Tambrands," *Business Week*, 28 August 1989, p. 28.

Spec's Music, Inc. (A)

Carol A. Reeves, University of Miami

Ann Spector Lieff, Chief Executive Officer of Spec's Music and Video, was excited but nervous about the changes that would be occurring in her company over the next few years. The Spec's of 1985 was far different from the Spec's that Ms. Lieff's father founded in Miami in 1948. The company had grown from a single store selling primarily records, to a sixteen-store chain selling records, tapes, compact discs, videotapes, and related products. The year 1985 was poised to be the most eventful year in Spec's history, as the company was scheduled to issue stock in order to raise funds for future expansion efforts. Ms. Lieff was enthusiastic about the future possibilities for the company but was concerned about whether the company could meet the growth projections management had made and, if the projections were met, whether Spec's could handle the growth. She knew that her decisions in the next year would have a tremendous impact on the future of the company.

SPEC'S HISTORY

After practicing law for a few years in the late 1920s, Martin Spector became a talent agent in the entertainment industry, a career that culminated with a two-year stint as Head of Talent for Universal Pictures after World War II. In 1948, Mr. Spector moved to Miami with his wife and young son and started a new career when he opened a retail store that sold records, cameras, and televisions. The store, which bore his nickname, Spec, provided a solid means of support for the growing Spector family, which soon included two sons and two daughters.

This case is intended for classroom discussion only, not to depict effective or ineffective handling of administrative situations. All rights reserved to the author and the North American Case Research Association.

A second Spec's store was opened in 1966, and a third was added four years later. The first three stores were located in the Miami area, but in 1972 Spec's extended its operations by opening a store in central Florida. From 1975 to 1984, Spec's added three more stores in the central region of the state and nine additional stores in the greater Miami area. All sixteen of these stores were financed from the operations of the company. However, Spec's could not support the increased rate of expansion management desired without the use of outside funds. At the prompting of a cousin who worked for an underwriting firm, Martin Spector and his daughters decided that they would make an initial public offering of stock in Spec's in October 1985. The funds received from the stock sale were to be used to fund the opening of stores outside of south Florida.

■ The Spectors and Spec's

All of the Spector children worked at Spec's on the weekends and during the holidays when they were growing up. The two sons worked for the company for a short period of time after graduating from college, but neither decided to pursue a career with Spec's. The daughters were a different story.

Martin Spector called his daughters into his office in 1980 and transferred all of his stock to them, primarily for estate-planning purposes. At the time, the stock transfer had little impact; the stock was not traded and Mr. Spector retained preferred stock, which gave him considerable decision-making power in the company. Now that stock in the company was going to be traded publicly, the daughters could become wealthy as a result of their father's generosity in 1980, as long as Spec's continued on its successful path.[1]

Ros, the oldest daughter, had begun working for Spec's full-time after graduating from Washington University with a degree in English in 1972. She moved away from Miami in 1975 but returned to the city and to Spec's in 1979. She has served as Treasurer since 1979 and Executive Vice President since 1980. In addition to her duties as Treasurer, she was in charge of human resources at the company.

Ann, the youngest Spector, earned a degree in Sociology from the University of Denver in 1974 and has been working for the company since that time. She worked in a variety of positions from 1974 to 1981, including buyer, store manager, regional supervisor, and Vice President. In 1980, she assumed the role of President and Chief Executive Officer from her father.

Mr. Spector and his daughters have developed a very comfortable working relationship over the past decade. Ann, 32, and Ros, 34, have a tremendous amount of respect for Mr. Spector's knowledge of the music industry and discuss all major decisions with him. Although Mr. Spector was 80 years old, he was very active in the business. He served as Chairman of the Board and has become the company's primary liaison with potential stockholders and the investment community. He was also primarily responsible for site selection for new stores, an area in which he has made few mistakes over the past 40 years.

The daughters still followed the business practices that their father established with his first store. Spec's was known in the industry for its high ethical

---

[1]Ann Lieff and Rosiland Spooner each owned 700,000 of the 1,400,000 shares of stock in the company at the end of 1984. An additional 600,000 shares were to be offered in the initial public offering (IPO), with provisions for 90,000 extra shares to cover overallotments. The daughters would each control 35 percent of the stock of the company after the IPO.

standards, a trait regarded as rare in the music business. Mr. Spector attributed the growth of the company to a philosophy based on paying the bills on time, taking care of key employees, and treating the customers well so that they would come back and also tell others about the store. According to Ms. Lieff, "We don't take shortcuts and we aren't greedy. We're more concerned about being ethical and profitable than with getting big."

PRERECORDED MUSIC INDUSTRY[2]

■ Record Producers

There were six major producers of prerecorded music in 1985: Warner Communications (Warner Brothers, Atlantic, and Elektra/Asylum labels), CBS (Columbia and Epic labels), RCA, EMI Ltd. (Capitol and EMI labels), MCA (MCA, Coral, and Infinity labels), and Polygram (Polydor, RSO, Casablanca, and Capricorn labels). These producers wield considerable power over music retailers due to several factors. Record producers determine shipments of inventory and preferential treatment is given to large customers. If a record store cannot stock hit albums as they are released, a prime profit opportunity for the store has been lost.

Effective advertising campaigns are critical to bringing customers into record stores. To promote their albums, record producers engage in cooperative advertising with retailers. However, cooperative advertising dollars go to larger retailers because of their ability to advertise on a large scale and reach more customers. Larger accounts are also able to participate in promotional appearances by recording stars. Smaller accounts do not enjoy these benefits, making it much more difficult for them to compete with regional and national chains.

■ Industry Rebound

After four of the worst years in the recording industry since the late 1940s, sales increased to $4.4 billion in 1984, exceeding the former record of $4.1 billion in 1978. Several factors influenced the decline and subsequent turnaround of the industry.

The tremendous increase in home taping during the late 1970s and early 1980s had a strongly negative impact on record sales. Unit sales of blank audiotapes grew from less than 65 million in 1978 to 215 million by 1983. It was estimated that at least 84 percent of blank audiocassettes were used to record music, costing the industry approximately $2.5 billion in lost retail sales in 1984. The record industry was arguing with members of Congress that music marketers should receive a royalty from blank audiotape sales. Congressional movement on this issue was uncertain, with the result that record retailers began to carry the items that had once been their archenemy—blank audiotapes. Blank tapes, with a profit margin that was typically two to three times higher than prerecorded music, helped retailers' bottom lines considerably.

[2]The primary sources of information for this section are Bob Marich, "Record Retailers Test Enemy Waters," *Advertising Age*, January 23, 1983, pp. 44–45; "New Technologies Spur Growth," *Standard and Poor's Industry Surveys*, February 1986, pp. L34–L36; "Sales Recover Strongly After Four-Year Decline," *Standard and Poor's Industry Surveys*, January 1985, pp. L32–L34.

The booming popularity of video games also hurt the recording industry during 1980–1982. Instead of adding to their record collections, 15–24-year-olds began channeling much of their energy and dollars toward video games. In an attempt to capture the dollars of one of their best customer groups, many record retailers began to stock video game software. The dramatic decline in the popularity of video games in late 1982 and early 1983 left these retailers with a large amount of obsolete inventory that had to be marked down to "firesale prices." Once the video game craze went bust, record sales increased, but not enough to offset the losses these retailers sustained from their video game inventory, and many smaller stores were forced to leave the record business.

As is typical of leisure industries, the record industry suffers when the economy declines. However, the low-price points of music items insulate the industry somewhat from economic declines. Record sales decreased during the recession years of 1980–1982 but increased again, with a slight lag, when the economy rebounded in 1983. Record sales continued to increase as the economy grew stronger in 1984.

In an effort to increase their profitability, record producers began to implement less generous return policies for record retailers in 1979. Until then, record outlets could order as many records as they desired and exchange those that didn't sell for new titles. Following increasingly large numbers of returns, record producers began limiting the number of copies of albums that could be exchanged for new titles to 20 percent. As a result, retailers were unwilling to assume the risk that came with a new, untried product. This risk aversion was exacerbated by a reluctance on the part of radio stations to give airtime to new artists, creating a Catch-22 situation: Record sales were declining because of a lack of exciting new artists, but new artists couldn't get exposure because record stores and radio stations didn't want to take a chance on unproven artists.

The profitability of both record producers and retailers is dependent on blockbuster hits from performers. It is estimated that only one in five records breaks even, making it critical to record companies that they sign the artist or groups that can go to the top of the charts. Retailers depend on hit records to draw customers into the store. Unfortunately for producers and retailers, hits were rare in the early 1980s.

In 1983, music videos, pioneered by MTV, created new excitement in the industry by reviving interest in established artists and exposing new artists and groups. Much of the new music originated in Britain and was a combination of rock, soul, and reggae. Groups such as Talking Heads, Eurythmics, the Thompson Twins, Culture Club, Cyndi Lauper, Billy Idol, and Duran Duran represented a great diversity of music styles and brought buyers back into record stores. In addition, record producers began to relax their return policies in 1983, making it easier for retailers to stock albums by new performers.

■ Changing Technology in the Record Industry

In addition to the improved economy, introduction of music videos, emergence of new artists, and declining popularity of video games, an exciting new technology, compact discs (CDs), spurred sales in 1984. Compact discs, introduced in 1982 by Sony, use a digitally encoded recording format that is read by a laser beam rather than a needle, making sound reproduction superior to that of vinyl albums and tapes. An additional benefit of the CD is its immunity from the effects of wear and tear and its freedom from sound distortion.

CDs were appealing to record producers and retailers because they were more profitable than LPs (long-playing records) and generated higher margins. Shipments of compact discs increased from 0.8 million units in 1983 to 5.8 million units in 1984. It was estimated that CD shipments would approach 15 million units in 1985 as new CD production facilities were brought on-line. Demand for CDs was expected to increase dramatically as the prices of CD players and CDs declined with increased production.

Another music format that was becoming increasingly popular was prerecorded cassettes. From 1978 to 1983 sales of cassettes rose 186 percent, from 61.3 to 236.8 million units, making them the most popular format for prerecorded music. Sales increased another 40 percent in 1984, to a record 332 million units. The increased sales of cassettes came at the expense of LPs and eight-track tapes. Shipments of eight-tracks declined 96 percent from 1978 and accounted for just 5.9 million units in 1984. Sales were expected to drop to zero in the next few years. LP sales declined steadily from 1978 to 1984, dropping from over 400 million units to approximately 200 million units in 6 years. This decline was expected to continue as CDs become more popular. Exhibit 1 presents annual shipments of music items for the years 1978–1984.

■ Outlook for the Industry

The long-term outlook for the record industry was favorable in early 1985 but was tempered by several factors. The industry is price-sensitive and prices were beginning to creep upward. In contrast, Paramount Pictures had just dropped prices for its best-selling videotapes to $24.95, causing concern that money would go toward these instead of prerecorded music, particularly during the critical Christmas season.

Seven-Year Summary of Annual Music Shipments: Units and Dollar Volume   **Exhibit 1**
(in millions of dollars at suggested retail list price)

	1978	*1979*	*1980*	*1981*	*1982*	*1983*	*1984*
Disk	190.0	195.5	164.3	154.7	137.2	124.8	131.5
Singles	$260.3	$275.4	$269.3	$256.4	$283.0	$269.3	$298.7
LPs/EPs	341.3	318.3	322.8	295.2	243.9	209.6	204.6
	$2473.3	$2136.0	$2290.3	$2341.7	$1925.1	$1689.0	$1548.8
CDs	—	—	—	—	—	0.8	5.8
	—	—	—	—	—	$17.2	$103.3
Cassettes	61.3	82.8	110.2	137.0	182.3	236.8	332.0
	$449.8	$604.6	$776.4	$1062.8	$1384.5	$1810.9	$2383.9
8-Tracks	133.6	104.7	86.4	48.5	14.3	6.0	5.9
	$948.0	$669.4	$526.4	$309.0	$49.0	$27.9	$35.7
Totals	726.2	701.1	683.7	635.4	577.7	578.0	679.8
	$4131.4	$3685.4	$3862.4	$3969.9	$3641.6	$3814.3	$4370.4

Source: Recording Industry Association of America Market Research Committee.

Note: Top line represents manufacturers' unit shipments. Bottom line represents manufacturers' dollar value of shipments.

Demographic changes were also a concern to the record industry. The prime 15-to-24-year-old age group, which accounted for 41 percent of sales in 1983, was projected to decline by 13.4 percent between 1984 and 1990. The 25-to-34-year-old group, which accounted for another 26 percent of sales, was projected to grow by only 6.1 percent, failing to offset the decline in younger consumers. The fastest-growing age group would be those from 35 to 44, a group that had traditionally not purchased much music. However, hope exists in the industry that as records from the 1960s and 1970s are rereleased on CDs, older, more affluent consumers can be persuaded to replace their worn albums with CDs.

There was also a growing backlash in the country against what many parents considered offensive lyrics in new records. Some parents alleged that several records, when played backwards, extol the virtues of devil worship. A group headed by Tipper Gore, the wife of a senator, was clamoring for Congress to ban the offensive records or, at a minimum, require them to carry warning labels. Recording artists were against regulation, citing their Constitutional right to free speech. It appeared that this issue would continue to be fought during the next few years.

COMPETITION

Spec's main competitors in 1984 were Musicland, Record Bar, Peaches Music, Q Records, and Vibrations and Coconuts, subsidiaries of Trans World Music Corp. Many "mom and pop" stores also operated in Florida.

Musicland, a subsidiary of American Can, was the largest record retailer in the country in 1984. Musicland, according to management, had "effected a dramatic turnaround in its 430-store chain by improving store productivity and mix and by implementing up-to-date inventory control systems."[3] American Can was in the midst of a restructuring program that encompassed selling off businesses and assets in slow-growing industries and investing in industries where the outlook was more favorable. Management had full confidence that Musicland would continue to dominate the record retailing industry and plans to give it the resources necessary to maintain its number one position.

The second largest record retailer in 1984 was Record Bar, a private company based in Durham, North Carolina. Sales for Record Bar totaled $102 million in 1984, and the company expected strong growth in the future.

Trans World Music was a publicly held company that competed in the Florida market with its Coconuts, Vibrations, and Record Town stores. Total sales for Trans World Music were $39.4 million in 1984, up from $24.7 million in 1983 and $6.7 million in 1982. Net income for these years was $76,000 in 1982, $396,000 in 1983, and $1.2 million in 1984. Trans World anticipated that the growth in sales and earning would continue in the future.

Spec's Florida-based competitors included Peaches Music, Q Records and Tapes, and small retailers. Neither Peaches nor Q were expected to grow substantially in the next few years. As small private companies, they lacked the resources for major expansion efforts. "Mom and pop" stores did not pose much of a threat to Spec's because of the preferential treatment in advertising and promotion that larger accounts, like Spec's, receive from record producers.

[3]1984 Annual Report, American Can Company.

With sixteen stores, Spec's was the largest record chain in south Florida in 1984 and the second largest chain in the state of Florida. However, this dominance was unlikely to continue unless the company grew. National chains such as Musicland, Record Bar, Camelot, and Trans World Music were beginning to appreciate that Florida's demographics, in terms of both age and disposable income, were favorable and had made plans to expand in the state. Florida's population was expected to continue growing at a rapid pace in the foreseeable future, making the state very attractive to the national record retailers.

The Spector family realized that if they failed to increase their presence in Florida, they would quickly be overwhelmed by the national chains. According to Ms. Lieff, "We have the name recognition and a foothold in the state. We want to grow and keep our market share and avoid getting swallowed up by the national chains." However, the growth that would be needed could not be financed from retained earnings, as all past growth had been. The family decided to lead Spec's through a dramatic change by raising money through the sale of stock.

SPEC'S MUSIC[4]

Spec's Music sold records, cassettes and compact discs, video movies, music videos, blank audio- and videotapes, personal electronics products, and a variety of audio and video accessories in its sixteen stores. Seven stores also rented video movies. Spec's prided itself on the appearance of its stores, the atmosphere, and the customer service found in them. Management felt that their prices were comparable to those of the competition but that their selection and service were superior.

Spec's warehouse and corporate offices were located in a 22,000-square-foot building in west Miami. The close proximity of the warehouse allowed Spec's to restock store inventories two to three times per week, much more frequently than their competition. Stores in the south Florida area were served by two company trucks, while those in central Florida were served by common carriers, which usually provided next-day service.

Spec's was one of the first record retailers to locate more of its stores outside of malls. By 1984, eight stores were in regional malls, six were in shopping centers, and two, including the original store, were in freestanding locations. Because of parking proximity and ease of access, customers prefer to rent videotapes in shopping centers and freestanding locations and management intends to open most new stores in these locations. Spec's aggressive movement into videotape rentals was appealing to many in the investment community, who predicted a boom in the popularity of video rentals. Spec's management, along with the investment community, felt that video products complemented their music products and would provide them with strong growth in the coming years.

Twelve of the Spec's stores were located in south Florida (Dade, Broward, and Palm Beach Counties), while the remaining four stores were located in cen-

[4]Information on Spec's was gathered through interviews with management and "Prospectus, Spec's Music," October 10, 1985.

Exhibit 2   **Existing and Proposed Locations**

tral Florida. Additionally, six leases have been signed for the central Florida area. (See Exhibit 2 for a map containing current and proposed Spec's locations.)

Each Spec's store operated with relative autonomy until mid-1984. Stores had their own buyers, and store managers were responsible for making sure that the store was operated in accordance with company guidelines and procedures. Four regional supervisor positions were created in 1984. Regional supervisors visited the stores regularly to provide on-site management and support to the store managers. The supervisors reported directly to Ms. Lieff.

■ Management[5]

In addition to Martin Spector, Ann Spector Lieff, and Rosiland Spector Spooner, two other Spector relatives work for Spec's. Dorothy Spector, Martin Spector's wife, has served as company Secretary since the company was incorporated in 1970. She served as company Treasurer from 1970 to 1978 but no longer played an active role in the company.

William Lieff, Ann Lieff's husband, had been with the company since 1975 and has served as Vice President of Development since 1978. His duties include facilities management, construction, and new-store planning.

---

[5]Information on Spec's personnel was derived from interviews and "Spec's: Music to Your Ears for Forty Years," *Billboard*, May 28, 1988, p. S4.

Although not a part of the Spector family, other members of the top management team are considered family by the Spectors. The opinions of these managers are carefully considered when decisions are being made. Mr. Spector is referred to by his last name by most members of the company but the daughters are on a first-name basis with the vast majority of employees.

Joe Andrules, Vice President of Advertising and General Manager of the company since 1978, began his retail career with the Tower Records chain. He began working for Spec's as a store manager in 1975 and quickly moved up the ranks. He supervised the central Florida stores briefly but became increasingly involved with the advertising end of the company. Mr. Andrules was in charge of all advertising and promotional activities for the company.

Peter Blei, Chief Financial Officer, was the newest member of the Spec's management team. Unlike the rest of the senior management team, Mr. Blei did not work his way up through the Spec's organization. Before joining Spec's in 1984, he was Executive Vice President of MJS Entertainment Corporation, a wholesale distributor of records and tapes. (MJS was owned by Michael Spector, the eldest Spector child.) Mr. Blei has an MBA from Barry University and worked as a CPA with Peat Marwick Main for seven years. At the end of 1984 Mr. Blei was given responsibility for inventory management, an area of the company that had not been updated in years.

Diane Eklund, Vice President of Purchasing, has been employed by the company in various supervisory and merchandising positions since 1968. She has served in her current position since 1978.

■ Personnel

At the end of 1984, Spec's had approximately 240 employees, 140 of whom were full-time workers. Temporary employees were added during peak sales periods, such as Christmas. All salespeople were compensated on an hourly basis and did not receive sales commissions. To encourage sales efforts, the company occasionally sponsored store sales contests. The company provided health and dental benefits for full-time employees. Spec's stressed promotion from within its organization; regional and store managers have been employed by Spec's in various positions for an average of seven years. Management believed that employee relations were good.

■ Product/Market Mix

Spec's main customer groups were high school and college students. Video sales and rentals were beginning to bring in older customers and management hoped that these individuals could be persuaded to buy music along with their videos. Although stores carried the same basic inventory, merchandise stocked in each store varied by customer buying patterns. For example, Spec's stores in the Miami area carried more music preferred by Hispanics. The company carried a broad range of music, including popular selections, rock, country, classical, and soul. Sixty percent of Spec's inventory was purchased from the six leading record producers.

Spec's sales by category type broke down in the following manner:

Cassettes	35%
Phonograph records	32

Compact discs	6%
Video sales and rentals	11
Other	16

Sales figures in Exhibit 1 provide a breakdown of sales for music stores on a national basis.

■ Advertising and Marketing[6]

The company's marketing strategy was to position itself as the dominant retailer of prerecorded music and video products in the geographical areas in which it operated. It provided a broad selection of inventory at competitive prices in order to appeal to customers' desires for new products and to respond to customers' demands for existing products.

To promote sales, the company placed a strong emphasis on store appearance, merchandising, and customer service. It sought to create a clean, friendly, and exciting atmosphere which would appeal to customers. Several of the stores had won awards for design and architecture.

The company pursued an aggressive mass-media advertising program through radio, television, and newspapers, and frequently offered specials and promotions. In addition, in conjunction with major record manufacturers, the company participated in special promotions for south Florida appearances of prominent recording artists. Twelve of the company's stores were located within a 60-mile area covered by the company's advertising on radio and television in the south Florida area, thereby maximizing its cost-effectiveness.

The company's advertising stressed promotional pricing, broad assortment and depth of merchandise, and the convenience of store locations. The company's approach was to be flexible in decisions regarding advertising and to make changes to advertising copy on short notice, when necessary, in order to publicize product promotions or to take advantage of new products or unexpected market developments. The company had in-house advertising capabilities but went outside the company for marketing expertise on occasion.

Most of the vendors from whom the company purchased prerecorded music and blank audio- and videotapes offered their customers an advertising allowance, which is often based on a percentage of the customer's purchases. These allowances usually required a participating customer to submit advertising campaigns to the appropriate vendor for approval prior to their use. Spec's took full advantage of vendors' advertising allowances.

■ Finance

All of Spec's growth had been financed internally and the company had no long-term debt on its balance sheet. (See Exhibit 3 for financial statements of the company.) Spec's had never found itself in financial difficulty and had always been able to take advantage of the discounts, typically 2 percent, offered by record producers for payment within 60 days. According to Ms. Lieff, "Paying our bills on time allows us to control our own destiny. Record companies love to work with us because they know they will receive timely payment for their

---

[6]The section on advertising and marketing is taken virtually verbatim from "Preliminary Prospectus, Spec's Music, Inc.," October 10, 1985.

Selected Financial Information (in thousands, except per share, store, and square-foot data)				Exhibit 3

	Years Ended July 31,			
	1981 (unaudited)	1982 (unaudited)	1983 (unaudited)	1984
Income Statement Data				
Net sales	$10,565	$11,950	$13,244	$15,028
Cost of goods sold	6,134	7,027	8,414	9,428
Gross profit	4,431	4,923	4,830	5,780
Store operating, general and administrative exp.	3,614	4,347	4,879	4,836
Other expenses (income)	(102)	(147)	(160)	139
Earnings before taxes and extraordinary item	919	723	111	805
Provision for income taxes	428	319	17	348
Earnings before extraordinary item	491	404	94	457
Extraordinary item	—	—	—	—
Net earnings	491	404	94	457
Net earnings per common share	0.32	0.26	0.04	0.29
Balance Sheet Data				
Working capital	$ 206	$ 565	$ 560	$ 733
Total assets	2,850	3,271	3,671	4,636
Common stockholders' equity	525	884	934	1,346
Operating Data				
Number of stores	14	14	15	16
Net sales per store	$ 778	$ 854	$ 903	$ 985
Sq. ft. of selling space	31,200	33,600	34,400	35,300
Net sales/sq. ft.	$ 339	$ 356	$ 385	$ 42

products." Spec's had a $500,000 unsecured bank revolving line of credit that had never been used. Although the company has not used debt in the past, management is not opposed to using debt in the future if it becomes necessary.

■ Management Information Systems

Spec's management information systems capability had not been upgraded for several years but progress was being made in this area. Inventory control was done manually through inventory cards on each item. The company was dissatisfied with the amount of time it took for cash to move from the stores and into interest-bearing central accounts. To help alleviate this problem, actions had been taken to install new cash registers and hand-held optical scanners in 1985. These would allow the company to collect more data regarding sales, inventory levels, returns, and product orders. The information would be transmitted on a daily basis to the company's central computer for processing and inventory replenishment. When fully operational, the system will permit a buyer in the central warehouse to place orders directly with vendors. The system will also be used to transmit daily cash and payroll information from the stores to the central computer. Peter Blei, CFO, had been given responsibility for overseeing the development and installation of the computer system.

THE PLAN FOR EXPANSION

Spec's planned to open six new stores in each of the next two years. The company had signed leases for four new stores scheduled to be opened by November 1985 and for two new stores scheduled to be opened by February 1986. These six stores were to be located in central Florida, near Spec's present locations in Lakeland and Daytona Beach. By clustering stores within a geographic market, the company can obtain economies of scale in merchandising, distribution, and administration. Advertising can also be utilized in a more efficient manner.

The costs associated with the opening of a new store, including leasehold improvements, fixtures, and initial inventories, were estimated to range from $200,000 to $500,000, depending on the size, type, and location of the store to be opened. Spec's planned to open the majority of new stores in freestanding locations or shopping centers to take advantage of lower rents and increased accessibility for video rentals. The company did not plan to expand outside the state of Florida.

■ Preparations for Expansion

Spec's had taken several steps to prepare the company for the IPO (initial public offering) and subsequent growth. Touche-Ross was hired in 1983 to give the company advice regarding expansion and to institute more sophisticated accounting records. A consultant from Touche-Ross played an important role in defining responsibilities for top management and establishing a better warehousing system.

Peter Blei was hired in mid-1984 as Chief Financial Officer. He had been instrumental in updating many of the systems in the company. Under his guidance, Spec's completed a five-year plan for the first time. He had also coordinated the upgrading of the computer system used by the company.

Spec's planned to move from its current 22,000-square-foot office and warehouse facility to a 30,000-square-foot facility in October 1985. The new building should be of sufficient size to support 50 stores.

Senior management believed that the trained managers and assistant managers in its stores would provide it with a pool of experienced managers with which to staff its future stores. The company was developing a formal training program for employees identified as potential store managers, and was preparing a handbook for managers on procedures and store operations. The training program will be conducted by officers and regional managers.

■ Expansion Concerns

Ms. Lieff knew that Spec's had made great strides in the past two years. The company had replaced much of its "seat-of-the-pants" management style with more formalized systems. Consultants had been hired and important positions in the company had been filled. Leases for a new warehouse and six new locations had been signed. In spite of these improvements, Ms. Lieff still had concerns about the future of the company. Could the company, after almost forty years of steady growth, handle the rapid expansion that was planned? Would they be able to find acceptable store sites, get the stores open, and find the managers and employees necessary to operate them? Would the automated inventory system be brought on-line in the next year and operate as planned?

Ms. Lieff also had concerns about the impact of the expansion on the culture of the company. Spec's had always been run as a family company. She had close contact with store managers and knew most of the sales personnel. If Spec's doubled in size in the next two years, how could she maintain these relationships? It was important to Ms. Lieff that the ethical standards and emphasis on customer service established by her father be preserved. Could the values of the company be communicated to new employees? Finally, what impact would the expansion have on her family? She knew that both she and her husband would be busier than ever in the next year but they had a three-year-old daughter who also demanded their time and attention.

Ms. Lieff was proud of the company that Spec's had become and was excited about the company's future. However, she knew that more work was needed if the company was to be prepared for the expansion of the next two years. The stock offering was planned for October 1985. Would Spec's be ready?

Spec's Music, Inc. (B)

Carol A. Reeves, University of Miami

Spec's Music made an initial public offering of its stock on October 10, 1985. The offering was oversubscribed, with 660,000 shares being sold at $6.00 each. The net proceeds from the sale were $3,457,254. As the company had stated in the prospectus, the proceeds from the sale were used to finance the company's expansion in Florida. From the 16 stores operating in October 1985, the company has grown to 48 stores in October 1989. Revenues for the company have increased from $16,638,000 in 1985 to $40,152,000 in 1989. During the same period, net income increased from $924,000 to $2,437,000. The company has been referred to as a "darling of Wall Street." It made *Forbes'* list of the 200 best small companies in the United States in 1987 and 1988. And it has been cited by the *Miami Herald* as one of Florida's leading 100 companies for three years in a row. The future of the company also looks bright, although Ann Lieff and other top managers must confront the increased magnitude of problems that have occurred with the firm's rapid growth and changes in the industry.

PRERECORDED MUSIC INDUSTRY

The year 1988 marked the sixth consecutive year of growth in the prerecorded music industry. Growth is expected to continue over the next five years at a rate of 5 to 10 percent annually. (See Exhibit 1 for unit and dollar values of shipments from record producers from 1974 to 1988. Exhibit 2 presents a breakdown of the type of music purchased by consumers, price categories, and a consumer pro-

Exhibit 1   Unit and Dollar Values of Manufacturers' Annual Shipments

Manufacturers' Unit Shipments (millions net after returns)

	'74	'75	'76	'77	'78	'79	'80	'81	'82	'83	'84	'85	'86	'87	'88	% Chg. '87–'88
Disc singles	204.0	164.0	190.0	190.0	190.0	195.5	164.3	154.7	137.2	124.8	131.5	120.7	93.9	82.0	65.6	−20%
LPs/EPs	276.0	257.0	273.0	344.0	341.3	318.3	322.8	295.2	243.9	209.6	204.6	167.0	125.2	107.0	72.4	−32%
CDs	—	—	—	—	—	—	—	—	—	.8	5.8	22.6	53.0	102.1	149.7	+47%
Cassettes	15.3	16.2	21.8	36.9	61.3	82.8	110.2	137.0	182.3	236.8	332.0	339.1	344.5	410.0	450.1	+10%
CD singles	—	—	—	—	—	—	—	—	—	—	—	—	—	—	1.6	NA
Cassette singles	—	—	—	—	—	—	—	—	—	—	—	—	—	5.1*	22.5	+341%
Total	592.0	531.8	590.9	698.2	726.2	701.1	683.7	635.4	577.7	578.0	679.8	653.0	618.3	706.8	761.9	+8%

Manufacturers' Dollar Value ($ millions at suggested list price)

	'74	'75	'76	'77	'78	'79	'80	'81	'82	'83	'84	'85	'86	'87	'88	% Chg. '87–'88
Disc singles	194.0	211.5	245.1	245.1	260.3	275.4	269.3	256.4	283.0	269.3	298.7	281.0	228.1	203.3	180.4	−11%
LPs/EPs	1356.0	1485.0	1663.0	2195.1	2473.3	2136.0	2290.3	2341.7	1925.1	1689.0	1548.8	1280.5	983.0	793.1	532.3	−33%
CDs	—	—	—	—	—	—	—	—	—	17.2	103.3	389.5	930.1	1593.6	2089.9	+31%
Cassettes	87.2	98.8	145.7	249.6	449.8	604.6	776.4	1062.8	1384.5	1810.9	2383.9	2411.5	2499.5	2959.7	3385.1	+14%
CD singles	—	—	—	—	—	—	—	—	—	—	—	—	—	—	9.8	NA
Cassette singles	—	—	—	—	—	—	—	—	—	—	—	—	—	14.3*	57.3	+301%
Total	2186.4	2378.3	2732.0	3500.8	4131.4	3685.4	3862.4	3969.9	3641.6	3814.3	4370.4	4387.8	4651.1	5567.5	6254.8	+12%

Source: RIAA Market Research Committee.
*1987 figures represent six-month sales only.

Type of Music Purchased, Consumer Profile, and Price Categories

Exhibit 2

	1985	1986	1987
Type of Music Purchased			
Gospel	4%	3%	3%
Jazz	3	4	4
Classical	5	6	5
Other	8	6	7
Country	10	10	10
Black/urban	10	10	12
Pop	17	14	13
Rock	43	47	47
Consumer Profile			
Age			
10–14	9%	9%	7%
15–19	25	23	24
20–24	15	20	19
25–29	14	14	15
30–34	11	10	11
35+	26	24	25
Race			
White	82%	82%	80%
Black	11	12	12
Hispanic	3	2	3
Other	3	3	3
NA/refused	1	1	1
Gender			
Male	53%	56%	57%
Female	47	44	43
Price Categories			
Current release/best seller	37%	35%	50%
Full-price catalog	41	38	25
Midline	10	16	13
Budget	9	7	6
Cutouts	3	4	6

file.) Shipments of recordings in 1988 rose 8 percent over 1987, to 762 million units. This surpassed the previous high, set in 1978, of 726 million units. The dollar volume of 1988 shipments, calculated by suggested retail price, was $6.25 billion, a rise of 12 percent from 1987 shipments of $5.56 billion.[1] When taking discounts by retailers into account, expenditures by consumers were approximately $5.4 billion.[2]

The sales growth in the music industry is mainly attributable to the increasing popularity of compact discs (CDs). Unit shipments of CDs rose 47 percent, and dollar value of CD sales rose 31 percent in 1988 and accounted for $2.09 billion of the $6.25 billion in total industry sales. It has been estimated that close to half of these CD sales were for music that consumers already had at home in

[1]Recording Industry Association of America, 1989.

[2]"Compact Discs Fuel Industry Growth," *Standard & Poor's Industry Surveys*, March 16, 1989, p. L26.

another form, such as LPs (long-playing records).[3] At present, approximately 15 percent of U.S. households own CD players, making analysts optimistic about future industry growth if consumers continue to adopt this technology. If, however, sales of CD players slow, sales of prerecorded music could decrease significantly.

A favorable trend for music retailers is the declining price of CDs. In the past, demand for CDs has exceeded production capacity, but manufacturing capacity is currently sufficient to meet CD demand. Also, record company costs of producing CDs have declined, and cost of production, including packaging and royalties, is under $5.00 per disc. Analysts believe that once the price of CDs falls to approximately $10.00, a new wave of consumers will replace their old record collections with CDs.

An exciting but controversial breakthrough in the recording industry is the digital audiotape (DAT). Digital audiotapes possess the audio clarity of CDs but have advantages over it, including compact size, the ability to be played by portable machines, and the ability to be copied. Additionally, DATs can hold up to 2 hours of continuous playing time, compared with the CD's 74-minute capacity. However, emerging CD technology is reducing DAT's advantages before it receives widespread acceptance. Portable CD players are being introduced, and Tandy is developing a CD machine with recording capability. And like any tape format, DATs wear down over time, while CDs do not.

Audio firms began marketing DAT machines in Japan in March 1987, but sales have been slow because the machines are expensive and record companies have been slow to offer music in DAT format. Record producers in the United States have fought the introduction of DAT machines until provisions are made to prevent the copying of music for which they are entitled to receive royalties. Although an agreement is not final, record companies and stereo manufacturers have tentatively agreed to a copy protection plan that will allow the consumer to make one copy of a tape but prevent unlimited copies by digitally encoding DAT tapes to prevent further copies.

It is unlikely that DAT machines will achieve widespread acceptance in the next few years because of their cost, estimated to be $1500. Once volume production of the machines allows lower costs and increased market acceptance, record retailers are likely to profit from the technology, assuming that copying can be limited. Even if the agreement between record producers and stereo manufacturers falls through, the copying of DATs should not pose as much of a problem to record producers and retailers as the copying of analog tapes. Blank analog tapes cost under $5.00, while blank DATs cost around $10.00, making unauthorized DATs much more expensive and less worthwhile for the consumer.

■ Record Producers

The six record producers who dominated prerecorded music sales in 1985 continue to dominate the industry in 1989. However, the ownership of several of the producers has changed hands, and there has been consolidation in the industry as a result of the buyout of several independent labels. The market share of the top six producers, in terms of pop albums, is as follows:

[3]Ibid, p. L26.

Warner-Electra-Atlantic	44.4%
CBS	14.2
BMG (RCA)	10.8
MCA Records	9.1
Capitol-EMI	7.8
Polygram	7.6 (after the purchase of Island Records, 9%)
Independents	4.1

The record unit of Warner Communications was one of the primary attractions to Time, Inc., which bought the parent company for $14 billion in July 1989. Sony added to its entertainment software division by acquiring CBS records in 1987, the same year that Bertelsman AG, a German company, purchased RCA records in 1987. Polygram is owned by N. V. Philips of the Netherlands.

The consolidation in the industry and the dominance of large conglomerates worries many veteran industry experts, who fear that creativity in the industry will decline. Independents have traditionally been the source of most new trends in the music industry, but with the exception of Geffen Records, independents have lost much of their clout in the industry. One analyst estimates that of the thirty major music publishers ten years ago, perhaps eight remain.[4] There is concern that if it hadn't been for the boost in sales provided by CDs, retail sales would have declined due to a lack of exciting recordings from new and existing artists. Music producers and retailers depend on blockbuster hits for a substantial portion of their sales, but without the innovative sounds that are often discovered and developed by independent producers, there is concern over whether new music interesting enough to stimulate substantial sales will be forthcoming.

VIDEO INDUSTRY

The video rental industry has grown sharply since the beginning of the decade. It is estimated that over 60 percent of U.S. homes own VCRs and that consumer expenditures on videocassette rentals and sales will reach $10.3 billion in 1990.[5] Most consumers want to rent blockbuster movies, with the result that stores able to stock a sufficient inventory of these hits have a tremendous advantage over competitors who must rely on older movies supplemented by a few copies of blockbusters. The mom-and-pop rental stores that dominated the video rental industry in its infancy are quickly being pushed out due to the high capital expenditures necessary to stock hot titles and advertise effectively.

The video rental industry has experienced considerable consolidation over the past few years. The largest national competitor is Blockbuster Video, with approximately 680 stores in 39 states. Blockbuster is a strong force in the Florida market but its success has come at the expense of mom-and-pop stores rather than strong regional competitors. West Coast Video, which has stores in 17 states, is almost the same size as Blockbuster and provides the main national competition. There are also several strong regional competitors in the video rental business.

---

[4]Billy Meshel, "Giant Mergers Hurt Music Publishing," *Billboard*, May 13, 1989, p. 75.
[5]"Blockbuster Video & the Wow Factor," *Shopping Center Age*, May 1988, p. 76.

Many music retailers, including Spec's, have found synergy with video rentals. Of the 3805 stores that are part of the major chains in the music industry, 3602 sell prerecorded video. In addition, 890 of these stores also rent videos, and it is expected that more music retailers will move in this direction in the next few years.

COMPETITION

Three trends have dominated the retail music industry since 1985: consolidation, public firms being acquired and taken private, and a growth in the number of retail outlets. Many regional companies have been bought out by the major players in the industry, who have grown much larger through these acquisitions and store openings. Three major music retailers, the Musicland Group, Wherehouse Entertainment, and Sound Warehouse, have been taken private since the beginning of 1988. Spec's and Trans World Music are two of the few attractive retail music companies whose stock is being traded publicly. Although retail music sales have increased 12 percent in the last year, the number of retail outlets has increased at twice that rate, causing concern about a glut in the market.

Spec's major competitors are profiled in the next sections. It should be noted that the majority of these companies are private, making information on them more limited.

■ The Musicland Group

Musicland, operating under the names Musicland, Sam Goody, Suncoast Pictures, and Discount Records, has 682 stores and is the largest music retailer in the United States. Musicland's management led a leveraged buyout from Primerica Corporation (formerly American Can) in 1988. The total price for the company was $410 million, or $36 per share, and Primerica was given $330 million for its 81 percent stake in the company. Although there was concern over the company's ability to continue its growth given the debt incurred in the buyout, after a slow initial six-month period, the company opened 51 stores from September 1988 through March 1989. Five hundred ninety-one of Musicland's 682 stores are located in mall locations. Although all of the stores sell videotapes, only 40 of the stores rent videos.

■ Trans World Music Corporation

The second largest music retailer is Trans World Music Corporation, which runs stores under 22 logos, including Record Town, Tape World, Great American Music, Coconuts, Good Vibrations, Midland Records, and the Music Co. Trans World grew from 64 stores in 1984 to 437 stores in 30 states in 1989. The company financed the growth with a public offering of its stock in 1986.

Trans World's stores are operated under four basic formats: two for mall locations, one for free-standing or strip stores, and one for licensing agreements with other retailers. The larger mall format accommodates a full line of home entertainment software. Trans World operates 182 of these stores, with an average of 2700 square feet. The other mall format is smaller and the selection in these stores is limited; no LPs are sold in the stores and there is limited catalog selection. The 101 stores operated under this format average 1200 square feet.

The largest stores operated by Trans World are located in strip centers or free-standing stores. These stores are designed for the more serious music shopper, have a more extensive collection of recordings, and are generally more competitively priced than the mall locations. Ninety-nine stores, with a range of 1400 to 18,000 square feet, and an average of 5000 square feet, are operated under this format.

The final store format that Trans World has been experimenting with is licensing agreements with other retailers. Currently, the chain has 41 stores operating under licensing agreements, but the company has been hurt because of the bankruptcy of one of the two retailers, Crazy Eddie, with which it had a licensing agreement. Although Trans World has lost at least 25 outlets in Crazy Eddie stores, it is still planning to expand its licensing agreements with other retailers in the future.

Trans World's Florida stores include 4 full-line mall stores, 7 specialty mall stores, and 10 free-standing stores. Approximately two-thirds of the company's stores nationwide are located in malls. Although almost all of the stores sell videotapes, only 32 rent them. There are plans to increase the number of stores renting tapes in 1989.

Trans World has experienced financial difficulties in 1989. In August, the company announced that its net income, after growing at an average annual rate of 66 percent over five years, had plummeted 56 percent from February through July, from an income of $3 million on sales of $105.8 million, to $1.3 million on sales of $127.5 million. Blame for the decline has been placed on several causes. The company has been criticized for paying too much to rent space and acquire companies and for failing to stock a broad enough selection in its stores. Critics contend that Trans World's centralized buying staff has led to cookie cutter stores that are insensitive to the regional differences in buyers' tastes. The most disturbing figure in Trans World's financial difficulties is comparable-store sales, which experienced a second-quarter drop of 6 percent. Trans World's CEO blamed the drop on a lack of hot-selling music releases and blockbuster movies that took business from music stores. The company plans to continue its ambitious growth plans. Exhibit 3 presents financial figures for Trans World Music.

■ Super Club (Record Bar and Turtles)

As further evidence of the trend toward consolidation in music retailing, Belgium-based Super Club acquired Record Bar and Turtles in October 1989. Although the deals are subject to approval by the U.S. government, they are expected to be completed before the end of 1989. In September, the firm acquired a 22-unit chain based in Dayton, Ohio, and a 21-unit chain based in New Orleans. Turtles is a 114-unit chain based in Marietta, Georgia, with sales estimated at $75 million. Up to this point, Turtles has not been a major competitor of Spec's.

Record Bar had been a privately held company based in Durham, North Carolina. It was the sixth largest music retailer, with 167 stores, 145 of which are located in malls. Sales were estimated at $125 million.

Record Bar has begun to erect a new type of store, called Tracks, in the last two years. These stores are free-standing and are able to rent videos. At present, only the Tracks stores have video rental capability. Over the next few years, all

Exhibit 3	**Trans World Music Financial Statements: Consolidated Statements of Income and Consolidated Balance Sheets (in thousands, except share amounts)**

	Fiscal Year Ended		
	January 28, 1989	*January 30, 1988*	*January 31, 1987*
Income Statement			
Sales	$268,325	$183,321	$130,443
Cost of sales	167,302	114,118	81,052
Gross profit	101,023	69,203	49,391
Selling, general and administrative expenses	76,108	48,657	34,661
Interest expense	2,614	1,560	1,378
	78,722	50,217	36,039
Income before income taxes	22,301	18,986	13,352
Income taxes			
Current			
Federal	7,500	6,947	5,622
State	1,725	1,374	986
	9,225	8,321	6,608
Deferred	(442)	(95)	(15)
	8,783	8,226	6,593
Net Income	$ 13,518	$ 10,760	$ 6,759
Earnings per share	$ 1.50	$ 1.20	$ .80
Weighted average shares outstanding	9,015	9,004	8,433

	January 28, 1989	*January 30, 1988*
Balance Sheet		
Assets		
Current assets		
Cash and short-term investments	$ 28,878	$ 11,585
Accounts receivable	1,363	622
Merchandise inventory	100,173	69,587
Prepaid expenses and other	920	615
Deferred tax asset	666	184
Total current assets	132,000	82,593
Fixed assets		
Buildings	3,930	3,930
Fixtures and equipment	26,712	18,150
Leasehold improvements	25,433	19,452
	56,075	41,532
Less allowance for depreciation and amortization	18,899	12,316
	37,176	29,216
Other assets	281	221
Total assets	$169,457	$112,030
Liabilities and Shareholders' Equity		
Current liabilities		
Accounts payable	$ 81,241	$ 52,445
Notes payable	3,170	1,160
Income taxes payable	4,847	3,491
Accrued expenses and other	2,245	1,932
Current portions of long-term debt and capital lease obligation	383	564
Total current liabilities	91,886	59,592

	Fiscal Year Ended	
	January 28, 1989	January 30, 1988
Liabilities and Shareholders' Equity		
Long-term debt, less current portion	21,862	11,053
Capital lease obligation, less current portion	4,352	3,772
Deferred income taxes	244	204
Shareholders' equity		
Preferred stock ($.01 par value; 5,000,000 shares authorized; none issued)	—	—
Common stock ($.01 par value; 20,000,000 shares authorized; 9,020,447 and 9,009,061 issued and outstanding, respectively)	90	90
Additional paid-in capital	12,055	11,869
Retained earnings	38,968	25,450
Total shareholders' equity	51,113	37,409
Total liabilities and shareholders' equity	$169,457	$112,030

Source: Annual Report.

existing stores will be remodeled and receive the Tracks name. The converted mall stores will sell, but not rent, video.

The CEO of Record Bar, Barrie Bergman, felt that the company will have to eventually abandon its favored strategy of opening stores in mall locations because of the difficulty of securing preferred sites. The venture into Tracks stores will prepare the company for further expansion into free-standing sites.

Record Bar was the first large retailer to phase out sales of LPs. This format accounted for only 2 percent of Record Bar sales in 1988, while cassettes accounted for 65 percent, and CDs accounted for 30 percent. The proposed name change from Record Bar to Tracks will reflect the change in product lines carried at the stores.

In the past, Record Bar has had trouble coping with rapid expansion. The company entered the extremely competitive California market in the early 1970s but quickly sold the 10 stores it had opened. In 1985, the company instituted a series of money-saving measures, including major layoffs, to cope with flat sales. In 1986, Record Bar sold a 36-unit subsidiary operating in California, Licorice Pizza, to Musicland. The company shrank from 193 stores in 1985 to 149 in 1989 but is optimistic about future growth, particularly under the new Tracks format.

Super Club management plans aggressive expansion over the next few years. Management wants the chain to surpass Musicland as the country's largest music retailer. Plans are for the stores to carry 40 percent audio, 40 percent video, and 20 percent other products, including books, magazines, games, and food.

■ Sound Warehouse

Sound Warehouse, headquartered in Dallas, is the seventh largest music retailer, with 123 stores in 13 states, including Florida. The company plans to operate 132 stores in 36 cities and 15 states by year-end 1989. The main areas of expansion outside the Southwest include Minneapolis, Detroit, Ft. Lauderdale, and Miami. At present, the company operates 3 stores in Miami and stores in Ft. Lauderdale and Orlando. At least four leases have been signed for stores not yet opened in Florida.

Exhibit 4   Sound Warehouse Financial Statements: Selected Financial Data (dollars in thousands except for per share and per square foot data) and Consolidated Balance Sheets (dollars in thousands except par values)

		Fiscal Year Ended May 31,			
	1988	1987	1986	1985	1984
Income Statement Data					
Net revenues					
Product sales	$161,833	$139,425	$115,609	$100,753	$89,267
Video rentals	19,757	18,499	15,574	8,813	2,534
	$181,590	$157,924	$131,183	$109,566	$91,801
Gross margin	$ 60,935	$ 53,808	$ 48,559	$ 38,540	$24,978
Income before income taxes	6,727	6,858	12,304	10,516	2,307
Net income*	4,229	3,301	7,528	6,053	1,481
Net income per common share*	0.80	0.62	1.36	0.97	0.24

		May 31,			
	1988	1987	1986	1985	1984
Balance Sheet Data					
Total assets	$71,500	$80,240	$66,037	$41,028	$32,990
Long-term debt, including current					
maturities	—	—	283	567	851
Stockholders' equity	38,176	35,867	32,626	11,115	5,298
Other Financial Data and Ratios					
Net cash flows from operating activities	$23,171	$ 5,154	$ 1,232	$ 6,889	$ 5,570
Working capital	$18,599	$14,494	$18,953	$ 5,570	$ 3,623
Ratio of current assets to current liabilities	1.6:1	1.3:1	1.6:1	1.2:1	1.1:1
Ratio of total liabilities to total stock-					
holders' equity	0.9:1	1.2:1	1.0:1	2.7:1	5.2:1
Operating Data (unaudited)					
Store square footage	1,154,480	1,039,053	794,974	623,618	596,323
Number of stores	107	102	82	69	64
Average per store revenues for weighted					
average number of stores open dur-					
ing the fiscal year	$ 1,746	$ 1,705	$ 1,753	$ 1,681	$ 1,479
Revenues per weighted average gross					
square foot	$164.64	$171.02	$190.21	$180.35	$160.27

		May 31,	
		1988	1987
Assets			
Current assets			
Cash and cash equivalents		$ 1,039	$ 1,785
Marketable securities, at cost, which approximates market		—	1,300
Inventories		48,026	51,576
Other current assets		1,334	2,390
Total current assets		50,399	57,051

	May 31,	
	1988	*1987*
Assets		
Video rental tapes, net of accumulated amortization	8,664	11,899
Property and equipment, net of accumulated depreciation and amortization	12,077	10,846
Other assets	360	444
Total assets	$71,500	$80,240
Liabilities and Stockholders' Equity		
Current liabilities		
Trade accounts payable	$25,015	$26,697
Note payable to bank	—	11,030
Other accrued liabilities	6,785	4,830
Total current liabilities	31,800	42,557
Long-term deferred income taxes	786	1,534
Deferred rent	738	282
Total liabilities	33,324	44,373
Commitments and contingencies		
Stockholders' equity		
Preferred stock, $1 par value; 5,000,000 shares authorized, none issued	—	—
Common stock, $.01 par value; 20,000,000 shares authorized, 5,157,326 and 5,362,014 shares issued and outstanding as of May 31, 1988 and 1987, respectively	52	54
Additional paid-in capital	21,397	23,315
Retained earnings	16,727	12,498
Total stockholders' equity	38,176	35,867
Total liabilities and stockholders' equity	$71,500	$80,240

Source: Annual Report.

*Pro forma and unaudited for fiscal 1984 and 1985.

Sound Warehouse differs from the retailers discussed above in the types of stores it operates. The stores are large, with an average of 10,800 square feet, and sell and rent videos in addition to traditional music software. Sound Warehouse's new stores are even larger, with an average retail space of 12,000 square feet. With a few exceptions, these stores are free-standing or are the anchors in strip malls. The company attributes its success to stores in convenient locations with ample parking, a large selection of merchandise, prices generally lower than the competition, and knowledgeable, helpful sales personnel. Stores are clustered in major metropolitan areas, leading to maximum benefits of advertising and decreasing costs of regional management and distribution.

In 1988, Sound Warehouse announced a series of changes designed to combat declining same-store sales. These included a reorganization of top management, an intensified store manager training program, an upgrade of the company's management information systems—specifically the support for financial, distribution, and point-of-sale activities—and an acceleration of the amortization of videotapes. New video releases were to be amortized over an accelerated 36-month schedule, with the tapes being amortized 75 percent in the first year. Nonnew releases were amortized over 36 months using the straight-line method. Financial information for Sound Warehouse is presented in Exhibit 4.

Sound Warehouse made an initial public offering (IPO) of its stock in August 1985. The original issue sold 1,350,000 shares at $19 each. In May 1989, the company was acquired by Shamrock Holdings, an entertainment concern controlled by the family of Roy Disney. The company was acquired for five times the orig-

Shamrock bought the 60-unit Music Plus chain, which operates in California, in 1988. The two chains will be run separately. With the exception of Chairman Kay Moran, Sound Warehouse's entire management team is expected to remain with the company. Management believes that Shamrock, which is trying to increase its presence in the entertainment field, will provide the capital necessary for further expansion in the Midwest, Southeast, and Detroit.

■ Peaches Entertainment Corporation

Peaches Entertainment Corporation, a subsidiary of URT industries, is ranked as the thirty-fourth leading retail music account in the country. It operates 17 stores, none of which are in malls. None of the Peaches stores rent videos. Peaches Entertainment grew out of a 10-store acquisition by URT in 1982. The acquisition was part of a breakup of the national Peaches chain following bankruptcy. Sales in 1988 were $31.22 million.

■ Q Records and Video

Q Records and Video is a private company operating 8 stores, ranking it forty-ninth in the retail music industry. All of the Q stores rent videos. Q has 2 stores in the Miami area.

SPEC'S MUSIC

Spec's Music is the largest specialty retailer of prerecorded music and video products in Florida. The types of products the company sells have remained basically the same since 1985, but some categories have greatly increased in importance while others' importance has decreased. The company sells cassettes, compact discs, records, video movies, music videos, blank audio- and videotapes, and audio and video accessories. Thirty-four of the company's 48 stores rent video movies.

The company's basic goals remain the same: Spec's strives to provide good service, extensive selection at competitive prices, and a pleasant shopping environment. The company's strategy for new stores has changed; most new stores will be free-standing or located in strip shopping centers and contain from 7000 to 10,000 square feet, as opposed to mall stores, which have from 3500 to 4500 square feet. Free-standing and strip stores allow Spec's to rent videos, which does not work well in mall stores because of parking limitations. An additional advantage of free-standing and strip stores is that they are cheaper to lease than mall locations. However, sales per square foot tend to be higher in malls. Spec's has continued to concentrate its stores around three hubs, southeast Florida, central Florida, and the Tampa/St. Petersburg area. A map of Spec's store locations is given in Exhibit 5.

Spec's Music Locations

Exhibit 5

North Central

Northwest 13th Street, Gainesville
Silver Springs Boulevard, Ocala
Route 200, Ocala
34th Street Plaza, Gainesville*

South Central

South Florida Avenue, Lakeland
Searstown Plaza, Lakeland
Spring Lake Square, Winter Haven
Walden Wood Shopping Center,
Plant City
Grove Park Center, Lakeland
Fairmount Plaza, Sebring
Winter Haven Mall, Winter Haven

Tampa Bay

Walmart Shopping Center,
Bradenton
Seminole Mall, Seminole
Dolphin Village,
St. Petersburg Beach
Highway 60, Brandon
Gateway Mall, St. Petersburg
66th Street, St. Petersburg*
Missouri Avenue, Clearwater
U.S. #19, Clearwater*
Fowler Avenue, Tampa
Carrollwood Center, Tampa
Town & Country, Tampa*

Southwest

Winkler Avenue, Ft. Myers
Gulf Gate Mall, Sarasota
Tamiami Trail, Sarasota*
Tamiami Trail, Naples

Central

Shoppes of West Melbourne,
Melbourne
Volusia Avenue, Daytona Beach
Bel Air Plaza, Daytona Beach
Woodland Boulevard, Deland
Seminole Center, Sanford
Westgate Center, St. Cloud
University Park Plaza,
Winter Park
Town Corral Shopping Center,
Kissimmee

Treasure Coast

Palm Beach Mall,
West Palm Beach
Luria Plaza, Vero Beach
Regency Plaza, Stuart

Market Place, Jensen Beach
Okeechobee Boulevard,
Palm Beach*
Congress Avenue,
Boynton Beach*

Southeast

South Dixie Highway,
Coral Gables
Westland Mall, Hialeah
Dadeland Mall, Miami
Miracle Center, Miami
South Dade Plaza, Miami
Mall of the Americas, Miami*
Biscayne Blvd., North Miami*
NE 209th Street, North Miami*
163rd Street Mall,
North Miami Beach
Hollywood Mall, Hollywood
Hollywood Fashion Center,
Hollywood
Galleria Mall, Ft. Lauderdale
Broward Mall, Plantation
University Drive, Coral Springs*
Towncenter, Boca Raton
Kennedy Drive, Key West
Homestead Boulevard,
Homestead*
Monty's Bayshore,
Coconut Grove*
Pompano Plaza, Pompano*
Suniland Shopping Center,
South Miami*
Sawgrass Mills, Sunrise*

* Opening soon.

Spec's warehouse and corporate offices were expanded in 1988 and now contain 36,000 square feet. All stores are stocked two to three times weekly from the warehouse in west Miami, from which 90 percent of new products are shipped. The proximity of the warehouse and the sophistication of the company's computer systems have allowed it to build stores in the last three years without back room storage. This decreases store costs and encourages staff to put new products on the shelves as soon as they arrive.

■ Management

The top management at Spec's has not changed since 1985 but new managers have been added to handle the growth of the company. In addition, the Board of Directors has added two outside directors to the four Spector family members. A list of Spec's executive officers is presented in Exhibit 6.

Exhibit 6   **Executive Officers**

All executive officers of the Company were elected to their present offices at the Annual Meeting of the Board of Directors held on December 7, 1988. The following table sets forth, as of October 1, 1989, certain information regarding the executive officers of the Company.

Name	Age	Principal Business Experience During the Past Five Years
Martin W. Spector	84	Chairman of the Board of Directors of the Company since 1980; President and Chief Executive Officer 1948–1980. Director since the Company's incorporation in 1970.
Ann S. Lieff	37	President and Chief Executive Officer of the Company since 1980; Director since 1979.
Rosalind S. Zacks	39	Executive Vice President and Treasurer of the Company since 1981; Director since 1979.
Dorothy J. Spector	70	Secretary and a Director of the Company since its incorporation in 1970.
William A. Lieff	45	Vice President–Development of the Company since 1975.
Joseph Andrules	41	Vice President–Advertising since 1978.
Peter Blei	40	Vice President since September 1987; Chief Financial Officer of the Company since 1984.
Jeffrey Clifford	38	Vice President since September 1987; Regional Supervisor 1985–September 1987; Store Manager 1978–1985.
Vicki Carmichael	39	Vice President since September 1987; Assistant to the President of the Company 1985–September 1987; Regional Director 1983–1985; Store Manager 1979–1983.

Source: 1989 10-K.

■ Personnel

Spec's has approximately 600 employees, 343 of whom work full-time. The company hires temporary employees during peak sales periods, such as Christmas. Retail sales clerks, who are referred to as customer service associates, are compensated on an hourly basis and do not receive sales commissions. The company occasionally sponsors store sales and display contests to encourage sales efforts. Employees receive discounts on store products and health insurance if they work more than 30 hours per week. The company has also made a profit-sharing plan available to all full-time employees who have completed 18 months of continuous service.

Spec's continues to stress promotion from within and several of the company's officers began their careers as customer service associates. The company recently hired a human resources manager and has been working on improving sales associate training. Management believes that it has good relations with its employees. However, the shrinking labor market has made the hiring of good associates one of the primary concerns of management.

■ Product/Market Mix

Video rentals and sales have become an increasingly important part of Spec's product mix. Video products have encouraged a new group of customers to come into the stores, which has translated into increased purchases of music products. During the past seven years the company has earned a reputation as a premier video chain.[6] The flagship store in Coral Gables has gained both local and national acclaim as a leading video outlet. Spec's video inventory policy follows its music inventory policy: Have a depth of inventory, and provide customers with fast, personable service. The store's automated systems have been critical in allowing the store to keep a sufficient stock of demanded videos in the stores.

Video products have become the company's fastest-growing product category. Video rentals increased 30 percent from 1988 to 1989 and 38 percent from 1987 to 1988. The company plans to expand on its expertise in this area in the future and most of the new store locations will contain video rental departments.

The company has changed its amortization schedule for new videotapes to more accurately reflect the tapes' useful product life. New titles are now depreciated on a 24-month accelerated schedule. Previously, videotapes had been amortized on an accelerated basis over four years, which resulted in outdated inventory being carried on the balance sheet. This change reduced net earnings by $160,000 in 1989.

While video products have been the company's fastest-growing product category, CD sales have been the company's fastest-growing product line. Compact disc unit sales rose by 70 percent in 1988 over 1987. CD sales accounted for 20 percent of the company's sales in 1987 and 28 percent in 1989. As with other retailers, CD sales have come at the expense of the sales of LPs, which declined from 19 percent in 1986 to 7 percent in 1989. The higher margins for CDs have more than offset the decreased demand for vinyl records. Growth in CD sales is expected to continue as the prices of CD players and CDs decline, increasing their popularity.

Another product that has been increasing in importance to the product line is the cassette single, the counterpart of the vinyl 7-inch single. Cassette-single sales increased significantly in 1989 and accounted for 2.2 percent of sales. For the industry, shipments of cassette singles increased 500 percent in the first six months of 1989, while shipments of vinyl 45s decreased 40 percent.

Spec's sales by product line for the past four years are as follows:

	1989	1988	1987	1986
Audio products				
Cassettes	36%	35%	34%	34%
CDs	28	26	20	14
LPs	7	13	19	26
Video products				
Video rentals	14	12	11	8
Video sales	6	4	4	6
Other products	9	10	12	12

Spec's purchases merchandise for its stores from approximately 150 vendors. Approximately 55 percent of the merchandise purchased in fiscal year 1988 came from the seven largest vendors. Ninety percent of the company's merchandise is delivered directly to the Miami warehouse and then distributed to

---

[6]"Video: The Combo Road to Total Entertainment," *Billboard*, May 28, 1988, p. S-10.

stores based on historical sales and model stock levels for each store. Inventory adjustments for customers' musical tastes are made easier by the company's advanced computerized systems.

■ Advertising and Promotion

Spec's promotional attack includes radio, newspaper, and TV ads, direct mail, and community-oriented contests. The company's advertising stresses promotional pricing, broad assortment and depth of merchandise, and the convenience of store locations. Spec's continues to participate in special promotions organized by the major record manufacturers for the appearance of recording artists. The company also take full advantage of vendors' advertising allowances.

Spec's is particularly aggressive in its advertising in the summer and during the Christmas season. Sales have increased as much as 40 percent in some stores as a result of summer promotional campaigns. In recent years, direct mail has become an important component of the company's advertising mix. Direct-mail advertising was not possible before the company expanded enough to warrant the costs associated with this type of campaign.

■ Finance

Spec's growth continues to be financed primarily from current operations, but the company plans to take advantage of debt in financing future growth. At the end of the 1989 fiscal year, the company carried $1 million of long-term debt on its balance sheet. The company has a $5 million unsecured revolving line of credit at prime rate and plans to continue to use this, as warranted, in the future.

Since the initial public offering, Spec's management has split its stock three times. In December 1986, the stock underwent a 5-for-4 split; in October 1987, a 3-for-2 split was undertaken; and a 4-for-3 split occurred in August 1989. All of these splits took the form of a stock dividend. Taking the splits into account, Spec's stock has appreciated over three times, from $2.40 to approximately $8.00.

■ Management Information Systems

Spec's management information systems continue to impress analysts and investors. The company began replacing hand-held optical scanners with point-of-sale systems this year and all stores now use the point-of-sale system. Prior to the installation of this system, employees had to remove inventory tags that had been scanned with the hand-held optical scanner. The point-of-sale systems represented a significant investment for the company, but management feels that the new system will help decrease checkout time, control inventory, increase margins at the stores, and help buyers in their ordering. Daily sales from each store are automatically transmitted to the company's central computer, allowing management to keep a close tab on sales in each store and throughout the entire organization.

Spec's is preparing to initiate computer-to-computer transactions with vendors that have established such systems. This will allow the company to expedite return authorizations, orders, and invoices.

■ Recent Financial Results

Spec's sales and profit gains in 1989 were strong, with significant increases over 1988. Perhaps more impressive than sales and profits increases were increases in same-store sales. Same-store sales for the first quarter increased by 7 percent, for the second quarter, by 12 percent, for the third quarter, by 11 percent, and for the fourth quarter, by 5 percent. For the year, same-store revenues increased 9 percent. Spec's financial statements for the past three years are presented in Exhibit 7.

Spec's Financial Statements: Consolidated Statements of Earnings and Consolidated Balance Sheets   **Exhibit 7**

	Years Ended July 31,		
Statement of Earnings	*1989*	*1988*	*1987*
Revenues			
Product sales	$34,604,504	$28,640,793	$23,769,160
Video rentals	5,547,404	3,890,276	2,817,280
	40,151,908	32,531,069	26,586,440
Cost of goods sold	24,545,110	19,755,800	16,366,479
Gross profit	15,606,798	12,775,269	10,219,961
Store operating, general and administrative expenses	12,329,574	10,209,717	8,279,045
Operating income	3,277,224	2,565,552	1,940,916
Other income (expense)			
Commissions and other	305,817	393,663	438,382
Interest income	41,969	25,185	48,562
Interest expense	(54,107)	(22,470)	(1,000)
Recovery of related party advances	—	6,288	101,012
	293,679	402,666	586,956
Earnings before income taxes and cumulative effect of a change in accounting principle	3,570,903	2,968,218	2,527,872
Income Taxes			
Current	1,050,400	959,612	1,009,000
Deferred	290,000	193,388	237,000
	1,340,400	1,153,000	1,246,000
Earnings before cumulative effect of a change in accounting principle	2,230,503	1,815,218	1,281,872
Cumulative effect of a change in accounting principle	205,988	—	—
Net earnings	$ 2,436,491	$ 1,815,218	$ 1,281,872
Earnings per common share before cumulative effect of a change in accounting principle	$ .41	$ .34	$ .24
Earnings per common share from cumulative effect of a change in accounting principle	.04	—	—
Net earnings per common share	$ .45	$ .34	$ .24
Weighted average number of common shares outstanding	5,299,000	5,152,000	5,151,000

(continued)

Exhibit 7   Spec's Financial Statements: Consolidated Statements of Earnings and
                                Consolidated Balance Sheets *(continued)*

	July 31,	
	1989	*1988*
Assets		
Current assets		
Cash and equivalents	$ 342,684	$ 365,890
Receivables	211,905	172,003
Inventories	9,139,138	7,538,320
Video rental tapes, net	3,968,012	3,083,106
Prepaid expenses	698,858	450,417
Deferred tax asset	242,000	—
Total current assets	14,602,597	11,609,736
Equipment and leasehold improvements, net	5,022,850	4,298,580
Other assets	269,915	415,545
	$19,895,362	$16,323,861
Liabilities and Stockholders' Equity		
Current liabilities		
Accounts payable	$ 4,249,659	$ 4,397,205
Accrued expenses	1,059,929	931,796
Income taxes payable	22,000	168,999
Preferred dividends payable	22,540	22,540
Total current liabilities	5,354,128	5,520,540
Long-term debt	1,000,000	—
Deferred income taxes	942,000	617,988
Stockholders' equity		
58 cumulative preferred stock, par value $1.00; 5,635 shares authorized, issued and outstanding	5,635	5,635
Common stock, par value $.01; 10,000,000 shares authorized; 5,158,242 and 3,864,300 shares issued and outstanding as of July 31, 1989 and 1988, respectively	51,583	38,643
Additional paid-in capital	3,462,720	3,453,170
Retained earnings	9,079,296	6,687,885
	12,599,234	10,185,333
	$19,895,362	$16,323,861

Source: Annual Report.

■ Company Philosophy

Spec's company philosophy has remained basically unchanged over the 41
years the company has been in existence. Martin Spector's original business
tenets still guide the company.[7] These include the following:

- Keep payables clean.
- Plow profits into growth.
- Deal with honesty and integrity, but don't be afraid to fight for what's right for the company.

[7]"Founder/Chairman Martin Spector: His Name (and Wisdom) Help Spell 40 Years of Spec's Success," *Billboard,* May 28, 1988, p. S-3.

- Keep your eyes open for new revenue opportunities.
- Take care of employees and show them that there's a payoff for good work.
- Buy products wisely but not at the expense of selection.
- And, above all, always keep the customer satisfied.

Although company growth has inevitably created a distance between top management and store employees, operations at company headquarters still resemble a family company in terms of the attitude of top management. During the Christmas rush, executives do whatever is necessary in the stores to help operations run smoothly. According to CEO Lieff, "Spec's was built on the foundation that nobody's such an executive that they can't open a box."[8] This participation gives managers and sales associates a morale boost and gives top management a chance to get a close look at the problems experienced by the stores.

Spec's is known in the industry for its high ethical standards and it will continue to abide by these standards in the future. The company is unwilling to compromise ethics for short-term growth. Spec's gives 2 percent of its pretax profits to charity. According to Mr. Spector, "We support anything, within reason, that breathes in the community, whether it's a university, a high school, a music performance organization, any charity. We give back to the community because I'm grateful."[9]

FIRST-QUARTER DOWNTURN

Spec's experienced its first quarterly downturn since the company went public during the first quarter of fiscal 1990, which ended October 31, 1989. Although sales increased from $8.08 million in the first quarter of 1989 to $9.83 million in 1990, same-quarter earnings declined to $103,000. Earnings for the first quarter of 1989 were $481,000, but $206,000 of this amount was due to an accounting change. Management attributed the decline to the high cost of expansion and store automation. Spec's opened 5 new stores during the period and has 10 more under construction. After the stores currently under lease have been opened, Spec's management plans to expand more slowly.

THE COMPANY'S FUTURE PLANS

Spec's plans to continue its growth in the future and has a goal of operating 100 stores by 1993. For the immediate future, the company plans to concentrate its sales efforts in Florida. However, other locations will be considered as the Florida market becomes saturated. The outlook for growth in Florida is positive because the state has five of the nation's fastest-growing areas, and the company has stores in four of these areas. With population growth, more sites within Florida will become economical over the next few years.

[8]"Spec's Execs Pitch in at Stores for Holiday Rush," *Billboard*, January 7, 1989, p. 34.
[9]"Founder/Chairman," p. S-22.

The question confronting CEO Lieff is how to manage the growth the company desires and avoid the mistakes made by so many companies as they expand their operations. The results of the first quarter are troubling to Ms. Lieff. Although she believes they are a result of a one-time cost to the company (the cost of automation), she knows that stockholders have high expectations for her company and that they will put demands on the company to maintain the company's past performance. What changes, if any, should she make to ensure the company's future success?

Kaepa Athletic Shoes, Inc.

John P. McCray, Juan J. Gonzalez, University of Texas at San Antonio

Tom Adams looked out his office window and thought about the long journey he had made from a regional tennis tournament in Milwaukee in 1965 to the Chief Executive Officer (CEO) of Kaepa Athletic Shoes, Inc. Last year in 1984 Kaepa had $20 million in sales and this year looked like $40 million. Production in the Pacific Rim countries of Taiwan and Korea was providing quality shoes at an affordable price. Sales in the United States were increasing and sales had recently started to grow in Japan which was a very pleasant surprise.

INVENTING A BETTER ATHLETIC SHOE

In 1965 Adams had been playing tennis in a regional tournament in Milwaukee when his right shoelace snapped during a serve. Wanting to get back in the game as soon as possible, he retied his shoe with the broken lace. But instead of tying the two loose ends together, he tied the laces separately, one half in the lower eyelets, and the other half in the upper eyelets, creating a shoe with two sets of laces and two bows. During the rest of the game he noticed that the right shoe was more comfortable than the left, so he broke the lace of the left shoe on purpose and tied it with two laces and two bows in the same fashion as the right. For some time after the game he thought about the improvement in the fit of his tennis shoes resulting from using two sets of laces in each shoe.

Adams moved to the South from Milwaukee in 1966 to obtain a masters degree in Latin American studies from a large southern university. After one year Adams graduated and began to sell real estate at a large lakeside development. But he continued to play tennis in the shoes with the broken laces. In the back of his mind he thought that a new type of athletic shoe might be valuable.

Later he bought two new pairs of canvas tennis shoes and began to experiment by using two pairs of laces and tying them separately, creating two sets of laces on each shoe. He also tried cutting down the side of the shoe known as the vamp. After lacing each shoe with two sets of laces he cut the vamp between the second and third eyelet on one pair of shoes, and between the third and fourth eyelet on the second pair. With the vamp cut almost to the soles, the shoes fit well but did not seem stable enough. To cure this problem Adams went to a cobbler and had an extension sewn on one side of the cut. This made the shoes stable and comfortable.

Adams then spoke with a patent attorney, Mr. Shaffer, who agreed to file a patent for the normal fee. The patent request, although acknowledged by the U.S. Patent Office, was misplaced during a move of patent office records and lost. Adams applied for the patent the second time in 1967 and on December 15, 1970, it was granted. In discussions with the patent attorney, Adams learned a great deal about patents and trademarks and the procedures used in the U.S. Patent Office.

When he received the patent, Adams decided to take action. He visited several shoe manufacturers and offered to sell his patent, but the firms did not accept his offer. Adams also sent the shoes to several other manufacturers and was surprised when his newly invented athletic shoes were returned, the boxes still unopened. All the firms informed Adams that they did not solicit new ideas outside their own firms. Adams decided this was a result of the manufacturers' aversion to risk. He sensed that marketing directors seldom get fired for not trying a new product.

For four years, 1971–1974, he tried to sell his patent in his spare time. Finally, Adams decided that the only way to receive any value for his invention was to start a company, have the shoe manufactured, and establish distribution. Since his graduation he had been moderately successful as a real estate salesman and had saved about $25,000, but much of this money had been spent trying to sell the patent. So taking $15,000 of his remaining savings and raising another $20,000 from friends and relatives through sale of stock, Adams started Kaepa Athletic Shoes, Inc., which was granted its charter on St. Patrick's Day, March 17, 1975.

THE ATHLETIC SHOE INDUSTRY

Between the beginning of 1981 and the end of 1986, sales of athletic shoes doubled in the United States. The environment was favorable to new firms competing in the industry. A strategic window of opportunity existed throughout the 1970s because the demand for leather athletic shoes grew rapidly but the traditional shoe firms did not adjust their strategies and technology to take advantage of this opportunity.

■ Manufacturing

Athletic shoe manufacturing in the 1980s is concentrated in the Pacific Rim. Hides come from the United States and Australia and are tanned in Taiwan,

Korea, and Japan. During the 1970s tanning was concentrated in Japan, but by 1982 Taiwanese and later Korean tanners became primary suppliers for the shoe factories in their respective countries. The shoes are manufactured in Taiwan, Korea, and to a lesser extent in China and other countries. Leather athletic shoe manufacturing in the 1970s was concentrated in Taiwan, but between 1981 and 1985 Korean manufacturers improved their quality and began to replace Taiwanese firms.

In Taiwan there were several excellent factories, which tended to be smaller than Korean factories and owned by separate families. These factories did not customarily commit more than 50% of their production to large firms such as Mitsubishi. In Taiwan it was possible for even a small firm such as Kaepa to order production directly from the factory.

In Korea there were a few very large shoe factories in the hands of a few owners. These owners tended to contract almost all their production to large firms such as Mitsubishi. These factories were primarily located in Pusan and Seoul. Mitsubishi did not own the Korean factories but would contract for several entire factories' output. Since they controlled so much of the production, small firms such as Kaepa were initially forced to do business with Mitsubishi.

It was very important to have an overseas agent who could be trusted and who would inspect and ensure quality at the factory. A shoe firm could hire excellent agents in Taiwan and Korea who would inspect the manufacture of the shoes at the plant. On some occasions these agents in Korea even pulled the wires out of switches to shut down a production line which was producing substandard shoes. Inspection agents in the Far East received $5000 to $10,000 monthly and 2 or 3% of the cost of production to inspect during manufacture and reject poor quality shoes at the factory.

■ Marketing

During 1978 and 1979 Kaepa became a popular athletic shoe in Texas. Some customers liked the comfortable fit and others felt that the shoe made an important fashion statement.

Advertising consisted mostly of Adams telling his two lace story across the country. He appeared on the CBS "Morning News," the "Merv Griffin Show," and other talk shows. They and other news media across the country were anxious to hear the story of Tom Adams, the entrepreneur CEO. Kaepa also gave shoes to celebrities and supported athletic events. With Berkhemar and Kline, a Los Angeles based PR firm, Kaepa developed a unique marketing concept known as a shoe party. They would send one shoe to media representatives and invite them to receive a free pair of properly fitted Kaepas if they would attend a press briefing.

Sales were developed through corporate marketing and agents in seven separate regions. Adams had learned that a firm could expand into new geographic areas by hiring salesmen, training them and maintaining a large standing sales force, or by contracting to independent agents.

Most firms expanded using regional agents in order to conserve capital. Like many small and some large firms, they did not have any salesmen working directly for the company. Regional agents were not employees of the firm, but solicited orders and sold products to retailers within their specified region. Shipment was made from the company warehouse or warehouses. Agents worked on a guaranteed advance against commissions, which were 6% to 8% of gross sales. Normally the books were cleared once each year and the agent owed nothing if his commission was less than his advance. Defective merchandise returns were deducted from the agent's sales for commission purposes.

As an example, compensation in the California region from a small to medium sized athletic shoe company like Kaepa would be six percent of gross sales with $200,000 per year guaranteed and paid in four quarterly payments, plus anything due over the guaranteed amount. This would provide $75,000 annually for the agent, $39,000 each for two outside salesmen, $32,000 for a product salesman and $15,000 for expenses.

Agents were free to manage their regions. They hired the salesmen and managed the regional sales program. Also, agents could often represent other products that did not conflict with the athletic shoes. Agents were not permitted to transship products overseas or to other regions.

▪ Competition

Nike

Philip H. Knight, the CEO and founder of Nike, like Tom Adams, was an athletic entrepreneur with zeal. Named for the Greek Goddess of Victory, Nike first sold shoes under its own trademark in 1972. In that year gross sales were less than $2 million. Nike became a publicly traded firm in 1980. In 1984 Nike sold millions of pairs of shoes below cost; in 1985 Nike sales were just under $1 billion, but they had losses in the first quarter of fiscal 1986. Nike, like Kaepa, emphasized performance and prevention of injury. However, Nike, unlike Kaepa, emphasized professional management and continual improvement and invention.

Reebok

In 1979, which was the same time that Kaepa was attempting to expand, Paul Fireman of Boston licensed the rights to sell Reebok Athletic Shoes in North America and established Reebok International. Reebok had been a well established athletic shoe in Great Britain for many years, and in fact had outfitted the British Olympic Team featured in the movie *Chariots of Fire*. Because Fireman realized that he could not provide the needed cash for rapid expansion in the United States, he was joined by Pentland Industries of Great Britain. Pentland not only could provide financing, but had experience in manufacturing in Asia and marketing new products in Europe and America, two major reasons that Reebok was able to expand so rapidly in the United States. In 1983 Reebok introduced their glove leather women's aerobic shoes which became an instant success. In 1984 and 1985 they introduced other lines of men's and women's shoes, which were also very successful. By 1985 annual sales were $66 million, and in 1986 they took over the sales leadership in the industry from Nike.

Avia

Avia was founded in 1980, a year in which Kaepa had gross sales of $670,000. It grew rapidly in 1984 as a result of introducing an aerobic shoe with a patented cantilever sole which was very popular. In 1986, Avia's sales grew from $23 million to $70 million.

▪ Retail Stores

There were three principal types of outlets for the sale of branded athletic shoes: sports and specialty stores, department stores, and discount stores. Sports and specialty stores such as Oshman's, Foot Locker, and Athletic Attic, and department stores dealt with regional contract agents. Large discount stores such as K-Mart and Wal-Mart tended to deal directly with the shoe company and cut out the agent whenever possible.

▪ New Product Development

During the time span of this case, 1970–1985, there were at least four important inventions brought to the athletic footwear industry: Adams' twin lace split vamp, Avia's cantilever sole which flared on impact to absorb shock, and Nike's waffle sole and later air cushion sole which absorbed shock by use of compartments of compressed gas imbedded in it.

The athletic shoe industry was subject to constant competition through innovation from 1970–1985.

THE BIRTH OF KAEPA

Tom Adams was granted the charter for his new company on March 17, 1975. He named his new company Kaepa, which was a combination of portions of the first names of his two daughters, Mikaela, whom family members called Kaela, and Paula.

Adams tried to interest several American shoe manufacturers in producing the new shoe because he wanted it to be made in the United States. Finally a small shoe manufacturer in Pennsylvania showed an interest in producing the shoe. After five visits to the plant, and after most of the $35,000 start up capital had been used, the plant owner, Mr. Foldus, introduced Adams to Paul Gross, who had retired from the Bata shoe company and was very familiar with marketing in the athletic shoe business. Gross helped Adams to manufacture samples of his new athletic shoe.

After samples were made, Adams placed a minimum order of 5000 pairs of shoes. Since payment was required with the order, Tom had to sell some of Kaepa's stock to raise money. Each time Tom needed another order more money had to be raised by selling additional stock to friends and family.

In August 1976 Adams went to the Dallas Tennis Show to market the shoes. They were made of canvas and would retail for $19–$23. Adams had a difficult time competing at the show with the large manufacturers such as Nike, but he had prospective dealers try on the shoes and they liked the fit. By 1977 he had orders for about 5000 pairs of shoes per month, and additional orders came in as a lady's model was developed. Doc Adams, Tom's brother, had watched the early growth of Kaepa and thought the firm had tremendous potential. He joined Tom in October of 1977, giving up his job in New York in the newspaper business which had paid twice the salary that Tom could afford to pay at Kaepa.

At this time the firm had four employees and a part-time accountant. Adams was the CEO and majority stockholder, Adams's brother Doc was in charge of marketing; Beverly, who also invested in Kaepa, was the secretary; and Stan was hired to work in the warehouse.

Kaepa was now a going concern, although it was a long way from being profitable.

MANUFACTURING PROBLEMS AND EARLY GROWTH

Because Mr. Foldus and the small factory in Pennsylvania could not provide the quantity nor the quality of shoes Kaepa demanded, Adams decided to look for another manufacturer.

At a sporting goods trade show in Cologne, Germany, Adams met Jonas Senter of the Consolidated International Trading Company (C.I.T.C.) of New York City, which was backed by the Mitsubishi Corporation of Japan. Mr. Senter liked the design of the Kaepa shoe and decided to back Adams and give Kaepa financial credit. This was a major turning point for Adams and Kaepa. Until now Adams had to secure an emergency loan or sell stock each time he ordered a factory run. Now, with the backing of the Mitsubishi credit line, Adams felt that he would be able to play with the big boys like Nike and Reebok.

Kaepa placed an order for $200,000 worth of athletic shoes that would be manufactured in California with Korean components in a plant controlled by Mitsubishi. The quality of these canvas shoes was very good, but because of the glue and chemicals that were used in the canvas, the shoes turned an ugly brown color. Disappointed that the shoes were discolored, Adams complained to Mr. Senter that the shoes were unacceptable. Mr. Senter persuaded Adams to accept the shoes on the promise that future production problems would be eliminated and that quality would be excellent. He assured Adams that the next run of athletic shoes would be manufactured in Korea by plants familiar to Mitsubishi.

Mr. Senter agreed to provide credit for orders placed through Mitsubishi at generous terms. Since Kaepa had few assets and virtually no other line of credit, manufacturing through Mitsubishi was a way for Adams to keep the firm alive financially. To receive this credit Adams had to pledge his patents, trademarks, and inventory to Mr. Senter and C.I.T.C. Adams, however, still needed to pay for the original $200,000 shoe order.

Luckily, Adams's brother-in-law, Carl Fisher, had received a sizeable amount of cash selling his part of an outdoor sign business. With Carl's signature and support, Adams was able to borrow $200,000. He did not like obligating his brother-in-law, but Adams felt that without this infusion of capital he would soon be out of business. This money was used to pay for the first order; Mitsubishi then opened Kaepa's line of credit, and Adams went to Korea to supervise the manufacture of the samples. C.I.T.C. wanted Adams to place a six-month order, but he was reluctant, wanting to order enough for one- or at most two-months' sales at a time. Currently, retailers were ordering about 30,000 pairs of shoes per month from Kaepa.

Adams finally ordered 60,000 pairs to be manufactured, which would be a two-month supply. He asked to visit the factories during production but C.I.T.C. officials replied that this was unnecessary since Adams had been satisfied with the samples and that the order would be made exactly the same.

When the first truck arrived with 30,000 pairs of athletic shoes, everyone was overjoyed. But a few days later another truck arrived with an additional 30,000 pairs of shoes. This second truck filled the warehouse to capacity. Additional trucks continued to arrive until a six-month supply, 180,000 pairs, was on hand. Extra warehouse space was rented and a complaint sent to C.I.T.C. for shipping the shoes before they had been requested. Renting the additional space and storing the additional shoes was eating up precious capital which Kaepa could ill afford. Also, since the 180,000 pairs of shoes cost Kaepa $8.50 per pair, there was no way that Kaepa could afford to pay C.I.T.C. $1,530,000.

Kaepa was still a small firm at this time with only five full-time employees and a temporary accountant, and everyone pitched in to do whatever was required. Anyone would use the fax machine, stock merchandise, inspect inventory, or do office work as needed.

Adams and the others inspected the shoes which had just arrived and discovered that 35% to 40% were defective. When Adams inspected these shoes more closely he observed that the split vamps of the defective shoes had been sewn together improperly at the Korean factory. When he told C.I.T.C. to take the shoes back, they refused.

Although Adams believed he would eventually get C.I.T.C. to give Kaepa credit for the defective shoes, their bill was still a huge liability on the balance sheet of a small firm. Also, C.I.T.C. still held Kaepa's patents and trademark rights as security for the line of credit they had extended.

Payment to C.I.T.C. for the 180,000 pairs of shoes created a cash drain that once again had Kaepa at the door of bankruptcy. Fortunately another contract with a different Mitsubishi affiliate, Bob Wolf and Associates, had been arranged to produce a leather shoe in Taiwan. The leather shoes made in Taiwan were of excellent quality and they provided a solid product and cash flow during this time.

In September of 1979 a lawyer named Frank Bradley recommended to his employer, Rand Development Corporation, the purchase of Kaepa. Rand appeared to have the necessary cash to settle Kaepa's debts and fund their growth. Tom Adams signed an agreement with Rand which gave them control, thus allowing Kaepa to escape from C.I.T.C. by paying off the debt owed to them. C.I.T.C. released Tom Adams' patents and trademarks and he assigned them to Kaepa. Pumping $400,000 into Kaepa, and arranging for a $2.5 million line of credit, Rand took over active management of Kaepa. They appointed Frank Bradley as president and Tom Adams became the Director of Special Projects. Adams was pleased with this new arrangement and thought once again that Kaepa would really grow. However, Rand turned out not to have enough excess cash to pay Kaepa's debts and to fuel expansion. Adams began to negotiate the terms of a buy back. Again Kaepa was cash starved and in trouble.

Fortunately, Adams's brother-in-law, Carl Fisher, could again come to his rescue. He had just learned that he was a 25% owner of a newly discovered, large producing, gas well. Adams convinced his brother-in-law to replace Rand as principal owner of Kaepa. In March of 1981 Fisher assumed the liabilities of Kaepa, which included debts to Mitsubishi for over $700,000, and received controlling interest in Kaepa. Adams promised Fisher that he would find another investor within six months.

Foot Locker, a national athletic shoe store, became Kaepa's largest buyer. Sales continued to grow and in 1980 were $670,000 and in 1981 $1,200,000. By 1981, Kaepa dominated the Texas market for leather athletic shoes.

Although Kaepa was now solvent, they never had enough money to order sufficient stock for resale, advertise properly, and grow. At this time, the company owed $1.8 million to creditors. Invoices for manufactured shoes which had been ordered became liabilities of the company when the shoes were delivered, yet retail firms selling the shoes would often take between two and four months to pay Kaepa after shipment.

RESCUE AND RAPID GROWTH

In 1982, Adams tried to find a buyer to relieve his brother-in-law, who had exhausted the cash that he could invest in Kaepa. Again it looked as though Kaepa would be bankrupt. Adams noticed that the Wolverine Worldwide Corporation, widely known as the manufacturer of Hushpuppies, had purchased Brooks, a small athletic shoe company. Adams thought Wolverine might be interested in Kaepa. He called Thomas Gleason, the CEO of Wolverine, explaining the potential and plight of Kaepa. Gleason invited Adams to make a presentation before the Wolverine Board of Directors and hired a sporting goods consultant named Frank Legacki to prepare a feasibility study to determine if Wolverine should invest in Kaepa. The Wolverine board agreed that Kaepa was a sound investment and put approximately $800,000 in Kaepa. Wolverine also established a line of credit for Kaepa and received from Kaepa an option to buy 80% of the firm.

Wolverine was unfamiliar with production in the Pacific Rim, long lead times due to overseas shipping, and the lengthy pay back periods, but their management began to learn these aspects of the Kaepa operation. The Wolverine management also began to assist Kaepa, most notably in marketing, and a plan was devised to expand Kaepa in the Sunbelt. The Wolverine agreement was signed in January 1982, and Adams promised Wolverine a profit in 18 months. By the end of 1982 Kaepa had fourteen permanent employees, and by May of 1983, 15 months after the deal with Wolverine was signed, eight years and two months after Adams had started the company, and thirteen years after he had gotten the patent, Kaepa showed a profit (see Exhibits 1, 2, and 3).

Wolverine exercised its option to buy 80% of Kaepa's stock. Tom Adams and the other stockholders would retain 20%. Adams was the CEO, but Wolverine had the right to appoint three of the five members of the Kaepa Board of Directors, giving Wolverine unquestioned control. Adams and the other minority stockholders also agreed to provisions for selling their stock at a percentage of Kaepa's average after tax income from 1982 to 1987.

MANAGING A LARGER KAEPA

Apparently, shoes left over from an early Kaepa production run in Korea were being marketed through discount channels in the United States. However, Kaepa was successful in defending its patents. On Monday, the fourth of October 1982, Kaepa won a preliminary injunction against Solo Serve, a discount store, Illinois Footwear Company, Kelly Footwear Sales Company, and MCF Footwear Corporation.

With the help of additional capital provided by Wolverine, in the summer and fall of 1983 Kaepa attempted to become more than a regional athletic shoe. Promotion of sales and distribution was successful to a limited extent in St.

Kaepa, Inc.: Balance Sheet (unaudited)   **Exhibit 1**

	Years Ended December 31,			
	1982	*1983*	*1984*	*1985*
Assets				
Current assets				
Cash	$ 225,310	$ 150,057	$ (182,608)	$ (384,622)
Accounts receivable—trade	564,254	1,613,697	3,189,377	2,950,936
Prepaid expenses	22,466	3,208	66,220	128,948
Inventory—finished goods	2,197,192	2,106,934	7,870,240	8,798,204
Inventory—in transit	-0-	1,001,689	850,625	956,681
Total current assets	3,009,222	4,875,585	11,793,854	12,450,147
Inner-company receivables	124,270	214,297	428,979	893,175
Property and equipment (at cost)				
Real property	-0	153,500	153,500	153,500
Furniture and equipment	64,159	280,417	353,210	607,261
Leasehold improvements	300	58,676	68,289	17,058
Automobiles	7,416	7,416	-0-	-0-
	71,875	500,009	574,999	777,819
Less: Accumulated depreciation	18,656	55,266	160,279	203,784
Net property and equipment	53,219	444,743	414,720	574,035
Other assets				
Unamortized patents and trademarks	198,658	159,205	119,751	80,298
Deferred income tax	-0-	-0-	-0-	-0-
Deposits and miscellaneous assets	7,945	15,150	25,593	51,810
Total other assets	206,603	174,355	145,344	132,108
Total assets	$3,393,314	$5,708,980	$12,782,897	$14,049,465
Liabilities and Equity				
Current liabilities				
Trade accounts payable	$ 208,511	$ 31,864	$ 26,367	$ 172,592
Deferred federal income tax	-0-	-0-	-0-	(664,659)
Bank credit line and borrowings	3,186,880	1,500,000	-0-	5,107
Exercised letters of credit	604,343	2,630,616	4,324,430	4,459,581
Accrued expenses	86,482	505,174	765,283	803,490
Current maturities, long-term debt	130,264	294,127	35,197	153,500
Total current liabilities	4,216,480	4,961,781	5,151,277	4,929,611
Long-term debt (net of current material)	1,102,264	163,376	276,140	166,558
Intercompany debt	-0-	987,267	5,502,073	7,933,934
Total liabilities	5,318,744	6,112,424	10,929,490	13,030,103
Stockholders' equity				
Common stock, no par	1,646,925	2,446,925	2,446,925	2,446,925
Retained earnings	(3,572,355)	(2,850,369)	(593,518)	(1,427,563)
Total equity	(1,925,430)	(403,444)	1,853,407	1,019,362
Total liabilities and equity	$3,393,314	$5,708,980	$12,782,897	$14,049,465

Louis, San Francisco, Los Angeles, and all of Florida. By the end of 1983, Kaepa had become the number one selling leather tennis shoe in Texas.

Kaepa now had a full line of athletic shoes with ten different styles; the leather shoes sold for $40 at retail. The shoes were sold primarily through athletic footwear chains like Athletic Attic and Foot Locker. Kaepa was very suc-

Exhibit 2   Kaepa, Inc.: Statement of Changes in Financial Position (unaudited)

	Years Ended			
	December 31, 1982	*December 31, 1983*	*December 29, 1984*	*December 28, 1985*
Funds Provided				
Net income	$ (872,525)	$ 721,986	$ 2,256,851	$ (834,045)
Charges not requiring funds				
Depreciation	4,042	36,610	105,013	110,664
Amortization	39,453	39,453	39,454	39,453
Funds provided (used) by operations	(829,030)	798,049	2,401,318	(683,928)
Intercompany borrowing	-0-	987,267	4,514,806	2,431,861
Long-term debt borrowing	800,000	-0-	112,764	-0-
Contributed capital	-0-	800,000	-0-	-0-
Book value of disposed assets	-0-	-0-	-0-	20,583
Decrease in working capital	177,041	-0-	-0-	-0-
Prior period adjustments	-0-	-0-	-0-	-0-
Funds generated from operations	$ 148,011	$ 2,585,316	$ 7,028,888	$1,768,516
Funds Used				
Payment of long-term debt	$ 44,450	$ 938,888	$ -0-	$ 109,982
Fixed asset additions	25,200	428,134	74,990	301,445
Additions to other assets	6,450	7,205	10,443	26,217
Increase in working capital	-0-	1,121,062	6,728,773	877,559
Inter-company loans	71,911	90,027	214,682	453,313
	$ 148,011	$ 2,585,316	$ 7,028,888	$1,768,516
Changes in Working Capital				
Increase (decrease) in current assets				
Cash	$ 218,834	$ (75,253)	$ (332,665)	$ (202,014)
Accounts receivable	355,303	1,049,443	1,575,680	(238,441)
Prepaid expenses	21,779	(19,258)	63,012	62,728
Inventory	1,937,096	911,431	5,612,242	1,034,020
	$2,533,012	$ 1,866,363	$ 6,918,269	$ 656,293
Increase (decrease) in current liabilities				
Accounts payable	$ (316,242)	$ (176,647)	$ (5,497)	$ 146,225
Deferred federal income tax	-0-	-0-	-0-	(664,659)
Bank credit line	3,186,880	$(1,686,880)	$(1,500,000)	5,107
Exercised letters of credit	604,343	2,026,273	1,693,814	135,151
Accrued expenses	48,081	418,692	260,109	38,207
Current maturities of long-term debt	(813,009)	163,863	(258,930)	118,303
	$2,710,053	$ 745,301	$ 189,496	$ (221,666)
Net change in working capital	$ (177,041)	$ 1,121,062	$ 6,728,773	$ 877,959

Kaepa, Inc.: Statement of Income, Expenses, and Retained Earnings (unaudited)   **Exhibit 3**

	Years Ended			
	December 31, 1982	*December 31, 1983*	*December 29, 1984*	*December 28, 1985*
Sales				
Gross sales	$ 3,250,388	$10,865,239	$23,041,801	$32,386,519
Less				
Stock returns	(1,908)	-0-	(358,003)	(768,910)
Defective returns	(36,332)	(37,701)	(88,784)	(156,996)
Discounts	(20,102)	(110,154)	(189,257)	(1,153,208)
Net sales	3,192,046	10,717,384	22,405,757	30,307,405
Cost of sales	2,013,995	5,673,233	11,623,569	19,238,890
Gross margin	1,178,051	5,044,151	10,782,188	11,068,515
Operating Expenses				
Public relations/promotional	-0-	-0-	580,998	815,192
Aviation	-0-	-0-	-0-	354,992
Product development	96,700	165,110	251,526	143,767
Kaepa van program	-0-	-0-	-0-	-0-
General and administrative	759,035	1,942,583	1,652,501	2,086,690
Product sourcing	-0-	-0-	-0-	299,776
Sales department expenses	828,105	1,273,262	1,614,674	2,481,077
Warehousing and distribution	148,600	288,781	436,909	553,503
Marketing	-0-	-0-	2,276,457	3,935,655
International sales	-0-	-0-	-0-	-0-
Customer service	-0-	-0-	94,504	84,249
Telemarketing	-0-	-0-	-0-	15,760
Accounting and finance	-0-	-0-	159,322	184,174
Credit and collections	-0-	-0-	-0-	-0-
Total operating expenses	$ 1,832,440	$ 3,669,736	$ 7,066,891	$10,954,835
Net operating margin	$ (654,389)	$ 1,374,415	$ 3,715,297	$ 113,680
Other Income and Expenses				
Interest income	$ -0-	$ -0-	$ 41,038	$ 46,400
Interest credit (expense)	(366,229)	(535,069)	(988,365)	(1,011,058)
Miscellaneous income (expense)	179,794	74,016	11,396	5,438
Federal income tax credit (expense)	-0-	-0-	-0-	664,658*
Minority stockholders' bonus	(31,701)	(107,174)	(204,030)	(228,909)
Corporate allocation	-0-	(84,202)	(318,485)	(424,254)
Total other income and expenses	(218,136)	(652,429)	(1,458,446)	(947,725)
Net income	(872,525)	721,986	2,256,851	(834,045)
Beginning retained earnings (deficit)	(2,699,830)	(3,572,355)	(2,850,369)	(593,518)
WWW adjustments to retained earnings	-0-	-0-	-0-	-0-
Ending retained earnings (deficit)	$(3,572,355)	$ (2,850,369)	$ (593,518)	$ (1,427,563)

*Income tax benefit from WWW. Kaepa's operating loss as a stand-alone company would have been $1,498,703.

cessful in Texas and Oklahoma, but despite the fact that the footwear chains sold them nationally, Kaepa remained basically a regional shoe.

In 1985 Kaepa spent $100,000 on a major advertising and sales campaign in St. Louis to break out of the Texas–Oklahoma market. Television, radio, and print advertising was purchased and an aggressive promotional campaign at St. Louis athletic equipment stores was put into place. One chain with seven stores, Casey's, sold over $150,000 worth of Kaepa athletic shoes, which were then selling for $25 to $60 a pair. Retailers commented that 70% of the people trying on a pair of Kaepas would buy them.

These advertising campaigns increased Kaepa's market share and total sales, but Kaepa remained a regional brand which was popular only in the Southeast and Southwest. It appeared that to make Kaepa a truly national shoe a lot more capital would be required.

In 1985, while trying to expand beyond the Sunbelt market, Adams received a recommendation from marketing that Kaepa should change its logo. Since its inception, Kaepa had used a swirled "K", but it was difficult to reproduce on an athletic shoe. Nike, Reebok, and other competitors had easy to recognize trademarks which were designed as part of their shoes. Adams agreed to changing the registered trademark and logo from the swirled "K" to a double delta. This logo was easily recognized and could be manufactured as part of any shoe design. On the shoes, the double deltas were snap-in colored plastic. However, some informed sources in the athletic shoe industry felt that changing the trademark of Kaepa was trying to fix something that was not broken. Also, there were over one million pairs of shoes in inventory that were made obsolete by the decision.

MISUNDERSTANDINGS WITH WOLVERINE

Between 1975 and 1980, twenty-eight friends and relatives invested $1.3 million in Kaepa, and at the end of 1983 Tom Adams owned only 4% of the stock. By 1986 he felt that there could finally be a happy ending after all of his struggles, but there was trouble on the horizon. Although they had recently spent $100,000 in a major campaign in St. Louis, Kaepa was still a regional shoe. With about 75% of total sales being generated in Texas and Oklahoma, Adams felt greater market penetration was a necessity. Wolverine just was not in the athletic shoe business and the CEO of Wolverine, Thomas Gleason, did not seem to want to make a major investment in Kaepa. Further, Adams and Gleason did not see eye-to-eye on many issues of corporate management. Also Wolverine had insisted on appointing its three members of the five member Board of Directors, giving them absolute control of Kaepa. If that wasn't enough, Adams felt that Wolverine might want to place a professional manager in the presidency of Kaepa, relegating Adams to Chairman of the Board.

Adams looked out of the window again. He thought about the struggles he had been through to keep his invention and his firm alive. He was faced with some serious problems. First and foremost, Kaepa was still just a regional shoe company. Significant market penetration was necessary if Kaepa was ever going to get out of the woods. He could put an offer together and try to buy the firm he had founded back from Wolverine. He could weather out the storm with Wolverine; he was still the CEO and if a professional manager was appointed by Wolverine, Kaepa might become even more successful. He could find a buyer for his portion of Kaepa and sell out. By January of 1986 Kaepa had 46 employees and Adams felt that he was responsible to each of them. He also felt responsible to his brother Doc, his brother-in-law Carl Fisher, and all the others who had had faith in him and had invested in Kaepa.

BIBLIOGRAPHY

Abell, Derek F., *Defining the Business: The Starting Point of Strategic Planning* (Englewood Cliffs, N.J.: Prentice-Hall, 1980).

Adams, "Doc," interview—San Antonio, Texas, June 28, 1988.

Adams, Thomas M., interview—San Antonio, Texas, June 28, 1988.

Adweek, "We Lost a Shoe in Las Vegas," *Adweek,* April 18, 1982, p. 54.

Cooper, Arnold C., and Schendel, Dan, "Strategic Responses to Technological Threats," *Business Horizons,* February 1976, pp. 61–69.

Footwear News, "Adams' Better Mousetrap Set for Goliaths," *Footwear News,* August 16, 1976.

Gay, Verne, "Starting a Company on a Shoe String," *Venture,* December 1983, p. 16.

Kobrin, Sandra, "Wolverine Funds Kaepa with Option to Buy Later," *Footwear News,* September 27, 1982.

Magiera, Marcy, "Avia Buy Puts Reebok on Nike Turf," *Advertising Age,* March 16, 1987, p. 12.

Mark, Toni, "A $3 Million Education," *Forbes,* December 19, 1983.

McAuliffe, Donald, "Kaepa," *San Gabriel Valley (California) Tribune,* November 10, 1983, p. A12.

Money, "Footloose Inspiration," *Money,* April 1984.

Selinkoff, Richard, "Kaepa, Inc.: Starting on a Broken Shoestring," *San Antonio Magazine,* October 1982, p. 16.

Silverman, Dwight, "Kaepa Sues Firms for Unfair Competition," *San Antonio Light,* October 8, 1982, p. 9.

Sizemore, Richard C., "Tennis Bug Is Still Contagious," *Footwear News,* August 16, 1976.

Stanush, Michele, "Kaepa Shoe Company Sues over Alleged Fakes," *San Antonio Express,* October 8, 1982.

Trachtenberg, Jeffrey A., "On the Margin," *Forbes,* July 1, 1985, p. 84.

Weiss, Cindy, "Kaepa Gearing Up for National Distribution," *Footwear News,* April 14, 1980.

Weldon, Michele, "Wolverine Exercising Option to Buy Kaepa," *Footwear News,* May 2, 1983.

■ ————————————————————————————— ■

Northern Telecom, Inc.

Lew G. Brown, Richard Sharpe, University of North Carolina

■ ————————————————————————————— ■

Hall Miller, Vice President of Marketing for the Central Office Switching Division of Northern Telecom, Inc., looked up from the magazine on his desk to a picture of a single, snow-covered log cabin with stately mountains rising in the background. The picture reminded him of his childhood in British Columbia.

His eyes moved from the picture to the window, where he could see traffic already starting to pile up on the portion of Interstate 40 which ran through Research Triangle Park, North Carolina, between Durham, Chapel Hill, and Raleigh. It was midafternoon in March 1988, and the traffic would be bumper to bumper in another hour.

Hall smiled as he realized that the picture on the wall represented his perception of Northern's performance in the United States, while the impending traffic jam reminded him of the changing market conditions he felt the company would soon be facing.

Hall had been reviewing the results of a survey conducted by *Communications Week* in the fourth quarter of 1987. The purpose of the study was to identify purchase trends and priorities in the selection of central office telephone switching equipment. The survey respondents were primarily telephone company planners who were directly involved with selecting and purchasing central office switches.

Hall was interested in the results of the *Communications Week* survey since he wanted to use the information to prepare for the quarterly meeting of the Regional Marketing Managers which would be held in early April. These managers were assigned to each of the seven regions into which Northern Telecom had divided the United States for marketing purposes. It was these managers' responsibility to work with the sales force in each region to develop overall marketing strategies. They also worked on quotations and new business development in their regions.

Hall felt the time had come to get the group to step back and assess the overall market situation faced by the Central Office Switching Division and to identify potential changes in the division's marketing strategy.

HISTORY

Northern Telecom, Inc. (NTI), the U.S. subsidiary of Canadian-based Northern Telecom, Ltd. (NTL), was originally part of the Bell System. Bell Canada, the parent company of NTL, was a subsidiary of AT&T until the late 1950s, when AT&T was ordered to divest its foreign subsidiaries. Prior to that divestiture and for some time afterwards, Northern Telecom was known as Northern Electric, the Canadian counterpart of AT&T's U.S. manufacturing arm, Western Electric.

Despite the divestiture, Northern Telecom still had a captive customer in its parent, Bell Canada; and this relationship gave it roughly 80% of the Canadian market. However, Northern's management realized that if it were to survive, it would have to design its own equipment. Previously, Northern had made copies of telephone equipment manufactured by Western Electric. To make its own equipment, Northern would have to be able to afford the massive research and development budgets required in the telecommunications equipment industry. The Canadian market alone would not support the required level of investment. Therefore, Northern broadened its market by establishing its presence in the United States in the 1960s and 1970s as a supplier of telephone switches.

A telephone switch is a device that routes individual calls from the person making the call to and through the telephone network. Once in the network, the call is routed from switch to switch until reaching the person being called. Initially, Northern Telecom had sold switches known as "private branch exchanges." These private branch exchanges were switches which were owned by the customer, such as a manufacturing company or a university, and were housed in the customer's facilities. Northern also sold the telephone sets which went with its systems.

Manufacturing and support facilities were established in West Palm Beach, Florida; Atlanta, Georgia; Richardson, Texas; Minnetonka, Minnesota; San Ramon, California; and Nashville, Tennessee, the U.S. headquarters of NTI. Northern's first facility in North Carolina opened in the early 1970s in Creedmoor, a small community north of Durham. It still amazed Hall to think that Northern had grown from 300 people at Creedmoor to 10,000 employees in the Raleigh area in less than a decade.

DEVELOPMENT OF THE DIGITAL SWITCH

Throughout the 1970s, Northern Telecom, in conjunction with Bell-Northern Research (BNR), Northern's R&D equivalent to Bell Labs, developed a process known as *digital switching.* Unlike *analog signals*—a continuous wave of electrical signals varying in amplitude and frequency in response to changes in sound—digital signals involve sampling the human voice at a rate of 8000 times per second and breaking it into a stream of thousands of bits of electrical pulses in a binary code. As the pulses are routed through the network, they are multiplexed, which involves coding each pulse and sending them together in streams. Because each pulse is coded, it can be sent immediately and followed by other pulses from other conversations. This allows transmission of multiple conversations simultaneously on the same line. At each telephone switch, the pulses are either routed to another switch or are multiplexed (put back together) into voice signals and sent to the appropriate terminating party for the call.

Digital technology offered a number of advantages over analog switching, including faster and "cleaner" transmission, lower costs per line, and decreased floor space requirements for switching equipment (a digital switch required less than 50% of the space of an analog switch).

In 1970, Northern developed the SP-1, a hybrid electromechanical switch whose functions were digitally controlled. In 1975, it introduced the first completely computerized telephone switch, the SL-1. The SL-1 was a significant technological advance over the analog and hybrid switches then in use and became a platform for a high-performance product line that allowed businesses to significantly reduce their telecommunications costs.

With its development of the digital switch, Northern entered the central office switch market. As opposed to private branch exchanges, central office switches are located in the telephone company's facilities. The customer's telephone sets are connected directly to the telephone company's switch rather than to its own switch located in its facilities. Thus, Northern's customer became the telephone company rather than individual businesses. Northern installed its first digital central office switch in 1979.

THE BREAKUP OF AT&T AND EQUAL ACCESS

Until the early 1980s, AT&T had a monopoly in the U.S. telephone market, providing local and long-distance telephone service through the Bell System to more than 85% of the United States. Western Electric was the only supplier of telecommunications equipment to AT&T. The remaining 15% of the telephone service market was served by 1200 "independent" telephone companies. Northern Telecom, along with other equipment vendors, sold its products to these independent telephone companies.

In 1982, through the provisions of the Modification of Final Judgment which ordered the breakup of AT&T, AT&T divested the 22 local operating companies comprising the Bell System. Although the "new" AT&T retained the long-distance portion of the business (called AT&T Communications), the newly formed Bell operating companies provided local telephone service and became distinct entities which were no longer tied to AT&T. As such, the Bell operating companies were now free to buy telecommunications equipment from suppliers other than Western Electric (renamed AT&T Technologies). For Northern Telecom and other vendors, divestiture was the end of a monopoly and the beginning of a highly competitive marketplace. Exhibit 1 shows how the 22 Bell operating companies, such as Southern Bell and South Central Bell, were grouped to form seven Regional Holding Companies, such as BellSouth.

The Modification of Final Judgment also included the provision that the local telephone companies must provide exchange access to all long-distance carriers

Exhibit 1   **Regional Holding Companies**

- Operating company headquarters

(such as MCI and US Sprint) "equal in type, quality, and price to that provided to AT&T and its affiliates." In order to provide "equal access," many telephone exchanges (central office switches) had to be replaced with digital technology switches. Northern Telecom was well positioned at that time for success in the U.S. central office switching market, having a product lead in digital switching and being able to compete in an open market driven by equal access.

Thus began an era for Northern known to some observers in the industry as "one of the great marketing successes of recent times." Northern's sales went from $2.7 billion (United States) in 1983 to $4.2 billion in 1985, and it ranked second only to AT&T.

NORTHERN'S PRODUCTS

▪ Hardware

Northern Telecom's digital central office switching components fell into four categories: systems, remotes, extensions, and lines. Systems equated to digital central office switches. Northern had three versions collectively known as the DMS Family (Digital Multiplex System)—the DMS-100, the DMS-100/200, and the DMS-200. The DMS-100 handled local lines only, the DMS-100/200 handled both local lines and toll trunks (trunks were lines between offices carrying long-distance traffic), and the DMS-200 handled toll trunks only. Each DMS had a maximum capacity of 100,000 lines.

Software which resides in the switch for each line allows for the "programming" of each telephone served by the switch to determine which features that telephone will have.

Exhibits 2 and 3 show Northern Telecom's U.S.-installed equipment base by customer type and by product category, and sales by year.

Remotes were digital switching units that extended central office features to remote areas. Northern's remotes ranged in size from 600 to 5000 lines. Unlike central office systems which were housed in buildings, remotes were often constructed in environmentally controlled cabinets and placed outside on concrete platforms in areas away from central offices. In addition to extending central office features and services, most remotes had some stand-alone capability (i.e., if the host central office switch went out of service for some reason, calls could still be made between customers being served by the same remote). Remotes also provided a cost savings in lines by performing a line-concentrating function, since all the subscribers who were served by a remote in a particular location were wired to the remote rather than to the central office. Thus, all the customers on the remote were served by a single pair of wires extending from the remote to the central office. Remotes could be located up to 150 miles away from their hosts.

Northern Telecom, Inc.: DMS-100 Family, Installed Base by Customer Type, as of Year-End 1987   **Exhibit 2**

Customer	Systems	Remotes	Extensions	Lines (000s)
Bell operating companies	658	248	1106	9841
Independent operating companies	434	1303	1120	5686
Total U.S.	1092	1551	2226	15,527

DMS-100 Family: U.S. Sales by Year   **Exhibit 3**

Year	Systems	Remotes	Extensions	Lines (000s)
1979	5			2
1980	13			75
1981	69	31	19	453
1982	51	86	41	492
1983	83	130	58	798
1984	116	210	152	1379
1985	266	304	332	3665
1986	235	359	604	3962
1987	254	431	1015	4701
Total	1092	1551	2226	15,527

Source: Northern Telecom data.

Extensions represented hardware additions and software upgrades to existing Northern switches.

Lines were reported in thousands; thus, as of year-end 1987, NTI had over 15.5 million lines in service. A line represented the ability to serve one customer.

■ Software

In addition to hardware, an important portion of Northern Telecom's product line was software. Northern Telecom's DMS switches were driven by both operating software (similar to DOS in a PC environment) and applications software performing specific functions (such as an accounting program to log and bill long-distance calls). Centrex (originally an AT&T brand name) had become a generic term describing any central office–based applications software package combining business-oriented voice, data networking, and control features bundled with intercom calling and offered to end users as a package. As a shared central office–based service, centrex was designed to replace applications served by equipment located at the customer's premises, such as key telephone systems and private branch exchanges. As opposed to investing in telephone switching equipment, the customer simply paid the telephone company a monthly fee per centrex line for access to a multitude of sophisticated business voice and high-speed data features. Call Forwarding and Call Waiting were examples of centrex basic voice features that had been offered to the residential market. Centrex (as an AT&T brand offering) was widespread throughout the 22 local Bell System telephone companies prior to divestiture. Centrex (as a generic product) was a major source of revenue for the telephone operating companies. The companies billed the customers each month for the features they had selected for use in their telephone systems.

AT&T'S STRATEGY

In the late 1970s, AT&T began what was known as a "migration" strategy, urging business customers to a private branch exchange (on-site) solution for their telecommunications needs as opposed to a central office–based solution. Implementation of this strategy, which was designed to "bypass" the local telephone companies, intensified during and following divestiture. Telephone companies were directly affected by this strategy, for end users began purchasing their own private branch exchanges directly from AT&T and other vendors, rather than paying the telephone company's monthly per-line fees for central office–based business services. Telephone companies did not like this migration strategy, since it threatened their revenues.

Northern Telecom introduced its digital centrex applications software and was able to capitalize on the resentment telephone companies felt towards AT&T. Meridian Digital Centrex (MDC), Northern's centrex software offering, was introduced in 1982, and sales grew significantly from 1985 to 1987. Exhibit 4 shows NTI's MDC statistics by customer type.

Telephone companies purchased Northern's MDC software for their DMS switches for the purpose of reselling to end users the business service features the applications software provided. The telephone companies often renamed the service for the purpose of developing brand identity and loyalty (just as Sears bought appliances made by Whirlpool and sold them under the Kenmore label). BellSouth, for example, used John Naismith, the author of *Megatrends*, to advertise centrex as ESSX service. Exhibit 5 provides a profile of some of the major MDC software end users by vertical markets served. Exhibit 6 provides a breakdown by line size of Northern's DMS systems that had MDC software.

Meridian Digital Centrex Status (U.S.A.) as of March 26, 1988 (first quarter 1988)   **Exhibit 4**

Customer	In Service		Shipped and in Service		In Service, Shipped, and Firm Orders		SRs
	Systems	Lines	Systems	Lines	Systems	Lines	
Bell operating companies	594	1,610,166	696	1,956,973	757	2,087,921	44
Independent operating companies	265	292,633	280	387,810	288	401,299	6
Total U.S.	859	1,902,799	976	2,344,783	1045	2,489,220	50

Source: Northern Telecom data.

Notes: Numbers are cumulative across the page. SRs = schedule requests; jobs not yet firm orders.

Meridian Digital Centrex Major End Users   **Exhibit 5**

Vertical Markets	Number of Major MDC End Users	Example
Universities	35	Indiana University
Government		
Municipal	30	City of Las Vegas
State	20	Suncom (Florida)
Federal	11	Senate/White House
Major businesses	50	Ford Motor Company
Airports	15	Los Angeles Airport
Banks	27	Citicorp
Hospitals	16	Marquette Hospital
Telephone companies	11	NYNEX headquarters

Source: Northern Telecom data.

Meridian Digital Centrex Line Size Distribution   **Exhibit 6**

Number of MDC Lines	Number of Installed Systems of This Size
1–1999	658
2000–9999	241
10,000+	71
MDC software, no lines	75
Total in service, shipped, and on order through first quarter 1988	1045

Source: Northern Telecom data.

Exhibit 7 Northern Telecom, Ltd., and Subsidiaries: Consolidated 11-Year Review (millions of dollars)

	1987	1986	1985	1984	1983	1981	1979	1977
Earnings and Related Data								
Revenues	$4,853.5	$4,383.6	$4,262.9	$3,374.0	$2,680.2	$2,146.1	$1,625.5	$1,149.7
Cost of revenues	2,895.8	2,730.5	2,078.9	2,074.1	1,713.3	1,542.5	1,117.0	821.4
Selling, general, and administrative expense	917.8	764.6	701.9	603.2	454.8	300.1	234.9	149.1
Research and development expense	587.5	474.5	430.0	333.1	263.2	151.8	117.6	64.2
Depreciation on plant and equipment	264.1	247.3	203.3	162.8	126.6	100.8	77.9	29.1
Provision for income taxes	141.5	127.9	132.8	120.3	79.3	29.8	30.3	45.5
Earnings before extraordinary items	347.2	313.2	299.2	255.8	183.2	92.1	97.4	76.3
Net earnings applicable to common shares	328.8	286.6	273.8	243.2	216.7	105.4	97.4	80.2
Earnings per revenue dollar (cents)	6.8	6.5	6.4	7.2	8.1	4.9	6.0	7.0
Earnings per common share (dollars)								
Before extraordinary items	1.39	1.23	1.18	1.06	0.83	0.45	0.53	0.48
After extraordinary items	1.39	1.23	1.18	1.06	0.98	0.50	0.53	0.51
Dividends per share (dollars)	0.23	0.20	0.18	0.16	0.16	0.14	0.12	0.11
Financial position at December 31								
Working capital	570.7	1,188.7	933.9	859.0	563.4	421.6	477.4	307.3
Plant and equipment (at cost)	2,345.6	1,975.2	1,737.5	1,458.0	1,152.2	829.8	602.4	356.9
Accumulated depreciation	1,084.2	877.3	672.4	591.5	506.4	355.0	237.8	184.3
Total assets	4,869.0	3,961.1	3,490.0	3,072.9	2,309.4	1,809.4	1,620.8	698.8
Long-term debt	224.8	101.1	107.6	100.2	102.3	207.5	165.0	48.0
Redeemable retractable preferred shares	153.9	281.0	277.5	293.6	—	—	—	—
Redeemable preferred shares	73.3	73.3	73.3					
Common shareholders' equity	2,333.3	1,894.9	1,614.6	1,379.8	1,178.3	719.5	793.5	431.0
Return on common shareholders' equity	15.6%	16.3%	18.3%	19.0%	21.7%	15.7%	14.6%	19.4%
Capital expenditures	416.7	303.8	457.3	437.3	305.7	174.9	148.4	42.1
Employees at December 31	48,778	46,202	46,549	46,993	39,318	35,444	33,301	24,962

Quarterly Financial Data (unaudited) (millions of dollars except per share figures)

	1st Quarter 1987	1st Quarter 1986	2nd Quarter 1987	2nd Quarter 1986	3rd Quarter 1987	3rd Quarter 1986	4th Quarter 1987	4th Quarter 1986
Revenues	$1,143.3	$969.6	$1,253.0	$1,067.4	$1,158.1	$1,032.2	$1,299.1	$1,314.4
Gross profit	403.8	323.1	489.9	389.4	479.1	404.5	584.9	536.1
Net earnings	60.1	50.1	77.6	64.9	69.5	66.0	140.0	132.2
Net earnings applicable to common shares	53.7	43.3	72.9	58.0	66.2	59.4	136.0	125.9
Earnings per common share	0.23	0.19	0.31	0.25	0.28	0.25	0.57	0.54
Weighted average number of common shares outstanding (thousands)	235,237	233,154	235,573	223,650	236,024	234,199	236,444	234,767

Revenues by Principal Product Lines (millions of dollars)

	1983	1984	1985	1986	1987
Central office switching	$981.9	$1,452.9	$2,141.3	$2,230.9	$2,577.2
Integrated business systems and terminals	985.8	1,162.9	1,256.6	1,284.7	1,302.0
Transmission	376.3	385.1	431.2	468.1	498.6
Cable and outside plant	275.5	314.9	373.4	348.4	408.2
Other telecommunications	60.7	58.9	60.4	51.5	67.5
Total	$2,680.2	$3,374.0	$4,262.9	$4,383.6	$4,853.5

FINANCIAL PERFORMANCE

Exhibit 7 is a consolidated review of the financial performance of Northern Telecom, Ltd., and its subsidiaries during the period 1979–1987. As indicated, revenues for 1987 were $4.8 billion, up 11% from 1986. Net earnings for 1987 rose 15% to $329 million, up from $287 million in 1986.

As noted in the bottom portion of Exhibit 7, Northern Telecom, Ltd., had five principal business areas: central office switching; integrated business systems and terminals; transmission; cable and outside plant; and other. Central office switching, Hall's division, accounted for $2.6 billion, or 53%, of total revenues in 1987.

The integrated business systems and terminals group sold on-premises customer equipment such as private branch exchanges, local area networks, data terminals, electronic and key telephone systems, residential telephones, and special-applications telephone systems. Many of the products sold by the business systems and terminals group were offered under the Meridian product line name.

The transmission group and cable and outside plant group sold digital subscriber carrier systems, microwave radio transmission systems, fiber optic systems and cable, and network management systems.

Exhibit 8 presents a summary of Northern's income statements by geographic area for the 1985–1987 period. Although sales outside of the United States and Canada represented only a small percentage of total sales, Northern had scored a major breakthrough in 1985 by landing a five-year, $250 million contract with Nippon Telegraph and Telephone (NTT) and becoming the first foreign company to sell switches to NTT.

NTL had 48,778 employees as of year-end 1987, and 1987 earnings per share were $1.39.

THE CHANGING MARKETPLACE

Hall felt that Northern's success through the 1980s had been driven by five major factors:

- A sustained product development lead in digital central office switching technology (AT&T did not introduce a digital central office switch until 1983).
- Access to a huge market which had previously been restricted due to monopolistic constraints.
- A willingness in that new market to be served by a vendor other than AT&T (AT&T had moved from the position of supplier and parent organization to that of a competitor).
- Equal-access legislation requiring product replacement of old-technology exchanges with new digital switches.
- The ability to dilute the effect of AT&T's migration strategy on the Bell operating companies by providing them with revenue-generating features in MDC applications software for the DMS.

Northern Telecom, Ltd.: Income by Geographic Area, 1985–1987 (dollars in millions) **Exhibit 8**

	1987	1986	1985
Total revenues			
United States	$3,103.0	$2,965.6	$2,967.3
Canada	2,140.3	1,771.1	1,792.8
Other	272.1	245.9	215.2
Less, interarea transfers	(661.9)	(599.0)	(712.4)
Total revenues	$4,853.5	$4,383.6	$4,262.9
Operating earnings			
United States	$787.0	$674.2	$699.6
Canada	491.6	383.8	319.8
Other	(11.1)	18.8	12.0
Total operating earnings	$1,267.5	$1,076.8	$1,031.4
Less, research and development	($587.5)	($474.5)	($430.0)
Less, general corporate expenses	($227.6)	($188.3)	($179.3)
Net operating earnings	$452.4	$414.0	$422.1
Plus, other income	36.3	27.1	9.9
Earnings before tax	$488.7	$441.1	$432.0
Identifiable assets			
United States	$1,807.2	$1,749.6	$1,868.2
Canada	1,297.5	1,189.3	1,389.8
Other	181.1	210.1	264.2
Corporate assets*	332.4	460.3	204.6

Source: Northern Telecom, Ltd., 1987 Annual Report.

*Corporate assets are principally cash and short-term investments and corporate plant and equipment.

Despite Northern's success, however, Hall realized that the marketplace was changing and that Northern needed to reconsider its strategy to respond to these changes.

■ AT&T's 5ESS

Demand for digital switches had exceeded supply in the early 1980s, and AT&T had not entered the digital switching marketplace until 1983 with the 5ESS switch. As a result, Northern Telecom had a substantial competitive lead in both product and feature development and in marketing its products to the telephone companies. AT&T had found itself in the unusual position of being an industry technology "follower" rather than the industry leader. Moreover, because of its monopoly position, AT&T had not been concerned previously with having to market its products.

Exhibit 9 compares Northern's DMS and AT&T's 5ESS shipments in half-year increments starting in 1985. Although only 13 of AT&T's 5ESS units were in service by the end of 1983, with an additional 72 being placed in service in 1984, pent-up demand in the telephone companies for additional products to help

Exhibit 9

Northern DMS and AT&T 5ESS System Shipments by Half Year

System	Northern	AT&T
1H85	144	169
2H85	145	141
1H86	108	152
2H86	139	144
1H87	128	135
2H87	127	130

Sources: Northern Telecom data; AT&T estimates.

satisfy equal-access requirements and the desire to have multiple suppliers helped sales of the 5ESS grow rapidly. Moreover, Northern experienced delivery problems in 1985 with one of its remote switch products and performance problems with a particular release of operating system software. Combined with the strong market demand for digital technology, these events helped to assure that AT&T's 5ESS would be a successful product. The U.S. telephone digital switching market became a two-supplier arena.

AT&T claimed to have 800 5ESS systems, 660 remotes, and 15 million lines in service as of September 1987 (these figures included some switches located outside the United States and some within the AT&T system itself). Northern Telecom had 1092 systems, 1551 remotes, and 15.5 million lines in service as of the end of 1987.

■ Pricing

Due to equal access, demand for digital switches exceeded supply from 1982 to 1986. During this period, delivery was the primary determinant of which vendor would be chosen. Volume sales agreements negotiated with each regional or local telephone company for multiple changeouts of old-technology switches were the norm rather than the exception. Price was not a key selection criteria.

However, with supply exceeding the demand for digital switches from 1986 onward, the situation had become one of competitive bidding for each switch replacement, with bidding parties offering aggressive discounts. The objective was to win the initial system even at the sake of short-term profits, for winning the switch meant additional opportunities for revenue through software and hardware upgrades and extensions.

In 1987, the industry average price of a digital switch was estimated at $326 per line of capacity. However, discounts of up to 30% on this price were not uncommon. A switch with a 20,000-line capacity might be bid in the $4.5 million range. Switch prices ranged from $1 million to $10 million, with an average price of $2.5 million.

Hall had concerns that the discounts the vendors were offering often resulted in the winner leaving large sums of money on the table (e.g., coming in with a bid at $500,000 less than the next-lowest competitor, when all that would have been necessary to win the switch was a $100,000 discount). Moreover, Hall did not want bids to be so low that the telephone companies would refuse to accept higher bids.

■ The End of Equal Access

In addition to increased competition and pricing pressures from AT&T, other factors were affecting the market. With the completion of the equal-access process, telephone company construction budgets were declining 3–4% annually. Along with the decline in capital budgets was a corresponding increase in the expense budgets. As a result of this shift, telephone companies were expected to allocate more budget dollars towards upgrading equipment and less towards the purchase of new switches.

■ The Analog Switch Replacement Market

Following equal access, the next major determinant of growth in the U.S. telecommunications market was replacement of analog switches. These switches were analog-stored program control (software-driven) AT&T switches that were installed in the late 1960s and the 1970s. Exhibit 10 shows historical information and projections of the central office switch market by technology from 1988 through 1991. As indicated in Exhibit 10, analog switches accounted for 57 million lines of the total installed base in 1987, or 46% of the market, compared to a total of 36 million digital lines. The "Other" category represents older analog switches, which were electromechanical switches (no software).

Numerous factors were involved in analog replacement, which was estimated to be a $30 billion market over the next 30 years. Unlike other switches that had to be replaced, analog switches had been upgraded to support equal-access requirements, since they were software-driven. With depreciation service lives of 15–20 years, they would remain in the network until the early 1990s, assuming that the depreciation rates and regulatory positions did not change (switch replacement required approval from the appropriate state public utility commission). The latest versions of these switches offered a comprehensive set of centrex features, and they were large in terms of line size (30,000–55,000 lines). As such, a digital replacement switch would require both sufficient capacity and an equivalent set of centrex features.

These analog switches were usually housed in "wire centers," which were simply buildings that housed more than one type of central office switch and were typically located in high-growth metropolitan areas. Northern had a number of strategies to establish a presence in these wire centers in the hope that this initial presence would provide a competitive advantage when an analog switch became available for digital replacement. Other vendors were marketing adjuncts for the analog switches, which were enhancements designed to prolong their life, while these same vendors worked to develop competitive digital switches. As such, these adjuncts were basically stopgap measures designed to meet a particular need and to buy additional time for R&D switch development.

■ ISDN

Beyond the replacement of analog switches, the next phase of telecommunications technology was called ISDN (Integrated Services Digital Network). ISDN would allow the transmission of voice, data, and video simultaneously over the same facilities. With existing technology, voice, high-speed data, and video had to be transmitted separately or over separate lines. While business telecommunications in 1988 were 90% voice and 10% data, this ratio was predicted to move to 50%/50%. Cost, space, and time constraints would require that voice and data be integrated over one network.

Exhibit 10   Central Office Equipment Market by Technology (thousands of lines)

	1986	1987	Projected 1988	1989	1990	1991
Total Market						
Installed base						
Digital	27,048	36,560	45,230	54,072	62,693	72,057
Analog	56,143	57,022	57,426	57,854	56,750	54,800
Other	38,175	31,322	25,613	19,826	15,933	12,293
Total	121,366	124,904	128,269	131,752	135,376	139,150
Percent						
Digital	22.3	29.3	35.3	41.0	46.3	51.8
Analog	46.3	45.6	44.8	43.9	41.9	39.4
Other	31.4	25.1	19.9	15.1	11.8	8.8
Demand						
Digital	10,066	9,508	8,670	8,844	8,620	9,365
Analog	1,591	881	417	429	36	0
Total	11,657	10,389	9,087	9,273	8,656	9,365
Total Bell Operating Companies						
Installed base						
Digital	14,509	21,341	27,389	33,553	39,997	46,966
Analog	53,899	54,729	55,114	55,451	54,317	52,379
Other	25,246	20,114	15,998	11,891	9,077	6,648
Total	93,654	96,184	98,501	100,895	103,391	105,993
Percent						
Digital	15.5	22.2	27.8	33.3	38.7	44.3
Analog	57.6	56.9	56.0	55.0	52.5	49.4
Other	27.0	20.9	17.2	11.8	8.8	6.2
Demand						
Digital	6,904	6,832	6,048	6,165	6,443	6,969
Analog	1,530	830	385	338	0	0
Total	8,434	7,662	6,432	6,502	6,443	6,969
Total Independent Operating Companies						
Installed base						
Digital	12,539	15,219	17,841	20,519	22,696	25,091
Analog	2,244	2,293	2,312	2,403	2,433	2,421
Other	12,929	11,208	9,615	7,935	6,856	5,645
Total	27,712	28,720	29,768	30,857	31,895	33,157
Percent						
Digital	45.2	53.0	59.9	66.5	71.0	75.7
Analog	8.1	7.9	7.8	7.8	7.6	7.3
Other	46.7	39.1	32.3	25.7	21.4	17.0
Demand						
Digital	3,162	2,676	2,622	2,679	2,177	2,396
Analog	61	51	32	91	36	0
Total	3,223	2,727	2,654	2,770	2,213	2,396

Source: Northern Business Information, *Central Office Equipment Market: 1987 Edition.*

ISDN would also allow standard interfaces between different pieces of equipment, such as computers; and it would free end users from concerns as to whether new equipment from one vendor would interface with equipment made by another vendor which an end user might already own.

Although universal standards for ISDN had yet to be resolved, useful applications were already apparent. Since ISDN phones were designed to display the calling number and the name assigned to the number on a small screen simultaneously with the ring, the party being called would know where the call was coming from prior to answering. This call-screening ability would provide opportunities to enhance 911 services (police, fire department, rescue squad, etc.) by immediately identifying the calling party's location and other useful information (such as a known medical condition or the location of the nearest fire hydrant) and by efficiently routing both the call and the information to all parties involved. A person served by ISDN could talk to her banker while looking at her account information on a computer terminal and send data instructions to move funds, simultaneously on the same line.

ISDN was flexible since from any ISDN telephone jack, one could connect a computer terminal, personal computer, file server, printer, facsimile or telex machine, or video camera. Equipment could be moved to any location without having to worry if a specific kind of cable were available. The various pieces of equipment could share a common ISDN loop for data and voice transmission, reducing or eliminating the need for modems and multiplexers. Data on an ISDN network could be transmitted at a rate up to six times faster than standard analog networks but at a comparable cost.

Northern was positioning ISDN as its premier Meridian Digital Centrex software offering, since it offered both business voice features and high-speed data capabilities over a single line. Northern's strategy was to "migrate" end users from MDC to ISDN, stressing that existing MDC feature capabilities could serve customer needs today while ISDN standards and applications were being developed by industry regulatory organizations and other telecommunications equipment and computer vendors. In addition, MDC integrated with ISDN, with ISDN combining existing voice and data services while adding additional new features and sophisticated applications.

AT&T, on the other hand, had been advertising ISDN heavily to end users and was attempting to position it as a technologically superior *replacement* to centrex, rather than as a centrex enhancement. AT&T was pursuing this strategy since BRCS, its digital centrex offering, was perceived as being much less feature-rich than its analog centrex systems or Northern's Meridian Digital Centrex.

Northern Telecom placed the first successful ISDN phone call in the United States in November 1987 and had a number of DMS sites in service offering ISDN capabilities. In addition, both Northern Telecom and AT&T had numerous ISDN field trials and commercial applications scheduled with telephone companies and business end users throughout the country at specific sites during the 1988–1990 time frame.

COMPETITION

In addition to the changing market and technological environments, Northern faced a number of strong competitors. Replacement of analog switches and

ISDN were two potential markets attracting other equipment companies into the U.S. digital central office telecommunications market. Also, most of the telephone companies were interested in having a third equipment supplier in addition to AT&T and Northern Telecom to ensure that pricing and product development remained highly competitive.

Another potential opportunity/threat for Northern was that the seven Regional Holding Companies (RHCs) had petitioned Judge Green, the presiding judge in the AT&T antitrust suit, to lift the restrictions barring them from providing information services, going into the long-distance business, and manufacturing terminals and central office switches through direct subsidiaries and/or joint ventures.

Finally, although the level of competition was increasing, the number of competitors was actually decreasing. In 1979, there had been 30 major telecommunications equipment manufacturing companies in the developed world. Estimates were, however, that this number would decrease to 15 by 1989. Some experts estimated that a firm needed a 10% worldwide market share to survive. The worldwide telecommunications construction market was estimated to be $109 billion for 1988, up from $100 billion in 1987, with the United States accounting for 22% of this market.

Following is a discussion of some of Northern's competitors and the inroads each had made into the Bell operating companies.

▪ Siemens

Siemens, a West German conglomerate, had sales of 8 billion German marks (DMs) for its telecommunications segment in 1987 (sales for the entire company in 1987 were $20 billion U.S.). Seventy-three percent of Siemens' total sales for the year were from Germany and Europe, with 10% from North America.

The headquarters for Siemens's U.S. telecommunications division was in Boca Raton, Florida. An R&D facility was also located at Boca Raton, while manufacturing sites were located at Cherry Hill, New Jersey, and Hauppauge, New York. Siemens had 25,000 employees in the United States.

Siemens's digital central office offering was the EWSD. It was available in three versions: DE3, with a maximum capacity of 7500 lines; DE4, with a maximum capacity of 30,000 lines; and DE5, with a maximum capacity of 100,000 lines.

Siemens had announced ambitious feature rollout plans for its offerings, promising both centrex and ISDN feature parity with both AT&T and Northern Telecom. However, whether it could effectively leapfrog the software development intervals incurred by the industry leaders remained to be seen.

Siemens had made inroads with five of the seven RHCs: Ameritech, Bell-South, Bell Atlantic, NYNEX, and Southwestern Bell. Siemens's progress had been based primarily on both competitive pricing and the desire of the Bell operating companies to increase competition in the central office switch market.

In spite of its recent success, industry consultants cited operational/maintenance problems with the EWSD regarding system reliability, architecture, and compliance to Bellcore standards. (Bell Communications Research, or Bellcore, was a standards organization jointly owned by the seven RHCs.) However, heavy R&D efforts were underway to resolve these issues at Boca Raton, and Siemens was fully committed to adapting its products to U.S. market specifications.

Siemens had a $2.1 million contract with West Virginia University to develop computer-based training courses in the operation of EWSD central office equipment. In terms of joint ventures and acquisitions, the company purchased 80% of GTE's foreign transmissions operations in 1986.

■ Ericsson

Ericsson, a Swedish-based telecommunications company, had consolidated international sales of $5.5 billion U.S. in 1987. Europe and Sweden accounted for 84% of the geographic distribution of total sales for the year, with the United States and Canada contributing 7%. Like Siemens, Ericsson was attempting to crack the hold that Northern Telecom and AT&T shared on the U.S. central office switch market. Ericsson had targeted the Bell operating company market in BellSouth, NYNEX, Southwestern Bell, and USWest.

Ericsson's digital central office offering was the AXE 10. Ericsson had already installed the AXE in 64 countries, had a worldwide installed base of over 11 million lines, and dominated markets in the developing world. Like Siemens, Ericsson had announced aggressive feature rollout plans (bypassing years of software development by AT&T Technologies and Bell-Northern Research), which it might not be able to deliver.

The AXE was manufactured in 16 countries and was being made available by Ericsson's Network Systems Division in Richardson, Texas. No plans were underway to construct manufacturing facilities for the AXE in the United States, although Ericsson was considered to have superior skills in setting up manufacturing plants in foreign countries and training local workers for skilled jobs.

Ericsson had made a number of recent strategic moves intended to strengthen its position in the United States. The company had reorganized by regions to serve the RHC markets more effectively; moreover, it had reorganized marketing for the division into the functional areas of Market Development, Marketing Communications, Systems Engineering, and Marketing Systems. Plans had been announced for a Technical Training Center at the company's U.S. headquarters in Richardson, Texas. In addition, Ericsson had announced that it would be working with IBM to develop private networking capabilities.

■ NEC

NEC had $13 billion U.S. in sales for 1987, $4 billion of which was from its communications segment. Geographic sales distribution percentages were classified as domestic (Japan) at 67% and overseas at 33%.

NEC's digital central office offering was the NEAX61E. The switch was primarily an ISDN adjunct that interfaced analog systems and grew into a full central office. As such, it was basically an interim offering that was designed to extend the life of analog switches while buying time to improve the product in the hopes of having a competitive offering ready when analog replacement began. NEC claimed that the NEAX61 was serving 4.8 million lines in over 250 sites in 40 countries.

NEC's U.S. headquarters was located in Irving, Texas, where production of the system was scheduled to begin by mid-1988. NEC had made inroads with four of the seven RHCs: Bell Atlantic, NYNEX, Pacific Telesis, and USWest.

The company had recently announced plans for a Switching Technology Center in Irving, Texas, dedicated to developing software for central office switches and customer premises equipment. A second facility in San Jose, California, would develop software for intelligent transport networks, transmission systems, data communications, and network management systems. NEC claimed that it was moving its software development closer to its customers.

A major problem that NEC had to overcome was one of perception. NEC's first attempt to enter the U.S. market with the NEAX61 in the early 1980s met with little success. The product was highly touted, launched, and subsequently withdrawn due to numerous performance issues. Many industry experts felt that NEC was again entering the market prematurely with a product that was not powerful enough to meet U.S. requirements to support advanced business features or large capacities.

▪ Stromberg-Carlson

Stromberg-Carlson was a division of Plessy, a British telecommunications corporation. Plessy had 1987 revenues of $2.45 billion from all product lines. Because Stromberg was a division, reliable data on its 1987 financial performance was not available. Stromberg-Carlson's product offering was the DCO (Digital Central Office). It was available in three versions: the DCO-CS, which was a toll version of the DCO (7000 trunks maximum); the DCO-SE (a 1080-line switch designed to serve as a rural central office); and the DCO (32,000 lines maximum). In addition, Stromberg-Carlson offered a full line of remotes, ranging in size from 90 lines to 10,000 lines.

Unlike Siemens, Ericsson, and NEC, Stromberg-Carlson had been a player in the U.S. telecommunications marketplace for a number of years. Stromberg was a primary supplier to the independent operating companies and was committed to maintaining strong ties with them. Stromberg's strategy was to target small to midsize central offices (5000–12,000 lines), focusing on rural applications. While Stromberg's lack of a large switch limited the market it could address, its niche strategy had served it well over the years in that it could economically provide digital central capabilities in small-line sizes.

However, Stromberg was now trying to crack the Bell operating company market as well. The company had made inroads with BellSouth and Pacific Telesis and had recently signed a volume supply agreement with South Central Bell for the 1989–1990 time frame.

Stromberg-Carlson's U.S. headquarters and DCO manufacturing facility were located in Lake Mary, Florida (a suburb of Orlando). While Stromberg stated that it had a manufacturing capacity of 1 million lines per year at the Lake Mary facility, less than half of this capability was being used.

In response to its agreement with South Central Bell, Stromberg-Carlson had recently opened sales offices in Birmingham, Alabama. The company had a small installation force and was negotiating with AT&T to arrange to install some of its switches in South Central Bell.

Stromberg-Carlson shipped its 1000th remote in December 1987 and placed its 2 millionth line in service in January 1988. Two hundred switches, 400 remotes, and 400,000 lines were shipped by Stromberg-Carlson to the U.S. market in 1987.

▪ Alcatel N.V.

Alcatel was established in France in 1985 as a subsidiary of Alcatel S.A. On December 1986, the firm's present name was adopted with the transfer of assets from its parent, Compagnie General d'Electricite (CGE). At the same time, CGE and International Telephone and Telegraph (ITT) combined their telecommunications activities, with ITT assuming 37% ownership of Alcatel. Alcatel offered digital switches, cable and fiber optic transmission networks, and radio and satellite transmission systems. Its 1986 sales were 10.6 million French francs.

The ITT deal allowed Alcatel to gain a position in West Germany, Italy, and Spain. While Alcatel had been insignificant in the world telecommunications market, the arrangement with ITT set the stage for it to become a major equipment manufacturer. Alcatel's strengths in transmission facilities offset ITT's weakness in this area. ITT contributed a dominant position in switching in the European market. Although the acquisition introduced Alcatel to the U.S. market due to ITT's presence, it was not clear what effect this would have on the U.S. market. ITT had been working unsuccessfully for several years to develop a switch for the U.S. market.

CONCLUSION

Musing over the status of Northern's potential competitors, Hall Miller's gaze returned to the magazine on his desk. Overall, the *Communications Week* study had given Northern high marks relative to most of the competitors. However, there were shortcomings in particular areas he wanted to address. (Exhibits 11 and 12 contain the results of the study, segmented by Bell and independent operating company respondents.)

In terms of the changing market and increased competition, Hall felt Northern had a competitive advantage in that the company had the largest installed base of digital switches of any vendor. This would help generate revenue through hardware and software extensions and new features prior to the replacement of analog switches. However, Hall had seen AT&T's 5ESS shipments reach parity in a relatively short period of time, and it seemed that com-

Summary of Vendor Performance Rankings by Bell Operating Company Respondents   **Exhibit 11**

Item	AT&T	Ericsson	NEC	Northern Telecom	Siemens	Stromberg-Carlson
Initial cost	3.12	3.37	3.42	3.83	3.51	3.76
Life cycle cost	3.55	3.26	3.29	3.53	3.48	3.26
Strength of financial backing	4.66	3.48	3.74	4.24	4.05	3.05
Availability	3.90	3.36	3.29	4.17	3.40	3.56
Service/support	4.07	3.21	2.97	3.39	3.22	3.50
Reliability	4.06	3.31	3.08	3.52	3.47	3.24
Delivery	3.76	3.18	2.80	3.71	3.21	3.39
Experience in industry	4.88	3.97	3.34	4.29	3.78	3.91
High-technology company	4.63	3.77	3.69	4.28	4.08	3.23
Sound technical documentation	4.32	3.24	2.67	3.50	3.37	3.10
Breadth of product line	4.07	3.24	3.14	3.90	3.33	2.80
International experience	3.19	4.08	3.83	3.58	4.20	2.64
Long-term commitment to R&D	4.44	3.81	3.83	3.99	3.91	3.04

Source: Courtesy *Communications Week*, "Central Office Switch Study," April 1987.

Note: Scale of 1–5: 5 = excellent, 1 = poor. N = 497.

Exhibit 12   Summary of Vendor Performance Rankings by Independent Operating
Company Respondents

Item	AT&T	Ericsson	NEC	Northern Telecom	Siemens	Stromberg-Carlson
Initial cost	2.40	2.67	3.70	3.67	3.12	3.96
Life cycle cost	3.24	2.74	3.17	3.71	3.04	3.61
Strength of financial backing	4.65	3.31	3.69	4.34	3.65	3.50
Availability	3.56	2.61	3.22	4.06	2.93	4.03
Service/support	3.79	2.81	2.98	3.81	3.02	3.75
Reliability	4.23	2.80	3.41	4.08	3.25	3.63
Delivery	3.46	2.61	3.16	3.83	2.91	3.80
Experience in industry	4.74	3.27	3.55	4.58	3.62	4.19
High-technology company	4.72	3.35	3.93	4.45	3.84	3.72
Sound technical documentation	4.47	2.78	2.95	4.08	3.32	3.63
Breadth of product line	4.16	2.83	3.43	4.12	3.27	3.47
International experience	3.84	3.48	4.04	3.84	4.03	3.27
Long-term commitment to R&D	4.67	3.21	3.80	4.29	3.69	3.57

Source: Courtesy *Communications Week*, "Central Office Switch Study," April 1987.

Note: Scale of 1–5: 5 = excellent, 1 = poor. N = 1047.

petitors were popping up everywhere. In addition, 1988 MDC sales had been sluggish. Hall felt this was largely due to customer confusion resulting from AT&T's hype of ISDN.

Hall glanced out the window towards the Raleigh-Durham Airport. It was 5:20 P.M., and the highway was packed with traffic. He decided that he would develop a presentation for the Regional Marketing Managers which outlined the division's position and presented a number of possible changes in the marketing strategy that the division could consider. This would generate discussion and help the group focus on the options that needed more in-depth study before a decision could be made.

Hall closed the magazine and placed it, along with several other pieces of information that had been gathered for him, in his briefcase. Despite the traffic and the work, he had to get home in time for his daughter's 6 P.M. soccer game. Perhaps he would be able to work on his analysis after supper.

Allied Stores Corporation

H. Allan Conway, University of Calgary

During 16 years as chief decision-maker at Allied Stores Thomas M. Macioce had deliberately and indelibly imprinted his managerial beliefs upon the operations of the company. In September of 1986, however, Mr. Macioce found his company the target of an unwanted takeover bid by Robert Campeau, a Canadian real estate developer. Because such a highly leveraged takeover by an industry outsider would cause significant adjustments in the company's long-term direction, Tom Macioce and his management were intent on finding a better alternative to Mr. Campeau's takeover.

Thomas Macioce had been well known throughout U.S. retailing for changing Allied's strategic orientation from a merchandising emphasis to a financially driven, return-on-investment emphasis. Macioce had always felt that this characteristic distinguished his leadership from that of other retail conglomerates, whom he felt were enamored with the glamour of the business, even though he was often credited with leading the whole industry toward a stronger financial orientation. Mr. Macioce felt that this difference in style meant that Allied, despite being one of the most consistent financial performers in the industry, was consistently undervalued by investors and markets:

> It's incomprehensible to me that we have never been able to gain the recognition of the analysts, the industry, and Wall Street for what we have accomplished.

In the Fall of 1986 Allied Stores Corporation was one of six (there had been seven until recently) major department store groups in the United States. Allied was comprised of such well-known regional department store chains as Jordan

---

Marsh in New England, Stern's in New Jersey, Joske's in Texas, as well as national specialty retail operations like Brooks Brothers and Ann Taylor (see Exhibit 1 for a listing of Allied's operating divisions). With a corporate staff of 550, Allied's sales for the previous full fiscal year were $4.5 billion with profits of $159 million.

THE TAKEOVER BID

Campeau's original offer of $58 per share was regarded as inadequate by most observers. In fact, some Wall Street pros were originally skeptical as to whether Campeau's "meager resources" would allow him to stay around until any bidding war that he might have ignited was concluded. Macioce and his management bitterly opposed the deal, making it clear that many of the top people might not stay on to manage the firm if Campeau wrested away control. Some industry experts felt that Allied's long-time business associate Edward J. DeBartolo, a U.S. shopping mall developer and partner with Allied in many projects over the years, might be a logical candidate to be encouraged by the Board of Directors to make a higher bid and thus act as a "white knight" in the

Exhibit 1   **Operating Divisions**

Division	Principal Geographic Location	Number of Stores	Gross Square Feet
Department Stores			
Block's	Indiana	10	1,411,000
The Bon	Pacific Northwest	39	4,538,000
Cain-Sloan	Tennessee	4	769,000
Day's	New York	4	621,000
Donaldson's	Minnesota	15	1,881,000
Heer's	Missouri	2	189,000
Herpolsheimer's	Western Michigan	6	527,000
Jordan Marsh	New England	19	4,090,000
Jordan Marsh	Florida	17	3,013,000
Joske's	Texas	27	5,029,000
Maas Brothers	Florida	21	2,785,000
Miller & Rhoads	Virginia	17	1,651,000
Miller's	Eastern Tennessee	12	1,192,000
Pomeroy's (2 divisions)	Pennsylvania	16	2,175,000
Read's	Connecticut	6	865,000
Stern's	Mid-Atlantic	24	4,501,000
		239	35,237,000
Specialty Stores			
Ann Taylor	National	91	293,000
Bonwit Teller	National	13	914,000
Brooks Brothers	National and Japan	57	882,000
Catherine's	National	210	631,000
Garfinckel's	Washington, D.C.	10	920,000
Jerry Leonard	Midwest and Southwest	26	103,000
Plymouth Shops	New York City and Washington, D.C.	51	221,000
		458	3,964,000
Overall total		697	39,206,000

takeover process. Experienced commentators on such hostile takeovers felt that an ensuing competition for control could raise the offered price as high as $68 or $69 per share.

Although any offer by Mr. Campeau was subject to his getting adequate financing, it was possible that a combination of investment banks and commercial banks might advance him sufficient money on a short-term basis to complete a bid even at the higher forecasts of a winning bid. A reasonable estimate would be that more than $1 billion of that would have to be repaid within the following two years allowing the rest to be financed by permanent means. Appendix 1 contains additional information on Campeau Corporation.

The consequences of the massive debt (in a 10 percent interest rate environment) required by Campeau or other possible competing buyers, if successful, to complete what could become a $3.5 billion deal were uncertain at that time. The possible financing complications led to estimates that commercial and investment bankers might make as much as $300 million in fees if Mr. Campeau were to become the winning suitor. Thus, the concern by Allied management about the operating consequences of the resulting financial structure.

Robert Campeau's exact plans if successful in taking over Allied were not clear. He had publicly stated that Allied's real estate assets were of little direct value. However, he had also stated that Allied's presence in 46 states was very attractive in his ambition to enter the U.S. market. Still, issues such as whether the real estate assets would be sold to help finance the retail stores or vice versa would not be decided until some time after any deal was closed.

CORPORATE HISTORY AND PERFORMANCE

Allied Stores had been established in 1929 by a combination of investment bankers and industrial entrepreneurs who combined 28 stores with total sales of $112 million into a department store group called Hahn Department Stores. The original Allied stores were typically not market leaders and tended to be dissimilar in size, image, and clientele. By 1950, however, Allied had become the largest and most profitable department store chain in the country.

Mr. Macioce had come to Allied in 1961 as Chief Financial Officer, becoming President in 1970 and Chief Executive shortly thereafter. At that time the firm was suffering from severely depressed profits. The sixties' strategy had been the general one pursued by department store chains of extensive expansion through building new stores in suburban shopping centers, often with the expectation that there would be up to a ten-year time lag before the population growth around the store justified its location. In fact, during the 1960s the company's selling space increased by 40 percent and suburban stores went from contributing 25 percent of sales to contributing almost two-thirds. A foray into the discount retailing sector had also been a drain on cash flow. Although exiting the discount business was one of Macioce's first decisions as Chief Executive, it took seven years to find a buyer for the two ailing discount chains.

Although there were those who would argue that Macioce had failed in his goal to inspire Allied to become the best retailer in the country, there was no question that his leadership restored fiscal stability to the company's operations. It continued to make steady, if not spectacular, returns during his tenure, a time when many changes were taking place that had far-reaching effects on

---

Exhibit 2   Allied's Financial Performance*

	1985	1984	1983	1982	1981
Net sales	$4135	$3970	$3676	$3216	$2733
Net earnings	159	141	128	91	88
Total assets	2772	2676	2530	2283	2179
Long-term debt	664	753	756	791	605
Shareholders' equity	1258	1063	964	868	798
Return on beginning shareholders equity	15.0%	14.6%	14.8%	11.4%	11.9%
Per Share					
Earnings (fully diluted)	$ 3.21	$ 2.99	$ 2.80	$ 2.16	$ 2.17
Dividends	1.07	1.00	0.925	0.90	0.875
Book equity	27.30	25.35	23.00	20.84	19.72
Market price range	25–36	19–28			10–12

*Dollar figures in millions, except for per share amounts. Year end actually February of the following year.

---

the department store segment of the retail industry. Shoppers were increasingly opting to divide their consumer dollar between specialty shops and discounters at the expense of the traditional broad-line department store.

Allied's sales in fiscal 1985 (ended January 31, 1986) were $4.2 billion with record profits of $159 million. With depreciation of $85 million, cash flow from operations was some $244 million before capital reinvestment.

Mr. Macioce's leadership years had generally been accompanied by rising profitability throughout. By 1979, the firm had reached sales of $2.2 billion and profits of $90.1 million. Exhibit 2 indicates that the nine-year record of increasing profits ended with the severe recession of the early 1980s but increasing profitability resumed again by 1983. During the strong economy and bull market of 1983–1986, Allied's stock price had risen from the $10–$12 range (adjusted for a stock split) to $49 just previous to the Campeau offer. With about 46 million shares actually issued, Allied's possible number of shares outstanding on a fully diluted basis was almost 53 million. The company returned between 11 and 15 percent annually on book equity over the 1980s.

PERFORMANCE IN THE DEPARTMENT STORE INDUSTRY

As of the early 1980s the large players in the industry had been relatively untouched by the phenomena of diversification and takeovers. Other than diversifying somewhat into other segments of retailing, the industry competitors tended to be single industry companies. However, the ownership structure of the industry was changing rapidly as of 1986. R. H. Macy had been taken private by its management in a $3.7 billion leveraged buy out. May Department Stores was in the process of paying $2.5 billion to take over the retail chains of Associated Dry Goods. Carter Hawley Hale had fought off an earlier takeover attempt by the Limited, Inc. by buying back half of its own shares and giving General Cinema (a theater and soft drink conglomerate) an option on 37 percent ownership.

Industry Performance, Year End, February 2, 1986					Exhibit 3
Firm	Sales ($ millions)	Net Profit ($ millions)	R.O.S.	R.O.E.	Average P/E
Allied Stores	4200	159	3.8%	12.4%	10.5
Associated Dry Goods	4385	120	2.7	12.8	11.5
Carter Hawley Hale	2890	18	0.6	*	n/a
Dayton Hudson	8790	284	3.2	15.4	13.5
Federated	9980	287	2.9	10.9	10.5
R. H. Macy	4653	206	4.4	21.4	n/a
May Stores	5080	235	4.6	17.2	9.5

*Returns to common were negative after preferred dividend payment.

Different industry competitors had lessened their dependence on the full-line department store segment in different ways. Carter Hawley Hale, for example, had made substantial investments in the bookstore business as well as in acquiring a number of very prestigious, upscale retailing establishments. Dayton-Hudson had emphasized the development of its two discount chains to the extent that 76 percent of its operating income came from this group. Federated, on the other hand, although active in the grocery business in California, continued to emphasize the department store segment in its expansion plans. Exhibit 3 includes comparative data on the seven firms that have traditionally been thought to make up the full-line department store industry.

ALLIED REPOSITIONS

After concentrating on ensuring Allied's survival in the early seventies, by 1977, Macioce had made growth and expansion of its traditional department store divisions—such as Jordan Marsh in New England, Maas Brothers in the Pacific Northwest, and Joske's in Texas—central to his strategy for Allied. Despite the seeming change in strategy, however, the store additions in the various company divisions continued to be of the smaller, suburban satellite variety, leveraging on the presence of an anchor store in a particular geographic area.

On the other hand, Allied management had adopted an ongoing strategy called "One-Step Up" in the late 1970s. Under this strategy, each retail chain aimed to move its merchandise mix toward a higher income, more fashion conscious clientele. Because the chains differed greatly in terms of geography and target market when the program was introduced, the program meant different things to different division managements. However, the strategy represented a movement away from discounting, for example, heralding the removal of the Bargain Basement departments from many of the stores.

Exhibit 4 summarizes information on Allied's expansion of store floor space in the 1980s. During the 1981–1985 period, Allied spent $538 million on capital investments (excluding the $233 million to take over Garfinckel, Brooks Brothers, Miller & Rhoads, Inc.).

During 1979, 1980, and 1981, Allied achieved some diversification from its dependence on the mid-market department store business by acquiring well-

Exhibit 4   Floor Space Expansion (sq. ft.) Since February 1, 1981

Year	Openings and Acquisitions	Closings and Dispositions	Total at Period End
1981	7,427,000*	828,000	36,291,000
1982	728,000	683,000	36,386,000
1983	959,000	243,000	37,102,000
1984	874,000	1,030,000	36,945,000
1985	1,637,000	897,000	37,685,000

*Includes the acquisition (260 stores, 5,458,000 sq. ft.) of Garfinckel, Brooks Brothers, Miller & Rhoads, Inc.

known specialty retailers like Brooks Brothers, Ann Taylor, and Bonwit Teller. These acquisitions had been conceived and executed largely by Mr. Macioce himself and not as part of an explicit overall strategy. The 1981 acquisition of Brooks Brothers (one of three divisions in Garfinckel's) was probably the single most important event during the years of Macioce's leadership. It is interesting to note that it occurred as a result of an extremely hostile, acrimonious takeover process that resulted in the top corporate management of the target bailing out. Following that acquisition, however, acquiring new retail chains became a conscious building block of the company's corporate strategy.

Allied planned to spend another $600 million on capital items in the next five years mostly to augment its specialty clothing operations. For example, it planned to open 100 more Ann Taylor and Catherine Stout's Shoppes stores. During 1985, Allied had acquired a six-store Los Angeles based chain of stores for large women, a six-department-store chain in Minneapolis, and the 26-store Jerry Leonard chain which markets apparel for big and tall men.

Exhibit 1 lists Allied's operations by division and geographic location. All of the specialty store chains had been acquired in the previous seven years although some had been expanded aggressively since being taken over. For instance, Plymouth Shops consisted of only 21 stores when acquired. Allied also managed six regional shopping malls, five of which it owned. Besides the divisional operations, Allied had a corporate staff of about 550 providing specialized services such as finance, personnel, legal, real estate, and private label development.

Information on the performance of some of Allied's chains is provided in Exhibit 5. While the seven chains listed as strong performers in Exhibit 5 accounted for under one-third of Allied's retail space, it was estimated that they generated 62 percent of sales, and delivered a staggering 87 percent of operating profits.

LEADERSHIP STYLE

Tom Macioce was proud of his Italian heritage and the fact that he grew up in the East Harlem section of New York City. A law graduate of Columbia University where he was captain of the basketball team, Macioce maintained a close relationship with the University and was a member of the Board of Trustees. Following service as a Lieutenant Commander in the navy during the Second

Weak and Strong Performers **Exhibit 5**

Weak Performers			Strong Performers		
	% Total Sales	Sales/ Square Feet		% Total Sales	Sales/ Square Feet
Department Stores			*Department Stores*		
Donaldson's	3.8	$ 83	The Bon	11.8	$107
Joske's	9.5	78	Jordan Marsh*	13.2	138
Miller & Rhoads	3.4	74	Jordan Marsh†	6.4	92
Pomeroy's	3.6	73	Maas Bros.	8.2	122
			Stern's	10.3	149
Specialty Stores			*Specialty Stores*		
Bonwit Teller	3.7	145	Ann Taylor	3.6	623
Catherine's	2.5	165	Brooks Brothers	5.6	272
Garfinckel's	2.7	122			

Source: *Business Week*, February 9, 1987.

*New England.

†Florida.

World War, Macioce was assistant Corporate Secretary for the Flintcote Company from 1946 to 1950. After that he was a Vice-President and Director of Bloomberg Mills for six years and President of L. F. Dommerich & Company, a factoring firm for four years. He joined Allied Stores as Vice-President for Finance in 1960.

The physically imposing, six-foot-six Macioce was well known throughout the industry as a tough, financially oriented executive. His disciplined, hard-working style was legend within the company. Macioce was a searching and persistent interrogator of those who brought proposals before him. Executives who slipped up on any detail of a proposal, generally found themselves the subjects of long, drawn-out lessons for onlookers of what not to do in Allied Stores.

Dedicated to what he described as a "hands-on" management style, Macioce often criticized leading business schools for putting too much emphasis on the role of the C.E.O. as an abstract strategist rather than an overseer of operational details. An Allied Vice-President explained: "Allied has no five-year plans. Macioce doesn't believe we can look forward that far." Another executive described the Allied culture as being one where "we put great emphasis on the immediate."

In fact, Macioce had, since his first day as President, embarked on an ongoing process to educate managers, throughout Allied's many divisions, to analyze carefully the profit impact of each possible decision affecting their businesses. Mr. Macioce felt that an enamorment with the glamour of "merchandising" could easily get in the way of sound management thinking. He introduced a rule that all capital expenditures had to show a 25 percent R.O.I. by year 3 to focus management's attention on the financials of a decision as opposed to earlier practices of doing whatever others in the industry were doing in order to avoid being left behind.

Mr. Macioce reinforced his emphasis on financial analysis of performance and decisions at every opportunity. In addition, he used the "One-Step Up" slogan to guide division executives as to how they should view and plan their businesses.

Despite the responsibility of running a 23-division retail conglomerate, Mr. Macioce spent a great deal of time in contact with individuals and institutions outside of the company's headquarters. He was a member of the Board of Directors of a number of other large companies as well as some prominent foundations. This meant that his schedule included a number of meetings of these bodies. In addition, he tried to meet regularly with Allied's major suppliers, as he wanted them to understand how closely Allied management monitored the fairness of its treatment by suppliers. Because of the nature of strategic development at Allied, Macioce was, of course, intently involved with the acquisition negotiations and early stages of integration of newly acquired chains. Historically, he had travelled a great deal to attend the annual two-day planning review sessions at each of his 23 independent department store and specialty chains spread across 46 states. These meetings Macioce regarded as an important opportunity to continue educating company management as to the importance of good financial analysis and of the need to remain committed to the "One-Step Up" strategy. There was usually a one-day follow-up meeting for each of these divisions at Allied's New York headquarters. Division management personnel prepared intently for these meetings as they knew that Tom Macioce would quickly zero in on any weakness or oversight.

EXECUTIVE SUCCESSION

From time to time the question of executive succession had become an issue at Allied. Macioce retained the title of President and Chief Executive with no Chairman of the Board throughout most of his tenure at Allied. This was in contrast to other major retailers who generally had a tandem top management team of Chairman and President. He had always maintained that any appearance of naming a successor before absolutely necessary would dampen the initiative of those other executives not chosen. Some of those who worked for Mr. Macioce, however, felt that he did not want to share any authority specifically because it would reduce his own control and power over the organization.

Certainly, Mr. Macioce had clearly spelled out his own approach to leadership in explaining why Allied had no management committees or regularly scheduled management meetings:

> I happen to believe that the answer to the operation of a company is a one-on-one relationship between the guy who is responsible for a certain area of the company and the President, whether it is a financial area, a store management area, a personnel area, or whatever it is.

Thus, group and division management ran fairly independently of the head office on a day-to-day basis. At the end of the period, however, they could be called on to account for unacceptable performance. And, of course, proposals for capital investments had to be approved by Mr. Macioce. This dominant leadership style carried over into Macioce's view of the appropriate relationship of the Board and C.E.O.

The function of the Board is to select the Chief Executive and, once it has made its decision, it is incumbent on the Board to stand back—watch, oversee, advise, correct, but not operate. And, really, that is what the Allied Board did. Its function is to select the Chief Executive and then to allow him to operate.

The Allied Board was comprised of sixteen members, six company officers and ten outsiders (see Exhibit 6). Because Allied was a widely held concern, no member of the Board was a significant shareholder. During its approximately nine meetings per year, the Board listened to reviews of operating group performance and presentations on major investment proposals. Members of the Board tended to concentrate their input on areas where they had particular insight or expertise—e.g., Mr. Thomas (President of the Ford Foundation) on social issues, Mr. Roeder (Chase Manhattan Bank) on financing issues. Just as Allied was operated without any regularly scheduled management meetings, there were also no meetings of the executive committee of the Board. Some of the corporate officers (for example, Executive Vice-President John Cullen and Chief Financial Officer Howard Hassler) had been senior executives and Board members since the early years of the Macioce leadership.

When asked what the Board should look for in a possible successor, Mr. Macioce stated his formula would be for "an executive with the same characteristics as I have. If I have a success formula there is no reason that I should not look to find the same ingredients that worked so well for me." Many on the Board agreed. For its part, Allied's Board of Directors included a particularly

Board of Directors			Exhibit 6
Name	**Major Affiliation**	**Director Since**	**Age**
Frank A. Bennack, Jr.	President and C.E.O., The Hearst Companies	1980	53
Lillian Berkman	President and C.E.O., General Alarm Corporation	1974	64
Milton P. Brown	Professor of Retailing, Harvard Business School	1967	67
John T. Cullen	Senior Executive Vice-President, Allied Stores Corporation	1973	60
John P. Diesel	President, Tenneco Inc.	1984	60
Donald F. Dunn	Senior Vice-President, Allied Stores Corporation	1977	60
Leonard H. Goldenson	Chairman and C.E.O., American Broadcasting Company	1969	80
Howard E. Hassler	Executive Vice-President (Finance), Allied Stores Corporation	1975	57
George C. Kern, Jr.	Partner (law firm), Sullivan & Cromwell	1971	60
Thomas M. Macioce	President and C.E.O., Allied Stores Corporation	1966	67
William A. Marquand	Chairman and C.E.O., American Standard Inc.	1983	66
Frank T. Reilly	Senior Vice-President, Allied Stores Corporation	1982	58
George A. Roeder, Jr.	Vice-Chairman, Chase Manhattan Bank	1968	65
Theodore C. Rogers	Chairman and C.E.O., NL Industries Inc.	1983	51
Franklin A. Thomas	President, Ford Foundation	1973	52
James A. Walsh	Executive Vice-President, Allied Stores Corporation	1980	63

Exhibit 7	Five Highest-Paid Officers, 1985		
Name	**Position**	**Salary**	**Bonus**
Thomas M. Macioce	President and C.E.O.	$690,000	$270,000
John T. Cullen	Senior Executive Vice-President	300,000	160,000
Howard E. Hassler	Executive Vice-President, Finance	220,000	130,000
Frank T. Reilly	Senior Vice-President of Brooks Brothers Div.	265,000	85,000
Elliot J. Stone	Vice-President, President of Jordan Marsh (New England) Div.	280,000	70,000

impressive group of accomplished individuals. Mr. Macioce had been the choice of the Board in 1970 when times were tough at Allied and new, strong leadership was deemed necessary. Subsequent events had made them strong supporters of their "iron-willed" C.E.O.

This strong support for Mr. Macioce's leadership by the Board was demonstrated by the fact that, in November of 1981, it had extended his employment contract to 1987 and that, in 1984, it had again extended it to January 1990. The Board stated that this would have Macioce at the helm for another five-and-one-half years "while providing for an orderly and gradual transfer of his responsibilities to his successor." At that time it was agreed that Mr. Macioce would recommend a successor by year-end. As a result of that process, James Walsh was installed as President in mid-1985 and Mr. Macioce took the title as Chairman and Chief Executive Officer. Exhibit 7 discloses the remuneration of Allied's five highest-paid officers. Although it shows that Mr. Macioce is paid substantially more than anyone else, it also shows that there are a number of well-paid senior executives at Allied, both at the corporate level and at the operating division level.

ONE UNFULFILLED OBJECTIVE

If there was one frustration throughout his years as head of Allied, it would be what Mr. Macioce described as the failure of the firm to receive what he deemed appropriate recognition for what had been accomplished since the precarious times of 1970 and 1971. Except for the economically depressed years of 1980 and 1981, Allied had achieved record levels of revenue and earnings in each year since 1971. Yet, its price-earnings multiple had been consistently inferior to that of most of the major retail operators. This even applied in cases where other retailers had much more varied and consistently worse operating results than Allied's. In fact, in its 1986 "Report on American Industry" Forbes had rated the stability of Allied's operating performance as "very high." For his part, Macioce believed that the industry and its analysts were still wedded to their merchandising past and did not appreciate good management for its own sake.

Mr. Macioce's current preoccupation was with devising a response to the Campeau takeover threat. However, if that situation is resolved satisfactorily, he will still be anxious to finally have external analysts and other industry watchers fully credit the strategic value of the company.

APPENDIX 1: CAMPEAU CORPORATION

■ ── ■

Robert Campeau was a native of Sudbury, a northern Ontario nickel mining town. He built his first house in Ottawa in 1949 at the age of 25. Between then and 1977 he had built 20,000 homes in Canada's capital. By 1977 he had abandoned the housebuilding sector for commercial and industrial development. His real estate company, of which Campeau owned 55 percent with 85 percent of the votes, in 1986 had assets of $2.4 billion. The company's financial history is reflected by the data in Exhibit 8.

Campeau had long considered himself an outsider in Canada's business establishment. Movement by certain of Toronto's financial institutions in 1980 to block him from taking over Royal Trustco, then Canada's largest trust company with $27 billion in assets, reinforced his resentment of what he considered a business elite in the country. Still, in 1983 Campeau moved from Ottawa to Toronto and built Toronto's largest house in its most exclusive district. Campeau's success in leasing substantial amounts of space to Canada's federal government departments had often been linked to his friendship with another prominent French Canadian, former Prime Minister Pierre Elliot Trudeau.

The offer for Allied represented a vehicle for Campeau's announced intention of developing or acquiring a number of shopping centers in the United States over the ensuing ten years. He reportedly saw the retail real estate market in the U.S. as offering good potential at a time when other real estate sectors were unattractive. Campeau was also quoted as saying that, had he entered the U.S. market earlier, he would have become ten times richer than he had by staying in Canada.

Historical Summary ($ thousands)   **Exhibit 8**

Fiscal Year	Total Assets	Long-Term Debt	Shareholders' Equity	Total Revenue	Net Income, Operating	Earnings per Share
1969	111,199	56,948	10,226	23,719	1,046	0.20
1973	334,600	218,121	57,991	94,173	5,985	0.88
1978	721,036	534,046	34,988	209,169	523	—
1983	1,795,648	1,463,171	172,784	183,339	21,266	1.20
1984	2,036,487	1,690,029	182,506	211,192	10,659	0.53
1985	2,377,913	1,946,735	228,423	213,470	27,878	1.37

6

CASE

■ ─── ■

Pier 1 Imports, Inc.

Mark Kroll, Jim Frierson, Fred Jacobson, University of Texas at Tyler

■ ─── ■

INTRODUCTION

Clark Johnson moves uneasily in his seat on the airplane. Down below, patches of greens and browns extend into the never-ending horizon. A string made of silver and blue appears to divide the fields underneath. "It has to be the Mississippi," his mind wanders for a few seconds from his thoughts about the company, as the airplane continues its course toward the Dallas/Fort Worth Airport. The papers and charts on the table bring his thoughts back to the future of the firm.

Clark is Chairman of the Board and Chief Executive Officer (CEO) for Pier 1 Imports, and he has just met with several investment bankers considering the possibility of issuing new stock to help finance an aggressive expansion program now under consideration. Pier 1 operates approximately 500 stores as of mid-1989, and plans to reach a corporate goal of 1000 by the year 2000. The company imports almost all of its goods from overseas, primarily from the Pacific Rim countries with about 23 percent coming from China.

In recent years, the company has enjoyed above average sales growth. This sales growth, coupled with what many believe is excellent corporate management, has resulted in a strong financial position.

As the 1990s begin, the company faces a number of important issues. The recent upheaval in China has depressed the market price of Pier 1's publicly traded stock. Another important issue is whether the company has the necessary means to develop its distribution system and its managerial staff to handle the proposed 1000-store operation.

─────────

This case is intended for classroom discussion only, not to depict effective or ineffective handling of administrative situations. All rights reserved to the authors and the North American Case Research Association.

Also, Pier 1's target market is another concern. The company has done extensive marketing research and identified its customer base. Consequently, Pier 1's product lines were modified to fit their customers needs. Would this target market change?

Profits are above average for the industry. The company is doing well. "The time to make a move is now," he thought. A sudden deceleration was felt. The "Fasten Your Seat Belt" sign came on. Finally, the aircraft began its approach into the Dallas/Fort Worth area.

IMPORTANT FACTS ABOUT PIER 1

■ Location

At first glance Fort Worth, Texas, may seem an unlikely place to headquarter North America's leading specialty retailer of decorative home furnishings. After all, most people would imagine that a worldwide importer of unique merchandise would locate perhaps in New York City, not Fort Worth. The company occupies six floors in the prestigious Bass Towers in the City Center Two complex located in downtown Fort Worth.

Pier 1 operates approximately 500 retail stores in 37 states and three Canadian provinces and franchises approximately 50 retail stores in 26 states. The stores are located near large shopping malls. They lease or own eight major distribution centers. Most of these centers have recently been upgraded to handle the increasing volume.

■ Size: Sales/Employees

In 1989, sales totaled approximately $414.6 million. The company employs over 7,500 people; 500 full-time employees at the home office, 4,400 part-time employees in its retail stores and distribution centers, and approximately 2,600 full time sales employees. A typical Pier 1 store contains about 1000 square feet and carries between 12,000 and 14,000 different items. About 8,000 of these products, called Stock Keeping Units (SKUs), are offered on a continuous basis. The remainder are seasonal or opportunistic buys.

■ Product

Pier 1 offers four major types of merchandise: decorative home furnishings (approximately 37 percent), wicker and rattan furniture (approximately 20 percent), housewares and kitchen goods (approximately 12 percent), and specialty clothing and seasonal items (approximately 20 percent).

Decorative home furnishings are imported from approximately 40 countries and include furniture made from pine, beech, rubber wood and selected hardwoods. This category also includes brass items, lamps, window covering, bedspreads, pillows, vases and numerous other decorative items, most of which are handcrafted from natural materials.

Wicker and rattan furniture, primarily used in dens, sun rooms and casual dining areas, is obtained from Taiwan, Hong Kong, China, the Philippines and Indonesia. These goods are handcrafted from natural fibers including rattan, buri and willow, and have either natural or painted finishes.

Housewares and kitchen goods include fine items, ceramics, dinnerware and other functional and decorative products. They are brought from India, the Far East and Europe.

Clothing items are shipped from India, Greece and Indonesia. They are primarily women's specialty clothing made from cotton and other natural fibers.

Of the merchandise Pier 1 imports, approximately 22.7 percent comes from China, 17.9 percent comes from India, 18.5 percent comes from Taiwan, and another 15.1 percent comes from Hong Kong, Japan, Thailand and the Philippines. The remaining 25.8 percent is not only imported from various Asian, European, Central American, South American and African countries, but also obtained from U.S. manufacturers, wholesalers, and importers.

■ Target Market

The customer base has evolved from the flower children of the Sixties to the baby boomers of the Eighties. Pier 1 implemented an extensive marketing research operation after changing from their in-house advertising department to the Richards Group, a premier Dallas advertising agency. This agency began a series of focus group interviews, followed by a random sample of 8,150 regular customers (Edmondson, 1986). Today, Pier 1 has a 1,500 "member" advisory board that answers four questionnaires a year. These surveys show that over 50 percent of Pier 1's customers are college graduates, and another 30 percent have some college education. The average household of the Pier 1 customer base earns over $38,000 a year. Approximately 88 percent of Pier 1 customers are women, 65 percent of whom are between the ages of 25 and 44 (*Chain Store Age Executive*, 1986). This group should continue to be a very desirable customer base.

AN AMERICAN SUCCESS STORY

■ The Beginning

Pier 1 began as a rattan furniture wholesaler which opened as a single Cost Plus store to liquidate excess inventory. In 1962, Charles Tandy, a Fort Worth businessman and founder of Radio Shack stores, obtained the rights to open and operate stores under the Cost Plus name. In 1965, the name was changed to Pier 1 Imports when the business had grown to 16 locations. In early 1966, Mr. Tandy sold Pier 1 to a group of 30 investors led by Luther Henderson, now a member of the Board of Directors. By 1969, when the company went public, the chain consisted of 42 stores. In 1970, Pier 1 began trading on the American Exchange, and in 1977, moved to the New York Stock Exchange. By this time, Pier 1 had 123 stores with a sales growth of 100 percent in four years.

In the Sixties, Pier 1 served a very specific customer group. This was the era of the flower children and Pier 1 provided their incense, sandals, and love beads. The personnel of Pier 1 reflected their clients' fashions: long hair and casual attire.

In 1973, worldwide inflation coupled with deregulated exchange rates radically increased the cost of foreign made goods. To further complicate matters, other retail chains began to stock many of the goods that were previously only offered by Pier 1. In the mid-Seventies, Pier 1 mounted several reorganization campaigns to enhance its performance capabilities. By 1977, the firm had grown to 280 stores, and in 1979, one store in Detroit achieved, for the first time in the history of the company, a million dollars in sales. That same year, Pier 1 merged with Cousins Mortgage and Equity Investments creating a company with three subsidiaries. In 1983, Intermark, a California-based holding company located in La Jolla, purchased a controlling interest in Pier 1. By 1985, the current management team headed by Clark Johnson was formed, and the other subsidiaries were sold. Since that time, sales have grown from $173.5 million to $414.6 million in 1989, which represents a 23 percent annual growth rate (see following table).

Net Sales (in millions of dollars)

1984	1985	1986	1987	1988	1989
147.3	173.5	203.9	262.3	327.2	414.6

Source: Pier 1 Annual Report 1989.

While expanding the number of stores from 300 to 500, Johnson and his team also closed unproductive stores and kept sales per square foot of store space constant. The firm has also not had to sacrifice gross profit margins in order to generate sales. Gross profits have continued to average better than 50 percent throughout the firm's period of rapid growth. Consequently, last year's net profit margin of 5.2 percent was slightly above the industry average.

PRESENT SITUATION

Pier 1 is confronted with numerous issues which keep reminding management of the inevitable interrelationship between the company's strengths and weaknesses and the environment. Furthermore, the international nature of the business exposes the company to a wide array of opportunities and threats. Following is a description of those external and internal factors that have a bearing on the firm.

■ External Factors

The external environment presents a number of opportunities and threats in both the domestic and international arenas.

Internationally, the European Economic Community (EEC) will form a new common market in 1992. Many U.S. firms are establishing operations in the European market now because of the anticipated restrictions on entering it after 1992. This market, comprised of 320 million people, will be the largest integrated market in the world. The Pier 1 expertise in international trade and import would be a significant strength if Pier 1 decides to pursue that market.

A number of countries with which Pier 1 deals are heavily indebted. The urge to acquire hard currencies to pay their debts has led to establishing incentive plans to promote exports. This is the case for many Asian and South American countries. For example, Columbia, after experiencing decreases in its export receipts has developed aggressive export promotion policies (*Business Latin America*, 1986), particularly of nontraditional products. Some of these nontraditional products fit the Pier 1 product profile. Therefore, such countries may offer an opportunity for Pier 1.

Because China provides approximately 23 percent of Pier 1's products, political stability of this country is critical to Pier 1. Recent actions taken by the Chinese government to stop a democratic movement may affect the business environment in which the company has operated for the last 12 years. Although the U.S. government has not formally restricted trade with China, the possibility still exists with respect to future Chinese governmental actions. However, of the percentage that is imported from China, "more than 90 percent of these items can be purchased from other countries where Pier 1 already does business" (*Drexel Burnham Lambert,* 1989).

Another important supplier of goods to Pier 1 is Hong Kong, which is scheduled to be returned to China by Great Britain in 1997. Under the current agreement, China will allow Hong Kong to retain much of its political and economic autonomy for a period of 50 years.

As an importer of all of its products, Pier 1 is affected by the Omnibus Trade and Competitiveness Act. Among the many provisions of this law, "Super 301" targeting countries that systematically use unfair trade practices, is seen as one of the most important. The effects of this legislation could be restrictions of the goods imported and sold by Pier 1.

The company competes for consumers' discretionary dollars with other specialty retailers offering similar lines of merchandise such as department stores (J.C. Penney, Dillards, Sears) and discount stores (Walmart, Target, K Mart). For example, analysts describe the "Sears factor," which refers to Sears' new "lower price" strategy, as a potential threat. If Sears can attract new customers, incremental sales will be taken away from other stores.

World Bazaar is the only specialty retailer similar to Pier 1. This competitor operates a small chain of stores in the Southeast United States. There is also a significant number of single store entrepreneurs offering a product line similar to that of Pier 1.

Additionally, Pier 1 competes with import wholesalers and other major retailers in the acquisition of merchandise abroad. Unlike the retailers of domestically produced merchandise, Pier 1's retail operation is subject to risks associated with its imported products. Some of these risks include:

1. Need to order merchandise from four to twelve months in advance of delivery and to pay for such merchandise at such time by letter of credit.
2. Dock strikes.
3. Fluctuations in currency values and exchange rates.
4. Restrictions on the convertibility of the dollar and other currencies, and duties.
5. Taxes and other charges on imports.
6. Import quota systems and restrictions generally placed on foreign trade (*Pier 1 10-K,* 1989).

■ Internal Factors

There are a number of internal issues confronting Pier 1, including: financial position, management and personnel, marketing and advertising, and distribution. Pier 1 enters the 1990s as a strongly capitalized and financially sound firm. The 1989 fiscal year ended on net earnings from operations of $21.9 million, up 36 percent from net earnings a year earlier of $16.1 million. Earnings per share were 70 cents, up 34.6 percent from 52 cents in the prior year. Also

Exhibit 1   Pier 1 Imports, Inc.: Financial Highlights ($ in millions, except per share amounts)

	1989	Change	1988	Change	1987
For the Year					
Net sales	$414.6	26.7%	$327.2	24.7%	$262.3
Gross margin	$217.5	27.6%	$170.5	25.4%	$136.0
Operating expenses	$175.6	26.2%	$139.1	25.2%	$111.1
Income before income taxes	$ 31.9	37.5%	$ 23.2	8.9%	$ 21.3
Net income	$ 21.9	36.0%	$ 16.1	34.2%	$ 12.0
Earnings per share of common stock	$.70	34.6%	$.52	26.8%	$.41
Return on average equity	20.6%	9.6%	18.8%	(3.6)%	19.5%
At Year End					
Common shares and equiv. outstanding (millions)	30.7	—	30.6	5.5%	29.0*
Number of employees	7,306	12.5%	6,493	44.3%	4,500
Number of stores	450	13.6%	396	13.1%	350
Retail square feet (millions)	3.1	14.8%	2.7	17.4%	2.3

Source: Pier 1 Annual Report 1989.

*Adjusted for stock split.

reported were record total sales of $414.6 million, which represented a 26.7 percent increase from a year earlier. These results leave the company with an attractive Return On Equity (ROE) of 20.6 percent (*Pier 1 Annual Report 1989*). However, adding another 500 stores in 10 years will require tremendous financial resources. (See Exhibits 1 through 6 for financial statements.)

Pier 1 directors and top management are an experienced group of team players who have collectively guided the affairs of the company to its present financial position. They have been responsible not only for successfully guiding it to its present position, but also for establishing the future direction of the company. Here too, however, the question has been asked whether the team can manage 1000 stores as successfully as it has 500.

The Board of Directors is guided by Clark A. Johnson, who serves as Chairman and Chief Executive Officer. (See Exhibit 7.) He previously served as President of the company and is largely credited with the company's recent success. Under his leadership, the company sold its unprofitable subsidiaries and increased sales. In addition, under Johnson's leadership, the company's goal of a 500-store chain was accomplished. The Vice Chairman of the Board of Directors is Charles R. Scott. He is President and CEO of Intermark, Inc., a diversified operating/holding company and Pier 1's largest shareholder. Another Director who also plays an important role in the company's management is Marvin Girouard. He is the company's current President and Chief Operating Officer. Formally, the Vice President of Merchandising, Girouard's efforts helped change the image and style of the stores. In addition, he is responsible for the plan to upgrade the stores' product line to include more collectibles and household items. In his present position, he directs the day-to-day operations of the corporation and is responsible for the company's financial performance. Luther Henderson is founding Chairman of the company. He has been with the company since 1966 and served as President of the company between December

Pier 1 Imports, Inc.: Financial Summary (see note) ($ in millions except per share amounts)   **Exhibit 2**

	5-Year Compound Annual Growth Rate	Year Ended in February					
		1989	*1988*	*1987*	*1986*	*1985*	*1984*
Earnings							
Net sales	23.0%	$414.6	327.2	262.3	203.9	173.5	147.3
Gross margin	24.5%	$217.5	170.5	136.0	101.0	82.8	72.6
Selling, general and administrative	24.0%	$163.0	130.3	104.8	78.3	65.8	55.7
Depreciation	30.0%	$ 11.5	8.8	6.3	3.9	3.1	3.1
Interest, net	28.1%	$ 10.0	8.2	3.6	3.6	3.0	2.9
Credit card costs, net		$ 1.1	—	—	—	—	—
Earnings before income taxes	24.0%	$ 31.9	23.2	21.3	15.2	10.9	10.9
Earnings for common shareholders	35.1%	$ 21.6	15.8	12.0	8.6	5.9	4.8
Common Share Results (adjusted for stock splits)							
Net earnings	28.5%	$ .70	.52	.41	.34	.25	.20
Cash dividends declared		$ .09	.06	.02	.01	—	—
Shareholders' equity	25.1%	$ 3.77	3.08	2.57	1.90	1.42	1.23
Weighted average number of shares outstanding (millions)	5.2%	30.7	30.6	29.0	25.5	24.2	23.8
Other Financial Data							
Working capital	24.9%	$117.2	87.2	96.8	43.4	38.6	38.5
Current ratio		2.9	2.3	3.3	2.4	3.5	4.4
Total assets	34.8%	$299.9	257.9	218.3	106.6	76.5	67.4
Long-term debt	35.2%	$121.3	96.5	101.5	26.7	26.7	26.9
Shareholders' equity	31.6%	$115.8	94.1	74.4	48.5	34.3	29.3
Tax rate		31.5%	30.8	43.7	43.2	46.0	51.2
Return on common shareholders' average equity		20.6%	18.8	19.5	20.8	18.6	22.5
Return on average total assets		7.7%	6.6	7.4	9.4	8.2	7.8
Pre-tax return on sales		7.7%	7.1	8.1	7.5	6.3	7.4

Source: Pier 1 Annual Report 1989.

Note: This financial summary is prepared on the basis of continuing operations after the distribution of the common shares of two subsidiaries to shareholders in December, 1985, and before the tax benefits of operating loss carryforwards fully utilized in fiscal 1986.

1979 and September 1983. Lawrence P. Klamon has been Director of the company since March 1983, and was Vice President during 1982 and 1983. Presently, he is President and CEO of Fuqua Industries, and also serves as Director of Advanced Telecommunication Corporation. Sally F. McKenzie has been a Director of the company since November 1985. She has served as civic leader on a local, regional and national basis for over five years. Thomas N. Warner has been a Director and Chairman of the Executive Committee of Intermark since 1975.

Exhibit 3 Pier 1 Imports, Inc.: Consolidated Statement of Operations (in thousands except per share amounts)

	Year Ended in February		
	1989	1988	1987
Net sales	$414,646	$327,226	$262,297
Cost and expenses			
Cost of goods sold	197,138	156,753	126,297
Selling, general and administrative expenses	162,994	130,235	104,762
Depreciation and amortization	11,452	8,826	6,299
Interest expense, net	10,022	8,194	3,662
Credit card costs, net	1,120	—	—
	382,726	304,008	241,020
Income before income taxes	31,920	23,218	21,277
Provision for income taxes	(10,070)	(7,143)	(9,307)
Net income	21,850	16,075	11,970
Cumulative dividends on preferred stock	250	250	—
Net income available to common stockholders	$ 21,600	$ 15,825	$ 11,970
Per common share	$.70	$.52	$.41

Source: Pier 1 Annual Report 1989.

Exhibit 4 Summary of Results of Operations (in millions except percentages and number of stores)

	1989		1988		1987	
	Amount	%*	Amount	%*	Amount	%*
Net sales	$414.6	26.7	$327.2	24.7	$262.3	28.6
Gross profit	217.5	52.5	$170.5	52.1	$136.0	51.8
Selling, general and administrative expenses	163.0	39.3	130.3	39.8	104.8	39.9
Depreciation and amortization	11.5	2.8	8.8	2.7	6.3	2.4
Interest expense, net	10.0	2.4	8.2	2.5	3.6	1.4
Credit card costs, net	1.1	.3	—	—	—	—
Income before income taxes	31.9	7.7	23.2	7.1	21.3	8.1
Provision for income taxes	10.0	31.5	7.1	30.8	9.3	43.7
Net income	21.9	5.3	16.1	4.9	12.0	4.6
Cumulative dividends on preferred stock	.3	.1	.3	.1	—	—
Income available to common stockholders	$ 21.6	5.2	$ 15.8	4.8	$ 12.0	4.6
Number of stores at end of period	450		396		350	
Sales gain for same stores	7.8%		12.1%		11.4%	

Source: Pier 1 Annual Report 1989.

*The percentages related to net sales represent increases in sales compared with the previous year's net sales. The percentages related to provision for income tax are expressed as a percentage of income before tax. All other percentages are calculated as a percent of sales.

Pier 1 Imports, Inc.: Consolidated Statement of Cash Flows (in thousands)   **Exhibit 5**

	Year Ended in February		
	1989	1988	1987
Cash Flow from Operating Activities			
Net income	$ 21,850	$ 16,075	$ 11,970
Adjustments to reconcile to net cash provided by operating activities			
Depreciation, amortization, deferred taxes and other	12,687	8,309	8,709
Increase in inventories	(26,698)	(20,954)	(21,069)
Increase in accounts receivable and other current assets	(12,125)	(2,472)	(2,137)
Change in other assets and other, net	150	(2,651)	(12)
Change in accounts payable and accrued expenses	12,362	6,607	8,410
Net cash provided by operating activities	8,226	4,914	5,871
Cash Utilized in Investing Activities			
Capital expenditures	(48,146)	(48,647)	(22,119)
Proceeds from disposition of property, plant and equipment	4,330	4,009	2,317
Investments in securities	19,507	3,794	(39,189)
Net cash used in investing activities	(24,309)	(40,844)	(58,991)
Cash Flow from Financing Activities			
Proceeds from sale of convertible debentures	—	—	49,266
Proceeds from sales of capital stock and treasury stock	2,971	8,648	14,628
Cash dividends	(2,970)	(2,021)	(557)
Proceeds from issuance of long-term debt, net of repayments and costs	18,593	(1,202)	21,783
Net borrowings (payments) under line of credit agreements	(6,604)	17,499	(8,000)
Purchase of treasury stock	(637)	(3,323)	(552)
Restricted cash for distribution center construction, net of receivables			
for reimbursable construction costs	255	16,890	(25,000)
Net cash provided by financing activities	11,608	36,491	51,568
Change in cash and cash equivalents	(4,475)	561	(1,552)
Cash and cash equivalents at beginning of year	8,219	7,658	9,210
Cash and cash equivalents at end of year	$ 3,744	$ 8,219	$ 7,658

Source: Pier 1 Annual Report 1989.

Pier 1's Board of Directors is backed up by the rest of the executive management team. This team includes, in addition to Clark Johnson and Marvin Girouard, Thomas A. Christopher, Executive Vice President and former Vice President of Operations. He has been with the company since 1980. Robert G. Herndon is the Chief Financial and Administrative Officer for the company, a position he has held since 1985. He is largely responsible for the provision of capital, as well as maintaining appropriate relationships with banks and other financial institutions. E. Mitchell Weatherly, Vice President of Human Resources, tends to the needs of Pier 1's employees. This management group works closely with the Board of Directors and is responsible for implementing and controlling the strategic plans developed jointly by the board and the management. Successive years of increasing sales and earnings have demonstrated management's ability to guide Pier 1. The following tables present the Board of Directors common stock holdings and management compensation. It is worth noting that Charles Scott, a member of the board, is also CEO of Intermark, Pier 1's controlling shareholder, which means controlling interest in Pier 1 is represented on the board.

Exhibit 6   **Pier 1 Imports, Inc.: Consolidated Balance Sheet (in thousands)**

	February	
	1989	*1988*
Assets		
Current assets		
Cash	$ 3,744	$ 8,219
Marketable securities	15,888	32,956
Accounts receivable, net	20,832	2,208
Inventories	130,224	103,526
Other current assets	7,714	6,358
Total current assets	178,402	153,267
Property and equipment		
Buildings	38,400	23,202
Equipment, furniture and fixtures	53,946	40,598
Leasehold interests and improvements	39,647	27,513
Construction in progress	1,175	2,977
	133,168	94,290
Less accumulated depreciation and amortization	30,679	22,857
	102,489	71,433
Land	8,963	7,681
	111,452	79,114
Other assets—restricted cash ($8,100,000 in 1988) and other	10,052	25,550
	$299,906	$257,931
Liabilities and Stockholders' Equity		
Current liabilities		
Notes payable and current portion of long-term debt	$ 16,267	$ 33,480
Accounts payable and accrued liabilities	44,951	32,589
Total current liabilities	61,218	66,069
Long-term debt	121,313	96,530
Deferred income taxes	1,605	1,191
Stockholders' equity		
Formula rate preferred stock, $1.00 par, 10 votes per share, 5,000,000 shares authorized, 1,500,000 outstanding	1,500	1,500
Common stock, $1.00 par, 100,000,000 shares authorized, 30, 399,000 outstanding	30,399	30,399
Paid-in capital	43,475	43,336
Retained earnings	40,895	22,015
Cumulative translation adjustments	568	153
Less—117,000 and 431,000 common shares in treasury, at cost, respectively	(1,067)	(3,262)
	115,770	94,141
	$299,906	$257,931

Source: Pier 1 Annual Report 1989.

Strategic Management Team at Pier 1   **Exhibit 7**

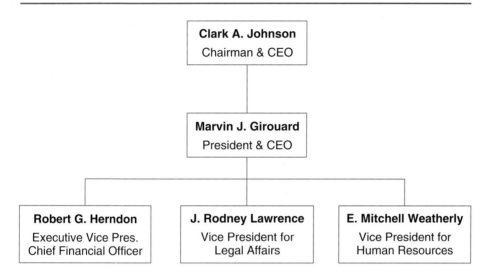

Board of Directors Stock
Ownership: Shares of Common
Stock Held

Clark A. Johnson	489,138
Charles R. Scott	47,912
Marvin J. Girouard	244,907
Luther A. Henderson	122,246
Lawrence P. Klamon	48,544
Sally F. McKenzie	23,941
Thomas N. Warner	58,023

Source: "Pier 1 Proxy Statement for Annual Meeting of Shareholders," 18 May 1989, p. 3.

Executive Cash Compensation

Clark A. Johnson	810,000
Marvin J. Girouard	412,250
Thomas A. Christopher	348,000
Robert G. Herndon	331,500
E. Mitchell Weatherly	135,725

Source: "Pier 1 Proxy Statement for Annual Meeting of Shareholders," 18 May 1989, p. 5.

Shortly after joining the firm, Johnson and the Richards Group adopted an intense marketing research program. This effort resulted in a clearly defined customer profile and suggested new methods of reaching them. These methods include enhancing the current advertising efforts and adding new mediums. Pier 1 adopted a slicker advertisement copy to reach their more affluent customers and incorporated magazine and television ads to supplement their weekly print advertising (Fisher, September 1988). "The company anticipates that television advertising will create double-digit increases over and above the increases normally seen during that period" (*Montgomery Securities*, 1989). Pier 1 has tried television advertising before (1975–1977), but now feels there is a large enough store base in metropolitan markets to be cost effective. "The company has increased its advertising effectiveness through improved creative execution and media placement and thus has been able to reduce the advertising-to-sales ratio, without reducing the impact of its advertising" (*Montgomery Securities*, 1989).

In order to maintain the orderly flow of merchandise, Pier 1 relies on its modern distribution centers. These centers are strategically located by region and provide the traditional functions of receiving, sorting, storing and delivering (*Transportation and Distribution*, 1988). The distribution centers are a critical element in the continued success of Pier 1 as it attempts to expand to 1000 store-objective by the year 2000. Pier 1 has four leased and four owned distribution centers. (See the following table describing their location and size.)

Distribution Center Location	*Facility (approx. sq. ft.)*
Rancho Cucamonga, California	419,010 sq. ft. warehouse space (1)
Fort Worth, Texas	104,000 sq. ft. office space (2)
Fort Worth, Texas	459,868 sq. ft. warehouse space (1)
Chicago, Illinois	297,552 sq. ft. warehouse space (1)
Chicago, Illinois	102,000 sq. ft. warehouse space (2)
Savannah, Georgia	393,216 sq. ft. warehouse space (1)
Montreal, Quebec, Canada	104,000 sq. ft. warehouse space (2)
Baltimore, Maryland	252,358 sq. ft. warehouse space (2)

Source: Pier 1 10-K Report, 1989, p. 14.
Note: (1) Owned; (2) leased.

Typically, buyers for Pier 1 are people promoted from the retail store operation who know their clients' wants and needs. Buyers are led by Marvin Girouard in their worldwide search for products. This intensive search has taken Mr. Girouard over 33 times to China since his first visit in 1977 (Fisher, October 1988). This group combs the world to import products suitable for their clientele.

The products are shipped by air and sea from over 60 countries. Some products, such as clothing, are exclusively shipped by air to take advantage of their inherent lightweight characteristics, which minimizes inventory by getting the product to market sooner and meeting seasonal demands.

The major points of entry into the United States are Rancho Cucamonga, California; Savannah, Georgia; and Fort Worth, Texas. Subsequently, these imported and domestic purchases are delivered to the distribution centers, unpacked, and made available for shipment to the various stores in the center's regions. The merchandise is then distributed to the retail stores by company owned trucks and contract carriers (approximately half and half). Because of the long shipping times involved, a high inventory level is required at these distribution centers.

STRATEGIC ISSUES

As Clark Johnson continues his reflection on the future of Pier 1, he concludes there are two sources of strategic issues confronting the firm: the ambitious expansion program and the securing of product sources from foreign markets. Following is a brief description of these issues as Johnson sees them.

1.   The goal of doubling its size in the next 10 years will require extensive development of Pier 1's distribution, data processing, and sales management as well as developing the capital to accomplish these goals. Currently, Pier 1 enjoys strong same-store sales and an experienced, successful marketing team. The

strategic issues result from the growth process itself and require the development of the appropriate management systems. Despite Pier 1's success, competitors entering this unique and profitable marketplace cannot be ignored. Pier 1 has the ability to enter the market with such penetration that it can discourage competitors, but not completely. However, the expertise that the company has gained in international procurement is not only hard to develop, but can only be achieved through experience. However, even with no new competition, good store location will be harder and harder to identify.

2.   The other strategic issue deals with the securing of quality products on a dependable basis at an acceptable price. The lack of control over foreign events leaves the company vulnerable to face disruptions in product availability. The significant amount of products imported from China may require the establishment of some alternative product sources if the Chinese or U.S. government for whatever reason restrict trade. Also, if the expansion of distribution outlets is successful the volume of purchases may exceed some suppliers capacities.

REFERENCES

"Colombia: Economic Outlook." *Business Latin America*, 1986, pp. 750–769.

"Company Update: Pier 1 Imports, Inc." *Montgomery Securities*, 28 April 1989.

Edmondson, Brad. "Pier 1 Keeps Up." *American Demographics*, May 1986, pp. 16–17.

"$8-million DC Under Construction for Pier 1 Imports." *Transportation and Distribution*, March 1988, pp. 61–64.

Fisher, Christy. "Girouard Combs World for Pier 1." *Advertising Age*, 26 September 1988, p. 78.

Fisher, Christy. "Pier 1 Sets Sail with TV Effort." *Advertising Age*, 24 October 1988, p. 54.

"Pier 1 Consumer Research Reshapes Strategy." *Chain Store Age Executive*, June 1986, pp. 75–77.

Pier 1 Annual Report 1989.

Pier 1 10-K, 1989.

"Pier 1." *Drexel Burnham Lambert*, 20 June 1989.

7

CASE

KLLM Transport Services, Inc.

M. Ray Grubbs, Susan M. Sharpe, Marian P. Simmons, Millsaps College

KLLM Transport Services, Inc., is an irregular-route common carrier that transports truckload quantities of various commodities throughout the United States. (An irregular-route carrier's trucks are dispatched to specific jobs, rather than simply running a standard route.) It specializes in providing temperature-controlled transportation and dependable and timely service to customers with specialized needs. KLLM management is committed to becoming the "biggest and best" in the temperature-controlled high-service market. This commitment has allowed the company to manage significant growth since deregulation. In fact, in 1986, the company made the decision to move from a mixed company-owned and owner-operated fleet to a solely company-owned fleet. William J. Liles, Jr., the company's Chairman and CEO, expects revenue growth in the 20% range in the near future.[1] In 1989, the company was well on its way with growth of 19%. This growth rate significantly exceeds long-run nominal GNP growth.

COMPANY HISTORY

In 1963, when KLLM began, the principals of the company were involved primarily in various aspects of the poultry business. As Liles has stated, the company was not begun because of some grandiose entrepreneurial plan but rather to simply "make a living."

---

[1]Interview with William J. Liles, Jr., Chairman, KLLM Transport Services, Inc.

When it began, the company operated as a broker, arranging transportation for poultry shippers to the West Coast, with backhauls of fruit and vegetables. The company saw an opportunity to buy a truck and then added more trucks slowly. Before deregulation, KLLM was able to carry only "exempt commodities." It was also able to carry loads on irregular routes, but only after obtaining permission from the Interstate Commerce Commission (ICC). With the advent of deregulation in 1980, the company was well positioned to expand its operations in the commodities area. Today, KLLM concentrates on the temperature-controlled markets in transporting foodstuffs, chemicals, and medical supplies. The company has grown from a small freight broker to a carrier with an operating fleet of 938 tractors and 1227 temperature-controlled trailers by the end of 1989.

KLLM operates primarily from its headquarters in Jackson, Mississippi, but also runs other terminal facilities in Houston and Dallas, Texas; Atlanta, Georgia; Fontana, California; and St. Louis, Missouri.

THE MARKET

The market for temperature-controlled, high-service freight transportation is highly fragmented, with companies ranging in size from single-rig owner-operators to large, multiline freight transporters. Many large shippers use what they refer to as core carriers (a small group of larger, better-financed truckers) to handle most of their transport needs. This allows them to choose and support quality shippers who can meet the high-service demands and who will provide continued good service. KLLM specializes in this market segment, concentrating resources on food (70% of revenue), medical supplies (9% of revenue) and chemicals (15% of revenue) (see Exhibit 1).

While the truckload (TL) transport market as a whole is not growing at a very rapid rate (3% annually, with annual sales of $120 billion last year), the temperature-controlled segment is expected to grow more quickly. This growth is due in part to changing demographics. With growing percentages in both two-income and single-person households, there has been an increased demand for convenience food items (frozen and other prepared food products) which are distributed nationally. Also, changing consumer tastes and continuing health consciousness have boosted demand for fresh produce year-round.

In the other revenue segments, specialty chemical producers have shifted many products from oil to water bases, which require temperature-controlled environments. Also, medical supplies are increasingly requiring refrigerated carriage.

COMPETITION

The high-service truckload (HSTL) carrier industry, of which KLLM is part, is highly fragmented. Competition is divided among other TL carriers, private fleet operators, and rail intermodal carriers.[2] The HSTL market is characterized

[2]Alex. Brown & Sons, *Prospectus for KLLM Transport, Inc.,* 1989.

KLLM Transport Services, Inc., Revenue by Product Groups **Exhibit 1**

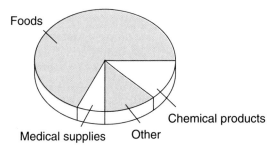

Foods

Medical supplies   Other   Chemical products

by little or no growth, with future gains in market share generated by taking market share away from owner-operators and private carriers. It is estimated that $10–$12 billion in transportation will move from private carriers to HSTL carriers over the next 5 to 10 years.

The cost and rate structures for the HSTL carriers allow them to be competitive with the rail intermodal carriers in the trailer on flat car (TOFC) and container on flat car (COFC) configurations.[3] However, in a double-stack configuration, rail intermodal transport operates at a lower cost, which allows them to offer lower rates. Under the team driver configuration, the HSTL carriers can provide significant advantages in transportation time in the high-service segment. Rail intermodal can only be competitive in high-density, long-haul freight corridors. Although the rail intermodal segment does provide a slight cost advantage, this segment is not likely to grow into a significant portion of the high-service transport market. Several factors contribute to this unlikely growth:

1. This mode of transport can only be competitive in high-density long-haul applications.
2. Quality in transit is reduced due to the rough ride experienced.
3. Transit time is often longer and does not meet the needs of many shippers.

The primary threats to the HSTL market are intense rate competition among all sectors of the market; a trend toward just-in-time inventory management, causing suppliers to move closer to major distributors; and the changing attitude of shippers concerning their delivered product cost.

THE COMPANY

■ Operations

KLLM operates its entire freight transport system from its dispatch office in Jackson, Mississippi. The dispatch function is set up by geographical areas. The dispatcher maintains positions for each tractor and sets routing for freight

[3]Ibid.

loads. He also acts in a supervisory capacity, contacting drivers, issuing purchase orders, arranging time off, and handling other problems as they arise.

The customer service group is primarily responsible for telemarketing. It secures the freight work with field sales representatives, makes appointments for shipping, and handles customer reports.

The operations area has access to important freight and shipping information made available through Electronic Data Interchange. This computerized service is provided to major customers to handle billing and ordering. KLLM is on the forefront in its industry sector in providing this added service to its customers. Another recently available technological advancement, Geostar, has further aided information retrieval. Geostar is a satellite transmission network which allows specially equipped tractors to be pinpointed and tracked. Because of the high unit cost per tractor, however, the Geostar system is unlikely to be installed on all tractors—unless the unit cost falls considerably. The trucks are also fitted with Rockwell Tripmasters which record equipment efficiency with respect to how well drivers manage their fuel through acceleration, top speed and idling time. This equipment allows the company to closely track fuel usage and spot consistent problems among drivers. A fuel efficiency bonus program to further encourage efficient fuel consumption is also tied to this system.

KLLM recruits new drivers from experienced driver pools and approved driver training schools. A lead driver for KLLM must have two years of driving experience, while a trainee is only required to have graduated from a qualified driving school and gone through company orientation. A trainee travels with a lead driver for several months before being tested as a lead driver. Salaries for these positions, including bonuses, range from $13,000 to $58,000. The drivers for long-haul carriers such as KLLM are limited to driving 10 hours, with an 8-hour break following. The typical driver spends 3 to 7 weeks on the road and receives one day off for each week away from home.

While away, a single driver drives an average of 2500 miles per week; a team of two drivers drives an average of 5000 miles, representing 22 hours per day on the road. Many drivers soon learn that trucking demands a very difficult lifestyle.

William S. Sullivan, Vice-President for Safety and Personnel, sees the biggest driver problem as time away from home, since KLLM drivers spend up to 90% more time away than do many other TL drivers.[4] KLLM experiences a turnover rate of over 100% annually. Sullivan adds that "last year KLLM hired 4.6 drivers [in order] to [ultimately] add one [driver to the employee roster]."

The driver supply problem is recognized by all levels of management. The company currently employs 1268 drivers of various skill levels. Management recognizes that with stated growth goals, the shrinking demographic base of the driver pool (males aged 24–39), and the relative unattractiveness of the truck driver's lifestyle, changes will have to be made to maintain and improve the levels of equipment utilization.

One recently introduced program designed to increase the recruitment of lead drivers is the Recruiting Bonus Program. Along with regular compensation and bonus programs, each lead driver who recruits another lead driver who is subsequently hired will receive a bonus of $100 per driver recruited. Addition-

---

[4]Interview with William S. Sullivan, Vice-President for Safety and Personnel, KLLM Transport Services, Inc.

ally, the driver who makes the most successful recruitments in a quarter will receive $500.

When questioned about the possibility of unionization of drivers, management and drivers are in agreement. Unionization at KLLM is unlikely. Reasons commonly offered for this are as follows:

1. Competitive pay.
2. Geographic dispersion of drivers.
3. The "free spirit" of long-haul truck drivers.

One driver responded simply, "We don't need one."

■ Maintenance

With maintenance costs representing around 10% of revenues,[5] Joseph M. Stianche, Vice-President of Maintenance, recognizes the critical role that his department plays in KLLM's operations. Stianche states that his goal is "to minimize long-term maintenance costs."[6] In order to achieve this goal, KLLM actively utilizes a preventive maintenance program, which also helps to minimize costly in-route repair expenses. The maintenance operation in Jackson and Dallas are computerized and fully integrated to aid in maintenance scheduling. The maintenance shops are manned 24 hours a day.

Stianche believes that his biggest management problem is "keeping people productive and motivated in the maintenance area." When questioned about unionization in the shop, he admits that there is a possibility, but that good managers eliminate the need for unions.

In order to keep operations running smoothly, KLLM has maintained consistent equipment specifications. The company uses only Freightliner and Kenworth tractors and Great Dane trailers. This facilitates easy and consistent handling of maintenance problems. Required specifications for company equipment stress fuel efficiency and safety. The company has recently fitted a number of trucks with antilock brakes to maintain their strong safety record.

■ Marketing

KLLM stresses quality service in marketing its transport services. Regardless of whether the customer's priority is quick transit time or special handling, the regional sales managers seek to tailor high-service transport quality to the customer's specific needs. James T. Merritt, Vice-President for Sales, comments that "the goal for KLLM is to select accounts among necessary growth industries which are interested in developing long-term relationships and which see quality transport as a value-added service."[7] In order to select these preferred accounts, the field salesperson must know what makes people buy and must identify the philosophy of the corporation with which he is dealing. He must know that the customer wants quality service and is willing to pay for it.

The marketing managers identify the criteria for carrier selection. Is the choice made by transit time, safety, clean trailers, or a timely claims depart-

---

[5]Reprinted by Allyn and Bacon with permission from *Commercial Carrier Journal,* July 1989, copyright Chilton Co.

[6]Interview with Joseph M. Stianche, Vice-President for Maintenance, KLLM Transport Services, Inc.

[7]Interview with James T. Merritt, Vice-President of Sales, KLLM Transport Services, Inc.

ment? Whatever the criteria, KLLM does not want accounts that stress price; the company offers high-service quality, which costs in terms of price. Merritt identifies the strengths of building these relationships:

- These accounts are easier to access for rate increases.
- KLLM's density in shipping lanes in the geographic area is increased.
- These relationships allow the company to reduce its debt overhead through better equipment utilization.

Liles has a goal of keeping all accounts under 10% of revenues. Its largest account was responsible for slightly over 10% in 1986 and 1987 and 10.7% in 1988. No accounts represented over 10% in 1989.

The company salespeople stress quality in transit. This means high product quality will be maintained in transit between the producer and distributor through high-service and specialized operations. KLLM concentrates primarily on the temperature-controlled sector of the TL market. The company will, however, handle dry freight in order to fill trucks in backhauls or to position the trailer for an important temperature-controlled load. In fact, 28% of revenues in 1989 were derived from dry-freight shipping.

■ Management

In 1986, Liles made Joseph H. Cherry President and Chief Operating Officer of the company and removed himself from the day-to-day operations of KLLM. However, Liles still plays an active role in the planning and implementation of policy. He is instrumental in financing decisions and broad operations decision making for KLLM.

Cherry terms his management style as "semidecentralized." He promotes individualized management on all levels.

Cherry attributes his management success to these factors:

- Hiring good people.
- Demanding quality work from his team.
- Delegating.
- Making the workplace as pleasant as possible.

"This approach tends to minimize personality pressures while maintaining a high level of personnel productivity."[8] William Sullivan characterized Cherry as a "working-style manager" and one who wants direct involvement from his staff.

Cherry communicates primarily by way of meetings. He meets with all the vice-presidents daily on an informal basis and conducts a formal staff meeting each week. In addition, he reports to Liles each day. Cherry is committed to his job, normally working from 7:00 A.M. until 7:00 P.M. on weekdays and on weekends as necessary. He exercises an open-door policy and is easily accessible. He can often be found conversing with employees in the hallways. Cherry takes one truck trip each year to maintain his "feel for the company."

A management training program develops future managers by exposing the trainee (typically a college graduate with a degree in transportation) to every

[8]Interview with Joseph H. Cherry, President and Chief Operating Officer, KLLM Transport Services, Inc.

aspect of the company, from dispatching to personnel. KLLM attracts and maintains highly motivated individuals; it has maintained a low management turnover for many years. Only one key management person has left the company since 1980. The company relies on this high motivation and a liberal compensation policy to keep turnover at a minimum. In 1986, senior managers were offered shares of the company at $3.25 per share. The company has also instituted a 401(K) plan and an ESOP (employee stock option plan) for many employees.

In addition, management participates in a bonus program which is based on the company's operating ratio. The bonus begins at a 90.0% ratio and increases incrementally as the ratio improves. The operating ratio for 1989 was 94.2% (see Exhibit 2).

KLLM Transport Services, Inc., and Subsidiaries: Selected Financial and Operating Data   **Exhibit 2**

	1989	1988	1987	1986	1985
Statement of Earnings Data (in thousands except per share amounts)					
Operating revenues	$115,745	$97,410	$75,230	$58,066	$46,850
Operating expenses					
Salaries, wages and fringe benefits	39,459	32,813	22,327	13,239	8,909
Operating supplies and expenses	42,538	33,600	24,191	13,118	8,913
Insurance, taxes and licenses	8,148	7,033	5,160	3,466	2,068
Depreciation and amortization	12,904	10,834	7,918	3,373	2,123
Operating leases for revenue equipment				2,629	2,200
Purchased transportation			4,720	15,478	18,453
Other	6,161	4,860	3,801	2,439	1,757
Gain on sale of revenue equipment	(176)	(121)	(79)	(112)	
Total operating expenses	109,034	89,019	68,038	53,630	44.423
Operating income	6,711	8,391	7,192	4,436	2,427
Interest and other income	9	26	3	74	27
Interest expense	(4,529)	(3,749)	(2,535)	(1,326)	(1,202)
Earnings before income taxes and cumulative effect of a change in accounting principle	2,191	4,668	4,660	3,184	1,252
Income taxes	800	1,725	1,750	850	379
Earnings before cumulative effect of a change in accounting principle	1,391	2,943	2,910	2,334	873
Cumulative effect of a change in accounting principle			103		
Net earnings	$ 1,391	$ 2,943	$ 3,013	$ 2,334	$ 873
Per common share amounts					
Earnings before cumulative effect adjustment	$ 0.54	$ 1.15	$ 1.14	$ 1.10	$ .46
Cumulative effect of a change in accounting principle			0.04		
Net earnings	$ 0.54	$ 1.15	$ 1.18	$ 1.10	$ .46

(continued)

Exhibit 2   **KLLM Transport Services, Inc., and Subsidiaries: Selected Financial and Operating Data (continued)**

	1989	1988	1987	1986	1985
Weighted average common shares outstanding	2,569	2,567	2,563	2,051	1,583
Balance Sheet Data (in thousands)					
Total assets	$ 89,003	$82,874	$67,907	$40,563	$19,307
Total liabilities	60,380	55,823	43,977	19,851	13,618
Net property and equipment	68,856	65,796	55,176	31,006	11,903
Long-term debt, excluding current maturities, and preferred stock	39,975	37,290	29,141	10,033	8,872
Stockholders' equity	28,623	27,051	23,930	20,712	4,239
Operating Data					
Operating ratio	94.2%	91.4%	90.4%	92.4%	94.8%
Average number of truckloads per week	1,678	1,437	1,083	840	662
Average miles per trip	1,253	1,234	1,298	1,306	1,300
Total miles travelled (000s)	109,310	92,195	73,090	57,027	44,757
Average miles per tractor	124,099	122,275	123,881	115,909	106,311
Average revenue per total mile	$ 1.06	$ 1.06	$ 1.03	$ 1.02	$ 1.05
Percentage loaded miles to total miles	90.1%	89.7%	90.1%	88.8%	91.7%
Equipment at year-end					
Company-owned tractors	938	831	646	400	221
Owner-operated tractors	0	0	0	121	216
Refrigerated trailers	1,227	1,090	932	675	490

Source: KLLM Transport Services, Inc., *Annual Report,* 1989.

■ Finance

In 1986, an initial public offering was made, raising $14 million in new capital. The proceeds from the offering were used to repay long-term debt and preferred stock obligations. The retirement of these securities has allowed KLLM to prepare for continuing its high growth rate without financial strain.

Company sales for 1988 and 1989 were $97,410,000 and $115,745,000, respectively. This is an indication of a long-run growth rate of 20–25%. Key factors influencing profitability are such things as fuel costs, driver costs, and depreciation. These costs averaged $0.16, $0.26, and $0.12 per mile, respectively, in 1988. Any changes in these costs have a major impact on profitability. A significant increase in fuel costs from the fourth quarter 1988 to the fourth quarter 1989 resulted in a decrease in net earnings of $0.27 per share (see Exhibits 3, 4, 5, and 6 for related financial information).

Although KLLM is not unionized, heavy competition exists for drivers. This fact, coupled with the fact that the demographic pool of available drivers is shrinking, has forced KLLM to recently increase its advertising for drivers. In July 1988 driver compensation rates were increased $0.02 per mile, reflecting these competitive measures. The company's costs are relatively stable ($0.80–$0.85 per mile), although they do demonstrate a seasonal trend. Revenues, on

KLLM Transport Services, Inc., and Subsidiaries: Selected Quarterly Data (unaudited) for the Years Ended 1989 and 1988 (in thousands, except per share amounts)

Exhibit 3

	First Quarter	Second Quarter	Third Quarter	Fourth Quarter
1989				
Revenues	$27,182	$29,700	$29,754	$29,109
Operating income	1,491	2,441	2,205	574
Net earnings (loss)	248	816	700	(373)
Earnings per share	$ 0.10	$ 0.31	$ 0.28	$ (0.15)
1988				
Revenues	$22,575	$23,737	$24,827	$26,271
Operating income	1,732	2,526	1,903	2,230
Net earnings	580	1,052	568	743
Earnings per share	$ 0.23	$ 0.41	$ 0.22	$ 0.29

Source: KLLM Transport Services, Inc., *Annual Report*, 1989.

Note: Fuel costs rose significantly in the fourth quarter of 1989 from the fourth quarter of 1988 resulting in a decrease in net earnings of approximately $700,000 ($0.27 per share).

In the third quarter of 1988, an equipment recall for replacement of power steering units idled approximately 10% of the fleet for four weeks. The Company settled with the manufacturer of the power steering units in the fourth quarter of 1988 resulting in an increase in net earnings of $90,000 ($0.03 per share).

the other hand, are largely determined in the freight lanes and are based on dry-freight rates, which increased in 1988. For example, freight rates into the Rust Belt—states around the middle Great Lakes—average around $1.60, while outbound rates run around $0.90.

When questioned about the company's relatively high use of financial leverage, Cherry responded by pointing out that the debt level has been higher and he is comfortable with the debt levels currently experienced. KLLM does, however, plan to seek new equity financing through a stock offering or through the issuance of convertible debentures (see Exhibit 2).

■ Strategy

KLLM Transport Services, Inc., plans to become the largest and best transporter in the temperature-controlled segment of the TL industry. To accomplish this, the company will concentrate on high-service quality and development of quality accounts. These goals will be accomplished through the following:

- Active management of company growth.
- Increased concentration on driver recruitment and retention.
- Customer service, both in handling and equipment availability.

When questioned about strategic planning, Liles remarked that KLLM has a "fluid five year plan," in the sense that management tries to remain aware of opportunities while keeping an eye on long-term goals. Top management is active in the strategic planning process and periodically engages in formal planning sessions outside a strict budget planning and review process. Cherry adds that he thinks "about strategic planning every day."

Exhibit 4   **KLLM Transport Services, Inc., and Subsidiaries: Consolidated Balance Sheets (in thousands)**

At Year End	1989	1988
Assets		
Current assets		
Cash and cash equivalents	$ 558	$ 612
Accounts receivable		
Customers (net of allowances of $36,000 in 1989 and 1988)	13,743	11,489
Advances to drivers	221	254
Other	393	459
	14,357	12,202
Inventories—at cost	919	692
Prepaid expenses		
Tires	2,934	2,234
Taxes, licenses and permits	816	701
Other	563	637
	4,313	3,572
Total current assets	20,147	17,078
Property and equipment		
Revenue equipment and capital leases	91,602	79,534
Land, structures and improvements	7,635	6,380
Other equipment	3,902	2,677
	103,139	88,591
Less accumulated depreciation	(34,283)	(22,795)
	68,856	65,796
	$ 89,003	$ 82,874
Liabilities and Stockholders' Equity		
Current liabilities		
Note payable to bank	$ 1,067	$ 787
Accounts payable	4,408	4,157
Accrued expenses	4,765	2,751
Deferred income taxes	175	950
Current maturities of long-term debt	5,660	6,583
Total current liabilities	16,075	15,228
Long-term debt, less current maturities	39,975	37,290
Deferred income taxes	4,330	3,305
Stockholders' equity		
Preferred stock, no-par value; authorized 5,000,000 shares; none issued		
Common stock, $1 par value; authorized 10,000,000 shares; issued and outstanding 2,571,583 shares in 1989 and 2,569,030 shares in 1988	2,572	2,569
Additional paid-in capital	14,051	14,022
Unearned compensation	(333)	(482)
Retained earnings	12,333	10,942
	28,623	27,051
Commitments and contingencies	$ 89,003	$ 82,874

Source: KLLM Transport Services, Inc., *Annual Report,* 1989.

KLLM Transport Services, Inc., and Subsidiaries: Consolidated Statements of Earnings (in thousands, except per share amounts)			Exhibit 5
For the Year	**1989**	**1988**	**1987**
Operating revenue	$115,745	$97,410	$75,230
Operating expenses			
Salaries, wages and fringe benefits	39,459	32,813	22,327
Operating supplies and expenses	42,538	33,600	24,191
Insurance, taxes and licenses	8,148	7,033	5,160
Depreciation and amortization	12,904	10,834	7,918
Purchased transportation			4,720
Other	6,161	4,860	3,801
Gain on sale of revenue equipment	(176)	(121)	(79)
Total operating expenses	109,034	89,019	68,038
Operating income	6,711	8,391	7,192
Other income and expense			
Interest and other income	9	26	3
Interest expense	(4,529)	(3,749)	(2,535)
	(4,520)	(3,723)	(2,532)
Earnings before income taxes and cumulative effect of a change in accounting principle	2,191	4,668	4,660
Income taxes	800	1,725	1,750
Earnings before cumulative effect of a change in accounting principle	1,391	2,943	2,910
Cumulative effect on prior years of changing to a different method of accounting for income taxes			103
Net earnings	$ 1,391	$ 2,943	$ 3,013
Per common share amounts:			
Earnings before cumulative effect adjustment	$ 0.54	$ 1.15	$ 1.14
Cumulative effect of a change in accounting principle			0.04
Net Earnings	$ 0.54	$ 1.15	$ 1.18

Source: KLLM Transport Services, Inc., *Annual Report*, 1989.

AN INTERVIEW WITH THE COO OF KLLM

The following is the text of a conversation the case authors had with Mr. Joe Cherry, President of KLLM. It provides good insight into the man and his management style.

Case Writer: Mr. Cherry, tell us something about your background.

Cherry: I graduated from Southern Mississippi University in Accounting in 1974 and worked with Touche-Ross (a CPA firm) for about 6 years—then I came to work here in 1980, in the financial area. I've worked in the general management area for the last 3 or 4 years. I guess my style is to hire good people and to be fairly demanding that they do their jobs, and then to follow up periodically to make sure that the job is being done—to delegate with restraint. I think our emphasis is on making the workplace a pleasant place. There is a certain amount of job pressure that is inherent in our business—but we don't want to add any personality pressures to that. We do set goals, and we demand that our people achieve goals. But we let them do their jobs in their own way, achieve the goals, and report back. I think that is our basic style.

Exhibit 6   **KLLM Transport Services, Inc., and Subsidiaries: Consolidated Statements of Cash Flows (in thousands)**

For the Year	1989	1988	1987
Cash Flows from Operating Activities			
Cash received from customers	$113,491	$93,253	$73,501
Interest and other income received	9	26	3
Cash paid to suppliers and employees	(94,592)	(76,095)	(60,381)
Interest paid	(4,416)	(3,139)	(2,535)
Income taxes paid	(590)	(588)	(804)
Net cash provided from operating activities	13,902	13,457	9,784
Cash Flows from Investing Activities			
Purchases of property and equipment	(16,920)	(12,545)	(24,917)
Proceeds from sales of equipment	890	551	469
Net cash flows used in investing activities	(16,030)	(11,994)	(24,448)
Cash Flows from Financing Activities			
Sale of common stock	32	29	56
Net change in borrowing under revolving line of credit	6,500	(6,000)	24,500
Proceeds from long-term borrowings		10,000	
Repayment of long-term debt and capital leases	(4,738)	(4,790)	(9,686)
Net change in borrowings under working capital line	280	(925)	190
Net cash flows provided from (used in) financing activities	2,074	(1,686)	15,060
Net increase (decrease) in cash and cash equivalents	(54)	(223)	396
Cash and cash equivalents at beginning of year	612	835	439
Cash and cash equivalents at end of year	$ 558	$ 612	$ 835
Reconciliation of Net Income to Net Cash Provided from Operations			
Net Income	$ 1,391	$ 2,943	$ 3,013
Noncash expenses and gain included in income			
Cumulative effect of accounting change			(103)
Depreciation and amortization	12,904	10,834	7,918
Deferred income taxes	250	1,095	1,205
Amortization of unearned compensation	149	149	149
Book value of equipment written off in accidents	242	68	100
Increase in accounts receivable	(2,155)	(4,460)	(1,648)
Increase in inventory and prepaid expenses	(968)	(110)	(1,130)
Increase in accounts payable and accrued expenses	2,265	3,059	498
Gain on sale of equipment	(176)	(121)	(79)
Other			(139)
Net cash provided from operations	$ 13,902	$13,457	$ 9,784
Noncash financing activities			
Capital equipment lease obligations		$ 9,407	$ 7,661

Source: KLLM Transport Services, Inc., *Annual Report,* 1989.

Now, I'm the chief operating officer. Various vice presidents report to me, and we meet informally every day. Also, we have a staff meeting once a week. I report to Billy Liles, who's the chairman of the board and the chief executive officer. I meet with him daily just to keep him abreast of what's going on.

We've got a basically young group of [management] people—that is, we started out with young people. We all came to work here when we were about 30 years old, and we had some business experience. Of course, Billy Liles and

Bennie Lee both started the company, so they were around 10 or 15 years before we were.

We put a lot of time into our jobs. I think a typical workday starts at seven in the morning and ends at seven at night. We have to do some traveling. And we have to work weekends.

The job is very demanding, physically and mentally. Sometimes you're away from your family. For instance, every year, I try to take at least one truck trip, or I drive a truck and visit the drivers. This year, I went to Los Angeles, from Los Angeles to Salt Lake City, then through Denver, and back to Jackson. I got to see some snow and ice on this trip. These trips help me to see what the drivers are experiencing.

Philosophically we take a great deal of pride in our company and our accomplishments. Since we put so much of our life into the job, it's a little bit like a masterpiece—or something like that—an artist has drawn.

I've got a financial background, so I can see expense relationships. But you must get past that step of seeing where the break-even point is and come up with the idea, the vision, of how you're going to do more than break even. Certainly, anybody can put the mechanical formulas together. But you've got to conceive some way to get the company growing.

For instance, we look at things on a per-mile basis. That's our variable. I can see what our variable costs are and what our fixed costs are. Then I say, I need X amount of revenue. And then I have to find a market—places that will need our services on a consistent basis and provide that revenue. And as we grow, some geographic areas or some niches become tapped out, and I have to find other markets. We also are challenged by the driver shortage in the industry, and we have to come up with a plan that gives us the proper number of drivers—a plan that compensates them adequately, but doesn't overcompensate them and make our operating performance suffer.

There are big challenges, and the answers don't just leap out at you. There's no consultant that walks in and says, "Hey, here's the way you do trucking." It just doesn't happen that way. So there are challenges, and you have to find your own answers. As a group, we [the managers] study the issues and the alternatives; we look at the industry and look at the country; and we come up with a plan that pushes us in the right direction.

Case Writer: You've talked before about your voice mail. Can anybody in the country (in the company) dial and communicate with you in that way?

Cherry: Yes, anyone in the company has access.

Case Writer: Are there any other ways that you communicate with these people in the outlying places?

Cherry: Yes. We have memos, of course, and telephone conversations. Also, I visit the places, as do the various department heads. We also use teleconferencing. We get everybody in the outlying locations of a particular job class on the line and we talk. That gives us a chance to discuss problems, rather than let them fester. We try to keep in touch with our people in the branches (the terminals), just as we keep in touch with our people here. It's a bit different, of course, because here we see each other all the time. We eat lunch with each other; we see our people in the hall. And we get problems worked out. But with the people outside, you don't see them. So you have to keep in touch in other ways.

Case Writer: Do you have formal times that you talk with these people?

Cherry: Yes, at the departmental levels, we do. The various vice presidents have specific responsibilities—Stan Sullivan handles recruiting; Ken Anders has the overall responsibilities for the terminals; Joe Stianchi has the maintenance responsibilities; and Rick Sheehan handles operations. They maintain daily contact; they keep abreast of what's happening.

Case Writer: Do you pretty much let people make their own decisions here? Is your management style centralized or decentralized? How do you *control* it?

Cherry: I guess our style is semidecentralized. I look at everybody—a vice president or a factory worker—the same way: as an individual. And based on past performance, I know how much rope to reel out or to reel in.

But I like to know a lot about what's going on. I read everything that comes in here. I think that's a tremendous asset in business: reading whatever needs to be read. I find that one weakness in a lot of people who are college-educated is their poor reading comprehension and their not liking to read.

I see all the V.P.'s every day several times, and I want to know everything that's going on. In the event an issue comes up, I expect a message. So we discuss significant transactions before we do them, and we get plenty of update. But it doesn't bother me at all to leave the place; I know everything's going to be OK. I'm going to take a week off this week and I don't have any worry about whether everybody knows what to do and will do it. If an emergency comes up, they'll handle it.

Case Writer: How was the management team put together?

Cherry: Well, Joe Stianchi, Stan Sullivan, Rick Sheehan, and myself were hired within a year of each other. Kirby and Jim Merritt were hired in the last 2 years. And Jack Liles has been with the company 4 or 5 years longer than that.

Case Writer: So as far as all the people that have been hired since you have been here, you have had an influence in selecting them?

Cherry: Yes. We look very carefully at the people we interview and make sure that we're hiring people who are motivated and aren't going to need a lot of supervision—so that we're not going to have a lot of turnover. We have very little turnover. I think that's from being selective at the outset.

Case Writer: This is on a different level. What about the driver turnover?

Cherry: OK, the driver turnover is probably a very serious industrywide problem, and I can talk for hours about it. But just to put it in a nutshell—we ask, in the 48-state trucking operations, for a very demanding job of an individual: that he be gone from home 3 or 4 weeks at a time, minimum; that he work whatever hours are necessary under any weather, any unfavorable shipper-receiver conditions.

Trucking is a dangerous occupation. The freight's got to move even if it's bad weather. But we leave it up to our drivers' discretion. If it's too bad for him to drive in, we tell him, "Do what you think best." But we know that he'll try to go—ice, snow, mountains, whatever. So it's a tough job. I think the three major reasons for driver turnover are

1. Time away from home
2. Money—salary
3. Interaction with our company and our shippers

The feeling of being involved—the same thing we were talking about for the terminal people—is accentuated with the driver. Drivers so often don't feel like they're a part of the team unless you really work at it hard. And that's a major problem. They have minimal contact; and if it's not going pretty good, then they think, "Here I am, out here killing myself, and these people don't even appreciate me."

Recognition or appreciation in any job is very important. If you don't feel appreciated, it's hard to do your best. We see that so often that it's a real demand. But we're constantly trying to change our systems to facilitate this kind of interaction. We'll be changing our operating systems so that we have more contact with the driver. Right now, the driver talks to different people, depending on where he is going geographically, but we're trying to change it so that he talks to only one individual wherever he is.

We see some potential for change in the industry, but it will only be brought about by dire circumstances. That's the way our industry reacts. Our shippers and our competitors will not react without some strong marketplace push. There will have to be some customers that can't be serviced at certain rate levels, and that'll get their attention.

Case Writer: What is your percentage of driver turnover?

Cherry: I would say somewhere around 100%.

Case Writer: What is the likelihood of unionization?

Cherry: I think in our industry at this time—probably remote. The drivers aren't based in the same places. Also, many of them have been unionized before, and they really don't want to be part of the union again. The guys I've talked to could work for Jones Trucking next door if they wanted to, but they really like the open-road structure—or they'd probably quit.

One time a year, around Christmas, we get a lot of the people in the same place. But otherwise, we just don't get many of them together. Union is just a bad word to them. I think you get a flavor of this out on the road. They laugh at union truckers. They think of them as less skilled and not as much of a cowpoke as they are.

Case Writer: How much of your strategic planning is not operational? Do you ever just sit back and think about where you are and where you want to go?

Cherry: Yes, I think we're forced to, periodically. There is a lot of day-by-day planning necessary to implement our goals. But I think when you do your annual plan—the 3- to 5-year projections—that that is a good time to sit down and think about those other things. Now, growth is on my mind constantly: seeing the problem you're having today and how it's going to impact you in a couple of years. Organizationally, how should we be structured to achieve the growth that we're planning?

You can't just pile people on top of people and expect things to go just as they've always gone. And you're not going to be able to go to the same markets indefinitely. At some point, that's over, and you're going to have to get into other markets.

So I would say that Billy and I think about the future on a constant basis, and we talk about it with the board of directors quarterly. Kirby is probably involved with it as much as anybody else—with the vision of where we're going to be. We ask, "Should we acquire companies?" We look at other companies periodically. So far we've found that there is really nothing we would want to buy. But there's a lot of informal planning at this level.

We structure the process at our board meetings through our annual planning process, when we update our other plans. But we don't have a strategic planner on board to do this kind of thinking.

And I guess, too, that you see things evolving so rapidly that you scrap a plan almost before it becomes operational—or you change it enough, to make things work out.

Case Writer: Do you monitor your strategic plan? Do you check for what went wrong?

Cherry: Yes, I think we're continually checking things. Of course, with our monthly plan, we can see how things are going. And the plotting of our results for a year will just about tell us which direction we have to go in. For instance, we phased out our owner-operators over the last 2 to 3 years (those are the people we leased the trucks from—and who worked as our drivers). The profitability really wasn't in this type of operation, so we phased out of it.

Five to 7 years ago, we were in a brokerage business. We solicited business and solicited trucks, and then we put the loads together, and someone else hauled them. We took a commission. But we phased out of that business. Its direction wasn't positive, so we got out of it.

We think that our niche as a refrigerated motor carrier is the one that has the most possibility for the future. We have a chance to be the biggest force in the nation in this niche. That's what turns us on—and it turns on the stock market people, too, the financing people.

We see that when we go to the shippers with this kind of resource, we attract more attention. We go in and say, "We've got 1000 refrigerated trailers." Nobody else has 1000 refrigerated trailers. It's typically a smaller-level business. With 1000 trailers you get a lot more attention. You get in doors you wouldn't get into with 100. And that's helping us increase our pricing: Our incremental revenue dollars are going up on a per-mile basis. We think size is going to be a big asset there.

Case Writer: How are rewards tied to the strategic performance, or are they tied to actual performance? How do they trickle down throughout the organization?

Cherry: Our incentive program is a profit-sharing situation. But it isn't something that can be monkeyed with too easily. It has more credibility that way. For instance, if you don't hit 90.0, you don't get anything; for 90.1 you get nothing. At 90.0, I get 10% of my salary—for that one tenth. At 89, it's 20%; at 88, it's 30%; and so on. It's open-ended. If we get an 81, I get 100% of my salary as bonus.

Case Writer: That's annual operating ratio?

Cherry: Yeah.

Case Writer: What is it operating at now?

Cherry: It was 90.4 for 1987.

Case Writer: You say you talk with the upper-level management. How do you get the message out to everybody?

Cherry: I put out memos to the staff. But I rely pretty heavily on the direct supervisor approach. The person who knows you best is the guy you work for, and good news or bad news ought to come from that same source. The person who gives you your money or takes your money ought to be the one who keeps you informed. Again, from my standpoint, I monitor things closely to see how people react. But I don't need to do everything. I think management needs to show a lot of respect for departmental people, because they're going to be giving the marching orders.

But I do see everybody regularly—everybody in the company—except the drivers. There are 1000 drivers out there, and I don't see them that regularly. But with everybody here on the premises, I go by and talk to them. You can read most people's reactions to life in general if you talk to them. If you've sent out a memo or something—usually, if it's bothering them, they'll bring it up. "What's going to happen here? Why didn't we get a bonus? We tried hard, you know. What happens now?"

You've got to face problems—you can't let things fester. A lot of times, people are just getting things off their chest. Give them an opportunity to tell you that they didn't like this or that. That doesn't mean they're jumping off the boat. It just means that they didn't like it.

But sometimes there are people with pent-up emotions, or someone who resigns unexpectedly. And you wonder: Maybe if you'd taken the time to talk to them or had given them a chance to talk to you, it wouldn't have happened.

That's a little bit of the driver problem, too. He doesn't have that opportunity for face-to-face discussion. We're hoping that with our new system, he'll have one person to dialogue with—to get things off his chest daily—so that he can go on about his business.

Case Writer: And the driver can call you directly?

Cherry: Yes. And they're usually very respectful. They can be mad. They can have just been in an accident. They can be laid over for 3 days. They can be calling from an outside phone at 20 below zero. But that opportunity to talk means a lot to them. If they're here on the premises, and they want to walk in the door and talk to me—and nobody else is talking to me—I say, "Sit down. Let's talk."

They like that. They feel like they're part of the company. And a lot of the time, when they're walking by and they see nobody's in here, they'll come on in.

Case Writer: When you go through your planning process, is that really a bottom-up situation or a top-down?

Cherry: We're trying to get to a more bottom-up situation. I think that we're probably more top-down at this stage. I think that 1988 was the first time we really solicited input from the bottom.

Case Writer: How much time do you spend in your meetings?

Cherry: I would say, with one meeting or another, 3 or 4 hours a day.

Case Writer: Is that the same with all the managers, the vice presidents?

Cherry: I don't think they spend as much time as I do in meetings.

Case Writer: Back to the labor for just a second: What is your driver cost per mile?

Cherry: In February, it ran between 27 and 30 cents a mile.

Case Writer: One of the analysts' reports that we got indicates that there is a possibility of an industrywide increase of 1 to 3 cents. What would that do if it happened?

Cherry: I don't think it would hurt us that much. We've got various ways to handle money. We can handle the drivers' money problems. We've got a Driver Trainer Program where the guy will make pretty good money. He'll make 40 to 50 thousand dollars a year in that program, which is substantially above the industry norm.

If money is what the problem is, we've got that trainer program. We've also got the single driver who drives the truck by himself, and we have a trainee student driver program. So I don't see that increase as hurting us very much.

The big key to our asset use is that we have team drivers who can run about 5000 miles a week and single drivers who can run about 2500. So we've got to run various analyses to see how many teams we've got and what the optimal level of team drivers is as opposed to single drivers.

Case Writer: We talked to Mr. Liles about a possible equity issuance. What's your plan?

Cherry: Well, given the market situation right now, I think we'll never need any more equity. (Chuckle.) But if we've got debt, we'll probably want to convert that to equity when the market's right. I think Mr. Lee and Liles have plans to sell more shares as the price goes up.

Case Writer: Would you do a convertible offering or something like that?

Cherry: I think we would probably like to hold out and then to do an equity offering. We had an idea in our mind—especially before the crash [in Fall 1987]—that we'd see $30 a share; and then we'd give the public another million shares to have and hold. (Chuckle.) But that time may not come very soon.

We've got the wherewithal to keep growing without additional equity; but for a public company, we've got pretty good leverage. I came to the company when we were very leveraged, and I lived through cash flow crunches. Leverage doesn't scare me that much.

As opposed to some public companies looking at 2 to 1 or 3 to 1—this company has had 10-to-1 debt to equity. That's the way we came up: by the bootstrap, with no capital.

In 1977, we did enter a venture capital deal, but we got out of it. It took us almost 10 years to get out of that venture deal.

Case Writer: What do you see as your threats and opportunities?

Cherry: I think one threat would be not planning adequately for the future. You can get involved in trying to optimize operating performance, which sometimes doesn't leave enough for the future.

You have to ask: What do you want? Do you want to make a big killing in year one and forget about the future? Or do you want to hire management trainees? Or do you want to use data base systems, or experiment with satellites and things like that? Or do you say, "If it doesn't contribute to the bottom line this month, I don't want to see any money spent on it."

I think that putting the necessary money forward is going to be important to a company like ours, especially from the standpoint of systems.

Other threats might come from insurance issues or from government socialization issues, like workman's compensation, or even health insurance—some of the laws do not favor corporations.

Some politicians are really going after corporations, as if they didn't understand what a corporation is. It's a good buzz word, you know, tax structure—so they really pound the corporation periodically.

Another threat, of course, is the drivers' situation.

Case Writer: Do you see another source of drivers than the drivers' school?

Cherry: Well, as other sources dry up, we'll have to redo the way we run our fleet. There are people out there who would probably do trucking work, but not like we'd like it done. So we'd have to modify our work rules.

Case Writer: You were talking about the size of your fleet and that the availability of your trailers and trucks makes you salable. Do you see that as a bigger point than service—or what do you see as the biggest benefit of contracting with your company?

Cherry: Certainly size without service is nothing in our market. We've got a very good reputation in the U.S. for good-looking, dependable equipment. We've spent a lot of time specifying our equipment, and this means a lot to transportation people. We're representing them to their customers at the dock, so they want the job handled right. I had it pointed out to me very recently in a sales call that size didn't matter to this particular shipper.

Corporations are being stretched to the point that upper management of a Kroger, a Pillsbury, or a Safeway doesn't want to hire people to watch us do our work.

In other words, they're saying, "KLLM, your job is to do it right the first time, and get me the information proving you did it right. It's not my job to check on you. I'll find somebody else if it is." That's the message the marketplace has given us. "We want a few good carriers and we'll make it worth their while. We're not going to spend a lot of overhead playing watchdog. We're going to go to the bargaining table every year and say, "Here's what we expect. Here's what we're going to pay. And here's the information we want."

Before 1980 and the deregulation of the transportation industry, there were big traffic departments. And they had regulations to follow through on: tariff filings, authority.

Today, we have a 48-state general commodity authority. We can haul anything we can fit in that tractor trailer, interstate. Intrastate, now, is a different story. That's still tightly regulated.

So before 1980 the shipper was beholden to whoever had the authority. After 1980, any man who could do the job had the authority. If you advertise yourself as the kind of carrier that can handle 50 truckloads a week, the customer expects you to handle it and let him know through systems—computer systems—how well you did, oftentimes billing him electronically. And if you don't have these abilities, sometimes you're not even asked to bid on the freight or be involved in freight. That's their way of getting your attention.

Case Writer: Where do you see the industry—refrigerated trucking industry— 5 years from now, in terms of geographical expansion of trucking into Mexico and Canada?

Cherry: We're doing a little bit of trucking in Canada right now, and we've got a little bit of interest in some cross-border arrangements in Mexico.

In the next 5 years we think we're going to have an advantage, because we went to the public market before the door closed, and there's very little public refrigerated transportation.

A lot of the boys got shut out just as they were thinking about going public. So we've got a jump on them in that direction.

We're the largest—essentially the largest now—and given our ability to be profitable, we should gain a lot of ground. It's going to be hard to take it away from us.

In 5 years we see our niche in the refrigerated end of temperature control. We may get into some nontrucking transportation–related areas that are tempera-ture-control related. We may get involved in some acquisitions. We think there will be a market with a couple of big players 5 years from now and we'll be one of them. There will still be some smaller players, but the major marketplace shippers are wanting us to do more and more.

So if we're able to hold up our end, there is growth possibility out there for us, and we'll get it at the expense of the smaller guys. There may be consolida-tion without acquisition. But we'll get the loads, and they'll go out of business.

Case Writer: Where will KLLM be in 5 years?

Cherry: Well, we anticipate we'll be about a $200-million-a-year company and a profitable company. We intend to keep up our service level and, organization-ally, be a nationwide company.

United Federal Savings and Loan Association

Cecelia L. Harper, John W. Simmons, Mark J. Kroll, University of Texas at Tyler

In late 1987, Arlin E. David, President and Chief Executive Officer of United Federal Savings and Loan Association of Longpoint, Texas, was preparing a report for the Association's monthly Board of Director's meeting. Several significant trends were affecting the Association's external environment, and it was essential to determine possible courses of action available in light of these trends.

United Federal could no longer rest on past successes. Much of the confidence traditionally placed in the savings and loan industry as a secure investment alternative has been lost because of negative publicity about the condition of the Federal Savings and Loan Insurance Corporation (FSLIC) and an unprecedented number of insolvent Texas institutions. David was also concerned about the entrance of a substantial number of new competitors into the mortgage lending field. Rapid expansion of mortgage securitization has made mortgage lending much more attractive to these firms.

Of further concern to David were poor regional economic conditions plaguing the Association with declining property values, escalating loan delinquency rates, and a rising rate of mortgage loan foreclosures. Although the outlook for 1989 suggests improvement, a sustained decline in oil prices to $15 per barrel or below could lead to another downturn in the oil patch and cause another fallout in the East Texas financial community.

Exhibit 1   Selected Financial Data for United Federal (dollars in thousands except for per share)

	1983	1984	1985	1986	1987
Selected Financial Condition Data					
Total assets	$115,592	$116,632	$124,454	$129,404	$131,534
Loans receivable	97,216	107,405	111,354	106,962	93,042
Mortgage-backed securities	—	810	775	2,768	14,190
Cash including interest-bearing cash	13,305	5,047	6,311	9,793	7,441
Investments	2,500	200	711	3,122	8,340
Deposits	109,262	110,373	108,629	115,766	115,194
Total borrowings	26	—	6,000	3,035	5,035
Stockholders' equity	4,489	4,167	7,763	8,355	8,931
Offices					
Full-service	2	2	3	4	4
Limited-service	0	0	1	1	1
Selected Operations Data					
Total interest income	$10,988	$11,845	$12,039	$12,053	$11,497
Total interest expense	11,513	11,487	11,075	9,811	8,756
Net interest income (expense)	(525)	358	964	2,242	2,741
Provision for loan losses	(4)	—	—	(22)	(60)
Loan fees and service charges	356	447	389	338	263
Net (loss) on sale of loans and investments	(1)	0	0	147	212
Net (loss) before income taxes and extraordinary item	(1,337)	(420)	(5)	979	1,123
Income tax (expense) or benefit	386	98	25	(284)	(270)
Extraordinary item	—	—	57	—	—
Net income (loss)	(951)	(322)	77	695	853
Earnings per common share					
Income before extraordinary item	—	—	0.45	1.81	2.22
Extraordinary item	—	—	—	—	—
Net income	—	—	0.45	1.81	2.22
Dividends per share	—	—	—	0.20	0.70
Financial Ratios and Other Data					
Interest rate spread during period	(1.0%)	(.1%)	0.5%	1.5%	1.8%
Interest rate spread at end of period	(.6%)	0.2%	1.5%	1.9%	2.2%
Return on assets (ratio of net income to average total assets)	(.9%)	(.3%)	0.1%	0.5%	0.6%
Return on equity (ratio of net income to average equity)	(19.2%)	(7.3%)	1.6%	8.5%	9.9%
Equity to assets ratio (ratio of average equity to average total assets)	4.5%	3.8%	4.0%	6.4%	6.5%

COMPANY HISTORY

United Federal Savings of Longpoint was chartered in 1934 as a federal mutual savings and loan association by a group of local citizens. Since there were no other savings and loans in the city, the Association grew rapidly, paralleling the growth of Longpoint. Today, United Federal is one of only two locally-owned financial institutions in Longpoint.

Historically, the Association, like many other S&Ls, offered relatively few products to consumers. Their primary business was to attract deposits from the

Analysis of Loan Portfolio (dollars in thousands) Exhibit 2

Type of Loan	1985 Amount	1985 Percent	1986 Amount	1986 Percent	1987 Amount	1987 Percent
Conventional						
Loans on existing property	$ 99,174	87.3%	$ 97,937	88.4%	$ 96,380	89.2%
Commercial property real estate loans	9,115	8.0	7,651	6.9	7,472	6.9
Construction	1,052	0.9	1,219	1.0	268	0.3
Insured by FHA or partially guaranteed by VA	43	0.1	37	0.1	21	—
Consumer loans	4,193	3.7	4,028	3.6	3,919	3.6
Total loans receivable and mortgage-backed securities (before net items)	$113,577	100.0%	$110,872	100.0%	$108,060	100.0%
Fixed-rate loans	79,714	70.2	73,185	65.6	68,712	63.6
Adjustable-rate loans	33,863	29.8	37,687	34.4	39,347	36.4
Total	$113,577	100.0%	$110,872	100.0%	$108,060	100.0%
Type of Security						
Residential						
1–4 family	$ 99,498	87.6%	$ 97,956	88.3%	$ 96,115	89.0%
Other dwelling units	82	0.1	492	0.5	473	0.4
Commercial real estate loans	9,115	8.0	7,651	6.9	7,472	6.9
Consumer loans	1,742	1.5	1,588	1.4	1,972	1.8
Property improvement loans	2,494	2.2	2,477	2.2	1,968	1.8
Land development	646	0.2	708	0.7	60	0.1
Total loans receivable and mortgage-backed securities (before net items)	$113,577	100.0%	$110,872	100.0%	$108,060	100.0%

general public and lend the funds for homes in the community. Until the deregulation of financial institutions began in the early 1980s, these products were strictly controlled by the government. Since only a limited number of traditional products were offered and those that were were largely governmental mandates, the industry was relatively simple before deregulation and did not require a high level of expertise. United Federal prospered in a stable economy and regulated environment, but circumstances now were changed.

Deregulation forced major changes in the environment in which United Federal operated. It had to pay high interest rates to keep its depositors, but on the income side of the ledger, the mortgages it had sold were fixed at low interest rates. As a result, the Association incurred significant operating losses during fiscal 1982 and 1983. A moderation of market interest rates returned the institution to profitability in 1985 (see Exhibit 1).

Originally, United Federal was organized as a mutual Savings and Loan. In early 1985, United Federal converted to a federal stock association by selling 383,445 shares of common stock at a price of $10 per share to local investors. United Federal's conversion to a public company has not changed management's strategies. The stock issue provided additional resources to develop the Association's market presence in Longpoint and made it possible to add new

---

Exhibit 3   **United Federal Savings and Loan Association of Longpoint, Texas: Investment Yields**

Item	1985	1986	1987
Weighted average yield on loan portfolio	10.6%	10.2%	9.3%
Weighted average yield on investment portfolio	12.2%	7.8%	7.4%
Weighted average yield on other interest-earning assets	8.6%	8.0%	8.2%
Combined weighted average yield on loan, investment, and other interest-earning portfolios	10.5%	10.0%	9.1%
Weighted average rate paid on savings deposits	9.0%	8.0%	6.9%
Weighted average rate paid on borrowings	8.9%	7.5%	7.4%
Combined weighted average rate paid on savings deposits and borrowings	9.0%	8.1%	6.9%
Spread	1.5%	1.9%	2.2%
Average yield on loan portfolio	10.1%	10.1%	9.5%
Average yield on investment portfolio	12.6%	7.8%	6.3%
Average yield on other interest-earning assets	10.8%	8.0%	6.9%
Combined average yield on loan, investment, and other interest-earning portfolios	10.2%	9.9%	9.1%
Average rate paid on savings deposits	9.7%	8.4%	7.2%
Average rate paid on borrowings	10.5%	8.6%	7.0%
Combined average rate paid on savings deposits	9.7%	8.4%	7.2%
Spread	0.5%	1.5%	1.9%
Net yield on average interest-earning assets (net interest-earnings divided by average interest-earning assets; net interest-earnings equal the difference between the dollar amount of interest earned and paid)	0.82%	1.83%	2.16%

---

products and services. However, a new responsibility was to manage the Association in order to earn an adequate return-on-equity (ROE) for stockholders.

During 1988, the Association completed its 54th year of operations. Since deregulation, the product markets served by United Federal can be classified into four areas: single-family residential mortgages; multifamily residential mortgages; commercial lending; and consumer products. Although the business has changed, United Federal is still dedicated to providing funds for building or purchasing homes. In general, United Federal's goal is to originate real property and consumer loans in the Simms and Harlison Counties market area of North East Texas. Total assets are now over $130 million and net operating profits for the year ending June 30, 1987, were $852,769. The firm has growth as a key objective for the future (see Exhibits 2, 3, 4, and 8 and 9 presented in this case).

THE TEXAS THRIFT INDUSTRY

In 1987, there were 281 thrift institutions operating statewide in Texas. Of these institutions 45 percent were under $100 million in assets, 39 percent were in the $100–500 million range, and 12 percent had assets of $1 billion or more. The state's thrift industry collectively held over $101 billion in total assets (*Standard & Poor's Industry Surveys*, 1989).

District Nine Statistics   **Exhibit 4**

	Third Quarter 1987	Second Quarter 1987	First Quarter 1987	Fourth Quarter 1986	Third Quarter 1986
Selected Balance Sheet Items ($ millions)					
Mortgage loans					
Construction	8,085	8,879	9,711	10,144	11,179
Permanent	62,701	64,616	66,421	68,529	70,877
Mortgage-backed securities	16,685	14,381	13,177	11,301	11,927
Net mortgage loans and contracts	80,534	81,385	82,911	83,084	86,395
Net nonmortgage loans	7,823	8,065	8,276	8,444	9,221
Repossessed assets	9,836	8,191	6,818	5,252	4,644
Cash and investments	15,872	16,431	15,272	15,919	13,526
Total assets	133,340	133,439	132,236	131,359	131,796
Total deposits	111,088	110,089	109,630	109,255	108,205
FHLB advances	11,988	11,523	10,600	10,655	9,134
Other borrowed money	11,322	10,962	9,465	7,535	8,002
Selected Sources and Uses of Funds ($ millions)					
Net new savings	(242)	(481)	(679)	(641)	257
Interest credited	1,242	1,189	1,211	1,301	1,346
Cash repayment of principal	2,633	3,656	3,315	4,909	4,603
Mortgage loans closed—total	3,991	5,062	4,713	6,539	7,355
Construction	778	720	691	857	1,080
Permanent (except land)	2,867	3,873	3,432	4,814	5,446
Land loans	346	469	589	868	830
Selected Ratios					
Yield on all financial assets	8.73%	8.92%	8.67%	9.08%	9.67%
Yield on mortgage loans	8.69%	8.83%	8.66%	9.10%	9.57%
Cost of funds	7.62%	7.38%	7.37%	7.89%	8.35%
Cost of deposits	7.46%	7.11%	7.15%	7.71%	8.19%
Asset growth rate	−0.30%	3.64%	2.67%	−1.33%	6.76%
Deposit growth rate	3.63%	1.68%	1.37%	3.88%	6.90%
Delinquent mortgage loans/net mortgage loans	20.67%	20.82%	20.22%	14.86%	11.97%
Delinquent nonmortgage loans/net nonmortgage loans	18.65%	18.36%	15.73%	14.76%	11.19%

Annual industry losses in 1987 amounted to over $6 billion, and Texas savings and loans at the close of 1987 held over $8.7 billion of repossessed assets. The collapse of energy and real estate prices, regulatory lenience, and large-scale fraud are blamed for the industry's lingering state of crisis (Klaiser, 1988). Complicating the issue has been the ease of entry into the S&L industry: Many new players have been able to enter the field, as capital and regulatory requirements have in the past been modest.

Survival has been the most pressing issue for most Texas thrifts. The crisis is such that of the state's 281 thrifts, 104 are bankrupt and 39 are under regulatory supervision for having net worth below what is considered safe by industry regulators (Klaiser, 1988).

Exhibit 5 Financial Performance of East Texas Thrifts

Thrift	Regulatory Net Worth as Percent of Assets, Second Quarter	Percent Change in Net Worth	Net Income (in thousands)	Repossessed Assets as Per-cent of Assets	Net Assets (in millions)
Sales County					
Oak Banc Savings	2.97	3.7	52	1.6	29
Gloria County					
Huntsville Federal Savings & Loan	5.63	2.4	143	1.5	108
Robert County					
Stillwater Federal Savings & Loan	−13.69	N/C	−1,594	6.4	30
Federal Savings Bank	2.56	2.9	30	1.7	42
Kilstone Federal Savings & Loan	8.73	3.1	252	0.1	96
United Federal Savings & Loan (Longpoint)	6.74	3.7	318	2.8	131
Longpoint Savings & Loan	−14.49	N/C	−5,502	7.3	162
Southside Savings (Longpoint)	1.88	−84.2	−3,313	24.1	33
Harleson County					
Sherriff Federal Savings & Loan	4.17	7	196	2.8	73
Sabine County					
Sabine Savings & Loan	12.32	1.6	301	0.3	56
Rust County					
Major Savings	3.31	−28.9	−749	5.9	57
Anderson Savings & Loan	4.41	0.9	−8	1.3	70
Jones County					
Northeast Texas Savings & Loan	5.14	−3.5	−650	2	345
First Federal Savings & Loan	9.51	2.1	199	0.1	102
Ussher County					
Gilmore Savings & Loan	4.26	17.1	173	0.7	29

Note: Most savings and loan institutions in East Texas posted ratios of regulatory net worth to assets above the 3 percent level considered healthy by the Federal Savings and Loan Deposit Insurance Corporation. The majority of the area's thrifts also reported low ratios of repossessed assets for the first two quarters of the year.

Savings and Loans' Yields and Costs  **Exhibit 6**

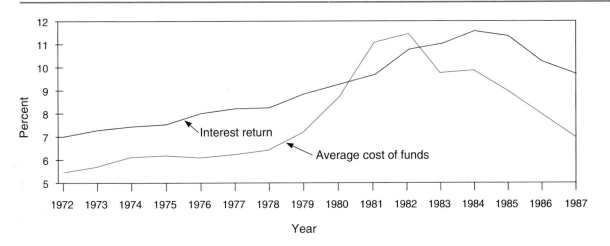

Unfortunately for the taxpayer, insolvent institutions often have offered high-rate deposits to cover overhead when their assets degraded and no longer generated sufficient cash flows. The result has been to drive up the cost of funds in the industry, leading to a phenomenon known as the "Texas premium" which runs up to one percentage point above the national average. Industry experts predict that if the "Texas premium" cannot be controlled, the entire domestic industry is in peril. It is rather common nowadays to read or to hear expressed the opinion that the S&L industry has outlived its usefulness and that other financial institutions can now complete the traditional S&L mission of providing home financing at least as efficiently (see Exhibits 5 and 6).

REGULATORY ENVIRONMENT

Federal thrift institutions such as United Federal are members of the Federal Home Loan Bank (FHLB) system and have their deposits insured up to $100,000 per account by the Federal Savings and Loan Insurance Corporation. Such institutions are subject to extensive regulation by the Federal Home Loan Bank Board (FHLBB), a chartering authority and the operating head of the FSLIC. As an insurer, the FSLIC issues regulations, conducts examinations, and generally supervises the operations of insured members. This supervision extends to promulgating a comprehensive set of regulations which covers a variety of operating issues, including the form of savings instruments issued by an insured institution; and certain aspects of an insured institution's lending activities, including appraisal requirements, maximum loan amounts, private mortgage insurance coverage, and related party transactions. In addition, the consent of the FSLIC must be obtained before any corporate reorganization, including a merger, bulk purchase, or any other disposition of assets, can take place.

The FSLIC attempts to reduce the risk of insuring deposits through a program of examination and supervision and by imposing a 3 percent minimum capital requirement. Financial reports are filed monthly with the Federal Home Loan Bank Board and examinations are conducted on an annual basis. Theoretically, if regulatory capital falls below the 3 percent level, federal regulators can still sell off an institution's assets and use the proceeds to pay off insured deposits without the insurance fund suffering a loss. However, by 1986 there was some doubt as to the effectiveness of the regulatory agency's performance in monitoring insured institutions. The FSLIC was $6 billion in the red. In August 1987, Governor Bill Clements startled the Texas industry by publicly predicting that the FSLIC would pay depositors at failed S&Ls only a fraction of their deposits in cash, with a piece of paper for the rest.

Depositor concern led Congress to pass the Competitive Equality Banking Act of 1987, to recapitalize the FSLIC and use the funds to liquidate or otherwise dispose of insolvent institutions. Repayment of the $10.87 billion in bonds, however, will have to come from a supplemental deposit insurance premium which will significantly increase the cost of deposit insurance to surviving institutions within the industry, an additional cost of funds to which competitor banks will not be subject. This cost is currently at .208 percent of deposits as compared to .083 percent for commercial banks insured by the Federal Deposit Insurance Corporation (FDIC) (Klaiser, 1988).

UNITED FEDERAL MANAGEMENT

United Federal is headed by Robert Plate, the Chairman of the Board of Directors. Plate, 71, has been a director since 1965 and retired as the owner-manager of a local construction company in 1980. In addition to his affiliation with United Federal, Plate is also a director of a competing commercial bank in Longpoint.

The Association is comprised of a hierarchy of executive officers, senior officers, junior officers, and employees. Arlin F. David, 57, and Rod Sojack, 46, jointly, are the executive managers of the company. Both David and Sojack are longtime employees of the firm and have been promoted "through the ranks." David handles investments and asset/liability management while Sojack, Executive Vice President and Chief Operating Officer, concentrates on internal operations, including personnel. David also does considerable public relations and civic work, in addition to serving on the Board of the Texas League of Saving Institutions. Although much of the day-to-day operating decision making is done through informal consultation between David and Sojack, all major decisions are made by the Association's Board of Directors and committees of the Board.

In addition to the two executive officers, the Association also employs five other senior officers. United Federal is functionally structured into four departments: mortgage lending; consumer lending; savings administration; and accounting. Consequently, the mortgage loan and savings areas are each headed by one Vice President, while two VPs head the consumer loan area. Dotty Renolds, who originally joined the Association in 1960 as a bookkeeper, currently is the Secretary/Treasurer. Renolds heads the Accounting Department as well as serving as the Secretary to the Board of Directors (see Exhibit 7 for Board of Directors data).

Board of Directors   Exhibit 7

Name and Position with the Organization	Number of Shares Owned	Percent of Outstanding Shares Owned	Director Since
Arlin David, President, CEO, and Director	5,000	1.3	1982
Robert Plate, Chairman of the Board	25,875	6.7	1965
Charles F. Grissome, Director	2,000	0.5	1976
Dr. F. R. Southrite III, Director	5,000	1.3	1985
John Tobbine, Vice Chairman of the Board	25,875	6.7	1970
John M. Riegle, Director	21,875	5.7	1966
John R. Topper, Director	33,700	8.7	1982
David R. Johnson, Director	25,875	6.7	1982
Peter Williams, Director	20,000	5.2	1986
Subtotal	165,200	43.0	

The Association is governed by a Board of Directors that includes David and eight local residents. The local members are business and professional people, including a dentist, several individuals in the petroleum industry, an insurance broker, the owner of a radio station, and several building contractors. The Board meets monthly and members also serve on various Board committees which meet throughout the year.

OPERATING POLICIES

United Federal has a conservative banking philosophy, a characteristic that has proven to be a strength in a weak economy. Underwriting guidelines are more stringent than those required under Federal Home Loan Bank regulations. For example, although an S&L is permitted to lend 100 percent of the appraisal value on commercial property, United Federal has chosen to lend only 80 percent in an effort to protect the firm from declines in property values and poor economic conditions. Clearly, many other savings and loans in the oil-producing states have not demonstrated such good judgement in recent years.

United Federal appears to have a secure financial position with Generally Accepted Accounting Practices (GAAP) net worth of over 6 percent. This is twice the 3 percent required net worth under Federal Home Loan Bank regulations. Also, the Longpoint thrift appears to be performing better than most of its competitors in the local market. The goodwill of the firm in the community also is in enviable shape. The deposit base of United Federal has grown steadily during recent years.

As with other thrifts, the role of United Federal as a home-financier is rapidly changing. The traditional 30-year fixed-rate mortgage is still originated, but there is an ongoing effort to diversify assets among the various lending categories as well as to better match asset and liability maturities. Mortgage loans comprise approximately 96 percent of the United Federal's loan portfolio.

Since mortgage loan assets consist primarily of long-term fixed-rate loans whose yields do not vary rapidly, the Association has implemented several strategic policy changes designed to match loan yields to the associated cost of funds. These changes include the following:

1. De-emphasis of 30-year fixed-rate mortgages.
2. Emphasis of adjustable-rate loans.
3. Disposal of long-term fixed-rate loans in order to invest in short-term adjustable-rate assets.

Approximately 37 percent of the mortgage loan portfolio is now made up of adjustable-rate loans, as compared to 22 percent just three years ago.

United Federal traditionally concentrated its lending activities in the residential real estate market. However, the Garn-St. Germain Banking Act of 1982 changed earlier industry regulations and provided new flexibility to institutions in the amounts, terms, and security for which loans could be underwritten. Mortgage loans were permitted to be written for shorter terms and with adjustable rates, in contrast to the long-term fixed-rate mortgages in use prior to the legislation.

The Association has taken advantage of industry deregulation to expand its commercial real estate lending, primarily to increase market-rate-sensitive assets in its portfolio. Commercial loans involve much larger amounts of money than residential properties, therefore, management has taken a conservative approach to this type of lending. In underwriting commercial real estate, the Association is permitted, under current regulations, to lend up to 100 percent of the appraised value, although the Association's general policy is to lend only 80 percent or less of the value in order to reduce the risk associated with this type of loan. The Association also thoroughly evaluates the debt coverage ratio in relationship to the income stream generated by the property in order to evaluate the credit risk to the Association.

Although the Association primarily originates mortgage loans, it also makes various types of consumer loans. These include home improvement loans, loans to depositors secured by deposit accounts, auto loans, marine loans, and secured personal loans. Management plans to further expand the amount of these types of loans in the future. With this strategy in mind, United Federal recruited an experienced consumer lending officer from a local competitor in July 1986. Although these loans offer greater risk, they generally yield much higher returns to the Association as well as providing a better asset/liability match.

In addition to its lending activities, United Federal is also involved in investment activities. The firm's major type of investment is government-guaranteed mortgage certificates, such as those issued by the Federal National Mortgage Association (FNMA, or Fannie Mae), the Government National Mortgage Association (GNMA, or Ginnie Mae) and the Federal Home Loan Mortgage Corporation (Freddie Mac). These securities are purchased for portfolio diversification as well as to invest excess cash when loan demand is insufficient in the local area. Although the yields available on these types of assets are below conventional security yields, management feels that the safety factors make them attractive investment opportunities for the Association.

As a member of the Federal Home Loan Bank system, United Federal is also required to maintain specified levels of liquid assets. The Association's liquid investments consist primarily of certificates of deposit, federal funds and overnight deposits, and U.S. government securities with maturities of five years or less. The Association is currently participating in a new Federal Home Loan Bank program which is designed to lower the cost of funds in the FHLB ninth district. By permitting those institutions that need to borrow funds to borrow from competing institutions in the district, the need to bid up rates on new deposits should be reduced. However, no significant change in the cost of deposits is yet evident.

Savings deposits are an important source of the Association's loanable funds. The Association offers several types of savings programs designed to attract both the short-term and the long-term saver. The interest rates on these accounts are established by the Association's Board of Directors after considering the rates competitors are offering as well as the level desired to support lending programs.

United Federal's earnings are highly dependent on its interest rate spread, which is the difference between average yields on its loan and investment portfolios and the average yields paid on its deposits and borrowings. The combination of the interest rate spread and the relative volume of interest-earning assets and interest-earning liabilities determines the net interest income of the Association. The result of the recent large number of foreclosures has been a reduction in the relative volume of interest-earning assets in the portfolio. In addition, although a larger percentage of mortgage loans are being originated with adjustable rates, these products will initially have a limited impact on the Association's earnings, primarily because low initial rates are offered to encourage consumers to consider this type of loan.

Most of United Federal's assets and liabilities are monetary in nature, and they are consequently very sensitive to interest rate shifts and poor economic conditions. During inflationary periods, the profitability of savings and loans generally declines as a result of accepting deposits on a short-term basis at increasing rates, while lending on a long-term basis at stationary rates. Furthermore, the S&L industry has traditionally been subject to declining demand for mortgages during inflationary periods due to buyers being priced out of the market. Despite the economic doldrums which have plagued Texas over the last several years, United Federal has managed to be a profitable lender during this period (see Exhibits 8 and 9).

Income and Expense as a Percentage of Average Assets				Exhibit 8
Item	**1984**	**1985**	**1986**	**1987**
Interest income—United Federal	10.84	9.67	9.31	8.74
Interest income—all FSLIC insured institutions	10.26	9.87	9.00	8.23
Interest expense—United Federal	−9.84	−8.89	−7.58	−6.65
Interest expense—all FSLIC insured institutions	−9.42	−8.55	−7.47	−6.52
Net interest income—United Federal	0.30	0.77	1.73	2.08
Net interest income—all FSLIC insured institutions	0.84	1.34	1.53	1.71
Net income—United Federal	0.27	0.06	0.53	0.64
Net income—all FSLIC insured institutions	0.12	0.38	0.09	−0.26

Exhibit 9   **Financial Ratios**

Ratio	1987
Yield on financial assets—United Federal	9.10%
Yield on financial assets—FHLB—District 9	8.92%
Cost of deposits—United Federal	7.20%
Cost of deposits—FHLB—District 9	7.46%
Asset growth rate—United Federal	1.64%
Asset growth rate—FHLB—District 9	3.64%
Deposit growth rate—United Federal	0.00%
Deposit growth rate—FHLB—District 9	1.68%

DEMOGRAPHICS OF THE HOME BUYER

According to the United States League of Savings Institution Home Buyers Survey of 1987, mortgage lenders can expect some changes in the next few years in the methods home buyers use to finance their purchases. The long-term fixed-rate mortgage is no longer the preference for the majority of home buyers and its popularity is expected to continue to decline. The impact of deregulation on the providers of mortgage credit as well as consumer demand are factors contributing to these changes.

In 1987, 46.7 percent of home buyers chose adjustable-rate mortgages (ARMs), 15.8 percent chose 15-year fixed-rate mortgages, and 34.4 percent chose 30-year fixed-rate mortgages. The older the buyer, the greater the likelihood that an adjustable-rate mortgage will be the choice. Middle-aged and older home buyers spend more time analyzing mortgage options which leads them to choose adjustable-rate or shorter term mortgages more often, according to the study (Brantley, 1988). The price of a typical ARM is generally 1–2 percentage points less than a fixed-rate mortgage and is tied to the T-Bill or District Cost of Funds Indexes.

In the long term, demographics are contrary to the interests of the housing industry because baby boomers are moving out of the 25- to 35-year-old age group in which many people buy their first homes. In 1987, the typical home buyer was approximately five years older than the typical buyer of ten years earlier. The median age of a home buyer climbed from 32.4 in 1977 to the present high of 37.0 in 1987 (Brantley, 1988). By the early 1990s, the typical home buyer is expected to be over 40 years old. As baby boomers reach middle-age, more of the market for mortgage lending is expected to be comprised of this segment.

MARKETING

United Federal Savings faces substantial competition in attracting and retaining deposits and in lending funds in their local market area. As of December 31, 1987, there were three thrift institutions and nine commercial banks in their primary market area. The Association estimates its market share of deposits and mortgage loans in this area to be 12 percent and 13 percent, respectively.

The managers of the Association feel that two factors are especially important in competing for savings deposits: office locations and rates offered to the customer. The Association is headquartered in the downtown Longpoint area in a modern building with ample parking facilities. However, since the early 1980s, the downtown area has declined due to new suburban shopping centers and the construction of a large mall in the northern part of the city. These new facilities attract the bulk of the shopping and pedestrian traffic. For this reason, United Federal has four full-service branch offices and one limited-service office located strategically throughout the city to provide customers with convenience in their banking transactions. The limited-service branch and two of the full-service branches have been added within the past five years (see Exhibit 10).

Direct competition on rates comes from other thrifts and commercial banks in the area. Additional significant competition also comes from money market mutual funds and corporate or government securities which are substitute products. These instruments may offer more attractive yields to consumers than those available at United Federal. However, it is generally felt that the firm offers a competitive rate, although it tends to lag behind other competitors in raising or lowering rates. Instead, United Federal prefers to monitor what local competitors are offering and follow with a midmarket pricing strategy.

The factors that management believes are most important in competing for mortgage loans are interest rates, loan origination fees, and the types of loan programs offered. Regional imbalances in the demand and supply equation for home mortgage money and bouts with tight money have led to the liberalization of secondary market-related regulations. This ability to buy and sell mortgages easily has increased competition from such entities as mortgage bankers, mortgage brokers, and insurance companies for new mortgage originations.

United Federal uses midmarket rates to price deposits and loans. For exam-

---

Major Traffic Arteries of Longpoint, Texas   **Exhibit 10**

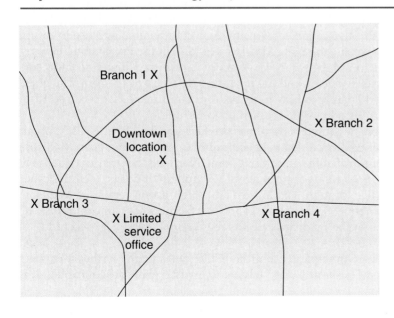

ple, the Association prices mortgage loans on rates quoted daily by the Federal Home Loan Mortgage Corporation. However, this market has no direct correlation with the Association's liability costs. Rather, it reflects the position of originations relative to rates in other locations around the country. All rates generally follow the buying of investors on Wall Street or other markets nationwide.

The Association has no well-defined plan for marketing or other promotional strategies, other than to run ads on local television stations and newsprint advertisements. These ads promote the safety and security of United Federal, stressing their positive net worth and their reputation in the community. However, deregulation has brought the company a number of new opportunities to diversify into related services and products that are largely fee-based. For example, credit cards, Automated Teller Machines (ATMs), and trust services are commonly provided by other financial providers and clearly are desired by modern financial consumers.

MERGER PROSPECT

In December 1987, the Federal Home Loan Bank Board announced a "Southwest Plan" in order to consolidate many of the insolvent Texas institutions. This plan would eventually reduce the number of Texas thrifts from 281 to approximately 160–180. The plan would also cut back the number of branch offices in the state from a present total of roughly 1800 to a new total of 1400. By consolidating troubled institutions, the FSLIC hopes to cut the operating cost of Texas institutions through economies of scale. The plan is also expected to reduce competition for funds.

United Federal has expressed an interest in this plan and has submitted a preliminary proposal. The qualities United Federal is looking for in a merger candidate are good geographic location and compatibility with existing systems. For example, a merger may include a host of hidden costs such as incompatibility of computer systems and unemployment benefits for redundant employees. Furthermore, any potential merger candidate's financial position is expected to be enhanced by yields guaranteed by the FSLIC. Additionally, tax loss carryforwards (also called carryovers) would be available to use in future periods. In other words, the merged firms would gain the tax benefit allowing it to apply losses to reduce future tax liability. Firms are allowed to carry forward capital losses five years and net operating losses up to 15 years. The question facing United Federal is how to respond to overtures it has received from the FSLIC concerning a possible acquisition in the area.

As just mentioned, United Federal has been approached by the FSLIC about acquiring another Savings & Loan, specifically, Northeast Savings in Madison, Texas, which is about 45 miles from Longpoint. Northeast Savings is a relatively small institution, with total assets of about $70 million. It has no facilities other than its main office, though it is located in a high-traffic region of Madison, which is a city of about 90,000 people. Northeast Savings has come under FSLIC management due to the inadequacy of its regulatory capital, and recent losses (see Exhibits 11 and 12).

United Federal is anticipating that the FSLIC will merge Northeast Savings into United Federal without United having to invest a great deal of capital. It is

Northeast Savings & Loan: Income Statement for the Year Ended December 31, 1987 **Exhibit 11**

Section D: Income

Operating income—total	1,711
Interest income—total	1,663
Mortgage loans and contracts—total	996
Interest	996
Adjustments	0
Mtg-backed pass-thru securities—total	93
Nonmortgage loans—total	181
Commercial	46
Consumer (open- and closed-end)	135
Investment securities and deposits—total	393
Income from financing leases	0
Fee income—total	53
Mortgage loan fees	15
Loan servicing fees	0
Other loans fees and charges	14
Service charges and fee income from transaction accounts	24
Accretion of deferred gains—total	0
Futures/options hedging assets	0
Futures/options hedging liabilities	0
Net income (loss) from	
Office building operations	0
Real estate held for investment	0
REO (other than sales)	8
Service corporations/subsidiaries	−17
Leasing operations	0
Other operating income	4
Nonoperating income—total	2
Profit on sale of	1
Foreclosed real estate (REO)	0
Other repossessed property	0
Other real estate held	0
Investment securities	0
Loans	0
Other assets	1
Accretion of deferred gains on	0
Loans sold	0
Other assets sold	0
Other nonoperating income	1
Total income	1,713

Section E: Expense

Operating expense—total	371
Directors fees	5
Officers and employees' compensation	162
Legal expense	1
Directors', officers', and employees' expense	21
Office occupancy expense	20
Furn/fixtures/equipment/and auto expense	33
Marketing	18
Professional services	10
Loan servicing fees	11
Amortization of goodwill	0
Amortization of deferred losses on	10
Futures/options hedging assets	10
Futures/options hedging liabilities	0
Other operating expenses	80
Cost of funds—total net	1,345
Interest on deposits—gross	1,145
Penalties on early deposit withdrawal	4
Interest on deposits—net	1,141
Interest on FHL bank advances	2
Interest on subordinated debentures	0
Interest on mortgage-backed bonds	0
Interest on other borrowed money	202
Interest on escrow accounts	0
Deduction: Capitalized interest	0
Nonoperating expense—total	68
Net provision for losses and losses on sale—total	58
Net provision for losses on assets	0
Losses on sale of	58
Foreclosed real estate (REO)	47
Other repossessed property	11
Other real estate held	0
Investment securities	0
Loans	0
Other assets	0
Amortized deferred losses on	6
Loans sold	6
Other assets sold	0
Other nonoperating expense	4
Income taxes—total	−21
Federal	−21
State, local, and other	0
Total expense	1,763
Current net income (loss)	−50
Adjustments to net income	0
Adjusted net income (loss)	−50

Exhibit 12　　Northeast Savings & Loan: Balance Sheet as of December 31, 1987 (amounts in thousands of dollars)

Section A: Assets

Mortgage loans and mortgage-backed pass-through	
Securities—total gross*	43,148
Total less contra-assets and valuation allowance*	42,869
Construction loans—total*	1,178
1–4 dwelling units	1,178
5 or more dwelling units	0
Nonresidential	0
Permanent loans—total*	37,286
1–4 dwelling units	36,091
5 or more dwelling units	217
Nonresidential (except land)	44
Land	934
Facilitating REO sales	0
Mortgage-backed pass-through securities—total*	4,184
Insurance guaranteed by an agency or instrument of the U.S.*	4,104
Conventional	0
Accrued interest receivable	500
Advances for borrowers' taxes and insurance	0
Contra-assets to mortgage loans—total*	279
Loans in process	286
Deferred loan fees, unamortized premium and loan discounts	−9
Valuation allowances—total*	2
Nonmortgage loans—total gross*	6,439
Total less contra-assets and valuation allowance*	6,131
Commercial loans—total*	1,917
Secured (other than mortgage)	1,917
Unsecured	0
Consumer loans—total*	4,488
Closed-end—total*	4,488
Loans on deposits	773
Home improvement loans	2,627
Education loans	0
Auto loans	635
Retail mobile home loans	0
Other closed-end consumer loans	453
Open-end total*	0
Financing leases—total*	0
Consumer	0
Nonconsumer	0
Accrued interest receivable	34
Contra-assets to nonmortgage loans—total*	308
Loans in progress	156
Deferred loan fees, unamortized premium and loan discounts	148
Valuation allowances—total*	4
Repossessed assets—gross of valuation allowance*	893
Total less valuation allowances*	868
Foreclosed real estate/real estate in judgment	869
Other repossessed assets	24
Valuation allowances	25
Real estate held for development inventory/resale—gross*	0
Total less valuation allowances*	0
Residential property	0

Section A: Assets

Nonresidential property	0
Valuation allowances	0
Service corporations/subsidiaries—total gross*	−218
Total investment*	−218
Appraisal increment	0
Cash, deposit, and investment securities (non-pass-through)—gross*	18,076
Total less valuation allowances*	18,076
Cash and noninterest-earning deposits	455
U.S. government and agency securities	3,300
Total other investment securities*	14,089
Equity securities, except FHLB stock	0
Other investments—total*	14,089
Accrued interest receivable	232
Valuation allowances	0
Fixed assets—gross*	830
Total less valuation allowances*	830
Office building (land and improvements)	689
Leasehold improvements	0
Appraisal increment	0
Furniture, fixtures, and equipment	141
Valuation allowances	0
Other assets—total gross*	2,217
Total less valuation allowances*	2,217
Initial margin for financial futures/options	0
Maintenance margin for financial	0
Financial options fees paid for financial futures options	68
Deferred net losses (gains) on futures/options hedging assets	720
Deferred net losses (gains) on loans sold	513
Deferred net losses (gains) on other assets sold	0
Purchased servicing and goodwill—total*	0
Consumer leased property	0
Nonconsumer leased property	0
Accounts receivable secured by pledged deposits	0
Other assets	916
Valuation allowances	0
Gross assets (including contra-assets and valuation allowance)*	71,385
Total assets less contra-assets and valuation allowance*	70,773

Section B: Liabilities

Deposits—total*	57,793
Balances less than $100,000*	55,966
Balances more than $100,000*	3,827
Borrowed money total*	9,257
FHL bank advances	400
Other borrowed money—total*	8,857
Commercial bank loans	0
Reverse repurchase agreements	8,857
Retail repurchase agreements	0
Overdrafts in transaction accounts	0
Commercial paper issues	0
Subdebentures not qualifying as capital	0
Mortgage-backed securities issued—total*	0
Other borrowings	0

(continued)

Exhibit 12

Northeast Savings & Loan: Balance Sheet as of December 31, 1987 (amounts in thousands of dollars) *(continued)*

Section B: Liabilities

Other liabilities—total*	778
Accrued interest payable	21
Interest accrued on deposits	105
Dividends payable on stock	0
Accrued taxes	5
Accounts payable	0
Advance payments by borrowers for taxes/insurance	265
Financial options fees received	0
Other liabilities and deferred income	382
Deferred net gains (losses) on futures/options hedging liabilities	0
Deferred income taxes	0
Total liabilities*	69,828

Memorandum items	
Pledged deposits	0
Deposit balances by type	
NOW, Super-NOW and other transaction accounts	2,563
Money market deposit accounts (MMDA)	5,798
Other accounts without fixed maturity	812
Total number of deposit accounts	6,122

Section C: Regulatory Capital

Preferred stock—total*	0
Common stock	737
Contributed capital	418
Qualifying mutual capital certificates	0
Qualifying subordinated debentures	0
Appraised equity capital	0
Net worth certificates	0
Accrued net worth certificates	0
Income capital certificates	0
Retained earnings	−210
Total regulatory capital excluding general loan valuation allowances	945
Total liabilities and regulatory capital excluding general loan valuation allowances	70,773

Memorandum items	
Cash dividends—total	0
Preferred stock	0
Common stock	0
Other capital instruments	0
Annual closing date (month/day)	06/30

* Denotes subtotal or total.

anticipated that the FSLIC will assume a portion of the bad loans on Northeast's books, and United Federal will have to invest enough capital to get Northeast's regulatory capital base up to the required 3 percent of assets.

However, several questions still haunt the management of United Federal. The one of greatest concern is whether the FSLIC will assume responsibility for enough of the bad loans that United Federal will be free of risk of further defaults. At present, about 10 percent of Northeast's loans are in default, with another 8 percent either not repaying principal or having to be renegotiated. United's management is afraid that should oil prices turn down sharply again, even more of Northeast's loan portfolio will turn bad, losses for which United will be responsible. In a very short period of time they must make an offer to the FSLIC. If they ask too much, the FSLIC may look for another suitor. If they ask too little, they may be stuck with a lot of bad loans.

Another concern to management is that of marketing and market share. They have never managed a unit outside of Longpoint, and are not certain they can effectively gain market share in the Madison market. At present, Northeast is the smallest of four S&Ls in the Madison market, which also has a number of large banks representing some of the Nation's largest banking corporations. If Northeast is to ever return to profitability it must attract new deposits and generate considerably greater loan volumes.

The FSLIC will have to receive an offer soon. Management must decide what it plans to do within the next few days.

REFERENCES

Brantley, Lamar R. "Retail Bankers Plan to Cut Costs and Boost Services." *Savings Institutions*, March 1988: 116–117.

Klaiser, Dennis L. "Aging Baby Boomers Reshape the U.S. Housing Market." *Savings Institutions*, January 1988: 58–62.

Standard and Poor's Industry Surveys 1 (January 1989): B33–B38.

American Airlines Deregulation Strategies

Hooshang Kuklan, Mei-Lung Chen, Youngil Cho, Raphael Thompson, North Carolina Central University

The Airline Deregulation Act of 1978 amended the Federal Aviation Act of 1958 and ended an era of far-reaching federal control over the operations of airliners. The law was intended to encourage price competition; eliminate restrictions on fare, route, and frequency of flight changes; remove several barriers of mergers and acquisitions; and, in brief, make the airline industry more competitive.

In late 1985, about seven years after the enactment of the deregulation law, an executive of American Airlines* characterized the impact of this legislation on American Airlines as follows:

> Deregulation, as anticipated, opened the industry to intense competition and made it highly cost-conscious. Only the low cost airlines had a chance to succeed. American Airlines just could not compete with such new low-cost carriers as People Express, New York Air, Northeast, and later the re-born Continental Airlines. American had to get its cost down to the new market place levels.
>
> In brief, American was confronted with a number of most challenging tasks. To survive in a highly competitive deregulated environment, American had to find ways of changing its fleet and route structure, expanding its ground facilities, lowering its cost to competitive levels, and changing the nature and scope of its operations.

*Brad Jensen, Managing Director of Schedules Planning; all quotations in this case for American Airlines are from Mr. Jensen.

HISTORY AND BACKGROUND

■ Company History

The first regularly scheduled flight of what was to become American Airlines was made on April 15, 1926, when Charles Lindbergh, chief pilot of Robertson Airline Company, flew the mail in a DH-4 airplane from St. Louis to Chicago. Robertson Company and several other small airline companies were consolidated in 1929 into Aviation Corporation. Aviation Corporation comprised Colonial Airways, the Embry-Riddle Company, Interstate Airlines, Inc., Southern Air Transport, and Universal Airlines System.

Colonial Airways consisted of Colonial Transport, Colonial Western Airways, and Canadian Colonial Airways. Colonial Air Transport, organized in 1923, won the contract to carry mail over the Boston–Hartford–New York route and began service in July of 1926. Passenger service was inaugurated on April 4, 1927, which is believed to have been the first night passenger flight in the United States. Colonial Western Airways started service in December 1927, linking Albany, Syracuse, Rochester, Buffalo, and Cleveland. Canadian Colonial Airways began service in 1928 between New York and Montreal via Albany.

Embry-Riddle, based in Cincinnati, operated the first scheduled service on the Cincinnati-Indianapolis-Chicago route starting in December 1927.

Interstate Airlines flew between Atlanta and Chicago starting in November 1928.

Southern Air Transport, a strong and successful airline, resulted from the merger of Texas Air Transport and St. Tammany Gulf Coast Airways. Texas Air Transport began scheduled service at Dallas, Fort Worth, and other Texas cities in February 1928. St. Tammany began flying between Atlanta and New Orleans in January 1929.

Universal Air Lines, having originated as Continental Air Lines, started scheduled service between Cleveland and Louisville in August 1928. After acquiring a number of other airlines, in June 1929, Universal joined with the New York Central and the Atchison, Topeka, and Santa Fe railroads to inaugurate the first transcontinental air-rail service.

To put together an airline system from this conglomeration, all airline subsidiaries of the Aviation Corporation were incorporated in 1930 into American Airways, Inc.

In February of 1934, the government abruptly canceled the airmail contracts and thus the first chapter of commercial airline history ended. American Airways became American Airlines that year, and the new company emerged with a more integrated route system. American Airlines quickly made itself known through its initiative in the development of an airways traffic control system, which was later adopted by all airliners and administered by the U.S. government. (See Exhibit 1.)

Ranking high among the important airline industry events of the mid-1930s was the development of an airplane, the DC-2. The DC-2, though a good airplane, was not an economical passenger-carrying aircraft. American Airlines collaborated with McDonnell Douglas, and the result was a new airplane, the DC-3, destined to become one of the most famous commercial airplanes in history. American inaugurated commercial flights with the DC-3 between Chicago and New York on June 25, 1936. By the end of the decade, American was the nation's number-one domestic air carrier.

Early Genealogy of American Airlines **Exhibit 1**

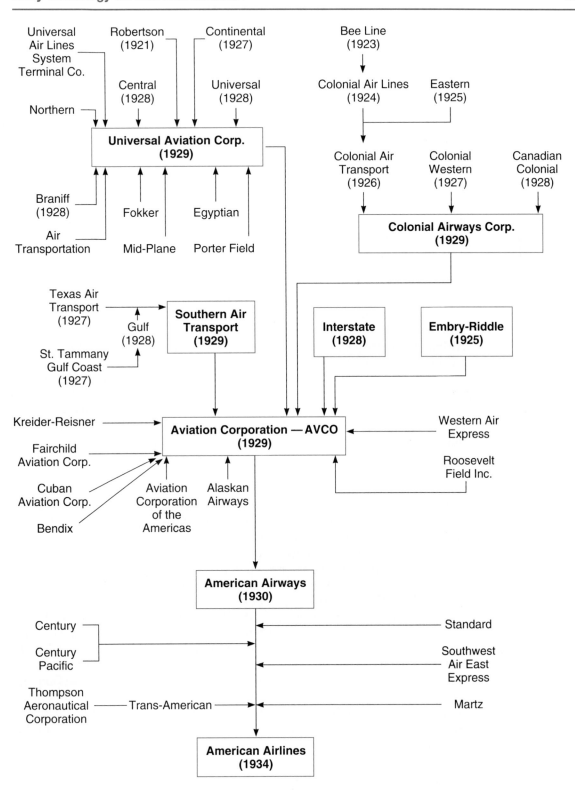

During the 1930s, American introduced a "sell and record" reservations system, which gradually became antiquated. Later in the early 1950s, American developed a new electronic reservations system, and in 1962 it took another step with installation of SABRE. This highly sophisticated airline reservations system was expanded in 1972 and again in 1975. In 1987 SABRE was the largest and most widely used computer reservations system in the industry.

Development of new commercial airplanes stopped during World War II, but with the end of the war came a series of famous airplanes to fill a greatly expanded need for air transportation. The first of 50 American DC-6s entered service in 1947. American retired its last DC-4 in 1948 and its last DC-3 in 1949. Thus, by 1949 American had become the only airline in the United States with a completely postwar fleet of pressurized passenger airplanes.

In 1953, American pioneered nonstop transcontinental service in both directions across the United States with the DC-7; and in 1959, the company began the first cross-country jet service using the new Boeing 707s. American's first-generation 707 jets shortly became second-generation jets with the introduction of the turbofan engine, another industry first for American.

In the mid-1950s, American became the first airline to establish a special facility for flight attendant training. The installation, built on a 40-acre tract between Dallas and Fort Worth, Texas, opened in 1957 as the American Airlines Stewardess College. It was later renamed the Flight Service College and subsequently the Learning Center. The size of the facility more than doubled from 1957 to 1987, and training activities widened to include instruction of other American Airlines personnel. The center is also made available to outside companies for meetings and other business functions.

As jets were added to the fleet—including, in 1964, the Boeing 727—piston equipment was phased out. American's last piston airplane, a DC-6, flew on December 17, 1966, at which time American already had placed an order with the Boeing Company for the 747, a wide-body jet capable of carrying 360 or more passengers. In 1968, American was the first to order the McDonnell Douglas DC-10, a big, versatile, quiet trijet that made its first scheduled flight on August 5, 1971, when it was introduced on the Los Angeles–Chicago route.

In 1977, American completed the final phase of a 1975 plan to consolidate its 11 U.S. mainland reservations offices into four regional centers: The Western Reservations Office at Los Angeles, the Southern Reservations Office at Dallas/Fort Worth, the Central Reservations at Cincinnati, and the Eastern Reservations Office in Hartford, Connecticut.

In October 1978, Congress passed the Airline Deregulation Act, and in November of the same year American announced that it would move its headquarters from the New York metropolitan area to the Dallas/Fort Worth region. The relocation took place over a period of two months in the summer of 1979.

American retired the Boeing 707 from its fleet in 1981. In the same year, Advantage, a marketing program to reward frequent travelers, was introduced. In 1982, American welcomed its 500 millionth passenger, began service to London, and introduced the Boeing 767 to its fleet. In 1983 the first 33 of McDonnell Douglas's Super 80s joined the American Airlines fleet, and in 1984 American ordered 67 additional Super 80s and placed options on 100 more (a total of 200 Super 80s) for the largest single aircraft purchase in U.S. aviation history. In the same year, American began the American Eagle program, a commuter feeder network at its major airports, and inaugurated nonstop jet service to Paris and Frankfurt.

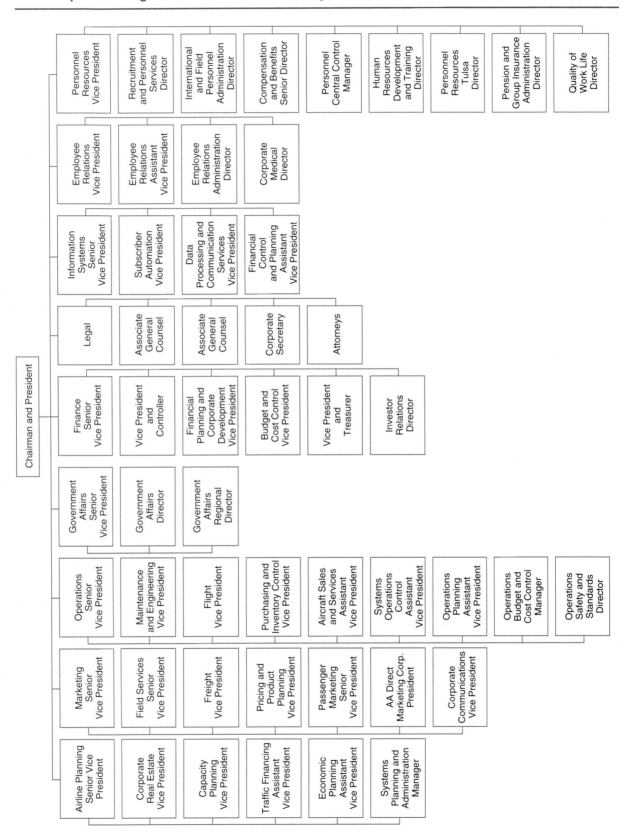

Exhibit 3   **American Employees Represented by Labor Unions**

Union	Categories	Number of Employees
Transport Workers Union (AFL/CIO)	Maintenance	12,655
	Stores	487
	Flight/ground instructors	157
	Dispatchers and assistants	86
	Simulator technicians	57
	Meteorologists	12
	Guards	12
Allied Pilots Association	Pilots	4,808
Flight Engineers International Association (AFL/CIO)	Flight engineers	299
Association of Professional Flight Attendants	Flight attendants	8,418

■ Organization Structure and Work Force

In 1982, American Airlines and its subsidiaries were incorporated into a holding company, AMR Corporation. The organizational components of AMR were American Airlines, Sky Chefs, American Airlines Training Corporation, AMR Energy Corporation, and AMR Services Corporations. American Airlines accounts for 95% of AMR's revenues.

By early 1986 American was organized on a functional basis consisting of nine functional departments—namely, Airline Planning, Marketing, Operations, Government Affairs, Finance, Legal, Information Systems, Employee Relations, and Personnel Resources. The first seven departments were headed by senior vice presidents and the last two by vice presidents (Exhibit 2). In January 1986, the upper organizational echelon of American included 50 senior executives, consisting of the chairman and president, 9 senior vice presidents, 17 vice presidents, 6 assistant vice presidents, and 14 directors.

By the end of 1985, the 44,000-member work force of American Airlines consisted of 6421 (15%) management/specialists, 5072 (12%) pilot/flight engineers, 8392 (19%) flight attendants, 12,159 (28%) ground service personnel, 10,608 (24%) agent/clerical staff, and 808 (2%) persons working in various other jobs. Labor unions represented about 62% of American's employees. Exhibit 3 lists unions representing different categories of American employees and their membership as of the end of 1985.

■ Operations

In terms of scheduled services in 1985, American had over 463,000 departures, with a daily average of 1271. This represented an increase of 17.5% over the performance in 1984. During 1985, over 41 million passengers boarded American flights. The daily average was about 113,000 passengers. Comparable numbers for 1984 were 34 million and 93,000 passengers, respectively. The available seat-miles (total seats available multiplied by miles flown) rose by 60% from 1979 to 1985. The increase was 11.9% in 1984 and 16.5% in 1985. The passenger

Operating Statistics, 1979–1985   **Exhibit 4**

Item	1979	1980	1981	1982	1983	1984	1985
Seat-miles flown (millions)*	43,109	40,672	41,756	44,605	48,203	58,667	68,336
Passenger load factor	67.4	60.4	61.4	63.5	65.0	62.6	66.8
Ton-mile load factor	56.6	51.4	53.3	54.3	56.0	53.7	NA
Break-even ton-mile load factor	55.9	53.7	52.0	54.7	52.1	49.4	NA
Domestic load factor							
American Airlines			61.4	63.9	64.5	62.0	64.2
Industry	NA	NA	57.8	58.3	59.9	56.9	60.9
Commissions paid to travel agents (as a percentage of passenger revenue)	NA	NA	6.5	7.2	7.8	8.2	8.6

Note: NA = not available.

*Scheduled service.

Commissions Paid to Travel Agencies   **Exhibit 5**

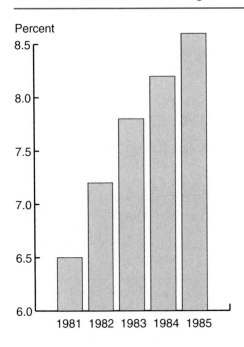

load factor (percentage of seats filled) went up in 1981, 1982, 1983, and 1985, but it dropped in 1980 and 1984. The load factor jumped from 62.6% in 1984 to 64.6% in 1985 (Exhibit 4).

The ton-mile load factor experienced a somewhat similar change during the period. In 1984, the break-even ton-mile load factor, an indication of the firm's profitability, was 6.5 points lower than in 1979. The difference between ton-mile load factor and break-even ton-mile load factor—a measure of operating cost efficiency—was positive in 1983 and 1984. It was 3.9 points and 4.3 points for

1983 and 1984, respectively (Exhibit 4). Further, total commission paid to travel agents, as a portion of the carrier's passenger revenues, increased consistently during the period, from 6% in 1981 to about 9% in 1985 (Exhibit 5).

From its inception through December 1985, a total of 623 million scheduled and charter passengers were boarded by American Airlines and its predecessor companies. From the start of scheduled jet service on January 25, 1959, through December 1985, American cumulatively had a total of over 18 million scheduled passenger departures and arrivals.

In January 1986, American served 99 points on the U.S. mainland and 31 points outside the U.S. mainland—namely, Alaska, the Caribbean, Canada, Europe, Mexico, and the Pacific. In total, American flew to 117 cities and 130 airports. Furthermore, through American Eagle—American's franchise partners to provide feeder traffic at major airports—American served 20 additional cities in Texas, Virginia, North Carolina, Arkansas, Louisiana, Oklahoma, and Missouri.

During the 12 months ending September 1985, American's top ten markets, ranked by revenue passenger-miles, were Los Angeles–New York, Dallas/Fort Worth–Hawaii, Dallas/Fort Worth–New York City, Chicago–Greater San Francisco, Dallas/Fort Worth–Greater San Francisco, Los Angeles–Hawaii, New York–San Juan, and Chicago–New York City.

International Services

American was primarily a domestic airline during the 1930s. Then, it began service to Toronto in 1941 and to Mexico in 1942. For a period of about five years—1945 to 1950—American operated a transatlantic division, American Overseas Airlines, which served a number of European countries. That division was sold to Pan American World Airways in September 1950.

American became an international airline again in August 1970, when flights were started from the U.S. mainland to Hawaii, American Samoa, the Figi Islands, New Zealand, and Australia. Service to all those points except Hawaii was suspended in March 1974 because of government-imposed route restrictions and limited profitability. In June 1975, American conducted a route exchange agreement with Pan American World Airways, under which American traded its Pacific routes (except Boston/St. Louis–Honolulu) for Pan Am's U.S.–Bermuda, New York–Santo Domingo, and New York–Barbados authority. In March 1978, American suspended its nonstop flight between Boston/St. Louis and Honolulu. However, nonstop service between Los Angeles and Honolulu and between Dallas/Fort Worth and Honolulu was inaugurated in December 1980 and June 1981, respectively. Dallas/Fort Worth–Maui and Chicago–Honolulu nonstop service began in December 1984 and May 1985, respectively.

American started service to Montreal, Jamaica, Guadeloupe, and Martinique in 1976 and 1977. And in early 1979, service on 19 new domestic and international routes was launched, including St. Maarten in the Caribbean and Nassau in the Bahamas. Joining the system later in the year were Guadalajara and Puerto Vallarta, Mexico.

In May 1982, American returned to the European market. It introduced service to London's Gatwick Airport with five 747 flights a week, increasing it to daily frequency in June of the same year. European service was expanded in the spring of 1985 to include nonstop service between Dallas/Fort Worth–Frankfurt and Chicago-Frankfurt.

Freight Services

In 1944, American introduced the first domestic scheduled U.S. freight service with two DC-3s. As the business grew, DC-4, DC-6A, and DC-7 freighters were put into service in the 1940s and 1950s.

By 1964, American was operating Boeing 707 jet freighters, each capable of carrying 90,000 pounds of freight over a range of 3000 miles. On November 5, 1974, American put into service the first 747 freighter on domestic routes. The airplane, capable of carrying 221,000 pounds of cargo, was introduced in New York, Chicago, Los Angeles, San Francisco, and Dallas/Fort Worth. By the summer of 1981, American was operating six 747 freighters, and the 707 freighters had been retired. American retired its freighter fleet in the fall of 1984.

The Fleet

As of the end of December 1985, American's fleet consisted of 39 Boeing 727-100s, 125 Boeing 727-200s, 56 McDonnell Douglas Super 80s, 46 McDonnell Douglas DC-10s, 10 McDonnell Douglas DC-10-30s, and 13 Boeing 767s. By January 1986, American had 79 aircraft on order, 5 Boeing 767-ERs, 10 Boeing 767s, and 64 Super 80s, to become available for service between 1986 and 1988. Exhibit 6 shows American's fleet mix by the end of 1986, with the seat configuration in each aircraft.

(Text continues on p. 426.)

Aircraft Fleet Mix at Year End   **Exhibit 6**

Aircraft	Fleet Count		Seat Configuration			
	1985	*1986*	*First Class*	*Business Class*	*Coach/ Economy*	*Total*
Boeing 727-100	36	36	10		105	115
	3	3	10		108	118
Boeing 727-200	125	125	12		138	150
McDonnell Douglas Super 80	56	56	12		130	142
McDonnell Douglas DC-10	2	2	16		297	313
	5	5	16		293	309
	8	8	34		256	290
	31	31	34		234	268
McDonnell Douglas DC-10-30	2	2	16		297	313
	2	2	16		288	304
	6	6	25	36	180	241
Boeing 767	13	13	24		180	204
	2	7	24		180	204
Total	291	296				

Aircraft on Order (as of 12/1/86)	Number	Available for Service
Boeing 767	10	No later than 1989
Super 80	64	No later than 1988

Exhibit 7 Consolidated Statement of Operations, 1979–1985 (in thousands except per share amounts)

	1985	Year Ended December 31, 1984	1983	1982	1981	1980	1979	Increase/ Decrease from 1979 to 1985 (%)
Revenues								
Passenger	$4,985,565	$4,335,779	$3,885,347	$3,414,222	$3,377,016	$3,154,426	$2,752,981	80
Other	1,145,463	1,017,492	877,960	762,752	731,752	666,552	602,310	90
Total operating revenues	6,131,028	5,353,721	4,763,307	4,176,974	4,108,768	3,820,978	3,355,291	83
Expenses								
Wages, salaries, and benefits	2,115,027	1,892,088	1,726,989	1,583,645	1,512,518	1,453,536	1,325,940	60
Aircraft fuel	1,141,848	1,091,799	1,038,556	1,070,236	1,115,733	1,114,812	801,506	42
Other operating expenses	2,337,520	2,001,306	1,716,280	1,513,956	1,408,231	1,338,885	1,197,434	95
Total operating expenses	5,594,395	4,985,193	4,481,825	4,167,837	4,036,482	3,907,233	3,324,880	68
Operating income	536,633	368,528	281,482	9,137	72,286	(86,255)	30,411	1664
Other income (expense)								
Interest income	131,898	134,678	77,012	65,857	63,361	52,507	62,043	126
Interest expense	(152,888)	(153,006)	(152,010)	(148,491)	(136,115)	(91,434)	(82,040)	86
Interest capitalized	19,726	19,964	11,254	16,160	13,877	9,145	7,670	157
Miscellaneous, net	(16,323)	29,426	81,345	27,380	23,731	(50,041)	28,445	(157)
	(17,587)	31,062	17,601	(39,094)	(35,146)	(79,823)	16,118	(210)
Earnings before income taxes	519,046	399,590	299,083	(29,957)	37,140	(166,078)	46,529	1015
Provision for income taxes	173,206	165,710	71,216	(10,344)	20,231	(14,418)	(29,450)	688
Earnings (loss from extraordinary items)								
Net earnings	345,840	233,880	227,867	(19,613)	16,909	75,868	11,466	295
Preferred dividend requirements	9,052	21,789	21,356	12,033	12,033	(75,792)	87,455	(25)
Earnings applicable to common shares	$ 336,788	$ 212,091	$ 206,511	$ (31,646)	$ 4,876	$ (87,825)	$ 75,412	347
Earnings per common share								
primary	$ 5.94	$ 4.37	$ 4.79	$ (1.00)	$ .16	$ (3.06)	$ 2.63	126
Fully diluted	$ 5.88	$ 4.16	$ 4.48	$ (1.00)	$ .26		$ 2.54	131

Exhibit 8 Selected Consolidated Financial Data (in thousands, except per share amounts)

	1985	1984	1983	1982	1981	1980	1979	Increase/ Decrease from 1979 to 1985 (%)
Total operating revenues	$6,131,028	$5,353,721	$4,763,307	$4,176,974	$4,108,699	$3,820,978	$3,355,291	83
Total operating expenses	5,594,395	4,985,193	4,481,825	4,167,837	4,036,482	3,907,233	3,324,880	68
Operating income	536,633	368,528	281,482	9,137	72,217	(86,255)	30,411	1665
Earnings (loss) before extraordinary item	345,840	233,880	227,867	(19,613)	16,840	(151,660)	75,979	355
Net earnings (loss)	345,840	233,880	227,867	(19,613)	47,440	(75,792)	87,445	295
Earnings (loss) before extraordinary item per common share								
Primary	5.94	4.37	4.79	(1.00)	.16	(5.70)	2.23	166
Fully diluted	5.88	4.16	4.48	(1.00)	.26	(5.70)	2.18	169
Net earnings (loss) per common share								
Primary	5.94	4.37	4.79	(1.00)	1.21	(3.06)	2.63	126
Fully diluted	5.88	4.16	4.48	(1.00)	1.16	(3.06)	2.54	131
Total assets	6,421,101	5,260,896	4,728,165	3,896,813	3,738,221	3,277,883	3,186,897	101
Long-term debt	920,542	774,821	726,580	751,798	717,873	669,386	680,019	35
Obligations under capital leases	910,183	766,585	784,961	764,811	798,553	601,727	509,590	77
Redeemable preferred stock	88,621	126,753	105,399	110,600	109,505	108,410	107,314	(17.4)
Convertible preferred stock	—	125,000	125,000				—	
Common stock and other stockholders' equity	2,180,914	1,513,407	1,299,627	836,155	731,199	695,064	785,746	177
Common shares outstanding at year-end	58,681	48,453	48,374	37,241	28,766	28,698	28,696	104
Book value per common share	37.00	30.98	26.59	22.07	24.88	23.64	26.77	38
Preferred shares outstanding at year-end								
Redeemable preferred stock	2,971	4,602	4,749	5,000	5,000	5,000	5,000	
Convertible preferred stock	—	5,000	5,000				—	

Exhibit 9 Consolidated Balance Sheet (in thousands)

	1985	1984	1983	1982	1981	1980	1979	Increase/Decrease from 1979 to 1985 (%)
Assets								
Current assets								
Cash and short-term investments	$1,357,016	$1,353,683	$1,070,042	$465,862	$459,884	$292,418	$455,374	198
Receivables, less allowances for uncollectible accounts	631,600	587,341	556,637	514,134	532,028	530,549	493,571	28
Inventories, less allowances for obsolescence	224,600	197,521	192,605	193,634	186,065	185,081	146,404	53
Other current assets	57,557	42,010	46,180	40,802	33,540	41,623	10,880	429
Total current assets	2,270,773	2,180,555	1,865,464	1,214,432	1,211,517	1,049,671	1,106,229	105
Equipment and property								
Flight equipment, at cost	3,190,404	2,411,932	2,411,737	2,157,106	1,879,668	1,686,847	1,967,776	62
Less accumulated depreciation	1,143,134	970,228	945,522	885,607	785,328	687,622	953,072	20
	2,047,270	1,441,704	1,466,215	1,271,499	1,094,340	999,225	1,014,704	102
Purchase deposits for flight equipment	141,279	133,148	73,382	89,993	103,946	102,829	111,179	27
	2,188,549	1,574,852	1,539,597	1,361,492	1,198,286	1,102,054	1,125,883	94
Other equipment and property at cost	1,407,752	1,196,052	1,049,753	953,777	861,638	775,326	671,819	110
Less accumulated depreciation and depletion	666,989	611,912	558,037	501,665	426,265	365,533	305,968	118
	740,763	584,140	491,716	452,112	435,373	409,793	365,851	105
	2,929,312	2,158,992	2,031,313	1,813,604	1,633,659	1,511,847	1,491,734	96
Equipment and property under capital leases								
Flight equipment	934,760	813,171	885,543	852,439	858,320	642,284	656,803	42
Other equipment and property	193,932	204,910	208,505	203,828	181,606	171,269	163,194	19
	1,128,692	1,018,081	1,094,048	1,056,267	1,039,926	813,553	819,997	38
Less accumulated amortization	409,271	363,443	439,554	382,470	335,053	290,622	370,490	10
	719,421	654,638	654,494	673,797	704,873	522,931	449,507	60
Other assets								
Route acquisition costs, net	36,054	37,146	38,238	39,330	40,423	41,515	42,608	(15)
Other	465,541	229,565	138,656	155,650	147,749	151,919	96,819	381
	501,595	266,711	176,894	194,980	188,172	193,434	139,427	260
Total assets	$6,421,101	$5,260,896	$4,728,165	$3,896,813	$3,738,221	$3,277,883	$3,186,897	101

Liabilities, Redeemable Preferred Stock, Convertible Preferred Stock, Common Stock, and Other Stockholders' Equity

Current liabilities								
Accounts payable	$ 516,307	$ 476,769	$ 494,697	$ 420,000	$ 404,354	$ 357,857	$ 313,558	65
Accrued salaries and wages	269,516	226,943	186,845	172,304	167,150	149,624	150,879	79
Other accrued liabilities	421,680	358,077	275,253	245,256	260,880	157,256	142,166	197
Air traffic liability and customer's deposits	452,207	382,420	368,665	305,332	280,296	300,522	260,531	74
Current maturities of long-term debt	99,666	66,823	64,215	48,921	55,105	50,824	57,696	73
Current obligations under capital leases	43,565	41,814	48,262	51,377	53,469	42,439	41,592	5
Total current liabilities	1,802,941	1,552,846	1,437,937	1,243,190	1,221,254	1,058,522	966,422	87
Long-term debt, less current maturities	920,542	774,821	726,580	751,798	717,873	669,386	680,019	35
Obligations under capital leases, less current obligations	910,183	766,585	784,961	764,811	798,553	601,727	509,590	77
Other liabilities								
Deferred federal income tax	299,718	241,384	131,330	81,374	99,469	112,322	118,239	153
Other liabilities and deferred credit	218,182	160,100	117,331	108,885	60,368	32,452	19,567	1015
	517,900	401,484	248,661	190,259	159,837	144,774	137,806	276
Redeemable preferred stock	88,621	126,753	105,399	110,600	109,505	108,410	107,314	(17)
Convertible preferred stock, common stock and other stockholders' equity								
Convertible preferred stock		125,000	125,000					
Common stock	58,681	48,453	48,374	37,241	28,766	28,698	28,696	104
Additional paid-in capital	1,030,123	709,632	708,022	461,309	333,182	332,522	332,511	210
Retained earnings	1,092,110	755,322	543,231	337,605	369,251	333,844	424,539	157
	2,180,914	1,638,407	1,424,627	836,155	731,199	695,064	785,746	178
	$6,421,101	$5,260,896	$4,728,165	$3,896,813	$3,738,221	$3,277,883	$3,186,897	101

423

■ The Financial Outlook

The airline industry experienced a back-to-back recession during 1981–1982. American Airline's financial performance slid in 1980–1982 but improved consistently from 1983 to 1985. The years 1983–1985 were American's best years since the deregulation.

From 1979 to 1985, total operating revenues rose by over 80%, but total operating expenses increased by under 68%. The operating income increased about 17 times, with net earnings rising by 29%. During the same postregulation years, American's current assets and its total assets more than doubled. Despite an $8 billion capital spending commitment for the period 1985–1991, the airline's operating earnings and net earnings rose by 74% and 52%, respectively, from 1983 to 1985 (Exhibits 7, 8, and 9).

Within the same time frame, American's current ratio and acid-test ratio improved slightly, while its fixed-asset turnover and debt to total assets experienced a modest drop. Return on total assets doubled. Return on net worth rose from 9.8% to 15%. The profit margin on sales more than doubled from 1979 to 1985 (Exhibit 10).

Over the three-year period from 1983 to 1985, AMR Corporation experienced significant profit growth. Operating revenues rose by 12.4% in 1984, primarily due to higher passenger revenues. The operating revenue for 1985 increased 14.5%, to $6131 million. During 1984 and 1985, operating income rose by $87 million (30.9%) and $168 million (45.6%), and net earnings advanced by $6 million (2.6%) and $111 million (47.9%), respectively. The 1985 operating margin was 8.8%, up from 1984's level of 6.9%. The revenue passenger-miles (one passenger flown one mile) realized an increase of 20.3% in 1985. Revenue ton-miles (one ton of cargo or mail transported one mile) also went up by over 10% in 1985. Despite strong traffic growth, the revenue yield per passenger-mile (the average amount received per passenger-mile) decreased by 4.3% in 1985. The decrease in yield was caused primarily by substantial fare discounting in the industry during this period.

Labor costs rose by only 1.5% in 1984, the lowest increase in more than 15 years and slightly below the U.S. industry average. Fuel costs, which typically account for about 25% of each revenue dollar, experienced a steady decline due to American's fuel management programs and the drop in worldwide oil prices.

Exhibit 11 provides a comparison of operating statistics for 12 major carriers for 1984 and 1985.

Exhibit 10	Financial Analysis Ratios						
Ratio	*1985*	*1984*	*1983*	*1982*	*1981*	*1980*	*1979*
Current ratio	1.26%	1.40%	1.30%	0.98%	0.99%	0.99%	1.14%
Acid-test ratio	1.13	1.28	1.16	0.82	0.84	0.82	0.99
Fixed-asset turnover	1.48	1.74	1.66	1.56	1.63	1.71	1.61
Profit margin on sales	5.6	4.4	4.8	(0.5)	0.4	(2.0)	2.6
Returns on total assets	5.4	4.4	4.8	(0.5)	0.5	(2.3)	2.7
Returns on net worth	15	12	14	(2.1)	2	9.4	9.8
Debt to total assets	28.1	29.5	30.4	31.9	32.7	32.2	30.3

Exhibit 11 Comparative Operating Results of 12 Major Carriers (in thousands of dollars)

Carrier	Revenues			Operating Expenses			Operating Income			Net Income[‡]		Revenue Passenger-Miles		Passenger Load Factor (%)	
	1984	1985	% Change	1984	1985	% Change	1984	1985	% Change	1984	1985	1984	1985	1984	1985
American*	6,087,382	6,859,334	+15.2	4,748,317	5,352,850	+12.7	339,065	506,484	+49.4	233,880§	345,840§	36,702	44,138	62.6	84.8
Continental	1,185,378	1,704,773	+43.8	1,077,278	1,548,110	+43.7	108,100	156,663	+44.9	50,270	60,884	10,923	18,405	62.7	64.8
Delta	4,458,837	4,690,194	+5.2	4,167,325	4,464,979	+6.9	291,512	235,215	-19.3	258,641	158,776	27,040	30,071	62.9	58.5
Eastern	4,383,898	4,815,070	+10.3	4,174,267	4,593,454	+10.0	189,631	221,616	+18.9	d37,927	5,875	29,409	33,140	68.9	60.3
NWA	2,444,974	2,055,491	+8.6	2,348,898	2,578,404	+9.0	96,276	77,087	-19.9	88,857	73,119	20,127	22,912	60.9	60.7
Pan Am*	3,304,218	3,090,324	-6.5	3,411,594	3,287,950	-3.6	d107,376	d197,626	NM	d206,826§	48,750§	28,406	27,332	64.4	63.0
Piedmont†	1,282,879	1,627,231	+19.0	1,143,599	1,407,003	+23.0	139,280	120,228	-13.7	58,175	66,712	6,352	8,307	62.4	65.7
Republic	1,547,232	1,734,397	+12.1	1,447,230	1,588,087	+8.3	100,002	186,330	+66.3	13,709	69,231	8,594	10,737	60.2	68.8
TWA	3,525,070	3,725,418	+5.8	3,447,939	3,787,827	+9.9	77,131	d82,409	NM	29,885	d208,433§	28,304	32,052	62.2	65.2
UAL*	6,218,720	6,291,609	-14.9	5,654,590	5,534,265	-2.1	564,130	d242,658	NM	235,857§	d88,223§	46,687	41,640	60.4	63.0
USAir	1,829,696	1,749,126	+7.3	1,436,972	1,582,204	+10.1	192,724	166,922	-13.4	110,331	109,850	8,191	9,732	58.1	59.2
Western	1,181,900	1,306,600	+10.5	1,170,500	1,230,000	+5.1	11,400	78,500	+571.1	d29,200	35,400	9,412	10,441	57.7	68.8
Total	36,230,184	38,149,467	+5.3	34,228,309	36,925,113	+7.9	2,001,875	1,224,354	-38.8	811,852	875,780	260,147	266,907	59.3	81.7

Sources: Company reports.

Note: NM = not meaningful; d = deficit.

* Airline operations only.

† Systems operations; includes nonairline subsidiaries.

‡ Before extraordinary items.

§ Corporate total.

■ **Distinctions**

In November 1975, the Flight Safety Foundation presented a special Distinguished Performance Award to American in recognition of the 6 million hours of safe flying the airline had compiled over a ten-year period. It was the greatest total of safe flying hours ever amassed by an airline in the history of aviation.

In 1982, American earned the distinction of being selected number one for domestic service in an International Airline Passengers Association survey for the fourth time. More than 14,000 of IAPA's members took part in the survey. American has finished first in every poll ever taken by the Association.

In January 1982, American was named Airline of the Year for 1981 by *Air Transport World* magazine. In February, the *Wall Street Transcript* announced that its annual gold award for outstanding airline industry management had been awarded to the American Airlines team of Chairman Casey and President Crandall. *Financial World* magazine in March named Chairman Casey the top airline management executive of the year.

DEREGULATION STRATEGIES

American Airlines responded to the deregulation of 1978 with four major strategies in order to improve its competitive posture:

1. Improve the aircraft mix and increase the seating density of the fleet.
2. Minimize labor costs.
3. Maximize revenues by expanding the use of American's computer reservations system, developing new frequent-flyer programs, establishing a system of feeder service to American's major cities, and initiating structural readjustments.
4. Restructure and strengthen the route system.

■ **Programs to Improve Fleet Mix and Increase Seating Density**

Fleet Mix Improvement

In 1978, fuel accounted for about 30% of American's total operating expenses. One of the biggest tasks confronting American at the time was to ground the inefficient portion of its fleet. Twenty-six of the 707s, a fuel-inefficient aircraft, were removed from service in January 1981, and the remaining 36 aircraft (including 9 707 freighters) were retired by the summer of the same year.

In anticipation of the retirement of the 707s, American placed an order in November 1978 to buy 30 transcontinental versions of twin-engine 767s. The 767 accommodates 204 passengers in a mixed first-class and coach arrangement and performs the same mission as the 707, but it does so providing greater comfort and fuel efficiency. The airplane carries up to 10,000 pounds of baggage and cargo. In November 1982, American introduced into service the first of 30 Boeing 767 jetliners.

In 1983, American further expanded its fleet with the acquisition of 20 Super 80 aircraft from McDonnell Douglas Company. Later, 13 more Super 80s were acquired. On February 29, 1984, American announced the largest airplane pur-

Exhibit 12   American Airlines Aircraft Fuel Statistics

Item	1981	1982	1983	1984	1985
Gallons consumed	1,087,364,643	1,106,763,564	1,169,938,000	1,277,845,000	1,411,146,045
January–December price-per-gallon spread	95.77¢–$1.031	$1.03–95.08¢	96.24¢–86.79¢	86.80¢–84.39¢	83.70¢–82.39¢
Average price per gallon	$1.026	96.70¢	88.77¢	85.44¢	80.96¢
Total fuel cost	$1,115,733,000	$1,070,236,000	$1,038,556,000	$1,092,614,000	$1,141,289,000
Total operating expenses	28.8%	26.8%	24.2%	23.0%	21.3%

chase in commercial aviation history up to that point when it placed an order for 67 Super 80s and acquired options to purchase an additional 100 planes.

From 1978 to 1985, the fuel-efficient percentage of American's fleet increased from 15 to 44, and the percentage of seats in the fuel-efficient fleet jumped from 29 to 53 during the same seven-year period following deregulation. The fuel-efficient portion of American's fleet and also of its seat capacity are anticipated to increase to 64% and 69%, respectively, by 1991.

The restructuring of the fleet mix resulted in a drop in fuel cost from about 30% of the airline's total operating expenses in 1978 to 21.3% by the end of 1985, a reduction of about 9%. This reduction occurred despite an increase of over 20% in fleet size from 1978 to 1985. American's aircraft fuel statistics for the period from 1981 to 1985 are given in Exhibit 12.

Increase of Seating Density

From 1978 to 1985, American undertook measures to increase seating density in DC-10 and B-727 aircraft through use of slimline seats, compact galleys, and centerline bins. During this period the number of seats in DC-10-10 aircraft was increased from 264 to 290 (an improvement of 9.8%). The increase in B-727-100 aircraft was from 100 to 118 seats, and in B-727-200 the number of seats was raised from 127 to 150, an increase of 18% in both cases.

■ Programs to Minimize Labor Costs

Deregulation required implementation of various cost reduction programs. The deregulation-generated competition made the industry significantly more cost-conscious than before. Brad Jensen of American Airlines characterized the situation as follows:

> After the deregulation, American Airlines just couldn't compete with the low cost carriers. We had to get our cost down to the new market-place levels. The cost differential was quite significant. The cost structure at some airlines was up to 22 to 35 percent lower than ours. Regarding the labor cost, there were two ways to go about getting the cost down. One way was to cut down the pay of existing employees which, we all agree, is a very painful and hard thing to do. Continental did it successfully. They filed for bankruptcy and took the position that they could not survive with their existing contractual obligations including their labor contracts. They arbitrarily proposed their own new conditions and pay scale. The Continental situation could never happen again the same way it happened for Continental. The strategy that the senior officers of American adopted was to seek a negotiated solution to the problem. American could not unilaterally lower wages and risk a strike. A strike could not achieve our goal. American negotiated with the unions to protect current employees at their existing salaries, but hire new employees at market rates. We succeeded in convincing our labor unions that this was the only way we could survive in the deregulated environment.

The collective-bargaining agreement signed by American and the Transport Workers Union and the pilots and flight attendants unions in 1983 was the first airline agreement to include the so-called "two tier," "new hire," or "market rate" wage scale. Under this system historical rates of pay for existing employees were preserved while providing that new employees be hired at market rates. In return for the union agreement to the two-tier scheme, American promised internal growth rather than growth through mergers and acquisitions. Labor costs rose by only 1.5% in 1984 (the lowest increase in more than 15 years), the first full year that American enjoyed the benefits of the new system. In September 1985, the Transport Workers Union agreed to a continuation of the market rate scales as approved in 1983.

An important statistical measure of airline employee productivity is the number of available seat-miles produced per employee. According to this measure, the productivity of American's personnel has consistently increased since 1981, with a 7% increase recorded in 1985. The available annual seat-miles per employee increased from about 1.25 million in 1981 to 1.65 million in 1985.

The two-tier pay scale has given American a strong incentive to grow and reduce cost through growth. By the end of 1985, the proportion of American's market rate employees had increased to 36% of its nearly 44,000-member work force. American expects 50% of its employees to be on the market rate pay scale by 1989.

In 1985, due to a tight market, American revised and increased its 1983 pay for the newly hired pilots by about 15–36%. To hold down labor costs, in August 1986, American was negotiating with its pilots' union, Allied Pilots Association, to almost double the time that it would take new pilots to reach the top of their pay scale.

In November 1986, AMR revealed plans to buy ACI, the parent company of AirCal, in an attempt to strengthen its market position on the West Coast. AMR's chairman and president, Robert L. Crandall, stated that this was not a departure from the company's commitment to internal growth. The decision was defended as a tactical move in response to the strong consolidation forces present in the industry.

In addition to the new cost-saving labor agreements that American reached with its unions, the airline also managed, as noted above, to reduce its fuel consumption as a percentage of total operating expenses from 28.8 in 1981 to 21.3 in 1985 through fleet mix improvement and fuel management programs.

▪ Programs to Maximize Revenue

American's efforts to maximize profits in the deregulated environment focused primarily on its SABRE computer reservations system, frequent-flyer program, American Eagle commuter airline, and programs of internal diversification and consolidation.

SABRE

The airline industry has five computer reservations systems (CRS) owned by American, United, TWA, Eastern, and Delta, which collectively generate a total annual revenue of over $800 million. American's SABRE is the largest in the industry; United's APOLLO ranks second. These two systems together account for 70% of the market. Computer reservations systems constitute sources of significant revenues for airlines. American's 1985 revenue from its SABRE was $338 million, representing an increase of 89% over the preceding year. United estimated the revenue from its APOLLO system would increase by 66% to $246 million in 1985.

By the end of 1985, SABRE had more than 11,000 subscriber locations, over 50,000 terminals, and about 1200 airlines for which the system had schedules

---

Exhibit 13	SABRE at a Glance	
	Number of locations (travel agency, corporate and government accounts)	Over 11,000
	Number of CRTs	Over 50,000
	Number of printers	Over 25,000
	Number of airlines for which SABRE has schedule information	1200
	Number of fares in SABRE	Over 13 million
	Number of participating carriers	291
	Number of hotel properties and condominium firms	Over 10,000
	Number of car rental companies	20
	Advance boarding passes available for	
	American Airlines	Ozark Airlines
	Delta Air Lines	Trans World Airlines
	Eastern Airlines	United Airlines
	Frontier Airlines	Western Airlines

---

information (Exhibit 13). In an effort to maximize their CRS-related revenues, by late 1986, American Airlines and United were aggressively pushing their sophisticated reservation systems into Europe.

Frequent-Flyer Program

Following deregulation, the low-cost airlines began promoting several forms of systemwide deep discount fares. Instead of offering such across-the-board discount fares, American responded to this challenge by introducing, in 1981, a focused discount program intended to reward loyal and frequent customers. The program was called AAdvantage. AAdvantage grew rapidly; by early 1986, its membership exceeded 3 million.

Another innovation of American in 1981 was AAirpass, a concept that guaranteed fixed personal and business air travel cost for periods ranging from five years to a lifetime.

American Eagle

American Eagle, a commuter airline, was formed in 1984—a network of regional airlines integrated into the American Airlines domestic route system. American Eagle provides franchise feeder service into American's major cities and also serves markets not economically feasible for service with American's aircraft.

The first partners in this marketing venture were Metro Airlines and Chaparral Airlines, which fed passengers through the Dallas/Fort Worth hub. American Eagle schedules are integrated into American's timetable. Eagle in-flight personnel are trained by American. Eagle reservations are handled through American's SABRE terminals, which can automatically print both tickets and boarding passes. American Eagle planes are painted in a color scheme complementing the American look. By January 1986, American Eagle served 35 cities.

Internal Diversification and Consolidation

American has experienced several structural changes since deregulation. During this period AA Training Corporation, AMR Corporation (a parent holding company), and AA Services Corporation were formed. Further, American sold its catering business, AA Sky Chefs.

American Airlines Training Corporation

AA Training Corporation (AATC) was created in 1979 to service various commercial and military contracts awarded to American for pilot and mechanic training. The subsidiary has its headquarters near the airline's pilot training center, the Flight Academy, at Dallas/Fort Worth. A new training facility at London's Gatwick Airport—operated by a subsidiary, American Airlines Training, Ltd.—was opened in 1981.

While 1985 was the third consecutive profitable year for AATC, revenues and earnings from continuing operations declined from the record highs of 1984 as activity on several major programs began to wind down.

Contributing to the decline in earnings was a $1.6 million loss realized on the sale of AATC's London-based training subsidiary. In 1985 a training contract with the U.S. Air Force continued to be AATC's principal source of revenue.

AATC also manufactures training equipment pursuant to contracts with NASA, the U.S. Navy, and Beech Aircraft. Lack of new markets for such equipment prompted a decision in 1985 to discontinue manufacturing operations following completion of the existing contractual commitments in 1986.

AMR Corporation

On May 19, 1982, American Airlines' stockholders voted to approve a plan of reorganization under which a new holding company, AMR Corporation, was formed and became the parent company of American Airlines, Inc. The holding company was established to provide increased flexibility for financing and investment.

American Airlines Services Corporation

AA Services Corporation, the ground services subsidiary, began operations in 1984. The company performed a variety of aircraft service functions, including loading and unloading, baggage handling, cabin cleaning, and deicing. Other services included freight warehousing, passenger processing, building cleaning, sky cap services, and security and ground transportation.

The company experienced substantial growth in 1985. Revenues were $15.8 million, up from $3.2 million in 1984. After-tax net income was $1.4 million. Apart from the work it performed under its own contracts, the company also administered American Airlines' ground-handling contracts, the revenues from which increased from $55 million in 1984 to $60 million in 1985.

American Airlines Sky Chefs

In 1942, American entered the airline catering business with the formation of Flagship International, known as Sky Chefs, to provide food service for American as well as other airlines. Starting with 218 employees at eight catering locations, Sky Chefs served about 1 million meals during the first year.

In 1985, American sold its food service subsidiary to Onex Capital Corporation, a diversified company based in Toronto, Canada. It was believed that because of its affiliation with American, Sky Chefs had limited chances of further growth in the future.

Sky Chefs' revenues amounted to $352.3 million in 1985. The net income was $15.9 million, compared with $13.6 million in 1984. Sky Chefs operated 29 airline catering kitchens and 238 airport restaurants and concessions at 30 airport terminals. At the time of sale, Sky Chefs catered over 43 million airline meals annually, served about 7 million airport restaurant meals, and catered approximately 449,000 flights.

Sky Chefs will continue to meet the majority of American's catering needs under a multiyear contract.

■ Programs to Strengthen and Restructure the Route System

Route Expansion

During the period from deregulation to mid-1985, American Airlines opened 72 new cities, including 6 cities reinstated and 2 Alaskan cities served through the American/Alaska Airlines interchange. During the same time, the airline started nonstop service in 114 new city pairs and increased the number of airports served from 65 to 129.

In addition to domestic routes, American also increased its daily service to Europe. In 1985, American carried more than 383,000 passengers between the United States and Europe. The company expects to operate a total of eight trips a day between the United States and Europe during the peak season.

Hub Expansion

Air travel can be either point to point or through a connecting hub supported by smaller feeder lines. In the point-to-point market, the airplane flies from point A to point B and so do all the passengers on that airplane. In a more complex system, passengers are taken from point A to an intermediate point, a hub, where they can connect to any of the many points on the other side of the hub. The hub system creates connections, making it less desirable than the nonstop service, but it serves many more markets. American Airlines adopted the strategy of evolving from a mostly point-to-point system to a primarily hub structure.

In 1981, American Airlines started major expansions at its two existing hubs in Chicago and Dallas/Fort Worth. In July 1982, a $76 million expansion program at Dallas/Fort Worth Airport was announced, and in September 1983, an additional $15 million was committed to expansion at this hub. A 75,000-square-foot terminal expansion was completed in 1984, permitting the addition of 1600 seats to the departure lounges. American also acquired an additional nine terminal gates in 1984 to handle future expansion. In 1985, American expanded the operations at its Dallas/Fort Worth hub to 321 daily nonstop flights to 94 destinations. In September 1983, American also launched a five-year $100 million expansion and improvement program at its Chicago hub. Forty-nine new flights were added to the Chicago hub in 1984, a 32% increase. Service to 15 new cities was introduced in 1984. The service grew in 1985 to 237 daily nonstop flights to 66 cities.

Hub Development

In addition to expanding its two east-west hubs at Chicago and Dallas, American concluded that as part of its deregulation strategies, it had to also establish a major new hub to serve the strong north-south market in the eastern part of the country.

ESTABLISHING A NORTH/SOUTH HUB

■ Growth Strategy

Under the deregulated system, carriers were free to decide which markets to enter and which to exit. The intense competition and cost-consciousness forced airlines to change their operating efficiencies and systems. In general, the industry's response to the deregulation centered around cost reduction measures, expansion of existing operations, and consolidation through mergers and acquisitions.

The senior officers of American Airlines concluded that without major adjustments the airline could not effectively compete in the new environment. Efficiency improvement through growth and expansion constituted the thrust of the American's coping response. As expressed by an American Airlines executive:

> Excellent deals we had struck on aircraft acquisition prices as well as the two-tier plan gave American a strong incentive to grow. The faster we grew, the more market rate employees we took in and the faster our average cost got down to market rate. Subsequently, we adopted an aggressive growth plan as a means of lowering the cost of our operations.
>
> To grow, we needed to expand the markets we served and take advantage of the growth economics. We defined some areas of the world that could bring us new business. We divided the country into sections—north/south services in the east, point-to-point services on both coasts, and east/west services. We concluded that the Eastern half of the country, where we did not have a strong presence, held the most promise.
>
> We thoroughly examined the north/south market in the East and gradually became convinced that the focal point of our growth strategy had to be this market. As part of our analysis, we did a study of Piedmont Airlines. Piedmont operates out of three major hubs, Charlotte, Baltimore, and Dayton. Piedmont has been a very successful carrier in that part of the country. We tried to determine why Piedmont was so successful. Piedmont had realized that there were some underserved markets out there. During deregulation, major carriers pulled back from a lot of these point-to-point services. Piedmont identified the fact that these areas provided a strong potential because they were not served by any carrier. Piedmont opened a hub and collected all the traffic from a lot of small markets which because of their size no other carrier was interested in. We concluded that we needed a hub in the East to serve the north/south traffic.

Exhibit 14   **Major Hubs in the United States**

- ■ International
- ● Domestic
- ▲ Planned

Exhibit 15   **Major Hubs for the Airline Industry**

American	Delta Western	Trans World
Chicago	Atlanta	New York
Dallas/Fort Worth	Cincinnati	St. Louis
Nashville	Dallas/Fort Worth	
Raleigh/Durham	Los Angeles	**USAir**
	Salt Lake City	Philadelphia
		Pittsburgh

Texas Air

Atlanta (Eastern)
Denver (Continental)
Houston (Continental)
Kansas City (Eastern)
Miami (Eastern)
Newark (People Express)
New York (N.Y. Air)

**MAJOR
AIRLINE
HUBS**

Piedmont

Baltimore
Charlotte
Dayton

Pan American

Miami
New York

Northwest

Detroit
Memphis
Minneapolis/St. Paul

United

Chicago
Denver
San Francisco
Washington, DC

Hubbing in the East was judged to be capable of providing American with access to wholly new sources of passenger and freight revenue, as well as to several ancillary benefits, including increased "frequent-traveler plan" coverage; better personnel, facility, and equipment productivity at many existing stations; and improved productivity of national advertising.

Hubbing

Throughout the country, there are 33 major hubs located in 25 cities (Exhibits 14 and 15). Predominantly north/south hubs are limited in number. The majority of the hubs are mostly east/west, with multidirectional hubs ranking second in number.

Typically, east/west hubs have a larger local traffic base. However, they are individually more competitive as well as substantially more competitive with other hubs for flow traffic. By contrast, north/south hubs are less competitive both individually and in relation to other hubs. On average, each east/west hub city faces strong competition from eight other hub cities. The comparable number for north/south cities is 2.3 (Exhibit 16). Exhibit 17 shows predominantly east/west, north/south, and multidirectional hubs broken down by the relative local O&D (origin and destination)—using Chicago as a base—and the complexing carriers for each hub.

As characterized by an aviation executive:

> Hubbing is, in fact, an economical way of market expansion. The math is simple, 10 airplanes in and 10 airplanes out take 10 gates. If it takes 10 gates, it takes 10 crew to feed them. Cost tends to go up with the number of aircraft on the ground at the time, but the revenue goes up with the product of the number of aircraft on the ground at the time. Ten airplanes at a time mean we have 100 markets served. Thirty airplanes at a time serve 900 markets. Roughly, three times more cost and nine times more revenue, so revenue builds exponentially with the size of the hub. A hub is like a heart-beat in the circulatory system pumping traffic from one side to the other.

■ The Selection Process

American Airlines used geography, market size, and competitive forces as the primary criteria for the selection of its intended north/south hub. More specifically, the selection criteria included the following:

- Geographic location relative to the area to be served.
- Potential flow traffic as well as potential local market size.
- Competitive environment.
- Facility options.
- Relative operating conditions such as weather and airport capability.

The new hub was to be centrally located to balance cities north and south of the hub, to minimize overlap, to optimize American's competitive positions, and to minimize long thin "spokes." American followed a process of elimination in selecting a hub city. In the beginning, there were 16 cities under consideration: New York's LaGuardia and Kennedy, Philadelphia, Newark, Pittsburgh, Baltimore, Washington's National and Dulles in the Northeast; Atlanta, Memphis, Nashville, Charlotte, Norfolk, Greensboro/High Point, Raleigh/

Exhibit 16 Level of Competition at East/West and North/South Hub Cities

East/West Hub City	Highly Competitive	Competitive Hubs											
		Chicago	Dallas/Ft. Worth	Houston	Denver	Atlanta	Detroit	Minneapolis/St. Paul	St. Louis	Pittsburgh	Kansas City	Salt Lake	Memphis
Chicago	(10)	|	X	X	X	X	X	X	X	X	X	X	O
Dallas/Ft. Worth	(8)	X	|	X	X	X	O	O	X	X	X	O	X
Houston	(8)	X	X	|	X	X	O	O	X	X	X	O	X
Denver	(10)	X	X	X	|	X	X	X	X	X	X	X	O
Atlanta	(8)	X	X	X	X	|	O	O	X	X	X	O	X
Detroit	(6)	X	O	O	X	O	|	X	X	X	X	O	O
Minneapolis/St. Paul	(6)	X	O	O	X	O	X	|	X	O	X	X	O
St. Louis	(11)	X	X	X	X	X	X	X	|	X	X	X	X
Pittsburgh	(8)	X	X	X	X	X	X	O	X	|	X	O	O
Kansas City	(11)	X	X	X	X	X	X	X	X	X	|	X	X
Salt Lake	(5)	X	O	O	X	O	O	X	X	O	X	|	O
Memphis	(5)	O	X	X	O	X	O	O	X	O	X	O	|
Average	(8)												

North/South Hub City	Highly Competitive	Competitive Hubs					
		Atlanta	Pittsburgh	Baltimore	Cincinnati	Memphis	Charlotte
Atlanta	(2)	|	O	O	O	X	X
Pittsburgh	(3)	O	|	X	X	O	X
Baltimore	(2)	O	X	|	X	O	O
Cincinnati	(2)	O	X	X	|	O	O
Memphis	(2)	X	O	O	O	|	X
Charlotte	(3)	X	X	O	O	X	|
Average	(2.3)						

Note: X = highly competitive; O = competitive.

East/West, Multidirectional, and North/South Hubs by Hub Location, Local O&D, and Complexing Carriers   **Exhibit 17**

Hub Locations	Local O&D* Index (Chicago = 100)	Carriers Complexing[†]
Predominantly East/West Hubs		
Chicago	100	AA, UA
Dallas/Ft. Worth	82	AA, DL
Houston	63	CO
Denver	50	CO, UA, FL
Detroit	37	RC
Minneapolis/St. Paul	33	NW, RC
St. Louis	28	TW, OZ
Kansas City	21	EA
Salt Lake City	14	WA
Multidirectional Hubs		
Atlanta	49	DL, EA
Pittsburgh	25	AL
Memphis	10	RC
Dayton	7	PI
Predominantly North/South Hubs		
Baltimore	19	PI
Cincinnati	12	DL
Charlotte	10	PI
Nashville[‡]	10	AA
Raleigh/Durham[‡]	10	AA

*O&D = origin and destination.

[†]AA = American Airlines; UA = United Airlines; DL = Delta; CO = Continental; FL = Frontier Airlines; RC = Republic Airlines; NW = Northwest Airlines; TW = TWA; OZ = Ozark Airlines; EA = Eastern Airlines; WA = Western Airlines; AL = Allegheny/USAir; PI = Piedmont.

[‡]Potential hub sites.

Durham, and Richmond in the Southeast. Data were collected on the 16 potential north/south hub cities, including such factors as local population base that would use the airport, industry O&D passengers to and from the city, industry passengers enplaned at the city, passengers per operation, load factor, and carriers with high enplanement shares at each airport (Exhibits 18 and 19).

Some cities were eliminated early in the process because they failed to meet all or most of the selection criteria. Several locations were difficult to eliminate because they met all or most of the selection criteria. At the end of the first phase of screening, seven cities were eliminated and nine remained in competition (Exhibit 20).

In the second phase, special attention was given to the local market and the connecting O&D flow (passengers per day each way, PDEW), using the city pairs likely to be served by each hub. The top five sites for connecting traffic flow were Nashville, Greensboro/High Point, Atlanta, Raleigh/Durham, and Charlotte. On the basis of local plus connecting flow, the top six choices were Atlanta, Nashville, Charlotte, Raleigh/Durham, Greensboro/High Point, and Washington Dulles (Washington National had slot problems and was taken out of consideration) (Exhibit 20).

Exhibit 18 Five-Year Plan: Status of the North-South Hub by Population and Historical Traffic for the Year Ending Second Quarter 1983

Area	(1) Population Base (1/1/84 estimate)	(2) Industry O&D Passengers PDEW*	(3) Industry Enplaned Passengers per Day	(4)[†] Annual Travel Rate (O&D trips per population)	Carriers with High-Enplanement Shares[‡]
Northeast					
LaGuardia	11,658,821	19,188	22,797	1.00	EA: 31%; AA: 14%; DL: 10%
Kennedy		12,605	17,484		TW: 20%; AA: 18%; EA: 18%; PA: 16%
Philadelphia	6,403,109	8,641	10,510	0.49	AL: 26%; EA: 18%; UA: 14%
Newark	5,610,795	17,423	16,594	1.13	PE: 18%; EA: 17%; AL: 15%; UA: 12%
Pittsburgh	3,728,852	6,805	3,747	0.67	AL: 75%
Baltimore	2,993,090	4,714	5,176	0.57	AL: 19%; EA: 16%; DL: 13%; UA: 12%
National	1,854,842	13,849	17,082	2.73	EA: 25%; AL: 12%
Dulles	1,544,695	2,115	3,121	0.50	UA: 30%; AA: 22%; NW: 12%
Southeast					
Atlanta	3,348,178	12,889	48,430	1.41	DL: 51%; EA: 41%
Memphis	2,063,733	2,858	6,292	0.51	RC: 44%; DL: 33%
Nashville	1,770,424	2,490	2,936	0.51	AA: 25%; RC: 20%; DL: 14%
Charlotte	1,642,418	2,636	8,863	0.59	PI: 68%; EA: 27%
Norfolk	1,446,731	3,068	3,435	0.77	PI: 45%; AL: 21%; EA: 16%
Greensboro/High Point	1,353,019	1,489	1,931	0.40	PI: 44%; EA: 31%; DL: 18%
Raleigh/Durham	1,311,595	2,276	2,737	0.63	EA: 35%; PI: 22%; DL: 20%
Richmond	1,079,327	1,112	1,275	0.38	PI: 55%; EA: 37%

* PDEW = per day each way.

[†] (4) = (2) × 365/(1).

[‡] See the footnote[†] in Exhibit 17 for the key for the airlines.

Five-Year Plan: Status of the North-South Hub by Historical Local Traffic for the Year Ending Second Quarter 1983 — **Exhibit 19**

Area	Industry O&D RPMs (000)* PDEW†	Industry Onboard RPMs (000)* PDEW†	Passengers per Operation	Load Factor
Northeast				
LaGuardia	14,420	14,578	84	59.6
Kennedy	19,760	26,653	118	65.1
Philadelphia	9,076	7,993	74	56.7
Newark	14,949	13,010	94	65.3
Pittsburgh	4,851	7,732	66	60.7
Baltimore	4,823	4,177	68	60.6
National	9,853	7,855	72	58.1
Dulles	3,396	5,601	90	62.1
Southeast				
Atlanta	9,075	30,942	80	56.6
Memphis	2,120	3,645	54	54.4
Nashville	1,850	1,568	64	55.9
Charlotte	1,696	3,991	64	57.1
Norfolk	2,050	1,430	62	54.6
Greensboro/High Point	1,044	866	53	48.7
Raleigh/Durham	1,617	1,211	54	58.3
Richmond	773	615	51	50.3

*RPM = revenue passenger-miles.

†PDEW = per day each way.

Five-Year Plan: Status of the North-South Hub by Local and Connecting O&D over Hub Passengers PDEW for the Year Ending Third Quarter 1983 (based on the city pairs likely to be served by each hub) — **Exhibit 20**

Hub City	Local Markets	Flow Markets	Nonstop in Flow Markets	Connecting Flow	Local Plus Connecting Flow
Atlanta	9524	32,980	20,701	12,279	21,803
Nashville	1695	43,351	28,701	14,650	16,345
Charlotte	1995	36,946	24,851	12,095	14,090
Raleigh/Durham	1817	38,283	26,033	12,250	14,067
National	5661*	29,661	21,576	8,085	13,746
Greensboro/High Point	1130	38,970	26,586	12,384	13,514
Baltimore	2322*	29,661	21,576	8,085	10,407
Dulles	2322*	29,661	21,576	8,085	10,407
Philadelphia	4329	14,144	8,584	5,560	9,889

*Local Washington traffic divided among three area airports on basis of airport preference shown in Washington Council of Governments 1981/1982 *Air Passenger Survey:* Washington National, 55%; Baltimore, 22.5%; Dulles, 22.5%.

The choices were then grouped under three broad sites:

1.   Nashville, Tennessee.
2.   Atlanta, Georgia; Raleigh/Durham, North Carolina; Charlotte, North Carolina; Greensboro/High Point, North Carolina.
3.   Washington Dulles.

Atlanta was already the hub city for Eastern and Delta. Piedmont had one of its hubs at Charlotte. Raleigh/Durham had higher local traffic and growth potential than Greensboro/High Point. Though not the main issue, Greensboro/High Point also presented some potential expansion problems. According to an executive of American Airlines who visited the Raleigh/Durham and Greensboro/High Point airports as part of the selection process:

> In Greensboro the airport configuration of the terminal is different from Raleigh/Durham. The Greensboro airport has a main concourse with two concourses off of it at 90 degree angles. The master plan designed for the airport included an extension at either end of the terminal. The airport authorities stated that it was a relatively easy matter to extend the terminal and create another concourse off of it. Our concern, however, was that because of leasing arrangements between the airport and the tenants such an extension required the approval of other airlines to the airport. That was a hindrance. We wanted to be able to go in and start the project. We did not want to be subject to perhaps competing airlines saying yes or no. Further, Greensboro did not have a second runway. At Raleigh/Durham a second runway was already in the process of being built and a new terminal did not require any consideration from the other airlines at the airport.

Thus, the final sites were reduced to Nashville, Raleigh/Durham, and Washington Dulles. After additional analyses and forecasts, Washington Dulles was also taken out of competition because its share of Washington local traffic was estimated to be less than Raleigh/Durham's for the foreseeable future. Further, the geography at Raleigh/Durham meant fewer connections in full-up hub comparisons.*

Subsequently, the process of elimination left American Airlines with two final choices: Nashville, Tennessee, and Raleigh/Durham, North Carolina.

■ Market Analysis

Nashville

The economy of Tennessee is expected to continue to grow at a healthy rate through the end of the century. Total employment in the state is expected to grow 1.33% a year, on the average, through 2005. Over that period, the state will create 709,520 new jobs, the eighteenth-largest increase of any state in the nation. The population of Tennessee is expected to grow steadily over the next two decades, increasing at an average rate of 0.9% a year. The total population of the state will grow from 4.68 million in 1983 to about 5.7 million by the turn of the century.

The Nashville metropolitan area led the state in durable-manufacturing job growth during the 1970s. Between 1983 and the year 2000, Nashville is expected

---

*Shortly after AA announced its north/south hub selection, three carriers (Continental, United, and Presidential) announced hubs at Dulles.

Examples of Comparative Service and Traffic: Nashville Versus Memphis and Raleigh/Durham Versus Charlotte   **Exhibit 21**

Reference City	Nashville			Memphis			BNA* O&D (as % of Memphis O&D)
	Nonstop	One Stop	Local O&D	Nonstop	One Stop	Local O&D	
Charlotte	4	—	52.2	2	2	34.0	153
New York	3	5	262.3	6	6	211.2	124
Washington	4	1	119.1	6	1	98.4	121
Philadelphia	2	1	66.8	2	3	55.7	120
Tampa	0	0	47.0	3	1	50.0	94
Kansas City	0	1	29.8	5	0	37.6	79
Houston	0	0	72.7	6	1	94.4	77
New Orleans	1	0	39.9	9	0	73.8	54

Reference City	Raleigh/Durham			Charlotte			RDU† O&D (as % of Charlotte O&D)
	Nonstop	One Stop	Local O&D	Nonstop	One Stop	Local O&D	
Washington	10	—	191.0	10	5	108.6	176
New York	15	3	567.7	15	9	366.9	155
Boston	2	6	113.8	5	3	81.4	140
Orlando	1	1	49.1	5	—	45.6	108
Chicago	2	2	108.9	9	3	126.5	86
Philadelphia	2	—	75.5	7	—	99.3	76
Miami	1	—	52.9	5	3	84.7	63
Pittsburgh	3	—	36.7	8	—	59.8	62

*BNA represents the Nashville airport.

†RDU represents the Raleigh/Durham airport.

to create approximately 100,000 manufacturing and service jobs. Nashville is a dynamic city with continued high-growth potential. The Association of American Geographers selected Nashville as one of the four "best places to live." *Advertising Age* ranked Nashville as one of the "top ten growth markets in the nation." During the height of the 1981–1982 recession, the unemployment rate in Nashville was 7%, versus the national average of 9%–10%. Nashville has a balanced work force: 23% manufacturing, 22% trade, 21% service, and 17% government. The area has 16 universities, colleges, and technical schools. There is low union membership. Nashville is famous for its music industry. It is the sixth-largest publishing center and the state capital.

The closest hub city to Nashville is Memphis. Using eight reference cities of Charlotte, New York, Washington, Philadelphia, Tampa, Kansas City, Houston, and New Orleans, the local O&D for Nashville—as opposed to that for Memphis—is larger in the first four cities and smaller in the remaining four. For each of the reference cities, Exhibit 21 shows the comparative nonstop, one-stop, and local O&D service as well as the Nashville O&D as a percentage of that of Memphis.

Serving the eastern half of the country diagonally through Nashville would provide American with a relative advantage in terms of travel time, mileage, and yield (Exhibit 22). Four examples of this comparative advantage are given

Exhibit 22   **Geographic Area Served North/South by Nashville Hub**

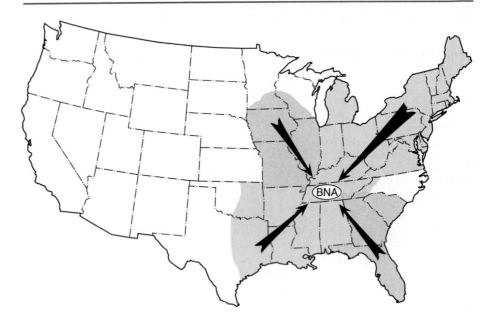

Exhibit 23   **Examples of Implied Cost and Yield Advantage for Nashville**

Carrier	Connect Station	Elapsed Minutes	Indexed	
			Mileage	Yield*
Detroit–Huntsville				
Eastern	Atlanta	204	100	100
Delta	Atlanta	210	100	100
Republic	Memphis	195	106	94
American	Nashville	153	75	133
Philadelphia–Little Rock				
TWA	Saint Louis	242	100	100
Delta	Atlanta	245	100	100
Republic	Memphis	210	91	110
American	Nashville	210	90	110
Minneapolis/St. Paul–Birmingham				
Delta	Atlanta	215	100	100
Eastern	Atlanta	224	100	100
Republic	Memphis	200	88	114
American	Nashville	182	84	119
Chicago–Huntsville				
Delta	Atlanta	205	100	100
Eastern	Atlanta	209	100	100
Republic	Memphis	175	89	112
American	Nashville	144	68	148

*Yield = percentage of $100 over mileage.

in Exhibit 23. This exhibit shows that for the sample pair cities of Detroit–Huntsville, Philadelphia–Little Rock, Minneapolis/St. Paul–Birmingham, and Chicago–Huntsville, American would enjoy a significant time, mileage, and yield advantage if it were to use Nashville as its connecting station. The time advantage can be as high as 65 minutes, with indexed mileage and yield superiority of 32 and 48 points, respectively.

Raleigh/Durham

The population of North Carolina is expected to grow at an average rate of 0.84% a year between 1983 and the beginning of the twenty-first century. In 2005, North Carolina will be the twelfth most populous state in the nation, with a population of 7.3 million. Total employment in North Carolina will grow at an average annual rate of 1.18% during the period from 1983 to the end of the century. It is estimated that by the year 2000, the state will have about 850,000 more jobs than it had in 1983.

Raleigh/Durham/Chapel Hill (Wake, Durham, and Orange counties) is also a highly dynamic and growth-oriented area. It experienced an annual population growth rate of 1.8% between 1983 and 1987, more than double the statewide rate for the same period. The average household income for the area rose from $25,000 in 1983 to $42,000 in 1987, an increase of 68%. In 1983, the gross retail sales in the three-county area exceeded $4.4 billion. The Rand McNally *Places Rated Almanac* ranks Raleigh/Durham number three in the category of "the most desirable area in which to live." The area has four major universities: North Carolina State University in Raleigh, Duke University and North Carolina Central University in Durham, and the University of North Carolina at Chapel Hill. Though the area has a diversified economic base, tobacco and textiles remain as strong industries in the region. Durham contains the Research Triangle Park, a nationally unique planned research center for private and public scientific/medical research and high-tech development. The park employs more than 22,000 people, with an annual payroll of over $700 million. During the height of the 1981–1982 recession, the unemployment rate was 4.2% in the area, versus the national average of 9%–10%. The area has the highest concentration of Ph.D.s per square mile in the nation. Raleigh is the state capital.

The closest hub city to Raleigh/Durham is Charlotte. The relative position of Raleigh/Durham and Charlotte in terms of nonstop, one-stop, and local O&D traffic is given in Exhibit 21 for the eight reference cities of Washington, New York, Boston, Orlando, Chicago, Philadelphia, Miami, and Pittsburgh. This exhibit shows that the true local O&D demand at Raleigh/Durham may well be larger than it is at Charlotte. Serving the most eastern north/south corridor through a potential Raleigh/Durham hub would give American a consistent time, mileage, and yield advantage over the competing carriers. Exhibits 24 and 25 provide examples of this comparative advantage for the four sample pair cities of La Guardia–Jacksonville, Philadelphia–Savannah, Pittsburgh–Ft. Meyers, and Baltimore–Orlando.

Nashville and Raleigh/Durham Versus Atlanta, Charlotte, and Memphis

American's new north/south hub had to compete with a number of established hubs in the east. Atlanta and Memphis (two multidirectional hubs) as well as Charlotte (a predominantly north/south hub) posed the highest level of com-

Exhibit 24   Geographic Area Served North/South by Raleigh/Durham Hub

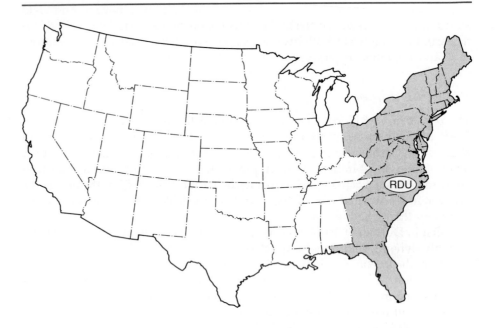

Exhibit 25   Examples of Implied Cost and Yield Advantage for Raleigh/Durham

Carrier	Connect Station	Elapsed Minutes	Indexed	
			Mileage	Yield*
LaGuardia–Jacksonville				
Eastern	Atlanta	234	100	100
Delta	Atlanta	240	100	100
Piedmont	Charlotte	209	82	121
American	Raleigh/Durham	192	81	123
Philadelphia-Savannah				
Piedmont	Charlotte	160	100	100
Eastern	Charlotte	163	100	100
Delta	Atlanta	217	133	75
American	Raleigh/Durham	155	95	105
Pittsburgh–Ft. Meyers				
Delta	Atlanta	215	100	100
Eastern	Atlanta	225	100	100
People Express	Newark, N.J.	305	133	74
American	Raleigh/Durham	200	96	105
Baltimore–Orlando				
Delta	Atlanta	215	100	100
Eastern	Atlanta	220	100	100
Piedmont	Charlotte	194	85	118
American	Raleigh/Durham	173	81	124

*Yield = percentage of $100 over mileage.

petition. A close review of the relative merits of Nashville and Raleigh/Durham suggested that collectively they would provide access to virtually all north/south markets of significance.

Among the five competing hub cities of Atlanta, Memphis, Nashville, Raleigh/Durham and Charlotte, Nashville and Raleigh/Durham had two of the highest population growth rates for 1970–1985. In terms of average daily local O&D, Charlotte, Nashville, and Raleigh/Durham experienced the sharpest growth during the five-year period of 1979–1984 (Exhibit 26). The Nashville and Raleigh/Durham flow markets were estimated to be competitive with 73 of Delta's top 100 revenue markets served via Atlanta, 70 of Eastern's top 100 revenue markets served via Atlanta, 78 of Piedmont's top 100 revenue markets served via Charlotte, and 75 of Republic's top 100 revenue markets served via Memphis.

Elapsed time from origin to destination has always been an important consideration influencing buyer selection of a particular airline or flight. In the existing computer reservations systems (CRS), both "screen presence" and "line position" are influenced by elapsed time. American's service through Nashville and Raleigh/Durham was estimated to involve less mileage in over 65% of the flow occurrences by an average of about 5% to 6%. American's scheduled elapsed time (flying plus ground time) would be shorter in over 78% of the cases due to (a) reduced circuitry, with the potential of resulting in lower costs, higher yield, and improved CRS positioning; (b) less congestion at the hub airports; and (c) reduced ground/connection time at smaller, less complex directional hubs.

Thus, American Airlines, already committed to the establishment of a hub in the East as an integral part of its deregulation and growth strategies, had to choose between Raleigh/Durham and Nashville, two equally attractive sites for a new north/south hub. The survival and prosperity of American Airlines during the highly competitive postregulation years was believed to depend on this strategic decision.

Population Growth and Average Daily Local O&D Among Potential North/South Hub Cities　　　　　　　　　　　　　　　　　　　　　　**Exhibit 26**

North/South Hub Cities	Population Growth Trends			O&D Growth Comparisons		
	Population, 1985 Estimate	1970–1980 Growth	1980–1985 Growth	Average Daily Local O&D, Year Ending 9/30/84	5-Year Growth, 9/79–9/84	3-Year Growth, 9/81–8/94
Atlanta	3,361,000	23.2%	6.4%	13,959	6.6%	10.2%
Memphis	2,137,000	10.9	3.8	2,925	(21.5)	(2.6)
Nashville	1,853,000	20.8	5.3	2,809	7.5	13.0
Charlotte	1,715,000	15.5	7.2	2,931	20.3	27.4
Raleigh/Durham	1,335,000	17.6	8.5	2,793	33.8	41.8

446

CASE 9

■ **Ranking in the Industry Seven Years After the Deregulation**

Among the major carriers in 1979, American ranked number eight in terms of its operating earnings and number two with respect to its net earnings. By 1985 the company had improved its position in both of these areas to number one in the industry. In terms of operating margin, American was number eight in 1979 but up to number two in 1985 (Exhibit 27). From an operational point of view, American's load factor ranking dropped from number one in 1979 to number three in 1985. However, when 1985 ended, not only was American the second-largest carrier in the nation in terms of fleet size and passengers carried, but also it ranked number one in available seat-miles, revenue passenger-miles, and profitability.

Exhibit 27   **American's Ranking Among the Major Carriers, 1979–1985**

Item	1979	1980	1981	1982	1983	1984	1985
Operating earnings	8	10	3	4	1	2	1
Net earnings	2	11	3	4	1	3	1
Operating margin	8	8	4	4	2	5	2
Load factor	1	5	2	1	1	3	3

Chaparral Steel Company

Mark J. Kroll, John W. Simmons, University of Texas at Tyler

In 1973 Texas Industries, Inc., of Dallas, also known as TXI, a construction materials (cement, aggregates, and concrete products) company, and Co-Steel International Ltd. of Canada determined to build a steel mill as a joint venture. The initial attraction of a small town 25 miles south of Dallas to the constructors of a steel "mini-mill" was its proximity to a major population center, large power supplies, highways, and railroads. At the time, Midlothian, Texas, seemed an unlikely choice, but, as the story goes, Co-Steel Chairman Gerald Heffernan saw a Midlothian Chamber of Commerce bulletin board notice which read, "Need money? Try working," and he was finally convinced that they had found the sought-after site for the new mill. The farm and ranch lands in the area are peopled with a hard working stock deeply imbued with the work ethic that management was seeking. Few of the locals had ever worked in a steel mill, and as one manager observed, "We didn't want people who had learned bad work habits."

TXI's decision to start its own steel company sprang rather naturally from its building materials business, since steel reinforcement is required in so much of construction. Forecasting a reinforcing bar shortage that never developed, the new TXI venture, christened Chaparral Steel Company, had its initial steel production greeted by a glut in the rebar market. Observed one member of Chaparral's top management: "We had to diversify, and fast." Fortunately for the new manufacturer, flexibility, a trait that has virtually eluded domestic "Big

Exhibit 1   **TXI Business Segment Information ($ in thousands)**

	1988	1987	1986
Net Sales			
Steel	$376,398	$318,807	$297,155
Cement/concrete	258,936	270,254	351,075
	$635,334	$589,061	$648,230
Operating Profit			
Steel	$ 60,496	$ 42,171	$ 37,178
Cement/concrete	3,233	14,150	32,431
	63,729	56,321	69,609
Corporate expense (income)			
Administrative and general	14,605	16,912	14,836
Interest expense	38,043	38,740	41,880
Other income	(998)	(2,262)	(14,107)
Income before taxes and other items	$ 12,079	$ 2,931	$ 27,000
Depreciation, Depletion and Amortization			
Steel	$ 21,566	$ 23,567	$ 22,433
Cement/concrete	29,339	31,347	33,221
Corporate	634	510	790
	$ 51,539	$ 55,424	$ 56,444
Capital Expenditures			
Steel	$ 22,265	$ 14,281	$ 7,019
Cement/concrete	17,443	14,422	40,969
Corporate	259	403	573
	$ 39,967	$ 29,106	$ 48,561
Identifiable Assets			
Steel	$313,452	$310,063	$298,666
Cement/concrete	281,635	299,874	323,510
Corporate	67,026	68,836	86,607
	$662,113	$678,773	$708,783

Steel" firms, is one of the drawing cards within the mini-mill segment of the steel industry. Unlike the bigger, more complex "integrated" mills, the mini-mills are basically recycling plants, albeit technologically sophisticated ones. Having scaled-down operations and including fewer steps in the manufacturing process provides the mini-mill with significantly more margin for error and therefore more flexibility than exists in the typical integrated mill.

The town of Midlothian (current population 3219) has achieved no small degree of acclaim as the setting for a very successful player in the nation's steel industry. Indeed, Chaparral has proven it possible to be profitable and competitive in an industry facing perhaps the most difficult period in its history (see Exhibit 1). When U.S. Steel (now USX) lost $2.5 billion in 1982, Chaparral had a profit of $11 million. In fiscal 1987, Chaparral produced and shipped a company record of over 1.2 million tons of steel, and for the first time, over half of sales for TXI, which became the 100% owner in November 1985, were represented by Chaparral. Pursuing market share amid its efforts to be the low-cost producer in the marketplace, Chaparral, in fiscal 1987, produced and sold more tonnage, in a greater variety and over a wider geographic market, than in any previous year. This record production was achieved in the face of what TXI's President and CEO, Robert D. Rogers, referring to Texas and surrounding states, TXI's locus of operations, called "the most stagnant economic growth since before Texas Industries was founded in 1951." In his letter to shareholders, dated July 15, 1987, Rogers announced that initial shipments of steel were made that same month to Western Europe and noted that Chaparral's impressive results were accomplished in "only an average market for structural products and a declining market during the year for bar products." Chaparral is one of the most productive steel firms in the world in terms of labor, and it is the nation's tenth largest steelmaker, providing steel products to 44 states, Canada, and now Western Europe. The firm has been the only U.S. mini-mill to lower costs enough to make a profit in foreign markets. Efforts have also been made to crack the bureaucratic obstacles of the Japanese market.

Since the first day of operations, May 5, 1975, Chaparral has used unorthodox managerial methods to achieve and maintain its competitiveness. According to Tom Peters: "If you wrote down the ten most widely believed principles about managing in this century, you would find that Chaparral violates every one of them." Peters, one of the authors of *In Search of Excellence*, writes that some business savants consider Gordon Forward, Chaparral's President and CEO, to be "the most advanced thinker in American management today." Notwithstanding such hyperbole, the Midlothian steel firm is ever-watchful of its competitive environment and looks to the future rather than resting on its impressive early accomplishments. Noting that this U.S. steel-producer is "one of the few profitable ones," Peters explains that Forward manages his firm "more as a laboratory than as a factory." Forward, a native of Canada, armed with a Ph.D. in metallurgy from M.I.T. and a healthy distaste for the traditional inefficiencies of Big Steel, has directed his company with managerial acumen, perceptive marketing, and a drive towards technological innovation. Company executives credit Chaparral's success to three major areas of concentration: A marketing strategy sympathetic to customer needs, an insatiable thirst for technological improvement, and, perhaps, most significantly, the application of participatory management techniques that encourage employee creativity.

At start up in 1975, Chaparral operated with only the basics of a mini-mill plant: A single electric arc furnace, a continuous billet caster, and a rolling mill, with an annual capacity of just over 400,000 tons. By 1978, the firm was a leader in mini-mill technology. From 1978 to 1981, Chaparral earned a pretax average of $18 million per year. Again, this was at a time when the U.S. steel industry as a whole was in the doldrums. Early in 1982, Chaparral's second phase of expansion brought on-line a second electric arc furnace, another continuous billet caster, and a larger rolling mill. This $180 million, largely debt-financed, expansion could not have become operational at a worse time, paralleling the start of the worst steel recession in 50 years. Steel prices tumbled 20–50%, the industry's operating rate fell below 40% of capacity, and much of Chaparral's debt, at floating rates, floated to the outer reaches of the biosphere. Fueled by high interest rates, the dollar climbed to new heights, imported steel flooded domestic markets, and Chaparral, due to merciless economic conditions, faced losses between 1982 and 1984, returning to profitability in mid-1985. Maintaining a long-term vision of its industry, the highly-automated mini-mill tripled its annual capacity between 1982 and 1987. With its new product development program, the firm shipped approximately 1.3 million tons of steel to more than 900 customers in fiscal 1988. Furthermore, Chaparral has added an average of 100,000 tons to its annual output during each of the past 13 years.

From the outset, TXI and Co-Steel wanted to build the most modern mini-mill that they possibly could. Not suffering from the myopia that has diminished Big Steel, Chaparral has changed and grown constantly, if only in incremental steps. The attitude at TXI and Chaparral is that it is possible to make money in nongrowth industries if you are good enough. As a result of its vision and diligence, the Midlothian firm currently produces and ships more tonnage than any single U.S. steel mill constructed in the past 30 years. Although future growth in the mini-mill segment is expected to slow somewhat from what it has been within the past decade or so, industry experts still see opportunities for additional mini-mill market growth. The "minis" are expected to retain an advantage because of lower raw materials costs, utilization of new technology, efficient operation, plant location, perceptive marketing, flexible work rules, and consequent higher productivity, but saturated markets and cheap imports are forcing the mini-mills to continue seeking new ways to grow. Prior to 1982, Chaparral was a part of the much-publicized mini-mill phenomenon, but the future holds ever-greater challenges. In 1985, 4 Sunbelt mini-mills closed their doors, and global overcapacity portends a continued threat of industry shake-out. Older, less technologically-competent minis are particularly vulnerable. Producers of steel are differentiated nowadays mostly by price, product mix, and service. State-of-the-art technology is so accessible around the world that quality is no longer optional. The challenge which Chaparral has successfully faced in the past and will continue to face in the foreseeable future is to maintain its responsive managerial style, marketing sensitivity, and technological currency and consequent productivity gains. It appears that Chaparral is not striving to become the new Big Steel but rather desires to maintain its status as a highly competitive niche-player.

CHAPARRAL MANAGEMENT

■ Robert D. Rogers, Chairman of the Board, Chaparral Steel Company

Robert Rogers, a graduate of Yale and Harvard Business School, has been with TXI for 25 years. Mr. Rogers, Chairman of the Board of TXI and a TXI Director since 1970, is Chairman of the Board for the Dallas Chamber of Commerce, the immediate past Chairman of the 11th Federal Reserve District, and has numerous additional professional and community associations. Another TXI Director, Edward W. Kelley, Jr., went to the Board of Governors of the Federal Reserve System in 1987.

In an interview, Mr. Rogers reflected back on the unlikely success of an upstart company in a declining steel industry:

> We went into the carbon steel business when everyone else was going out of it. The biggest advantage we had was that we didn't have any plant, didn't have any customers, didn't have any employees or management and we didn't really know anything about how to make steel. We're still learning. Once we learn it, we're going to be in big trouble.

Pondering further the benefit of being the new kid on the block, Rogers observed:

> If we would have known the steel business, we would have known that the only way you could go forth with a company of any size would be to be unionized. Not knowing the steel business and being the largest nonunion cement company in the U.S., we felt it was far better to represent the legitimate interests of employees ourselves rather than turn it over to some outside partner.

Concluding his remarks on Chaparral's unorthodox approach, Rogers said:

> Another thing was to hire employees who by and large did not come from industrial backgrounds. They came from rural backgrounds. The steel plant is next door to our largest cement plant and we have the same type of employees there. We knew they were hard-working and imaginative, so they didn't know you were supposed to spend 3 to 4 man-hours per ton of steel. When we got to 1.8 or 1.6 and were working to get down substantially less than that, they didn't know that there's a limit on how many tons of steel you can get per man-hour.

Despite recent economic setbacks for TXI as a whole, Chaparral remains strong and is moving forward, and Rogers and the TXI Board of Directors are still planning for the long-term. Fiscal 1988 was the 26th consecutive year of increased cash dividends to TXI shareholders. Notwithstanding the virtual absence of earnings, due in large part to the regional construction slump and the dumping in TXI markets of imported cement, the Directors maintained cash dividends at the annual rate of $0.80 per year with a year-end stock dividend of 4% (see Exhibit 2).

■ Chaparral Steel Company Board of Directors

The Chaparral Board of Directors provides a wealth of educational, professional, and cultural experience. Past and present directors have served as university trustees and in other capacities of institutional leadership and most have other corporate affiliations. Co-Steel Chairman Heffernan, who is involved with several Canadian mining and metallurgical professional groups, has been a TXI Director since 1986 and is also a Chaparral Director. In October 1987, the board was reduced in number and reorganized to have a nonTXI majority. New board members are John M. Belk, Chairman, Belk Stores Services, Inc., Charlotte, North Carolina; Dr. Gerhard Liener, Chief Financial Officer, Daimler-Benz AG, Stuttgart, West Germany; and William J. Shields, President and CEO, Co-Steel International Ltd., Toronto, Ontario, Canada.

■ Gordon E. Forward, President and CEO, Chaparral Steel Company

Gordon Forward is described as the architect of the winning Chaparral formula and has received from various quarters the lion's share of credit for making the formula a success. After leaving a successful career with Big Steel, Forward has come up through the ranks of the mini-mill industry and has displayed a great willingness to undertake managerial experiments. Forward claims the legen-

Exhibit 2	Selected Financial Data, TXI and Subsidiaries ($ in thousands except for per share)							
	1988	**1987**	**1986**	**1985**	**1984**	**1983**	**1982**	**1981**
Results of Operations								
Net sales	635,334	589,061	648,230	343,688	335,381	321,468	282,713	285,003
Net income	13,053	1253	22,114	17,597	12,300	18,691	18,332	30,411
Return on common equity	6.8%	0.6%	11.9%	9.9%	7.2%	11.4%	11.9%	22.4%
Per Share Information								
Net income	1.09	—	2.26	1.93	1.32	2.00	1.96	3.22
Cash dividends	0.80	0.76	0.73	0.70	0.67	0.64	0.62	0.60
Stock dividends, distributions	4%	4%	4%	4%	4%	4%	4%	4%
Other Information								
Average common shares outstanding (in 000's)	10,160	10,039	9574	9074	9285	9299	9339	9427
Number of common stockholders	5632	5975	5508	5811	6111	6286	6605	6785
Common stock price (high/low)	40–24	31–22	31–23	29–21	38–25	36–15	30–14	31–18

dary Captain Bill "Scrap Heap" Jones, a 19th century steel mill superintendent, is a role model for his approach. Of Jones, Forward says:

> If there was a better machine to do a job, the old one went quickly on the scrap heap. He also fought for his men's welfare and inspired them to set world steel production records. And they loved him for it. I think the industry ought to take a new look at Captain Jones' ideas. (Kantrow, 1986, p. 96)

The operating philosophy at Chaparral of concentrating on technological improvement, as well as on marketing and participatory management, emerged as early as 1974.

Mr. Forward, a native of Vancouver, B.C., has been referred to as "a refugee from Big Steel bureaucracy." He was hired as Chaparral's Executive Vice President in 1974. A vocal critic of the stagnated domestic steel industry, Forward, in an interview, remarked:

> U.S. steel producers had no real competition after the war. Every time the unions demanded more wages or whatever, the managers said, "Fine, we'll simply pass the costs on to the consumer." Well, this went on for more than 20 years and had a real effect on how managers thought about staying on top technologically . . . Of course, they spent money on improvement. But they went about it the way that bureaucracies are likely to go about something like that: They kept tacking new things on to their established operations. (Kantrow, 1986, p. 102)

As steel labor costs rose in the 1970s, the mini-mills, quickly adopting foreign technological improvements, were able to seize new markets, and Chaparral was a leader of the pack. Says Forward: "In our end of the business, we can't afford to act like fat cats."

NATURE OF THE STEEL INDUSTRY

▪ Big Steel

The term "Big Steel" generally refers to the large traditional "integrated" steel mills, so named because they have the capability of processing coke and iron ore into a number of steel products of a wide range of size and shape. Steel mill products are consumed by industries touching virtually every aspect of daily life, principally transportation, construction, machinery, and containers. Prior to 1970, the United States had long been the world's leading steel producer, but, by that time, the domestic steel industry had been declining for over 20 years. Most U.S. steel mills were of pre-World War II vintage, and, despite periodic renovation, the mills lacked the efficient layouts, the economies of scale, and the more productive technologies utilized in the "greenfield" mills of Japan and Western Europe.

After World War II, domestic steel negotiations with the United Steelworkers began an upward spiral of wage rates, disproportionate to the growth of labor productivity, thereby increasing unit labor costs. Wishing to reduce escalating wage increases, which averaged 6.6% annually between 1947–57, a period of relatively low inflation, Big Steel accepted a long strike (July–November 1959). Foreign producers consequently filled the gap, and the United States became a net importer of steel in 1959. Imports grew to an average 15% of consumption in the 1970s, 19% in 1981, and over 20% in 1982.

The world steel industry was becoming much more competitive and internationalized as world exports of finished steel products increased dramatically during the 1960s, prompted by declining raw material and shipping costs, and powered by foreign investment in modern facilities. U.S. steel exports tumbled as Japanese and Western European exports shot skyward. State-of-the-art technology became available to any producer willing to pay for it, and product quality became essentially uniform across geopolitical boundaries. During the 1970s, domestic steel production grew only modestly, profits remained depressed as competition from imports grew, and, as a result, the U.S. industry's ability to add new capacity was severely constrained. Domestic industry employment began a steady decline in 1972, and, in 1982, reached the lowest levels since data collection began during the Great Depression. In 1982 the U.S. steel industry lost a record $3.2 billion. By mid-1987 the industry's operating losses had reached some $6 billion.

In March 1982, testifying before the U.S. Senate, Dr. Donald F. Barnett, speaking for the American Iron and Steel Institute (AISI) regarding international competitiveness in the domestic steel industry, stated:

> Perhaps the most significant determinant of international competitiveness is labor productivity. . . . However, even if labor productivity is low, a product can still be competitive if there are other compensating advantages, e.g., lower labor rates as persist in many developing countries. Alternatively, an investment which raises productivity can actually decrease cost competitiveness if the capital cost of the investment outweighs the labor savings. Hence, improved labor productivity cannot be the ultimate goal in and of itself. International competitiveness in the steel industry, therefore, must also look at capital efficiency, e.g., capacity use, labor costs, raw material costs, yield rates, and energy efficiency. . . . (Bureau of National Affairs Special Report)

Exhibit 3

Average Man-Hours to Produce One Ton of Steel

Mill	1977	1986	1988
U.S. integrated mills	10.04	6.91	—
Japanese integrated mills	8.94	8.61	—
U.S. mini-mills	—	2.00	—
Chaparral	—	1.60	1.50

Other factors which determine industry competitiveness include regulatory costs and materials availability. Despite recent turmoil, the domestic integrated mills have increased their productivity in the last decade considerably vis-à-vis the Japanese mills (see Exhibit 3). By 1986, AISI reports, the U.S. steel industry had become the most efficient in the world. Generally speaking, while the domestic steel industry is competitive in energy and materials costs and use, it is less competitive in terms of labor costs and productivity as compared to foreign competitors.

Clearly, the integrated mills were attempting to respond to the changing market conditions as indicated by improved productivity rates. The big mills have gradually improved their marketing techniques by specializing in limited ranges of higher-quality, cost-competitive products. In a word, the Big Steel firms are no longer able to function as steel "supermarkets". The emphasis in recent years has been on "restructuring", what one industry executive referred to as a "state of accelerating self-liquidation". Yet, the "great shake-out" has had a positive side, that is, corporate reorganizations, steel unit spin-offs, forced mergers, management or employee buyouts, and Chapter 11 bankruptcies have required firms to pare costs and exit from unprofitable markets. In 1987 the domestic integrated mills began to emerge from this period of price-war activity, prices firmed for the first time in years as the dollar declined in relation to other currencies, earnings improved amid productivity gains, and export activity began awakening. Unfortunately, the stock market crash of October 19, 1987, occurred just as the moribund steel industry was reviving. Despite the 33% drop in steel stocks, analysts predict sharp increases in earnings, due to a falling dollar and steel import quotas legislated through September 1989. Despite recent difficulties in earning, attracting, and borrowing sufficient investment capital, the domestic integrated firms have retained a large share of the U.S. market.

The growth of U.S. production is projected to remain relatively low due to trends in consumption and output. Projections of world steel production indicate a continuing malaise in the industrialized nations contrasted with rapid growth in the developing countries. Steel production capacity, by one estimate, had increased by 20% in developing countries and had eroded by 3% in the United States by 1990.

The hard times which domestic steel has been facing have many causes, including: poor management, labor squabbles, obsolete technology, foreign competition, and product substitutes such as aluminum and fiber-reinforced plastics. Many of U.S. Big Steel's problems can be attributed to their own sluggishness and complacency in technology and marketing matters, but the problems of integrated mills are proving to be somewhat systematic as the industries in Japan and Europe have begun to face problems similar to their American counterparts. As Dr. Barnett foresaw, developing countries are entering the steel industry with relative ease and success, and some experts doubt whether the large, inflexible integrated mills will survive the 20th century.

■ Mini-mills

The steel industry can be divided into 3 segments of different economic and technical profiles: the integrated mills, the mini-mills, and the specialty steel mills. Domestically, the minis are the chief competitors of the integrated mills. The specialty steel mills account for only 5% of U.S. output, but they manufacture much more expensive products than do the minis and account for a much higher percentage of total revenues. The minis and specialty steel mills have avoided the worst of the recent industry turmoil, but it is the mini-mills that are expected to make the greatest gains in the domestic market into the 1990s, at the expense of the integrated mills.

The mini-mill concept was relatively slow in arriving in the United States. The method had thrived in Japan and Western Europe for over 20 years when Chaparral was founded as one of the United States' first operations of its kind in 1973. Interestingly enough, North America's first mini-mill was established in Canada in 1962 by a former manager of Co-Steel, the Canadian holding company that played a seminal role in the creation of Chaparral. Since the 1960s, when 10–12 mini-mills shared roughly 2% of the domestic steel market, the number of domestic mini-mills has grown to around 55, with a market share just over 20%.

The mini-mill segment has been able to remain relatively profitable by restricting product range and therefore the level of capitalization required, by utilizing locally-generated scrap and thereby lowering transportation costs, and by marketing in the vicinity of the mill. Furthermore, the mini-mills have typically concentrated on relatively high-volume, low-cost steels. Unlike Big Steel, the minis, in order to increase productivity, have relied on innovative processing technology, much of which comes from abroad and which they can adapt to suit their individual purpose. In contrast, the specialty steel industry has typically developed its new technologies in-house. Whereas the specialty steel mill invests in its own R&D and the integrated mill is constrained by relatively larger capital investment requirements and must work under restrictive union labor contracts, the mini-mill is more able to invest capital in new technology, and, by so doing, the mini-mills have recaptured markets that Big Steel had abandoned to imports.

The significance of potential foreign competition in the mini-mill segment is mitigated by the dominant role played by transportation costs. On this topic, Mr. Forward has said of Chaparral:

> We adopt certain goals. In our beams, for instance, the Koreans are the most efficient producers. So we just adapt so that we will have a lower labor content than the shipping costs of beams from Korea to the West Coast. If they have zero labor costs, we'll still have a competitive advantage. (Melloan, 1988, p. 29)

Furthermore, as mentioned earlier, the minis have the advantage of relatively low raw material costs and flexible work rules. In addition, firms such as Chaparral, Nucor, and Birmingham Steel have much lower base wage rates, but provide generous bonus programs for high levels of team productivity.

Exhibit 4   **Steelmaking process**

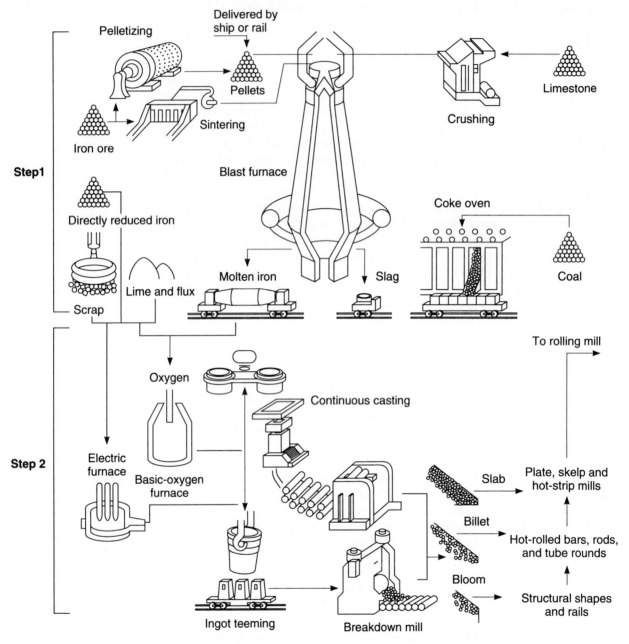

Integrated steel mills produce steel using both Steps 1 and 2; beginning with iron ore, coal, and limestone, they go through most of the steps presented here. Mini-mills use scrap as their raw material and complete Step 2, using either an electric furnace or a basic-oxygen furnace. Most recently built mini-mills use an electric furnace and continuous-casting technology.

The "mini-mill" is so-named, not so much because it is small, but because its operations entail only a part of the integrated steelmaking process (see Exhibit 4). The mini-mill avoids almost entirely the integrated mill's energy- and capital-intensive "front end" of steelmaking, that is, the iron-smelting process, including the mining and preparation of raw materials and the blast-furnace operation. The mini-mill begins with steel scrap, flux, and occasionally directly-reduced iron. The scrap is melted in an electric furnace, poured into ladles, and then transferred to a continuous-casting machine. Continuous casting is the casting of billets, blooms, or slabs directly from the molten steel. The success of domestic minis is due in part to the use of continuous billet-casting, which has been standard practice in minis since around 1970 and which increases yield 18% over ingot-casting, common to conventional steel mills. Only about half of the domestic integrated mills utilize continuous casters. Continuing to emphasize innovation, Chaparral has a recently-commissioned horizontal casting machine which came on line in 1988 and should add materially to productivity (see Exhibit 5).

Recycling scrap, or the processing of secondary materials, results in less waste and reduces overall raw materials requirements. All 3 segments of the domestic industry use scrap to one degree or another but only the mini-mills are almost wholly dependent on it. The United States was estimated to have had a scrap inventory of 620 billion metric tons in 1982, and, with annual accumulations, supply is expected to meet demand for at least several decades. Chaparral processes some 300,000 cars per year, or one every 20 seconds, and this provides roughly 30% of the firm's raw material. The use of steel substitutes (plastic, etc.) in automobiles is cause for some concern in the industry, but Mr. Forward maintains a sense of humor:

> There is a possibility we may have to go back to an iron ore base some day. For the moment, however, we are all right. We keep on importing Toyotas, which have a 7-year life. It takes us 7 years to get a new Toyota into our furnace. (Melloan, 1988, p. 29)

In the meantime, there is what some call a "ubiquitous availability" of domestically-generated scrap. Another dimension of the problem concerns the impurity content of the scrap, which prevents production of certain high-quality grades of steel.

The mini-mill products of the recent past have been simple and limited in variety. They have included wire rods, reinforcing rods, and various bar prod-

Horizontal Continuous Caster: Baltimore Works, Armco   **Exhibit 5**

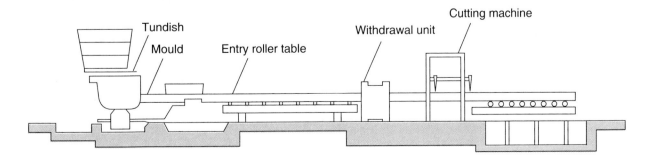

ucts. The bar forms, classified by cross-sectional shape, include flats, rounds, and squares. Mini-mills may also manufacture light I beams, T beams, angles (with 90 degree cross section), and channels (with a shallow "U" in cross section). A product is a light section if the longest part of a shape viewed in cross section is 75 mm or less; a heavy section measures greater than 75 mm. Merchant bars are bars made of carbon steel and rolled hot. An alloy steel is made when small amounts of manganese, chromium, nickel, etc., singly or in combination, are added to the melt. A product made increasingly by mini-mills is termed SBQ (special bar quality) grade. Recently, mini-mills have been venturing into lines of higher-grade products. These items are mainly for the construction industry, but Chaparral and other minis also sell such products to the automakers.

Steel sheet and large structural girders have long been the mainstay of integrated steelmakers and out of the province of the minis. Until now, mini-mills haven't been able to manufacture sheet, but Nucor Corporation, the most successful of the minis, is building a sheet mill that will use a new technology to make sheet in mini-mill quantities and of mini-mill thicknesses. Furthermore, Nucor, which already owns a number of mini-mills, has announced a joint venture with Yamato Kogyo Company, a large Japanese steelmaker, to build a mill in Arkansas that will manufacture large structural girders. Similarly, Chaparral has voiced an interest in buying or building a plant that can turn out large structural beams. With continued adaptation of new technologies, the mini-mill segment of the industry is expected to continue to increase market share at the expense of the less efficient, older mills. Estimates for the mini-mill share range as high as 40% of domestic output by the end of the century. The locations of many of the larger mini-mills are presented in Exhibit 6.

Exhibit 6   **Mini-mill Sites in the United States**

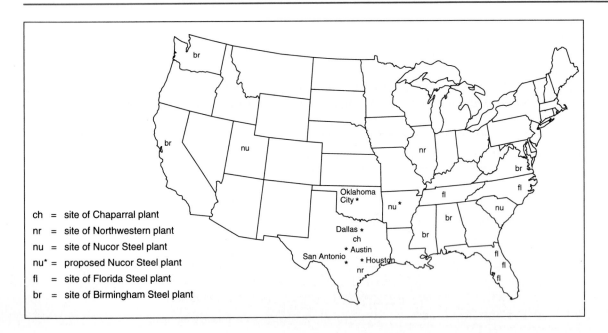

ch = site of Chaparral plant
nr = site of Northwestern plant
nu = site of Nucor Steel plant
nu* = proposed Nucor Steel plant
fl = site of Florida Steel plant
br = site of Birmingham Steel plant

Comparison of Cost Structures **Exhibit 7**

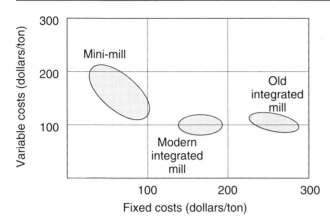

Typical range of costs per ton of annual capacity for an old integrated mill, a modern integrated mill, and a mini-mill can be expressed in terms of fixed and variable costs. Fixed costs are expenditures for such items as capital, manpower, and maintenance, which do not vary significantly once a plant is operating. Variable costs include expenditures for raw materials, other supplies, and energy, which may change from year to year. Since mini-mills do not have to wait as long as integrated mills to recoup the investment in setting up operations, they can consider replacing old equipment with new sooner.

Clearly, mini-mills have natural cost advantages over the integrated mills. Indeed, minis are sometimes referred to as "money-mills". The capital cost of building an integrated plant is approximately $1600 per ton of annual capacity, whereas for a mini-mill, it is only $200–300. The capital outlay for an integrated steel plant can easily approach several billion dollars. As mentioned, the man-hours per ton are also substantially different (Exhibit 3). Likewise, raw materials costs and energy costs favor the minis. For a comparison of mini-mill and integrated steel mill cost structures, see Exhibit 7.

THE CHAPARRAL WAY OF RUNNING A PROFITABLE BUSINESS

■ Market Responsiveness

In 1987, Gordon Forward set forth Chaparral's marketing goal: That was to become the "easiest steel company to buy from." The strategy for accomplishing that objective is to provide service by developing new products, raising quality levels, and extending shipping capabilities. Flexibility and responsiveness to changing customer needs is crucial. As a recent example, Forward recalls how the company Quality Control Department introduced a micro-alloy steel production capability and began marketing the resultant product in an unconventional way and thereby expanded the firm's SBQ customer base. As an additional service, Chaparral customers have full access to the Marketing and Quality Control Departments. Furthermore, the Midlothian firm offers flexible rolling schedules and newly developed remote shipping points.

The classic mini-mill concept is grounded in the strategy of locating where the mill can take advantage of locally available markets and sources of labor and scrap. Subcategories of mini-mills include the "neighborhood mill", the strategy of which is to locate in an area where the demand for steel is expected to grow, and the "market mill", which concentrates on 1 or 2 specific products to meet a given market. When Chaparral began operations 14 years ago, it was essentially a market mill, producing rebar for the regional construction market. Richard T. Jaffre, Chaparral's VP-Raw Materials, noting that domestic and global mini-mill capacity was being overbuilt in the late 1970s, has written:

> It became clear that if Chaparral was to continue to prosper and grow, we had to rethink our place in the market. From the beginning, our focus has always been on steel. We had no interest in diversifying into oil, insurance, or whatever. We believe the steel business can and should be both profitable and fun. So, in 1979, Chaparral decided that our primary opportunity for growth was to expand our product mix and transcend the traditional mini-mill size range (structural shapes up to 6 inches in cross section).The problem with this strategy is that the cost of building a facility for larger shapes can flatten a mini-mill's wallet. The price of steel mill equipment tends to rise exponentially with the cross-sectional dimensions of its products. (Jaffre, 1986, p. 21)

Nevertheless, the perception of Chaparral as a market mill persisted at least through the mid-1980s, but a recent comment by Forward is quite revealing in this respect:

> Although Chaparral is classified as a mini-mill, this year we began producing a range of steels traditionally supplied only by larger, integrated steel mills. And when the recently commissioned horizontal casting machine comes on line in 1988, Chaparral will have even greater opportunities to serve customers more completely. (Texas Industries Annual Report, 1987, p. 7)

Indeed, the horizontal caster is expected to facilitate getting Chaparral down to "micro-mill" size. Rejecting the prospect of making the Midlothian plant bigger or increasing its 950-member employee roster, Forward asserts that his firm is steadfast in its intent to remain relatively flat organizationally, acknowledging that small is better in today's steel industry. After looking hard at microtechnology and studying how McDonald's fast food chain does what it does, Forward claims: "We figured out how to build something small enough you could literally put it on a barge and run it with only 40 people." Says Forward: "We could almost franchise it."

■ Technological Currency

A scientist by training, Mr. Forward views his mill as a laboratory and encourages experimentation. Saying that research is too often mistakenly isolated as a staff position, Forward explains:

> We've tried to bring research right into the factory and make it a line function. We make the people who are producing the steel responsible for keeping their process on the leading edge of technology worldwide. If they have to travel, they travel. If they have to figure out what the next step is, they go out figure out what the next step is, they go out and find the places where people are doing interesting things. They visit other companies. They work with universities. (Kantrow, p. 99)

According to the AISI, the integrated steel industry spends an average of 4–7% of annual sales on modernizing plant and equipment. Chaparral, by contrast, spends 15% of annual gross profits on upgraded equipment and new technologies. As a matter of policy, the Midlothian firm has an annual summer shutdown in order to make the necessary capital improvements. Having labor costs at 9–10% of sales, compared with an integrated steel industry average of 40%, is another factor that makes technology funding an easier task for Chaparral.

Chaparral has fought to maintain a work environment that nourishes people, innovation, and accomplishment. The total involvement of the work force is critical, because, as one writer notes:

> This is really the heart of the matter, because high tech is something people create, implement, and maintain. You can't just go out and buy it. Bodies and dollar bills aren't enough. Big Steel went out and hired thousands of researchers, industrial engineers, corporate planners, and staff specialists and the world still passed them by. (Jaffre, 1986, p. 22)

What are typically staff functions at other mills are dovetailed with line functions at Chaparral. For example:

> When there's a need for new production equipment, a line manager is put in charge of the entire project, including conceptual design, budgeting, purchasing, construction, installation, and start-up. Maintenance people are also included in the conceptual design stage, with the result that the equipment is easier to maintain. We've found that when forces shaping the design come from our production managers—when their egos get hooked—the odds of success are greatly enhanced. They make it work. (*Fortune*, April 13, 1987, p. 9)

People who are involved in the decision process are more likely to be committed to the decision when reached.

Naturally, computers are a major technology which any efficient steel mill will utilize. According to Mr. Jaffre, Chaparral uses computers in "planning, forecasting, inventory management, control of receipts, control of purchase orders, issuance of purchase orders, extensions, payables . . . the whole nine yards". Because the Chaparral operation consumes 100 million tons of junk automobiles, refrigerators, stoves, etc., per year, Jaffre notes that the computers are most useful as repositories of historical cost-trend information. Like most firms, Chaparral tries to minimize its investment of cash in inventory, but the mini-mill must buy numerous lots of scrap, and frequently. Therefore, observes the VP: "We're bound by the market." In conclusion, Jaffre states: ". . . in the main, the computer is for short-term, medium-, and long-term planning. It's the data base for our formal planning—the corporate financial forecast, done typically once a year with quarterly updates." The firm not only relies on a talented motivated work force but also on its investment in sophisticated computerized systems and production facilities.

■ Participatory Management

During the 1970s, U.S. Steel (USX) had as many as 11 layers of management. The quintessential Big Steel firm subsequently "evolved down" to 4 layers. A key initial Chaparral decision was to create only 4 layers. Decision making at Chaparral is forced down to the shop floor where the actual production takes place. It has been said to Gordon Forward that he is "a man of many slogans", including: "Participatory management means taking decision making to the lowest competent level—and making the lowest level competent." Says Chaparral's CEO: "We believe that people want to work and do a good job if you give them some responsibility and reward them with more than a paycheck." Chaparral's pioneering participatory management strategies appear to bear fruit for the firm as well as for the employees. A clear indication is the fact that a 1977 attempt by the United Steelworkers of America to unionize the mill was soundly rejected by 73% out of the 98% of the work force voting. A former worker at U.S. Steel's South Works mill in Chicago was quoted as saying: "At the other mill I was stuck in a craft line. I couldn't help somebody in a different job, and he couldn't help me. That was because of the union. Here we do what we have to do to get the job done."

Described by some in the business literature as a "maverick mini-mill", the "us"-versus-"them" mentality that haunts so many of the older mills is largely absent from the Midlothian firm. Rather than "steelworkers", some employees prefer to refer to themselves as "Chaparral people". Chaparral is quite simply a people-oriented firm, whether dealing with employees or with customers. The Chaparral work force is governed by an *esprit de corps* which is hospitable to risk taking and forgiving of setbacks. Although such incidents are not unique to Chaparral nor common there, one $15,000 mistake, which at a less dynamic firm might have cost the melt shop superintendent his job, has been stoically dubbed a "$15,000 paper-weight". Along these lines, the company has a no-layoff policy and claims never to have laid off an employee, not even during the difficult 1982–84 period. In fact, during that time, employees with construction skills were lent to the construction of Chaparral's second mill rather than bringing in outside builders and having to sack superfluous steelmakers.

Numerous other policies and programs distinguish Chaparral as a steelmaker. For instance, the seniority system, common at Big Steel mills, was never adopted at the Midlothian firm, and promotions are made based upon job performance. There are no time clocks to punch, and all Chaparral employees have been salaried since 1981. Furthermore, there are no assigned parking spots, no dress codes or color-coded hard hats, and no executive lunchroom. Claims one Chaparral manager: "We've eliminated every barrier to communication, every barrier to identification with management and company goals." Of Chaparral, Peters writes:

> Imagine a $300-million company where the Vice President of administration fills in on the switchboard, where there are no formal personnel and purchasing departments and no personal secretaries. There isn't much for secretaries to do because executives are discouraged from writing memos. For that matter, there aren't that many executives. (Peters, 1987, p. 2)

Moreover, Peters declares, "You won't find a corporate organization chart like that in any business text." Team spirit is further promoted by the company-wide practice of communication on a first-name basis, decentralized offices, and the minimization of formalized meetings.

Although Chaparral workers have not been paid extravagant wages, job security and other benefits take up the slack. Bonuses and profit sharing were introduced from the start and together have run as high as 20% of wages. Management further shows its trust in labor by delegating to every member of the firm responsibility for quality control and sales, thus removing what they see in their company as two inessential managerial layers. Says Forward:

> Everyone in the company pays attention to our customers. Everyone in the company is a member of the sales department. Literally. About four years ago, we made everyone in the company a member of the sales department. That means people in security, secretaries, everyone. (Kantrow, 1986, p. 100)

Actually, at Chaparral there is a conscious effort to "bash barriers between jobs". Security guards, for example, are paramedics, run the company ambulance, administer employee hearing tests, and enter safety and quality-control data into the computer. Foremen remain responsible for hiring, education, training, and benefits. To prevent employee burnout, Chaparral has a compulsory annual sabbatical program that permits people at the front-line, supervisor level to visit other mills, customers, etc., for a period from 2 weeks to 6 months.

THE FUTURE OUTLOOK FOR CHAPARRAL

Asked if Chaparral would "swallow hard and scrap unamortized equipment and put in new technology—and if (the firm) didn't feel competition nipping at (its) heels," Forward responded:

> Absolutely. We simply can't wait until we've been forced into a corner and have to fight back like alley cats. In our end of the business, we can't afford to act like fat cats. We have a system that's tough by its own definition. If we succeed in making our business less capital-intensive, we'd be naïve not to expect a lot of others will want to get into it. If we succeed at what we are trying to do as a mini-mill, we'll also lower the price of entry. So we have to go like hell all the time. If the price of what we sell goes up too high, if we start making too much money on certain parts of our product line, all of a sudden lots of folks will be jumping in. And they can get into business in 18 months or so. They can hire our people away. . . . This makes us our own worst enemy. We constantly chip away the ground we stand on. We have to keep out front all the time. Our advantages are the part of the industry we're in, but also the kind of organization we have. We have built a company that can move fast and that can run full out. We're not the only ones—there are others like us. Nucor does many of the same things, but it has a slightly different personality. And there's Florida Steel. There are a number of quality mini-mills. We are all a bit different, but we all have to run like hell. (Jaffre, 1986, p. 27)

And today's steel industry is increasingly dichotomized into two segments: the quick and the dead. Forward likens firms that don't utilize ever-improving technologies with Forest Lawn: "Not because there are no good ideas there, but because the good ideas are dying there all the time."

Observing that mini-mills are no longer very labor-intensive, Forward, taking a cue from Dr. Barnett, believes that the next big step for Chaparral is to use new technology to drastically cut energy usage. Technological developments in the forging process are also receiving close scrutiny. Jaffre states that Chaparral maintains a competitive edge thusly:

> . . . by never forgetting the magnitude and strength of international competition; by maintaining our capacity to anticipate and manage change; by continuously

developing our skills in the application of new technology and the service of our markets; by providing an environment that taps our greatest natural resource—our people. (Jaffre, 1986, p. 27)

Furthermore, Jaffre asserts that Chaparral has aggressively chosen not to be a part of any "deindustrialization" but rather to be a forceful player in the new "industrial renaissance."

The question before Chaparral management now is: "How do we grow in the future?" Do they keep expanding the Texas facility, or expand into a new area and attempt to duplicate their success? With the opening of the Nucor plant in Arkansas, the competition in both the structural steel and scrap markets in the North Texas, Eastern Oklahoma, Arkansas area will heat up. This is especially true given the reopening of a Houston plant by Northwestern Steel. The regional market may be reaching saturation with these additions. On the other hand, with the dollar declining against other major currencies, both a greater share of the domestic market and export opportunities will be expanding. For all of these reasons, the possibility of a new mill will have to be addressed. Problems may develop if Chaparral continues expanding the present plant. The firm will have to go further and further for scrap. More importantly, Chaparral's management feels that their success formula is susceptible to diseconomies of scale. As Forward has pointed out, small is beautiful in terms of the Chaparral formula. The firm cannot continue to grow and stay small indefinitely. By the same token, it may not be able to reproduce its magic everywhere it goes. At this juncture the real question facing Chaparral is "which way to grow?"

BIBLIOGRAPHY

Carey, David, "Forecast: Industry Analysis—Metals," *Financial World*, January 5, 1988, p. 40.

"Chaparral Steel Company," in *Making America Competitive: Corporate Success Formulas* (Washington, D.C.: Bureau of National Affairs Special Report, n.d.).

Eichenwald, Kurt, "America's Successful Steel Industry," *Washington Monthly*, February 1985, pp. 40–44.

The Elements of Leadership: Texas Industries Inc. 1987 Annual Report, July 15, 1987.

Flint, Jerry, "Help Wanted: Stakhanovites Only," *Forbes*, September 7, 1987, p. 82.

Forward, Gordon E., "Wide-Open Management at Chaparral Steel," interview by Alan M. Kantrow, *Harvard Business Review* 64, no. 3 (1986), pp. 96–102.

Freeze, Karen, "From a Casewriter's Notebook," *HBS Bulletin*, June 1986, pp. 54–63.

How We Compete: Texas Industries Inc. 1988 Annual Report, July 13, 1988.

Jaffre, Richard T., "Chaparral Steel Company: A Winner in a Market Decimated by Imports," *Planning Review*, July 1986, p. 20.

Keefe, Lisa M., "Forward's March," *Forbes*, April 20, 1986, p. 20.

Lee, Robert E., "How They Buy Scrap at Chaparral," *Purchasing*, August 22, 1985, pp. 98A1–98A4.

May, Todd, Jr., "The Economy: Surprising Help from the Crash," *Fortune*, January 18, 1988, pp. 68–87.

McManus, George J., "Horizontal Casting: A New Direction for Steel," *Iron Age*, April 5, 1985, p. 29.

——— , "Mini-Mill Report: The Honeymoon Is Over," *Iron Age*, March 1, 1986, p. 26.

Melloan, George, "Making Money Making Steel in Texas," *The Wall Street Journal*, January 26, 1988 (southwest ed.), p. 29.

Miller, Jack Robert, "Steel Mini-Mills," *Scientific American*, May 1984, pp. 32–39.

"Mini-Mills Up the Heat on the Maxis," *Fortune*, April 13, 1987, pp. 8–9.

Peters, Tom, "On Achieving Excellence," *Monthly Newsletter*, San Francisco, May 1987.

Stundza, Tom, "Steel: Making More with Less," *Purchasing*, February 1987, pp. 50–57.

Szekely, Julian, "Can Advanced Technology Save the U.S. Steel Industry?" *Scientific American*, July 1987, pp. 34–41.

United States Department of Commerce, *Critical Materials Requirements of the U.S. Steel Industry* (Washington, D.C.: March 1983).

Northrop Corporation: The Tigershark Dilemma

Thad Munnerlyn, Robert McNamara, Frank Leibold, University of South Carolina, James J. Chrisman, Louisiana State University

Los Angeles, May 15, 1985—Thomas V. Jones, chairman and chief executive of the Northrop Corporation, said that Tuesday's crash of an F-20 Tigershark jet fighter would not deter the company from promoting the plane to prospective buyers, including the Air Force. The crash, which killed the pilot, David Barnes, was the second of an F-20 in eight months and leaves only one Tigershark in operation. "Our belief in it [the F-20] has not changed," Mr. Jones said at a news conference after Northrop's annual shareholder's meeting in Hawthorne, California. Northrop has not received any orders for the plane, which has cost the company more than $800 million to produce (*New York Times*).

The second fatal crash of an F-20 fighter plane was unfortunate, but such crashes were hardly unexpected. Test pilots often flew new planes to the limit of their capabilities, and many times serious accidents were the result. Indeed, pilot error would be ruled as the cause of both Tigershark crashes rather than problems with the plane itself.

However, his confident comments to the stockholders aside, Northrop's CEO had other reasons to worry. Northrop had developed the F-20 Tigershark for export to Third World and European allies. Despite high praise from the aviation press and pilots alike, not one had been sold. The plane was Thomas Jones's brainchild, but the program's costs, which were approaching $1 billion, were

Exhibit 1	Northrop Corporation: Consolidated Statements of Income (year ended December 31) (in millions, except per share)				
	1984	*1983*	*1982*	*1981*	*1980*
Net sales	$3687.8	$3260.6	$2472.9	$1990.7	$1655.4
Cost of sales	−3444.4	−3120.1	−2539.5	−1977.6	−1548.3
Operating costs	−3005.5	−2725.0	−2260.2		
Administrative and general expenses	−438.9	−395.1	−279.3		
Operating margin	243.4	140.5	−66.6	13.1	107.1
Other income and deductions	6.1	26.5	33.0	62.1	35.5
Interest expense	−7.5	−14.3	−3.1	−7.5	−2.9
Income before taxes	242.0	152.7	−36.7	67.7	139.7
Federal and foreign taxes (benefits)	−75.1	−52.0	42.1	−19.8	−53.6
Net income	$166.9	$100.7	$5.4	$47.9	$86.1
Per-share stock prices					
High	$39.50	$32.75	$25.88	$21.00	$20.63
Low	$23.75	$21.88	$13.13	$11.00	$12.50
Book value per share	$15.72	$12.64	$10.87	$11.32	$11.27
Earnings per share	$ 3.63	$ 2.21	$ 0.12	$ 1.10	$ 2.01
Cash dividend per share	$ 0.90	$ 0.60	$ 0.60	$ 0.60	$ 0.60
Number of employees	41,500	37,200	35,500	31,400	30,200

Sources: Northrop Corporation, *Annual Report,* 1986: *Moody's Industrial Manual,* 1982; Standard and Poor's *NYSE Reports,* 1985.

adversely affecting the company's financial performance (see Exhibits 1–3 for Northrop's consolidated financial statements).

Late in the 1970s the Carter administration put out a call for an inexpensive, easy-to-maintain aircraft to be produced primarily for export and to be designed and built without Department of Defense (DOD) funding. The F-20 was Northrop's answer to that call. However, by 1985 the political sands had shifted, and the F-20 was faced with competition from frontline U.S. fighters previously reserved for domestic use. It was becoming increasingly apparent that sales to foreign customers were going to be contingent upon either getting the Tigershark into the inventory of some branch of the U.S. military, a purpose for which it was not designed, or competing with some of the world's finest and best-known fighter planes in the international marketplace. The question facing Mr. Jones was easily stated even if the answer was not. Should he continue costly development of a potentially profitable program, or should he close the project and divert the funds to other uses?

NORTHROP CORPORATION: COMPANY BACKGROUND

The Northrop Corporation was founded in 1939 by John K. Northrop. Mr. Northrop had previously been an engineer for Douglas Aircraft, where he became a preeminent designer, doing most of the work on the Lockheed Vega, which

Northrop Corporation: Consolidated Statements of Financial Position (as of December 31) (in millions)

Exhibit 2

	1984	1983	1982	1981	1980
Assets					
Cash and cash items	$ 3.7	$ 60.2	$ 124.6	$ 194.3	$ 311.2
Accounts receivable	306.7	205.4	137.6	193.0	131.0
Inventoried costs	418.0	301.0	238.6	327.5	390.4
Prepaid expenses	15.0	10.7	10.8	11.4	9.0
Total current assets	$ 743.4	$ 577.3	$ 511.6	$ 726.2	841.6
Land and land improvements	105.6	78.6	70.6		
Buildings	575.5	479.8	375.4		
Machinery and equipment	981.5	777.9	610.8		
Leasehold improvements	19.3	16.6	17.8		
Accumulated depreciation and amortization	−510.9	−379.5	−278.0		
Net property, plant, and equipment at cost	$1171.0	$ 973.4	$ 796.6	$ 490.3	$ 343.5
Investments in and advances to affiliates	22.7	11.9	16.9		
Net investment in aircraft direct financing leases	17.1	19.2	17.9		
Notes and accounts receivable	2.3	14.2	9.5		
Total other assets	$ 42.1	$ 45.3	$ 44.3	$ 40.9	$ 48.6
Total assets	$1956.5	$1596.0	$1352.5	$1257.4	$1233.7
Liabilities					
Notes payable	$ 43.4	$ 0.0	$ 0.0		
Trade accounts payable	233.7	214.1	177.3		
Accrued employees' compensation	149.9	133.1	114.4		
Advances on contracts	187.0	192.7	159.0		
Income taxes payable	25.3	26.7	16.9		
Deferred income taxes	331.5	255.1	224.2		
Other current liabilities	175.1	108.6	84.1		
Total current liabilities	$1145.9	$ 930.3	$ 775.9	$ 666.8	$ 660.2
Long-term debt and capital leases	7.7	10.5	14.5	14.5	19.4
Long-term liabilities	31.7	29.1	32.0	40.5	43.6
Deferred income taxes	46.4	49.2	36.2	28.6	28.1
Total liabilities	$1231.7	$1019.1	$ 858.6	$ 750.4	$ 751.3
Shareholders' Equity					
Paid-in capital	$ 150.7	$ 133.3	$ 128.0	$ 116.2	$ 84.4
Retained earnings	596.7	471.1	397.9	419.7	398.0
Unvested employee restricted award shares	−22.6	−27.5	−32.0	−28.9	0.0
Total shareholders' equity	$ 724.8	$ 576.9	$ 493.9	$ 507.0	$ 482.4
Total liabilities and shareholders' equity	$1956.5	$1596.0	$1352.5	$1257.4	$1233.7

Sources: Northrop Corporation, *Annual Report*, 1986; *Moody's Industrial Manual*, 1982; Standard and Poor's *NYSE Reports*, 1985.

aviator Wiley Post flew around the world. While at Douglas he also did pioneering work on the DC-1, DC-2, and the popular DC-3 passenger planes. As would be expected, his new company manufactured aircraft, producing several lesser-known and unexceptional designs prior to World War II. Although it was not the manufacturer of the glamour planes of the wartime period, such as the P-51 Mustang or P-38 Lightning, Northrop did produce the P-61 Black Widow

Exhibit 3

Northrop Corporation: Consolidated Statements of Changes in Financial Position (year ended December 31) (in millions)

	1984	1983	1982
Operating Activities			
Sources of cash			
Sales, net of change in accounts receivable	$3586.5	$3192.8	$2528.3
Other income and deductions, net	(1.5)	19.6	13.5
Change in progress payments	125.6	(95.3)	146.1
Changes in advances on contracts	(5.7)	33.7	65.9
Cash provided by operating activities	$3704.9	$3150.8	$2753.8
Uses of cash			
Cost of sales, net of inventoried costs, payables, and accruals	$3583.5	$3010.1	$2508.8
Depreciation and amortization	(138.1)	(109.8)	(60.9)
Amortization of unvested employee share awards	(13.7)	(6.4)	(5.8)
Income taxes	2.9	(1.7)	(6.1)
Cash used in operating activities	$3434.6	$2892.2	$2436.0
Net cash provided by operating activities	$ 270.3	$ 258.6	$ 317.8
Investment Activities			
Additions to property, plant, and equipment	($ 345.3)	($ 293.1)	($ 376.8)
Carrying value of disposals of property, plant, and equipment	9.6	6.5	9.6
Change in other assets	3.2	(1.0)	(3.4)
Net cash used in investment activities	($ 332.5)	($ 287.6)	($ 370.6)
Financing Activities			
Change in indebtedness	$ 44.1	$ 1.4	$ 1.9
Issuance of common stock	8.6	3.4	2.9
Net interest income/expense	0.1	(7.4)	(16.4)
Repayment of long-term debt	(5.8)	(5.3)	(10.9)
Net cash provided by (used in) financing activities	$ 47.0	$ (7.9)	$ 10.3
Cash dividends	(41.3)	(27.5)	(27.2)
Change in cash and cash items	($ 56.5)	($ 64.4)	($ 69.7)

Source: Northrop Corporation, *Annual Report,* 1986.

that appeared later in the Pacific theater. Painted all-black and designed to fly at night with the aid of radar, the sleek aircraft was technologically advanced for its time but was built in limited numbers. Northrop also produced one of the world's first production jet fighters, the F-89 Scorpion. It enjoyed moderate success in the Korean War era as an all-weather fighter.

Shortly after the end of World War II, Northrop commenced its B-35 Flying Wing program. Extraordinarily daring in design, the bomber was a culmination of many of John Northrop's ideas and dreams. The company invested heavily in the boomerang-shaped plane, only to have the program canceled in favor of the B-36 developed by Convair, a forerunner of General Dynamics. The Air

Force ordered all the remaining prototypes destroyed in what became a bitter loss for Northrop. The cancellation left the company near bankruptcy in 1953.

It was in 1953 that Thomas V. Jones joined the company as a planner and assistant to the Chief Engineer. Five years later he was Senior Vice-President of Development Planning. In 1960 he became Northrop's CEO, and in 1963 he was named Chairman of the Board. In the early 1960s, the company developed and manufactured the Snark intercontinental ballistic missile, but rapid advances in technology soon rendered it obsolete. More importantly, during his early tenure as CEO, Jones helped return Northrop to profitability with the F-5 Tiger series, a relatively unsophisticated and inexpensive fighter plane that Jones correctly saw as filling a need for Third World countries. Dismissed by one critic as "toys for sheiks," the F-5 was nevertheless one of the premier success stories in aviation history. The F-5 and its variations became the most widely used fighter plane in the world, with more than 2500 planes sold to nearly 30 countries. The F-5 dominated the export fighter market from its inception in the early 1960s through the late 1970s. Its trainer derivative, the T-38 Talon, was extremely successful as well, with 1000 sold worldwide. Used by tens of thousands of aspiring pilots, it became the most widely used jet trainer in history. Although Northrop had remained afloat after the B-35 cancellation, it was the cash revenues generated by the F-5 program that rallied the company to its current level of success. Using these funds, Northrop entered into more advanced aerospace research and development and expanded its operations into several areas of military electronics.

Northrop made two attempts to build new military aircraft during the 1970s. Bidding against other companies for domestic business, it first lost out to Fairchild Aviation's A-10 Thunderbolt in a battle to obtain a product on contract for an antitank aircraft. Northrop then bid on contracts with the Air Force and Navy to produce a domestic fighter. Northrop approached McDonnell Douglas, offering to make it the prime contractor on the Navy program and major subcontractor on the Air Force program. Northrop expected to be named the prime contractor for the Air Force project and thought the combined proposal would strengthen its overall bargaining position with DOD. Unfortunately, its F-17 prototype was rejected by the Air Force in favor of the F-16, designed by General Dynamics. The Navy, by contrast, accepted the McDonnell Douglas bid for the plane, which was designated as the Navy's F-18 strike fighter. McDonnell Douglas then subcontracted the F-18 fuselages to Northrop, leaving Jones's company without a prime contract on the plane that it had originally designed.

Boeing designated Northrop as the main subcontractor for its 747 commercial airliner in 1966; it continued to build the fuselage center section for Boeing through 1985. Despite the financial success of these programs, however, Northrop was still known mainly for its subcontract work for other companies and for the F-5.

THE DEFENSE INDUSTRY

The defense industry consisted of thousands of companies of many different types and sizes which produced a wide variety of weapons and military products. The industry was dominated by two groups of firms: large diversified commercial companies, like General Electric, Westinghouse, IBM, and Litton; and large aerospace companies, such as General Dynamics, Boeing, McDonnell

Exhibit 4   **Top 10 Defense Aerospace Companies in 1980 (dollars in millions)**

Company	Ranking in Value of Defense Contracts	Value of Defense Contracts	Total Sales	Net Income	ROE	Assets	Major Defense Products
General Dynamics	1	$3518	$ 4,645	$195	21.0%	$2242	F-16, Trident subs, SSN-668 submarines, Tomahawk missiles
McDonnell Douglas	2	$3247	$ 6,086	$145	9.9%	$3900	F-18, F-15, and KC-10 planes, Trident II missiles
United Technologies	3	$3109	$12,324	$393	17.5%	$7326	UH-60 helicopters, jet fighter engines
Boeing	4	$2386	$ 9,426	$601	28.8%	$5931	AWACS, Stealth bomber, B-52 bomber
Lockheed	6	$2037	$ 5,396	$ 28	7.5%	$2443	C-5A and C-5B cargo planes, Trident II missiles
Hughes Aircraft*	7	$1819	$ 2,610	NA	NA	NA	AH-64 helicopters, defense electronics
Raytheon	8	$1745	$ 5,002	$282	22.7%	$2929	Hawk missiles, defense electronics
Grumman	10	$1322	$ 1,729	$ 31	9.5%	$ 906	F-14 and A-6E planes, aircraft carriers
Northrop	11	$1227	$ 1,655	$ 86	19.0%	$1234	F-20 and F-5 planes, F-18 fuselage, Stealth bomber
Rockwell	14	$ 969	$ 6,907	$280	17.3%	$4431	B-1 bomber

Source: J. J. Chrisman, "Note on the Defense Electronics Industry," University of Georgia, 1982.

*Privately held.

Douglas, and Lockheed (see Exhibit 4). Like its counterparts, Northrop competed for a limited number of large, long-term contracts (e.g., aircraft) as well as for numerous smaller, short-term contracts.

The industry supplied essentially one customer—the U.S. military, which consisted of the Army, Navy (including the Marines), and Air Force. The Department of Defense managed the military and was responsible for preparing the national defense budget for the various military services, a complicated, consensus-building process that involved hundreds of agencies. While only about half of the military budget actually went towards weapons procurement (salaries and supplies represented the other half of the budget), increases in defense spending generally resulted in banner years for the major defense contractors both in terms of sales and profits.

Ten-Year Defense Market Forecast (dollars in billions) **Exhibit 5**

Year	1982 $	Annual % Change	1982 $	Annual % Change	Electrical Content in DOD Budget (%)
1982	214.0	10.5	34.7	18.0	23.4
1983	221.6	3.6	37.3	7.5	24.2
1984	232.4	4.9	41.1	11.0	25.2
1985	243.4	4.7	44.6	8.5	25.9
1986	253.2	4.0	47.9	7.4	26.6
1987	261.4	3.2	50.6	5.6	27.1
1988	269.0	2.9	53.7	6.1	27.8
1989	274.6	2.1	55.7	3.7	28.2
1990	280.2	2.0	56.8	5.2	29.1
1991	286.0	2.0	60.6	3.4	29.5

The funds available to the military each year were controlled by the Congress. The defense budget was determined both by the administration's policy with regard to defense spending and by the funds required for other programs. Money spent on defense could not be spent on other programs such as welfare and social aid, and some weapons were politically less popular than others (the MX strategic missile program, for example). The military competed with these other programs for funds, and if Congress deemed it necessary to reduce the President's proposed budget, some programs might be drastically reduced in scope or cut altogether.

With military policies changing from administration to administration, the President and his views on defense and international politics were of critical importance. The interplay between Congress and the administration in regard to the proposed defense budget obviously had a great impact on contractors. For example, under President Carter defense spending sank to its lowest real levels since the end of World War II. In 1980 Ronald Reagan won a landslide victory over Jimmy Carter. As part of his election campaign Reagan had promised to increase the political presence of the United States on the international scene, which many felt had been significantly weakened by the Carter administration. Reagan also planned to increase military spending by 9% per year (in real terms), as opposed to Carter's more moderate 4.6% per year. Exhibit 5 provides projected budgets for defense electronics for the years 1982–1991.

Almost all defense sales were made through contracts between the DOD and the prime contractor. These contracts were usually made on either a fixed-fee or cost-plus basis and often included incentive clauses to encourage the contractor to complete the contract under the target price. Almost all production contracts were issued on a yearly basis (development contracts were typically multiyear), with the contractor's performance and funding status being reviewed each year.

The acquisition process in the defense industry was long and complex. Most defense contracts were for high-technology items which required long development periods. In 1979 John H. Richardson, President of Hughes Aircraft, estimated that the time required to develop a major new defense item was eight to nine years, from the initial development stage to the start of full production. These development costs were usually paid by the military under development contracts. The military typically paid a number of companies to develop various designs for the item and then contracted one company to perform full-scale engineering development (FSED) on the best design. Once FSED was complete, the military then asked for bids on the production contract. The company which carried out the FSED did not always get the production contract, which often led to inefficiencies in the early production stages. Historical buying patterns seemed to indicate a tendency for the DOD to award production contracts to the major aerospace manufacturers that had lost out on previous contracts.

Another source of inefficiency in this process was that at the time the initial production began, the final size of the production run could only be estimated. Therefore, contractors could never be certain if or when investments in plant and equipment would be recovered on a project, because the size of the production run might change from year to year. The size of the total production run was an especially important concern for aerospace manufacturers whose profitability depended on experienced-based cost reductions.

Furthermore, the government did not allow the contractor to recover costs that were not directly tied to the particular program involved. Such conditions tended to discourage defense contractors from investing capital in new plant and equipment. Given this uncertain operating environment and the ponderous bureaucracy of the military, inefficiencies in the industry and the "padding" of defense contracts were common results.

Another problem inherent in the defense industry was the military's desire to compromise cost in favor of improved performance. The desire for better performance often led to product design changes halfway through the production run. These changes made it necessary for the contractor to have to go back and "refit" all the previously produced items, which often were in different stages of completion. Delays of this sort were costly. Many contractors tried to pass these costs onto the military, and disagreements between the contractor and the military over who should bear these costs often ensued.

It was in this environment that Northrop and other defense contractors operated. They produced very expensive, high-technology products with long development times for, essentially, a single customer. That customer's requirements could fluctuate considerably, depending on the policies of the existing administration and the mood of Congress.

THE FX ENVIRONMENT

Late in the 1970s, the Carter administration became alarmed at the number of foreign requests for frontline military aircraft, particularly fighters. Nations with severe domestic problems were clamoring for planes that were costly and had capabilities greatly exceeding their security needs. These planes often presented maintenance problems that taxed the Air Force support crews on U.S. bases; they were likely to present even greater problems to Third World owners. Sales to such countries were seen as politically and economically destabilizing. Thus, the Carter administration approached the defense industry and asked for a privately funded and developed aircraft specifically designed for foreign customers. The aircraft was to be simpler, less expensive, and less capable than frontline U.S. fighters. In return, the administration promised to refuse to license frontline planes for sales overseas, virtually forcing the potential buyers to purchase the foreign export fighter, or FX, as it was known.

The details were worked out and the program was put into place in late 1979. With a ready-made customer base of previous F-5 users and substantially improved performance, Northrop executives figured they had a "hot" aircraft in their new F-20 Tigershark. Less than a year later, however, Carter lost his reelection bid to Ronald Reagan, and a new administration took office in January 1981. Within two years, the Reagan administration, walking a political tightrope between Red China and Nationalist China, had blocked the sale of approximately 150 F-20s ordered by the Taiwan government. The reason given for this move was that the F-20 was too advanced, and therefore, the plane would be destabilizing for the region. Three years later that would still be the only firm order for the Tigershark. Similarly, negotiations with India were quashed on the grounds that the plane and its advanced electronics would be too close to "too many Russians," a reference to India's relations with the Soviet Union.

Of equal significance to Northrop, in 1982 the Reagan administration, reacting to what it believed to be an increased threat from the Soviet military presence in Third World areas, overturned long-standing U.S. policy and began to sell U.S. inventory fighters to less developed countries. The exports included some of McDonnell Douglas's F-15s and F-18s but consisted primarily of the General Dynamics F-16. An American fighter became a highly charged symbol of friendship and support, and the Reagan administration dangled the planes like political bait to sway Third World countries. Nations with U.S. planes were dependent for parts and technical support. Also, the advisors, who necessarily accompanied the planes, provided an important American presence in these countries. Thus, the FX policy, for which the F-20 was built, was all but officially dead, even though this policy change was reversed by Secretary of Defense Carlucchi three months later in December 1982.

■ Competition

At the outset of the FX program Northrop believed it had few competitors in its effort to sell the F-20 to the export market and was relatively free of political problems at home. However, along with the policy changes invoked by the Reagan administration, significant competition from both domestic and foreign aerospace firms had developed.

The least troublesome competitors in the "affordable" fighter market from Northrop's viewpoint were the foreign producers. Several had been improving their position, however, the most notable being Dassault of France with its Mirage 2000. Even though Dassault had made inroads into Third World markets, it was still considered an also-ran in the industry behind competing U.S. firms. Perceived as not having the glamour or performance of an American fighter, the Mirage was more expensive to fly and lacked the large support network that U.S. companies had worldwide. Still, the French plane was a choice for countries that found it politically expedient to appear neutral in terms of Soviet or American influence. For example, in 1983 the United Arab Emirates bought Mirage jets from the European consortium PANAVA, rather than F-20s or F-16s.

McDonnell Douglas had two frontline domestic aircraft that were being exported, the Air Force's F-15, an extremely sophisticated and expensive air-superiority fighter, and the Navy's F-18 strike fighter, built with the assistance of Northrop. These planes were considered too sophisticated and expensive for

Exhibit 6

General Dynamics's F-16 Multinational Program Organization

Prime Contractor

General Dynamics

Suppliers-Subcontractors

Engines: Pratt & Whitney Aircraft (government-furnished equipment) (Pratt & Whitney supplied by Fabrique Nationale, Philips, Korgsburg, and Disa)

Airframe (wings): SABCA
Airframe (center fuselage): Fokker
Airframe (aft fuselage): SONACA
Airframe (parts and equipment): Other European suppliers
Avionics and equipment: U.S. supplier (supplied by European industry)
Other: Government-furnished equipment

all but the most well-heeled allies. Canada, Australia, and Spain were examples of friendly nations which were interested in these planes.

Northrop's main competition in the export fighter market was General Dynamics Corporation and its well-received F-16. General Dynamics was the nation's largest defense contractor. The F-16 was its biggest aviation success, having dominated the U.S. inventory in numbers since its introduction in the 1970s. In terms of performance, it was nearly equal to the F-15, the most capable U.S. fighter. The F-16 was, however, priced considerably lower than the F-15, although at $14 million or more per plane, it was not inexpensive.

General Dynamics was well suited to compete in the export market. It had in place an elaborate supply system for manufacturing the F-16 (see Exhibit 6), a system that included both American and European subcontractors. It also had considerable experience producing the F-16 and had benefited from learning curves of approximately 80% for assembly and fabrication labor and of 95% for materials, including subcontracted items.

General Dynamics responded early to President Carter's FX request, but without much enthusiasm. In 1980, it offered a version of the F-16 known as the F-16/J79, so named because it had an older, less sophisticated engine, the J79. In addition, it had fewer electronic refinements. The F-16/J79 suffered from comparisons with the more sophisticated U.S. Air Force version of the F-16, the availability of which had made the F-16/J79 almost extraneous. In 1984, General Dynamics made a request to designate its current series of F-16s as FX fighters and essentially abandoned the F-16/J79.

■ **Comparison of the F-20 and F-16**

While the F-16/J79 was an old plane with "detuned" technology, Northrop's export fighter was a completely new aircraft. Although initially built for the FX market, the F-20 was the first U.S. fighter plane to be designed with 1980s technology. Even the newer F-15s and F-16s were built with 1960s and 1970s hardware. Except for physical appearance, the F-20 bore little resemblance to its forerunner, the F-5, and was a legitimate rival to the top U.S. fighters. Despite costing at least $2.5 million less per plane, the F-20 was equal in most areas, and actually superior in some others, to the F-16 (see Exhibit 7).

Specifications, Performance, Armaments, and Costs of the F-20 and F-16   **Exhibit 7**

	F-16	F-20
Specifications		
Length	49 ft, 6 in	47 ft, 3 in
Height	16 ft, 9 in	13 ft, 10 in
Wing span with two AIM-9 missiles	31 ft, 0 in	27 ft, 11 in
Empty weight (pounds)	18,496	12,049
Takeoff weight with two AIM-9 missiles (pounds)	22,264	18,540
Combat weight—50% fuel, two AIM-9 missiles (pounds)	18,348	16,015
Combat thrust/weight ratio	1.1 to 1	1.12 to 1
Maximum weight	33,000	28,000
Maximum external weapons carriage (pounds)	12,000	10,000
Engine thrust (pounds)	25,000	18,000
Number of weapon pylons	6	6
Performance Estimates		
Scramble time (seconds)	120	60
Sortie rate (in 12 hours)	Not available	12
Maximum speed at 40,000 feet	Mach 2 +	Mach 2 +
Sea level rate of climb (feet per minute)	72,834	53,800
Takeoff distance (feet)	1200	1475
Combat ceiling	50,000	55,000
Maneuverability	Essentially equivalent	
Weapons delivery accuracy	Essentially equivalent	
Range ratio F-16/F-20		
General Dynamics estimate	1.34–1.56/1.00	
Northrop estimate	1.12/1.00	
Costs (in millions)		
Annual operating and support costs (including fuel)	$5.7	$12.2
Procurement costs for 20 aircraft in flyaway condition		
Without spares	$280.0	$228.0
With spares	$420.0	$315.0
Armaments		
Cannon	20 mm	20 mm
Ammunition per cannon	500 rounds	450 rounds

Northrop had designed the new plane from the ground up, starting with the engine. Its engineers used General Electric's new F404 engine, which sacrificed a small amount of power in exchange for increased reliability and repairability, as well as an uncanny ability to recover from stalls. The F-16 was powered by the Pratt & Whitney F100, a powerful but problematic and expensive-to-maintain engine. The F-20 engine held one more advantage over the engine used on the F-16: It could start in under 20 seconds, less than half the time of the F-16. The Tigershark also had the fastest scramble time (the time an aircraft needed to become airborne after an alert) of any fighter in the world. The Tigershark could be in the air in less than 60 seconds, at least twice as fast as the F-16 or any other frontline fighter. That was owed in large part to a new laser-controlled inertial guidance system that replaced the traditional mechanical gyroscopes, as well as the faster starting engine.

In terms of electronics, the F-20 was, in many respects, superior to any other American fighter, including the supersophisticated F-15. The radar, equal to the F-16 in performance, had twice the reliability of the unit used by General Dynamics.

In other areas of performance the two planes were essentially equivalent. Maneuverability and weapons accuracy were approximately equal. The F-16 did hold a slight edge in sustained turns, although the F-20's smaller size could offset the advantage in aerial combat. The F-20 was designed primarily as a defensive aircraft and, as a consequence, did have less payload capacity (the amount of armaments—e.g., missiles and bombs—that a plane can carry aloft on one mission) than the F-16, which had been designed as an offensive fighter. The F-20 also had a shorter flight range than the F-16, a fact that prompted one General Dynamics salesman to say, "[The F-20 is] a good plane if you want to bomb the end of your runway." Northrop countered by explaining that the F-20 was designed for Third World countries whose enemies were nearby, making range less critical and scramble time of far greater consequence. In test flights the F-20 set records for the number of missions that could be performed in a day, presumably an important attribute to nations with limited aircraft and manpower. However, Northrop had decided to modify the plane to correct some minor design flaws and better differentiate the F-20 from the F-5, a decision that was soon leaked to the aerospace community. These modifications included increasing the F-20's wing area by 29% and modifying the plane to accommodate a larger engine.

Just as significant to Third World countries as performance, in the view of the F-20's designers, was the Tigershark's ease of maintenance and reliability. Air Force data suggested that the mean number of hours in the air between failures was 4.2 for the F-20 versus 3.2 for the F-16. The F-20 required slightly less than half the man-hours of routine maintenance per hour of flight as the F-16; a squadron of 20 Tigersharks required a maintenance staff of only 180; the F-16 required 380. Northrop officials felt both these figures would take on added significance in Third World countries with limited numbers of trained personnel. According to company figures, lower fuel consumption and lower maintenance requirements reduced the cost per flight hour of the F-20 to $1575 while the F-16 cost $3497 per flight hour. The other savings in terms of support and maintenance were highly in favor of the F-20.

The lower price of the Tigershark also gave it a strategic advantage as well as an economic one, since more planes could be bought for the same amount of money. During the Arab-Israeli wars the Israeli Air Force had found that a high density of aircraft offset performance differences between adversary aircraft during aerial combat.

MARKET FOR THE TIGERSHARK

Initially, the FX policy was not meant to apply to all overseas customers, and the export market was divided into two segments. The first, or "high," segment included NATO allies and some other countries, such as Israel and Japan. Countries in this group usually had State Department approval for frontline aircraft.

The second, or "low," segment consisted of all remaining noncommunist countries. It was this second group to which the FX program applied.

With the demise of the Carter policy, however, a third group of countries previously included in the FX group emerged. This "medium" segment included nations that wanted, and some that could afford, frontline fighters like the F-16 and were felt to have legitimate defense threats. Examples were Pakistan, Afghanistan's border neighbor and tacit ally to that country's anticommunist guerillas, and South Korea, whose border was with North Korea, a recent benefactor of Soviet air technology (see Exhibit 8).

The newly created medium segment of previously FX-only fighter buyers such as Venezuela, South Korea, and Pakistan represented a substantial number of potential orders, in part because the U.S. government helped finance their purchases through direct aid programs consisting of grants and long-term, low-interest loans. Linked with other foreign aid packages, these arrangements greatly reduced initial costs. Essentially, the United States paid for the military aircraft of its less affluent allies. An extreme example was Israel's purchase of 150 F-16s worth $3.3 billion. Through 1984, Israel had actually paid $22 million, or roughly the price of one F-16. In fact, over half of the $8.1 billion worth of F-16s sold to foreign countries through 1984 was paid by grants from the U.S. government or by loans that were later forgiven.

In the three years after the FX policy went into effect, approximately 1100 planes had been sold to foreign customers. Not one was an F-20. In fact, not one was an FX fighter. Those nations in the medium category which were seen as potential customers for the Tigershark opted for the Air Force issue F-16 after it became apparent that it would be made available to them. Pakistan, one of the poorest nations in the world, bought 40 F-16s at a cost of $1 billion. Venezuela, another potential F-20 customer, purchased 24 F-16s. Turkey, viewed by the Reagan administration as an important line of defense against a growing Warsaw Pact threat to NATO's southern flank, received special political consideration. A request on behalf of the Turkish government for $755 million in aid was put before the Congress for review in 1985. The aid was to be earmarked for military hardware and included specific mention of F-16s. Thailand was originally tagged as a FX country, but the threat from Vietnam had it arguing for F-16s, with a large number of its regional neighbors anxiously awaiting the outcome before making their own decisions. Thailand had the potential to purchase up to 75 planes. Saudi Arabia, the best hope for a large order, was high on the F-20 but insisted that Northrop have the plane in production and that it be in the U.S. Armed Forces system before it would place an order. It already had some F-15s and F-16s in its inventory.

It was an all-too-familiar refrain for Northrop executives. Despite the high performance of the Tigershark, it had what one expert called a "training wheels" image. It was still associated with the concept of an underpowered FX fighter, lacking the aura of an U.S. Air Force or Navy plane. Technological glamour and the political prestige of owning a frontline U.S. fighter appeared to be paramount concerns for Third World countries, despite the higher price and operating costs, as well as their inability to keep the planes in the air. As California Congressman Mervyn Dymally noted, "They want the best. It doesn't matter if it works."

The countries that remained classified in the low segment of the export market consisted of smaller, even less affluent nations that could afford only limited orders or whose needs dictated fewer planes. For example, the tiny kingdom of

---

Exhibit 8   **The Export Fighter Market**

Country	Market Segment	Remarks
Australia	High	Never classified as FX country. Entitled to frontline equipment as major Pacific ally. Received F-16s and F-18s.
Austria	Medium	Neutrality stance led to purchase of French Mirages.
Canada	High	Traditional ally entitled to frontline planes such as F-15s and F-18s.
Egypt	Medium	Initially seen as big F-20 purchaser, but was allowed F-16s by Reagan administration. Sales possibilities for F-20 still existed.
European participating group	High	European allies entitled to frontline fighters. Involvement with successful coproduction agreement for previous F-16s made reorders likely.
Greece	Medium	Status as NATO ally allowed frontline aircraft purchases. Indicated interest in F-16s.
India	Medium	U.S. government prohibited sales talks due to possibility of F-20 technology falling into the hands of Soviet military advisors. Bought Russian MIGs.
Indonesia	Low	Strong possibility for F-20 order, but national economy delayed purchase plans.
Israel	High	Close relationship with U.S. allowed access to frontline fighters and substantial foreign aid. Ordered F-15s and F-16s.
Jordan	Medium	Sale of F-16s to other Middle Eastern countries created pressure to sell to Jordan, which was needed in Middle Eastern peace talks. Purchase of F-20s still possible.
Malaysia	Low	Potential buyer of 50 planes. Would strongly consider F-20, but is very cautious and would not be a likely lead buyer in the region.
Pakistan	Medium	One of first FX countries to get approval to purchase F-16s. Proximity to Afghanistan figured in administration's decision.
Portugal	Medium	NATO ally, but favored French Mirage 2000.
Singapore	Low/Medium	FX country considered F-20s and F-16/J79, but purchase of F-16s by Thailand caused reconsideration.
South Korea	Medium	Previously FX country. Seen as F-20 customer, but Reagan administration allowed F-16 sales due to North Korean threat.
Spain	Medium/High	Potential member of NATO. Would probably seek F-16s for commonality with other NATO members.
Taiwan	Medium	Seen as first buyer for F-20, but potential sales of 150–200 planned stopped by Reagan administration to avoid diplomatic problems with Red China.
Thailand	Low/Medium	Previously FX country. Was given clearance to purchase F-16s due to threat from Vietnam. Important country in terms of setting precedent for region.
Turkey	Medium	NATO member. Receiving large amounts of military aid from the United States. Likely to include F-16s.
Venezuela	Medium	One of first FX countries to be allowed frontline fighters. Purchased F-16s.

Bahrain wanted four Tigersharks but had to settle for F-5s because the F-20 was not yet in production. A significant problem now faced Northrop. The company had stated that it would have to have firm orders for 300 to 400 planes before the F-20 could be put into production. These smaller countries could not afford a frontline U.S. fighter, but it was unclear whether or not this low segment of the FX market could collectively support the F-20 program. While some analysts believed that the low segment might ultimately hold sales potential for 300 or more planes over a period of years, it remained to be seen whether enough of the countries in the low category would place sufficient initial orders to justify the start-up of the F-20 production line. Most observers believed that obtaining orders for the F-20 from the middle segment, the one contested by General Dynamics, was the more likely route to success. Nearly all these nations, as well as some NATO countries, were considering the purchase of F-16s and some had already placed orders.

NORTHROP CORPORATION: CURRENT OPERATIONS

In 1985 Northrop was a diversified company consisting of business units in the fields of aviation and aerospace, electronics, and technical and management support. The company was divided into three groups: aircraft, electronics, and services. Exhibit 9 lists the divisions and major products of each group. Exhibits

---

Northrop Corporation: Products and Services by Group and Division   **Exhibit 9**

Aircraft Group

Advanced Systems Division
(Pico Rivera, California)
Stealth bomber
AFT development

Aircraft Division (Hawthorne, California)
F-20 fighters
F-5 fighters
747 midsections
F-18 fuselages
T-38 trainers
Aerospace research and development

Ventura Division (Newbury Park, California)
Aeronautical target systems
Aircraft subassemblies
Aeronautical tactical systems

Electronics Group

Defense Systems Division
(Rolling Meadows, Illinois)
Electronic countermeasures
Laser warning receivers
Infrared countermeasures

Electro-Mechanical Division
(Anaheim, California)
Sensor systems
Tactical missile systems
Tracking systems
Fabricated products

Electronics Division (Hawthorne, California)
Peacekeeper missile guidance system
Navigation system for AWACS

Precision Products Division
(Norwood, Massachusetts)
Gyroscopes
Inertial guidance and control subsystems
Accelerometers

Services Group

Aircraft Services Division
(Hawthorne, California)
Maintenance training and technical support
Logistics and on-the-job training

Northrop Services, Inc. (Anaheim, California)*
Managerial and technical support services

Northrop Worldwide Aircraft Services, Inc. (Lawton, Oklahoma)*
Military base operations and aircraft maintenance specialist
Helicopter and aircraft maintenance contractor

Source: Northrop Corporation, *Annual Report,* 1983.

*Wholly owned subsidiary.

Exhibit 10   Northrop Corporation: Group Sales (year ended December 31) (in millions)

	1984	*1983*	*1982*	*1981*
Aircraft				
Net sales to customers	$2563.9	$2119.9	$1452.5	$ 985.7
Intersegment sales	0.7	3.3	0.3	0.6
Other income (deductions)	−2.5	0.1	4.4	14.7
Total	$2562.1	$2123.3	$1457.2	$1001.0
Electronics				
Net sales to customers	$ 702.4	$ 669.2	$ 525.0	$ 427.0
Intersegment sales	55.5	16.2	5.6	29.8
Other income (deductions)	0.6	−0.2	−0.6	2.6
Total	$ 758.5	$ 685.2	$ 530.0	$ 459.4
Services				
Net sales to customers	$ 421.5	$ 457.7	$ 454.8	$ 519.6
Intersegment sales	0.3	0.1	0.2	0.0
Other income (deductions)	0.2	0.3	0.0	0.1
Total	$ 422.0	$ 458.1	$ 455.0	$ 519.7
Construction				
Net sales to customers	—	13.8	40.6	58.4
Other income (deductions)	—	−6.7	0.0	0.3
Total	—	$ 7.1	$ 40.6	$ 58.7

Source: Northrop Corporation, *Annual Reports,* 1984–1987.

10 and 11 provide group sales and operating profits, respectively. Contract acquisitions, funded-order backlogs, identifiable assets, capital expenditures, and depreciation and amortization for each group are shown in Exhibit 12. Exhibit 13 provides sales breakdowns by geographic areas and customer groups.

■ Aircraft Group

Northrop's largest and most important business segment was the aircraft group, which contributed over $2.5 billion of 1984 sales. The group consisted of three divisions: Aircraft, Advanced Systems, and Ventura.

Aircraft

The Aircraft Division handled production of the F-5s and the prototype F-20s. Sales of the F-5 were dwindling, notwithstanding a brief flurry of final orders. The final sales would have to be used to cover the costs of the write-down of inventory as the F-5 program came to an end. As for the F-20 program, one Prudential-Bache security analyst felt that it could "yield higher profits than any other major weapons production program in history," with pretax profit margins of 15% to 20%. Jones still believed a potential market of over 2000 planes existed, as numerous countries were going to have to replace their aging F-5s and other outmoded aircraft.

Northrop Corporation: Group Operating Profits (year ended December 31) (in millions)

Exhibit 11

	1984	1983	1982	1981
Aircraft	$203.3	$ 90.0	−$114.9	−$ 75.6
Electronics	81.7	77.3	54.1	51.8
Services	62.8	68.6	49.2	101.2
Construction	—	−22.7	−0.4	2.6
Total operating profit (loss)	$347.8	$213.2	−$ 12.0	$ 80.0
Less				
Other income (deductions) included in total revenue	−1.7	−6.5	3.8	17.7
State and local income taxes	18.3	11.4	2.2	9.9
General corporate expenses	87.8	67.8	48.6	39.3
Operating margin (loss)	$243.4	$140.5	−$ 66.6	$ 13.1

Source: Northrop Corporation, *Annual Reports*, 1984–1987.

The division's F-18 subcontract with McDonnell Douglas brought substantial cash flow to the company. Once thought politically vulnerable, the program had substantial backing in Congress and was far enough along in its production curve to survive. With approximately $623 million in 1984 sales and a backlog of over $1.1 billion, its future appeared secure. The division had also been involved with the assembly of the fuselage midsection of Boeing's 747 airliner since the start of the plane's production in 1966. Sales from that product reached $125 million in 1984 and were expected to increase modestly into the 1990s.

Advanced Systems

In 1981, the aircraft group's Advanced Systems Division, along with team members Boeing, LTV/Vought, and the General Electric Aircraft Engine Group, was awarded the development contract for the Air Force's top-secret Advanced Technology Bomber, better known as the Stealth. The Stealth had been widely discussed in the media, but little was actually known about the secret plane. A large strategic bomber with a radical shape and the technology to render it undetectable to radar, the Stealth was expected to cost nearly $500 million per plane. If it was put into production that price would make it the most expensive aircraft ever built. The Stealth was, as a consequence, politically vulnerable; its astounding price was a liability in Congress.

The development contract for the Stealth bomber had boosted company sales substantially. Although the exact figures were classified, analysts believed that the contribution to revenues from the development contract was nearly $1 billion in 1984 and would increase in 1985. While there was no assurance of Northrop being awarded the production contract, such a contract could produce sales of up to $35 billion over the next decade.

Perhaps as profitable would be the contract for the Air Force's Advanced Technology Fighter (ATF). Northrop's Advanced Systems Division had begun preliminary research and development on this project without the benefit of government funding. However, the ATF was as much of a gamble as the Stealth

---

Exhibit 12	**Northrop Corporation: R&D Expenditures and Group Operating Characteristics (year ended December 31) (in millions)**			
	1984	*1983*	*1982*	*1981*
R&D Expenditures				
Contract	$1339.6	$ 858.5	$ 489.6	$ 289.5
Noncontract	238.6	266.0	312.9	192.2
Total R&D expenditures	$1578.2	$1124.5	$ 802.5	$ 481.7
Contract Acquisitions				
Aircraft	$2903.6	$2719.3	$1513.9	$1376.7
Electronics	1335.7	715.9	591.1	402.8
Services	194.8	288.0	828.0	260.1
Construction	−2.8	3.0	8.7	28.3
Total acquisitions	$4431.3	$3726.2	$2941.7	$2067.9
Funded-Order Backlog				
Aircraft	$2492.4	$2152.7	$1553.3	$1491.9
Electronics	1273.6	640.3	593.6	527.5
Services	218.3	445.0	614.7	241.5
Construction	0.0	2.8	13.6	45.5
Total backlog	$3984.3	$3240.8	$2775.2	$2306.4
Identifiable Assets				
Aircraft	$1306.5	$1001.9	$ 783.5	$ 693.6
Electronics	370.4	264.1	223.6	181.7
Services	49.6	41.6	31.9	43.4
Construction	0.0	8.7	7.5	20.1
General corporate	230.0	297.7	306.0	318.6
Total assets	$1956.5	$1596.0	$1352.5	$1257.4
Capital Expenditures				
Aircraft	$ 232.6	$ 201.2	$ 246.9	$ 103.2
Electronics	68.0	40.9	59.7	44.6
Services	3.5	2.3	1.9	4.5
Construction	0.0	0.0	0.1	0.8
General corporate	41.2	48.7	68.2	36.6
Total expenditures	$ 345.3	$ 293.1	$ 376.8	$ 189.7
Depreciation and Amortization				
Aircraft	$ 105.8	$ 75.2	$ 33.3	$ 21.5
Electronics	22.9	19.8	12.2	10.1
Services	2.3	1.6	1.6	1.9
Construction	0.0	0.0	0.2	0.2
General corporate	7.1	13.2	13.6	7.3
Total depreciation and amortization	$ 138.1	$ 109.8	$ 60.9	$ 41.0

Source: Northrop Corporation, *Annual Reports,* 1985–1987.

in some respects. Designed to be a "superfighter" for the twenty-first century, the ATF was targeted to replace the F-15s and F-16s as America's top fighter. The competition for the contract, however, was expected to be long and costly. Teams consisting of a prime contractor and major subcontractor were required to put in bids to build the plane. The two winning teams would be selected in the early 1990s and each would then construct a prototype of their own design.

Northrop Corporation: Net Sales by Geographic Areas and Major Customers (year ended December 31) (in millions) **Exhibit 13**

	1984	1983	1982
Net Sales by Geographic Area			
U.S. government domestic agencies	$2670.5	$2185.9	$1429.4
Foreign military sales (FMS) through U.S. government			
Near/Middle East	276.1	264.8	336.1
Other areas	158.1	185.7	107.7
Other domestic sales	210.7	247.0	219.8
Direct foreign sales			
Near/Middle East	35.7	43.1	28.4
Other areas	336.7	334.1	351.5
Net sales	$3687.8	$3260.6	$2472.9
Net Sales by Major Customer			
U.S. government (including FMS)			
Aircraft	$2018.6	$1575.7	$ 946.9
Electronics	675.4	626.1	486.1
Services	410.7	434.6	440.1
Construction	0.0	0.0	0.1
Total U.S. government sales	$3104.7	$2636.4	$1873.2
Kingdom of Saudi Arabia (mainly FMS)			
Aircraft	$ 64.4	$ 30.9	$ 20.7
Electronics	0.2	7.1	29.3
Services	221.5	254.8	274.4
Total Saudi Arabian sales	$ 286.1	$ 292.8	$ 324.4

Source: Northrop Corporation, *Annual Report*, 1986.

One of these prototypes would be chosen for full-scale production by the team that created it. Northrop was the prime contractor on its team; McDonnell Douglas was the major subcontractor. Vying with Northrop and McDonnell Douglas for the contract were Lockheed, Rockwell Industries, and Boeing.

Although managements at both companies believed they had an excellent chance of being one of the two winning teams, financial analysts saw such a possibility as a mixed blessing. Each winning team would receive $691 million from the Defense Department but would probably have to spend several times that amount again in order to complete a prototype. The stakes were high, however, as the total production contract was expected to generate sales of $35 to $45 billion and extend into the next century. On the other hand, the loser could come away with nothing but substantial research and development costs.

Ventura

The aircraft group's Ventura Division had contributed sales of $350 million in 1984 and was the dominant producer of unmanned drones (self-propelled targets). Basically small monoplanes driven by turbojets, the drones were typically used to train pilots and antiaircraft crews in the operation of various weapons systems. A derivative of these drones had also been used by the U.S. Navy as a remotely piloted reconnaissance vehicle with infrared or high-resolution television. Several variants had been produced. Northrop's UMVs (unmanned vehicle) and RPVs (remotely piloted vehicle) were being used by every branch of the U.S. Armed Forces and numerous NATO countries as well.

The experience gained with unmanned flight vehicles helped land the Ventura Division a contract for a joint U.S. Air Force and Navy radar suppression missile system known as Tacit Rainbow. Designed to seek out and attack enemy radar-warning systems, it had the capability to loiter over an area until a transmitter activated and presented itself as a target.

■ Electronics Group

Northrop had used its cash inflows to build the electronics group into a business that, standing alone, would have ranked in the top 300 industrial companies compiled by *Fortune* in 1984. The group consisted of four divisions: Defense Systems, Electro-Mechanical, Electronics, and Precision Products. Group sales were $750 million in 1984.

Defense Systems

By 1985 the Defense Systems Division of the electronics group was on its way to becoming the nation's largest producer of airborne jamming equipment. Broadly defined as electronic countermeasures (ECMs), this equipment protected aircraft and crew by confusing and disrupting enemy radar-guided weapons systems. Enormously successful for a program of its type, Northrop's ECM equipment was typically installed on various aircraft such as the McDonnell Douglas F-15 fighter and the Boeing B-52 bomber. In addition, the division had attracted some foreign customers. Northrop was under contract with Denmark, Spain, and Canada to provide jamming systems for their armed forces. Britain had also purchased several ECM components for its Harrier aircraft.

Electro-Mechanical

Both the Electro-Mechanical and the Precision Products Divisions performed research and development in several areas that had led to contracts for Northrop. The Electro-Mechanical Division had become an important producer of passive sensor devices. These devices used electro-optical television and infrared technology to enable pilots and antiaircraft crews to locate targets without the telltale emissions of radar. Both the U.S. Army and the U.S. Navy had placed orders. The Navy refitted its F-14 Tomcat fighter squadrons with Northrop TV systems. These systems permitted visual identification at distances ten times greater than possible with older equipment.

Precision Products

Northrop's Precision Products Division pioneered the development of "strapdown" guidance and navigation systems. The name was derived from the method of bolting the systems' gyroscopes to a vehicle frame, rather than mounting the devices in complex gimbals, as was previously done. The design had applications in multiple areas including tactical missiles, airplanes, helicopters, spacecraft, and torpedoes. It was already being used on the F-20. Northrop expected to receive a guidance system contract for the advanced, medium-range, air-to-air missile from the U.S. Air Force and Navy, as well as the contracts for the Navy's Harpoon and Tomahawk antiship missiles.

Electronics

The Electronics Division was involved in two major projects. The first was the development and manufacture of the navigation system for the Air Force's AWACS (early warning) plane. The other project involved a long-term contract to produce the Advanced Inertial Reference Sphere (AIRS), the primary element of the MX Peacekeeper missile's internal guidance system. About the size of a basketball, the AIRS contained nearly as many parts as an entire fighter plane and had to be built to exacting tolerances. The program had the potential to last into the early 1990s, and it was expected to be worth in excess of $1 billion in future revenues. The MX was, however, a politically unstable program. Budget deficits and arms control talks made its future unclear.

■ Service Group

Service was the smallest group in terms of sales ($422 million in 1984). It was a no-growth business that lacked the excitement and glamor of Northrop's other groups. It consisted of one division, Aircraft Services, and two wholly owned subsidiaries, Northrop Services and Northrop Worldwide Aircraft Services.

Aircraft Services

The Aircraft Services Division provided on-the-job training in management and support for civil and military aviation personnel.

Northrop Services

The subsidiary Northrop Services provided environmental studies and general consulting to a number of federal agencies such as NASA and the Environmental Protection Agency.

Worldwide Aircraft Services

Northrop's Worldwide Aircraft Services subsidiary was the major revenue generator of the service group. It provided maintenance, support, and property management for military bases and for F-5s sold throughout the world. It had received a continuing maintenance contract for the famed U.S. Navy "Top Gun" fighter pilot school. A large portion of the group's operating profits were derived from this subsidiary's Peace Hawk/ATTS, a support services project for the Saudi Arabian Air Force. This project, however, was scheduled to end in 1986.

NORTHROP'S CORPORATE STRATEGY

With Thomas Jones leading the company, Northrop used a six-pronged strategy with aspects that distinguished it from many of its defense competitors. In the main, this strategy shaped the formulation of the F-20 program.

1. *High level of spending on research and development.* Research into radar avoidance won Northrop a profitable development contract for the Stealth bomber. Research in electronics, reinvestment, and the purchase of existing companies, such as the Hallicrafters Electronics Company, made Northrop the industry leader in ECM and other military electronics. The Tigershark became the first fighter with 1980s technology. By using avionics and electronics garnered from company research, the F-20 had some capabilities beyond those of its competitors, including the F-15, F-16, and F-18.

2. *Use of company funds for plant and equipment.* Northrop owned 94% of its plants, putting it above the industry average in terms of capital spending as a percentage of sales. The DOD owned half of all other defense aerospace manufacturing facilities. Northrop's ownership of its plants allowed more flexibility and made the F-20 project possible without government funding.

3. *Conservative financial and accounting practices.* Northrop employed a financial policy described by one analyst as reactionary. The company chose to expense development costs as they occurred. For example, all of the costs of the Tigershark program, including fixtures and tools, were charged against earnings in the year incurred. So far the F-20 write-offs had amounted to $258.5 million in 1982, $168.1 million in 1983, and $148.5 million in 1984, with a like amount expected for 1985.

4. *Focus on defense aerospace and electronics.* Exclusive of its 747 subcontract, Northrop had no significant commercial business, a characteristic that it had in common with some of its competitors. Northrop's sales of F-5s to foreign governments, however, did give it a degree of protection from domestic budget cuts and political swings that might affect defense spending. Northrop hoped the F-20 would allow it to keep this advantage.

5. *Competing for major frontline contracts.* In 1985, Northrop was competing for major domestic defense contracts and was building prototypes of the F-20.

6. *Willingness to take risks and reinvest cash flow.* Jones was adamant in his belief that private contractors should accept the risks inherent in developing new technology. The F-20 was the most visible symbol of Jones's entrepreneurial beliefs and was the only modern fighter ever developed solely from private funds without a government contract.

Not everyone was comfortable with these policies, however. There was little doubt that some Wall Street analysts would be happier if the Tigershark program was scrapped. Their predictions were that a decision to drop the program would add as much as $1.55 per share to the value of a Northrop stock. They also felt that the company would better off refraining from investment in manufacturing equipment for the F-20's production at a time when the company was recovering from earlier capital expenditures.

CONCLUSION

Northrop was clearly not prepared for the change in policy invoked by the Reagan administration, nor did it anticipate the political symbolism Third World countries would attach to having a top-quality U.S. Air Force inventory plane.

Relegating itself to the foreign market, Northrop had, in the past, managed to avoid most of the political infrastructure characteristic of the domestic defense market. It was unclear whether that approach would continue to be possible. Northrop's main competitor, General Dynamics, had the largest share of the industry, but many believed it also had an intangible advantage that went beyond its research and development prowess. General Dynamics built the F-16 in Texas, the home of Senate Armed Services Committee Chairman John Tower (R) and within the district of Jim Wright (D), House Majority Leader. Both controlled key votes concerning foreign military aid packages. As one anonymous Air Force officer joked, "It rolls off the assembly line faster if it's built in Texas."

Another obstacle Northrop had to overcome was the Defense Department itself. The Pentagon acted as middleman for all export sales and disseminated information and performance data to interested parties. DOD officials had privately stated that both the Air Force and the Navy preferred to promote the sales of their own fighters overseas "to amortize costs and to keep production lines open." Other officials allowed that the Pentagon "procurement community" preferred planes it had ordered to privately designed aircraft like the F-20, even if the aircraft were capable. In addition, the Air Force received $745,000 for each F-16 sold to export to cover flight preparation and testing. Northrop officials had complained that data comparing the F-20 and F-16 had not been given to prospective buyers and that the State Department had done little to represent their fighter. In fact, Jones publicly asked that the Air Force be ordered to inform other governments of the low cost and high performance of the Tigershark.

The current success of Northrop was due in large part to the cash flows generated by the F-5 Tiger. For decades, it had bankrolled Northrop's entry and growth in military electronics and higher levels of research and development in aerospace. The F-5 and T-38 had virtually created the export fighter and trainer markets and had claimed the lion's share for Jones and his company. Now, American and foreign export fighters alike were outperforming the aging Tigers, which were approaching obsolescence. To fail with the Tigershark would be tantamount to abandoning the market for export planes that Northrop had created and exploited for so long.

Ultimately, the future of Northrop's aircraft business rested on risky and uncertain programs: the Stealth (Advanced Technology Bomber), the Advanced Technical Fighter (ATF), and the F-20 Tigershark. The Stealth and ATF projects held great promise, and Jones wondered if Northrop would be better served by writing off the F-20 program and diverting the funds to these new projects. On the other hand, he knew that a successful F-20 program could help fund these projects and more, as the F-5 had before it. In 1981, Jones had remarked that "If we didn't make this investment [in the Tigershark], I would be telling you our future in fighter planes is less secure. It's riskier to do nothing." Four years later, with no orders in hand, Jones had to decide if that was still true.

REFERENCES

Air Cal, "Northrop Corporation: The Sky's the Limit," May 1986.

Air Force Magazine, "Trials of the Tigershark," January 1985, pp. 72–77.

Asian Defence Journal, "Revving Up for the Big Flyoff: F-20 vs. F-16," April 1986, pp. 1–7.

Atlantic Monthly, "The Airplane That Doesn't Cost Much," August 1984, pp. 46–55.

Aviation Week & Space Technology, "U.S. Will Assist Turkey in Improving Air Defense," February 20, 1984, p. 68.

Berstein & Company, "General Dynamics," August 6, 1981.

Business Week, "Look Who's Heading for No. 1 in Defense," April 19, 1982, pp. 70–75.

Business Week, "Northrop's Campaign to Get a New Fighter Flying in the Third World," June 18, 1984, pp. 74–75.

Chrisman, J. J., "Note on the Defense Electronics Industry," University of Georgia, 1982.

Cunningham, R., Dampier, J. D., Fuqua, A., Gill, E., Pannell, D., and Turner, L., "General Dynamics Corporation: Defense Electronics Industry Analysis," University of Georgia, 1984.

Dun's Business Month, "Northrop: The Rewards of Risk," December 1985, p. 36.

Electronic Industry Association, "Defense Electronics Market: Ten Year Forecast 1982–1991," October 1981.

Financial World, "A Cloudy Future for Northrop Corp.," February 20, 1985, pp. 38–39.

Flight International, "Tigershark Tour Raises Sales Hopes," October 6, 1984.

Flight International, "Stealth Specialists Win ATF Contracts," November 8, 1986, p. 2.

Forbes, "High Roller," March 2, 1981, pp. 38–39.

Fortune, "Northrop Aims for a Killing with the Tigershark," June 24, 1985.

Fox, J. R., with Field, J. L., *The Defense Management Challenge: Weapons Acquisition* (Cambridge, Mass.: Harvard Business School Press, 1988).

General Dynamics, *Annual Reports,* 1974–1984.

Insight, "Northrop Uses Spit and Polish to Keep an Untarnished Image," June 16, 1986.

Interavia, "The Affordable Fighter Market," January 1985, pp. 23–26.

International Defense Review, "East Asian Tactical Fighter Markets," December 1985.

Jurkus, A. F., "Requiem for a Lightweight: The Northrop F-20 Initiative," *Strategic Management Journal,* 11 (1990), pp. 59–68.

Leslie, J., "Northrop Corporation," University of South Carolina, 1988.

Moody's, *Moody's Industrial Manual,* 1980–1985.

Newsweek, "Northrop's F-20 Goes Begging," March 26, 1984, p. 71.

New York Times, "Dispute over Fighter Imports," April 5, 1985.

New York Times, "Northrop Backs Tigershark Jet," May 15, 1985.

Northrop Corporation, *Annual Reports,* 1982–1988.

Northrop Corporation Public Relations, *Northrop News,* 1989.

Shearson/American Express, "Aerospace/Defense Outlook," March 17, 1983.

Standard and Poor's, *NYSE Reports,* 1980–1985.

United Airlines, Inc.

Robert A. Orwig, Barbara A. Spencer, Mississippi State University

Captain Roger Small sat in his car overlooking Washington, D.C. Had it really been over 20 years since he applied for a job at United Airlines? When he left Bradley University in 1965, he had never expected to build a career as a pilot. It was a strange twist of fate that had led him to give up that job as an electronic engineer with G.E. for what would turn out to be one of the highest paid jobs in America.

But the good pay was only part of the picture. In his years at United, Roger had made many good friends. And he had enjoyed having plenty of time to raise a family. Still, Roger had not been satisfied just to put in his time. He had gotten involved in the pilot's union. It wasn't long before those wonderful committee assignments had started rolling his way. Of course, someone had to do them. Well, one thing had led to another and the darned union had voted him onto the Master Executive Council (MEC). Who could've predicted he would have been in the eye of some of United's most difficult moments? But before you can understand his story, you need to have a little background.

HISTORY

In many ways, the story of United Airlines is a tale of scientific conquest. This company has seen technological advances in its primary business that rival the computer industry's learning curve of today. Innovations regularly rock the industry and strain management's ability to adapt. Over the years, pressurization systems that allow pilots to bring their own atmosphere ten miles high, electronic beams that are as reliable as railroad tracks, and radio that allows constant contact with the ground, all have burst upon the airline industry bringing advancement and change. Today's jet engine technology ensures reliable operations at a level unheard of a few years ago. Radar sees through rain and fog, allowing flight-following over huge areas while ensuring safe spacing between aircraft transiting the most congested airports in the world.

Over 60 years ago, a man named Vern Gorst ventured into this fledgling industry with $40,000 of his own money and a little over $100,000 in investment capital. Known as a "promoter without peer" (Taylor, 1951:17), Mr. Gorst brought a marketing touch to what was then called the Pacific Air Transport Company.

On March 6, 1926, the Postmaster General handed over the Pacific Coast Route to this new company, ensuring its survival. Flying the mail during this period of our country's history was not for the fainthearted. Of Gorst's original 10 pilots, 3 lost their lives during the first winter of operations.

In 1927, Boeing Air Transport of Seattle rocked the airline industry with a major technological advancement—the air-cooled engine. This new engine technology slashed engine failure rates and as a result, company overhead, allowing Boeing to become the country's model airline. Eventually, Pacific Air Transport and Boeing merged with each other and with two other smaller firms all under the banner of United Airlines. In this way, United Airlines became the first coast to coast air transport giant.

In 1934, 45% of the airline's revenue still came from airmail delivery for the post office. Suddenly that year, all contracts were canceled and given to the Army to fly. This surprise move by the Postmaster General and President Roosevelt, which caused an incredible amount of name calling, reshuffling, and political maneuvering, turned out to be a mistake. After one disastrous winter in which 12 Army pilots lost their lives, President Roosevelt reinstated commercial air service. However, many airlines, including United, were forbidden to bid for the contracts for five years.

A loophole in the Airmail Act allowed United to get back into the mail delivery business, but the cost was high. To do so, it had to divest the Pratt and Whitney engine works, the Sikorsky and Vaught airplane plants, and the Boeing Airplane Company (Taylor, 1951) all of which were part of United at that time.

The United system that exited from this period has grown steadily over the years. In 1978, United was the largest airline in the United States. Because of its large size, the government refused to grant the airline any new routes; therefore, United's management was the first to support the move towards industry deregulation. They believed that this alternative would give them the chance to expand that they did not enjoy under government regulation (Zeeman, 1988).

Ironically, deregulation changed the rules of the competitive game in ways that United executives did not foresee. One major change was the flood of new entrants into the business. These upstarts achieved labor advantages of 25–30% over the established carriers (Meyer and Oster, 1984). From the beginning, they competed almost entirely on price, thereby placing ample pressure on established carriers such as United.

Other major effects of deregulation included a broader range of fares and services offered, increased productivity, lower cost structures, and increased service to small communities. In essence, deregulation stimulated cost, price and service innovation (Meyer and Oster, 1984). If United hoped to prosper in this new environment it would have to make adjustments on each of these fronts.

Unfortunately, United failed to aggressively move with the new changes. Mr. John Zeeman, executive vice president for marketing at United remembers, "We rocked along all right for 7 or 8 years with a rather inconsistent profit and growth." He recalls it as a time of frustration for the entire management team as they sought to realign with the changing environment.

THE AIRLINE INDUSTRY TODAY

Ten years have gone by since deregulation plowed through the airline industry. Although many changes have occurred, most analysts still view the industry as being in a state of disequilibrium. The expectations at the time of deregulation were that equilibrium would be reached in a relatively short period of time. A host of environmental variables acted to slow these adjustments. Among these were the labor unions, the air traffic controller's strike, the increase in fuel prices, and the immediate, but limited, success of the new entrants.

The most noticeable trend for the airlines over the last 10 years has been the growing reliance on the hub and spoke system of operations. This method establishes a number of routes connected to a central hub where passengers can be collected from feeder flights, transferred to other flights of the same line, and taken to their ultimate destination. This route structure has cost advantages and also provides an effective entry barrier for competitors. It is widely held that passengers prefer not to change planes. Given that a change of planes is required, the preference would be an on-line change versus an interline change. The hub system allows the major carrier to collect passengers from outlying, less traveled locations and send them to their final destinations on the larger more economical aircraft, thus improving average revenue per passenger. It also allows for advantageous connections with a host of commuters who work in collaboration with each major to feed into the hub from locations that are traveled too lightly for the major to service. A synopsis of these systems and the relationships among the majors is in Exhibit 1.

Labor issues have also gained importance over the last 10 years. The airlines are heavily unionized. Prior to deregulation, unionized labor had been very successful in raising salaries. Although the airline pilot still rates among the top 10 paying jobs in the United States, the salary for pilots has faced continual downward pressure since deregulation. At that time, the appearance of new entrants with dramatically lower cockpit costs became an industry-wide concern.

The major way of dealing with this development has been the use of the "B–scale". The "B–scale" allows airlines to hire pilots at a much lower rate than the going union contract with a promise to transfer them to the "A–scale" after a specified experience level is reached. The use of this technique has split the union's bargaining power and has caused dissension among the various labor factions within the larger airlines. Although, this unrest is alleged to affect safety, no measurable, negative impact has been noted thus far.

The high level of merger activity within the industry also illustrates the airlines' continued disequilibrium. In attempts to expand and solidify market positions, most of the smaller majors have sought acquisition targets. Texas Air is the dean of merger mania. Texas Air has combined Peoples Express, Continental, Eastern and several smaller airlines into one highly leveraged megacarrier. As this is written, Eastern has filed for bankruptcy protection, resulting

Exhibit 1   **Major Airlines Code Sharing Agreements (as of March 1987)**

American Airlines
  Air Midwest
  AV Air
  Chaparral
  Command Airways
  Executive Air Charter
  Metro Airlines
  Simmons Airlines
  Wings West

Continental Airlines
  Air New Orleans
  Britt Airways
  Colgan Airways
  Emerald Airlines
  Gulf Air
  Mid Pacific
  PBA
  Presidential Airways
  Rocky Mountain Airways
  Royale Airways
  Trans-Colorado

Delta Airlines
  Atlantic Southeast
  Business Express
  Comair
  Skywest

Eastern Airlines
  Air Midwest
  Atlantis Airlines
  Aviation Associates
  Bar Harbor
  Britt Airways
  Metro Airlines
  Precision Valley Aviation

Northwest Airlines
  Big Sky Airlines
  Express Airlines
  Fisher Brothers
  Mesaba Aviation
  Simmons Airlines

Pan American
  Air Atlanta
  Pan Am Express (Ranscome)
  Presidential Airlines

Piedmont Aviation
  Brockway Air
  CC Air
  Henson Aviation
  Jetstream Int'l.

Trans World Airlines
  Air Midwest
  Piedmont
  Resort Air
  Resort Commuter

United Airlines
  Air Wisconsin
  Aspen Airways
  Westair Commuter

USAir
  Air Kentucky
  Chautauqua Airlines
  Crown Airlines
  Pennsylvania Airlines
  Pocono Airline
  Southern Jersey Airlines
  Suburban Airlines

Note: Data from *Industry Averages*, 1988.

from a strike of its machinists supported by its pilots. The position they hold in the market may be drastically affected (see Exhibit 2).

Mergers affect the hub positions of the carriers involved in two important ways. First, they allow the carriers to build a position in a market and second, they allow carriers to consolidate a market position at the hub. An example of the first would be Delta's entrance into the western markets such as Salt Lake City through its acquisition of Western. An example of the latter would be the combination of TWA and Ozark who were both important in St. Louis. The latter type of consolidation must meet federal standards concerning antitrust violations. However, to date, the government has been very liberal in the interpretation of the antitrust statutes. In fact, no merger proposal has been turned down during the deregulated period (Dempsey, 1988).

It was recognized early in the deregulated period that strong route networks would be of significant importance; however, the vigorous marketing efforts necessary to compete in this highly competitive environment were not so read-

---

Market Share   **Exhibit 2**

1987 Rank	Company	Market Share (%)	United's Market Share Since Deregulation				
			Year	Revenue (in billions)	Earnings (Loss) (in millions)	No. of Planes	Market Share (%)
1	Texas Air System	19.0	1978	3.55	284.5	336	20.4
2	United	16.7	1979	3.30	(99.1)	351	17.2
3	American	14.1	1980	4.46	(14.1)	324	19.0
4	Delta	11.7	1981	4.54	(104.0)	314	17.3
5	NWA	10.0	1982	4.70	(17.3)	318	18.4
6	TWA	8.3	1983	5.37	120.8	329	18.7
7	USAir	7.3	1984	6.22	238.0	319	18.4
8	Pan Am	6.6	1985	5.29	(95.3)	325	14.9
9	Southwest	1.7	1986	7.11	(112.8)	364	17.2
10	America West	1.5	1987	8.29	(4.2)	382	17.1
	Others	3.1	1988 (est.)	9.14	255.0	403	17.2*

Source: Wall Street Journal (7/28/88).

*Through June.

ily apparent. The frequent flier programs, red carpet programs and affinity club plans are all ways for an airline to reward the businessperson for choosing its service over the competitors (Zeeman, 1988). These programs and competitive pricing policies work to draw buyers. They also cut deeply into profits. For an airline to succeed, it must use these methods judiciously.

Another trend that cuts across all players in this industry is an increased use of debt. The airline industry is capital intensive. The purchase price of a new Boeing 747 is approximately $150 million. Expansion at airports is very costly. These costs have increasingly been financed with techniques that have placed the firms in a more leveraged position. One preferred means of financing is to lease the aircraft as needed. This increases management's flexibility in the face of an uncertain economic environment.

Safety continues to be an important concern in the airline industry. In the unhappy event of an accident, all major news media descend on the company. The large number of people involved in an airplane accident coupled with the general public's fear of and respect for flying makes the coverage highly desirable from the news agency's view. Unfortunately, from the company's point of view, the coverage is almost surely negative.

Managing the negative impact of this coverage becomes important for all major carriers. The majors counteract this media pressure with active public relations departments. This threat is potentially more damaging for smaller carriers that cannot afford to divert resources into such departments.

Two recent examples illustrate this point. First, Delta's loss of two aircraft at Dallas, both caused by pilot error, has negatively affected the company's ability to compete with American at that hub. Yet Delta's public relations personnel have performed admirably in limiting the damage to the Dallas market. Second, on February 11, 1989, nine people lost their lives due to a structural failure of the aircraft on United flight 811. In this case, the pilot was instrumental in saving the aircraft and the remaining passengers. The public relations department has sought to focus the public's eye on the expertise demonstrated by the pilot rather than the significant maintenance questions arising from such a structural failure.

Another aspect of the negative media attention associated with an accident is the pressure brought to bear on federal regulatory powers, most notably the Federal Aviation Administration (FAA). Even though airline safety rates are much higher than those of automobiles, the shock value of multiple deaths involved in the typical airline crash could influence the FAA to become more restrictive. Almost certainly, this result would have negative economic results for the majors.

At present, safety regulations include the inspection of maintenance facilities, rule making for operations, licensing of pilots, and the inspection of the flying operations for compliance. This type of regulation constrains competition for the public good. After deregulation occurred, some feared that, in the name of competition, airlines would slash their maintenance and training budgets resulting in unsafe flying practices. The point at which these cuts might become dangerous is viewed as too important to allow the industry to determine through trial and error. For this reason the public requires the federal government to regulate this area of the airlines' business.

Quality of life issues are certain to be an increasingly important trend for the airline industry. Airplanes are noisy and, like most transportation forms that use engines, they dirty the air with their exhaust. *Fortune* magazine identifies environmental protection as the number 1 issue of the 1990s (Kupfer, 1988:45). This constraint will affect the expansion of old airfields, the location and building of new airfields, and the type of aircraft allowed in the various airports around the country. The impacts on those firms which compete with less modern equipment could be significant.

Advances in computer technology and communications allow firms to react more quickly to developments abroad. Major airlines are becoming more enmeshed with foreign customers, competitors, and suppliers (Main, 1988:55). Two upcoming events illustrate this shift towards globalization. In 1992, the European Economic Community will remove most of the remaining trade barriers among member nations. In addition, Hong Kong is to be taken over by China in 1997. International business travel should increase as firms compete for these global markets.

The airlines are tied to the business cycle through their dependence on oil prices. If fuel prices rise one cent, the industry sees a cost rise of $100 million annually (*Industry Surveys*, 1988). A shift upward in fuel prices will give an advantage to established carriers who fly newer, more fuel efficient equipment.

Another factor that ties the industry to the business cycle is the businessperson. Business travel is typically price insensitive yielding the highest profit margins in the business. However, during general recessions, business people have lighter travel requirements or replace travel with other means of communications. Presently, the rate of business travel is growing, but the threatened recession could shut it down.

Finally, the baby boom generation will move through the economy with two major effects on the industry. First, it will leave a scarcity of entry level job seekers making it difficult for airlines to attract quality pilots, mechanics and other workers. Second, baby boomers share a growing interest in vacation travel domestically and abroad. As a group, these vacationers may be comparatively price insensitive because so many come from dual career families. Fewer price sensitive customers would mean fewer deep discounted fares, possibly increasing profits.

THE COMPETITION

Key competition for United comes from 4 transportation groups. First and foremost are the other major airlines which include American, Delta, USAir, Texas Air Corporation, and Northwest. Second, the new entrants, commuters, national and regional airlines offer competition as the low cost operators, though the percentage of passengers on these carriers is relatively small. Third, the international carriers, such as Japan Air Lines, British Airways, and KLM are increasingly a factor as they pursue their global strategies. The last major competitive group includes other transportation and communication methods.

American is United's strongest competitor. Upon deregulation, American pursued a contrarian strategy. It ignored the merger strategy pursued by most carriers and elected to grow from within. The results have been impressive. American's route structure is strong and growing. It has been an innovator in the fields of marketing and finance, and was first to introduce a frequent flier program. Even its labor problems have been minor, compared to other carriers. In 1988, it became the carrier with the biggest fleet and the highest traffic in the United States (Ellis, 1989).

The other major airlines have many of the same strengths and weaknesses as United. They are financially strong. They have healthy, multihub route structures. Their computerized systems enable them to adjust fares on a capacity basis. They have good marketing plans and have seen consistent growth, if not consistent profits, in the deregulated period.

The smaller carriers have neither the wide route structures, nor the capitalization of the majors. Their advantage lies in their use of a less expensive, nonunionized work force. These carriers have little trouble attracting pilots at $1500 a month salaries, although they do have some difficulty in keeping experienced ones. One problem for the smaller carriers is the public's view of their safety. Though the commuters are still safer than car travel, they are 3 to 20 times less safe than the majors (Meyer and Oster, 1984). Most of the new entrants and commuters have connected with the established carriers and now support the larger carrier's hub system in order to enjoy the benefits of increased passenger load factors.

International competitors pose a growing threat. Consisting of national firms that enjoy almost total control of their nation's air assets, these national airlines are a source of pride for their governments. As a result, the governments will not allow outside competition that would be a threat to the national airline's business. Moreover, some governments subsidize their national airlines, if necessary. These subsidized firms are thus granted significant advantages when in competition with a U.S. firm.

Often overlooked competitors for the airline industry are alternative forms of travel and communications. Cars, buses, trains, and other transportation forms compete with airlines for customers. Communications also can substitute for airline travel, especially among that most important target for the major airlines, the business traveler. The facsimile machine, capable of quick, efficient, inexpensive communications is an excellent example of a cost saving communication technology. Telephone conferences and video tapes also take the place of face-to-face meetings in some situations.

CASE OF THE MISSING EXECUTIVE

On February 17, 1987, United announced a change in name and a major change in emphasis. Chief executive officer (CEO), Richard Ferris was leading the company in a radical new direction. His plan was to turn United into an integrated travel company, concentrating on the special needs of the businessperson.

Ferris envisioned a travel empire in which the customer could be taken to the airport from his or her place of business via rental car, flown to the appropriate destination, driven to the company's hotel in another rental car, and returned to his or her place of business in the same manner. He hinted about plans for corporate travel packages that would produce high volumes of full-fare business. He described schemes to provide dual check-ins and frequent flier bonuses for hotel and rental car customers (Labich, 1987:44). He argued that each division would be more valuable as part of the team than standing alone. Even the company's new name, Allegis, was viewed as a means of marketing the new travel conglomerate.

A scant 4 months later, Mr. Ferris was fired. His undoing actually began in March of 1987 when the Coniston Partners, a New York investment partnership, began their involvement with Allegis. On May 13, 1987, the partnership decided to buy out the company. In their opinion, the management at United had put the company in a position where the investment group could become "a catalyst to improve shareholders value and actually improve the fundamentals of the company for the other constituencies" (Tierney, 1988).

According to Paul Tierney of the partnership, several company moves precipitated the buy-out attempt (Tierney, 1988). First, no convincing argument was ever offered by management as to when the proposed conglomerate strategy was going to payoff. As a result, major shareholders were becoming increasingly hostile towards United's management in general and Mr. Ferris in particular. They felt that Allegis stock, then selling in the $55–$60 range, was vastly undervalued. Some analysts judged that the company would be worth $100 a share if its operations were sold separately. What was needed were immediate steps to improve stock price. Despite these sentiments, Ferris made precisely the opposite move. In late March and early April, he issued over 8 million new shares of stock at $56.50 in order to finance his purchase of Hilton International. The move baffled investment professionals and prompted widespread take-over speculation.

These take-over rumors caused Ferris to begin defensive action. He arranged a deal in which Boeing Company would pay $700 million for notes convertible to 16% of Allegis' shares. The idea was that the increased leverage would make a take over more difficult. Management then proposed to further leverage the company with a recapitalization. The recapitalization included, among other things, $7 million to implement the Allegis name change. Some investors viewed this series of actions as the efforts of an inept management to defend against the possibility of a hostile take-over bid. The Coniston partnership began buying the stock in earnest.

The partnership accumulated a 14% stake in UAL. According to Mr. Tierney, the partnership faced two alternatives to force the restructuring change that they wanted: a proxy contest or a consent proceeding. The partnership decided on the consents method "soliciting written consents from shareholders to oust all but 3 of the company's directors, and to elect 6 of our own nominees" (Tierney, 1988:A–34).

On May 26, the partnership went to court to block management's proposed Boeing deal and the recapitalization plan. On the ninth of June, Richard Ferris resigned. The board agreed to the Coniston plan in return for the discontinuance of the consent proceeding. Coniston's restructuring plan simply suggested the sale of nonairline parts, a distribution of the cash on a one-time basis and a continuation of the company with a renewed focus on their core business (Labich, 1987).

The Coniston moves overshadowed significant labor developments during this same period. The pilot's union wrote a letter offering to buy the airline company by means of an Employee Stock Ownership Plan (ESOP), the sale of all nonairline assets, and a recapitalization of the airline. Labor's suggestions formed the basis for the board's actions subsequent to Mr. Ferris' dismissal. Labor's view of the travel-service company was strongly negative. "In today's highly competitive industry environment, a first-class airline cannot afford the drain of financial capital and corporate commitment that results from excessive diversification," the letter stated. "In our view, an airline should not be operated as part of a diversified enterprise" (Kaizer, AP news release April 1987) (see Exhibit 3).

UNITED TODAY

■ Top Management

The year following Ferris' resignation was a busy one. Frank Olson, of Hertz, was named interim CEO. Mr. Olson announced that the company would restructure by selling off the parts associated with nonairline operations, exactly as the union had proposed. A group of executives, led by Mr. Olson announced their intention to purchase Hertz in partnership with Ford Motor Company. Hilton International was sold to Ladbroke PLC of Britain for $1.07 billion. The deal was finalized on October 14, just prior to the stock market crash of 1987. The Westin Hotel chain was sold to the Bass Group and Aoki of Japan for $1.3 billion. Labor's ESOP was formally rejected.

The harvesting of these business interests was not the only thing United had to accomplish. Mr. Ferris had been a hotel man and Mr. Olson, a rental car man. What was needed was a new executive who had exemplary credentials in the airline business. Mr. Steve Wolf was selected to be that man.

Hired from the Flying Tigers, a West Coast cargo carrier, Mr. Wolf understands the business. He has become known as a turnaround expert in the airline industry. Perhaps his most notable achievement was the revitalization of Republic in the early years of deregulation. While at Republic, he won concessions from employees, consolidated the route structure, and laid the groundwork for the company's merger with Northwest. Next, he spent 23 months at Flying Tigers, where he supervised another corporate success. The cargo line

Exhibit 3　　　　　　　　**Financial Review**

	June 30, 1988	December 1987	December 1986
Statements of Consolidated Financial Position (in thousands)			
Assets			
Current assets			
Cash and cash equivalents	857,145	2,208,016	102,396
Receivables, net	902,891	816,547	717,807
Inventories, net	203,290	221,744	198,497
Prepaid expenses and other	148,842	180,711	122,146
Refundable federal income tax			61,118
	2,112,168	3,427,018	1,201,964
Net assets of discontinued operations		426,747	1,102,886
Operating property and equipment			
Owned	7,548,851	7,214,028	6,444,981
Accumulated depreciation and amortization	(3,672,387)	(3,534,297)	(3,144,748)
	3,876,464	3,679,731	3,300,233
Capital leases	521,642	643,134	642,959
Accumulated amortization	(210,698)	(316,981)	(283,569)
	310,944	326,153	359,390
	4,187,408	4,005,884	3,659,623
Other assets			
Intangibles, net	251,084	287,096	393,090
Other	125,770	79,524	68,965
	376,854	366,620	462,055
	$6,676,430	$8,226,269	$6,426,528
Liabilities and shareholder's equity			
Current liabilities			
Short-term borrowings	$ 297,577	$1,010,311	$ 747,698
Advance ticket sales	747,734	581,333	561,322
Accounts payable	510,782	496,216	474,970
Other	1,448,263	1,322,001	792,703
	3,004,356	3,409,861	2,576,693
Long-term debt	1,902,371	996,553	663,010
Long-term obligations under capital leases	415,166	430,742	450,725
Other liabilities, deferred credits and redeemable preferred stock	557,313	467,026	443,852
Common stock and other shareholder's equity			
Common stock	116,331	292,354	251,118
Other (additional capital and retained earnings)	680,893	2,629,733	2,041,130
	797,224	2,922,087	2,292,248
Commitments and contingent liabilities (see notes)			
	$6,676,430	$8,226,269	
	$6,676,430	$8,226,269	$6,426,528
Statement of Consolidated Operations (in thousands, except per share)			
Operating revenues			
Passenger	$3,707,516	$6,855,750	$5,958,144
Cargo	252,789	488,828	413,532
Contract services and other	481,869	948,212	733,465

	June 30, 1988	December 1987	December 1986
Statement of Consolidated Operations (in thousands, except per share)			
Operating expenses			
Salaries and related costs	1,390,812	2,777,618	2,557,673
Aircraft fuel	616,996	1,243,579	1,099,441
Traffic commissions	528,397	907,049	714,667
Depreciation and amortization	258,157	548,990	501,086
Purchased services	273,309	480,443	436,663
Rentals and landing fees	191,145	342,871	287,905
Maintenance materials	130,505	251,452	224,698
Food and beverages	97,499	183,001	156,661
Advertising and promotion	93,246	174,914	207,207
Personnel expenses	78,389	159,123	147,268
Other	482,382	992,502	698,591
	4,140,837	8,061,542	7,031,860
Earnings from operations	301,337	231,248	(73,281)
Other deductions (income)			
Interest expense	106,591	238,502	208,762
Interest capitalized	(15,025)	(16,399)	(11,925)
Interest income	(55,787)	(51,031)	(19,344)
Other, net	25,226	67,266	110,685
	61,005	238,338	288,178
Earnings (loss), continuing operations before taxes	240,332	(7,090)	(214,897)
Provisions (credit), for taxes	88,243	(2,896)	(102,062)
Earnings (loss) from continuing operations	152,089	(4,194)	(112,835)
Discontinued operations			
Earnings from discontinued operations, less taxes	457	68,817	124,435
Gain of sale of discontinued operations, less taxes	548,478	270,494	
Net earnings	701,024	335,117	11,600

	1983	1984	1985	1986
Airline Industry Financial Averages				
Sales	523.35	588.09	549.28	543.89
Operating income	45.71	69.74	54.33	55.78
Profit margins	8.73	11.86	9.89	10.26
Depreciation	35.22	38.06	37.86	39.12
Taxes	1.53	12.46	6.43	5.20
Earnings	6.30	13.10	15.48	1.24
Dividends	1.51	1.53	1.94	2.09
Earnings as % of sales	1.20	2.23	2.82	.31
Dividends as % of earnings	23.97	11.68	12.53	168.55
PE ratios				
High	28.41	14.07	13.97	184.09
Low	20.83	9.14	10.46	143.72
Book value	125.42	137.70	146.63	147.43

Notes: The companies used for this data are AMR Corp., Allegis Corp., Delta Airlines, NWA Inc., Pan American, and USAir Group (added 12-17-86).
Data based on *Industry Surveys* (28 April, 1988), A–41.

reported earnings of $45 million for the first 9 months of 1987 versus a loss of $55 million just a year earlier.

Wolf's turnaround skills are currently in demand at United—a company unaccustomed to playing second fiddle to anyone. His mandate is to overtake arch-rival American and return United to the number-1 spot in the airline industry. His 1988 plans include $1.6 billion in capital investments designed to revamp United's aging fleet, improve terminal and baggage facilities, and increase capacity. He is also focusing on cost-cutting measures by pushing his employees to accept wage cuts while making painful changes in work rules. Wolf claims that unless he wins these concessions, United will never catch up with American (Ellis, 1989).

A shrewd, tough bargainer, Wolf is likely to give the unions a run for their money. Says one former Tiger International Union member, "He doesn't like us. He views us as another fixed expense, like food and fuel . . . Those United boys are in for a real fight" (Perry, 1988).

However, given United's stellar earnings in 1988, many employees do not see the need for concessions. In the first 9 months of 1988, the company's operating earnings rose 89%, to $40.6 million. After cutting United's debt by a third, Wolf still has $1.1 billion in cash (see Exhibit 3). In addition, he repurchased a large chunk of United's stock, raising share prices 60%, to $112.

■ Other Changes at United

In addition to the company's overall goal of being the best airline in the world (Zeeman, 1988), United has 3 primary objectives: (1) To provide the best and safest service for customers; (2) to provide fair compensation and growth opportunities for employees; (3) to produce a fair return to investors (*United Times*, 1988).

In order to meet these objectives, the company is utilizing the Introspect initiative. This process, which is run by an external consulting group, aims to build a more efficient, cost-effective and focused organization. Through Introspect, the United managers intend to restructure the organization allowing each department or division to better focus on company goals and objectives. Some of the structural changes include the following:

1. The elimination of unnecessary management layers. For example, the station managers of the 6 largest airports now report directly to a senior vice president, instead of to regional vice presidents. The hoped for result is better communication and faster decision making.
2. Increased spans of control. Introspect found 500 managers who managed 5 or fewer employees. Span of control was increased by 30%.
3. An improved succession system. This system establishes new career paths, recognizing that not all employees need or want to be managers.
4. A reallocation of employees to meet strategic business needs. Areas such as market analysis and operations research were dramatically increased in size. In human resources, a larger staff was added to focus on employee training and career development. In marketing, a market development department was added to gain better understanding of customers. The corporate sales force was expanded to gain more revenue from key corporate accounts (*United Times*, 1988).

United is also making changes in its internal operations. Operations in the airline business include almost all customer contacts. United has reinforced its focus on this vital area with a "best airline" program. According to John Dansdill, director of systems operations control, the purpose of the program is to process customers in a professional way (Dansdill, 1989).

The program began with an organizational study on how operations could enhance dependability and service, the keys to a quality product. Representative areas identified for improvement were departures, arrivals, and baggage handling. Standards for these and other areas were established, enabling management to improve organizational control.

United has a well-developed route structure that is the envy of most of its competition. The extension of that system is certainly an objective. Priorities include, strengthening the existing hubs, as in the recently completed terminal in Chicago, and expanding into new areas. One statistic concerning United's hub system illustrates it's strength: United is the number 1 airline at 4 out of 5 of their key hub cities (*Annual Report*, 1987).

United is presently laying the groundwork for a global strategy. The company sees the international theaters as particularly lucrative and in line with its business strengths. The recently finished Covia Partnership is a major move in this direction. Under this partnership United has sold partial ownership of its computer system, Apollo, to 5 large international airlines. British Airways, Swissair, USAir, KLM, and Alitalia have joined with United as the airline industry moves towards global distribution systems (*UAL Corporation Second Quarter Report*, 1988).

CONCLUSION

Captain Roger Small smiled as he considered the changes that had recently taken place at United. Every one of those changes had been masterminded by the pilot's union, he gloated. Wolf might be a smart cookie but he wasn't doing one thing that the pilots couldn't do themselves . . . except for his confounded demand for wage cuts.

But the pilots' union still had a few tricks up its sleeve, he thought. For one thing, the machinists had received an 11% raise from United in 1987—a fact that even Wolf couldn't overlook. The developing shortage of mechanics had helped the machinists' union in that situation, and the growing shortage of pilots, due to increasing retirements (see Exhibit 4), should serve the same purpose now. The pilots had grounded the airline when they went on strike in 1985 and they could strike again.

In addition, the pilots had not given up on their bid to take over the airline. And indeed, Small had high hopes in that regard. Although management had tried to thwart their plans by inserting a "poison pill" in the machinist's contract, the courts had already ruled 2 of the 3 points to be illegal and a similar ruling was anticipated for the third. When the decision was finalized, the union planned to revise its offer. The recent rise in stock price had made its last offer obsolete.

The union's ace-in-the-hole for its take-over plan was Mr. William Howard, former CEO of Piedmont Airline. The union had hired Mr. Howard to head its take-over attempt and to run its airline. In Small's opinion, Howard was eminently qualified. He had done for Piedmont, what Wolf had done for Republic, but without gouging labor in the process. In fact, Howard had paid the pilots at

---

Exhibit 4   **Pilot Retirement, 1988–99**

Company	Year											
	88	89	90	91	92	93	94	95	96	97	98	99
American	61	70	136	150	221	235	269	226	225	226	252	203
United	143	191	209	198	241	271	273	253	256	263	222	285
Delta	53	62	75	70	98	95	147	260	286	248	341	309

Notes: Figures are based on age 60 attrition only. Data does not include professional flight engineers. Information obtained from Future Airline Pilots of America.

Piedmont, then a regional carrier, the same wages earned by pilots at the majors. He was obviously the man to run United.

With this thought in mind, Roger turned the key and headed his Porsche into the city. He had a 3:00 P.M. meeting with the MEC. The topic: strategy.

REFERENCES

Dansdill, John. Personal interview (January 27, 1989). Director, Systems Operations Control.

Dempsey, Paul Stephen. (November 21, 1988). "Deregulation Has Spawned Abuses in Air Transport." *Aviation Week and Space Technology* pp. 147–151.

Ellis, James E. (February, 1989). "Will the Carrot and Stick Work at United?" *Business Week,* pp. 56–57.

Kaizer, Hank. Personal interview (November 4, 1988). Pilot at United and unofficial historian. Internal letters and Communications from 1987 and 1988.

Kupfer, Andrew. (September 26, 1988). "Managing for the 1990s." *Fortune,* pp. 44–50.

Labich, Kenneth. (July 6, 1987). "How Dick Ferris Blew It." *Fortune,* pp. 42–45.

Main, Jeremy. (September 26, 1988). "Winning Organizations." *Fortune,* pp. 50–62.

Meyer, John R., and Clinton V. Oster, Jr. *Deregulation and the New Airline Entrepreneurs.* The MIT Press, Cambridge, Mass., 1984.

Perry, Nancy J. (January 18, 1988). "A Wolf from Tiger." *Fortune,* p. 145.

Taylor, Frank J. *High Horizons.* McGraw-Hill Book Co., New York, 1951.

Tierney, Paul, Jr. (June 6, 1988). "Someone Said, 'Let's Tear It Up in Front of Ferris' Face.' " *Crain's Chicago Business,* p. A–34.

UAL, Inc. *Annual Reports,* 1985, 1986, 1987.

UAL Corporation Second Quarter Report. (July 1988).

United Times. (September 1988).

Zeeman, John. Personal interview (November 4, 1988). Executive vice president for marketing.

Note on the Motion Picture Industry

Marilyn L. Taylor, University of Kansas; Natalie T. Taylor, Babson College

The U.S. theater industry is part of the broader motion picture industry. Exhibit 1 summarizes the major periods in the history of the motion picture industry. In 1981 the theater industry faced a diversity of opinion as to its future. On one hand was the relative stability that the industry had experienced over the prior two decades. On the extreme other side were prophets of doom who predicted that the theater industry would fall victim to changing demographics and advancing use of new technologies such as videocassettes, videodiscs, cable TV, and pay TV.

Major Periods of the Motion Picture Industry **Exhibit 1**

Years	Characteristics
To 1905	"Archeology"
1905–1914	Silent short
1915–1927	Silent feature
1927–1934	Coming of sound
1934–1941	Hollywood's golden age
1941–1948	The war and its effects
1948–1955	Hollywood beleaguered
1955–1962	Blockbuster years
1963–	New Hollywood

Source: Charles F. Altman, "Towards a Historiography of American Film," in Richard D. MacCann and Jack C. Ellis, eds., *Cinema Examined* (New York: E. P. Dutton, Inc., 1982), pp. 103–129.

PRE–WORLD WAR II

The motion picture industry from its inception in the late 1800s until World War II was characterized by immense strides in film technology, the development of a film distribution network, the emergence of large chains of movie theaters, and, finally, vertical integration of the industry.

▪ Film Technology

Motion picture technology was originally developed in the later nineteenth century. The technology was the result of dozens of inventions primarily in the United States, England, and France. Most notable among American inventors was Thomas A. Edison. Edison's kinetoscope, an unwieldy peep show machine, gave way to the cinematograph. This lighter and more compact mechanism was developed in France and first shown in Paris in 1895. Moreover, the cinematograph was hand-cranked—a boon in an era when electricity was not universally available and what was available was not standardized output. The machine functioned as camera, projector, and printer. The cinematograph used Edison's invention of a sprocket-wound film and the idea of projecting successive frames on screen. From this early beginning France dominated filmmaking until World War I, when German restrictions forced the French industry to give way to the United States.

▪ Early Films

Early showings of silent shorts occurred in carnival peep shows. Under the direction of the first important film artist, Edwin S. Porter, such great classics as the 15-minute *The Great Train Robbery* (1903) were filmed by Edison Manufacturing Company of New York. Edison agreed to invest in technical equipment and set aside space when it became clear that moving pictures were indeed profitable; in 1906 the Edison studio was established. The company made a number of innovations during these years. For example, through Edison's efforts, the width-to-length proportion for screens became standardized at 4:3, as did the width of film stock at 35 mm, although 70 mm became an option in the 1950s.

Early films were viewed by audiences in storefront theaters called nickelodeons and later in vaudeville theaters. At the turn of the century vaudeville had been the preeminent American popular entertainment. In 1908 at the vaudeville height there were 300 touring companies and 1500 legitimate theaters coast to coast. Some of the theaters organized into chains with centralized management for booking. But by the mid-1920s most vaudeville theaters had been closed or converted to movie theaters.

Early silent shorts were fill-ins between live vaudeville acts. Later, as filmmaking became more sophisticated and feature films developed, the vaudeville acts became the fill-ins. A ready supply of films became available after 1903. It took some time, however, for distribution networks to form. At first, exhibitors purchased films directly from producers and took their film "library" on the road. Later, "exchanges" sprang up to handle distribution of the shorts. Paramount Pictures Corporation, an amalgamation of 11 state exchanges, was formed in 1914. Paramount helped finance and advertise films and charged producers 35% of gross. As sound technology was produced, filmed "stage shows" or vaudeville shorts replaced the live acts.

The talkies came into vogue with *The Jazz Singer* (1927), the first major sound motion picture. This movie, starring Al Jolson, was an enormous commercial success. Many of the early silent film stars, however, were not capable of making the transition into sound films. Even Charlie Chaplin was never satisfied with his voice on the sound track.

■ Development of Theaters

By the 1920s nickelodeons and converted vaudeville theaters had evolved to become the downtown movie palaces. In these theaters, musical accompaniment for the silent films was provided by pianists, organists, and even orchestras, often improvising from movie scores. Regional chains of theaters developed. This development coincided with the development of the chain store strategy, the major marketing innovation from 1900 to 1920.[1]

The 1920s witnessed an unprecedented boom in theater construction and a beginning of consolidation into chains. One of the largest chains was First National Exhibitors Circuit, a franchise initiated in 1917 and initially subscribed to by 26 of the country's most important exhibitors.

Another large chain was the Paramount chain. This chain originated in Chicago under the name B&K. In 1926 B&K merged with Paramount, which consisted of Paramount distribution and the Famous Players production studios. At its peak in 1930–1931, this chain was the largest motion picture circuit in film history.

■ The Effects of Sound Technology

Sound equipment was initially developed by American Telegraph and Telephone. The first company to take a risk with the new technology was Warner Brothers, which produced *The Jazz Singer.* With the profits from the film Warner Brothers acquired First National and another chain of theaters and thus established itself as a major integrated company. A competing sound system was developed by RCA, which founded RKO, a holding company of theaters, a booking (distribution) office, and production facilities.

The introduction of sound led to layoffs of musicians, organists, and stagehands. With the coming of sound, Paramount began in 1929 to produce sound vaudeville shorts to replace the live stage extravaganzas for which the B&K chain had been so noted. Thus, Paramount developed into a fully integrated movie production, distribution, and theater chain that was able to survive the Great Depression. Size and operating techniques in this and other firms led to Hollywood's monopoly power and the national chain domination from 1930 to 1950.

The positive effect of the talkies on movie theater attendance diminished by 1931, and the Depression took its toll on the industry. Admission prices rose and audiences shrank from 80 million in 1929 to 60 million in 1932 and 1933.

---

[1]Douglas Gomery, "The Movies Become Big Business: Public Theatres and the Chain Store Strategy," in Richard D. MacCann, ed., *The First Tycoons* (Metuchen, N.J.: Scarecrow Press, 1987), pp. 130–143.

None of the majors emerged unscathed from the Depression. Depressed profits and even bankruptcy forced the ownership from the colorful figures of the founders or other early industry leaders to Wall Street and public ownership.

POST–WORLD WAR II

World War II brought prosperity to most of the industry. However, there were differential effects. General Cinema, which had pioneered the drive-in theater concept in 1935, was made up largely of drive-ins during World War II. By 1981, General Cinema had been the nation's largest theater circuit for some time. Richard Smith, CEO of General Cinema, explained that during World War II his firm had "just barely survived the effects of gas rationing and daylight saving time."

After World War II a number of profound changes took place in the movie industry. Immediately after World War II the industry was restructured with changes imposed by the 1948 and 1952 Consent Decrees. During the 1950s the increasing popularity of television eroded movie audiences. The 1960s brought significant change in the location and format of theaters. Throughout the period the number and kind of films produced also encountered changes.

■ The Consent Decrees

The Consent Decrees of 1948 and 1952 were reached after the Supreme Court found that the ownership of theaters and other distribution arrangements violated the Sherman Anti-Trust Act. Up until this time the industry had been dominated by the Big Five—Paramount, Twentieth-Century Fox, Warner Brothers, Loew's, and RKO—all fully integrated movie companies which possessed production, distribution, and exhibition facilities. The strength of the Big Five was clearly evident. For example, in the 1920s at the time of the introduction of sound technology, the crisis was whether the independent theaters were going to have access to talking pictures.

In the late 1940s the Big Five were releasing approximately 80% of all feature films and a significantly higher percentage of box office successes. Although the Big Five controlled only 17% of the nation's theaters in 1945, they accounted for 45% of domestic film rentals. In particular, they were the dominant factor in downtown theater districts, as they operated more than 70% of the first-run movie houses in cities with populations exceeding 100,000. As much as 80% of the profits reported by these integrated companies were thought to come from their exhibition activities.

The Big Five and the Little Three (Columbia, United Artists, and Universal) were enjoined in the antitrust suits. Although none of the Little Three owned theaters, all eight companies had practiced "block booking," a practice of selling the entire season's output on one contract. The Consent Decrees, reached after a decade of litigation, required that each picture be rented on a picture-by-picture, theater-by-theater basis. In addition, each existing integrated company was to be divided into a theater-exhibition and a production-distribution company. The court ordered certain theaters to be divested, and during divestiture some of the larger chains were broken up. Divestiture under the Consent Decree contributed significantly to the drop in the number of theaters held by the Big Five, from 2765 in 1948 to 1223 in 1958.

The decree also prohibited the chains from buying new theaters without court permission, although this restriction was later liberalized. Film rental could no longer be set on the basis of how much it grossed nationally, nor could the chains determine how various theaters used a package of films.[2]

■ The Effect of Television

The growing postwar popularity of television greatly affected the movie industry (see Exhibit 2 for penetration of television, color TV, and cable TV). The number of TV sets rose in startling numbers, and by the end of the 1950s, 90% of homes had TV sets, while the number of TV stations had risen from 7 to 517.

The commercial war between the movie and television industries was largely over by the mid-1950s, although Hollywood still withheld all but a trickle of its oldest films from TV for several more years. Clearly, the movie industry had lost. In addition, population shifts to the suburbs, the growth of alternative leisure activities, and a decline in the number of feature films from over 400 to between 200 and 250 (see Exhibit 7a later in this case) all contributed to a decline in both industry revenues and the number of theaters. The total number of theaters dropped from 18,631 in 1948 to 16,354 in 1958.

In contrast to the decline in indoor theaters from 17,811 in 1948 to 14,714 in 1954, drive-ins increased from 820 to 3775 during the same period. (See Exhibit 4.) The greatest commercial year for the movie industry was 1946, with box office receipts of $1.7 billion. By 1958 admission receipts had dropped to $1 billion. Movie exhibition receipts declined from 19.8% of U.S. recreational expenditures to 6.3% during that same period. (See Exhibits 3 through 7 for selected industry statistics.)

Penetration of Television, Color TV, and Cable TV   **Exhibit 2**

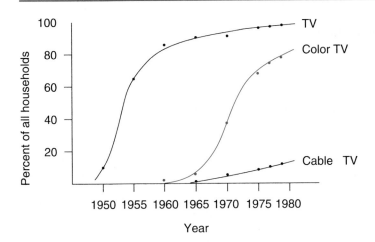

---

[2]"Justice Agency Weighs Relaxing Curbs on Theater Ownership by 8 Film Firms," *The Wall Street Journal*, October 22, 1981, p. 4.

Exhibit 3   **Statistics on the Motion Picture Industry**

Year	Admission Receipts (millions)*	Average Admission Price	Percent of U.S. Recreational Expenditures*	Percent of U.S. Spectator Amusement Expenditures	Number of Feature Films[†]
1946	$1692	N.A.	19.8	81.9	N.A.
1948	1506	$0.44	15.5	78.5	N.A.
1954	1228	0.55	9.4	73.4	N.A.
1958	992	0.65	6.3	64.5	N.A.
1960	951	0.69	5.2	59.2	155[‡]
1961	921	0.69	4.7	56.7	185[‡]
1962	903	0.70	4.4	54.9	145
1963	904	0.74	4.1	53.4	150
1964	913	0.76	3.7	51.8	150
1965	927	0.85	3.5	51.2	165
1966	964	0.87	3.3	50.1	168
1967	989	1.19	3.2	47.7	215
1968	1045	1.31	3.1	49.1	230
1969	1099	1.42	3.0	48.6	325
1970	1162	1.55	2.9	48.0	267
1971	1198	1.65	2.8	47.3	281
1972	1203	1.70	2.5	45.1	273
1973	1292	1.76	2.5	44.6	229
1974	N.A.	1.90	N.A.	N.A.	223
1975	N.A.	2.03[‡]	N.A.	N.A.	182
1976	1742		3.84	53.4	N.A.
1977	2376		4.12	34.8	N.A.
1978	2811	2.34	N.A.	35.8	N.A.
1979	2946	2.52	N.A.	N.A.	138
1980	2899	2.69	N.A.	N.A.	171
1981	2751		N.A.	N.A.	N.A.
1982	3450	2.93	N.A.	N.A.	280

Source: U.S. Department of Commerce, Motion Picture Association of America, *Film Daily Yearbook of Motion Pictures.*

Note: N.A. = not available.

*International Motion Picture Almanac, various years through 1984.

[†]Approved by the Code Administration. From 1970 through 1975 reissues of old films had become more common, averaging 39 per year.

[‡]Estimated.

The chairman of the nation's seventh-largest theater circuit in 1981, Carl Patrick of Martin Theatres, explained the effect of the postwar period on his firm:

> Back then in Hollywood, the producing companies owned theaters. Paramount, the biggest chain, had 1,500. Fox had probably 600 or 800. Loews and Metro Golden Mayer [had theaters]. . . . Then the Consent Decree came along in 1948. The producing companies had until 1951 to divest themselves of these theaters. No longer did they have pictures in bunches like bananas because they did not have to feed their own theaters any more. They could sit back and look, pick, and choose the pictures they wanted to make. So we went from 500 to 600 pictures a year to 140 pictures a year. So we had all of this come along, television and the Consent Decree, back to back.

Number of Screens (1977–1978) per Number of Theaters

Exhibit 4

Year	Total	Indoor	Drive-ins
1981*	18,040	14,732	3308
1980[†]	17,600	14,030	3570
1978–1979	16,965	13,329	3636[‡]
1977	16,494	12,692[†]	3802[§]
1976	15,969	12,169	3800
1973–1974	14,650	10,850	3800
1970	14,300	9,700	4600
1968	13,196	9,500	3690
1963	12,652	9,150	3502
1958	16,354	12,291	4063
1954	18,491	14,716	3775
1948	18,631	17,811	800

Sources: 1973–1981: *Motion Picture Almanac,* various issues; prior to 1973: *Box Office Magazine.*

*10% of indoor screens are multiplexes; 80% of these have 2 screens; the rest have 3–7. The average number of seats is 550; in 1950 the average was 750.

[†]Estimated. From 1968 to 1973 new theaters opened at an annual rate of close to 300. They required an average investment of $400,000 per theater in 1973. In the early 1980s new indoor screens represented demolishing of older theaters and replacement by new multiplex theaters with two to eight screens each.

[‡]Average capacity was 550 cars.

[§]Number of theaters: 3536.

U.S. Theatrical Film Admissions, 1946–1980

Exhibit 5

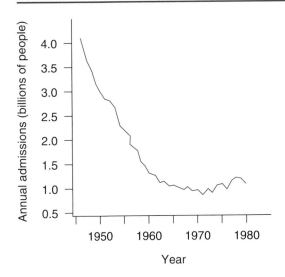

Exhibit 6   **Box Office Receipts and Ticket Prices (base year 1946)**

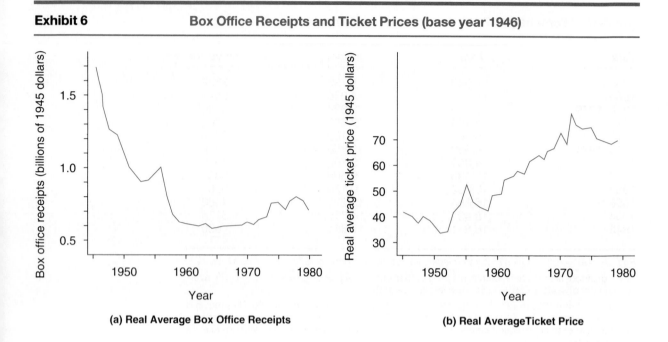

(a) Real Average Box Office Receipts   (b) Real AverageTicket Price

. . . 1953 was a very bad year for us. There was a stampede out of the theaters to watching TV at home. You must remember that it was a novelty. You spent a few hundred dollars for the set, [so] you had to sit there and watch it. And, of course, the neighbors would come too. . . . Then after '55 business started picking up again [as] we got acclimated to television.

In contrast, General Cinema fared well during this period, as its president Richard Smith explained:

Television was devastating to the indoor theater operator and the large chains were beset with legal problems. On the other hand, we found that we attracted a different kind of audience—families and young people—and benefited from laws which lowered driving ages, just as downtown theaters were penalized by inadequate parking facilities.

With the diminishing U.S. audiences in the 1950s, non-U.S. markets began to be taken into account. For almost 50 years the United States had so dominated the world film supply that admission prices for U.S. films in some other countries were fixed above domestically produced films, and there were also mandatory quotas. In addition to turning attention to non-U.S. markets, the motion picture industry introduced new gimmicks, such as 3-D, Cinerama, and Smell-O-Vision. Cinemascope—an invention of the late 1920s, where an image is "squeezed" onto a standard 35-mm film and then projected on a large screen with a special projector in such a way that the image is not distorted—was introduced in the 1940s. A number of box office hits were filmed in Cinemascope. The 1950s saw the conversion to Technicolor. All of these innovations were introduced as the industry was attempting to find new ways of attracting audiences.

Films Released, Film Production, and Film Production Cost   **Exhibit 7**

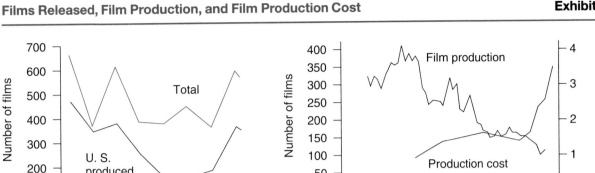

(a) Number of Films Released in America

(b) Film Production by Major Studios and
Real Film Production Cost

■ Theater Relocation

The movie industry reached its nadir in the 1960s. The number of screens reached a low of 12,652 in 1963. (See Exhibit 4.) Attendance continued to decline. (See Exhibit 5.) Shopping center and suburban theater attendance, however, increased. The largest company in the industry, General Cinema, pioneered the shopping center theater concept. Beginning in the 1960s the company built its new theaters largely in or near regional shopping centers. By mid-1976, for example, over 90% of General Cinema theaters were less than ten years old and were located in shopping centers.

In contrast, the traditional 2000-to-3000-seat downtown "movie palace," penalized by inadequate parking facilities and the population shift to the suburbs, lost audiences. Carl Patrick described the large theaters, especially in the smaller towns:

> We had these big theaters, like in Americus, Georgia, where there were 15,000 people and we had a 1500-seat theater there. We had 1600 seats in Opalaka because you wanted to get everybody in town in one theater, under one roof to see a movie. [At that time] you changed movies three times a week.

Shopping center and new suburban theaters began to command a greater share of movie audiences and were often able to obtain higher ticket prices. These theaters broke the dominance of downtown theaters in securing first-run movies. Mr. Wintman, Executive Vice President of General Cinema, explained why his company encouraged shopping center construction:

> Although General Cinema pioneered the shopping center theater concept, it made no attempt to preempt the marketplace. As early as October 1963, the president of General Cinema publicly urged exhibitors to seek locations in suburbia. It was sincerely felt that an influx of new and viable theaters would serve as an inducement to film producers to increase their investments in films.

By the mid-1970s the rate of increase in shopping center construction began to decline. In 1980 there were about 22,00 locations nationwide, and the rate of annual increase had dropped from a high of almost 10% to about 6%. Shopping center rental costs had risen significantly, and an increasing number of new theaters were being built on independent parcels of land in high-traffic areas, usually near existing mall sites.

Ease of entry proliferated the numbers of screens and theaters, as Wintman explained:

> Any exhibitor or entrepreneur with acceptable credit had only to furnish the theater facilities leased to him by the shopping center and built to his specifications. An exhibitor desiring further leverage could lease equipment and enter the marketplace at little or no cost.

By the mid-1970s competition was considerable. Wintman explained:

> Most marketplaces today are fairly saturated and expansion is limited to the relatively few new shopping centers being built, which in most instances will draw upon patronage already attending existing theaters. There exists virtually no market in which there is not already a competitive situation, and General Cinema faces strong competition in every one of its markets. Future expansion will of necessity be limited to marketplaces in which existing movie facilities are either old, poorly maintained and operated, or badly located with respect to population growth and highway accessibility. New shopping center theaters in these places could well prove extraordinarily successful.

■ Multiplexes

In addition to the move to the suburbs and the shopping center theaters, the theater industry began to build multiple theaters in one location. (See Exhibit 8b.) Carl Patrick of Martin Theatres recalled his introduction to multiple theaters.

> I had a call from a guy by the name of Bob Lippard who used to do pictures for Century Fox. Bob had some theaters. He said, "Pat, let me tell you a new wrinkle. I got a penthouse—a theater downstairs and a theater upstairs. I can show two pictures at the same time with the same crew and everything. I think this is a wave of the future. You might want to think about it." And I said, "That guy is crazy, you know."

As early as 1963, General Cinema had experimented with Cinema I and II theaters, two 500-to-1000-seat auditoriums under one roof instead of one 1200-to-1400-seat auditorium. The test proved successful on several counts. First, there were some operating cost savings in personnel, advertising, and maintenance. Second, the twin auditoriums provided a means of dampening the effect of increasing construction costs while at the same time increasing revenues.

In the mid-1970s, for example, General Cinema's investment in a shopping center twin was approximately $100,000–$150,000, as compared with $75,000–$125,000 for a single auditorium; the average revenues per location were 50%–80% higher. Although a few auditoriums had been built with as few as 400 seats, the company had not pursued minitheaters (i.e., theaters with less than 300 seats). During the early 1970s, General Cinema had continuously converted sin-

Number of Movie Theaters and Screens

Exhibit 8

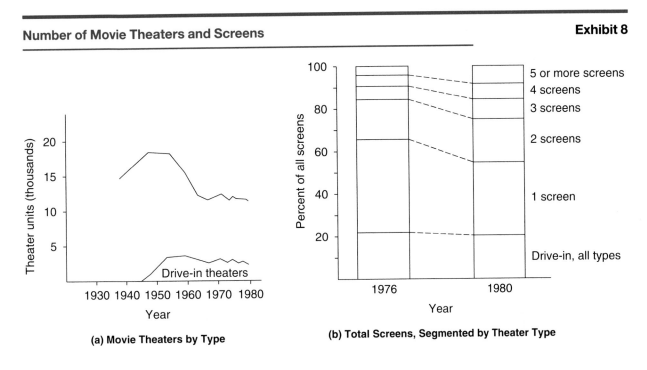

(a) Movie Theaters by Type

(b) Total Screens, Segmented by Theater Type

gle theaters to twins and twins to triples. By 1976 multiple theaters dominated the General Cinema chain.

The results of conversion to multiplexes increased the number of screens markedly (see Exhibit 4), although the number of locations did not increase significantly (see Exhibit 8a). Carl Patrick explained the results in his company:

> But we started in with multiple theaters and we built a number of new theaters in Atlanta in the early sixties. One of them was a twin. It made four times as much money as single theaters because you had that extra money coming in with one overhead. . . . And that's the way everything goes today. Like here in Columbus, we have the eightplex in a shopping center: eight auditoriums, eight screens, under one roof and all under one management. The booths are automated. You just turn them on and turn them off and the whole thing goes. So that's the economies that you work [with] now. There is no way that you could run these old big theaters like we did in the late forties and early fifties; I think [back then] the longest I ever saw a film run in Columbus was like two weeks, something like the *Outlaw*. It ran two weeks in Columbus. Now pictures run eight months. You have these multiple-screen theaters and you open up *ET*. Let's say you have eight screens and two of them have 800 seats, two of them have 600, two of them have 400, and two of them have 300. Well you open up in those 800-seat auditoriums and after about a month and a half it starts to slow down, so you drop it to a 600 or a 400 and open up something else. And then you can sit there and let them run, because you have no overhead much except film rental and personnel.

THE 1970s TO THE EARLY 1980s

As the 1980s opened, the industry was beset by a number of issues. Among these were film availability; the increasing costs of film production; relationships among production, distribution, and exhibition; and changing sources of revenue. In addition, the industry was confronting a number of new competitors, such as video; this new competition is covered in the final section of this case.

■ Film Availability

The number of films available to theaters had declined markedly from the heyday of the 1940s. By the end of the decade the production from large U.S. companies was about 25% of what it had been in the pre-1950 era. Film availability had increased somewhat in the latter part of the 1970s due to strong demand for pornographic films and increasing production from small, independent filmmakers. (See Exhibits 3 and 7a for film production.) Hollywood was no longer the center of the U.S. industry, and internationalism had largely occurred by the middle of the decade. Foreign films accounted for a substantial, though decreasing, share of all films released in the United States.

■ Film Costs

Films became increasingly expensive to produce (see Exhibit 7b). In 1980 production costs averaged about $6.8 million per film for the first negative, including script, equipment, studio facilities, and labor. Direct distribution costs added another $3–$5 million and included advertising and the making of multiple negative prints at about $1100 each. Production and direct distribution costs were capitalized and written off when the film began to generate revenues.

In the past movies were introduced area by area, but a trend had started toward opening nationally. Increasingly, advertising for movies had appeared on television. Columbia pictures, for example, had devoted nearly 30% of the production budget for marketing *Only When I Laugh*, including $4 million on TV advertising and hundreds of sneak previews in more than 600 theaters. Overall the amount spent on TV advertising in 1979 was about $206 million, nine times the amount spent in 1970. Indeed, advertising of movies was the fastest-growing advertising revenue source for television.

And high investment did not guarantee box office success. *Heaven's Gate*, a $36 million western epic, opened in the summer of 1980 to disastrous reviews. The United Artist release was the only major film to be withdrawn within days of its limited release. Theater owners were so incensed that at least one simply left the theater screen dark as a protest.

Moreover, interest rates, as high as 20% in early 1981, increased concern that the number of films produced would be sharply curtailed or that the artistic quality would be compromised. Alan Ladd, Jr., formerly of Warner Brothers and then head of his own studio, observed that movies were so expensive that the studios could not take the chances they once did.

■ Distribution

The number of movie studios had proliferated in the late 1970s, although distribution still remained concentrated. Indeed, six major distributors controlled 75% of the films released in the United States. The major distributors had sales offices and salesmen in nearly all the 30 exchange cities in the late 1970s. The distributor's fee was about 30% in the United States and Canada and 40% in other countries. Virtually all of the major film companies distributed their own products as well as those of independents. Distributors required advanced guarantees of as much as $100,00 for an expected blockbuster. These guarantees could severely curtail the revenues available to the theater owner.

Exhibitors negotiated with film distributors, in competition with other exhibitors, for the right to show films. The terms of these arrangements were influenced not only by competition among exhibitors but also by the availability of popular films. A product shortage had gradually shifted the bargaining power to the distributors. By the seventies rentals for the popular films sometimes caused theater operating losses. Terms also had stiffened with respect to the number of weeks that a movie had to be shown, the guarantee of a minimum payment for which the exhibitor was obligated, payment conditions, dates when movies were to be shown (distributors tended to concentrate introductions during the Christmas and summer seasons), and the pressure on exhibitors to take several pictures from the same distributor.

In spite of this shift in bargaining position, film producers had found their business to be extremely volatile. For example, by the end of the sixties, the large old-line production-distributed companies, which continued to dominate film releases, had incurred massive write-offs of $250 million. These write-offs were caused by excessive inventories of high-budget films. This volatility in producers' performance greatly affected the supply of films, which, in turn, influenced the operating results of the exhibitors.

The supply of product became a major concern. The 1975 General Cinema *Annual Report* stated: "Over the past few years, the number of major new feature films produced has declined. Conversely, as we continue to expand our theater circuit, our requirements for these films are increasing." Not only the supply but also the cost of film rentals was of concern to management. In the mid-1970s theaters might play 80%–85% first-run pictures, compared to 40%–50% in the sixties. As a result, film rentals had escalated from 35%–40% of box office receipts to over 50%, and operating margins had declined to around the 10% level.

Gross revenues usually referred to exhibitors' box office receipts but were also applied to total film rentals distributors received from exhibitors. Film rentals was that portion of the box office receipts owed to the distributors. It could be calculated in a number of ways. One method was a sliding scale which was usually tailored to the particular theater and provided that exhibitors pay an escalating percentage as determined by the success of the film. Another method was a minimum-percentage agreement which required that the distributor receive a fixed percentage, often as much as 90% of box office receipts after theater overhead had been deducted. In other instances a flat price was charged.

■ Revenue Diversification

As a result of the profit squeeze, a number of theater companies had diversified. For example, General Cinema Corporation, with 1000 screens, was the largest U.S. theater chain. However, $412 million of the company's $759 million in revenues came from its bottling operations.

In addition, movie theater owners, squeezed by higher film costs, were increasingly reliant on refreshment revenues. Theater operators were in a "catch-22." If they didn't play the "big picture," they didn't gross enough to cover operating deficits. If they paid high rental, they simply had to hope that refreshment revenues and margins would compensate. The low proportion of the box office dollar that they retained, the large guarantees and advances that they had to pay, and the shift in the supply/demand ratio experienced over the prior decade had forced many of the "mom and pop" theater owners out of the business. Even the large chains made more money on sales of popcorn, soft drinks, and other concessions than on ticket sales. For example, in 1975 General Cinema's refreshment revenues amounted to $28 million, or $0.40 per capita, compared to an average admission price of $2.20.

■ Blind Bidding

In the late 1970s and on into the decade of the 1980s, studios and distributors, on one hand, and theater owners, on the other, were at odds over the practice of blind bidding.[3] Blind bidding was also called advance bidding or advance licensing and was a practice requiring theater owners to commit to renting a film before viewing. Films for key seasons (Christmas, Easter, and summer) were often licensed months ahead, perhaps even before production was begun.

In April 1978 Alabama put the first law against blind bidding into practice; 22 states enacted similar laws prior to 1982. The battle was led by the National Association of Theatre Owners (NATO), on the one hand, and the Motion Pictures Association (MPAA), on the other. Studios maintained that blind bidding was necessary in order to share the risks of production costs. MPAA maintained that for the theater owners to require previewing before committing to rental contracts would add prohibitive time and cost. Theaters, on the other hand, maintained that they had to take films sight unseen, even if the film ended up R-rated, and had to guarantee studios a fixed sum, sometimes as much as $100,000, for blockbusters plus a share of box office receipts, which averaged 40% in 1979.

In response to the enactment of the laws against blind bidding, the studios threatened no filmmaking in those 22 states which had passed such laws. NATO indicated clearly that it planned to push ahead, especially in the nearly 20 states which were considering similar legislation. The *Heaven's Gate* fiasco heightened theater owners' bitterness at blind bidding.

OTHER COMPETITION

During the 1970s more new competitive forces sprang up. These included production of movies by television, cable and pay TV, and home video. Reaction to these new competitive entrants varied over time and with the background of the observer.

■ Television-Made Movies

In the early 1970s the major television networks had begun the production of feature-length pictures for original release. This move was undertaken because

---

[3]"Blind Bidding at a Glance," *Variety*, December 13, 1982.

recent box office successes were not generally available to television and inventories of older films were being rapidly depleted. Lurking in the background was the prospect of pay TV, which conceivably could offer competitive rental fees to conventional film distributors for first-run pictures. A third possibility was the videocassette or disc. The viewer would buy or rent a film on videotape or disc and replay it at his or her convenience on a recorder incorporated in or attached to the television set.

■ Cable and Pay TV

Cable TV had been introduced in the early 1960s, and it was estimated that about 16 million U.S. homes received cable TV in 1980. About 6 million subscribed to pay TV.[4] However, the penetration of cable had been slower than experienced with television in the 1950s.[5] The effect of the cable boom had been to factionalize the commercial-television mass audience and reduce the number of homes using any particular television station.

The first, national, satellite-interconnect pay network was initiated by Home Box Office (HBO), Inc., in September 1975, an event which drew little attention at the time.[6] About 50%–60% of basic-cable subscribers also purchased pay TV. By 1981 the number of pay TV networks had proliferated; however, HBO, a Time subsidiary, and Showtime, which was owned by Viacom International and Teleprompter Corporation, supplied 80% of the pay TV programming. The two companies produced their own sports and other programming. However, movies represented about half of their programming. Another leading pay TV company was The Movie Channel, a Warner Amex subsidiary. All three companies were national pay-cable services.

Interactive networks, such as Warner's QUBE, were expected to spur cable penetration. Interactive capabilities included banking, computing, home protection, and pay for view. The pay-for-view capability threatened a first-run film exhibition alternative to theaters. However, a significant first-run film release on pay-for-view cable was not projected until about the year 2000.[7] Pay TV was expected to represent about 10% of film revenues in 1981 and 14% in 1982.[8] The growth rates in these various industry segments were substantial. The number of pay TV customers was up 50% per year, and the market for video recordings of movies was up 25%.

The theater industry represented $3 billion in box office receipts. However, when pay-cable reached 20% of all TV homes (about 20 million homes), it would also represent $3 billion in film rental revenues. At $12.95 per month the cost to each home would be approximately three movie tickets per month. Theater owners were expected to have to increase prices if admissions declined when pay TV became relatively cheaper.[9]

[4]Thomas J. Murray, "Hollywood Battles for New Markets," *Dun's Review*, June 1980, pp. 70–75.

[5]Fuqua Industries, *Consulting Report*, p. 17.

[6]*Broadcasting Yearbook*, 1981.

[7]Fuqua Industries, op. cit.

[8]"Why the Film Industry Is Singing the Blues," *Business Week*, December 14, 1981, p. 26.

[9]Philip Lowe, "Warning Cable TV and Popcorn Don't Mix," *Variety*, December 14, 1981, p. 140.

▪ Home Video

Home video technology consisted of videocassettes and videodiscs. Videocassette technology had existed since the early 1970s,[10] while videodisc technology had been introduced only recently. It was surmised that the videocassettes were for people who wanted to "time-shift" TV viewing or make video home movies. Videodisc players, on the other hand, could not record material and were thus only for those interested in viewing prerecorded material.

The market for home video equipment had been expanding at a breakneck pace. Sales of videocassette recorders (VCR) totaled 804,663 units in 1980, up from 475,396 units in 1979, and VCR sales during 1981 were expected to approach 1.2 million units. Indeed, sales through the first seven months of the year totaled 652,490, nearly 86% above sales a year earlier.

However, the home video market had not developed as rapidly as had been predicted. It was estimated that there were about 2 million units in use, although not all these videotape machines were compatible. The average price of units was about $1000. Tape rentals were running way ahead of tape sales. It was estimated that 20%–50% of all prerecorded videocassette sales were pornographic material, but a decline in pornographic sales was foreseen as more family-oriented movies became available on cassette.[11] It appeared that Europe and the Far East were more interested in home video than cable. It was estimated that there were 2 million cassette decks in the United States, 1 million in Japan, and another 250,000 in Germany.[12]

It was expected that 350,000 videodisc players would be sold in 1981, compared with fewer than 50,000 in homes at the end of 1980, and that another 500,000 players could be sold in 1982. Sales for 1985 were forecasted at 2.5 million units. MCA, Inc. (parent of Universal Pictures), and NV Phillips had developed the initial technology. Magnavox had introduced its videodisc system in 1978, while RCA had introduced its set in 1981 after investing $150 million in the development of the technology. As another entrant in this industry, Pioneer had sold 20,000 units since introduction of its unit in early 1981.

There were basically two kinds of videodisc technologies. One used laser technology and grooveless discs. The other, such as the RCA and JVC systems, had a contact stylus. There were also two basic price points. The higher-priced units had more features and were priced at $750 or more. Other units, such as RCA's unit, retailed at $500 and lacked the features of the other systems retailing at $750. However, the newly introduced JVC unit was priced at $500 and, unlike the RCA system, had random access, still frames, and various speeds. Its rpm, however, was slower than RCA's. MCA had priced its videodiscs from $24.95 to $29.95 for feature films, with $19.95 for music titles from MCA Disco-Vision.[13] Home video products found their greatest market in the over-25-year-old age group.

A major problem for the home video industry was piracy. As one observer put it, "Piracy is an on-going disaster for the entertainment industry. . . . If the major entertainment suppliers lowered the cost of prerecorded cassettes, coun-

[10]Kathleen K. Weiger, "Video Fever," *Forbes*, September 1, 1980, pp. 35–36.

[11]Weiger, op. cit.

[12]Michael F. Goldman, "New Technology Destructive or Not?" *Variety*, January 14, 1981, p. 15.

[13]"Videodisks," *Broadcasting*, February 2, 1981, p. 34.

terfeiting and continued piracy becomes a more marginal practice and might not be worth the risk."[14]

The comparison of the videocassette and videodisc industries indicated that videodiscs could be produced more cheaply and were more difficult to copy. It was estimated that the distribution channel revenues were as follows:[15]

Customer	Videocassette	Videodisc
Retailer	$20	$ 8
Distributor	30	9
Program supplier	10	3
Retail price	60	20

▪ Early Industry Entrant Reactions

In 1971, Mr. Wintman had indicated that in his opinion these new sources of competition would not have a serious impact on theater operators:

> The economics of the business work against other means of exhibition. A feature-length picture can be shown on television once or maybe twice during prime time, no matter how good it is, while we can offer guarantees of 10–15 weeks for a picture like *Love Story*. As a result, television can afford perhaps $500,000 to $600,000 per picture, about the equivalent of a double-length regular hour TV program. That is a million or so less than the cost of a good low-budget film. In fact, we support the networks: the more films produced, the better. If they strike a good one, they may bring it to theaters first, or, if not, we are always interested in less expensive fillers. Pay TV, on the other hand, could be a problem if a large enough audience could be attracted. However, the public hasn't accepted the pay-TV concept. We also suspect that the moviegoer really wants to get out of the house, especially the woman, to see a show. For this reason, I bet, except for pornography, cassettes won't generate much of a market for recreational films either, though they may be great for educational purposes.

In 1975, Mr. Smith reiterated this theme:

> As happens with each new technological advance in the telecommunications field, a new round of speculation about the future of movie theaters takes place. Currently two such advances, the satellite-linked pay-TV movie service network and the video-disc players, the visual equivalent of the phonograph, are in the news. In spite of these and other remarkable technical advances, nothing major has changed or will change the basic marketing of motion pictures. According to Paul Kagan Associates, a leading authority on pay TV, there are currently 10 million cable subscribers and the number should grow to 20 million by 1980. Their projection contemplates that there might be 3 million pay-TV subscribers by 1980. There is no way that an audience of this size can produce the income necessary to obtain first-run pictures in competition with movie theaters. We are talking about a small audience overlap in any event, without considering demographic, economic, and geographical limitations. We still feel that free home television, offering a choice from about 50 movies a week, is our principal competition, although supplemental income to film suppliers from pay TV after theatrical exhibition may eventually be a further stimulant for film production.

---

[14]Hy Hollinger, "Homevideo Boom: More Sizzle Than Steak," *Variety,* January 14, 1981, p. 226.
[15]Ibid.

As to the video-disc players, it is beyond our comprehension how any but the most wealthy 1% or 2% of the population would spend the money to buy a player for more than $500 and then pay $10 to $20 to see a picture on a TV screen perhaps two or three times at the most. This device will have to find its market in something much cheaper than motion picture features or in material suitable for repeated viewing if it is to be economically viable.

■ The 1980–1981 Situation

As the decade of the eighties opened, the movie industry faced considerable uncertainty. On one hand were the dire predictions of some that the number of movie screens could decrease by a third to half and small-town theaters would be wiped out altogether. Even those theaters that remained could expect decreased customer bases because of the onslaught of technological innovation and changes in demographics and film industry practices. As one observer put it, "The motion-picture industry is in desperate trouble and I don't think there's very much the exhibitors can do to protect a position that isn't very tenable in the first place. The tide is going against them. They'll have to redeploy their assets or face total destruction."[16]

It was unclear what effects cable TV, pay TV, and home video would have and in what time frame. Hollywood executives were convinced that growth of new markets, including cable, home video, and pay-per-view, would have an increasingly beneficial impact. But some acknowledged that rising costs and recent high interest rates coupled with a slow growth in theatrical business and network sales had forced companies to put brakes on costs wherever possible. There was a growing risk in the making of films because the movie tax shelters that provided financing might also begin to disappear. For example, the 1981 tax act lowered the top income tax rate to 50% and made tax shelters in general less attractive.[17]

Indeed, it was speculated that sometime in the next ten years these ancillary markets (cable TV, pay TV, and home video) might be "the tail wagging the dog."[18] Observers asked "whether these new technologies are destructive or supportive to the industry's future. The destructiveness is quickly seen in admission statistics."[19] Indeed, the flat attendance and lower operating profits experienced by the theaters in 1980 were considered the first impact of the in-home entertainment revolution.[20]

In order to combat the new technologies, theater owners were beginning to introduce Dolby sound systems. By the early 1980s, however, only about 2000 theaters had converted. Direct beaming of signals from satellites to theaters and some method for exhibiting high-resolution videotapes of digitally encoded tape were expected.[21] Also, 70-mm tape with its clearer picture was being intro-

---

[16]Theodore Levitt, professor at Harvard Graduate School of Business, quoted in Stephen J. Sansweet, "Coming Attractions: Analysts See Bleak Future for Movie Theaters," *The Wall Street Journal,* August 19, 1981, pp. 1:6, 19:1.

[17]"Why the Film Industry Is Singing the Blues," *Business Week,* December 14, 1981, p. 26.

[18]Goldman, op. cit.

[19]Ibid.

[20]Lowe, op. cit.

[21]Goldman, op. cit., p. 120.

duced, although prints costs $12,000 each, as contrasted to somewhat over $1000 for 50-mm tape.

On the other hand, others maintained that "Hollywood studios are drooling over the possibilities of this home market of 77M households."[22] Indeed, producers were making "presales" to the TV networks and thus decreasing their risk somewhat. These advance sales were sometimes made even before production had begun. In spite of the interest commanded by the home entertainment market, however, there was argument that the studios would maintain their interest in keeping the theaters viable. "Theatres are and for the foreseeable future will remain, the prime market for us," said Richard Kahn, the Senior Vice President of Marketing for Metro-Goldwyn-Mayer Film Company. Overall, however, the combat involved the big movie studios (who wanted more control), the major pay TV networks, and the nation's 17,000 theater owners, "which are fighting to defend their hard-won markets."[23]

BIBLIOGRAPHY

"Big Deal in Big D: Warner Wins Cable Race," *Broadcasting,* November 3, 1980, pp. 26–27.

Boyum, Joy Gold, "Independent Film Makers; Will Unity Bring Success?" *The Wall Street Journal,* March 13, 1981, p. 23:3.

"Columbia Pictures: Lionised and Loathing It," *Economist,* October 4, 1980, p. 85.

"Daly Jumps Ship for Warner Bros," *Broadcasting,* November 24, 1980, p. 32.

"Davis Buys Fox for $720 Million," *Broadcasting,* June 15, 1981, pp. 62–63.

"Gearing Up for 'Theme Week' at ABC Video," *Broadcasting,* April 6, 1981, p. 131.

Grover, Stephen, "Film Makers Turn to TV Ads, Research to Help Sell Movies," *The Wall Street Journal,* October 1, 1981, p. 29.

Harris, William, "See It Again, Sam," *Forbes,* May 10, 1982, p. 164.

"*Heaven's Gate* Leaves Theater Owners Fuming," *Business Week,* December 8, 1980, pp. 29–30.

"Heller, Columbia Close to Deal for Media Venture," *Broadcasting,* January 19, 1981, p. 36.

Hollinger, Hy, "Film Survival Years Lie Ahead," *Variety,* January 14, 1981, p. 11.

"Hollywood Fights Blind Bidding Bans," *Duns Business Month,* September 1981, p. 77.

"Hollywood's Cure," *The Economist,* August 11, 1979, pp. 26–28.

"Pay-Cable World in an Uproar as Movie Firms and Getty Make Move into the Business," *Broadcasting,* April 28, 1980, pp. 22–23.

Pryor, Thomas M., "If Consent Decree No More, Then What? Majors Won't Rush to Buy Theatres," *Variety,* January 13, 1982, p. 11.

"Rogers Bid for UA-Columbia Cable Carries the Day; Columbia Pictures Outlet Talking," *Broadcasting,* June 15, 1981, pp. 30–31.

Sansweet, Stephen J., "Movie Makers Worried by Sag in Ticket Sales," *The Wall Street Journal,* December 18, 1981, p. 25:3.

"Star Bores," *Forbes,* January 21, 1980, p. 46.

"Theater Owners Blame Box Office Blues This Summer on Lower Quality of Movies," *The Wall Street Journal,* July 18, 1980, p. 15.

"Twentieth Century Fox: Reel Two," *Economist,* April 4, 1981, p. 81.

---

[22]Weiger, op. cit.

[23]Murray, op. cit., p. 70.

Carmike Cinemas, Inc.

Marilyn L. Taylor, University of Kansas

Mike Patrick, President of Carmike Cinemas, Inc., put the September 1986 month-end reports in his drawer. He glanced at the pile of notes he had hand-written as he went through the reports. He would ask his secretary, Jo, to distribute them to various company managers. For the most part, the notes asked for the reasons behind specific expenditures in September or gave directions regarding expense reduction.

In half an hour Mike planned to join Carl Patrick, his father, Chairman of Carmike. The father and son team had purchased Carmike, then named Martin Theatres, in 1982. At the time of the purchase Martin was the seventh-largest U.S. theater circuit and had been a Fuqua Industries Inc. subsidiary for over 12 years. Fuqua was a large diversified company. The equity in Carmike was held entirely by Carmike, Inc., a private Georgia company owned by the Patrick family and a New York investment company.

Mike knew his father would spend some time on the issue of taking the company public. There were a number of issues to be considered before making the decision. Jay Jordan and others at the investment company wanted to withdraw all or a major part of their investment. His own family would be likely to be able to reduce their investment in Carmike by offering some of their stock in a secondary issue. However, the Patrick family owned 51% of Carmike's stock, and Mike felt strongly that he wanted to be clearly in charge of the company. Mike wondered how the broader investment community would view the various strategic and operational moves undertaken at Carmike over the previous four years. He thought briefly of the acquisition of the video movie chain. An infusion of cash and reduction of debt would position Carmike to take advantage of other potential acquisitions on a timely basis. Mike also realized that resiliency was important, as the company faced numerous challenges, including difficult industry conditions and continuing capital requirements. However, going public entailed some costs, including potentially more scrutiny by share-holders, public disclosure of company moves, and the costs of required reports and public relations with shareholders, the investment community, and the general public.

Whether to go public was a dilemma. He began to jot some notes under the heading "Pros and Cons of Going Public in Fall 1986."

HISTORY OF THE COMPANY

Carmike Theatres was originally founded as the Martin Theatres circuit in 1912. Mr. C. L. Patrick, the company's Chairman of the Board, joined Martin Theatres in 1945, and became the General Manager and Director in 1948. Fuqua Industries Inc. purchased the Martin family business holdings, including Martin Theatres, in 1969. Mr. Patrick served as President of Fuqua from 1970 to 1978 and as Vice Chairman of the Board of Directors of Fuqua from 1978 to 1982.

During the 13 years that Martin was a part of Fuqua the subsidiary had been a cash generator for its parent company. Fuqua sold a number of Martin properties. In 1981 Fuqua completed the sale of three TV stations which had come with the original purchase. Only the theater circuit remained.

Mike strongly felt that the executives at Martin had largely kept the theater chain in a holding pattern during its time as a Fuqua subsidiary. The Treasurer, for example, had been promoted because he was "sort of in the right place at the right time, . . . when the previous treasurer, a brilliant man," had a stroke in 1969. Further, when Carl Patrick moved to Atlanta in 1970 as President of the parent company Fuqua, Ron Baldwin as next Martin President was "good in real estate but very poor in accounting."

The purchase price for Martin Theatres was $25 million. Financing arrangements for purchasing Martin Theatres were very favorable. The total investment by the Patrick family was less than $250,000. However, the purchase of the theaters was highly leveraged. (See the financial statements in Exhibit 1.) Early efforts were directed toward improving the company's cash flow in order to reduce the debt. At the same time the company had significant capital improvement requirements. To make the venture viable, the Patricks undertook a number of changes in operations, which are described in the ensuing sections of this case. Success was by no means assured, as Mike Patrick explained:

> When we bought Martin, Martin was going downhill. It looked bad. And I want you to know that it looked pretty bad for us for a while. I mean it really did. For a while there we were asking ourselves, "Why are we in this mess?" Not only were we leveraged 100%, but we realized that we had to spend somewhere in the neighborhood of $25 million more dollars to renew the company.

At the time of Carmike's acquisition of Martin Theatres, the circuit had 265 screens (excluding 26 drive-in theater screens) located in 128 theaters. Carmike had acquired or constructed an additional 215 screens and closed or disposed of 44 screens since 1982.

Carmike Cinemas, Inc.: Financial Statements   **Exhibit 1**

	Fiscal Years Ended				
	March 25, 1982	March 31, 1983	March 29, 1984	March 28, 1985	March 27, 1986
Income Statement Data					
Revenues					
Admissions	$33,622	$40,077	$43,778	$49,040	$42,828
Concessions and other	13,595	15,490	16,886	19,917	18,150
	47,217	55,567	60,664	68,957	60,978
Costs and expenses					
Cost of operations (exclusive of concession merchandise)	36,436	39,981	44,760	50,267	45,902
Cost of concession merchandise	2,695	2,703	3,117	3,566	3,004
General and administrative	2,522	2,878	3,008	2,702	2,760
Depreciation and amortization	2,348	1,964	2,868	3,140	3,385
	44,001	47,526	53,753	59,675	55,051
Operating income	3,216	8,041	6,911	9,282	5,927
Interest expense	380	2,569	2,703	2,337	2,018
Income before income taxes	2,836	5,472	4,208	6,945	3,909
Income taxes	1,323	2,702	1,615	3,054	1,745
Net income	$ 1,513	$ 2,770	$ 2,593	$ 3,891	$ 2,164
Earnings per common share	—	$ .65	$ .61	$ .92	$ .51
Weighted average common shares outstanding	—	4,200	4,200	4,200	4,200
Balance Sheet Data (at end of period)					
Cash and cash equivalents	$ (1,317)	$ 433	$ 767	$ 770	$ 786
Total assets	34,742	27,754	35,324	34,953	40,665
Total long-term debt	3,656	18,853	22,125	16,969	18,843
Redeemable preferred stock	—	405	405	405	405
Common shareholders' equity	27,752	2,829	5,382	9,233	11,357

MIKE PATRICK'S BACKGROUND

Mike Patrick had worked in Martin Theatres first as a high school student in Columbus, Georgia, later in Atlanta as a student at Georgia State University, and still later back in Columbus as he finished his studies in economics at Columbus College. He explained these time periods in his life and how he became acquainted with the company:

> Movie theaters was the only business in which I wanted really to work . . . it's a fun business. If you are in construction, no one cares about your business. But if you tell someone that you are in the theater business, then everybody has seen a movie. Everyone has something they want to talk about. So it's an entertaining industry. Plus when I got into it, I was in the night end of it. I wasn't into administration. So I got captured, as I called it. If you have never worked at night, then you don't understand. I really went to work at 8 A.M. and got off at 10 A.M. and then went back at 2 P.M. and got off at 11 P.M. at night. So your whole group of

friends is a total flip flop. You have nighttime friends. Before you know it, you are trapped into this life. All your friends work at night. So your job becomes a little more important to you because that's where you spend all your time. Working in a theater . . . is a lot of fun. It really is, especially when you are 19 and you get to handle the cash. A theater is a cash business.

My father was President of Martin. In 1970 he became President of Fuqua and moved to Atlanta. My father wanted to sell the house in Columbus and my mother did not want to. I was very homesick for Columbus. . . . So I said, "I will go to Columbus College and I will live in the house." I moved back here in the summer of 1970 and worked in the accounting department because I wanted to understand the reports, why I filled out all these forms, and where they went. I learned then that the Treasurer of the accounting department did not understand the paper flow at all.

The Patrick family and a limited number of investors acquired Martin Theatres in April 1982 in a leveraged buyout for $20 million in cash and a 10% note in the principal amount of $5 million. Mike Patrick became President of Carmike Theatres, as the new company was called. He explained the advantage of working so long in the company:

I had done every job in this company except that of Marion Jones, our attorney. But my brother is an attorney, so I have someone in the family to talk to if I have a question. No one can put one over on me. . . . I've fired them too, and I want to tell you something—I do my own firing . . . and firing a man who is incompetent when he doesn't know it is hard. He breaks down because he thinks he's good. When I first became President, there was a member of my family who had to go. The other management noticed that.

POSTBUYOUT: STREAMLINING THE ORGANIZATION

In considering the purchase of Martin, Mike Patrick had described the firm to his father as "fat." Mike described what he did after purchase of the firm:

It appeared that each layer of management got rid of their responsibilities to the next echelon down. For example, I could not figure out what the President did. . . . I kept looking at senior management trying to figure out what they did. I sort of took an approach like you call zero budgeting. Instead of saying my budget was $40,000 last year and I need 10% more this year, I required that each individual justify everything he did. For example, there is now only one person in our financial department. The young man in there makes less than the guy that had the job as Vice President of Finance three years ago, and the current guy does not have a subordinate. The advertising department went from a senior-level vice president to a clerk. You are talking about the difference between an $80,000 and a $19,000 salary.

When we got hold of the company, we let go the President, the Financial Vice President, and the Senior Vice President. At the same time the film procurement people retired, because they were over 65. So I have streamlined the organization tremendously. When we got Martin, Martin had 2100 employees. Since then we bought a circuit called Video out in Oklahoma. They had 900 employees. Today I have 1600 employees. Let me double check that number. As of October 31, I had 1687 and the year before I had 1607. So I actually have 80 more employees than I had last year. But when I got the company, it had 2100 and the other company had 900.

Of the employees approximately 65% were paid minimum wage. Another 9% were paid subminimum wage. About 8% of the employees were in a managerial capacity, and the company was totally nonunion. Employee relationships were generally good. Initially, however, there were difficulties. Mike Patrick recalled the initial time period:

> Management was not well disciplined when we came into Martin. I had to almost totally clean house: I eliminated all of top management, but it took about six months to get second-level management to where it felt secure and at the same time develop a more aggressive attitude. I call it a predator attitude. But that first year we had some great hits, such as *E.T.* We did so well that first year breaking all previous records, so that the management team, even though it was new, became really confident, maybe too confident. Today they don't believe we can lose. Here's a list of the directors and key employees. [See Exhibit 2.]

The company also implemented improved technology in order to trim the number of employees. Mike Patrick explained what happened in one city when he wanted to replace the projectionists with totally automated projection booths. He consulted with the company attorney regarding action the projectionists could take in retaliation:

> I called our attorney in and I asked him, "What is the worst that could happen?" The attorney said, "You might have to reinstate the projectionists and pay them the back pay." I said, "You mean there is no million dollar fine?" He replied, "No, you just got to worry about reinstatement and back pay." He went on to say, "Well, why are you going to get rid of the projectionists?" I said, "There is automated projectionist equipment for showing movies that will work very similar to an eight-track tape player. If we convert the theaters, we won't need projectionists." And he said, "Well, you can do it."
>
> However, the city had a code which said that to be a projectionist, you must take a test from the city electrical board to be certified. That law was put in about 1913, because back in the old days, they didn't have light bulbs. A projector then used two carbon arcs and it was a safety issue back then, because film was made out of something that burned. That was before my time that film burned like that. Often they had fires in the lamp house. Now we have Zenith bulbs. The projectionists hadn't . . . gotten their certification from the electrical board for years. But the rule was on the books. So I figured the only problem we had was the city. As soon as we fired projectionists, they went to the council. They complained that the managers were doing the projectionist job without certification from the electrical board. The police raided my theater. I sued the city of Nashville. . . . In the meantime we sent an engineer up from Columbus and started teaching all our managers how to pass the electrical board test. As they began to pass the board, the rule became a moot question.

Martin had already leased and installed all the needed equipment except for an automatic lens turner. The cost of $15,000 per projector was not justified when it took only a few seconds to change the lens. The new equipment eliminated the position of projectionist. The theater managers took over the job of changing the lens. Mike explained how he was able to get the theater managers to cooperate.

> I told our managers that once the automated projectionist booth was in operation and the job of projectionist eliminated, I would give them a raise consisting of 40% of whatever the projectionists had made. So all of a sudden the manager went from

Exhibit 2   **Backgrounds of Directors, Officers, and Key Employees**

C. L. Patrick (61) who has served as Chairman of the Board of Directors of the company since April 1982, joined the company in 1945, became its General Manager in 1948, and served as President of the company from 1969 to 1970. He served as President of Fuqua from 1970 to 1978, and as Vice Chairman of the Board of Directors of Fuqua from 1978 to 1982. Mr. Patrick is a director of Columbus Bank & Trust Company and Burnham Service Corporation.

Michael W. Patrick (36) has served as President of the company since October 1981 and as a Director of the company since April 1982. He joined the company in 1970 and served in a number of operational and film-booking and -buying capacities prior to becoming President.

Carl L. Patrick, Jr. (39), has served as a Director of the company since April 1982. He was the Director of Taxes for the Atlanta, Georgia, office of Arthur Young & Co. from October 1984 to September 1986, and is currently self-employed. Previously, he was a certified public accountant with Arthur Andersen & Co. from 1976 to October 1984.

John W. Jordan II (38) has been a Director of the company since April 1982. He is a cofounder and managing partner of The Jordan Company, which was founded in 1982, and a managing partner of Jordan/Zalaznick Capital Company. From 1973 until 1982, he was Vice President at Carl Marks & Company, a New York investment banking company. Mr. Jordan is a director of Bench Craft, Inc., and Leucadia National Corporation, as well as the companies in which The Jordan Company holds investments. Mr. Jordan is a director and executive officer of a privately held company which in November 1985 filed for protection under Chapter 11 of the Federal Bankruptcy Code.

Carl E. Sanders (60) has been a Director of the company since April 1982. He is engaged in the private practice of law as Chief Partner of Troutman, Sanders, Lockerman & Ashmore, an Atlanta, Georgia, law firm. Mr. Sanders is a Director and Chairman of the Board of First Georgia Bank, and a Director of First Railroad & Banking Company of Georgia, Fuqua Industries Inc., Advanced Telecommunications, Inc., and Healthdyne, Inc., and a former governor of Georgia.

David W. Zalaznick (32) has served as a Director of the company since April 1982. He is a cofounder and general partner of The Jordan Company, and a managing partner of Jordan/Zalaznick Capital Company. From 1978 to 1980, he worked as an investment banker with Merrill Lynch White Weld Capital Markets Group, and from 1980 until the formation of The Jordan Company in 1982, Mr. Zalaznick was a Vice President of Carl Marks & Company, a New York investment banking company. Mr. Zalaznick is a director of Bench Craft, Inc., as well as the companies in which The Jordan Company holds investments. He is a Director and executive officer of a privately held company which in November 1985 filed for protection under Chapter 11 of the Federal Bankruptcy Code.

John O. Barwick III (36) joined the company as Controller in July 1977 and was elected Treasurer in August 1981. In August 1982 he became Vice President–Finance of the company. Prior to joining the company, Mr. Barwick was an accountant with the accounting firm of Ernst & Whinney from 1973 to 1977.

Anthony J. Rhead (45) joined the company in June 1981 as Manager of the film office in Charlotte, North Carolina. Since July 1983, Mr. Rhead has been Vice President–Film of the company. Prior to joining the company, he worked as a film booker for Plitt Theatres for 1973 to 1981.

Lloyd E. Reddish (58) has been employed by the company since 1948. He served as a District Manager from 1971 to 1982 and as Eastern Division Manager from 1982 to 1984, when he was elected to his present position as Vice President–General Manager.

Marion Nelson Jones (39) joined the company as its General Counsel in December 1984 and was elected Secretary of the company in March 1985. Prior to joining the company, Mr. Jones was a partner in the law firm of Evert & Jones in Columbus, Georgia, from 1979 to 1984.

---

being against the program of converting to automated projectionists booths to where I got a flood of letters from managers saying, "I passed the projectionist test. I'm now certified by the electrical board. Fire my projectionist."

■ Improving Theater Profitability

At the time that they purchased the Martin Theatre circuit, the Patricks were well aware that some of the theaters were losing money and that much of Martin's facilities were quickly being outmoded. A 1981 consulting report on Martin underscored that during the 1970s Martin had not aggressively moved to multiplexing. In addition, one of the previous presidents had put a number of theaters into "B locations," where, according to Mike Patrick, there were "great leases . . . but the theaters were off the beaten track." Mike explained his approach for handling the situation:

> I looked at all the markets we were in, the big markets where the money was to be made, and I said, Here's what we will do. First, let's take the losers and make them profitable. At the time the losing theaters were a $1.2 million deficit on the bottom line. So I decided to experiment . . . Phenix City is a perfect example. I took the admission price from $3.75 to $0.99. Everybody said I was a fool. The first year it made $70,000, which I thought was a great increase over the $26,000 it had been making. . . . The people in Phenix City are poor, very poor, blue collar workers, but the theater is as nice as anything I have over here (in Columbus). So as word of mouth got going that theater kept getting better and better. Now it almost sells out every Friday, Saturday, and Sunday. And I still charge $0.99. That theater will make over $200,000 this year.

As Mike put it, the conversion to "dollar theaters" was "a new concept. No one else is doing that." By 1986, Carmike had twenty 99¢ theaters. The company also offered a discount in admission prices on Tuesdays and discount ticket plans to groups. Two facilities called Flick 'n' Foam had restaurants and bar services in the theater.

In addition, Mike Patrick continued to consider potential acquisitions.

> I'm looking at a circuit of theaters in a major metropolitan area. Now the owner hasn't told me that it is for sale yet. He wants me to make him an offer and I won't do it. I want him to make me the first offer. He has no new facilities. All his theaters are twins except one, and that's a triple. He's getting killed. A large chain is coming against him with a twelveplex. He's located all around the metro area and he's getting killed. He had that town for years, and now he's almost knocked out of it. His circuit is going to be worthless. I've been up there. There are no 99¢ or dollar theaters anywhere. His locations are good for that. You see for a 99¢ theater, the location must not be a deterrent. It cannot be downtown, because downtown cannot support a night life, so that's a deterrent.

■ Facility Upgrading

When the Patricks purchased Martin Theatres in 1982, its facilities were quickly becoming outmoded. As Mike put it, "We were basically noncompetitive. . . . We were just getting hit left and right in our big markets. . . . The biggest thing we had was a twin, and we had competitors dropping four- and sixplexes on us." One reason for Martin's earlier reticence to convert to multiscreen theaters was the tendency to put emphasis on the number of theaters rather than screens. In addition, management of the theater company, although not so required by the parent company, had managed the circuit for its cash flow. Patrick explained, "Ron (Baldwin) really never understood working for a $2 billion company. He still managed the firm as though it were privately owned."

Mike Patrick explained the difficulties in the early 1980s:

> Oh, we were just outclassed everywhere you went. Ron Baldwin told me that Columbus Square was doomed. . . . I made it an eightplex. With our nice theater, the Peachtree, I added one screen but I didn't have any more room. But I took the theater no one liked and made it an eightplex. It is also one of our most profitable theaters we have today.

New theaters, either replacements or additions, were undertaken usually through build, sale, and leaseback arrangements. Carl Patrick explained that in 1985 the theaters were about 75% leased and about 25% company-owned.

By 1986 the company had become the fifth-largest motion picture exhibitor in the United States and the leading exhibitor in the southern United States in terms of number of theaters and screens operated. The company operated 156 theaters with an aggregate of 436 screens located in 94 cities in 11 southern states, with a total seating capacity of 125,758. (See Exhibit 3.)

All but 22 theaters were multiscreen. Approximately 95% of the company's screens were located in multiscreen theaters, with over 62% of the company's screens located in theaters having three or more screens. The company had an average of 2.79 screens per theater. The company's strategy was designed to maximize utilization of theater facilities and enhance operating efficiencies. In the fiscal year ending March 27, 1986, aggregate attendance at the company's theaters was approximately 15.3 million people.

The company owned the theater and land for 37 of its 156 theaters. The company owned 30 other theaters which were built on leased land. Another 78 theaters were leased. In addition, Carmike shared an ownership or leasehold interest in 11 of its theaters with various unrelated third parties.

The following table describes the scope of the company's theater operations at the indicated dates:

Date	Theaters	Screens
March 25, 1982	128	265
March 31, 1983	126	283
March 29, 1984	158	375
March 28, 1985	160	407
March 27, 1986	156	415

Carmike's screens were located principally in smaller communities, typically with populations of 40,000 to 100,000 people, where the company was the sole or leading exhibitor. The company was the sole operator of motion picture theaters in 55% of the cities in which it operated, including Montgomery, Alabama;

Carmike Cinemas, Inc.: Data for 1986　　　　　　　　　　　　　　　　　　**Exhibit 3**

State	Number of Screens per Theater						Total	Percent of Total Screens
	1	2	3	4	5	6–8		
Alabama	1	16	9	12	0	15	53	12.2
Florida	1	0	3	0	0	0	4	0.9
Georgia	3	12	15	4	10	16	60	13.8
Kentucky	0	2	0	4	5	6	17	3.9
New Mexico	0	2	0	0	0	0	2	0.4
North Carolina	0	28	9	4	0	0	41	9.4
Oklahoma	9	24	3	12	10	18	76	17.4
South Carolina	0	10	6	0	0	0	16	3.7
Tennessee	6	24	12	32	0	18	92	21.1
Texas	2	16	3	28	0	18	67	15.4
Virginia	0	8	0	0	0	0	4	1.8
	22	142	60	96	25	91	436	100.0
Percent of total screens	5.0	32.6	13.8	22.0	5.7	20.9	100.0	

Note: The company currently operates 156 theaters with an aggregate of 436 screens located in 94 cities in 11 southern states, with a total seating capacity of 125,758.

Albany, Georgia; and Longview, Texas. The company's screens constituted a majority of the screens operated in another 22% of such cities, including Nashville and Chattanooga, Tennessee, and Columbus, Georgia. The location of the company's theaters is indicated in Exhibit 4.

Carmike gave close attention to cost control in construction, as Mike Patrick explained:

> Under Fuqua Martin usually owned the theater. In some instances the land was also owned; in others the company had a ground lease. Since theaters were basically the same from one site to another, the cost of construction of the building was fairly standardized once the site, or pad, was ready.

Mike Patrick built his first theater in 1982 at a cost of $26 per square foot. At the time the usual price in the industry was $31 per square foot. He explained that even his insurance company had questioned him when he turned in his replacement cost estimate. In order to reduce his costs, Mike Patrick had examined every element of cost. Initially the Patricks worked with the E&W architectural firm, as Martin Theatres had done for years. Mike Patrick explained that their costs were so favorable that other theater companies began to use E&W. Eventually E&W costs went up. In 1985 Mike employed a firm of recent University of Alabama graduates to be the architects on a new theater in Georgia.

Costs were also carefully controlled when a shopping center firm built a theater Carmike would lease. The lease specified that if construction costs would exceed a certain amount, Carmike had the option of building the theater. Without that specification there was, as Mike Patrick explained, no incentive for the development firm to contain costs. Carmike's lease payment was based on a return on investment to the development firm. On a recent theater the estimated costs had come in at $39 per square foot versus the $31 per square foot that the

Exhibit 4   **Theater Locations**

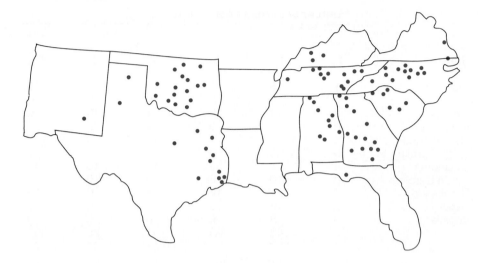

lease specified. Mike Patrick convinced the development company to use one of his experienced contractors in order to reduce the $39 per square foot.

■ Zone Strategy

The orientation under Martin management in the 1970s had been a systemwide operations approach. Mike Patrick's approach to theater location and number of screens was zone by zone and theater by theater.

Mike explained that the basic strategic unit in a theater chain was a geographic area called a zone. A small town would usually be one zone. Larger cities usually had two or more zones. Considering competitive activity in a zone was critical. Mike explained what happened over a period of two years in one major metropolitan area.* (See Exhibit 5.)

> This city has a river which divides it in two. There is only one main bridge and so there are automatically two zones. There is also a third zone which is isolated somewhat. When we first bought Martin there were seven theaters and fourteen screens.
>
> Let me tell you what happened in zone A. A strong competitor came in and built a sixplex against me in a shopping center. [See #1 in Exhibit 5.] I leased land, built a sixplex theater [#2], and did a sale leaseback. I built the sixplex here right off one of the two shopping centers. I leased the equipment and I leased the building. I actually have no investment. Last year that theater made $79,000. Think about the return you have with no investment!
>
> I took the single theaters in the shopping center [#3] and put a wall down the middle of it. That cost me $30,000. I added an auditorium to a triple [#4]. Both of these theaters are near the competitor's sixplex. Now it's 6—4 here and 2 here. So that is 6 against his 6. So now I have 12 screens in zone A. That's about the number of screens the population in zone A can support. So no one else can come in. My

*The river separating zone A from zone B was considered a natural geographic division within a city.

Map of the City with Three Zones   **Exhibit 5**

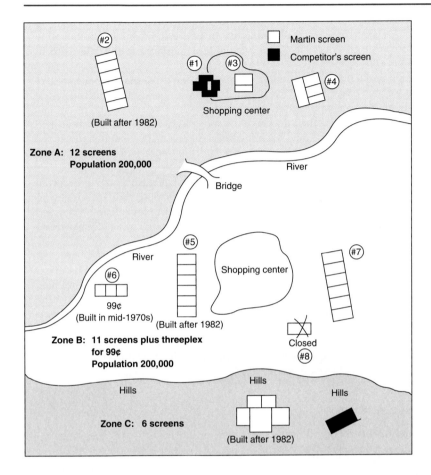

competitor has no advantage over me in negotiations with Warner Brothers and Paramount. In fact, I have an advantage over him. He's only here in one location and I am in three.

In the other zone I took a twin and added three auditoriums [#5]. Then I took a triple theater and made it a dollar house, $0.99 discount.... It was way off the beaten track, way off [#6]. So I had eight screens against the competitor's theaters [#7]. There was an opposition single screen, but he closed [#8]. We now have 20 screens in those two zones.

If you are playing *Rocky*, you can sell three prints to this town. If you choose your theaters carefully as to where you show it, you can make a lot more money. That's something the previous President (of Martin) never understood.

EXPANSION

In May 1983 Carmike acquired the outstanding stock of Video Independent Theatres, Inc. The purchase price included $1.1 million in cash and $2.7 million in a note. The note was at 11%, payable in three equal installments. Mike talked about the acquisition:

During the 1970s Martin had not been aggressive. In our industry if you are not on the attack, you are being attacked. Then you are subject to what the industry does. We believe in making things happen.

Video was owned by a company which had bought Video for its cable rights. In the mid 1970s the management was killed in an air crash. I went up and talked to the guy in charge of video. He told me the parent company wasn't interested in theaters.

The circuit had a lot of singles and a lot of profitable drive-ins. We borrowed $1 million as a down payment, and the parent accepted a note for the remainder, due in three equal yearly installments.

We immediately looked at all the drive-ins and sold two drive-ins for about $1.5 million. So immediately we paid back the down payment. We planned to use the cash flow to meet the installment payments and the depreciation to rebuild the circuit. Today Video is completely paid for.

In some of the towns we went into a tremendously aggressive buying program for film which was very successful. In another we bought out an independent who was building a fiveplex. In others we converted twins into fourplexes. We closed singles and in some instances overbuilt with four-, five-, or sixplexes. Our revenue per screen as a result is low.

In one town we went in with a new sixplex which cost $620,000. We had used basic cement block construction and furnished the facility beautifully. An independent had put in a fourplex, about the same-size facility, which has cost $1.1 million. A large circuit also had a twin. I attacked with a sixplex during a time when the state economy was down. In addition, there were a lot of bad pictures. The two companies really beat each other up during the period bidding up what pictures were available. The independent went under. We'll pick up that theater from the bank. The circuit was bought by a larger company which wants to concentrate on larger cities. They've offered us their twin.

■ Control Systems

The company also put considerable emphasis on budgeting and cost control. As Mike Patrick explained, "I was brought up on theater P&Ls." The systems he set in place for Carmike theaters were straightforward. Every theater had what Mike called "a P&L. . . . I call them a Profit or Loss Statement." Results came across Patrick's desk monthly, and results for the theaters were printed out in descending order of amount of profit generated for that month. No overhead was charged to the theaters. As Mike explained, "If you can charge something to an overhead (account), then no one cares, no one is responsible." Rather, each administrative department had a monthly statement. Mike Patrick explained his approach:

> I used something like zero budgeting on every department. For example, here's the Martin building. It cost me $18,700 for the month. The report for the Martin building even has every person's name. . . . What they made last year, what they made this year, what they made current month, every expense they have. . . . For example, I know what my dad's office cost me each month and mine also.
>
> Everyone must answer, be responsible, for everything they spend. They can't come to me and say, "Well, we've done it every year this way." Since 1982 we have become more and more efficient each year.

Every department head received a recap each week. Mike noted that in a recent weekly report he had a charge for $2000 for new theater passes reading Carmike instead of Martin. Charges for business lunches appeared on the statement of the person who signed the bill. Mike checked the reports and required explanations for anything out of line. Theater expenses also received close scrutiny, as he explained:

> Then I go a step beyond that. All district managers have a pet peeve. They all want their facilities to look brand new. You can write them letters, you can swear, you can cuss. It makes no difference. They are in that theater and that's the only thing they see. It's their world. They want new carpet every week. They want a new roof every week. They want a new projector and a new ticket machine every week. . . . The government says you have to capitalize those expenditures [but] I hate to capitalize expenses. The government says if the air conditioning breaks, you capitalize it. . . . [But] I wrote the check for $18,000. The money is gone.
>
> So, now I give every district manager a repair report. It shows anything charged to repairs. Yes, I could probably accomplish the same thing with a cash flow statement, but they wouldn't understand it.

■ Managing the Theaters

The company did not have a nepotism policy. Indeed, Mike Patrick encouraged the hiring of family. Especially in smaller towns where there might be several family members in visible positions, hiring family was seen as a deterrent to theft. As Mike Patrick explained:

> I will let them hire family for two reasons: One, they don't want to quit. . . . They're married to me as much as they are the family. Second, you get people who just would not steal. They have more to lose than just the job. None of the family will steal from me because it would have a direct bearing on the father, the uncle, the whole family. I am in a lot of little towns, and in a small town a son is either going to work on a farm, a grocery store, a filling station, or a theater, because there is no industry there. The cleanest job in town is the theater manager. Also, in a small town we allow the manager to look like he owns the theater. . . .
>
> Theater managers are paid straight salary. Under Fuqua ownership the manager's salary was linked to theater performance. But changes in company operations led to the change. Theater managers don't make the theater profit; the movie does. Theater managers used to select the movies. But now they don't have anything to do with selection. I am the only theater chain in the United States in which the booking and buying for the circuit is done by computer from right here on my desk. This computer is hooked to Atlanta and Dallas, which are my two booking offices.

Mike Patrick had hired both booking managers after the retirement of the previous incumbents. He explained how one came to work for Carmike:

> Let me tell you how I got Tony Reed. . . . He was the booker in a small city and that circuit was the best in town. He used to give me fits. And I used to spend more time trying to figure out how to get prints away from him than anybody else. So what did I do? I hired him. He made $19,000 a year working for a competitor and he makes $65,000 working for me. That's a lot of difference.

The planning system for booking films was set up so that past, current, and future bookings could be called up by theater, zone, or film. In addition, competitor's bookings were also available. The system allowed interaction between home office and the two booking offices, one in Atlanta and the other in Dallas.

■ The Outlook in 1986

As the 1985 year came to close, Carmike, like much of the industry, faced disappointing year-end results. Part of the problem was attributed to the number of executive turnovers in the movie production companies. Mike explained:

> A number of production executives changed jobs within a 90-day period. That meant that production stopped. Production is like developing a shopping center. It takes 18 months from the time you decide to do it to the time it opens. This year is off because there were no pictures out there. I believe that it will get better. . . . *Rocky IV* has just come out so we will end the year on an upbeat.

The industry faced a number of challenges that affected Carmike. Lack of films was a negative factor. However, the increase in ancillary markets for films, such as video purchase and rental, was viewed as a positive factor, as Mike explained:

> By 1979–1980 the ancillary market became very big. I understand the ancillary market is now about $3 billion and our side is $4 billion, . . . [but] I talked to a man in Home Box Office when he first started. He told me that they could not figure a way to sell a movie on its first run at all. If it was a bad movie, he couldn't give it away. If it was a good movie, he had all the attendance watching it he needed. He told me, "Mike, I want you to do better every year. The more blockbusters you get, the more demand I have. If you get *Who Shot Mary* and it dies in your theater, no one will watch it on Home Box Office." The theater is where you go to preview a movie. That establishes the value. So I realized then that CBS will pay more for a big movie than they will a lousy one, so anything that comes through the tube is no problem with me. I love it because [the revenues] help create more new movies.

An increase in films might be offset by the unabated increase in number of screens. However, the Patricks did not, as others did, foresee the demise of the movie theater. Mike especially felt that the difficult times offered opportunities to those who were prepared:

> There is more opportunity in bad times than in good times. The reason is that no one wants to sell when business is good, and if they do, the multiples are too high. So you want to buy when business is bad (and) . . . you got to plan for those times.
>
> I have to know where my capital is. I run this company through this set of reports. This is every financial thing you want to know about Carmike theaters— construction coming up, everything we are going to spend, source of cash, where it's going to go, everything. One of the critical things we are thinking about is how to expand. I know that if industry business goes bad, within 90 days, three or four more circuits are going to come up for sale. I must be in a position to buy them and I must have the knowledge to do it with. I will not bet the store on any deal.
>
> I am trying to buy a theater circuit right now—[it's priced] at $16 million. At $16 million I am paying a premium for that circuit—a big premium, because it loses money every year—but I am going to fire its management. I could buy it as part of Martin, [but] if Martin would buy it, then Martin would be liable for the money, so I don't want to do that. So what's my alternative? . . . I will take $2 or $3 million out of Carmike or have Carmike borrow $13 million and purchase the theater circuit. Then we expect that the cash flow from the purchased circuit will pay back the $13 million.

Mike Patrick was on the continuous outlook for new opportunities. One of those opportunities was outside the theater industry, as he explained:

> Our new office building is 100% financed with an industrial revenue 20-year bond issue. In case the theater business goes bad, I want to own an asset that is not a theater.

Cineplex Odeon Corporation

Joseph Wolfe, University of Tulsa

In mid-February 1989 Jack Valenti, head of the Motion Picture Association, reaffirmed the American film industry's basic health by citing 1988 movie theater attendance figures surpassing 1.0 billion people for the seventh year in a row. While this magnitude translated into box office revenues of over $4.4 billion, there are indications that the industry is in a state of both absolute and relative decline. It is also undergoing a restructuring that is fundamentally changing the nature of competitive practices for those in the film exhibition business. In the first instance a lower proportion of America's aging population attends the movies each year, partially due to the use of VCRs for film viewing, the presence of television in both its broadcast and cable versions, and to other uses of the consumer's leisure time dollars. In the second instance a great degree of owner concentration is occurring due to separate actions by both the Hollywood producers of films and their exhibitors.

Despite the apparent decline of the motion picture theater as the major supplier of America's needs for mass entertainment, the Toronto-based firm of Cineplex Odeon has quickly become North America's second-largest and most profitable theater chain through a series of shrewd and adventuresome acquisitions while creating a large number of upscale, multiscreened theaters in key cities and market areas. With 482 theaters and 1809 screens in 20 states, the Washington, D.C., area, 6 Canadian provinces, and the United Kingdom, the firm posted record sales of $695.8 million and profits of $40.4 million in 1988 while on the verge of developing and operating more than 110 screens in the United Kingdom by 1991. Central to Cineplex Odeon's success is the firm's driven and often abrasive chairman, president and CEO, Garth Drabinsky. It is against the backdrop of the industry's fundamental changes and basic decline that Drabinsky must chart his firm's future actions to insure its continued growth and prosperity.

THE MOTION PICTURE THEATER INDUSTRY

■ Early Operations and Competitive Strategies

The motion picture theater industry [Standard Industrial Code (SIC) 783] has undergone a number of radical transformations since its turn-of-the-century beginnings. The first movies were shown in cramped and hastily converted storefront locations called nickelodeons, so-named for their 5¢ admission charges. Their numbers grew rapidly, because the costs of entering this industry were relatively low and a plentiful supply of films was available in both legal and illegal, pirated versions. By 1907 it was estimated that the United States had about 3000 movie theaters concentrated in the larger cities. Rural areas were serviced by traveling film shows which made their presentations in the local town meeting hall.

The typical show lasted only 15 to 20 minutes augmented by sing-along slides or lectures. As the film medium's novelty declined, audiences began to clamor for more lavish and ambitious productions using recognizable actors and actresses. Feature-length movies replaced one-reel short subjects and comedies in the 1910s, and the theater industry's greatest building period began. Opulent, specially built structures soon became the focal point of every major city's downtown area. Often possessing more than 5000 seats, they came complete with a pit orchestra with vocalists and chorus, baby-sitting facilities, elevators, and grand staircases to a heavenlike balcony, numerous doormen, and a watchful and attentive fleet of uniformed ushers.

By the mid-1920s over 19,000 theaters were in operation, and Hollywood's film producers began what was a continuing attempt to control the first-run exhibitors of their films via acquisitions. The battle for theaters was initially waged between Paramount and First National, but soon Loew's (MGM), Fox, and Warner Brothers joined in, with First National being the major loser. By 1935 the twin realities of the Great Depression and the advent of sound films caused the number of theaters to plummet to about 15,000. Because of the nation's bleak economic outlook, many theaters had become too run-down or too costly to convert to the greater demands of sound films. Many Americans also substituted radio's free entertainment for their weekly lemminglike trek to the movies. Surviving theaters introduced the double feature to create more value for the entertainment dollar while obtaining the major source of their profits from candy, soft drink, and popcorn sales.

During World War II motion picture attendance and Hollywood's profits reached their all-time highs, with about 82.0 million people a week going to the nation's 20,400 theaters. This pinnacle did not last long, however, as postwar incomes were spent on new cars, television sets, and homes built in the newly emerging suburbs. Motion picture attendance began its precipitous fall in 1947, with attendance reaching its all-time low of 16.0 million per week in 1971. The number of theaters followed the same downward trend, although a steady increase in the number of drive-in theaters temporarily took up some of the slack.

The postwar period also saw the effects of the government's 1948 Consent Decree. By the early 1940s Hollywood's five major studios had obtained control or interests in 17.0% of the nation's theaters. This amounted to 70.0% of the important large-city, first-run theaters. Although certain studios were stronger in different parts of the country—Paramount dominated New England and the South, Warner Brothers the mid-Atlantic region, Loew's and RKO the New York–New Jersey area, and Twentieth Century Fox the western states—each controlled all stages of the distribution chain from its studios (manufacturing), its film exchanges (wholesaling), to its movie theaters (retailing). Under the Consent Decree the studios could either divest their studios and film exchanges or get rid of their movie theaters. Hollywood chose to sell their cinemas, thereby opting to control the supply side of the film distribution system.

In an effort to arrest the decline in attendance and to counter the relatively inexpensive and convenient medium of black and white television in the 1950s, the film studios retaliated by offering movies that dealt with subject matter considered too dangerous for home viewing, shown in formats and hues beyond television's technical capabilities. Moviegoers heard the word "virgin" uttered for the first time, women "with child" actually looked pregnant rather than merely full-skirted, and couples were shown in bed together without having to put one foot on the floor. From 1953 to 1968 about 28% of Hollywood's films were photographed and projected in a bewildering array of wide-screen processes such as Cinerama, CinemaScope, RegalScope, SuperScope, Technirama, VistaVision, Panavision, Techniscope, and even three-dimensional color.

■ Current Competitive Conditions

As movie attendance stabilized in the mid-1980s to a little more than 20 million patrons per week, two new trends established themselves in the movie theater business. The first was the creation of multiple-screened theater sites (see Exhibit 1), while the second trend was Hollywood's reacquisition of theaters and theater chains as part of a general consolidation within the industry. Many theater chains rediscovered the glitz and glamour of old Hollywood by rejuvenating old theaters, while existing single-screen theaters were subdivided and multiplexes were constructed from scratch in suburban malls and shopping districts. The economies of multiple-screened operations are compelling at the local level. Rather than needing a separate manager and projectionist for each theater, a number of variously sized auditoriums can be combined and centrally serviced. Box office operations and concession stands can also be centrally managed and operated. The availability of a number of screens at one location also yields programming flexibility for the theater operator. A "small" film without mass appeal can often turn a profit in a room seating only 300 people, while it would be unprofitable and would be lost in a larger auditorium. Having a number of screens in operation also increases the likelihood that the complex will be showing a hit film, thereby generating traffic for the other films being shown at the site. Multiple screens also allow the operator to outfit various rooms with different sound systems (the THX System by Lucasfilm versus the standard four-track optical stereo system) and projection equipment (at least one 70-mm, six-track magnetic sound projector in addition to the usual 35-mm projector), thereby offering the very finest possible viewing.

Exhibit 1   **Number of U.S. Movie Theaters (selected years, 1923–1989)**

Year	Theaters	Drive-ins	Total	Screens
1923	15.0		15.0	
1926	19.5		19.5	
1929	23.3		23.3	
1935	15.3		15.3	
1942	20.3	0.1	20.4	
1946	18.7	0.3	19.0	
1950	16.9	2.2	19.1	
1955	14.1	4.6	18.7	
1965	9.2	4.2	13.4	
1974	9.6	3.5	13.2	14.4
1980	9.7	3.6	13.3	17.6
1981	11.4	3.3	14.7	18.0
1984	14.6	2.8	17.4	20.2
1985	15.1	2.8	17.9	20.7
1986	16.8	2.8	19.6	22.8
1987*	17.9	2.8	20.7	23.6
1988*	18.1	2.7	20.8	24.3

Sources: Joel W. Finler, *The Hollywood Story* (New York: Crown Publishers, 1988, p. 288); "The Motion Pictures Rides into Town, 1903," *The Wall Street Journal*, February 7, 1989, p. B1; *1989 U.S. Industrial Outlook* (Washington, D.C.: U.S. Department of Commerce/International Trade Administration, 1989, p. 57-1).

*Estimated.

The second trend towards consolidation is occurring at all levels of the film distribution chain. A number of studios recently purchased major theater chains after sensing a relaxation of the enforcement of the Consent Decree (in 1984 the Justice Department offered advance support to any studio financing a lawsuit to reenter the movie theater business) plus their promise to limit their ownership to less than 50.0% of any acquired chain. MCA, owner of Universal Studios, has purchased 49.7% of Cineplex Odeon, the Cannon Group purchased the Commonwealth chain, and United Artists Communications acquired the Georgia Theatre Company, the Gulf States and Litchfield chains, and in 1988 alone, the Blair, Sameric, Commonwealth (from the Cannon Group) and Moss theater chains. Gulf & Western's Paramount Studios purchased the Mann Theaters and Festival Enterprises, while Columbia and Tri-Star (owned by Coca-Cola) bought the Loew's chain. On the retailing side Cineplex Odeon purchased the Walter Reade, Plitt, RKO, Septum, Essaness, and Sterling chains, Carmike Cinemas purchased Stewart & Everett, while AMC Entertainment purchased the Budco Theatres. Through these actions and others the top six chains now own nearly 40% of America's screens, which is a 67.0% increase in just three years.

Wholesaling operations were drastically reduced over the years on a scale unnoticeable to the public but very significant to those in the business. When film going was in its heyday, each studio operated as many as 20 or so film exchanges in key cities across the country. Hollywood's studios have since closed many exchanges, until they are now operating only five to eight branch offices each. Paramount recently merged its Charlotte and Jacksonville branches into its Atlanta office, while Chicago now handles the business once serviced by its Detroit, Kansas City, Des Moines, and Minneapolis branches. As observed by Michael Patrick, president of Carmike Cinemas, "As the geographical regions serviced by these offices increase, the ability of smaller exhibitors to negotiate bookings is diluted relative to the buying power of the larger circuits."[1]

THE INDUSTRY'S PRODUCT AND COMPETITIVE STRUCTURE

Despite the glamour associated with Hollywood, its stars, its televised Academy Award show, and such megahits as *Who Framed Roger Rabbit?*, *Rain Man*, and *Batman*, theater operators are basically in the business of running commercial enterprises dealing with a very perishable commodity. A movie is a merchandisable product made available by Hollywood and various independent producers to commercial storefront theaters at local retail locations. Given the large degree of concentration in the industry, corporate-level actions entail the financing of both acquisitions and new construction, while local operations deal with the booking of films that match the moviegoing tastes of the communities being served.

To the degree a movie house merely retails someone else's product, the theater owner's success lies in the quality and not the quantity of products produced by Hollywood. Accordingly, the 1987–1988 Christmas season did not produce any blockbusters, while 1987's two big hits were *Beverly Hills Cop II* and *Fatal Attraction*; and 1986's hits were *Top Gun*, *Crocodile Dundee*, and *The Karate Kid, Part II*. Under these conditions of relatively few real money-makers the bargaining power shifts to the studios, leaving the exhibitors with more screens than they can fill with high-drawing films. Although the independent producers (the "indies")—such as the DeLaurentis Entertainment Group, New World, Atlantic, Concorde, and Cannon—are producing proportionally more films every year and the majors are producing fewer, their product is more variable in quality and less bankable. Additionally, theaters often pay a premium for the rights to show first-run movies on an exclusive basis in a given area or film zone, such as the May 1989 release of *Indiana Jones and the Last Crusade*. This condition hurts the smaller chains especially hard, as they do not have the resources to outbid the giant circuits.

Marketing research conducted by the industry consistently found that young adults are the prime consumers of motion picture theater entertainment. This group is rather concentrated but not organized. A study by the Opinion Research Corporation in July 1986 found those under the age of 40 accounted for 86.0% of all theater admissions. Frequent moviegoers constitute only 21.0% of the eligible film goers, but they account for 83.0% of all admissions. A general downward attendance trend has been occurring, as shown in Exhibit 2, where 43.0% of the population never attended a film in 1986. The long-term demographics also appear to be unfavorable, as America's population is moving towards those age categories least likely to attend a movie. Those 40 and over make up only 14.0% of a typical theater's admissions, while they account for

---

[1]Michael W. Patrick, "Trends in Exhibition," in Wayne R. Green, ed., *The 1987 Encyclopedia of Exhibition* (New York: National Association of Theatre Owners, 1988), p. 109.

Exhibit 2

Frequency of Attendance by Total Public Ages 12 and over

Attendance*	1986	1985	1984
Frequently	21.0%	22.0%	23.0%
Occasionally	25.0	29.0	28.0
Infrequently	11.0	9.0	8.0
Never	43.0	39.0	39.0
Not reported	0.0	1.0	2.0

Source: 1988 International Motion Picture Almanac (New York: Quigley Publications, 1988), p. 29A.

*Frequently: at least once a month; occasionally: once in 2 to 6 months; infrequently: less than once in 6 months.

44.0% of the nation's population. Those from 12 to 29 years of age make up 66.0% of admissions while accounting for only 36.0% of the population.[2] (See Exhibit 3.)

It appears that certain barriers to entry into the motion picture theater industry exist. Economies of scale are present, with the advantage given to operations concentrated in metropolitan areas where one omnibus newspaper advertisement covers all the chain's theaters. As shown in Exhibit 4, the largest chains in the United States lost the least during the period July 1984 to June 1985. (These specific chains are listed in Exhibit 5.) Based on these results, scale economies appear to exist in the areas of operating costs, executive compensation, advertising, and rental expenses. Those choosing to enter the industry in recent years have done so through the use of massive conglomerate-backed capital. The possibility that an independent can open a profitable movie theater is very remote. "There's no way the small, independent operator can compete against the large screen owners these days," says John Duffy, cofounder of Cinema 'N' Drafthouse International of Atlanta, Georgia.[3] As a way of carving a niche for himself, Duffy's chain charges $2.00 for an "intermediate-run" film but serves dinner and drinks during the movie, thereby garnering more than $5.00 in food revenue, compared to a theater's average $1.25 per admission.

Despite attempts by various theater owners to make the theater-going experience unique, customers tend to go to the most convenient theater showing the film they want to see at the time which is best for them. Accordingly, a particular theater chain enjoys proprietary product differentiation to the degree it occupies the best locations in any particular market area. Additionally, the cost of building new facilities in the most desirable areas has increased dramatically. Harold L. Vogel, of Merrill Lynch, Pierce, Fenner and Smith, observed that the average construction cost comes to over $1.0 million per screen in areas such as New York or Los Angeles.[4]

[2]Presented in 1988 International Motion Picture Almanac (New York: Quigley Publications, 1988), pp. 29A–30A.

[3]Quoted by Peter Waldman, "Silver Screens Lose Some of Their Luster," The Wall Street Journal, February 9, 1989, p. B1.

[4]Harold L. Vogel, "Theatrical Exhibition: Consolidation Continues," in Wayne R. Green, ed., The 1987 Encyclopedia of Exhibition (New York: National Association of Theatre Owners, 1988), p. 62.

U.S. Population by Age Group for 1980, with Projections for 1990 and 2000

Exhibit 3

Age Range	Year	Number (in millions)	Percent of Total*	Percent Change
5–17	1980	47.22	20.7	
	1990	45.14	18.1	–4.4
	2000	49.76	18.6	10.2
18–24	1980	30.35	13.2	
	1990	25.79	10.3	–15.0
	2000	24.60	9.2	–4.6
25–44	1980	63.48	27.9	
	1990	81.38	32.6	28.2
	2000	80.16	29.9	–1.5
45–64	1980	44.49	19.5	
	1990	46.53	18.6	4.4
	2000	60.88	22.7	31.1
65 and over	1980	25.71	11.3	
	1990	31.70	12.8	23.3
	2000	34.92	13.0	10.2

Source: Adapted from U.S. Department of Commerce, Bureau of the Census, *Statistical Abstract of the United States, 1985* (Washington, D.C.: Government Printing Office, 1985), pp. 26–27.

*1980 total: 227,705,000; 1990 total: 249,675,000; 2000 total: 267,955,000.

Average Operating Results for Selected Motion Picture Theater Corporations by Asset Size, July 1984–June 1985

Exhibit 4

Operating Results	Small-sized		Middle-sized		Large-sized	
Revenues	$224,171	100.0	$4,476,042	100.0	$151,545,455	100.0
Cost of operations	93,917	41.9	1,780,066	39.8	54,707,909	36.1
Operating income	130,254	58.1	2,695,976	60.2	96,837,546	63.9
Expenses						
Compensation of officers	6,788	3.0	150,647	3.4	2,121,636	1.4
Repairs	5,497	2.5	74,134	1.7	2,438,504	1.6
Bad debts	170	.1	4,196	.1	82,661	.1
Rent	32,195	14.4	315,841	7.1	11,489,901	7.6
Taxes (excluding federal taxes)	12,904	5.8	179,881	4.0	5,689,843	3.8
Interest	8,045	3.6	117,216	2.6	8,031,909	5.3
Depreciation	8,866	4.0	269,122	6.0	8,954,959	5.9
Advertising	16,004	7.1	152,745	3.4	5,689,843	3.8
Pensions and other benefit plans	—	—	42,622	1.0	771,504	.5
Other expenses	70,971	31.7	1,682,992	37.6	55,245,207	36.5
Net profit before taxes	(31,186)	(13.9)	(293,460)	(6.6)	(3,678,421)	(2.4)
Current ratio	1.0		1.3		.7	
Quick ratio	.6		1.0		.5	
Debt ratio	140.6		52.9		74.2	
Asset turnover	3.0		1.3		1.0	

Exhibit 5   **North America's Largest Theater Circuits**

Circuit	Headquarters	Screens
United Artists Communications	Denver, Colorado	2677
Cineplex Odeon	Toronto, Canada	1825
American Multi-Cinema	Kansas City, Missouri	1531
General Cinema	Chestnut Hill, Massachusetts	1359
Carmike Cinemas	Columbus, Georgia	742

Source: 10-Ks and various stockholder's reports for 1988.

Just as the motion picture was a substitute for vaudeville shows and min-strels at the turn of the century, radio and now television are the major, somewhat interchangeable substitutes for mass entertainment in America. More recently, cable television, pay-per-view TV, and videocassettes have eaten into the precious leisure time dollar. Estimates are that 49.2 million homes now subscribe to cable television, 19.0 million homes have pay-per-view capability, and 56.0 million homes have a VCR, with 20.0% of those homes having more than one unit. The greatest damage to theater attendance was accomplished by videocassettes, which deliver over 5000 titles to viewers at a relatively low cost in the comfort of their own living rooms. Sumner Redstone, owner of the very profitable National Amusements theater chain, remarked, "Anyone who doesn't believe videocassettes are devastating competition to theaters is a fool."[5]

Although the motion picture medium has been characterized as one that provides visual mass entertainment, those going to movies must ultimately choose between alternative forms of recreation. In that regard skiing, boating, baseball and football games, books, newspapers, and even silent contemplation vie for the consumer's precious time. Exhibit 6 shows that the movie theater industry has declined in its ability to capture both America's total recreation dollars and its thirst for passive spectator entertainment. During the period from 1984 to 1987 the greatest increases in consumer recreation expenditures were for bicycles, sports equipment, boats and pleasure aircraft, and television and radio equipment and their repair.

Different marketing strategies are being employed in an attempt to remain viable in this very competitive industry. Some chains, such as Cinemark Theaters and Carmike Cinemas, specialize in $1.00 or low-price, second-run multiplexed theaters in smaller towns and selected markets. In a sense they are applying Wal-Mart's original market strategy of dominating smaller, less competitive rural towns. Others, such as General Cinema, United Artists Communications, and AMC Entertainment, favor multiplexed first-run theaters in major markets. Within this group AMC Entertainment has been a pioneer as a multiscreen operator. It opened its first twin theater in 1963 and its first quadplex in 1969. As of mid-1988 AMC was operating 269 complexes with 1531 screens, with most of its expansion in the Sunbelt. General Cinema has been diversifying out of the movie theater business through its nearly 60% interest in

[5]Quoted by Stratford P. Sherman, "Movie Theaters Head Back to the Future," *Fortune,* January 20, 1986, p. 91.

Motion Picture Exhibitors' Share of Entertainment Expenditures: Receipts as a Percent of Total for Selected Years, 1929–1989

Exhibit 6

Year	Consumer Expenditures	Recreation Expenditures	Spectator Expenditures
1929	0.94	16.6	78.9
1937	1.01	20.0	82.6
1943	1.29	25.7	87.6
1951	0.64	11.3	76.3
1959	0.31	5.6	61.0
1965	0.21	3.5	51.2
1971	0.18	2.7	47.7
1977	0.56	5.8	34.8
1983	0.16	2.4	41.9
1986	0.14	1.9	37.3
1987	0.14	1.8	36.9
1988	0.13	1.8	36.5
1989*	0.13	1.7	36.1

Sources: Joel W. Finler, *The Hollywood Story* (New York: Crown Publishers, 1988), p. 288; U.S. Bureau of Economic Analysis, *Survey of Current Business,* July issues; U.S. Bureau of the Census, *Statistical Abstract of the United States: 1989,* 109th ed. (Washington, D.C.: U.S. Government Printing Office, 1988).

*Estimated by the case writer.

the Neiman-Marcus Group (Neiman-Marcus, Contempo Casuals, and Bergdorf Goodman) and 18.4% interest in Cadbury Schweppes. Most recently, General Cinema sold off its soft-drink-bottling business to PepsiCo for $1.5 billion, to obtain cash for investments in additional nontheater operations.

A great amount of building has occurred in the theater industry in the past few years. Since 1981 the number of screens has increased about 35%, but the population proportion attending movies has actually fallen. Additionally, the relatively inexpensive days of "twinning" or quadplexing existing theaters appears to be over, and the construction of totally new multiplexes is much more expensive. Exhibit 7 shows that operating profit margins peeked in 1983 at 11.7%, and they have fallen dramatically since then as the industry has taken on large amounts of debt to finance the construction of more and more screens now generating 24.6% fewer admissions per screen. Many operations are losing money, although certain economies of scale exist and laborsaving devices have allowed industry employment to fall slightly, while the number of screens has increased substantially. The Plitt theaters were money losers before being acquired by Cineplex Odeon and AMC Entertainment lost $6.0 million in 1987 and $13.8 million in 1988 on theater operations. Carmike was barely profitable in 1986, and General Cinema's earnings from its theater operations have fallen for the past three years, although the operation's assets and sales have been increasing. Generally speaking, about half the nation's motion picture theaters and chains were unprofitable in the 1980s, while numerous chains have engaged in the illegal practice of "splitting," wherein theater owners in certain markets decide which one will negotiate or bid for which films offered by the various distributors available to them.

Exhibit 7

Per-Screen Admissions, Capital Expenditures, and Operating Profits Margins (selected years, 1979–1987)

Item	1979	1981	1983	1985	1987
Tickets sold (000,000)	1,121	1,067	1,197	1,056	1,086
Average admission per screen	65,575	58,422	63,387	49,936	47,797
Capital expenditures (000,000)	$19.0	$57.4	$77.6	$164.0	$515.7
Profit margin	9.3%	9.1%	11.7%	11.6%	8.8%

Source: Peter Waldman, "Silver Screens Lose Some of Their Luster," *The Wall Street Journal,* February 9, 1989, p. B1.

BUILDING THE CINEPLEX ODEON CORPORATION

Today's exhibition giant began in 1978 with an 18-screen complex below the parking garage of a Toronto shopping center. Garth Drabinsky, a successful entertainment lawyer and real estate inventor, joined with the Canadian theater veteran Nathan Aaron (Nat) Taylor in this enterprise. After three years and dozens of new theaters, Cineplex entered the American theater market by opening a 14-screen multiplex in the very competitive and highly visible Los Angeles Beverly Center. Despite the chain's growth, however, it was only marginally profitable. When the fledgling chain went public on the Toronto Stock Exchange in 1982, it lost $12.0 million on sales of $14.4 million.

Cineplex nearly went bankrupt, but not through poor management by Drabinsky or Taylor. Canada's two major theater circuits, Famous Players (Paramount Studios) and the independent Odeon chain, had pressured Hollywood's major distributors into keeping their first-run films from Cineplex. But in 1983 Drabinsky, who as a lawyer had written a standard reference on Canadian motion picture law, convinced Canada's version of the U.S. Justice Department's antitrust division that Famous Players and Odeon were operating in restraint of trade. Armed with data gathered by Drabinsky, the Combines Investigative Branch forced the distributors to sign a consent decree, thus opening all films to competitive bidding. Ironically, without the protection provided by its collusive actions, the 297-screen Odeon circuit soon began to lose money, whereupon Cineplex purchased its former adversary for $22.0 million. The company subsequently changed its name to Cineplex Odeon.

In its development as an exhibition giant the chain always was able to attract a number of smart, deep-pocketed backers. Early investors included the since-departed Odyssey Partners, and with a 30.2% stake, Montreal-based Claridge Investments & Company, the main holding company of Montreal financier Charles Bronfman. The next major investor was the entertainment conglomerate MCA, Inc., of Universal City, California. MCA purchased 49.7% of Cineplex's stock (but is limited to a 33.0% voting stake because of Canadian foreign ownership rules) in January 1986 for $106.7 million. This capital infusion gave Cineplex the funds to further pursue its aggressive expansion plans. As Drabinsky said at the time, "There's only so much you can do within the Canadian

---

Cineplex Odeon Theater Acquisitions   **Exhibit 8**

Odeon	Septum
Plitt Theatres	Essaness
RKO Century Warner Theaters	Sterling Recreation Organization
Walter Reade Organization	Maybox Movie Centre Limited
Circle Theaters	

---

marketplace. It was only a question of when, not where, we were going to expand."[6] In short order the company became a major American exhibitor by acquiring six additional chains. (See Exhibit 8.) Some rival and fearful exhibitors, because of Drabinsky's quest for growth via the acquisition route, have been tempted to call him Darth Grabinsky, after the *Star Wars* protagonist.

■ Operating Strategy

Despite these rumblings, Cineplex Odeon reshaped the moviegoing experience for numerous North Americans. Many previous theater owners had either let their urban theaters fall into decay and disrepair or sliced larger theaters into unattractive and sterile multiplexes. Others had built new but spartan and utilitarian facilities in suburban malls and shopping centers. When building its own theaters from the ground up or when refurbishing an acquired theater, Cineplex's strategy is to make the patron's visit to the theater a pleasurable one and thereby obtain a top-dollar return per admission.

The Olympia I and II Cinemas in New York City typify the scope of the renovations undertaken. Originally built in 1913, the theater seated 1320 and was billed as having "the world's largest screen." In 1939 it was remodeled in an art deco style, and in 1980 it was renovated as a triplex, with a fourth screen added in 1981. As part of Cineplex's renovation, the four smaller auditoriums were collapsed into two larger, 850-seat, state-of-the-art, wide-screened theaters featuring Dolby stereo sound systems and 70-mm projection equipment. Its art deco design was augmented by postmodern features such as marble floors, pastel colors, and neon accents.

Whether through new construction or the renovation of acquired theaters, many Cineplex cinemas feature entryways of terrazzo tile, marble, or glass. The newly built Cinema Egyptien in Montreal has three auditoriums and a total seating capacity of 900. It is replete with mirrored ceilings and hand-painted murals rendered in the traditional Egyptian colors of Nile green, turquoise, gold, lapis lazuli blue, and amber red. Historically accurate murals measuring 300 feet in length depict the daily life and typical activities of the ancient Egyptians.

Toronto's Canada Square office complex features a spacious, circular, art deco lobby with a polished granite floor and recessed lighting highlighted by a thin band of neon encircling the high, domed ceiling. On the lobby's left side moviegoers can snack in a small cafe outfitted with marble tables, bright red chairs, and thick carpeting. In New York City the chain restored the splendor and elegance of Carnegie Hall's Recital Hall as it was originally conceived in 1891. The

---

[6]Quoted by David Aston, "A New Hollywood Legend Called—Garth Drabinsky?" *Business Week*, September 23, 1985, p. 61.

plaster ceilings and the original seats were completely rebuilt and refinished in the gold and red velvet colors of the great and historic Carnegie Hall. (See Exhibit 9.)

Just to make the evening complete, and to capture the high profits realized from concession operations, patrons of a Cineplex theater can typically sip cappuccino or taste one of 14 different blends of tea served in Rosenthal china. Those wanting heavier fare can nibble on croissant sandwiches, fudge brownies, or carrot cake, while freshly popped popcorn is always served with real butter. An unsuccessful innovation was the creation of in-theater boutiques which sold movie memorabilia. Although designed to obtain additional revenues from the moviegoer, operating costs were too high.

This glamor does not come cheaply, as the chain usually charges the highest prices in town. For those in a financial bind the American Express credit card is now honored at many of the chain's box offices. Cineplex broke New York City's $6.00 ticket barrier by raising its prices to $7.00, incurring the wrath of then-Mayor Ed Koch, who marched on picket lines with other angry New Yorkers. Cineplex's action also caused some to suggest that the New York State legislature pass a measure requiring all exhibitors to print admission prices in their newspaper advertisements. When justifying the increased ticket price, Drabinsky said the alternative was "to continue to expose New Yorkers to filthy, rat-invested environments. We don't intend to do that."[7] Approximately $30 million was spent refurbishing Cineplex Odeon's 30 Manhattan theaters.

Exhibit 9   **One of Cineplex Odeon's Recently Opened Theaters**

[7]Quoted by Richard Corliss, "Master of the Movies' Taj Mahals," *Time,* January 25, 1988, pp. 60–61.

Another unpopular and somewhat incongruous action, given the upscale image engendered by each theater's trappings, is the running of advertisements for Club Med and the California raisins before feature films. Regardless of the anger and unpopularity created among potential patrons, Cineplex is not interested in catering to the "average" theater patron. Rather than trying to attract the mass market, the theater chain aims its massive and luxurious theaters at the aging baby boomers, who are becoming a greater portion of America's population.

■ The Man Behind the Screen: Garth Drabinsky

Over the years Cineplex Odeon and Garth Drabinsky have received high marks for their creative, show business flair. As observed by theater industry analyst Paul Kagan, "Garth Drabinsky is both a showman and a visionary. There were theater magnates before him, but none who radiated his charisma or generated such controversy."[8] These sentiments are reiterated by Roy L. Furman, president of Furman Selz Mager Dietz & Birney Inc., one of Drabinsky's intermediaries in the Plitt acquisition: "Too many people see the [theater] business as just bricks and mortar. Garth has a real love for the business, a knowledge of what will work and what won't."[9] When a new Cineplex Odeon theater opens, it begins with a splashy by-invitation-only party, usually with a few movie stars on hand. Besides his ability to attract smart investors, Drabinsky believes moviegoers want to be entertained by the theater's ambience as well as by the movies it shows. Accordingly, about $2.8 million ($450,000 per screen) is spent when building one of the chain's larger theaters, in contrast with the usual $1.8 million for a simple, no-frills sixplex. "People don't just like coming to our theaters," says Drabinsky. "They linger afterward. They have another cup of cappuccino in the cafe or sit and read the paper. We've created a more complete experience, and it makes them return to that location."[10] "This company has attempted to change the basic thinking. We've introduced the majesty back to picture going."[11]

Drabinsky dates his fascination with the silver screen to his childhood bout with polio, which left him bedridden much of the time from the ages of 3 to 12. His illness also imbued him with a strong sense of determination; this resolution has helped to drive Cineplex Odeon forward. No one speaks for the company except Drabinsky, and he logs half a million miles a year visiting his theaters and otherwise encouraging his employees. The energetic CEO likes to drop by his theaters unannounced to talk with ushers and cashiers, and he telephones or sees 20 to 25 theater managers a week. His standards are meticulously enforced, often in a very personal and confrontational manner. He has been known to exemplify his penchant for detail by stooping in front of one of his ushers to pick up a single piece of spilled popcorn.

The combative nature that helped Drabinsky break the Famous Players and Odeon cartel in the early 1980s still resides in him. When Columbia Pictures

---

[8]Ibid., p. 60.

[9]Aston, op. cit., p. 62.

[10]Quoted by Alex Ben Block, "Garth Drabinsky's Pleasure Domes," *Forbes*, June 2, 1986, p. 93.

[11]Mary A. Fischer, "They're Putting Glitz Back into Movie Houses," *U.S. News & World Report*, January 25, 1988, p. 58.

temporarily pulled its production of *The Last Emperor* out of distribution, he retaliated by canceling 140 play dates of the studio's monumental bomb, *Leonard Part 6*, starring Bill Cosby. "Some people are burned by his brashness," says Al Waxman, formerly of the television series "Cagney & Lacey." "There's no self-denial. He stands up and says, 'Here's what I'm doing.' Then he does it."[12] His longtime mentor Nat Taylor observed, "He's very forceful, and sometimes he's abrasive. I think he's so far ahead of the others that he loses patience if they can't keep up with him."[13] This nature may have long-term negative consequences for Cineplex, however, as Drabinsky recently had heated arguments with Sidney Jay Sheinberg, president of MCA, Inc., the head of the circuit's largest shareholder group.

■ Other Product and Market Ventures

In addition to its motion picture theater operations, Cineplex Odeon engaged in other entertainment-related ventures such as television and film production, film distribution, and live theater. In the latter area the company is restoring the Pantages Theatre in downtown Toronto into a legitimate theater for the housing of its $5.5 million production of Andrew Lloyd Webber's *The Phantom of the Opera*, scheduled for fall 1989.

Cineplex also began a 414-acre motion picture entertainment and studio complex in Orlando, Florida, as a joint venture with MCA, Inc., but sold its stake to an American unit of the Rank Organization PLC for about $150 million in April 1989, after having invested some $92 million in the project. Various industry observers felt Cineplex withdrew from the potentially profitable venture to help reduce its bank debt, which had grown to $640 million.

In August 1988, the firm also created New Visions Pictures as a joint venture with a unit of Lieberman Enterprises Inc. to produce ten films over a two-year period. Cineplex Odeon also owns Toronto International Studios, Canada's largest film center. This operation licenses its facilities to moviemakers and others for film and television production. In a related motion picture production move, Cineplex acquired The Film House Group Inc. in 1986 to process 16-mm and 35-mm release prints for Cineplex Odeon Films (another one of the company's divisions) and other distributors. After doubling and upgrading its capacity in 1987, it sold 49.0% of its interest to the Rank Organization in December 1988 for $73.5 million. Rank has a one-year option to buy the remaining portion of The Film House Group by December 1989.

The company also engaged in various motion picture distribution deals and television productions, none of which have been commercially successful. Cineplex distributed such films as Prince's *Sign o' the Times*, Paul Newman's *The Glass Menagerie*, *The Changeling* with George C. Scott, and *Madame Sousatzka* starring Shirley Maclaine. Its television unit contracted 41 new episodes of the revived "Alfred Hitchcock Presents" series for the 1988–1989 television season. The series, however, was canceled. For future release Cineplex is financing five low-budget ($4.0 to $5.0 million each) films, joint-ventured with Robert Redford's Wildwood Enterprises through Northfork Productions Inc. The five movies will be distributed through Cineplex Odeon Films.

---

[12]Block, op. cit., p. 92.

[13]Aston, op. cit., p. 63.

■ Finances and Accounting Practices

Garth Drabinsky's financial dealings and his ability to attract capital to his firm has always been very important to its success. Serious questions have been raised, however, about the propriety of some of Cineplex's financial reporting methods. Charles Paul, a vice-president of MCA, Inc., and Cineplex board member, noted that various board members are very concerned about the company's financial reporting practices and procedures. In a highly critical report distributed by Kellogg Associates, a Los Angeles accounting and consulting firm, a number of questionable practices were noted. Most frequently cited was Cineplex's treatment of the gains and losses associated with asset sales, with the overall effect creating an overstatement of operating revenues. As an example, Cineplex treated its gain of $40.4 million from the sale of The Film House Group as revenue rather than as extraordinary income. The report also criticized (1) Cineplex's $18.7 write-off on the value of its film library, which "postponed" losses on the sale of American theaters, and (2) its inclusion of the proceeds from the sale of theaters as nonoperating income in its cash flow statement, but calling it operating revenue in its profit and loss statement. In 1988 alone Cineplex reported a profit of $49.3 million from the sale of certain theater properties.

Also of concern is the role asset sales play in the company's revenue and cash flow picture. Jeffrey Logsdon, a Crowell Weedon analyst, believes Cineplex has

---

Cineplex Odeon's Revenue Sources, 1985–1988   **Exhibit 10**

Revenue Source	1988	1987	1986	1985
Admissions	51.1%	62.5%	64.5%	68.0%
Concessions	16.5	18.2	20.0	20.0
Distribution and other	22.5	11.1	8.6	7.0
Property sales	9.9	8.0	6.8	5.0

Sources: Various 10-Ks and *1988 Annual Report.*

Selected Summary Financial Data (in millions except when presented as percents)   **Exhibit 11**

	1989*	1988	1987	1986	1985	1984
Revenue	$710.0	$695.8	$520.2	$357.0	$124.3	$67.1
Net profit	$43.0	$40.4	$34.6	$22.5	$9.1	$3.5
Net profit %	6.1%	5.8%	6.6%	6.3%	7.3%	5.3%
Long-term debt	$720.0	$600.0	$464.3	$333.5	$40.7	$36.1
Interest	$52.6[†]	$40.2[†]	$33.8	$16.4	$3.9	$2.1
ROE %	10.2%[†]	10.3%	11.0%	18.1%	40.7%	30.5%

Sources: Value Line Report, no. 1756, prepared December 9, 1988; *Standard NYSE Stock Reports* vol. 55, no. 176, sec. 6, September 12, 1988, p. 536F.

*Estimated by Value Line.

[†] Estimated by the case writer.

been selling its assets just to keep operating, citing as evidence the sale of both The Film House Group and its 50.0% stake in MCA's Universal Studios tour project to the Rank Organization. Exhibit 10 demonstrates how Cineplex's revenue sources have changed since 1985, with box office receipts constantly falling and property sales constantly rising. Over the period shown the sale of theater assets has increased 98.0% as a source of corporate revenues. Additionally, the return on those sales, based on selling price over acquisition costs, has fallen every year from their high of 139.1% in 1985 to their low of 13.3% in 1988.

There is also a question as to whether Cineplex can continue its current growth rate via acquisitions and debt financing. The cost of acquisitive growth

---

Exhibit 12   **1988 Per-Capita Attendance Rates**

Country	Rate (%)
United States	4.4
Great Britain	1.4
Canada	2.8
France	1.9
West Germany	1.9
Italy	1.6

Source: "Movies 'Held Firm' Last Year," *Tulsa Tribune,* February 16, 1989, p. 9C.

Exhibit 13   **Cineplex Odeon Corporation: Unaudited First-Quarter Consolidated Statement of Income (in thousands of U.S. dollars)**

	1989	1988
Revenue		
Admissions	$ 85,819	$ 80,389
Concessions	26,657	24,082
Distribution, postproduction and other	70,033	28,782
Sale of theater properties	5,731	1,600
	188,240	134,853
Expenses		
Theater operations and other expenses	133,158	97,733
Cost of concessions	5,085	4,466
Cost of theater properties sold	5,837	550
General and administrative expenses	8,035	6,310
Depreciation and amortization	11,207	7,923
	163,322	116,982
Income before the undernoted	24,918	17,871
Interest on long-term debt and bank indebtedness	12,257	9,138
Income before taxes	12,661	8,733
Minority interest	978	—
Income taxes	968	727
Net income	$ 10,715	$ 8,006

Source: First Quarter Report 1989, pp. 12–13.

may become more expensive, as many of the bargains have already been obtained by Cineplex or other chains. The early purchase of the Plitt Theater chain (in November 1985) cost about $125,000 per screen, although the bargain price for Plitt may have been a one-time opportunity, as it had just lost $5.0 million on revenues of $111.0 million during the nine months ending June 30, 1985. To get into the New York City RKO Century Warner Theaters chain in 1986, Cineplex had to pay $1.9 million per screen, while it paid almost $3.0 million a screen in 1987 for the New York City–based Walter Reade Organization. Overall, Cineplex Odeon paid about $276,000 each for the screens it acquired in 1986.

Some analysts are questioning the prices being paid for old screens as well as the wisdom of expanding operations in what many see as a declining and saturated industry. A past rule of thumb has been that a screen should cost 11 times its cash flow, but some experts feel a more reasonable rule should be 6 to 7 times cash flow, given the glut of screens on the market. The changing effects of Cineplex's acquisition and debt structure since 1984 have been summarized in Exhibit 11.

Cineplex Odeon Corporation: Consolidated Statement of Income (in thousands of U.S. dollars)   **Exhibit 14**

	1988	1987	1986	1985
Revenue				
Admissions	$355,645	$322,385	$230,300	$ 84,977
Concessions	114,601	101,568	71,443	24,949
Distribution, postproduction and other	156,372	61,216	30,846	7,825
Sale of theater properties	69,197	34,984	24,400	6,549
	695,815	520,153	356,989	124,300
Expenses				
Theater operations and other expenses	464,324	371,909	258,313	89,467
Cost of concessions	21,537	18,799	13,742	5,980
Cost of theater properties sold	61,793	21,618	11,690	2,736
General and administrative expenses	26,617	17,965	15,335	5,701
Depreciation and amortization	38,087	23,998	14,266	3,678
	612,358	454,289	313,346	107,562
Income before the undernoted	83,457	65,864	43,643	16,738
Other income	3,599	—	—	(330)
Interest on long-term debt and bank indebtedness	42,932	27,026	16,195	3,961
Income before taxes, equity earnings, preacquisition losses, and extraordinary item	44,124	38,838	27,448	12,447
Income taxes	3,728	4,280	6,310	5,032
Income before equity earnings, preacquisition losses, and extraordinary item	40,396	34,558	21,138	7,415
Add back: Preacquisition losses attributable to 50% interest Plitt not owned by the corporation	—	—	1,381	—
Equity in earnings of 50% owned companies	—	—	—	1,021
Income before extraordinary item	40,396	34,558	22,519	8,436
Extraordinary item	—	—	—	9,096
Net income	$ 40,396	$ 34,558	$ 22,519	$ 17,532

Source: Company annual reports for 1987 and 1988.

Given the maturity of the North American market and Cineplex Odeon's penchant for growth, the company is currently implementing a planned expansion into Europe. Cineplex is scheduled to build 100 screens in 20 movie houses throughout the United Kingdom by 1990, with additional expansion plans in Europe and Israel for the early 1990s. Exhibit 12 lists the comparative per-capita motion picture attendance rates found in various European countries. Other exhibitors are also interested in bringing multiscreened theaters to Europe. In addition to Cineplex, Warner Brothers, American Multi-Cinema, Odeon, and

Exhibit 15

Cineplex Odeon Corporation: Unaudited First-Quarter Consolidated Balance Sheet (in thousands of U.S. dollars)

	1989	1988
Assets		
Current assets		
Accounts receivable	$ 229,961	$ 151,510
Advances to distributors and producers	18,334	26,224
Distribution costs	9,695	10,720
Inventories	7,781	7,450
Prepaid expenses and deposits	6,756	5,505
Properties held for disposition	23,833	25,557
	296,360	226,966
Property, equipment and leaseholds	844,107	824,836
Other assets		
Long-term investments and receivables	35,169	130,303
Goodwill (less amortization of $3545; 1988—$2758)	53,589	53,966
Deferred charges (less amortization of $8456; 1988—$7724)	30,222	27,100
	118,980	211,369
Total assets	$1,259,447	$1,263,171
Liabilities and Shareholders' Equity		
Current liabilities		
Bank indebtedness	$ 37,185	$ 21,715
Accounts payable and accruals	98,876	107,532
Deferred income	38,167	21,967
Income taxes payable	3,726	5,651
Current portion of long-term debt and other obligations	12,174	10,764
	190,128	167,629
Long-term debt	625,640	663,844
Capitalized lease obligations	14,213	14,849
Deferred income taxes	10,920	10,436
Pension obligations	6,847	6,326
Stockholders' Equity		
Capital stock	284,533	283,739
Translation adjustment	12,473	13,348
Retained earnings	88,571	77,856
	385,577	374,943
Total liabilities and shareholders' equity	$1,259,447	$1,263,171

Source: First Quarter Report 1989, pp. 14–15.

National Amusements have announced their intentions of opening a total of more than 450 screens in the United Kingdom.

While few deny the attractiveness of the theaters owned and operated by Cineplex, the firm may have overextended itself both financially and operationally. (Key financial data are provided in Exhibits 13, 14, 15, and 16.) Is Cineplex Odeon on the crest of a new wave of creative growth in North America and Europe, or does it stand at the edge of an abyss? Is consolidation or a thorough review of past actions in order? What next moves should Garth Drabinsky and Cineplex make to continue their firm's phenomenal success story?

Cineplex Odeon Corporation: Consolidated Balance Sheet (in thousands of U.S. dollars)　　　　　　　　　　　　　　　　　　　　　　**Exhibit 16**

	1988	1987	1986
Assets			
Current assets			
Accounts receivable	$ 151,510	$ 42,342	$ 20,130
Advances to distributors and producers	26,224	10,704	4,671
Distribution costs	10,720	10,593	4,318
Inventories	7,450	8,562	6,978
Prepaid expenses and deposits	5,505	4,683	4,027
Properties held for disposition	25,557	22,704	16,620
	226,966	99,588	56,744
Property, equipment and leaseholds	824,836	711,523	513,411
Other assets			
Long-term investments and receivables	130,303	49,954	14,292
Goodwill (less amortization of $2758; 1987—$1878)	53,966	52,596	40,838
Deferred charges (less amortization of $7724; 1987—$1771)	27,100	12,015	6,591
	211,369	114,565	61,721
Total assets	$1,263,171	$925,676	$631,876
Liabilities and Shareholders' Equity			
Current liabilities			
Bank indebtedness	$ 21,715	$ 20,672	$ 30
Accounts payable and accruals	107,532	74,929	47,752
Deferred income	21,967	755	—
Income taxes payable	5,651	4,607	1,926
Current portion of long-term debt and other obligations	10,764	5,965	6,337
	167,629	106,928	56,045
Long-term debt	663,844	449,707	317,550
Capitalized lease obligations	14,849	14,565	15,928
Deferred income taxes	10,436	13,318	11,142
Pension obligations	6,326	4,026	3,668
Minority interest	25,144	—	—
Stockholders' equity			
Capital stock	283,739	289,181	212,121
Translation adjustment	13,348	1,915	(3,591)
Retained earnings	77,856	46,791	19,113
	374,943	337,887	227,643
Total liabilities and shareholders' equity	$1,263,171	$926,413	$631,976

Source: Company annual reports for 1987 and 1988.

BIBLIOGRAPHY

Finler, Joel W. *The Hollywood Story.* New York: Crown Publishers, 1988.

Gertner, Richard, ed. *1988 International Motion Picture Almanac.* New York: Quigley Publishing Company, Inc., 1988.

Green, Wayne R., ed. *Encyclopeda of Exhibition.* New York: National Association of Theatre Owners, 1988.

Hall, Ben M. *The Best Remaining Seats: The Story of the Golden Age of the Movie Palace.* New York: Bramhall House, 1961.

Harrigan, Kathryn Rudie. *Managing Mature Businesses.* Lexington, Mass.: Lexington Books, 1988.

Harrigan, Kathryn Rudie. "Strategies for Declining Industries," *The Journal of Business Strategy* 1, no. 2 (Fall 1980), pp. 20–34.

Musun, Chris. *The Marketing of Motion Pictures.* Los Angeles: Chris Musun Company, 1969.

1989 U.S. Industrial Outlook. Washington, D.C.: U.S. Department of Commerce/International Trade Administration, 1989.

Tromberg, Sheldon. *Making Money, Making Movies.* New York: New Viewpoints/Vision Books, 1980.

Troy, L. *Almanac of Business and Industrial Financial Ratios.* Englewood Cliffs, N.J.: Prentice-Hall, 1988.

U.S. Bureau of the Census. *Statistical Abstract of the United States: 1989,* 109th ed. Washington, D.C.: U.S. Government Printing Office, 1988.

U.S. Department of Commerce, Bureau of the Census. *Statistical Abstract of the United States, 1985.* Washington, D.C.: Government Printing Office, 1985.

Waldman, Peter. "Silver Screens Lose Some of Their Luster," *The Wall Street Journal,* February 9, 1989, p. B1.

Hands Around Our Jobs

Marilyn Young, C. Ray Gullett, Mark J. Kroll, University of Texas at Tyler

Carl Roberts, manager and CEO of Falcon Industries, walked into the restaurant to meet with two management consultants. He had known one of them, Frank Coats, since he first became CEO at Falcon. Frank recently introduced him to his partner, Mike Johnson. Carl had asked the two to talk with him about a major career decision. He greeted them both and sat down rather nervously. As he glanced at the menu, he said thoughtfully, "I don't know where to go from here. I have invested three years of my time and energy at Falcon, but it seems to be a losing battle. I have everything including my reputation riding on this company." He leaned across the booth and whispered, "Falcon has been offered a contract from a really big outfit, Liz Claiborne. They want us to make their women's jeans which would double our volume. I would give anything to take the deal, but I doubt that my employees can meet the deadline, given their low productivity levels. I have to decide, and soon, whether to take the order or throw in the towel and resign. The union leadership is putting heavy pressure on me not to turn down the work."

Mike, who was unacquainted with the company, responded with surprise, "But I thought this was an employee-owned company. If these people are the owners, I would expect them to be motivated and have pride in their work. Although I have never worked with such a firm, I have seen research that concludes that employee-owned companies grow faster and are more profitable than their traditional counterparts. I was showing Frank a summary of these findings just before you came in [see Exhibit 1]. You have a pending contract with a prestigious company like Claiborne, and you don't know whether to take it?" He shook his head and stated, "Carl, I don't understand."

Exhibit 1

Summary of Research on Employee-Owned Companies

As an employee-owned firm, Falcon should reap certain benefits. Research has shown that the most effective employee-owned companies have annual employment and sales growth rates twelve to seventeen points higher than their competitors. One study found that employee-owned firms were 1.5 times as profitable as the average firms in their industries. Also, another study discovered that ESOP firms had twice the average annual productivity growth rate of nonESOP firms. Before/after studies show that ESOP companies did better than their competitors before they set up their plans as well as afterwards.

A survey of 2800 employees found that employees in an ESOP were more enthused and motivated. Employees were clearly proud to be owners which caused them to be more interested in their company's financial performance. Also, they want to stay with the company longer. However, employees will only feel and act like owners if the notion of ownership is constantly reinforced. Also, regular sharing of information about the company, participation in decisions affecting their jobs, and a management attitude that sees workers as partners are important to successful employee-owned companies.

According to the National Center for Employee Ownership, the higher a company's annual contribution to its ESOP, the more committed employees are to their company. Also, the more satisfied they are with their jobs, and the happier they are with their ownership plan. Also, management philosophy toward ownership is extremely important in that the employees must be treated like owners. The most successful ESOPs were the ones with the highest levels of employee participation regarding their work.

People are drawn to ESOPs because of tax benefits; however, there is much more to an ESOP insofar as motivation, commitment, turnover, and participation. Research has shown that effective employee-owned companies can achieve sales growth rates twelve to seventeen points higher than their competitors. As mentioned earlier, however, employees will only feel and act like owners if the notion of ownership is constantly reinforced. A method found to be successful in accomplishing this is to make large annual contributions to the plan. Also helpful is regular sharing of information about the company, participation affecting their jobs and a management attitude that sees workers as partners. There must be a constant effort on the part of management to reinforce the idea of ownership.

Sources: National Center for Employee Ownership, Inc., *Beyond Taxes: Managing an Employee Ownership Company* (1987); Corey Rosen and Michael Quarrey, "How Well Is Employee Ownership Working?" *Harvard Business Review*, pp. 126–128, 132.

Sadly, Carl continued, "Sometimes I wonder if they really feel like owners. I am not sure they are really different from other employees." Frank interrupted, "Wait, Carl, before you go on, you had better start from the beginning if you want us to help you. Tell us how you got started with this company."

"About three years ago, a union regional director contacted me. She was conducting a national search for a plant manager/CEO to head up a new employee-owned company. She told me the employees planned to buy out the local facility of a large jeans manufacturing company. It sounded exciting and challenging.

Sandra Rameriz was not your "typical" union leader. She was very sensitive to the needs of the company as well as the employees. I found her to be extremely intelligent, articulate, and assertive. I liked her immediately and respected her dedication to this project. I felt she really wanted this effort to succeed for the sake of the employees. I had never worked with a union before

Number of ESOP Plans and Number of Employees **Exhibit 2**

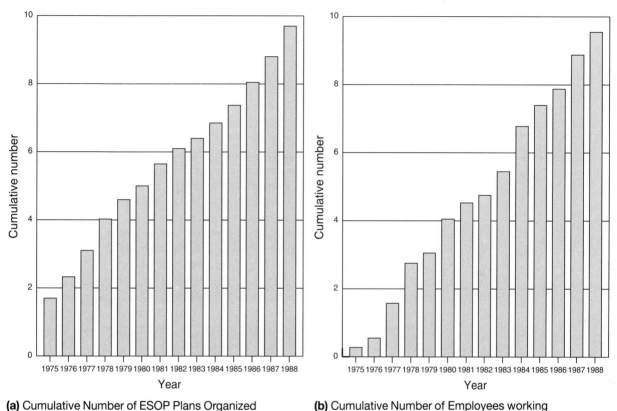

(a) Cumulative Number of ESOP Plans Organized in the United States (thousands)

(b) Cumulative Number of Employees working in ESOP Organized Firms (millions)

Source: Data used to prepare the exhibit was supplied by the National Center for Employee Ownership.

and knew nothing about an employee-owned company, though I was aware that ESOPs (Employee Stock Ownership Plans) had increased significantly over the past ten years." (See Exhibits 2a and 2b.)

BACKGROUND

■ The Closing of a Plant

Frank continued his story by telling the consultants how the firm was founded. He noted that the company which previously owned the plant had been a strong influence in the local economy, employing over 500 workers and occupying an 84,500 square foot facility. It announced the closing of the plant in order to consolidate production and eliminate excess manufacturing capacity. Employees and community leaders were dismayed at the announcement, especially in light of the ongoing economic recession, numerous bankruptcies, and high unemployment rates in the area. The 500 employees affected by the closing were provided with thirteen weeks advance notice or equivalent pay plus severance allowances. Initially, counselors from the union were available to help employees locate other employment and thus ease the impact of the shutdown. The work force was composed mainly of women; approximately two thirds of the employees were ethnic minorities (Black and Hispanic). Most of the workers' only skills were those learned in the sewing plant. With the local economy floundering and the plants' work force lacking other skills, most joined the ranks of the unemployed. As the closing drew nearer, community business leaders began to look for ways to interest out-of-town firms in the soon-to-be vacant building.

The rallying point for most of these workers was their union. It was seen as the only "safe harbor" in what appeared to them as a community either unconcerned about their plight or unable to give much help.

The union's strength was personified in Sandra Rameriz, the District Director. Although based in San Antonio, Ms. Rameriz was very active at the local plant and was a visible presence throughout its closing.

Sandra Rameriz was properly labeled a "charismatic leader." A college graduate and the widow of a long-time union activist, she had dedicated her career to the union cause. Articulate, tough minded, and ideologically devoted to unionism, she was a formidable opponent of those who opposed her. Yet she was not an ideologue. Ms. Rameriz could best be described as a pragmatist who recognized the need for prosperous companies as well as a strong union.

Sandra was also active in state and national politics. Her connections at these levels convinced her that there was an excellent chance that the plant could be reopened through the formation of an Employee Stock Ownership Plan (ESOP). Under federal tax and pension laws, it was possible for employees to form an ownership trust to which funds could be contributed for the formation and/or expansion of a business.

For this company a leveraged ESOP would be created since borrowed money would be obtained by the trust to largely finance its opening and operation. Tax advantages would be allowed for both the company and the lender with the employees eventually owning all of the company's stock.[1]

With encouragement from Sandra and other union leaders, a number of employees agreed to pursue a reopening strategy. However, the workers faced major challenges in securing financing, hiring a manager, and obtaining manufacturing contracts. The first step in this effort was raising $20,000 for a feasibility study to be conducted by an outside consulting firm. This study would determine product costs, cost improvement opportunities (methods to produce cheaper and perhaps a better product), future leadership requirements, and potential work and contract availability.

With the help of the union, the employees planned a buyout of the plant. Union and employee leadership enthusiastically launched a fund-raising campaign called "Hands Around Our Jobs" to raise money for the feasibility study. Officials of the company which previously owned the plant agreed to match each $50 contribution made for the study up to $10,000, and the Governor's Office of Economic Development as well as the local community committed funds to the project. The study received further assistance from the National

---

[1]For a thorough discussion of the ESOP mechanism, see Joseph Blasi, *Employee Ownership* Cambridge, Mass: (Ballinger Publishing Company, 1988).

Cooperative Bank in Washington, D.C. Some 129 employees each donated $50 for the feasibility study. With help from all the sources, the money was raised. When the announcement was made that the goal was reached, employees rallied at a local cafeteria and carried signs which read: "We Won't Give Up" and "Our Jobs are in Our Hands." As a result of this collective effort of committed groups (employees, union, community and political leaders), the feasibility study for Falcon Industries was begun.

■ The Feasibility Study

The results were generally optimistic. Citing trends in the industry, the final report forecast an overall stable demand for denim garments through the year 2000. Given Falcon's capabilities and the trends in the market, the production of women's and girls' slacks and of men's and boys' jean-cut and work slacks showed the most promise.

Production was to be primarily contract (production for other manufacturers) with the possibility of manufacturing directly for retailers as an option. The company would have no products with its own brand for the foreseeable future.

The new firm was feasible, but with fewer jobs than its predecessor. Eventually capacity was predicted to reach 200 employees, or about 40 percent of previous employment. Pay rates would have to average about $2.00 per hour lower than union scale in other unionized plants.

■ Full Speed Ahead

Given the qualified approval, the union retained legal counsel to help draft the ESOP documents, an investment advisor (The National Cooperative Bank), a valuation appraisal firm, and an executive recruitment agency to search for a general manager.

Several candidates were referred to Sandra Rameriz for interviews. After talking with each of them, she chose Carl Roberts whose title was to be Chief Executive Officer/General Production Manager. Roberts had over 20 years of managerial experience in the textile industry in both the marketing and production. But perhaps most important was the way he and Sandra felt about the interview. Both later commented that they felt the "chemistry was right" between them. Thus, they believed that they could work well together. Sandra was tacitly acknowledged by both as a member of the management team. She was clearly the person to whom the workers continued to look for leadership and guidance.

■ Financing the Enterprise

As the recruiting of Roberts was taking place, efforts to obtain financing were also underway. Of all the issues confronting the leadership, none was more important than obtaining appropriate financing. Indeed, all other matters hinged on the availability of adequate funding for the fledgling business. Employee contributions were to make up a minor part of the total financing with 80 percent of the necessary funds to be obtained from outside sources.

Several sources of funds were considered including the Small Business Administration. In the end, the financing of the ESOP was made up of $1000 pledges from the initial 120 workers/owners hired and a $500,000 loan from the

National Cooperative Bank. In order to help those workers who needed financing for their contributions, a local bank offered personal loans for this purpose. Each $1000 employee contribution purchased one share of Falcon Enterprises common stock.

■ The ESOP Mechanism

The financing structure of a leveraged ESOP is diagrammed in Exhibit 3. Falcon's ESOP was to provide the employees with total ownership of the stock of the company and full voting rights. All employees were required to participate in the plan and hold voting rights.

Shares were held in trust for the employee/owners similar to a pension or profit sharing plan, except that the shares were only in Falcon Industries' company stock. The employees' accounts were designed to accumulate shares of Falcon stock and upon death, retirement, or other termination of employment, the employee would receive the value of stock and other assets vested in his/her account. The value of the stock was determined by Falcon's success or failure. If the company was profitable, the stock value would increase. A new employee was to contribute $1000 within seven days of the day of being hired.

■ A Falcon Is Born

Once financing had been obtained, an announcement was made that Falcon would open its new plant in the downtown area. Because of its age and location, the cost of leasing the downtown site was approximately one third less than that of the original building. Carl Roberts also felt that new surroundings might

---

Exhibit 3 **Leveraged ESOP**

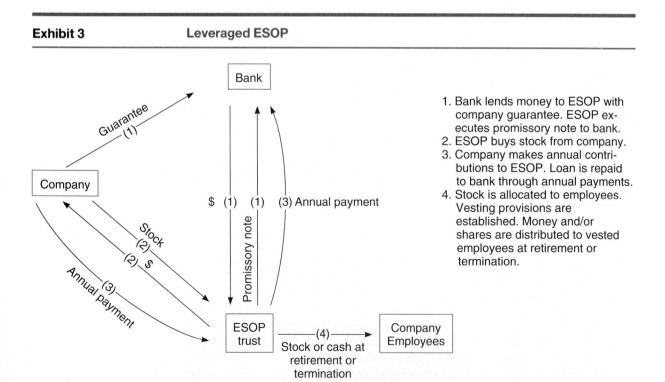

1. Bank lends money to ESOP with company guarantee. ESOP executes promissory note to bank.
2. ESOP buys stock from company.
3. Company makes annual contributions to ESOP. Loan is repaid to bank through annual payments.
4. Stock is allocated to employees. Vesting provisions are established. Money and/or shares are distributed to vested employees at retirement or termination.

be helpful in creating a feeling of employee ownership. A return to the previous building might encourage a "business as usual" feeling and work against the new worker-owner culture to be developed at Falcon.

After the downtown site was selected, equipment was purchased, and the first orders were obtained for production. The new name, Falcon Industries, was selected and voted on by the employees—the new owners. The Falcon was born, and the union leader, Sandra Rameriz, went on local television and declared, "This Falcon will soar to new heights."

■ The Collective Bargaining Contract

The initial contract between the union and the company was negotiated in approximately two days. Prior to production start-up, Sandra Rameriz, Carl Roberts, and two local union officers met in Carl's motel room to write the one-year agreement.

Most standard contract clauses such as exclusive union recognition, grievance procedure steps, wage rates including incentives, and contract renewal procedures were included. Little actual negotiation, however, took place. Sandra essentially dictated the terms that she and Carl had informally agreed upon earlier. More specifics would be added when the employee handbook was later written.

■ High Hopes

Production began slowly, and employees were hired a few at a time. The company produced small orders for three large contractors. Initially, 60 workers were hired; another 20, a month later with a total employment of 120 after six months of operation.

During this time, the company also began developing a handbook of policies and procedures. Sandra Rameriz suggested a nontraditional format using infor-

Employees celebrate the reopening of their plant.

mal wording and a few cartoons. However, the end result was a typical document consisting of company rules and regulations. After several revisions, those who participated in the design (management, employees, and union steward) approved it, and the handbook became a part of the collective bargaining agreement. The Falcon made its first flight.

ORGANIZATION STRUCTURE

Falcon Industries was created to be entirely owned by the employees who would have a voice in the operation of the company. The Board of Directors, elected by the owners, was composed of seven elected members: 1 Union Representative (the District Director); 3 Employee/owners; and 3 outside business and professional members.

Falcon functioned as a contract manufacturer—producing garments for other firms. Three departments were established at the plant: cutting, sewing, and shipping. Initially, Carl Roberts attempted to manage everyone. Additionally, he spent considerable time performing the marketing and finance functions during his 12-hour a day work week. After a few months, he hired an experienced assistant manager to directly supervise the three departments. "Floor ladies" were also given supervisory duties in the cutting and sewing departments. The plant manager/CEO chose employee/owners for these positions based on their experiences and skills.

A person was hired to perform clerical duties as well as bookkeeping and to maintain personnel records. One of the original "Hands Around Our Jobs" leadership members, Karen Holt, became an informal assistant manager to the CEO. Another leadership member, Thelma Rhodes, announced she did not want to be on the Board of Directors but desired to continue as local union president. However, she also assumed various managerial duties on an informal basis. Karen Holt and two other employees were elected by the employee/owners to serve on Falcon's Board of Directors.

■ Organizational Culture

Despite the largely mechanistic organization structure, the leadership made a verbal commitment to high levels of employee participation in the new firm. As a demonstration of this commitment, a brief orientation program was provided for the new owners on the first day of work. Its purpose was to explain the philosophy of Falcon Enterprises and the ESOP mechanism. The sessions emphasized the importance of commitment, good communications, trust, and employee participation in decision making. As agreed to by both management and the union, the trainers emphasized the following:

> Falcon Industries, an employee-owned company, the union, and the employees desire to create an environment of mutual understanding with the owners/employees. We see ourselves as partners working together, realizing that the success of Falcon Industries will result in increased stock values for the ESOP.
>
> The key values at Falcon are intended to be ownership, participation, commitment, and teamwork. Falcon will seek to develop common goals, good communication, and trust among all participants. Knowledge sharing, experimentation with new ideas, and high expectations from coworkers will be operating premises.

Although Carl Roberts saw himself as a participatory leader, no follow up to these initial sessions were made. No formal participation programs such as quality circles were instituted. No training or rewards were ever given for making innovative suggestions. Carl maintained, however, that he always encouraged employees to discuss new ideas and to suggest solutions to work problems on their own time before and after work.

Once the plant opened, little or no enthusiasm appeared to exist among the workers. Carl blamed it on general employee apathy stemming largely from their traditional reliance on union leadership to protect them from the company. "They just can't seem to think like owners," he continually said. "Why can't they see that they are only hurting themselves when they don't give 110 percent all the time?"

He seemed genuinely stunned when he called an employee meeting after work to vote on the newly developed employee handbook. Sandra, three employees, the union president, and he had worked long hours to cover many crucial issues such as discipline, job bidding, and promotion. At the meeting, only a few people attended. They approved the new work rules without comment. A similar turn out greeted the Board of Directors at the annual stockholders' meeting on the firm's first anniversary.

Given the seeming apathy of the work force and the pressure for sales and production, Carl settled into a "benevolent autocratic" style of management in order to "keep the ship afloat," as he put it. Shortly after the plant opened, Sandra Rameriz was promoted to Regional Director of the union and was transferred to St. Louis. Her contacts with Falcon decreased significantly as a result.

Local union leaders seemed increasingly to identify with Carl and rarely questioned his judgment. Although a few employees voiced resentment at what they said was a sellout, most simply did their jobs perfunctorily and said little. Sometimes Carl wistfully compared the electricity in the air when the buy out was taking place with the turned off attitude he perceived after operations began.

After Sandra's transfer to St. Louis, Carl felt that their relationship began to deteriorate. When disagreements arose, they seemed to have more difficulty resolving them. Carl saw Sandra as reverting back to a much more traditional and "hard-line" unionist approach on some issues and as apathetic on others. "I feel as if I'm the only one who really cares about the future of the company," Carl told the consultants.

■ The First Two Years

Various problems have confronted the fledgling company, such as securing contracts, difficulty in meeting loan obligations, producing a quality product in a timely fashion, and low productivity. However, they have survived over two years, secured numerous contracts and have been able to convince lenders to allow postponement of loan payments. After six months of operation, employees were working only a 4-day work week due to lack of contracts and had to take a pay cut, sometimes postponing pay days altogether. As time went by, enough contracts were secured that a 5-day week was reinstituted, and the work force rose to 120.

Sales at Falcon have been sporadic as shown in Exhibit 4. Sales in 1987 were 106,000 units (approximately 2000 units per week). Sales increased by 33.7 percent to 124,300 in 1988, and sales were stable for the first quarter of 1989. The

Exhibit 4   **Sales at Falcon Industries, 1987–1989 (thousands of units)**

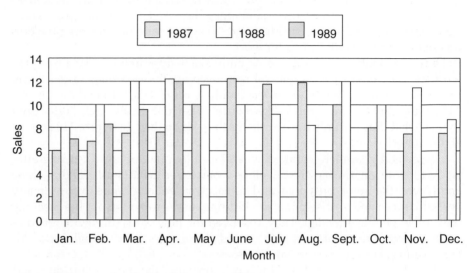

Note: 1989 sales only reflect the first quarter at Falcon.

company manufactured the jeans at a cost of approximately $4 per unit which includes the direct and indirect costs. Falcon total sales for 1987 were $530,000 and $626,500 in 1988. The units sold for $5 per unit which results in a profit of $1 per unit with a 25 percent markup.

After two years in operation, the CEO at Falcon stated, "We now have more work than we know what to do with." However, he outlined the typical problems of low productivity rates and other personnel problems. Productivity was far below industry standards and grievances were filed frequently.

Employee morale continued to decline since the strong solidarity of "Hands Around Our Jobs." This low morale was attributed to several factors. Layoffs during the first year of operation, the reduction of operations to a 4-day work week, and the postponement of paychecks were significant factors. But even when these problems were overcome, Carl felt that the overall attitudes were no better. Productivity had remained at 70 percent of industry standards ever since, and apathy among the employees had been continuous. The CEO and union representative were amazed at how little interest the employee/owners continued to show in the firm's performance. Meetings continued to be very poorly attended.

Originally, the company borrowed $500,000 to finance the ESOP. However, about eighteen months after operations began, it found it could not pay debts to suppliers. To obtain additional funding, Falcon issued $100,000 in newly created preferred stock to an outside individual who supported the cause. Within six months the national union quietly purchased $500,000 in additional preferred stock, leaving the employee/owners with approximately 40 percent of total equity. On the positive side, sales continued to increase with orders received from a variety of customers. The sales of Falcon are shown in Exhibit 4.

Toward the end of the first two years, Frank Coats, was called in to measure the attitudes of the company employees by using the National Center for Employee Ownership (NCEO) questionnaire. Norms were developed from thirty-seven ESOPs studied by NCEO. The questionnaire was translated into Spanish and given to both English and Spanish speaking employees. The final results were compared to universe norms. (The Universe is defined as thirty-seven other ESOPs). Also, Falcon employee attitudes were compared to a similar ESOP which was also a distressed buy out. The results are shown in Exhibits 5, 6, and 7. Attitudes of Falcon employees were quite similar to other ESOPs. However, significant differences in perceptions were noted among Falcon employees in several crucial areas as shown in the exhibits cited below.

Many of the employees also told Sandra Rameriz that they felt "left out" and even threatened to file grievances regarding job related problems at Falcon. It was Rameriz's belief that the workers appeared to have some pride in their jobs. In support of this she pointed out that one employee designed a unique pair of women's jeans called "The Flamingo," hoping that the company would manufacture them. He even had a local market research group prepare a business plan for marketing the jeans. However, she indicated management showed little interest in the idea. Carl's response was that the proposed product could not be produced economically because of the small volume needed to match sales projections.

Measurement of Job Satisfaction in Employee-Owned Companies　　　　　**Exhibit 5**

Criteria	Falcon	37 ESOPs	Other
Job satisfaction	5.3	5.6	5.4
Commitment	5.1	5.1	4.7
Turnover intention	3.6	2.7	2.5
Pay satisfaction	3.7	4.3	3.7
Job freedom	4.0	5.3	4.9
Job variety	4.6	4.7	4.6
Task feedback	5.3	5.4	
Task completeness	3.9	4.9	
Task impact	5.6	5.8	
Task significance	5.4	5.6	
Task quality	5.8	5.7	5.4
Role conflict	4.0	4.0	3.9
Role clarity	5.3	5.6	5.7
Role overload	4.2	3.3	4.1
General ESOP satisfaction	5.2	4.9	4.7
ESOP influence	4.0	3.4	3.1
ESOP effort	4.9	4.1	4.8
Perceived worker influence*	2.4	2.2	2.0
Desired worker influence*	3.3	3.1	3.3
Discrepancy-perceived/desired	0.9	0.9	1.3
Supervisor participation	3.7	4.6	4.2

Note: Mean scores on scales of 1–7.

*Scales of 1–5.

Exhibit 6   **Statistical Analysis of Job Satisfaction**

Criteria	Z Values Falcon/37	Falcon/Other
Job satisfaction	−1.66	0.34
Commitment	−0.01	−1.21
Turnover intention	3.40*	−3.48
Pay satisfaction	−2.04*	−0.03
Job freedom	−4.35*	−2.54*
Job variety	−0.39	−0.07
Task feedback	0.44	
Task completeness	−3.31*	
Task impact	−0.83	
Task significance	0.80	
Task quality	0.30	−1.67
Role conflict	−0.22	−0.16
Role clarity	−1.26	1.47
Role overload	3.06*	−0.14
General ESOP satisfaction	1.40	−1.69
ESOP influence	2.06*	−2.78
ESOP effort	3.00*	−0.13
Perceived worker influence*	0.85	−1.61
Desired worker influence*	1.23	0.10
Supervisor participation	−2.81*	1.36

*Significant at the .05 level.

■ Carl's Dilemma

While talking with the two consultants, Carl refocused on the situation at hand and the decision he had to make. Here was the kind of order the young firm had previously only dreamed about. Yet, now that the opportunity actually presented itself, he said he felt very uncertain about Falcon's ability to make good. If Falcon failed to meet the terms of the contract, Liz Claiborne could hold it financially responsible for resultant losses it sustained. Such an outcome would destroy Falcon. On the other hand, for Falcon to have any hope of ever rehiring all of the ex-employees and establishing itself as a permanent force in the garment industry, this was the kind of contract Falcon would have to produce.

Exhibit 7   **Analysis of Variance for Falcon and 37 ESOPs**

Source of Variation	Degrees of Freedom	Calculated Value	F Ratio
Between groups	1	0.03364	$F = 0.034$
Within group	38	0.996	

Note: The critical value of F at the .05 level for 1 and 38 degrees of freedom indicates an F of 4.41 would be required to reject the null hypothesis. Therefore, the two groups are not independent.

Unfortunately, Carl was having real doubts as to whether the average Falcon employee had the commitment and determination to see the Liz Claiborne contract through. He certainly did not want to be around if Falcon failed to deliver. Neither did he see how he could argue for turning down what on the surface appeared to be the best offer Falcon had ever received.

Club Med Inc.

Robert P. Vichas, Florida Atlantic University

A NEW BEGINNING FOR THE 1990s

Asked for their impressions of Club Med, those who had never been said:

- A college student: "Sand, sun, sex, and lots to drink."
- A family vacationing in Orlando, Florida: "We prefer family-oriented vacations. Club Med is for swinging singles."
- A retired couple: "That's like those Playboy Clubs, isn't it?"

Travel agents offered opinions, too:

- A New Jersey travel agent, in 1988: "The idea of free sex and a lot of drinking really turns off the older, more sophisticated people Club Med is trying to reach."
- A New York travel agent, in 1989: "Club Med's marketing efforts have really neglected us. Some agents find them offensive."
- A Florida travel agent, in 1990: "In the past, Club Med has been reluctant to pay commissions. Now they're improving the commission rate, and they're telling us now about new tour offerings."

A professional American couple, who had many times visited properties in Europe, the United States, and the Caribbean, said, in 1990:

They seem to be growing for the sake of expansion. There's no quality growth. I think village managers need more training. Club Med is trying to be all things to all people, and, I believe, the increased competition, especially in the U.S., has created some corporate panic. We like the European villages better.

Club Med Inc., a U.S.-based subsidiary of Club Méditerranée, a French-headquartered multinational corporation (MNC), still marketing a 40-year-old product, ran into an ever-widening circle of fierce competition as it developed new products for new markets. To cope with end-of-the-decade challenges, the parent company was restructured organizationally. It initiated a strategic shift from an international to a global concept. It refocused its North American marketing strategies. It developed a worldwide growth strategy for the 1990s.

Will its strategy for the 1990s steer the firm through the straits of adversity or did management build a castle of sand? Serge Trigano, Chief Executive Officer (CEO) of Club Med Inc., understood the challenge well. He said, "We are beginning 1990, the fortieth year of the Club Med concept, with an aggressive strategy for growth. The challenge will be to execute this strategy effectively while rapidly adapting to changes in our markets."

A NEW CONCEPT FOR POSTWAR EUROPE

In the early days, a manager's life might have been characterized as idyllic, albeit a primitive, tranquil life, on a Mediterranean island. Gerard Blitz, a Belgian, dreamed of providing war-weary continentals a vacation ambience away from the afflictions and adversities found in a post-World War II Europe, which emphasized sports and love. Gilbert Trigano's family business sold army surplus tents—the ideal guest accommodations for communal bliss.

On the Spanish island, Majorca, in Alcudia, Blitz established the first Club Méditerranée village in 1950, where guests helped cook meals and wash dishes and during balmy evenings, under the blue savannah of Mediterranean skies speckled with white stars of universal love, discussed the harsh realities of capitalism before snuggling down into sleeping bags. Despite its "escape from civilization" concept, Club Méditerranée was predestined for growth from the day Blitz first approached Trigano, the tent seller.

A French Communist, of Moroccan-Jew parentage, Gilbert Trigano fought in the communist resistance during World War II, became a reporter with the communist daily, *L'Humanité*, after liberation of France, then drifted into the family tent business (Moskowitz, 1988, p. 146). He joined Club Med in 1954 as Managing Director (MD).

Transforming the back-to-nature dream of primitive paradise into a concept of uninhibited play in the sun, a romp in the sand, and discarding the cares, and clothes, of civilization, Trigano forged a highly profitable chain of resort-villages in France, Italy, Greece, and Africa. Polynesian-styled huts and bungalows replaced tents and sleeping bags. Today, pampered guests, in luxurious accommodations nestled on hilltops along the French Riviera, no longer needed to cook, and wash dishes.

Chronologically, the firm opened its first straw hut village in 1954, its first ski resort in Leysin, Switzerland in 1965, and in the American Zone its first village in 1968, and the first family "Mini Club" in 1974. In 1976, the company acquired a 45 percent interest in Valtur, an Italian company, which had holiday villages in Italy, Greece, and Tunisia mainly for an Italian market. (Club Med either leased or operated many of its villages under management contract.) Also, Club Med maintained time-sharing apartments and hotels. Most members were French in the 1950s; by 1980 the proportion of French visitors had dropped to 45 percent. It began offering its Rent-a-Village Program in 1981 to large corporations for meetings and market incentives. From global headquarters in Paris (France), Club Méditerranée marketed its products worldwide.

In late 1981, when the firm again attempted decentralization, Serge Trigano, Gilbert's son, assumed leadership of the American Zone. Then, on May 17, 1984, the firm incorporated its American Zone in the Cayman Islands (B.W.I.) as Club Med Inc. (CMI), a wholly owned subsidiary of Club Méditerranée S.A. It hoisted a new slogan: "The perfect climate for body and soul."

With Serge Trigano as its CEO, CMI was chartered to develop markets and operate in the United States, Canada, Mexico, The Bahamas and rest of the Caribbean, Southeast Asia, South Pacific, and parts of the Indian Ocean Basin; while Club Méditerranée, retaining responsibilities for marketing and operations in the rest of the world (Europe, Africa, and South America), mainly focused its marketing strategy toward a European market. In September 1984, CMI signed an agreement with the Seibu Saison Group, a large Japanese retail, real estate and development firm, to create resorts in Japan. A summer mountain resort and winter ski village, Club Med-Sahoro opened on the island of Hokkaido, Japan, in December 1987. Worldwide, Club Méditerranée and its subsidiaries maintained operations in 35 countries on 5 continents.

NEW FINANCING FOR AN OLD CONCEPT

Club Méditerranée, founded as a nonprofit sports organization in 1950, and incorporated as a *societé anonyme* (S.A.) in 1957 in France, went public in 1965. Effective November 1, 1983, most of Club Méditerranée assets in the American Zone were transferred at book value to Club Med Inc. (CMI). Incorporated in the Cayman Islands in 1984, CMI, a majority-owned (74 percent by October 31, 1989) subsidiary of Club Méditerranée S.A., sold 3,400,000 common shares through a public offering in the United States and 300,000 common shares in a private offering to certain club officers, directors, and employees. CMI maintained financial records in U.S. dollars prepared in conformity with generally accepted U.S. accounting principles.

Summary financial data appear in Exhibit 1; for detailed balance sheet data, refer to Exhibit 2. Of property and equipment shown in the balance sheets, on the basis of cost, less than 5 percent represented land value of the villages. Buildings plus leasehold improvements accounted for most of the value of villages.

With international transactions conducted in several currencies, CMI had suffered exchange rate losses. For several years it endured the negative impact from net French franc-based costs and expenses. Despite a 10 percent worsening of the dollar in international markets, those losses stabilized in 1988 partly due to a 35 percent increase in customers from European countries who paid for visits to American Zone villages with stronger currencies. The firm also had experienced the adverse effects of Mexico's decision to maintain a fixed exchange (below market) rate of pesos for dollars.

Exhibit 1		Club Med Inc.: Financial Highlights, 1984–1989 (millions of U.S. dollars)				
	1989	*1988*	*1987*	*1986*	*1985*	*1984*
Income Statement Data						
Revenues	468.8	412.4	370.4	337.0	279.7	235.3
Gross profits	159.4	133.2	125.1	115.3	92.4	81.5
Depreciation	17.9	16.4	13.5	11.5	7.8	6.1
Operating income	25.4	11.2	20.0	19.8	16.0	15.1
Income before extraordinary items	20.4	8.7	16.8	17.4	14.2	11.5
Extraordinary items*	0.7	0.1	0.6	0.7	1.4	0.6
Net income	21.1	8.8	17.4	18.1	15.6	12.0
Balance Sheet Data						
Working capital	27.5	42.5	4.6	30.9	31.9	34.6
Long-term debt	100.1	131.1	89.4	91.2	76.1	39.3
Shareholders' equity	207.6	189.4	184.2	159.0	142.5	129.5
Total assets	415.5	403.2	353.4	313.8	269.1	212.1

Sources: Club Med Inc. *Annual Reports,* 1988, 1989.

*The firm is taxed under many jurisdictions, some of which do not impose an income tax. Resulting from negotiated tax reductions for periods ranging from 1991 to 2005, the firm received incentive concessions from the Dominican Republic, Turks and Caicos Islands, Haiti, Saint Lucia, Mauritius, Thailand, and Indonesia. Also, the firm had net operating losses and various tax credit carryforwards, as well as tax loss carryforwards expiring mostly 1990 through 1994.

OLD AND NEW PRODUCTS

The original Trigano formula was to construct villages in exotic places and operate the business as a membership organization. Subsequently, Club Med entered the corporate meeting and incentive market with its Rent-a-Village. Some villages added NAUI and PADI certification scuba diving programs as well as an English-style riding instructional workshop and lectures. In later years the organization added ski, mountain and other scenic settings to appeal to a diversity of tastes.

June 1989 marked the opening of Club Med Opio, a 1000-bed village near Cannes on the French Riviera. The model for future Club Med villages, Opio offered luxury rooms, full convention and seminar facilities. Also brought on line in 1989, the firm promoted a new Mini Club at St. Lucia for children. The Caribbean resort offered horseback riding for children ages 8 to 12 and flexi-vacations to encourage visitors to take long weekends at Club Med or combine a village stay with visits to nearby tourist attractions. In 1990, Club Med spread sail on luxury packages aboard the s/v Club Med I, the world's largest automated sailing vessel.

The 442-passenger ship boasted 8 decks of Burmese teak and the latest maritime technology. Created by world-famous designer, Alberto Pinto, its interior comprised a small casino operated by Casinos Austria; 197 guest quarters; "2 posh restaurants; 4 cocktail lounges; a nightclub; a large boutique with a duty-free shop; a health center with massage, sauna, and U.V. tanning machines; a beauty salon; and a multi-purpose hall for conferences, movies, shows, and spe-

Club Med Inc.: Financial Statements, 1986–1989 and 1987–1989   **Exhibit 2**

	1989	1988	1987
Consolidated Balance Sheet (Year ended October 31; in thousands of dollars)			
Assets			
Current assets			
Cash and cash equivalents	$ 56,881	$ 33,697	$ 24,741
Marketable securities	15,506	35,000	4,990
Accounts receivable	24,488	19,568	23,474
Due from affiliates	6,108	4,846	3,428
Inventories	14,074	14,276	11,872
Prepaid advertising and marketing	8,259	9,571	6,344
Other prepaid expenses	6,564	4,668	6,004
Total current assets	131,880	121,626	80,853
Property and equipment			
Villages	307,633	291,222	265,742
Other	10,287	9,367	9,960
Construction in progress	6,289	12,588	13,646
	324,209	313,177	289,348
Less accumulated depreciation and amortization	85,426	69,970	56,865
Net property and equipment	238,783	243,207	232,483
Other assets			
Investments in and advances to affiliates	9,767	6,778	8,337
Deposit on equity interest	4,778	4,778	4,778
Long-term investments	17,189	17,520	17,530
Other	13,115	9,326	9,408
Total other assets	44,849	38,402	40,053
	$415,512	$403,235	$353,389
Liabilities and Shareholders' Equity			
Current liabilities			
Due to banks	418	8,180	13,528
Accounts payable	13,133	10,249	8,806
Due to Club Méditerranée	6,393	4,107	8,365
Due to affiliates	—	220	243
Accrued expenses	42,120	27,373	17,700
Amounts received for future vacations	30,992	25,066	24,709
Total current maturities in long-term debt	11,307	3,956	2,939
Total current liabilities	104,363	79,151	76,290
Long-term debt			
Club Méditerranée	—	1,501	1,425
Other	100,103	129,606	87,935
Total long-term debt	100,103	131,107	89,360
Minority interest and other	3412	3575	3490
Shareholder' equity			
Common shares	14,096	14,087	14,146
Additional paid-in capital	115,036	114,921	115,501
Retained earnings	79,061	60,782	54,829
Foreign currency translation adjustment	(559)	(388)	(227)
Total shareholders' equity	207,634	189,402	184,249
	$415,512	$403,235	$353,389

(continued)

Exhibit 2   Club Med Inc.: Financial Statements, 1986–1989 and 1987–1989
                                 (continued)

	1989	*1988*	*1987*	*1986*
Consolidated Statement of Income				
(Year ended October 31; in thousands of dollars, except share data)				
Revenues	$468,817	$412,423	$370,443	$336,950
Cost of revenues	309,419	279,204	245,376	221,613
Gross operating profit	159,398	133,219	125,067	115,337
Selling, general, and administrative expenses	116,127	105,688	91,557	83,989
Depreciation and amortization	17,851	16,378	13,517	11,544
Operating income	25,420	11,153	19,993	19,804
Interest income	9,685	7,236	4,580	5,250
Interest expense	11,443	9,730	6,056	4,832
Foreign currency exchange, net	(1,464)	802	(1,061)	(1,135)
Income before income taxes and extraordinary item	22,198	9,461	17,456	19,087
Provision for income taxes	1,768	785	657	1,714
Income before extraordinary item	20,430	8,676	16,799	17,373
Extraordinary item, utilization of operating loss carryforwards	668	94	552	682
Net income	$ 21,098	$ 8,770	$ 17,351	$ 18,055
Net income per common				

Source: Club Med Inc. *Annual Reports,* 1988, 1989.

cial events (Club Med, 1990). Rooms and suites had local and closed circuit tele-vision (mostly in French), other extras, plus 24-hour-a-day room service for a price.

With a broader product line, added amenities, plus 110 vacation villages in 35 countries, Club Med (the global organization) expected to appeal to a wider range of clientele: singles and couples, retired persons and children, organiza-tions and businesses, professionals and the wealthy, the adventurer and the timid. By comparison, CMI, in 1990, owned, operated, or managed 26 vacation villages throughout its geographical area, 5 archeological villas in Mexico, 2 in Beijing, PRC, and retained the exclusive rights to sell vacation packages at resorts operated by Club Mediterranée.

MARKETING TO NEW GENTLE MEMBERS

Typically, the firm marketed to its GMs (*Gentils Membres,* or Gentle Members) an all-inclusive prepaid vacation package. Additional fees for liquor, golfing, and horseback riding increased total vacation expenditures. Worldwide the global firm claimed about 1.2 million GMs.

The key to success in the 1980s lay in effective implementation of a marketing and ad campaign begun in 1980 to convey the message that Club Med was for everyone. Management aimed to penetrate an up-scale vacation market. New 30-second television ads in the United States presented vignettes of vacation possibilities available to singles, couples, and families. The American Zone pro-motion budget exceeded that of its European counterpart about fourfold.

Paris had its own strategic decisions to make with respect to Europe. Serge Trigano said, "We decided that we had three options: to remain a French company and lose markets elsewhere; to compete in each market; or to become European." The first option was inconsistent with the firm's global perspective. The second option would have led to catastrophic results. Trigano said, "If we had built a village just for, say, the German market, we would have had huge occupancy problems. The German market is at its peak in May and June and falls off in July and August." The third option meant acceptance of Europeanization. "In 1992, 1993, or whenever, we will all be Europe. So why not try to be European before Europe?" asked Trigano (Wood, 1990, pp. 68–69).

The new brochure would market five levels of products. Level One would market a half-board holiday at a low basic price to overcome price resistance. Level Two would be the classical Club Med product. Level Three would appeal to those who travel business class, want a single room with telephone, and eat breakfast anytime before midday. Level Four consisted of a new product, packaged tours for people who wanted to explore a country. Serge Trigano said, "In the 1991 brochure we will introduce our own tour operator. The margins won't be high, but these tours will bring new customers, more traffic to airlines, and better occupancy in our hotels and villas." Level Five represented a combination of new products and new marketing.

CMI identified families as a fast-growing market segment. (See Exhibit 3 for a profile of the North American membership.) By late 1989, CMI had opened 8 Mini Clubs and 2 Baby Clubs, which offered child care and activities up to 12 hours a day and one or two nurses 24 hours each day. The Baby Club, debuted in April 1985 at Club Med Fort Royal in Guadaloupe, was for infants and toddlers. Management estimated that more than 100,000 children worldwide shared vacations with parents each year.

To develop a marketing style appropriate for the 1990s, Paris management decided to be European rather than compete in each separate market. Seventeen villages were selected for an international flavor, where the MNC would guarantee to customers a welcome in their own language. Instead of a single package, several options surfaced during the 1980s to appeal to different customer segments. Forty new villages were planned for 1990–1995.

In Asia, the marketing slogan was "Absolutely Paradise." The fastest growing Asian segment, the Japanese market between 1984 and 1988 grew 200 percent. Links with the giant retail firm, Seibu Saison, gave Club Med crucial distribution outlets through its stores. New destinations in Florida and The

---

1989 Survey of North American Membership | **Exhibit 3**

Married members	40%
Single, divorced, or widowed	60%
Members with children	40%
Members who are children	8%
Members between ages 25 and 44	71%
Members who are college graduates	72%
Percentage holding postgraduate degrees	28%
Professionals, executives, managers	68%
Median age	35
Median household income (annual)	$60,000
Percent reporting incomes exceeding $75,000	36%
Percent reporting incomes exceeding $100,000	21%

Source: Club Med Facts (New York: Club Med, April 1989).

Bahamas were promoted to the Japanese during 1989, and its Mexican villages in 1990.

Travel agents sold about 85 percent of CMI's vacation packages, on which they typically earned 10 percent commission. (By contrast, Club Méditerranée in Paris direct-booked about 70 percent of its business.) Despite implementation of a U.S. travel agent marketing program, some agents claimed that Club Med's efforts tended to neglect, even offend, them. Club Med responded by increasing its sales force to 23 regional and district sales managers with plans to double its sales force by the end of 1991 (Levine, 1989, pp. 136–137).

Two Florida travel agents interviewed in 1990 said that in the past Club Med had been reluctant to pay commissions. Now, they said, the MNC was increasing commissions (which could reach 18 percent on selected packages), and had improved communications regarding new tour offerings. A New Jersey travel agent, who sold many Club Med vacation packages, in 1988, believed that the firm had difficulty selling itself to older clientele in an increasingly competitive market. The agent said, "The idea of free sex and a lot of drinking really turns off the older, more sophisticated people Club Med is trying to reach" (Phalon, 1988, p. 61).

Club Med offered a variety of vacation packages: custom-tailored vacations; honeymoon specials; length-of-stay and transportation flexibility; sailing ship cruises; family villages; singles vacations; luxury packages; as well as standard ones. Advance bookings, when confirmed, required a 25 percent prepayment per person plus membership fees. Final payment for air fare, housing, meals, and entertainment was due 30 days prior to departure. Club Med earned additional income on the float. Although guests could settle accounts for beverages, sports equipment, and rentals when they checked out, not all villages accepted all credit cards for personal expenses, and none accepted personal checks. More than one-half of the firm's business derived from repeat customers, some of whom were frequent visitors.

ORGANIZING A NEW GLOBAL APPROACH

Club Méditerranée began with a very simple and informal organizational structure: Gilbert Trigano appointed some friends, and original vacationers, to manage different vacation spots in Europe. Gradually, a more complex, functional structure was established and remained in place until 1971. Between 1971 and 1976, the organizational structure was modified. Area managers had 10 to 15 village managers reporting to each. Because operationally it seemed as though several Club Meds had been created, management reverted to the pre-1971 structure after 1976 (Horovitz, 1986). The pre-1971 structure prevailed until the early 1980s, at which time management considered reorganization.

Five key goals dominated the organization:

1. Trigano wanted to double capacity every 5 years either by adding new villages or increasing the size of existing ones.
2. Innovation drove decisions to make Club Med different from other hotel chains and to respond to changing customer needs.
3. The firm sought to internationalize personnel and its strategy because the proportion of French customers was diminishing.

4. To remain price competitive, management sought ways to improve productivity and control rising costs by standardization of procedures.

5. Trigano insisted on retaining the original concept: protect the villages from the outside world and yet identify with each local environment as closely as possible (Horovitz, 1986).

However, as markets changed, new products introduced, and geographical diversification occurred, the organizational structure hindered efficient implementation of the corporate strategy. For instance, Serge Trigano, Managing Director of Operations, discovered that reporting to him were corporate managing directors, 16 country managers, 100 chiefs of village plus 8 product managers. The structure was too centralized: information overload; too much detail; difficult to adapt to the international character of customers; bottlenecks in assignments and supervision of personnel.

The corporation still recruited its GOs* from France, despite that Americans accounted for 20 percent of business—a potential language and cultural barrier. Additionally, poor communications existed between marketing and operations (Horovitz, 1986). Consequently, the company was reorganized. Some aspects of the old structure remained, *viz.*, the Chief Executive Officer (CEO) and his Managing Directors (MDs) of financial affairs and new development. At the next level, titles of functional MDs were changed to Joint Managing Directors (JMDs) to suggest unity among functional activities.

In another major change management combined the MDs of marketing and operations. The new MD participated both in operations and promotions of vacation programs, according to Jean-Manre Darbouze, a CMI manager in New York City. Instead of assigning responsibilities for managing all product directors, country and village managers directly, a new level of managers, closer to actual areas of operation, now reported to the JMD of marketing and operations.

Two regional JMDs of marketing and operations assumed responsibility to internationalize these activities. The JMD for the American Zone controlled activities in North and South America, the Caribbean, and Tahiti. The JMD of the European Zone controlled activities in Europe, Australia, and the Far East. Geographical regions were subdivisionalized by country for each of which a country manager was appointed.

To avoid duplication, Club Med layered product directors between the corporate JMD of marketing and operations and regional JMDs to facilitate global coordination of products through product directors at an upper management level, who could examine challenges worldwide instead of the more narrow country focus.

The *Chef de Village* (Chief of Village), at the heart of implementing Club Med's marketing and operations strategies, dealt with daily operations: The *chef* managed the many GOs, coordinated GO activities with the various programs, and was the direct link between customers and upper management. Through regionalization, problems surfaced at the village level were dealt with at a lower level in the new organizational hierarchy. Further, the *Chefs de Village* were selected from many countries to multinationalize operations.

At the top of the organization, the Triganos sustained control. Gilbert Trigano, aged 69, remained Chairman of the Board of CMI, and Chairman of the

---

*(GOs, or "gentils organisateurs," specialized by function, had the task of helping people making this vacation the best. They both organized and participated in events. Typically there were 80 to 100 GOs per village.)

Board, CEO, and MD of Club Mediterranée S.A. His son, Serge Trigano, born in Paris, May 24, 1946, headed CMI as Vice Chairman of the Board and CEO.

Serge worked as a GO during college breaks from the Faculté de Droit et Science (Paris), where he earned a degree in economics. After serving as *Chef de Village* in six villages, in 1981, following some decentralization, Serge assumed leadership of the American Zone and became CEO in 1984 of the newly incorporated CMI. Between 1985 and 1987 he was, also, Club Mediterranée S.A.'s MD for development and operations of Europe and Africa. In 1987 he became its Chief Operating Officer (COO), dividing time between world headquarters in Paris and offices and villages around the world. Serge concentrated mostly on operational matters, his father on strategic issues.

The President, COO, and Chief Financial Officer (CFO) of CMI, Jean-Luc Oizan-Chapon, who had begun as a GO sports instructor with Club Mediterranée in its early years, later followed Serge Trigano to the American Zone. Other CMI corporate officers included: Alexis Agnello, Executive Vice President; Jacques Ganin, Secretary; and Joseph J. Townsend, Treasurer.

CMI Board of Directors included: Gilbert Trigano, Chairman; Serge Trigano, Vice Chairman; Jacques Giraud, Vice Chairman; Alexis Agnello; Evan G. Galbraith, former U.S. Ambassador to France, now Director International and Senior Advisor, Morgan Stanley & Company; Harvey M. Krueger, MD, Shearson Lehman, Hutton, Inc.; Stanley Komaroff, Partner, Proskauer, Rose, Goetz & Mendelsohn; Richard A. Voell, President, CEO, The Rockefeller Group.

Business writer Stephen Wood described the global organization as too small, too French, with a management system characterized by worship of a 69-year-old guru and a product that was 40 years old (Wood, 1990). President Jean-Luc Oizan-Chapon admitted that Americans and the French did not always get along well.

NEW VILLAGES, NEW CHALLENGES WORLDWIDE

The basic operating unit, village or villa or comparable unit, was headed by a *Chef de Village,* who linked customers and joint managing directors. The life of a *Chef de Village* might be described in the name of Janyck Daudet, the youngest appointed *Chef* at age 26 in 1983. A native of Nîmes, France, he began as a ski instructor in Yugoslavia and worked in clubs from Morocco to Thailand as a GO. (Staff members were reassigned every 6 months not only to keep them motivated but also because some seasonal villages were closed part of each year. Typically, a GO earned low wages, plus room and board, was under age 30 and unmarried. A U.S. GO earned less than $500 a month in 1990. *Chefs* could earn considerably more.) As a chef, Daudet worked 18 hours a day, on call 24 hours, seven days a week, mingled with guests, performed in after-dinner shows, called midnight staff meetings, and maintained a high level of enthusiasm and energy.

For approximately every five GMs there was one GO. Having remained firmly intact since inception, the GO concept afforded the firm a competitive advantage, according to management. Worldwide there were more than 8000 GOs, from 32 countries, in 1990, 25 percent of whom were employed by CMI. About 3000 new GOs were selected each year from an applicants' pool of 100,000. Roughly one-half of the GOs were former GMs.

Toward the end of the 1980s, hiring French GOs was virtually halted as international teams were employed from the U.K., West Germany and Italy plus cheaper talent discovered in some less developed countries. In early 1990 Club Mediterranée engaged around 250 British GOs to service 17,000 British GMs in popular villages such as Marbella, Kos, Turkey and Sardinia. Management also considered opening a London Club Med.

The American Zone suffered setbacks during fiscal year 1987–88. Construction delays in Mexico resulted in lost revenue. Construction delays in The Bahamas postponed reopening of Paradise Island. An adverse political environment resulted in the closing of Magic Isle in Haiti. Occupancy rates declined. The following fiscal year witnessed more problems. Hurricane Gilbert shutdown Cancun; Hurricane Hugo caused temporary closings of Caravelle on Guadeloupe and Turkoise in the Turks and Caicos Islands; Eleuthera, closed in May 1989 for renovations, reopened in December 1989; and St. George's Cove in Bermuda ceased operations while a sale was negotiated.

On the upside, occupancy rates in the American Zone reached a new high of 66.3 percent. The number of GMs from France and other European countries rose nearly 50 percent; and the number of GMs from Mexico, the Caribbean, and South America increased modestly. Inauguration of the newest 700-bed CMI village, under construction on San Salvador (The Bahamas), was anticipated in 1992, in time for the five-hundredth anniversary of Columbus' landing on that island.

Likewise, the Asian Zone in 1989 achieved new records. Occupancy rates attained 73.2 percent. Hotel days increased by 24.4 percent. The Japanese not only visited Sahoro—a Winter ski resort and Summer mountain resort—in record numbers (70.9 percent occupancy), but traveled in large numbers to locations throughout the Asian and American Zones. The Tahitian villages of Moorea and Bora became more accessible via direct Air France flights between Tokyo and Papeete. (Bora had been closed for several months during 1989 for renovation but reopened in September.) During 1990, CMI expected to increase aggregate bed capacity by nearly 500 at these villages: Sahoro, Bali in Indonesia, Phuket in Thailand, and La Pointe aux Canonniers. A new village in Vietnam was planned for the early part of the decade. On the other hand, the number of European visitors to Asia actually decreased from 1987 levels.

CONFRONTING NEW COMPETITORS

Club Med had fashioned its worldwide profile during the 1950s. Because its style, and 40-year-old product, might not carry it through the century, management unfurled a strategy of market segmentation for implementation during the late 1980s, and 1990s. Despite global coverage, Club Med was still a small company, based on number of clients, compared with such European rivals as Thompson Travel and the German group, TUI. As a tour operator, Club Med fell from third to seventh place between 1984 and 1988. With growth in its French home market of less than 3 percent annually, the company faced rather limited potential in France (Wood, 1990). When it launched its Europeanization program, Club Med selected 17 villages for conversion to an international flavor because its biggest competitor, Robinson, had 16 of them.

Trigano waxed philosophically on the changing markets:

When we started, 99 percent of the people in the Paris region had never seen the Mediterranean. I hadn't. Just to see the sea was a considerable emotional event. And in my first year we had a water-ski boat . . . and you could walk on the water. When the Club offered wonders like that, you didn't worry about the accommodation—in U.S. Army surplus tents. We were all together, sharing these wonderful experiences, so we became friends; and that friendship was a sort of powerful cement.

But the sense of discovery has gone now. People just want the best. Club Med can't be the same because life is not the same.

By the end of the 1980s, CMI had encountered customer price resistance, especially apparent in the Winter 1988 season, when it raised prices 13 percent. Political unrest and labor problems, coupled with temporary closings, gave competitors an edge during 1988–1989.

Additionally, for many, Florida, with its own attractions such as Disney World and Universal Studios, represented the gateway to the Caribbean. Because CMI was also in the vacation business, the term, "vacation," which conjured up different images for vacationers, resulted in yet a broader definition of competition for CMI. Resorts, catering to an up-scale business clientele, represented a lucrative segment of the lodging industry. Firms, such as the Marriott Corporation, Holiday Inn, and Hyatt Regency, created luxurious up-scale resorts in different environmental settings. Conference centers, meeting rooms, quarters for executives, and getaway packages surfaced among American competitors.

Other competitors, such as Hedonism II, Club Paradise, and Jack Tarr Village, in imitation of Club Med, packaged lower priced vacations. Club Med judged these numerous copycat villages to be inconsequential competitors. Nevertheless, Thomas J. Garzelli, Vice President of Fly Fare Vacations said, "There's no question that the people who are filling up these resorts are the right demographics to go to Club Med" (*Business Week*, 1987, p. 120). Most copycats, usually located in the Caribbean, were not global players; but they competed effectively in limited markets.

Similarly, in Japan, competition for the leisure yen was triggered by success of Tokyo Disneyland: 15 million people had visited the theme park by March 31, 1990. Japanese corporations seeking to diversify mostly focused on the Japanese amusement park industry when industry revenues jumped from $1.4 billion (U.S. dollar equivalent) in 1982 to $2.5 billion anticipated for 1990.

Nevertheless, the newest and fastest growing wave of competitors, the cruise ship industry, generated all-inclusive trips and tours, not unlike Club Med's, and frequently traveled to the same exotic destinations. Multinational companies, such as Carnival Cruise Lines, Royal Viking, and Norwegian Caribbean, packaged multi-price level programs that appealed to young singles and marrieds, families, as well as leisure trips for retirees. Robert H. Dickenson, Vice President of Sales and Marketing for Carnival Cruise Lines said, "Cruising was once the domain of the rich. Now cruising is open to everyone" (*Business Week*, 1987, p. 120).

A NEW STRATEGY FOR THE REST OF THE CENTURY

Club Méditerranée began as an international firm with headquarters in Paris, operations in the Balearic Islands, and customers predominately French. As operations spread across the globe, management largely maintained the original strategies of Trigano. Nevertheless, changing demographics and customer tastes could not be denied.

CMI President Oizan-Chapon insisted, "Only part of the market is maturing. Part of it is growing." He pointed out, "We are following a life cycle plan." With respect to losses, he said, "In business you take the risk; you cannot control everything." He mentioned two major factors that hurt Club Med in 1988: (1) political unrest, which precipitated closing its Magic Isle village in Haiti and negatively impacted occupancy rates in New Caledonia; (2) construction problems, which delayed opening of a big new village in Huatulco, Mexico. (Business writer Richard Phalon estimated that the Mexican misadventure cost Club Med around U.S. $7 million in reimbursements and debits (Phalon, 1988).

Product diversification efforts met with limited success. The North American market encountered problems: west coast U.S. customers were less attuned to French culture than east coast ones. *Chef de Village* Jean-Luc Olivero thought that the problem was even more basic: Americans were puritanical. For instance, when Club Med bought the Sandpiper property in Florida from Hilton Hotels, management ordered removal of TVs and telephones from rooms. Americans preferred them. They were replaced in 1989. (See Exhibit 4 for data on operating results by market segment.)

CMI developed a three-part growth strategy for the 1990s:

Club Med Inc.: Operating Data by Market Segment, 1987–1989 (in millions of U.S. dollars)
    Exhibit 4

Regions, by Years	Consolidated Regional Revenues	Operating Income (Loss)	Identifiable Assets
1989			
North America	103.4	(8.4)	48.1
Mexico-Caribbean	175.4	10.8	264.5
Asia-Pacific	157.9	22.9	102.9
Consolidated	468.8	25.4	415.5
1988			
North America	133.1	(11.7)	55.5
Mexico-Caribbean	151.6	8.2	241.6
Asia-Pacific	127.7	14.7	106.2
Consolidated	412.4	11.2	403.2
1987			
North America	124.6	(1.6)	48.1
Mexico-Caribbean	143.6	12.0	223.3
Asia-Pacific	102.2	9.7	82.0
Consolidated	370.4	20.0	353.4

Source: Club Med Inc. *Annual Report,* 1989, p. 41.

Note: Consolidated revenues eliminate revenues between geographic areas and revenues originating in another area. Therefore, although the North American area generated nearly twice the revenues shown above, these were spent in another region. By the same token, about 75 percent of revenues attributed to the Mexico-Caribbean region were generated elsewhere. In the Asia-Pacific area, most revenues generated there were spent in the region.

1. Broaden the appeal: increase market penetration of the core product, the Club Med village vacation.
2. Expand the reach: introduce the Club Med concept to countries with growing economies and desires for new vacation opportunities.
3. Widen the concept: develop new vacation products, particularly in the rapidly growing cruise market (Club Med, 1989, pp. 4–5).

Success during the 1990s depended upon effective implementation of this strategy.

REFERENCES

Club Med Inc. *Annual Report*, 1989.

Club Med Inc. (promotion catalog), Summer/Fall 1990.

Horovitz, Jacques, "Club Mediterranée [A]," in Leslie Rue and Phyllis Holland, *Strategic Management: Concepts and Experiences* (New York: McGraw-Hill, 1986), pp. 636–655.

Levine, Joshua, "I Am Sorry, We Have Changed," *Forbes* (Sept. 4, 1989): 136–137.

Moskowitz, Milton, *The Global Marketplace* (Chicago: 1988), pp. 146–148.

"Now Club Med Wants an Antidote for Competition," *Business Week* (Nov. 2, 1987): 120–121.

Phalon, Richard, "Trouble in Paradise," *Forbes* (Sept. 19, 1988): 56, 61.

Wood, Stephen, "Club Med's Global Villages," *Business* (U.K.) (Jan. 1990): 64–71.

General Dynamics: The Chrysler Tank Decision

John Leslie, University of South Carolina; James J. Chrisman, Louisiana State University

On December 10, 1981, *The Wall Street Journal* announced that Chrysler Corporation, the third-largest automobile manufacturer in the United States, had decided to sell its tank manufacturing subsidiary. The cash-hungry corporation was considering selling its only profitable business as part of an effort to stave off impending bankruptcy. Although it may have caught some observers unaware, the article could hardly have been a surprise to David Lewis, Chairman and CEO of General Dynamics Corporation. General Dynamics was one of the "several interested companies" which were alluded to in the article.

In November 1981 General Dynamics (GD) had been approached by brokers representing Chrysler to see if they had any interest in purchasing the tank manufacturing subsidiary. Since GD's major line of business was defense contracting, it expressed an interest in the deal. Following the initial meeting with Chrysler, Lewis sent some senior GD people to tour Chrysler Defense's two plants and to talk with people from the Pentagon and AVCO Corporation, the main subcontractor for the M1 tank.

General Dynamics was not the only company to express an interest in Chrysler Defense, however. Industry observers speculated that Chrysler was playing it smart by offering the profitable tank business (1981 profit was expected to be about $73 million on sales of $846 million) to all the major defense contractors in an effort to increase the selling price. Lewis knew that several other companies had also met with Chrysler, and that LTV Corporation and Teledyne, Inc., were likely to submit bids. (See Appendixes 1 and 2 for brief descriptions of LTV and Teledyne). Chrysler had asked that sealed bids for Chrysler Defense be submitted no later than January 19, 1982.

General Dynamics was already heavily reliant on defense sales. Over the past several decades senior management had expressed the goal of balancing the company's defense and commercial operations. Purchasing Chrysler Defense would increase GD's defense business to over 80% of total sales; however, the outlook for defense spending was very good. Over the next month GD had to decide whether to submit a bid and for how much. It was a major decision and certainly among the toughest the 64-year-old Lewis had faced in his 11 years as CEO of General Dynamics.

COMPANY BACKGROUND

Currently considered the number-one primary contractor in the industry, General Dynamics had long been involved in the defense business. The firm, originally called the Electric Boat Company, had been supplying the U.S. Navy with submarines since 1899. In 1934 it acquired Electro-Dynamic, a producer of electric motors. However, submarine building remained Electric Boat's (EB) primary line of business until after World War II. The transformation of the company into a major defense contractor was led by its President at that time, John Jay Hopkins. Hopkins was a daring, driving man with ambitious plans for the company. He envisioned building EB into a major supplier of defense equipment for all branches of the military, not just the Navy. The first major move toward that goal came in 1947 when EB acquired Canadair, a defense aerospace company owned by the Canadian government.

In 1950 Hopkins accepted the request from Captain Hyman G. Rickover of the U.S. Navy to design and build for the Navy the world's first nuclear-powered submarine, the Nautilus. While Electric Boat had more expertise building submarines than anyone else in the world, incorporating the relatively unknown technology of atomic power into what would be the largest sub ever built was a monumental job. Hopkins committed EB to the task, and almost five years later the nuclear-powered Nautilus was launched from the EB yard in Connecticut.

In 1952 Hopkins decided that the name The Electric Boat Company did not match the vision and scope of the company and renamed it the General Dynamics Corporation. He also felt that the company should have a large commercial presence, to balance its defense business. Guided by Hopkins, General Dynamics began a major effort to diversify through acquisition and internal development.

In 1954 Convair, an aviation company with both commercial and military products, was purchased. Stromberg-Carlson, a long-established electronics and communications company, was acquired in 1955. In the same year General Dynamics formed a separate division called General Atomic to perform pure research in the new and exciting nuclear power field, with the expectation of developing profitable spin-off products from the research.

Hopkins died of cancer in 1957, and Frank Pace succeeded him as CEO. Pace continued Hopkins's strategy of expanding into the commercial sector by purchasing Liquid Carbonic, one of the world's largest suppliers of compressed gases, in 1957. Pace also set forth a directive that GD should achieve equal earnings from its commercial and defense businesses to protect its overall earnings from the cyclical nature of the defense industry.

By 1960, Convair had become GD's largest division. It made primarily military products, such as B-58 bombers, Terrier missiles, fighter jets, and Atlas rockets for the Mercury space program. The division was located in California and operated almost as a separate company. In the late 1950s Convair attempted to diversify into the commercial jet field with two midrange jets. This ambitious program was a disaster from the start and cost the company $425 million.

The Convair disaster brought General Dynamics to the brink of bankruptcy and cost Pace his job. After losing money in 1960 and 1961, GD lured Roger Lewis away from Boeing to succeed Pace as CEO. Lewis was picked by the executive committee, headed by the chief shareholder, Chicago industrialist Henry Crown. Crown had merged his Material Service Company, made up of three Chicago area construction companies, into GD in 1959 in exchange for a 20% share of the combined company and three seats on the Board of Directors.

Roger Lewis shifted the company's attention back to defense and returned GD to profitability. During the sixties, programs such as the Atlas booster rockets, Polaris submarines, and the controversial, but profitable, F-111 fighter bombers accounted for about 75% of General Dynamics' sales and were its main source of profits. GD's only major commercial venture under Lewis was the purchase of the aging Quincy naval shipyard from Bethlehem Steel in 1963 for $5 million. Lewis hoped to convert Quincy into a successful commercial yard; but handicapped by labor problems and aging facilities, the yard became a constant cash drain on General Dynamics. Bethlehem officials were later quoted as saying that they would have paid GD $5 million to take Quincy off their hands.

In 1969 GD was able to post only a $2.5 million profit despite sales of $2.2 billion. Henry Crown publicly challenged the reported profit, stating that had Lewis not employed some optimistic accruals on GD's defense business and switched depreciation methods, the company would have recorded a $40 million loss. In fact, Crown was right; GD's defense operations were now in poor shape. The Pomona missile division was losing money, and the U.S. Air Force had recently issued an order grounding all F-111 jets until further safety tests could be carried out. Crown was also displeased that the market share and profits of his Material Service Company had steadily eroded during the ten years that it had been part of GD. With spending for the Vietnam War winding down, Crown felt that it was time for the company to become more oriented towards the commercial sector.

In 1970, with four of the company's ten divisions losing money, David S. Lewis, President of McDonnell Douglas, was brought in to replace Roger Lewis as CEO (the two were not related). David Lewis moved GD's headquarters from New York to St. Louis, in order to exercise closer control over the company's geographically dispersed divisions. Under his leadership GD also implemented tighter cost controls, adopted more conservative procedures for accruing profit, and invested heavily in some of the company's unprofitable divisions. David Lewis employed a centralized style of management from the St. Louis headquarters. A former aeronautical engineer, he kept tight personal control over the largely engineering-oriented company and took a close interest in the company's key development projects, such as the F-16 jet.

Lewis acknowledged the company's defense business as its traditional strength, but he also tried to bolster GD's commercial activities through acquisition and capital investments. By 1973, General Dynamics' commercial operations accounted for one-third of its sales and almost half of its earnings. As a result of Lewis's efforts, the company's dying defense business also began to turn around. The company's F-16 fighter jet won the final fly-off against Northrop's F-17 in 1974, which enabled the Fort Worth division to convert to F-16s just as F-111 production was being terminated. In early 1975 the Air Force ordered the first batch of 650 F-16s, worth $4.3 billion. And in 1976, GD's Electric Boat division was awarded the contract for the first Trident submarine, giving it both the Trident and SSN-668 submarine programs.

The F-16, Trident, SSN-668, and Pomona missile programs provided GD with a substantial sales base in the late seventies and returned General Dynamics to prominence as a major defense contractor. In 1979 and 1980 GD led all companies in defense contracting. However, in 1981 it slipped from this position largely due to disputes with the Navy. Exhibit 1 provides financial data and lists important defense products for the top aerospace defense contractors in 1980.

In 1981 Lewis was 64. Although he had no plans to retire, many felt that President Oliver Boileau, 55, who had been hired from Boeing in 1980, would eventually succeed Lewis as CEO. Both Lewis and chief shareholder Henry Crown maintained that they wanted to reduce GD's dependency on the military and expand its commercial operations. Top management at General Dynamics was still committed to the goal of obtaining "equal profits from defense and civilian industries"—a goal expressed by former GD management almost 30 years earlier.

Exhibit 1　　　　　　　　Financial Information for the Top Ten Defense Aerospace Companies (all data for 1980 are dollars in millions)

Company	Ranking in Value of Defense Contracts	Value of Defense Contracts	Total Sales	Net Income	ROE (%)	Assets	Major Defense Products
General Dynamics	1	3518	4,645	195	21.0	2242	F-16, Trident subs, SSN-668 subs, Tomahawk missiles
McDonnell Douglas	2	3247	6,086	145	9.9	3900	F-18, F-15, KC-10 planes, Trident II missiles
United Technologies	3	3109	12,324	393	17.5	7326	UH-60 helicopters, jet fighter engines
Boeing	4	2386	9,426	601	28.8	5931	AWACS, Stealth bomber, B-52 modifications
Lockheed	6	2037	5,396	28	7.5	2443	C-5A, C-5B cargo planes, Trident II missiles
Hughes*	7	1819	2,610	NA	NA	NA	AH-64 helicopters, defense electronics
Raytheon	8	1745	5,002	282	22.7	2929	Hawk missiles, defense electronics
Grumman	10	1322	1,729	31	9.5	906	F-14, A-6E planes, aircraft carriers
Northrop	11	1227	1,655	86	19.0	1234	F-20, F-18, F-5G, Stealth bomber
Rockwell	14	969	6,907	280	17.3	4431	B-1 bomber

Source: James J. Chrisman, "Note on the Defense Electronics Industry," Working Paper, Department of Management, University of Georgia, Athens, 1982.

*Privately held.

INDUSTRY PROFILE

The defense industry consisted of literally thousands of companies of many different types and sizes which produced a wide variety of weapons and military products. To a large extent the industry was dominated by two groups of firms: large diversified commercial companies, like General Electric, Westinghouse, IBM, and Litton, and large aerospace companies, such as General Dynamics, Boeing, McDonnell Douglas, and Lockheed.

The industry supplied essentially one customer—the U.S. military, which consisted of the Army, Navy (including the Marines), and Air Force. The Department of Defense (DOD) controlled the military and was responsible for preparing the national defense budget for the various military services, a complicated, consensus-building process that involved hundreds of agencies. While only about half of the military budget actually went towards weapons procurement (salaries and supplies represented the other half of the budget), increases in defense spending generally resulted in banner years for the major defense contractors both in terms of sales and profits.

The funds available to the military each year were controlled by Congress. The defense budget was determined both by the administration's policy with regard to defense spending and by the funds required for other programs. Money spent on defense could not be spent on other programs such as welfare and social aid, and some weapons were politically less popular than others (the MX strategic missile program, for example). The military competed with these other programs for funds, and if Congress deemed it necessary to reduce the President's proposed budget, some programs might be drastically reduced in scope or cut altogether.

Almost all defense sales were made through contracts between the DOD and the prime contractor. These contracts were usually made on either a fixed-fee or a cost-plus basis and often included incentive clauses to encourage the contractor to complete the contract under the target price. In 1981 almost all production contracts were still issued on a yearly basis (development contracts were typically multiyear), with the contractor's performance and funding status being reviewed each year. The acquisition process in the defense industry was long and complex. Most defense contracts were for high-technology items which required long development periods. In 1979 John H. Richardson, President of Hughes Aircraft, estimated that the time required to develop a major new defense item was eight to nine years, from the initial development stage to the start of full production. These development costs were usually paid by the military under development contracts. The military typically paid a number of companies to develop various designs for the item and then contracted one company to perform full-scale engineering development (FSED) on the best design. Once FSED was complete, the military then asked for bids on the production run. The company which carried out the FSED did not always get the production contract, which often led to inefficiencies in the early production stages.

Another source of inefficiency in this process was that at the time the initial production began, the final size of the production run could only be estimated. Therefore, contractors could never be certain if or when investments in plant and equipment would be recovered on a project, because the size of the production run might change from year to year. Furthermore, the government did not allow the contractor to recover costs that were not directly tied to the particular program involved. Such conditions tended to discourage defense contractors from investing capital in new plant and equipment. Given this uncertain operating environment and the ponderous bureaucracy of the military, inefficiencies in the industry and the "padding" of defense contracts were common results.

Another problem inherent in the defense industry was the military's desire to compromise cost in favor of improved performance. The desire for better performance often led to product design changes halfway through the production run. These changes made it necessary for the contractor to have to go back and "refit" all the previously produced items, which often were in different stages of completion. Delays of this sort were costly, especially in the inflationary environment of 1981. Many contractors tried to pass these costs on to the military, and disagreements between the contractor and the military over which party should bear these costs often ensued.

It was in this air of uncertainty that General Dynamics and other defense contractors operated in 1981. They produced very expensive high-technology products (e.g., Trident subs, F-16s) with long development times for a single customer. That customer's requirements could fluctuate considerably, depending on the existing administration's policies and the mood of Congress.

PATTERNS OF U.S. DEFENSE SPENDING

The defense industry was cyclical in nature. Exhibit 2 shows the level of U.S. defense spending in constant dollars for the years 1960 through 1985. There had been a buildup in U.S. military force during the Korean War and Cold War years. By the late 1950s, however, defense spending had begun to decline. Political confrontations with the Soviet Union and Cuba, followed by the escalation of U.S. involvement in Vietnam, led to increased defense spending in the 1960s. Military spending in the United States peaked in 1969 and then began to

Exhibit 2   **U.S. Defense Spending, 1960–1985 (in constant dollars)**

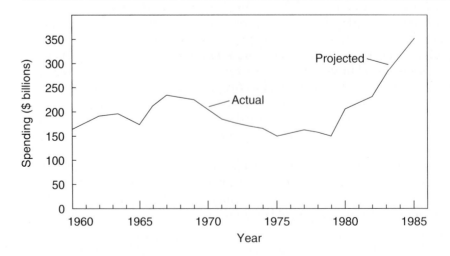

Year	Total Defense Budget	% Change	Procurement and RDT&E* Authorized	% Change	% of Defense Budget	Procurement and RDT&E* Expenditures	% Change
1981	178.4[†]	—	64.6[†]	—	36%	50.5	—
1982	211.4[†]	+18%	84.2[†]	+30%	40%	61.0	+21%
1983	240.5	+14%	104.7	+24%	44%	76.6	+26%
1984	274.1	+14%	123.7	+18%	45%	94.5	+23%
1985	322.4	+18%	151.8	+23%	47%	115.9	+23%
1986	357.2	+11%	170.5	+12%	48%	136.3	+18%

Projected Defense Spending, 1981–1986 (dollars in billions)   **Exhibit 3**

*RDT&E = research, development, testing, and evaluation.

[†]Actual approved amount.

decrease in the 1970s as the United States slowly withdrew manpower and equipment from Vietnam. Under President Carter defense spending sank to its lowest real levels since the end of World War II.

In 1980 Ronald Reagan won a landslide victory over Jimmy Carter. As part of his election campaign Reagan had promised to increase the political presence of the United States on the international scene, which many felt had been significantly weakened by the Carter administration. Reagan also planned to increase military spending by 9% per year (in real terms), as opposed to Carter's more moderate 4.6% per year. Exhibit 3 provides the projected defense budgets for the U.S. military for the years 1982–1986.

There were obstacles to Reagan's plans, however. The economy was sluggish; and with this fact combined with proposed tax cuts, many wondered where the funds for increased defense spending would come from. As interest rates climbed in 1980–1981, concern about an increasing federal deficit and the high cost of servicing the debt began to surface in Congress. At the same time the Pentagon was arguing that higher defense budgets were necessary to prevent the United States from falling further behind the ever-increasing military strength of the Soviet Union.

Nevertheless, with the commitment of the President and the Pentagon's support, the outlook for the defense industry in the 1980s appeared bright. The industry had received over $90 billion in defense contracts in 1981, and this figure was expected to jump to $110 billion in 1982. Thus, despite the many problems and uncertainties in the defense business, the lure of getting a big piece of the growing Pentagon budget was sufficient to keep all the big players in the game in 1981. Many of the aerospace companies were relying on profits from their defense divisions to compensate for losses incurred in the depressed commercial aircraft field during the late 1970s.

CURRENT OPERATIONS

In 1981 General Dynamics consisted of four lines of business: aerospace, shipbuilding, building products and resources, and telecommunications. GD's military business sectors, aerospace and shipbuilding, accounted for about 75% of total sales. Exhibits 4 through 7 present financial data for GD.

Exhibit 4   General Dynamics: Consolidated Balance Sheets, 1977–1981 (dollars in millions)

	1981	1980	1979	1978	1977
Assets					
Current assets					
Cash and equivalents	13.8	16.2	42.3	62.6	47.4
Accounts receivable					
United States and other governments	109.5	96.3	71.8	65.4	50.0
Commercial customers	213.2	195.3	202.0	174.7	111.7
Government contracts in progress	605.6	600.0	475.6	412.1	560.8
Commercial contracts in progress	96.1	92.0	21.0	55.3	32.8
Inventory	233.5	241.8	252.6	221.3	181.2
Prepaid expenses	19.6	16.5	12.8	12.1	8.6
Total current assets	1291.3	1258.1	1078.1	1003.6	992.6
Investments in unconsolidated subsidiaries	266.7	233.7	130.7	98.1	29.6
Other assets	68.6	71.0	62.4	63.4	29.1
Net property, plant, and equipment	700.2	679.2	733.6	613.6	549.8
Total assets	2326.8	2242.0	2004.8	1778.7	1601.1
Liabilities and Shareholders' Equity					
Current liabilities					
Short-term borrowings	134.0	170.1	24.5	27.6	23.0
Accounts payable	316.2	306.8	321.2	271.6	190.1
Accrued salary and wages	119.9	116.8	82.8	210.6	208.4
Other accrued expenses	171.0	166.7	143.7	16.5	155.3
Loss provision for SSN-668	62.4	100.7	146.6	245.0	0.0
Total current liabilities	803.5	861.1	724.9	771.4	576.8
Noncurrent liabilities					
Long-term debt less current maturities	26.9	29.0	66.9	70.6	52.4
Deferred income taxes	310.2	239.4	235.9	123.3	97.4
Other	87.6	84.3	60.1	52.3	85.2
Total noncurrent liabilities	424.7	352.7	362.9	246.2	235.1
Equity					
Minority equity in subsidiary	0.0	0.0	61.1	57.7	56.3
Redeemable preferred stock	27.1	28.8	29.5	29.5	0.0
Common shareholders' equity	1071.5	999.4	826.4	674.0	732.9
Total equity	1098.6	1028.2	917.0	761.2	789.2
Total liabilities and shareholders' equity	2326.8	2242.0	2004.8	1778.7	1601.1

Source: General Dynamics, *Annual Reports,* 1978–1981.

The outlook for General Dynamics in late 1981 was generally optimistic. The company was well positioned to take advantage of the proposed increases in defense spending and was sitting on a $10.5 billion backlog of funded orders. However, despite the prospect of future sales, 1981 was not an outstanding year. Although sales for the year had increased 9% from 1980 to over $5 billion, net income was down 36% to $124 million. Slow economic growth had led to a poor showing by GD's commercial operations, and the otherwise strong performance of its defense divisions was hurt by a $45 million write-off taken by the Electric Boat Division to cover cost overruns on two submarine contracts. Substantially

General Dynamics: Consolidated Statements of Earnings, 1977–1981 (dollars in millions except per share amounts) — **Exhibit 5**

	1981	1980	1979	1978	1977
Net sales	5063.4	4645.0	3912.5	3205.2	2901.2
Cost of sales	− 4539.0	− 4039.8	− 3317.9	− 3344.5	− 2709.0
Selling, general, and administrative	− 350.1	− 349.8	− 318.5	0.0	0.0
Total operating costs	− 4889.1	− 4389.6	− 3636.4	− 3344.5	− 2709.0
Operating profit	174.3	255.4	276.1	− 139.3	192.2
Other income, net	42.7	10.9	15.3	1.1	1.3
Earnings before interest and taxes	217.0	266.3	291.4	− 138.2	193.5
Interest expense	− 20.8	− 9.5	− 6.9	− 17.1	− 10.8
Earnings before income taxes	196.2	256.8	284.5	− 155.3	182.7
Provision for income taxes	− 72.1	− 61.8	− 99.3	107.2	− 79.3
Net earnings	124.1	195.0	185.2	− 48.1	103.4
Dividends	41.3	36.3	34.4	0.0	0.0
Net earnings per common share	2.25	3.58	3.43	− 1.80	3.80

Source: General Dynamics, *Annual Reports,* 1978–1981.

all the profit for 1981, even before the fourth-quarter write-offs, was derived from the aerospace sector. A breakdown of the four business sectors is presented below.

▪ Aerospace

The aerospace section consisted of four divisions: Fort Worth, Convair, Pomona, and Electronics. Exhibit 8 lists the major products produced by each division.

The Fort Worth division accounted for almost 40% of GD's sales in 1981 and 70% of the operating profit (before the fourth-quarter write-offs). Almost all the sales resulted from the F-16 Fighting Falcon program, developed in the mid-1970s as the low-cost alternative to McDonnell Douglas's F-15 jet. The F-16 program was in the peak of its development. Deliveries and profit margins were increasing each year, and the outlook for the future was very good. The Air Force had increased its total planned procurement to almost 2000 planes (351 had been delivered at the end of 1981). GD was also developing a high-performance version of the F-16, the F-16/XL, which would compete against the more expensive F-15 and F-18 (both Northrop and McDonnell Douglas made F-18s).

The F-16 was also well positioned for foreign sales. GD had developed the slower, less expensive F-16/79, which competed with Northrop's F5-G in the low-cost end of the foreign market. Depending on each country's budget and the level of sophistication that the administration wished each Allied Air Force to have, the country was offered the F-16, the F-16/79, or a mixture of both. The cost for the F-16/79 was about $14 million per plane, versus $15 million for the standard F-16. Allied Air Forces were planning to purchase a total of 560 planes from General Dynamics.

Exhibit 6   General Dynamics: Consolidated Statement of Changes in Financial Position

	1981	*1980*	*1979*
Cash Provided from Operations			
Net earnings	124.1	195.0	185.2
Costs and expenses not requiring cash			
Depreciation	122.5	106.9	89.4
Deferred income taxes	70.8	46.8	96.3
Other	18.5	20.8	7.4
Total cash available from operations	335.9	369.5	378.3
Dividends	(41.3)	(36.3)	(34.4)
Total cash provided from operations	294.6	333.2	343.9
Cash Used for Operations			
Capital investment			
Property, plant, and equipment	146.1	205.1	201.6
Goodwill from acquisitions	0.0	0.0	0.0
Unconsolidated subsidiaries	29.4	11.1	31.5
Total capital investment	175.5	216.2	233.1
Working capital			
Accounts receivable	31.1	52.0	40.6
Contracts in process	9.7	195.4	29.2
Inventories	(8.3)	50.8	23.9
Accounts payable	(9.4)	(1.4)	(52.4)
Accrued salaries and wages	(3.1)	(35.3)	(8.8)
Other accrued expenses	(4.3)	(22.8)	(9.3)
Provisions for loss on SSN-668 program	38.3	45.9	98.4
Total working capital investment	54.0	284.6	121.6
Other	21.3	21.9	6.3
Cash used for operating transactions	250.8	522.7	361.0
Financing Transaction			
Short-term borrowings	(36.1)	162.8	(2.6)
Long-term debt	3.0	(0.5)	(2.8)
Preferred stock issued	0.0	0.0	0.0
Stock options exercised	10.9	9.9	8.9
Treasury shares	(24.0)	0.0	(10.9)
Cash provided (used) for financing transactions	(46.2)	172.2	(7.4)
Increase (decrease) in cash and equivalents	(2.4)	(17.3)	(24.5)

Source: General Dynamics, *Annual Reports*, 1978–1981.

Additionally, the Defense Department was considering awarding a multiyear procurement contract to cover the Air Force's projected requirements over the next five years. This award would be the first of its kind and, if successful, might pave the way for other multiyear defense contracts. It was a tribute to the efficiency of the F-16 program that the military was considering it for the first contract of this type.

The Convair division was very successful as well. Its main program, the Tomahawk cruise missile, was completing the last of its performance tests and would likely enter full-scale production in 1982. Large orders for the sea-

General Dynamics: Business Segment Contributions to Sales and Operating Profits (dollars in millions)   **Exhibit 7**

	1981	1980	1979	1978	1977
Net Sales					
Military aircraft	1978	1744	1281	808	488
Tactical missiles and gun systems	747	667	557	423	304
Space systems	138	106	97	96	106
Commercial aircraft	100	133	128	94	78
Goverment shipbuilding	1030	902	678	655	943
Commercial shipbuilding	110	176	256	287	206
Material services	406	422	430	341	298
Telecommunications	305	262	271	183	165
Data products	139	140	109	85	70
Other	107	94	107	103	104
Total sales	5063	4645	3913	3075	2762
% military sales	77%	74%	67%	64%	67%
Operating Profits					
Military aircraft	181	127	74	52	38
Tactical missiles and gun systems	46	38	32	29	35
Space systems	8	9	10	10	11
Commercial aircraft	0	12	17	21	17
Government shipbuilding	(12)	23	19	(338)	31
Commercial shipbuilding	(34)	1	48	35	0
Material services	16	37	44	14	24
Telecommunications	(27)	(10)	13	(2)	(12)
Data products	(6)	12	10	9	6
Other	2	6	10	13	9
Total operating profits	174	256	276	(157)	159
% military profit (loss)	128%	77%	49%	(157%)	72%

The Aerospace Section   **Exhibit 8**

Division	*Location*	*Major Products*
Fort Worth	Fort Worth, Texas	F-16 jets; also F-16/79s, F-16/XLs
Convair	San Diego	Missiles: Tomahawk, SLCM, GLCM, MRSAM; space systems: Atlas/Centaur upper-stage shuttle booster rockets; commercial: DC-10 fuselages, 767 engine struts
Pomona	Pomona, California	Navy: Standard, RAM, and Sparrow missiles, Phalanx gun systems; Army: Stinger and Viper antitank guns
Electronics	San Diego	Testing equipment for F-16s and F-111s

launched (SLCM) and the ground-launched (GLCM) versions of the missiles had been placed by the Navy and the Army, respectively. Convair was also developing a medium-range surface-to-air missile (MRSAM) which management believed had great earnings potential.

In addition to its military operations Convair also included two smaller commercial operations. The Space Systems group produced the Atlas/Centaur upper-stage rocket booster for the space shuttles. The commercial aircraft group produced fuselages for the DC-10 engine and struts for the 767. Although both commercial operations were profitable, neither accounted for a significant portion of total sales. Orders from McDonnell Douglas and Boeing were down in 1981 due to a slowdown in the U.S. commercial aircraft industry. This slowdown was expected to continue for the next few years.

The Pomona division was entirely military-oriented. It produced four different lines of ship defense systems for the Navy. Three of these, the Standard surface-to-air missile, the Sparrow air-to-air missile, and the Phalanx shipboard gun system, were in full production, with the assurance of steady orders in the future. The fourth system was the RAM missile. Although still in the full-scale engineering stage, it looked very promising. Pomona also produced the Stinger antiaircraft gun and the Viper antitank gun for the Army, both of which were in full production.

The fourth aerospace division was the Electronics division. It produced testing and support systems for F-16s and F-111s already in service. Although profitable, it did not contribute significantly to revenues or profits.

■ Shipbuilding

The shipbuilding sector consisted of two divisions, Quincy and Electric Boat (EB). Exhibit 9 lists the major products of each division.

The poor performance of the Electric Boat division, with its Trident and SSN-668 submarine programs, was in sharp contrast to the performance of the Fort Worth division. While the F-16s rolled out of Fort Worth consistently ahead of schedule and below cost, Electric Boat was plagued by late deliveries, quality problems, and massive cost overruns. While the Fort Worth operation drew praise from the military, EB and the Navy were constantly feuding over costs, quality control, and late deliveries.

After fighting for a number of years over who would pay what share of the cost overruns on the first 18 SSN-668 submarines, General Dynamics and the Navy reached a settlement in 1978. The settlement required GD to split the extra

---

Exhibit 9   **The Shipbuilding Section**

Division	Location	Major Products
Electric Boat	Groton, Connecticut	Trident strategic submarines, SSN-668 attack submarines
Quincy	Quincy, Massachusetts	Commercial shipbuilding, small Navy vessels, Navy repair work

costs with the Navy, and this resulted in a $359 million write-off in 1978, giving the company an overall net loss of $48 million for that year. The situation at EB continued to deteriorate. In 1980, the Navy awarded three 668 contracts to EB's only competitor, Newport News Shipping and DryDock Company, a division of the Tenneco Company. The Navy claimed that the 668s built at EB cost 50% more and took 14 months longer to build than those built at Newport. Although performance at EB had recently improved, the company still had to write off an additional $45 million in 1981 to cover cost overruns on the first two 668s which were not covered by the 1978 settlement.

While the Trident program was more profitable, it was also plagued by late deliveries and charges of defective welding and painting. The first Trident, the *Ohio*, was launched in October 1981, almost 2.5 years late, although it performed well in its trials. General Dynamics and the Navy were essentially locked into the Trident program together. No other yard was equipped to build the Trident, and it was considered too important strategically to the nation's defense for the Navy not to proceed with the program. However, continued quality problems prompted the Navy to break off negotiations with General Dynamics for the ninth Trident in March 1981, leaving the future of the program in doubt.

The disputes with the Navy had also hurt the company's public image. Given its concern over rising defense spending, the general public was only too willing to believe horror stories of defense contractors padding costs to inflate revenues. Too often, General Dynamics was singled out in the news as a prime example of a big defense contractor wielding too much control over a helpless, bureaucratic military.

The Quincy division was struggling to stay profitable. The conversion of Quincy from a Naval yard into a commercial yard had been difficult. From 1963 to 1972 Quincy had lost a total of $330 million. The yard's performance had turned around in the 1970s, with contracts for eight LNG tankers, but future contracts for these ships were doubtful. The last tanker had been delivered in 1980, and although Quincy had provisional contracts for six more, these contracts were dependent upon the construction of a proposed LNG terminal in California. The future of this entire project was in serious doubt. Even if approved, environmentalists were expected to block the project, which might delay the contract decision for another two or three years.

The U.S. commercial shipbuilding industry was generally in poor shape, but Quincy's high labor costs and militant unions made its position even worse than some of its competitors'. Furthermore, Quincy was not equipped to build large, sophisticated Naval destroyers and carriers. It tried to compensate for this by building small Naval ships and doing Navy repair work. High overhead and past cost overruns at Quincy resulted in a $31 million write-off in 1981 for GD.

■ Building Products and Resources

The building products and resources sector consisted of three wholly owned subsidiaries and a 54.6% interest in a fourth, the Asbestos Corporation Ltd. (ACL). Exhibit 10 lists the major products of each division.

Asbestos Corporation Ltd. consisted of a number of asbestos mines and mills in Northern Quebec. Since 1977 the Quebec provincial government had been trying to appropriate GD's share in ACL, as part of an effort to gain control of

Exhibit 10   **Building Products and Resources Section**

Division	Location	Major Products
Material Service	Chicago	Aggregates, concrete, concrete products
Marblehead Lime	Chicago-based: mines in other areas	Commercial lime to the steel industry
Freeman United Coal	Chicago-based: mines in other areas	Coal for domestic and foreign markets
Asbestos Corporation Ltd. (ACL)	Quebec (Canada)	Asbestos mining

the resources within the province. General Dynamics had fought the move in court but by 1981 had all but given up hope of keeping ACL and was negotiating a price with the Quebec government. Negotiations were expected to be completed in early 1982. GD expected to break even on the deal.

The three other resource divisions were essentially the same companies which Henry Crown had merged into GD in 1959. Material Service was the largest supplier of sand, gravel, and concrete in the Chicago area. Marblehead Lime was the country's largest lime producer, supplying steel companies such as U.S. Steel and Bethlehem Steel. Freeman United mined low-grade coal for power generation and coking. About 80% of its output was dedicated to electric utility companies via long-term contracts.

All three Material Service divisions were heavily reliant on overall economic conditions. As a result, 1981 had not been a particularly good year for any of them. In recent years they had accounted for 5%–10% of General Dynamics' sales and profits.

■ Telecommunications and Information Systems

The telecommunications section consisted of four divisions, as shown in Exhibit 11. The three telephone-related divisions accounted for only 5%–6% of General Dynamics' total sales and had lost money in five out of the last six years. Unfavorable economic conditions and a weak competitive position had led to a total loss for these divisions of $27 million in 1981.

The future of these three divisions was not bright either. Most of their sales were to the independent (non-Bell) telephone companies, which were smaller and more widely dispersed than AT&T. Moreover, while the telecommunications industry was growing rapidly, the technology was changing just as rapidly. Stromberg-Carlson could not match AT&T's research and development efforts and hence often lagged behind in new technological developments.

Datagraphix controlled about 30% of the world market for computer output microfilm and related products. Despite competing with large companies such as 3M and Kodak, the division was well established and generally performed well. Start-up costs and poor economic conditions, however, had hurt the division's performance in 1981.

Telecommunications and Information Systems

Exhibit 11

Division	Location	Major Products
Stromberg-Carlson	Orlando, Florida	Digital phone-switching equipment
American Telecommunications	El Monte, California	Telephones and accessories
GD Communications	St. Louis, Missouri	Telephone exchanges and equipment
Datagraphix	San Diego	Computer output microfilm and related equipment

CHRYSLER DEFENSE, INC.

In 1981, almost all of Chrysler's nonautomotive business consisted of its tank manufacturing subsidiary, Chrysler Defense Inc. The tank division was a product of Chrysler's defense efforts during World War II. Like Ford and General Motors, Chrysler converted its plants from automobiles to defense products for the war effort. Throughout the war Chrysler factories churned out guns, Army trucks, engines for B-29 bombers, and many other military products, including tanks which were built at a special facility which was constructed just outside of Detroit in 1940. During the war years over 25,000 tanks were produced at the Detroit facility.

The Detroit tank plant continued operations after World War II, producing more advanced generations of tanks for use in Korea and Vietnam. Chrysler began production of the Army's current main battle tank, the M60, in 1959. In 1971 the Army received funds to develop a new tank, the M1. Despite improvements to the original design, the M60 was considered inferior to the Soviets' first-line tank. In 1973 both Chrysler and General Motors were called upon to submit a design for the M1.

In 1976 both companies submitted bids for full-scale engineering and design (FSED). Chrysler's bid was accepted amid controversy that the bid was incomplete and hence lower than it should have been. FSED of the M1 began at Chrysler in 1977. Eleven pilot vehicles were produced during the FSED phase. These vehicles were put through performance tests, and although many problems were encountered, in 1979 the Army gave Chrysler a contract to proceed with the first production models. The M1s were to be built at the Army's new tank plant in Lima, Ohio, which was owned by the military and leased to Chrysler for M1 production. Initial plans called for the M1s to be built in Lima and assembled in Detroit, with the Detroit plant eventually converting from M60 to M1 production.

In June 1980 the tank division was made a consolidated subsidiary of Chrysler, called Chrysler Defense Inc. This move was made primarily at the insistence of the Pentagon. Chrysler was the sole supplier of both the M1 and M60 tank to the U.S. Army. Because of this, the Pentagon wanted the tank business to be separate, so that if Chrysler declared bankruptcy, Chrysler Defense could be easily sold off. The Pentagon did not want the uncertain financial position of the parent company jeopardizing the vital production of tanks. The Pentagon also insisted that Chrysler Defense be excluded from any liens against the parent company, and that no assets of Chrysler Defense be used as collateral for any of the loans that Chrysler was seeking.

■ Current Operations

Chrysler Defense employed about 7000 people in 1981. In addition to the Lima and Detroit plants, Chrysler Defense also produced components for the M1s and M60s at government-owned plants in Sterling Heights, Michigan, and Scranton, Pennsylvania. All the plants were leased by Chrysler through government facilities contracts.

Although all of the plants were unionized, because of the important nature of the tank business, the UAW had been able to resist the concessions made at other Chrysler plants. Chrysler's defense business was somewhat isolated from the problems facing the rest of the parent company. In fact, in 1981 Chrysler Defense was the only profitable section of Chrysler Corporation, with profits of about $73 million before taxes on sales of $846 million. Chrysler as a whole, though, lost about $500 million in 1981. This loss followed almost $2.8 billion in losses for the previous two years. Exhibit 12 shows some financial data for Chrysler Corporation and for Chrysler Defense for 1980–1981.

Chrysler officials denied that the desperate financial position of the company had anything to do with their desire to sell off the tank subsidiary. They claimed that the company did not need the cash and would sell Chrysler Defense only if the offer was "too good to pass up." At the time, however, observers estimated that Chrysler's cash position was only enough to cover about two days of its normal operating expenses.

The M1 and M60 programs accounted for almost 98% of Chrysler Defense's sales. The cost to the military in 1981 was about $2.8 million per tank for an M1 and about $750,000 for an M60. These prices were expected to remain relatively

---

Exhibit 12	**Chrysler Financial Data, 1980–1981 (dollars in millions)**		
		1981	*1980*
Chrysler Corporation			
Sales		10822	9225
Net income (loss)		(476)	(1708)
Chrysler Defense			
Sales		846.0	625.0
Operating income		72.5	61.9

Source: Chrysler Corporation, *Annual Reports*, 1980–1981.

Note: Chrysler Corporation data includes Defense group data.

constant over the next several years. Chrysler Defense received approximately 50% of the total contract price for each tank, with the Army paying the remainder directly to major subcontractors, such as AVCO (supplier of turbine engines for the M1).

Even though it was profitable, Chrysler Defense had several critical problems. There was a 20-tank backlog of M1s at Lima, and the Army had returned many of the tanks already completed for further work. Some of the tanks required almost two months of reworking before they were acceptable. The planned production rate was 30 M1s per month, but the actual rate of production was only about 15–20 tanks per month in 1981. Production was expected to jump to 60 per month when the Detroit Arsenal plant converted to M1 production, scheduled for early 1982. Exhibit 13 shows production data for the M1 and M60 programs.

While the Army had increased its expected requirements to 7058 M1s (through 1988), it had not yet received full approval by Congress for this order, and there was much criticism of the entire M1 program. Many of the problems which had surfaced during the performance tests in the FSED phase had not yet been corrected. The revolutionary turbine engines which gave the M1 advantages in speed and low noise were clogging with dust and seizing, sometimes after only a few miles. There were also problems with the transmissions (GM-supplied) and the firing-control computers (supplied by Hughes). Chrysler officials were embarrassed when, during the official unveiling of the first M1 off the line, the tank's transmission jammed and the machine would not go into forward gear.

Perhaps wary of large cuts to the M1 program, the Army continued to praise the new tank and downplayed its operating problems. When functioning properly, the M1 was, in fact, far superior to the old M60 in almost every way. The big problem was keeping the tanks running. As the M1 repeatedly failed its durability and combat-readiness tests, criticism mounted. The cost per tank had risen from $507,000 in 1972 to $2.8 million in 1981. Many critics, calling for budget cuts to the M1 program, were dubbing the M1 "the Army's Edsel."

Chrysler Defense, Inc.: Production Data, 1979–1984   **Exhibit 13**

Item	1979*	1980*	1981*	1982*	1983[†]	1984[†]
M1s authorized by DOD	—	310	570	665	775	1080[‡]
M1s delivered	—	56	216	—	—	—
M60s authorized by DOD	438	560	400	360	360	360[§]
M60s delivered	1016	695	600	—	—	—

Sources: G. D. Shapiro, *General Dynamics Corporation—The Defense Department's "Prime" Contractor* (New York: Salomon Brothers, Inc., June 24, 1982); General Dynamics, *Annual Report*, 1982.

*Actual approved quantity

[†] Proposed quantity

[‡] Total stated Army requirement was for 7058 tanks.

[§] DOD planned no procurement of M60s beyond 1984. Additional foreign sales of M60s could extend production.

CONCLUSION

Although David Lewis had recently stated that he felt General Dynamics was too reliant on the military for business, Chrysler Defense was an attractive opportunity. The acquisition would fit in well with GD's existing defense businesses and would give the company major defense programs with the Army, Navy, and Air Force, thus solidifying its position as the number-one defense contractor. An opportunity to get into the ground floor of a large program like the M1 tank did not come along everyday. Only 260 out of a potential 7058 tanks had been produced so far, and if GD could turn the program around, it might be very profitable. Lewis, therefore, was faced with the difficult choice of whether to further tie General Dynamics to the military or pursue an alternative strategy which would move the company back towards management's long-standing goal of balancing military and commercial earnings.

REFERENCES

Aviation Week & Space Technology, April 6, 1981, pp. 57–58.

Aviation Week & Space Technology, April 27, 1981, pp. 200–201.

Barron's, April 6, 1981, pp. 11 ff.

Barron's, August 30, 1982, pp. 37 ff.

Barron's, February 7, 1983, pp. 16 ff.

Business Week, July 11, 1970, pp. 17–18.

Business Week, April 15, 1972, pp. 38–39.

Business Week, June 3, 1972, pp. 74–75.

Business Week, July 1, 1974.

Business Week, February 3, 1975, pp. 58–59.

Business Week, April 6, 1981, pp. 33–34.

Business Week, July 13, 1981, p. 32.

Business Week, May 3, 1982, pp. 102–106.

Business Week, June 28, 1982, p. 54.

Business Week, September 13, 1982, pp. 39–40.

Business Week, March 31, 1986, pp. 50–54.

Chrisman, J. J., "Note on the Defense Electronics Industry," University of Georgia, Athens, 1982.

Chrysler Corporation, *Annual Reports,* 1980–1983.

Chrysler Corporation, *Report to Shareholders,* 1980–1981.

Cunningham, R., Dampier, J., Fuqua, A., Gill, E., Pannell, D., and Turner, L., "General Dynamics Corporation," University of Georgia, Athens, 1984.

Forbes, October 15, 1964, pp. 16–17.

Forbes, May 11, 1981, pp. 199–200.

Fortune, February 22, 1986, p. 7.

Fox, J. R., with Field, J. L., *The Defense Management Challenge: Weapons Acquisition* (Cambridge, Mass.: Harvard Business School Press, 1988).

Gardner, M., *Aerospace Defense Outlook* (New York: American Express, March 17, 1983).

General Dynamics, *Annual Reports,* 1974–1984.

General Dynamics, *10-K Reports,* 1974–1982.

Gilmore, J. S., and Coddington, J. S., "Diversification Guides for Defense Firms," *Harvard Business Review.* May-June 1966, pp. 144–159.

Hanisee, R. M., *Defense Electronics Highlights* (Los Angeles: Amdec Securities, April 16, 1982).

LTV, *Annual Reports,* 1980–1981.

Moody's Industrial Manual, "General Dynamics, 1968–1982."

Nisbet, P. H., *Aerospace/Defense Review: Current Events Continue to Favor Defense Industry Fundamentals* (New York: Bache, August 25, 1982).

Scherer, F. M., *The Weapons Acquisition Process: Economic Incentives* (Boston: Harvard University Graduate School of Business Administration, 1964).

Shapiro, G. D., *General Dynamics Corporation—The Defense Department's "Prime" Contractor* (New York: Salomon Brothers, June 24, 1982).

Teledyne, *Annual Reports.* 1980–1981.

The Wall Street Journal, February 18, 1981, p. 29.

The Wall Street Journal, April 2, 1981, p. 6.

The Wall Street Journal, April 20, 1981, p. 1.

The Wall Street Journal, November 18, 1981, p. 4.

The Wall Street Journal, November 23, 1981, p. 4.

The Wall Street Journal, December 10, 1981, p. 56.

The Wall Street Journal, January 6, 1982, p. 46.

The Wall Street Journal, January 8, 1982, p. 6.

The Wall Street Journal, January 20, 1982, p. 4.

The Wall Street Journal, January 22, 1982, p. 2.

The Wall Street Journal, January 25, 1982, p. 2.

The Wall Street Journal, January 28, 1982, p. 2.

The Wall Street Journal, February 8, 1982, p. 35.

The Wall Street Journal, February 17, 1982, p. 4.

The Wall Street Journal, February 22, 1982, p. 14.

The Wall Street Journal, March 17, 1982, p. 37.

The Wall Street Journal, May 18, 1984, pp. 1 ff.

The Wall Street Journal, January 8, 1987, p. 15.

APPENDIX 1: LTV CORPORATION

■ ──────────────────────────────── ■

LTV was a large industrial company, operating primarily in steel, energy, defense aerospace, and ocean shipping. It was the third-largest producer of steel in the United States. In 1981 steel accounted for 59% of LTV's sales; energy, 26%; aerospace, 10%; and shipping, 5%. Exhibit 14 summarizes LTV's operations by business segment for 1980 and 1981.

LTV had an outstanding year in 1981. Sales were up 30% from 1980 to $7.5 billion, and net income had more than doubled to a record $386 million, largely due to the boom in the oil and gas exploration industry, to which LTV's energy division supplied drilling and production equipment. Much of LTV's steel business was also oil field–oriented.

Well positioned for an acquisition in 1981, LTV management was trying to become less reliant on steel. They were looking to the potential high-growth areas of energy and aerospace. With this in mind they had acquired Wilson Oil Rig Manufacturing earlier in the year. They had also unsuccessfully tried to acquire Grumman Corporation, a large aerospace company.

LTV was an active defense contractor. Their military contracts totaled $510 million in 1980, making them the 25th-largest defense contractor. Most of the products produced by the company's aerospace division were defense-oriented, such as the A-7 plane and the multiple launcher rocket system (MLRS), which was just beginning full-scale production. LTV also produced antisatellite rockets, space shuttle parts, fuselages for the B1-B bomber, and various electronic products and services.

LTV Corporation: Business Segment Contributions, 1980–1981 (dollars in millions)

Exhibit 14

	1981	1980
Net Sales		
Steel	4786	3800
Energy products and services	2081	1218
Aerospace/defense	797	652
Ocean shipping	457	413
Intersegment eliminations	(610)	(340)
Total sales	7511	5743
Operating Profits		
Steel	336	69
Energy products and services	220	114
Aerospace/defense	39	58
Ocean shipping	29	36
Total operating profits	624	277
Identifiable Assets		
Steel	2925	2696
Energy products and services	755	466
Aerospace/defense	369	333
Ocean shipping	280	230
Corporate and other	73	51
Intersegment eliminations	(69)	(55)
Discontinued operations	—	105
Total assets	4333	3826

Source: LTV, *Annual Reports,* 1980–1981.

APPENDIX 2: TELEDYNE, INC.

Teledyne, Inc., was a diversified company based in Los Angeles, California. Exhibit 15 summarizes Teledyne's operations by business segment for 1980 and 1981. Teledyne enjoyed a good year in 1981. Sales were up 10% from 1980 to $4.3 billion, and net income had increased 20% to $412 million. The company had a strong cash position, had low debt, and, because of its wide diversification, was insulated from the adverse effects of changing business cycles in any one industry. Teledyne's divisions produced a wide array of products: diesel and turbine engines, machine tools, welding equipment, oil-drilling and exploration equipment, tungsten coatings for cutting tools, titanium alloys, audio speakers, and Water-Pik shower accessories, to name but a few.

In 1980 Teledyne ranked 33rd among defense contractors, with almost $400 million in military sales. They had two prime defense programs: remotely piloted planes (RPV) for unmanned flight testing and target practice; and diesel and turbine engines for a variety of military vehicles, including the M60 tanks assembled by Chrysler Defense, Inc.

The GM design for the M1 tank, which had lost out to the Chrysler design in 1976, had used a diesel engine designed by Teledyne. With the M1's turbine engines currently experiencing so many problems, Congress had asked Teledyne to submit an advanced turbo-charged version of the original M1 diesel engine design. Critics argued that the turbine engine was not doing the job. Army officials, however, were not eager to redesign the tank to incorporate a new engine. They argued that long delays would result, at an additional cost of $300 million. It was a long shot, but if Teledyne could acquire overall responsibility for the M1 program (by buying the profitable Chrysler Defense), it would have a much stronger lobbying position with the Army. Hence, for Teledyne, the Chrysler Defense acquisition was a potentially attractive opportunity.

Teledyne, Inc.: Business Segment Contributions, 1980–1981

Exhibit 15

	1981	1980
Net Sales and Revenues		
Industrial	1204	1017
Specialty metals	870	899
Aviation and electronics	865	727
Consumer	299	284
Total sales	3238	2927
Insurance and finance	1104	985
Total revenues	4342	3912
Operating Profits		
Industrial	216	156
Specialty metals	148	147
Aviation and electronics	112	86
Consumer	41	36
Total operating profits	517	425
Identifiable Assets		
Industrial	354	333
Specialty metals	281	274
Aviation and electronics	197	179
Consumer	71	79
Unconsolidated subsidiaries	1464	1420
Corporate	501	267
Total assets	2868	2552

Source: Teledyne, *Annual Reports,* 1980–1981.

Note: Insurance and finance interests are unconsolidated.

Browning-Ferris Industries, Inc.

Robert McGlashan, University of Houston at Clear Lake; Timothy Singleton, North Georgia College

The company has become more and more involved in the public, political and regulatory arenas [1].

Harry J. Phillips, Sr., September 7, 1988

In a double fiscal 1988 milestone, Browning-Ferris Industries reached $2 billion in revenues, and Harry J. Phillips, Sr., Chairman and CEO . . . stepped aside.

Browning-Ferris Industries
1989 Annual Report

In 1988, a barge carrying tons of New York garbage journeyed the high seas and traveled thousands of miles, seeking a final resting place for its polluted cargo. Initially, the barge and its contents became an international joke and an American embarrassment, as the world witnessed the wanderings of this peripatetic waste. Far more important, however, was the fact that this event focused on a significant problem, as it heightened the American public's consciousness to the seriousness of waste disposal and created an awareness of an associated multibillion-dollar industry.

Later that year, William D. Ruckelshaus, former Director of the Environmental Protection Agency (EPA), was elected Chairman and Chief Executive Officer of Browning-Ferris Industries, Inc. (BFI), the nation's second-largest solid and industrial hazardous waste company, with interests throughout the United States and abroad.

Ruckelshaus inherited the leadership of an extremely successful corporation, and it will be his responsibility to lead it into the 1990s and beyond. He has already acknowledged that the industry is operating in "a climate of escalating public demand and concern for their safety and protection of their environment" [2]. Government intervention is likely to become more stringent in response to public demand; competition could become intense; and public attitude provides the ultimate complication. After all, garbage by any other name is still garbage; it must be gathered, processed, compacted, trashed, or otherwise dumped—in someone else's back yard.

Thus, William Ruckelshaus must pursue a strategy that will attract investors and delight stockholders while placating a vocal American public. It's a tough business, and it's a dirty job; but apparently, Ruckelshaus wants to do it.

COMPANY HISTORY

In 1967, two friends reacted to a neighborhood nuisance when garbage collection at their homes appeared to be sporadic and inconvenient. The men took charge, bought an old truck, and were hired to collect the garbage in their Houston subdivision. From this early start, American Refuse Systems evolved, and two years later was sufficiently successful to acquire a controlling interest in Browning-Ferris Machinery Company, a distributor of heavy construction equipment. The company changed its name to Browning-Ferris Industries and embarked upon an impressive expansion program. By the end of 1970, BFI had acquired 16 waste collection firms and set the stage for an ongoing strategy of "growth through acquisition" [3].

In its 20-year existence, BFI has grown into one of the largest U.S. publicly held companies in the waste services industry. Though company literature claims its primary business continues to be the collection and disposal of solid wastes both for residential and industrial customers, expansion has catapulted BFI into diversity. Today, interests include chemical and hazardous wastes, medical/infectious waste disposal, and asbestos abatement.

Browning-Ferris Industries maintains its corporate headquarters in Houston, Texas, but its 360 subsidiaries and affiliates operate in locations throughout the United States and foreign countries on every developed continent. The company's growth took place under the leadership of Harry J. Phillips, Sr. (1977–1988), and by the end of fiscal year 1988, BFI had total assets of $2.3 billion and had produced a net profit of $227 million on sales of $2.1 billion [4].

On October 1, 1988, William D. Ruckelshaus assumed the leadership of Browning-Ferris Industries.

THE U.S. GOVERNMENT AND THE ENVIRONMENT

In 1965, with the passage of the Solid Waste Disposal Act, the U.S. Congress recognized the threat posed by wastes to water and land resources and to human health [5]. By the end of the decade, public awareness of a polluted environment was apparent, and in 1970, the Environmental Protection Agency (EPA), under the leadership of William D. Ruckelshaus, was formed to monitor and enforce the steady stream of laws that would follow in the decade of the seventies. Most significant of these was the 1976 Resource Conservation and Recovery Act (RCRA) that gave the EPA the authority to identify hazardous waste materials and to establish standards to which facilities must adhere in their treatment, storage, disposal, and transportation of those materials [6].

In 1978, the Love Canal disaster caused the evacuation of dozens of families from a contaminated section of New York State and drove the problem of hazardous waste to the forefront of American consciousness. In response, Congress appropriated $1.6 billion for the 1980 Comprehensive Environmental Response, Compensation and Liability Act (CERCLA), commonly known as the Superfund, to be administered by the EPA to clean up 1200 previously identified, abandoned toxic-waste sites [7].

In the early years of the Reagan administration, governmental influence on private industry was de-emphasized, a policy that placed severe constraints on the EPA's effectiveness. At the same time, the EPA's credibility was being heavily scrutinized, primarily as a result of the leadership of Anne Gorsuch Burford and Rita Lavell [8]. In 1983, however, Reagan selected Ruckelshaus to lead the EPA once again, in the expectation that he could revitalize its programs.

BFI OPERATIONS

Browning-Ferris Industries uses a decentralized management structure which the company feels allows it to remain focused on its primary business of solid waste collection and disposal but allows it also to diversify quickly [9]. (Exhibit 1.)

SOLID WASTE COLLECTION

Waste disposal is considered by many to be virtually a recessionproof industry, averaging 15 percent annual growth [10], and Browning-Ferris has capitalized on the technology that has created a "throwaway mentality" in American society. By the late 1960s, government intervention and numerous clean air acts had begun to affect the garbage disposal business. Garbage collection was no longer simply a matter of gathering refuse, carrying it out of town, and dumping it in open ground to be burned; now, it had become "solid waste management" that demanded a major capital investment and the ability to adhere to increasingly stringent laws and regulations [11].

BFI found that many small family businesses were willing to sell, rather than cope with numerous changes and government red tape. By 1973, BFI had acquired 157 subsidiaries and net income reached $15 million [12].

Among those early acquisitions were five companies owned by Harry Phillips, who joined BFI in 1970 and guided the company as its Chairman from 1977 to 1988. During Phillips's tenure, BFI's collection from businesses and industry comprised approximately 59 percent of BFI's annual revenues, and BFI's commitment to commercial and industrial solid waste collection remained the foundation of its services. By 1988, waste disposal subsidiaries were responsible for residential contracts to provide service to more than 4.5 million customers [13].

BFI's growth has depended largely on its concentration on and development of landfills; and by the end of 1988, the organization and its subsidiaries owned,

Exhibit 1   **Corporate Management and Operations**

Officers

William D. Ruckelshaus	John E. Drury
Chairman of the Board	President and Chief Executive Officer
Chief Operating Officer	
	Harry J. Phillips, Jr.
Norman A. Myers	Executive Vice President
Vice Chairman	Solid Waste Operations
Chief Marketing Officer	North America
4 Senior Vice Presidents	Secretary
8 Vice Presidents	Treasurer

Seven Board Committees

Audit	Finance	Pension Benefit
Compensation	Nominating	Strategic Planning
Executive		

14 Divisions (each headed by a Divisional Vice President)

Asbestos Abatement	Medical Waste Systems
Corporate Finance	Operations and Training
Engineering Services	Portable Services
Environmental Affairs	Public Affairs
Government and Industry Affairs	Recycling Systems
Landfill Operations	Risk Management/Loss Control
Marketing and Sales	Street Sweeping

Other Divisions

International Operations	Victor H. Webb, Vice President
	Mark P. Lowrey, Vice President
America Ref-Fuel Company	Clifford F. Jessberger, President
(Joint Venture)	
CECOS International	Robert V. Price, President
Browning-Ferris Overseas, Inc.	Arthur W. Johnson, President and CEO
Browning-Ferris Services (U.K.) Ltd.	Gerald F. Murphy, Managing Director

Source: Browning-Ferris Industries, *1988 Annual Report.*

leased, or operated 180 sanitary landfills. Some are used both by the company's collection companies and by competitors from the private sector and municipal sanitation services [14].

Currently, the entire industry must deal with proposed regulations that could eventually close a third of the nation's commercial and city landfills. At Browning-Ferris, Michael Lawlor, Vice President of Landfill Operations, claims that the company is heeding community opposition but is predicting the opening of 30 new landfills in the next three years [15]; this, in conjunction with the expansion of existing sites, will double the company's capacity.

Indeed, as recently as January 1989, it was noted that Browning-Ferris might actually become a "beneficiary of the landfill crisis" [16] which was promulgated by spiraling real estate prices in many areas and resistance by communities toward having new acreage designated for this purpose. With insight, however, BFI has been spending about $200 million annually to acquire and develop new sites. In addition, the company has acted to combat impending federal regulations and could garner even higher returns on their landfill assets if competing operators divest rather than conform to more stringent government regulations [17].

Such expansion can be a tedious challenge, as exemplified by BFI's recent venture near Memphis, Tennessee, which required eight governmental approvals or permits, six public hearings, and consultants with 11 separate specialties prior to completion. The site, however, complies with all existing and contemplated regulations [18].

Meanwhile, BFI must try harder or settle for second place in the solid waste business. Waste Management retains the profit/size leadership role. Though solid waste management is currently the company's acknowledged major strength, alternative challenges abound. Achieving continued growth and profit must be reconciled with the undeniable demands of increasing governmental regulations and increased public awareness. It appears doubtful, however, that solid waste can sustain the company's incredible growth into and beyond the next decade [19]; and William Ruckelshaus must look to the future.

HAZARDOUS (CHEMICAL AND TOXIC) WASTE

In 1983, Browning-Ferris broadened the scope of its services by acquiring CECOS International, Inc., the first private company to be involved in remedial action at the Love Canal chemical dump site. CECOS functions as an independent corporation, operates a variety of facilities throughout the United States, and has assumed essentially all collection, processing, and disposal service for BFI's chemical and hazardous waste customers [20].

However, the path to hazardous waste glory is fraught with pitfalls and problems, both for the industry and for Browning-Ferris. Though many Americans appear to understand and even forgive the seamier side of the hazardous waste industry [21]—one that is no stranger to accusations of bribery and corruption—it is less accepting of close proximity to a disposal site. If it is difficult to woo a skeptical American public to support maneuvering of solid waste, the same task in terms of hazardous waste is awesome, if not impossible. When debating the placement of landfills or other facilities to deal with toxic and chemical waste, few would disagree with the generally held sentiment: Not in *my* back yard (the NIMBY syndrome).

In 1983, BFI's entry into the hazardous waste business was hailed as a positive step for the company, particularly in light of "an improving legislative climate" [22] and BFI's participation in a $1.6 million federal appropriation for hazardous waste cleanup. The following year, CECOS predicted a 15–20 percent increase in sales as the U.S. government renewed its efforts to clean up hazardous wastes as a result of the public's growing concern, while increasingly more businesses—both large and small—came under regulatory scrutiny [23].

Since 1984, Browning-Ferris has experienced a series of setbacks in its hazardous waste operation, as revenues from CECOS have fallen 19 percent, primarily because regulatory problems have led to temporary shutdowns and slowdowns at two of its three hazardous waste sites. In 1985, state and federal agencies repeatedly closed down BFI's hazardous waste landfill in Ohio, and in the same year, the company was charged with criminally dumping contaminated water into a nearby creek—an accusation denied by BFI's management

[24]. A year later, BFI reported a $2.5 million loss for its hazardous waste division [25]; in 1987 the company was a target of "grand juries in Alabama, Tennessee, Ohio, Arizona, California, and possibly other states" [26]; and the current BFI *Annual Report* informed the stockholders that "CECOS International underwent a troublesome year in fiscal 1988." Thus, in the last five years, BFI appears to have fallen victim to those very regulations that it had once seen as a major key to the company's future growth.

Regardless, BFI seems to have made a commitment to hazardous waste, and as recently as September 1988, Harry Phillips, Sr., acknowledged that the company was considering making a bid for Environmental Systems Company, a waste incineration and cleanup company. In addition, BFI has invested heavily in American Ecology Corporation, the leading operator of low-level radioactive waste dumps [27].

Apparently, Ruckelshaus supports the company's planned commitment in this area, though he is not unmindful of BFI's problems in hazardous waste, acknowledging that to be successful in that area, BFI will have to be "very, very, pure" [28]. As have other organizations in the industry, BFI has embarked upon a vigorous public relations campaign, in an attempt to convince the public of a predominant concern for the environment and to gain support. In addition to recruiting former professional hockey star Derek Sanderson to address groups about his personal struggle with "toxic waste"—alcohol and drugs—the company has launched a new and hopefully persuasive slogan: BFI Cares [29].

But William Ruckelshaus will have to face the reality that the U.S. government and state officials demand more than slogans and speeches. In late 1988, CECOS was denied a permit in Louisiana because of groundwater contamination, and the company has been described as "the Amish of the hazardous-waste industry—they're still using buggies, whips and wagons" [30].

It will take a determined, charismatic, and influential leader to convince America that Bob Price, President of CECOS, is offering more than support for BFI's public relations program when he claims that his division "runs the most . . . secure landfills in the country" [31].

MEDICAL WASTE SYSTEMS

In the late 1980s, infectious and pathological wastes emerged as one of the newest environmental and social concerns. In 1986, Browning-Ferris entered the field of infectious waste treatment and disposal with the purchase of two tiny companies—and did $3.5 million in business [32]. Within a year, BFI Medical Waste Systems was conducting collection services from 46 different locations and had established 15 regional facilities to treat the collected wastes [33]. By the end of fiscal year 1988, revenue from medical waste services reached an annualized rate of $50 million, and the company currently serves a 42-state market from its 18 treatment centers [34].

The need for responsible and environmentally sound treatment and disposal of medical waste was reaffirmed in the summer of 1988, when hypodermic needles washed up on New Jersey coastlines, and medical waste appeared on seashores as far apart as the Gulf Coast and the Pacific Ocean in Southern California. Public outrage was immediate, and politicians rushed to regulate infectious waste [35]. In November 1988, a new federal law went into effect, requiring that medical waste be traceable from its point of generation to final disposal; but Browning-Ferris was prepared. Earlier in the year, the company had implemented a system of tracking to provide just such "cradle to grave" records [36]. In addition, BFI is the only commercial firm to participate in the EPA's development of guidelines for infectious waste disposal [37].

Medical waste disposal does not appear to be a diminishing industry. Large hospitals, research facilities, and small clinics are becoming increasingly more alert to the dangerous consequences of the by-products of their industry. Cancer clinics generate huge quantities of chemotherapy-related waste (both as residual therapeutic chemicals and the waste excreted by humans after treatment); pathology laboratories must dispose of infectious waste products from patients; and nuclear pharmaceuticals are now part of the armamentarium used in treating patients and require special handling and disposal.

With the right laws in place, Harry Phillips, Sr., has predicted that the infectious waste market will grow to $1 billion annually in five years [38]; thus, it appears that William Ruckelshaus has inherited at least one potential star.

FACING THE FUTURE

While BFI has never abandoned its "roots" and still maintains a thriving and sophisticated residential curbside collection division, its phenomenal growth reflects a company far from content to rest on its laurels. In addition to its three major components—solid waste, chemical waste, and infectious waste—BFI now has operations in seven related or semirelated services: resource recovery (waste-to-energy) plants, portable services, public transportation services, street sweeping, transfer stations, asbestos abatement, and recycling. It would seem, to paraphrase an old cliche, that they've got *most* of the bases covered.

■ Resource Recovery (Waste-to-Energy)

In 1984, studies indicated that the overall market for trash collection and landfill was expected to grow at only 4 percent per year through 1989 [39]. BFI, looking for future alternatives, joined forces with Air Products and Chemicals, Inc., of Allentown, Pennsylvania, establishing the American Ref-Fuel Company, to market waste-to-energy facilities. The company snared the exclusive North American rights to utilize the mass-burning technology of a West German company, allowing it to use a proven technique for converting the combustible portions of solid waste to steam and/or electricity [40].

However, four years later, American Ref-Fuel has yet to complete its first large-scale recovery system, though BFI indicates that operations are due to begin in 1989 at the American Ref-Fuel facility in Hempstead, New York. In addition, a second site is under construction in New Jersey, and negotiations on four other facilities are underway.

In 1984, Harry Phillips, Sr., predicted that within ten years, up to 10 percent of BFI's revenue would result from such waste-to-energy plants [41]. William Ruckelshaus has just half that time to convert this prediction into a reality—though an outside company has shown interest in the purchase of American Ref-Fuel. At this time, discussions are continuing.

■ Recycling

A little more than a decade ago, gathering materials for recycling was often viewed by the American public as a means for community or youth groups to raise funds, rather than as a potential profit center for a major corporation. Today, recycling is one of BFI's rapidly expanding divisions [42], aimed at the limitless amount of household waste. The company indicates that the average household generates almost 720 pounds of recoverables (waste materials that can be recycled) annually, and BFI appears to view this opportunity as a natural complement to its residential garbage collection service. By the end of 1988, six recycleries were in operation, with several more in the planning stage, while a major contract had allowed expansion as far as Alberta, Canada.

Yet the paradoxical nature of recycling could present BFI's management with the need to resolve a major contradiction: While recycling is, intellectually, a socially acceptable alternative to the use of garbage dumps, the success of the program is dependent on the cooperation of a public that must be persuaded that there is nothing distasteful about sorting its trash; that investing the time to participate in the program is preferable to dumping everything into the closest landfill; and that the social benefits of recycling are far more important than the resulting corporate profits for Browning-Ferris.

■ Asbestos Abatement

From pre–World War II through the early 1970s, an estimated 300 million tons of asbestos was used in construction [43]. Ultimately, researchers pointed to asbestos fibers as a possible health hazard, and public concern focused on this newly identified danger. In 1986, the Asbestos Hazard Emergency Response Act (AHERA) required all school districts to analyze their asbestos problems and develop management plans either for its removal or containment. A year later, the asbestos abatement market grew by 50 percent, with predictions indicating that it will be a $6 billion industry by 1992 [44]; in 1988, BFI acquired a Houston asbestos abatement company.

Currently, BFI is licensed in 40 states and perceives this as a service opportunity with apparently great growth potential. BFI expects to make a significant penetration of this market in the future.

■ Other Interests

Less significant but thriving BFI interests are street and highway sweeping contracts, including five government contracts acquired by company subsidiaries during 1988; transportation contracts in 32 locations in 6 states, providing services to handicapped and elderly passengers; 55 transfer stations where waste disposal materials can be brought and loaded onto larger trucks to be hauled to their final resting place; and portable services, operating in 56 markets, to provide portable restrooms as conveniences for construction sites and outdoor recreational events.

INTERNATIONAL OPERATIONS

As a multinational organization, Browning-Ferris is in its infancy. As recently as 1980, the company recorded zero profits from international activities; three years later, foreign operations accounted for approximately 5 percent of pretax profits; and in 1984, BFI was pursuing the Saudi Arabian and Kuwaiti markets, as was Waste Management, but still had only one European interest.

In the last five years, however, BFI has expanded its foreign interests and is now represented in Canada and nine countries outside North America.

By the end of 1988, Browning-Ferris reported major inroads into the foreign market, with a 20-year contract in The Netherlands; the acquisition of three companies in Spain; the assumption of 100 percent ownership of a former joint venture plus two new acquisitions in Australia; and entry into a joint venture in Hong Kong, a 15-year contract won against international competition and BFI's first venture into the Far East [45]. Since this contract will be in force when Hong Kong is relinquished by the British to the Chinese, the international implications of such a venture are potentially awesome.

As a multinational organization, BFI will be faced by the same laws, regulations, taxes, and constraints familiar to students of international marketing. Yet the very nature of this company's business raises a myriad of questions for its leadership.

If it is unacceptable to pollute American air, land, and water, is it also wrong to do so in a foreign land where no controlling government agency exists? Since Europeans are permitted to burn about 50 percent of their hazardous waste [46], will BFI's Spanish acquisitions be allowed to follow suit, even though U.S. standards limit burning of such materials to about 15 percent?

During his years as Director of the Environmental Protection Agency, William Ruckelshaus vowed, "We are going after all polluters" [47]. As Mr. Ruckelshaus leads Browning-Ferris toward greater expansion through international markets, will those words return to haunt him?

STRATEGY AND STRIFE

In a way, we really have two separate businesses. One is just operating the $1.2 billion business we have. The other is expanding the company [48].

Harry J. Phillips, Sr.

Since its inception, Browning-Ferris has embarked upon a vigorous program of expansion and is now the second-largest publicly owned waste management organization in the United States. Growth has been largely through acquisition, but with growth has come intense competition, and BFI has sought new strategies to maintain or improve its market share.

Joint ventures, diversification, and international expansion are now very much a part of the BFI scene, but garbage is a very difficult business to manage. Investigations of the waste disposal industry have brought accusations of bribery, organized crime influence, and a variety of suspect business practices. Since 1984, BFI has defended itself against a stream of charges, ranging from unethical practices to violation of antitrust laws.

Browning-Ferris is seemingly in continuous litigation and must employ a small army of lawyers. Within the last year, BFI has pleaded guilty to price-fixing ($1.35 million fine) and faced criminal pollution charges in Ohio; it has paid $2.5 million to settle state and federal suits for environmental violations in Louisiana; and in April 1989, the U.S. Supreme Court rejected BFI's appeal of a lower court's findings ($6.1 million in punitive damages), the result of an antitrust suit in Vermont.

Exhibit 2　　　　　　**William Doyle Ruckelshaus: Biography**

William Doyle Ruckelshaus is Chairman and Chief Executive Officer of Browning-Ferris Industries, Inc., of Houston, Texas. BFI is one of the nation's largest waste disposal companies.

Born in Indianapolis, Indiana, on July 24, 1932, Mr. Ruckelshaus graduated cum laude from Princeton University in 1957 with a Bachelor of Arts degree and obtained his law degree from Harvard University in 1960. He began a career in law with the Indianapolis firm of Ruckelshaus, Bobbitt and O'Connor in 1960 and was associated with the firm for eight years. In addition, he was Deputy Attorney General of Indiana from 1960 through 1965 and Chief Counsel of the Office of Attorney General of Indiana from 1963 to 1965. He served as a minority attorney for the Indiana Senate from 1965 to 1967 and was a member of the Indiana House of Representatives and its majority leader from 1967 to 1969. In 1968, he ran for the Indiana seat in the United States Senate and lost by a narrow margin to Senator Birch Bayh. He was appointed by the President for the years 1969 and 1970 as Assistant Attorney General in charge of Civil Division for the U.S. Department of Justice.

Mr. Ruckelshaus became the United States Environmental Protection Agency's first Administrator when the agency was formed in December 1970, where he served until April 1973. He was appointed by President Reagan to become the fifth EPA Administrator, in which capacity he served until joining Perkins Coie in 1985. His appointment as the fifth EPA Administrator was unanimously confirmed by the United States Senate by a vote of 97–0 in May 1983.

In April 1973, he was appointed acting Director of the Federal Bureau of Investigation, and in the same year was named Deputy Attorney General of the United States Department of Justice.

From 1974 through 1976, Mr. Ruckelshaus was a senior partner in the Washington, D.C., law firm of Ruckelshaus, Beveridge, Fairbanks and Diamond.

In 1976, he joined the Weyerhaeuser Company in Tacoma, Washington, as Senior Vice President for Law and Corporate Affairs, responsible for policy setting and coordination of the company's key external relationships and its legal service function.

Mr. Ruckelshaus serves as a director of several corporations, including Cummins Engine Company, Monsanto Company, and Nordstrom, Inc.

He is a member of the Board of Trustees of The Conservation Foundation/The World Wildlife Fund; the William and Flora Hewlett Foundation; The Urban Institute; The National Wildlife Research Center and Scientist's Institute for Public Information. He is also a member of the Board of Trustees of Princeton University.

He was also the United States Representative to the United Nations World Commission on Environment and Development.

Mr. Ruckelshaus and his wife, Jill, have five children and reside in Houston, Texas

---

Source: Browning-Ferris Industries, Inc., Office of Public Affairs.

Considering BFI's record of incredible growth under the leadership of Harry Phillips, Sr. (1977–1988), his replacement in October 1988 might have raised many an eyebrow. However, the appointment of William Ruckelshaus as Chairman and CEO of Browning-Ferris Industries has placed at the highest management level someone with deep insight into the regulatory process [49], and this should enhance his chances of success as he strives to ensure that BFI stays clean. In addition, his past experience and involvement with the mechanisms of the EPA should help BFI "spot early the regulatory trends that create hot growth areas in the waste management industry" [50] as BFI solidifies its future. (See Exhibit 2.)

CORPORATE FINANCES

Browning-Ferris Industries has not experienced a decline in net earnings since 1975, and in the past five years, its net earnings have increased more than 20 percent per year, from $89 million in 1984 to $226.8 million in 1988. In the same period (1984–1988), revenues have grown by more than 16 percent annually, surpassing the $2 billion mark in fiscal 1988, while earnings per share rose from $0.68 to $1.51 [51]. (See Exhibits 3 and 4.)

In spite of adverse economic conditions in Texas, Louisiana, and other petroleum-producing states during the mid-1980s, BFI's gross profit margin, net profit margin, and return on equity have been consistent and have even exceeded the company's expectations. (See Exhibit 5.) Equally important, however, is the 30 percent annual increase in operating costs (1986–1988), but since such increments are generic to the industry, BFI's management expects to maintain current levels of operating profits through price increases [52].

Selling, general, and administrative expenses have risen significantly, but a major portion of these increases is attributed to the company's continuing acquisitions program, expanded selling and marketing efforts [53], and other strategies aimed at ensuring competitive success.

The company's revenue growth continues to center principally on BFI's solid waste business segment; 80 new acquisitions accounted for approximately half

---

Balance Sheet Statement for Fiscal Years 1985–1988 Browning-Ferris Industries and Subsidiaries: (in thousands) **Exhibit 3**

	1988	1987	1986	1985	1984
Current assets	$ 532,369	$ 507,033	$276,131	$222,893	$209,261
Current liabilities	386,087	311,415	245,600	225,211	204,343
Working capital	146,282	195,618	30,531	(2,318)	4,918
Property and equipment, net	1,428,957	1,193,399	793,145	652,086	554,760
Other assets	110,097	75,572	54,412	53,281	56,221
Net tangible assets	1,685,336	1,464,589	878,088	703,049	615,899
Intangible assets, net	186,691	161,572	101,997	71,624	49,482
Net assets	$1,872,027	$1,626,161	$980,085	$774,673	$665,381
Long-term debt, net of current portion	$ 284,701	$ 245,744	$101,824	$115,621	$107,272
Convertible subordinated debentures	345,000	345,000	—	—	—
Common stockholders' equity (net worth)	1,043,476	874,473	746,867	550,256	465,736
Total capital	1,673,177	1,465,217	848,691	665,877	573,008
Deferred items and other	198,850	160,944	131,394	108,796	92,373
Total	$1,872,027	$1,626,161	$980,085	$774,673	$665,381

Source: Browning-Ferris Industries, *1988 Annual Report.*

Exhibit 4	Browning-Ferris Industries: Consolidated Income Statement (in thousands except for per share amounts)				

	Year Ended September 30,				
	1988	1987	1986	1985	1984
Revenues	$2,067,405	1,656,616	1,328,393	1,144,509	1,000,814
Cost of operations	1,307,037	1,036,784	836,413	729,345	641,475
Gross profit	760,368	619,832	491,980	415,164	359,339
Selling, general and adminis- trative expenses	375,383	296,056	243,077	207,384	189,653
Income from operations	384,985	323,776	248,903	207,780	169,686
Interest expense	37,417	22,361	12,359	11,177	11,641
Interest income	(12,534)	(5,773)	(4,257)	(4,166)	(3,491)
Income before income taxes	360,102	307,188	240,801	200,769	161,536
Income taxes	133,238	135,163	103,948	88,941	72,368
Net income	$ 226,864	$ 172,025	$ 136,853	$ 111,828	$ 89,168
Number of common and common equivalent shares used in comput- ing earnings per share	150,275	149,410	144,006	139,340	137,460
Earnings per common and common equivalent shares	$1.51	$1.15	$0.95	$0.80	$0.68
Cash dividends per common share	$0.48	$0.40	$0.32	$0.27	$0.24

Sources: Browning-Ferris Industries, *Annual Reports,* 1988 and 1986; *Value Line,* December 30, 1988, p. 341.

of the company's 26 percent increase in revenues in 1988. In the same period, the chemical waste segment registered a mere 1 percent increase, reflecting the organization's inability to secure the appropriate permits from state and federal agencies in Ohio [54].

All the company's long-term debt is, by design, at fixed interest rates; however, variable-rate interest could be used, as in the past, for short-term or interim financing needs. In its 1988 *Annual Report,* BFI notes that the company believes that cash provided by operations, the sale of short-term investments, credit agreements, banks and other external sources are more than sufficient for its financing needs.

Additionally, BFI's concern regarding resolution of litigation is minimal, as it declares, "Management believes that the ultimate disposition of these matters will not have a materially adverse effect upon the business or consolidated financial position of the Company" [55].

AND FINALLY...

For 11 years, Harry J. Phillips, Sr., presided over BFI's successes and failures [56], its phenomenal growth in the United States and its development as a multinational corporation, and its metamorphasis from a million-dollar company

| Browning-Ferris Industries: Key Financial Ratios | | | | | Exhibit 5 |

	Year Ended September 30,				
	1988	1987	1986	1985	1984
Gross profit margin	36.8%	37.4%	37.0%	36.3%	35.9%
Income from operations	18.6%	19.5%	18.7%	18.2%	17.0%
Income before income taxes	17.4%	18.5%	18.1%	17.5%	16.2%
Net income	11.0%	10.4%	10.3%	9.8%	8.9%
Pretax, preinterest return on total equity	24.5%	28.0%	34.4%	33.5%	31.3%
Return on common stockholders' equity	23.7%	21.4%	21.7%	22.2%	20.7%
Average net assets per dollar of revenue	$.84	$.79	$.66	$.63	$.63
Current ratio	1.4:1	1.6:1	1.1:1	1.0:0	1.0:0
Days' sales in receivables (trade)	50	49	49	50	53
Long-term indebtedness as a % of total capital	38%	40%	12%	17%	19%
Net tangible assets as a % of long-term indebtedness	268%	248%	862%	608%	575%

Source: Browning-Ferris Industries, *Annual Reports*, 1988 and 1986.

to a billion-dollar enterprise. Following the selection of his successor, Phillips commented, "What I can do for the company is largely done, frankly" [57].

The British writer and philosopher John Ruskin believed that one should always be striving to reach for something slightly beyond one's grasp. Harry J. Phillips, Sr., appears to have been motivated by such a philosophy; and that, for William D. Ruckelshaus, will be the challenge.

REFERENCES

1. Browning-Ferris Industries, *1988 Annual Report.*

2. Ibid.

3. "Cashing in on Trash," *Industry Week,* February 16, 1976, pp. 22–24.

4. Browning-Ferris Industries, *1988 Annual Report.*

5. "Hazardous Waste Cleanup and Disaster Management," *Environment,* vol. 28, no. 3, August 1986, p. 2.

6. "New Law Tackles Hazardous Wastes," *The American City & Life,* vol. 28, no. 3, December 1976, p. 10.

7. "Superfund: The Search for Consistency," *Environment,* vol. 28, no. 3, April 1986, p. 6.

8. "Who Will Clean Up?" *Fortune,* March 17, 1986, p. 99.

9. Browning-Ferris Industries, *1988 Annual Report.*

10. Ibid.

11. "One Man's Garbage," *Forbes,* June 26, 1978, p. 37.

12. Ibid.

13. Browning-Ferris Industries, *1988 Annual Report.*

14. Ibid.

15. "A New Top Broom," *Forbes*, November 28, 1988, p. 202.

16. Joel Galbraith, *Value Line*, December 30, 1988.

17. Ibid.

18. Browning-Ferris Industries, *1988 Annual Report*.

19. "A New Top Broom," *Forbes*, November 28, 1988, p. 202.

20. "BFI Lands a Big One in CECOS International," *Chemical Week*, February 9, 1983, p. 21.

21. "Browning-Ferris: Plowing into Toxic Waste and Overseas Markets," *Business Week*, April 23, 1984, p. 108.

22. "Vast Wasteland," *Barron's/Investment News and Views*, November 21, 1983, p. 64.

23. Ibid.

24. "Par for the Course," *Forbes*, September 9, 1985, p. 70.

25. "Who Will Clean Up?" *Fortune*, March 17, 1986, p. 101.

26. "U.S. Targets Waste Haulers in Big Inquiry," *The Wall Street Journal*, June 4, 1987.

27. "A New Top Broom," *Forbes*, November 28, 1988, p. 202.

28. Ibid.

29. "The Big Haul in Toxic Waste," *Newsweek*, October 3, 1988, p. 39.

30. Ibid.

31. Ibid.

32. "A New Top Broom," *Forbes*, November 28, 1988, p. 200.

33. Browning-Ferris Industries, *1988 Annual Report*.

34. Ibid.

35. "A New Top Broom," *Forbes*, November 28, 1988, p. 202.

36. Browning-Ferris Industries, *1988 Annual Report*.

37. *Medical Waste Systems* (BFI literature).

38. "A New Top Broom," *Forbes*, November 28, 1988, p. 202.

39. "The Big Haul in Toxic Waste," *Business Week*, April 23, 1984, p. 106

40. Browning-Ferris Industries, *Backgrounder* (1989).

41. "Browning-Ferris: Plowing into Toxic Waste and Overseas Markets," *Business Week*, April 23, 1984, p. 106.

42. Browning-Ferris Industries, *1988 Annual Report*.

43. *Residential Curbside Collection of Source Separated Recyclables* (BFI literature).

44. "Cleanup Dollars Flow Like Water, but Industry Is Awash in Problems," *ENR*, March 9, 1989, p. 43.

45. Browning-Ferris Industries, *1988 Annual Report*.

46. "The Hidden Liability of Hazardous-Waste Cleanup," *Technology Review*, vol. 89, no. 2, p. 60.

47. "Powerful New Environmental Agency," *The Oil and Gas Journal*, November 1970, p. 119.

48. "Par for the Course," *Forbes*, September 9, 1985, p. 70.

49. Joel Galbraith, *Value Line*, January 6, 1989, p. 641.

50. "A New Top Broom," *Forbes*, November 28, 1988, p. 202.

51. Browning-Ferris Industries, *1988 Annual Report*.

52. Ibid.

53. Joel Galbraith, *Value Line*, January 6, 1989.

54. Browning-Ferris Industries, *1988 Annual Report*.

55. Ibid.

56. "A New Top Broom," *Forbes*, November 28, 1988, p. 200.

57. Ibid.

Babbitt Brothers Trading Company

Jon Ozmun, Northern Arizona University

Bill Galis stood at the window of his office and gazed out. It was late March 1986. At the moment, the sun shone in a cloudless, brilliant blue Arizona sky. The weather forecast was calling for precipitation, however. Below, on the Flagstaff streets, a mix of early arriving tourists and local residents were on the move, some shopping for Native American rugs, jewelry, or pottery, others just on their way to lunch. Bill was a relative newcomer to Flagstaff. Less than a year before, he had accepted the President and Chief Operating Officer position for the Babbitt Brothers Trading Company (BBTC), a diversified, multimillion-dollar operation doing business throughout the vast but sparsely populated Northern Arizona trade region. Bill's office was located in Flagstaff's Babbitt's Department Store (BDS), one of the seven full-service stores which comprised the Department Store Division of BBTC. It was this division of the business which was on his mind now. During the past year, a majority of his time and energy had been consumed by the problems in this division. In two weeks, Bill would be making a recommendation to the BBTC Board of Directors on an issue that would determine the future of the Babbitt's Department Stores.

Bill began to reflect on the events which had transpired since he had first heard of BBTC. In January 1985, he had received a call from Kermit Halden, President of Halden and Associates (H&A), a consulting firm located in Minnetonka, Minnesota (a suburb of Minneapolis). Halden explained that he was trying to identify candidates who would be interviewed for the President and Chief Operating Officer position of a diversified business in Arizona. Halden further explained that he had gotten Bill's name from a common acquaintance, Jim Hamlin, Vice President of Retail Operations for Smitty's Inc. in Phoenix.

Halden and Hamlin had been business associates years earlier when Halden was the Personnel Manager for Dayton-Hudson. Hamlin knew Bill Galis from their days together at Smitty's, where Galis had been the Vice President of Finance for almost three years (1979–1981). After determining that Galis was interested in learning more about the opening, Halden suggested that they meet for lunch. At the lunch meeting, Halden gave Galis a brief historical sketch of the Babbitt Brothers Trading Company.

BABBITT BROTHERS TRADING COMPANY

The story of BBTC is the story of five imaginative, energetic brothers from Cincinnati, Ohio, who came West in the late 1800s. These brothers had widely diverse interests, but with hard work and dreaming they parlayed a handful of cattle and a small lumber and hardware store into what was, in 1984, a $70 million a year mercantile and ranching empire. Between 1889 and the present, the Babbitts fed, clothed, equipped, transported, entertained, and buried four generations of Arizonans. They also did it more profitably than anyone else.

The year was 1884. After listening to colorful tales of the western United States from a close friend who had just returned from an extended tour, David, George, William, Charles, and Ed Babbitt decided to investigate the West as a future home. Their family had been successful in business in Cincinnati. They were looking for the one best place in the West where they could settle and invest the capital they could collectively realize from the sale of their grocery store and family home and farm. On April 2, 1884, David, the eldest, embarked on an "exploratory journey" to gather information about opportunities and places. After four months of travel, he had eliminated Kansas, Colorado, and Wyoming and had begun to focus on the territories of New Mexico and Arizona. David ended his tour of the West in Tucson. He returned to Cincinnati and spent the next 14 months convincing the other four Babbitt brothers that their future lay in the American Southwest.

In early 1886, David and younger brother William arrived in New Mexico with $20,000. Their intention was to buy a herd of cattle, acquire water rights and grazing permits, and locate near Springer, New Mexico. Conditions had become unfavorable since David's previous visit, so on a tip from a railroad clerk, the brothers set out to investigate Flagstaff and northern Arizona. In Flagstaff, they were able to get the cattle, water, and grazing rights they wanted for $17,640. Within a month, the cattle were branded with the "CO Bar" (for Cincinnati, Ohio) and the Babbitt empire had begun.

After the cattle business had become established, David returned to Cincinnati to marry his childhood sweetheart, Emma VerKamp. Emma's father, a wealthy Cincinnati mercantilist, thought ranching was too risky and that the life would be too harsh for his daughter. He agreed to finance David in a mercantile venture if one became available. Upon his return to Flagstaff with his bride, David encountered a range war and an Apache uprising and decided to look into his father-in-law's offer. The other brothers also believed that it made good business sense to diversify. David's expertise was in the grocery business, but this industry was crowded, so he bought an existing lumber and hardware business. Babbitt's Department Store stands on this location today.

The lumber and hardware business prospered. David expanded the business and in addition offered Flagstaff's only banking services. He eventually founded the Citizen's Bank of Flagstaff in December 1888. On December 31, 1889, David formed a partnership with his four brothers and BBTC was formed. Other significant events in the history of BBTC follow.

1891	The Babbitt store building was enlarged to house the Babbitt Opera Hall, the cultural center of Flagstaff life.
1892–1922	Babbitt's Mercantile stores were opened in Winslow, Williams, Ashfork, Kingman, Oatman, and Yucca. All but the Winslow store were later closed or sold.
1892	The Flagstaff Undertaking Parlor was opened for business.
1893–1905	Babbitt's ranching operations were expanded with the purchase of the Circle S, A-1, Hashknife, and Apache Maid ranches. The Babbitts were shipping cattle eastward to Dodge City, and at one time owned 100,000 acres in five Kansas counties which were used to fatten the cattle.
1904	Flagstaff Ice Plant was built.
1909	Flagstaff's first garage and automobile agency was built.
1918	The loosely organized partnership of 1889 was dissolved and BBTC was incorporated with a capitalization of $5 million.
1928	A new store was built at the Grand Canyon.
1931	A retail lumber yard was opened in Flagstaff.
1955	Thriftway Grocery Stores were opened in Flagstaff and Winslow.
1958–1983	Babbitt's Department Stores were introduced in Page (1958), Cottonwood (1975), Kingman (1978), Prescott (1981), and Yuma (1983).

From its beginnings in 1899 until 1984, BBTC had always had a Babbitt at the top. David Babbitt's two sons, Ray and Joseph, succeeded him in the top management position and this started the tradition. By 1984, Paul Babbitt, Jr., a great-grandson of Charles Babbitt, was CEO and Chairman of the Board of Directors of BBTC.

During the 1970s, BBTC was organized into six divisions: Ranching, Real Estate, Grand Canyon Stores, Home Centers, Trading Posts, and Department Stores. The Grand Canyon Stores consisted of a grocery store, restaurant/cafeteria, and a specialty (hiking, climbing, and general outdoor supplies) store. The Home Centers sold a complete line of building materials, from lumber, to plumbing and electrical supplies, to basic hardware items. The Trading Posts, located on the Indian reservations, supplied the Indians with a variety of food, clothing, and miscellaneous items.

By 1984, annual sales for the six divisions of BBTC had grown to over $70 million. Financial information is shown in Exhibits 1 and 2.

WILLIAM R. (BILL) GALIS

Following the luncheon meeting with Kermit Halden, Bill sent his resume to H&A and became a candidate for the position at BBTC. Within two weeks, he received a call from Halden, who scheduled a formal interview session. During the four-hour interview, Halden went over Bill's resume, gathering in-depth

Exhibit 1

Babbitt Brothers Trading Company: Consolidated Statement of Income for the Year Ended December 31, 1984

Revenues		
Department Stores	$14,628,637	
Trading Posts	3,571,169	
Home Centers	44,226,221	
Grand Canyon Stores	6,684,650	
Ranches	914,417	
Real Estate	1,224,713	
		$71,249,807
Cost of operations		
Department Stores	$16,106,369	
Trading Posts	3,305,392	
Home Centers	41,857,025	
Grand Canyon Stores	5,712,274	
Ranches	551,621	
Real Estate	359,972	
		67,892,653
Income from operations		3,357,154
Other expenses		
General and administrative	$3,772,831	
Net interest	721,506	
Income tax benefit	(773,000)	
		3,721,337
Income (loss) before extraordinary item and cumulative effect of change in accounting principles		(364,183)
Extraordinary item—recovery from termination of employee pension plan		216,000
Cumulative effect of prior years of changing depreciation method		201,215
Net income		$53,032

information on his education, professional experience, and personal life. H&A wrote up the content of the interview session and their appraisal of Bill. These comments and Bill's resume were sent to BBTC along with those of several other candidates. In less than a month, Bill was informed that BBTC wanted to interview him in Flagstaff.

To prepare himself for the interview, Bill asked to be furnished with BBTC financial information for the past three years of operation. To his surprise, he was told that the information was not available. Bill was informed that Touche Ross & Company was conducting a complete audit of BBTC for 1984 and the report was still in process. BBTC agreed to have Touche Ross & Company furnish Bill with any information he needed to form an opinion about the operating and financial performance of BBTC. The information that Bill obtained from Touche Ross & Company was essentially the same as what is shown in Exhibits 1 and 2.

Bill made two trips to Flagstaff in March and April. On the first, he spent a day interviewing with the BBTC CEO and a former Dillard's Department Store

Babbitt Brothers Trading Company: Consolidated Balance Sheet, December 31, 1984

Exhibit 2

Current assets		
Cash	$ 84,611	
Receivables	7,317,213	
Other	2,928,310	
Prepaid expenses	124,595	
Inventories	7,494,791	
Total current assets		$17,949,520
Operating property and equipment		
Land	419,563	
Buildings and improvements	7,132,717	
Furniture and equipment	5,934,971	
Less: Accumulated Depreciation	6,855,262	
Total		6,631,989
Investment and rental property		
Land and rental property	5,547,113	
Less: Accumulated depreciation	3,017,932	
Total		2,529,181
Notes receivable		1,042,215
Total assets		$28,152,905
Current liabilities		
Accounts payable	$2,102,578	
Short-term debt	5,400,000	
Accrued compensation	1,550,085	
Current portion of long-term debt	180,822	
Total Current Liabilities		9,233,485
Long-term debt		1,059,643
Deferred income		767,245
Stockholder's equity		
Preferred and common stock	2,115,200	
Retained earnings	14,977,332	
Total stockholder's equity		17,092,532
Total liabilities and stockholder's equity		$28,152,905

executive who was working as a consultant to BBTC. Bill's wife Diana accompanied him on his second trip to Flagstaff. This visit lasted three days and during that time, Bill and Diana met with other members of the extended Babbitt family and were generally "wined and dined." Bill was then offered the position and asked to make a decision within 30 days. While in Flagstaff for the second interview, Bill was asked to consult on the hiring of a person to fill the position of Company Controller. He interviewed three candidates and recommended one, who was subsequently hired. So even before he had accepted a position with the company, Bill had made his first personnel decision. On May 1, 1985, Galis agreed to a two-year contract to serve as President and Chief Operating Officer (COO) for BBTC.

Bill had a BSC in Accounting from DePaul University and was a registered CPA. He had completed his MBA at the prestigious University of Chicago. After four years as an audit supervisor at Peat, Marwick, Mitchell & Company, he

Exhibit 3   **Employment History of William R. (Bill) Galis**

Time Period	Firm	Title
1953–1956	Peat, Marwick, Mitchell & Company	Audit Supervisor
1956–1968	Helene Curtis Industries	Corporate Controller
1968–1977	Fingerhut Corporation	Senior Vice President, Corporate CFO
1977–1979	Council Laboratories, Inc.	President (part owner)
1979–1981	Smitty's Supervalu, Inc.	Vice President Finance and Operations
April 1981–July 1982	Hub Distributing, Inc., dba Miller's Outpost Stores	Vice President Finance and Operations
September 1982– January 1985	Team Central Inc.	Executive Vice President (part owner)

moved steadily to positions of higher responsibility in the consumer products industry, as is summarized in Exhibit 3.

The President and COO position at BBTC was interesting to Bill for a number of reasons. During his employment with Smitty's he had lived in Phoenix and had enjoyed the Arizona climate and lifestyle. But more important, Bill believed that running the diversified operations of this historic Arizona family business would be challenging and rewarding and that he had the training and experience to do the job. The Home Center and Cattle Ranching Divisions were the most interesting to Bill because these would be new and unique challenges.

During the interviews and negotiations that led up to his accepting the position, Bill became aware that his first priority would be to deal with the problems surrounding the ailing Department Store Division. He needed to either make the division profitable within a short time horizon or develop an alternative course of action.

THE FIRST YEAR

Bill had learned enough during the interview process to determine an action agenda for his first few weeks on the job. Even before arriving in Flagstaff in mid-May, he developed the following "must do" list:

1. Begin the process of developing an up-to-date management information system.
2. Familiarize himself with the management, operations, and facilities of the six Divisions of BBTC (Real Estate, Ranching, Department Stores, Grand Canyon Stores, Home Center Stores, and Trading Posts).
3. Develop an in-depth understanding of the Department Store Division by visiting each of the seven stores to determine strengths and weaknesses in terms of its market, personnel, and facilities.

Based on what he found in agenda items 2 and 3 above, he would decide what immediate actions would be taken and what he would recommend to the Board of Directors regarding the Department Stores Division. Bill gave himself six weeks for his "must do" list and set July 1 as his deadline to have these activities accomplished.

UPGRADING THE MANAGEMENT INFORMATION SYSTEM

During the interview process, Bill became aware that the quality and degree of detail coming from the management information system (MIS) was totally inadequate to support rational, objective decision making. For example, separate historical income statements were not available for each division. As a result, it was not possible to accurately determine which of the divisions were profitable, which were not, and why. Within the Department Store Division, detail was unavailable to determine which lines (e.g., furniture, ladies fashions) were generating profits and which were not. This lack of accurate, detailed financial information would be a severe handicap in making initial assessments as well as follow-up decisions. In an attempt to eliminate this severe weakness, the following actions were taken:

• The Corporate Controller (whom Bill had hired during his second on-site interview) and the MIS Director were assigned the task of generating separate income statements for each of the seven stores. Data for the first five months of the year would be estimated using corporate-level financial information. This would be combined with actual information on store revenues and expenditures for the remainder of 1985.

• The Retail Sales Analyst (hired in April 1985) was assigned the task of building a computerized system for determining the sales volume and gross margin for each item in each product line for each location. This was done on a PC using sales tickets, manual reports, and personal interviews. Bill knew that this information would be crude, but it would be a start and set the wheels in motion for the development of the system he would need for the future.

The target date for producing the separate income statements was January 1986. For the information on sales volume and gross margin by store and product line, the goal was to have 1985 information for one store (Flagstaff) compiled by early 1986.

THE DIVISIONS

During a three-week period in May, Bill held a series of meetings with each manager of the six divisions and visited all of the facilities. He determined that some shifting of management responsibilities was in order for the Real Estate and Trading Post Stores Divisions. Ranching, Grand Canyon Stores, and Home Center Stores operations were operating in a satisfactory manner and could be allowed to continue in the short run without changes. Bill's first session with the General Merchandise Manager (head of the Department Store Division) confirmed his initial impressions made during the interview process. This division was being badly managed and would require most of his attention and energy in the months to come.

THE DEPARTMENT STORE DIVISION

The BBTC Board of Directors and Division Managers who were familiar with sketchy company financial information believed that the Department Store Division had been and was continuing to lose money. Lack of financial information made it impossible to determine which locations had been profitable and which had suffered losses and the magnitude of profits and losses. Shortly after Bill arrived, an audited income statement for 1984 was made available. The quality of the accounting information was so poor that it took the accounting firm over five months to produce the audit. The results showed that the Department Store Division lost almost $1.5 million during 1984 (see Exhibit 4). The losses could be traced to poor performance in gross margins and sales performance. BDS gross margin for 1984 was just 27.5%, compared to the industry average of 40%, and sales performance was $86 per square foot of store space, compared to the industry average of $140.

Bill suspected that a major reason for the poor performance of the division was inadequate leadership by the General Merchandise Manager (GMM). The GMM was in his early sixties and had been with Babbitt's Department Stores for 17 years. He had retired in 1984, but a satisfactory replacement could not be found so he had been rehired just a few months before Bill arrived. Bill and the GMM both agreed that he did not have the energy and drive to oversee the reorganization ahead. With no hard feelings, the GMM reentered retirement.

On a structural level, Bill was concerned with the number of merchandise "buyers" employed. Based on his experience at Miller's Outpost, he was convinced that 18 buyers were excessive in a department store chain that annually sold less than $15 million. With the idea that he should try to understand why

---

Exhibit 4   **Babbitt Brothers Trading Company: Department Store Division Income Statements, 1984 and 1985**

	1984	*1985*
Sales	$14,622,766	$10,204,589
Cost of goods	10,598,367	6,484,627
Gross margin	4,024,399	3,719,962
Other income	5,871	104,971
Total income	4,030,270	3,824,933
Total expenses	3,821,881	3,136,269
Store operations income	208,389	688,664
Cost of support operations	1,686,121	1,439,123
Income (loss)	($ 1,477,732)	($ 750,459)

the sale-to-buyer ratio was so low and what he might do about it, Bill interviewed the entire staff. From these interviews, the following picture developed:

- Buyers did not travel to "markets." Instead, they solicited information and advice from the sales representatives who called on them in their Flagstaff offices. Merchandise for all seven Department Stores was purchased in this manner.
- Buyers did not regularly visit each of the individual stores to interact with managers and salespersons.
- Buyers were not informed of customer complaints regarding items that were within their sphere of responsibility.
- Buyers were generally unhappy with the way that their jobs were structured.
- The General Merchandise Manager, who developed this system and supervised the 18 buyers, saw no reason for any changes.

Bill then visited the seven individual Department Stores in order to assess the strengths and weaknesses of the markets, facilities, and the personnel. Demographic information that was available for the seven markets is shown in Exhibit 5. A summary of information for individual store facilities is shown in Exhibit 6. In addition, Bill made the following determinations: Each store needed some degree of renovation, either general remodeling or replacement of

---

Babbitt Brothers Trading Company: Demographic Information for Individual Markets　　　　　　　　**Exhibit 5**

Area	1980	1985	Estimated 1990	Median Household Income	Population Characteristics
Cottonwood	4,550	5,025	5,975	$16,114	26% in 65 years and over
Flagstaff	34,743	38,247	44,610	16,867	47% in 20–44 years
Kingman	10,249	10,515	11,041	16,413	24% in 35–54 years
Page	4,907	6,469	7,665	10,812	—
Prescott	20,055	21,336	24,000	19,935	Median age is 55 years
Winslow	7,921	8,240	9,295	14,592	29% in 20–39 years
Yuma	42,481	49,980	52,795	15,770	36% in 20–44 years
United States				19,902	38% in 20–44 years

Other information

Arizona population grew from 2,224,000 in 1974 to 3,135,000 in 1984.

Employment

Cottonwood	Wholesale retail trade
Flagstaff	Government (Northern Arizona University), Peabody Coal Company (administrative offices), W. L. Gore (medical equipment manufacturer), tourism, wholesale retail trade
Kingman	Tourism, wholesale retail trade
Page	Navajo Generating Station (coal-fired electricity), tourism
Prescott	Government, tourism, wholesale retail trade
Winslow	Santa Fe Railroad, tourism, wholesale retail trade
Yuma	Military (U.S. Marine Corps Air Station, U.S. Army Proving Ground), agriculture, wholesale retail trade

---

Exhibit 6   **Information on Individual Stores**

Store	Store Established	Size (Square feet)	Store Location and Condition/Ownership	Department Store Competition
Cottonwood	1975	15,000	Poor; strip shopping center/BBTC	None
Flagstaff	1887	42,000	Good; downtown/BBTC	Penney, K Mart, Sears
Kingman	1978	18,000	Poor; downtown/leased	Penney, Sears catalog
Page	1958	13,000	Poor; strip shopping center/BBTC	None
Prescott	1981	32,000	Fair; downtown/leased	Penney, K Mart, Sears
Winslow	1899	11,000	Poor; strip shopping center/BBTC	None
Yuma	1983	40,000	Good, new mall/leased	Penney, Sears

fixtures. A building contractor who consulted for BBTC estimated the costs of the renovations at $800,000. Personnel was a mixed bag; several of the stores had good management and sales clerks, others did not. Two managers (Yuma and Winslow) would need to be replaced. Overall the stores were poorly merchandised primarily due to the lack of input from the buyers. The individual markets were dissimilar in demographics and climate.

With the number and magnitude of the problems, Bill gave strong consideration to making a proposal to the board that the Department Store Division be sold or liquidated. There were several factors mitigating against this, however: First, three of the stores were located in facilities that were owned by other parties and had long-term lease obligations. Second, if the stores in company-owned strip shopping centers (Cottonwood, Page, and Winslow) were closed, there was the problem of subleasing the space to other businesses. The downtown Flagstaff store location, covering almost one-half of a city block, had no alternative use. In fact, businesses were migrating away from downtown in favor of the Flagstaff Mall. Third, there was strong support from the Board of Directors and Babbitt family stockholders for a continuation of the Department Store Division. For many, the department stores were the only part of the diversified business that they could identify with. Fourth, and most compelling, was that in every market served, Babbitt's Department Stores had virtually no direct competition. Bill knew from experience that there were few such opportunities in retailing.

After carefully considering all of the factors involved, Bill decided that a turnaround/reorganization strategy was appropriate for the division. As a first step, he made several personnel changes in the Department Store Division. These changes were designed to improve operations while at the same time reducing administrative overhead. Bill first terminated eight of the buyers. He then reorganized some of the responsibilities of the previous GMM into two new job categories:

Divisional Merchandise Manager 1	Ready-to-Wear Division Junior, Missy, Sportswear Dress Buyer
Divisional Merchandise Manager 2	Mens and Homestore Division Menswear and Furniture Buyer

The two new Divisional Merchandise Managers were promoted from within the buying organization. Both had previously been buyers. The buyers jobs were redefined. All buyers were to become actively involved with store managers and sales personnel. Buyers were to spend at least one day a week visiting stores. Finally, buyers were to attend the "market" which was appropriate to their product line.

Bill then assumed the remaining responsibilities of the GMM and began the process of finding a replacement. In his role as "acting" GMM, he set up a meeting schedule for store managers (once a month) and buyers (once a week). Bill used these meetings to discuss problems, exchange ideas, plan promotions, improve store merchandise offerings, plan markdowns, and work on improving costs and cost controls. He also stressed the importance of developing and maintaining adequate gross margins as opposed to simply generating increased sales revenue. This partial reorganization was completed by the end of June 1985 and was expected to produce significant cost savings.

Bill contacted H&A and asked them to develop a candidate pool for the open GMM position. After a difficult search process that took almost a full year, the position was filled in March 1986. The new GMM was scheduled to begin employment on April 1. He would bring five years of experience managing a 12-unit Tulsa, Oklahoma, retail chain which had gross sales of over $16 million annually.

During the search process, Bill had interviewed six other well-qualified candidates only to be turned down by each. The basic reasons for the candidates' disinterest were the difficulty of the situation, the small size of the store chain, and the lack of alternative employment in the area. Candidates also expressed concern about being able to attract and retain the qualified middle-level managers and buyers who would be essential human resources for the revitalization of the division.

UNANTICIPATED DEVELOPMENT

Early in September 1985, Bill got what was his biggest surprise in his first year at BBTC. A small group from the BBTC Board of Directors informed him that they intended to terminate the present CEO (a member of the Babbitt family) and asked for Bill's approval. Bill explained that he was too new to the company to have formed an opinion on a matter of this magnitude. Further, he explained that he had no problems with the CEO and was still accumulating operating information about BBTC from him. Bill asked that the board members delay action on this issue for 3–6 months to allow him to develop a more substantial foundation regarding the operations of BBTC.

Approximately three months later, the board acted and voted to remove the CEO from his position. The major duties and decision-making responsibilities of the CEO were assumed by a subcommittee of the board, which included Bill. Bill began to make more and more decisions by himself as the months went by. The action to remove the CEO was approved by a majority of the board. The ousted CEO, who retained his position on the board, and another Babbitt family stockholder were quite unhappy with this change. They expressed dissatisfaction with the new management structure and a desire to liquidate their shares of stock in the family corporation. Since ownership of the corporation was "closed" to the Babbitt family and stock was not traded on any market, no easy solution was available to the board for dealing with the dissatisfied stockholders. The two dissatisfied stockholders, in a maverick action not sanctioned by the board, then began a campaign to interest outside buyers in purchasing the company.

DEPARTMENT STORE OPERATIONS, 1985

In January 1986, one of Bill's initial actions paid off. Financial information for the Department Store Division for the previous year became available. This was the first time that separate income statements were produced for each of the seven Department Stores (see Exhibit 7). Not surprisingly, the data showed that the Flagstaff store was the most profitable, followed by the Prescott, Cottonwood, and Kingman. The Page and Winslow operations were about break-even, while the Yuma store showed a loss for the year. The major surprise was that the Prescott store had done so poorly. A comparison of the income statements for 1984 and 1985 showed that although sales revenues had declined sharply in 1985, losses had been cut by almost $750,000 (see Exhibit 4). The drop in sales volume between 1984 and 1985 was due primarily to a "liquidation" pricing policy assumed by the chain in late 1984. For example, gross margin in the holiday selling period was under 15%. In 1985, realistic sales prices were reintroduced. Sales revenues declined, but gross margins increased. The management reorganization and cost-cutting strategies implemented during 1985 had been in effect for only six months of the accounting period, so Bill could anticipate further improvement in 1986.

Since this was the first year that such financial information had been available, it was difficult to make objective assessments concerning individual store performance. The 1985 data became the benchmark for further years' comparisons. A second goal for the management information system was to provide a breakdown of financial information (e.g., dollar value, gross margin) for individual department/product lines for each store. With this level of detail, management could determine the optimal product mix for each location and evaluate buyer and sales performance. The MIS target objective was to have complete detail on department/product lines for one store available at the beginning of 1986. Data for 1985 for the Flagstaff store are shown in Exhibit 8.

Exhibit 7	Babbitt's Department Stores: 1985 Income Statements						
	Cottonwood	*Flagstaff*	*Kingman*	*Page*	*Prescott*	*Winslow*	*Yuma*
Sales	$727,802	$3,349,307	$908,835	$853,305	$1,688,420	$608,611	$2,068,308
Cost of goods	461,932	2,130,602	568,313	584,012	1,049,768	402,861	1,286,639
Gross margin	265,870	1,218,705	340,522	269,012	638,652	205,750	781,669
Other operating income (Expenses)	1,093	96,985	275	61	2,413	155	3,989
Total income	266,963	1,315,690	340,797	269,354	641,065	205,905	785,658
Variable expenses	149,295	630,760	223,406	166,504	399,221	119,335	499,025
Fixed expenses	67,530	193,408	89,382	102,792	114,347	84,820	296,434
Store income	$ 50,138	$ 491,522	$ 27,999	$ 58	$ 127,497	$ 1,750	$ (9,801)

Babbitt's Department Store: Flagstaff 1985 Performance by Department/ Product Line   **Exhibit 8**

Department/Product Line	Sales (000)	Gross Margin (000)	Inventory at Cost (000)
Men's casual dress	$ 253.0	$ 56.8	$114.2
Men's furnishings/accessories	194.6	90.7	49.2
Women's casual dress	703.0	271.7	90.2
Women's furnishings	121.7	50.7	32.1
Women's accessories	53.4	24.7	7.6
Boy's clothing	70.9	23.0	19.8
Girl's clothing	83.5	32.6	17.7
Infant/toddlers	88.7	38.7	14.3
Shoes	385.6	154.7	120.4
Jewelry	145.9	57.9	37.7
Cosmetics	328.0	127.2	122.5
Toys	31.8	10.0	6.8
Electronics	117.3	−28.7	71.7
Furniture	347.5	162.9	67.3
Textiles	137.5	52.0	34.7
Luggage	25.2	10.2	9.4
Gifts	97.6	23.0	72.0
Stationery	76.8	30.7	22.2
China	19.8	4.2	25.1
Housewares	60.4	25.3	11.6
Total	$3342.2	$1218.3	$946.6

THE MALL DECISION

At about the same time as the board terminated the CEO, another ominous event in the history of BBTC occurred. In late November, 1985, Dillard's Department Stores, headquartered in Little Rock, Arkansas, announced that they would become an "anchor store" in the five-year-old Flagstaff Mall. Dillard's had decided to build a new 72,000-square-foot addition to the present 284,000-square-foot structure. Dillard's therefore would soon enter into competition in the Babbitt's Department Stores' largest market area. Dillard's Flagstaff Mall opening was scheduled for November 1986.

When the Flagstaff Mall was opened in 1980, the BBTC Board had considered moving their downtown Flagstaff operations into the Mall. They also considered opening a branch outlet in the mall. The board decided against both alternatives, opting instead to continue operations out of their downtown Flagstaff facility. Originally built in the early part of the century, it had not been remodeled since 1962. At the time the decision was made, the BBTC's board did not believe that any Phoenix-based chain would move into Babbitt's home territory. This position was based on the assumption that the market was simply too small to support still another major retailer. The board knew that the mall would bring a new Sears store into the competition and the downtown Penney store was being relocated to the mall. These were not considered insurmountable threats to Babbitt's continued strong position in the Flagstaff market. Furthermore, the board believed at the time (1980) that Babbitt's did not have the management expertise to compete in the mall environment and the cost of a mall store would be excessive.

The move by Dillard's took everyone by surprise. Bill now had to analyze a completely unanticipated situation and formulate a strategy to respond to the entry of Dillard's. It was apparent to Bill that several alternatives were worth considering. The major options were the following:

1. A "no location" strategy. This would mean closing down the Babbitt's stores in downtown Flagstaff.
2. A "one location" strategy. Either maintain the present downtown location or develop a new mall store, but not both.
3. A "two location" strategy. Maintain the downtown location and develop a new mall store with fixed-space commitments.

To help sort out the complexities of the various alternatives, Bill hired the consulting firm Management Horizons of Columbus, Ohio, to do a marketing study for Babbitt's. In particular, Bill wanted an assessment of how Dillard's entry into the Flagstaff market would affect Babbitt's downtown store.

In late March 1986, Bill received the consulting report from Management Horizons (for an executive summary of the report, see Exhibit 9). Of special interest to Bill was the conclusion that sales revenues at Babbitt's downtown Flagstaff store would decline by approximately $1–1.5 million annually as a result of the Dillard's entry.

While the consulting report was helpful, Bill felt that he should evaluate the alternatives from a financial perspective before making a recommendation to the board. The monetary and logistical considerations for putting a store in the mall were formidable. Babbitt's would have to quickly commit to a long-term lease to acquire a recently available 15,000-square-foot space in the mall. In order to enter the mall at approximately the same time as the new Dillard's store opened, a decision would have to be made within the next month. The "up front" costs to put a store in the mall were as follows:

Remodeling, fixtures, and personnel	$ 500,000
Inventory	500,000
	$1,000,000

In addition, to lease the space in the mall, BBTC would have to agree to an eight-year lease costing approximately $8000 per month. Finally, personnel to staff the facility would have to be recruited and trained. After careful analysis, Bill estimated that the downtown Flagstaff store should generate sales of approximately $2 million during 1987. He made this estimate using the most recent annual level of sales ($3.35 million in 1985) adjusted for the impact of Dillard's entry into the market.

Bill sat down at his desk and turned his attention to a review of the events of his first eleven months as COO:

1. The essential first steps toward developing an effective management information system had been accomplished. Better financial information was available now than at any previous time in the history of BBTC.
2. The reorganization of the Department Store Division had been accomplished. Early indications were that division performance was improved.

Management Horizons Report: Executive Summary	**Exhibit 9**

Research Findings

A considerable amount of research has been done, including an extensive secondary-market analysis, an in-depth review of Babbitt's performance, and an on-site audit of Dillard's Farmington, New Mexico, store. Highlights of this research are given below.

The Flagstaff Market

Compared to the United States, it is younger and less affluent.

After adjusting for the influence of Northern Arizona University, the area still has a sizeable young family, household formation population of average means.

Flagstaff is a small metro market, with some regional shopping attractiveness.

Expenditures are skewed toward necessities, as well as reflective of transient tourist purchases (e.g., gas, meals, lodging).

In terms of retail space, the area is clearly well above the average U.S. saturation index

Area	Gross Leasable Area (Square feet per capita)
Flagstaff	27.0
Arizona average	21.3
U.S. average	14.3

For department store merchandise, the market is growing but already well represented (not necessarily well served), with very little upscale potential.

Babbitt's Performance

The company enjoys a 7% market share overall for its merchandise lines.

There is an incredible degree of variation and inconsistency between departments; the essential point, however, is that in considering the combination of sales, market share, market size, and market growth by category, space and inventory productivity, and profit contribution, only a few categories are reasonably well situated as a base upon which to build at the mall and against Dillard's.

In general, the combination of market and performance analysis suggest that in the past, Babbitt's has taken sales from the market wherever a void existed. Market forces, rather than planning, have defined strategy. This may have been good enough. The result today, however, is an unfocused offer exacerbated by events such as the last year's sell-off of inventory.

Dillard's Market Entry

As is documented in the body of this report, Dillard's will present Flagstaff retailers with formidable challenges.

Dillard's is, in brief, broadly assorted in moderate to better brands, competitively priced and aggressively promotional, an excellent marketer, very complete in apparel and related merchandise, attractive to a broad consumer segment, organized, strong in the financial and resource markets, and experienced in secondary city locations.

Dillard's entry, while a challenge to Babbitt's in itself, can serve to highlight and motivate Babbitt's to deal with a broader set of challenges and focus on opportunities which in the end may strengthen the total Babbitt's retail operation.

Over the past few years, Dillard's merchandising emphasis has shifted from a full-line, moderate department store operation to a department store focusing on moderate to better soft lines.

In 1985, Dillard's average square footage performance was estimated by the company at $125 and projected to be $140 for 1986.

Dillard's assortment emphasizes apparel over all other categories. While apparel represents 71.3% of Dillard's sales, Babbitt's performance in apparel categories represents 61.1% of Flagstaff volume and 66.4% of all locations volume (based on preliminary estimates of 1985 operations).

(continued)

Exhibit 9   **Management Horizons Report: Executive Summary** *(continued)*

Among apparel categories, Babbitt's junior/children category appears to be more developed than Dillard's.

While Dillard's emphasizes the soft aspect of home over hard home, Babbitt's features a developed hard-line area. Furthermore, it is expected that Dillard's Flagstaff volume will be even less dependent on home, as the furniture category is not expected to be a part of the assortment.

Dillard's projected sales volume for the Flagstaff Mall store in 1987 is approximately $7.2 million ($100 per square foot). The volume will originate from three sources: the natural market expenditure growth; a portion of dollars currently spent outside Flagstaff and especially in Phoenix at Diamond's; dollars which until now were spent at Babbitt's and other Flagstaff retail outlets carrying similar types of merchandise.

The impact from the Dillard's entry into the Flagstaff market is estimated to be a $1–$1.5 million annual loss in sales revenues for Babbitt's downtown Flagstaff store.

---

3. A new GMM had been hired and would be on the job within a few days. This would free Bill's time for other responsibilities. During the past 11 months, he had spent about 40% of his time in various activities associated with the Department Store Division.

4. Budgeting as a planning and control tool had been introduced starting in 1986. This was a milestone in proactive management for the company. For the first time, Division Managers were conscious of revenue forecasts, cost containment, gross margins and other performance criteria.

While Bill was pleased with the progress that he had made in his first year, he could not be sure about the Board of Directors' assessment. The episode involving the two dissatisfied stockholders had bothered him a great deal, and he wondered how the board evaluated the accomplishments of his first 12 months on the job.

Looking ahead to his second year, Bill could see that in addition to his responsibilities for the other BBTC Divisions, continuing attention would be required to keep the MIS improvements on track. Also, he would have to monitor the activities of the new GMM and the Department Store Division. Of most immediate concern, however, was the mall decision. Bill had to evaluate all of the information and make his recommendation to the board within the next two weeks.

As he glanced up to the window, Bill noticed that a spring snow had begun to fall. "This will please the skiers," he thought to himself.

McMaster Group

Jon Ozmun, Northern Arizona University;
David Atchison, University of Utah

The blinking light on the phone console told Mark Spencer that his administrative assistant, Mary Yard, had important business to discuss with him. Mark was entering his third year as Chief Executive Officer (CEO) of the diversified businesses of the McMaster family. The "McMaster Group" was comprised of three divisions doing business in the city of Rock Springs and surrounding Sweetwater County, Wyoming. In 1988, the McMaster Group had achieved sales revenues of over $9 million, but net income was only $185,000 and two of the divisions had sustained large losses. Mark finished his call and then walked out into the adjacent reception area to see what was going on. Mary saw him coming and motioned that they go back into his office.

"Richard just called from Cheyenne," she said. Richard McMaster was Mark's father-in-law and the previous CEO of the McMaster Group. Richard had held that position for over twenty years before stepping down in 1986. He was still a major shareholder and Chairman of the Board of Directors for the McMaster Group. Mary continued, "The legislative schedule has been changed and he now has the entire weekend off. Richard said to contact the Governor's office and let him know if you want to meet with him to discuss the strategy proposal you've been working on. He can leave Cheyenne in time to meet with you here at 4 P.M. today."

Mark checked the time; it was 10 A.M. He needed a few minutes to gather himself and determine if he could get ready for a meeting with Richard by 4 P.M. "Hold my calls and cancel my lunch meeting," he told Mary. Mary acknowledged his instructions and went back to her desk.

Mark sat down at his work console and opened the file marked "The McMaster Group—Strategic Directions." He had started the project about four weeks ago, working on it as he could, given his busy schedule. Mark knew that breaks in Richard's schedule were both scarce and irregular. If they didn't take advantage of this opportunity, it could be several weeks before they could get together. Richard was working in Cheyenne for the Governor of Wyoming. He had been instrumental in convincing the Governor to run for office, was active in generating financing for the campaign, and had agreed to assist in the Governor's legislative agenda following his election in November, 1986. Richard was now in his third year as Legislative Liaison, a seven day a week job when the Wyoming Legislature was in session.

Mark knew what he had to do. He asked Mary to call the Governor's office and set up a meeting with Richard later that afternoon. Mark then poured himself some coffee and walked into the conference room. He looked at the numerous plaques, pictures, and framed certificates that adorned the walls and visually told the story of the McMaster family businesses. The three divisions, McMaster Construction Company, Valley Concrete Company, and Basin Asphalt Company were facing some significant threats.

Throughout its forty year history, the business divisions of the McMaster Group had been differentiated from their competitors through the quality of their products and services. Historically, there had been a sizable segment of the market that was willing and able to pay a premium for products and services of higher quality. By employing more highly skilled employees and managers, owning and operating more modern and expensive equipment, and focusing on availability and on time delivery and/or completion of products and services, the McMaster Group had dominated the quality sensitive (and less price sensitive) segment of their markets. During periods of sluggish business activity, emphasis on quality would decline and the market would become more price competitive. Because of their higher costs of operations, such periods were relatively more difficult for the McMaster Group than their competitors. Until the 1980s, the duration of the economic downturns had been short enough that the McMaster Group's financial strength had sustained them until a revival of activity resulted in a resurgence of quality consciousness. However, Mark was now coping with a recession that had lasted for seven years. McMaster's historic market niche had gradually shrunk to the point that they were being forced to compete on the basis of price alone. This was uppermost in Mark's thinking as he went back to work on the "McMaster Group —Strategic Directions" report.

Working without interruption, Mark completed a working draft of the report by 3:30 P.M. The following sections present Mark's draft.

THE McMASTER GROUP—STRATEGIC DIRECTIONS

■ Mission Statement

The McMaster Group exists to serve the needs of its three major stakeholder groups; customers, employees, and stockholders. The needs of the customer are served through the creation of the highest quality products and services. Further, the highest priority is placed on availability and on-time delivery of those

Rock Springs: Demographic and Economic Statistics, 1981–1988   **Exhibit 1**

Year	Population	Building Permits: No. of Units	Total Value of Building Permits ($ millions)	Housing Vacancy Rate (%)
1981	35,000	431	30.7	2
1982	35,400	181	22.1	2
1983	35,600	239	19.0	3
1984	36,700	162	12.7	4
1985	35,900	135	13.6	6
1986	35,700	93	14.2	7
1987	35,500	76	13.3	8
1988	35,200	31	9.9	7

products and services. All personnel are encouraged to place the needs of our customers at the highest level of priority. The needs of employees are served through the provision of a safe, secure, challenging, and financially rewarding work environment. Through the efficient operation of the businesses comprising the McMaster Group, stockholders can expect both growth and above average return on their investment.

■ Economic Environment

The economic base for Rock Springs and Sweetwater County, Wyoming is provided by three major industrial sectors together with area retail trade and government service activities. The industrial sectors are: electric power generation, coal mining, and oil and gas exploration, drilling and production. The electric power generation and coal mining sectors have been growing slowly and steadily throughout the 1980s. Economic activity resulting from the oil and gas sector declined precipitously throughout the 1980s, apparently reaching a trough in 1987. Exhibits 1 and 2 show demographic and economic data for both Rock Springs and Sweetwater County.

Sweetwater County: Demographic and Economic Statistics, 1981–1988   **Exhibit 2**

Year	Total Employment	Unemployment Rate (%)	Gross Receipts, Retail Trade ($ millions)
1981	33,422	7.5	473.9
1982	31,075	11.5	394.8
1983	28,683	16.1	385.0
1984	28,741	12.9	402.6
1985	30,057	13.7	444.2
1986	29,074	16.1	404.2
1987	27,500	15.7	403.9
1988	29,050	12.2	431.1

■ Economic Forecast

A forecast for the Rock Springs and Sweetwater County economies must be generally based on a forecast for the oil and gas industry. The business divisions of the McMaster Group depend either directly (McMaster Construction) or indirectly (Basin Asphalt and Valley Concrete) on the activity generated by the oil and gas industry.

Oil and gas drilling activity reached a trough in 1987 and has been in a general slow recovery period since, due in large part to "coal-gas" exploration. Beginning in 1987, the Federal Government made a tax credit available to companies who develop "coal-gas" reserves through drilling and production. This tax incentive is responsible for increased drilling activity in the Rock Springs area since mid 1987. The tax incentive program expires on December 31, 1990.

Apart from the government subsidized drilling for "coal-gas", a recovery of the oil and gas industry in the Rock Springs area will require an increase and stabilization of the price of oil and an increase in the market for natural gas. The average drilling cost for an oil or gas well is $500,000. There are considerable risks associated with such an investment. First, there is the possibility of drilling a "dry hole"; that is, no oil or gas is found. Second, the well may contain oil or gas, but in insufficient quantities to recover the drilling and exploration costs incurred. These risks have always been a part of the oil and gas business and by themselves are not responsible for fluctuations in exploration activities. Since the early 1980s, a new problem has plagued the oil industry—extreme price volatility. Since 1981, the spot price of oil has fluctuated between $11.00 and $20.00 per barrel. With such wide movements in price, the market is considered too unstable for the undertaking of expensive drilling projects. Industry experts believe that a *stable* spot price for oil of at least $21.00 per barrel is necessary for a recovery of oil drilling programs.

Two major problems confront the natural gas segment of the industry, low prices and foreign competition. The current price per "unit" (a "unit" is 1 million standard cubic feet of gas) is $1.20 and experts believe that a price nearer $2.00 is required for full recovery of drilling costs. In addition, the short run demand for natural gas is quite limited and a decline in price will not significantly impact the market. Gas produced in the Rock Springs area is sold primarily in the state of California. Presently, the California market is being served by gas from the Rock Springs area, Canada, and Mexico. In general, the short-term increases in demand are met by additional gas from Canada and Mexico. In the longer run, industries in Southern California must switch from their present coal and heavy oil fuels to natural gas. As this process occurs, the market for natural gas from the Rock Springs area is expected to steadily increase.

Virtually all of McMaster Construction's business is the result of drilling for oil and natural gas wells. This work consists primarily of maintenance of existing roads and the construction of new well sites. With thousands of miles of dirt roads providing access to producing oil and natural gas wells within the company's area of operations, the maintenance necessary to keep them passable in all weather conditions is significant. New construction generally consists of building a short section of dirt road and leveling the drilling site. The drilling site itself is a level rectangular area a few hundred feet on each side, with two large pits on one side to contain water or "drilling mud" used to lubricate the string of drill pipe as the well is bored. Revenues generated by this type of project can vary from a few thousand dollars to hundreds of thousands of dollars

Forecast of Total Market for Construction Services, Asphalt, Aggregate, and Concrete ($ millions)   **Exhibit 3**

Year	Construction Services	Asphalt	Aggregate and Concrete
1989	8.0	1.8	7.0
1990	9.0	2.0	7.5
1991	4.0	1.7	6.0
1992	4.5	1.8	6.0
1993	5.0	1.8	6.0

depending on the size of the individual job, and the terrain upon which it is built.

On the other hand, business activity for Basin Asphalt and Valley Concrete is dependent on the general level of economic activity and in particular on housing and commercial construction activity. While the general economy is substantially influenced by oil and natural gas drilling activity, it has some underlying stability provided by the other industrial sectors, government and the retail economy.

Exhibit 3 shows a five year forecast of the total market for oil and gas construction services, asphalt, aggregate and concrete. This forecast represents a consensus of the present management of the McMaster Group. For 1988, the total market for construction services was approximately $9 million.

■ Current Situation Analysis

The McMaster Group is comprised of three separate operating divisions, McMaster Construction, Valley Concrete, and Basin Asphalt, with total 1988 sales of over $9,000,000. Financial information for 1988 for each of the divisions is shown in Exhibits 4 through 9.

The McMaster Group's types of business in order of size are oil and gas drilling site excavation, concrete, road building, paving, aggregates, and dump trucking. The groups product lines can be basically described by the following four categories: asphalt (Basin Asphalt), aggregates and concrete (Valley Concrete), and oil field (McMaster Construction). The Group's types of customers in order of size are: oil companies, governmental agencies, commercial builders, heavy construction and highway contractors, precast manufacturers, mines, commercial property owners, residential builders, individuals and developers. The Group offers some overlapping products and has considerable overlapping customers, especially for the concrete and paving business. There is very little sharing of support groups, except in the administrative area.

Basin Asphalt's paving is the strongest product line. It has a high value added portion, a very good public image with high customer loyalty, and very little competition. Basin Asphalt has good management in place which excels at performing high quality work. The equipment fleet is in very good shape. Sales are not difficult to obtain as the product essentially sells itself. The division currently enjoys a 100% share of the market. Treating depreciation, interest, office,

Exhibit 4

McMaster Construction Company: Balance Sheet, Year Ending August 31, 1988

Assets

Current Assets
Cash	$ 175,961
Accounts receivable	469,375
Prepaid expense	5,961
Inventory	41,100
Other current	260,204
Total current assets	952,601

Property and equipment
Land	39,421
Equipment	4,081,847
Less accumulated depreciation (equipment)	2,648,692
Net property and equipment	1,472,575
Other assets	207,754
Total assets	$2,632,931

Liabilities and Equity

Current liabilities
Accounts payable	391,452
Accrued expenses	114,785
Notes payable	265,854
Total current liabilities	772,091
Long-term debt	1,507,880

Stockholders equity
Common stock	36,206
Retained earnings	384,472
Current income (loss)	(67,718)
Total liabilities and equity	$2,632,931

Exhibit 5

McMaster Construction Company: Income Statement, Year Ending August 31, 1988

Service revenue	$3,560,064

Operating expenses
Bad debt expense	2,949
Depreciation	249,346
Equipment rental	71,598
Fuel and oil	157,823
Insurance	150,538
Interest	112,215
Professional services	53,670
Materials and supplies	313,774

Office	29,835
Rent	84,000
Royalties	38,422
Repairs and maintenance	330,238
Subcontracts	992,976
Payroll taxes	92,902
Salaries	
Division manager	50,000
Officer personnel	60,000
Wages	733,921
Other	119,374
Total operating expense	3,643,581
Net operating income	(83,517)
Other income*	18,847
Net income (loss)	($64,670)

*Other income includes gain on the sale of assets and rental income.

Valley Concrete Company: Balance Sheet, Year Ending December 31, 1988   **Exhibit 6**

Assets

Current Assets	
Cash	$ 82,090
Accounts receivable	359,311
Prepaid expenses	16,385
Inventory	344,736
Other current	27,214
Total current assets	829,736
Property and equipment	
Land	893,652
Equipment	4,795,639
Less accumulated depreciation (equipment)	3,905,410
Net property and equipment	1,783,881
Other assets	903,529
Total assets	$3,517,146

Liabilities and Equity

Current liabilities	
Accounts payable	148,193
Accrued expenses	73,828
Notes payable	142,958
Total current liabilities	364,979
Long-term debt	327,001
Stockholders equity	
Common stock	78,109
Retained earnings	2,803,154
Net income (loss)	(56,097)
Total liabilities and equity	$3,517,146

Exhibit 7

Valley Concrete Company: Income Statement, Year Ending December 31, 1988

Sales	
Sales	$3,711,257
Less: Cost of goods sold	713,984
Gross profit	2,997,273
Operating expenses	
Depreciation	195,120
Fuel and oil	242,779
Insurance	262,044
Interest	108,635
Office	37,912
Payroll taxes	142,830
Professional services	60,566
Repairs and parts	429,648
Subcontracts	70,295
Salaries	
Division manager	50,000
Office personnel	70,000
Wages	1,028,504
Other	454,924
Total operating expense	3,153,257
Net operating income (loss)	(155,984)
Other income*	99,916
Net income (loss)	($56,068)

*Other income includes rent income for equipment and land.

rent and salaries as fixed or period costs and all other costs are variable, the division's contribution margin for 1988 was 32.4%.

Valley Concrete's aggregates and concrete product lines are extremely weak. The division's single strength is the ability to make a high quality product. This is almost completely mitigated by the price sensitive market and the high cost of quality control. During 1988, Valley Concrete lost sales due to the retirement (in February 1988) of the long-time, respected division manager, a lack of effective marketing effort, and the growing strength of the major competitor (Con-Co). The equipment fleet is aging to the point of being counterproductive. It will be necessary to purchase new equipment in order to produce gravel (aggregate) cost effectively. Finally, the product lines are not cost competitive, as labor costs per unit are approximately double those of the major competitor. Valley Concrete's contribution margin for 1988 was 8.2%. Aggressive measures have been taken to measure and improve the productivity of the labor force, such as cutting back on excessive use of overtime. These measures are expected to reduce wages as a percentage of sales by about 5% beginning in 1989.

There are currently three firms competing in the aggregates market. Valley Concrete is the market leader with 50%, but market share has declined gradually since 1981 when the division had about 70% of total area sales. The largest competitor (Con-Co) currently has a 40% market share, up from 20% in 1981.

Sand and gravel (aggregates) production is of special importance to both Valley Concrete and Basin Asphalt. Aside from the revenues generated for Valley Concrete by the sale of aggregates, the ability to produce concrete and asphalt

Basin Asphalt Company: Balance Sheet, Year Ending August 31, 1988   **Exhibit 8**

Assets

Current Assets
Cash	$ 12,404
Accounts receivable	479,109
Prepaid expenses	695
Inventory	41,343
Other current	296,275
Total current assets	829,826

Property and equipment
Land	-0-
Equipment	768,699
Less accumulated depreciation (equipment)	187,394
Net property and equipment	581,305
Other assets	300,000
Total assets	$1,711,131

Liabilities and Equity

Current liabilities
Accounts payable	153,724
Accrued expenses	52,100
Notes payable	117,741
Total current liabilities	323,565
Long-term debt	526,751

Stockholders equity
Common stock	10,000
Retained earnings	541,739
Current income (loss)	309,076
Total liabilities and equity	$1,711,131

is dependent on the supply of aggregate materials. As a necessary component of final products, asphalt and concrete, the aggregate products available must fall within specific quality control limits with respect to average size of gravel elements and ratio of "fines" (sand) to crushed rock. Suitable raw materials for the crushing and mixing of aggregate products are only found in fossil river-beds, or in riparian environments. Only after the raw material has been mined, crushed to specified size, screened, and mixed, does it become a raw component input to concrete or asphalt when combined with cement or asphalt tar.

Three other firms compete with Valley Concrete in the concrete market. Valley Concrete is the largest in terms of assets and is the market share leader with 50%. Con-Co, the largest of the competitors, holds a market share of 40%, with the remainder divided among the two remaining firms. The division's market share has declined significantly during the last several years, from a high of about 70% in 1981.

The asphalt, aggregates, and concrete product lines share a common problem—excessive materials hauling costs. Ideally, all materials should be located contiguous to production facilities and production facilities located near final customers in order to minimize handling and transportation costs.

McMaster Construction's oil field product lines (drilling site excavation and access road construction) have improved during the past two years, but are still

Exhibit 9

Basin Asphalt Company: Income Statement, Year Ending August 31, 1988

Service revenue	$1,880,876
Operating expenses	
Bad debt expense	25,054
Depreciation	108,759
Equipment rental	10,146
Fuel and oil	69,892
Insurance	79,771
Interest	70,960
Professional services	6,123
Materials and supplies	396,428
Office	6,494
Rent	39,000
Royalties	161
Repairs and maintenance	86,792
Subcontracts	121,051
Payroll taxes	56,535
Salaries	
Division manager	50,000
Office personnel	25,000
Wages	355,964
Other	64,013
Total operating expense	1,572,143
Net operating income	308,733
Other income	343
Net income (loss)	$ 309,076

operating far below break-even and are subject to the volatile domestic oil market which in turn is strongly influenced by the world oil market. The local market should remain stable at its present level due to the artificial profits resulting from the tax advantages of "coal-gas" drilling programs. The recent negative publicity resulting from the Exxon oil spill at Valdez, Alaska may eliminate any chance that Congress will extend the subsidy for domestic drilling programs. The market for these product lines is very price competitive when the volume of business declines. There are numerous competitors of varying sizes, most of whom have reduced prices to recover only variable costs during recent downturns. The division's contribution margin for 1988 was 14.1%.

McMaster Construction is the largest of ten competitors of widely varying size in this market. The division has increased its market share somewhat during the last three years and is the current market leader with 30% of total sales.

For each of the product lines, the necessary business competencies for successful competition are quality service and cost control. For the oil field and concrete product lines, effective marketing is also a necessary business competency. In order to provide quality service, the divisions must recruit, train and retain productive personnel, both at the production and managerial level. Cost control is essential if the divisions are to remain price competitive. The major controllable components within total product cost are labor and transportation costs. Neither of these costs is being effectively managed by the Division Vice-President of Operations at McMaster Construction and Valley Concrete. Lack of adequate information systems and effective incentives is the major cause of this failure. The recent development of an effective management information system, which is now in place, should alleviate one of the causes of ineffective cost management. The adoption of a performance-based compensation plan for Division Managers, which is described in the next section should also be considered.

■ Strategic Directions

At the last Board of Directors' meeting, tactics designed to address the problem of cost control were discussed. The Board unanimously agreed that an incentive should be created to encourage Division Managers to use the new management information system as a tool for better understanding and control of costs. In response to this directive, the following performance-based compensation plan is suggested for implementation:

Performance-Based Compensation (PBC)

The following tactical approach to creating a strong incentive for improved cost control by the Division Managers is based on the premise that management actions which yield more profitable results to the company should result in income enhancements to the manager. Implementation of this tactic would require tying a significant portion of the manager's compensation to his division's profitability. A PBC policy could be implemented as follows, using McMaster Construction's Division Manager annual compensation as an example:

Current	*Proposed Under PBC*
$50,000 salary only	$40,000 + PBC

The PBC portion of annual compensation would be equal to 30% of all improvement in controllable costs. Using the McMaster Construction Company 1988 Income Statement (Exhibit 5) as a reference, controllable costs from the point of view of the Division Manager are:

Category	*Amount*
Equipment rental	$ 71,598
Fuel and oil	157,823
Materials and supplies	313,774
Repairs and maintenance	330,238
Wages	843,921
Total	$1,717,354

Improvement could be defined in a number of ways. For instance, these controllable costs equalled 48.23% of Service Revenues in 1988. The Division Manager's PBC would be based on the reduction in this percentage during future years. If 1989 Service Revenues were $4,000,00 and these controllable costs were $1,880,000, then the controllable costs would represent 47% of Service Revenues. The manager's PBC would be calculated as shown below:

$$(\% \text{ Improvement}) \times \text{service revenues} \times 30\% = \text{PBC}$$
$$(48.23 - 47.00) \times \$4,000,000 \times 30\% = \$14,760$$

Investment Alternatives

In addition to the PBC, several alternative investment strategies have been discussed at planning sessions during the past year. These alternatives involve moving production facilities, purchasing and developing new aggregate pits, and purchasing additional production equipment. The alternatives are described below in an unprioritized order.

1. *Move the Basin Asphalt production facilities ("hot plant") from its present location to the Quealy pit.* The aggregate pit at the present Basin Asphalt production facility was depleted about two years ago. Since that time, Basin Asphalt has purchased aggregate from Valley Concrete. This aggregate has been produced at the La Plata pit located about two miles from Basin's production facility. The La Plata pit has less than two years supply of aggregate remaining based on expected usage. The Quealy pit is owned by Valley Concrete and has a twenty to thirty year supply of river rock used to produce aggregate for asphalt and concrete production. The approximate cost to move the hot plant is $70,000. Savings in transportation costs would be about $1.50 per ton. In 1988, approximately 30,000 tons of aggregate were used by Basin Asphalt.

This move could be made immediately. Approximately two weeks of production and sales would be lost while in the process of relocating. To minimize this revenue loss, the move could be scheduled during our slowest period, the months of November and December. Based on historical records, these two months together account for only 10% of annual sales revenues.

2. *Move the Valley Concrete crusher and batch plant from their present location to the Quealy pit.* Valley Concrete is currently using aggregate mined from the Valley pit. The Valley pit is located one mile from the present plant location and has two to three years supply of aggregate remaining based on current usage. The approximate cost to move the crusher and batch plant is $100,000. Savings in transportation costs would be about $1.50 per ton. In 1988, Valley Concrete used approximately 25,000 tons of aggregate from the Valley pit.

This move could also be made immediately. However, Basin's and Valley's production facilities could not be moved simultaneously. Approximately three weeks of production and sales would be lost while in the process of relocating. As with Basin Asphalt, the months of November and December are the slowest in terms of revenue production, together accounting for only 8% of annual sales revenue. A move during this time period would minimize revenue loss.

3. *Establish a competitive advantage for the aggregate and concrete product lines through geographic diversification.* Present management believes that a competitive advantage can be achieved by locating *point of sales* production facilities in areas of strong current and/or expected future demand for the asphalt, aggregate and concrete product lines. The competitive advantage generated would be a combination of lower cost and better service to customers. This would result in increased market share and profit. The complete strategy requires aggregate pits and production facilities at three different locations within the present market area. The locations in order of priority are: Farson, Superior, and Green River, Wyoming.

To achieve the competitive advantage, an aggregate pit would have to be purchased and developed at each location. There are several pits situated near each prospective location. In addition, a concrete batch processing plant would be required at each location. A portable crusher would move to each location on an as needed basis to maintain sufficient inventory levels of crushed aggregates. A portable *hot plant* would be required to produce asphalt at each location. As a result of this geographic diversification, aggregate materials as a final product would be closer to customers, which would reduce costs of hauling. These savings would reduce costs for the aggregate product line.

By locating concrete batch processing plants at each new pit, hauling costs for the concrete product line would be reduced in two ways: First, no trucking would be required to move the aggregate from the pit to the batch processing plant. Second, as the processed concrete would be closer to the customer, cost of hauling from the plant to the customer would be reduced. Similar savings would result from the ability to produce asphalt closer to customers. The McMaster Group has one portable concrete batch processing plant, one portable crusher, and one portable *hot plant* on hand. The purchase of three additional pits and two portable batch processing plants would be required to make the full blown strategy operational.

The achievement of the competitive advantage in location would result in substantial savings in hauling costs. However, additional costs of operations would also be incurred. The increased operations costs would be for additional labor to operate the pits and plants and moving expenses for the batch plants, crusher and scales. To maximize the hauling cost savings a substantial increase in market share must be achieved. Some of this will be accomplished through our closer proximity to the customer. To further increase market share, prices would be reduced and advertising promotion would be increased. After about one year, prices would be gradually increased in order to reestablish profit margins, and after two to three more years, prices would be back at their present level. It is anticipated that this gradual increase in price would not result in a substantial reduction in market share.

Taking all of these savings and cost impacts together, the estimated net savings that would result from the investment in the competitive advantage alternative is as follows:

First year of operation	$300,000
Second year of operation	350,000
Third year of operation	400,000
Subsequent years of operation	400,000

This project will take about six months from start to completion, primarily due to the time required for purchase of the leases for the aggregate pits. Lead times on equipment purchases are all less than three months, and not a critical path issue. The project could be begun in the fall of 1989. The cost of acquisitions associated with the achievement of a competitive advantage is $1,250,000 and is shown in Exhibit 10.

■ Analysis of Capital Requirements

The *risk adjusted* cost of capital for the McMaster Group is presently 12.5% and is expected to remain at this level unless there are significant fluctuations in the general level of interest rates. Existing credit lines appear to be sufficient to cover all anticipated capital needs shown in Exhibit 10; thus it would not be necessary to arrange for additional borrowing capacity. For capital budgeting

---

Exhibit 10   **Capital Requirements by Product Line**

Use of Capital	Asphalt	Aggregate	Concrete	Oil Field
Real property				
Pits	$300,000*	$300,000*	$300,000*	
New equipment				
Paving	415,000[†]			
Crushing		200,000[‡]		
Construction				230,000[‖]
Concrete			640,000[§]	
Two batch plants			350,000*	
Total	$715,000	$500,000	$1,290,000	$230,000

Note: For accounting purposes, average life of new equipment is ten years with no salvage value. Depreciation schedule for new equipment is straight line.

Capital requirements for continuing operations	$1,485,000
Capital requirements for competitive advantage	1,250,000
Total capital requirements	$2,735,000

No increase from the present level of working capital is anticipated for the next five years.

*The capital requirement is associated with the achievement of a competitive advantage.

[†] $200,000 in 1990; $215,000 in 1992.

[‡] $100,000 in 1990; $100,000 in 1993.

[§] $100,000 in 1989; $300,000 in 1990; $240,000 in 1992.

[‖] $100,000 in 1990; $130,000 in 1993.

---

purposes the McMaster Group utilizes a 30% marginal tax rate as a standard policy.

Capital requirements for the McMaster Group by product line are shown in Exhibit 10. The capital needs are further disaggregated by type (either real property or equipment) and whether they are required for continuing operation or are related to the achievement of a competitive advantage.

THE FRIDAY AFTERNOON MEETING

As was his habit, Richard arrived early for the 4 P.M. meeting. Since Mark was ready, the two immediately got to work. Three hours later, they emerged from the conference room and Richard left the McMaster Group office complex. Mark went into his office and mentally reviewed what had transpired.

The meeting had been very productive. Richard had carefully read the entire report and then gone through it with Mark, page by page and item by item, raising questions and making constructive comments. Richard had been impressed with the overall scope of the report and had complimented Mark on this. The report had served its major purposes: First, it had focused the thinking of the two executives on developing a strategic direction for the three divisions and second, it had promoted a discussion of the investment alternatives to be considered by the McMaster Group.

Both Richard and Mark felt confident that the information in the report was complete and accurate and would serve as the basis for the next logical step in the process—the development of recommendations for operating the divisions for the next several years. Mark agreed to complete this final portion of the report and have it ready by the following Sunday afternoon. He and Richard would then discuss and evaluate the recommendations with the intention of presenting the report at the upcoming Board of Directors' meeting.

As Mark left the darkened office complex and headed home, he knew that he had plenty of work to do in the next couple of days.

Liz Claiborne, Inc.

Barbara A. Spencer, Lisa K. Rowe, Mississippi State University

At 20 years of age, a young woman determined to enter the fashion industry won a *Harper's Bazaar* design contest and headed for New York to begin a new career. After working in the apparel industry for 26 years, Elisabeth Claiborne Ortenberg and her husband, Arthur Ortenberg, started Liz Claiborne, Inc., on January 19, 1976, with $50,000 of their own savings and another $200,000 from family and friends. In 1986, Liz Claiborne, Inc., moved into the Fortune 500 list of the largest industrial companies in the United States. Today, Claiborne (as she is known professionally) is one of the most successful entrepreneurs in the world.

Liz Claiborne, Inc., concentrates primarily on providing apparel that meets the needs of the professional women in a business environment. It offers its customers an array of related separates including blouses, sweaters, skirts, jackets, tailored pants, and matching accessories. On a more casual basis, customers can find jeans, jumpsuits, knit tops and skirts, dresses, and sportswear. In 1985, the company introduced a menswear collection that has been making steady gains in the marketplace.

The company's clothing lines are designed by its own staff under Claiborne's personal supervision. Most items are manufactured by independent suppliers, about 12% in the United States and the remainder abroad, mainly in the Far East. Claiborne's products are marketed under various trademarks to over 3500 accounts throughout the United States, operating approximately 9000 department and specialty stores. Sales are also made to direct-mail catalogue concerns, foreign customers, and other outlets.

In addition to its apparel lines, Liz Claiborne, Inc., has licensees in such areas as shoes (Marx and Newman), eyewear (Tropi-Cal), hosiery (Kayser Roth), optics (Pal Optical), and patterns (McCall). These licensing agreements allow other firms to use the Claiborne trademark on their products. Generally, licensees pay a fixed sum when signing the agreement and then pay a royalty over the life of the contract. In 1986, the company acquired the Liz Claiborne Accessories division of Wickes Cosmetics, Inc., which had previously operated under a licensing agreement. Later that year, in a joint venture with Avon Products, the firm introduced a Liz Claiborne perfume with its first national advertising campaign. In yet another venture, Claiborne announced the establishment of a new retail operation in 1987.

The common threads underlying each of these product lines are style and practicality. Claiborne believes that a limited number of clothing items can be arranged into a multitude of different outfits with the help of accessories like belts, hats, shoes, and scarves. The result is clothing that meets the needs of the New York customer and the middle-American customer too (Skolnik, 1985). As one industry expert notes, "It's not the cutting edge of fashion, but it's where fashion really sells" (Skolnik, 1985).

This formula has pushed Liz Claiborne, Inc., to the top of the apparel industry. Since the firm went public in 1981, sales have grown at an average compounded annual rate of more than 40%, while earnings have soared tenfold (Deveny, 1989) (see Exhibit 1).

THE APPAREL INDUSTRY STRUCTURE

The apparel industry includes the manufacture of children's clothing; men's and boys' sportswear; men's, youths', and boys' trousers and slacks, shirts, nightwear, suits, coats, and overcoats; women's, misses', and juniors' blouses, dresses, suits, skirts, coats, sportswear, undergarments, and sleepwear. It has an enormous structure with millions of employees whose main objectives are to generate profits and keep customers in suspense from season to season. The industry is only a little over 100 years old but has already developed into a multibillion-dollar business which allows individuals to express themselves to the world. The apparel industry's trends as well as its clothing designs are almost constantly changing to cater to a society of self-expression, imagination, and power. It is one of the few industries whose success is determined by so many climates: social, economic, political, and cultural.

The U.S. Department of Commerce estimates that the domestic apparel manufacturing industry consists of about 5000 firms utilizing 21,000 facilities throughout the United States. Out of the 21,000 operating units, nearly 25% employed fewer than 5 workers, and more than half employed fewer than 50 workers (*Standard and Poor's Industry Surveys*, 1987). Most of these companies produce a narrow range of products, frequently under contract for a larger diversified firm or retailer. The competition, on both domestic and foreign fronts, is fierce. This has kept apparel prices relatively low, with price increases consistently lagging inflation (*Standard and Poor's Industry Surveys*, 1987).

New York is the main market center for the apparel industry. In this city are located an estimated 5000 apparel firms where almost all of the leading fashion designers work. Overall, about 60% of the apparel industry is concentrated in

Company Performance   **Exhibit 1**

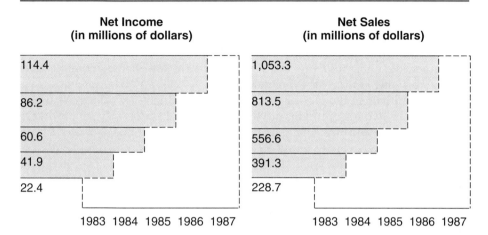

New York, California, Pennsylvania, and New Jersey (*Standard and Poor's Industry Surveys*, 1987). Most high-fashion and tailored clothing producers are located in the metropolitan areas of the Mid-Atlantic states and in California. Factories making products such as jean-cut casual slacks are usually located in the South and Southwest.

As apparel manufacturing has shifted overseas, the population of U.S. apparel companies has been shrinking through bankruptcies and acquisitions (*Standard and Poor's Industry Surveys*, 1987). According to the American Manufacturers Association, failures of companies making apparel and related products have been increasing since the late 1970s. Because they frequently provide labor cost savings, imports have been increasing.

The apparel industry has been particularly vulnerable to foreign competition because of the high labor content of its products. Because detailed and often repetitive tasks are the norm in this industry, semiskilled or unskilled workers are typically employed. Until recently, wage rates in such textile and apparel nations as Taiwan, China, Hong Kong, and South Korea have ranged from $0.20 to less than $2.00 per hour. Moreover, many importers say that they cannot get the quality, reliability, price, and quick delivery from domestic sources that are available abroad.

Yet in 1988, the falling dollar and trade agreements that sharply restricted growth in Asian clothing imports may provide apparel makers with incentives to return to the United States. Production expenses, especially in the Far East, have risen sharply. And importing is getting trickier. For example, Chaus Inc., a New York–based women's clothing maker recently had $12 million dollars worth of blouses barred from entering the United States due to import quotas.

The domestic apparel manufacturing industry does have at least one advantage over foreign producers—direct access to U.S. markets. Domestic producers are turning this to their advantage by using new techniques and technology to shorten the long product line from supplier, to producer, to retailer. Not only does new technology enable the industry to speed up the manufacturing process and shorten the distribution line, it also reduces labor time per garment.

Presently, larger manufacturers utilize technological innovations because of their great impact on labor costs. Computer-aided garment design is being upgraded and refined using better software and faster computers. Computer inspection of fabrics, scanning and measurement of fabric width variance, and automated marker-making systems are widely used. In the fabric-cutting area, water-jet and laser methods have been used with some success. New programmable sewing units utilizing microprocessors are faster and more flexible, thereby reducing labor costs even more.

More than half of the U.S. apparel industry production workers are union members. The two major unions are the International Ladies Garment Workers Union (ILGWU) and the Amalgamated Clothing and Textile Workers Union (ACTWU). Workers earned about $5.85 an hour in 1986, an increase of almost 28% since 1980 (*Standard and Poor's Industry Surveys*, 1987). Despite these increases, apparel workers' earnings are significantly less than those of the average manufacturing worker. Possible explanations for this discrepancy include the low wage rates paid by foreign apparel-producing countries, the low level of skill required for the job, and the fact that 81% of all apparel production workers are women.

Entrance into the apparel industry is not easy. Start-up costs and capital required for inventories and fixed facilities are relatively low compared to those of other industries; yet the new competitor must have a sufficiently large financial base to overcome the effects of product differentiation. It is difficult for someone just getting into the business to overcome brand loyalty among consumers. In order for apparel to sell, it must have a better quality and price than that existing in the market. In the fashion industry, a company must be knowledgeable about production procedures, marketing, research and development, and monitoring structural and cultural changes. If a new competitor lacks these qualities, his or her company will be more likely to lag behind in the industry. A new entrant may gain access to a distribution channel, but if it is not the right channel at the right time, profits will be hard to come by.

Suppliers of raw materials, particularly of fabrics, abound. Almost 7000 fabric-producing plants operate in the United States, yet no particular plant controls the industry. Furthermore, inexpensive textiles can be easily imported to the United States from numerous countries.

It is difficult to pinpoint competitors in the apparel industry because of the large number of different target markets, price levels, and quality levels. Liz Claiborne products, for example, are marketed as "designer" items, as are those of Donna Karan, Ralph Lauren, Yves St. Laurent, and Giorgio Armani, among others. Yet Claiborne prices her clothing in the "better" apparel range, which is generally less expensive than many designer lines. Mass market styles like those of Bernard Chaus fall slightly below Claiborne's in price.

Ralph Lauren targets upper-income buyers but does not have a strong career focus. His line has a more casual, relaxed look than those of his competitors. Lauren's outfits are basically separates which can be mixed and matched, unlike the fully coordinated outfits that many working women desire.

Donna Karan learned designing tips from Anne Klein and went on to become chief designer of Anne Klein and Company after Klein's death in 1974. Later she began her own business. Two of Karan's key strengths are convenience and knowledge of what the consumer wants. She markets her entire line, including accessories, at a single location. Karan's clothes are expensive: a blazer costs approximately $250, and a crocodile purse can cost as much as $2000 (Fierman, 1985).

Karan played a big part in the development of a collection called Anne Klein II which is considered a major competitor of Liz Claiborne. In 1985, a typical blazer from the former Anne Klein collection cost around $115 to make and was sold to the consumer for twice that amount. In contrast, Anne Klein II blazers cost the company about $45 and retailed for $175 (Fierman, 1985). Anne Klein II and other derivative lines cut costs by using inexpensive labor and less expensive fabrics. They sometimes leave out linings and add less detail, making clothing items less expensive (Fierman, 1985). The moderate prices of Liz Claiborne and Anne Klein II appeal to their target markets because these women desire affordable clothing with the style, sophistication, and comfort to be worn in an everyday working atmosphere.

The level just below Liz Claiborne has a large target market which demands good-quality clothing at a lower price. Bernard Chaus's designs fit into this category and can be found in the same department stores as those of Liz Claiborne and Anne Klein. His womenswear line targets business and professional women who cannot afford to pay high prices for clothing. His clothes have great appeal to this market since they are well made and are not trendy but can be worn from year to year.

ENVIRONMENTAL TRENDS

The Bureau of the Census estimates that from 1960 to 1990 the number of women in the labor force will more than double, with the largest gain among women ages 24 to 44.

For apparel makers, the influx of women into professional occupations has resulted in the sale of billions of dollars in clothes a year. In the past, designers took a man's pin-striped suit and changed it a little so it would fit a woman (Smith, 1986). These days, clothes in the workplace are becoming more feminine, reflecting women's security in business, as well as their quest for individualism and personal identity. The majority of these women work in jobs that do not require extremely formal executive wear. Many can go to work more casually dressed in a wider range of styles. At the same time, the daily task of dressing for work requires a wardrobe with depth and versatility as well as affordability (*Madison Avenue*, 1986).

With the growing number of two-income families, shoppers are finding their time increasingly valuable. One way that apparel makers are attempting to reach these busy consumers is through the mail order business. Direct marketing appeals to the needs of consumers who are less interested in going into stores because of traffic and parking problems. In 1984, according to a Direct Marketing Association study, at-home mail and phone orders brought in $170 billion to retailers, double the amount of five years before (Schneider, 1985).

Today, direct-mail sales are growing so fast that some industry observers expect direct mail to be pulling in 20% of general merchandise sales by 1990 (Schneider, 1985). More and more companies are getting in on the action. Bloomingdale's, for example, started sending catalogues after finding that mailings designed to increase store traffic actually resulted in a considerable increase in phone and mail sales (Schneider, 1985). Recently, however, so many new catalogues have appeared that some consumers have reached their limit. They may carefully pursue a few favorites, while tossing out the rest.

The retail industry is also experiencing problems that directly affect apparel firms. First, many stores lack a clear identity. Since consumers can choose from a large number and variety of stores, retailers need apparel that differentiates them in the mind of the consumer. Consequently, they are putting pressure on manufacturers to shorten time cycles in order to provide more varied and timely deliveries. Retailers feel that the manufacturing process must be accelerated to keep up with the constantly changing tastes of customers. This has also increased the pressure to shorten the lead time from ordering to delivery.

Second, in 1988, many department stores found themselves saddled with excess inventory due to sluggish sales. Female customers, in particular, stopped buying in the summer of 1987. Some say that they rebelled against the resurrection of the miniskirt. As of mid-1988, they had not yet returned to former buying levels, and both retailers and manufacturers were faced with declining orders (see Exhibit 2).

Third, many stores are increasingly emphasizing house brands, putting them in direct competition with makers of designer-label goods. As a result, some manufacturers are cutting wholesale prices. Others are abandoning their own labels and becoming contractors for retailers' private-label clothing. Moreover, analysts predict that many smaller apparel makers will be forced out of the business altogether (Agins, 1988).

Fourth, there has been a growing trend toward consolidation among retail department stores. Larger stores place larger orders and favor vendors who can meet their needs. They are also likely to seek "one-stop shopping," buying from manufacturers who provide a broad range of styles and sizes, as well as give assistance in merchandising the goods in the store (Agins, 1988). Manufacturers who do not meet these needs are being dropped.

In an attempt to reduce their dependency on department stores, some of the larger manufacturers are opening their own retail stores. Ralph Lauren, for example, has over 70 stores that showcase his entire collection under one roof—providing exposure he would never get in a department store. Other newcomers to retail include Calvin Klein, Christian Dior, Adrienne Vittadini, Williwear, and Liz Claiborne. Vertical integration has already proved to be quite successful for such firms as Espirit, Bennetton, Laura Ashley, and The Gap.

INTERNAL ENVIRONMENT

Elisabeth Claiborne Ortenberg was born in Brussels to American parents and spent much of her childhood traveling in Europe with her banker father. Claiborne later lived in New Orleans and Baltimore but returned to Europe before completing high school (Sellers, 1987). After studying art for several years in Paris, she won a *Harper's Bazaar* design contest at age 20. She then moved to New York, where she found work drawing and modeling, and married an art director from the Bonwitt Teller specialty store.

Claiborne met Arthur Ortenberg in the mid-1950s when he was running the junior-dress division of the women's sportswear company. He hired her as a designer. They ended their first marriages and wed each other (Sellers, 1987).

Exhibit 2

Unit Purchases of Women's Sportswear (first 5 months of 1988 compared with first 5 months of 1987)

Category	Change in Unit	Change in Dollars
Women's shirts/ blouses	−10%	−10%
Sweaters	−14	−16
Slacks	−6	0
Blazers	−31	−24
Jeans	−7	+1
Skirts	−5	−13
Total (women's sportswear)	−9	−10

Source: The Wall Street Journal, August 3, 1988.

Claiborne then went to work as chief designer of Jonathon Logan's junior-dress division. In that capacity, she tried continually to convince her bosses to create clothes for highly paid working women. She made limited progress but remained unsatisfied. She wanted to strike out on her own, but she waited until her son, Alex, turned 21. In her words, "If we were going to lose everything we had, I wanted him to be old enough to handle it" (Sellers, 1987). Her fears were unfounded. The business showed a profit in the first nine months.

Presently, Claiborne serves as chairman, president, and chief executive officer of the organization. Although she no longer designs clothes herself, a point she regrets, she personally oversees all designs. Her past experience in art and her keen eye for fashion serve her well in these roles. Within the industry, she is widely credited with having a deep understanding of her working woman customer (*Sales and Marketing Management*, 1987).

Claiborne's husband, Arthur Ortenberg, has served in various senior executive positions and as one of the directors of the company since its incorporation in 1976. His 20 years of experience in textiles and apparels include a stint as director of Fashion Products Research, Inc., a textile consulting firm. His strengths in finance, administration, and organization have also served the firm well. In 1985, he was elected vice-chairman of the board along with a third key member of the management team, Jerome (Jerry) Chazen.

STRENGTH:
The company's management and Liz Claiborne herself are very knowledgeable of the fashion industry.

Chazen formally joined the company in May of 1977. With 20 years' experience in the women's sportswear area, Chazen's major strengths are in sales and marketing. He has served in various executive positions, including executive vice-president of marketing. In addition to his position as vice-chairman, he presently sits on the Board of Directors.

Leonard Boxer served as the fourth senior executive of the firm from 1976 to 1985. With seven years' prior experience in running production at Susan Thomas Apparel Company, he had the contacts to help line up overseas manufacturing operations. Although Boxer is officially retired, he still serves as a director and as a special consultant to the corporation.

The top managers at Liz Claiborne, Inc., have always worked as a team. Claiborne and Ortenberg particularly seem to complement each other in many ways. She is shy, whereas he's outgoing. She looks at details, while he sees the big picture (Sellers, 1987). The marketing of Liz Claiborne, Inc., reflects both of their personalities. "Both are intense, a bit arrogant and obsessed about the high quality image of Liz Claiborne clothes" (Sellers, 1987).

Claiborne and Ortenberg describe their most important mission as preparing successors (Sellers, 1987). Ortenberg is developing managers who will be able to run the company with the same team approach that has worked so well from the beginning. Claiborne is working with several designers to take her place.

STRUCTURE/CULTURE

Liz Claiborne, Inc., is well managed without being extremely formal. Many of the employees are young, and many sport Liz Claiborne's hippest attire (Deveny, 1989). Claiborne's personal style can be felt throughout the organization—from the decor to the creative process (Deveny, 1989).

Generally, managers and designers use their own discretion when carrying out their tasks. Few restrictions are needed because Claiborne believes in hiring employees who are the best at what they do. Claiborne, Ortenberg, and Chazen oversee the vice-presidents of all divisions, with Chazen having more authority over the men's line. Until recently, the structure was comprised of three levels, with the Board of Directors at the top, the management team in the middle, and a horizontal level of product and design divisions (Collection, Lizsport, Lizwear, Dresses, Dana Buchman, Accessories, Cosmetics, Menswear, and Retail).

In 1987, the three sportswear divisions, Collection, Lizport, and Lizwear, were brought together as the Sportswear Group and placed under the direction of a single president. This move was intended to bring a sharper focus and more dynamic direction to the major portion of the business on a daily basis (*Liz Claiborne Annual Report*, 1987).

A number of other structural changes were also made in 1987. First, the Executive Committee, which had advised the board on strategy and policy issues, was replaced by a new, pared-down Policy Committee (*Liz Claiborne Annual Report*, 1987). The old Executive Committee had grown fairly large partially because it had been used as a development tool for younger managers who served alongside seasoned executives. In addition, a Strategy Planning Committee was established to evaluate new business opportunities, monitor market share, and identify growth areas within the business. This committee includes employees from key areas throughout the company.

Two additional executive positions were also created, again to help train new managers for their eventual role in replacing the original Claiborne team. The first position, executive vice-president of operations and corporate planning, consolidates all production planning, raw materials acquisition, manufacturing, and distribution in one office (*Liz Claiborne Annual Report*, 1987). The second, senior vice-president of corporate sales and marketing, coordinates these efforts across divisions (*Liz Claiborne Annual Report*, 1987).

Liz Claiborne, Inc., considers its staff as one big family. It devotes more time and effort to the development of employees than any other activity. In training, great emphasis is placed on understanding the consumer and seeing clothing through "Claiborne eyes" (*Liz Claiborne Annual Report*, 1987). Claiborne herself believes in hard work and conveys this belief to her employees through her own actions on the job.

The first commandment at Liz Claiborne, Inc., is, "Satisfy thy consumer." The second is, "Support thy retailer" (Skolnik, 1985). Yet the company has no sales force on the road. From the beginning, retailers have come to New York several times a year to get Liz Claiborne merchandise. This enables Claiborne's marketing team to deal directly with top executives and to be readily accessible to major customers. It also adds a measure of control to the company's sales operation. Each of the company's divisions is responsible for marketing its own products, but the entire sales effort reflects the format of the buying organizations of its major customers.

Many of the salespeople at Liz Claiborne, Inc., have worked as buyers for retail outlets. Because the company often helps department stores in planning their merchandizing programs, the salespeople have to be at least as knowledgeable as the buyers they work with. Moreover, most of the salespeople are women who "look like the typical Claiborne customer" (*Sales and Marketing Management*, 1987).

The company claims that its salespeople are not pushy. But in one sense, they are demanding. Buyers are required to take an entire line, not choose selected items from those shown. Liz Claiborne's clout with retailers stems from the fact that its clothes generate annual sales of more than $400 per square foot, while the average is less than $200 per square foot. As a result, the company claims that it is the number 1 or 2 vendor at most of the department stores it supplies (Deveny, 1989).

In yet another innovative move, Claiborne was the first to transcend industry standards by offering six seasonal lines per year, as opposed to the usual four. As a result, retailers can buy six smaller chunks of fresh merchandise a year instead of four larger ones. This not only cuts inventory costs for the stores but also enables Claiborne's overseas suppliers to operate more efficiently with two extra cycles filling their slack period (Rudnitsky, 1984).

Although Claiborne has no traveling sales force, the company does provide a group of retail consultants who travel from store to store and work with retail salespeople. According to Jerry Chazen, one of the biggest problems in retail today is the "lack of trained people on the floor" (Skolnik, 1985). Claiborne's consultants try to combat this problem by running seminars and clinics for store employees. They explain the company's goals and fashion perspective, and stress good customer service.

Liz Claiborne, Inc., maintains a cooperative advertising program under which it generally matches a customer's advertising expenditures up to 2% of its apparel purchase and up to 3% of its accessories purchases. The company does no significant direct advertising to the public other than this cooperative advertising. In fact, the firm actually discourages retailers from listing the Liz Claiborne label in sale ads. Moreover, Liz Claiborne, Inc., rarely gives credits or discounts that other apparel companies typically offer. Chazen estimates that 60% of the company's clothes are sold at full price, versus around 40% for the average apparel firm (*Sales and Marketing Management*, 1987).

In 1987, the company opened its first store-within-a-store in the Jordan Marsh department store in Boston. Organized like a women's specialty shop, it is a personalized selling space where knowledgeable salespeople can help shoppers find the Liz Claiborne products they need to complete their wardrobe. Several more of these shops are planned for the future.

RESEARCH AND DEVELOPMENT

Claiborne regularly makes trips across the country to visit department stores and talk to customers. This gives her immediate feedback on how customers view her clothing. Information is also gathered using the firm's Systematic Updated Retail Feedback (SURF) System. In this system, reports come in weekly from a sample of department stores across the country that represent a cross section of store sizes and geographical locations. Using this data, computer programs generate outputs that indicate how consumers are reacting to recent merchandise shipments. Claiborne has discovered that there's often no relationship between what the retailers think and what the consumers buy.

As noted earlier, Claiborne personally oversees the creation of new designs. She has the ability to sense various moods in her mostly female, business-oriented target market and creates her design statements accordingly. To assist her in this task, the company is planning to open a limited number of Liz Claiborne prototype and presentational specialty shops in key markets across the United States. The stores will allow consumers to view a specially coordinated selection of Liz Claiborne merchandise in an ideal setting. They will also allow the firm to track sales, styles, colors, and customer perceptions to better plan future offerings.

MANUFACTURING

In the manufacturing area, Liz Claiborne, Inc., has been able to stabilize production prices over the years because it owned no factories. Instead, company managers have made agreements with independent suppliers located mostly in the Orient. All finished goods are shipped to the company's New Jersey facilities for reinspection and distribution.

Currently, manufacturing operations are run by a production administration staff which overseas product engineering, allocation of production among suppliers, and quality control. This staff constantly seeks additional suppliers throughout the world. Liz Claiborne, Inc., does not have formal or long-term arrangements with the suppliers who manufacture its products. Because it is often the largest customer of many of its manufacturing suppliers, its power over them is relatively high.

Liz Claiborne, Inc., buys materials such as the fabrics and trimmings used in its apparel in bulk from various suppliers in the United States and abroad. Until recently, the company has criticized U.S. textile mills for their reluctance to produce small orders of custom fabrics. To get such materials, used in 80% of its clothes, it had to go abroad, usually to Asia. Now the company is buying more fabrics custom-ordered from U.S. mills and has renovated two factories in New York's Chinatown to sew women's shirts, skirts, and slacks. Although it costs more to make the clothes in Chinatown, the New York location permits better quality control and faster turnarounds (*Business Week*, 1988).

The company schedules a great portion of its products and manufacturing commitments late in the production cycle in order to deliver on time clothes that reflect current tastes. By doing this, it favors suppliers who can make quick adjustments in response to changing production needs. In order to support and continue sales growth, Liz Claiborne, Inc., has to make substantial advance commitments with its suppliers, often as much as seven months prior to the receipt of firm orders from customers for the items to be produced. Yet management is very careful when doing this because misjudging the market could cause the company to face excess inventory supplies and/or manufacturing commitments.

HUMAN RESOURCE MANAGEMENT

As of December 1987, Liz Claiborne, Inc., employed approximately 3800 full-time employees. Claiborne feels that all jobs are important and she has good relations with her employees. This reflects the company's informal, decentralized structure which allows for smoother operation and communication between employees.

Liz Claiborne, Inc., is a member of the Manufacturers' Association and has been bound by a collective bargaining agreement with an affiliate of the International Ladies Garment Workers Union. The company also has an agreement with the Joint Board of Shirt, Leisurewear, Robe, Glove, and Rainwear Workers Union of the Amalgamated Clothing and Textile Workers Union.

FINANCE

In 1987, the company's net sales were $1053 million, up from $813 million in 1986 and $557 million in 1985. Net income expressed as a percentage of net sales in 1987, 1986, and 1985 was 10.9%, 10.6%, and 10.9%, respectively. The increase in 1987 as compared to 1986 was primarily due to a reduced provision for income taxes as a percentage of net sales. The decline in 1986 as compared to 1985 was caused by lower gross profit margins and higher selling, general, and administrative expenses, offset by a reduced provision for income taxes. Liz Claiborne's balance sheet and income statement are shown in Exhibits 3 and 4.

CURRENT SITUATION

Liz Claiborne, Inc., has been moving forward on a number of fronts. In September of 1986, the company entered the "bridge" sportswear market with a new Dana Buchman clothing label. The bridge category bridges the gap between designer and better sportswear (Gill, 1987). Although the distinctions among these categories are somewhat fuzzy, bridge merchandise is priced lower than designer labels, while still providing a fashionable designer look. The Dana Buchman line earned over $5 million in sales in its first four months in the marketplace. Company executives are pleased with these results because through

Exhibit 3   Liz Claiborne, Inc., and Subsidiaries: Consolidated Balance Sheet (dollar amounts in thousands)

	12/26/87	12/27/86	12/28/85
Assets			
Cash	$ 2,704	$ 2,628	$ 955
Short-term investments	157,762	101,441	55,225
Accounts receivable	80,591	57,718	58,940
Inventories	156,375	114,879	72,846
Deferred income tax benefits	6,563	2,861	—
Other current assets	19,994	14,860	12,109
Total current assets	423,989	294,387	200,075
Property and equipment			
Building	15,002	13,702	—
Machinery and equipment	22,085	13,599	6,341
Furniture and fixtures	8,916	6,007	4,124
Leasehold improvements	23,900	14,608	8,447
	69,903	47,916	18,912
Less—accumulated depreciation and amortization	16,763	11,118	7,721
	53,140	36,798	11,191
Investment in joint venture	3,767	3,392	3,460
Other assets	1,473	925	7,838
	$482,369	$335,502	$222,564
Liabilities			
Long-term debt due within 1 year	$ 357	$ —	$ —
Note payable	—	4,900	—
Advances from developer	—	2,409	—
Accounts payable	53,044	39,820	$ 26,804
Accrued expenses	43,374	26,166	15,574
Income taxes payable	6,412	7,921	3,527
Total current liabilities	103,187	81,216	45,905
Long-term debt	14,464	—	10,000
Deferred income taxes	7,762	6,499	3,930
Stockholders' equity			
Preferred stock, $0.01 par value; authorized shares—50,000,000 in 1987 and 1,500,000 in 1986; outstanding shares—none			
Common stock, $1 par value; authorized shares—250,000,000 in 1987 and 125,000,000 in 1986; outstanding shares—87,135,873 in 1987 and 43,279,361 in 1986	87,136	43,279	42,904
Capital in excess of par value	29,889	21,404	12,865
Retained earnings	239,931	183,104	106,960
	356,956	247,787	162,729
	$482,369	$335,502	$222,564

Dana Buchman, they have gained entry into a new price category with a name not associated with Liz Claiborne that can be developed independently (*Liz Claiborne Annual Report*, 1987).

The menswear division is also growing rapidly. When first introduced, the men's clothes, particularly the pants, were too baggy. With this problem taken care of, sales of men's clothing increased 79% in 1987. In 1988, the company expanded its offerings in this area with a new line of dress shirts, ties, hosiery, and underwear.

In December of 1987, Liz Claiborne, Inc., ended its joint venture with Avon to develop and market fragrances. The company charged that Avon failed to meet its obligations for the fall/Christmas seasons, which together account for

| Liz Claiborne, Inc., and Subsidiaries: Consolidated Income Statement (all dollar amounts in thousands except per share data) | | | | **Exhibit 4** |

	Fiscal Year Ending		
	1987	*1986*	*1985*
Net sales	$1,053,324	$813,497	$556,553
Costs and expenses			
Cost of goods sold	655,569	502,247	341,700
Selling, general, and administrative expenses	194,686	146,289	97,325
Interest expense	670	1,122	71
Interest and other income—net	(5,626)	(5,463)	(2,143)
	845,299	644,195	436,953
Income (before income taxes)	208,025	169,302	119,600
Income taxes	93,611	83,108	59,020
Net income	$ 114,414	$ 86,194	$ 60,580
Earnings per common share	$ 1.32	$ 1.00	$ .71
Dividends per common share	$ 0.16	$ 0.12	$ 0.08

over 70% of annual sales. In a suit filed in the New York Supreme Court in Manhattan, Liz Claiborne, Inc., complained that this gaffe would "irreparably harm and likely destroy the business" (*The Wall Street Journal*, 1988). Despite these problems, however, the Liz Claiborne fragrance is selling well. A men's cologne is now being developed, but industry analysts caution that a second success is not automatic.

In February of 1988, Liz Claiborne, Inc., opened the first of a chain of stores called First Issue Boutiques. These stores sell a collection of relaxed sportswear bearing the merchandise label First Issue. Although the clothes are said to have the Liz Claiborne look, they are priced just below the Liz Claiborne collections. Ideally, the new stores will compete with The Limited, The Gap, and Banana Republic while not antagonizing retailers who already carry the Liz Claiborne line. Like Dana Buchman, First Issue provides Claiborne with an entrance into a new market and a new label to develop and expand. Jerome Chazen predicts that the stores could eventually become a bigger part of Liz Claiborne, Inc., than apparel. The company opened 13 stores in 1988 and about 20 more are planned for 1989.

The company also plans to introduce a line of large-size women's clothing in 1989. The line, which will be named Elisabeth, will be aimed at the 400 million U.S. women who wear a size 14 or larger. With its strong presence in department stores across the country, Liz Claiborne, Inc., hopes to gain a major share of this market.

Although all of these moves appear to be positive, not everything the company touches turns to gold. In 1987, Liz Claiborne, Inc., phased outs its Girls' Sportswear Division, which could not compete with the lower prices charged by other children's clothing producers. In addition, the company brought out a line of miniskirts, midriff-baring tops, and prewashed denim clothing that customers rejected (Deveny, 1989).

Problems with the clothing line combined with flat sales throughout the industry caused the company to predict that its full-year 1988 earnings would fall 10% from 1987. It indicated that the abundance of inventory in the industry had made it unable to obtain anticipated prices (Agins, 1988). Management addressed the problem by maintaining price points for fall 1988 and by absorbing higher costs (particularly for fabrics) and so narrowing operating margins. As a result, for the first time in its seven years of covering Liz Claiborne, Inc., *Value Line* ranked Claiborne stock as a likely below-average performer in 1988 (*Value Line*, 1988).

Although sales did rebound during the holiday season at the end of 1988, there are indications that the Liz Claiborne label may be maturing. The tremendous growth rates of the past may no longer be feasible. Given the present conditions in the apparel industry, continued diversification may be required if growth is to continue. Yet there are numerous risks.

One obvious risk is that management may not have the skills to prosper in industries outside of apparel. The First Issue stores, for example, compete in a market that has been even more lackluster than the company's core business (Deveny, 1989). Moreover, the competition from such entrenched firms as The Limited and The Gap is fierce. Does Claiborne's management team have the expertise to beat these players at their own game?

Another risk is that the Liz Claiborne name may become overused. The use of the Dana Buchman and First Issue labels seems to reveal a sensitivity to this possibility. But do these new products actually serve different market segments or will they simply cannibalize the original Liz Claiborne line?

Another question to consider is whether the company can continue to prosper without the guidance of Elisabeth and Arthur Ortenberg. Recently, they have been trying to limit their role in daily operations. They had hoped to shift to a one-month-on, one-month-off schedule, but the plan fell through when the stock market crashed in October 1987 (Deveny, 1989). Another sign that they may be reducing their involvement with the firm was their sale of over 900,000 shares of their company stock in 1988. Some analysts are worried about this large sale, while others note that their holdings in the firm (valued at $82 million) are still substantial.

Elisabeth Claiborne Ortenberg and her company appear to have reached a critical juncture in their development. What strategies should they utilize to maintain their number 1 position in the apparel industry? How can they convince skeptical investors that the bloom is not off the rose?

REFERENCES

Agins, T. "U.S. Apparel Makers Face Tough Times," *The Wall Street Journal*, August 3, 1988, pp. 20, 22.

"Claiborne Comes Home," *Business Week*, January 11, 1988, p. 73.

Deveny, K. "Can Ms. Fashion Bounce Back?" *Business Week*, January 16, 1989, pp. 64–70.

Fierman, J. "High Fashion Names Knock Themselves Off," *Fortune*, June 10, 1985, p. 73.

Gill, P. "Bridge-(Wo)manship," *Stores*, October 1987, pp. 20–25.

Liz Claiborne Annual Report, 1987.

Liz Claiborne, Inc., "Business Brief," *The Wall Street Journal*, March 1, 1988, p. 44.

"Liz Claiborne's Pattern for Success," *Sales and Marketing Management*, June 1987, p. 54.

"Liz Is Big Biz," *Madison Avenue,* October 1986, pp. 28–31.

Rudnitsky, H. "What's in a Name?" *Forbes,* March 12, 1984, pp. 43–44.

Schneider, J. "Direct to the Consumer," *Nation's Business,* June 1985, pp. 29–32.

Sellers, P. "The Rag Trade's Reluctant Revolutionary," *Fortune,* January 5, 1987, pp. 36–38.

Skolnik, R. "Liz the Wiz," *Sales and Marketing Management,* September 9, 1985, pp. 50–52.

Smith, A. "How Liz Claiborne Designed an Empire," *Esquire,* January 1986, pp. 78–79.

Standard and Poor's Industry Surveys, August 27, 1987, pp. T82–T88.

Value Line, June 3, 1988, p. 1608.

Sears, Roebuck and Company

John E. Oliver, Valdosta State College

On March 8, 1989, Sears, Roebuck and Company, the largest retailer in the world with over 800 stores, reopened after being closed for 42 hours. The prices of 50,000 products in every store had been marked down to reflect lower, discounted prices. After many years of competition with discount department store chains like K Mart, Wal-Mart, Toys "R" Us, and Target, Sears had changed its philosophy. The basic strategy of advertising frequent sales to attract customers was replaced with a policy of "everyday low prices."

"We recruited an army of retirees and high school students, armed them with 29,000 label guns, and sent them in to change the price tags on $1\frac{1}{2}$ billion pieces of inventory. We sold twice as much on our first day under the new policy as we did on an average day under our old strategy," said one Sears executive. "This is an important change for us. We haven't just changed the way we do business. We've changed the business we're in. We did it because of changes in what customers want and what our competitors are doing. Mr. Brennan, our CEO, is making some tough decisions."

SEARS HISTORY

Discount pricing is not new to Sears. The cover of its 1894 catalogue, then called *Consumer's Guide*, was illustrated with a globe and the inscription "Cheapest Supply House on Earth." In fact, Sears began as a mail order business in 1886. By 1894, it had offices in Minneapolis and Chicago. It was not until 1925 that Sears operated its first retail store. Soon after, it began to acquire existing retail

establishments in Temple, Oklahoma; Chicago, Illinois; New Orleans and
Shreveport, Louisiana; and locations in North Dakota. In 1931, Allstate Insurance Company was established. In 1934, Sears Finance Corporation was formed
to finance home modernization loans under the Federal Housing Program, and
Sears International was formed to sell merchandise in other countries. During
the late 1930s, the 1940s, and the early 1950s Sears acquired, and sometimes sold
off, various manufacturing firms that supplied the retailer with some of its merchandise. The firm manufactured a wide range of products, including appliances, plumbing fixtures, encyclopedias, pianos, wallpaper, textiles, furniture,

paint, trading stamps, shoes, and electronics. In 1943, Sears gave its investment in Encyclopedia Britannica to the University of Chicago.

Many people believe that the best strategic decision ever made at Sears came near the end of World War II. General Robert E. Wood predicted that the buying habits of Americans would change as the war ended. Service personnel would return to civilian jobs and family life. Manufacturers would switch from producing war materials to producing consumer goods. People would use automobiles to drive to stores rather than ordering from catalogues. These predictions allowed Sears to develop a "vision." Sears rapidly expanded the number of retail stores to tap the new markets. Montgomery Ward, where Robert Wood worked before moving to Sears, Sears' largest competitor at the time, did not. Sears soon surpassed the competition and has continued its retail expansion ever since.

In 1956, Sears Roebuck Acceptance Corporation was organized to finance the complex operations of the parent company, and in 1959, Homart Development Company began to develop shopping centers with Sears stores as the focus or anchor stores. By 1981, real estate development and financing had been supplemented by the acquisition of several savings and loan and mortgage banking companies in Washington, California, New York, and other states. Some of the savings and loan and mortgage banking subsidiaries carry their own names, while some are under the Allstate banner. In addition to its full line of insurance services and its mortgage banking operations, Allstate operates a motor club, travel bureau, and several banks.

In 1981, Sears acquired Coldwell Banker & Company, a real estate brokerage firm, and Dean Witter Reynolds Organization, Inc., a financial services firm. Both subsidiaries have grown both internally and through additional acquisitions.

More recent acquisitions included Eye Care Center of America in 1987, Pinstripes Petites, Inc., in 1988, and Western Auto Supply Company also in 1988.

INTERNATIONAL OPERATIONS

Although Sears had sold some merchandise to foreign customers, including Canadians, through its catalogue operations since the 1880s, it was not until 1942 that the company actually located a store on foreign soil. This Cuban operation was expropriated by the Castro government in October 1960. However, subsidiaries in Mexico, Brazil, Columbia, Peru, and Venezuela, opened during the 1940s and 1950s, fared somewhat better. In 1955 the Sears Roebuck Overseas, Inc., subsidiary was formed to facilitate the purchase of foreign-made merchandise. By 1958, a subsidiary was needed to finance installment accounts of foreign customers and Banco de Credito Internacional, S.A., was formed in Panama. A Spanish subsidiary was formed in 1964, and stores were opened in Barcelona in 1967 and Madrid in 1970. An interest in Galeries Anspach, S.A., was acquired in Belgium in 1971 but sold in 1976 after an $18 million injection of capital that failed to turn the unit profitable. In 1982, Sears World Trade, Inc., a world trading company, was formed for exporting and importing, third-country trading, and countertrading not only consumer goods but industrial goods and services as well. About the same time, Sears sold its Spanish retail operations in Madrid and Barcelona but maintained an agreement for Sears World Trade, Inc., to supply the new owners, Galerias Preciados, S.A., until 1992. In 1983, the Brazilian and Venezuelan retail, manufacturing, and service subsidiaries were sold.

JOINT VENTURES

Throughout its history, Sears has entered joint ventures with other companies as a way of investigating the feasibility of new lines of business and developing technology. Beginning with its manufacturing ventures in the 1930s and 1940s, Sears has participated in ventures involving insurance services, land development, telephone communication, and more. Its most recent joint venture was Videotec, with IBM and CBS, Inc., to develop a home-shopping and order service for consumers utilizing personal computers, television, and telephone technologies.

CURRENT ORGANIZATION AND OPERATIONS

Sears' organization structure changes constantly. Exhibit 1 is an approximation of the current corporate structure of Sears. The four principal groups of enterprises include the Merchandise Group, the Allstate Group, the Dean Witter Financial Services Group, and the Coldwell Banker Real Estate Group.

■ The Merchandise Group

The Merchandise Group conducts merchandising and credit operations in the United States, Canada, and Mexico. Based on sales of merchandise and services, it is the largest retailer in the world. A broad line of merchandise and services (see any Sears catalogue) is offered through three types of department stores: over 400 full-line stores in major metropolitan areas, over 350 medium-sized stores which carry an extensive assortment of merchandise, and over 60 hard-line stores which serve neighborhoods or smaller communities with a limited selection of appliances, hardware, sporting goods, and automotive supplies. In addition, over 300 specialty stores (including Sears Business Systems Centers, Paint and Hardware Stores, Eye Care Centers, Pinstripes Petites, and Western Auto Stores) are operated by the Merchandise Group, along with the catalogue order operation, which consists of over 640 catalogue sales offices and 1700 independent sales franchises. The Western Auto Stores consist of almost 400 company-owned stores and over 1500 independently owned and operated dealer stores nationwide. Sears merchandise is supplied by 9950 domestic suppliers and is purchased by 27 buying departments.

Approximately 60% of the Merchandise Group's sales are credit sales. Sears has over 27 million active customer credit accounts, over $14 billion in receivables. Sears sells some revolving charge account balances to other financial institutions instead of borrowing to finance them. Over $830 million in such balances are outstanding. Sears credit operations provide collection processing service for other credit grantors.

Sears Roebuck Corporate Structure **Exhibit 1**

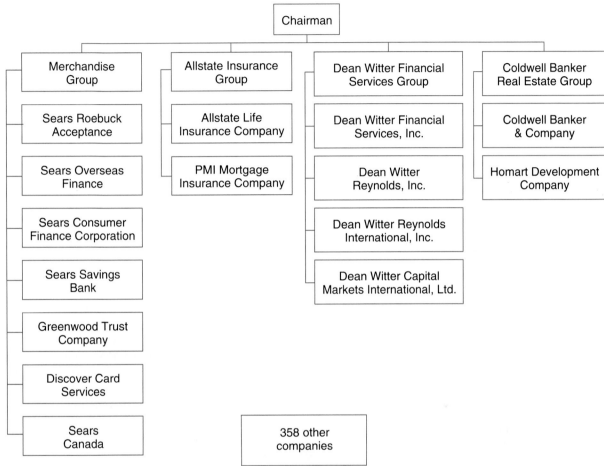

Sears Mexican and Canadian subsidiaries are a part of the Merchandise Group and have over 100 stores and 1600 catalogue sales offices with 55,000 personnel.

Sales and profits of the Merchandise Group have been slipping in recent years. Intense competition from discounters such as Wal-Mart and specialty retailers such as Toys "R" Us has chipped away at Sears' traditional middle-America customer base.

■ The Allstate Group

The Allstate Insurance Group provides property, liability, life, and health insurance to individuals, businesses, and other groups primarily in the United States and Canada. Over 70% of property and liability insurance premiums come from auto insurance and over 16% come from homeowners' policies. Allstate has over $93 billion of life insurance in force, with approximately $58 billion on individuals and $35 billion in group plans. The company has 51 offices and operation centers, 320 claim service offices, and almost 7000 sales locations, including Sears stores. Sales and profits of the Allstate Group have been growing steadily in the past few years.

■ Dean Witter Financial Services Group

The Dean Witter Group provides a broad range of securities-related and consumer banking services, including securities brokerage, principal trading, formation and sale of mortgage-related securities, investment banking, credit card services, mortgage banking, and consumer deposit and lending services. The largest subsidiary, Dean Witter Reynolds, Inc., has over 2 million individual and corporate accounts. It is a member of every major securities, futures, and options exchange in the United States. Interest from securities, repurchase transactions, and client margin accounts provide over 35% of securities-related revenues, with another 27% coming from commissions on securities transactions for clients. The balance of securities-related revenue comes from trading and investment banking.

Consumer banking income comes 42% from credit card services, 15% from mortgage banking, 29% from deposit and loan operations, and 14% from consumer finance services. The Discover Card, issued by Greenwood Trust Company (a wholly owned subsidiary of Sears Consumer Finance Corporation and a Delaware state bank), is intended to be a general-purpose credit card to compete with American Express, Master Card, and VISA, as well as a vehicle for delivering services of the Sears Financial Network. Over 22 million cards are outstanding and may be used at over 750,000 locations. Discover Card Services, Inc., Sears Payment Systems, Inc., Hurley State Bank, Sears Mortgage Securities Corporation, Sears Savings Bank, Sears Mortgage Corporation, and Sears Consumer Finance Division also contribute to financial service income. Unfortunately, the Dean Witter Group is not contributing to Sears' profit on a regular basis.

■ Coldwell Banker Real Estate Group

The Coldwell Banker Group is a broker in residential and commercial real estate; invests in, develops, and manages commercial real estate; and performs services for owners, developers, investors, and users of real estate. Services are offered through more than 1000 company-owned offices and 1000 franchised offices. Homart Development Company develops and operates shopping centers, office buildings, and other commercial properties both through 100% ownership and through joint ventures. The Coldwell Banker Group accounts for about 5% of Sears' total profits.

■ Leadership

Sears' chief executive officer (CEO) is Edward A. Brennan, a tall, robust man who has been with Sears for over 33 years. His brother, his parents, and his grandfather were all Sears employees at one time. At age 22, Mr. Brennan started his own Sears career as a salesman in men's furnishings. He is energetic, intelligent, and knowledgeable in merchandising. In 1980, at the age of 46, Mr. Brennan was promoted to chairman and chief executive officer of the Merchandising Group by the former Sears Chairman Edward R. Telling. Brennan ran the Merchandising Group for eight years. He has been characterized as a formal, tough, no-nonsense executive with a friendly manner, an enormous reservoir of self-confidence, and an endless ability to absorb detail. He once broke Sears' tradition by laying off employees based on performance rather than seniority. Brennan's positive attitude is reflected in the following quotes he has made at various times when confronted by the press concerning current problems faced by Sears:

- "The most important growth opportunities come from within."
- "We're moving past the investment stage to the harvest stage."
- "Sears is not only the biggest, it is the best."
- "I don't see any huge problems. I feel very good about how we're positioned strategically."
- "I really don't think consistency is a problem in our stores."
- "Bigness has disadvantages and it has advantages. . . . Over the years, in general, bigness has served Sears well."
- "This is the most stimulating time of my life."

■ Sears Corporate Culture and Home

Brennan, of course, is a product of the Sears corporate culture, which has been described as methodical, lumbering, and even lethargic. The company has a promotion-from-within policy that assures opportunity for those who stay with the firm and do a good job. Both Edward R. Telling, the former chairman, and Edward A. Brennan, the current chairman, rose through the ranks of the Merchandising Group of Sears to become chairman. In the past, Sears people believed that their company was the biggest and the best, and that steadiness would win the game. They respected authority and procedure. Employees were expected to be orderly and punctual and to be attentive to detail. They worked long hours and strived to satisfy the customer at all costs. Initiative in serving customers was admired, but ambition was to be controlled. Respecting the supervisor, performing your duties, serving your customers, and putting in your time were important to advancement.

The 110-story Sears Tower in Chicago is the world's tallest building and home to the largest retailer in the world. It is also a symbol of the company and its culture, both of which have been called monolithic.

But even monoliths can be changed. In December of 1988, the Sears Tower was put up for sale at an asking price of over $1 billion. It has cost $200 million to build in 1972. The reason given for selling the Tower was that Sears could cut its costs of operation by moving into less expensive facilities.

The Sears culture has changed a great deal in the last decade. All of the changes were for good reasons, but together they do not form a clear and understandable pattern of movement from one set of coherent values to another. In the years following World War II (1940–1960), Sears' cultural values clearly were aimed at satisfying customers with quality goods and services. Shares of Sears stock were used as an incentive to encourage these values. Employees were viewed by the public, and viewed themselves, as knowledgeable professionals who were capable of advising and serving customers making buying decisions, whatever unique needs the customer might have.

Exhibit 2 Sears, Roebuck and Company: Ten-Year Summary of Consolidated Financial Data
($ millions, except per common share data)

	1988	1987	1986	1985	1984	1983	1982	1981	1980	1979
Operating Results										
Revenues	$50,251	$45,904	$42,303	$39,349	$37,898	$35,257	$29,559	$27,243	$25,082	$24,301
Costs and expenses	45,617	41,222	38,139	35,384	33,766	31,751	26,866	25,182	23,170	22,323
Nonrecurring expenses	751	105	—	—	—	—	—	—	86	—
Interest	2,937	2,721	2,653	2,629	2,528	1,703	1,628	1,520	1,133	918
Operating income	946	1,856	1,511	1,336	1,604	1,803	1,065	541	693	1,060
Other income	157	239	282	277	246	66	28	101	(11)	43
Income from continuing operations before income taxes, minority interest and equity in net income of unconsolidated companies	1,103	2,095	1,793	1,613	1,850	1,869	1,093	642	682	1,103
Income taxes										
Current operations	54	521	444	306	498	565	238	10	98	317
Fresh start and deferred tax benefits	—	(172)	—	—	(60)	—	—	—	—	—
Income from continuing operations	1,032	1,726	1,336	1,280	1,422	1,326	866	646	604	820
Income (loss) from discontinued operations	(122)	(93)	3	14	30	11	(5)	4	6	10
Cumulative effect of change in accounting for income taxes	544	—	—	—	—	—	—	—	—	—
Net income	1,454	1,633	1,339	1,294	1,452	1,337	861	650	610	830
Percent return on average equity	10.5	12.3	10.8	11.4	14.0	14.4	10.1	8.2	8.1	11.4

Financial Position

Investments	$29,136	$25,120	$22,183	$19,249	$17,203	$15,434	$13,497	$12,229	$11,336	$ 9,985
Receivables	28,685	26,026	21,417	18,942	17,565	15,511	11,532	10,827	8,956	8,967
Property and equipment, net	5,179	4,790	4,593	4,541	4,361	3,938	3,396	3,312	3,153	3,061
Merchandise inventories	3,716	4,115	4,013	4,115	4,530	3,621	3,146	3,103	2,715	2,680
Total assets	77,952	75,014	66,009	66,426	57,073	46,177	36,541	34,406	28,218	26,904
Insurance reserves	17,329	13,169	10,014	8,090	6,919	6,262	5,667	5,161	4,407	4,075
Short-term borrowings	8,978	7,055	4,306	3,996	3,887	4,596	2,820	3,233	4,436	4,293
Long-term debt	9,736	9,562	10,067	9,907	9,531	7,405	5,816	5,324	2,965	2,966
Total debt	18,714	16,617	14,373	13,903	13,418	12,001	8,636	8,557	7,401	7,259
Percent of debt to equity	133	123	110	118	123	123	98	103	97	97
Shareholders' equity	14,055	13,541	13,017	11,776	10,903	9,782	8,812	8,269	7,665	7,446

Shareholders' Common Stock Investment

Book value per share (year end)	$37.75	$35.77	$33.90	$31.66	$29.46	$27.59	$25.08	$23.77	$24.32	$23.44
Shareholders (Profit Sharing Fund counted as single shareholder)	351,999	328,446	319,686	326,201	340,831	339,644	350,292	354,050	349,725	339,459
Average shares outstanding (millions)	379	378	369	363	358	353	350	316	316	320
Net income per share										
Income from continuing operations	$2.72	$4.55	$3.57	$3.47	$3.92	$3.76	$2.47	$2.05	$1.91	$2.57
Income (loss) from discontinued operations	(0.32)	(0.25)	0.01	0.04	0.08	0.03	(0.01)	0.01	0.02	0.03
Cumulative effect of change in accounting for income taxes	1.44	—	—	—	—	—	—	—	—	—
Net income	3.84	4.30	3.58	3.51	4.00	3.79	2.46	2.06	1.93	2.60
Dividends per share	$2.00	$2.00	$1.76	$1.76	$1.76	$1.52	$1.36	$1.36	$1.36	$1.28
Dividend payout percent	52.1	46.5	49.2	50.1	44.0	40.1	55.3	66.0	70.5	49.2
Market price (high-low)	46-32¼	59½-29¾	50⅜-35⅞	41⅛-30⅞	40⅜-29½	45⅛-27	32-15¾	20¾-14⅞	19½-14½	21⅝-17⅞
Closing market price at year end	40⅞	33½	39¾	39	31¾	37⅛	30⅛	16⅛	15⅜	18
Price/earnings ratio (high-low)	12-8	14-7	14-10	12-9	10-7	12-7	13-6	10-7	10-8	8-7

Source: Annual report.

Exhibit 3   **Sears, Roebuck and Company: Five-Year Summary of Business Group and Segment Financial Data**

	1988	1987	1986	1985	1984
Revenues					
Sears Merchandise Group					
Merchandising	$24,252	$22,894	$22,092	$21,549	$21,671
Credit	2,260	2,011	2,068	2,098	1,894
International	3,744	3,180	2,914	2,905	2,943
Sears Merchandise Group total	30,256	28,085	27,074	26,552	26,508
Allstate Insurance Group					
Property-liability insurance	13,197	11,730	9,827	8,368	7,640
Life-health insurance	1,656	1,261	896	701	532
Noninsurance	71	64	56	46	34
Allstate Insurance Group total	14,924	13,055	10,779	9,115	8,206
Dean Witter Financial Services Group					
Securities-related	2,481	2,747	2,563	2,031	1,840
Consumer banking	1,277	699	248	154	125
Dean Witter Financial Services Group					
total	3,758	3,446	2,811	2,185	1,965
Coldwell Banker Real Estate Group	1,444	1,399	1,344	1,242	1,005
Corporate and other	198	176	489	424	359
Intergroup transactions	(329)	(257)	(194)	(169)	(145)
Total	$50,251	$45,904	$42,303	$39,349	$37,898

Income from Continuing Operations Before Income Taxes, Minority Interest and Equity in Net Income of Unconsolidated Companies

	1988	1987	1986	1985	1984
Sears Merchandise Group					
Merchandising	$ (312)	$ 807	$ 885	$ 738	$ 1,196
Credit	517	463	502	582	483
International	128	132	98	94	16
Sears Merchandise Group total	333	1,402	1,485	1,414	1,695
Allstate Insurance Group					
Property-liability insurance	671	702	441	261	363
Life-health insurance	192	191	166	150	112
Non-insurance	3	(1)	3	(1)	1
Allstate Insurance Group total	866	892	610	410	476
Dean Witter Financial Services Group					
Securities-related	104	148	154	(3)	(92)
Consumer banking	45	(192)	(174)	(5)	23
Dean Witter Financial Services Group					
total	150	(44)	(20)	(8)	(69)
Coldwell Banker Real Estate Group	119	186	85	130	79
Corporate and other	(365)	(341)	(367)	(333)	(331)
Total	$ 1,103	$ 2,095	$ 1,793	$ 1,613	$ 1,850

In the early 1970s, however, Sears added levels of management and controls while allowing its store-level work force to erode. Many of its experienced, professional salespeople retired or left the company. In many cases, the exodus was due to the falling value of Sears stock as an incentive. One reason for the drop in stock value was the increased cost of excessive hierarchy and control. Sears became a high-cost retailer. About this time (early 1980s), the emphasis at Sears shifted from serving the customer to cutting costs.

	1988	1987	1986	1985	1984
Net income (millions)					
Sears Merchandise Group					
Merchandising	$ 194	$ 488	$ 458	$ 447	$ 656
Credit	289	263	253	294	243
International	41	36	25	25	6
Sears Merchandise Group total	524	787	736	766	905
Allstate Insurance Group					
Property-liability insurance	979	928	631	490	505
Life-health insurance	(29)	18	105	105	152
Non-insurance	3	—	2	1	1
Allstate Insurance Group total	953	946	738	596	658
Dean Witter Financial Services Group					
Securities-related	63	76	80	—	(45)
Consumer banking	23	(116)	(93)	—	14
Dean Witter Financial Services Group total	86	(40)	(13)	—	(31)
Coldwell Banker Real Estate Group	90	129	66	99	74
Corporate and other	(199)	(189)	(188)	(167)	(154)
Total	$ 1,454	$ 1,633	$ 1,339	$ 1,294	$ 1,452
Assets					
Sears Merchandise Group					
Merchandising	$ 8,111	$ 8,253	$ 8,233	$ 8,240	$ 8,332
Credit	12,844	12,706	12,070	11,887	11,825
International	2,752	2,257	2,068	1,917	1,881
Sears Merchandise Group total	23,707	23,216	22,371	22,044	22,038
Allstate Insurance Group					
Property-liability insurance	19,382	17,217	15,442	13,372	11,913
Life-health insurance	10,250	7,234	4,848	3,529	2,591
Non-insurance	76	69	66	53	49
Allstate Insurance Group total	29,708	24,520	20,356	16,954	14,553
Dean Witter Financial Services Group					
Securities-related	9,015	13,952	12,600	18,720	12,508
Consumer banking	8,742	6,059	2,962	1,184	1,359
Dean Witter Financial Services Group total	17,757	20,011	15,562	19,904	13,867
Coldwell Banker Real Estate Group	6,780	6,551	7,880	7,552	6,849
Corporate and other	1,335	1,907	2,300	1,981	1,627
Intergroup eliminations and reclassifications	(1,335)	(1,191)	(2,460)	(2,009)	(1,861)
Total	$77,952	$75,014	$66,009	$66,426	$57,073

Source: Annual report.

Replacing experienced, professional salespeople with younger, cheaper, inexperienced workers led to erosion of the service ethic and customer satisfaction. This happened at about the same time that discount marketers like K Mart and Wal-Mart were gaining solid footholds in department store markets.

Sears tried to reposition itself in the market only to compound the confusion. First, the company tried to take middle-class customers back from the specialty shop competition by marketing brand names like Reebok, General Electric, Sony, and Toshiba. The firm even developed labels like McKids in partnership with McDonald's to show how trendy it was. Later, the company tried to pre-

---

Exhibit 4   Sears, Roebuck and Company: Consolidated Statements of Income (millions, except per common share data)

	Year Ended December 31		
	1988	*1987*	*1986*
Revenues	$50,251.0	$45,904.1	$42,302.8
Expenses			
Costs and expenses	45,616.5	41,222.5	38,138.8
Nonrecurring expenses	751.1	105.2	—
Interest	2,937.4	2,720.6	2,653.3
Total expenses	49,305.0	44,048.3	40,792.1
Operating income	946.0	1,855.8	1,510.7
Other income	156.8	239.4	282.2
Income from continuing operations before income taxes, minority interest and equity in net income of unconsolidated companies	1,102.8	2,095.2	1,792.9
Income taxes			
Current operations	53.5	520.5	443.8
Fresh start and deferred tax benefits	—	(172.4)	—
Minority interest and equity in net income of unconsolidated companies	(17.0)	(20.9)	(13.5)
Income from continuing operations	1,032.3	1,726.2	1,335.6
Discontinued operations			
Operating income (loss), less income tax benefit (expense) of $34.7, $97.0 and $(8.6)	(64.2)	(93.4)	3.0
Loss on disposal, less income tax benefit of $30.2	(58.6)	—	—
Income before cumulative effect of accounting change	909.5	1,632.8	1,338.6
Cumulative effect of change in accounting for income taxes	544.2	—	—
Net income	$ 1,453.7	$ 1,632.8	$ 1,338.6
Net income per common share			
Income from continuing operations	$ 2.72	$ 4.55	$ 3.57
Discontinued operations	(.32)	(.25)	.01
Income before cumulative effect of accounting change	2.40	4.30	3.58
Cumulative effect of change in accounting for income taxes	1.44	—	—
Net income	$ 3.84	$ 4.30	$ 3.58
Average common shares outstanding	378.8	377.9	368.8

Source: Annual report.

tend it was a discount store like K Mart or Wal-Mart. By late 1988, customers were confused, employees were confused, managers were confused, and the Sears culture was confused.

FINANCIAL POSITION

Sears financial position has been both a cause and a result of the confusion the firm has experienced lately. Exhibits 2 and 3 contain consolidated income and expense information for Sears for the years 1979–1988 and 1984–1988. Trends in

---

The Top Five Retailers, 1971, 1979, 1988   **Exhibit 5**

1971		*1979*		*1988*	
Company	*Sales (in billions)*	*Company*	*Sales (in billions)*	*Company*	*Sales (in billions)*
Sears, Roebuck	10.1	Sears, Roebuck	17.5	Sears, Roebuck	30.2
J.C. Penney	4.8	K Mart (Kresge)	12.7	K Mart	27.3
Kresge (K Mart)	3.1	J.C. Penney	11.2	Wal-Mart	20.6
Woolworth	2.8	Woolworth	6.7	J.C. Penney	15.2
Montgomery Ward	2.3	Federated	5.8	Dayton-Hudson	12.2

Costs of Sales for Several Large Retailers   **Exhibit 6**

Company	*Percent of Sales*
Sears	32
J.C. Penney	25
K Mart	24
Wal-Mart	23
The Limited	17

operating revenues and net income indicate some very significant changes, weaknesses, and challenges taking place at Sears. Sears' sales, for example, add to 1% of this nation's GNP.

Consolidated balance sheets for the period 1984 to 1988 also reveal several basic changes, strengths, and opportunities occurring. With total assets of $75 billion, and equity of more than $13 billion, as shown in Exhibit 4, Sears could lose a billion dollars a year for many years before going bankrupt (assuming no one intervened).

To fully grasp what is happening at and to Sears, financial statements and trends should be compared to those of its competitors like K Mart, Wal-Mart, J.C. Penney, and others. For instance, the examination of the five largest retailers presented in Exhibit 5 indicates the gains made by competitors in Sears' markets. In 1989 it is anticipated that K Mart will become the world's largest retailer, with Wal-Mart close behind. In another comparison, Sears' costs as a percent of sales is high for the industry (see Exhibit 6).

At a recent stockholders meeting, it was pointed out by a stockholder that the market price of Sears stock was so low it would tempt corporate raiders to buy up enough stock to allow them to take over the company and liquidate the assets and/or separate parts of the company at a huge profit.

Later, Wall Street analysts began publishing reports showing how Sears could be broken up profitably at stock prices as high as $90 a share when Sears stock was selling at less than half that amount. Rumors of takeover plans by R. O. Perelman of Revlon, Donald Trump, and others caused the stock price to fluctuate in time to the rumors.

At the 1989 annual meeting, one stockholder criticized Sears' management: "You lost me a long time ago. And you lost the focus of Middle America 10 or 15 years ago." Brennan replied, "Give us a try. We want you back."

BRENNAN'S CHALLENGE

Imagine you are Edward Brennan, chairman and CEO of Sears. Do you think the "everyday low prices" strategy of the Merchandising Group will solve some of the problems the group faces? What other alternatives do you see for Sears? What will you do to get "Middle America" back?

KNP Paper N.V.

Alan Bauerschmidt, Daniel Sullivan, University of South Carolina—
Columbia

Koninklijke Nederlandse Paperfabrieken N.V. (KNP), or Royal Dutch Papermills, specializes in the production and sale of paper and board products to
serve the printing and packaging industries throughout the world. The firm
originated in 1850 as a small papermill on the Maas River in the Province of
Limburg in The Netherlands, and this location in the city of Maastricht continues to be the site of one of the three modern Dutch papermaking mills operated
by the firm. Another papermill containing two papermaking machines is
located across the Maas in Belgium, while the firm also produces packaging
materials at various European locations and has investments in paper merchant
operations in a number of countries.

These activities reflect a progressive expansion of the firm that requires a
degree of centralized control, and the corporate headquarters for the management of the domestic and international activities of the firm occupies a modern
office building located at Erasmusdomein 50, in a newer portion of the ancient
and historic city of Maastricht. It is here that Mr. Wilmer Zetteler, the Commercial Director of KNP België, considers his response to an interviewer's questions
concerning the emerging international business strategy of KNP and the decisions that will be necessary to meet the challenges faced by the firm he represents. Mr. Zetteler appreciates that any reply he might make must be understood in the context of the emerging position of his firm in the paper industry
and the European Community.

KNP AND THE WORLD PAPER INDUSTRY

The evolution of the papermaking industry and the emergence of the modern European economic system has shaped the development of KNP. In the year immediately following World War II, the relatively undamaged but depreciated plant at Maastricht produced only 10,000 tons of paper, but by 1950 the firm had begun its pioneering effort in the production of coated paper and became the first European producer of such papers, using technology obtained under a license from the Consolidated Paper Company in the United States. A companion plant, also producing the top-grade coated paper used in the printing of brochures, art books, and catalogues is located at Nijmegen on the Waal River, the extension of the Rhine in the Gelderland province of the Netherlands. Another mill at Meerssen, a town outside the city limits of Maastricht, produces uncoated papers that are world-renowned in the markets for colored and water-marked paper, although the overall demand for such traditional forms of paper remains small and the capacity of the three papermaking machines at this plant only totals 27,000 tons per year.

The oil price shock of 1973 led the firm to reconsider its fundamental strategy and further specialize in the production of high-grade coated papers to gain prominence in international markets. This is a field of activity in which the firm was already well known and it has expanded that position in the specialized grades of paper it now produces. A mill was constructed at Lanaken, across the Maas in Belgium, just north of the Albert Canal, to further advance this niche strategy in the area of lightweight coated paper. The products of this plant, incorporated as KNP België, are used mainly in the printing of magazines, brochures, catalogues, and promotional material. This plant became the site for the addition of a second papermaking machine in 1986, increasing the capacity of the plant by 175,000 tons of paper each year. The original Fourdrinier machine at this location has an annual capacity of 145,000 tons, and the combined capacity of the four mills operated by KNP in the two countries is approximately 700,000 tons per year, with a total of six papermaking machines in addition to the three small machines at the Meerssen plant.

The separate packaging division of KNP has 9 plants that produce various forms of carton board for the packaging industry and other industrial applications. These products include solid, folding, corrugated, and other board products for the converted manufacture of boxes. In addition, the plants at Oude Pekela and Sappemeer produce a greyboard used in the manufacture of files, jigsaw puzzles, books, and various types of deluxe packaging. This product of KNP's Verpakkingsgroep is exported to manufacturers in 35 countries under the Kappa board trade name, and the firm is one of the world's largest manufacturers of this product.

The plant at Oude Pekela in The Netherlands' northern province of Groningen also produces the solid board that is used in the manufacture of boxes that are necessary for the export of packaged products, as well as some typical products such as flowers, vegetables, and fruit. This board product is manufactured on machines similar to those used in the manufacture of paper, but the board machines of KNP use purchased wastepaper, rather than virgin pulp, as a raw material in the manufacturing process. The firm owns and operates 8 wastepaper collection firms that have a capacity to provide 250,000 tons of this raw material each year. Some 30,000 tons of this capacity were added during 1986, with the acquisition of two firms.

A factory in the Dutch town of Eerbeek produces folding box board. This product consists of thin layers of board used mainly for boxes and packaging, and the pharmaceutical and food industries create a heavy demand for this product of KNP. Again, as with all the carton board manufacturing conducted by KNP, wastepaper is the raw material used in the manufacture of this product. Overall, KNP processes 500,000 tons of wastepaper in the course of a year's operation, and there is strong price competition due to financial aid from nearby firms in West Germany for this essential raw material.

In 1986, KNP acquired the German firm of Herzberger Papierfabrik Ludwig Osthushenrich GmbH and Company KG that manufactures boxes in four locations in West Germany. The Oberstrot plant gained in the Herzberger acquisition also produces liner and corrugated board used in the manufacture of boxes and other packaging applications. The Herzberg and Oberau plants that were acquired also produce the corrugated materials used in box converting operations, while the Herzberg location joins the Eerbeek plant in The Netherlands in producing the folding board used in the manufacture of boxes. These acquisitions increased the capacity of the packaging division of KNP by 60 percent, and the Herzberger plants draw on the board stocks of KNP for a portion of their required raw materials. It might be noted that the Herzberger operations convert 70 percent of their board output into boxes.

In addition to the four German packaging plants gained in this recent acquisition, KNP has ownership positions in box-making operations in The Netherlands, Italy, and Spain, and each of these is supplied with board stock manufactured by other divisions of the firm. KNP is also a partner in a joint venture with Buhrmann-Tetterode N.V. in the operation of a mill at Roermond, on the Maas River just north of Maastricht, which is capable of producing 350,000 tons of paper by using wastepaper as raw material for use in the manufacture of corrugated board. With the addition of a fourth machine at the mill in 1986, this joint venture has become one of the principal suppliers of packaging paper for the European market.

The third organizational component of KNP resulted from a series of acquisitions of paper merchants beginning in the late 1970s that served to complete the forward integration of the value chain associated with papermaking, converting, and distribution. Each of these acquisitions involved a defensive strategy to prevent competitors from capturing existing channels of distribution for KNP products. At the present time KNP conducts a paper merchant operation in Belgium, France, and the United Kingdom. In addition, the firm owns an approximate 35 percent interest in Proost en Brandt, one of the two largest paper merchants in The Netherlands, located in Amsterdam, and 51 percent in Scaldia Papier B. V., located in Nijmegen.

Exhibit 1 displays the group structure of KNP, while Exhibits 4 and 5 summarize the plant capacity of the principal divisions of the company. Exhibits 2 and 3 provide a financial summary of the activities of the firm as drawn from the current annual reports. Exhibit 6 shows the location of the facilities of the firm in The Netherlands.

■ Internationalization of the Firm

The extension of KNP's activities outside of its home country is not surprising; along with most other Dutch manufacturers, the firm has always been an exporter and maintained an international perspective. The market for paper in

Exhibit 1   **KNP N.V. Group and Divisional Organization**

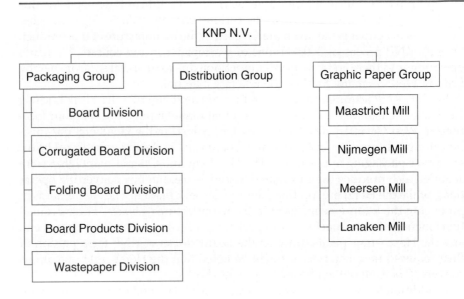

the Netherlands is insufficient to support a plant dedicated to that market, and any firm manufacturing paper in The Netherlands must visualize a market that extends beyond the borders of its home country. Europe is KNP's principal market, and in 1986, 75 percent of its paper product and 45 percent of its packaging materials were sold outside The Netherlands.

In fact, all of the products produced by the firm are manufactured for the larger European market, as there is no distinct market for paper in The Netherlands. The portion of the total product of the firm sold outside the European market consisted of output similar to that produced for the primary market, although the firm is willing to meet the specifications of purchasers in every market that is within the capability of the firm. Therefore, it is impossible for anyone in the firm to recall that first sale of any product in a foreign country; however, the location of the original mill on the Maas between Belgium and Germany would lead to the belief that sales of paper products to printers in each of these nations must date from the origin of the firm.

The portion of Belgium immediately adjacent to the province of Limburg is included in the Belgian province of Limburg, and the people of that province are largely Flemish, with close ethnic and cultural ties to the Dutch. A similar situation exists to the east where there are relatively strong cultural links with the inhabitants of those portions of Germany adjacent to the Dutch border, as no natural barriers divide the two nations in this portion of the Rhine lowlands that fringe on the Ardennes. The history of these two portions of Europe includes a strong common link that is connected with the defensive positions held by the Romans on the Rhine and Charlemagne's capital in Aachen, immediately to the east of Maastrict.

Because of these demographic and geographic features, KNP identifies Europe and the European Community as its principal market. The modern manufacture of paper products depends upon sufficient demand to permit

Exhibit 2 KNP N.V.: Balance Sheet (figures in thousands of Dutch guilders)

	1986	1985	1984	1983	1982	1981	1980	1979	1978	1977
Assets										
Tangible fixed assets	1,156,529	606,237	433,024	397,588	384,692	382,035	341,651	332,083	323,274	334,550
Financial fixed assets	51,848	55,252	43,826	7,337	17,752	20,067	18,603	19,720	43,716	54,239
Inventories	289,363	201,059	203,194	182,381	178,384	185,376	163,377	157,340	130,188	117,327
Accounts receivable	418,355	260,556	267,031	227,434	203,701	199,923	162,865	162,105	123,938	116,868
Cash	185,307	195,864	10,938	8,311	—	—	—	—	5,471	9,572
	2,101,402	1,318,968	958,013	823,051	784,529	787,401	686,496	671,248	626,587	632,556
Liabilities and Equity										
Issued share capital	82,810	74,180	70,943	70,943	59,185	56,909	56,909	56,909	56,909	56,909
Share premium account	103,691	58,784	41,644	41,644	31,420	33,696	33,696	33,696	33,696	33,696
Other reserves	421,543	330,634	255,009	206,545	173,966	168,820	165,382	165,322	168,871	164,501
Shareholders equity	608,044	463,598	367,596	319,132	264,571	259,425	255,987	255,927	259,476	255,106
Minority interests in group companies	104,918	70,786	2,215	123	123	140	106	103	103	103
Equalization fund (subsidiaries)	180,434	70,858	61,451	47,677	39,464	34,135	22,325	10,037	3,894	—
Group equity	893,396	605,242	431,262	366,932	304,158	293,700	278,418	266,067	263,473	255,209
Provisions	198,743	102,802	105,403	92,809	118,259	117,348	109,842	114,348	112,826	118,911
Long-term liabilities	535,398	271,398	137,988	147,820	166,002	147,535	110,017	121,448	130,684	108,578
Current liabilities	473,865	339,526	283,360	215,490	196,110	228,854	188,219	169,385	119,604	149,858
	2,101,402	1,318,968	958,013	823,051	784,529	787,437	686,496	671,248	626,587	632,556

Exhibit 3 KNP N.V.: Profit and Loss Statement (figures in thousands of Dutch guilders)

	1986	1985	1984	1983	1982	1981	1980	1979	1978	1977
Net sales	1,581,491	1,616,344	1,496,887	1,213,461	1,174,308	1,164,384	1,065,293	950,886	816,592	717,514
Changes in inventories	4,079	11,301	3,587	−9,165	8,870	8,387	4,326	11,504	5,439	2,762
Own work capitalized	7,191	6,573	4,077	5,274	5,609	5,782	5,214	3,573	2,879	1,263
Other operating income	8,672	2,583	475	796	2,241	1,331	652	2,318	1,949	529
	1,601,433	1,636,801	1,505,026	1,210,366	1,191,028	1,179,884	1,075,485	968,281	826,859	722,068
Raw materials and consumables	855,784	917,468	944,217	717,926	722,904	742,812	627,443	524,025	419,638	411,239
Work subcontracted and other external costs	89,073	82,489	63,485	59,173	52,316	51,036	53,421	50,912	42,925	33,238
Labor costs	316,833	314,731	288,278	283,633	290,399	287,311	289,270	273,932	250,956	205,788
Depreciation of tangible fixed assets	74,809	71,547	55,113	54,758	52,836	51,524	51,290	50,132	47,685	44,675
Other operating costs	69,786	59,666	49,572	42,649	38,245	39,891	39,842	36,867	32,136	25,563
Total operating costs	1,406,285	1,445,901	1,400,665	1,158,139	1,156,700	1,172,574	1,061,266	935,868	793,340	720,503
Operating results	195,148	190,900	104,361	52,227	34,328	7,310	14,219	32,413	33,519	1,565
Profit on financial fixed assets	131	167	201	0	0	0	0	0	0	900
Interest income	5,101	11,558	3,437	2,139	2,609	2,527	1,478	1,351	1,297	784
Interest expense	13,871	27,624	18,443	17,603	22,236	19,854	15,716	14,200	12,226	6,564
Results on ordinary operations before taxes	186,509	175,001	89,556	36,763	14,701	−10,017	−19	19,564	22,590	−3,315
Taxes thereon	68,720	66,140	27,643	10,457	4,014	−5,959	−143	10,284	9,637	−3,245
	117,789	108,861	61,913	26,306	10,687	−4,058	124	9,280	12,953	−70
Share on results of partly owned companies	15,103	8,397	1,481	−1,672	−2,070	−2,128	55	1,813	920	1,446
Results on ordinary operations after taxes	132,892	117,258	63,394	24,634	8,617	−6,186	179	11,093	13,873	1,376
Extraordinary income (expense) net	0	0	0	11,764	−97	0	−14,443	0	0	0
	132,892	117,258	63,394	36,398	8,520	−6,186	−14,264	11,093	13,873	1,376
Minority interests	297	−21	−16	0	0	0	0	0	0	0
	132,595	117,279	63,410	36,398	8,520	−6,186	−14,264	11,093	13,873	1,376

KNP N.V. Plant Capacities of Packaging Group (in tons per annum)   **Exhibit 4**

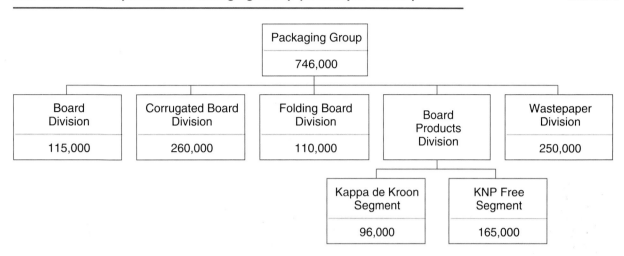

capacity operation of large-volume paper machines. Each of the paper machines operated by KNP reflect state-of-the-art technology, and the firm has made a great effort and investment in the greenfield development of modern plants or the rebuilding of existing machinery to permit it to effectively compete in its specialized niches. The Netherlands has a population of approximately 15 million, and this is a woefully inadequate number to provide the demand that would absorb the capacity of a single modern paper machine manufacturing lightweight coated paper for the printing trades that is the premier product of the firm. On the other hand, the European Community has a population of approximately 275 million and a modern economy that can easily support a number of competing firms manufacturing the types of paper products produced by KNP. Exhibit 7 shows the makeup of the European Community.

It should be understood that in most European countries paper is traditionally marketed through paper merchants who serve to distribute the various products of papermills to converters and printers. These merchants serve national or subnational markets. Although the original relationship of KNP with a foreign market is lost in history, its typical pattern of market development has been to establish a relationship with paper merchants in the various national markets it chooses to serve.

KNP N.V. Plant Capacities of Graphic Paper Group (in tons per annum)   **Exhibit 5**

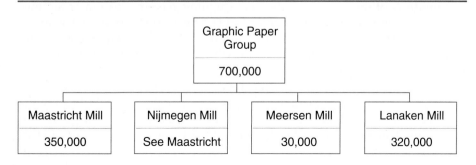

Exhibit 6   KNP Plant Locations

Sometimes this pattern of market development is not quite as straightforward. When the demand for lightweight, mechanical machine-coated paper in the United States emerged, KNP already maintained a relationship with a paper merchant on each coast to serve the U.S. market for the other products of the firm, but the lightweight coated product required a more direct approach to the printing customer. KNP skirted the traditional distributors and developed an exclusive relationship with the Wilcox-Walter-Furlong Paper Company, a paper merchant in Philadelphia, to stock and sell KNP's product in the eastern portion of the United States. The firm followed a somewhat different but equally effective route to the burgeoning market for lightweight coated paper in the western portions of the United States; there it markets the product to printers through the offices of MacMillan Bloedel, a firm that holds a 30 percent stock interest in KNP, and whose Chairman and Director of International Operations both serve on the Supervisory Board of KNP.

The firm has progressively increased the capacity of its plants to meet increased demand in its committed markets. KNP makes a commitment to a market when it contains the potential for a continuing demand for the specialized products of the firm. Such demand can only exist in a nation or an integrated group of nations with a modern and sophisticated economy. The European Community is an example of such a market, and the emergence of the community in the years following World War II paralleled the development of KNP's international ventures.

The foreign activities of KNP can be divided basically into two segments and two stages. The first stage included a segment that existed since the beginnings of the firm in the nineteenth century, with the transport of the products of the firm to immediately adjacent localities that by force of political circumstances

The European Community

Exhibit 7

happened to be in other nations. At the same time the special products of the firm were entering into the more extensive foreign trade that are historically typical of firms in The Netherlands. There is no clear separation of these two segments of the initial foreign trade of this firm.

The second stage of the international business activity of the firm was a simple elaboration of the trade conducted across national political boundaries. This was the broader cross-national trade permitted by the development of the European Community. Thus the international business activity of KNP can be divided into a pre– and post–Word War II period, with the more worldwide export activity of the firm overlapping these two periods.

As indicated above, the establishment of the European Community appears as the most important factor in the development of KNP. The history of growth and development of KNP following World War II is not untypical of that of other manufacturers throughout the various industries of Europe. However, this apparent motivation for the expansion of international activity does not account for the management knowledge and skill that had to be present to permit the firm to grasp the opportunity provided by the reconstruction of the European economy under the new economic confederation.

The operating capacity of modern papermaking mills is the key factor in the extension of markets. The trend has been toward larger and larger capacity as the technology of papermaking has evolved. One can only speculate as to the course of actions that firms would take if technological developments advanced an opportunity for minimills such as has occurred in the steel industry. Paper-making is only one example of an industry that requires a highly developed economy to absorb efficient production.

The European Community is a unique design to overcome the various barriers that prevent the extension of economic activity to permit efficient production. As the community emerged, firms in the paper industry among others used skilled sales agents that were proficient in dealing with the new market. At the same time firms that were extending their activities throughout the growing market became expert in meeting the different needs of the various component national economies. Language provides no barrier to a firm such as KNP, where executives typically speak a number of the European languages. It is also apparent that residual differences in the cultures of the various nations that make up the European Community provide a negligible barrier to the international business of firms in the papermaking industry.

As far as the extracontinental trade of KNP is concerned, it exported its specialized products to Africa and the Middle East initially. After the beginning of the present decade it began exporting its products to Australia and the Far East, along with an emerging export activity to the United States and Canada. These new locations for trade presented no special problems, and the penetration of new markets depends more on the level of economic development of the country than any other factor. For example, language barriers are unimportant, as managers in the firm have the necessary language skills, and the firm is accustomed from its earliest days to the language necessities and cultural appreciations associated with foreign export.

The inclusion of the United Kingdom in the European Community provides insight on the way in which KNP goes about extending its international market. The firm considered its traditional markets as including France and Germany, in addition to the Benelux countries, and it was committed to this combination of markets. It then began to develop a similar long-term commitment to the paper market in the United Kingdom, which began with the unusual measure of first working through a sales agent to reach the outlets to the printing trades. At a later point the firm established a more permanent position in the United Kingdom by having Contract Papers Limited, a large English paper merchant, distribute its paper products. KNP now owns a 45 percent interest in this company.

As indicated previously, KNP moved to the acquisition of paper merchants in many of its committed markets under the pressure of competitive actions that threaten to control such channels of distribution. This has occurred in The Netherlands, Belgium, France, and the United Kingdom. It has not taken place in Germany, which represents the other major national market of KNP in the European Community. While competitive pressures have not induced such an extension of the firm in the German market, KNP is monitoring this situation very carefully.

KNP is now one of Europe's largest producers of coated paper as well as one of the leading producers of board. Both of these activities are highly specialized and internationally oriented fields, and it should be noted that The Netherlands imports over half its total paper requirement while exporting 60 percent of its total paper and board production. While only 31 percent of KNP's 1986 sales were in The Netherlands, 55 percent were to other European countries, and 14 percent were made elsewhere in the world.

■ Globalization of the Firm

KNP has not reached a stage of globalization characterized by intermediate production in various localities and final production in the specific markets served. While the specialized paper products of KNP are global products, their manufacture does not lend itself to the global integrated strategy as described by Yves Doz and other theorists of international business. Therefore, KNP would be best described as following a multifocal international business strategy.

Following the theoretical distinction made between the concepts of internationalization and globalization it might be noted that the paper industries in Europe and North America have different configurations. American firms tend to be more fully integrated vertically and horizontally in respect to the full range of forest products. European firms, with the exception of the Scandinavians, have little opportunity to integrate backward and acquire extensive woodlands in their home countries. Because North American firms can command woodlands adequate to supply the raw materials for paper production and have a large domestic or regional market for their products, globalization of production is generally a moot point and of only theoretical interest in strategic planning. Because European paper manufacturers lack a wider forest products orientation, there is little inclination to consider the opportunities to exploit comparative advantage in many global manufacturing locations. Globalization, therefore, is oriented toward forward integration of distribution activities. The Swedes and Finns, on the other hand, have forest resources but are handicapped by lack of a domestic market for finished paper products and face firm competitors in the markets for paper products in developed nations where high-value-added products might be sold.

KNP appears among those European firms on the leading edge of globalization of distribution activities in the paper industry. As indicated previously, KNP has seen fit to acquire foreign paper merchants that are involved in the warehousing of paper products for sale to converters and printers in various domestic markets. At present KNP owns Papeteries Libert S.A. in Paris; the firm also has a 51 percent interest in Scaldia Papier N.V. in Wilrijk, Belgium, and a 45 percent interest in Contract Papers (Holdings) Ltd. in London. At home the firm holds a 35 percent interest in Proost en Brandt N.V. in Amsterdam, acquired in the early 1970s, and a 51 percent interest in Scaldia Papier B.V. in Nijmegen.

These acquisitions took place during 1978 and 1979 as a defensive move to protect vital channels of distribution in the European Community from competitors, and Mr. Zetteler denies that the firm was principally interested in capturing profits from distribution or promoting growth through constraints on channels. Competitors began acquiring paper merchants that sold KNP products and threatened to promote the stock of goods manufactured by their own firms. The paper merchants acquired by KNP continue to stock a full range of goods, including those produced by competitors.

Paper merchants are the traditional extension of the distribution system in the paper and board industry. Paper manufacturers receive orders from paper merchants for the range of common products that are intermediate goods used by final producers. They also may enter into various forms of cutting and sheeting operations as an adjunct to distribution. Occasionally a paper manufacturer will sell directly to the larger printing and converting firms, but the operation of direct sales offices can be considered as the more modern development. Nevertheless, all three of these arrangements are extant and viable methods of distribution.

Paper merchants serve national markets through a fleet of trucks that transport the warehoused products to printers and manufacturers of converted paper products, who either distribute products to final consumers or supply manufacturers producing products with a paper or board component. Generally paper merchants cater to the needs of users in their own country, and the paper merchant operations of KNP are each national firms with wide distribution in their respective nations.

No distinct figures exist in published reports as to the results of KNP's foreign ventures in distribution channels. Overall, distribution provided 7.9 percent of operation revenues of the firm and 2.0 percent of operating results, while the paper group provided 62.9 percent of operating revenues and 71.7 percent of operating results, and the packaging group produced 29.2 percent of operating revenue and 26.3 percent of operating results. These figures ignore the influence of internal transfers, which made up 8.2 percent of the total operating activity of the firm and may have had an important part to play in the reported results in respect to distribution.

■ Other Aspects of Globalization

While the acquisition of an ownership position in paper merchant operations is a major thrust of the international marketing strategy of KNP, it does not mark the initial globalization of the activities of the firm. The purchase of shares in Celupal S.A., a manufacturer of paper products for the packaging industry in Spain, took place some 20 years ago. The global connotations associated with the construction of the Lanaken plant can also be debated.

In many respects the creation of KNP België N.V. in Lanaken is a prime example of the establishment of a greenfield manufacturing operation in a foreign country. The Lanaken paper manufacturing operation was established at the point when the business strategy of the firm shifted toward the production of special grades of coated paper for the printing trades. This decision, made just before the energy crisis in the early 1970s, has let the firm exploit those grades of specialty paper that had a higher value added in manufacture. It was largely distinct from the move to acquire paper merchant operations outside the country, although the two strategic moves took place during the same decade and generally support the strategy of focusing on a segment of the overall line of products in the paper industry. The creation of the greenfield operation at Lanaken was in support of an offensive European niche strategy, while the acquisition of paper merchants in France, Belgium, and the United Kingdom was a defensive maneuver to prevent erosion of existing channels of distribution that supported the more extensive range of products produced by KNP.

Some portion of the lightweight coated paper produced at Lanaken is shipped to The Netherlands; however, it is obvious that the Lanaken plant was established to serve the European market that is the principal focus of the firm. Nevertheless, it is clear that the plant might have served the same purpose if located in The Netherlands, and although the Belgian government did provide certain assistance and cooperation during the establishment of the plant, this was not a prime consideration in the location of the new mill.

It can be supposed that the plant that was finally constructed at Lanaken would have had to be located somewhere in the heavy industrial triangle of northwest Europe to minimize the transportation costs of final distribution to key European markets. The Liege-Limburg-Aachen area is close to the heart of this triangle and is well served by the infrastructure necessary for paper production. The location of Lanaken adjacent to the Albert Canal provides direct access to the facilities of the port of Antwerp and pulp shipments from worldwide sources. It therefore is likely that any other decision to locate this plant would have been close to the actual location, and the actual site is quite ideal. The Lanaken plant does draw a small portion of its coating material requirements from the Maastricht plant, producing some economies of sca' this aspect of the operation, but otherwise the papermaking plants are sel nt and completely independent.

The situation is somewhat different in respect to the packaging als operations of KNP in Germany, Italy, and Spain. The packaging converters of the firm draw on the packaging board manufactured by KNP in The Netherlands and Germany to fulfill or supplement their raw material requirements, and economies of scale in the production of packaging paper and board are the principal reason for the production of these intermediate products at central locations. It is necessary that such locations be strategically situated to minimize transportation costs, and the firm is contemplating some restructuring of activities at a later point in time to rationalize production at the acquired packaging plants.

Although the paper production facilities of KNP are largely freestanding in each of the two national operations, distribution of paper products remains in part dependent on owned paper merchants and sales offices in host country locations. The packaging material production facilities of KNP depend upon multinational operations of specialized components of the manufacturing value chain. The company, therefore, provides an illustration of the use of two types of global strategy.

▪ Future Globalization of Activities

Given the past strategic development of KNP it is obvious that the firm will adopt the form of global production and distribution strategy dictated by the present state of the art at any point in time. The firm is somewhat more judgmental about the degree to which it would internationalize its activity. For example, KNP will not seek to enter the American market on a short-term basis simply because a temporary shortfall in supply exists in this market ist-ing capacity of the firm is temporarily underutilized. It must be rea e a long-term commitment of capacity to this market before it wou er exporting any product.

It also appears that KNP has no intention of specializing production po-nents in various parts of the world to capture the benefits of comparative advantage in various locations, but this is more likely the result of the nature of the integrated operation of paper manufacturing; the industry is limited in the amount of global specialization that can be practiced. On the other hand, the firm does specialize the production of board and its conversion into packaging materials in separate national locations.

A more important question is whether KNP would ever consider entering into the upstream, extractive portion of the paper business that would provide for the globalization of the firm, given the limited opportunity to manufacture pulp in The Netherlands. American observers have the example of the major papermakers in their countries being backwardly integrated into the extractive portion of the business and consider it a competitive advantage. Some American and Japanese firms have been enticed into participation with foreign governments in the development and harvest of forest resources to obtain sure sources of supply for pulp.

Theorists suggest from empirical evidence provided by certain industries that the evolution of globalization and internationalization includes the backward and forward integration of the firm into global arrangements. The previous example of some American and Japanese firms integrating backward into the forests of less developed nations to gain assured sources of cheap raw materials for paper manufacture is one instance of an evolutionary development in globalization. Other examples of globalization include the shipment of antiquated paper machines or converting equipment to less developed countries where they can be operated in a somewhat economic fashion with low-cost labor or energy resources.

FUTURE STRATEGIC DEVELOPMENTS

There is no doubt that the top management team of KNP is aware of these developing features of the worldwide paper industry, and it is somewhat obvious that Mr. Zetteler will take these features into account as he contributes to the decisions that will shape the future of KNP. It is already apparent within his own division of the firm that technological developments at hand will shortly begin to modify the marketing and production strategies of the firm and the industry. For example, early in 1987 the firm started a 70,000-ton-capacity chemical thermomechanical pulp line in integrated operation with the new Paper Machine 8 at the Lanaken mill. This marks the first integrated paper production operation for KNP, using softwood drawn from the Ardennes, and replacing the chemical pulp purchased in the international commodity markets. The firm contemplates doubling this integrated capacity with a second pulp line in the next couple of years. It is rumored that chemical thermomechanical pulp (CTMP) operations of this sort have the potential to permit reduction of the minimal efficient scale (MES) of production of high-value-added paper products such as lightweight, machine-coated papers that are produced in bulk in the around-the-clock operation of high-speed paper machines.

The emergence of KNP and firms that follow its lead as an integrated European producer of special papers for the printing trades would undoubtedly enhance the opportunity to compete in various world markets. The United States has already witnessed the penetration of its domestic markets for printing papers as a result of the declining value of the dollar and the superior quality of certain paper products that has been the result of innovations in production by European firms. However, any firm that wished to make a committed entry into the U.S. market would have to consider the costs of transportation of finished paper goods and the comparative advantage of U.S. producers resulting from available forest resources.

Buckeye Glass Company in China

James A. Brunner, University of Toledo

In November, 1988, Buckeye Glass sent a highly skilled team to Qinhuangdao, People's Republic of China to negotiate a joint venture for the manufacture of glassware. The team consisted of John Brickley, Vice-President of Marketing; Bob Caines, Production Manager; and Steve Miller, Chief Engineer. Brickley had carefully selected an interpreter, Ling Sida who knew Mandarin Chinese, the dialect spoken in Northern China, as he was concerned that a language barrier might arise.

COMPANY BACKGROUND

Buckeye Glass headquartered in Columbus, Ohio, produced glassware, including wide and narrow mouth containers, and glass prescription ware. It had over 25,000 customers worldwide in diverse industries such as food processing, liquor, beer, wine, cosmetics, soft drinks, and proprietary and prescription drugs. Its 10 month worldwide sales in 1988 were $3.0 billion, and had plants in Europe, Asia, North and South America, employing 44,000 people. Its earnings have been flat for the past 5 years and management was exploring new avenues for growth of sales and earnings. The plant being considered for construction in China would produce all types of glassware under the name of Buckeye, its brand name worldwide. It is known as a high quality producer and a leader in its field.

Year	Sales (billion)	Profits (million)
1988*	$3.0	$120
1987	$3.4	$138
1986	$3.0	$140
1985	$3.0	$136
1984	$2.8	$135

*10 months.

QINHUANGDAO

Qinhuangdao is a Chinese international port city in Northern China. Located on the Bohai Sea, it is only 277 kilometers (166 miles) southeast of Beijing and serves as the gateway to the capital as it has a large, modern harbor, which is ice and salt free. The weather is milder than inland, and its beaches at Beidaihe attract thousands annually, including leading government officials from Beijing.

By 1988 Qinhuangdao had developed into an important economic center and was the glass capital of the People's Republic of China. It is one of 14 coastal cities opened to the outside world in 1984; and has a new economic and technical development site which has attracted foreign investors from the United States, Australia, and several other countries. This site had a 12,000-unit Swedish program controlled telephone system. One of the companies located there manufactured silicon solar batteries, and another, special tubing for refrigerators and buses. There were 25 glass factories in the area producing laminated glass, thermal glass, medical glassware, fiberglass, and heat-absorbing glass. These companies engage in lateral economic cooperation and pool both technologies and skilled personnel, thereby enhancing the quality and efficiency of production. The area is rich in quartz, a major ingredient in the manufacturing of glass.

TRIP TO QINHUANGDAO

The Buckeye Glass team had flown for 26 hours and stayed overnight in Beijing at the Great Wall Hotel. The next morning they traveled by train for 6 hours to Qinhuangdao. Enroute they discussed their plans and were anxious to meet the Chinese and begin negotiating as soon as possible.

When they arrived there, they were greeted warmly by their Chinese hosts and escorted to the Jinshan Hotel, expressly reserved for foreigners. They found to their surprise that their accommodations were comparable to those of first-class hotels in the United States. The rooms were complete with comfortable beds, baths, TV, and telephones. Wake-up service and a dining room were available for meals, which were served in both Chinese and Western styles.

Pleased by their surroundings and encouraged by the congeniality of their hosts at dinner that night they retired; confident that the meeting scheduled for the next day would establish a beneficial working relationship with the Chinese. At 10 PM strains of Brahm's lullaby flowed from the intercom system, and the negotiators slept peacefully after their arduous journey as they began to adjust to their jet lag.

The Chinese arrived promptly at 9 A.M. The Chinese delegation was led by Tien Chao, the Deputy Director of the Foreign Affairs Office. Through his interpreter, he introduced the others in his party. Pi Zhao, Director of the Xia Xian Glass Factory, the leading glass manufacturer in China, and Mah Ai-qi, his personal secretary and interpreter. Tien Chao was tall, thin, erect, and very dignified in bearing. After formal introductions and an exchange of pleasantries, the group left for a tour of Xia Xian Glass Factory's manufacturing facilities.

Arriving at the factory, the group was greeted by Poh Jiwei, the Managing Director, who escorted them on a tour of the facilities. The Americans were surprised by what awaited them. The floor of the factory was dirty, and there was a large number of glass container crates located haphazardly on the floor. Groups of employees were loitering, playing cards, conversing, and laughing, while others were engaged in various work activities. Surprised at the minimal level of activity in the plant, Caines asked through their interpreter, Ling Sida, "Why aren't all these people working or are some of them on break?"

Poh Jiwei smiled and replied proudly, "Our plant has met its production quota for the year; but these men report in each day to be with their friends and do whatever work is planned for that day. You know, in China we provide jobs for all our people and unemployment is nonexistent. When we receive our new quota from the government, production will begin again at a higher level."

Caines, still perplexed, replied, "Wouldn't it be more profitable to close down some of the production facilities and lay off at least some of the workers until the new quotas are announced and thereby increase the profits of the company?"

Poh Jiwei replied politely as he smiled, "In China, we do what is best for the workers in order to give them steady incomes. Our concern is more about the workers, than the income of the factory."

Caines, noting that some workers were arriving late, asked, "I've known that Chinese factories practice this *iron rice bowl* concept whereby all workers are assured they will have jobs. But some of them are late in arriving for work. Aren't they expected to be on time?" Poh Jiwei smiled and replied, "Well, in the past we have not enforced your Western-style work ethic of being punctual, but we are beginning to change. But please understand that the middle-aged and elderly workers are hard to change and they resist this new approach. The younger workers, however, agree that punctuality should lead to increased productivity, and are willing to accept these changes. In fact we now give bonuses to those who exceed their quotas and stay on their jobs until closing time. You may be interested to know that our workers retire when they reach the age of 55, and we have only a few older workers in the factory."

As the tour progressed, Caines continued to be amazed by the antiquated machinery in operation, but was startled when they came to an installation which had the latest container glass manufacturing technology. When he openly praised the equipment, Poh Jiwei smiled broadly and replied humbly to the surprise of the Americans, "Oh, our factory is very ill-equipped, with few modern machines unlike those you have in your country." Brickley, confused by Poh Jiwei's statement since they had just viewed a great deal of modern machinery, quickly assured Poh that the plant was indeed impressive and very well equipped.

After the tour of the plant, the Buckeye executives were escorted to a conference room which was plainly decorated, had 24 chairs arranged around the walls of the room, and a conference table with 10 chairs. They were invited to be seated at the table, and were served tea by their hosts. Pi Zhao thanked the Buckeye team for visiting the plant and commented for 5 minutes upon their proposed relationship with Buckeye Glass. He elaborated upon the economic development plans of the People's Republic of China and noted that even though the government had not given top priority to glass container production, he assured them it looked favorably upon the possibility of building a plant in Qinhuangdao for that purpose. He stressed the need for the development of a long-term relationship and hoped those present could become "old friends." After elaborating further for 20 minutes, he sat down.

John Brickley immediately stood up and responded by expressing his sincere appreciation for the plant tour, and also his hope that a close relationship could be developed with the Chinese in this endeavor. He stressed how a glass manufacturing plant would be beneficial to the economic progress of the country as well as the living standards of the Chinese. He profusely thanked Poh Jiwei for the tour of the factory and continued to elaborate for about 10 minutes on this relationship and its mutual benefits.

After he finished, Tien Chao proposed that after lunch they should tour Qinhuangdao and visit the eastern section of the Great Wall of China. He proudly stated that the sea end of the wall was in Qinhuangdao and at one time had been over 23,000 meters long, but that only 2300 meters of it still existed. He stated it had been originally constructed by Emperor Qin Shi Huang of the Qin dynasty, commencing in 221 B.C. He also announced, "We should visit other features of interest, such as the "Old Dragon's Head" at the sea end of the wall, the park and, of course, the beach in Beidaihe."

The rest of the afternoon was, therefore, spent touring the area. A photographer went with the party to photograph the Americans at the various points of interest, which were proudly described in detail by Tien Chao through an interpreter. (Appendix 1 provides a brief review of Chinese culture and negotiating styles.) Brickley was frustrated as he wanted to discuss the proposed joint venture. He attempted not to show his impatience, and expressed interest in the special features of the region. At 6 PM they returned to the hotel. The Chinese joined them for dinner and left promptly at 8 PM.

▪ Initial Meeting

The next morning, the Chinese delegation arrived promptly and escorted the Buckeye team to the hotel's meeting room. The Chinese delegation now consisted of 12 members including Pi Zhao, the Director of Xin Xian Glass Factory, its plant manager, two assistant plant managers, several engineers, and the interpreter. The Chinese arranged themselves on one side of the table and the Buckeye Glass team was seated opposite them. After they were served tea, Brickley rose, thanked the Chinese for inviting them, and described the services of his company.

Brickley then introduced Caines who elaborated for approximately 20 minutes upon the history of Buckeye Glass, its premier position in the worldwide market in the production of containers for a wide range of industries such as food, soft drinks, beer, cosmetics, and pharmaceuticals, and how profitable they had been internationally. He then turned to Steve Miller who introduced the engineers. As a team, they presented a slide presentation of the company's production and sales facilities, and a statistical review of sales and profits for the previous decade. They continued by elaborating on the technological capabilities of Buckeye Glass. Brickley then rose and commented at length about the strong managerial team which the company had. He elaborated upon the integration of the marketing, finance and production activities at Buckeye Glass, which he explained had been highly effective in thrusting the company into a leading position in the international glass container industry.

He commented briefly upon his opinions concerning observations made the previous day in the factory, and noted that his company could assist the Chinese by introducing its production workers and managers to Western concepts of production and marketing. He emphasized the need for management to introduce Western management know-how and methods in the Xia Xian Glass Factory in order that it could effectively serve the needs of the Chinese people.

During his presentation, the Chinese seemed somewhat passive, but occasionally asked questions and probed for information. Brickley and the other members of the Buckeye Glass team carefully and patiently answered the questions raised. They also endeavored to sense the priorities of the Chinese concerning the various types of problems that they had and what they wanted the American team to do. In their discussions, it became evident that breakage was a major problem as the Chinese workers were not well trained in the use of the equipment. Further, they learned the Xia Xian's customers wanted different types of glass containers than were being produced in this plant, but the company was still manufacturing ware no longer in heavy demand. They had a sizable overaged inventory of these outmoded containers.

Further, the Chinese noted that their products were not meeting the quality specifications demanded by foreign buyers. Thus, it was evident that a quality control training program was essential. Poh Jiwei observed further that the corregated shipping containers for the glass products were inferior and oftentimes broke in shipment, which then led to damaged merchandise.

While Brickley was aware of these problems, he had no idea of the order in which the Chinese would prioritize them, and specifically, which of Buckeye's services were considered to be the most important to the Chinese.

After the discussion had continued for 3 hours, Pi Zhao suggested that they break for lunch; and that after lunch they should go on a sightseeing tour of Yanshan University, a new educational institution founded in the 1980s to train engineering and technical students in the latest scientific developments and technology. Pi Zhao assured the Buckeye team that he would like to meet the next day to discuss the possibility of signing a letter of intent. The meeting then adjourned.

The next morning promptly at 9 AM Tien Chao, Pi Zhao, and Poh Jiwei arrived with their interpreter, and 3 engineers. They escorted the Buckeye Glass executives to the conference room and they arranged themselves on one side of the table while the Americans occupied the other. Through his interpreter, Tien Chao expressed his appreciation to the Americans for their informative presentation and announced that they were interested in signing a letter of intent. Tien Chao observed that the Xia Xian Glass Factory had inadequate equipment, and elaborated on a low level of skill possessed by the production workers as well as the managers. Brickley silently concurred with Tien Chao's observations concerning the workers, but he was surprised to hear this comment concerning the managers as some of them were present at the meeting. Further, Tien Chao expressed his admiration of the Buckeye Glass executives, acknowledging that the company was one of the leading glass manufacturers in the world, and that his company was humbly appreciative of the opportunity to join them in a joint venture. Brickley was amazed at this sense of humbleness by the Chinese as he didn't feel that they were as inferior as Tien Chao was suggesting.

Tien continued, "We feel that the time has arrived for us to sign a letter of intent and to express the general principles under which our venture will operate. Our objective is the modernization of the Xia Xian plant in Qinhuangdao and propose that it be located in the new economic and technical development zone. Further, Buckeye Glass will provide for managerial training of the Chinese managers and also for the factory workers and service staff of the joint venture." He paused and then announced, "Further, Buckeye Glass will provide for the transfer of technology to improve the product's quality and performance, reduce production costs and conserve energy and materials. This technology should also enable the company to expand the exportation of glass containers and thereby increase the foreign exchange revenues of the Xia Xian Glass Factory. Finally Buckeye will be the marketing agent for the joint venture, not only in China but on a worldwide basis."

Brickley was silently pleased. On second thought, he was somewhat perplexed as the objectives proposed were very broad and outlined the general principles of the accord without spelling out the specific details. Nevertheless, he thanked Tien Chao and added, "I think it's important that we also include the specific details of our mutual obligations in order to avoid any misunderstandings in the future."

Tien Chao smiled and replied, "We appreciate your concern, but it is not necessary to specify the particulars of the joint venture at this point. But we need to reach a general agreement on the principles in your letter of interest."

As the executives of Buckeye Glass were surprised at the Chinese proposed letter of intent, they began to fire questions concerning the specific details. Tien Chao again smiled and asserted, "The details can be worked out later but first we must come to an agreement on general principles. We propose that we break for a period of time in order that you may have an opportunity to review our broad objectives, I propose that we meet again after lunch."

The meeting adjourned and the 2 groups went to separate meeting rooms. The Buckeye team met in Brickley's room and after pouring each a cup of tea, Brickley, exasperated, stated, "Well this certainly isn't what I expected. I thought we could reach some general agreement on the specific details. Evidently the Chinese are only interested in general principles. Frankly, I'm concerned they didn't specify the time period for the joint venture and the financial details. How much each of us is going to have to put up front is also up in the air. What products are to be produced? This is certainly different than any joint venture I've ever written in the United States. I propose that we come up with recommendations so that we can get this show on the road." Brickley noted further, "After listening to their monologue, I'm sure glad that I took notes, but I'm not certain what their priorities are. There is a lot we can bring to the table, but it would be helpful if we knew their priorities. I will press that issue after lunch."

At noon, Tien Chao and his team met Brickley and his associates and they went to the dining room. While the Chinese remained reserved and occasionally talked among themselves, the atmosphere was still friendly. After lunch they adjourned again to the conference room and Brickley stated their concern about the missing details and made some specific suggestions. Tien Chao commented, "I know we are old friends, but you are insisting upon being very specific about the details, and are not willing to agree only on the general principles. We regret this and don't understand why." Brickley's interpreter told him the Chinese felt he was behaving dishonorably and acted as though he did not trust the Chinese. Brickley feeling intimidated quickly responded, "I'm disappointed we can't agree. However, if it is not customary in China to be specific in a letter of agreement but only to reach agreement only on the general principles, we will go along to demonstrate our sincerity. After we have signed it, I would like to give it to the press in order that my company may publicize it in the United States as it will be good publicity and will demonstrate Buckeye's interest in economic development in the People's Republic of China."

Tien Chao agreed, but asked that no dates be stated concerning when it was to commence, and that no mention be made of the investment that would be involved, nor the city in China in which it was to be located.

Brickley knew that the Chinese had mixed feelings about publicity and preferred to maintain secrecy in the negotiating process as they had a mistrust of publicity and perceived it as a form of pressure. Moreover, he sensed that they were concerned that their superiors might feel they were endeavoring to promote themselves. On the other hand, he thought that if he didn't publicize the agreement, the Chinese might be offended. He was aware that they might sense a violation of confidentiality if he revealed too much. It was a minor dilemma for him. Brickley paused, and then agreed to all of these stipulations with the exception that the city should be specified as it was known in the United States that his company had representatives in Qinhuangdao. Tien Chao agreed reluctantly.

The next day they met again and signed a joint agreement, which Brickley recognized was not binding on either parties, but at least served as a basis for commencing the substantive negotiations. He personally felt quite gratified with the progress made, as the Chinese indicated that they were now willing to work out the specific details.

■ Formal Banquet

That evening the Chinese team escorted the Buckeye Glass representatives to a Chinese banquet to celebrate the signing of the letter of intent. Brickley was surprised to observe that place cards had been arranged on the tables in order to facilitate the seating arrangements. He was seated next to Tien Chao's left and the Chinese were interspersed among the Americans around 2 tables. When the first course consisting of braised prawns were served, the Chinese to the right of a Buckeye executive served him a portion of the prawns. While they were awaiting the second course, Tien Chao gave a speech lauding Sino-American relations and the signing completed that afternoon. As he closed he offered a toast of Mao Tai wine to the Buckeye Glass team. Brickley, aware of the effect of Mao Tai which has a 40% alcoholic content, toasted cautiously.

Following this, in sequence, scallops fried in tomato sauce, sautéed conch, fillet of fish stir-fried, pork steak fried, crabmeat stir-fried, heart of rape with mushroom, and sea slugs were served. During each of these 7 courses, the Chinese served the Americans saying, *"Quing, Quing"* ("please, please").

During the course of the 2 hour banquet, innumerable toasts were made by the Chinese and the Buckeye team reciprocated, oftentimes going from table to table to present toasts. Both teams used the white wine on the table for their toasts on these occasions, rather than the Mao Tai. However, when Tien Chao offered his toasts, Brickley followed protocol, and drank the complete glass of wine, on the urging by Tien Chao, who proposed, *"Ganbei"* ("bottoms-up").

During the dinner, the conversation naturally turned to the different cuisines of the various regions of the People's Republic of China. Miller asked facetiously if it was true that the Chinese in Southern China ate dog, snake and monkey brains. Tien Chao smiled broadly and replied affirmatively. Encouraged by Tien Chao's smile, Miller began joking about some of the other delicacies that appeared on the menu; such as heart of rape on mushrooms and the sea slugs. The Chinese apparently enjoyed this humorous approach as they were grinning and nodding their heads in response. Encouraged, the Americans began to tell Western jokes. Apparently, the atmosphere was friendly and relaxed.

Brickley, encouraged by this feeling of cordiality, sensed that the time was appropriate to again address the subject of the joint venture. Turning to Tien Chao, he said, "With our technology and investment, Buckeye Glass can pull China from its backwardness and make it a world power." Tien Chao replied, "Yes, yes, Buckeye Glass is a world leader, and a very powerful company from the United States. Xia Xian certainly must make use of a liaison with it."

Encouraged by Tien Chao's reply, Brickley continued, expounding upon the mutual benefit which this joint venture would provide both parties. He observed that Buckeye Glass could train the management of Xia Xian in modern managerial techniques and assist them in training their workers to use Western technology. He noted further that their close contacts would enable Buckeye to establish a foothold in the Chinese market and become a major power in the glass industry in the Pacific Basin countries.

While the guests were eating the stir-fried crabmeat course, Tien Chao rose and commented on the close ties being established with Buckeye Glass. He then presented Brickley a gift of 2 Chinese exercise balls, which he stated had been in use in China since the fourteenth century and were used to stimulate important acupressure points below the wrist. He then demonstrated that they emitted soft chiming sounds in two different pitches to calm the nerves and soothe the soul. Tien Chao then gave Brickley a 4 × 6 foot tapestry of the Great Wall. Brickley thanked him profusely, but was embarrassed as he had no gifts to reciprocate this show of friendship and cordial relations.

After the pastry had been served, the next course consisted of soup, rice and fruit. The Americans found the soup to be delicious and each took two servings of the rice as they especially enjoyed it. Tien Chao listened politely as Brickley sipped his tea. After a third cup, Tien Chao rose and thanked the Buckeye executives for attending the dinner. The hosts escorted them back to their room and quickly departed.

POLITICAL AND ECONOMIC ENVIRONMENT

That night, Brickley reflected on the economic and political environment of China in order to gain a broader perspective. He was aware that the PRC had a population of over a billion, and that its economic system was being developed aggressively by the government. He noted that labor was inexpensive, and quite abundant without any problem of labor strikes. Further, he was aware that although raw materials and other supplies were less costly than in some countries, there were some difficulties in their procurement. He had heard that in the PRC the availability of materials and supplies was oftentimes dependent upon connections which one had with others. These relationships in China were referred to as *guanxi* and Brickley was aware that if one formed such ties, they signified close bonding. This permitted either party to call upon the other for any favors if they were within the power of a *guanxi* member to grant and he would be obligated to do so. Further, he knew that *guanxi* ties were also important for getting things done when working with the governmental bureaucracy as the PRC does not have an institutionalized legal system. Therefore, getting favorable interpretations by bureaucrats was dependent largely upon whom one knew and who had *guanxi* with whom.

Moreover, he noted that the PRC had a culture which traditionally shunned legal considerations and stressed rather the ethical and moral principles of everyday living; and that formal agreements were based more upon moral obligations than the law. He also recognized that although the People's Republic was a socialist country, it suffered from political instability, and the recent *open door* policy was primarily the endeavor of their senior leader Deng Xiaoping. Brickley knew that in November, 1983, Deng had launched a movement to put his mark on China's new emerging economic development. He had devised a 5 year plan to purge the Communist party's 40 million members of 1 million leftists, most of whom were ill educated. This had been accomplished through a reedification program of self criticism and prescribed study. Deng endeavored to clear the way for his protégés to rise to positions of power in order to ensure continuation of his economic, political and open-door policies.

In October, 1987, Zhao Ziyang became the party general's secretary succeeding Deng and a sixth 5 year plan was announced. Deng, however, remained a paramount figure in the decision making process and was encouraging some capitalistic practices to be adopted in China, such as, using quotas and holding managers accountable for the profitability of their factories.

In general, China's semiclosed economy was modified to an open economy with international exchanges encouraged. In moving toward a market mechanism for setting prices, however, inflation surged in 1988 to an unofficial but acknowledged annual rate of nearly 50% in cities. There was evidence that government officials were capitalizing on entrepreneurism by accepting bribes and engaging in other unsavory activities. The economy was clearly overheated and industrial output had risen 7% in the first half, and investment in capital construction had increased 14%. China's inefficient factories were unable to keep up with the demand for goods and thereby added to the inflationary pressures. Demand for consumer goods was far outstripping supply and black market activities were thriving with inflationary price rises as a consequence.

The government attempted to slow the economy by controlling the money supply, but this had proven to be ineffective as the money supply rose 30% in the first 5 months of 1988. Finally, in order to get better control on the economy and slow down the inflationary pressures, the state council in October 1988, announced that as of December 1, it would reduce investment in a variety of nonessential industries, ranging from textile processing to consumer electronics and plastics. However, this would not apply to projects involving foreigners or those in priority areas such as energy and transportation. It was anticipated that the roll back would be huge, and that Beijing would cutback capital investment in 1989 by 50 billion Chinese yuan (13.5 billion dollars). Fortunately for Buckeye Glass, this would not pertain to glass containers but rather involved such products as cotton textiles, rubber goods, tractors, television sets, and those which consumed too much energy such as irons, vacuum cleaners and rice cookers. The crux of the problem was that the Chinese enterprises were state owned and the managers were not inclined to think in terms of economic efficiency.

■ Substantive Negotiations

Negotiations commenced promptly the next day and continued for 2 days. Both teams had copies of the Law of the People's Republic of China on Joint Ventures. (See Exhibit 1.) On occasion, the Chinese would engage in detailed questioning about topics which apparently were not too significant. Brickley sensed that this stalling tactic was used to gain time to enable the Chinese to elicit the comments of their superiors concerning various parts of the contract. He observed that when points requiring clarification arose, the Chinese during informal breaks would gather around the Buckeye Glass interpreter in order to attempt to persuade her to get concessions for the Chinese or to clarify Buckeye's proposals. Further, when the Americans expressed their views on a point under negotiation, Tien Chao would say, "We'll take note of your position," but then go on to the next issue under discussion. Brickley sensed that this indicated that the Chinese did not agree, but wished to avoid confrontations.

He also noted that the Chinese were extremely sensitive when pricing was being discussed and were apparently concerned that they might be given unfavorable treatment or were being cheated. From his interpreter, Brickley learned that this was true and that the Chinese were apprehensive that their superior would deal with them harshly if favorable terms were not obtained. Brickley also noted that in order to gain concessions from the Chinese, it was necessary to give one in return, thereby engaging in a face-saving action.

■ American Hosted Dinner

That evening, the Buckeye Glass executive hosted a dinner for the Chinese. The menu was simpler than the Chinese banquet as the Buckeye executives felt that the Chinese meal was too exotic for their tastes and digestion. Speeches were again given by Tien Chao and Brickley and frequent toasts were offered. Miller again told some Western jokes accompanied by friendly backslapping. The Buckeye executives attempted to lighten the ongoing formal conversation by steering it to familiar topics, such as, the families of the Chinese, personal tastes and ideas, and sexual patterns in China. The Chinese responded with much smiling and laughter even though their replies to the questioning were vague.

■ Proposed Joint Venture Contract

After a long weekend, during which the Americans and Chinese separately developed proposals for the joint venture, the Buckeye team were the first to present their terms for negotiations. Brickley submitted the financial requirements as he and his team perceived them (see Exhibit 2) and their terms for the joint venture (see Exhibit 3).

The Law of the People's Republic of China on Joint Ventures Using Chinese and Foreign Investment (adopted in 1979 at the second session of the Fifth National People's Congress)	Exhibit 1

1.   Foreign companies and individuals within the territory of the People's Republic of China may incorporate themselves into joint ventures with Chinese companies or other Chinese entities with the objective of expanding international economic cooperation and technological exchange.

2.   The Foreign Investment Commission must authorize joint ventures, and if approved, ventures are required to register with the General Administration for Industry and Commerce of the PRC, which will then issue a license within 3 months.

3.   Joint ventures shall have limited liability and the foreign parties will contribute not less than 25% of the registered capital.

4.   The participants will share profits, risks, and losses of the joint venture in proportion to their capital contributions.

5.   The equity of each party may be capital goods, industrial property rights, cash, etc., in the ventures.

6.   The contributors of technology or equipment contributed run the risk of forfeiture or damages if the technology or equipment contributed is not truly advanced and appropriate for Chinese needs. If losses are caused by deception through the intentional provision of outdated equipment or technology, compensation must be paid for the losses.

7.   Investments by the Chinese participants may include the right of use of a site but it shall not constitute a part of the investment as the joint venture shall pay the Chinese government for its use.

8.   A joint venture will have a Board of Directors and the Chairman of the board is to be appointed by the Chinese participants. The foreign parties may appoint 2 Vice-Presidents. These do not necessarily have to be Chinese but must be approved by the partners to the joint venture.

9.   A joint venture agreement must stipulate procedures for the employment and discharge of the workers and staff members and comply with Chinese laws.

10.   The net profit of a joint venture shall be distributed in proportion to the parties' respective investment shares after deductions for reserve funds. Bonuses and welfare funds for the workers and the expansion funds of the venture and the profit or losses shall be in accordance with the capital investment of the parties involved and be subject to the tax laws of the People's Republic of China and expatriation.

11.   Joint ventures must maintain open accounts in a bank approved by the Bank of China.

12.   All foreign exchange transactions shall be in accordance with the foreign exchange regulations of the People's Republic of China.

13.   Joint ventures may borrow funds directly from foreign banks. Appropriate insurance will be provided by Chinese insurance companies. A joint venture equipped with up-to-date technology by world standards may apply for a reduction of or an exemption from income tax for the first 2 or 3 profit-making years.

14.   A joint venture is encouraged to market its products outside China through direct channels, its associated agencies, or Chinese foreign trade establishments. Its products may also be distributed on the Chinese market.

15.   The contract period of a joint venture must be agreed upon by both parties and may be extended subject to authorization by the Foreign Investment Commission.

16.   Disputes which cannot be settled through consultation may be settled through consultation or arbitration by an arbitral body of Chinese or arbitral body agreed upon by the parties.

■ Negotiations Concluded

As Brickley was willing to negotiate and make concessions, he was puzzled that the Chinese did not present their terms. He commented on the key issues of the joint venture agreement and the Chinese listened intently. As they were passive and remained silent, Brickley couldn't tell whether they agreed or not with his

Exhibit 2

Proposed Joint Venture, Dragon Glass Company: Financial Requirements (U.S. $000)

First year capital			Loan from Bank of China	$200
Working capital		$898	Long-term debt	400
Installations and equipment		790	Total liabilities	600
New	$450			
Old	40			
Factory		800	Net worth	
Land			First 2 year loss	200
Technology		550	Initial capital	2338
Total		$2738	Total	$3038

Partners' Investments

Xia Xian Glass Company		55%	Buckeye Glass		25%
Factory		$400	Factory		$400
Installations and equipment		490	Technology		550
New	$750		Cash equivalent		102
Old	40				
Cash/equivalent		396			
Total		$1286	Total		$1052

proposal, and the team was perplexed about how to cope with these periods of silence. Tien Chao thanked him and proposed they continue their discussions at 2 PM that afternoon. He was most concerned about the confidentiality of the transfer of technology in China as he knew there were no comprehensive commercial laws to protect his company, and China did not have trade secret laws. He had been told that the Chinese, on occasion, take technology and copy it. Moreover, he was aware margins initially would be nonexistent for goods sold on the world markets, and the joint venture would undoubtedly incur losses until the company could become more efficient.

In the afternoon session, the Chinese were cordial but remained passive. Tien Chao observed, "We have reviewed your proposal and can agree on most of its provisions. However, the value placed on the technology is far greater than we believe can be justified. As you have already paid for its development, we insist that in the spirit of friendship, a much lower figure be used. Further, we believe that Buckeye Glass should contribute all of the money for the investment in installations and equipment as we are providing labor at a considerably lower level than can be obtained elsewhere. We will cover the cost of the factory in our investment. We believe that 80% of the goods should be sold in the export market. Before proceeding, we wish to resolve these issues."

Brickley then endeavored to explain that although his company had already invested in the glass technology, that on world markets it would be valued at this level. Further, he was quite puzzled by the large percentage of output which was to be destined for the export market as he had assumed the Chinese were interested in raising the standards of living of the people in the PRC. Obviously the need for foreign hard currency was more paramount. Discussion continued for another hour, at which time Tien Chao then proposed they adjourn and meet the next morning.

Proposed Joint Venture

Exhibit 3

Name: Dragon Glass Company.

Capital Contributions: 55% of the capital for the venture should be provided by the Xia Xian Glass Factory and 25% by the Buckeye Glass Company. In meeting this requirement, the Chinese were to obtain the right to use a site in the Qinhuangdao Economic Development Zone. It was agreed that the joint venture should rent the property from the Chinese government. Buckeye Glass was to invest $400,000 in the building and installations.

Training: Buckeye Glass was also to provide for training of the joint venture's managers and engineers in the United States for a period of 3 months.

Marketing: Buckeye Glass shall be the sole sales agent in the world market and provide for the maximum market penetration by its products internally in China and in the Pacific Basin countries, with the objective of 40% being sold domestically and the remaining 60% in the export market.

Pricing: The prices established in the world market would provide a 20% after tax return on the total investment of each party to the contract.

Technology: Technology provided by Buckeye Glass shall comply with the technology transfer regulations of the People's Republic of China and provide for the improvement of product quality and performance, reduce production costs, and increase foreign revenues. The value of the technology in the first year shall be $550,000.

Imported Materials: All silica and related production materials imported will not be subject to the standard 12% import duty if used for exported products, but a duty will be applied to those used for glassware produced for domestic sales. An 18% tax of value-added nature on domestic sales shall be levied. Sales in the world market shall provide a 20% after-tax return on the total investment of each party to the contract.

Work Force: The work force shall consist of the normal staff of production workers and include staff employees including engineers, office workers and managers. The joint venture shall not hire additional workers for the factory or office workers without the approval of the Board of Directors.

The initial work force for the plant shall be limited to 200 factory workers and 50 service employees in the offices, including the managers.

Wage Compensation: The direct salary and benefits for the workers shall be determined by the Chinese government. The range for factory workers in the first year will be for 1200 Yuan and in the second year 1800 Yuan and will be for 2000 hours annually.

The annual wage rate for the production workers will include direct and fringe benefits. The wage rate will be modified after the first year in conformity with those paid in other Chinese corporations for production workers by the Board of Directors.

Technology Confidentiality: The joint venture partners will be obliged to maintain confidentiality of the technology and shall be required during the life of the joint venture and beyond. Damages for the breach of contract will be pursuant to the Foreign Economic Contract Law and recoverable against a contract transferee who discloses the confidential information.

Expansion: The joint venture should secure from the Chinese government an additional 10 acres for expansion of this manufacturing facility.

Board of Directors: The management of the joint venture shall consist of 7 members on a Board of Directors, 4 of whom will be appointed by the Chinese and 3 by the Buckeye Glass Company. The board will follow modern management principles and establish a 5 year marketing and production plan. A planning budget shall be developed for the same period of time. It will be the responsibility of the joint venture board to specify the types and numbers of workers and managers for the venture.

Taxation: With approval of the tax authorities, the joint venture may be exempt from taxation for the first 2 profit-making years and granted a 50% tax reduction for the following 5 years. A profit-making year shall be defined as the year in which a joint venture realizes profits after the accumulated operating losses from prior years have been deducted. Further, as this joint venture is in a Special Investment Zone, the tax rate applicable to the enterprise shall be 15%, and no withholding tax on repatriated profits shall be levied.

Currency: This joint venture will use Reminbi (RMB) to calculate its income and tax liabilities. It may maintain its accounting records and books in dollars.

XIA XIAN'S PROPOSAL

At the meeting, Tien Chao presented Xia Xian's proposal. Buckeye Glass was to invest 35% of the capital in the form of cash, installations, and technology. He specified that the technology must be advanced, lead to improved product quality and performance, and contribute to export expansion.

Brickley thereupon assured him that the technology proposed would do all these things, but insisted that the most advanced technology would not be appropriate at this time in China. He agreed that the value of the property in the buildings should be fixed by the People's government of Qinhuangdao according to a relative industry index. When Brickley inquired concerning the availability of silica and other raw materials for this project the Chinese were evasive, but assured him their "connections" would be able to find the necessary materials at reasonable prices.

To relieve some of the tension, Mr. Brickley and his team avoided the topics about which the 2 groups were in most disagreement; and again emphasized the great mutual benefits which would result from this venture. The afternoon meeting ended well. There were still some disagreements remaining, however, much ground had been covered. The remaining differences were considered by the Buckeye Glass negotiators to be minor, and they agreed to go back over them for the discussion on the next day, but Brickley was becoming impatient as he thought about the considerable investment his company had made in order to conduct these negotiations in Qinhuangdao. Buckeye had already committed over $25,000 for lodging, food, transportation and other expenses, and at least another million could be required for the equity capital.

The next morning the negotiators met again and to Brickley's dismay, the Chinese were adamant and refused to modify their terms. However, Tien Chao proposed that production be expanded to include containers for the wine and soft drink industries rather than only for food. This astounded Brickley as these industries were expanding rapidly and naturally he wanted to be involved in the early phase of development of these markets. He knew that the Chinese had strong loyalty to their initial suppliers and it was essential to establish these relationships before other foreign competitors entered the Chinese market. "What do we do now to break this impasse?" he agonized to his team. "What concessions can we make to enable the Chinese to save face and alter this position?"

Brickley was aware that any joint agreement proposal would be subject to review by not only the Chinese government but also his legal department. At least another year would be required to formalize the agreement. His team had been in China for 2 weeks and the potential for profit in the long run was in the millions after the shakedown period in the first 2 years. He perceived several options at this point. They could drop the idea and move on to more promising ventures in the short run, make some concessions, and bring in an agent who resided on a permanent basis in Beijing who had strong Chinese ties, as he was a successful Chinese negotiator; they could offer to invite the Chinese to come to America as Buckeye's guests in order to visit the corporate plant and observe the technology and training facilities, or they could set a date for departure with the objective of forcing the Chinese to move off dead center and reach an agreement on the terms. He murmured to himself, "Patience, John, getting a joint venture signed in the PRC is like building Rome—it takes longer than a day! Freight trains move faster than negotiations in the PRC!"

APPENDIX 1: CHINESE CULTURE AND NEGOTIATING STYLES

■ ────────────────────────────────── ■

FACE

Paramount to an understanding of Chinese behavior in relationships is an understanding of face behavior. In China, *face* has two forms: *lien* and *mien-tzu*. Lien refers to one's moral character and is a person's most precious possession. Without it, one cannot function in society. It is earned by fulfilling one's duties and other obligations. Mien-tzu refers to a person's reputation or prestige and is based on personal accomplishments, political status or bureaucratic power. It also refers to one's ability to deal smoothly with people face-to-face. Face enhancement can be attained by acts of generosity in terms of time or gifts, or praise of others.

Face is the cooperative manner in which people behave toward one another in order to avoid loss of self-respect or prestige by either party. While the concept of *face* is often a fiction in practice, it retains its importance in actual dealings. For example, given a situation where 2 people are bargaining with each other, 1 must win and the other must lose. Each side expects that the other will consider *face* in the transaction. In reality, both sides know at the end who has won and who has lost, but the winner makes token concessions to save the loser's *face*. This is important in that it allows the loser to win in that he or she has been respected by the other, the winning party. Without the saving of *face*, the loser will be justly offended and avoid dealing with the winner in the future. This avoidance reaction carries with it obvious consequences and hinders any potential ongoing business relationship.

Another aspect of *face* is similar to the Western concept of *being a good sport*, or *being a good winner*. Modesty over one's own achievement and appreciation of the loser's skill and effort are central to saving *face*.

Face most often requires little effort but merely an attention to courtesy in relationships with others, yet will have a great positive effect upon the recipient. If lost, *face* will have a negative effect; which, if shown by the loser, results in still further loss of *face*. With the exception of a show of controlled anger by a person in authority, such as by a policeman, loss of self-control, sulking, and displays of anger or frustration create further loss of *face* rather than drawing respect or conciliation.

Once *face* has been lost, the loser will prefer to avoid the winner and ignore the face-losing incident as though it never occurred. In circumstances where the 2 parties must continue a relationship, the loser will return to formal and polite etiquette, pretending that the incident had not occurred. The other party should accommodate the loser's preference and not refer again to the incident. *Face* involves a high degree of self-control, social consciousness, and concern for others.

SMILING AND LAUGHTER

Laughter and smiling in Chinese culture represent the universal reaction to pleasure and humor. In addition, they are also a common response to negative occurrences, such as death and other misfortunes. When embarrassed or in the wrong, the Chinese frequently respond with laughter or smiling which will persist if another person continues to speak of an embarrassing topic or does not ignore the wrong. Westerners are often confused and shocked by this behavior, which is alien to them. It is important to remember that smiling and laughter in the above situations are not exhibitions of glee, but are rather a part of the concept of *face* when used in response to a negative or unpleasant situation.

GUANXI (THE VALUE OF AN ONGOING RELATIONSHIP)

Guanxi is the word that describes the intricate, pervasive network of personal relations which every Chinese cultivates with energy, subtlety and imagination. *Guanxi* is the currency of getting things done and getting ahead in Chinese society. *Guanxi* is a relationship between 2 people containing implicit mutual obligation, assurances and intimacy, and is the perceived value of an ongoing relationship and its future possibilities that typically govern Chinese attitudes toward long-term business. If a relationship of trust and mutual benefit is developed, an excellent foundation will be built to future business with the Chinese. *Guanxi* ties are also helpful in dealing with the Chinese bureaucracy as personal interpretations are used in lieu of legal interpretations.

Due to cultural differences and language barriers, the visitors to China are not in a position to cultivate *guanxi* with the depth possible between 2 Chinese. Regardless, *guanxi* is an important aspect of interrelations in China and deserves attention so that good friendly relations may be developed. These connections are essential to get things accomplished.

FORMAL AND INFORMAL RELATIONS

At present it is likely that the majority of social contacts foreigners have with the Chinese are on a more formal than informal level. Informality in China relates not to social pretension or artifice, but to the concept of *face*. Great attention is paid to observance of formal, or social behavior and corresponding norms. The social level is the level of form and proper etiquette where *face* is far more important than fact. It is considered both gauche and rude to allow one's personal feelings and opinions to surface here to the detriment of the social ambience. It is much more important to compliment a person or to avoid an embarrassing or sensitive subject than it is to express an honest opinion if honesty is at the expense of another's feelings. Directness, honesty, and individualism that run counter to social conventions and basic considerations of politeness have no place on the social level; emotions and private relationships tend to be kept private in Chinese society.

CHINESE ETIQUETTE FOR SOCIAL FUNCTIONS

Ceremonies and rules of ceremony have traditionally held a place of great importance in Chinese culture. Confucianism perpetuated and strengthened these traditions by providing the public with an identity, mask, or persona with which a person is best equipped to deal with the world with a minimum of friction. Confucianism consists of broad rules of conduct evolved to aid and guide interpersonal relations. Confucius assembled all the details of etiquette practiced at the courts of the feudal lords during the period c. 551–479 B.C. These rules of etiquette are called the *li* and have long since become a complete way of life for the Chinese.

The *li* may appear overly formalistic to Westerners at first glance. Upon closer inspection it is apparent that the rules of etiquette play a very important role in regulating interpersonal relations. Some basic rules of behavior are as follows:

- A host should always escort a guest out to his car or other mode of transportation and watch until the guest is out of sight.
- Physical expression is minimal by Western standards. A handshake is polite, but backslapping and other enthusiastic grasping is a source of embarrassment.
- At cultural functions and other performances, audience approval of performers is often subdued by American standards. Although the accepted manner of expressing approval varies between functions and age groups, applause is often polite, rather than roaring and bravo-like cheers.
- A person should keep control over his temper at all times.
- One should avoid blunt, direct, or abrupt discussion, particularly when the subject is awkward; delicate hints are often used to broach such a topic.
- It is a sign of respect to allow another to take the seat of honor (left of host), or to be asked to proceed through a door first.
- The serving of tea often signals the end of an interview or meeting. However, it is also served during extended meetings to quench the thirst of the negotiators.

ISM Engineering

Lester A. Neidell, University of Tulsa

Paul Olson, Director of Marketing for ISM Engineering, leaned back in his chair, and looked at the telephone. For the past ten minutes he had listened to a tirade from Jean Moret, Purchasing Agent for Snecma (France), one of ISM's largest customers. Snecma maintained all of Air France's jet engines and provided similar services to other European airlines. ISM's first quarter 1987 sales figures, which were displayed prominently on a wall sales chart, did little to alleviate his foul mood. He thought about the situation he faced, and the options open to him:

> April 1987—we're 27 percent under the sales forecast for the year, and Pete Adams (acting CEO) has put a hold on $328,000 of completed parts scheduled to be shipped to Snecma. I've got one angry customer on my hands.

Paul pressed his intercom button, "Jessica, better book us on an early flight to Paris tomorrow, and make hotel reservations for two nights . . . no, better make it until Saturday . . . at the Orly Hilton."

THE COMPANY

ISM Engineering is a repair facility for aircraft turbine (engine) parts. Its customers include the United States Armed Forces and major airlines in the United States and around the world. A list of ISM's ten largest customers for each of

Exhibit 1	Yearly Sales by Top Ten Customers			

	Percent of Annual Sales			
Customer	*1983*	*1984*	*1985*	*1986*
U.S. Armed Forces	35.9	44.9	32.6	11.5
KLM (Holland)	12.1	11.7	24.2	32.9
Snecma (France)	9.1	12.8	16.1	16.7
McDonnell Douglas	6.9	5.5	4.1	2.4
Korean Airlines (Korea)	5.4	1.8	—	—
Alitalia (Italy)	2.2	1.8	2.3	3.7
Avianca	2.2	—	—	—
General Electric	1.9	—	—	—
Western Airlines	1.5	4.6	3.4	4.4
Rolls-Royce (England)	1.4	—	—	—
American Airlines	—	1.8	1.9	—
Varig Airlines (Brazil)	—	1.7	1.2	—
Republic Airlines	—	1.7	1.7	2.4
Pacific Southwest	—	—	1.5	1.5
Continental Airlines	—	—	—	6.1
Air Ground	—	—	—	1.3
Total company sales ($ millions)	11.8	11.3	13.6	16.8

the preceding four years is contained in Exhibit 1. Financial statements for the two previous years are contained in Exhibit 2. ISM is a subsidiary of Air Services, Inc., a publicly traded company with 1986 sales of $125 million.

■ Company History

In 1961, three former college roommates from Georgia Tech founded a specialty steel fabrication business, Automatic Welding, in Atlanta, Georgia. John Isom, Vice President of Sales, and Elliott Stevens, Treasurer, had obtained business degrees, while Lawrence Martin, President, was a mechanical engineer.

Exhibit 2	ISM Engineering: Consolidated Statements of Income and Retained Earnings and Consolidated Balance Sheets, Years Ended December 31, 1985 and 1986	

	1986	*1985*
Income Statement and Retained Earnings		
Net sales	$16,781,317	$13,620,979
Cost of sales	12,246,093	10,136,844
Gross profit	4,535,224	3,484,135
Selling, general and administrative expenses	2,422,979	1,729,426
Operating income	2,112,245	1,754,709
Other income (expense)*	—	1,007,437
	(544,100)	(435,807)
	(544,100)	571,630

	1986	1985
Income Statement and Retained Earnings		
Income before income taxes	1,568,145	2,326,339
Provision for income taxes	557,715	850,247
Net income	1,010,430	1,476,092
Net loss for the period from December 9, 1984, through December 31, 1984[†]	—	(25,967)
Retained earnings, beginning of year	3,123,122	1,672,997
Dividends paid	(678,928)	—
Retained earnings, end of year	$ 3,454,624	$ 3,123,122
Balance Sheet		
Assets		
Current assets		
Cash	$ 317,033	$ 362,341
Accounts receivable	3,460,616	2,113,485
Due from parent	—	1,010,412
Claim for income tax refund	73,559	—
Inventories	4,627,351	2,370,824
Other	47,289	42,024
Total current assets	8,525,848	5,899,086
Property and equipment, less accumulated depreciation	4,620,012	2,948,608
Due from parent	—	415,000
Other assets	340,705	405,081
	$13,486,565	$ 9,667,775
Liabilities and Stockholder's Equity		
Current liabilities		
Note payable	$ 250,000	$ 250,000
Accounts payable	1,232,929	514,834
Accrued payroll	496,206	398,188
Other accrued liabilities	163,240	273,270
Due to parent	335,304	—
Income taxes payable	—	716,552
Current maturities of long-term debt	3,743,506	680,974
Total current liabilities	6,221,185	2,833,818
Long-term debt	2,566,787	2,609,279
Deferred income taxes	555,732	413,319
Stockholder's equity		
Common stock, $1 par—shares authorized, 1,000,000; outstanding, 688,237	688,237	688,237
Retained earnings	3,454,624	3,123,122
Total stockholder's equity	4,142,861	3,811,359
	$13,486,565	$ 9,667,775

Related party transactions: The company purchased approximately $300,000 of raw materials from its parent in each of the years 1986 and 1985. The company paid $478,680 in 1986 and $80,056 in 1985 to an affiliate in sales commissions. In 1985, the company received $1,007,437 in sales commissions from its parent. A management fee of $81,804 and $72,608 was paid to its parent in 1986 and 1985, respectively.

[†]*Accounting period:* Beginning in 1985, the company changed its year end from a 52–53 week fiscal year to a calendar year. The 1984 fiscal year was a 53 week period ending December 8, 1984. This change was made to conform the company's year end with that of its parent.

Shortly after startup, Mr. Martin was in the machine shop of Delta Airlines, where Delta machinists were trying to repair a jet engine part. After watching several failures, Mr. Martin asked if he could take the part back to his shop for repair. In about a week's time, a superior repair was developed. News of this spread rapidly by word of mouth through the U.S. commercial aircraft industry, and the small welding business was soon overwhelmed with orders from other airlines. In 1966, Specialty Welding became ISM Fabrication. The informal business objective of this new company was to repair an aircraft engine part so that it met or exceeded all OEM specifications, and to do it for less than half the price of a new part.

In 1969, the largest customer of ISM was the U.S. Army. Business with the army began when the army purchased a repairable part from KLM Airlines, but was not able to complete the repair to its satisfaction. ISM's expertise provided a solution, with the result that almost all U.S. Army aircraft turbine repair work was routed to ISM. When KLM heard of the repair through its army contacts, ISM received its first international order.

Two years later, John Isom spent one hundred consecutive days in Europe, marketing ISM's know how to European airlines. Toward the end of this time period, because of his lack of cultural knowledge and contacts, Mr. Isom decided to hire a European manufacturer's representative. Kirk Dhouw, a Swiss citizen fluent in six languages, was selected.

While the European market was being opened, there were significant sales problems in the United States and in other foreign markets. The sales organization was unable to market repairs as fast as Larry Martin developed them. Seven manufacturer's representatives were added, three for the U.S. market and four for international sales. The 1971 "rep" organization and the commission structure is shown in Exhibit 3.

By 1980, ISM had lost its technical differential advantage. Other repair facilities developed similar repair procedures for older jet engines, while the three Western OEM engine manufacturers, General Electric, Pratt and Whitney, and Rolls-Royce, warranted their new products in such a way that many of ISM's

Exhibit 3	Representatives and Their Commission Structure, 1971	
Location of Representative	**Territory**	**Commission (%)**
Switzerland	Europe (except Portugal)	5
Rio De Janeiro, Brazil	Brazil	7
Bogata, Colombia	Colombia	7
Miami, Florida	U.S. east of Mississippi, Canada (except house accounts)	5
Bombay, India	India	5
Buenos Aires, Argentina	Argentina	7
St. Louis, Missouri	McDonnell Douglas	5
Lisbon, Portugal	Portugal	7
Los Angeles, California	United Airlines	5

Resume of Paul Olson

Exhibit 4

Birth Date: September 12, 1944

Career Objective: Senior Sales Management in Aircraft Industry

Education: University of Georgia; BBA 1965
Major: Corporate Finance
Minor: Transportation
Graduated top 15% of class

Georgia State University
10 hours towards MBA

Florida International University, MBA, 1981
Major: International Business

Experience

March 1978—December 1983	Eastern Airlines, Miami, Florida Purchasing Agent, Repair and Overhaul Section
June 1977—January 1978	Great Lakes Dredge & Dock Company Jebal Ali, United Arab Republic On-Site Administrative Manager/Diving Superintendent
January 1976—March 1977	Gulf Standard Dredging Company Manama, Bahrain Operations Manager
December 1974—December 1975	Gulf Standard Dredging Company Basra, Iraq Welder
March 1971—November 1974	Brussels Development Company Limited Atlanta, Georgia President (site developers of real estate)
January 1966—February 1971	United States Army Medical Corps Company commander of combat medical company in Vietnam Honorably discharged with rank of Major

repairs would have voided the warranty. Repair volume was maintained due to an increase in air travel, but the company's market share declined. More frequently ISM was winning orders based on price and turnaround time instead of on technology.

The three partners disagreed on how to compete in this new environment. John Isom wanted to expand to take advantage of volume pricing, but Elliott Stevens and Larry Martin were more conservative. Stevens finally decided that he had had enough and offered to sell his share of the partnership. Unable to come up with the money to buy out Stevens, and unable to find a new investor/partner, the three founders agreed to sell ISM.

In July 1984, Air Services, Inc., purchased all outstanding stock of ISM, and established a subsidiary, ISM Engineering. John Isom remained as Marketing Director of the new subsidiary until March 1985, when he was replaced by Paul Olson. Mr. Olson was experienced in international marketing, and had a broad background in the airline and heavy equipment industries. (See Exhibit 4 for a

---

Exhibit 5   **Organizational Chart, March 1985**

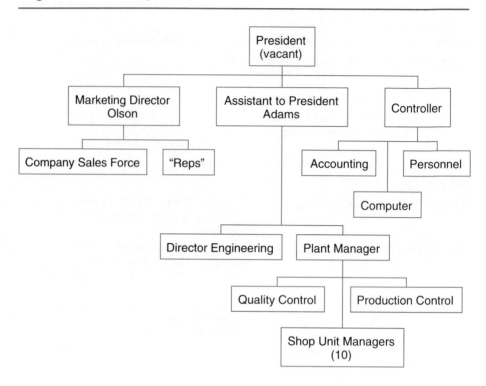

summary of his experience.) Shortly before Olson was hired, the other of the two remaining original owners, Larry Martin, resigned from the presidency. Peter Adams, formerly Contract Administrator and Director of Purchasing of the parent company, was appointed acting CEO but was not given the title of President. Instead, a new position, Assistant to the President was created for him, and the President's position was left vacant. Adams had no prior line experience and had not traveled outside the United States. His primary responsibility was to oversee the financial side of the company. Exhibit 5 shows the organizational hierarchy of the new company.

■ Paul Olson Talks About His New Job

When I first came to ISM it was apparent that I was an unwanted outsider. Larry Martin, the former President, had just left the company, and there was much fear of the unknown. Martin had managed the company very conservatively. Everyone seemed to move in slow motion and no one wanted to make a decision. Group management existed, which is good for the communication factor, but unfortunately even minor issues were hashed to death. It was a very close group, a family; each member covering the other's mistakes when necessary, and each very skeptical of new ideas. For many years these people had worked under no pressure. Sales volume had increased very little, and the emphasis was on efficiency, especially on the Snecma project. The learning curve for Snecma had been long and costly, but this customer was now producing a profit.

I was enthusiastic and ready to help this company grow. My idea was to involve everyone, to develop a full team effort. I held a meeting to introduce myself and to

---

Sales Territory and Representative Structure, July 1985   **Exhibit 6**

Position	Territory	Payment
Director of Marketing (Paul Olson)	Far East, Middle East, Africa	Salary
Company salesman	Europe, Canada	Salary
Company salesman	West of Mississippi	Salary
Company salesman	East of Mississippi	Salary
Company salesman	Special large accounts	Salary
Company salesman	U.S. government	Salary
Representative	South America, Mexico	Commission of 10 percent

---

spread my enthusiasm. Few people laughed at my jokes. I felt like a Democrat in a Republican Congress.

New Strategy

Paul Olson began immediately to revamp the sales force. During his first six months on the job, four new sales people were hired, and the manufacturer's representative network that Isom had developed was largely disbanded. The world was divided into six territories (see Exhibit 6), and the new sales force went on the road.

From Olson's standpoint:

> Sales growth in this industry requires frequent direct contact with the customers. Reps sell everyone's services, and have little or no loyalty. We have no control over their time or efforts. I use them only in developing markets or when absolutely necessary to penetrate the market, as in South America.
>
> ISM's reputation in the industry was not good. Previous promises had not been fulfilled. We had to convince lost customers that our organization was under new leadership and things would be different. I begged, borrowed on old friendships and called in markers for a chance to prove this.

Frequent company meetings were held in which Mr. Olson explained his operations, marketing and sales goals:

> I was determined that everyone in the organization would be prepared to service the increased volume. Sarcastically, I was told, "Bring it in; we'll get it out." Six months after I initiated the new sales program, the backlog had tripled. Production just wasn't prepared for the new surge in orders.

Advertising and Sales Promotion

For the first time in the company's history, ads were placed in trade publications. Promotional activity, which had been largely the domain of the now terminated manufacturer's reps, became a major thrust. Professional consultants were hired to develop trade show booths, and to instruct the new sales force on how to "work" trade shows. Customer giveaways and organized outings, fishing trips in Mexico and Hawaii, a hunting trip in Canada, also became part of the communication program.

■ Key Current Problems

A summary of the company's major problems, developed during a staff meeting in December 1986, is contained below:

- Pricing: There is a trend towards cutthroat competition among U.S. airlines as a result of deregulation. This fare competition is reflected in the airlines' efforts to reduce costs elsewhere. Profits on domestic repairs will become more limited.
- Production: Lack of computer capability limits ability to control and track material. Scheduling is manual and ineffective. Poor employee attitude due to inconsistent management policies and turbulent union contract negotiations has hurt job commitment. There have been isolated incidences of slowdown and sabotage.
- Engineering (R & D): Innovations have been slow, and the area is understaffed.

COMPETITION

Mr. Olson discussed the competition:

Only one "noncaptive" competitor exists in the United States—Chromalloy, Inc. Other competition is from airlines' in-house repair facilities, from the OEM's and from engine overhaul shops. But these companies are also customers. ISM gets overflow from all, and in the case of the airlines and OEM's, gets business for processes that they have not developed internally. Quality is not a major competitive issue, as all work must meet specifications. Inspection is very involved and tedious; all parts not meeting standards are returned for rework. The most important competitive factor, now that technology is about even, seems to be "turn time," how quickly the job can be done. Price occasionally becomes a marketing issue, but an acceptable price range is typically dictated by the market. A company must decide if repairs can be profitable within that price range. Price is more important internally; at different times it's necessary to give extremely low prices in order to obtain volume necessary to cover overhead. We marketing people are often at odds with accounting, which continually complains about low margin items.

MARKETS

For much of its history, ISM depended on three accounts for one half to two thirds of its annual volume. These were the U.S. military, typically contributing 30 to 40 percent of annual volume, and KLM and Snecma, which combined for 20 to 25 percent each year. Olson was determined to reduce this dependence, and was particularly fearful of losing American military contracts as defense budgets came under pressure. A massive marketing campaign, targeting the entire world except the Eastern Bloc nations, commenced. Olson had no qualms about selling to the Eastern Bloc, but it was unlikely that the U.S. government would approve such transactions. As a result of the new marketing emphasis, several new accounts were developed, and older, smaller accounts were expanded, lessening dependence on the three major customers. While the largest single air travel market is the United States, several factors favor expanded international marketing efforts.

List of ISM's International Accounts   **Exhibit 7**

Alitalia	Pakistan International Airlines
Canadian Pacific Airlines	Caledonian Airmotive, Ltd (England)
Pratt & Whitney of Canada	Iberia Air Lines (Spain)
Cruzeiro do Sul S A—Servicos Aereos (Brazil)	KLM (Holland)
	Lufthansa German Airlines
VASP (Brazil)	South African Airways
Ansett Industries, Australia	Air France
Air India	Scandinavian Airlines System
Far Eastern Air Transport	Swissair
Japan Air Lines	Transportes Aereos Portuguese
Air New Zealand	

Note: From company accounts receivables, August 1986.

First, air travel in many third world countries is underdeveloped. As incomes increase so will air travel. Second, as mentioned earlier, there are three jet engine manufacturers in the Western world: General Electric, Pratt and Whitney and Rolls-Royce.[1] The first two are headquartered in the United States, and it is likely that foreign airlines will look to the United States for repair of their GE and P&W engines.[2] Third, ISM has been successful in obtaining foreign business, as Exhibit 7 indicates. In 1986 more than twenty foreign accounts were active.

Mr. Olson's assessment of foreign markets follows:

• *Europe:* Europe has the greatest potential of the international markets. There are some nationalistic tendencies, but most airlines, even though state-owned, will go where they get the best combination of price and turn-around time.

• *The Far East:* This is a tough market. Most routes are long haul, which carry a smaller per mile seat cost and require less maintenance. Most engine wear occurs during take-off and low atmospheric travel. Low atmospheric travel produces more sand, dust and other engine pollution. Engines used for long haul may fly 10,000 hours before repairs are required, and the extent of repairs are less. Short haul carriers normally overhaul their engines after approximately 4000 hours flight time. Nevertheless, the Far East remains a priority market for ISM because we see a significant increase in air travel. Some countries' markets are more promising than others.

• *Japan:* Japan is extremely nationalistic. The government provides protective trade policies, and the country has overhaul companies that get most of the repair business.

---

[1] A joint venture between GE and Snecma, CFM International, is producing GE designed engines in France for Airbus Industrie, a European consortium.

[2] Transportation of entire engines to and from the United States is usually accomplished by *hanging* a nonoperating engine on the wing of an aircraft that is regularly scheduled to the United States. That is, regularly scheduled passenger aircraft *ferry* engines back and forth.

• *Korea:* Korean Airlines is a small, long-time, solid account. There are prospects for additional work when some of the R and D we are working on becomes usable.

• *Singapore:* Little business can be obtained here because of internal airline policies. Aircraft are usually replaced in four or five years, when the manufacturer's warranty runs out.

• *Indonesia and Thailand:* There is good potential here, especially when the individual airlines develop in-house overhaul capability. Currently, these airlines send the entire engine to a major overhaul company, where it is broken down, repaired, and parts sent out to a company like ISM for repair. As these airlines begin to disassemble their own engines, they will require more outside repair work than the overhaul companies.

• *Australia and New Zealand:* Currently ISM has a limited amount of work from both countries. Distance is an important factor governing turn time. These airlines freight their own parts, and shipments wait at their docks until there is a cargo vacancy. Australia, in particular, has a policy of keeping work at home as much as possible, but volume and lack of technology requires that some repairs be sent outside of the country.

• *South and Central America:* Unlike other parts of the world, local sales reps are a must. Most deals are "under the table," involving large commissions and kickbacks, and cannot be handled by U.S. personnel. Also, many countries are extremely nationalistic, and governments typically restrict or tax any currency transactions. We have paid as much as 25 cents on the dollar surcharge. Even though technology is limited, each airline tries to keep as much work in the country as possible. Aircraft flown in South America are typically flown in worse condition than allowed in the United States. Despite this, ISM has had small but steady business from Brazil and Venezuela. However, receivables collection can run as long as six months, and we need to consider this when pricing in this market. A list of accounts receivable (see Exhibit 8) shows the difference between foreign and domestic payments.

• *Africa:* South Africa is the only country where local overhaul capability exists. Olson has no reservations about South African business. "Business is business and I don't confuse business with politics." In all other African countries, engines are sent to the country of old colonial rule for repair. Corruption and government regulation cause problems.

THE SNECMA DISPUTE

As noted earlier, Snecma had been one of the company mainstays. This was achieved from the R&D efforts the founding CEO, Larry Martin, had expended and from the close personal relationship that had developed between Snecma personnel and another of the company's founders, John Isom. However, the French were also shrewd negotiators, and it wasn't until 1983 that ISM had achieved satisfactory profits from the Snecma account. The French were continually trading volume for price. Through the years, the French had never contracted to the price or volume terms requested by ISM, but had always sent the required number of parts once ISM agreed to the French price. In other words,

Status of Accounts Receivables **Exhibit 8**

Status	Domestic Accounts	Foreign Accounts
Current (percent)	48.5	21.1
31–60 days (percent)	26.5	21.0
61–90 days (percent)	9.4	16.3
Over 90 days (percent)	15.6	41.6

ISM had always capitulated to a price without receiving volume guarantees. The French always met the desired, but informally agreed upon, volume. It was a risky game but ISM management accepted this method in order to retain the business.

■ Jean Moret, Snecma Purchasing Agent

Jean Moret assumed the position of Snecma Purchasing Agent in 1980. He was a tough negotiator and very nationalistic. One of his primary goals was to build a comprehensive turbine repair source within his native France. In addition to servicing all of Air France's turbine repair needs, Snecma also performed work for other European airlines. It was an important gesture to have as much French content as possible.[3] But, due to Snecma's volume, it was necessary for them to go outside of France for many different repairs. Also, ISM's specialized repairs were weak points in Snecma's R&D efforts. As a result, funds and manpower were routed to more profitable areas within Snecma. Despite this, Moret continued to use the threat of in-house capability in his annual contract negotiations with ISM. Thus, the *game* followed for several years was as follows: Moret was probably bluffing, but the founders of ISM, and last year, Olson, were unwilling to call his bluff.

■ 1987 Contract

Olson and Adams were well aware of this *game* when they arrived in Paris in November 1986 to negotiate the next year's contract. They were determined to obtain a long-term volume commitment from Snecma, one that extended several years. In this way, ISM could plan better for facilities expansion, for the purchase of new equipment, and for the hiring and training of new personnel.

The proposal they planned to present to Moret was:

1. Continue to repair units at the rate of twelve per month at $20,500 per unit until current orders were completed.
2. Reduce the price to $18,500 per unit based on receiving a multiyear commitment of a minimum of 16 units per month.

Moret opened the meeting with the following information. He had promised his superiors a $2000 per unit price decrease for 1987. Before Paul Olson could respond, Peter Adams, who had not previously participated in the French con-

---

[3]Snecma was wholly owned by the French government.

tract negotiations, assumed control. Adams responded that he would agree to this price reduction if the annual repair was increased from 144 units to 192 units. As in the past, Moret refused to sign such a contract, but gave broad assurances that the need was there for 192 units. Adams held firm. Snecma would sign a contract guaranteeing the volume increase or the previous price stood.

No contract was signed, and the ISM contingent returned unhappily to Atlanta.

Orders and shipments continued to flow without a signed agreement. ISM billed at the $20,500 price; Snecma paid $18,500. After 90 days of underpayments, the Controller brought the situation to Adams' attention. Adams sent a telex to Moret, informing him that all work in house for Snecma was to be terminated, and no completed product would be shipped until Snecma paid the additional $2000 per unit for all 1987 work, which amounted to 21 units or $42,000.

Moret called Olson on Monday, April 6, 1987. However, Olson was not in the office and his assistant, Jessica Winters, who had accompanied Olson and Adams on the November trip, took the call. Jessica was an "old friend" of Moret's; she had also been assistant to John Isom and had known Moret ever since ISM began business with Snecma.

Tuesday morning Jessica relayed the conversation with Moret to Paul Olson:

> I can't believe how angry Jean was. He said that he had never been so insulted in all his life, and he refuses to negotiate with Pete Adams. However, after talking for a while, Jean did authorize release of payment of $2000 additional for twenty units.
>   Paul, in my opinion we're in serious danger of losing the Snecma business.

Paul Olson then called Jean Moret. The conversation was entirely one-sided; Moret shouted in the telephone at Paul for ten minutes, sometimes in English and sometimes in French:

> I have never been so affronted. First, my contract with you remains unsigned. Then, Monsieur Adams sends me a telex telling me that our orders are being stopped. We have been doing business for eight years, and never do I get such an insulting message. Monsieur Isom was a gentleman—a man of honor. I can't do business with someone with no honor.

Then Jean Moret dropped a bombshell:

> You know, my friend Paul, that we just lost two large contracts, UTA (Union de Transports Ariens) and LTU (Luftransport-Unternehmen, West Germany). Many of my employees will be leaving this division to work repairing cases. I know we're not competitive with your work, but *mon dieu,* I can't fire any workers. So I don't know if we'll be needing any more work done by ISM.

It was after this conversation that Paul called Jessica and asked her to book the both of them for Paris.

Caterpillar Inc. in Latin America

Robert P. Vichas, Florida Atlantic University;
Tomasz Mroczkowski, American University

Although Caterpillar's presence in Latin America dated to 1914, when the U.S.-based multinational corporation (MNC) opened its first dealership in Panama, manufacturing in Latin America did not commence until 1960, when the company initiated assembly operations in Brazil, its fourth-largest national market.

A giant in the global construction equipment industry, Caterpillar was challenged in the early 1980s by Komatsu Ltd, a Japanese multinational corporation. Having grown from a weak rival one-tenth the size of Caterpillar in 1961 to the world's second-largest supplier of construction equipment, Komatsu confronted Caterpillar on the latter's home turf in the United States as Caterpillar had done 20 years earlier in Japan.

In 1988 Komatsu renewed its assault by forming a strategic alliance with Dresser Industries of Dallas, Texas. The Komatsu-Dresser joint venture presented the latest threat to Caterpillar's Latin American markets. Although Caterpillar, with a strategy of competitive renewal and its "plant with a future," had successfully defended itself from Komatsu's strategic thrusts in the 1980s, the company would face a new set of challenges in the 1990s.

CATERPILLAR INC.

A U.S. multinational corporation headquartered in Peoria, Illinois, Caterpillar could trace its origins to two inventors who, in the late 1800s, independently had developed leading-edge technology of that era. Their inventions led to automation of agricultural production in the state of California. Subsequently the two formed the Caterpillar Tractor Company.

Although the company for years had exported its products from the United States, globalization began in 1950 when the firm announced formation of its first foreign subsidiary in the United Kingdom. By the end of the 1950s, it had established manufacturing subsidiaries in the United Kingdom, Australia, and Brazil. Before the end of the 1960s, the MNC had expanded operations into France, Belgium, South Africa, and Mexico, with sales subsidiaries in Europe and the Far East to service those dealerships.

Historically, Caterpillar had led the global construction equipment industry with a strategy of broad and deep market penetration within two main categories of heavy equipment: (1) earthmoving, construction, and materials handling machinery, and (2) engines. Several subsidiaries serviced the Latin American markets.

■ Caterpillar Americas Company

To support its 34 dealers who sold Caterpillar machines, engines, lift trucks, paving products, parts, and repair service in Latin America and the Caribbean, Caterpillar Americas Company (also headquartered in Peoria, Illinois) controlled four district offices.

Two of these district offices were located in Plantation, Florida. The Northern District Office supported dealers in Colombia (1985), Ecuador (1925), French Guiana (1973), Guyana (1975), Netherland Antilles (1987), Suriname (1941), and Venezuela (1927). (Numbers in parentheses represent the year the dealership was established.) The Caribbean/Central America District Office serviced 16 dealers, the first of whom was appointed in Panama (1914), the most recent in Jamaica (1987).

In Santiago, Chile, a third district office served dealers in Argentina (1971), Bolivia (1969), Chile (1940), Paraguay (1951), Peru (1942), and Uruguay (1927). Located in Houston, Texas, the fourth district office assisted customers and dealers in Mexico.

■ Caterpillar Americas Exporting Company (CAMEC)

Yet another subsidiary, CAMEC, called Florida home. The Miami Lakes operation exported Caterpillar parts on behalf of its Latin American and Caribbean dealers. These replacement parts and components might have been manufactured in Latin America, shipped to the United States, and then reexported to still another Latin American country.

■ Caterpillar World Trading Corporation

Another subsidiary, Caterpillar World Trading Corporation, arranged for the acquisition of Caterpillar products through countertrade or barter for a variety of products. This type of trade permitted Caterpillar to penetrate markets where inconvertibility of foreign currency remained a problem.

Of its 15 manufacturing plants outside the United States, both Brazilian and Mexican subsidiaries were wholly owned. The only other Latin American manufacturing plant, an independent manufacturer in Argentina, produced under a licensing agreement with Caterpillar. Altogether, Caterpillar marketed over 100 models of earthmoving, construction, and materials handling machines, 40 paving/compaction products, 80 lift truck models, and 25 basic engine models.

Brazil

Caterpillar Brasil S.A. (CBSA) opened a parts distribution center in 1954 in Santo Amaro. To support Brazilian exports, it initiated assembly operations in 1960. Inaugurated in 1976 in Piracicaba, a second plant manufactured track-type tractors, motor graders, wheel loaders, and scrapers. Brazil represented the company's fourth-largest national market [1, p. 4].

To maintain market dominance, Caterpillar Brasil strengthened its manufacturing presence during the latter 1970s in response to competitive challenges of Komatsu, Dresser Industries, Case, Fiatallis, VME, and TEREX. Caterpillar expanded both manufacturing capacity and product lines. In 1973, it had purchased nearly 1000 acres of land, about one-half of the new industrial park, Unidade Industrial Unileste, north of Piracicaba, which was the largest land acquisition Caterpillar had ever made outside of the United States.

By 1989, the firm had enlarged the Piracicaba operation to almost 1 million square feet, with ambitions to nearly double the physical size again by 1992, at which time it planned to close the Santo Amaro plant. Altogether the two facilities in Brazil employed about 5000 persons [2, p. C9].

CBSA management had to cope not only with the competitive thrusts of Komatsu and Dresser but also with various constraints imposed by Brazilian government policies and regulations, such as local content laws. In order to obtain more duty- and tax-free import privileges, benefits its competitors were already receiving, CBSA signed an accord with the government in 1980. CBSA agreed to export $2.0 billion worth of equipment between 1980 and 1990. [*Note:* All monetary values are stated in U.S. dollars.] The commitment was predicated on projections that domestic and export demand for the 1980s would at least equal or better the demand in the 1970s.

However, demand declined. CBSA Project Manager Bill Cook said that the world market for construction equipment collapsed after Caterpillar had entered into the agreement. "Both the export market and the domestic market declined. So we couldn't export what we said we would, nor did we need to import what we thought."

Of the 1980 export pact, CBSA Vice President Don Coonan said, "There was a very real threat there. We had a contractual agreement that we weren't meeting. In fact, it looked like we would only get about 40 percent of that amount. We agreed we ought to have a strategy for CBSA."

Facing a potential penalty of $335 million for not meeting the export target, management reevaluated goals and strategies, both short- and long-term, then ranked the goals in the following order:

1. Become more cost effective.
2. Increase management effectiveness.
3. Emphasize quality in the production processes.
4. Develop a more export-driven organization.
5. Comply with local content laws.
6. Meet aggressive market challenges of Komatsu and Dresser.

Several task forces were created. Coonan headed an export task force. Its objective was to increase exports from Brazil. Another group focused on a new strategy for CBSA. They found that CBSA had noncurrent product, volatile demand, complex operations, deteriorating manufacturing facilities and excess costs.

During the mid-1980s, corporate headquarters had compiled an in-depth study and evaluation of Komatsu. Management reevaluated its Latin American presence. Caterpillar had realized a 16 percent gain for all of Latin America during 1986; much of that headway was attributable to the Brazilian operations. In 1987, corporate headquarters opted to strengthen its commitment in Brazil and support changes required by CBSA.

The new strategy embraced several significant elements. First, the new strategy called for renegotiation of the contract with the Brazilian government. CBSA management succeeded in renegotiating export requirements from $2 billion down to $816 million.

Second, to meet the goal of making CBSA a more export-driven organization, Brazil would become the new world source for scraper bowls (except elevating scrapers). A new motor grader series, as well as the D4H along with a newer model of the track-type tractor, would be dual-sourced, with Brazil designated as one of two manufacturing sites. Also, CBSA would manufacture the 3116 engine and countershaft transmission for use in Brazilian-built machines. Over the long term CBSA wanted its exports to account for 35 percent of total sales.

Third, modernization to achieve better cost and quality control became part of the manufacturing plan. Consolidation included expansion of the Piracicaba plant to accommodate increased production. Chuck Gladson, Technical Director, added, "We upgraded and simplified our processes through use of technology and layout."

Factories were reorganized to improve materials handling. Cook said, "We positioned ourselves with new manufacturing philosophies."

Fourth, because cost-effectiveness was essential to remain competitive, CBSA planned to reduce the number of different models it built. At that time CBSA built two distinct versions of each model: one for the domestic market that complied with local content requirements, and another version for export.

Fifth, in order to increase the allowable volume of products for domestic sale, CBSA intended to improve supplier capabilities in Brazil. Cook said, "We explained to our suppliers that we're looking at things from a world class perspective—that means higher volumes, lower costs and high expectations for quality and reliability from them." Reaching its local content goal would permit CBSA to expand Brazilian sales. Without greater domestic sales, CBSA's earning power would be considerably restricted.

Sixth, to meet efficiency goals, CBSA management reorganized its reporting structure in 1988 to implement consolidation of the two-plant operations. The departments of manufacturing, industrial relations, quality control, and materials at each plant were merged under one department head, who held simultaneous responsibility for the departments in both plants. Management created the new organizational structure in Exhibit 1 to improve accountability and efficiency.

Implementation of the new strategy, consolidation, modernization and new-product programs were scheduled over a five-year period. However, CBSA faced a number of environmental challenges:

Partial Organization Chart of CBSA, 1988

Exhibit 1

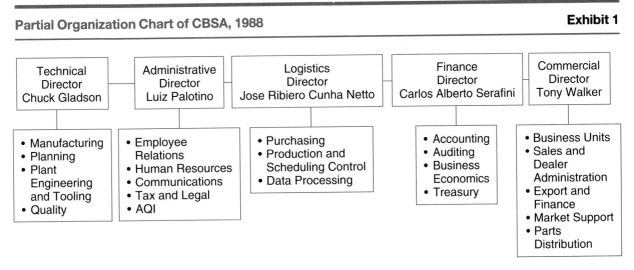

Source: "A Letter for Caterpillar Management," April 1989, p. 3.

- A volatile Brazilian market.
- Inflation of 1000 percent a year.
- Price controls that limited prices of final outputs but not necessarily the cost of raw material inputs and labor.
- Government-owned and -protected industries.
- Brazilian debt crisis that restricted availability of foreign exchange for imports and profit repatriation.
- Local content regulations.
- A massive governmental bureaucracy.
- Political uncertainty and capital flight.
- An aggressive foreign competitor, Komatsu.

On the positive side, Brazil, the world's seventh-largest economy with abundant natural resources, offered potential opportunities in mining, agricultural, and construction markets, as well as growing infrastructure needs. Brazil had the most highly developed industrial structure in South America; many multinationals considered it a potentially attractive investment; and should Brazil resolve its political and fiscal problems, established companies would have first crack at newly emerging opportunities. However, even from a perspective of late 1988, realization of market projections were subject to considerable variance. Since uncertainties continued into 1989 for Brazil, Mexico seemed to offer greater promise.

Mexico

During the early part of the decade of the 1980s, Caterpillar suffered a precipitous decline in Mexican sales due in part to lower oil prices. (Mexico was a net exporter of petroleum, an important generator of foreign exchange.) Caterpillar blamed a challenging economic environment, high foreign debt, and high interest rates in the United States for its problems in Latin America.

Despite operating losses, Caterpillar preserved a strong relationship with its Mexican dealers in Chihuahua (1945), Monterrey (1981), Ciudad Obregon (1929), Mexico City (1926), and Guadalajara (1974). This established dealership network was costly to sustain. Caterpillar typically turned around requests for parts within 48 hours—an important consideration in the purchase of heavy equipment—a service that competitors could not always match. In addition to its dealerships, the firm maintained manufacturing facilities in Monterrey.

Of Caterpillar's seven wholly owned foreign subsidiaries, two of them were located in Latin America: one in Brazil; the other, Conek SA de CV, in Mexico. For the first time in company history Caterpillar had accepted a minority interest of 49 percent in a joint venture formed in 1981 with the Mexican chemical producer, CYDSA, which owned the other 51 percent of Conek. (The name *Conek* is derived from the two words *construction* and *equipment*.) Caterpillar believed that a partnership with CYDSA was a good match; CYDSA had operations throughout Mexico; and Mexican law required a local partner.

Caterpillar had decided to locate the plant in Monterrey, Nuevo Leon, for several reasons.

1. CYDSA recommended the location.
2. Monterrey was the second-largest industrial city in Mexico.
3. It was near raw material sources: natural gas, steel, and trained labor and technical people educated at Monterrey Institute of Technology.
4. There was stability of state and local governments.
5. Fewer labor problems arose here than in some border areas where organized labor had disrupted work.
6. The work ethic and business philosophy seemed more akin to that of the United States.

With the crash of the Mexican economy in 1982, CYDSA found itself under financial constraints due to its U.S.-dollar-denominated debts and wanted to divest its interest in Conek. Caterpillar searched for a new Mexican partner. Partners which Caterpillar preferred had insufficient capital; those who came forward with sufficient capital Caterpillar did not want. Consequently, in December 1983, Caterpillar requested exemption from Mexican law and permission from the government for 100 percent ownership of the subsidiary. (*Note:* Current Mexican law allows 100 percent foreign ownership; however, for foreign investments exceeding $100 million, the foreign investor must have a Mexican partner.)

In August 1984 the government gave its permission for the company to assume 100 percent ownership of its Mexican subsidiary. In November 1984 Caterpillar completed the transaction and acquired CYDSA's interest in Conek; in that month Conek became a wholly owned subsidiary of Caterpillar Inc. in Peoria, Illinois. Until that point in time, Conek's operations had been essentially an assembly plant. Beginning in early 1985, the subsidiary began full-scale manufacturing to produce components and parts primarily for sale to the United States.

Conek chiefly shipped its output to corporate headquarters in Illinois or to other Caterpillar sales companies in the United States for reexport. By mid-1989, export production at Conek was about 40 percent finished products and 40 percent components and replacement parts; the remaining 20 percent of manufacture was destined for production of lift trucks and parts for the Mexican market.

Local content varied according to the product; heavy manufactures requiring substantial steel usage might have 99 percent local content.

Products were transported by truck to Texas. Ing. Adan J. Pena Guerrero, Treasury Manager at Conek, said that by clearing customs in Monterrey prior to shipment, the paperwork required about 24 hours versus three days at the Texas border. He also said that with anticipated construction of the Colombia Bridge between Nuevo Leon and Texas, built exclusively for the expedient movement of exports and imports, the new 10-mile bridge near Laredo would save the firm considerable time and money. Currently, strong labor unions required expensive and delaying off-loading and reloading to cross the border. Additionally, the Mexican government sought private investors to construct a 15-mile toll highway direct to the bridge to bypass Nuevo Laredo.

Caterpillar maintained three industrial locations near Monterrey. Nearly 3.3 million square feet, the main manufacturing plant sat on 272 acres of industrial land. A second location, used for parts warehousing and some electronics manufacture, comprised almost 100 acres, plus a third site at Santa Catarina about half that size.

With a 1989 total of 1700 office and plant workers (whose average age was 23 years) on a three-shift schedule, Conek operated at full capacity. Ing. Pena Guerrero proudly pointed out that office workers followed the American system of 8:00 to 5:00, with a 30-minute lunch break in the plant cafeteria. He said, "Most office employees usually arrive 15 or 20 minutes before 8 and do not leave until 10 or 15 minutes after 5." This contrasted sharply with Mexico City, where the workday traditionally might begin at 9:00, with a two-hour midafternoon lunch, and end at 7:00 P.M.

Although Ing. Pena Guerrero was born in Monterrey, he preferred the efficiency of a U.S.-styled system. He had earned his M.S. degree in engineering at the Monterrey Institute of Technology (ITSEM), a private university, and an M.B.A. from the University of Wisconsin at Milwaukee. At age 31, he managed 5 supervisors and a total of 42 employees, over whom he kept a watchful eye. He reported directly to another Mexican, Juan Gamez, Finance Manager, who, in turn, reported to the General Manager, Jim Palmer.

Conek paid plant workers slightly above market rates and generated employee loyalty and cooperation by using the following tactics:

- Providing a complaint and suggestion system to which management usually reacted within one week.
- Publishing a monthly employee newsletter entitled "Conexion."
- Holding periodic plantwide meetings to inform employees of news, progress, and events.
- Maintaining close supervision over all employees.
- Implementing an intense training program to improve quality and productivity.
- Offering free bus service to employees from the city to the plant.

Because the manufacturing facility was some distance from urban Monterrey, a daily bus picked up employees at designated points and times. Several advantages derived from this program:

1. Employee costs for transportation were reduced.
2. People arrived at work on time.

3. Riders could either rest or develop friendships during the ride.
4. Employees were less likely to talk casually with unionized workers from other plants.

The training program helped achieve corporate goals of greater productivity (lower costs of production) and higher quality. For example, welders must be adept at using a technique not employed in typical manufacturing. Conek required an intense six-week training course. Pena said that Conek had sent some employees to Texas for special welding training. After two weeks the welding school had sent them back to Mexico, because Conek had already trained them better for specific tasks than the school could. Pena added, "Conek also pays employees for college courses and for M.B.A. degrees."

Conek used Just-in-Time (JIT) inventory control and Duran Quality Control techniques. To resolve minor problems at the shop level, small quality control (QC) circles were activated. For larger problems Conek employed an annual quality improvement program (QIP), which, according to Pena, excelled over QC. Functioning like a task force, QIP focused on specific problems and on how to save money. All of this effort had paid off for the manufacturer. Pena said, "Conek has had no delivery or quality problems [since 1986]."

In Mexico, Caterpillar's chief competitor, Komatsu, was number two in the construction equipment market. Clark Equipment ranked as an unimportant third-place competitor; and all remaining competitors together represented only a minor threat to Caterpillar.

Conek and its parent had many strengths: It was well established in the market. It maintained a costly dealership network. It had built an international reputation. Its trademark, CAT, and the distinct yellow color of its equipment were instantly recognizable. Conek, as one of several sourcing points for components in a worldwide network, was assured of continued demand for its manufactures. Additionally, in its manufacture of finished products and components, Conek pursued the following practices:

- It used a high-grade heavy steel, from a Mexican source, not readily available everywhere.
- It maintained very good relations with its local steel supplier and had experienced no sourcing problems.
- It manufactured high-quality products which required less refabrication and, therefore, lowered overall costs.
- It tested all equipment thoroughly at the plant site and before shipment.
- It maintained careful quality control in its highly integrated operations.
- It insisted upon quality workmanship (e.g., welding) not necessarily found in all competing products.
- It achieved good cost control and continued to strive for higher productivity to maintain price competitiveness.

Financially the operation had not achieved payback of investment due to large start-up costs. A typical payback period in this industry would be on the order of 10 to 15 years. CYDSA, Conek's former partner, used payback projections of 18 years. By taking advantage of its experience curve, training employees for quality and productivity, and achieving a careful mix of exports and imports, Caterpillar expected to shorten the payback period of its Mexican subsidiary.

To test possibilities of diversification, Conek modestly invested in a small plant to assemble tractor electronics. The project had not been financially successful, due, in part, to sourcing problems for electronic chips. Its foreign source provided chips only twice yearly, which generated an inventory problem between overinvesting in inventory or a stock-out which would shut down the production line. The chip manufacturer needed longer production runs to bring down its costs. Since Conek was not a major purchaser, it had little influence on the supplier.

Peter Donis, President of Caterpillar, in early 1989 had said that profitability was constrained by higher material costs, higher start-up costs incurred by the factory modernization program, and higher-than-expected short-term interest rates to finance working capital needs.

Nevertheless, with a turnaround expected by 1990 in the Mexican economy, Caterpillar anticipated an increase in sales of construction machinery. The new President of Mexico seemed to have considerable popular support for his economic development strategy, which was to (1) open the economy to foreign competition; (2) privatize most public enterprises; (3) move toward creating a market economy; and (4) encourage foreign direct investment. Despite Caterpillar's aggressive stance, Komatsu's yellow (in imitation of CAT products) bulldozers could be seen excavating sites for construction of new commercial buildings in the heart of Monterrey, not many miles from Caterpillar's production facilities.

KOMATSU LTD.

Caterpillar's chief competitor was the Japanese multinational corporation Komatsu Ltd. Within most Latin American markets, Caterpillar's and Komatsu's other competitors were frequently a distant number three or four in a particular country, often market spoilers; but altogether they did account for a respectable volume of business. Komatsu had to concern itself not only with Caterpillar but also with those competitors whose presence in individual markets were most threatening to the Japanese firm.

Originating as the Takeuchi Mining Factory in 1894, Komatsu Ltd. manufactured and marketed a full line of construction equipment, industrial presses, and machinery such as robots and laser machines to customers in over 150 countries. The parent organization of the Komatsu Group, comprised of 60 affiliated companies, Komatsu Ltd. maintained world headquarters in Tokyo, Japan.

Komatsu had faced a major crisis in 1961 when Caterpillar announced a joint venture in Japan with Mitsubishi Heavy Industries Ltd. With one-tenth the sales of Caterpillar, Komatsu recognized that survival was problematic unless the prices and quality of its products were competitive. Komatsu signed a license agreement with Cummins Engine Inc. (U.S.) to manufacture and sell diesel engines, and subsequently entered into several other joint venture agreements (later terminated) with U.S. firms.

Nevertheless, Komatsu did not establish its first foreign subsidiary until 1967: N.V. Komatsu Europe S.A. in Belgium. Global expansion began in earnest with creation of Komatsu America Corporation and the establishment of Brazilian and German subsidiaries. Bulldozer production commenced at Komatsu do Brasil in 1975, at Dina Komatsu Nacional S.A. in Mexico in 1976, and at P.T. Komatsu Indonesia in 1983.

■ Brazil

Formed in 1970 in São Paulo, Komatsu do Brasil initiated the first overseas bulldozer production in 1975. In those early years the Brazilian operation neither figured prominently in Komatsu's corporate global plans nor had been successful financially. Because corporate net income in 1983 had declined about 20 percent from 1982, management blamed the Brazilian subsidiary for a significant share of those corporate losses and attributed them to unfavorable economic conditions in Brazil.

Of Third World countries, Shoji Nogawa (President of Komatsu) wrote: "Developing countries, also important markets for the industry, generally experienced economic difficulties, with their burdens of extensive debt further aggravated by the high level of U.S. interest rates" [3, p. 3]. (The Middle East had been Komatsu's most important foreign market.)

In 1985 corporate management communicated, "Internationalization for Komatsu means not only establishing more efficient corporate management in overseas marketplaces but, more importantly, pursuing more effective customer-focused operations as the Company continues to expand its worldwide customer portfolio" [4, p. 10]. Despite management's stated commitment to globalization, the firm continued to manufacture principally in Japan for export to its foreign markets. Even as late as 1986, foreign manufacturing represented only 5 percent of company total, while 95 percent of manufacturing was still done in Japan.

Then, in 1987, under leadership of Komatsu's new Corporate President, Masao Tanaka, the company sped up globalization of its operations. Setting a new target, management wanted foreign manufacturing to account for 35 percent of total production and pushed to integrate its manufacturing bases in Brazil, Mexico, and Indonesia into a framework of strategically defined roles.

■ Mexico

Komatsu's Mexican subsidiary, Dina Komatsu Nacional, SA de CV, also experienced a change during 1987 when the Japanese MNC's share in this joint venture rose from 40 to 68 percent ownership [5]. Dina Komatsu Nacional, a joint venture with Nacional Financiera, the government-owned Mexican development bank, began to manufacture bulldozers in 1976; but it produced no profit in its nearly 13-year history. The Mexican government, under President Salinas de Gotari, had been trying to privatize much of the public sector and divest itself of unprofitable joint ventures. Although the government's investment in Komatsu had been on the sale block since early 1988, potential private investors showed little interest in the offer.

Primarily, Komatsu's global strategy had been one of export development. The Mexican venture figured in a defensive move to counter Caterpillar in Mexico. Perceiving the Mexican market as a subunit of the larger North and South American market, Komatsu chose to do battle on U.S. soil and in 1988 sought to strengthen its presence in the Americas' markets with a joint venture (JV).

■ The United States

Management of the world's second-largest integrated maker of construction machinery stated that competitive strength "lies in its versatile technological base and its tradition of quality first" [1, cover]. Entry into the U.S. construction equipment market was a cornerstone in Komatsu's global market penetration strategy [6].

When Komatsu opened its manufacturing facility in Chattanooga, Tennessee, in 1965, it had an 8 percent share of the U.S. market, which it had hoped to double. Nobuo Murai, President of Komatsu America Corporation, said, "Our goal is a market share of 15 percent in the near term and 20-to-25 percent in the long term" [7]. Komatsu faced increasing obstacles in its exports to the United States due to the depreciated value of the dollar coupled with trade conflict issues between the United States and Japan.

Masao Tanaka (Corporate President) in 1988 wrote: "Strategically, we are committed to establish a competitive operational system on a global scale, by setting up a worldwide manufacturing/sales network capable of flexibly and effectively responding to changes in the economic climate" [8, p. 2].

Komatsu Dresser Company

To strengthen its competitive position in both North and South America, Komatsu and Texas-based Dresser Industries, Inc., announced, in February 1988, the formation of a strategic alliance in which the two companies would combine their construction equipment manufacturing and engineering facilities in the United States, Canada, and Latin America. In operation September 1, 1988, the 50–50 JV, Komatsu Dresser Company, constituted an initial capitalization of $200 million for machinery and automation plus $50 million to refurbish manufacturing plants. Sales for 1989 were projected at $1.5 billion. The strategic alliance also called for the creation of Komatsu Dresser Finance Division to finance sales both to wholesale and retail customers [9].

An essential element of the agreement was that Komatsu and Dresser would share equally in the management of Komatsu Dresser, which had exclusive manufacturing and marketing rights for North, Central, and South America. The JV also would distribute replacement parts, engage in engineering, and establish training and test centers as well as sales and administrative offices [10, p. 121].

The new alliance also required consolidation of three foreign subsidiaries—Komatsu America Corporation, Komatsu America Manufacturing Corporation, and Komatsu do Brasil—together with Dresser's Construction Equipment and Haulpak Divisions and Dresser's manufacturing subsidiary in Brazil. Of this 1988 joint venture, Komatsu management wrote:

> The venture clearly symbolizes one successful outcome of Komatsu's internationalization strategy to establish the three-core comprehensive operations in Japan, the U.S. and Europe. It also advances Komatsu's commitment to further promote international cooperation with other firms for mutual business expansion as an equal partner [11, p. 18].

Based in Libertyville, Illinois, a Chicago suburb, Komatsu Dresser Company began operations in late 1988 with 5000 workers employed at eight plants in the

United States, Canada, and Brazil. It had more than 3.5 million square feet of factory space. One of these plants, the Haulpak Division (which produced mining trucks), was only 22 blocks down Adams Street from Caterpillar's Peoria, Illinois, corporate headquarters.

The new strategic alliance allowed Komatsu to shift much final assembly from Japan to the Americas and fight the battle for Brazil and the rest of Latin America right in Illinois. The new company would become number two in the Americas in the construction equipment industry.

FIGHTING FOR MARKET DOMINANCE

When battle lines between the two firms were drawn in 1961, Komatsu developed Total Quality Control (TQC) to become competitive in price and quality, broadened its product offerings to match Caterpillar's, reduced manufacturing costs, increased exports, and, by 1980, became recognized as the world's second-largest manufacturer of construction machinery. It dominated the Japanese market with a 60 percent share.

Generally, in every country-market the Japanese had entered in recent decades, they applied a market share pricing strategy, which meant using a low entry price to build market share and, in the long run, dominate the targeted market. However, shifts in exchange rates and the debt-laden economies of Brazil and Mexico dampened that success pattern for Komatsu.

Komatsu's exports to the United States had doubled in 1983. Its world market share rose to around 20 percent; and its U.S. market share had been expanded to 8 percent by the mid-1980s. The Japanese firm managed to boost volume by 40 percent with very little escalation in employment by the heavy application of robotics. Management was spending $80 million a year alone on automation while continuing to diversify products in order to become a major producer of automated production systems and robots. By 1985, the firm had erected three large R&D laboratories, established five foreign production facilities—including a plant in the United States and in the United Kingdom—and added plastics, electronics, robots, metal presses, and other products to its line.

Prior to 1985 a high dollar exchange rate and price-cutting strategy gave Komatsu a 40 percent price advantage over Caterpillar. Its export ratio was 64 percent. But environmental factors swung against Komatsu. The dollar-yen relationship turned in favor of the dollar. Due to the strong yen, export-oriented Komatsu had to raise prices by 18 percent in 1986, while Caterpillar raised their prices an average of 3 percent, the first increase since 1984; Komatsu lost a 2 percent market share to Caterpillar. Komatsu's 1986 profits plummeted by 33 percent, exports fell nearly 5 percent, and in 1987 its president, Shoji Nogawa, resigned in the midst of unfavorable rumors. Komatsu's battle cry had been "MARU 'C' " ("Encircle CAT") to put Caterpillar in a defensive position.

However, Caterpillar maintained a solid financial position, held significant leadership in many areas of construction equipment technology, and by its size and global network was well positioned to take an offensive, rather than a defensive, position. Management initiated a strategic analysis.

Asked to assess strengths and weaknesses of Caterpillar and Komatsu, middle managers from various functional activities developed a comparative competitive analysis between Japan and the United States. By rating the two firms

Komatsu Versus Caterpillar: Competitive Advantages as Perceived by U.S. Executives (summary of responses)

Exhibit 2

| | ADVANTAGE/SAMPLE MEAN | | | | | | | ADDITIONAL STATISTICS | | |
| | Komatsu | | | | Caterpillar | | | | | |
AREA	1	2	3	4	5	6	7	$S_{\bar{x}}$	M_C	M
1. Cooperative labor-management relations		1.52						.16	1.25	1.00 (18)
2. Cooperative business-government relations		1.59						.15	1.34	1.00 (16)
3. Labor costs		1.82						.26	1.34	1.00 (16)
4. Work force trained in statistical and quality control			2.07					.17	2.05	2.00 (10)
5. Strong organizational culture			2.22					.25	1.02	1.00 (11)
6. Pressure of management for short-term profit			2.64					.26	2.43	2.00 (7)
7. Better-trained blue-collar workers			2.92					.32	3.69	4.00 (8)
8. Capital charges				3.32				.27	3.68	4.00 (11)
9. Responses to international markets				3.65				.29	3.79	4.00 (7)
10. Better-trained white-collar workers				3.67				.32	3.60	4.00 (8)
11. Overall management				4.04				.25	4.06	4.00 (8)
12. Superior marketing intelligence				4.52				.36	4.63	4.00 (6)
13. Modern equipment and machinery					4.78			.21	4.71	4.00 (7)
14. Advanced manufacturing technology					5.15			.28	5.64	6.00 (17)
15. Product research and development						5.78		.19	5.94	6.00 (17)
16. Technologically more advanced products						5.96		.16	6.03	6.00 (16)
17. Superior design and product development capabilities						6.00		.21	6.13	6.00 (12)

on a 7-point scale, they developed comparative analysis on 17 factors. Professors Tomasz Mroczkowski and Marek Wermus tabulated the summary of responses appearing in Exhibit 2. On the 7-point scale, a rating of 1 was most favorable to Komatsu; a rating of 7 most favorable to Caterpillar. The arithmetic mean represented the management group's averages. Additional statistics are included in the exhibit.

Caterpillar's managers perceived Komatsu as operating in a lower-labor-cost environment and enjoying access to lower-cost capital, a cooperative industry-government relationship, and a cooperative labor force that had extensive skills in statistical process control. Caterpillar's managers also felt that Komatsu's managers were not under pressures to produce short-term profits.

Caterpillar's managers saw their own superiority in design and product development, R&D, the technological level of products, and a worldwide reputation for quality products supported by a dealer network.

To counteract Komatsu's drive, Caterpillar reduced production capacity 25 percent, cut inventories 37 percent, slimmed down its labor force, and closed plants. With the plant closures Caterpillar was no longer a vertically integrated company. It defended market share with deep price discounts and offered smaller machines to smaller-sized contractors. The heart of the turnaround decision was to cut operating costs by 22 percent, give more price authority to local managers, and diversify into other product areas.

PLANT WITH A FUTURE

In October 1986, Caterpillar President Peter Donis said:

> Although we've reduced costs by more than 20 percent, we're not stopping there. We've returned to profitability, but we expect cost and price pressures to continue. Our costs are still 15-to-20 percent higher than our foreign competitor's, and in spite of the dollar weakening, transaction prices for our products are about the same now that they were in 1981. So, Caterpillar's long-term profitability will not be secure until we do, in fact, become the industry's low cost producer. We've developed a strategy for achieving the additional cost reduction. We call it our Plant with a Future [12].

For Caterpillar, the Plant with a Future (PWAF) concept portrayed in Exhibit 3 embraced all elements of manufacturing as well as product design, supplier relationships, and logistics. Although this new manufacturing strategy went beyond simple cost cutting, its implementation and integration of facilities would continue for the rest of this century. At the heart of PWAF was automation, new factory layouts, and continuous work flow. Caterpillar Executive Vice President, Pierre Gueridon, said, "We believe computer-integrated manufacturing is our supreme weapon for cost reduction. It's the area where we have the largest long term advantage over the Japanese."

Based on a cell manufacturing concept, plants and equipment were arranged to process families of components from start to finish. For example, machining, welding, heat treating, and painting might all be functions within a single cell. Work flow was continuous. Since all cells fed the assembly line Just-in-Time, it required JIT delivery to the cells. Immediate objectives were to simplify and integrate.

Computer-integrated manufacturing (CIM) linked self-contained manufacturing cells (i.e., independent islands of automation) to a material, tooling, and information network to allow for electronic communication between engineering, logistics, and the factory floor. By the next decade, interplant communication would be routine through a corporate information center coupled with global marketing and financial data bases. With complete implementation of the strategy and integration of operations, all systems, from the plant's host computer to personal computers on the shop floor, could communicate to result in unprecedented coordination and optimization of all manufacturing functions: supplier delivery, scheduling of equipment, tooling, quality control, maintenance, and troubleshooting.

PWAF and Its Three Basic Components   **Exhibit 3**

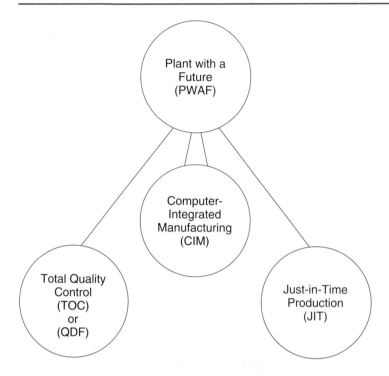

Gueridon said, "At our Gosselies [Belgium] plant, for example, we expect PWAF changes to result in a 22 percent reduction in material costs and a 31 percent reduction in labor costs by 1990."

Conek, the Mexican subsidiary, exemplified successful execution of this new strategy. Management implemented JIT and Duran Quality Control techniques, small QC circles at the shop level, and an annual QIP to resolve bigger challenges. Critical to success at Monterrey were cost and quality control.

On the other hand, CBSA, the Brazilian subsidiary, best reflected "gradualism": Caterpillar's chief approach to automation and implementation of the PWAF. PWAF automation was conceived as a self-financing program with highest priorities for capital investments. Funds generated from reduced inventories and improvement in efficiencies would finance these investments. Caterpillar management expected its manufacturing plants to migrate from present systems to a hybrid system and to end up with PWAF, a purely customer-driven manufacturing philosophy.

RETURN TO PROFITABILITY AND A NEW CHALLENGE

The Japanese invader was not invincible. Komatsu's exports decreased because most were dollar-denominated; and the dollar was overpriced in terms of yen. Its profits fell by a third in 1986.

On the other hand, Caterpillar's competitive position sharply improved. Profits in 1986 were $76 million ($0.77 per share) and in 1987 were $350 million

Exhibit 4   **Estimated Shares of World Construction Machinery Sales, 1987**

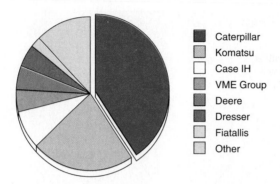

Caterpillar
Komatsu
Case IH
VME Group
Deere
Dresser
Fiatallis
Other

($3.51 per share). Sales were up; employment at Caterpillar increased by 732 persons in 1987; and market share rose. Exhibit 4 depicts global market shares in 1987.

Caterpillar still had the best recognizable and respected name in the construction equipment industry. Its products commanded a price premium. It had a worldwide dealership and parts distribution network. Project teams were working on quality improvement projects. A massive program of statistical process control training had been successfully launched to transfer the responsibility for quality control to employees. The PWAF strategy, now in place, seemed to function well. Certainly 1988 would be a good and trouble-free year.

A banner year, 1988 witnessed not only a 25 percent rise in revenue but also a 76 percent leap in profits. (See Exhibit 5 for summary financial data and other statistics.) Alexander Blanton of Merrill Lynch said "I estimate the company's earnings power at between $8 and $10 per share by 1990." Exhibit 6 graphically illustrates quarterly changes in net income during the decade.

Komatsu had not been especially successful in Latin America. Its Mexican joint venture had never produced a profit. Brazilian losses severely affected corporate profitability. It did not have the dealership network that Caterpillar had long ago established throughout Central and South America as well as the Caribbean.

Nevertheless, the Komatsu Dresser strategic alliance presented a serious challenge to Caterpillar in Latin America. With both Komatsu and Dresser, along with Caterpillar, having a strong manufacturing presence in Brazil, the market might become a strategic battleground for Latin America. Although all companies had older, less efficient manufacturing facilities, Caterpillar had already initiated its program of modernization to cut costs, improve quality, and consolidate product line—the PWAF strategy.

In its 1988 JV agreement, Komatsu would give up to $300 million to Dresser to upgrade factories, which prior to the agreement had been running at 50 percent capacity. Although both Komatsu and Dresser continued to introduce new products, they maintained separate, yet competing, dealerships.

By July 1989, Caterpillar had registered strong gains in sales outside of the United States; approximately 52 percent of business now derived from foreign sources. (See the data in Exhibit 7 for foreign versus domestic sales, 1984–1988.) Global revenues of $5.7 billion marked a 15 percent increase over the compara-

Caterpillar: Consolidated Financial Position and Income Statement at December 31 (in millions of U.S. dollars)

Exhibit 5

	1980	1981	1982	1983	1984	1985	1986	1987	1988
Financial Position									
Current assets	2933	3544	3433	3383	2915	2982	3363	4006	5317
Intangible assets	—	147	117	99	96	77	60	47	71
Other fixed assets	3165	3594	3651	3486	3212	2957	2865	3578	4198
Total assets	6098	7285	7201	6968	6223	6016	6288	7631	9586
Current liabilities	1711	2369	1197	1576	1939	1742	2180	2758	3435
Long-term debt	955	1059	2508	2055	1432	1206	959	1308	2138
Equity	3432	3857	3496	3337	2852	3068	3149	3565	4013
Total debt/equity	6098	7285	7201	6968	6223	6016	6288	7631	9586
Income Statement									
Revenue	8598	9154	6469	5424	6576	6725	7321	8180	10255
Operating profit	831	903	(253)	(310)	(339)	233	137	498	924
Net profit (loss)	565	579	(180)	(345)	(428)	198	76	350	616
Dividends per share of common stock ($)	2.325	2.40	2.40	1.50	1.25	0.50	0.50	0.50	0.75
Average number of employees	86,350	83,455	73,249	58,402	61,624	53,616	53,731	54,463	60,558

Source: Figures derived from annual reports.

Caterpillar Quarterly Net Income

Exhibit 6

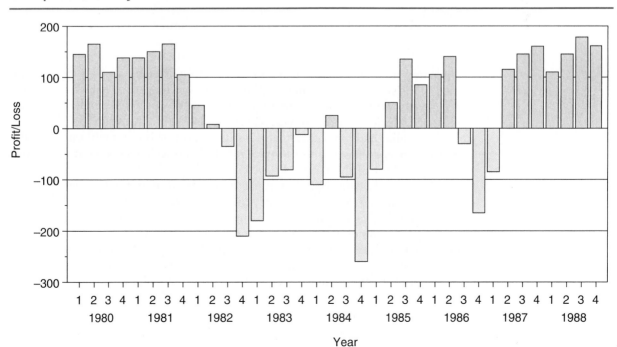

Exhibit 7   **Caterpillar Sales, Foreign and Domestic**

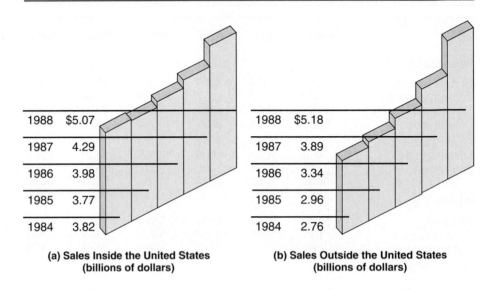

1988	$5.07
1987	4.29
1986	3.98
1985	3.77
1984	3.82

**(a) Sales Inside the United States
(billions of dollars)**

1988	$5.18
1987	3.89
1986	3.34
1985	2.96
1984	2.76

**(b) Sales Outside the United States
(billions of dollars)**

ble six-month period in 1988. Net income for the first half of 1989 of $282 million resulted in a $2.78 profit per share of common stock compared to $2.60 per share the first six months of 1988. Employment rose to 60,881 [13].

Early 1989 recorded no further major changes in the Latin American environments for either MNC. Considerable uncertainty reigned in most key Latin American markets. Argentina experienced yet another economic crisis as a new President was about to assume office. Peru's hyperinflation and Communist terrorism produced a chaotic situation as the country entered a campaign year for the presidency. Brazil's economic condition continued to deteriorate; national elections were scheduled for late 1989. The most stable economies appeared to be in Chile, which had successfully implemented a program partially consistent with free-market philosophy, and in Mexico, which was trying to move toward a market economy. Chile would elect a new President by year's end; and Mexico's President was still in the first half of his term.

Caterpillar had parried Komatsu's strategic thrust but not without difficulty. For instance, during the three-year 1986–1988 period, decreases in production costs fell short of the targeted 5 percent annual rate of reduction. Part of the problem could be attributed to translation losses due to unfavorable swings in foreign exchange rates. During 1989 the PWAF program experienced cost overruns exceeding $300 million. Uncertainty still characterized Latin American markets. A new competitor, Komatsu Dresser Company, was in training for yet another round. In early 1989, the Strategic Planning Committee, comprised of senior managers from various functional areas, was charged with the task of evaluating strategic options for the 1990s. The challenge to Caterpillar continued.

REFERENCES

1. "A Letter for Caterpillar Management," April 1989 (internal document).

2. "Cat Unit Merges Brazilian Facilities," *Journal Star* (Peoria, Illinois), December 10, 1988.

3. Komatsu *Annual Report 1983.*

4. Komatsu *Annual Report 1984.*

5. "Komatsu Raises Stakes in Mexico Venture," *Japanese Economic Journal,* 25 (August 29, 1987).

6. "Komatsu Digs Deeper into the U.S.," *Business Week,* September 22, 1985.

7. Clyde Farnsworth, "Chattanooga Reviving Itself with Foreign Capital," *Chattanooga Times* (October 10, 1985).

8. Komatsu (Quarterly) *Financial Report* (March 31, 1988).

9. *The Wall Street Journal,* August 17, 1988.

10. "Dresser, Komatsu Form Joint Venture," *Pit & Quarry,* March 1988.

11. Komatsu *Annual Report 1987.*

12. Speech by Peter Donis at the General Electric/Northwestern University Executive Dialog Series on October 14, 1986.

13. Caterpillar 1989 (Quarterly) *Financial Report.*

27

CASE

Citicorp

Randall K. White, Auburn University at Montgomery

Because Americans want to succeed, not just survive.

The above advertising theme has been frequently displayed over national TV across the United States. Yet this may understate the magnitude of this banking giant's operations as a major global power. With assets spread over five continents—North America; Caribbean, Central, and South America; Europe, Middle East, and Africa; Asia/Pacific—Citicorp has surpassed all other U.S. banks in terms of asset size (see Exhibit 1). It also ranked as the 50th-largest corporation in the United States and, based on *Business Week*'s criterion of market value,* Citicorp ranked 161 in the global 1000 firms.

Described as a global financial services company [1], the firm has characterized its uniqueness in three areas:

- In our commitment to serve a broad range of customers, from consumers to corporations and institutions, with a full range of financial services.
- In the balance and distribution of our activities globally.
- In our human, managerial, and financial resources drawn from worldwide marketplaces.

Moreover, it attempts to build shareholder value through the following financial objectives:

- Sustained growth of 12–18% in earnings per share.

*To determine this index, *Business Week* used the stock price as of May 31, 1988, multiplied by the latest available number of shares outstanding. This was translated into U.S. dollars at May month-end exchange rates. (*Business Week*, July 1988, p. 141.)

Exhibit 1   Top Twenty U.S. Banks by Asset Size, as of December 31, 1988 (in millions of dollars except ROE and ROA)

Rank		Assets ($)	Net Income ($)	Return on Equity ($)	Return on Asset (%)
1.	Citicorp, New York	207,666	1698.0	21.4	0.77
2.	Chase Manhattan, New York	97,455	1058.9	27.8	1.52
3.	BankAmerica, San Francisco	94,647	547.0	16.8	0.51
4.	Morgan (J.P.), New York	83,923	1001.8	19.1	1.20
5.	Security Pacific, Los Angeles	77,870	638.9	18.9	0.82
6.	Chemical Banking, New York	67,349	753.6	27.7	0.91
7.	Manufacturers Hanover, New York	66,710	751.6	29.4	0.96
8.	First Interstate Bancorp, Los Angeles	58,194	102.4	4.7	0.16
9.	Bankers Trust New York, New York	57,942	647.7	20.3	1.12
10.	Bank of New York, New York	47,388	213.0	15.6	0.78
11.	Wells Fargo, San Francisco	46,616	512.5	24.0	1.09
12.	First Chicago, Chicago	44,432	513.1	29.3	1.05
13.	PNC Financial, Pittsburgh	40,811	442.7	19.3	1.18
14.	Bank of Boston, Boston	36,061	322.3	18.3	0.91
15.	Bank of New England, Boston	32,200	281.7	18.6	0.93
16.	Mellon Bank, Pittsburgh	31,153	−65.0	−11.7	−0.34
17.	Continental Bank, Chicago	30,578	315.8	26.4	0.91
18.	NCNB, Charlotte, N.C.	29,848	252.5	15.5	0.86
19.	Suntrust Banks, Atlanta	29,771	308.7	17.4	1.13
20.	Fleet/Norstar Financial Group, Providence	29,052	335.8	18.1	1.21

- Superior rates of return on equity of 18–20%.
- A strong balance sheet with equity grown from earnings.

The above has been further amplified by its Chairman and CEO, John Reed:

> The year was very much in line with what we told you back at our first meeting in 1984. Our priorities then were to continue to build the core businesses, to strengthen the balance sheet, and to work on the sovereign debt issue [2].

Indeed, Citicorp posted significant results for 1988; e.g., net income exceeded $1.86 billion in contrast to a $1.12 billion loss in 1987; return on equity was 23.6% compared to a negative 19.6% in 1987; its earnings per share improved from a deficit $4.41 in 1987 to an impressive $4.87 for 1988. Although these results appear to indicate effective returns, its cross-border and foreign currency outstanding deserve comment.* For example, its debt exposure to Brazil and Mexico totaled $4 billion and $2.3 billion, respectively, with each country's debt exceeding 1% of Citicorp's total assets (see Exhibit 2). (It should be noted that Brazil declared a moratorium in February 19, 1987, on the interest payments due on its foreign debt [3].) Other country debts included several other Latin and South American governments; e.g., Argentina ($1.4 billion), Venezuela ($7 billion), Ecuador ($0.3 billion), Uruguay ($0.3 billion). (See Exhibit 3 for additional details.)

---

*These are funds that "are loaned, placed, or invested across a national border or in a currency that is foreign to the customer." There are obviously risks as exchange controls or other restrictions could affect a country's ability to obtain foreign exchange to serve its debt—notwithstanding the creditworthiness of the country regarding its local currency [1].

Citicorp: Cross-Border and Foreign Currency Outstandings; Countries with Outstandings Exceeding 1% of Total Assets, 1986–1988 (in billions of dollars at year-end)

Exhibit 2

	Cross-Border Claims on Third Parties			Investments in and Funding of Local Citicorp Franchises	Equity Investments	Total Outstanding		
Country	Banks	Public Sector	Private Sector			1988	1987	1986
United Kingdom	$0.5	$0.1	$1.2	$5.2	$—	$7.0	$5.4	$5.0
Brazil	0.4	3.0	0.5	0.1	—	4.0	4.3	4.6
Japan	1.0	—	1.0	1.2	—	3.2	4.2	5.7
Mexico	0.4	1.6	0.1	0.1	0.1	2.3	2.6	2.8
Canada	0.2	—	0.9	1.1	—	2.2	1.6	2.8
Federal Republic of Germany	0.1	—	0.6	1.1	—	1.8	2.9	2.8

Source: 1988 Annual Report.

Notes: Outstandings are presented on a regulatory basis and include all loans, deposits at interest with banks, acceptances, other interest-bearing investments, and other monetary assets. Adjustments have been made to assign externally guaranteed outstandings to the country of the guarantor and outstandings for which tangible, liquid collateral is held outside of the obligor's country to the country in which the collateral is held.

Legally binding cross-border and foreign currency commitments, including irrevocable letters of credit and commitments to extend credit, after adjustments to assign externally guaranteed commitments to the country of the guarantor, amounted to $4.7 billion in the United Kingdom, $0.6 billion in Japan, $0.8 billion in Canada, and $0.6 billion in the Federal Republic of Germany at December 31, 1988. Commitments were less than $0.1 billion in Brazil and Mexico.

At December 31, 1988, there were no countries with cross-border and foreign currency outstandings between 0.75% and 1.0% of total assets other than the Federal Republic of Germany. At December 31, 1987, the only such country was Canada. At December 31, 1986, the only such country was the Philippines ($1.8 billion).

Equity investments obtained in debt-for-equity swaps.

Although the preceding have shown a firm closely monitoring its worldwide operations, several questions have emerged: Given the changing world political environment, can Citicorp continue to cope with its foreign debt exposure and remain a financially stable global financial services firm? What should its role be with respect to its international lending? Are the internal controls for domestic and international lending adequate in terms of its risk?

THE BUSINESSES OF CITICORP

Citicorp, a holding company incorporated in 1967, consists of its wholly owned subsidiary, Citibank, N.A., and other majority-owned subsidiaries. It provides an array of financial services to individuals, businesses, governments, and financial institutions. Services are provided in over 3200 locations, which includes branches and offices in 39 states, Washington, D.C., and 89 other countries. These locations are staffed with 89,000 employees, with domestic and overseas offices accounting for 50,000 and 39,000 employees, respectively.

The parent is organized into three core sectors: individual banking, institutional and investment banking, and information business and corporate items. (See Exhibit 4.)

Exhibit 3   Citicorp: Details of Refinancing Countries, December 31, 1988 (in billions of dollars)

Country	Cross-Border Claims* on Third Parties		Investments in and Funding of Local Citicorp Franchises	Equity[†] Investments	Cash Basis Loans[‡] (in millions of dollars)	
	Medium and Long-Term	Trade and Short-Term			Amount at[§] Year-End	Estimated After[‖] Tax Impact of Cash Basis Loans on Earnings
Argentina	$1.1	$0.2	$0.1	$—	$ 800	$ (36)
Brazil	3.5	0.4	0.1	—	3275	264
Chile	0.3	0.1	—	0.1	—	1
Ecuador	0.2	0.1	—	—	260	(10)
Mexico	1.9	0.2	0.1	0.1	35	—
Nigeria	0.1	—	—	—	145	1
Philippines	0.1	0.7	0.4	—	44	5
South Africa	0.7	—	—	—	—	—
Uruguay	0.3	—	—	—	—	—
Venezuela	0.7	—	—	—	16	2
Yugoslavia	0.2	—	—	—	—	—
All others[#]	0.4	—	—	—	241	(7)
Total	$9.5	$1.7	$0.7	$0.2	$4816	$220

Source: 1988 Annual Report.

Note: Refinancing countries are defined as those countries that are currently in the process of refinancing their external debt or have completed such refinancings.

*Legally binding cross-border and foreign currency commitments, including irrevocable letters of credit and commitments to extend credit, after adjustments to assign externally guaranteed commitments to the country of the guarantor, amounted to $0.2 billion in the Philippines and $0.1 billion in Venezuela at December 31, 1988. Commitments were not material in any other refinancing country.

[†]Equity investments obtained in debt-for-equity swaps.

[‡]Its "policy of placing loans on a cash basis embraces all commercial loans on which interest or principal is 90 days past due, as well as those on which payment of interest or principal is determined to be doubtful of collection. Even if a cash payment may be anticipated, accrued interest is reversed and the loan is put on a cash basis after a 90-day period" [1, p. 32].

[§]Includes both local and foreign currency loans; includes $1152 million in bank replacements.

[‖]Parentheses reflect a reduction of earnings.

[#]The remaining 17 countries are as follows: between $50 million and $100 million of cross-border and foreign currency outstandings, Dominican Republic, Jamaica, Morocco, and Poland; less than $50 million, Bolivia, Costa Rica, Gabon, Honduras, Ivory Coast, Liberia, Malagasy, Mozambique, Panama, Peru, Senegal, Zaire, and Zambia.

■ Individual Banking

This sector provides a wide range of consumer financial services in 41 major economies worldwide; e.g., branch banking, mortgages,* consumer finance, insurance, mutual funds, travelers checks, money orders, student loans,[†] and Bankcards. The sector's objective is to increase earnings to $1 billion within the next five to seven yers. At year-end 1988, earnings totaled $626 million compared to $556 million in 1987, a 12.5% increase.

Citibank, its wholly owned subsidiary, provides MasterCard and Visa—the nation's largest—accounting for over 23 million cards in use. The increase was helped through marketing programs which were tied to American Airlines and

*Citicorp is the largest servicer of home mortgages, totaling over $52 billion.

[†]Its student loans are the largest in the United States.

Citicorp: Sector Performance, 1987–1988 (in millions of dollars)

Exhibit 4

	1988	1987*	Variation
Individual Banking			
Customer net revenue	$6899	$6476	$423
Total expense	6041	5532	509
Other income expenses	92	65	27
Income before tax	950	1009	(59)
Net income	626	556	70
Return on assets (%)	0.64	0.65	
Return on equity (%)[†]	16.1	16.3	
Institutional and Investment Banking			
Total revenue	$5514	$4596*	$918
Provision for possible credit losses	127	3344	(3217)
Operating expenses	3195	2990	205
Net income (loss)	1329	(2580)	3909
Return on assets (%)	1.19%	(2.27%)	3.46
Return on equity (%)[†]	29.8%	(56.7%)	86.5
Information Business and Corporate Items			
Total revenue[‡]	$305	$262[§]	$43
Operating expenses	459	396	63
Net income (loss)	($105)	($89)	($16)
Total revenue[‡]	($48)	$721[‖]	
Operating expense	233	146	
Net income (loss)	$8	$931	

[*] Prior-year results have been adjusted to reflect organizational and tax allocation changes, as well the restatement for the adoption of SFAS No. 91.

[†] Return on equity is based on dividing net income by a standard imputed average equity, reflecting Citicorp's internal target.

[‡] Net of interest expense.

[§] Prior-year results have been adjusted to reflect tax allocation changes and to conform to the current year's presentation.

[‖] Prior-year results have been adjusted to reflect organizational and tax allocation changes.

the National Football League. The size of its credit operations allows the bank to achieve significant economies of scale through three Bankcard processing centers located in Sioux Falls, South Dakota; Hagerstown, Maryland; and The Lakes, Nevada. Overseas, Citicorp has begun to issue Bankcards in Germany, Belgium, Indonesia, and Greece; at the same time, it has continued to emphasize Bankcard growth in Brazil and Puerto Rico. It also introduced Bankcards in Japan, the Philippines, and Canada in 1987, and bought Bank of America's Visa business in Hong Kong. Moreover, the U.S. government chose its Diners Club travel and entertainment card, a contract estimated by the General Services Administration (GSA) to be worth approximately $600 million. In addition, GSA chose Citicorp for its travelers checks.

The bank is well positioned for additional growth in its U.S. branching systems. For example, it added to its distribution network in Utah, California, and Maryland. Likewise, the merger of Citibank Arizona with the United Bank of

Arizona resulted in the fourth-largest bank in Arizona with assets of about $3 billion; the merger increased the number of Arizona branches to 60. Citicorp acquired United Bank from Standard Charter PLC of London [4]. It also bought Caribank, a commercial bank with 14 branches in south Florida, thus providing the impetus for futher expansion in the state. Hence, it has relatively good positions in New York (the corporate headquarters are located in the state), Illinois, Florida, California, and Arizona, but a more modest presence in other states. In the United States, it has a network of about 700 bank branches.

As a product innovator for its consumer business, Citicorp introduced several new products. Its CitiOne, marketed domestically and overseas, (e.g., Singapore, Malaysia, and Taiwan), is a multiproduct retail account which offers a Bankcard and a single integrated statement for account consolidation. Another is CitiFunds:

> A multi-currency deposit and investment account that gives customers a chance to move their money into a number of investment funds in different currencies [1].

Initially introduced in Hong Kong, it is now available in other world markets. Its Mortgage-Power program was designed to promote first mortgages through real estate brokers, builders, and developers.

Citicorp is also attempting to provide a hookup with Japan's huge postal savings system through its electronic international payments service. The postal savings system "is the world's biggest financial institution," with deposits estimated at $894 billion—about one-forth of Japan's total personal savings.

> About two-thirds of all Japanese keep savings accounts at more than 20,000 post offices nationwide, and they transfer . . . $118 million over seas through the system annually [5].

The tie-up with Citicorp would expedite money transfers and payments to the United States and many other countries from about two weeks to two or three days. The bank expects to earn a small fee on each money transfer; moreover, it wants to expand its six-office Japanese operations. As expected, however, the proposal has brought bitter controversy between two Japanese ministries—the Ministry of Posts and Telecommunications, a supporter, and the Ministry of Finance, a staunch opponent; the latter regulates commercial banks.

Citicorp has also advanced its technological base with a new generation of automated, full-service banking machines (ATMs) using touch-screen technology. Installing over 1000 machines in its New York branch system, these ATMs have already been put in use in Taiwan and Hong Kong, with plans to expand this process into other countries in 1989.

In summary, it is estimated that the sector has access to more than 25 million households worldwide, thus providing Citicorp the opportunity to promote and sell new services to its customers worldwide.

■ Institutional and Investment Banking*

The worldwide delivery of this sector's products is targeted to local and multinational corporations, governments, financial institutions, real estate develop-

---

*The distinction between institutional and investment banking is primarily an internal means of assigning responsibilities, as the two businesses operate as a single sector.

ers, and capital markets. Products and services offered are extremely varied and are shown below as seven segments—or in Citicorp's terms, the segments are "customer franchises" because of the bank's unique competitive advantages.

1. *Core lending:* Focuses on traditional lending activities as working capital loans and other long-term loans. In 1988, for example, seven separate Citicorp units in four countries completed the financing which led to the construction of Europe's tallest building in West Germany.

2. *Foreign exchange and hedging:* As the world's largest foreign exchange dealer, the service is extended to clients whose business activities cross national borders; for example, services include interest rate and foreign exchange swaps, futures, etc. An example of an innovative transaction was a debt/equity swap in Chili in which Citicorp "arranged for a New Zealand forest products company to invest in the largest" Chilean company.

3. *Debt products/money market services:* In addition to its position as one of the top dealers in U.S. government securities, the bank also underwrites, trades, and/or distributes securities of many foreign nations and U.S. municipal governments. It may also assist corporations and financial institutions in raising short-term funds through notes, commercial paper, and interbank money market instruments. Its European and domestic commercial paper market was broadened with the acquisition of Paine Webber's commercial paper business in late 1987.

4. *Specialized finance:* Deals with a variety of activities such as wholesale buying of corporate assets, equipment financing, and vendor financing to assist manufacturers or sellers of capital equipment. An illustration of this was leveraged buyouts and corporate restructuring; e.g., Citicorp handled 64 transactions either on its own or by syndication (i.e., through participation of other financial institutions), thus allowing management groups to assume direct ownership of the business.

5. *Liquidity insurance, financial guarantees, and asset intermediation:* Covers fees earned on loan commitments, as a guarantor for performance by another party, from financial guarantees with respect to its U.S. municipal bond business, and from brokering and asset sales.

6. *Equity products:* Provides venture capital for new companies in the United States, Great Britain, Canada, France, Germany, Italy, Australia, Mexico, Argentina, and Brazil; regarding Brazil, it has become a major equity underwriter employing innovative financing such as debt/equity swaps.

7. *Advisory, trade, transaction processing, and other:* Provides and maintains merger and acquisition assistance through documentary collection. An imaginative deal was Citicorp's participation in financing a $5 billion acquisition of over 80 U.S. and Canadian properties; this transaction included multiple currencies, financial instruments, and interest rate pricing options—services for which Citicorp was well recognized.

Teams of Citcorp personnel combine their financial expertise to tailor specific services to their worldwide clients. Exhibits 5 and 6 illustrate the global business and geographic mix of the sector and the net income by product.

Exhibit 5

Citicorp: Institutional and Investment Bank Portfolio, 1987–1988 (in millions of dollars)

	Net Income (Loss)	
	1988	1987*
OECD economies†	$ 780	$ 513
Emerging economies‡	287	195
Cross-border refinancing portfolio	262	(3288)
Total	$1329	$(2580)

Source: 1988 Annual Report.

*Prior-year results have been adjusted to reflect organizational and tax allocation changes, as well as the restatement for adoption of SFAS No. 91.

†Organization for Economics Cooperation and Development (includes the United States, Canada, the major European countries, Japan, Australia, and New Zealand).

‡All other countries where Citicorp has a presence.

■ Information Business and Corporate Items

Begun in the mid-1980s, this sector gathers, analyzes, and distributes financial data-base services worldwide as well as integrates banking electronic publishing and telecommunication services. Its acquisition of Quotron in 1986, one of the world's largest suppliers of on-line, real-time financial information services, gave Citicorp the opportunity to enhance its worldwide banking activities. Moreover, other new services included a travel information service to help corporations control their travel costs, and a point-of-sale information network to help packaged goods manufacturers and retailers market their products. The sector recorded net losses for the two-year period 1987–1988—i.e., $89 million, and $105 million, respectively.

Exhibit 6

Citicorp: Net Income by Product, 1987–1988 (in millions of dollars)

	1988	1987
Core lending	$ 353	$(3049)*
Foreign exchange and hedging	308	81
Debt products/money market services	300	216
Specialized finance	179	130
Liquidity insurance, financial guarantees and asset intermediation	115	102
Equity products	(96)	
Advisory trade, transaction processing, and other	170	
Advisory trade, transaction processing, equity products, and other	—	247
Total	$1329	$(2273)

Source: 1988 Annual Report.

*Core lending results include the $3.0 billion addition to the allowance for possible credit losses.

Corporate items include unallocated corporate costs and other items, e.g., gains from the sale of investment securities or gain on the sale of a condominium interest in its headquarters complex. The business showed a loss of $75 million in 1986 and gains of $931 million and $8 million in 1987 and 1988, respectively.

THE THIRD WORLD DEBT*

■ Citicorp's Position

As shown in Exhibit 2, both Brazil's and Mexico's total outstandings have been declining since 1986. With respect to Brazil, ending its moratorium (i.e., Brazil stopped interest payments on its loans) in September 1987 was a significant milestone in the debt crisis. For one thing, it reflected a more cooperative attitude towards its bank creditors and, moreover, was a necessary precondition for a new financing package negotiated in 1988 estimated at $82 billion, the "largest ever on international markets" [1]. The moratorium was a costly decision for the country, as it affected Brazil's ability to obtain new funds or receive debt service reduction which could have been obtained through bank negotiations. Additionally, its action precipitated capital flight from the country. Complicating matters more, Mexico and Peru also declared a similar moratorium.

As can be seen from the above discussion, debtor countries only exacerbate cross-border lending when banks are compelled to take heavy losses on their loans or when banks are pressured to "forgive" the debt. (See Exhibit 7.) Obviously, these "forced solutions" to the debt problem will only stop or limit future borrowings by debtor countries, thus affecting their economic development.

Concerning Mexico, a major restructuring of its debts was begun in 1984 when lenders negotiated debt/equity conversion clauses in their loan contracts. Under this proposal, Mexico

> exchanges portions of its foreign currency debt for local currency, which is invested in its economy. The country thereby reduces its foreign debt, and its debt service, while the investing party—normally from the private sector—creates new economic activity [1].

At year-end 1988, Mexico also announced a securitization offer,†

> under which creditor banks could voluntarily exchange, at a discount, Mexican public-sector debt for Mexican securities on which the principal is backed by zero-coupon bonds issued by the U.S. Treasury [1].

Debt/equity solutions were also undertaken by Chile; similar programs were made by Argentina and the Philippines. However, these innovative financial transactions can only be taken when these developing countries continue to take the necessary steps to restore their economies to stable and sustained growth.

---

*See the Appendix for further discussion.

†"Under securitization, a country raises new money, or substitutes for portions of its existing debt, by issuing bonds or notes. Bank Creditors gain flexibility in managing their loan portfolio to the country because they can trade the securities in the secondary market" [1].

Exhibit 7   **Bank Holding Companies Ranked by Risk Indicator, 1988**

Rank	Holding Company	City	Risk Indicator	LDC Coverage	Market/ Book
1	Corestates Financial	Philadelphia	10%	68%	153%
2	First Union	Charlotte, N.C.	12%	53%	138%
3	Fleet/Norstar	Providence	12%	72%	163%
4	Barnett Banks	Jacksonville, Fla.	12%	N.A.*	158%
5	Suntrust	Atlanta	13%	21%	187%
6	Banc One	Columbus, Ohio	14%	67%	179%
7	Sovran Financial	Norfolk, Va.	15%	35%	164%
8	First Wachovia	Winston-Salem, N.C.	15%	36%	163%
9	Bank of New England	Boston	18%	66%	135%
10	NBD	Detroit	21%	50%[†]	127%
11	NCNB	Charlotte, N.C.	22%	35%	116%
12	PNC Financial	Pittsburgh	30%	53%	172%
13	National City	Cleveland	31%	50%	144%
14	First Fidelity	Newark, N.J.	32%	51%	118%
15	Norwest	Minneapolis	34%	52%	126%
16	First Bank System	Minneapolis	38%	46%	106%
17	Bank of New York	New York City	47%	29%	91%
18	Bank of Boston	Boston	52%	55%	108%
19	Security Pacific	Los Angeles	68%	45%	113%
20	Wells Fargo	San Francisco	72%	31%	144%
21	First Interstate	Los Angeles	74%	45%	90%
22	J.P. Morgan	New York City	81%	25%[†]	136%
23	First Chicago	Chicago	108%	37%	96%
24	Bankers Trust	New York City	109%	25%	95%
25	Citicorp	New York City	121%	25%	89%
26	Irving Bank	New York City	146%	28%	117%
27	Chemical	New York City	155%	24%	63%
28	Chase Manhattan	New York City	164%	23%	59%
29	BankAmerica	San Francisco	185%	20%	54%
30	Manufacturers Hanover	New York City	195%	22%	53%

Source: Terence P. Paré, "How Banking Will Shake Out," *Fortune,* April 25, 1988, p. 216.

Note: The indicator represents the sum of problem loans (including those to less developed countries, LDC) as a percentage of the total shareholders' equity and reserves for bad loans. The stock market has not failed to recognize which banks are in trouble or don't have sufficienct reserves to cover LDC loan losses.

*N.A. means that the company has no LDC loans.

[†]*Fortune* estimate

▪ A "Gutsy" Decision [6]

Faced with its foreign debt exposure, Citicorp in 1987 announced a significant move to increase its allowance for possible credit losses to $3 billion (see Exhibit 8). This action was a clear indication that a sizeable portion of its foreign debt might be uncollectible. Moreover, it signaled a management philosophy with respect to its credit portfolio which emphasized

> the importance of asset and earnings diversification, the immediate recognition as losses of all credits judged to be uncollectible, and the building of a credit loss allowance for additional losses thay may exist in the portfolio at a point in time but that have not been specifically identified.

Citicorp: Allowance for Possible Credit Losses, 1986–1988 (in millions of dollars)			**Exhibit 8**

	1988	*1987*	*1986*
Attributable to			
Consumer credits	$ 786	$ 819	$ 769
Commercial credits			
Refinancing countries	2876	3275	
Other	543	524	929
Total	$4205	$4618	$1698

Since all identified losses are immediately written off, no portion of the allowance is specifically allocated or restricted to any individual loan or group of loans, and *the entire allowance is available to absorb any and all credit losses* [emphasis added] [1].

According to one source, the move

was pure John Reed. Bold. Brash. And infuriating to some very important people. . . . The 48-year-old chairman of Citicorp announced that he was setting up a gigantic $3 billion reserve to cushion the bank against bad loans. . . . Citi will lose about $2.5 billion in the second quarter—the largest loss ever in the industry [7].

In fact, Reed's decision would result in a $1 billion loss for the year.

Because of the impact of this decision, Citicorp informed a number of government agencies in the United States, including the Securities and Exchange Commission, the Federal Reserve Board, the Treasury Department, in addition to several senior U.S. bank officials and Citi staffers in Europe and Japan. Simultaneously, Citicorp's Third World senior bank officers were flown in to New York "so that personal letters from Reed could be hand-delivered to the Presidents of Mexico, Venezuela, Argentina, Brazil, and the Philippines" [7]. Indeed, the key issue would be the effect on other major banks with foreign debt such as BankAmerica, Manufacturers Hanover, Chase Manhattan, and J.P. Morgan [8].

Reed insisted that the decision should not be viewed as an attempt to discontinue loans to the less developed countries (LDC) nor as a negotiating tactic. It reflected more Citicorp's concern about the world economic picture and that the LDCs debt problems may not improve. However, he added that Brazil's moratorium on its interest payments was a catalyst for Citicorp's decision. He noted that refinancing these debts "to keep countries current on their payments" was not a viable "long-term strategy."

▪ What About Reed?

Joining Citibank in 1965, John Reed was Walter Wriston's (Mr. Wriston was Reed's predecessor) top planner in the Overseas Division. With an engineering degree from Massachusetts Institute of Technology, Reed's first major achievement: Unraveling the bank's back-office problems. Charged at age 35 with pulling together Citi's retail banking businesses, which he turned into the only truly national consumer bank in the U.S.

Strengths: Strategic visionary, risktaker, deep understanding of the technology that will increasingly be the key to delivering Citi's financial services.

What his selection as CEO will mean: . . . press on with Citi's ambitions to become the global power in all facets of financial services [9].

Prior to his selection as Chairman and CEO in 1984, Reed served as Vice Chairman in charge of the individual bank.

After about a year in office, he moved "cautiously" to avoid any suggestion that Wriston did anything wrong. Wriston was a strong advocate of lending to developing countries, insisting that "countries don't go broke" [10]. Reed also kept a "low profile":

Whereas Mr. Wriston met frequently with reporters and was given to irreverent public pronouncements on major banking issues, Mr. Reed has largely avoided the media . . . .

Mr. Reed . . . has made explicit his views on media exposure. "We certainly do not measure our success by the amount of newspaper space we occupy" [11].

Coming from the consumer banking unit where he made his reputation, Reed took special effort to avoid any favoritism to his former unit as well as "soften his image as an abrasive, tough-minded hatchet man" who lacked a "concern for people." Several careful moves characterized Reed's tenure during this period. He broke with tradition

by throwing a Christmas dinner in the bank's 39th floor dining room for senior vice presidents and top executives—in addition to the one customarily held for top officials and directors. In the past, Mr. Wriston had held Christmas gatherings at the exclusive River Club, but senior vice presidents went home after cocktails and before senior management and directors sat down for dinner.

Similarly, when Mr. Wriston moved out of his 15th floor corner office to smaller quarters, Mr. Reed granted vice chairman Hans Angermueller, another competitor to succeed Mr. Wriston, his longstanding wish to occupy Mr. Wriston's office [11].

He also appointed a woman "to head the Personnel Department and serve on the policy committee, the first time a woman had held either post." According to one woman officer,

"He's more tuned in to the complexity of the bank, the dual career situations, and the large numbers of women and minorities" [11].

THE RISK MANAGEMENT PROCESS AT CITICORP

Their approach to risk management stressed several factors:

1. Diversification—by products, customers, currency, and geographic areas, which allows "hedging" against political and currency risks.
2. Management decentralization—as Citicorp's businesses were geographically dispersed worldwide, decision making is kept as close to the marketplace as possible.

3. Solid financial and operating controls—their monitoring system would make diversification and management decentralization feasible.

4. A conservative accounting policy—rapid identification of problem loans and their subsequent write-offs were aggressively implemented.

5. An independent review process by its internal audit staff coupled with further examination by external auditors and government regulatory bodies.

All enhanced credit quality.

■ Commercial (Business) Loans

In order to implement the preceding, line business managers were held accountable with respect to well-defined product/markets and credit quality. In addition, staff credit analysts monitored and insured that loan policies and procedures were followed. Hence, "documentated operational procedures that specify levels of approval authority, separation of duties, and other sound practices" were carried out.

Each loan required approval of three lending officers who exercised independent judgment. The loan size dictated the composition of this loan committee; e.g., large loans* required that two of the three officers must be senior credit officers. Two-thirds of these senior credit officers would have hands-on "business management responsibility," while the remaining one-third would be experienced in several areas as "managing credit policy and audit staffs" plus "direct business management responsibilities." These officers were reviewed annually.

Large or "unusual transactions" required approval of a 17-member Credit Policy Committee which was made up of "Citicorp's most senior officers." This committee "monitored risk by industry and geographic area" to insure that sound financial and operating controls and standards were met. An in-house Risk Asset Review group (a part of Citicorp's audit division) conducted the independent review process at the unit lending level and focused on credit quality, lending procedures, and pinpointing problem loans "not yet indentified by the line management."

■ Consumer Loans

The preceding process was also applicable to consumer loans, with some modification. For example, Citicorp monitored *monthly* the credit quality of this *overall* portfolio on the following bases: loan trends, delinquencies, and write-offs by product. Hence, deviations from standards were identified and corrective action taken. The monthly review enabled line businesses to "fine tune and improve their credit criteria."

THE FUTURE

As 1989 came to an end and the next decade approached, Citicorp appeared to be poised for the future as a major global financial services company serving a

---

*Information was unavailable as to loan benchmarks.

Exhibit 9

Citicorp: Selected Ratios, 1986–1988

Ratios	1988	1987*	1986*
Return on average total assets[†]			
Before extraordinary item	.82%	(.60)%	.56%
After extraordinary item	.90%	(.60)%	.56%
Return on common stockholders equity[‡]			
Before extraordinary item	21.4%	(19.6)%	13.7%
After extraordinary item	23.6%	(19.6)%	13.7%
Return on total stockholders equity[§]			
Before extraordinary item	18.8%	(14.7)%	12.4%
After extraordinary item	20.5%	(14.7)%	12.4%
Average common stockholders equity as a percentage of average total assets	3.59%	3.28%	3.79%
Average total stockholders equity as a percentage of average total assets	4.36%	4.05%	4.47%

Source: 1988 Annual Report.

*Prior-year ratios have been restated to reflect the adoption of SFAS No. 91.

[†] Income (loss) before extraordinary item and net income (loss) as a percentage of average total assets.

[‡] Income (loss) before extraordinary item and net income (loss) less total preferred stock dividends as a percentage of average common stockholders equity.

[§] Income (loss) before extraordinary item and net income (loss) less redeemable preferred stock dividends as a percentage of average total stockholders equity.

broad range of customers including consumers, corporations, and governments. However, its top management was faced with several critical issues.

First, competition will become stronger as banks compete on a global basis. Second, the ability of its foreign borrowers—notably, Mexico and Brazil—to service their foreign debt may be impaired due to economic, social, and governmental pressures in those countries. With respect to the latter, recall Mexico's decision to suspend its interest payments and the request by some foreign borrowers to seek "debt forgiveness." Hence, should Citicorp curtail its international lending activities and, therefore, make a significant change in its strategic orientation? Lastly, are their internal credit controls for its domestic and international lending adequate?

THE FINANCIAL PICTURE

Exhibits 2 through 6 and 9 through 14 show the total financial condition of Citicorp. A brief explanation of typical financial indicators is presented below.

• Return on assets (ROA)—an overall indicator of management efficiency in using assets to generate a profit. The national average ranges from 0.60% to 1.40%; bankers tend to use a 1% ROA to distinguish the highly profitable banks.

Citicorp and Subsidiaries: Selected Financial Information, 1984–1988 (in millions of dollars except per share data)					Exhibit 10
	1988	*1987*	*1986*	*1985*	*1984*
Net interest revenue	$ 7,605	$ 6,337	$ 5,984	$ 5,342	$ 4,246
Fees, commissions, and other revenue	5,413	6,016	4,306	3,018	2,251
Total revenue	$ 13,018	$ 12,353	$ 10,290	$ 8,360	$ 6,497
Provisions for possible credit losses	$ 1,330	$ 4,410	$ 1,825	$ 1,243	$ 619
Operating expense	8,981	8,231	6,820	5,475	4,428
Total expense	$ 10,311	$ 12,641	$ 8,645	$ 6,718	$ 5,047
Income (loss) before taxes and extraordinary item	$ 2,707	$ (288)	$ 1,645	$ 1,642	$ 1,450
Income taxes	1,009	894	617	683	608
Income (loss) before extraordinary item	$ 1,698	$ (1,182)	$ 1,028	$ 959	$ 842
Extraordinary item—Carry forward tax benefit	160	—	—	—	—
Net income (loss)	$ 1,858	$ (1,182)	$ 1,028	$ 959	$ 842
Per Share*					
Earnings (loss) per share[†]					
Income (loss) before extraordinary item	$ 4.87	$ (4.41)	$ 3.46	$ 3.40	$ 3.04
Net income (loss)	$ 5.36	$ (4.41)	3.46	$ 3.40	$ 3.04
Dividends declared per common share[‡]	$ 1.45	$ 1.32	$ .92	$ 1.13	$ 1.03
Total assets	$207,666	$203,430	$195,954	$173,474	$150,510
Debt[§]	$ 23,998	$ 24,364	$ 23,383	$ 18,255	$ 14,682

Source: 1988 Annual Report.

Note: Prior-year amounts have been restated to reflect the adoption of SFAS No. 91.

*Per share amounts reflect the two-for-one stock split declared on October 5, 1987.

[†]On net income (loss) available for common stockholders after deducting total preferred stock dividends of $105 million in 1988, $92 million in 1987, $63 million in 1985, and $60 million in 1984.

[‡]Beginning in the second quarter of 1986, common dividends are considered for declaration in July, October, January, and April, instead of June, September, December, and March. As a result, only three dividends were declared in 1986.

[§]Includes long-term debt, subordinated capital notes, and redeemable preferred stock.

- Return on equity (ROE)—the after-tax profit to shareholders as compared to other investment opportunities. ROE tends to fluctuate from 10% to 20% for most banks. Generally, the bank's equity position is a smaller portion of its total asset base, about 4–7%.

- Reserve for loan losses—a contra-asset account appearing on the balance sheet, the reserve measures management's judgment regarding the adequacy of the reserve to the overall criteria are used, such as loan experience with the debtor country, the overall country risk and economic situation, and the likelihood of collectability. The size of the reserve varies from 0.90% of total loans outstanding and is affected by the quality of the loan portfolio.

- Nonperforming loans—as mentioned earlier, these are loans whose interest payments are past due 90 days or more and generally indicate poten-

Exhibit 11   Citicorp: Selected Information, 1984–1988 (in millions of dollars except per share data)

	1988	1987	1986	1985	1984
Results					
Earnings (loss) per share*					
Income (loss) before extraordinary item	$ 4.87	$ (4.41)	$ 3.46	$ 3.40	$ 3.04
Net income (loss)	$ 5.36	$ (4.41)	$ 3.46	$ 3.40	$ 3.04
Net income loss					
Income (loss) before extraordinary item	$ 1,698	$ (1,182)	$ 1,028	$ 959	$ 842
Net income (loss)	$ 1,858	$ (1,182)	$ 1,082	$ 959	$ 842
Return on common stockholders' equity	23.6%	(19.6)%	13.7%	14.7%	14.4%
Common Dividends					
Cash dividends declared[†]	$ 461	$ 379	$ 250	$ 290	$ 259
Annual dividend rate per share at year-end*	$ 1.48	$ 1.35	$ 1.23	$ 1.13	$ 1.03
Capital					
Common equity	$ 8,274	$ 6,994	$ 7,513	$ 6,398	$ 5,674
Percentage of total assets	3.98%	3.44%	3.83%	3.69%	3.77%
Total stockholders' equity	$ 9,864	$ 8,584	$ 8,878	$ 7,613	$ 6,314
Percentage of total assets	4.75%	4.22%	4.53%	4.39%	4.20%
Primary capital	$ 17,386	$ 16,545	$ 13,308	$ 10,710	$ 8,737
Percentage of total assets	8.21%	7.95%	6.73%	6.13%	5.77%
Year-End Balances					
Total assets	$207,666	$203,430	$195,954	$173,474	$150,510
Consumer loans, net of unearned discount	90,356	79,705	68,751	55,795	42,812
Commercial loans, net of unearned discount	58,841	58,210	61,988	60,584	60,738
Total deposits	124,072	119,561	114,689	104,959	90,349
Common stockholders' equity per share*	25.93	22.12	27.30	24.73	22.47

Source: 1988 Annual Report.

Note: Prior-year ratios and amounts have been restated to reflect the adoption of Statement of Financial Accounting Standards (SFAS) No. 91.

*Per share amounts reflect the two-for-one stock split declared on October 5, 1987.

[†]Beginning in the second quarter of 1986, common dividends are considered for declaration in July, October, January, and April, instead of June, September, December, and March. As a result, only three dividends were declared in 1986.

tial write-off and subsequent loss. The national average is about 1.94% of total assets.

• Primary capital—represents the total of a bank's equity capital position and its reserve for loan losses. Based on federal regulation, banks are required to maintain a level of at least 5.5% to 6%, depending on stock and debt issue.

Citicorp and Subsidiaries: Consolidated Balance Sheet as of December 31, 1987–1988 (in millions of dollars)

Exhibit 12

	1988	1987
Assets		
Cash and due from banks	$ 4,818	$ 5,029
Deposits at interest with banks	10,706	14,706
Investment securities (market value $15,464 in 1988 and $15,438 in 1987)	15,217	15,396
Trading account assets	3,924	5,594
Federal funds sold and securities purchased under resale agreements	6,441	7,552
Loans, net		
Consumer (net of unearned discount of $2685 in 1988 and $3844 in 1987)	90,356	79,705
Commercial (net of unearned discount of $490 in 1988 and $598 in 1987)	58,841	58,210
Loans, net of unearned discount	$149,197	$137,915
Allowance for possible credit losses	(4,205)	(4,618)
Total loans, net	$144,992	$133,297
Customers' acceptance liability	3,839	5,219
Premises and equipment, net	3,337	3,365
Interest and fees receivable	3,448	3,223
Other assets	10,944	10,049
Total	$207,666	$203,430
Liabilities		
Non-interest-bearing deposits in domestic offices	$ 12,190	$ 11,241
Interest-bearing deposits in domestic offices	50,819	44,731
Non-interest-bearing deposits in overseas offices	4,065	4,004
Interest-bearing deposits in overseas offices	56,998	59,585
Total deposits	$124,072	$119,561
Purchased funds and other borrowings	32,889	31,690
Acceptances outstanding	3,856	5,250
Accrued taxes and other expenses	5,037	4,349
Other liabilities	7,950	9,632
Long-term debt	20,709	21,076
Subordinated capital notes	3,249	3,248
Redeemable preferred stock	40	40
Stockholders' Equity		
Preferred stock	$ 1,590	$ 1,590
Common stock ($1.00 par value) Issued shares: 346,322,787 in 1988 and 343,995,863 in 1987	346	344
Surplus	2,901	2,866
Retained earnings	5,451	4,215
Common stock in treasury, at cost Shares: 27,260,266 in 1988 and 27,767,138 in 1987	(424)	(431)
Total stockholders' equity	$ 9,864	$ 8,584
Total	$207,666	$203,430

Source: 1988 Annual Report.

Exhibit 13   Citicorp and Subsidiaries: Consolidated Statement of Operations, Years Ended December 31, 1988, 1987, and 1986

	1988	1987	1986
Interest Revenue			
Interest and fees on loans	$20,575	$17,164	$15,531
Interest on deposits with banks	1,362	1,261	1,072
Interest of federal funds sold and securities purchased under resale agreements	1,234	725	692
Interest and dividends on investment securities	1,234	1,236	1,033
Interest on trading account assets	2,206	1,479	752
Total	$26,611	$21,865	$19,080
Interest Expense			
Interest of deposits	$10,612	$ 9,109	$ 8,191
Interest on other borrowed money	5,783	3,920	2,828
Interest on long-term debt and subordinated capital notes	2,611	2,499	2,077
Total	$19,006	$15,528	$13,096
Net interest revenue	$ 7,605	$ 6,337	$ 5,984
Provision for possible credit losses	$ 1,330	$ 4,410	$ 1,825
Net interest revenue after provision for possible credit losses	$ 6,275	$ 1,927	$ 4,159
Fees, Commissions, and Other Revenue			
Fees and commissions	$ 3,887	$ 3,518	$ 2,958
Trading account	277	177	162
Foreign exchange	616	453	412
Investment securities transactions	108	195	214
Other revenue	525	1,673	560
	$ 5,413	$ 6,016	$ 4,306
Other Operating Expense			
Salaries	$ 3,483	$ 3,213	$ 2,699
Staff benefits	744	663	492
Total staff expense	$ 4,227	$ 3,876	$ 3,191
Net premises expense	844	707	612
Equipment expense	797	759	630
Other expense	3,113	2,889	2,387
	$ 8,981	$ 8,231	$ 6,820
Income (loss) before taxes and extraordinary item	$ 2,707	$ (288)	$ 1,645
Income taxes	1,009	894	617
Income (loss) before extraordinary item	$ 1,698	$ (1,182)	$ 1,028
Extraordinary item—Carryforward			
Tax benefits	160	—	—
Net income (loss)	$ 1,858	$ (1,182)	$ 1,028
Earnings (Loss) Per Share			
Income (loss) before extraordinary item	$ 4.87	$ (4.41)	$ 3.46
Net income (loss)	$ 5.36	$ (4.41)	$ 3.46

Citibank, N.A., and Subsidiaries: Consolidated Balance Sheet as of December 31, 1987–1988 (in millions of dollars)

Exhibit 14

Assets	1988	1987
Cash and due from banks	$ 3,639	$ 4,193
Deposits at interest with banks	10,488	14,757
Investment securities (market value $11,101 in 1988 and $12,457 in 1987)	10,947	12,328
Trading account assets	2,413	3,303
Federal funds sold and securities purchased under resale agreements	6,657	7,407
Loans (net of unearned discount of $2507 in 1988 and $2362 in 1987)	$ 97,141	$ 93,650
Less: allowance for possible credit losses	(3,248)	(3,528)
Loans, net	$ 93,893	$ 90,122
Customers' acceptance liability	4,064	5,441
Premises and equipment, net	2,040	2,119
Interest and fees receivable	2,553	2,379
Other assets	6,226	5,982
Total	$142,920	$148,031

Liabilities		
Non-interest-bearing deposits in domestic offices	$ 9,933	$ 9,670
Interest-bearing deposits in domestic offices	34,185	30,122
Non-interest-bearing deposits in overseas offices	4,012	3,972
Interest-bearing deposits in overseas offices	54,315	59,370
Total deposits	$102,445	$103,134
Purchased funds and other borrowings	16,416	18,132
Acceptances outstanding	4,081	5,472
Accrued taxes and other expenses	2,789	2,551
Other liabilities	5,535	7,524
Long-term debt	3,486	3,670

Stockholder's Equity		
Capital stock ($20.00 par) Outstanding shares: 37,534,553 in 1988 and 1987	$ 751	$ 751
Surplus	3,220	3,203
Retained earnings	4,197	3,594
Total stockholder's equity	$ 8,168	$ 7,548
Total	$142,920	$148,031

Source: 1988 Annual Report.

APPENDIX: THE LATIN AMERICAN DEBT*

■ ─────────────────────────────────── ■

A number of U.S. banks faced serious problems as a result of their holdings of foreign debt—particularly debts to the less developed countries (LDCs) of the world where their economies faced uncertain stability, high unemployment, increasing population growth, rising poverty levels, increasing debt service ratios, and inflation. With respect to the latter, Bolivia at one time had a 10,000% inflation rate, while Mexico was projected to reach an annualized rate of about 1800% in 1988 [12].

Since the onset of the debt crisis in 1982, estimates of Latin America's foreign bank debt are projected to decline slightly in 1989 to $1.3 trillion from $1.32 trillion in 1988; in 1987, the total was $1.28 trillion [13]. Indeed, the U.S. government became concerned, as lenders attempting to minimize their losses began to use various innovative financing techniques. An explanation of these various approaches are provided below.

1. *Debt/equity swaps.* Specifically, the bank will swap its loans at a discount[†] for local currency or an equity investment in the debtor country; e.g., an equity investment in Chilean gold mines or Brazilian paper pulp companies. Brazil's first debt/equity conversion included swapping with creditors "$150 million of payments due to them for a smaller amount of local currency to be invested in Brazil."

> Half the auctioned debt was swapped for Brazilian cruzados that can be invested anywhere in the country. The discount on these conversions was 27% on $73 million and 26.5% on the remaining $2 million. The other half of the debt was swapped for cruzados that will be channelled into projects in the underdeveloped northern and western regions of the country. The discount on these conversions was 10.5%, reflecting the shortage of viable investment alternatives in the targeted areas [14].

Similarly, Citicorp acquired a 15% equity investment in Mexico's largest beer producer; $103.5 million of its Mexican government debt was converted into $50 million cash for the acquisition [15]. The risk, of course, to the lender is that the bank may "get involved in businesses they don't know well and may arouse nationalist antipathy to foreign ownership" [3].

A novel approach was the debt-for-nature swap involving $5.6 million in bank debt in Costa Rica. In essence,

---

*This discussion is adapted from several sources.
†"In debt/equity swaps, the discount on the debt is effectively shared by borrower and lender" [3].

a non-profit conservation group buys, or is given, commercial bank debt owed by a hard-pressed developing country. The group converts that debt into the local currency of the debtor country and uses it for environmentally related projects. Such programs require the prior approval of the debtor nation's government and central bank [16].

2. *Buy-backs.* The debtor country buys back its bank debt at a discount; e.g., Bolivia "bought back just under half its $670 million bank debt at 11 cents for each dollar of debt" [3]. In a similar fashion, Chile and Argentia have entered into buy-back agreements; the former would be able to use about $500 million of its reserves for buy-backs, while Argentina bought back its debts at approximately 22 cents for a dollar of Argentine debt. It should be noted that this approach has been feasible for only the very poor LDCs (e.g., Bolivia) and, moreover, all bank creditors needed "to waive certain loan covenants."

In Chile's case, its loan agreement required the approval of two-thirds of its bank creditors. Chilean debt—the country is generally recognized as having the best economic track record compared to other Latin American debtors—was priced in late 1988 at "60 cents for each dollar of debt, bid, and 60.5 cents for each dollar of debt, offered" [17]. It should also be noted that many bankers conclude that buy-backs "tend to discourage banks from future lending" [17].

3. *Collateralized loans.* Chile instituted an imaginative debt program to raise about $500 million in new bank loans that "would be collateralized with Chilean goods, 30% of which would be exports" [18].

4. *Bond swap.* This is basically exchanging debt for new bonds (often called exit bonds) and are attractive to the borrower as "they carry a lower interest rate or a lower face value than the loans they replace" [3]. For example, the U.S. Treasury assisted in a unique transaction [19]. J.P. Morgan, a noted investment firm, devised a plan whereby Mexico "would pay up to $2 billion for $10 billion of zero-coupon U.S. bonds"; hence, Mexico could issue as much as $10 billion new bonds of its own backed by U.S. Treasury bonds. With U.S. support, some "would accept the new bonds and would then write off about double their amount in old, riskier debt." In essence, Mexico "could use that $10 billion of bonds to get rid of $20 billion of debt." With the backing of the U.S. Treasury, banks would be able to get back some of their money; in addition, Mexico could obtain a lower interest rate on the debt, thus improving its ability to service the debt. The Mexican government "would still have to come up with the interest due every six months."

When banks incur a loss as a result of these financing options, the losses could offset their tax bill, and, of course, affect government revenues, which could ultimately be passed "indirectly to taxpayers." However, a recent Internal Revenue Service ruling stated

that for purposes of calculating foreign-tax credits, a bank must apply any loan losses against its income in proportion to the split between its foreign and domestic business. For instance, a bank that earns 10% of its interest income from foreign loans would apply interest income from foreign loans would apply 10% of the loan losses to its foreign portfolio and 90% to its domestic portfolio.

Some big banks have been applying a large portion of their foreign-loan losses against domestic income to make their foreign profits as large as possible; the big-

Exhibit 15

Debtor Nations Debt Service Ratio (in billions of dollars)

Country	*Debt**	*Service†*	*Ratio (%)‡*
Argentina	$ 49.4	$23.7	33.1%
Brazil	114.5	61.4	30.2
Chile	20.5	9.8	29.5
Mexico	105.0	44.9	32.7
Nigeria	27.0	12.2	11.6
Philippines	29.0	12.0	19.0
Venezuela	33.9	15.9	22.5
Yugoslavia	21.8	10.2	7.7

Source: Clyde H. Farnsworth, "Poor Nations Getting Poorer—World Bank," *The Orange Country Register,* January 19, 1988, p. D3.

*Total debt outstanding in 1987.

†The estimated interest and principal due between 1987 and 1989.

‡The percentage of export revenue devoted to interest payments in 1987.

ger their foreign profits, the more they can use foreign-tax credits to reduce their U.S. tax bills [20].

Increasingly, lenders are confronted with two options: debt relief or reduction, which both the Reagan and Bush administrations have endorsed—providing it is voluntary [21]; and extension of new credit. Both entail negotiations, which, according to a panel of senior bankers, can be an " 'effective means for easing the debt burden of developing countries' " [3].

Brazil's decision to suspend interest payments on its foreign bank debt certainly made lending to LDCs extremely risky and unattractive. With Argentina $1 billion in arrears on interest payments, and smaller debtor countries such as Peru, Nicaragua, and Bolivia making no interest payments, bank credit will likely diminish further. Yet these LDCs, faced with higher interest rates and continual pressure from their growing population for economic assistance, can only bring even greater pressure on lenders to seek more extensive debt relief programs. These external forces, indeed, provided the catalyst to Citicorp to increase its loan loss reserves by $3 billion in order to cope with this problem.

Exhibits 15 and 16 present information with respect to LDCs debt service ratio and the most recent quotes for discounted LDCs debt.

REFERENCES

1. *Annual Reports,* 1988, 1987; and 10-Ks.

2. Citicorp publication covering its Fifth Annual Presentation to Institutional Investors by John Reed and other senior executives, January 23, 1989.

3. Peter Truell, "Latin American Debt Prompts Action," *The Wall Street Journal,* September 22, 1988, p. 12.

4. "Citicorp to Acquire Bank in Arizona from London Firm," *The Wall Street Journal,* January 29, 1988, p. 10.

5. Marcus W. Brauchlo, "Citicorp Proposal Stirs Dispute in Japan Between Banks, Postal Savings System," *The Wall Street Journal,* September 22, 1988, p. 35.

Discount Debt of Selected Debtor Countries, 1988 (in cents on the dollar)

Exhibit 16

Country	May 1988		12-Month	
	Bid	Ask	High	Low
Argentina	28.0	29.0	60.5	25.0
Bolivia	10.5	12.0	12.0	6.0
Brazil	55.0	56.0	65.5	38.0
Chile	61.0	62.0	72.5	50.0
Mexico	53.5	54.5	59.5	46.5
Nicaragua	2.0	4.0	6.0	2.0
Nigeria	29.0	30.0	35.0	25.0
Peru	4.0	9.0	15.0	4.0
Philippines	50.0	51.0	72.0	49.0
Venezuela	55.0	56.0	74.0	49.5

Source: George Anders and Peter Truell, "For Investors Who Are Strong of Heart, Third-World Debt Holds Some Allure," *The Wall Street Journal*, May 17, 1988, p. 41

6. "A Gutsy Move at Citicorp," *Business Week*, June 1, 1987, p. 146.

7. Sarah Bartlett, William Glasgall, Blanca Riemer, and John Templeman, "A Stunner from the Citi," *Business Week*, June 1, 1987, pp. 42–43.

8. Peter Truell, "Since '87 Loss Reserves, Latin Debt Crisis Has Grown," *The Wall Street Journal*, May 19, 1988, p. 6.

9. For an excellent treatment concerning Walter B. Wriston, who was Reed's predecessor, see "The New Shape of Banking," *Business Week*, June 18, 1984, pp. 104–110.

10. Edward Boyer, "Citi Corp: What the New Boss Is Up To," *Fortune*, February 17, 1986, pp. 40–44.

11. Phillip L. Zweig, "Citicorp Chairman Avoids Wholesale Change," *The Wall Street Journal*, July 3, 1985, p. 6.

12. "Brazilian Plan to Cut Inflation Seen Inadequate," *The Wall Street Journal*, November 17, 1988, p. A12.

13. Walter S. Mossberg, "World Bank Seeks New Debt Strategy on Third World, Evolution of Baker Plan," *The Wall Street Journal*, December 19, 1988, p. B2.

14. "Brazil Holds First Auction to Swap Debt for Equity," *The Wall Street Journal*, January 30, 1988, p. 15.

15. "Citicorp Buys Stake of 15% in Producer of Beers in Mexico," *The Wall Street Journal*, December 9, 1988, p. A4.

16. Alvaro Umana, "Costa Rica's Debt-for-Nature Swaps Come of Age," *The Wall Street Journal*, May 26, 1989, p. A11; see also "A Debt-for-Nature Swap in Costa Rica Biggest Yet," *The Wall Street Journal*, January 13, 1989, p. A8.

17. Peter Truell, "Chile Buy-Back of Foreign Debt at Discount Set," *The Wall Street Journal*, September 22, 1988, p. 4.

18. Peter Truell, "Chile Markets Debt Plan to Its Creditors That Use Goods as Collateral for Loans," *The Wall Street Journal*, May 4, 1988, p. 19.

19. "Sanity at Last on Third World Debt," *Fortune*, February 1, 1988, p. 8.

20. David Wessel and Robert Guenter, "IRS Ruling Limits the Tax Advantages Banks Get on Foreign-Loan Write-Offs," *The Wall Street Journal*, May 4, 1989, p. A5.

21. Peter Truell and Matt Moffett, "The Brady Plan for Third World Debt Gets Off to a Bad Start in Latin America," *The Wall Street Journal*, May 10, 1989, p. A14.

Crystal Lawn Service

JoAnn K. L. Schwinghammer, Mankato State University;
Thomas M. Rieff, Owner, Crystal Lawn Service

Looking back over the past season, Tom Rieff was thinking about how his lawn care business, Crystal Lawn Service, had progressed in the five years he'd been in business.

"Someone told me that any small business that makes it five years has been through the most difficult times," he commented to his wife, June. "I don't think that person was in the lawn care business! With all of the uncertainty in this business, it really helps to have the wintertime to sit back and plan for the next season."

With his spreadsheets before him on the kitchen table on this January night in 1988, Tom reflected on his previous season's growth and pondered the direction his company should take next season. He wondered whether Crystal Lawn Service would ever attain the size or profitability necessary to provide the level of income that he had given up to start the business.

BACKGROUND OF CRYSTAL LAWN SERVICE

Thomas M. Reiff started Crystal Lawn Service (CLS) in March of 1983 as a part-time business in Mankato, Minnesota. At the time, Tom also was employed in a full-time position for Polar Industries as a farm fertilizer–LP gas plant manager in Lake Crystal, 12 miles from Mankato. He felt that, with his fertilizer and chemical expertise, lawn care would be an interesting twist to what he was already doing, and he saw a growing need for lawn care services in the area. Realizing a conflict in that both businesses were spring season–intensive, Tom immediately enlisted the services of a personal friend to help in getting CLS's work done. A used pickup truck was initially purchased, and spraying equipment was built from extra parts purchased from the fertilizer plant. Tom's initial goals for CLS were to build a customer base and maintain minimal debt, although he wasn't quite sure how many customers it would take or how large that debt should be. CLS ended the first season with 90 accounts and approximately $5000 in sales.

In 1984, more people became aware of CLS, and its customer base grew. To accommodate this growth, Tom's brother was hired part-time to help with fertilizer and herbicide applications. An ATV sprayer was also added to handle the larger-application jobs. The 1984 season ended with 210 accounts and $15,000 in sales.

CLS's excellent growth in customers and sales continued in 1985. Tom's brother was hired on a full-time basis and a second part-time individual was added. A second spray truck was also added to meet the needs. All of the employees were paid on a per-lawn basis to eliminate the headaches of the time clock. The 1985 season ended with 465 accounts and $30,000 in sales.

On September 1, 1985, Polar Industries, Tom's employer, sold all of its fertilizer plants to Cenex, which in turn sold the Lake Crystal branch to Crystal Co-op, also based in Lake Crystal. While Tom's employment was continued at Crystal Co-op, he felt that his future with respect to CLS was at a turning point. How was he going to continue operating Crystal Lawn Service, which had gone from a part-time operation to a full-time lawn care service, while working for another employer? Feeling that his freedom would be severely limited with both responsibilities, Tom decided to pursue CLS on a full-time basis in March 1986.

This decision created a new set of concerns for Tom. In order to achieve the level of income for the job he had left, he believed that continuous growth in CLS's customers, sales, and net profit was needed. Growth was of utmost concern. To gain the customer base needed, CLS purchased a small lawn company in Nicollet (12 miles northwest of Mankato) and opened a branch in LeSueur (28 miles northeast of Mankato). These two expansions, with the aid of newspaper advertising, pushed CLS to a level of 1036 customers and $72,000 in sales for 1986.

In 1987, Tom felt that CLS's geographical expansion should be slowed and that growth within each individual market/city should be emphasized. Promotion was done through the Yellow Pages, home improvement shows, newspapers, and shopper-type advertising tabloids. Adverse weather conditions during the summer of 1987 caused dry growing conditions not encountered since Tom had begun his business. Specifically, high heat and lack of rainfall in April, May, and June resulted in lost applications and an increase in lawn problems (insects, crabgrass, and thin turf). This affected overall sales, customer growth, and costs for 1987. Also, there was a concern over customer retention for 1988 because of these adverse conditions. With customers numbering 1260 and sales reaching $96,000 by the end of 1987, Tom observed that growth in sales revenues typically lagged growth in customer accounts by one year. Now in January of 1988, Tom was at the planning stage for CLS's 1988 lawn care season.

A TYPICAL LAWN CARE PROGRAM

Lawn care services typically provided proper application of fertilizer and pesticides to residential and commercial lawns. The results of these applications provided the homeowner with a lush green lawn. Lawn care consisted of a series of applications or treatments that had to be completed on a timely basis. The timing and quantity of fertilizer or herbicides were usually left to the discretion of the lawn care firm with whom the customer had contracted. The lawn care firm began by giving the customer a complete lawn analysis, noting existing weed problems, density of turf, the general condition of turf, thatch, and the underlying compaction. The number of treatments ranged from three to five, depending on the lawn care firm's program. The average price of a program ranged from $150.00 to $200.00 per year.

The fertilizer application was designed to meet the needs of the turf for each particular season. The herbicide treatment, made in conjunction with the fertilizer application, was commonly known as "weed and feed." Since different species of weeds thrived during different seasons of the year, the proper herbicides would be added to alleviate the specific weed problems. Insect and disease problems were treated on an individual lawn-by-lawn basis. During a programmed application, the lawn technician would survey the lawn and determine if any additional problems needed treatment. Following a fertilizer treatment, the lawn owner would usually be asked to water the lawn at specified intervals to ensure that the fertilizer was activated.

Aeration was a service completed on a periodic basis. This process removed cores of soil to reduce the thatch level, relieve soil compaction, and aid weed control. Another service, lawn renovation, was usually completed on a problem-only basis. In this process, the existing lawn was actually destroyed and reseeded, eliminating certain diseases, weed problems, and poor turf quality.

A typical lawn care program was as follows:

- Early spring: Liquid lawn fertilizer with crabgrass weed control. This application promoted early spring green-up of turf and provided herbicide treatment to prevent crabgrass germination.
- Late spring: Liquid lawn fertilizer with broadleaf control. This application followed six weeks after the first, continued strong grass growth, and eliminated weeds such as dandelions, plantain, and clover.
- Midsummer: Liquid lawn fertilizer with insect control. Turf was again fertilized after six weeks; insects, such as billbugs, chinchbugs, and grubs, were treated as diagnosed.
- Early fall: Liquid lawn fertilizer with broadleaf control. Lawn fertilization and broadleaf weeds were retreated. The fall was the best time to treat such weeds as dandelions to prevent spring recurrence.

THE LAWN CARE INDUSTRY

The professional lawn care industry consists of firms that provide services to care for residential and commercial lawns. The industry had been growing at a rate of 15% per year over the past 20 years and was by 1988 $1.5 billion strong.

The growth rate could be explained in part by Americans' desire to devote greater time to recreational activities, by the increase in two-income families, and by their growing appreciation for a beautifully landscaped yard. In addition, some homeowners had learned that do-it-yourself lawn care could cost as much as professional care, when the costs of materials, applicators, and time for preparation and planning were considered.

With the maturation of the industry had come competitiveness and consolidation of smaller companies into larger regional operations. Even so, *The Wall Street Journal* reported that the market was not near the saturation point. Industry experts said that in 1987 there were approximately 8 million residential customers in the United States, leaving 51 million single-family home lawns still cared for by their owners. There were an estimated 81.4 million residential structures and about 240 million residents in the United States.

The Professional Lawn Care Association of America (PLCAA), of which Crystal Lawn Service was a member, was the largest and most widely recognized trade association for lawn care service providers. It served 1350 member companies with regulatory, technical, safety, marketing, and financial information assistance.

CRYSTAL LAWN SERVICE

■ Product/Service Mix

During the 1987 lawn care season, Crystal Lawn Service operated as a full-time, complete-service lawn care firm. CLS's product/service mix consisted of a program of up to five, rather than the normal four, applications, in order to provide flexibility to each individual homeowner in designing a program to meet the owner's needs, budget, and social aesthetics. CLS had arranged these five applications into three common packages: deluxe (five applications), standard (four applications), and basic (three applications). Other services offered in 1987 were aeration, tree and shrub care, lawn seeding and industrial/commercial spraying. A typical lawn served by CLS was approximately 7000 square feet. All pesticide products used by CLS were licensed by the EPA and registered with the Minnesota Department of Agriculture.

■ Customer Profile

CLS had both residential (90%) and commercial (10%) accounts, a breakdown common in the industry. Exhibit 1 provides a listing of all cities and towns served by CLS, populations of those cities, and the number of all accounts in each city. A map of this service area appears in Exhibit 2.

A typical residential account was a homeowner, 30 years of age or older, with an annual adjusted household income of over $25,000. All homeowners, however, were not potential lawn care service users. About 40% of all homeowners, nationally, did nothing to their lawns but mow. In Mankato, 32.3% of families had incomes greater than $25,000, and approximately 37% of all Mankato residents were between the ages of 30 and 79.

Commercial accounts had the same needs as most residential accounts with respect to their lawns; occasionally industrial spraying was needed for treating bare ground and controlling weeds in parking lots and around buildings.

Crystal Lawn Service: 1987 Market Summary   **Exhibit 1**

City	Number of Accounts	Percent of Accounts	Sales	Percent of Sales	Population
Amboy	0	0.0	$ 0.00	0.0	627
Belle Plaine	1	0.1	190.00	0.2	2,940
Cleveland	3	0.2	65.00	0.1	726
Courtland	0	0.0	0.00	0.0	397
Eagle Lake	34	2.7	2,473.42	2.6	1,504
Garden City	7	0.6	740.00	0.8	275
Good Thunder	1	0.1	36.04	0.0	553
Hanska	2	0.2	143.60	0.1	417
Henderson	16	1.3	985.51	1.0	737
Janesville	1	0.1	252.30	0.3	1,896
Kasota	3	0.2	438.21	0.5	702
Lafayette	0	0.0	0.00	0.0	521
Lake Crystal	235	18.7	17,214.72	17.9	2,130
LeCenter	28	2.2	1,590.26	1.7	1,957
LeSueur	257	20.4	17,967.52	18.7	3,700
Madelia	6	0.5	423.20	0.4	2,081
Madison Lake	4	0.3	632.12	0.7	556
Mapleton	0	0.0	0.00	0.0	1,519
Mankato	310	24.6	27,007.28	28.1	28,871
New Ulm	15	1.2	1,158.51	1.2	13,751
Nicollet	31	2.5	2,298.72	2.4	728
North Mankato	258	20.5	18,905.86	19.6	9,626
Pemberton	0	0.0	0.00	0.0	221
St. Clair	2	0.2	238.60	0.2	699
St. James	1	0.1	118.40	0.1	4,267
St. Peter	24	1.9	1,719.34	1.8	9,146
Sleepy Eye	19	1.5	1,592.32	1.7	3,539
Vernon Center	2	0.2	82.00	0.1	353
Total	1260	100.0	$96,272.93	100.0	94,439

Whether for residential or commercial accounts, personal contact seemed to be an important factor. "People certainly are interesting, there's no doubt about that," Tom commented. "They're the heart of this business. But sometimes they're funny. Over the year, you can almost predict how they're going to react—in the spring they're happy and excited about the plans for their lawn, wanting to be involved. In the summer, they're distressed and tend to complain and focus on the things that go wrong—that's probably just their reaction to the heat and humidity. In the fall, they're rather indifferent; many haven't remembered what they've ordered, and they've lost interest in their lawns. But they like to talk, and that personal contact goes a long way in this business. Many of our customers have gotten to know me and expect to see me at some point during the summer."

■ Pricing

CLS had a philosophy of providing the best available products/services at a competitive price. " 'Competitive' doesn't mean that I am cheaper nor more expensive than the others; it means that I will provide the best value for the

Exhibit 2   **Crystal Lawn Service: Service Area**

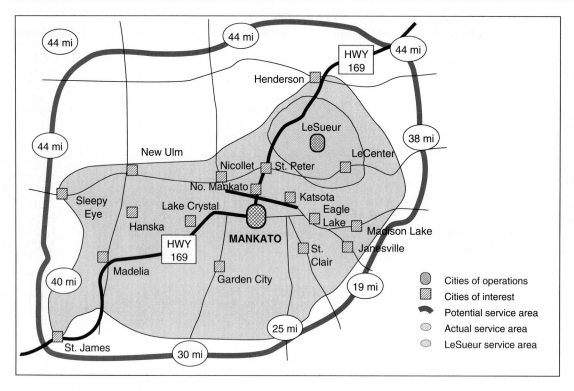

Source: D. B. Hulse, MAP Production Co., Inc. Tyler, Texas.

customer's dollar spent," Tom says. "If I can buy the better products efficiently and at the right times, I can provide a quality service to my customers without having to charge them a higher price."

Tom believed that price sensitivity was perhaps moderate. "It surprises me sometimes. When I send out the preseason renewal notices, many people will select the basic, three-application program. Then, when I go by their lawn in the summer, and I suggest to customers that they should have four or five applications, instead of three, quite a few will say, 'Yes, I suppose I should. Go ahead and do that next year.' "

The pricing of lawn care in the Mankato market was typically lower than in the larger urban markets, sometimes with a difference of as much as $10 per application. Tom believed this was due to demand that was based on a more rural, conservative perspective, less influenced by social pressure for a green, weed-free, visually pleasing lawn. Whereas major companies nationally averaged $150 to $200 per customer for their full programs (four or five applications), CLS's averages ranged between $135 and $170. CLS's overall customer average (for all customers and all services) was $76.40. This lower average was due to the flexibility with which services were tailored to customers' needs. A summary of CLS's applications follows.

Type	Number of Applications	1987 Sales	Application Average
Lawn care			
Early spring	753	$26,427.99	$35.10
Late spring	789	26,844.58	34.02
Middle summer	130	3,842.10	29.55
Early fall	656	21,397.62	32.62
Late fall	253	8,999.66	35.57
Aeration	22	792.80	36.04
Subtotal	2603	$88,304.75	$33.92
Miscellaneous	119	7,968.18	66.96
Total	2722	$96,272.93	$35.37

Miscellaneous services performed by CLS included nonprogram applications such as weed control only, tree care, and industrial spraying, for which there was a limited market and the cost per application was higher. For these reasons, they were separated from the normal program applications.

Invoices were left with customer at the time of the application. Normal payment was expected within 30 days of treatment, but a 5% discount was given for payment within 10 days. CLS also offered a 10% discount for prepayment of all services.

■ Promotions

Promotions for CLS were more extensive in 1987 than for previous years because of Tom's belief that informing customers of his service was of prime importance. The message presented in the ads did not change substantially from medium to medium. An example of an ad appears in Exhibit 3. CLS utilized several media, though the most extensively used were newspaper and shopper tabloids (63.6% of CLS's advertising expenditures). Additional forms were displays at home improvement shows (18%). Yellow Pages (11.4%), radio (3.8%), and other miscellaneous promotions (3.2%). A brief description of the specific media is given below.

   • Newspaper and shopper tabloids: These were local weekly and regional daily newspapers covering a 30-mile range of the area from Mankato. Ads were run from the middle of March to the end of May.

   • Home improvement shows: These shows consisted of February and March "home and garden" shows held at the two regional shopping malls in Mankato and at a community center in New Ulm, and "farm and home" shows at a community center in LeSueur and an entertainment facility in Sleepy Eye. Participation involved setting up a booth and being available to discuss the company's services, which were also discussed in literature available for the customers' taking.

   • Yellow Pages: Use of these media consisted of the Yellow Pages through the Mankato Citizens' Telephone Company, a privately held telephone company, and *Fronteer's,* a wide-area telephone directory which included all of the towns in CLS's service area except Belle Plaine.

Exhibit 3   **Sample Advertisement**

The **EASY, LOW COST** Way
To A **HEALTHY, BEAUTIFUL** Lawn

Complete Maintenance Programs For
LAWNS, TREES & SHRUBS

• Fertilization • Weed Control
• Insect & Disease • Aeration

Call US Today For A
FREE ESTIMATE

Mankato Ph.
LeSueur Ph.

CRYSTAL LAWN SERVICE
Locally Owned & Operated

• Radio: This medium was used on a limited basis in the LeSueur area only during April.

• Miscellaneous: These were ads placed in program booklets for local organizations and/or public schools and the purchase of candy for local parades. These were considered by Tom to be "goodwill" donations more than advertising.

While Tom believed he had chosen a good mix of media for 1987, he believed it might be helpful to rethink his media choices for 1988. In considering new advertising plans, Tom recalled that industry experts at a PLCAA meeting had mentioned that approximately $35 in advertising expense was needed to attract one new account over and above the customer base of the previous year.* Tom knew that he had not spent this much per new account and doubted that the rate was that high in the Mankato area. Available media alternatives are presented in Exhibit 4.

---

*For example, if a firm had 100 accounts in 1986, and at the end of 1987 had lost 5 accounts but gained 10, the total number of accounts at year-end 1987 would be 105, with a net gain of 5, upon which the $35 new account expense was based. Therefore, it would have taken 5 × $35 = $175 in total marketing expenditures to win this net gain. The $175 figure ignores the benefit of the marketing expense on the present customer base (retained accounts).

Types of Media Available for 1988   **Exhibit 4**

Name	City	Type	Coverage	Rate (per 12 column inches)
Newspapers				
Lake Crystal Tribune	Lake Crystal	Weekly	Local	21.00
News Herald	LeSueur	Weekly	Local	50.40*
Madelia Times & Messenger	Madelia	Weekly	Local	28.80
Lake Region Times	Madison Lake	Weekly	Local	14.28
Free Press	Mankato	Daily	Regional	$81.72
Star & Tribune	Minneapolis	Daily	Statewide	N/A
The Journal	New Ulm	Daily	Regional	78.00
Plain Dealer	St. James	Weekly	Local	30.00
St. Peter Herald	St. Peter	Weekly	Local	12.00*
Herald Dispatch	Sleepy Eye	Weekly	Local	12.00*
Shoppers				
The Valley	LeSueur/St. Peter	Weekly	39,007	†
The Peach	Madelia	Weekly	N/A	35.00
Home Magazine	Mankato	Weekly	N/A	74.40
New Ulm Shopper	New Ulm	Weekly	N/A	N/A
Watonwan County Shopper	St. James	Weekly	N/A	35.00

Radio (call letters)	City	Type	Audience (years of age)	Rate (30 sec)
KDOG-FM	Mankato	Pop/rock	20–34	$7.50
KEEZ-FM	Mankato	Pop/rock	20–34	N/A
KTOE-AM	Mankato	Contemporary	25+	7.50
KYSM-AM	Mankato	Oldies	25–54	3.40
KYSM-FM	Mankato	Country	25+	9.00
KXLP-FM	New Ulm/Mankato	Adult/contemporary	25–49	9.00
KNUJ-AM	New Ulm	Old time/country	30+	7.25
KXAX-FM	St. James	Country	25+	N/A
KRBI-AM/FM	St. Peter/LeSueur	Contemporary	25+	9.00

Television (call letters)	City	Type	Rate (30 seconds)
KEYC	Mankato	CBS affiliate	$30.00 ($50–$100 production)
Quest Advertising	Mankato	Cable TV	4.70 ($200 production cost)

Billboard

Vogel Outdoor Advertising, Mankato, $260–1760 per sign, depends on placement

Other Forms of Advertising

Telemarketing of prospective, present, and past customers

Direct mail: target mailing of potential lawn accounts; cost of list, brochure, and postage averages $0.242 per piece

Company image: logos on trucks, signs, uniforms, etc.

Flyers and/or coupons with invoice and renewal letter

Posting signs on CLS-treated lawns

---

*The *St. Peter Herald* and the *Herald Dispatch* are sister papers of the *News Herald*. This results in the reduced rate shown when the same ad is placed in all three papers through the *News Herald*.

†*The Valley* is also included in the rate for the *News Herald*.

■ Company Organization

While Tom organized and oversaw all of the company's operations from the office in his home, the day-to-day activities were flexibly scheduled utilizing seven part-time and seasonal full-time employees. Besides Tom, CLS had no formal full-time employees. While this could have presented problems for some companies, the seasonal nature of this business required unique organizational and planning practices. Actual application work began at the beginning of April and continued strong through May. Through June and into the hot months of the summer, work tapered off. In middle August, the early-fall season started, with applications continuing until the end of October. After this, Tom spent time planning for the following season and repairing equipment. Part of this planning involved evaluating the efficiency of operations for the previous season and attending to customer details such as sending out renewal notices to current customers. All customer information was kept in a computer database program, which allowed the tracking of services ordered by each customer and preprinting invoices for scheduled treatments.

Since the business was very seasonal, Tom's flexibility in scheduling had allowed him to employ competent people as applicators whose work or school schedules were also flexible. For instance, one employee had another small business whose spring schedule provided him the freedom to work for Tom during April and May, two of CLS's busy months. Another employee worked a swing shift for a local plastics company, allowing him to work six additional hours each day for CLS. Some of the employees were students who, by planning their schedules carefully, could work for CLS during the day and attend classes at night or vice versa. When the busy season was over, these employees welcomed the time off, alleviating any unemployment problems. All employees who performed pesticide applications were required to be licensed by the State of Minnesota. All employees were paid by the hour. In addition to these seven lawn applicators, Tom employed his wife as a bookkeeper and his sister-in-law as an accounts receivable clerk.

CLS used a local 24-hour answering service which received all calls and forwarded messages via pager to Tom, eliminating the need for a full-time secretary or receptionist. He returned the calls at his convenience, usually the same day he received the message. In addition, Tom used an incoming 800-number telephone service. This functioned as a collect-call service, for which Tom paid a monthly fee ($2.00) and a charge for each incoming call. This service was provided to accommodate those accounts residing outside of Mankato's local telephone-calling area.

When Tom answered a page from a prospective customer, his procedure was to arrange a time most convenient to both parties to conduct a lawn analysis and estimate. At the time of the analysis, Tom gave the customer a written lawn care proposal estimate based on the needs of the lawn and customer. While most customers accepted or rejected the proposal at that time, some would later contact CLS to accept the proposal. With an accepted proposal, Tom would indicate an approximate application date, coordinated with the customer's wishes and other planned applications in that neighborhood. The estimate then served as a contract between CLS and the customer.

During the "building years" between 1983 and 1987, Tom had continued to improve on his existing trucks and equipment and to add new equipment as necessary. By 1988, that equipment included four spray trucks, each with two hoses, allowing for two applicators per truck. Each truck possessed the capacity to accommodate an average of 400 accounts per year. If a new truck was necessary, it would cost between $12,000 and $20,000, depending on whether a used or new chassis was purchased.

CLS also had a trailer spray unit available to fill excess demand and an ATV sprayer particularly useful for large-application areas, such as schools, parks, and farmyards. Other equipment CLS utilized on a regular basis were aerators, hand sprayers, and dry spreaders. All solutions were blended at a warehouse in Lake Crystal. Products and equipment not used on a daily basis were stored there also. Trucks were parked overnight at a storage lot in North Mankato.

■ Financial Aspects

One of Tom's goals when he started CLS was to maintain minimal debt and keep careful track of his financial condition. Accounting procedures were done on a cash basis using a checkbook template on a computerized spreadsheet pro-

---

Crystal Lawn Service: Income Statement, 1987   Exhibit 5

Item	Dollars	Percent of Sales
Total sales	$96,272.93	
Cost of goods sold		
Fertilizer	$ 9,740.59	10.1
Chemicals	16,207.32	16.8
Seed, etc.	1,227.76	1.3
Total cost of goods sold	27,175.67	28.2
Gross profit from sales	69,097.26	71.8
Operating expenses		
Salaries	17,016.55	17.7
Payroll taxes	1,389.52	1.4
Commissions	342.52	0.4
Depreciation	0.00	0.0
Insurance	2,651.02	2.8
License	447.55	0.5
Gas, L.P. and oil	3,815.06	4.0
Truck repair	1,980.93	2.1
Equipment repair	4,247.64	4.4
Shop supplies	347.62	0.4
Equipment rental	741.97	0.8
Office supplies	1,215.59	1.3
Property rent	1,790.00	1.9
Postage	594.00	0.6
Telephone	1,617.49	1.7
Bank charges	42.09	0.0
Accounting, legal fees	386.00	0.4
Seminars, dues, magazines	681.96	0.7
Travel, lodging, meals	621.50	0.6
Uniforms, safety equipment	458.17	0.5
Advertising	4,063.65	4.2
Interest	757.30	0.8
Minnesota sales tax	5,222.37	5.4
Total operating expenses	50,430.41	52.4
Net income	$18,666.85	19.4

gram. The program provided records of individual checks written, check/deposit coding by prespecified accounts, monthly cash flows, and an income statement. A 1987 income statement is provided in Exhibit 5.

CLS had no formal balance sheet but maintained an asset list enumerating assets with a fair market value totaling approximately $50,000. Each year Tom reviewed his own personal financial statement, which helped him determine if he was better off "today" than he was a year ago. CLS had a 10% debt-to-asset ratio for equipment, and the operating line of credit had a zero balance at year end.

■ Competition

In the Mankato area, there were several full-time, complete-service lawn care firms, some limited-service firms, and a few part-time, one-person, limited-service lawn care companies. All known lawn care firms are listed below, ranked by market share and prominence, based on such information as approximate amount of Yellow Pages and newspaper advertising, promotional effort, and their presence as seen by CLS employees on a regular basis when servicing accounts.

- Lawn Pro: A private company based in Mapleton (17 miles south of Mankato); offered a complete five-application program at a medium price; slogan, "For a Beautiful Lawn."
- Green Touch: A private company based in Mankato; offered a complete program and maintenance services including lawn mowing and landscaping; slogan, "Everything We Touch Turns to Green."
- ChemLawn: A public company based in a suburb of Minneapolis, approximately 90 miles to the northeast; offered a complete program at a high price; slogan, "ChemLawn Guarantees."
- Amlawn and Garden Services: A private company based in Mankato that offered fertilization, weed control, and mowing only; no slogan.
- Evergreen: A private company based in Worthington, 90 miles to the southwest of Mankato; offered a complete program of lawn care at a high price; slogan unknown.
- Randy's Pest Control: A private company based in St. Peter, 12 miles north on Mankato on a major artery (Highway 169); offered a complete program, with a low-price appeal; no slogan.
- Equity Supply: A privately owned farm store located in Mankato, not serving the lawn care market in 1987, but planning to enter the market in 1988; depth of their intended program unknown.
- Nitrolawn: A private firm, based in Nicollet; in 1987 conducted mowing services only, but planned to add fertilization and weed control services in 1988; no slogan.
- Doran Turf: A private company based in LeSueur, serving the LeSueur area and northeast; considered by Tom to be *the* competition in the LeSueur market, but not the Mankato market.

There were numerous other part-time companies that offered various limited services. In Tom's estimation, Lawn Pro was clearly number one in market share in the Mankato area, with CLS number two. Green Touch and ChemLawn were probably of equal share in this market area, ranking in a tie for third. The remaining competitors had minor market shares individually.

■ Objectives and Goals

Tom was satisfied with his basic product/service line: full-service lawn care. He believed that to add lawn mowing would be more of a nuisance than a source of profits. There was a great deal of competition in that line, since many people liked to hire their children, grandchildren, or neighbor's children for that task. And Tom felt that he had neither the interest nor the expertise in landscaping to add that line. While Tom wished to find a profitable addition to his services that could be done in the wintertime, he was not interested in snow removal because of the destructive effects of snow and ice on his vehicles. However, a wintertime service would enable him to retain year-round employees.

Tom's ultimate goal for CLS had been to achieve a level of income ($26,000) relative to the job position he left in 1986. Along with that, however, he recognized that a business should have adequate compensatiion, over and above a normal salary, for the risk taken. As he began his preparation for the coming season, he jotted down several questions to be investigated:

1. What was the market potential for lawn care services in the area CLS served? Was there room for him to grow?
2. If there was enough potential, what levels of dollar sales/number of customers would be needed to meet his (a) income expectations and (b) income expectations plus a reward for the risk taken?
3. Given a potential level of sales/customers, what marketing actions would he have to take to achieve that level of sales?

REFERENCES

"Lawn Care Companies Add New Services as Growth Rates Slow," *The Wall Street Journal*, April 30, 1987, p. 1.

Leckey, Andrew. "Growth Strong in Lawn-care Biz," *The Free Press* (Mankato, Minn.), April 22, 1988, p. 12.

"State of the Industry," *Lawn Care Industry*, June 1988, p. 1.

"Where the Grass Is Greener," *Forbes*, April 21, 1986.

Harry's Pizza, Spirits, and So Forth

Ken Gardner, John Leslie, University of South Carolina;
James J. Chrisman, Louisiana State University

"I really don't know what I'm going to do Jim," said Steve Warner, owner and general manager of Harry's Pizza, Spirits, and So Forth, a popular student bar and restaurant in Athens, Georgia. "I opened this place four years ago and it's finally beginning to show a profit. But when the drinking age goes up to 20 this September, I stand to lose a lot of business, which I may not be able to replace."

"I don't know what to tell you Steve," commented the customer. "Maybe you should just sell out now before everyone starts to panic and the value of your business drops."

"I know, I know. I've thought of that," Warner responded. "I hate to give up without a fight though. There just has to be some other alternative."

Warner turned away and filled a pitcher of beer for some customers. It was the night of May 8, 1985, and through the local news on the bar's TV, Warner had been reminded that the Georgia State Legislature had recently passed a bill that would raise the legal drinking age in the state from 19 to 21. This change was going to occur in two stages. The drinking age would first be raised to 20 in September 1985 and then to 21 in September 1986. Although Warner had known this for several months, hearing the news again disturbed him.

Nearly 50% of Harry's business came from the sale of alcohol, and of this amount, approximately 60% was to individuals under the age of 21. Most of these customers were students at the University of Georgia, which was located within walking distance of the restaurant. The potential 30% drop in overall revenue was an obvious concern for Warner. However, Warner was also wor-

---

Exhibit 1   **Harry's Income Statements, 1983–1984**

	1984		*1983*	
Sales		$415,784		$344,000
Food	$220,332			
Alcohol	186,354			
Machines	9,009			
Other	89			
Cost of goods sold		150,529		127,000
Food	$ 75,270			
Alcohol	68,225			
Machines	4,719			
Other	2,315			
Gross margin		$265,255		$217,000
Operating expenses		$256,239		$212,700
Hourly wages			$58,800	
Administrative salaries			28,000	
Payroll taxes			8,100	
Rent			13,000	
Advertising and promotion			14,700	
Supplies			12,700	
Utilities			21,000	
Telephone			5,000	
Automobile			1,800	
Repairs and maintenance			2,100	
Spoilage			1,600	
Insurance			6,000	
Taxes and licenses			7,500	
Legal			2,200	
Bank			4,700	
Interest			11,300	
Depreciation (equipment)			10,300	
Miscellaneous			3,900	
Net income (before taxes)		$ 9,016		$ 4,300

ried that the change in the legal drinking age would cause a loss of food revenue; if students under 21 could not drink, they might stop eating at Harry's too. Although the full impact of the change in the drinking age would not be felt for 18 months, Warner knew he had to start considering alternative plans. Harry's had recorded a small profit in both 1983 and 1984, and Warner had thought that the bar was "turning the corner" profitwise (see Exhibits 1 and 2 for financial information). A 30% drop in sales, however, could be too much to take. Warner knew that he had to find a way to replace the anticipated loss of revenue or else risk losing his restaurant.

BACKGROUND

Harry's Pizza, Spirits, and So Forth began operation in April 1981 under the ownership of Steve Warner. Warner had considerable experience in the restaurant and bar business dating back to 1974 when he underwent an extensive

Harry's Balance Sheet, February 28, 1985

Exhibit 2

Assets

Current		
Cash on hand	$ 250.00	
Petty cash	200.00	
Bank	(5,175.00)	
Returned checks	661.00	
Accounts receivable	100.00	
Inventory	6,896.00	
Deposits (utilities)	1,460.00	
Prepaid interest	697.00	
		$ 5,089.00
Fixed		
Furniture and equipment	93,414.00	
Less accumulated depreciation	(71,164.00)	
Building	56,253.00	
Less accumulated depreciation	(22,032.00)	
Signs	1,526.00	
Less accumulated depreciation	(1,258.00)	
Leasehold improvements	11,686.00	
Less accumulated depreciation	(4,493.00)	
		63,932.00
		$69,021.00

Liabilities

Current		
Accounts payable	$ 8,011.00	
FICA payable	1,282.00	
Federal withholding	309.00	
State withholding	65.00	
Sales tax payable	1,308.00	
Taxes payable	237.00	
Accumulated state tax	380.00	
Notes payable	10,880.00	
		$22,472.00
Long-term		
Notes payable	160,000.00	
Loan	(110,056.00)	
		$49,944.00
Equity		
Common stock	500.0	
Paid-in capital	(444.00)	
Retained earnings	(3,451.00)	
		(3,395.00)
		$69,021.00

nine-month training program for a large national chain of family-style restaurants. Upon completion of the training program, Warner operated one of the chain's franchised restaurants for two years. This experience, and his desire to own his own restaurant, led Warner to become a partner in two distinctly different restaurant operations: a French restaurant and a pizza operation. After two years, disagreements among the partners caused Warner to sell his share of the businesses, although both had been profitable. With a new partner, Warner

Exhibit 3   **Population by Age and Sex in Clarke County, 1984**

Age Group	Male	Female	Total	% of Total
0–5	3,014	2,970	5,984	7.8
6–11	2,440	2,433	4,873	6.4
12–17	2,687	2,611	5,298	6.9
18–24	10,180	10,507	20,687	27.0
25–34	7,513	7,086	14,599	19.1
35–44	3,757	4,257	8,014	10.5
45–54	2,518	2,824	5,342	7.0
55–64	2,250	2,865	5,115	6.7
Over 65	2,224	4,364	6,588	8.6
Total	36,583	39,917	76,500	100.0

launched another venture in Florida called Mr. G's Pizza. Although the restaurant was successful, after a year and a half Warner began looking for a suitable location to start his own restaurant.

After conducting demographic studies on several southern cities, Warner selected Athens, Georgia, as a prime location in which to open a restaurant. Warner and his wife Beth soon moved to Athens and purchased an existing establishment. It had been a popular student bar, located just off the main campus of the University of Georgia (UGA). Warner renovated the old building extensively, and in April 1981, Harry's Pizza, Spirits, and So Forth opened for business.

Harry's was directly across the street from three of the school's main dormitories, which together housed over 3000 students. Warner thought that the students would find the combination of good pizza and spirits attractive; and since its opening, Harry's had developed a reputation as a student hangout. Warner also believed that the restaurant had built a reputation for quality pizza. Harry's sales had increased moderately each year, and until threatened by the change in the drinking age, Warner had been confident that the future of the business was bright.

ATHENS, GEORGIA

Located in northeast Georgia, about 65 miles to the east of Atlanta, Athens was the principal city of Clarke County (see Exhibits 3 and 4 for a demographic profile of Clarke County). In 1983 the median household income in Athens was over $18,000. Residents of Athens spent over $45 million eating and drinking out in 1983.

One of the reasons Warner had chosen Athens was the presence of the University of Georgia's main campus. The campus was an important part of life in Athens. The UGA student population was over 25,000, while the population of the entire city was only about 45,000. Due to the large student body, the 18–24-year-old age group was the largest population subgroup in the city.

The population of Clarke County was expected to increase 7.6% by 1988. On the other hand, the student population at UGA was expected to remain relatively stable for the next three years. The student population was tightly con-

Households by Effective Buying Incomes (EBI) in Clarke County, 1984   **Exhibit 4**

EBI ($)	No. of Households	% of Total
Under 5000	3,469	12.2
5000–9999	4,232	14.8
10,000–14,999	4,188	14.7
15,000–19,999	3,736	13.1
20,000–24,999	2,927	10.3
25,000–34,999	4,184	14.7
35,000–49,999	3,686	12.9
Over 50,000	2,078	7.3
	28,500	100.0%

Note: Median EBI = $18,068.

trolled by the University's admissions policy, and the change in enrollment was expected to be small from year to year. Exhibit 5 provides the 1980–1984 enrollment by class at UGA.

The economy of Athens was heavily dependent upon the student population. Virtually every business in the city was affected to some extent by the seasonality of the academic year. The student population dropped considerably during the summer months and in December. The holiday sales that stores in other areas traditionally relied upon during December were severely reduced in Athens because of the number of students who returned home for the holidays.

INDUSTRY TRENDS

The short-term outlook for eating and drinking establishments was positive. Americans spent 37% of their food dollars at restaurants in 1984, and industry sales had increased 55% since 1979 (*U.S. Industrial Outlook*). Furthermore, sales were projected to increase by another 10% in 1985 as restaurants continued to

Enrollment at the University of Georgia, 1980–1984   **Exhibit 5**

Class	1980	1981	1982	1983	1984	Historical % Male
Freshman	3,298	4,393	3,904	3,662	4,028	44.9
Sophomore	3,771	4,067	4,552	4,559	4,352	47.1
Junior	3,775	4,325	4,190	4,183	4,108	50.0
Senior	4,469	4,357	4,663	4,443	4,786	51.8
Graduate	4,163	4,319	4,504	4,671	4,568	49.8
Professional	1,603	1,577	1,570	2,102	2,172	47.0
Other	2,391	2,603	2,526	1,422	1,171	NA
Total	23,470	25,641	25,909	25,402	25,185	

Note: NA = information not available.

Exhibit 6

Average Common-Size Income Statements for Restaurants and Drinking Places in the United States with Assets of Less Than $1 Million in 1985

	Restaurants (N = 500)	Drinking Places (N = 38)
Sales	100.0%	100.0%
Cost of goods sold	44.4%	39.8%
Gross profit	55.6%	60.2%
Operating expenses	50.6%	55.1%
Other expenses	2.2%	2.5%
Net profit before taxes	2.8%	2.6%

Source: Robert Morris Associates, *'85 Annual Statement Studies.*

expand and diversified their menus. Salad bars and dishes with chicken and fish were the most popular menu additions.

Exhibits 6 and 7 provide common-size income statements and balance sheets, respectively, for restaurants and drinking places with assets of less than $1 million in 1984. Exhibit 8 shows selected 1984 financial ratios for these businesses.

Despite favorable sales trends, increasing legal pressure had been placed on owners of establishments which sold alcoholic beverages. Georgia state law held the owner of an establishment liable for damages caused by a patron (e.g., drunk-driving accidents) if it was shown that the patron had become intoxi-

Exhibit 7

Average Common-Size Balance Sheets for Restaurants and Drinking Places in the United States with Assets of Less Than $1 Million in 1984

	Restaurants (N = 500)	Drinking Places (N = 38)
Assets		
Cash and equivalents	11.1%	10.7%
Trade receivables (net)	4.1%	2.0%
Inventory	7.4%	11.4%
All other current assets	2.7%	4.2%
Total current assets	25.3%	28.2%
Fixed assets (net)	58.6%	54.9%
Intangibles (net)	4.5%	6.4%
All other noncurrent assets	11.6%	10.4%
Total assets	100.0%	100.0%
Liabilities and Owners' Equity		
Current liabilities	39.6%	35.5%
Long-term debt	32.6%	32.7%
All other noncurrent liabilities	2.5%	1.1%
Total liabilities	74.7%	69.3%
Owners' equity (net worth)	25.3%	30.7%
Total liabilities and owners' equity	100.0%	100.0%

Source: Robert Morris Associates, *'85 Annual Statement Studies.*

Financial Ratios for Restaurants and Drinking Places in the United States with Assets of Less Than $1 Million in 1984　　　　**Exhibit 8**

Ratios	Restaurants			Drinking Places		
	Upper Quartile	Median	Lower Quartile	Upper Quartile	Median	Lower Quartile
Current	1.3	0.6	0.3	1.7	0.8	0.3
Quick	0.8	0.4	0.1	0.7	0.3	0.2
Cost of sales/inventory	46.9	27.4	17.5	37.3	19.3	12.0
Sales/working capital	62.8	−30.3	−10.4	18.6	−60.8	−10.1
Asset turnover	4.9	3.4	2.1	3.8	2.2	1.5
Return on equity (%)	66.0	24.4	3.0	43.7	22.5	0.7
Return on assets (%)	17.8	6.7	−0.7	15.7	4.9	−1.5

Source: Robert Morris Associates, '85 Annual Statement Studies.

cated at the owner's establishment. The enforcement of such laws was becoming more strict, largely due to the influence of groups such as Mothers Against Drunk Driving (MADD) and Students Against Drunk Driving (SADD). An establishment found guilty in a case involving an intoxicated driver could be fined, lose its license to sell alcohol, and even face a civil law suit. Furthermore, the number of these actions was increasing.

There were, however, steps that could be taken to reduce the likelihood of involvement in legal actions. The most common precaution was the purchase of a liquor liability insurance policy which protected the owner from civil suits. The cost of such policies was rising dramatically, however, because of the increase in the number of cases. In many instances the cost of the policy was so high that the establishment chose to operate without any insurance. This practice was risky, though, because one lawsuit could potentially bankrupt a small restaurant as well as ruin its owner.

LOCAL COMPETITION

Competition in the restaurant and bar business in Athens was intense in early 1985. There were over 130 eating and drinking establishments in the city, all of which competed with Harry's to varying degrees. Exhibit 9 shows a breakdown of the restaurants and bars in Athens by number of employees.

Number of Establishments by Employment-Size Class　　　　**Exhibit 9**

Type	Total	Number of Employees						
		1–4	5–9	10–19	20–49	50–99	100–249	250–499
Eating and drinking places	134	33	20	29	45	6	1	0
Eating places	121	27	16	27	44	6	1	0
Drinking places	13	6	4	2	1	0	0	0

Source: Country Business Patterns. Georgia, 1982, Department of Commerce.

Exhibit 10   Pizza and Beer Prices of Competing Restaurants and Bars

Restaurant	Small Cheese Pizza	Large Cheese Pizza	Restaurant or Bar	Pitchers of Beer
Harry's	$4.50	$8.40	Harry's	$3.00–3.50
DaVinci's	4.75	8.00	DaVinci's	3.50
Express	4.85	6.95	Express	2.25
Classics	4.20	8.20	Classics	2.25–3.00
Domino's	5.25	7.75	Papa Joe's	3.25
Pizza Pronto	5.90	8.45	TK Harty's	3.75
			Uptown Lounge	2.00

Because Harry's had a bar upstairs, a restaurant downstairs, and offered pizza delivery, it competed with area restaurants, bars, and food delivery operations. Exhibit 10 provides pizza and alcohol prices for selected competitors in 1984.

■ Competing Pizza Restaurants: Eat-in

Although Harry's offered chicken, sandwiches, and a variety of snacks, most of its food revenue came from pizza sales. Its primary food competitors, therefore, were the eight pizza restaurants (not including their satellite stores) in the city. These included national chain stores like Pizza Hut and Pizza Inn and local establishments such as DaVinci's, Express, Steverino's, and Maxwell's.

Located only a block away, Express Pizza was perhaps Harry's closest pizza competitor. Express catered to an older crowd, offered a wide variety of food, and served less expensive draft beer than Harry's. It did not have a liquor license, although it had recently applied for one. Express was also planning to remodel its facility slightly in anticipation of the changes in the drinking age to further appeal to the older crowd.

■ Competing Pizza Restaurants: Delivery

In addition to the more traditional, sit-down establishments there were two major pizza delivery operations, Domino's and Pizza Pronto. Although most pizza restaurants in Athens, including Harry's, offered delivery, these two operations were unique because delivery was their specialty; neither competitor provided space for in-store dining.

Domino's was a nationally franchised operation which had established the trend towards faster delivery service with its guarantee that customers would get "hot pizza in less than 30 minutes" or the pizza would be free. With its reputation for fast service, Domino's had become the leader in pizza delivery nationwide, although the quality of its pizza was generally considered average. The Domino's store in Athens took advantage of the chain's strong national advertising and kept its costs low by using centrally purchased materials.

■ Competing Bars

Since many people went to Harry's primarily to drink, it also competed with other local bars and nightclub operations, such as Papa Joe's, O'Malley's, the

Mad Hatter, Uptown Lounge, and TK Harty's. These operations served alcohol and light snack food, rather than full meals. O'Malley's, Mad Hatter, Uptown Lounge, and TK Harty's also provided live musical entertainment on the weekends to attract customers.

Although all of these bars would be affected by the change in the drinking age, few had formulated definite plans for the future. The managers of O'Malley's and Papa Joe's, for instance, were "just sitting back and waiting to see what happens" and "didn't intend to change anything." On the other hand, nightclubs such as the Mad Hatter had toyed with various ideas, including starting an "all ages" club which would not serve alcohol and changing the entertainment format to attract an older crowd.

Harry's closest bar competitor was Papa Joe's. Located two blocks up the street from Harry's, Papa Joe's employed 13 part-time employees, including 12 bartenders and a janitor. Papa Joe's catered to the campus's "Greek" crowd; 85% of its business came from fraternities and sororities. Approximately 60% of its customers were under 21, and about 90% of its revenues came from the sale of beer and liquor. Besides alcohol, Papa Joe's offered its customers a limited menu of "snack" foods, a jukebox, and a large variety of video games.

According to its owners, the bar had enjoyed its most profitable year in 1984. Although Papa Joe's sales were still somewhat lower than Harry's, they had doubled over the previous year. Its before-tax profits were also considerably greater than Harry's. Low overhead, a strong regular clientele, an expanded product line, and daily drink specials were among the factors to which the owners attributed their success.

HARRY'S PIZZA, SPIRITS, AND SO FORTH: RESTAURANT AND BAR OPERATIONS

In addition to the pizza, Harry's offered chicken fingers (also very popular), a variety of sandwiches, french fries, and snacks such as nachos, fried vegetables, and potato skins. Warner had also considered adding hamburgers to the menu. Exhibit 11 shows Harry's menu items and prices.

In late 1984 Harry's began offering a lunchtime buffet featuring "all-you-can-eat" pizza for a single price. Warner believed that the buffet had been successful in increasing lunch business. He wanted to try the same idea to attract dinner business and had recently started an all-you-can-eat pizza and salad special between 5:30 and 7:30 P.M. Since it had been offered for only one month, it was too early to determine if the dinner buffet would benefit sales as much as the lunch buffet.

The bar offered a large selection of alcoholic beverages. Draft and bottled beers were available, as well as wines, liqueurs, a wide variety of spirits, and specialty drinks, such as Long Island tea and shooters. Exhibit 12 shows Harry's alcohol items and prices.

■ Facilities

Harry's had a seating capacity of approximately 250. This capacity was divided among the three sections of the restaurant: the downstairs restaurant, the upstairs bar, and the outdoor deck. The floor plans for the restaurant, bar, and deck are shown in Exhibits 13–15, respectively.

Exhibit 11   **Harry's Menu Items and Prices**

Salad Bar $2.75 ($1.25 with meal)
Lunch pizza buffet $3.25

Snacks

Nachos	$2.75	Chicken fingers	$3.50
Bean nachos	2.95	Sandwiches	3.25
Mucho nachos	3.25	Smoked ham	
Fried veggies	2.25	Chicken	
Potatoe skins	3.50	Meatball	
French fries	0.85		

Pizza	*Cheese*	*Extra Toppings*	*Harry's Special**	*Vegetarian Special†*
Thick crust				
Small (9 inches)	$4.50	$0.85	$ 7.05	$ 6.20
Medium (12 inches)	6.40	0.95	9.25	8.30
Large (14 inches)	8.40	1.05	11.55	10.50
Thin Crust				
Small (12 inches)	4.75	0.85	8.15	6.45
Large (16 inches)	7.70	1.05	11.90	9.80
Soft drinks, coffee, tea, and milk	$0.45			

*Includes six toppings.

†Includes four toppings.

The restaurant was located on the first floor and could seat approximately 100 people. The second floor housed the main bar and had a capacity of 80. Food items ordered upstairs were prepared in the downstairs kitchen and transported to the second floor via a dumbwaiter. The outdoor deck, which could accommodate about 70 people, was a popular addition to Harry's and was used frequently by customers from late April through early October.

- **Delivery**

Harry's also delivered its pizza, chicken fingers, and sandwiches to the immediate area. The primary customers for this service were the students that lived

Exhibit 12   **Harry's Alcohol Prices for the Upstairs Bar**

Wine	$1.25/glass	Special drinks	
Draft beer (16 ounces)	1.00/glass	Frozen margarita	2.50
	3.00–3.50/pitcher	Daquiri	2.50
		Piña colada	2.50
Bottle beer		Long Island tea	3.00
Budweiser	1.35	Shooters	1.75–2.50
Miller Lite	1.35	Bar brand highballs	1.75
Michelob/Lite	1.60	Bar brand cocktails	2.00
Imports	1.85	Canadian Club, Seagrams, etc.	2.25
		Jack Daniels, Crown Royal, etc.	2.50
		Chivas, Grand Marnier	2.75

Harry's Downstairs Restaurant (not drawn to scale) **Exhibit 13**

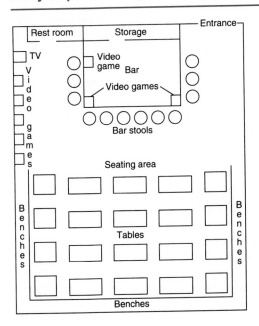

on or very near campus. Warner felt it was necessary to offer delivery in order to compete with the other delivery stores. He had advertised the delivery service in local student papers and through flyers to generate more delivery business. Although he felt the delivery service was doing all right, he had never separated the sales and costs of the delivery operation from the overall restaurant's.

Harry's Upstairs Bar (not drawn to scale) **Exhibit 14**

Exhibit 15   Harry's Outdoor Deck (not drawn to scale)

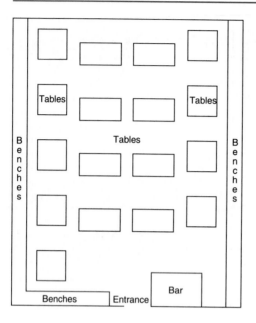

■ Food Sales and Costs

Pizza was Harry's most popular item, accounting for around 55% of total food sales. Exhibit 16 provides average pizza sales breakdowns for January through April, 1982–1985.

Although Harry's pizza prices had risen twice since 1981 (see Exhibit 17), they were competitive with other Athens restaurants. In 1985, a small cheese pizza cost $4.50, while a large cheese pizza was $8.40. These prices put Harry's in the medium-to-high bracket among competing pizza restaurants. Warner justified the higher prices because he felt the quality of the pizza at Harry's was superior to his competitors'. Since pizza was Harry's most popular food item, Warner had worked hard to develop and maintain the quality of his pizza. After four years in business, Warner felt that Harry's reputation for quality had begun to spread.

The cost of goods sold for pizza generally was around 28% of sales. The cost of goods sold for food overall was usually about 35% of sales. Food costs had been relatively stable and Warner believed they would remain so for at least the next year. Exhibit 18 gives a breakdown of sales and cost of goods sold by food item for the last 15 months of business.

■ Alcohol Sales and Costs

Warner felt that Harry's alcohol prices were competitive with other bars catering largely to students, such as O'Malley's and Papa Joe's. The cost of goods sold for alcohol was slightly less than 40% of sales (see Exhibit 19). Warner did not foresee any dramatic increases in prices from his alcohol distributors.

Warner held a liquor liability policy that was due to expire in July 1985. He was currently paying about $750 per year for the policy and was concerned that

Harry's Pizza Sales Breakdowns: January Through April (1982–1985 average)   **Exhibit 16**

		Percent of Unit Sales Volume			
Size	Total	Mr. Harry's*	Vegetarian†	Cheese	Average Number of Toppings per Cheese Pizza
Small	51.28	7.02	0.46	43.80	1.346
Medium	34.14	6.04	0.26	27.84	1.255
Large	14.58	2.56	0.20	11.82	1.656
Total	100.00%				

Item	1982 Jan.–Apr.	1983 Jan.–Apr.	1984 Jan.–Apr.	1985 Jan.–Apr.
Sales (dollars)	$51,834	$51,561	$51,023	$36,826
Average price	$6.52	$6.68	$6.68	$7.20

*Includes six toppings.

†Includes four toppings.

the premium would rise at renewal. He had heard of other establishments the size of Harry's having to pay three to four times this amount.

■ Sales Fluctuations

Exhibit 20 provides monthly sales figures for Harry's from April 1981 through March 1985. Sales were the lowest in June, July, August, and December, when there were few students on campus. In 1984 summer sales accounted for only 16% of total annual sales and were about evenly split between food and alcohol. Warner had considered closing the restaurant during the summer, but he was not sure if this was a good idea.

Sales were highest from September through November. High sales during this period were due to the return of the students and to the college football season. The University of Georgia football team was very successful and attracted crowds of over 70,000 when they played in Athens. Therefore, football weekends were always extremely busy at Harry's. During the fall the students also had more money to spend eating out, after having worked during the summer.

Harry's Pizza Price Changes, September 1981–April 1985   **Exhibit 17**

	Cheese			Mr. Harry's			Vegetarian			Toppings		
Size	9/81	8/82	6/84	9/81	8/82	6/84	9/81	8/82	6/84	9/81	8/82	6/84
Small	$4.10	4.10	4.50	6.35	6.65	7.05	5.61	5.81	6.20	.75	.85	.85
Medium	5.81	5.81	6.40	8.35	8.65	9.25	7.51	7.71	8.30	.85	.95	.95
Large	7.61	7.61	8.40	10.46	10.76	11.56	9.51	9.71	10.50	.95	1.05	1.05

Exhibit 18 **Harry's Sales and Cost of Goods Sold by Food Item, January 1984 through March 1985**

| Month | Sales | | | | Cost of Goods Sold | |
	Pizza	Finger Food	Sandwiches	Other Food, Beverages*	Total Food	Total Cost of Goods Sold
January 1984	$ 12,918	NA	NA	NA	$ 21,984	$ 8,284
February 1984	13,163	NA	NA	NA	22,785	7,473
March 1984	13,398	NA	NA	NA	22,311	8,133
April 1984	11,543	NA	NA	NA	21,435	7,420
May 1984	12,191	$ 6,818	$1,136	$1,940	22,085	7,466
June 1984	8,298	3.475	928	1,169	13,870	4,758
July 1984	6,678	1,755	447	651	9,531	3,369
August 1984	7,215	2,093	506	760	10,574	3,814
September 1984	14,272	6,999	2,040	2,452	25,763	7,240
October 1984	12,293	6,822	1,729	2,056	22,900	8,159
November 1984	10,710	5,575	1,309	1,587	19,181	6,551
December 1984	3,953	2,598	693	669	7,913	2,603
Total 1984	$126,632	NA	NA	NA	$220,332	$75,270
January 1985	$ 10,884	$ 6,005	$1,436	NA	NA	$ 7,546
February 1985	9,022	5,627	1,207	NA	NA	6,200
March 1985	8,860	5,493	1,208	NA	NA	5,759
Total first quarter 1985	$ 28,766	$17,125	$3,851	NA	NA	$19,505

Note: NA = information not available.

*Does not include alcohol.

Exhibit 19 **Harry's Alcohol Sales and Cost of Goods Sold, January 1984–March 1985**

Month	Sales	Cost of Goods Sold
January 1984	$ 12,451	$ 4,462
February 1984	13,323	4,605
March 1984	16,489	6,021
April 1984	19,332	6,526
May 1984	22,806	7,977
June 1984	10,325	4,507
July 1984	9,981	4,101
August 1984	10,564	4,511
September 1984	21,351	7,517
October 1984	25,090	8,893
November 1984	19,372	6,869
December 1984	5,270	2,236
Total 1984	$186,354	$68,225
January 1985	$ 21,786	$ 8,637
February 1985	18,247	6,928
March 1985	18,241	7,064
Total first quarter 1985	$ 58,274	$22,629

| Harry's Monthly Sales ($000) | | | | | Exhibit 20 |
Month	1981	1982	1983	1984	1985
January		42.0	42.5	34.0	40.0
February		34.0	30.0	35.0	34.0
March		31.5	32.5	38.0	34.0
April	25.0	33.0	34.0	41.0	
May	27.0	33.0	33.0	43.0	
June	21.0	22.0	19.0	23.0	
July	15.0	14.0	11.0	19.0	
August	15.0	16.0	14.0	20.5	
September	33.0	40.0	34.0	44.5	
October	37.0	48.0	41.0	46.0	
November	25.0	30.0	32.0	37.0	
December	18.0	16.0	15.0	13.0	
Average	21.0	29.9	28.0	32.8	

■ Advertising and Promotion

Harry's advertising and promotion was handled by Warner's wife, Beth. Because of its reputation for quality pizza, pizza was emphasized in advertising and promotions. Advertisements were placed in the University newspaper, *The Red and Black,* and other small circulars in Athens. These ads often included money-off coupons for pizza. Warner had also distributed fliers with pizza coupons throughout the UGA residence halls. Warner, however, was not sure if any of this advertising was effective.

In addition to advertising food items, Harry's offered drink specials for each night of the week except Sunday (alcohol sales were prohibited on Sundays). These specials were intended to attract students to Harry's on less popular nights such as Monday and Tuesday. For example, on Tuesday nights, Harry's offered tequila for $1.00 per shot and margaritas for $1.50.

Harry's offered a 15% group discount with the purchase of four or more pizzas, if 24-hour notice was given. Harry's also allowed a 10% discount for law and graduate students, and a 10% discount to all softball teams in uniform. This softball team discount was featured in an ad that the restaurant had run on local TV the previous summer.

■ Personnel

Harry's currently employed 22 people including Warner and his wife Beth, two managers, five waitresses, four bartenders, three cooks, two drivers, two doormen, and two cleanup people. Warner was the only full-time salaried employee. All employees were paid on an hourly basis. Managers earned $5.00 per hour, cooks were paid $3.75 per hour, and cleanup people made $3.35. The bartenders, doormen, and drivers made $3.35 plus tips. The food servers were paid $2.05 per hour plus tips. The number of employees fluctuated during the year according to sales volume. Less labor was required during the summer months than in the spring and fall.

Harry's suffered from high employee turnover. Warner had difficulty maintaining a stable work force for any period of time. Many students lasted only a few weeks, and even some of the more reliable students quit in December when final exams were being held. The average length of service for employees during 1984 was about six months. Warner felt the constant training of new personnel was costing the restaurant money, both in terms of actual training time and lost sales due to inexperienced serving personnel.

The problem was further complicated by the fact that Harry's busy season coincided with the time when the most new employees had to be trained. Students rarely returned to Harry's to work after the summer vacation, and therefore, Warner had to deal with the problems of large fall crowds and inexperienced employees at the same time. Football games were especially bad, because employees often did not show up for their assigned shifts, leaving the restaurant short-staffed during the busiest days of the year.

ALTERNATIVES FOR THE FUTURE

The increasing legal risks involved in operating a bar had prompted Warner to consider concentrating on food sales, even before the drinking age change was announced. Most of his experience was in the restaurant side of the business, and he admitted that he was more interested in the restaurant than the bar. He felt confident that Harry's had a good reputation for pizza, but he was unsure how to capitalize on this strength.

One idea Warner had considered was opening other Harry's stores. These other locations would be smaller, satellite stores with limited dining space and would be used primarily for takeout orders. In order to cut down on the expense of opening and operating the new locations, Warner had considered preparing the food at the current location and transporting it to the satellite operations. The food would be kept warm and reheated if necessary at the outlets. Warner recognized that preparing food at one location and transporting it to another might compromise the quality, but he felt future competition would be based more on speed of delivery than quality. Furthermore, this approach would eliminate the need for expensive cooking equipment in the new stores. The only equipment that would be required would be two or three food warmers and one or two microwave ovens. Warner was fairly sure he could obtain food warmers for about $600 each (half the price of a new food warmer) and microwaves for less than $350 apiece.

Warner had also considered renovating the upstairs bar and opening some other type of restaurant. A customer survey conducted the previous year by some UGA business students (see Exhibit 21) had indicated that an oyster bar would be popular, and there was only one other oyster bar in the area. An oyster bar would require the purchase of coolers, steamers, and shuckers. Warner figured that $5,000–$10,000 would cover all the equipment and the renovation costs. However, he was concerned that having an oyster bar upstairs might have a bad effect on pizza sales downstairs.

A third possibility that Warner had considered was to try to change Harry's current image as a student bar and attract the 21–30 crowd. Such customers would include Athens locals, professionals, UGA faculty, and graduate students. Warner knew that one reason why Harry's was popular with students

Customer Survey Results (N = 100)   Exhibit 21

Frequency	Food and Alcohol Consumption Away from Home		Most Liked Feature of Harry's	%
	% Eating Out	% Drinking Out		
Never	2	13	Atmosphere	47
Less than once per week	5	10	Food	44
Once per week	19	17	Drinks	9
Twice per week	29	27		
More than twice per week	45	33		

Age	Age Distribution		Favorite Restaurant/Bar	%
	Overall %	Bar Only %		
18	32	—	Bennigans	33
19	35	28	Harry's	17
20	19	27	Classics	14
21	5	27	Express	9
22–25	8	17	Maxwells	9
Over 25	1	1	Steverino's	3
			Other	15

Frequency	Frequency of Visits to Harry's		Preferred Renovation for Upstairs Bar	%
	Restaurant (%)	Bar (%)		
Never	32	42	Oyster Bar	46
Seldom	32	37	Wine & Cheese Shop	17
Once/Month	20	6	Deli	21
Twice/Month	11	9	Dessert Bar	10
Once/Week	3	1	Game Room	4
More than once/week	2	5	Dancing	1
			Wide Screen TV	1

was its high visibility and proximity to the campus. He knew he couldn't necessarily rely on his location if he was going after the older crowd, which would be spread out over the city. Some sort of extra advertising and promotion would likely be required.

Warner was aware that Harry's reputation as a student hangout had hurt his sales to local residents and that reacquiring their business would be difficult. On the other hand, Warner reasoned, his business might be better off in the long run catering to such customers. Furthermore, because area families had at one time accounted for a substantial proportion of Harry's food sales, Warner believed that changing the image of the bar might have a positive carryover effect on his food business.

Warner had also considered going after the local sports teams to increase his bar business. Summer sports, especially softball, were very popular in Athens, and many teams went to a bar to relax after the game. The people who played on these teams were generally in the 21–30 age range, and attracting their business would also help increase summer sales.

CONCLUSIONS

Steve Warner topped off the pitcher of beer and looked over at the table of students who had ordered it. None looked 21 to him. There was little question that something had to be done to change Harry's image and its customer base. Warner enjoyed living in Athens, and he had put a lot of effort into Harry's over the past four years. He still felt that Harry's could have a good future, and he resolved to come up with a plan to ensure it.

Doorstep Video, Inc.

John Dunkelberg, Wake Forest University; Robert Anderson, College of Charleston

BACKGROUND

The growth of the video and electronic industry had always interested twenty-one-year-old Clay Lindsay. Clay was more than one year away from finishing his education, and he planned to start and run his own business after graduation. He constantly thought about different business ventures which he felt could be profitable. He also wanted to start a business that had never been tried before. While on Christmas break, Clay came up with an idea for what he thought could be a very successful business venture—a video rental store that delivered movies, similar to the established pizza delivery service.

Clay discussed this idea with his parents and close friends. They criticized the concept and doubted that such a business could be profitable. Clay's father, who had owned and operated a drugstore in downtown Salisbury, North Carolina, for over thirty years, was one of those who doubted its profitability. He thought that Clay should finish his education before becoming involved in a new, time-consuming business venture. Clay, however, did find support from a couple of friends. One, Brent Snipes, whom Clay had known for about eight years, was very interested and recommended that they pursue the idea as a team. Brent would graduate from college that May, although Clay would not finish for another year.

Brent and Clay planned to start the business in June, with Brent controlling the everyday operations; Clay could come home when necessary since there was only a forty-five-minute drive between college and home.

Exhibit 1   **Doorstep Video's Logo**

"FROM OUR STORE TO YOUR DOOR"

■ Name and Logo

The two budding entrepreneurs immediately began to brainstorm for ideas on what to name the business, and Clay came up with the name Doorstep Video. After discussing other possibilities, they adopted Doorstep Video as a name that was easy to remember and one that conveyed the concept of what the business would be.

The next step, the design of a logo, took the two planners a little longer. They wanted a logo that would stick in the minds of their customers and one they would be proud to display. They decided that red and white would be the store colors as they felt these very dominant colors would demand attention. The design they finally adopted is shown in Exhibit 1. Brent and Clay felt details like this were necessary to project a professional image. In particular, Clay wanted this store to be an independent store that operated with the efficiency of a chain store.

■ Location

The next order of business was to determine where to locate the business. Brent and Clay had lived in Salisbury, North Carolina, all of their lives and felt that the contacts they had established in the area would be a major factor in the success of their planned business. Clay's father owned the building in the downtown shopping district which housed his drugstore. Clay was able to convince his father to rent them a small vacant space in the back of the store that was completely separate from the drugstore.

Brent and Clay knew that they must establish a basic plan of operation including name, location, and a business plan in order to gain the support of their parents. This would be a key to the success of their new business. After evaluating the preliminary steps the two had taken, Clay's parents seemed a little more positive about the idea than they had been at first. Brent's parents, however, remained very skeptical, and Brent decided not to pursue the business venture.

Clay, who strongly believed in the idea, continued to develop a business plan by learning more about the video industry. He conducted an extensive search of the existing literature using a computer data-based search program located at the college library. Although the number of existing articles on the videotape rental industry were few in number, Clay found several articles that gave him some ideas about the industry, the competition, and what the future might be like. A capsule summary and his findings indicated that the industry was passing from the pioneering stage into the fast-growth stage, and the future seemed to belong to the large, well-funded chain stores that would contain thousands of titles. In addition, he spent many hours visiting existing video stores to see what features they had that he liked.

About two months later, during his spring semester, Clay mentioned his idea to a fraternity brother, Garret Barnes, whom he had known for about two years. Garret thought the idea was worthwhile and something with which he would like to become associated with. Like Brent, Garret would graduate in May and would be able to begin work on a full-time basis. Clay had already developed a preliminary business plan that included an estimate of the start-up costs. These figures indicated that an investment of approximately $14,000 was required to open the doors. After talking with their parents, Garret and Clay decided to explore the business venture further.

■ The Entrepreneurs

Clay Lindsay, from Salisbury, North Carolina, was a business major at a nearby private university. He was active in his fraternity and had always been interested in assuming leadership positions. His goals were to be self-employed and to start a business that offered a better product and/or service than its competitors. He also wanted to establish a business that was interesting and that had the potential for rapid growth. Clay's business experience involved working at his father's retail drugstore and gift shop. He began janitorial work there when he was twelve. He was soon handling everyday functions such as personnel management, special promotions, the purchasing of imported goods, and advertising. Clay later managed a gift shop for his father during the Christmas season.

Garret Barnes, a twenty-two-year-old native of Florida, was active in the student legislature and intramurals, and he served in leadership positions within his fraternity. Garret's interests included competitive sports and other extracurricular activities. His goal was to start his own company which he could develop and nurture to a point that it would yield healthy returns for his future.

Prior to his involvement with Clay, Garret had no business experience; however, he was completing his Bachelor of Science degree in business. Garret thought this opportunity suited his needs perfectly and that it had the potential for a good career. He made friends easily and worked hard to make a good first impression on the people he met. In his fraternity, Garret was known as a hard worker and one who handled public relations very well.

■ Video Industry

During the latter part of the 1970s, videocassette recorders (VCRs) became popular. By the end of 1980, approximately 2 million homes had VCRs. At that time, the national sales rate of videocassette recorders was only 17,000 units per month, but by 1981, VCR sales rose to over 140,000 units per month. In 1984, nearly 7.5 million VCRs were sold, and by the end of that year VCRs were in 20 percent of the homes in America. By the end of 1987, 52 percent of American homes had at least one VCR.[1]

The rise in VCR sales was enhanced by an increase in the availability of prerecorded cassettes. In the late 1970s, the thought of selling prerecorded cassettes to consumers frightened the major movie and television studios in the United States. Many were afraid revenues from both television and movie theaters would be greatly decreased as viewers turned from movies and television to cassette tapes. However, a small number of studios decided to gamble on the idea of selling prerecorded cassettes to the home viewer. In the spring of 1978, there were only about 100 prerecorded cassettes available through studio distributors.

After some thorough market research, several other studios decided to enter the market. The market research indicated that consumers preferred renting prerecorded cassette tapes to buying by a margin of seven to one. At that time, cassette tapes sold for about $50 and rented for about $5 per day. Since then the cost of renting videotapes has dropped from $5 per day to as low as $1 per day. This, of course, was caused by the increased competition within the industry. On the other hand, the price of prerecorded cassettes has risen to as much as $70 and sometimes even higher for the biggest hits.

The home video market changed rapidly. Rental and sales outlets seemed to pop up in every shopping area. The industry enjoyed incredible growth over the next five years, but with growth came change. When home video first started, there were two formats available, beta and VHS. Beta and VHS competed with each other in software and hardware and neither was interchangeable with the other—a beta VCR could only show beta tapes and vice versa. However, over the past several years the VHS format became the dominant choice of consumers, and beta now accounts for only a small percentage of the market. At first, many video stores handled both the VHS and beta software; however, today it is almost impossible to find a beta rental store.

In 1983, 11 million prerecorded video cassettes were sold to retailers. By 1984 that number rose 100 percent to 22 million cassette tapes. As a result, rental stores can offer a large selection of titles. The smaller stores carry as few as 500 titles, while the superstores may have 10,000 or more titles for the consumer to select from. Today, the average video specialty store carries about 2600 different titles.[2]

The prerecorded cassettes are divided into two categories, A and B titles. The A titles are the "hit" videos and the most costly to produce. The B titles are those that are lesser known and are considered budget films. Examples of A titles would be *Top Gun* or *Fatal Attraction*; B titles would include *Creepozoids* or *The Curse*. Since the B titles were less expensive than the A titles, video rental stores did not have to rent them as often as the A titles to earn a profit. In the United States, the average number of rentals, per tape, for an A title was 108 and 62 rentals for B titles.

The videotape rental industry was one of the nation's fastest growing and one of the most fragmented. Nationwide there were over 25,000 video rental stores, mostly small entrepreneurial-type operations. In addition, there were about 32,000 rental outlets, such as convenience stores, that rented videotapes as a sidelight to their major business. These rental outlets usually carried only the newer movies, which they received three to four weeks after the release date, and stocked less than 250 titles.

As often happens in fast-growth industries, a shakeout seemed inevitable. Chain stores had started to exert pressure on the smaller, undercapitalized stores and the growth of the superstore chains, carrying more than 6500 titles, seemed to be just around the corner.[3]

BUSINESS PLAN

Clay and Garret planned to operate their business in the back of a warehouse owned by Clay's father. Since they planned to take telephone orders for rental tape deliveries, the only space requirement was space for the storage of tapes and enough room for the order taker and the driver. The existing warehouse area would require the construction of some walls to create a separate area for Doorstep Video's operations. (For the store layout, see Exhibit 2.) The rental business would operate much like a pizza delivery service with customers calling and placing orders for videotapes which would be delivered in thirty minutes or less. The planned hours of operation were Monday through Friday from 4 P.M. until 12 A.M., and Saturday and Sunday from 12 noon until 12 midnight.

Clay and Garret also planned to deliver popcorn and cokes along with the videos to allow customers to receive some of the full effects of a movie theater without leaving their homes. Videos would be returned by the customer to one of four return boxes positioned strategically throughout the town. The videos would be delivered by part-time drivers who could make approximately seven deliveries per hour. Drivers, students from a local small private college, would be paid the minimum wage of $3.35 per hour plus an incentive rate of 40 cents per delivery. Clay and Garret thought that by delivering the videos, the possibility for theft should decrease since they would actually know the customers' correct address.

Although they did not attempt any marketing research, Clay and Garret saw the potential for rapid growth in rental videotape delivery. Their goal was to test the concept in Salisbury, and if successful, expand to locations in other rel-

---

Doorstep Video's Floor Plan   **Exhibit 2**

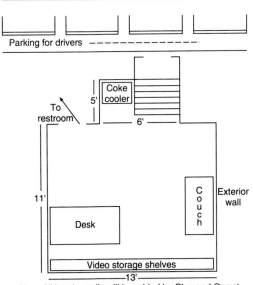

Note: All interior walls will be added by Clay and Garret to minimize cost. Total cost of the project will be $400.

atively small cities. The reason for operating in small cities was that major chains only located in larger cities, and Doorstep Video could gain strength in the video industry through growth in the less competitive markets.

■ Salisbury's Video Market

Salisbury, a small city located in the center of North Carolina, had a population of about 25,000. Doorstep Video's delivery area included the city and a few areas outside the city, with a total market of about 28,000 people. The per capita income in this area was approximately $10,000, while the average total house-hold income was $28,000. Currently there were 14 video rental stores in Salis-bury and an additional 14 convenience stores and other outlets that rented a small selection of videos. No major video chains had located in Salisbury.

■ Purchasing

A major factor to consider in any business is where to obtain merchandise. Since he was interested in buying used as well as new videocassettes, Clay contacted several sources across the country. One source, International Movie Merchants (IMM) in Dallas, Oregon, was a used-video distributor, and it agreed to supply Doorstep Video. IMM sent Clay a list of 500 used videos that would be available and suitable to the needs of Doorstep Video. IMM quoted a price of $13,000 for the 500 videos for an average cost of $26. After several changes, the list was approved. According to Clay, "You never settle for paying what the seller is asking;" therefore, the bargaining process began. After a short time the cost was finally agreed upon and set at $20.30 per video.

Doorstep Video also needed a source for new releases. Baker and Taylor Video, a major nationwide distributor, soon became that source. Baker and Tay-lor provided weekly catalogs which included all the new releases scheduled for the next several weeks. The average cost of a new release was $65.00 plus ship-ping, which usually added another $3.00. Garret later found another source, Schwartz Brothers, which offered savings of $1 to $2 per video, but shipping costs remained approximately $3.00. Schwartz Brothers also offered weekly cat-alogs which included all new releases and some special deals.

A key to buying new releases is knowing how many of each title to purchase. Garret took on this task, which included a lot of guesswork. He could only base purchases on how similar titles had sold in the past and how popular the title had been in the theater. Interestingly, Garret's research indicated that what was popular in the theater was not always popular in video. On the other hand, some titles that were sleepers in the theater were in high demand in the rental stores. There seemed to be no real formula to use when buying new releases. However, there is a lot of gut feeling involved in the selection process. Doorstep Video set its new-release budget at $1500 per month. Since there are no returns on opened merchandise, if Doorstep Video bought too many of a new release, they could only sell the used video to a used-video distributor like IMM. Unfor-tunately, these distributors purchase the video for about one-third of its original cost.

Doorstep Video also needed a source for the purchase of VCRs suitable for renting and the plastic cases which were needed as protective carrying cases for the videos. Commtron, a major distributor in Atlanta, was contacted, and they offered to sell Doorstep Videos the rental-type VCRs for $239 each. The plastic cases could be purchased at prices that ranged from $0.49 to $0.55 each, depending on the quantity ordered.

■ Inventory System

The inventory system used by Doorstep Video would be an index card system. Each video would have a card which would be placed in the out file when the movie was rented. The customer's number would be written on the card as well as the date rented. This was not the most advanced or efficient system; however, due to lack of funds, a computer system seemed out of the question.

As should be expected in a new-technology-oriented industry, several very complete computer software inventory programs were available for video rental stores. Interestingly, one of the best in the nation was produced and sold by a firm located in Salisbury. These systems are capable of handling 40,000 members and 100,000 videos. All transactions are handled by a bar code reader which makes the system efficient and accurate. The systems created statistics such as customers with debit balances; rentals per day, month, and year; rentals by customer; rentals per title; and many other management features. The cost for a system, including the computer and printer, was about $5500.

■ Financing, Legal, and Insurance

The total start-up cost for Doorstep Video was estimated to be about $15,500 (see Exhibit 3). Based on an estimate of daily rentals, Clay and Garret estimated weekly rentals of 513 titles over the first three months (see Exhibit 4). Rental price was $2.99 for one title and $2.50 each for two or more titles. Based on what they had observed in other stores and from what they had read in *Video Store*, a trade magazine, Clay estimated that the revenue from the average rental would be $2.63. In addition, they estimated that they could rent the VCRs on an aver-

---

Doorstep Video: Start-up Costs   **Exhibit 3**

Inventory	
500 used videos	$10,150
New videos	1,500
Rental VCRs, 2 @ $239	478
Opening advertising	
Flyer insert	$450
Printing	416
Newspaper ads	198
Furniture and equipment	900
Leasehold improvements	400
Return boxes, 4 @ $50	200
Insurance	300
Shirts for employees	170
Telephone installation	95
Office supplies	60
Plastic cases for videotapes	73
Licenses	60
Legal and professional	49
Total startup costs	$15,499

Exhibit 4   **Average Projected Video Rentals per Day**

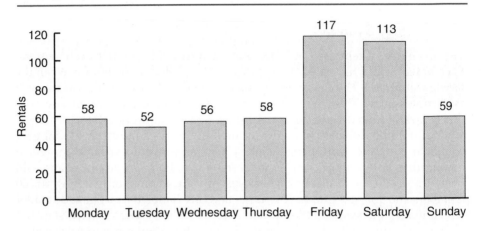

age of seven times per week at $5 per day. Monthly expenses were estimated to be $3635 (see Exhibit 5). During the first year of operation, Garret, who would be managing the store, would receive $700 a month salary and Clay, who would only work part-time, would not receive any compensation. Any profits would be used to purchase additional inventory. To finance the start-up and leave funds available to cover any possible cash flow problems over the start-up period, Clay and Garret each agreed to put up $10,400 from their personal savings.

Due to the potential liability problem, Clay and Garret thought they should organize Doorstep Video as an S corporation. This form of business allows small businesses to enjoy the limited liability benefits of the corporate form of organization yet obtain the benefits of being taxed as a partnership. They talked to an attorney, who agreed to handle the necessary incorporation paperwork for $49. In addition, a membership application form was designed to provide a measure of protection for Doorstep Video and serve as a contract between Doorstep and its customers (see Exhibit 6).

Clay talked to a local insurance agent about the coverage that would be needed by Doorstep Video. The agent recommended a comprehensive policy that would cover the contents of the store in the amount of $30,000 in case of

Exhibit 5   **Projected Monthly Expenses**

Videos	$1500
Gross payroll	1100
Advertising	300
Taxes	370
Telephone	115
Rent and Utilities	100
Miscellaneous expenses	120
Insurance	30
Total projected monthly expenses	$3,635

Membership Application Form **Exhibit 6**

"FROM OUR STORE TO YOUR DOOR"

Membership Application

Member # _____

Last Name _____ First Name _____ NCDL # _____

Address _____ City _____

Home
Phone _____

Relative
Phone _____

Relative
Name _____

Employer _____ Dept. _____

Work Phone _____ SS # _____

Remarks: _____

I, the undersigned, do hereby accept the videotape(s) and/or equipment for the purpose of previewing same in my home, and acknowledge that they are in good working condition, and agree to pay a stipulated handling charge therefore, and to take care of all said tapes and/or equipment and to use them in a proper manner and agree that in the event any of the tapes and/or equipment are lost, destroyed, or stolen before they are returned, to promptly pay the full cash value of such value, in cash and if damaged or injured in any way to pay an amount equal to the reasonable cost of repairing the same, and further do hereby exonerate, indemnify, and save harmless the company from all claims or liabilities to all parties for damage or loss to any person, persons, or property in any way arising out of or during the use of said videotape(s) and/or equipment. I, the under-signed, further understand that this agreement is binding for all videotape(s) and/or equipment rented during the duration of my membership.

It is understood that *federal law prohibits the reproduction of all copyrighted videotapes.*

Signed _____ Date _____

fire or water damage. Theft insurance was not included. In addition, the drivers were covered by a rider which provided Doorstep Video with liability insurance for any claim that was in excess of the liability coverage from the driver's own insurance—since the drivers would use their own cars for deliveries.

DECISION TIME

During the last week in April, with the spring semester almost complete, Clay and Garret had to decide whether to go ahead with the start-up of Doorstep Video or abandon their plans. They contacted students at a local college and found several willing to work part-time. In addition, the local telephone company agreed to give them a local number that helped describe the purpose of their business—636 = FAST.

They both felt that the idea of home delivery of rental videos was a good one and one that could be built into a profitable business. Clay, however, has one more year of college before joining the business full-time. To further complicate the decision, Garret received a job offer in sales with a nationally known firm. They agreed that a decision must be made no later than the first week in May.

REFERENCES

1. Subrata Chakravarty, "Give 'em Variety," *Forbes,* May 2, 1988, pp. 54–57.

2. "Video Marketing" published by *Video Store,* Hollywood, Calif., 1987.

3. Ron Stodghill, "Will Video Chains Push Small Stores Out of the Picture?" *The Charlotte Observer,* February 15, 1988, pp. 1, 13c.

31
CASE

Shades of Black, Inc.

Lester A. Neidell, University of Tulsa

Alex Corbbrey cleared space on his desk to study the initial fiscal year financial results of Shades of Black, Inc., a company whose primary mission is to produce greeting cards and social expression items for black consumers in the United States. In 1987, operating as an unincorporated sole proprietorship, sales of 15,239 cards ($9640) were achieved. In 1988, the first year of incorporation, 28,188 cards were sold, and revenues reached $42,396 for all product lines.

Alex had high expectations for his product line and was somewhat disappointed in the 1988 results. The Shades of Black retail store was located in the Greenwood shopping area, a renovated and attractive, predominantly black business district adjacent to the Tulsa, Oklahoma, downtown business zone. Even though he personally, and Shades of Black as a business, had received good publicity in the local media, it just didn't seem that the black population of Tulsa was large enough to support the retail store he envisioned. In particular, Alex contrasted the limited and somewhat depressed black community in Tulsa with the vibrant one he had recently visited in Atlanta, Georgia. This visit to Atlanta made him wonder if perhaps a location other than Tulsa would better fit with Shades of Black's needs.

But his first concern was development of a product line strategy for his young company.

THE PRODUCT/MARKET DILEMMA

It was unseasonably warm in Tulsa for a February. Alex had to force himself to study the "financials" (which are contained in Exhibits 1 and 2); his mind was

Exhibit 1

Shades of Black: Income Statements

	Year Ending	
	12/31/87	12/31/88
Sales	$ 9,640	$42,396*
Cost of goods sold	8,337	20,224
Gross margin	1,303	22,172
Expenses		
Rent and utilities	4258	5696
Travel	2682	4863
Advertising	1590	204
Auto expense	209	277
Taxes and license	2155	20
Maintenance	701	109
Meetings	191	348
Professional services	6324	2000
Office	655	1235
Interest	426	2232
Freight and postage	546	0
Dues and subscriptions	150	101
Miscellaneous	421	294
Depreciation	1440	2606
Insurance	306	692
Donations	0	115
Trade shows	0	4790
Wages	0	50
Telephone	0	2453
Total expenses	$ 22,054	$28,085
Net income (loss)	$(20,751)	$ (5,913)

*Distribution of sales by product category: cards—distributors, 68.9%; cards—retail, 7.1%; art, 3.3%; clothing, 20.8%.

brimming with ways to expand his business. He and his small staff had discussed four options for the 1989–1991 period.

- *Option 1: Expand retail coverage.* The greeting cards produced by Shades of Black currently are sold only in a limited number of black-owned shops in a few scattered cities in the United States. Chain drugstores, discount stores, and supermarkets combined have the greatest market share and are also the most rapidly growing retail outlets in the United States for greeting cards. None of these retailers were carrying any Shades of Black product. Sales expansion could thus be achieved by expanding market coverage in the U.S. retail market.
- *Option 2: Military market.* A possible untapped market is the American military. An estimated 594,000 black Americans serve in the armed forces. Many are away from family and friends for extended periods, which would seem to auger well for a company whose principal products are designed to communicate to loved ones.
- *Option 3: Black colleges.* Another market segment contains primarily black colleges and universities. Over 100 predominantly black colleges and universities exist in the United States, with a student body in excess of

Shades of Black: Balance Sheets   **Exhibit 2**

	Year Ending	
Assets	12/31/87	12/31/88
Current assets		
Cash	$ 305	$ 145
Accounts receivable	1,797	7,956
Accounts receivable—employees	0	14,029
Inventory	3,883	17,060
Total current assets	5,985	39,190
Fixed assets		
Equipment	20,149	16,751
Furniture and fixtures	0	3,477
Leasehold improvements	0	754
Less: accumulated depreciation	−1,440	−4,045
Total fixed assets	18,709	16,937
Other assets		
Deposits	610	660
Total other assets	610	660
Total assets	$25,304	$56,787
Liabilities and Owner Equity		
Liabilities		
Accounts payable	8,327	11,156
Sales tax payable	0	572
Notes payable	16,190	0
Note payable—TEDC	0	14,000
Note payable—Phippe	0	10,000
Note payable—Alex	0	4,692
Note payable—Jackson	0	1,000
Total liabilities	24,517	41,420
Equity		
Owner's draws	−5,043	0
Equity	24,543	0
Capital stock	0	4,686
Paid-in capital	0	16,595
Current earnings	−18,713	−5,914
Total equity	787	15,367
Total liabilities and equity	$25,304	$56,787

173,000. Both campus bookstores and alumni could be reached. For example, it might be possible to "customize" greeting cards for alumni associations to use as fund raisers. One such "package" is currently being designed for Morehouse College, in Atlanta, Georgia.

- *Option 4: Funeral homes.* Finally, the product line could be expanded even further in order to reach black-owned, or black-community-served, funeral homes. A mailing list of 12,348 black-owned funeral homes was available. This did not include those funeral parlors that serviced the black community but were not black-owned.

Alex knew he had to act quickly. The Christmas season, during which approximately 31 percent of all greeting cards were sold, had a design lead time of four to six months. And any market expansion would also require some new designs, although degree and type would vary according to which of the four markets he directed his company's efforts. Also, there was increasing interest on the part of both major and minor competitors in segmenting the greeting card industry. At the moment, no strong national competition existed for black-oriented greeting cards, but a flurry of recent news articles about the segment seemed to indicate that this would not be true for very much longer.

THE GREETING CARDS INDUSTRY IN THE UNITED STATES

Written greeting messages originated in ancient Egypt, following the discovery of papyrus and the development of hieroglyphics and inks. "Standardized" greetings probably stem from the time of Christ and the pen of Paul. Paul began his letters with "Grace to you and peace." During the Dark Ages of Europe, when chivalry reigned, letters and messages of good cheer were widely exchanged. Thoughts were conveyed not only by written expression but by symbols such as a handkerchief or knot of ribbon. These more durable message forms were hurled over the walls of besieged castles or through windows to gain entrance.* Today, retail greeting card stores in the United States also sell more permanent remembrances.

Greeting cards are more than pretty designs, pictures, or messages of greeting. They mirror the expressions and personalities of their senders. About 7 billion greeting cards of all types were purchased in the United States in 1988, with retail sales exceeding $9 billion. Industry data at the manufacturers' level for the period 1984–1988 are contained in Exhibit 3. Real growth is expected to be approximately 3 to 4 percent through 1992, but it could increase dramatically as baby boomers age. Market studies have shown that the heavy purchasers of greeting cards and related products and services are women in the 35–54 age group. Retail prices of greeting cards range from $0.35 to $7.50. The high price is for a sophisticated "musical" card; more typically, adult consumers pay between $1.00 and $1.25 per card purchase.

Greeting cards sales have been highly seasonal. About 31 percent of all cards are sold in the Christmas season, while Valentine's Day cards add 12 percent of sales. Other seasonal "holidays" (Easter, Mother's Day, Halloween, etc.) each

---

Exhibit 3   **Greeting Card Publishing Industry Data (in millions of dollars)**

Item	1984	1985	1986	1987	1988
Value of all products and services sold by the greeting card publishing industry	2394	2588	2793	3022	3294
Value of above (1982$)	2276	2843	2532	2596	2674
Value of products sold by the greeting card publishing industry	1679	1809	1948	2112	2306
Value of imports	14	15	19	23	27

Source: U.S. Department of Commerce, Bureau of the Census, Bureau of Economic Analysis

---

*Earnest D. Chase, *The Romance of Greeting Cards,* (University Press of Cambridge, 1956).

Greeting Cards Sales by Card Category, 1987 — Exhibit 4

Seasonal Sales	Percent	Nonseasonal Sales	Percent
Christmas	31.5	Birthday	22.9
Valentine's Day	12.2	Alternative and/or nonoccasion (not in sales order: birth, wedding, sympathy, retirement, congratulations, new home, friendship, love)	24.3
Easter	2.6		
Mother's Day	2.1		
Father's Day	1.3		
Graduation	1.2		
All other seasonal (decreasing sales order: Thanksgiving, Halloween, St. Patrick's Day, Jewish New Year, Hanukkah, New Year's, Grandparent's Day, Sweetest Day, Secretary's Day, National Bosses' Day, Mother-in-Law Day, April Fool's Day)	1.8		

Source: Data from Greeting Card Association, Washington, D.C.

contribute less than 3 percent. Nonseasonal sales are primarily birthday cards, with almost a 23 percent market share. The distribution of 1987 sales by card category is shown in Exhibit 4.

Nonoccasion or "alternative" cards are becoming more popular.* These products often have blank interiors, to allow the sender to write personal sentiments. Hallmark Cards, Inc., the overall market share leader, recently innovated a product line targeted for parents to send to their children simply to express caring. Hallmark's advertisements for these particular alternative cards depict children discovering the cards in their lunch boxes and textbooks. This approach by Hallmark also bypasses one of the problems the industry has encountered. Postal rate increases negatively impact the sales of cards. While actual cross-elasticity indices are not available, increases in postage have in the past most affected Christmas and other holiday cards. Alternative card sales, however, seem to have been least affected by postage changes.

Although the possibility of more rapid sales growth exists as baby boomers age, the general consensus is that the greeting cards industry is mature. Historically, major competitors created demand by capitalizing on "self-promoted" holidays, such as Bosses' Day, Secretary's Day, and Grandparents' Day. For these occasions, the suppliers, led by Hallmark, created designs and promoted as if everyone knew of the holiday, which were typically joint creations of the

*The term *alternative card* has had varied meanings in the greeting card industry. Originally this phrase was applied to cards that were not supplied by the three major competitors. These cards were often of an innovative design, although aimed at the standard seasons. When these nonstandard designs proved popular with consumers, Hallmark and the other national producers began to produce alternative designs for the standard seasons. Today, nontraditional seasonal cards are commonplace, with the result that the term *alternative* seems to be principally a synonym for nonoccasion cards.

florists, the greeting card industry, and organizations such as the National Secretary's Association. But the public seems to have become sated with these "events."

General consensus in the industry is that the cards themselves are the best promotional vehicle and that advertising tends to stimulate industrywide sales rather than promote brand loyalty. Nevertheless, Hallmark and American Greetings each spend about $60 million annually on advertising.

■ The Black or Afro-American Segment

As competition increased and market growth slowed, product strategies of the "majors" began to emphasize segmentation. Social expression merchandise targeted at minorities is being offered to those traditional outlets that have minority bases from which to draw. A black American, or other minority, has had a difficult time choosing a greeting card, or other social expression merchandise, suitable to his or her particular culture. The black population of the United States numbers about 12 percent of the total and by 2080 is expected to account for almost one in five Americans. In terms of retail greeting cards receipts, blacks, in 1986, spent about $360,000,000. By 1988, Afro-Americans' expenditures on greeting cards and other social awareness merchandise approached $600,000,000.

In 1986, 64 percent of the black population was under the age of 35, while 27 percent of all blacks were under 15 years of age. Thus, a large number of blacks will shortly enter the prime card-buying years of 35 to 54. In general, black buying patterns differ somewhat from those of white Americans. Blacks tend to be more brand-loyal and often prefer to patronize black-owned businesses. Blacks tend to make less than whites in comparable jobs and have lower savings rates than whites. However, there are a growing number of "Buppies" (Black Urban Professionals). Career patterns of Buppies mirror those of Yuppies, with increased mobility and the increased need to communicate with family and friends left behind.

■ Industry Competition

Exhibit 5 illustrates greeting cards market shares. Three competitors, Hallmark Cards, American Greetings, and Gibson Greetings, control 87 percent of the market. As many as 500 publishers vie for the remainder.

Each of the three "majors" has a unique strategy.

• *Hallmark Cards, Inc.,* privately owned, distributes its products principally through 22,000 specialty retail outlets, all of which are privately owned except for about 300 company-owned stores. Hallmark also uses selected department stores for distribution. Hallmark is a fully integrated producer and is reputed to have the most efficient production facilities. Hallmark's strengths are its size and financial strength, its efficient distribution system,

Exhibit 5   Competitive Market Shares, 1987

Hallmark	40%	Gibson Greetings	12%
American Greetings	35%	All others	13%

its quality image and "recognition" factor, and its licensed characters—Shirt Tale line, Rose Petal Place, Huga Bunch, and Rainbow Bright.

Hallmark's unique distribution is also a potential weakness. Recent studies show that mass merchandisers and chain food stores and drugstores now account for about 53 percent of retail greeting card sales. This trend is expected to continue, given the societal changes of single-parent families, dual-career families, and the popularity of one-stop shopping. Another potential weakness has been the inability to produce in-house an authentic ethnic greeting card, although it obviously has the financial capacity to acquire this capability.

Hallmark's principal approach to serving the ethnic market segments has been via a "Minority Vendor Resource List," which is provided to its stores. These are vendors who have met certain minimum quality standards. Shades of Black has submitted several designs to Hallmark for evaluation. Hallmark's reaction so far has been that Shades of Black's designs have a nice style; several have been picked for a test market which has not yet been completed. Concerns expressed by Hallmark about Shades of Black are of two types. First, Hallmark is hesitant to include Shades of Black on the vendor list because of its uncertainty about the company's ability to service any quantity of orders. Second, while acknowledging that Shades of Black's designs are of high quality for a company of its size, they are not yet at a level which Hallmark sets for products included on its vendor lists.

• *American Greetings Corporation* is the world's largest publicly owned manufacturer of greeting cards and social expression merchandise. Since 1975, American Greetings has been an aggressive competitor, with a marketing strategy designed to outflank Hallmark. Its primary weapon has been inexpensive cards distributed through mass merchandise outlets. American Greetings cards are carried by more than 90,000 retailers worldwide. Thirty-five percent of their sales are through drugstores and, in decreasing order of importance, mass merchandisers, supermarkets, stationery and gift shops, military post exchanges, and department stores. American Greetings initiated the practice of developing licensed characters. Its characters include Holly Hobbie, Ziggy, Strawberry Shortcake, and Care Bears.

• *Gibson Greetings, Inc.,* is the fastest growing of the three major competitors, although quite obviously its base is much smaller. Its principal distribution channels are (in decreasing order of importance) mass merchandisers, drugstores, and supermarkets. Gibson has also been very aggressive in licensing characters. The company has exclusive rights to the Walt Disney characters and also has licensed Garfield,* the Sesame Street characters, and the Looney Tunes and D.C. Comics comic book creations. Gibson has also moved aggressively into the ethnic market with licensing arrangements. One result has been a line of cards directed towards the black market, licensed from Cousin Mattie's Daddy's Sister's People of Oakland, California. Cousin Mattie's cards feature "soft sculpture characters" of black folksy people set in humorous domestic scenes of yesteryear. Begun in 1984, Cousin Mattie's was distributed in about 350 retail outlets prior to its agreement with Gibson. Gibson is expected to distribute Cousin Mattie cards in more than 1200 of its regular outlets.

---

*Beginning January 1989 Hallmark became the Garfield licensee. Major in-store promotions were planned around the Garfield character.

An important competitor in the black market is L'Image Graphics, Inc., of Culver City, California. This six-year-old, privately held company's investors include Sidney Poitier and also Don Clark and Barry Gordy of Motown Records. As of July 1988, L'Image cards were carried in 1500 retail outlets in the United States, Canada, Puerto Rico, and England. About 50 sales representatives carry their line in the United States. L'Image has over 225 designs, generally of a "fantasy-oriented" contemporary design. Originally sold in exclusive, top-of-the-line department stores, with a clientele over 90 percent white, L'Image created "crossover" designs using tan (rather than white or black) characters. This middle-of-the-road approach created a company whose sales doubled each of the last four years.

Over 20 black-owned and -operated greeting card companies are reputed to exist in the United States. These are all small, are regional in scope, and currently lack financial and production resources to be major players in the market for black customers.

HISTORY AND OPERATIONS OF SHADES OF BLACK

In late 1986, Alex Corbbrey sketched a black Santa Claus and one other greeting card, which he then had printed and distributed to a few friends. Soon afterwards, inquiries were received about the possibility of purchasing these cards. During this first Christmas season over 4000 cards were sold. Alex Corbbrey has had a varied and rich background, as his artist's vita (Exhibit 6) illustrates. During his five years of employment by I. Magnin, Alex managed the Sherman Oaks, California, store, with 15 employees. His duties included daily store management, public relations, headquarters coordination, and budgeting and cost control. Shades of Black is located in Tulsa, Oklahoma, with a small retail store and headquarters (total 718 square feet) in one building and a moderate amount of warehouse space in another facility. In addition to the founder, Shades of Black employs two full-time and one part-time person. Important professional and managerial input is provided by the Board of Directors, including legal and accounting help.

■ Marketing Mix: Product

All designs produced so far have been the inspiration of the founder, although several have been "farmed out" to contract artists for completion after initial sketches were completed. Five contract artists are now working on new designs. Shades of Black currently produces 27 copyrighted designs, equally divided between seasonal and alternative cards. One of its best-selling cards has been one that celebrates *Kwanza*, an African harvest festival that occurs near the Christmas season. Kwanza card sales were concentrated on the East Coast; the celebration is largely unknown in many other American cities with large black populations.

Production is provided by four different printers in Oklahoma and Kansas. Only fine linen paper is used, and the print quality is excellent. As an artist, Alex Corbbrey prides himself on the quality of product produced by Shades of Black.

Other items sold by Shades of Black in 1988 included original artwork, framed copies of the cards, and apparel.

Mr. Alex A. Corbbrey, founder of Shades of Black, Inc., took his formal training in art at Oklahoma State University at Stillwater and Chinourd Art Institute in Los Angeles, California.

Upon completing his academic training, Mr. Corbbrey, seeking employment as an Illustrator with I. Magnin's, an exclusive department store in the Los Angeles area, found himself instead working as a Buyer Trainee in retail. Having had virtually no college experience in marketing, Mr. Corbbrey returned to college, studying retail marketing, accounting, statistics, and business law.

During his five years with I. Magnin's, three years as Assistant Buyer and two years as Buyer for the Southern District, which included seven stores throughout Southern California, Mr. Corbbrey decided to also apply his marketing experience to the business of Art.

Realism, expressed through such mediums as oils, watercolors, acrylics, pastels, and pen and inks were the focus of his creative interest during this period. His work drew wide attention from many people, some of whom had become his personal customers at I. Magnin's, in the entertainment industry. During the years 1966–1968, he was exhibited in private showings throughout Southern California. In 1973, Mr. Corbbrey was commissioned to do several portraits of prominent citizens in the Los Angeles area, including Mayor Thomas Bradley.

After much success in the more traditional media, Mr. Corbbrey became fascinated with the possibilities of engraving. He experimented with many different types of materials, finally narrowing his efforts to wood and Plexiglass. The detail expressed in his wood and drypoint engravings has attracted the attention of collectors across the United States. One of his limited-edition prints entitled "Call to Arms" hangs in the White House. He has displayed his work in such respected galleries as Jim Settle's Art Galleries in Southern California and Scottsdale, Arizona; Variations of Palm Springs; L'Academie, Southern Cost Village, Costa Mesa, California; Old House Gallery, Orange, California; and several other galleries throughout the greater Southwest.

Since returning to Tulsa, Oklahoma, in 1978, Mr. Corbbrey has added to his fine list of credits such galleries as Fields Art Gallery, The Art Market, Up Against the Wall Graphics, and Accessory Street Gallery, Houston, Texas. His wildlife studies won him a first-place Blue Ribbon in the 1978 Ducks Unlimited Art Show in Tulsa. However, his study of the late Mrs. Freddie Martin Rudisill, on display at the Rudisill North Regional Library, is one of his proudest achievements. An 8′ × 10′ sculpting by Mr. Corbbrey is also prominently displayed at Westview Medical Clinic of Tulsa, Oklahoma.

With such an impressive list of collectors as Dick Van Dyke, actor and producer; H. B. "Toby" Haliciki, director, producer, and star of "Gone in Sixty Seconds"; Greg Morris of "Mission Impossible" and "Vegas" fame; Stevie Wonder, Diana Ross, and Nancy Laviska of Motown Recording Industries; Tulsa is proud to call Alex A. Corbbrey a native son.

■ Marketing Mix: Distribution

Shades of Black uses independent distributors to service its markets. Distributorships were originally sold by Alex at the fall 1987 National Black Caucus, held in Washington, D.C. Despite having a display of only seven designs, three distributorships were sold at that time. Distributorships cost $125, which included up to $75 of product. Through fiscal 1988, 35 distributorships have been sold. A list of distributorships and their sales activity is shown in Exhibit 7. Distributorships are no longer being offered as Shades of Black reevaluates its distribution policies. However, all current distributorship agreements will be honored.

■ Marketing Mix: Price

The trade discount given by Shades of Black to its current distributors is two-thirds (66.7 percent). Thus, for a $1.25 retail card, Shades of Black receives $0.42. Product is shipped UPS COD. Sales to nonprofit organizations are conducted at a 50 percent discount from suggested retail price. The package of cards and stationery for Morehouse College will be sold for $4.20 and carries a "list price"

Exhibit 7   **Unit Sales by Distributor**

Name	Location	Date Registered	Sales 1987	1988
Age	Missouri City, Texas	11/87	580	1,480
Atkins	Ferndale, Michigan	11/87	1,980	0
Allen	Shawnee, Oklahoma	11/88	—	170
Burk	Broken Arrow, Oklahoma	02/88	—	430
Colbert	College Park, Georgia	10/87	970	0
Cassett	Somerset, New Jersey	09/88	—	0
Copeland	Hyattsville, Maryland	09/87	4,435	9,530
Curry	Tulsa, Oklahoma	12/87	0	525
Davis	Birmingham, Alabama	12/87	0	0
Evans	Tulsa, Oklahoma	02/88	—	320
Exciting Cards	Ft. Lauderdale, Florida	10/87	500	0
Floral Creat	Omaha, Nebraska	11/88	—	170
Francis	Jacksonville, Florida	11/88	—	0
Ford	Tulsa, Oklahoma	11/87	1,800	200*
GSD Distributor	Cushing, Oklahoma	03/87	600	0
Hall	Morene Valley, California	09/88	—	1,422*
Holman	Tulsa, Oklahoma	12/87	60	0
Harriott	Huntsville, South Carolina	08/87	300	0
Joshua Enterprise	Nashville, Tennessee	09/88	—	750*
J&L Enterprise	Tulsa, Oklahoma	03/88	—	0†
Johnson, A.	E. Elmhurst, New York	12/87	664	2,470
Johnson, E.	Tulsa, Oklahoma	02/88	—	0
LaCour	Tulsa, Oklahoma	03/87	260	0
Marshall	Austin, Texas	09/87	300	0
Martin	Philadelphia, Pennsylvania	09/88	—	4,960*
Mayo	Chicago, Illinois	10/87	360	0
Morans	Houston, Texas	10/88	—	480*
Perkins	Baton Rouge, Louisiana	10/87	300	0
RLWD Distributor	Dallas, Texas	10/88	—	370
Smith	Chicago, Illinois	10/88	—	750
Simmons	Severna Park, Maryland	10/87	1,570	980
SB Marketing	Tulsa, Oklahoma	09/88	—	774
Unique Collection	Wheaton, Illinois	11/88	—	112*
Weathers	Kansas City, Missouri	10/88	—	1,180
Washington	Cushing, Oklahoma	11/87	560	1,115
Total units sold			15,239	28,188

*Purchased apparel.

†Purchased letterhead.

of $20.00. The package price to funeral homes is $13.95 per unit. All prices to organizations are FOB Tulsa. Shipments under 70 pounds go UPS unless the customer specifies otherwise. Orders exceeding the UPS weight limit are shipped by truck.

Currently, Shades of Black's average manufacturing cost of an existing black and white card is $0.07. Economies of scale are important in the industry. Hallmark probably produces the typical $1.25 retail card for $0.03. New designs are expensive. For Shades of Black, an initial production run of 5000 units for a new design will cost $0.35 per unit, which includes all initial setup costs.

■ Marketing Mix: Communication

Other than attendance at several trade shows, Shades of Black, Inc., has generated little in the way of paid communication activities. Publicity has been received in Tulsa and Oklahoma newspapers, and Sylvia Porter plans a feature in a forthcoming issue of her national publication, *Personal Finance*.

PRODUCT/MARKET EXPANSION OPPORTUNITIES

■ Enhanced Distribution

Primary targets are food and drug chains in the more heavily populated black cities and states. Contacts have already been made with the Food Lion chain (North and South Carolina and Virginia), Tom Thumb stores, Homeland supermarkets (Oklahoma), Giant Food Stores, Kroger, and Peoples' Drug Stores. As an example of requirements for these outlets, Food Lion requires a one-time "slotting fee" of $240 per card rack, which will initially be stocked with 1008 cards, 84 seasonal and alternative designs. Smaller aisle-end and counter display racks are also possibilities. Production costs for the racks range from $20 to $300 apiece; slotting fees for aisle-end and counter displays are negotiable. Based on talks with chain drug and supermarket executives, it seems reasonable to Alex that Shades of Black could have access to 325 stores by the Christmas season 1989. The number of supermarkets and drugstores carrying Shades of Black cards would then be expected to double in 1990 and to increase another 10 percent in the third year of this market expansion strategy.

■ The Military Market

Black men and women comprise over 27 percent of the armed forces. Distribution by service is shown in Exhibit 8. While blacks account for 12 percent of the U.S. population, only 8.8 percent of the American college population is black, and the number of black high school graduates continuing on to college is actually decreasing. Thus, black enlistment in the military is expected to continue to be high. If black military personnel would purchase cards at the national "average" rate of approximately 35 cards per year, military sales would exceed 40 million units. The Army and Air Force Exchange Service (AAFES) operates nearly 6000 retail facilities on military installations worldwide, with annual 1986 sales exceeding $6.2 billion. The AAFES buys goods and services from

---

Blacks in the Armed Forces, 1987　　　　　　　　　　　　　　　　　**Exhibit 8**

Branch of Service	Total Active Duty	Number of Blacks
Army	781,000	305,698
Air Force	608,000	132,388
Navy	581,000	104,804
Marines	199,000	51,876

Source: Statistical Abstract of the United States, 1987.

about 40,000 U.S. producers, 88 percent of which are classified as small businesses. Card racks available in AAFES facilities are identical to those in the U.S. chain stores. However, no slotting fees are charged. The three-year goal is to obtain distribution in 10 percent of the AAFES outlets.

■ Black Colleges

One hundred twenty-nine predominantly black colleges exist in the United States, with total enrollment approaching 175,000 students. A list of the 17 largest is contained in Exhibit 9. Currently Shades of Black has a contract with Morehouse College in Atlanta for its cards and is preparing a special "packet" for that school. Negotiations are under way for a similar display and material with Spelman College, also in Atlanta. Several other predominantly black colleges are located in Atlanta, whose black college and university population is about 17,000.

The Shades of Black product program for Morehouse is to develop a packet of cards and stationery displaying the college seal, a sketch of a campus landmark or of a famous alum, or a collage of unique school features. These items will be marketed to current students and, perhaps more importantly, will be targeted at graduates and for use by the alumni association, which could use the packets for fund raising. Similar materials could be developed for other predominantly black colleges. The sales goal is to place materials in 25 percent of these outlets by spring 1990 and to achieve 75 percent penetration by the third year. In terms of the special college packets, designs will be prepared for a minimum order of 100 units.

■ The Funeral Home Program

As mentioned earlier, 12,348 black-owned funeral homes exist in the United States. Currently there are no stationery-type products specifically tailored to

---

Exhibit 9   **Largest Predominantly Black Colleges and Universities**

School	Location	Size
University of D.C.	Washington, D.C.	14,107
Howard University	Washington, D.C.	11,650
Southern University & A&M College	Baton Rouge, Louisiana	9,177
Tennessee State University	Nashville, Tennessee	8,556
Norfolk State University	Norfolk, Virginia	7,400
Jackson State University	Jackson, Mississippi	6,900
North Carolina A&T State University	Greensboro, North Carolina	5,200
North Carolina Central University	Durham, North Carolina	5,000
Grambling State University	Grambling, Louisiana	4,775
Alabama State University	Montgomery, Alabama	4,044
Ft. Valley State College	Ft. Valley, Georgia	3,970
Tuskegee Institute	Tuskegee, Alabama	3,768
Hampton Institute	Hampton, Virginia	3,200
Virginia State University	Petersburg, Virginia	3,000
Spelman College	Atlanta, Georgia	3,000
Morehouse College	Atlanta, Georgia	3,000
University of Arkansas, Pine Bluff	Pine Bluff, Arkansas	3,000

the grieving black family and their culture. Shades of Black intends to fill this need by marketing, via a direct-mail campaign, a package of products which the funeral homes would then resell to their customers. This package would contain a registration book, acknowledgment cards, things to remember booklets, and so on. Initial informal reaction from the funeral home trade has been very encouraging. Letters of endorsement have been received from the National Funeral Directors & Morticians Association, Inc., and from the State Embalmers and Funeral Directors of Oklahoma.

Sales projections are to achieve distribution in 10 percent of this market by the end of the year, with a minimum order of 25 units per customer.

ADDITIONAL CONCERNS

Alex realizes that these grand ambitions are dependent on raising additional capital. He has already received a $16,300 development loan from the Tulsa Economic Development Authority, while a private investor has put up $10,000. One of his pressing problems is to prepare a business plan which could be submitted to venture capitalists. Another problem he continually wrestles with is the hiring of competent people. It seems that he personally is required to handle every problem that arises, whether it is in design, production, or sales. Finally, another matter that began to assume prominence is the possibility of moving the company headquarters to Atlanta. Retail sales in Tulsa have been much less than expected. On his visits to Atlanta he was very impressed with the vitality of Atlanta's black community and with the large number of black entrepreneurs, which are a rarity in Oklahoma. Alex had recently obtained a list of those areas in the United States with the largest number of black-owned businesses (Exhibit 10). But the most immediate matter is to determine in what market segments his young company could most profitably compete.

Metropolitan Areas with the Largest Number of Black-Owned Businesses   **Exhibit 10**

Area	*Number of Businesses*
Los Angeles/Long Beach, California	23,520
New York City, New York	20,242
Washington, D.C.	18,805
Chicago, Illinois	13,660
Houston, Texas	12,206
San Francisco, California	9,388
Detroit, Michigan	8,731
Philadelphia, Pennsylvania	8,581
Dallas/Ft. Worth, Texas	7,825
Atlanta, Georgia	7,077

Source: Data from *Statistical Abstract of the United States, 1988.*

Spottiswoode & Spottiswoode Ltd.

Robert Anderson, College of Charleston; John Dunkelberg, Wake Forest University

By Christmas of 1984, Spottiswoode & Spottiswoode Ltd., a specialized software house and consultancy in London, had been in existence for just over nine months. The company, founded by two sisters, Clare and Alison Spottiswoode, was formed to take advantage of a major new software market which was rapidly opening up within the business microcomputer sector. Although many companies were producing software packages for large clients, smaller-business customers were being neglected. Smaller businesses were poorly served by the computer industry because general business software was not directly applicable to their own individual requirements.

Spottiswoode & Spottiswoode developed high-quality software packages for markets composed of similar business users. These were vertical markets, and the software packages were referred to as Vertical Market Software Packages. The same package could be sold many times over to different businesses within the same market. Clare Spottiswoode realized that her company had to produce reasonably priced, high-quality software, but it also had to provide good documentation. The company had been able to do both in its first year; however, if it were to continue its success, Spottiswoode & Spottiswoode needed a large cash infusion. The company needed £200,000 in order to accomplish its short-term and long-range goals.

HISTORY

Clare Spottiswoode had the education and experience (see Exhibit 1) necessary to start her own business. She had a degree in economics from Cambridge University and a master's degree in the same field from Yale University. She worked at the Treasury for three years before starting her first business, which supplied 400 retail outlets with oriental gift items; that business was sold when Clare decided to open her software company. Her primary responsibilities in the new company included overall management and direction of the company and financial control. The other major shareholder and director of the company was Alison Spottiswoode.

Alison, Clare's younger sister, is officially the Company Secretary. Like Clare, Alison was a graduate of Cambridge University (see Exhibit 2), where she majored in natural science. Before entering Cambridge, Alison worked for IBM in the development of point-of-sale software. Alison also worked for Shell UK for three years after graduating from Cambridge. At Shell she was involved in the development of microcomputer applications software, and she advised small-garage (gas station) owners.

The other original shareholder was Nicholas Page, who was employed by a leading Accepting House (specialized bank). Mr. Page provided assistance and advice in overall company strategy and direction, and he assisted with financial matters and management control. Nicholas, a graduate of Oxford University, was an accountant who had worked for Deloitte Haskins & Sells for four years.

Exhibit 1   **Curriculum Vitae**

Clare Spottiswoode, M.A. (Cantab), M.Phil. (Yale).

1972–1975	Read Mathematics and Economics at Clare College, Cambridge, obtaining a II.I.
1975–1977	Won a Mellon Fellowship to Yale University, and read for a Masters of Philosophy (M.Phil.) in Economics.
1977–1980	Economist at H.M. Treasury, edited the 1978 Budget, and was one of two economists responsible for running the world economic prospects model (a very large econometric model run on the Treasury mainframe computer), with specific responsibility for the EEC and less developed countries. She also gave general economic advice on the EEC and North Sea oil.
1980–1983	Set up Spottiswoode Trading to import cotton and silk gift items from Thailand. Built company to point where it was selling to 400 shops and department stores nationwide. The company was administered with the aid of a microcomputer. A team of five agents covering the country sold the products. The business was sold in May 1983 to another company in a similar line of business.
1983–1984	Director of Trinity Resource, a company specializing in software support for microcomputer business applications. Responsible for the consultancy operation and for jointly running Trinity Resource, a subsidiary of Patrick and Leach Limited, which also administers two ICL microcomputer traderpoint outlets.

Exhibit 2

Curriculum Vitae

Alison Spottiswoode, B.A. (Cantab).

1978–1979	Worked for IBM helping to develop its point-of-sale software for a large supermarket chain. Learned to program in Assembler, APL, Cobol, and CMS command languages.
1978–1981	Read natural sciences at Clare College, Cambridge, where she was both a music and an academic scholar.
1981–1984	Employee of Shell on their Graduate Marketing Scheme. She has gained extensive experience with microcomputers advising on and specifying a system for use on garage forecourts, and more recently using the Hewlett Packard graphics system for presentations to marketing managers nationwide. She spent a year looking after the Shell garages in Derbyshire, and has benefited from extensive training in small-business management while with Shell.

■ Capitalization

Spottiswoode & Spottiswoode was formed as a corporation with 10,000 shares (£1 par value) distributed in the following manner:

Ordinary shares of £1 each
Executive Directors

Clare Spottiswoode	4,750
Clare Spottiswoode Trust	1,900
Alison Spottiswoode	2,850

Nonexecutive Director

Nicholas Page	500
	10,000

In addition to the £10,000 contributed by the three directors, initial capital included a £35,000 unsecured loan at 10.5 percent interest and a £40,000 loan from the Small Firms Loan Guarantee Scheme.

■ Vertical Markets

When Clare and Alison decided to start a computer software business, they felt that the vertical market would be the most lucrative. The rationale used to justify that decision is summarized below:

Hardware and software prices are falling while at the same time the sophistication of both is rising: it is likely that the costs of both hardware and software for business microcomputers will continue to fall. This trend will bring microcomputers within the reach of many more small businesses, further accelerating the already steep growth in the size of the market.

At present, many small businesses wanting to use a computer effectively must employ software specialists to adapt a generalized software package on a one-off (customized) basis. This is prohibitively expensive for many smaller concerns, since development of such an application can cost thousands of pounds.

The small-business market does, however, divide into a large number of sub-groups, often referred to as "vertical markets," in which businesses operate in a similar manner to each other. The reduction in microcomputing costs in relation to the increased computing power of microcomputers is now creating a market large enough to justify the costs of package production and marketing for an increased range of these vertical markets.

The Spottiswoodes were convinced that there was a large and growing market for good software programs. They also knew that theirs would not be the only company trying to capture a significant portion of that market. In order to develop plans to venture into this market of small businesses, Clare and Alison needed to identify and evaluate their competition. It would also be necessary to explain why Spottiswoode & Spottiswoode's software would be better than that which already existed.

■ Competition

There are many existing companies (the exact number could not be determined) which provide software programs for vertical markets. Most of the companies fall into one of the following broad categories:

 • Traditional computer programmers who, although technically competent, rarely have an understanding of the business they are addressing, and who develop systems which are difficult to use and are badly documented.

 • Professionals in a particular business sector who are computer hobbyists and who have only written systems for themselves. They then attempt to sell the systems to other businesses.

 • Producers or distributors of generalized software packages who wish to sell more of their basic software. The skills required, however, to write the initial program in a complex "machine code" are generally not suited to writing vertical market software, and these programmers rarely have a thorough understanding of both the industry sector and the needs of its members. Alternatively, such companies often approach others (like Spottiswoode & Spottiswoode) to write packages for them to market under their own name, but there is little or no systemic control over specification, quality, or test sites.

The Spottiswoodes were of the opinion that there was no extant competition which could keep their company from being successful in its goal of writing and selling quality computer programs. A number of other companies have already created Vertical Market Packages. Approximately 3500 business packages, both vertical market and others, are available in the United Kingdom. Only a small number of these packages will be successful (many will only sell a couple of packages), for the following reasons:

 • Dealers and consumers have insufficient time and expertise to evaluate all but a few of the available packages.
 • Dealers tend to remain with well-known suppliers with established products.
 • The majority of package designers do not understand the business problems which they are addressing. End users are not sufficiently involved in

developing packages, with the result that packages often do not overcome the business problems they claim to solve.
- Accompanying documentation is generally poor.
- The packages are written in outdated computer "languages" which are inflexible and difficult and expensive to develop or adapt.
- The good products are often overpriced, and inadequate marketing has led to small volume sales.

Despite the competition, Clare and Alison are confident that Spottiswoode & Spottiswoode will be successful. Their confidence seems justified when one examines the company's customer list. The following are some of the companies which are Spottiswoode & Spottiswoode customers:

Amec PLC	Lloyds Merchant Bank
Bank Line Limited (The)	Metzler Bank
Blade Corporation	Midland Bank PLC
Cable and Wireless	Nelson Steavenson
Centra Investments	Redland PLC
Compower	Samuel Montagu & Co.
Electronic Rental Group PLC	Scorpion Investments
Esso Petroleum Co. Ltd.	Shell Oil PLC
Hays Group Limited	Sinclair Research PLC
Korn/Ferry International Ltd.	Venturelink Monitoring

■ Products and Services

For Spottiswoode & Spottiswoode to be able to become a significant force in the vertical market, Clare and Alison knew that the company would have to develop some high-quality computer programs. They felt that their company could produce excellent, reasonably priced software because of the following competitive advantages it enjoyed: management and staff had considerable expertise in the use of microcomputers for business and management applications; they had the ability to write understandable documentation for computer neophytes; and software tools were available to simplify the technical processes of writing business software.

Books

To acquire both market recognition and essential experience of documentation and of the publishing process, Spottiswoode & Spottiswoode negotiated a contract with Century Communications to write a series of five books on the Xchange business software developed by Psion. The books would be written and produced to a very high standard, and would demonstrate both the technical skills and the presentation expertise of the company. Spottiswoode & Spottiswoode selected the authors, the cover designer, the book designer, the editor, and the cartoonist. To date, four books have been written, and three of those have been published.

The books went on sale in bookstores across the country in October and were very well received. The following are the reactions to the books of some well known computer experts:

An astonishing contribution to the QL—a wonderfully intelligent and creative approach to the user's needs (Sir Clive Sinclair).

An imaginative way of bringing to life abstract ideas and practical tools which can help all of us in our work and at home (David Potter, Managing Director of Psion).

Software

The management of Spottiswoode & Spottiswoode felt that they needed a name, one that could be registered, which would immediately identify the company's computer programs. After much deliberation, the name Blueprint was selected to be the company's trademark. In addition to several bespoke (customized) programs written to satisfy customers' specific needs, Spottiswoode & Spottiswoode developed a major Vertical Market Program, Blueprint Portfolio International, a multicurrency portfolio management system. Microcomputer-based, the software is designed to handle a wide range of investment management functions to help manage businesses with speed and accuracy. The package was designed for portfolio managers, stockbrokers, banks, and solicitors. A less sophisticated version of the program was available for personal investment management. A description of the program follows.

Description of Blueprint Portfolio International

The package is designed to deal with all information associated with investment management. The system currently developed is particularly suited for large international portfolios where not only management information but also client accounting is necessary. The system produces both client accounts and management reports such as balance sheets, bank statements, valuations, client holdings, and portfolio analyses by various criteria.

The package is very complex and specialized, so it will be sold to limited numbers of customers at a high price. It will be able to be modified to meet individual requirements and can be extended to multiuser operation; however, it currently runs on an IBM XT which is not a multiuser station.

The system can handle any number of clients, investments, and bank accounts in any currency, within the limits of the hardware. Client accounting is done automatically, as each transaction is entered. End-of-period client accounts and portfolio valuations are simply produced by running the relevant reports.

To facilitate use by people not familiar with computers, there are simple menus to guide the user through the system. To increase speed, one can bypass the menus and access the required screen directly. Screens are specially designed to handle each type of transaction. For example, investment purchases and sales can involve up to three currencies and three dates per transaction.

Consultancy

Consultancy experience would be essential to the company's success in writing Vertical Market Programs. In addition to providing experience, consultancy work also generates revenue. Spottiswoode & Spottiswoode completed projects for Monk Publications, Scorpion Investments, Blade Corporation, and National Film Finance Corporation. The company also did some work for Psion, mainly in the evaluation and improvement of the Psion Xchange package.

In addition to consultancy fees, the company obtains introduction fees (approximately 20 percent) from microcomputer hardware dealers for most hardware sold. Hardware introduction fees could become a significant source of revenue if Spottiswoode & Spottiswoode introduces many buyers to hardware dealers.

■ Turnover (Revenue)

In the first year, a substantial proportion of management time was devoted to establishing the company and developing its strategy and products. Turnover during that period was £72,000. Expenses exceeded turnover, resulting in a net loss of £12,000. Net cash outflow was £21,000. Spottiswoode & Spottiswoode currently has available to it undrawn facilities of around £64,000 (£85,000 original capitalization minus £21,000). The company's net loss from the first few months of operation had been anticipated. Spottiswoode & Spottiswoode was expected to be profitable in its third year of operation; however, if the company was to grow and become profitable, it needed an additional infusion of cash. Clare and Alison estimated that the company needed £200,000 to meet its expansion goals. They were not sure how difficult it would be to raise that amount of capital or where it would come from.

GROWTH

Spottiswoode & Spottiswoode's first year in business had been relatively successful. Three of five books had been published, several consulting contracts had been negotiated, a number of customized computer programs had been written, and one Vertical Market Package had been developed. While these accomplishments were significant, they were not enough to propel the company into the ranks of the major software producers. To do that, Spottiswoode & Spottiswoode would need more Vertical Market Packages, which could significantly increase its turnover. To produce those packages, Spottiswoode & Spottiswoode needed a capital infusion of £200,000. Management began developing a business plan which it could present to potential funding sources. The first item of the business plan was a description of the company's proposed new products.

■ New Products

Spottiswoode & Spottiswoode had one Vertical Market Package in the development phase, and it had several others that it was investigating. These packages, when made available to users, would account for a substantial portion of the company's turnover.

Blueprint Settlements

This system would be a microcomputer-based package for securities settlement. Spottiswoode & Spottiswoode programmers and staff felt that this system would offer the following advantages:

- *Single-trade entry:* Each trade would be entered only once by the dealer of the back-office staff.
- *Automatic multiple contracts:* From the single-deal entry, as many contracts as necessary could be issued automatically.

- *Automatic multiple telex:* Telexes would be produced automatically and queued for transmission via a telex manager module.
- *Clearing house instructions:* Fully automatic communications links to EURO-CLEAR and CEDEL would be incorporated.
- *Accounting:* The package would provide a complete double-entry accounting system. Each automatic posting would be documented on a full audit trail.

Blueprint Dentist

This Vertical Market Package was being developed for dentists and the people who managed their offices. Blueprint Dentist was being designed to assist with financial administration and clerical tasks. The program would simplify the job of running a busy practice by accomplishing the following:

- Provide up-to-the-minute calculation of all claims from the DEB (the government agency responsible for paying medical claims in the United Kingdom).
- Automatically calculate patient charges.
- Monitor individual dentists' performance.
- Issue letters.
- Store patients' records.
- Print receipts.

Proposed promotional information intended to encourage dentists to adopt the package would include the following message:

Blueprint Dentist provides a neat solution to your administration:
You'll know at once the DEB contribution that is due.
You can check that the DEB has sent you what it owes you.
You can keep running totals of money received and in the pipeline.
You can print bills to send to any patients with outstanding balances.
You can find out at any time the exact balance of your accounts.

Spottiswoode & Spottiswoode estimated that it would take one person-month to write the program, and another person-month would be needed to write the documentation and test the program. Development costs and initial promotional expenses would be recovered if the company could sell only 30 systems. Clare was confident that it would be relatively easy to sell, because, as she said, "We have been in discussion with a variety of different organizations who are keen to sell any system we produce, from private and national health dentists, microcomputer dealers, specialist financial advisors to dentists, and stationers. These organizations have a wide national spread with good marketing potential."

Blueprint Forecourt

This system was being developed to automate the activities of garages (gas stations). Spottiswoode & Spottiswoode planned to introduce a forecourt (service area) management and accounting package to satisfy the needs of retailers. This will be marketed directly to retailers, but the oil companies will take a large hand in recommending the package and will provide training courses on the system.

The considerable benefits to be derived from automation of forecourt management and accounting are at present generally unrealized. The major oil companies have for some years been searching for a package to suit their requirements. Alison Spottiswoode was involved with Shell in such an attempt some three years ago. Alison's experience would enable Spottiswoode & Spottiswoode to develop a package that could be recommended by the major oil companies.

Miscellaneous Programs

In addition to the proposed Vertical Market Packages being contemplated by Spottiswoode & Spottiswoode, the company also planned to develop some customized programs for the Sinclair QL, a popular, British-made microcomputer. The programs being considered included the following:

QL Card Index/Mail Box	QL Phone
QL Organizer	QL Business Budgeter
QL File	QL Home Budgeter
QL Portfolio Management Package	The Expert Gardener

■ Pricing Policy

Spottiswoode & Spottiswoode needed to increase sales volume in order to capture a significant share of the software market. The company would initiate the following pricing policy:

> The principal aim of the company is to achieve volume sales. As the cost of the hardware falls, the cost of the software must also fall proportionally. Many micro users are extremely price-sensitive; therefore, correct pricing of the packages is crucial. Pricing policy will be designed to take a large share of the market without provoking a price war. It is expected that prices for Vertical Market Packages will generally fall within the range of £400 to £5000. It is believed that this will offer a significant price advantage over the competition.
>
> Prices could nevertheless range from around £30 for basic software packages which could be sold in bookshops, to £10,000 for a complex multiuser investment manager's package where there is a relatively small market and the perceived value is high. The price of the packages will vary substantially from market to market.

■ Marketing

Clare and Alison are aware of the need to develop a marketing program that will enable Spottiswoode & Spottiswoode to sell the Vertical Market Packages developed by its staff. The company will spend £90,000 next year, £140,000 the following year, and £210,000 the year after that. Approximately half of the marketing budget will be allocated to Vertical Market Packages. Clare realizes that the company needs to hire marketing experts to design and implement an effective program.

> Spottiswoode & Spottiswoode is conscious of the critical role of marketing in the development and sales of software. The company will appoint a marketing manager as soon as a suitable candidate can be found. The company is actively looking for a marketing manager.

Spottiswoode & Spottiswoode has obtained the services of Robin Kinnear, one of the most experienced and capable Public Relations consultants in the computer field. He has advised Sinclair for the past seventeen years, and was also head of public relations at ICL. Mr. Kinnear now has his own company which services Sinclair and Psion among others. He will assist in the design and coordination of the marketing campaigns for Blueprint software.

• *Promotion:* The company's general promotional budget covers the costs of Kinnear and Partners, general promotional literature, the launch of additional books, and product launches as appropriate.

• *Advertising:* General advertising will be used to promote the concept of Blueprint; however, a more specialized package-by-package approach will also be used, which will vary from market to market. For example, effective targeting of dentists will require quite different tactics from those needed to target garages or portfolio managers. Trade newspapers will be used extensively to promote Vertical Market Packages.

• *Trade association and host company:* Wherever possible, Spottiswoode & Spottiswoode will obtain trade association or government seal of approval for its products. Host companies (those which assist in the development and testing of programs) will also aid sales by providing contacts, giving recommendations, and in some cases actively supporting the marketing effort.

• *Microcomputer dealers:* Microcomputer dealers are an excellent source of sales. Spottiswoode & Spottiswoode will establish a small network of key dealers nationwide who are particularly experienced in demonstrating and selling Blueprint packages. A complete package of hardware and software may be an appropriate method of selling in some areas, making the task of buying a system much easier for the customer.

• *Direct sales:* In some markets, direct sales might be appropriate. Carefully targeted mail and trade magazine advertising could be cost-effective in some areas. Spottiswoode & Spottiswoode will ensure that direct selling will not undercut the price charged by software dealers and retailers.

• *Support:* Good products and well-written documentation are necessary to increase turnover and profits; however, a reliable support system is also essential.

• *Postsales support:* Good support is essential for Vertical Market Packages. Spottiswoode & Spottiswoode will assemble a team of support staff as the packages go to market. The support staff will use a "hot line" to answer customer queries. If the staff cannot successfully answer queries over the phone, they will visit the customer or refer him or her to the nearest dealer. Service costs will be covered by maintenance fees paid by customers.

• *Training:* Training courses for dealers and customers will be provided either by the company's own support staff or by training specialists subcontracted by the company. Company operating manuals and its published books will be used for training materials whenever possible.

■ Personnel

When Clare and Alison formed Spottiswoode & Spottiswoode, they knew they would need good employees and reputable outside advisers.

Spottiswoode & Spottiswoode has recognized the importance of obtaining the very best professional advice. This is reflected both in its strategy of selecting prominent and reputable professional partners to develop the accounting and Vertical Market Packages, and in the current professional advice it has obtained.

The company's professional advisers are as follows:

Legal	Simmons and Simmons
Accountancy and Audit	Arthur Young
Public Relations	Robin Kinnear and Partners
Bankers	Barclays Bank, Islington
Publishers	Century Communications

Whenever necessary, Spottiswoode & Spottiswoode will rely on outside professionals to provide expertise not available in-house. The company does not want to become too dependent on outside experts; therefore, Clare plans to increase the company's staff to 30 people over the next three years. In addition to hiring office staff and general programmers, Spottiswoode & Spottiswoode will also need programmers to work on specific Vertical Market Packages (see Exhibit 3 for projected personnel additions).

■ Finances

Clare and Alison know that most lenders or investors will carefully scrutinize the financial projections included in their business plan. While financial projections are vital, Clare and Alison know that theirs will be quite inaccurate because they have so little historical data to use as the basis of future forecasts.

> The business plan covers the next three years. The projections constitute the best estimates of the company's future trading performance, they are, however, subject to considerable uncertainty and the fulfillment of certain assumptions that have been made.

(See Exhibits 4 and 5 for financial projections.)

■ Funding Sources

Clare and Alison have put together a business plan which covers the past and the next three years. They are very optimistic about the future of Spottiswoode & Spottiswoode; however, Clare and Alison know that their plans cannot become reality unless they can acquire £200,000 in new capital. It is time for Clare and Alison to decide how they should acquire the necessary £200,000.

Exhibit 3   Projected Personnel Additions

Staffing Analysis	1984 Q2	1984 Q3	1984 Q4	1984	1985 Q1	1985 Q2	1985 Q3	1985 Q4	1985	1986	1987
Customer support	4,050	4,200	4,200	12,450	4,200	4,200	4,700	4,700	17,800	20,000	25,000
Administrative assistance	3,644	3,600	3,600	10,844	3,600	3,600	4,000	4,000	15,200	17,000	21,000
New-product development				0		1,000	1,000	1,000	3,000	4,000	4,000
Marketing relations	1,838	2,050	2,050	5,938	2,100	2,100	2,100	2,100	8,400	12,000	15,000
Dealer training/support		1,333	2,000	3,333	2,000	2,000	2,000	2,000	8,000	10,000	12,000
Program writers		1,112	1,750	2,862	2,000	2,000	2,000	2,000	8,000	10,000	12,000
Marketing					2,000	4,000	4,000	4,000	14,000	20,000	25,000
Portfolio programmer					1,500	3,000	3,000	3,000	10,500	15,000	15,000
Portfolio support						3,000	3,000	3,000	9,000	12,000	12,000
Garage sales							6,000	6,000	12,000	24,000	24,000
Garage support						3,000	6,000	6,000	15,000	36,000	45,000
Dentist sales and support						3,000	3,000	3,000	9,000	12,000	24,000
Accounting programmer					1,000	3,000	3,000	6,000	13,000	36,000	36,000
Other programmer						2,000	2,000	2,000	6,000	10,000	12,000
Other support							1,000	2,000	3,000	24,000	40,000
Office support						2,000	2,000	2,000	4,000	16,000	32,000
Recruitment costs	722	1,228	1,420	3,371	6,000	6,400	4,800	1,600	18,800	11,200	12,800
Employee benefits					1,751	3,416	4,643	5,024	14,833	26,450	33,681
Total	10,254	13,523	15,020	38,798	26,151	45,716	58,243	59,424	189,533	315,650	400,481
No. of staff	3	5	5	5	9	13	16	17	17	24	32
Subcontractors	3,861	905	170	4,936	306	442	544	578	1,870	3,264	4,352

Trading Projections for the Next Three Years (£000s)

Exhibit 4

	Year 1	Year 2	Year 3
Turnover	£618	£1342	£2323
Net contribution			
Consultancy	60	60	60
Books	5	10	10
QL packages	27	144	288
Maintenance	40	92	165
Vertical markets	330	826	1560
Purchase invoices	156	210	240
	618	1342	2323
Direct costs	280	525	890
Overheads	360	600	750
Net profit/(loss)	(22)	217	683

Exhibit 5 Spottiswoode & Spottiswoode Business Plan, Christmas 1984

	1984 Q2	1984 Q3	1984 Q4	1984	1985 Q1	1985 Q2	1985 Q3	1985 Q4	1985	1986	1987
Overhead Costs											
Staff costs	10,254	13,523	15,020	38,798	26,151	45,716	58,243	59,424	189,533	315,650	400,481
Subcontracted staff	3,861	905	170	4,936	306	442	544	578	1,870	3,264	4,352
Office space	2,457	2,457	2,457	7,371	3,000	7,478	9,527	9,720	29,726	51,634	65,510
Leasing	452	452	452	1,356	904	904	904	904	3,615	6,000	8,000
Travel/subsistence	696	679	700	2,075	1,219	2,131	2,714	2,769	8,833	14,710	18,664
Office sundries	364	460	500	1,324	871	1,522	1,939	1,978	6,309	10,507	13,331
Communications	2,411	868	1,000	4,279	1,741	3,044	3,878	3,956	12,619	21,015	26,663
Sales/promotion	1,645	2,108	2,250	6,003	4,046	7,073	9,012	9,194	29,326	48,839	61,965
Legal/professional	1,574	885	2,800	5,259	4,875	8,522	10,857	11,077	35,332	58,842	74,656
Bank charges/interest	176	2,204	2,500	4,880	2,500	2,500	2,500	2,500	10,000	12,000	12,000
Bad debts		150	400	550	2,250	2,250	2,250	2,250	9,000	9,000	9,000
Depreciation	810	864	918	2,593	2,377	4,710	6,710	7,043	20,840	50,173	64,840
Sundries	200	300	300	800	522	913	1,163	1,187	3,786	6,304	7,999
Total operating expenses	24,900	25,854	29,467	80,222	50,761	87,204	110,241	112,581	360,787	607,939	767,460
Staff as % of expenses	41%	52%	51%	48%	52%	52%	53%	53%	53%	52%	52%
Fixed Assets											
Computers	4,590		500	5,090	5,500	12,000	9,000	3,000	29,500	21,000	24,000
Other equipment	544	174	150	869	1,000				1,000		
FF&F	4,590	470		5,060	3,000	4,000	3,000	1,000	11,000	7,000	8,000
Cars				0	8,000	12,000	12,000		32,000	38,000	12,000
Other				0					0		
Acquired assets	9,725	645	650	11,019	17,500	28,000	24,000	4,000	73,500	66,000	44,000
Cumulative assets	9,725	10,369	11,019	11,019	28,519	56,519	80,519	84,519	84,519	150,519	194,519
Less cumulative depreciation	810	1,675	2,593	2,593	4,969	9,679	16,389	23,433	23,433	73,606	138,445
Total assets	8,914	8,695	8,427	8,427	23,550	46,840	64,130	61,087	61,087	76,914	56,074

Lakeshore, Incorporated

George S. Vozikis, The Citadel; Timothy S. Mescon, Salisbury State
University

INTRODUCTION

Lakeshore, Incorporated, once a tuberculosis sanitarium, has been operating as
a rehabilitation facility since 1973 and offers rehabilitation of the whole person.
Social and psychological needs are met as well as physical needs. The 50-acre
Lakeshore campus, located near Birmingham, Alabama, was donated by the
city of Homewood, a Birmingham suburb, and is the flagship facility for the
comprehensive network of rehabilitation services. The 90-bed inpatient institution is part of a network which includes prosthetic and orthotic services, outpatient rehabilitation facilities, vocational training, a durable medical equipment company, a 36-bed transitional living unit, a sheltered workshop, and a
specialized rehabilitation services unit for individuals injured in industrial accidents. The system is designed to provide continuing services and benefits for
physically disabled individuals at every stage of the rehabilitation process.

Lakeshore's Transitional Living Unit is the utopian dream of Dr. John Miller,
a former Medical Director of Lakeshore, who has a vision of a complete rehabilitation process which includes the patient's reintegration into the community.
The unit allows the patient to practice using facilities encountered in daily life
such as the kitchen, bathroom, and bedroom. It is designed as an intermediate
step between the hospital and the outside world. Rehabilitation services are
designed to restore the disabled individuals, following disease or injury, to the
highest physical, social, vocational, and economic usefulness of which they are
capable. Rehabilitation can be viewed as the third phase of the medical care

continuum, with the first being the prevention of illness, and the second the actual treatment of disease. This third phase involves rehabilitation or a constructive system of treatment designed to enable individuals to attain their highest degree of functioning.

Comprehensive/specific services are provided for persons with the following conditions:

Back pain	Arthritis	Stroke
Spinal cord injury	Orthopedic impediment	Parkinson's disease
Chronic and acute pain	Peripheral nerve injury	Head injury
Industrial and sports injuries	Multiple sclerosis	Amputation
Circulatory problems	Cerebral palsy	Pediatric speech
Speech and language disorders	Musculoskeletal conditions	Hearing disorders

The following types of services are offered at the Lakeshore facilities:

Physical therapy	Social work services	Patient education
Functional evaluation	Occupational therapy	Family education
Speech therapy	Language therapy	Hearing assessment
Psychosocial counseling	Disability evaluation	Rehabilitation
Work injury rehabilitation	Community education programs	Nutritional counseling
Sports injury	Prosthetics and orthotics	Respiratory therapy
Durable medical equipment		

Lakeshore also houses the George C. Wallace Recreation Center. The concept of the recreation center was created by Lakeshore's present CEO, Michael Stevens, who designed the barrier-free center for "leisure therapy." The $1.2 million building has over 26,000 square feet and consists of a full-size gymnasium with a regulation-size basketball court which can also be used for volleyball and indoor racquet sports. The court is the home of the Birmingham Chariots wheelchair basketball team. Other organized activities at the facility include adapted training classes, team sports, Red Cross/YMCA programs, advanced lifesaving, personal safety courses, arts and crafts, and therapeutic exercises.

The facility also includes an indoor pool which has a transfer wall that allows a wheelchair patient to enter the pool from the height of the chair and reenter the chair without the aid of a hoist. Lakeshore hopes one day to host the state competition, then the regional and national, and perhaps even the world, handicapped Olympics in the pool. Paraplegic scuba diving is another of the planned activities.

Lakeshore has earned national respect because it is one of the few facilities which provides acute care and services all the way through job training in a single location. The Vocational Guidance and Training Facility, operated by the Alabama Vocational Rehabilitation Service, offers job placement counseling and opportunities in computer programming, dispatching, microfilming, switchboard operation, small-engine repair, engraving, and driver education.

Referral to the Lakeshore Hospital can be made by any physician. Patients may be referred for a specific prescribed treatment or for an evaluation and therapy plan to be developed by the center's therapy management team. Referrals can also be made by discharge planners, insurance companies, industry representatives, and rehabilitation counselors. A patient may also be accepted without a referral following an evaluation by a staff physician.

The Lakeshore Mobile Rehabilitation Center is an outpatient facility that opened in the spring of 1986. The company has leased the entire first floor of the five-story Providence Hospital School of Nursing. The Lakeshore Center is Mobile's second comprehensive rehabilitation center, the other being Rotary Hospital, which provides inpatient and outpatient services. Lakeshore did a feasibility study and determined that more rehabilitation centers were needed in the Mobile area because of increased population in the area. The Center, with its professional staff of ten specialists, provides basically the same type of services as the main division in Homewood.

In the fall of 1985, the Huntsville Rehabilitation Center joined forces with Lakeshore to provide comprehensive outpatient services to the north Alabama area. Additionally, projected for completion in May 1987 are plans that include a 50-bed inpatient addition to Huntsville Hospital, which was based on a Certificate of Need awarded in 1984. The hospital will own the new wing but it will be managed by Lakeshore. The building design will allow the hospital to share many of its services with Lakeshore, such as radiology and medical specialities.

Lakeshore is a United Way Agency, so keeping its costs down is an important factor. Patients referred by the Alabama Vocational Rehabilitation Service receive the vocational development portion of their services at no charge. The center is reimbursed by private insurance companies and Medicare, but those who do not have insurance are not turned away. Fees are adjusted on a sliding scale to ensure that health care services are available regardless of a person's level of income.

MAJOR ISSUES

One of the major issues that the rehabilitation industry will face in the future, due to changing demographic trends, will be an increase in the average-age category. More disabled people will be in the 65-years-old-and-above category than in the less-than-44-years-old category. Studies have shown the younger age category to have decreased in number as much as 17% during the past decade.[1] The overall aging of the population is due to a decreasing birth rate. Currently, Lakeshore's concentration in their rehabilitation services is for the less-than-44-years-old category, since statistics have shown that the highest percentage of disabled people is in that age category.[2]

The changing demographic trends indicate that Lakeshore will have to focus its services more toward the 65-years-old-and-above category. For example, Lakeshore currently gears its environment for the younger patients who are more likely to be interested in competitive sports and activities which help them

[1]Jeanne Saddler, "Low Pay, High Turnover Plague Day Care Industry," *The Wall Street Journal*, 19 February 1987, p. 27.
[2]Alabama State Health Planning Agency, "Alabama State Health Plan," Montgomery, 1986 (mimeographed).

to become rehabilitated sooner. In contrast, the focus in the future should be on psychological and sedentary activities.

Legislation now being studied would provide insurance for catastrophic illness to those who could not otherwise afford coverage. This will mean that a larger number of the elderly and poor will enter the market for rehabilitative services, since they will no longer need to worry about making any kind of payment. Many of these patients do not seek out rehabilitative services now because they think they cannot afford it or because they are too proud to accept welfare assistance.

Another issue that Lakeshore might face in the future is a decrease in the percentage of physical impairments and disabilities in the state of Alabama. Currently, according to a survey sanctioned by the State Health Plan, Alabama has a higher percentage of physical impairments and disabilities than both the United States and the South and this prevalence rate is higher in the nonwhite population. According to statistics in the State Health Plan, 5% of all Alabamians, or 177,800 persons, are estimated to be disabled.[3] A small decrease in the prevalence rate could affect the continued growth of Lakeshore, Incorporated.

Another major issue that the rehabilitation industry may be forced to deal with is the reclassification of reimbursement procedures by the government. Until about four years ago, before Prospective Payment, hospitals were reimbursed by Medicare based on what it cost them to treat a disability such as a stroke or amputation. The Prospective Payment System implies that the facility is paid prospectively and health care administrators know beforehand how much per discharge will be paid based on the standard cost structure. The government then established a formula for reimbursement based on Diagnostic Related Groups (DRGs). The formula tells a hospital exactly how much it will be reimbursed for specific condition, regardless of how much the treatment actually costs. Rehabilitation units are exempt from DRGs and are reimbursed on what it actually costs them to treat a patient. What this means is that a rehabilitation center is in a better position to provide the kind of intensive therapy that disabled patients may require after being discharged from a hospital. A new Prospective Payment System is currently under study which would provide standard cost structures for rehabilitation facilities and remove this competitive advantage.

INDUSTRY COMPETITIVE STRUCTURE

A comprehensive rehabilitation center is a specialty hospital that deals specifically and exclusively with those disability conditions that result in permanent and long-term impairments. The Lakeshore Rehabilitation Complex is a privately held, specialty service system, as are each of its two competitors in the state of Alabama. Each of these systems operates under a license granted to them under the State Health Plan. The licenses specify such operating characteristics as the number of beds that can be set up and staffed, the number of registered nurses and licensed practical nurses per patient, the number of other specialists per patient, and the types of records that must be kept of programs operated by the facility.

[3]Ibid.

Two other institutions operate in Alabama under the same type of license as Lakeshore: Spain Rehabilitation Center in Birmingham is a 78-bed state-owned and -operated rehabilitation center of University Hospital, and Rotary Rehabilitation Hospital in Mobile is a 50-bed, private, nonprofit hospital. Each of these facilities provides inpatient rehabilitative care in addition to outpatient services.

Spain Rehabilitation Center places major emphasis on teaching and research in addition to patient care. The Center is one of seven regional spinal cord injury centers designated and funded by the National Institute of Health. Its patients come from throughout the Southeastern United States. Another special program at Spain is pulmonary rehabilitation and rheumatology.

Each of the three rehabilitation facilities in Alabama offer the following therapies or services: physical, occupational, respiratory, psychological, speech and hearing, rehabilitation nursing, drug-administered therapies, and social services, including discharge planning and follow-up services. Recreation therapy services are also provided at each of the three facilities. Custom prosthetic and orthotic devices are prepared by the Prosthetic Shop at the Lakeshore Rehabilitation Complex. The Lakeshore Complex is the only one of the state's rehabilitative hospitals which provides custom orthotic and prosthetic services on-site. The other hospitals use the services of prosthetic and orthotic vendors located in the Birmingham area. The Lakeshore Prosthetic Shop was purchased from Spain Rehabilitation Hospital in 1980. Lakeshore also complements the rehabilitation process through the delivery of services of its Transitional Living Unit, Independent Living Unit, sheltered employment, and supportive resources for the patient within Alabama's comprehensive rehabilitative continuum of care. Vocational rehabilitation counseling is provided at both Spain and Lakeshore by employees of the Alabama Vocational Rehabilitation Service. The Lakeshore Complex also offers vocational evaluation and a range of other vocational rehabilitation services which would generally be utilized by patients in the Transitional Living Unit or on an outpatient basis.

Discharge data from the "Utilization" section of the *Annual Report for Hospitals and Related Facilities,* as submitted to the State Health Planning Agency, indicates that all the patients served by the three facilities can be grouped into one of six major disorder or disease classifications under the ICDA Code, 8th revision. These are cerebrovascular disease, pulmonary disorders, arthritic disorders, neuromuscular disorders, spinal cord injuries, and amputations. This seems to indicate that the state's three inpatient rehabilitation hospitals are all serving basically the same type of customer needs.

STRENGTHS, WEAKNESSES, OPPORTUNITIES, AND THREATS

The rehabilitative health care industry in the state of Alabama is relatively young, and limited opportunities for growth exist. Of course, any additional beds will have to be approved by the State Health Board, upon formal submission of a Certificate of Need. As was mentioned earlier, Lakeshore has only been in existence for 14 years, and four years ago, neither Lakeshore in Mobile or Huntsville was in existence. Prior to this time, the patients in Alabama had to be served either by Spain Rehabilitation Hospital in Birmingham or by one of the outpatient systems, or they were forced to go out of state.

A major strength which results from being located in the Birmingham area is that it is possible to draw upon the resources of the University of Alabama in Birmingham Medical College, which is located less than five miles away. The major strength which Lakeshore has is the enormous resources available to it in a single location. Lakeshore is a fully integrated facility, which can offer the patient everything from prosthetics, to minor surgery, to participative sports for the handicapped, to job counseling and placement.

The weakest point appears to be its dependence on the State Health Agency, which rules over all health care services in the state. A minor consequence is the fact that the same agency also rules over every other health care facility in the state. A threat exists in the proposed government regulations, which could play a vital role if the Prospective Payment System should be modified to include the rehabilitation industry under the DRG system.

Many opportunities exist for growth in the rehabilitation area if the corporation should strategically decide to pursue them. It has already committed to manage the facility in Huntsville; it is managing the Mobile facility; and it could possibly expand into other growth areas such as Dothan, Gadsden, or Tuscaloosa. Additional growth could come in the way of patients from the border states of Tennessee, Florida, Georgia, and Mississippi. Lakeshore might also decide to expand its role as a vendor to supply prosthetic and orthotic devices to other rehabilitation units, either in or out of state. Currently eight such units are located in the Birmingham area alone; the general rule of thumb is one rehabilitation unit per 100,000 people.

GENERAL ORGANIZATION AND MANAGEMENT

Until 1984, the organization was structured much like any other not-for-profit hospital would be (Exhibit 1). The different functional groups—the Sheltered Opportunities Workshop, Rehabilitation Services, Transitional Living Unit, Medcore, System Services, and Lakeshore Hospital—each operated as separate entities; and Lakeshore, Incorporated, the parent holding company, was charged with responsibility for each of the operations.

Exhibit 1   **Lakeshore: Organizational Structure, 1984**

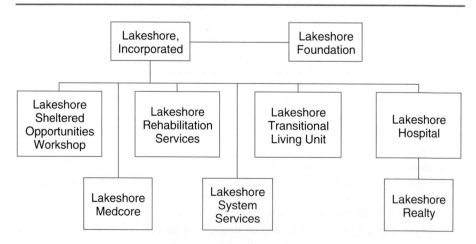

In the latter part of 1984, immediately prior to the opening of the satellite facilities program, the strategic plan entailed the reorganization of the for-profit and not-for-profit sections of the corporation. Part of the organization remained a nonprofit group, while the remainder became a for-profit group and was placed under Systems Services (Exhibit 2). This fundamental change was the result of long-range strategic thinking on the part of the Executive Board and would allow the corporation to grow at a more controlled rate, as well as to benefit from the profits projected from the growth.

Lakeshore's Board of Directors is a volunteer group with 17 members. It is made up of bankers, lawyers, doctors, educators, and the Mayor of Homewood. The Board functions as most hospital boards do and is charged with guiding the overall direction of the company. The Executive Council functions independently of the Board of Directors. The Executive Council is charged with formulation and implementation of the strategic plan of the corporation. It is made up of nine people:

Chief Operating Officer
Chief Executive Officer
Vice President of Corporate Finance

Vice President of System Services
Vice President of Corporate Development
Regional Medical Director

Corporate Medical Director
Coordinator of Medical Services
One other physician

The Executive Council meets on the second and last Fridays of each month. Meetings on the second Friday are held on the Lakeshore campus, and the last Friday meeting is held at a local state park in order to separate the Council from the workplace and any interruptions that might occur. The meetings are based

---

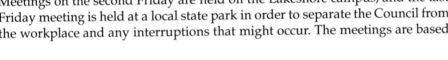

Lakeshore: Organizational Structure, 1987 **Exhibit 2**

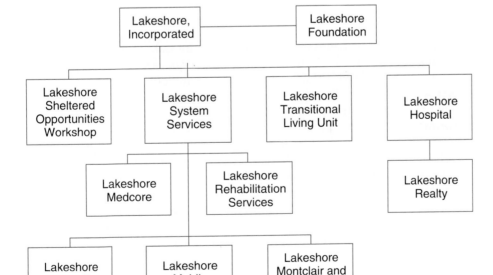

on a planned agenda, which must be approved by the President and Chief Executive Officer. However, the Council members can make additions to the agenda by submitting them to the President's Office no later than the day before the meeting is to be held. The off-site meeting is held primarily as a strategy planning meeting, and policy items discussed may include such things as new programs, new facilities, and financial decisions.

Lakeshore's Chief Executive Officer, Michael Stevens, is a graduate of both Spain and Lakeshore Rehabilitation Centers. Stevens was injured in a diving accident in 1973, which left him paralyzed from the neck down. Following his discharge from Spain Rehabilitation Center, he was still not fully recovered and eventually entered Lakeshore as a patient. He has fully recovered now, and a slight drag to his walk is the only evidence that remains of his accident. After his discharge, Stevens, who was employed in legal services at Prentice-Hall, Inc. (a publishing company), decided to pursue his Master's Degree in Hospital Administration.

After he graduated, he did part of his residency at Lakeshore, and when the administrator resigned, he became the acting Executive Director. Stevens is a man who is driven by goals and objectives. He has led the corporation for ten years now, and operations have improved as a result of his leadership. He has a keen business mind as well as a solid background in hospital administration, and he cares about people. This combination has helped to make him a leader.

The information system in place at Lakeshore includes the data-based office automation system recently purchased and installed. The system uses a Data General mainframe computer and handles everything from payroll functions, to patient data, to information management (including appointments, messages, electronic mail, word processing, etc.). The system has been in place for about one year, and the corporation plans to have the entire system performing at its most efficient level within five years. The Information Services System is the responsibility of the Vice President of Corporate Finance, because he has a background in computers.

MARKETING

The market served by Lakeshore includes the entire state of Alabama, in addition to the border states of Florida, Tennessee, Georgia, and Mississippi; but its primary market includes the four-county area including Jefferson, Shelby, Walker, and Talladega. This four-county area makes up 76.6% of Lakeshore's patient base and is projected to have 2.2% growth rate between 1986 and 1990. The primary service area also contains 33% of Alabama's total population.[4]

Lakeshore is comprised of a group of interrelated services and products for the rehabilitation of the physically disabled. Among its services are a comprehensive rehabilitation hospital and outpatient facilities for patients who have completed their stay at Lakeshore Hospital or for those who do not require hospitalization. Through its Medcore Clinic, Lakeshore provides services for those individuals who are injured on the job. These services include not only rehabilitation but also vocational evaluation, counseling, and case management.

[4]Alabama State Health Planning Agency, "Alabama Certificate of Need Application: Carraway Methodist Medical Center," Montgomery, 1986 (mimeographed).

Other related rehabilitation activities offered at Lakeshore include the fabrication and fitting of prosthetic and orthotic devices and the distribution and sale of durable medical equipment. Special services for the housing, vocational training, and employment of disabled individuals are provided. Also, for those who wish to participate, Lakeshore offers one of the finest handicapped athletic programs in the United States.

Although Lakeshore's main facility is located near Birmingham, it is affiliated with a growing network of inpatient and outpatient facilities. These include comprehensive rehabilitation hospitals designed to meet the needs of communities and cities beyond the greater Birmingham area. Lakeshore also offers management contracts and joint ventures to expand its quality programs to existing or new facilities.

These and other support programs offered through Lakeshore's network of rehabilitation services allow patients to be taken from the first stages of recovery through rehabilitation, job training, and employment to the point where they reach their full potential. The system is unique and provides a synergy of corporate services, based on the belief that to be successful, rehabilitation must ensure that patients are equipped in every way to function in society.

The majority of Lakeshore's promotion and advertising is handled by an outside marketing agency. However, a Director of Public Relations for the corporation has been hired recently. Her name is Dell Witcher, and she was employed as a news anchor for WBRC, the Channel 6 television station in Birmingham, for several years prior to joining Lakeshore. Ms. Witcher's responsibility is to improve the image of the corporation through public relations, including speeches, videotapes, and slide presentations, which are made available to area doctors, educators, hospitals, and civic groups.

Lakeshore's pricing of its services is generally less than the average in the state of Alabama and the Southeast. Lakeshore's cost containment strategy requires the corporation to strive to remain a low-cost producer by carrying out aggressive cost containment strategies and by promoting increased productivity. Costs can be controlled further by keeping abreast of changes in medical education, technology, new practices, and knowledge through the establishment of new programs, acquisitions of new equipment, and changes in medical practice. Lakeshore will also consider participation in any multi-institutional sharing ventures that will enhance its ability to provide existing or new services in a more effective and efficient manner. These and other strategies will allow Lakeshore to reduce costs and improve both its price structure and its profits.

As evidence of Lakeshore's cost containment strategy, the following information is given in the State Health Plan: as of October 1, 1985, the per diem rate for Alabama's three comprehensive rehabilitation hospitals was $496.61 for Spain, $424.44 for Lakeshore, and $387.12 for Rotary.[5] These data are based on Medicaid cost reports.

PRODUCTION AND OPERATIONS

The major capital asset at Lakeshore, Incorporated, the hospital building and 50 acres on which the main campus is located, was donated to Lakeshore by the city of Homewood in 1973. Prior to that time, the building had been condemned

[5]Alabama State Health Planning Agency, "Alabama State Health Plan."

Exhibit 3   Lakeshore: Hospital Management

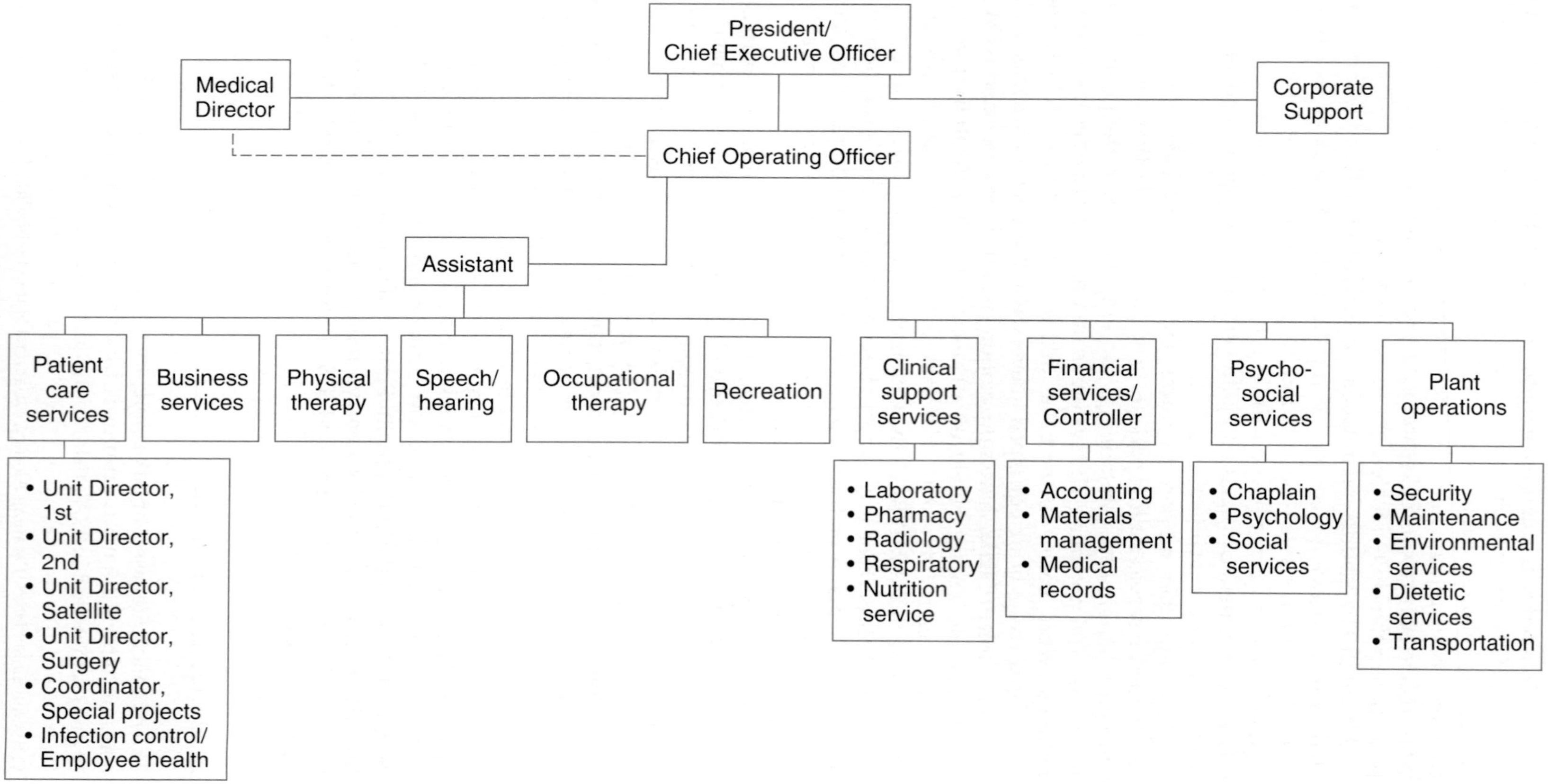

President/Chief Executive Officer

Medical Director

Corporate Support

Chief Operating Officer

Assistant

- Patient care services
  - Unit Director, 1st
  - Unit Director, 2nd
  - Unit Director, Satellite
  - Unit Director, Surgery
  - Coordinator, Special projects
  - Infection control/Employee health
- Business services
- Physical therapy
- Speech/hearing
- Occupational therapy
- Recreation
- Clinical support services
  - Laboratory
  - Pharmacy
  - Radiology
  - Respiratory
  - Nutrition service
- Financial services/Controller
  - Accounting
  - Materials management
  - Medical records
- Psycho-social services
  - Chaplain
  - Psychology
  - Social services
- Plant operations
  - Security
  - Maintenance
  - Environmental services
  - Dietetic services
  - Transportation

by the city (in 1970), after operating as a tuberculosis sanatorium for 50 years. The main building has since been remodeled and does not look like a 67-year-old structure; in fact, it looks like a very modern hospital. With the addition of the prosthetic and orthotic shop building in 1980 and the $1.2 million gymnasium and pool in 1981, the facility is an impressive one.

Lakeshore operates as a nonunion shop employing about 400 people, mostly skilled professionals. Its business operations are separated into nine different areas:

Patient care services   Clinical support services
Business services   Financial services
Speech and hearing therapy Psychosocial services
Occupational therapy   Plant operations
Recreation

For more detailed information on the organizational chart, see Exhibit 3.

Production capability in the orthotic and prosthetic shops has been in place since Lakeshore purchased the unit from Spain Rehabilitation Hospital in 1980. The shops employ seven technicians. Each technician is certified in either orthotics or prosthetics or both. Certification requires having a four-year college degree in addition to one year of training and successful completion of the certification exam. Presently eight other shops which fabricate orthotic and/or prosthetic devices are located in the Birmingham area.

The fabrication process begins with a psychological meeting with the client to assess his or her needs and develop a definitive prosthesis. The first step in the prosthetic process is to wrap the stump and produce a plaster casting. The casting will be used for analysis of stress points, nerves, muscle compositions, etc. Next the plaster casting is used to vacu-form a test socket of thick plastic, which is placed on the patient for static and dynamic alignment. The test socket and casting are then placed in a stand and built up with several layers of poly-felt material. The patient's skin color is then matched, the resin is mixed, and the limb is poured. Further alignment takes place at this point if necessary.

The fabrication of orthotic devices takes place here as well. The bracing is designed to assist those who only have partial control of their limbs or muscles, whether the result of defects, deformities, or injuries. The patient's needs are kept in mind at all times by the staff, since they realize that motivation to learn to use the artificial limb or orthotic bracing is critical for it to be successfully used by the client. Follow-up is provided to the client in all cases.

Requirements for the quality of services provided by Lakeshore are spelled out in the State Health Plan, which requires all comprehensive rehabilitation hospitals to meet or exceed the certification requirements for the Medicare program. Lakeshore recognizes that in all levels of rehabilitation care, it is essential that the patient be exposed to the highest level of expertise and quality service available. It also realizes that the quality of care rendered is largely dependent on the qualifications of those rendering the services. To this end, Lakeshore strives to maintain a highly trained group of professionals and has a ratio of 60% registered nurses to 40% licensed practical nurses employed on its staff.

The cost of producing goods and services offered at Lakeshore is a major concern to management. Managers realize how important the sharing of services with other health care institutions and group purchasing arrangements are to effective cost containment. It has been demonstrated that the cooperative efforts of the Spain Complex and Lakeshore have resulted in the effective, efficient delivery of rehabilitative goods and services.

FINANCIAL INFORMATION

Lakeshore, Incorporated, is a private institution and is not required to make public its financial data. The only information made available is the statement of income and expense contained in the Certificate of Need for Carraway Methodist Medical Center, as required by the State Health Planning Agency. This data covers the period from January 1985 through November 1986 and shows that Lakeshore Hospital incurred a $9494 loss in 1985, a $10,652 profit in the first 11 months of 1986, and is projected to make profits of $59,557 in 1987 and $65,432 in 1988.

HUMAN RESOURCES

Lakeshore employs 400 people at its main campus in Birmingham, 120 at the Huntsville facility, and 10 in Mobile. None of the corporation's employees are represented by a labor union. Lakeshore recognizes that its human resources are its most valuable asset and treats its employees accordingly. Each of Lakeshore's employees is a guide in a way: a guide toward new hope, functioning minds and bodies rebuilt through rehabilitation, and attainable goals. New employees are given adequate time to become oriented to the Lakeshore way of helping people. They spend an entire day viewing videos, reviewing corporate policies and procedures, and getting to know their way around the campus so that they will be able to give information or directions to anyone who asks. In this sense, they are guides and valuable marketing assets.

Turnover is the biggest personnel issue in the health care industry due to the high demand for skilled employees. Even though Lakeshore makes every attempt to promote from within its organization, it often resorts to the use of external sources to find the qualified personnel needed. Lakeshore accepts applications two days per week, conducts on-campus interviews, runs advertisements in newspapers and medical publications, and maintains personal contacts through various personnel associations. The result is a successful recruiting program.

Lakeshore's employee pay and benefits program is comparable to any in the area. This is due in part to the need to remain competitive in the labor segment of the health care industry. Different benefit packages are offered to the hourly employees, to the salaried nonexempt employees, to exempt, salaried employees, and to top-level management. For example, salaried employees have their health care benefits paid for by the company; top-level managers receive increased levels of disability, health, and life insurance; and hourly employees receive paid sick leave and are allowed to accumulate any unused vacation or sick leave from one year to the next.

Lakeshore initiated a wellness program for its employees in January 1987. The program is open to participation by all employees and is designed to improve their physical conditioning. Employees participate in activities during their scheduled working hours, and awards are given to those who achieve their predetermined goal.

In keeping with its policy of requiring its employees to remain current on technology and education in the health care field, Lakeshore offers its employees leave of absence to continue their education. A job transfer policy also helps keep employees satisfied with the jobs they occupy. When a job becomes available, the opening is first communicated to the Department Managers, who make their employees aware of the opening. Individuals may then bid for the job, and the most qualified applicant will be awarded the job. An attempt is made to fill all jobs internally, where qualified applicants exist, before going to the outside for candidates.

Lakeshore has a formal salary administration program which is based on job descriptions and is reviewed annually. The present system has been in effect for three years and has been revised and improved each year. Individuals fit into a job family grade and salary range. The salary administration formula is based on the individual's experience and education and the job description. Salary levels are reviewed on an annual basis and as needed to maintain a competitive position in the Birmingham area health care industry.

The performance appraisal form rates the employee on job-based criteria as objectively as possible, applying measurable goals and objectives which are set by the department head and communicated to the employees. The form is used for all but top-management-level employees. The performance appraisal form used for top management has some subjectivity built into it, which includes such immeasurable things as good will and granting interviews to students.

The appraisal form is completed and discussed with the employee once a year. At this time the employee has the opportunity to write comments on the form and has the choice of signing it or protesting the appraisal to the department head. If not satisfied with the department head's response, the employee can protest to the Director of Human Relations and finally to the Chief Operating Officer. Once the form is complete and signed, the Human Resource Department will review it, weighing the response and assigning points to the job criteria. Within two weeks the merit increase is granted based on total points, and the appraisal process is complete.

CONCLUSIONS

As a full-service comprehensive rehabilitation institution, Lakeshore has developed a good relationship with area doctors and hospitals. Its system is designed to provide continuing services and benefits for physically disabled individuals at every stage of the rehabilitation process. The Lakeshore system is unique and provides a synergy of corporate services, based on the belief that to be successful, rehabilitation must ensure that patients are equipped in every way to function in society. It is one of the few facilities in the country which provides acute care and services all the way through job training in a single location.

BIBLIOGRAPHY

Aiding Independence Rehabilitation Center. *Huntsville Business*, 1st Quarter 1986, pp. 16–26.

Alabama State Health Planning Agency. "Alabama Certificate of Need Application, Carraway Methodist Medical Center." Montgomery, 1986 (mimeographed).

Alabama State Health Planning Agency. "Alabama State Health Plan." Montgomery, 1986 (mimeographed).

Caspell, Richard E., Vice President of Corporate Services, Lakeshore, Incorporated, Birmingham, Alabama. Interview, 24 February 1987.

Doremus, Harvey, Joseph W. Benoy, and Ronald Zallocco. "Strategic Market Planning for Hospitals." *Journal of Health Care Marketing,* Vol. 4, No. 2 (Spring 1984), pp. 19–28.

Elliot, Carolyn Payne, Director of Corporate Relations, Lakeshore, Incorporated, Birmingham, Alabama. Interview, 11 February 1987.

Hart, Sylvia. "New Rehab Center Offers Service for Outpatients." *Mobile Register,* 3 April 1986, sec. B, p. 2.

Jones, Alice, Director of Planning and Development, Lakeshore, Incorporated, Birmingham, Alabama. Interview, 11 February 1987.

Easten, Bernard L., Jr. *The Physician's DRG Handbook.* Cleveland: Lexi-Comp Inc., 1986.

Peters, Joseph P., and James Webber. *Strategic Thinking: New Frontier for Hospital Management.* Chicago: American Hospital Association, 1985.

Russell, Ammy, Staff Administrative Assistant, Lakeshore, Incorporated, Huntsville, Alabama. Interview, 4 February 1987.

Saddler, Jeanne. "Low Pay, High Turnover Plague Day Care Industry," *The Wall Street Journal,* 19 February 1987, p. 27.

Swiers, Clark, Prosthetic Technician, Lakeshore, Incorporated, Birmingham, Alabama. Interview, 24 February 1987.

Vann, Lauralee. "Rehabilitation: Dealing with Human Life." *The Birmingham News,* 21 March 1983, p. 19.

Watson, Eugene, Vice President of Corporate Development, Lakeshore, Incorporated, Birmingham, Alabama. Interview, 17 February 1987.

Witcher, Dell, Director of Public Relations, Lakeshore, Incorporated, Alabama. Interview, 11 February 1987.

Strategic Planning at Davy Crockett University

Mark Kroll, University of Texas at Tyler

It was already dark when Clark King, a professor of strategic planning at Davy Crockett State University (DCU), walked out of the administration building and onto the sidewalk. He gazed across the dimly lit, winter-swept campus, and the cool air dissipated some of the anger-generated heat from his face. He had just concluded an hour and a half visit with the vice president of academic affairs, and little of what he had heard did he like. Clark headed down the hill toward the business administration building trying to untangle his emotions as he went. While he very much wanted to be the cool, detached professional who was observing what he thought to be a classic case of how not to undertake the strategic planning process, he could not escape the disappointment and frustration of seeing eighteen months of committee work go for nothing. Still worse, he thought he might be watching DCU, his alma mater, fall further behind its competition.

THE HISTORY OF DAVY CROCKETT STATE UNIVERSITY

Davy Crockett State University has been, and is today, a relatively small liberal arts school which has a long, but not especially noteworthy, history. The school was founded well over a hundred years ago as a normal institute, or teacher training school. Over time, as student demand warranted, the school added other programs in the arts, sciences, vocational areas, and business administration. The net result? No clear focus or direction for the university. Its tradition as a teacher's college prevented Davy Crockett from having either a strong research or technical orientation. The absence of any of the traditional professional programs, such as engineering, law, or medicine, precluded more than lukewarm alumni support.

The student body is drawn largely from the immediate area surrounding the university. The single most important market the university serves is one of the five largest cities in the United States, which is just fifty miles to the south. As the university has few programs which have regional or national reputations (notable exceptions are social work and music), it draws relatively few students from out of state or even from distant areas of its own state. Generally, the students admitted to DCU score slightly below the national average on standardized admission exams (e.g., the ACT and SAT). DCU's students are not aggressively recruited by major industrial concerns, and many eventually find their way into smaller firms, teaching positions, or entry-level service industry positions.

■ Structure and Administration

The university is made up of four colleges. The largest college is the College of Arts and Sciences, created a few years earlier by the merger of two schools. Arts and Sciences is a hodgepodge of programs—areas as diverse as physics and drama are included in the college. However, the college has relatively few majors because many of its departments service the freshman and sophomore course requirements of other colleges.

The largest college in terms of majors is the College of Education. Given the university's history as a "teacher's college," it is not surprising that the College of Education accounts for the largest number of degrees granted. The college offers degrees in the traditional teaching fields, such as elementary and secondary education, guidance counseling, and school administration. Most of these programs have been in place since the university's inception, though they have been modified to reflect changes in teaching theory and legislative mandates for teacher training. In addition, the college houses several vocational programs (e.g., agriculture, farm technology, office automation, and printing). These programs were the result of the strong vocational training orientation of William Bennett, the president of the university immediately after the Second World War. The college does not offer a doctorate and does not have a national or regional reputation for excellence.

The College of Business Administration is the second-largest college in terms of majors. Unfortunately, as is the case with the College of Education, it is not regionally recognized, nor is it accredited by the American Assembly of Collegiate Schools of Business. It has grown primarily as a result of the national trend of student interest in business. While the Business School has existed since the early 1950s, and has offered an MBA since 1960, its rapid growth did not begin until the early 1970s.

Finally, the College of Social Work, the newest and smallest of the four colleges, was founded in 1969. It has achieved some regional, if not national, prominence, and does offer a doctorate. Exhibit 1 lists key dates in the university's history.

Historical Sketch of Davy Crockett State University

Exhibit 1

1872	Davy Crockett School for Teachers is founded.	1955	Enrollment declines to 6000 students.
1900	Enrollment tops 600 students.	1960	College of Business is replaced the Master of Science degree in business with the MBA.
1922	Colleges of Education and Liberal Arts are formed.		
1930	Enrollment tops 3000.	1967	Enrollment climbs to 10,000 students.
1932	Name is changed to Davy Crockett State Teachers College.	1968	Name is changed to Davy Crockett State University.
1949	Enrollment tops 7500 students.	1975	College of Fine Arts and College of Science and Mathematics are recombined to form the College of Arts and Sciences.
1950	College of Business Administration is formed.		
1952	Vocational programs in agriculture, automotive and farm technology, and printing are introduced.	1977	Enrollment peaks at 10,800 students.
		1980	University undertakes a $47 million building program.
1954	Name is changed to Davy Crockett State College.	1984	University enrolls 10,500 students for the fall.
1954	College of Fine Arts and College of Science and Mathematics are formed.	1988	University enrolls 11,500 students for the fall.

The administrative structure of DCU is presented in Exhibit 2. The administration is, for the most part, a product of DCU. In conversations with the various university officers, it was learned that all of the vice presidents and the president gained most of their teaching experience at DCU, and some are graduates of DCU. None of the top administrators have ever been involved in university administration elsewhere. The president of the university, P. T. Barham, has held that office for the past fifteen years. The vice president for academic affairs, Ricky Malthus, took over in that capacity after serving for many years as dean of the College of Education. The other vice presidents have been in their respective positions for many years. Faculty representation to the administration is provided by the faculty senate, which is made up of four representatives from each college for a total of sixteen senators, plus a chairman.

THE STRATEGIC PLANNING COMMITTEE

Early in the academic year, about eight months after becoming vice president of academic affairs, Ricky Malthus read a book on strategic planning for colleges and decided it was something that was sorely missing at DCU. The literature he had been exposed to suggested that collegiate strategic planning should be comprehensive in nature, meaning all parts of the college should be involved

Exhibit 2   **Organization Chart for Davy Crockett State University**

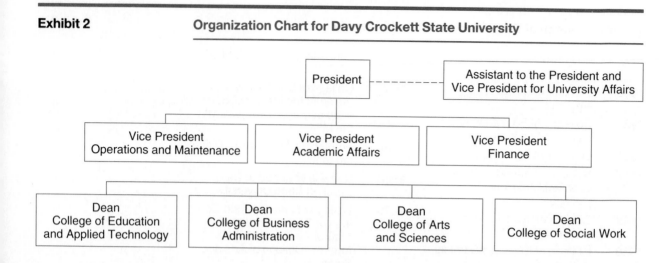

(everything from the student union, to the football team, to the physics department). However, when he attempted to share his enthusiasm with the other vice presidents, they balked at the idea. They did not feel that such an effort would, for political reasons, result in any concrete improvement in the university. They then challenged him to undertake such an effort on the academic side of the university, and if successful, they would consider such an effort in the other areas of the university.

Malthus, convinced of the merits of strategic planning, decided to go it alone and push ahead with planning. He knew that this was an opportune time for such an effort because the university had just completed a state-mandated review of its purpose and mission as an institution of higher education, and the governor had just formed a task force to examine what the future of higher education should be in the state. Malthus felt that DCU could demonstrate its innovativeness to the state and the governor's panel if it could present a comprehensive plan based on the recently revised mission statement.

■ Committee Formation

In order to develop a plan, Malthus decided to seek the aid of his longtime confidant, and the head of the Management Department, Rose Loreal. Malthus felt that Loreal was someone who could navigate the treacherous political waters the planning effort would have to go through and also someone with whom he could work. After some discussion, Loreal and Malthus decided that a faculty committee made up of highly respected members of each college headed by Loreal would be the best mechanism for developing an academic master plan. Rose was instructed by Malthus to choose persons she thought she could work with, who would be willing to put in the effort required to complete the project, and who had credibility with the faculty. After some thought and consultation with Malthus, Loreal asked the persons listed in Exhibit 3 to be on the committee.

The committee met for the first time on September 20, with an agenda of trying to decide how to tackle a job none of them had any experience with. The committee arrived at three conclusions as a result of their meeting:

Bill Start: Longtime professor of philosophy; active in committee work, professional organizations, and research.

Paula Friendly: Full professor of psychology; active in committee work and program development for the School of Social Work.

Davy Kaiwee: Head of the Physics Department; active in research and university committee work.

Sammy Kaye: Longtime member of the Drama Department faculty and former head of the department; nationally recognized for his work in college drama production.

Bob Unison: Longtime member of the Government Department faculty; heavily published; the current president of the faculty senate.

Doug Papst: Full professor of history; active in university committee work, faculty government, and research.

Clark King: Fairly recent addition to the Management Department faculty, after having completed his doctorate in management; teaches strategic planning almost exclusively.

1. Rob Angelia, a widely respected expert in the area of university planning, should be brought in to help give the group guidance.
2. The vice president of academic affairs should be made a member of the committee.
3. The committee wanted the administration's assurance that it was in fact committed to the effort and was prepared to make the hard choices that would be involved.

The committee felt it was important for the vice president to be on the committee for two reasons: (1) It would be the vice president who would ultimately have to live with the political and organizational consequences of whatever emerged; and (2) it was felt that his perspective would be invaluable to the committee.

Loreal then went to see Malthus for what was to be one of many such trips to communicate the committee's feelings. In response to the committee's request that Rob Angelia be brought in for a help session, Malthus thought it was a good idea. In response to the other two issues, however, Malthus felt he had better approach the president. When Malthus discussed the situation with the president, he asked to visit with Loreal in order to develop a more complete understanding of what the entire effort was all about.

At the meeting between Loreal, Malthus, and the president, Loreal was able to impress upon the president the importance of planning for business organizations and how she felt that a similar effort in universities could be highly beneficial. As a result of Loreal's persuasive arguments, the president left the meeting very enthusiastic about the process and suggested that a university-wide plan might be appropriate, an idea the other vice presidents had already rejected. He also assured Rose that the committee's recommendations would be given serious consideration and that the administration was prepared to "take the political heat" that might result. As for the request that Malthus join the committee, Malthus later told Loreal that after talking it over with the president, he felt his participation would unduly suppress the committee's openness and would give the impression that the committee's recommendations were final when it made its report.

THE COMMITTEE'S METHODOLOGY

About one month after Rose Loreal's meeting with the president and Malthus, the committee had a daylong workshop with Rob Angelia. In addition to the committee, all of the deans and vice presidents were invited to attend. Beside the committee members, only one dean participated. None of the vice presidents or the president attended. While Angelia made a number of suggestions and shared with the committee many of the possible pitfalls associated with strategic planning for a university, the following are some of the points which highlighted the workshop:

1. The planning process should be comprehensive in that all facets of the university should be involved.
2. The president and other top administrators should be actively involved in the planning effort and, in fact, guide the process.
3. The planning task force should select a series of internal and external environmental variables to use in measuring the relative merits and likely future direction of the various academic programs offered at the university.
4. The task force should try to produce a final report which spells out which programs the university presently offers should be enhanced (given additional resources), maintained (continue to be provided resources at present levels), reduced (be given fewer resources in the future), or phased out (closed out within a three-year period). The final report should also make an assessment of the overall academic climate of the university and outline suggestions for organizationwide changes which might lead to improvements in this area.
5. After the report is completed, the programs which are adversely effected should be given a period of time (about one month) in which to provide rebuttal evidence, showing why their programs should not be reduced or phased out. It should be understood by all parties affected that disagreements with the methodology used in arriving at the recommendations cannot be used as a basis for an appeal of the findings.
6. With the completion of the appeals process, the top administrators should finalize the plan and develop a schedule for its implementation. In instances where layoffs will be required, the persons involved should be given ample time to find a new position, and whenever feasible, retraining and reassignment should be attempted.

■ Committee's Strategy

At a meeting held shortly after the Angelia presentation the committee concluded that while Angelia had provided some useful ground rules for their effort, given the uniqueness of DCU, it was going to be necessary for the committee to create much of its methodology from scratch. However, the committee did feel that two points made by Angelia did need to be addressed before the

Program Evaluation Variables

Exhibit 4

Item	Score
1. Rate of change (slope) in total hours taught from 1979 to 1988–1989	1 2 3 4
2. Rate of change (slope) undergrad advanced hours taught 1979–1980 to 1988–1989	1 2 3 4
3. Rate of change (slope) in graduate credit hours 1979–1980 to 1988–1989	1 2 3 4
4. Net revenues earned hours taught 1979–1980 to 1988–1989	1 2 3 4
5. Absolute percentage of university's (undergrad advanced and grad) hours taught	1 2 3 4
6. Teaching load ratio	1 2 3 4
7. Teaching course ratio	1 2 3 4
8. Employment outlook	1 2 3 4
9. Departmental scholarship and research performance	1 2 3 4
10. Centrality to the university's mission	1 2 3 4
11. Potential service to the community	1 2 3 4
12. Does program have a competitive advantage in the region? Yes or no?	No Yes
13. Potential for externally funded research grants	1 2 3 4
14. Potential for external program support	1 2 3 4
15. State reimbursement per hour taught	1 2 3 4
16. Locational advantage	No Yes
17. Teaching effectiveness of program faculty	1 2 3 4

committee could move forward: At least the vice president of academic affairs should be on the committee, and the committee would have to first define a set of variables it wished to look at in making its program assessment. At the same meeting the committee decided to use a standardized questionnaire developed by a national testing service to measure the university's academic climate, or culture.

At the following meeting, Loreal reported that Malthus had again declined to join the committee. The committee expressed its disappointment about Malthus's refusal, but then went on to discuss what variables should be used in the review of the various programs offered by the university. The discussion about what variables should be used was a long and difficult one, as the various committee members had their own perspective as to what information was truly relevant in assessing the merits of a given program. After some debate, the variables listed in Exhibit 4 were the ones finally decided upon.

During the same meeting, it was decided that the committee would be divided into two subcommittees, one to gather data necessary to assess each program in terms of the seventeen variables to be used in the analysis, and the other to gather data used to forecast future trends the university would likely face in the coming years and to conduct an analysis of the university's academic climate using the questionnaire discussed earlier.

Exhibit 5   **Memo to Administrators**

To: Department Chairs or Program Coordinators

From: R. T. Malthus
                Vice President for Academic Affairs

Subject: Strategic Planning Committee

The Strategic Planning Committee has begun its work of evaluating the programs of the university with a view toward recommending directions for the long-range development of university programs, including the enhancement and reduction of programs. The committee will utilize all relevant data and studies as a basis for its recommendations. It is important that this basis include an evaluation of each program by the faculty members directly responsible for the program. In order to obtain these evaluations in a standard form, the committee has drawn up the enclosed "Program Evaluation Instrument."

The committee requests that you, as a department chair or program coordinator, complete a "Program Evaluation" for the degree program for which you are responsible. In the event you direct two or more programs (for instance, a bachelor's and master's program), you are asked to complete a separate instrument for each program.

Please complete the instrument using the guidelines provided and return it to: Clark King, College of Business Administration, chair of the subcommittee on program evaluation. If you have any questions concerning the completion of this instrument, feel free to contact Dr. King. Please try to return the instrument by March 17, 1986.

Exhibit 6   **Program Evaluation Instrument**

On the last page of this document, you will find a series of rating scales which we would appreciate your using in evaluating the program you direct. Please use the following instructions and guidelines in responding to the items on the last page. If you need additional copies of this instrument, please contact Dr. Clark King, ext. 1932. When completed, return your reply to Dr. King, College of Business.

Instructions

Please circle the response to each item that you feel is most appropriate and then write out or type on a separate sheet of paper, in a paragraph or two, why you feel your response is appropriate. We would appreciate your keeping the discussion of your scoring on the eight items to less than five single-spaced, typewritten pages (but please feel free to attach any supporting documentation which would validate your choice on any of the scales).

Item 1   In responding to this question, please base your choice on the following questions: What is the employment outlook for your program's majors for the next five years? Do a high percentage of your majors secure work in their major area? Do they secure jobs in areas in which their major skills are directly relevant? Please provide as documentation any statistical or expert opinion you feel is appropriate.

Item 2   In responding to this question, please base your choice on the following criteria:

   4   Very productive: all or most of the faculty of this program have produced relevant journal articles or appropriate publications, showing, exhibitions, etc., in the past three years

   3   Productive: one-half of the faculty of this program have produced relevant articles, etc., in the past three years

   2   Somewhat productive: a quarter of the faculty of this program have produced relevant articles, etc., in the past three years

   1   Nonproductive: no apparent productivity within the past 3 years

Attach bibliographic citations to justify your response.

Instructions

Item 3   Please develop your response in terms of the current mission of the university as stated in the University Mission Statement, a copy of which accompanies this document.

Essential   Mission cannot be accomplished without the program
Desirable   Not essential, but contributes significantly to programs which are essential to the University Mission

Marginal   Makes some contribution to programs which are essential to the University Mission

Not needed   University Mission can be accomplished without this program

Explain why you made the choice you did.

Item 4   In response to this question, please make your evaluation in terms of whether programs have been or could be developed which would appeal to adult learners in either an off-campus or on-campus format. You might take into consideration whether such programs have been successfully developed for nontraditional students by other colleges or universities in the region.

Item 5   In responding to this question, if you circle "yes," please provide a description of those structural features of your program which you feel give it an advantage over similar programs in the region. In doing this, indicate the region you serve and your chief competition in the region.

Item 6   In responding to this item, please use the following rating criteria:

4   Good track record already in place

3   Some money has been secured within the past three years

2   At least one externally funded grant was received within the last three years, or a number of possibilities for future funding exist

1   No grants secured within the last three years, and prospects for securing grants are dim

Please document available grants.

Item 7   In responding, please base your evaluation on two key questions: (1) Has your program received external financial support in the past? If so, provide dollar estimates. (2) If no funds have been raised in the past, is there any reason to believe that external funding would be possible in the future? Please briefly outline any fund-raising efforts you have mounted and their success. Attach documentation if appropriate.

Item 8   In responding to this question, if you circle "yes," please describe how the location of DCU provides your program with an advantage over other regional programs. Examples: (1) Being close to a large industrial research laboratory might be an advantage to an electrical engineering program because of opportunities for students. (2) Being close to major defense contractor's facilities might be an advantage to a marine engineering program because of the large number of potential students there.

■ Work of the Subcommittees

The subcommittee charged with gathering data on the seventeen variables decided upon a two-step process. The subcommittee would ask the program chairs and coordinators to provide input on eight of the variables—those which were of a qualitative nature and could be influenced by one's perceptions of the evidence. It was decided that program administrator input would be requested on variables 8, 9, 10, 11, 12, 13, 14, 16, and 17. The remaining variables, it was felt, could be objectively assessed using university reports and documents. Packets were then prepared consisting of a Likert-scale-type instrument requesting the program administrator's assessment of the eight variables along with a set of criteria the administrators were to use in making their assessments (see Exhibits 4, 5, 6, and 7). The program administrators were not only expected to respond to the survey but also to provide supporting documentation as to why they gave the response they did. Each packet was accompanied by a cover

---

Exhibit 7   **Program Evaluation Matrix**

Item	*Score*			
1. Employment outlook for majors	Excellent	Good	Fair	Poor
2. Departmental scholarship and research performance	Very productive	Productive	Marginally productive	Nonproductive
3. Centrality to the university's mission	Essential	Desirable	Marginal	Not needed
4. Potential service to nontraditional students	Great potential	Potential	Little potential	No potential
5. Does program have special features (other than location) which give it competitive advantage in the region served?	Yes			No
6. Potential for externally funded research grants	Great potential	Potential	Little potential	No potential
7. Potential for external program support	Great potential	Potential	Little potential	No potential
8. Does program have a locational advantage in region served?	Yes			No

---

letter from the vice president of academic affairs requesting the program administrators' participation.

After the subcommittee received the reports from the program administrators, it made its own assessment of the merits of each program in terms of variables 8, 9, 10, 11, 12, 13, 14, 16, and 17. This assessment was based on a review of the evidence presented by the program administrators and other sources available to the subcommittee. Other sources used consisted of such things as enrollment records for the various programs, analysis of the surplus or deficit history of the programs, and secondary sources which assessed the outlook for various majors. The assessments, along with the reports submitted by the administrators, were combined with the subcommittee's analysis of the remaining variables. All of the variables for each of the programs were then assembled in files—for each program offered by the university, a file was created.

The files were then presented to the committee as a whole, along with some summary documentation, including copies of a sheet which listed all of the university's programs and how they scored on each of the variables (see Exhibit 8). In order to reduce the variables to a four-point scale, such variables as state reimbursement per student credit hour earned by the various programs were ranked highest to lowest. Then, they were divided into four groups. Programs receiving the greatest reimbursements were coded with a 4, the lowest group received a 1. These files provided the basis for the entire committee's assessments of the various programs and later became a source of great curiosity for the university community. As the committee's work progressed, a number of faculty members made attempts to "get a peek" at the files. However, the committee maintained complete secrecy throughout the deliberation process.

For both subcommittees the months of November through April were busy, as they finished getting the survey completed, the responses back from the program administrators, and the quantitative-variable data collected and processed. The committee had originally hoped to give a finished report to the vice

Program Ratings for Seventeen Evaluation Variables **Exhibit 8**

Program	Variable																
	1	2	3	4	5	6	7	8	9	10	11	12	13	14	15	16	17
Accounting	3	3	4	4	4	3	1	4	2	4	3	No	2	4	2	Yes	3
Administration/super-vision/counseling	3	3	3	2	4	2	3	4	3	4	2	No	3	3	2	No	3
Agriculture	3	1	1	3	4	2	3	2.5	2	3	3	No	2.5	3	3	No	2
Automotive technology	3	3	—	1	2	1	1	2	3	3	3	No	—	3	3	No	2
Art	2	3	2	2	3	1	2	3	4	4	3	Yes	1	2	4	No	3
Biology	1	2	2	3	3	4	2	3	2.5	4	3	No	3	3	2	No	4
Business analysis	4	1	2	4	3	3	1	2.5	3	4	3	No	3	3	3	No	2
Business education	3	—	—	1	—	4	4	2	3	2	2	No	2	2	See GBA	No	4
Chemistry	2	1	2	2	3	2	2	4	2	4	2	No	3	4	2	No	4
Computing science	4	4	4	4	4	4	1	4	1	4	2	No	2	2	3	No	3
Dance	4	3	None	4	2	2	2	2.5	3	2	2	Yes	1	3	4	Yes	4
Drama	2	2	3	1	2	1	3	2.5	3	3	2	No	1	3	4	No	4
Economics	3	4	3	4	4	4	1	2.5	3	4	3	No	3	3	1	No	1
Elementary education	4	4	3	2	4	2	2	4	3	4	2	No	3	3	3	No	1
English	1	1	4	3	4	3	1	3	2	4	2	No	2	2	1	No	1
Environmental science	4	2	None	3	1	4	4	4	2	3	2	No	2	3	2	No	2
Farm technology	2	1	2	1	1	1	4	3	1	2	3	No	2	3	4	No	2
Finance	4	4	4	4	4	4	1	3	2	4	3	No	2	2	3	No	1
French	3	3	None	1	1	3	4	2.5	2	2.5	1	No	2	2	1	No	2
General business administration	1	4	2	4	1	4	1	2	2	3	3	No	3	3	3	No	2
Geography	1	4	None	2	3	3	2	2	2	2	1	No	1	2	1	No	1
Geology/geoscience	4	1	3	4	1	4	4	2	2.5	3	2	No	2	3	2	No	1
History	1	1	3	3	3	3	2	2	2.5	4	2	No	3	3	1	No	4
Home economics	1	2	1	2	1	2	4	3	2	3	3	No	3	3	3	Yes	4
Home economics education	2	2	—	1	1	1	—	3	2	3	3	No	1	2	3	No	2
Industrial education	3	4	None	1	1	1	—	4	2	3	3	Yes	2	3	4	Yes	2
Printing	2	1	2	2	3	1	4	3	1	2	3	No	2	3	4	No	1
Journalism	2	2	None	1	2	1	4	3	2	3	2	No	1	3	1	No	4
Library science	NA	NA	NA	NA	NA	NA	NA	NA	NA	NA	NA	NA	NA	NA	NA	NA	NA
Management	4	2	1	4	4	3	1	3	3	4	2.5	No	2.5	2	2	No	3
Marketing	3	4	1	4	4	4	1	3	3	4	2.5	No	1	2	2	No	2
Mathematics	4	1	3	3	3	4	1	—	—	—	—	—	—	—	1	—	2
Music	2	4	3	1	3	1	3	3	4	4	4	Yes	2	3	4	Yes	4
Office automation	1	1	None	3	3	4	1	4	2	3	2.5	No	2	2	2	No	3
Philosophy	2	3	—	2	2	3	4	NA	2	3	2	No	2	1	1	No	3
Physical education	1	1	2	2	3	2	3	3	2	4	3	No	1	3	2	No	2
Physical rehabilitation	2	3	4	1	2	1	4	3	2	3	3	Yes	2	3	4	No	1
Physical science	2	2	—	3	—	3	2	4	3	4	1	No	3	3	2	No	2
Physics	2	1	2	2	2	2	3	4	3	4	2	No	4	3	2	No	1
Political science	3	4	4	3	3	4	2	2	3	4	2	No	3	2	2	No	4
Psychology	1	1	3	3	4	4	2	2	2	4	2	No	2	2	2	Yes	4
Radio/television/film	4	4	—	4	4	3	3	3	2	3	3	Yes	3	3	4	Yes	1

(continued)

Exhibit 8   Program Ratings for Seventeen Evaluation Variables *(continued)*

Program	Variable																
	1	*2*	*3*	*4*	*5*	*6*	*7*	*8*	*9*	*10*	*11*	*12*	*13*	*14*	*15*	*16*	*17*
Russian	3	3	None	1	1	1	4	2	3	2	1	No	2	2	1	No	3
Secondary education	4	3	4	2	4	2	1	—	—	—	—	—	—	2	—	—	2
Social work	1	4	1	3.5	4	3	3	3	3	4	4	Yes	4	4	4	Yes	3
Sociology	1	2	2	2	2	4	3	1	1	4	2	No	1	1	1	No	2
Spanish	3	4	None	2	1	4	2	3	4	3.5	3	No	1	2	1	No	4
Special education	1	2	2	2	2	1	3	4	3	4	3	Yes	2	2.5	3	Yes	1
Speech	4	4	None	2	2	2	2	—	1.5	4	2	No	1	1	1	No	3
Photography	3	1	3	4	1	2	3	3	2.5	3	3	Yes	1	4	4	No	3
Small business administration	1	4	2	4	1	4	1	2	2	3	3	No	3	3	3	No	3

Note: NA indicates not available or not included in the study.

president in early May, but it was not until then that all of the variable data had been collected and the organizational climate survey results tabulated. However, on the week of final exams for the spring semester, Rose Loreal scheduled what she knew would be a very crucial meeting. It was time to decide which programs to enhance, to maintain, to reduce, and to terminate. It was expected to be a long, difficult meeting.

On May 12, the committee worked through a session which lasted from 8:00 A.M. to about 6:00 P.M. The committee, through what one committee member later described as a "jury deliberation" type of process, categorized each of the programs into one of four groups (the groupings originally suggested by Angelia): programs to enhance, to maintain, to reduce, and to phase out. While each committee member had access to all of the data available on each program, and each program was discussed at length at the meeting before a vote was taken, it was left up to committee members to weigh the relevance and importance of each variable for themselves. While academic quality of programs was weighed and debated extensively, so too was the financial performance of the programs. Programs with declining enrollments also often had heavily tenured faculties with a high percentage of full professors. Given that the state funds the university based upon a specified dollar amount for each student hour produced, times the number of hours, it was easy for the committee to determine which programs were losing heavily and which were "earning a profit" after instructional salaries have been covered. The results of the meeting were interesting in that after each program was discussed, the votes were generally unanimous.

The program recommendations made by the committee, along with the external environment subcommittee's conclusions, were then combined into a single document. A table listing the programs which were placed into the four categories is provided in Exhibit 9.

In early June a draft of the final report was then delivered to the vice president for academic affairs by Rose Loreal, with the request that he examine it and make whatever suggestions he would like before it was sent to the president. After only minor changes, the document was finalized and sent to the president.

Summary of Academic Program Priorities   **Exhibit 9**

Programs to Be Enhanced	Programs to Be Maintained at Present Level	Programs to Be Reduced	Programs to Be Phased Out
Accounting	Administration/supervision/counseling	Agriculture	Botanical science
Computer science	Art	Drama	German
Finance	Biology	English	Russian
Management	Business analysis	General business administration	Physical rehabilitation
Marketing	Chemistry	Geography	Farm technology
Secondary education	Criminal justice	History	Automotive technology
	Dance	Mathematics	Office automation
	Economics	Music	Home economics
	Elementary education	Physical education	Printing
	Environmental science	Political science	
	Geology/geoscience	Sociology	
	Industrial education		
	Journalism		
	Library science		
	Philosophy		
	Photography		
	Physical science		
	Physics		
	Psychology		
	Radio/television/film		
	Secondary education		
	Social work		
	Spanish		
	Special education		
	Speech		
	Small business administration		

THE FIRE STORM

On July 1, Loreal and Clark King met with the president to present the document and discuss its implications and recommendations. Both Loreal and King attempted to impress upon the president the severity of the political fallout they anticipated. They encouraged the president and the vice president to act decisively and have a limited review process after which a final, definitive set of decisions would be made public. They also encouraged the president to immediately begin an in-depth analysis of the nonacademic portions of the university, as Malthus had suggested almost one year earlier. The president assured Rose and Clark that he would begin moving on a review of the nonacademic side of the university, and that Malthus would have his support in implementing whatever portion of the report Malthus thought appropriate.

Malthus, in a quandary as to how the review process should be carried out, decided to wait until the beginning of the fall semester and ask the original committee how he should proceed. In effect, nothing of substance occurred until the beginning of the fall semester. By this time, some of the committee's conclusions were starting to leak out, and the rumor mill was quite active. In order to replace rumors with facts, Malthus decided to act. He first sent copies of the committee's report to all of the program administrators and coordinators. He then called a press conference which was intended to head off what he anticipated being an adverse reaction in the community. At the press conference, which was attended by the local media, Malthus presented the members of the committee to the press and explained the rationale for the entire effort.

▪ University Community Reaction

The committee had anticipated a hostile reaction by the faculty and students whose programs were adversely affected by the report, but no one had anticipated the fire storm which swirled around the report after its release. Exhibit 10 provides some sample headlines and article titles taken from the school paper, *The Pioneer*.

The level of tension for the committee members and Malthus became very great. The relationships between the committee members and their colleagues whose programs were adversely affected became, in many instances, quite strained. The motives of the committee members were questioned with rumors that the committee had set out with various hidden agendas and a "hit list" of programs. Many of the committee members were openly attacked or confronted in public situations.

Students in the affected programs did such things as have bumper stickers printed which called for the preservation of their programs. Some of the programs slated for phaseout rallied their alumni and started letter-writing campaigns. Other programs went to the media to plead their cases. The report itself was subjected to extremely close scrutiny, and there were many demands that the files prepared for each program, containing the committee's assessment of the seventeen variables, be made public.

One of the key issues in the debate was the enhancement of four programs in the College of Business. The planning committee felt that these four programs would have to be enhanced if the college was to ever have a chance of achieving accreditation by the American Assembly of Collegiate Schools of Business (AACSB). The committee had concluded in its final report that the College of Business needed to be accredited, given the large number of majors it accounts for, along with the fact that all of the major universities in the region have already achieved AACSB accreditation. Many on campus countered that to invest so heavily in the College of Business would require draining away significant resources from other parts of the university, especially the liberal arts area. It was feared that, given the relatively high salaries commanded by business professors, there would be few resources left for anything else.

Selected Newspaper Headlines Exhibit 10

Ag Tech Students Are Spurred by Plan

Agriculture technology students are mounting a campaign against the recommendations of the Academic Master Plan that calls for the demise of their program. . . .

Auto Tech Students: Don't Kill Our Program

On a campus which has traditionally been without much student interest in planning, the Master Plan seems to have struck a few raw nerves among students who think their studies would be affected by some of its proposals. No group of majors have shown more outrage over the plan's recommendations than have the auto technology majors. . . .

Plan Questioned; Senate Wants Methods, Raw Data

In its first meeting since the release of the Master Plan, the faculty senate decided to review the methodology used in writing the report to determine if errors were made and to assure that the recommendations in the plan are in line with the mission of the university.

To facilitate the review of the plan, the senate appointed a three-member subcommittee and passed a resolution requesting access to the analysis of raw data used by members of the committee that wrote the report.

Johnson Says Cuts Heartless

A recent proposal to reduce the scope of the History Department, which according to the History Department Chair Dr. Bill Johnson, "was cold and heartless," has created some negative feedback from students and faculty. The 10-member faculty committee, which devised this master plan, is suggesting a cut in specialized courses through the process of a two-tier system.

Baldwin: Language "Must" in Liberal Arts

The chairman of the Foreign Languages Department "emphatically opposes" the recommendation that Russian and German majors be dropped at DCU. He termed such a move as a "detriment to the school."

Baldwin said, "I can't imagine the university claiming to support the liberal arts without a viable foreign languages program."

■ Planning Scope Expanded

In the midst of all of the controversy, the vice president for administration, liking the results of the academic planning effort, encouraged the president to formulate a committee to undertake an analysis of the nonacademic side of the university. Initially Clark King was asked to head up this effort. However, when King suggested that such a committee must be headed by the vice president for administration if it were to have any credibility at all, the president asked to meet with King to "hear for himself how King thought the effort should be handled." In a private meeting with the president, King tried to impress upon the president the necessity of top administrators becoming involved with the planning process. King's meeting with the president took place in early October. In early December, King called the vice president of administration to see what was happening. King was told that the entire process was "dead in the water."

Meanwhile, in response to all of the controversy, Malthus, with the committee's approval, decided to begin the rebuttal process in October by first making available to the program administrators the files which had been prepared for their programs. With this data, and whatever else they chose to use, the program administrators were invited to present reports either refuting the committee's findings or presenting evidence which would cast a new light on the merits of the program. The reports were to be turned in to Malthus by the middle of November. By the time the deadline rolled around, over 700 pages of rebuttal had been submitted. Some of the replies were emotional appeals; some were carefully thought-out, effective counterarguments. The question Malthus then had to answer was how to carry out the review process in a politically acceptable way. Once again, he requested that the committee meet and develop recommendations as to how he should proceed.

■ Faculty Senate's Response

In the meantime, the faculty senate had been debating the entire affair and decided to assign a committee to review the validity of the methodology used by the committee. Three members of the senate were assigned this task, with a charge to report to the senate as soon as possible their conclusions as to the credibility of the plan. The senate committee requested and got access to all of the program files and the raw data. The senate committee also requested a meeting with the planning committee, which was granted. At that meeting, the senate committee members expressed concerns over a number of issues. Some of their concerns centered around statistical techniques used, while other questions focused on the committee's interpretation of the university's mission as to what constituted a "regional advantage," and what flaws the committee itself saw in what was done.

The senate committee's final report held that the methodology used by the planning committee was so flawed and inappropriately applied as to render the report useless, though the senate committee did suggest that the concept of planning was a good one. When the senate committee reported back to the full senate, a long, trying debate ensued which centered on whether any plan which called for cutting programs would be given the senate committee's blessing. Conspicuously absent in the debate was Bob Unison. He had taken himself out of the senate deliberations given his position on the Strategic Planning Committee. The final resolution voted out of the senate recommended that another committee, made up of a mixture of administrators and faculty, examine the plan and correct its flaws. Some of the members of the Planning Committee took exception to the suggestion that the report was flawed. Bob Unison, who was also a member of the faculty senate, commented during the debate that "if God himself had designed the methodology the senate would still say it was flawed!"

Shortly after the senate subcommittee report was made public, Loreal called the Planning Committee together for one final time. The emotions displayed by the committee members at the meeting were varied—ranging from introspection in terms of what errors the committee might have made, to indignation over the charges made by the senate committee. The purpose of the meeting was to develop a recommendation for Malthus as to how he should proceed. The final draft of the memo sent to Malthus is presented in Exhibit 11. The most important points the committee felt it needed to make with Malthus was that the review process should not be a rehash of what it had already done but a relatively expeditious review of the rebuttals followed by a set of definitive action plans.

Memo to Malthus Exhibit 11

Memo To: Dr. R. Malthus, Academic Vice President

From: The Strategic Planning Committee

Subject: Recommendations for Future Action

The committee sees the development of an Academic Plan passing through three phases.

Phase 1   The first phase is the collection of information on the environmental factors, university culture, and university programs. This information then would be evaluated and formulated into a preliminary Academic Master Plan. We feel that this was the task that you assigned to our committee and that task was completed when we presented you with our committee report.

Phase 2   In this phase, all interested parties are given a chance to respond to the preliminary plan. This information along with the preliminary plan would then be evaluated and final recommendations developed. Our committee does not feel that it would be appropriate for us to be a part of phase 2. We would recommend that a new committee be formed, chaired by the academic vice president. The committee should include the academic deans, representation from the Academic Master Plan and Strategic Planning Committee, and representation from the faculty senate. We feel that this committee would provide continuity in the planning process and provide a broader base for the review phase. Due to the volume of responses received in the review phase, we recommend that the completion of this phase be extended into the spring semester.

Phase 3   The final phase would be the implementation phase. In this phase, the academic vice president and the academic deans would formulate and execute an implementation plan approved by the president of the university.

Shortly after Malthus received the recommendations of the committee, he announced the formation of a new "review" committee. The new committee was made up of the deans of the colleges, some program administrators, the members of the senate committee, and three members of the original committee; Malthus would chair the committee. The three original committee members asked to serve on the review committee were Bob Unison, Davy Kaiwee, and Clark King. The reason these three were asked to join was because they were the ones most responsible for developing the original program files used by the Planning Committee.

■ Review Committee Formed

The vice president sent a memo to all of the prospective members (see Exhibit 12 for an example of the letters sent) outlining a two-point charge:

1. Review the Planning Committee document to determine its validity.
2. Formulate recommendations to be forwarded to President Barham with regard to program offerings at DCU.

Shortly after receiving the invitation, Clark King went to see Davy Kaiwee to see just how Davy interpreted the committee's charge. Davy said that he basi-

---

Exhibit 12   **Malthus's Letter to the Members of the Review Committee**

Dr. David Kaiwee, Chair
Department of Physics
Davy Crockett State University
Roxton, AR 32518

Dear Dr. Kaiwee:

The Academic Planning Committee has recommended to me that a separate committee be established to review the responses to the document developed during the first phase of the Academic Master Plan study. I have accepted the recommendation and will chair the Plan Review Committee. The new committee will be made up of the four academic deans, three members from the former Planning Committee, three members from the university faculty senate, and three members from the Academic Policy Council.

The charge to the Review Committee is as follows:

1.   Review the Planning Committee document to determine its validity.

2.   Formulate recommendations to be forwarded to President Barham with regard to program offerings at DCU.

I am asking you to serve on the Review Committee as a representative of the former Planning Committee. If you cannot accept this very important appointment, please let me know at your earliest convenience.

Sincerely,

J. T. Malthus
Vice President

DK: ldr
cc: Dr. E. T. Barham

---

cally felt that Malthus was running scared, and that he wanted to essentially let the new committee do with it whatever it wanted. He went on to point out that given the relatively hostile composition of the new committee (e.g., the senate committee members, and some program chairs who had been adversely affected were involved), he felt that the Planning Committee's report would probably be picked apart. His major concern was that the new committee would essentially reexamine each program and the evaluations made by the original committee and change the results more to their liking. Given that the three from the original committee would be three against many, their odds of stopping this from happening were slight. Clark agreed and wondered aloud if it would not be best for the three of them to go see Malthus prior to the new committee's first meeting and outline their fears. Kaiwee agreed, and a meeting with Malthus was scheduled for 5:00 that evening.

Clark and Davy knew going into their 5:00 P.M. meeting that it was critical they not back the vice president into a corner by forcing the issue of his support of the committee's original recommendations. On the other hand, they were very much concerned that Malthus had essentially "gotten cold feet" and was looking to the new committee to reshape the report into a more politically palatable document. They saw the consequences of this being a move away from enhancing those programs which needed it and an unwillingness to close programs which had outlasted their usefulness.

Their fears were in no way alleviated by what they heard in the meeting. First, while Malthus understood that Davy and Clark feared the consequences of a complete reproduction of the earlier committee's work, he would not try to steer the committee away from such an approach, if that is what it wanted to do. Second, he outlined his reasons for taking exception to some of the committee's recommendations for closing programs. His rationale seemed, at least to Davy and Clark, to completely ignore the reasons given by the committee for its recommendation. Malthus also expressed regret that the committee had raised the issue of AACSB accreditation in its report, suggesting that accreditation was "not a major issue at this time." Finally, Malthus impressed upon them his feeling that whatever plan is adopted, it should have the full support of the faculty senate. When Davy and Clark told Malthus that in their estimation, the senate would never back a plan that involved closing programs or accrediting the College of Business, he simply said that he was not prepared to go against the will of the senate. At that point, King and Kaiwee told the vice president that they had said all they came to say, and they thanked Malthus for his time.

When they walked out of the office and looked at each other, Kaiwee asked King for his reaction. King simply responded, "It's over."

Pardon Me, Boys, Is That the Chattanooga Aquarium?

R. L. Driggans, Marilyn M. Helms, University of Tennessee

Communities across America are replacing manufacturing jobs with service jobs as companies move production offshore to locations with lower labor costs. This case looks at the situation of one midsized city as it tries to plan for its future economic vitality.

Chattanooga is the fourth-largest city in Tennessee with a population of 178,465. It is located in the southeastern portion of the state near the Georgia and Alabama state lines and is the center of a six-county Metropolitan Statistical Area (MSA) with a combined population of 445,000. Chattanooga's central location in the South makes it a perfect distribution center for the eastern United States. Supplies and products for industry flow easily into and out of the Chattanooga area through its extensive system of highway, railroad, river, and air transportation.

Chattanooga is one of the nation's oldest manufacturing cities. In 1979, 31.4 percent of its employment was in the manufacturing sector. By 1988, manufacturing's proportion of the area's employment had fallen to 24.1 percent (Exhibits 1, 2, and 3), providing 19 percent of the MSA population's income.

This decrease in the manufacturing sector is not unique to Chattanooga. The major employer in Tennessee is now the health services industry, with travel and tourism ranking second. Between 1980 and 1986, U.S. manufacturing employment decreased by 6 percent, while total employment increased by 10 percent (Exhibit 4). During this same period, manufacturing's contribution to U.S. gross national product (GNP) decreased from 21 percent in 1980 to 19 per-

---

Exhibit 1 Chattanooga MSA Nonagricultural Employment, 1979–1988

	1979	1980	1981	1982	1983	1984	1985	1986	1987	1988
Employment (in 1000)										
Manufacturing employment	54.8	50.2	48.4	44.4	43.3	43.7	43.7	43.8	45.5	46.5
Nonmanufacturing employment										
Trade	34.1	33	36.5	35.1	36.6	39.2	40.1	41.2	43.7	44.7
Services	27.9	28.2	29.8	29.7	31.1	31.7	33.3	35.2	36.7	37.5
Other nonmanufacturing	57.8	57.3	56.5	55.4	55.2	56.7	57.8	59.4	62.4	64.2
Total nonmanufacturing employment	119.8	118.5	122.8	120.2	122.9	127.6	131.2	135.8	142.8	146.4
Total employment	174.6	168.7	171.2	164.6	166.2	171.3	174.9	179.6	188.3	192.9
Percent of Employment										
Manufacturing	31.4%	29.8%	28.3%	27.0%	26.1%	25.5%	25.0%	24.4%	24.2%	24.1%
Trade	19.5%	19.6%	21.3%	21.3%	22.0%	22.9%	22.9%	22.9%	23.2%	23.2%
Services	16.0%	16.7%	17.4%	18.0%	18.7%	18.5%	19.0%	19.6%	19.5%	19.4%
Other	33.1%	34.0%	33.0%	33.7%	33.2%	33.1%	33.0%	33.1%	33.1%	33.3%
Total	100.0%	100.0%	100.0%	100.0%	100.0%	100.0%	100.0%	100.0%	100.0%	100.0%

Chattanooga MSA Employment, 1979–1988

Exhibit 2

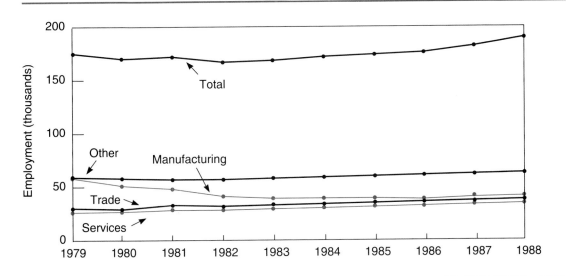

Chattanooga MSA Employment, 1979–1988 Percentages by Sector

Exhibit 3

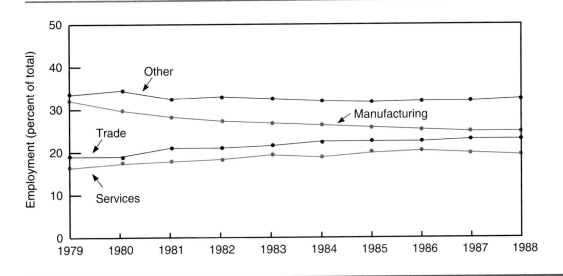

U.S. Nonagricultural employment, 1980–1986

Exhibit 4

Employment	1980		1986		
	Number (in 1000)	*% of Total*	*Number (in 1000)*	*% of Total*	*% Change Since 1980*
Total	90,406		99,610		10.2
Manufacturing	20,285	22.4	18,994	19.1	−6.4
Services	17,890	88.2	23,099	121.6	29.1
Retail Trade	15,035	84.0	17,845	77.3	18.7

Exhibit 5   **GNP Contribution for Selected Sectors (current dollars in billions)**

Sector	1980	1983	1984	1985	1986	% Increase 1980–1986	% of GNP	
							1980	1986
Total	$2732	$3406	$3772	$4010	$4235	55.0		
Manufacturing	$581	$683	$772	$799	$824	41.9	21.3	19.5
Retail trade	$245	$316	$351	$382	$408	66.5	9.0	9.6
Services	$374	$516	$580	$644	$700	87.2	13.7	16.5
Hotels	$19	$24	$27	$30	$32	68.8	0.7	0.8
Amusement	$12	$17	$18	$20	$21	72.6	0.5	0.5

cent in 1986, while the service sector's contribution increased from 14 to 17 percent of GNP (Exhibit 5).

Chattanooga still ranks as the 21st most industrialized city in the United States (based on industrial jobs as a percentage of the total work force) and offers manufacturers relatively low labor, energy, and basic living costs. However, since 1983 more than 50 businesses either left Chattanooga or were purchased by outside interests. Today, decisions as to where to create, locate, or maintain businesses are increasingly being based more on the quality of life in an area rather than just its proximity to raw materials, markets, or transportation factors. Recognizing this fact, Chattanooga's leaders set a goal of making Chattanooga the finest midsized city in America.

EARLY BEGINNINGS

In 1815, Cherokee descendent Chief John Ross built a trading post on the banks of the Tennessee River. The settlement that grew up around the trading post became known as Ross's Landing and was a center for farming, trade, and river traffic. In 1839, the community was incorporated as Chattanooga, an Indian name describing the "rock rising to a point" that was Lookout Mountain. Chattanooga prospered as a link between producers in the South and manufacturers in the North. Development of an extensive network of railroads to transfer goods consequently made the city a valued occupation prize during the Civil War. After the war, the nation's first military park was established and became Chattanooga's first tourist attraction.

Chattanooga built its industrial base thanks to its position as a railroad crossroads, its abundant supply of raw materials, and its river access. In the 1930s, the Tennessee Valley Authority (TVA) was established and brought low-cost electricity, flood control, and recreational water facilities to the Chattanooga area. The TVA system of dams also improved the Tennessee River as a navigable waterway. Three major interstate highways (I-75, I-24, and I-59) intersect in the Chattanooga area.

THE SCENIC CENTER OF THE SOUTH

From its beginning after the Civil War, tourism has grown into a major industry in the Chattanooga area. In 1986, travelers to Tennessee numbered over 39.1

million and spent $4.1 billion. This generated 89,300 jobs in Tennessee and provided nearly $894 million in income. Chattanooga had 6.8 million visitors in 1986 who deposited over $229 million in the local economy. Hamilton County's tourism industry provided $48.9 million in payroll for the industry's 5100 employees.

Chattanooga sits in a valley surrounded by Lookout, Signal, Elder, and Raccoon Mountains and Missionary Ridge. This adds to the scenic beauty of the region but also causes frequent temperature inversions, which contribute to air-quality problems. Due to its location and heavy industrialization, in the 1960s Chattanooga suffered from severe air pollution. With the advent of stricter air-pollution regulations and the loss of some manufacturing plants, air quality has improved. But it is still very seldom that one can actually "see seven states" from the top of Lookout Mountain, as the tourist brochures boast.

ECONOMIC DEVELOPMENT

To achieve the goal of becoming the nation's finest midsized city, Chattanooga's leaders have initiated efforts to revitalize the downtown core and to develop the long-neglected potential of Chattanooga's extensive river access. This revitalization is seen as a key factor in efforts to attract businesses and to stimulate visitor-based economic development. In 1985, a 20-year master plan for the development of 20 miles of the Chattanooga riverfront was announced, which included public recreation and fishing areas, a riverfront industrial park, housing, and the $30 million Tennessee Aquarium, which is expected to serve as the catalyst for an additional $70 million of public and private investments in hotels, office space, and retail establishments at Ross's Landing, where downtown Chattanooga meets the river. At the time the Tennessee Aquarium was proposed, it was expected to have great economic appeal as a tourist attraction since there were no aquaria between Baltimore and Orlando. Annual attendance of 570,000 was projected for the facility.

An issue concerning the aquarium is the entire riverfront development project being proposed for Chattanooga. Proponents want to close a half-mile section of Riverfront Parkway, a downtown bypass spoke which separates the aquarium from the Tennessee River. Closing the road would cost $3 to $5 million and result in poorer traffic patterns but is seen as important to the entire riverfront development effort (Exhibit 6). The roadway was constructed in 1973 to provide a route for 5000 Combustion Engineering employees. Layoffs at Combustion's Chattanooga plant have reduced the need for the parkway, but it is still used to handle tractor-trailer traffic at a loading terminal operated by Southern Railway.

Some industry leaders see the road closing as another sign that Chattanooga is turning its back on its industrial base in pointing to a future based on tourism. With the decrease in manufacturing in the Chattanooga area and the competition among midsized cities to attract new industry, some residents feel that it may be time to seriously investigate the tourism option. Chattanooga has some of the top tourist attractions in the state, including Rock City, Ruby Falls, the Tennessee Valley Railroad, and the Chattanooga Choo Choo Vacation Complex (for a more complete list of attractions, see Exhibit 7). Chattanooga has the largest shopping mall in Tennessee; outdoor recreation opportunities, including white-water rafting, boating, and fishing; and seasonal events, including the summer Riverbend Festival, a week of outdoor concerts by national and local

Exhibit 6   **Map of Riverfront, with Proposed Parkway Closing Shown in Gray**

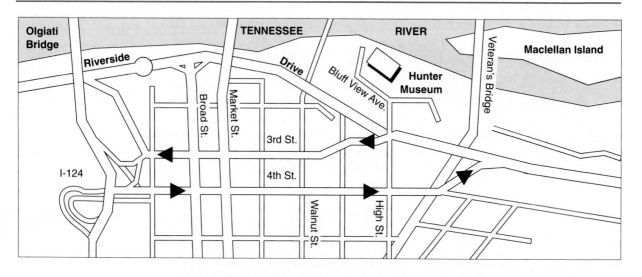

Exhibit 7   **Chattanooga Tourist Attractions**

Chattanooga Nature Center

Southern Belle Riverboat

Chickamauga-Chattanooga National Military Park

Confederama

Lake Wimnnepesauka Amusement Park

Ruby Falls

Lookout Mountain Flight Park

Incine Railway

Rock City Gardens

Tennessee Valley Railroad

Chattanooga Choo Choo

Raccoon Mountain Caverns and Adventure Park

Ocoee Rafting

Lake Chickamauga

Harrison Bay State Park

Chester Frost Park

Tennessee Valley Authority Energy Center

entertainers, and the Annual Fall Color Cruise and Folk Festival, featuring boat and train tours. By tying in with the proposed aquarium, Chattanooga intends to promote itself as the "National Sports-Fishing Center," a position it hopes to justify by luring fishing tournaments and fishing equipment manufacturers to the area. The success of this activity would in part depend on the continued health of area lakes, which had recently been threatened by a multiyear drought and widespread growth of milfoil.

Chattanooga is within one day's drive (500 miles) of nearly one-third of the major U.S. markets and half of the nation's population. The interstate highway system provides Chattanooga with a strong supply of pass-through travelers going north or south, and there are 9 million people within 150 miles of the Chattanooga area. Nearly 93 percent of all visitors to Chattanooga arrive by automobile, with most coming from areas close to Chattanooga. Atlanta produces the most overnight stays, followed by Nashville, Birmingham, Knoxville,

Memphis, and Huntsville. Almost 98 percent of the travelers to the Chattanooga area stay less than five days, with over 76 percent staying only one day. Also, most travelers are not repeat visitors, with 69 percent having made only one visit to Chattanooga.

Demographic studies of present visitors to the Chattanooga area show that there are two major classes of traveler: One group is made up of retirees (28 percent of all visitors), and the other consists of families in the 25–34 age group. The typical traveler has a high school education (only 17 percent have completed college), and only 23 percent of travelers have incomes greater than $40,000.

In 1988, a survey was commissioned to determine the travel habits of vacationers and potential vacationers to the Chattanooga area. The study involved telephone interviews with persons from the general drawing markets of Chattanooga tourism, including Atlanta, Nashville, Knoxville, Birmingham, and Huntsville. All of the 1303 interview subjects had traveled during the past year and had taken a day trip of at least 75 miles, a one- or two-night trip of more than 50 miles, or any trip lasting three or more nights.

The study found that 75 percent of those surveyed had visited Chattanooga, but only 5 percent had done so during the past year. The study indicated that one of the major difficulties in marketing Chattanooga to travelers is that there is not a sharply defined, central attraction that brings and holds visitors for more than a short time. Chattanooga competes with Nashville, Gatlinburg/Pigeon Forge, Atlanta, and Disneyworld for short-trip travelers and has only a modest market share.

The survey asked respondents to rank nine qualities of potential vacation destinations. Scenic beauty, shopping, and outdoor recreation where the top three qualities, all of which are advantages of Chattanooga. However, aquariums and Civil War history were near the bottom of the list (Exhibit 8). When respondents were asked to indicate the first thought that came to mind when they hear of Chattanooga, 42 percent said they thought of trains and the song "Chattanooga Choo Choo," with Lookout Mountain being the second-mentioned association and scenic beauty coming in third (Exhibit 9); while Atlanta was associated with shopping and sports, Gatlinburg was associated with scenic beauty and shopping, Nashville with country music, and Memphis with Elvis and Graceland. Respondents rated Chattanooga eighth out of nine southern cities as a place they would like to return to on vacation.

Scenic beauty is an important attribute to vacationers that the Chattanooga area offers. However, it was the opinion of the study authors that Chattanooga would benefit from an attraction which cannot be found in any competing market. Presently, Chattanooga has a lot of two- and three-hour attractions and no three-day attractions. They indicated that the Tennessee Aquarium being built in Chattanooga should help to create "a unified and distinctly favorable impression on the potential vacationer." (This opinion was made in spite of the fact that only 9 percent of survey respondents had heard that Chattanooga was building an aquarium, and aquariums were ranked seventh out of nine qualities considered by potential visitors to the Chattanooga area.) However, it has recently been announced that an aquarium project is being considered for Atlanta.

An editorial in the *Chattanooga News Free Press* on January 19, 1989, stated that Chattanooga needs to avoid a shotgun approach but should, rather, combine its many facilities, attractions, assets, and efforts into a single package of

---

Exhibit 8   General Attributes with Appeal

We read respondents nine qualities and asked them to rate their importance in a potential vacation destination. When ranked by those that are "very" or "somewhat" important to consider, the nine qualities provide an indication of the things which will have the most appeal to those travelers from markets we tested. While all qualities have appeal, scenic beauty, shopping, and outdoor recreation were each important to three-fourths or more of all respondents.

The table presented below shows the ranking of these qualities both in total and by age, income, and the presence of children in the household. As one might expect, younger respondents are more likely to prefer outdoor recreation, water sports, or nightlife; and older respondents are more likely to prefer cultural or historic activities.

Question: I'd like to read you a short list of things some people consider when making travel plans. For each I'd like you to tell me whether or not it is very important, somewhat important, or not very important to you that your destinations include these qualities.

		Age			*Income*			*Children*		
	Total	*Under 35*	*35–64*	*65+*	*$20,000*	*$20,000–$40,000*	*Over $40,000*	*Any Under 12*	*Only Over 12*	*None*
Total	1303	542	630	107	209	565	431	411	158	734
Attractions Ranked by Very or Somewhat Rating										
A. Scenic beauty	92	91	92	95	92	90	94	94	90	92
H. Shopping	78	82	75	76	82	79	75	79	80	76
C. Outdoor recreation or water sports	74	88	67	47	67	78	73	83	78	68
I. Fairs and festivals	69	73	68	53	69	75	63	70	73	67
D. Museums	67	61	69	82	71	64	68	68	61	67
G. Nightlife	60	78	52	22	56	61	63	59	72	59
E. Aquariums	47	46	47	49	54	46	45	53	44	44
B. Civil War history	42	34	48	53	48	42	39	40	35	45
F. Theater, opera, or symphony	41	40	40	47	44	37	43	34	39	45

Exhibit 9   Attributes Associated with Chattanooga

For Chattanooga, top-of-mind awareness generated much recall related to the popular song lyric, at 42 percent. Second and third most mentioned were Lookout Mountain and general "scenic beauty," mentioned by 22 and 13 percent, respectively.

Of the entire sample, 82 percent had some top-of-mind association for Chattanooga. The categorical responses of these individuals is presented in the table below.

Question: What is the first thought that comes to mind when you hear this place?

Total Responding to "Chattanooga"	1068
Train, song, choo-choo	42%
Lookout Mountain	22
Countryside, mountains, rivers, scenic beauty	13
Rock City, Ruby Falls	10
Other positive response	13
Any negative	2

Note: Percentages add to more than 100% because respondents could provide multiple responses.

U.S. Production Worker Employment, 1980–1986 Hourly Earnings **Exhibit 10**

Sector	1980	1986
Manufacturing	$7.27	$9.73
Retail Trade	$4.88	$6.03
Services	$5.85	$8.16
Hotels	$4.45	$5.96
Amusement	$5.52	$6.88

visitor-attracting excitement that will "guarantee good times for visitors who come here and provide jobs for those who live here." The article warned that Chattanoogans are good at thinking of projects and bringing them into being without contriving means to assure their continuing financial support, thus ending up with economic losers. The Chattanooga/Hamilton County Convention and Trade Center, Engel Stadium, the UTC Arena, the Soldiers and Sailors Memorial Auditorium, the Tivoli Theatre, the proposed Bessie Smith Hall, the planned restoration of the Walnut Street Bridge, and talk of installing trolley cars on downtown streets are cited as examples of projects with enthusiastic supporters but which do not have financial support sufficient to assure a positive cash flow.

In deciding how far it should go in courting tourism, Chattanooga should consider both its chances of success and the results of that success. Chattanooga faces strong competition from surrounding cities and from other eastern U.S. vacation destinations. Since 93 percent of Chattanooga tourists arrive by car, Chattanooga will likely continue to miss out on upscale and long-term visitors. In Tennessee in 1985, there was one tourism job for every $41,600 in tourist expenditures. However, the average hourly wage rates for U.S. production workers in the hotel and recreation sectors are $5.96 and $6.88, respectively, versus $9.73 for the manufacturing sector (Exhibit 10).

Chattanooga's leadership has stated that its economic development efforts would be aimed at both business and tourism. However, it is inevitable that there will be conflicts between the needs of business and tourism that will have to be decided in favor of one or the other. The Aquarium and Riverfront Parkway closing are just the first of many issues which will divide residents along lines of business versus tourism.

REFERENCES

"The Aquarium: Accentuating the Positive," *Chattanooga Life & Leisure*, May 1988.

Chattanooga Area Convention and Visitors Bureau. *Chattanooga's Story.*

Chattanooga Area Convention and Visitors Bureau. *1988/1989 Marketing Plan.*

Chattanooga Area Convention and Visitors Bureau. *Picture Yourself in Chattanooga: 1989 Visitors Guide.*

"Chattanooga's Industrial Parks," *Chattanooga Life & Leisure*, September 1988.

"Citizens Debate Parkway Closure," *Chattanooga Times*, February 22, 1989, p. 1.

"City Lacks Trademark Attraction, Marketing Study Says," *Chattanooga Times,* January 19, 1989, p. 1.

"How Vital Is the Riverfront?" *Chattanooga Times,* February 11, 1989, p. 8.

"Most Outsiders Unaware of Aquarium," *Chattanooga News Free Press,* January 19, 1989, p. 1.

"Portland Goes for Broke," *Planning,* February 1989.

"Putting Our Best Foot Forward," *Chattanooga News Free Press,* February 19, 1989, p. 5.

"The RiverCity Co.: A Private Non-Profit Corporation to Implement Development Initiatives in Chattanooga, Tennessee." March 1986.

R. L. Associates. *Chattanooga Regional Tourist Market Analysis: A Study Conducted for Chattanooga Area Convention and Visitors Bureau.* Princeton, N.J.: January 1989.

Tennessee Department of Employment Security, Labor Market Information Unit, Research and Statistics Division. *Tennessee Labor Force Estimates.*

University of Tennessee. *1988 Tennessee Statistical Abstract.* Knoxville: 1988.

U.S. Department of Commerce. *Statistical Abstract of the United States.*

U.S. Department of Commerce. *1985 OBERS BEA Regional Projections,* Volume 1, State Projections to 2035.

Mud Island

George S. Vozikis, The Citadel; Timothy S. Mescon, Ernst P. Goss, Salisbury State University

The city of Memphis Park Director, Bob Brame, pondered the future of Mud Island, the city's river park on the banks of the Mississippi River. Things did not look upbeat, especially since the sixth person to serve as general manager of Mud Island in as many years had just resigned the month before. Brame realized that Mud Island is a seasonal attraction and during 1987, it drew the second-highest number of tourists in Memphis, attracting almost 33,000 more tourists than Elvis Presley's Graceland during the April 15–August 31 season. However, the cold-weather months, especially after Thanksgiving, caused the number of visitors to drop dramatically. The facility was closed from January 1 to March 12 during 1988, and Brame thought that a plan to stretch the closing for seven weeks longer during the cold off-season made sense and would save the city about $233,000, reducing the island's budget to about $1.5 million. Memphis Mayor Dick Hackett, however, had already rejected a 1987 Park Commission proposal to close Mud Island for five months during the fall and winter. Brame decided to try once again and resubmit his request to the City Council Operating Budget Committee in May 1988.

HISTORY

Mud Island, a 53-acre island offshore from downtown Memphis in the middle of the Mississippi River, was built up from mud and silt carried downriver after the Civil War and deposited around a sunken Union gunboat. The island has been used as farmland, a racetrack, and even an airstrip, but because of flooding it was never considered to be a particularly valuable piece of property until recently. The Corps of Engineers in Memphis tried different ways of destroying it in the early 1900s, but the island just kept growing. In 1923, E. H. Crump, the Mayor of Memphis, finally said, "Well, if we can't get rid of this thing, we'd better make a park out of it" (Mud Island Press Release, 1987:5). Fifty short years later, Roy Harrover and Associates were selected to design the park. Construction of what was to become known as Mud Island, America's only Mississippi River Museum and Park, began in 1974. The city of Memphis raised the money for the entire project with general obligation bonds, except for federal funds used for dredging to raise the island above flood level. Total costs for the project had come to $63 million by the time Mud Island opened on July 3, 1982.

The money for the project was partially spent on construction of a monorail/walkway connecting the island with the Memphis mainland. Visitors can also get to the island on a riverboat, the *Memphis Queen II.* The main attraction is a scale model of the Mississippi River, the only one of its kind on public display anywhere and only the second one ever built. The other scale model, a 40-acre-long hydraulic model of the entire Mississippi River, was built by German laborers during World War II in Clinton, Mississippi, for American engineers. The scale model at Mud Island, known as the River Walk, is five city blocks long and illustrates the bends and curves of the Mississippi River, as well as the major riverside cities and watersheds from Cairo, Illinois, to the Gulf of Mexico.

The other main attraction, the Mississippi River Museum, includes a three-story reproduction of an 1870s paddle wheeler "afloat'" within the museum, reconstruction of a Civil War battle, memorabilia tracing the development of river music, and other exhibits featuring historical depictions of the Civil War era and river history. Three restaurants on Mud Island offer foods and snacks ranging from sandwiches at Paddy Meagher's, seafood at Crawdaddy's on the Gulf, and Creole specialities at the River Terrace Restaurant. Retail stores offering souvenirs and handicrafts are River Mercantile, the Delta Drummer, River Crafters, and a shop known as the Just for Fun Store.

The most recent addition to Mud Island's permanent exhibits was put in place in May 1987. The *Memphis Belle,* a B-17F World War II bomber, was restored in 1986 through public fund-raising and corporate contributions, then dedicated at the Memphis Belle Pavillion on May 17, 1987, where it will remain on permanent display. Another outdoor attraction, thought by some to have the greatest money-making potential of any attraction on Mud Island, is the amphitheater, which seats 5000 and has featured in the past the Beach Boys and Chicago, as well as Broadway performances. (See Exhibit 1.)

Plans for the future of Mud Island under the most recent General Manager's tenure had included European-style open-air cafes and beer gardens on the promenade-level terrace of the River Center, the removal of a hillock that blocked the view of the river behind the main stage in front of the River Center, and more events to attract black Memphians.

THE LEISURE TIME/RECREATION INDUSTRY

Leisure-time spells big business. During 1986, a U.S. population of about 240 million spent more than $11 billion to attend movies and/or watch home video, another $4 billion on pre-recorded music, and lost more than $20 billion in various

Mud Island in Memphis, Tennessee

Exhibit 1

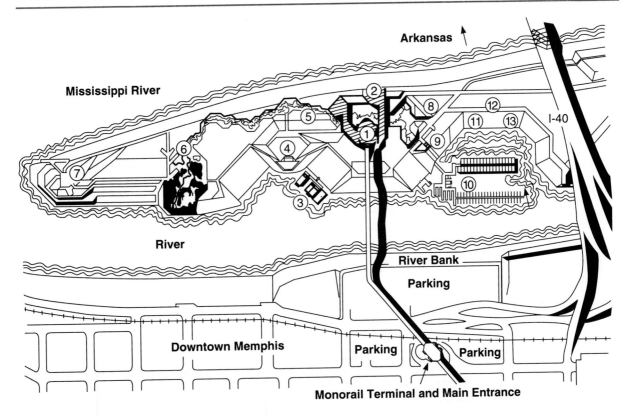

FEATURE ATTRACTIONS ON MUD ISLAND

(1) River Center housing west Monorail terminal, Mississippi River Museum, gift shops. (2) River Terrace Restaurant. (3) Island Queen Excursion Dock. (4) 5000 seat Amphitheater. (5) River Walk, a five-block-long flowing scale model of the Mississippi River. (6) Crawdaddy's on the Gulf Restaurant. (7) Lookout Point. (8) Huck's Backyard Playground. (9) Harbor Landing Catering Facility. (10) Marina. (11) Picnic Grounds. (12) Memphis Belle Pavilion. (13) Tented Catering Facility.

TOURS AVAILABLE

Island Queen — Tour the mighty Mississippi River on a 1-1/2 hour riverboat ride leaving from Mud Island's Island Queen Excursion Dock daily:

1:30 P.M. (April 15th–October 15th)
3:30 P.M. (Memorial Day through Labor Day)
Tickets may be purchased at the dock. $6 ages 12 and over; $3 ages 4–11; no charge ages 3 and under with parent. Reservations required for groups.

Mississippi River Walk — Catch a tour of our block-long scale model of the lower 900 miles of the Mississippi River daily (tours begin at the Cotton Patch concession stand). Check sign in front of River Center for exact times.

Memphis Belle Pavilion — Daily tours available of World War II's most famous B-17 bomber. (Check at the front of the pavilion for exact times.)

River Walk and Belle Pavilion Tours included with regular park admission.

gaming activities. Hundreds of billions more were expended on hotels, restaurants, sporting equipment, reading material, toys, and other diversions (Graves, 1987).

The gross national product has risen from $3132 billion in 1980 to $3548 billion in 1985 (as measured in constant 1980 dollars). Overall recreational spending for 1985 came to $176.3 billion. Recreational spending was basically in line with overall personal consumption expenditures during the ten-year period between 1975 and 1985, and rose about 165% during that time period, largely because of inflation (Graves, 1987). Of this amount, the *Statistical Abstract of the*

United States reports that $13.7 billion was spent on amusement and recreational services in 1980, increasing to $17.4 billion in 1985 (in constant 1980 dollars).

According to *Forbes,* earnings per share for the group of leisure and recreation stocks were up 7.7% in 1986, compared with only 2.8% for all of American industry. Average revenues for the group more than doubled the all-industry median, reaching 10.4% (Frank, 1987).

The forecast for further growth of leisure time and recreational spending is generally good, because of rising growth in consumer disposable income, lower unemployment, and more favorable federal income tax laws for American consumers' disposable income (Graves, 1987). Because of the recent stock market upheaval, however, some analysts are predicting slower growth in leisure and recreational spending because of the possibility of a recession (Zweig, 1987). *Forbes* analysts also comment on a different reason for a slowdown in the leisure and recreational spending market. They feel that the large gains in this particular market have already been made because of the growth in recent years of mergers and acquisitions that have saturated the market (Frank, 1987).

The types of establishments making up the leisure time/recreational industry are more varied, perhaps, than any other service industry. It may include billiard parlors, bowling alleys, skating rinks, amusement parks, golf courses, motion picture theaters, sight-seeing tours, and museums. Almost anything which can be done in one's leisure time that money can buy can be classified as belonging to the leisure time/recreational industry. (See Exhibit 2.)

Amusement parks are now attracting more people than ever. "Last year, theme parks had at least 215 million visitors, up from more than 170 million a decade ago" (Jeffrey, 1987: 21).

A *Public Participation of the Arts Survey* reports that the following numbers of adults attended the specified forms of recreational activities at least once in the previous 12 months:

Jazz performances	14.8–16.3 million
Classical music performances	20.5–22.5 million
Opera performance	4.7– 5.5 million
Musical plays	29.6–31.4 million
Plays (nonmusical)	18.7–20.3 million
Ballet performances	6.7– 7.2 million
Art museums or galleries	35.2–37.3 million

The survey also found that 61% of adults surveyed did not participate at all in any of the above activities. Level of education achieved by those surveyed was the most important factor involved in an analysis of which adults participated in which activities (National Endowment for the Arts, 1984).

The diversity of activities involved in the leisure time/recreational industry makes it difficult to generalize about competing companies and pricing policies. Each recreational-type organization is basically in competition with other local and/or national organizations offering leisure/recreational services. Their pricing policies are determined by these factors, as well as the locale and the particular type of consumers within the locale. (See Exhibit 3.)

INDUSTRY ISSUES

One factor which has had a definite impact on the attendance at museums and parks in recent years has been the phenomenal growth of in-home electronics

Share by Type of Recreational Services (in millions of 1980 dollars)   **Exhibit 2**

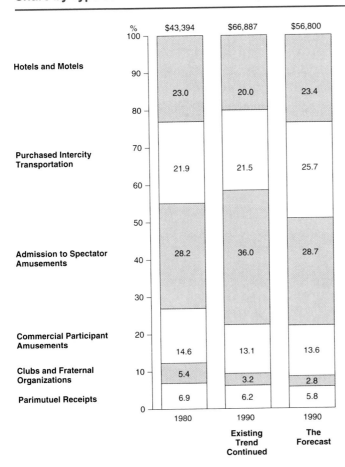

	$43,394	$66,887	$56,800
Hotels and Motels	23.0	20.0	23.4
Purchased Intercity Transportation	21.9	21.5	25.7
Admission to Spectator Amusements	28.2	36.0	28.7
Commercial Participant Amusements	14.6	13.1	13.6
Clubs and Fraternal Organizations	5.4	3.2	2.8
Parimutuel Receipts	6.9	6.2	5.8
	1980	1990 Existing Trend Continued	1990 The Forecast

and videocassette recorders. VCRs, now present in 40% of American homes, have created a $7 billion cassette business. Home video and pay television now generate more revenue for the movie industry than theaters do (Graves, 1987). Some surveys report that the average household has a television set going about seven hours a day.

Masses of Americans are now living in electronic cocoons, and there are indications that this passive leisure style may become even more popular in the future (Cornish, 1986: 58).

Nevertheless, tourism will probably become the world's biggest industry by the year 2000. Constant improvements in all forms of transportation make traveling more enjoyable and increasingly less expensive for tourists who travel great distances. More advanced communications systems will also make it easier to transfer money and confirm hotel reservations (Cornish, 1986).

One major issue facing the leisure time/recreational industry, which has only recently been recognized as a major problem, is the lack of long-range strategic planning. Tindell (1986:33) states:

Long range planning—a process sometimes called "futuring"—is a methodology completely accessible to the leisure industry, yet rarely applied at the operational

Exhibit 3   Participation in Outdoor Recreation Activities, by Selected Characteristics, 1983

Activity	All persons	Sex		Race		Age				Education			Family income (dollars)				
		Male	Female	White	Black	12–24 years	25–39 years	40–59 years	60 years and over	Did Not Finish High School	High School but not 4-Year College	4-Year College	Under 5000	5000–14,999	15,000–24,999	25,000–49,999	50,000 and Over
Walking for pleasure	53	45	61	54	49	57	58	53	42	35	56	67	45	46	54	61	62
Swimming	53	56	51	56	32	79	65	41	16	19	52	66	34	39	57	68	72
Visiting zoos, fairs, amusement parks	50	50	51	51	40	65	62	41	26	26	51	61	32	40	55	62	62
Picnics	48	45	51	49	42	52	59	46	29	29	51	61	36	41	53	62	62
Driving for pleasure	48	47	49	50	35	48	59	46	35	31	54	59	29	43	53	56	58
Sight-seeing	46	45	46	47	36	46	54	47	31	27	50	63	27	38	48	57	60
Attending sports events	40	44	36	41	33	55	44	36	16	15	39	51	24	30	43	51	61
Fishing	34	47	23	35	27	43	40	31	17	26	35	30	24	30	38	38	35
Bicycling	32	33	32	33	29	55	37	22	7	11	28	37	23	24	35	41	42
Boating	28	32	24	31	6	38	35	25	9	11	28	41	16	20	27	39	43
Canoeing or kayaking	8	10	7	9	1	14	9	6	1	1	7	13	6	5	8	12	10
Sailing	6	7	5	7	1	9	7	5	2	1	4	14	4	3	5	9	14
Motorboating	19	22	16	21	3	25	23	17	7	8	19	25	10	13	18	27	32
Running or jogging	26	30	23	26	30	51	31	13	2	6	20	34	21	20	27	33	37
Attending concerts, plays, etc	25	25	26	26	21	34	29	22	12	10	24	40	17	21	24	32	38
Camping	24	28	22	27	6	36	30	19	6	10	25	27	15	19	29	31	25
Backpacking	5	6	3	5	1	9	5	2	(z)	(z)	4	7	3	3	5	7	5
Outdoor team sports	24	30	18	24	27	50	26	11	2	7	19	23	22	20	25	29	28
Tennis	17	18	16	17	13	32	20	10	1	2	13	31	12	11	18	22	37
Day hiking	14	15	13	15	3	19	17	12	5	3	13	25	10	10	13	18	25
Golfing	13	20	7	14	3	16	13	13	7	4	12	24	6	6	13	20	27
Birdwatching, nature study	12	11	12	13	5	10	12	12	13	6	13	17	9	10	12	14	19
Hunting	12	22	3	12	7	15	13	13	5	10	13	7	8	12	14	14	8
Off-road vehicle driving*	11	14	8	12	3	20	11	6	2	3	10	10	9	8	10	15	13
Sledding	10	12	9	12	2	22	11	5	(z)	1	7	11	9	6	12	13	15
Waterskiing	9	11	7	11	(z)	17	12	4	(z)	2	8	12	5	6	10	13	14
Snow skiing	9	10	7	10	1	15	11	5	1	1	6	18	5	5	7	13	21
Horseback riding	9	8	10	10	4	18	10	5	1	2	8	9	7	6	9	11	15
Ice skating	6	6	6	7	1	15	6	3	(z)	1	4	8	5	3	7	10	11
Other activities	4	4	3	4	1	3	4	4	3	2	4	5	4	3	4	10	9
No participation	11	8	14	10	18	3	5	13	30	29	9	5	28	18	6	4	3

Source: National Park Service, press release.

z less than .5 percent.

Note: Represents percent of respondents who said they participated once or more during 12 months prior to interview. Covers persons 12 years old and over and period from September 1982 to June 1983. Based on a sample survey of 5,757 conducted by the Bureau of the Census.

*Includes motorcycles; excludes snowmobiles

level in most of its organizations. While academics, researchers, and state or federal parks and recreation planners do trend analysis and recreation participation projections, few local municipalities have formally adopted "5-year strategic business plans" or "20-year comprehensive long range plans" to guide their daily work. They are without the anchor of having articulated a creative, inspiring vision of the future they dream of and prefer for their communities, with their services and facilities cornerstone contributions to the quality of life there.

"Quality of life" has to be understood by recreation and park officials as a 24-hour-a-day process, where all aspects of an individual's life come into focus during the fairly brief impact on that life of leisure activities.

GENERAL ORGANIZATION AND MANAGEMENT

Mud Island is owned by the city of Memphis and operated by the Memphis Park Commission. The city of Memphis was incorporated in 1826 and operated under a commission form of government until January 1, 1968. Since that time, the city has functioned under a strong Mayor-Council form of government and is organized into the following divisions: Executive, Finance and Administration, Fire, Police, Parks, Sanitation, Public Works, Personnel, Public Service, General Service, Community Development, and Legislative and Community Affairs.

The Mayor of the city of Memphis is an elected chief executive who prepares the budget, approves and removes department heads and other principal officials, and is responsible for both the political and the administrative functioning of the city.

The City Council is an elected body which performs the legislative functions of the city. The council reviews and approves the proposed budget as well as the administrative appointees of the Mayor. In addition, the council passes all ordinances and laws affecting the area of the city.

A centralized organizational structure exists in all city of Memphis government entities. The decision making at Mud Island moves from the bottom up, all the way to the Mayor. Bob Brame, Director of the Park Commission and interim General Manager of Mud Island, reports directly to Jim Broughton, Chief Administrative Officer of the city of Memphis, who reports directly to Mayor Hackett. The City Council approves the budget and other capital improvements designated for Mud Island. (See Exhibit 4.)

The General Manager of Mud Island has authority over all the island employees and is responsible for their performance appraisals. He is the communication link between Mud Island and the city of Memphis government. The General Manager's degree of control is narrow and limited, largely because of the restrictions of city of Memphis policies, particularly in relation to the Mud Island budget and capital improvement plans for the future.

MARKETING

The marketing function of Mud Island could be considered to be the most important. The budget for the marketing function is $639,000 per year, with $365,000 of that budget contracted out to a local, independent advertising

Exhibit 4   **City of Memphis: Administrative Structure**

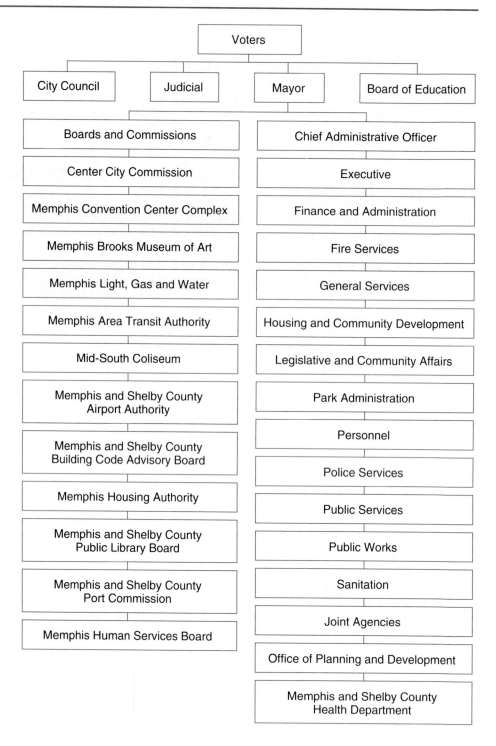

Mississippi River Museum   **Exhibit 5**

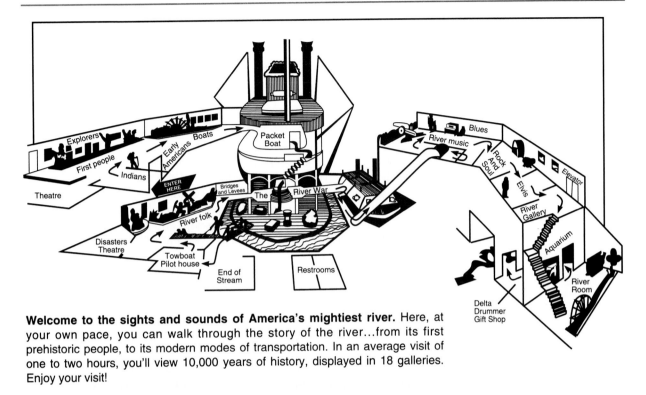

Welcome to the sights and sounds of America's mightiest river. Here, at your own pace, you can walk through the story of the river...from its first prehistoric people, to its modern modes of transportation. In an average visit of one to two hours, you'll view 10,000 years of history, displayed in 18 galleries. Enjoy your visit!

agency. Mud Island is now doing more advertising in-house than it did previously. Services offered by Mud Island are extremely diverse in nature. The park is billed as the only attraction in the world to showcase a river from all aspects—recreational, educational, cultural, historic, and scientific. The services offered by Mud Island include the following:

- *River Center,* housing the monorail terminal, Mississippi River Museum, and gift shops. (See Exhibit 5.)
- *Restaurants:* The River Terrace, Crawdaddy's on the Gulf, Paddy Meagher's, and Harbor Landing, a catering facility.
- *Outdoor attractions:* River Walk, Observation Deck, 70-boat public marina and picnic areas, Memphis Belle Pavillion, River Boat Tours, and Amphitheater.

Because Mud Island features such diversified types of entertainment, it is difficult to classify Mud Island's current or potential visitors.

To find out what types of people visited Mud Island during a special occasion (dedication of the *Memphis Belle*) and during a typical weekday, a survey was conducted by the American Marketing Association during a Sunday in May 1987. It was found that on the special occasion, 52% of the respondents received their information about the dedication of the *Memphis Belle* from newspaper advertising, 25% from friends. Only 3% were notified of the dedication from street banners, and only 1% from billboards. Eighty percent of those surveyed had visited Mud Island before (32% of those within the last 6 to 12 months, 24%

within the last one to two years, and 12% within the last month). The majority of respondents were from Tennessee (73%), and 90% of the Tennesseeans were from Shelby County, where the city of Memphis is located. The adjacent counties of Lauderdale and Gibson, as well as Nashville's Davidson County, were the other most represented counties (2.3%, 1.7%, and 1.3%, respectively). The most prevalent age groups at the time of the *Memphis Belle* dedication were 25 to 34 years of age (166 individuals out of a total of 230 surveyed) and 35 to 44 years of age.

Information about the regular weekday visitors was obtained on three separate occasions during different weeks in the month of June 1987. Out of approximately 1440 visitors to the island on these three days, 420 people participated in the surveys.

It was found that only 29% of the respondents were from Tennessee. Shelby County was still the most represented county, with 18%, and Nashville's Davidson County next with 5% representation. Out-of-state representation accounted for 71% of the visitors, with 11% coming from Arkansas, 7% Texas, 6% Missouri, 5% Mississippi, and 5% California. Thirty-five states and foreign countries were also represented, including Canada, Mexico, the Grand Cayman Islands, Germany, England, Switzerland, Finland, and the Netherlands.

Forty-four percent of these individuals came to Mud Island because of word of mouth, 12% because of television advertising, 10% because of newspaper advertising, and 5% because of radio advertising. Billboards and street banners were still the least effective method of promotion, with only 4% and 1% effectiveness, respectively. Seventy percent of the respondents to the average weekday interviews were visiting the island for the first time. Of the 30% who had been previously, 50% had been within the last year, and 60% had been to the island within the last two years. Twenty-one percent of respondents were back at Mud Island after more than three years had elapsed since their previous visit.

This survey indicated that a very large difference exists between Mud Island's special events and/or weekend customer and the regular weekday customer, and between the national tourist market and local residents. Special services for local residents include festivals and special events, lectures and demonstrations, and a changing exhibit gallery in the River Gallery, so that local residents can see new exhibits for a reduced price without having to tour the entire museum again. In addition, Mud Island officials now lead field trips for schoolchildren as well as summer day camps. Attendance of local tourists has gone up because of these special events and festivals like the Budweiser Challenge Cup (a boat race held in September 1987), the British Car Festival, and special Halloween festivities for local children. (See Exhibit 6.)

The advertising budget is split in half between these two target markets. The management of Mud Island feels that Memphis is a pass-through city, not a destination city for tourism. If a tourist visits Memphis and does not visit Mud Island, then they believe that their marketing efforts have failed. As a result, Mud Island has joined forces with other Memphis attractions to promote the city of Memphis as an entire tourist package. When visitors to Memphis tour the city, it is hoped by the newly formed Attractions Association that these tourists will explore all the local attractions, not just one. Additionally, the new Crowne Plaza Hotel will offer discounts in conjunction with a visit to Mud Island.

By teaming up with other local businesses such as the Crowne Plaza, Mud Island hopes to gain an edge over other local attractions. The island's major

---

Mud Island Special Event Advertising   **Exhibit 6**

ON THE ISLAND

AMERICA'S ONLY MISSISSIPPI RIVER MUSEUM & PARK

- *MUD ISLAND OPENS TOMORROW ON A HIGH NOTE!*

A musical note, that is. Help us kick off our 1988 season as **Strings and Things presents Memphis Music Day.** Hear the best of Memphis' musical talent as they play and sing their way into your heart along the River Walk. It will be a treat to your ears!

And *you'll be the judge* of who's the best. Every visitor to the Island gets to vote for their favorite performer. The grand-prize winner will receive: a $500 gift certificate from Strings and Things; one hour of recording time at Cotton Row Recording; and an opportunity to perform at this year's Neighborfest.

OUR MUSEUM COMES TO LIFE WITH MUSIC!

On a different note, our 18-gallery Mississippi River Museum will have professional musicians—including a dulcimer player, bluegrass band and others— performing tomorrow only in several of the galleries. If you haven't been through the museum in a while—or ever—now is a great time to visit!

- *FREE CRACKER BARREL COBBLER!*

Throughout our entire 1988 season, every Mud Island ticket stub is good for a free regular cobbler at both Memphis Cracker Barrel restaurants: 6081 Shelby Oaks Dr. and 3919 American Way.

- *EASTER IS ON ITS WAY!*

Plan now to join us for our PAAS Easter Eggstravaganza, Saturday, March 26. Three Easter egg hunts with 20,000 eggs. PAAS prizes, free balloons, Disney goodies and much more! Sponsored by PAAS. Official Stations: WRVR 104–FM and Memphis Cablevision.

---

competitors for the local market are other local attractions such as Graceland, the Pink Palace Museum, Libertyland, and the Memphis Zoo. They are also in competition with these attractions for the tourist and convention business. In addition, other leisure time activities such as shopping, going to the movies, and eating out are diversions which rob Mud Island of a possible customer market.

Operating hours for the restaurants as well as the Mississippi River Museum may vary according to season. In the peak season, April 11–October 31, the hours are 10 A.M.–10 P.M. Off-season, November 1–April 10, the hours are 10 A.M.–5 P.M. The island is closed from January 1 to March 5.

Though the weather has a lot to do with the operating schedule, the multi-level programming and the broad target market, along with the contracted businesses, help determine when the island will be open and for how long it remains in operation. The major controlling factor is the city. Though the Park Commission does not like to think of itself in terms of organizational charts, the city owns Mud Island, and therefore, the city has the final say about operational decisions.

Pay-one-price admission was adopted only two years ago in order to resolve long-term consumer confusion about overly complex pricing. The comprehensive admission price includes the 18-gallery River Museum (including the changing exhibits gallery), the *Memphis Belle*, River Walk, and monorail travel to and from the island. Admission for adults is $4 and is $2.50 for children, senior citizens, and disabled persons.

Regular park admission includes the changing exhibits gallery, *Memphis Belle*, River Walk, and monorail travel to and from the island. Admission for adults is $1.50 and is $1.00 for children, senior citizens, and disabled persons. Children under four years of age get in free under both pricing policies, and group rates are available for groups of 25 or more.

OPERATIONS

Mud Island, as mentioned earlier, is a nonprofit organization owned by the city of Memphis. It is maintained and operated under the direction of the Memphis Park Commission, which is chiefly funded through property taxes. The organization is a service operation, whereby its primary mission is to provide intangible services (leisure and recreation) instead of physical products for the city of Memphis. These services are intended to be available to all people from all walks of life. In the words of Bob Brame, Park Commission Director, "We try to be all things to all people."

The goal of all nonprofit organizations in the city of Memphis is to try to cut costs by reducing expenditures and generate enough funds to cover expenses. Therefore, the operational budget policy set for Mud Island by the city is that of cost minimization rather than profit maximization.

The number-one priority of Mud Island is customer satisfaction, closely followed by cost efficiency. The city, and in particular the Park Commission, striving to ensure customer satisfaction and quality of services, encourage the collection of customer feedback. Any complaints, which are few in number, are monitored, examined, and acted upon immediately, to alleviate the problem.

On the other hand, cost efficiency measures necessary to reduce expenditures have already been implemented. Many of the services needed to maintain the operations of the island were previously contracted out. Management has begun, in its effort to reduce costs, a preventive maintenance program. Mud Island workers are now better able to perform many of these maintenance tasks themselves.

Another cost reduction tactic considered by Mud Island is additional dependence upon the private sector. An example of this is the island's attempt to reduce the advertising budget by suggesting to TV Channel 3 (the Memphis CBS affiliate) that Mud Island should not buy advertising but instead co-op with Channel 3 to help promote an event intended to be a public service. The management officials of Mud Island are trying to stress to the community that they have a social responsibility, since they provide a recreational facility for the public to enjoy that without community support would not otherwise exist.

The construction budget is an important part of the city's capital improvement program. A ten-year plan is drafted, yet the City Council approves the individual items on a yearly basis. For the next ten years, the Park Commission has a ranking of 46 projects. Three of these projects pertain to Mud Island. Ranked eighteenth is Mud Island improvements, covering fiscal years 1988 through 1992.

The state is presently funding the construction of the Auction Street Bridge over to the area just north of the Mud Island boundaries. To capitalize on this, funds are presently being used to add a parking lot, turnstiles and ticket booths, and eventually (1991) a new retail facility. In 1989 there are plans to recaulk the River Walk and construct sheltered and nonsheltered picnic areas to replace existing areas currently covered by tents. Finally, 1992 may bring an expansion of office space and the creation of a storage facility at the east terminal.

Project improvements to the Mud Island River Center from 1990 to 1993 include enclosing the entire west terminal. At present, only a few of the floors are enclosed, and a great deal of heating/cooling escapes at great cost to the island. Also, due to exposure to the elements, the escalators will need to be replaced. Finally, another elevator needs to be added; originally, two shafts were built, but only one elevator was installed in an effort to cut costs during the initial phase of construction of the island.

The chief purpose of a proposed retail warehouse would be for the storage of purchased merchandise and display fixtures. This would eliminate the high costs of storage and split storage, and better security would be provided for the merchandise.

The three major sources of revenue for Mud Island are admissions, retail sales, and promenade lot parking (54%, 20%, and 17%, respectively, for the period ending October 31, 1987). Each of these areas is expected to increase in the future. As more people learn about Mud Island through local and national publicity, more people are expected to visit the park. The new retail stores that are planned in the near future—one at the new north gate and one at the east end of the tram—are an effort to "catch" visitors just before they leave the park. Parking revenues will also increase, as the new lot to be built at the north gate will have room for between 2000 and 3000 more parking spaces. In addition, existing parking spaces are now being leased to downtown businesses, and the continuous influx of new development will ensure maximum parking usage.

PERSONNEL

The Director of Personnel for the city of Memphis is responsible for administering the employment and promotional procedures for all divisions of the city of Memphis government, including Mud Island employees, as set forth in the city of Memphis Charter and Code of Ordinance. The Director of Personnel is also responsible for the development and maintenance of all policies related to employment, wages and salaries, benefits, records, and other employee services. The personnel policies of the city of Memphis provide a uniform system of discipline and work rule expectations so that all city employees, their supervisors, department heads and division directors know exactly what is expected of them in the performance of their duties. The Compensation Bureau, located within City Personnel, is responsible for the design and maintenance of the city's pay plan, providing uniform salary guidelines and related policies and procedures.

Permanent full-time employees in the divisions of the city of Memphis government are subject to a performance appraisal review during the initial and/or administrative probationary period. The employee's appointing authority or designee is responsible for monitoring the employee's performance during the critical and/or administrative probationary period. Written documentation is maintained that records the employee's ability and willingness to competently perform the assigned job duties as well as the employee's adaptability, dependability, and attitude.

Finally, centralization of employment and promotional procedures in the office of the City Personnel is required in order to monitor necessary and pertinent documentation in compliance with Equal Employment Guidelines and to reduce the amount of time expended by the separate city divisions in the processing and screening of applicants for positions that are to be filled. The Personnel Division serves the various divisions and agencies of the city by establishing registers and providing initial screening of applicants.

The critical strength of the personnel policies of the city of Memphis is the uniformity in the interpretation and the administration of the provisions of the City Charter, the Code of Ordinances, and the policies, decisions, and directions of the city administration. The personnel policies provide guidance to supervisory personnel on issues such as leave, pay and benefits, retirement, disciplinary procedures, and the employee termination process. This ensures consistency in employee-manager relations across the divisions of the city government.

This strength may, however, prove to be a weakness to those given the responsibility to manage Mud Island. The General Manager and his staff must utilize recruitment and employee compensation procedures which make no distinction for the nature of Mud Island. The island's management does not have the flexibility to hire employees with the unique skills necessary to market the park as an entertainment or "theme" park. Job descriptions and classifications, although tailored to the needs of the island, still resemble those within the current Park Commission organizational structure. Since few, if any, of the current positions within the Park Commission are engaged in profit-generating activities, it is doubtful that the recruitment and selection of employees for Mud Island will identify those traits necessary for the employees of a profit-making enterprise. (See Exhibit 7.)

In addition, once employees are in place, the General Manager of the island is limited as to the incentives which can be provided to reward performance. It is doubtful that the island could attract the caliber of employees needed to transform the park into a profit-making facility, when those employees would receive the same pay raise and benefit package voted to all regular city employees.

Exhibit 7　　　　　**Parks and Recreation Authorized Positions, Fiscal Years 1986–1988**

Bureau	1986 Actual	1987 Original	1987 Amended	1988 Proposed
Administration	18	20	20	20
Recreation	134	134	134	134
Mud Island	68	63	63	63
Maintenance	134	132	132	132
Special services	156	156	156	156
Rangers	6	6	6	6
Mallory Neeley	0	0	0	1
Total division	516	511	511	512

Mud Island was cited as an "economic catalyst" upon its opening five years ago. In addition to possible further downtown revitalization, it was also expected to change Memphians' perception of their city. Among the major economic impacts expected of Mud Island were the following:

1. The creation of about 5000 jobs—both full-time and part-time.
2. An infusion of new money into the city. The Convention and Visitors Bureau estimated that a visitor spends about $50 per day. If each out-of-town visitor spends one night in Memphis, $25 million in revenue could be generated, changing hands three to four times within the community.
3. Purchases of local goods and services—paper goods, retail store items, gasoline, restaurant foods, and beverages.
4. Marketing strategies which would promote the entire city of Memphis while selling the sponsoring attraction (Clubb, 1982).

Mud Island is a line item of the Memphis Park Commission's budget, which falls under the jurisdiction of the city of Memphis's budget for parks and recre-

---

1987–1988 City of Memphis Budget   **Exhibit 8**

Where the Money Comes From

Property taxes	95,329,232	24.8%
Other local taxes	78,032,996	20.3%
Charges for services	56,335,665	14.6%
State shared	49,027,000	12.7%
Intergovernmental	45,659,432	11.9%
License and privileges	31,110,000	8.1%
Federal grants	12,425,038	3.2%
Investment interest	9,646,150	2.5%
Fines and forfeitures	3,950,000	1.0%
Other	3,126,286	0.8%
Total operating revenues	384,641,799	100.0%

Where the Money Goes

Police services	60,131,329	15.6%
Fire services	53,905,975	14.0%
Special accounts	53,110,811	13.8%
Debt service	51,582,144	13.4%
Public works/sewer	50,409,982	13.1%
Sanitation	24,793,220	6.4%
Park commission	21,044,916	5.5%
Other funds	20,992,889	5.5%
General services	16,336,738	4.2%
Community development	13,131,156	3.4%
Executive services	7,113,385	1.8%
Finance and administration	3,711,575	1.0%
Public services	3,484,400	0.9%
Judicial and legislative	2,868,040	0.7%
Personnel	2,025,239	0.5%
Total operating expenditures	384,641,799	100.0%

ation. The Park Commission received 5.5% of budgeted expenditures for fiscal year 1988, an amount just over $21 million. (See Exhibit 8.) Whereas the city budget for Parks and Recreation proposed expenditures of $21,044,916 and net expenditures of $14,663,891 (See Exhibit 9), Mud Island received a budget of $3,478,517, a 16.5% share of the Park Commission budget (See Exhibit 10).

Even though Mud Island is subsidized by property taxes, the majority of its resources are supplied through admission, parking, and retail sales. There are other functions on the island which generate funds, as can be evidenced by the financial data presented in Exhibit 11. It should be mentioned, however, that during the 1985–1986 fiscal year when the city subsidy peaked at $1.9 million, the land budget was trimmed and revenue increased, resulting in a decrease from 66% to less than 50% of the current $3.4 million budget (Gaither, 1987).

The most solid hope for the future of Mud Island is probably its amphitheater, a 5000-seat auditorium. Another source of revenue for the island is Midland Food, a division of Coca-Cola, an independent company that has exclusive

---

Exhibit 9 **Parks and Recreation: Budget Summary**

	Actual Expenditures 1986	Budgeted Expenditures 1987	Forecasted Expenditures 1987	Proposed Expenditures 1988
Full-time salaries	8,587,972	8,869,267	9,073,000	8,859,598
Other salaries	459,841	481,352	389,430	457,017
Fringe benefits	1,884,683	1,939,641	1,928,419	1,873,507
Full-time subtotal	10,932,496	11,290,260	11,390,849	11,190,122
Part-time/temporary	2,945,224	3,267,085	3,196,367	2,910,320
Total personnel	13,877,720	14,557,345	14,587,216	14,100,442
Intragovernmental	482,533	496,880	390,249	490,954
Telephone	212,836	209,186	213,496	201,574
Data processing	11,480	11,800	11,145	10,658
Operating supplies	1,576,856	1,715,965	1,628,824	1,379,424
Repairs/maintenance	183,108	222,874	169,029	169,600
Professional services	1,569,848	1,378,817	1,157,428	1,284,414
Travel	24,743	24,200	25,569	24,199
Transportation	57,263	77,900	59,284	58,097
Utilities	2,316,081	2,529,459	2,629,146	2,793,524
Miscellaneous services/charges/ contracts	307,666	579,305	497,488	504,230
Total material/supplies	6,742,414	7,246,386	6,781,658	6,916,674
Capital outlay	0	0	0	0
Lump sums	522,739	93,966	29,249	0
Goods purchased for resale	25,114	109,725	155,600	150,000
Contingency	0	0	0	0
Gross expenditures	21,167,987	22,007,422	21,553,723	21,167,116
Expense recovery	190,615	113,600	142,655	122,200
Total city expenditures	20,977,372	21,893,822	21,411,068	21,044,916
Departmental revenue	6,727,096	6,396,936	6,136,883	6,331,808
Grant revenue	768,310	995,302	957,490	49,217
Net city expenditures	13,481,966	14,501,584	14,316,695	14,663,891

Exhibit 10 Mud Island: Budget Summary, 1986–1989

	Actual 1986	Budgeted 1987	Forecast 1987	Actual 1987	Budgeted 1988	Forecast 1988	Actual 10/31 Year to Date	Annualized 1988	Forecast 1989
Full-time salaries	1,044,589	1,133,695	1,135,411	1,168,823	1,102,105	1,212,889	420,444	1,681,776	1,192,972
Other salaries	20,132	45,426	31,304	46,959	44,083	61,183	25,507	102,028	59,739
Fringe benefits	238,531	272,988	256,830	267,527	256,359	286,855	100,339	401,356	292,548
Full-time subtotal	1,303,252	1,452,109	1,423,545	1,483,309	1,402,547	1,560,927	546,290	2,185,160	1,545,259
Part-time/temporary	589,017	557,155	550,600	563,238	557,155	580,433	286,714	1,146,856	585,000
Total personnel	1,892,269	2,009,264	1,974,145	2,046,547	1,959,702	2,141,360	833,004	3,332,016	2,130,259
Intragovernmental	44,229	47,461	51,571	58,542	46,130	48,352	24,377	97,508	48,000
Telephone	42,472	38,782	40,072	925	35,155	33,306	313	1,252	33,300
Data processing	0	0	0	0	0	0	0	0	0
Operating supplies	213,443	196,783	199,394	186,041	193,710	183,098	51,007	204,028	184,950
Repairs/maintenance	103,333	112,850	73,564	68,324	67,600	68,001	23,595	94,380	69,000
Professional services	884,583	703,183	516,631	536,973	533,035	530,830	106,060	424,240	530,000
Travel	11,369	11,350	6,566	4,388	0	0	2,949	11,796	0
Transportation	3,366	10,950	5,935	7,208	4,831	4,735	1,264	5,056	4,900
Utilities	452,506	501,400	486,709	475,962	510,779	510,211	168,946	675,784	545,000
Miscellaneous services/ charges/contracts	124,110	183,500	113,757	86,981	21,575	19,965	7,835	31,340	19,700
Total material/supplies	1,879,411	1,806,259	1,494,200	1,425,344	1,412,815	1,398,498	386,346	1,545,384	1,434,850
Capital outlay	0	0	0	0	0	0	0	0	0
Lump sums	0	0	0	0	0	0	0	0	0
Goods purchased for resale	25,114	109,725	155,600	160,397	150,000	186,549	74,899	299,596	170,000
Contingency	0	0	0	0	0	0	0	0	0
Gross expenditures	3,796,794	3,925,248	3,623,945	3,632,288	3,522,517	3,726,407	1,294,249	5,176,996	3,735,109
Expense recovery	44,216	53,000	58,297	60,586	44,000	38,885	9,444	37,776	39,000
Total city expenditures	3,752,578	3,872,248	3,565,648	3,571,702	3,478,517	3,687,522	1,284,805	5,139,220	3,696,109
Departmental revenue	1,761,671	2,054,500	1,789,122	1,819,969	1,881,124	1,909,060	945,979	3,783,916	1,888,000
Grant revenue	13,368	3,550	7,527	6,480	0	19,908	3,480	13,920	0
Net city expenditures	1,977,539	1,814,198	1,768,999	1,745,253	1,597,393	1,758,554	335,346	1,341,384	1,808,109

Source: City of Memphis FY '88 Proposed Operating Budget and Appropriation Statements, fiscal years 1986 through 1989.

Exhibit 11   Mud Island: Revenue Summary, 1986–1989

	Actual 1986	Budgeted 1987	Forecast 1987	Actual 1987	Budgeted 1988	Forecast 1988	Actual 10/31 Year to Date	Annualized 1988	Forecast 1989
Summer day care				6,237	8,299	7,732	5,652	22,608	8,000
Mud Island admission				855,573	935,000	945,048	510,147	2,040,588	930,000
Amphitheatre admission				89,835	86,600	80,570	39,976	159,904	81,500
Mud Island retail				364,599	339,666	356,551	185,722	742,888	354,000
Restaurant revenue				60,994	59,500	61,029	24,680	98,720	56,500
Amusement revenue				4,356	5,285	3,178	1,810	7,240	3,000
Excursion boat revenue				8,996	8,746	9,333	7,789	31,156	10,000
Sponsorships				59,000	60,000	55,750	42,750	171,000	55,000
Marina income				9,582	0	14,769	5,669	22,676	14,500
Promenade lot parking				354,306	370,028	368,737	160,852	643,408	370,000
Camp fees				0	6,000	0	225	900	0
Folkfest rentals				3,226		0	0	0	0
Miscellaneous revenues				4,212	2,000	6,781	5,635	22,540	5,500
Sales tax commission				1,038	0	(417)	(266)	(1,064)	
Overage/shortage				(1,985)	0	(1)	(566)	(2,264)	
Accounts receivable and prior year collections				0	0	0	(44,096)	0	0
Total departmental revenues	1,761,671	2,054,500	1,789,122	1,819,969	1,881,124	1,909,060	945,979	3,960,300	1,888,000
Mac grant				3,000	0	0	0	0	0
Local other revenues	13,368	3,550	7,527	3,480	0	19,908	3,480	13,920	0
Grant revenues				6,480	0	19,908	3,480	13,920	0
Total revenues	1,775,039	2,058,050	1,796,649	1,826,449	1,881,124	1,928,968	949,459	3,974,220	1,888,000

Source: City of Memphis FY '88 Proposed Operating Budget and Appropriation Statements, fiscal years 1986 through 1989.

Exhibit 12 Schedule of Changes in General Fixed Assets by Source, for the Fiscal Year ended June 30, 1986

	Land and Buildings	Improvements Other Than Buildings	Equipment and Furniture	Construction Work in Progress	Totals 1986	Totals 1985
Total investment in general fixed assets, July 1	$352,387,979	48,029,090	122,009,326	38,512,109	560,938,504	517,706,407
Add:						
Net equipment and furniture increases from operating fund						
General city government	—	—	7,486,664	—	7,486,664	3,803,681
Board of education	8,300,287	—	8,590,380	—	16,890,667	16,997,996
Expenditures from capital projects fund						
General city government	—	—	—	14,952,418	14,952,418	20,566,780
Board of education	—	—	—	12,805,306	12,805,306	7,162,834
Transfer capital projects fund projects to general fixed assets						
General city government	5,909,198	908,070	668,756	(7,486,024)	—	—
Board of education	1,280,759	—	—	(1,280,759)	—	—
Reclassification of assets of Mud island	50,852,684	—	3,050,589	—	53,903,273	—
Less disposal of general fixed assets						
General city government	—	—	(4,863,633)	—	(4,863,633)	—
Board of education	(763,193)	—	(3,141,818)	—	(3,905,011)	(5,299,194)
Total investment in general fixed assets, June 30	$417,967,714	48,937,160	133,800,264	57,503,050	658,208,188	560,938,504

catering rights and pays 5% of its on-land gross sales to Mud Island. Revenues derived from contracts through restaurant sales are computed on a progressive scale. The more the restaurants earn, the larger the percentage of their revenues which go to the island.

The four retail shops contribute a small portion of the revenue of the island (3.3% for the 1987 fiscal year). Mud Island does the purchasing for these retail shops. In an effort to reduce additional operational costs, management has budgeted the building of a warehouse to store their inventory, thereby reducing inventory costs.

Other items necessary for the operation of Mud Island are supplied by the city through City Hall. A request is made by the General Manager of Mud Island and works its way up the organizational ladder until it is approved by City Hall.

The finances of the city are reported under a modified accrual basis of accounting. This method records revenues in the accounting period in which they may become susceptible to accrual—that is, when they are both measurable and available (City of Memphis, *Annual Report*, 1986). The Mud Island accounting reporting also falls under fund accounting, with the general fund being the most important. These funds are entirely or predominantly supported by user charges. Mud Island was originally classified as an Enterprise Fund. "Effective June 30, 1986, the City determined that the activity of this fund was more properly accounted for in the General Fund due to the inability of user charges to cover the majority of the operating expenses of Mud Island. As a result, the city finances the majority of these expenses" (City of Memphis, *Annual Report*, 1986). Consequently, the general fixed assets of the city now include a $53.9 million reclassification of Mud Island's fixed assets from enterprise assets. This represents the original or estimated original cost. (See Exhibit 12.) This figure consists of mostly land and buildings, with smaller portions allocated for furniture and equipment. These assets comprise just over 8% of the city's total investment in general fixed assets. No depreciation is taken on these assets.

In addition to reclassifying fixed assets, long-term debt of $32,221 was reclassified to the general long-term debt account group. This comprises much less than 1% of outstanding long-term debt, which is funded through general obligation debt and revenue bonds.

EPILOGUE

As is common with most other attractions, both local (Memphis Zoo, the Pink Palace Museum, etc.) and national, Mud Island operates at a deficit, even though the deficit has been decreasing. Annualizing from October 1987 figures, the deficit for 1987 will be $600,000 less than that for 1986. Part of the reason for the decrease was the presence of complementary local attractions during 1987, such as the Rameses exhibit and the Zoo's panda bear exhibit, as well as the new addition of the *Memphis Belle* to the island. While nothing of this magnitude is planned for fiscal years 1988 or 1989, park officials do hope that they can maintain the increased level of admissions and revenues.

REFERENCES

American Marketing Association. *Dedication of the Permanent Home for the Memphis Belle: Survey Results.* Memphis, Tenn.: Memphis State University, June 1987.

Beifus, J. "Cottam Quits as Mud Island Chief." *The Commercial Appeal,* April 13, 1988, p. B1.

Brame, B., Assistant Director, Memphis Park Commission and Interim General Manager, Mud Island. Personal interview, November 20, 1987.

City of Memphis. *Annual Report.* Memphis, Tenn.: 1986.

City of Memphis Fiscal Year Proposed Operating Budget and Fiscal Year 1988–1997 Capital Improvements Program. Memphis, Tenn.

Clubb, D. "Model Shows a Mile of River for a Step." *The Commercial Appeal,* June 27, 1982, p. J3.

Comprehensive Annual Financial Report/Year Ended June 30, 1986. Memphis, Tenn.: City of Memphis, Division of Finance and Administration.

Cornish, E. "Free Time." *Parks and Recreation,* May 1986, pp. 57–60.

Frank, A. D. "Leisure and Recreation," *Forbes,* January 12, 1987, pp. 158–159.

Gaither, S. "Island's Lure of Residents Increasing, Ogle Says." *The Commercial Appeal,* October 11, 1987, p. B4.

Graves, T. "Leisure-Time: Current Analysis." *Standard and Poor's Industry Surveys,* July 30, 1987, pp. L1–L60.

Humphrey, F. "The Future of Leisure Services: Will We Be Architects or Reactors?" *Parks and Recreation,* May 1986, pp. 38–39.

Jabbour, C., Financial Manager, Memphis Park Commission. Personal interview, November 19, 1987.

Jeffrey, N. "Joy Rides: Theme Parks Introduce More High-Tech Thrills and Chills." *The Wall Street Journal,* July 2, 1987, p. 21.

Jordan, T. "Seasonal Closing of Island Urged." *The Commercial Appeal,* May 5, 1988, p. B1.

Kotler, P. *Marketing Management: Analysis, Planning, and Control.* 5th ed. Englewood Cliffs, N.J.: Prentice-Hall, Inc., 1984.

Lollar, M. "Opening Day at Mud Island." *The Commercial Appeal,* March 11, 1988, pp. E12–E13.

May, E. G., Ress, C. W., and Salmon, W. J. *Future Trends in Retailing.* Cambridge, Mass.: Marketing Science Institute, 1985.

Mud Island Press Release. "Mud turns to millions." Memphis, Tenn.: 1987.

National Endowment for the Arts. *Five-Year Planning Document: 1986–1990.* Washington, D.C.: U.S. Government Printing Office, 1984.

Nave, M. "Park Officials Seek Way to Market Mud Island." *Memphis Press Scimitar,* February 22, 1984, p. D1.

Obermark, J. "Economic Catalyst Cited Among Island's Benefits." *The Commercial Appeal,* June 27, 1982, p. J4.

Personnel, Policies, and Procedures for the City of Memphis. Memphis, Tenn.: City of Memphis, 1987.

Roberts, N., Marketing Director, Mud Island. Personal interview, November 18, 1987.

Tindell, J. P. "The Art and Science of Futuring." *Parks and Recreation,* May 1986, pp. 32–35.

Zweig, P. L. "Panic/Industry Analysis." *Financial World,* December 1, 1987, pp. 21–26.

The Tragic Crash of Flight 191

Joseph Wolfe, University of Tulsa

Shortly before 3:00 P.M. on May 25, 1979, American Airlines Flight 191 bound for Los Angeles calmly taxied from its gate at Chicago's O'Hare International Airport. Ground personnel monitoring the McDonnell Douglas DC-10's engine start, pushback, and runway maneuvers observed nothing unusual. But with the words "American one ninety-one under way" announced by Captain Walter Lux, 273 lives would be lost within the next four minutes in a blazing crash that directly and indirectly changed the lives of thousands and would result in economic costs of over $260 million to the airline industry and lawsuits approaching $500 million against American Airlines, McDonnell Douglas, and General Electric, the airplane's engine manufacturer. Ensuing legal wrangling over liability claims for the nation's greatest aircrash would pit interdependent but now hostile corporate giants against each other. The accident's aftermath would also destroy the engineering career of Joe White, a whistle-blowing maintenance supervisor who had repeatedly warned American Airlines that their shortcut maintenance practices were dangerous and contrary to the servicing methods suggested by the airplane's manufacturer. While the ordeal of many of the parties was to last only a few seconds or days, White's ordeal was to last almost ten years.

THE CRASH OF FLIGHT 191

The doomed McDonnell Douglas DC-10-10 was delivered to American Airlines on February 25, 1972, at a purchase price of about $37 million. Over the airliner's history, 37 Airworthiness Directives were applicable to the airplane itself and six Directives were pertinent to its engines, which were three General Electric CF6-6Ds rated at 40,000 pounds of thrust for takeoff. A postcrash investigation of N110AA's repair and maintenance records found its history to be very routine. The aircraft's last C check had been accomplished at American Airlines' Tulsa, Oklahoma, maintenance facility on March 28, 1979, during which each engine pylon's forward and aft spherical bearings had been replaced in conformance with the manufacturer's Service Bulletins Nos. 54-48 and 54-59. By the time of the crash 341 flight hours and 166 flights had elapsed since the check had been conducted.

The fatal flight began in a normal fashion on the Friday of a Memorial Day weekend. The airplane was fully loaded with 258 passengers and its 13-member crew. Based on partially recovered flight recorder information, Flight 191 thundered down runway 32R for about 6000 feet, whereupon all thrust was lost from its No. 1 (port) engine. The takeoff continued, however, even though the left engine and pylon assembly, as well as about 3 feet of the wing's leading edge, had been torn away and was falling towards the ground. During the breakaway, many of the DC-10's vital systems and monitoring devices were destroyed—all the flight instruments used by Captain Lux, the left-stall warning computer, the stickshaker motor, the No. 1 engine's instruments, the slat disagree warning light system, and portions of the flight control indicator systems. Additionally the flight crew was bombarded by a vast array of multicolored warning lights and buzzers as they struggled to keep the airplane aloft.

During the next few seconds the airplane's port lift flap began to retract as the hydraulic fluid used to drive the wing's outboard slats drained from the lines which had been torn open during the engine/pylon separation. With the left flap now retracted the crew was in a "split flaps" condition, thus pitching the DC-10 into a violent left bank at about 325 feet of altitude. The flight crew did not respond to the control tower's question, "Do you want to come back?" as it tried to control the aircraft's roll by raising the right wing's aileron and applying the right rudder. After climbing a few more feet, the airplane's nose pitched down and Flight 191 crashed and exploded in an open field just short of the Oasis Mobile Homes trailer park about 4600 feet northwest of the runway's departure end. Two men in a parked truck were also killed, and an old aircraft hangar, several automobiles, and a mobile home were destroyed by ground fire.

THE DC-10 GROUNDING AND NTSB INVESTIGATION

Within hours of the crash both Langhorne M. Bond, FAA head and former Illinois Transportation Secretary, and Elwood T. Driver, head of a "go" team from the National Transportation Safety Board (NTSB), prepared to fly to Chicago to investigate the accident. A split bolt due to metal fatigue was initially thought to have been the accident's cause. As a precautionary measure the NTSB recommended that mandatory, emergency inspections be carried out on "all pylon attach points" of the nation's domestically operated DC-10s. In independent actions, however, McDonnell Douglas quickly issued an "alert bulletin" which covered in minute detail the set of inspections it recommended should be completed within 50 flight hours or seven days, while American Airlines had already inspected 12 of its DC-10s within two days of the accident. No defects were found.

Although it had been felt the original minimal inspection of the pylon's attachment bolts would be sufficient, Bond dramatically changed the FAA's policy of brief postaccident inspections by grounding all domestic DC-10s because "grave and potentially dangerous deficiencies" had been found in a plate which reinforced the wing's engine mountings. By this order the nation's fleet of 141 DC-10s, or 12 percent of available airline seats, as well as the rest of the world's 137 DC-10s were taken out of service until they had been inspected.

Bond's decision was prompted by the actions of a conscientious United Airlines mechanic. As Ernest Gigliotti came on duty, a DC-10 that had just passed its emergency inspection did not seem correct in "the way the fairing fit over the pylon," as well as the unusual presence of metal powder on the aft end of the pylon. Exhibit 1 presents a diagram of the airplane's entire wing, pylon, and engine components with their three attachment devices. Gigliotti and Lorin Schluter, another mechanic, laboriously removed over 100 connectors to obtain a better look at the pylon's innards. What they found was a crack in a key pylon support as well as the absence of numerous fasteners. Because of this finding, as well as the determination that some other calamitous event and not metal fatigue caused the suspected connecting bolt to break, many experts felt the DC-10 should not return to the air until a final determination of the accident's cause had been found. Despite these urgings most DC-10s were placed into service after passing their FAA-mandated inspections.

Over the next few days disturbing reports continued to come from the field. The FAA reported 68 "from serious to minor" flaws in the nation's DC-10s instead of the 37 originally cited, and two American Airlines planes had to be taken out of service due to severely cracked aft pylon bulkheads—one received preventive maintenance and was ferried without passengers to American's overhaul base in Tulsa, Oklahoma, while another airplane was so severely damaged it had to be jury-rigged in Bermuda before it could be ferried to Tulsa. More importantly, information emerged that many domestic airlines were not following the engine maintenance procedures recommended by McDonnell

The Pylon-Wing Assembly   **Exhibit 1**

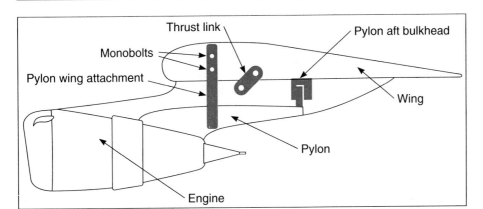

Douglas. As prescribed in Chapter 54-00-00 of the manufacturer's *Maintenance Manual,* the airplane's 11,612-pound GE CF6-6D turbofan engine was to be removed from the pylon followed by the removal of the 1865-pound pylon itself in two separate steps. Rather than employing this procedure, the engine and pylon were being removed in one forklift-assisted maneuver, thereby saving $8000–$12,000 in labor charges per engine removal. Engineers watching the reinstallation of an engine pylon had concluded that a vertical misalignment of merely a fraction of an inch could have caused the 2-inch and 5-inch cracks that had just been discovered in two American Airlines DC-10s on the ground in San Francisco. Accordingly, the NTSB urged the FAA to formally advise airlines "to immediately discontinue the practice of raising and lowering the pylon with the engine still attached."

Twelve days after the fatal crash Langhorne Bond deferred to the constantly emerging evidence as well as to pressure exerted by the Airline Passengers Association and Federal Judge Aubrey E. Robinson, Jr., who attempted to restrain Bond "from permitting the continued operation of the McDonnell Douglas DC-10 aircraft until such time as the cause for the loss of the left engine on American Airlines DC-10 Flight 191 is identified and sufficient corrective measures have been taken to prevent future occurrences of this type." The FAA Chief ordered an immediate and open-ended grounding of all DC-10s by suspending the aircraft's design certificate until either tests pinpointed any basic design flaws in the airplane or it was proven the McDonnell Douglas aircraft met rigorous airworthiness criteria. This suspension effectively grounded the world's fleet of DC-10s, as foreign operators traditionally cooperate with the FAA. As shown in Exhibit 2, European operators employed 75 wide-bodied jets, while Asian operators used an additional 43 DC-10s.

With the prospect that the airplane would be grounded for weeks if not months, chaos broke out in the world's air service as passengers, airlines, and travel agents sought alternative seating capacity for the over 65,000 daily users of the craft. The grounding order, however, did not affect all airlines equally. World Airways was the domestic carrier hit hardest, as all its airplanes were DC-10s; for sheer volume United Airlines was also hurt, as 23 percent of its seats were provided by DC-10s and the carrier was just emerging from a costly strike. Among foreign carriers the British-based Laker Skytrain was completely shut down due to its exclusive use of the jumbo jet. Sir Freddie, the Director of Skytrain, was especially incensed because the cracks were found on "aircraft belonging to two carriers that have put engines and pylons onto aircraft using a maintenance procedure that is not recommended. We have found no cracks and there cannot be any cracks because we have abided by the procedures."

The FAA grounding would last for 37 days, during which time over 100 special investigators would operate in the six cities with facilities for servicing the DC-10—San Francisco/Oakland (United Airlines, Trans International Airlines, and World Airways), Los Angeles (Continental Airlines, and Western Airlines), Tulsa (American Airlines), Minneapolis (Northwest Airlines), and Miami (National Airlines). The search, however, was centered in Tulsa at American Airlines' Maintenance and Engineering Center and was coordinated by John M. Cyrocki, a retired former chief of the FAA's Midwest region. Cyrocki said he would "attempt a very comprehensive review of maintenance, especially work on the pylon assembly, including all the repairs ever made, information as to what prompted them, when and by whom, and all the correspondence between the companies, the manufacturers and suppliers."

Worldwide DC-10 Fleets

Exhibit 2

Country	Airline	Number
North America		141
Canada	Wardair	1
Mexico	Aeromexico	2
United States	United	37
	American	30
	Northwest	22
	National	16
	Continental	15
	Western	9
	World	6
	Trans International	3
South America		10
Brazil	Varig	5
Venezuela	Viasa	5
Europe		75
Belgium	Sabena Belgian World	3
Finland	Finnair	3
France	U.T.A.	6
Great Britain	British Caledonian	3
	Laker	6
Iceland	Icelandic	1
Italy	Alitalia	8
Netherlands	KLM Royal Dutch	6
	Martinair	3
Spain	Iberia	7
	Spanlax	1
Sweden	S.A.S.	5
Switzerland	Balair	1
	Swissair	9
W. Germany	Lufthansa German	11
Yugoslavia	Yugoslav (J.A.T.)	2
Africa		6
Ivory Coast	Air Afrique	2
Nigeria	Nigeria	2
Zaire	Air Zaire	2
Asia		43
Indonesia	Garuda	4
Japan	J.A.L.	9
Malaysia	Malaysian	2
New Zealand	Air New Zealand	7
Pakistan	Pakistan International	4
Philippines	Philippine	4
Singapore	Singapore	4
South Korea	Korean	5
Thailand	Thai International	2
Turkey	Turk Hava	2

Source: McDonnell Douglas, cited in Fred Ferretti, "Worldwide Air Service Still Hampered by DC-10 Curb," *The New York Times,* June 8, 1979, p. A16.

From the NTSB's final report, as well as from testimony delivered before the five-member board, a number of facts emerged and the following conclusions could be drawn:

1.   William S. Fey, an American Airlines supervisor, suggested in September 1978 that a forklift-assisted, combined engine/pylon removal method be used to meet a company deadline for replacing all monoball bushings. This was a labor-saving procedure that completed the job in 36 hours rather than the normal 80 hours and required the removal of only 27 fittings instead of the 80 fittings required under the McDonnell Douglas two-stage procedure. A Hyster forklift, Model 460B, with a load capacity of 42,500 pounds, was especially equipped with extralong forks for the task. Fey examined the method in Los Angeles, where he said the test "went off beautifully." Three Los Angeles mechanics were then dispatched to Tulsa to begin the monoball replacement program, as these workers were the only ones with experience in the method's use.

The newly devised procedure was first used on four foreign DC-10-30s. The mechanics assigned to the task found, while working on a Varig Airlines DC-10, that reversing McDonnell Douglas's worksteps was more practical, although this change in workstep order was not reported to management. Exhibit 3 illustrates the disassembling order recommended by McDonnell Douglas. The extemporaneous method used on the DC-10-30s was adopted for all subsequent DC-10-10s in Engineering Change Order (ECO) R-2693 written by Herbert H. Cunningham, Tulsa's Senior Maintenance Engineer. The ECO said to remove the forward bulkhead's attach assemblies before removing the aft bearing bolt and bushing. The forklift operator was then instructed to insert the truck's forks into an engine shipping stand and to attach the support stand to the engine. The ECO continued with the directions, "Adjust the engine support adapter aft so that the centerline of the lifting forks are centered with the centerline on the (engine's) thrust reverser." The lifting forks were 5 feet apart, but no mark on the forklift designated the midpoint between the forks. Alignment was therefore a visual estimate.

Exhibit 3   **McDonnell Douglas Disassembly Order**

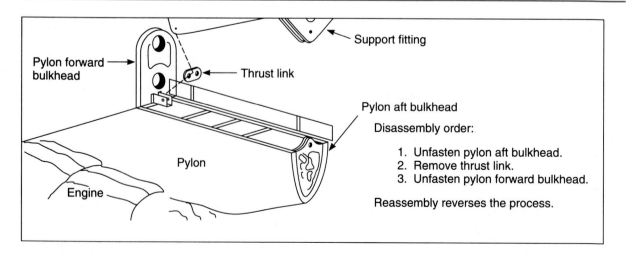

In common practice a loaded forklift experiences a bleedoff or pressure loss of about 2000 to 3000 pounds during a 15-minute period, although there is no perceptible movement in its load. It is also normal for mechanics to manipulate the controls to restore the forklift's original pressure gauge reading. When this is done, a loaded forklift "jumps" as lowering begins, and this jumping motion moves the forks about 1 or 2 inches at a time.

As part of the review of all maintenance procedures used by United States carriers flying DC-10s, the statistics shown in Exhibit 4 were collected by the NTSB for engine/pylon maintenance work. It was apparent to the Board that the maintenance method was accident-prone, although an American Airlines spokesman described the forklift used in the procedure as a "super device." Of the nine damaged airplanes discovered in subsequent ground checks, four American Airlines and four Continental Airlines aircraft had been damaged by the procedure.

2. Although the NTSB judged that faulty maintenance procedures were the main cause of the crash, the Board felt McDonnell Douglas was not decisive enough regarding the impropriety of the unitary removal procedure and that the airplane should have been designed so that maintenance errors would not cause fatal damage to the airplane's structure. In its defense of the forklift method American Airlines claimed that McDonnell Douglas officials Chuck O'Connell, J. C. McCarthy, and J. T. Moran were familiar with the procedure and voiced no objections to its employment. Fey, however, gave somewhat conflicting testimony in this regard by stating he "got the feeling" that McDonnell Douglas did not like American's use of the procedure but that O'Connell "did not advise me that they did not approve [and merely] gave me an indication that the clearances were tight. That's the only thing he conveyed to me." Fey also admitted that American Airlines did not officially ask McDonnell Douglas to evaluate its new maintenance procedure.

In sworn testimony McDonnell Douglas personnel said they saw the engine and pylon assembly after it had been lowered from the wing. None of them, however, had observed the actual mating, separating, raising, or lowering of the unit, and those who had seen the unit resting on the hanger's floor stated they attached no significance to what they saw. Tolerances were very tight on

Damage Results by Engine/Pylon Removal Method **Exhibit 4**

Method	Number
Sequential-unit removals	87
Cracks and impact damage	0
Single-unit removals	88
Overhead crane use	12
Cracks and impact damage	0
Forklift truck use	76
Cracks and impact damage	9
Total removals	175

Source: Aircraft Accident Report—American Airlines, Inc., DC-10-10, N110AA, Chicago-O'Hare International Airport Chicago, Illinois, May 25, 1979, Washington, D.C.: U.S. National Transportation Safety Board, December 21, 1979, p. 31.

the DC-10-10, although less so on the later DC-10-30s and DC-10-40s mostly flown by foreign airlines.

3.   The NTSB found that American Airlines operated within its authority when it altered the maintenance procedures it employed. The FAA has no authority expect for "major" repair alterations, and an airline does not have to notify the FAA when it changes its maintenance procedures. Aircraft owners have routinely superseded the builder's recommended procedures and they need not report these changes to the FAA.

4.   The NTSB determined that the doomed aircraft was mortally damaged while undergoing a spherical-bearing modification from March 29 to March 31, 1979. The midnight shift started the modification and removed the aft spherical bearing's bolt and bushing before going off duty on March 30. When the day crew constituting Raymond Lattanzia, Jr., William Robinson, and Hank King (a five-man crew of mechanics was usually assigned to the task) took over, two of them saw the upper lug of the aft bulkhead come in contact with the bolts attaching the clevis to the wing. The forklift's engine was running at the time, no one was at the controls, and its pressure gauge was reading 18,000 pounds. After working 15 or 20 minutes with great difficulty at removing the forward attach assemblies, they discovered the engine stand had been misaligned. The clamps holding the stand's cradle were loosened, and the lifting forks and engine stand were shifted to the left and forward on the engine about 12 inches until proper alignment was obtained. The forward upper and lower attach assemblies were then removed, and the engine and pylon assembly was lowered as a unit to the hanger's floor.

During the reassembly operation the forklift ran out of gasoline, and during a 30-minute delay it lost about 6000 pounds of pressure and the forklift jumped and jerked occasionally upon its being restarted. Ralph W. Osborn, a mechanic working nearby, said he heard heavy hammer pounding and swearing coming from the direction of the airplane as the three-man crew struggled with the assembly. They were "having difficulty in installing the rear hanger and bolt. I did notice that they were putting quite a bit of pressure on the left wing."

This testimony, plus an examination of the badly damaged tools that were used in the operation, indicated to the NTSB that the mechanics had trouble with the assembly and that the rearmost attaching mechanism was probably cracked at this time. The fissure increased its size in subsequent flights due to metal fatigue until the attaching device could no longer stand the stresses being exerted. Exhibit 5 shows the creation of a 10-inch crack in the flange area of a damaged aft bulkhead with attendant fatigue areas.

The NTSB also concluded that American's mechanics had received little or no training in the use of the unitary removal method—American Airlines allowed 40 pylons to be removed and reinstalled via the new procedure before initiating formal training in the operation. Between November 1978 and June 3, 1979, 46 engine-pylon combinations were removed at the Tulsa facility, of which only three of the many mechanics assigned possessed the experience which the work required.

5.   In an explanation of its actions Donald J. Lloyd-Jones, a Senior Vice President for American Airlines, felt its maintenance procedures were not the main cause of the engine tearaway. Other factors they felt should be considered were whether the doomed aircraft had been built with the proper clearance or gap in

Damaged Aft Bulkhead

Exhibit 5

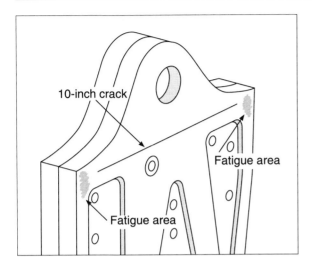

the area where the 10-inch crack developed; whether the cracked part, which was a flange on the forward part of the aft bulkhead, had been designed thickly enough; and the significance that could be attributed to the manufacturer's insertion of a gap-narrowing shim not called for in the airplane's blueprints just above the cracked area. As testified by Lloyd-Jones, "It may be that we did cause the crack. It also may be that the existence of shims in the aft bulkhead created an interference fit that made the creation of the crack inevitable, no matter what procedure was used." Upon hearing the NTSB's statement of probable cause, Rocco J. Masiello, Vice President of Maintenance and Engineering stationed at the Tulsa facility, said:

> We feel it is shoddy, premature and unfair for anyone to prejudge why that aircraft crashed. American Airlines does not believe any employee is responsible for that accident and we will stand by them, defend them, and support them until this matter is resolved. American Airlines also does not believe (the crash) result[ed] from a crack in the manner which has been described and although we do not have a better explanation of what might have caused the incident, we will continue looking until we find that answer. This type of premature judgment is very harmful and unfair to our employees. It is a knee-jerk reaction. This matter is still under investigation and until it is resolved it is extremely unfair to blame our Tulsa employees.

Ironically, the crash of Flight 191 did not have to occur for other reasons. Precrash indications showed clearly that the engine-changing procedure was harmful to the airplane's safety. On two occasions Continental Airlines' mechanics had damaged their DC-10s by using the forklift procedure. They notified McDonnell Douglas about cracked flanges, although the problem was cited as a maintenance or personnel error rather than as an incorrect procedure. Even though the builder accepted Continental's explanation for the cracking and did not pursue the matter independently after two separate damage incidents, American Airlines was duly warned on January 5, 1978, in Operational Occurrence Report No. 10-7901 that the use of the procedure was creating cracks in pylon bulkheads. Lloyd-Jones of American Airlines said his company received the report, but such information has very little clout when distributed as an operational occurrence report. "To show you how significant it was the warning about the cracks was under an item about a stewardess stubbing her toe. I hardly call that an emergency warning." In addition to the toe-stubbing incident, the report contained a number of items including the report of an air-conditioning pack malfunction, a lightning strike, and the collapse of a passenger-loading stand.

More relevant to Flight 191's immediate survival, however, was the fact that American Airlines had deactivated the DC-10's engine vibration detection system via Maintenance Alert No. 79-16 dated March 15, 1979. Had this sensing system been operational, it is unlikely the airplane would ever have left its departure gate. Minus the McDonnell Douglas–installed vibration detection system the aircrew's only means for detecting excessive vibration was now through the shaking of the airplane's frame or engine controls, rather than through the early warning system provided by the sensors.

AMERICAN AIRLINES MAINTENANCE CENTER RESPONSES

A great deal of postcrash pressure from many sources was applied and felt by those working at American's Tulsa, Oklahoma, maintenance facility. Langhorne Bond flew to the center to view the engine/pylon assembly, Cyrocki set up operations, and sworn testimony was obtained from various mechanics regarding the facility's methods. Tensions soon cracked, and over 830 employees felt compelled to create a full-page advertisement in their defense (see Exhibit 6), while four anonymous mechanics, claiming they were afraid to go to the FAA, telephoned a local television station in separate disclosures. They asserted the facility's inspection personnel had been reduced and that the company's training procedures were inadequate. Art Jackson, an American spokesman, responded that "we may make mistakes but in no way are any of our procedures improper. When you have an unidentified person complaining, you have no way of knowing if he is qualified to judge." While touring the plant a few days later, Michael Synar, a member of the congressional subcommittee investigating the crash, spoke with three mechanics who had worked on the ill-fated plane. They said they were not encouraged to engage in unsafe practices and that they felt free to report possible maintenance faults to the FAA or the NTSB. In a brief press conference Synar pointed out the "real issue is not the mechanics but the Federal Aviation Administration" because the FAA had only six inspectors available to monitor the work of the facility's 2600 mechanics.

In NTSB testimony ten mechanics said they received absolutely no training before they began performing the tricky engine/pylon removing process, and it was determined that American used the method on 40 DC-10s before any formal training was given to the mechanics. A 40-hour training course (Number 9320) was begun on March 12, 1979. Trainees receiving as little as half the course were cited as having completed the entire course; thus it was possible that mechanics could have missed the portion of the course that taught how to use the forklift removal method. Although the Board concluded that "American ini-

---

Advertisement Used by American Employees　　　　　　　　　　　　　　**Exhibit 6**

Notice to the People of Tulsa and Surrounding Communities:

We are your friends, your neighbors, members of your schools, churches, and your clubs. We bank in your banks, shop in your stores, attend your sporting events, and live in your community. We are the employees of American Airlines. We represent nearly 6,000 employees of American Airlines in Tulsa.

We had a terrible tragedy occur in Chicago that we all regret, but we also have a tragedy of a different type occurring daily here and nation-wide. We are being misrepresented by some of the news media and being maligned by two so-called American Airlines employees who wish to remain anonymous.

We are not anonymous. We are the employees of American Airlines. You know us. We do not perform careless maintenance or inspection on our airplanes, and safety is always our number one priority. We know that our friends, our neighbors, and our own families fly on our airplanes; therefore, it logically follows (and is true) that we would not put anyone on a flight that is in any way unsafe. We think it is only fair that you hear our side of the story, and if you have any questions ask [any] one of us.

This ad paid for by donations from the employees of American Airlines in Tulsa, Oklahoma.

Note: This full-page advertisement appeared in the Sunday, July 1, 1979, *Tulsa World*, p. 8H. The text was superimposed on the names of over 830 individuals.

---

tiated a practice and placed it into operation without giving adequate consideration to the equipment and training requirements necessary to carry out the function properly," R. J. Masiello said, "What is considered proper training by one man may not be perceived as proper training by another." He added that the company was reexamining all its training standards and teaching systems. (See Exhibit 7.)

An additional pressure source came from American's own internal investigation of the accident's cause and the anticipation of the filing of many liability lawsuits. Immediately after the crash Rocco Masiello informed personnel that his office would assemble all records, files, memos, and any other written materials pertaining to the aircraft and its maintenance procedures. Additionally, Mac Eastburn, Senior Director of Safety for American, was directed by Donald Lloyd-Jones on July 17, 1979, to prepare an investigation and report the facts, circumstances, and cause of the May 25, 1979, crash. Eastburn created teams and held two in-house briefings in September 1979 about the results of his investigation. Upon the instructions of Richard Malahowski, House Counsel for American, Mac Eastburn prepared one copy of the draft report and sent it to Lloyd-Jones while destroying the notes of his team chiefs. Eastburn also instructed his chiefs not to make any copies of their notes. After reviewing the report, Lloyd-Jones testified he threw it in his wastebasket, thereby becoming a party to the overall disobedience of a court order entered on May 29, 1979, by Judge Gilberto of the Circuit Court of Cook County, Illinois. This order required the preservation of all records relating to, or which might be relevant to, the airplane crash in anticipation of the discovery of liability for the numerous lawsuits that were certain to appear before the courts.

Exhibit 7

Partial Organization Chart for the Technical Advancement Program at American Airlines

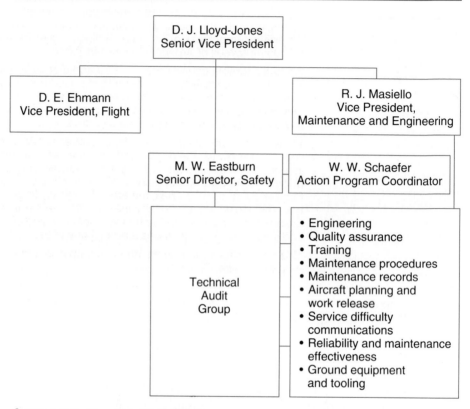

Source: Adapted from Plaintiff's Exhibit 45.

American Airlines was later sanctioned by the United States District Court, Northern District of Illinois, on June 23, 1981, and ordered to pay all costs and fees incurred in depositions, motions, or court appearances necessitated by the destruction of the Eastburn Report. While not judging whether American knew of the cracked pylon before flying the airplane, the "adverse inference" rule was found to apply. This rule operates under the presumption that a party attempts to withhold information that is unfavorable to itself and accordingly one could conclude the report contained information that demonstrated that American was at least partially responsible for the accident.

THE FAA AND PASSENGER SAFETY IN THE DEREGULATED AIRLINE INDUSTRY

Although regular airline travel began in 1914 in the United States with a $5.00, 20-minute ride between Tampa and St. Petersburg, Florida, the original versions of the airline giants of today were not formed until the mid-1920s. The airmail and the airfreight business dominated passenger service, however, and passenger volume during this period was merely 100,000 people per year. Charles

Lindbergh's famous Atlantic Ocean crossing quickly piqued the public's interest in air travel, and by 1936 the industry served over a million passengers.

At about this time the Civil Aeronautics Board (CAB) was created to bring order to the three federal agencies holding conflicting power over the airline industry—the Post Office Department, the Commerce Department, and the Interstate Commerce Commission. Through the creation of the Civil Aeronautics Act of 1938 the CAB was placed in charge of airline safety as well as becoming the industry's economic regulator and caretaker. Most importantly, the law was aimed at fostering the industry's growth by insuring the existence of safe air travel. Airline safety had become a major public concern, as between 1929 and 1933 the industry generated a fatality rate that was 900 times that of bus travel and 1500 times that of railroad travel. In 1932 alone the airline industry experienced over 100 reported accidents.

By the mid-1950s air travel's jet age was about to begin, and the CAB realized the greater speeds attained by these aircraft, plus the increased crowding of the skies, required the creation of another agency having control over all aviation affairs, both civil and military. Congress subsequently created the Federal Aviation Administration (FAA), which gained overall regulatory powers in the industry. Under the current structure the FAA possesses the legal mandate to insure the highest degree of public safety while simultaneously encouraging and promoting the development of civil aeronautics. Although many argue the agency has more often favored the short-term profit needs of the airline industry and its suppliers over the long-term safety needs of the public, the economic costs and limited benefits of increased FAA surveillance mitigate the argument for a stronger watchdog agency within many circles. A large number of skilled engineers would have to be hired to oversee the construction and maintenance of the industry's airplanes as well as to corroborate the large number of inspections required to keep an airplane airworthy—approximately 42,000 inspections are required on the DC-10, and its major C check requires one week of work from 10 to 15 inspectors. Additionally there is no assurance that the FAA's separately controlled engineers would generate an economically justifiable improvement in safety over the agency's current Designated Engineer Representative (DER) system, in which the FAA appoints manufacturer's employees to carry out the majority of the inspection and design approvals required by the airworthiness certification and retention process.

In addition to the increased complexity of the aircraft being flown and safety problems associated with the crowded airspace found around many American cities, the airline industry has also had to deal more recently with the results of the Airline Deregulation Act of 1978. This act was initiated under the Carter administration as part of the President's anti-inflation plan. The act was designed to bring marketplace pressures to bear on the industry by eliminating fare controls and removing almost all barriers to market entry. Accordingly, the industry became more susceptible to business cycle swings. Widespread changes in route structures occurred, and a number of airlines, both young and old, became financially distressed, as shown in Exhibit 8. Of greater potential concern for the flying public, however, has been the apparent disregard for safety standards set by the FAA.

A report prepared by the General Accounting Office (GAO) in 1979 documented a number of dangerous attitudes and concerns that had been detected. Many smaller carriers have found ways to circumvent the FAA's safety monitoring system through the use of leases and the location of their home offices.

Exhibit 8   **Noncommuter Airline Chapter 11 Bankruptcy Filings**

Year	Number of Airlines
1977	0
1978	0
1979	5
1980	0
1981	3
1982	4
1983	3
1984	13
1985	1

Through the use of dry leases—i.e., leasing an aircraft without a flight crew—the lessee assumes the responsibility of an operator and is responsible for compliance with *private* aircraft regulations, which are less stringent than the *commercial* regulations associated with a wet lease—i.e., the aircraft's owner provides an air crew with the lease. The GAO report cited two airplane crashes killing a total of 43 passengers that most likely would not have occurred had the carriers been operating with wet leases. In each instance the airplanes were operating within private aircraft rules, but both airplanes would have been grounded under commercial safety regulations.

The other method used by air carriers to avoid the most stringent safety requirements entails the headquartering of the firm in a foreign country. The FAA requires that all foreign carriers comply with private safety regulations. In many cases a particular carrier merely files a statement that it is a foreign carrier and records that statement in the foreign country of choice. This method is especially prevalent in southern Florida, where many claim their headquarters are located in the Caribbean yet they compete with domestic carriers throughout the United States. The FAA classifies operators who illicitly avoid commercial safety regulations as "uncertified," and thus far 90 such operations have been found within the Miami area alone. These uncertified carriers are using aircraft ranging from ancient twin-engined DC-3s to huge Boeing 707s and DC-8s.

The overall effects of these schemes are threefold. They keep the public uninformed regarding the potential hazard of flying any particular airline, cause suspicion of all airlines even though many are in strict compliance with the law, and place complying airlines at a competitive cost disadvantage vis-à-vis those who have avoided conformity to the FAA's safety regulations.

THE DC-10 AND THE MCDONNELL DOUGLAS CORPORATION

Although Exhibit 9 shows that the DC-10 has been one of the safest airplanes ever flown worldwide, it has also been a very controversial aircraft. Many critics have charged that McDonnell Douglas rushed the airplane into production in reaction to the new Boeing 747s and Lockheed L-1011s being offered by its major competitors. Accordingly, inadequate or nonexistent backup control mechanisms were provided for emergency situations. The most prominent example of the consequences of this hastiness involved the world's second-worst crash—

Percentage Rate of Fatal Accidents for Commercial Airliners, 1968–1977   **Exhibit 9**

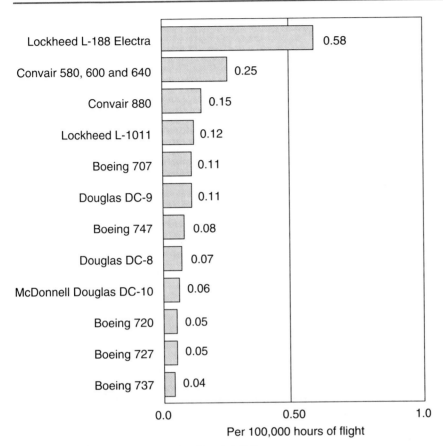

Per 100,000 hours of flight

Source: National Transportation Safety Board statistics.

346 lives were lost in 1974 when a Turkish Airlines DC-10 plummeted into a forest outside Paris.

In this instance the airplane had been crippled when its cargo door opened accidentally and the resulting loss of cabin pressure caused the floorboards to collapse, smashing the airplane's control cables embedded therein. Various experts felt the cables should have been placed in the airplane's hull, where they would have been less susceptible to damage. Aggravating the safety concerns of various individuals, however, was the conduct of McDonnell Douglas in response to an earlier near-crash which occurred in 1972. A similar cargo door blew off during a flight near Windsor, Ontario, and not all the corrections in the door's latching mechanism dictated by that close call had been made on the Turkish DC-10. Most importantly, after the Windsor, Ontario, accident, the McDonnell Douglas Corporation prevailed upon the FAA to allow it to inform its customers of the need for correcting the door-latching mechanism via an advisory bulletin rather than a government-endorsed field directive. Many felt this notification method minimized the importance of the correction to the extent that many other worldwide DC-10s had still not been altered after more than two years of postcrash service.

As a business entity, the McDonnell Douglas Corporation (MDC) was created in 1967 through the amalgamation of the financially troubled Douglas Aircraft Corporation of Santa Monica, California, and the McDonnell Company of St. Louis, a manufacturer of armed forces aircraft. At the time of the merger Sanford ("Sandy") N. McDonnell said the acquisition provided a desirable balance between commercial and military sales. Unfortunately, commercial aircraft operations resulted in losses of $49.6 and $60.3 million in the two years before the DC-10's crash, and commercial sales had fallen to less than 20 percent of the combined corporation's overall sales during the 1976–1978 period.

As an airplane, the McDonnell Douglas DC-10 had yet to make money by 1979; the design and construction of a modern-day jetliner is an extremely complicated and hence expensive affair. The DC-10 contains 210,000 parts, employs 1,750,000 fasteners, and has 50 miles of electrical wire snaking through its superstructure. Its wings are made in Canada, its body panels are made in Italy, its evacuation slides are produced in Australia, and its tailcones come from Japan. Originally designed at a cost of $1 billion, it was developed in 1970 in a race against Lockheed's L-1011 for a fleet contract with American Airlines. Lockheed had a head start in the race but stumbled when Rolls Royce, the L-1011's engine manufacturer, went bankrupt.

Initial slow sales of the DC-10 made it look like a money loser for a number of years, and in 1977 McDonnell Douglas's outside auditor issued a qualified opinion of the corporation's health due to the DC-10's slow sales growth. This opinion was removed the following year, however, as sales began to increase to levels approaching the 400-unit break-even point. At the time of the crash the McDonnell Douglas Corporation had 335 firm orders for the DC-10, with 277 airplanes delivered and 70 additional "committed orders" in hand. John N. Simon, aerospace analyst with Crowell, Weedon & Company, felt that the DC-10 crash would not be a great problem for the corporation and said that he had not heard of any airlines canceling their orders. A McDonnell Douglas spokesman believed the company would still receive orders for the DC-10, as "there is only so much manufacturing capacity in the world and airlines are in need of replacement planes." On June 15, 1979, however, Alitalia suspended its plans to buy six DC-10s for $310 million because of the airplane's safety problems.

As a corporation MDC had over 105,000 employees in 1988, with major American operations in Missouri, California, Florida, Arizona, and Oklahoma, as well as numerous worldwide support operations. Additionally the corporation has had a longtime commitment to ethical values and the role that ethics should play in corporate decision making. Upon his assumption of the role of Chairman and Chief Executive Officer in 1980, Sandy McDonnell provided a strong impetus for MDC's work in ethics by leading the development and publication of the company's *Business Ethics and Conduct* guide. This guide was revised in 1983 and 1985 and was revised and reissued again in 1987 in booklet form as *The McDonnell Douglas Code of Ethics* and the *Standards of Business Conduct*. He also instituted "The Five Keys to Self-Renewal," which was the codification of MDC's formula for success in the competitive climate found in the mature aerospace industry. Although five individual keys were enumerated, the last key, "Ethical Decision Making," was considered to be the glue that held all other keys together.

Top management's commitment to the concept of ethical decision making has been reinforced through some of the following methods:

1.   Every employee receives a copy of the above-cited booklets.

2. An all-day meeting of MDC's 19 top managers was convened to discuss questions of ethics faced by all management levels in the corporation.

3. All-day workshops throughout the organization are conducted using a specially prepared videotape and workbook. By mid-1987 about 35,000, or 60 percent, of the company's salaried employees had participated in the program.

4. A half-day workshop for hourly (unionized) employees was begun in late 1987.

5. The company created an ombudsman program. To this date only about 1 percent of the cases have been concerned with "waste, fraud or abuse."

JOE L. WHITE VS. AMERICAN AIRLINES

Although the crash of Flight 191 had a significant impact on the aviation industry, the wreck also had a similar impact on the career and fortunes of Joe L. White, the supervisor of a DC-10 engine-changing crew at the time. In late December 1978 White was assigned to a task force studying the maintenance methods being used on the McDonnell Douglas DC-10. Joe was placed on the task force because of his diverse background in many company maintenance operations—he had worked his way through various jobs as a production tool designer, a methods engineer, a work measurement analyst, and as an industrial engineer. After concluding the task force's work, he authored a lengthy "Request for Engineering Evaluation" report that was highly critical of the "unit concept method" of removing engines and pylons simultaneously from the DC-10s at American Airlines.

Over the next five months White submitted a series of memos which continued the critical vein established in the task force report. As late as May 1, 1979, 24 days prior to the crash of Flight 191, Joe personally delivered a critical memo to William Fey, the creator of the unit concept method and his supervisor at the time. Although American Airlines would later state they received the memo on May 29, 1979, White this time detailed how the forklift being employed on the DC-10 was hanging and jumping erratically. Additionally, the Hyster's "engine seem[ed] to load up or idle too fast."

As the crash-associated turmoil at the Maintenance Center died down, Joe White's career continued in a normal fashion until the spring of 1981. During the month of March lawyers for McDonnell Douglas began to seek depositions from nearly 150 American Airlines maintenance personnel, as the manufacturer was attempting to determine liability for some 118 pending lawsuits associated with the crash. Before he could be deposed, however, White was interviewed for nearly eight hours by American's Los Angeles attorney, David Wheeler. During that interview White alleged he was told to perjure himself by forgetting he ever wrote any memos, that he was to forget anything he had seen, as well as to forget what happened to the memos or whether anyone had ever seen them. Joe refused to aid in what he felt was a cover-up, and on July 17, 1981, he was fired by the company for falsifying his time cards, being absent from his workstation, demonstrating poor judgment, and exhibiting an overall deterioration in his work performance. White was discharged without written notice or a hearing regarding his unsatisfactory work performance, and he was denied the usual termination hearing. In a secretly obtained tape recording (which is legal under Oklahoma law) of the dismissal made by Darrol Davison, Vice President of Power Plants, White admitted some of the entries on his time cards were not completely accurate. In the recording, however, Davison also acknowledged that most employee time cards were somewhat in error (for a summary of American's maintenance organization, see Exhibit 10).

Although Joe White was carried on the American Airlines payroll until September 18, 1981, he was unable to find employment within the airline industry despite 14 years of experience with his former employer and additional manufacturing experience with both Cessna and Boeing. Feeling he had been treated unfairly and that remarks about his character had prevented him from finding work, White filed a $9.5 million civil lawsuit against American in July 1982 for lost wages and benefits. His case took five years to come to trial after a number

Exhibit 10   **DC-10/B747 Organization, March 1, 1979**

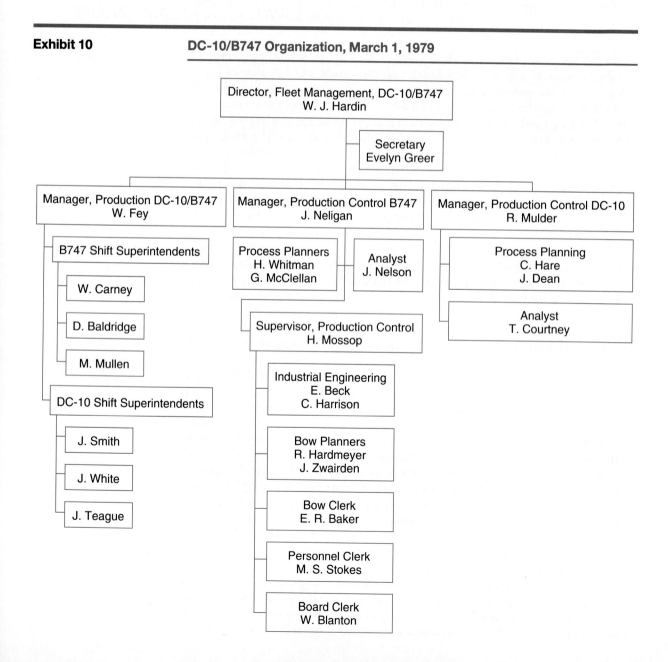

of delays by American Airlines. During the intervening years Joe lost his farm, his house went into foreclosure, his children were tormented at school, hundreds of supporting documents and microcassette recordings disappeared from his lawyer's office, and he spent every dime he owned pursuing his case.

During his 12-day trial, which began September 24, 1987, a number of facts emerged. Gordon O'Dell, who was the Maintenance and Engineering Center's comptroller for 12 years before his retirement in December 1982, testified he had conducted between 40 to 50 investigations of time card falsifications and "only Mr. White's case did not come to my office." Joe White's firing also seemed to be different to O'Dell:

> I have never heard of a foreman fired from American who had been so damned, and there were certainly dishonest foremen fired from time to time. I spent some time looking into Mr. White's background [as] Mr. White worked for me at one time and I do that to everybody transferred into my office. I reviewed all his personnel records, I talked to all the people Mr. White had worked with and for. I examined all his expense reports and they all were very honest. He was a very good employee and had performed well.

Larry Bonner, a labor/management specialist at American Airlines, also felt the White firing was unusual. To his recollection White was the only person fired without written notice and a hearing advising him of his unsatisfactory work performance. Bonner stated, "My impression is that Mr. White was being railroaded," and nothing existed in American's files to indicate that White was terminated for deteriorating work performance. "I saw [his] performance evaluation reports and all of them demonstrated to me that he was an excellent employee. In fact, a few months before he was terminated he was given a merit increase." A review of White's personnel evaluations for July 1979, February 1980, and February 1981 revealed that of 21 criteria he had been awarded ten 1s or 2s (outstanding or exceeding requirements) and no 5s (the lowest possible rating). Joe was rated below average on writing ability; behavioral flexibility; effective relations with associates, subordinates, and superiors; dependability; occupational knowledge; and leadership. He was highly rated in quantity of work, organization, oral communications, self-confidence, energy level, resistance to stress, general aptitude, and decision making.

American's contention that White falsified his time cards was challenged by handwriting expert Jessie Will, who said that whoever doctored the time cards made "an obvious effort to write as he did, but the numbers are not the right size . . . they are at the wrong angle. There are very obvious discrepancies." Through the use of a microscope and indirect lighting the expert was able to determine that the eight hours of overtime the company claimed were fraudulently represented by White were not in his handwriting. "With indirect lighting you can see there is an '8' beneath the '12' on Sunday of the second week and an '8' beneath the '12' of Monday for the second week. It appears that when the '8' underneath was eradicated, they got water or coffee and spilled it on it." For the time card's total hours Alma Clark, a secretary with 36 years of experience at the airline, had written a second 0 on top of the 0 in 80, thereby turning the total into 88 hours of work. (See Exhibit 11.)

In defending its firing of Joe White, American Airlines said it began an intensive review of his performance in the spring of 1981 after receiving an anonymous note about his poor attendance. In May and June 1981 spot checks of his attendance were conducted, and he was found with his crew on only one of 11

Exhibit 11 **Joe White's Time Card**

AA FORM C128-J	REFER TO AA REG 110-2	PRINTED IN U.S.A.

ADMINISTRATIVE TIME CARD

EMPLOYEE NBR.	EMPLOYEE NAME	JOB CODE
11181	J.L. White	1600

STATION CODE NBR.	ORG. CODE NBR.	WORK PERIOD ENDING
241	685	6/12/81

REMARKS:

SUPERVISORY APPROVAL

R. G. Rumbaugh

TITLE

Manager, JT8

CODE	ELAPSED TIME IN	OUT	OVER-TIME HOURS	SICK TIME	HOLIDAY WORKED	S-2	S-3	S-4	S-5	NON PRO-DUCTIVE
SAT DO										
SUN VC								8		8
MON VC								8		8
TUE	2300	0700						8		
WED	2300	0700						8		
THU	2300	0700						8		
FRI DO										
SAT DO										
SUN	1900	0700	4					12		
MON	1900	0700	4					12		
TUE	2300	0700						8		
WED	2300	0700						8		
THU	2300	0700						8		
FRI DO										
TOTALS HRS	8							88		16
TOTALS TNS	0							0		0
	72	33	29	30	34		36	56		97

FORWARD TO EMPLOYEE

Source: Plaintiff's Exhibit 10.

occasions. It was later determined, however, that White was on vacation on three of the days in question and that his crew was divided between two hangars 900 feet apart. American also challenged the portrait of White being a model employee. Fey said:

> Mr. White was probably the most disliked shift supervisor that I've ever had work for me. Every time I turned around, somebody was coming to me, upset because he did not have an A & P (Airframe and Power Plant) license, was not schooled in aeronautical technology, that he had to have everything explained to him in troubleshooting. He was not well liked by his peers.

Although Joe White admitted that the hours on his time cards may have been inaccurate, evidence was produced that extensive time card abuse existed at American. In violation of company policy and not condoned by upper management, certain supervisors made "deals" with crews to repair aircraft in a given time period in return for signing out early. Mechanics commonly falsified time cards, sometimes leaving early and at other times charging overtime to another pay period. When the airline stopped paying double time for overtime hours, supervisors began to allow mechanics to work double time and make it up on other time cards. In a typical ploy, a mechanic would work six hours overtime on a regular workday with two hours of double time being placed in the following day's time card as time and one-half.

The decision to fire Joe White was a stressful one for a number of individuals at the maintenance facility. One of White's closest friends felt he finally had to make the recommendation that Joe be fired. As he sobbed on the witness stand, Ken Harding, American's former labor relations manager, said:

> I have lost total respect for this man to tell the truth. His conduct has totally destroyed my belief that Joe White knows what the truth is. I'm still touched by Mr. White's situation, but I'm not touched by what this situation has driven him to. I have known Joe White for some time. I have known his family. It was not easy. I have been involved in other cases that were stressful but I knew Joe White very well.

For Darrol Davison the firing was less emotional but just as necessary because of White's pattern of dishonesty. "I thought it was probably the most flagrant abuse of time cards, the most dishonesty, that I had seen in the aviation business." Davison said very little documentation was put into White's personnel file because "I knew he was in law school, and I didn't want to make his termination any worse."

The trial's four-woman, two-man jury deliberated for five hours, whereupon it awarded Joe White $1,516,000 in damages plus attorney fees and court costs for wrongful discharge. The lawyers for American Airlines immediately said they would ask a U.S. District Court judge to set aside the verdict. In response to the award American Airlines attorney Reuben Davis said, "American Airlines has abiding faith in our system of justice. The trial judge did an excellent job in a very complicated trial, and the basis for the action we plan to take is that the verdict is just not supported by the evidence." Regarding the verdict for the plaintiff, White's lawyer said, "I think it vindicates Joe White. Here's a man of honesty and integrity and American Airlines tried to destroy him. This trial was all about a man's attempt to tell the truth, and had we been able to get into evidence all the truth of this case, the jury would have been calling for an adding machine."

*APPENDIX 1: WHISTLE BLOWER LAWS**

■ ────────────────────────────────── ■

Since 1981 various states have begun to create so-called Whistle Blower Laws to protect individuals who have suffered retaliatory discipline for "going public" about their employer's illegal actions. A whistle blower could report, for instance, their company's failure to conform to state licensing or labeling laws, their firm's involvement in a price fixing scheme, or a company violation of a consumer protection law. In each of these instances the employee is considered to be acting in the public's good by trying to stop the employer from committing acts which have been determined to be against society's general well-being.

Although the state of Oklahoma does not have a whistle blower statute, personal legal action for retaliatory discipline is possible under other laws. Accordingly many experts recommend, despite the existence or nonexistence of whistle blower laws, it is in the employer's best interests to create a positive environment of honesty and trust within the firm. This is usually accomplished by establishing and monitoring a set of practices and procedures which encourage the raising of issues of company wrongdoing before the employee feels forced to seek a public forum as the only method for insuring correct company behavior. These practices and procedures, in turn, provide management with the opportunity to investigate the claims of incorrect behavior, and to take corrective action if necessary.

When operating in a state that provides whistle blower protection, it is advised that employers should consider the following questions:

1. To whom does the law apply—Private-sector workers only, public-sector employees, or any employee in the state?
2. What disclosure requirements are imposed upon employees if imposed at all? Under what conditions are such requirements waived?
3. What kinds of employee conduct are protected? Need an employee possess only "reasonable belief" that wrongdoing is being committed?
4. Must employers post public notice of worker protections and obligations under the law?
5. Must employees seek relief through internal complaint procedures before filing a retaliatory discharge lawsuit? What legal remedies are available to the whistle blower once all internal procedures have been depleted?

**Abstrated from *Personnel Management: BNA Policy and Practice Series*. Washington, D.C.: Bureau of National Affairs, 1987, pp. 207, 583–586.*

APPENDIX 2: OFFICIAL FINDINGS OF THE NATIONAL TRANSPORTATION SAFETY BOARD, DECEMBER 21, 1979*

The National Transportation Safety Board determines that the probable cause of this accident was the asymmetrical stall and the ensuing roll of the aircraft because of the uncommanded retraction of the left wing outboard leading edge slats and the loss of stall warning and slat disagreement indication systems resulting from maintenance-induced damage leading to the separation of the No. 1 engine and pylon assembly at a critical point during takeoff. The separation resulted from damage by improper maintenance procedures which led to failure of the pylon structures.

Contributing to the cause of the accident were the vulnerability of the design of the pylon attach points to maintenance damage; the vulnerability of the design of the leading edge slat system to the damage which produced asymmetry; deficiencies in Federal Aviation Administration surveillance and reporting systems which failed to detect and prevent the use of improper maintenance procedures; deficiencies in the practices and communication among the operators, the manufacturer, and the FAA which failed to determine and disseminate the particulars regarding previous maintenance damage incidents; and the intolerance of prescribed operational procedures to the unique emergency.

*Aircraft Accident Report—American Airlines, Inc., DC-10-10, N110AA, Chicago-O'Hare International Airport, Chicago, Illinois, May 25, 1979. Washington, D.C.: National Transportation Safety Board, Bureau of Accident Investigation, December 21, 1979, p. 69.

APPENDIX 3: THE BUSINESS ROUNDTABLE: LESSONS TO BE LEARNED REGARDING THE DEVELOPMENT AND CONDUCT OF ETHICAL BUSINESS PRACTICES*

■ ─────────────────────────────────── ■

The Business Roundtable has noted that the question of ethical business conduct has become one of the most important challenges to this era's corporate community. Because of this, the Roundtable obtained material from one hundred American companies, and conducted in-depth investigations of the practices of ten firms possessing different histories, industries, and geography to determine how American firms can better deal with this challenge. The study group's findings and major observations are summarized below:

1. Top management's role should be one of commitment, leadership, and example. To achieve results, the Chief Executive Officer and those around that individual must be openly and strongly committed to ethical behavior, and give constant leadership in tending and renewing the organization's values. This commitment must be communicated in directives, policy statements, speeches, company publications, and especially by the actions of the company's top executives.

2. Expectations should be clear and a code of conduct should exist. Companies take various approaches to the establishment of sound principles for business conduct. Some accomplish this through a long and largely unwritten tradition of integrity while others adopt variously detailed written documents. The importance of a "code" is twofold: it clarifies the company's expectations regarding employee conduct, and it makes clear that the firm intends and expects its people to recognize the ethical dimensions of their corporation's policies and actions.

3. Mechanisms must be created to make ethics operable in everyday work situations. Human consciences are fragile and they need the support of the company, while a strong corporate culture and high ethical standards are strategic keys to a firm's survival and profitability.

4. Personnel must be involved and committed at all organizational levels. Ethical decision making comes about through decentralized involvement which in turn leads to a better adherence to the firm's standards of conduct.

5. Results should be measured. There is no precise way to measure the end results of efforts to develop effective corporate ethics programs. Accord-

*Quoted and abstracted from *Corporate Ethics: A Prime Business Asset* (New York: The Business Roundtable, February 1988), pp. 4–10; and press release from The Business Roundtable, February 4, 1988.

ingly companies use various methods such as surveys and auditing procedures to monitor compliance with standards of conduct. Company executives can also make personal judgments about the effectiveness of their corporate ethics programs. These judgments can be based on their own observations of the corporation's climate, their appraisal of the company's community reputation, and its performance in the marketplace.

Union Carbide of India: The Bhopal Gas Incident

Arthur Sharplin, McNeese State University

I can say that I have seen chemical warfare. Everything so quiet. Goats, cats, whole families—father, mother, children—all lying silent and still. And every structure totally intact. I hope never again to see it (Mayor of Bhopal).

In reality, there is but one entity, the monolithic multinational, which is responsible for the design, development and dissemination of information and technology worldwide (Indian government lawyer).

A corporation is not liable for the acts or omissions of another corporation by reason of ownership of stock (Union Carbide Corporation lawyer).

December 2, 1984, began as a typical day in the central Indian city of Bhopal. In the northern sector of town, shoppers moved about a bustling, open-air market. Here and there a customer haggled with a merchant. Beasts of burden, donkeys and oxen, pulled carts or carried ungainly bundles through the partly paved streets. Children played in the dirt. In the shadow of a Union Carbide India Limited (UCIL) pesticide factory, tens of thousands of India's poorest citizens milled about the shantytown they called home.

Inside the plant, several hundred Indian workers and managers went about their duties, maintaining and operating the systems that produced the mildly toxic pesticide Sevin. The plant was running at far below capacity and most of it was shut down for maintenance. Poisonous methyl isocyanate (MIC) was used in making Sevin, but the system which produced MIC had been idle for six weeks. The Sevin unit was using MIC from a 1-ton charge pot, which was periodically resupplied from either of two 15,000-gallon tanks (tanks 610 and 611). The tanks were half-buried and covered with concrete. Tanks 610 and 611, respectively, contained 41 and 20 metric tons of MIC at the time. A third storage tank (tank 619) was available for emergencies and for dumping off-specification MIC.

Sometime before midnight, several hundred gallons of water entered tank 610. News accounts would suggest the cause was improper maintenance procedures. But an Arthur D. Little consultant, hired by UCIL's U.S. parent, Union Carbide Corporation (UCC), would conclude the water probably entered through a hose which a "disgruntled operator" connected to the tank during a 10:45 P.M. shift change.[1]

Whatever the source of the water, it reacted with the MIC, producing heat and gas. A relief valve soon lifted, and MIC vapor began flowing through vent headers and out a discharge stack. Several of the workers noticed that their eyes started to water and sting, a signal that indicated an MIC leak. They reported this to the MIC supervisor and began to search for the leak. At about midnight, they found what they believed was the source, more than 200 feet from the tanks. They set up a fire hose to spray water on the suspected leak. It was 12:15 A.M. then, time for tea. The supervisors retired to the company canteen. A "tea boy" came to serve tea to the workers who remained on watch. The gas fumes were getting stronger, though, and the tea boy later said some refused to stop for tea. There were apparently other signals: The reaction in the tank was growing more violent, and pressure gauge readings were increasing.

Within a few minutes, an operator called the supervisors back from the canteen. About a ton of MIC was transferred to the Sevin unit in an attempt to relieve the pressure. But the tank pressure gauge was soon pegged. A worker later said the concrete above tank 610 was moving and cracking. Someone sounded the alarm siren and summoned the fire brigade. As the futility of their efforts became apparent, many of the workers evacuated upwind, some scaling the chain-link and barbed-wire fence at the plant perimeter. At about 12:45 A.M., the vapor could be seen escaping from an atmospheric vent line 120 feet in the air.

The cloud of deadly white gas was carried by a northwest wind toward the Jai Prakash Nagar shanties, on the south side of the plant. In the cold December night, the MIC settled toward the ground (in the daytime, or in the summer, convection currents probably would have raised and diluted it).

As the gaseous tentacles reached into the huts, there was panic and confusion. Many of the weak and elderly died where they lay. "It was like breathing fire," one survivor said. As word of the gas leak spread, many of Bhopal's affluent were able to flee in their cars. But most of the poor were left behind. When the gas reached the nearby railroad station, supervisors who were not immediately disabled sent out word along the tracks and incoming trains were diverted. This diversion cut off a possible means of escape but may have saved hundreds of lives. The whole station was soon filled with gas. Arriving trains would have been death traps for passengers and crews.

By 1:00 A.M., only a supervisor and the fire squad remained in the area of the MIC leak. The supervisor stayed upwind, donning his oxygen-breathing appa-

---

[1]Ashok S. Kalelkar (Arthur D. Little, Inc.), "Investigation of Large-Magnitude Incidents: Bhopal As a Case Study" (Paper for presentation at The Institution of Chemical Engineers Conference on Preventing Major Chemical Accidents, London, May 1988), 26.

ratus every few minutes to go check the various gauges and sensors. The fire squad sprayed water on the vent stack.

Of Bhopal's total population of about 700,000, tens of thousands fled that night, most on foot. An estimated 2000 or more died and over 200,000 were injured.[2] An Indian appeals court later set the number of seriously injured at 30,000–40,000.[3] The surrounding towns were woefully unprepared to accept the gasping and dying masses. Confused crowds waited outside hospitals for medical care. There was no certainty about how to treat the gas victims, and general-purpose medical supplies were in hopelessly short supply. Inside the hospitals and out, screams and sobs filled the air. Food supplies were quickly exhausted. People were even afraid to drink the water, not knowing if it was contaminated.

The second day, relief measures were better organized. Several hundred doctors and nurses from nearby hospitals had been summoned to help medical personnel in Bhopal. Just disposing of the dead was a major problem. Mass cremation was necessary. Islamic victims, whose faith allows burial rather than cremation, were piled several deep in hurriedly dug graves. Bloating carcasses of cattle and dogs littered the city. There was fear of a cholera epidemic. Bhopal's mayor said later, "I can say that I have seen chemical warfare. Everything so quiet. Goats, cats, whole families—father, mother, children—all lying silent and still. And every structure totally intact. I hope never again to see it." A U.S. appeals court would later call Bhopal "the most devastating industrial disaster in history."[4]

By the third day, the city had begun to move toward stability, if not normalcy. The plant was closed and locked. A decision was made to consume the 20 tons of MIC in tank 611 by using it to make pesticide. Most of the dead bodies had been disposed of, however inappropriately. The injured were being treated as rapidly as the limited medical facilities would allow, although many people simply sat in silence, stricken by an enemy they had never known well enough to fear.[5]

COMPANY BACKGROUND

The Ever-Ready Company, Ltd. (of Great Britain), began manufacturing flashlight batteries in Calcutta in 1926. The division was incorporated as the Ever-Ready Company (India), Ltd., in 1934 and became a subsidiary of Union Carbide Corporation (UCC) of New York. The name of the Indian company was changed to National Carbon Company (India), Ltd., in 1941 and to Union Carbide India Limited in 1959. The 1926 capacity of 6 million dry-cell batteries per year had expanded to 767 million by the 1960s. In 1959, a factory was set up in India to manufacture flashlights.

By the 1980s, UCIL was involved in five product areas: batteries, carbon and metals, plastics, marine products, and agricultural chemicals. Exhibit 1 shows production statistics for UCIL products. Eventually, there were 15 plants at

---

[2]In Re Union Carbide Corp. Gas Plant Disaster, 809 F.2d 195 (2nd Cir. 1987).

[3]Union Carbide Corporation v. Union of India, Regular Civil Suit No. 1113 (High Court of Madhya Pradesh, Bhopal, India, 4 April 1988), 2.

[4]In Re Union Carbide Corp. Gas Plant Disaster, 809 F.2d 195 (2nd Cir. 1987).

[5]Except where noted, information in this section was obtained from anonymous sources in India and from dozens of news accounts which appeared in the months following the disaster.

Exhibit 1   **Production Statistics**

Item	1989 Capacity	1988–1989	1987	1986	1985	1984	1983	1982	1981	1980
Batteries (000,000)	917	718	536	572	528	510	510	512	411	459
Flashlights (000,000)	8	10	7	8	6	7	7	7	7	7
Arc carbons (000,000)	9	10	8	8	8	7	8	7	7	7
Carb. electrodes (000,000)	3	1	1	1	1	1	1	1	1	0
Printing plates (metric tons)	1200	450	358	416	393	376	412	478	431	399
Metal castings (metric tons)	150	31	22	18	19	17	18	13	16	15
Mn dioxide (metric tons)	4500	4186	3620	4023	3670	3069	3335	3085	3000	2803
Chemicals (000 metric tons)	14	—	—	3	6	6	7	6	7	8
Polyethylene (000 metric tons)	20	—	1	7	19	17	18	17	20	19
Pesticides (metric tons)	—	—	—	—	18	1240	1647	2308	2704	1542
Marine products (metric tons)	—	—	—	—	—	272	424	649	642	601

eight locations (including the headquarters operation in Calcutta) which employed over 2000. UCIL's petrochemical complex, established in Bombay in 1966, was India's first petrochemical plant.

The marine products operation of UCIL was begun in 1971 with two shrimping ships. The business was completely export-oriented and employed 15 deep-sea trawlers. Processing facilities were located off the east and west coasts of India. The trawlers harvested deep-sea lobsters in addition to shrimp. This division was closed in 1984 and the facilities were sold in 1986.

In 1979, UCIL initiated a letter of intent to manufacture dry-cell batteries in Nepal. A 77.5 percent–owned subsidiary was set up in Nepal in 1982, and construction of a rupees (Rs.) 18 million plant was begun. The Nepal operation was solidly profitable by 1986.

The agricultural products division of UCIL was started in 1966 with only an office in Bombay. A letter of intent was issued by the Indian government that year to allow UCIL to set up a pesticide formulation plant at Bhopal. Land was rented to UCIL for about $40 per acre per year.

The initial investment was small, only $1 million, and the process was simple. Concentrated Sevin powder was imported from the United States, diluted with nontoxic powder, packaged, and sold. While UCC had no explicit technology transfer agreement with the Indian government, there was continuing pressure under the Foreign Exchange Regulation Act to limit imports. This translated into demands by the government for UCIL to manufacture Sevin and its components, including MIC, in India. A UCC executive said later, "The last thing we or UCIL wanted to do was build a pesticide plant in India." Another UCC executive later explained, "UCIL did not wish to incur the substantial capital investment of building a pesticide manufacturing plant in India because it was far less expensive to import finished pesticide from the U.S. and formulate

The UCIL Pesticide Factory at Bhopal

Exhibit 2

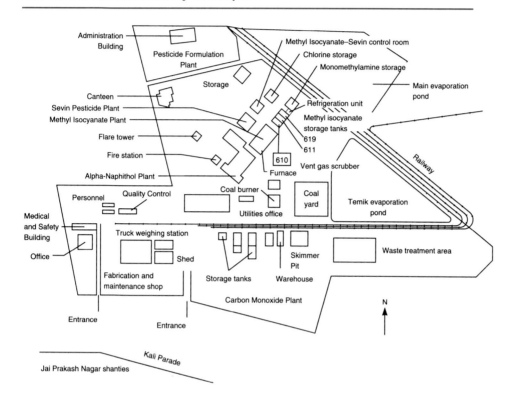

The Methyl Isocyanate Manufacturing Process

Exhibit 3

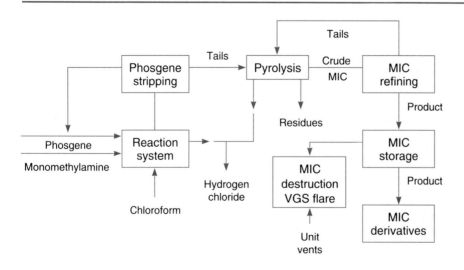

it in India."[6] Eventually the investment at Bhopal exceeded $25 million, and the constituents of Sevin were made there. Another Union Carbide insecticide, called Temik, was made in small quantities at Bhopal. Exhibit 2 is a map of the Bhopal plant as it existed in 1984. Exhibit 3 is a flow diagram of the MIC production process.

The assets of UCIL grew from Rs. 558 million in 1974 to Rs. 1234 million in 1983 (the conversion rate stayed near 9 rupees to the dollar during this period, moving to about 12 as the dollar strengthened worldwide in 1984 and 1985, then staying near 12 until 1989). The *Economic Times* of India ranked UCIL number 21 in terms of sales among Indian companies in 1984.

Primarily as a condition attached to permission to construct the MIC project, UCIL had voluntarily diluted UCC's equity from 60 percent to 50.9 percent in 1977–1978.[7] At the time of the Bhopal incident, UCC still held 50.9 percent, financial institutions owned by the Indian government held 25 percent, and the remaining 24 percent or so was in the hands of about 23,000 Indian citizens. The Indian Foreign Exchange Regulation Act (see Exhibit 4) generally limited nonresident interest in multinational corporations operating in India to 49 percent. However, UCC was exempted from this provision based on its being a high-technology company.

Starting in 1967 an Indian served as chairman of the 11-member UCIL board of directors. And foreign membership on the board was limited to four. In 1985, an expert on Indian industry affairs said, "Though the foreigners on the board are down to four from six in previous years, they continue to hold sway over the affairs of the company." However, UCC's chief litigation counsel, Robert A. Butler, wrote:

> None of Union Carbide Corporation's Directors are on the Board of the Indian Company. All of the employees and officers of the Indian Company, including its Chairman and Managing Director, are Indian residents and citizens.

UCC said UCIL was not required to get its approval for even major capital investments, which were controlled by the UCIL board.[8] Monthly reports detailing operations and safety procedures were submitted by the Bhopal plant to UCIL headquarters in Bombay. UCC said these reports were not provided to the U.S. parent, although certain periodic operating reports were submitted by UCIL to Union Carbide Eastern, a separate corporation charged with monitoring UCC investments in the Far East.[9]

UCC said it had conducted three safety audits at Bhopal at UCIL's request. The first two, in 1979 and 1980, were audits of personnel safety practices. The third was an evaluation of process safety in May of 1982. UCIL performed many safety audits itself.[10]

After the gas incident, UCC maintained it had never "had a presence in

[6]Robert A. Butler to author, 17 July 1989, 5.

[7]"Amended Written Statement and Set Off and Counterclaim," Union of India v. Union Carbide Corporation and Union Carbide Corporation v. Union of India, Regular Civil Suit No. 1113 of 1986 (Court of the District Judge, Bhopal, India), 10.

[8]Robert A. Butler to author, 17 July 1989, 5–6.

[9]Robert A. Butler to author, 19 July 1989, 6.

[10]Robert A. Butler to author, 19 July 1989, 6.

The Foreign Exchange Regulation Act	Exhibit 4

The act was originally enacted as a temporary measure in 1947. It was made permanent in 1957, then revised in 1973. The act covers various aspects of foreign exchange transactions, including money changing, buying or selling foreign exchange in India or abroad, having an account in a bank outside India, and remitting money abroad.

The purpose of the act is to restrict outflow of foreign exchange and to conserve hard-currency holdings in India. One provision requires that any company in which the nonresident interest is more than 40 percent "shall not carry on in India or establish in India any branch or office without the special permission of the Reserve Bank of India." But the Reserve Bank of India has authority to exempt a company from the provisions of the act. The 40 percent requirement was changed to 49 percent by Rajiv Gandhi's government.

High-technology companies are frequently exempted from the equity-ownership provisions of the act. Other companies that have operated in India for many years are sometimes exempted if they agree not to expand their Indian operations.

Policies in India regarding nationalization of foreign-owned companies have varied. A number of major oil companies have been nationalized. For example, Indian Oil Corporation, Bharat Petroleum, and Hindustan Petroleum used to be, respectively, Burmah Shell, Mobil, and Stanvae (Standard Vacuum Oil Company, an Esso unit).

More typically, a multinational company is asked to reduce its holdings to 49 percent or less by offering shares to the Indian public and Indian financial institutions. Multinationals that have diluted equity to meet the 49 percent requirement include CIBA-GEIGY, Parke-Davis, Bayer (aspirin), Lever Brothers (which operates as Hindustan Lever in India), Lipton, and Brooke-Bond.

When Indira Gandhi was voted out of office in 1977, the Janata (Peoples') Party strengthened the act. As a result, IBM and Coca-Cola pulled out of India. IBM's business in India was taken over by ICIM (International Computers Indian Manufacturers), a domestic firm. Another similar firm was set up to perform the maintenance services for the existing IBM computers.

India"[11] and that UCIL was an essentially autonomous operation. A UCC executive said, "UCIL has been subject to less control by Union Carbide than any subsidiary I know of anywhere in the world."

OPERATIONS AT BHOPAL

On the surface, the UCIL insecticide factory was a typical process plant. A wide diversity of storage tanks, hoppers, and reactors were connected by pipes. There were many pumps and valves and a number of tall vent lines and ducts. Ponds and pits were used for waste treatment, and several railway spur lines ran through the plant.

Sevin is made through a controlled chemical reaction involving alpha-naphthol and MIC. Alpha-naphthol is a brownish granular material, and MIC is a highly reactive liquid that boils and becomes a gas well below usual daytime temperatures. In 1971, when plans were first made to make alpha-naphthol

[11]Robert A. Butler to author, 26 May 1989, 9.

at Bhopal, a pilot plant was set up. A full-size alpha-naphthol plant (in fact, the world's largest) was finished in 1977.

In the meantime, work had begun on the ill-fated MIC plant. UCC provided the process design for part of the plant. Twenty senior Indian engineers went to UCC's Institute, West Virginia, pesticide facility in 1978 to study that plant's design and operation. An engineering company headquartered in Bombay, Humphreys and Glasgow, Pvt. Ltd., was retained by UCIL to produce the detail drawings for the plant and serve as general contractor. All the subcontractors were Indian firms. In 1979–1980, five Americans were sent to assist the thousand or so Indian employees of UCIL in starting up the plant. All except one of the Americans left in 1980. The last one, with the title of Works Manager, stayed on until December 1982, when he also left.

UCC was a world leader in MIC technology and provided much of the process design for the plant. But a UCC attorney later stated, "UCC was not involved with [the MIC plant's] construction and did not send engineers to supervise the construction."[12] A U.S. appeals court agreed, finding: "The plant has been constructed and managed by Indians in India."[13] The attorney said UCC was uninvolved "both because UCIL was an autonomous company and because the Indian governmental regulations prohibited foreign involvement if Indians were capable of performing a given task."[14]

Even before 1980, when the MIC facility began operating, problems began to crop up with the alpha-naphthol unit. The latter system continued in various stages of shutdown and partial operation through 1984. V. P. Gokhale, Managing Director of UCIL, called the decision to make alpha-naphthol a "very large mistake." But he noted that the company was forced to do it to retain its operating license. The Bhopal factory was designed to produce 5000 tons per year of Sevin but never operated near capacity; in the early eighties, UCIL was generally the third-largest producer of pesticides in India, sometimes slipping to number 4.

Annual profits of several million dollars from the Bhopal operation were originally predicted by 1984. But that was not to be, for several reasons. First, an economic recession made farmers more cost-conscious and caused them to search for less expensive alternatives to Sevin. Second, a large number of small-scale producers were able to undersell the company, partly because they were exempt from excise and sales taxes. Seventeen of these firms bought MIC from UCIL and used it to make products virtually identical to Sevin and Temik. Finally, a new generation of low-cost pesticides was becoming available.

With sales collapsing, the Bhopal plant became a money loser in 1981. By late 1984, the yearly profit estimate had been adjusted downward to a $4 million *loss* based on 1000 tons of output, one-fifth of capacity. To forestall what might have seemed inevitable economic failure, extensive cost cutting was done. The staff at the MIC plant was cut from 12 operators on a shift to 6. The maintenance team was reduced in size. In a number of instances, faulty safety devices remained unrepaired for weeks. Though instrumentation technology advanced at Union Carbide's other pesticide plants, the innovations were only partly adopted at Bhopal.

[12]Robert A. Butler to author, 26 May 1989, 6.

[13]In Re Union Carbide Corp. Gas Plant Disaster, 809 F.2d 195 (2nd Cir. 1987).

[14]Robert A. Butler to author, 17 July 1989, 7.

Upon reviewing the above paragraph, UCC's Chief Litigation Counsel, Robert A. Butler, wrote:

> This . . . suggests that the incident was due to cost-cutting, faulty maintenance, and understaffing. The facts do not support that claim. In fact, at the time of the incident the plant was well overstaffed.[15]

However, UCC Chief Executive Warren Anderson and Director of Safety and Health Ron Van Mynen had expressed a different view shortly after the incident. Anderson said, "I feel badly about it now, that we could have an operation within the Union Carbide complex that was running the way it [the Bhopal facility] was running—in total disregard for operating procedures." Van Mynen remarked:

> I had never been to Bhopal earlier, but some members of my team had been there. And I must admit that they were shocked at what they saw. When they had been there earlier the [safety] equipment was running according to s.o.p., and when we did get there in '84, after the event, it was not running, and it had not been running. And it was a surprise to those gentlemen who had worked so hard in the startup of the plant.[16]

On the night of the disaster, several safety systems failed to work adequately or were at least suspect. For example, the flare tower, used for burning carbon monoxide, had been taken out of service to repair corroded piping a few days earlier. UCC recommended maintaining MIC at temperatures below 5 degrees Celsius (41 degrees Fahrenheit) because it was an unstable liquid that reacted unpredictably to changes in temperature. But the refrigeration unit cooling the three MIC storage tanks had repeatedly malfunctioned and had been shut down since June.

The UCIL directors, like the UCC parent, disclaimed fault for the incident. The "Report of Directors," included in UCIL's 1984 annual report, stated:

> At no time had any significant fault been found with the working or safety precautions taken by your company. Your company had taken all safety precautions to avoid any accident in the Plant, which had been operated all along with trained and qualified operators.

In early 1985, the government of India canceled the operating license of the Bhopal plant, clearing the way for the plant's dismantlement. The likelihood that this would happen provoked a Bhopal political leader to remark, "We've lost 2000 lives, now must we lose 2000 jobs?"

FINANCE

Exhibit 5 provides financial summaries for UCIL. Exhibit 6 gives selected comparative financial statistics for the United States and India. During the months before the Bhopal disaster, UCIL's common shares, listed on the Bombay and

---

[15]Robert A. Butler to author, 26 May 1989, 6.
[16]Kenneth Brooks, "Carbide's Report: How Bhopal Happened," *Chemical Week*, 27 March 1985, 9.

Exhibit 5   **Financial Statements (Rs. 000,000 except as noted)**

	1984	1985	1986	1987	1988–1989*
Balance Sheet					
Funds employed					
Fixed assets	467	324	294	286	302
Investments	14	10	14	80	32
Net current assets	472	534	805	803	416
Deferred revenue expenses			9	9	9
Bhopal Company deposit					690
	953	868	805	803	1448
Financed by					
Share capital and Reserves	686	687	698	706	776
Loan funds	268	181	107	97	672
	953	868	805	803	1448

	1979	1980	1981	1982	1983	1984	1985	1986	1987	1988–1989
Summary of Operations										
Income	1465	1720	1881	2092	2122	2245	2444	2175	2010	2578
Materials consumed	598	757	847	955	916	980	1057	874	803	971
Operating expenses, employee-related	188	199	218	246	272	283	337	325	347	438
Other operating expenses	228	265	315	364	395	391	382	385	315	390
Depreciation	32	37	41	42	48	50	56	39	22	24
Interest	20	32	28	53	58	47	31	24	19	33
Excise duty	261	270	258	287	286	340	431	420	431	623
PBT	138	161	175	147	148	153	65	90	73	100
Income tax	73	80	80	50	55	71	64	40	25	30
Net profit	65	81	95	97	93	82	13	50	48	70
Dividends	35	46	49	49	49	16	—	39	39	—
Share price (in rupees)										
High	30.9	36.0	31.7	28.1	28.3		29.8		37.0	43.0
Low	25.5	22.0	24.9	23.3	21.5		18.5		17.1	20.0

Note: Column totals may not check, and amounts less than 500,000 Rs. are shown as zero, due to rounding.

*Financial data is for the period 12/26/87 to 3/31/89.

Calcutta stock exchanges, hovered around Rs. 30. They dropped to a low of Rs. 15.8 on December 11, recovering only slightly in succeeding months. The shares reached a high of Rs. 43 in January 1986 but then fell steadily to the middle teens by late 1987, rising again to the midtwenties in July 1989. The exchange rate was Rs. 16.38 per U.S. dollar on July 16.

In 1975, the United States Export-Import Bank, in cooperation with First National Citibank of New York, approved loans of $2.5 million to UCIL for the MIC project. Also, the Industrial Credit and Investment Corporation of India (ICICI), a government agency, authorized a Rs. 21.5 million loan, part of which was drawn in 1980. Finally, long-term loans were provided by several other Indian financial institutions and insurance companies. Some of these loans were

Exhibit 6

Comparative Financial Statistics for the United States and India

Year	U.S. Producer Price Index*	India Wholesale Price Index†	Conversion Rate‡
1974	161.1	169.2	8.111
1975	175.1	175.8	8.914
1976	183.6	172.4	8.985
1977	195.8	185.4	8.703
1978	197.1	185.0	8.189
1979	215.8	206.5	8.108
1980	244.5	248.1	7.872
1981	269.8	278.4	8.728
1982	280.7	288.7	9.492
1983	285.2	316.0	10.129
1984	291.1	338.4	11.402
1985	293.7	357.8	12.352
1986	289.7	376.8	12.680

*Wholesale Price Index before 1978. Arithmetic average of monthly figures. Base year, 1967.

†Arithmetic average of April–March monthly figures. Base year, 1970 (April 1970–March 1971).

‡Arithmetic average of monthly figures (rupees per dollar).

guaranteed by the State Bank of India. UCC guaranteed none of the loans of UCIL.

UCC stock was listed on the New York Stock Exchange. It traded near $50 in the months before December 1984, down from its historical high of $74, reached in 1983. When news of Bhopal reached the United States, the stock fell to near $30, to remain there until takeover rumors would propel it upward six months later. The rumors would soon subside, though, and the stock would trade near $30 throughout most of 1989.

THE GAF RAID

GAF Corporation increased its holdings of UCC stock in 1985 and announced a takeover effort. The two companies had markedly different corporate cultures. GAF had a reputation for legal toughness, if not ruthlessness, having been successfully involved in massive toxic tort litigation (related to asbestos) for decades. GAF Chairman Samuel J. Heyman, an attorney, had muscled his way into control of the company in a bitter proxy fight in 1983. *The Wall Street Journal* reported a widespread belief that Heyman was likely to fire all the top managers of UCC if he ever gained control.

In contrast to what might have been expected from GAF, UCC Chairman Warren Anderson had expressed extreme sympathy for the victims of Bhopal and had even gone there to try to help. Though most of his attempts at providing financial and medical aid were rebuffed, he continued to assume major responsibility for the incident, saying it would be his main concern for the rest of his working life. Anderson also admitted the MIC plant should not have been operating in its condition at the time, one of several statements he made which later complicated his company's legal defenses. Anderson said, "Right from the beginning . . . we said that we'd accept moral responsibility," but from a legal standpoint, he noted, "It's their company, their plant, their people."[17]

Union Carbide managers rushed to erect takeover barriers and took actions to make the company less desirable as a merger candidate. Golden parachutes worth at least $8.8 million were adopted for 42 of the executives. Two operating divisions were set up, one for chemicals and plastics and the other for everything else. Various assets were written down by nearly $1 billion. The employee retirement plan was amended to free the $500 million "surplus" in the pension fund "for general corporate purposes." Union Carbide repurchased 56 percent of its outstanding common stock, issuing $2.52 billion in high-interest (average 14.2 percent) debt in the transaction.

The Wall Street Journal later reported 3.2 million of the shares were purchased by UCC in a private deal with Ivan Boesky. Boesky's UCC machinations figured prominently in his subsequent conviction for various securities violations. GAF, too, was later charged with stock manipulation and other offenses growing out of its efforts to take over UCC and, having failed in that, to profit from the adventure. Boyd Jeffries, also later convicted of stock manipulation, was involved in the alleged GAF crimes. There was never any suggestion UCC was involved in these alleged offenses.

After the takeover attempt was thwarted, much of the UCC debt was repaid. Money for the repayment came from three major sources. First, the sale of Union Carbide's agricultural products and electrical carbon units and the sale and leaseback of the Danbury, Connecticut headquarters building provided $875 million. Second, 30 million new common shares brought $651 million. Third, the divestiture of UCC's Consumer Products Division provided substantial funds. Within months, Union Carbide stock recovered to predisaster levels. After a three-for-one split in 1986 the shares continued to climb, reaching the low thirties (high eighties, corrected for the split) by early 1989.

PERSONNEL

In 1984, all of UCIL's approximately 9000 employees were Indians, according to UCC.[18] The Bhopal plant accounted for 10 percent of these. In general, the engineers at Bhopal were among India's elite—better educated, according to a UCC official, than the average American engineer. Most new engineers were recruited from the prestigious India Institute of Technology and were paid wages comparable with the best offered in Indian industry. Successful applicants were given two years of training before being certified for unsupervised duty.

Until the late 1970s only first-class science graduates or persons with diplomas in engineering were hired as operators at Bhopal. New employees were given six months of theoretical instruction, followed by on-the-job training. As cost-cutting efforts proceeded in the 1980s, standards were lowered signifi-

---

[17]Kenneth Brooks, "Carbide's Report: How Bhopal Happened," *Chemical Week*, 27 March 1985, 10.

[18]"Amended Written Statement and Set Off and Counterclaim," Union of India v. Union Carbide Corporation and Union Carbide Corporation v. Union of India, Regular Civil Suit No. 1113 of 1986 (Court of the District Judge, Bhopal, India), 11.

cantly. Some persons with only high school diplomas were hired, and training was said to be less rigorous than before. In addition, the number of operators on a shift was reduced, and many supervisory positions were eliminated. UCC officials have said that there is no evidence that lowered educational standards had any impact on the incident.[19]

The Indian managers at UCIL developed strong ties with the local political establishment. A former police chief became the plant's security contractor. A local political party boss, who was also President of the Bhopal Bar Association, got the job as company lawyer. *Newsweek* reported that a luxurious guest house was maintained by UCIL, and "lavish" parties were thrown there for local dignitaries.

In general, wages at the Bhopal factory were well above those in domestic firms. Still, as prospects continued downward after 1981, a number of senior managers and junior executives began to abandon ship. The total work force at the plant dropped from a high of about 1500 to about 900. This reduction was accomplished through voluntary departures rather than layoffs. An Indian familiar with operations at Bhopal said:

> The really competent and well-trained employees, especially managers and supervisors, got sick of the falling standards and indifferent management and many of them quit despite high salaries at UCIL. Replacements were made on an ad hoc basis. Even guys from the Consumer Products Division, who only knew how to make batteries, were drafted to run the pesticide plant.

A UCC attorney disputed this, writing:

> This is wholly inaccurate. Any individuals who left were replaced by competent, well-trained and experienced individuals. In addition, the reduction in the work force resulted primarily from the shut down of the alpha-naphthol unit rather than any alleged disillusionment on the part of the employees.[20]

In May 1982, a team from UCC headquarters audited the safety status of the MIC plant. The team listed as many as ten major deficiencies in the safety procedures that the plant followed. The high turnover in plant personnel was noted and commented upon. (A UCC official later commented, "The plant addressed all of these deficiencies well before the incident. None had anything to do with the incident."[21]) The team declared it had been impressed with the operating and maintenance procedures at Bhopal.

MARKETING AND DEMOGRAPHICS

The population of India was over 700 million persons in the 1980s, although its land area was only about one-third that of the United States. Three-fourths of India's people depended on agriculture for a livelihood. Only about one-third of the population was literate. Modern communications and transportation systems connected the major cities, but the hundreds of villages were largely untouched by twentieth-century technology.

[19]Robert A. Butler to author, 19 July 1989, 9.
[20]Robert A. Butler to author, 19 July 1989, 10.
[21]Robert A. Butler to author, 26 May 1989, 9.

English was at least a second tongue for most Indian professionals, but not for ordinary Indians. There were 16 officially recognized languages in the country. The national language was Hindi, which was dominant in 5 of India's 25 states. The working classes spoke hundreds of dialects, often unintelligible to neighbors just miles away.

India's farmers offered at best a challenging target market. They generally eked out livings from small tracts of land. Most had little more than subsistence incomes and were reluctant to invest what they had in such modern innovations as pesticides. They were generally ignorant of the right methods of application and, given their linguistic diversity and technological isolation, were quite hard to educate. To advertise its pesticides, UCIL used billboards and wall posters as well as newspaper and radio advertisements.

Radio was the most widely used advertising medium in India. The state-owned radio system included broadcasts in local languages as well as in Hindi. Companies could buy advertising time on the stations, but it was costly to produce commercials in so many dialects. Much of the state-sponsored programming, especially in rural areas, was devoted to promoting agriculture and instructing farmers about new techniques. Often the narrators mentioned products such as Sevin and Temik by name.

Movies provided another popular promotional tool. Most small towns had one or more cinema houses, and rural people often traveled to town to watch the shows. Advertisements appeared before and after main features and were usually produced in regional languages, though not in local dialects.

Until the eighties, television was available only in the cities. During 1984, a government program spread TV relay stations at the rate of more than one each day, with the result that 80 percent of the population was within the range of a television transmitter by the end of the year. Still, few rural citizens had ready access to television receivers.

Pesticide sales were highly dependent on agricultural activity from year to year. In times of drought, like 1980 and 1982, UCIL's pesticide sales suffered severe setbacks. In 1981, abundant rains helped spur sales.

India had a very extensive network of railways; the total track mileage was second only to that of the Soviet Union. The road and highway system criss-crossed the areas in between the railway lines. The railway system was especially significant to UCIL's pesticide operation because Bhopal lay near the junction of the main east-west and north-south tracks in India. An Indian familiar with the agricultural economy remarked, "Overall, physical distribution of pesticides is not too monumental a task. Getting farmers to use them and teaching them how are the real problems."

The marketing division for agricultural products was headquartered in Hyderabad, in southern India. Eight branch offices were scattered all over the country. Sales were made through a network of distributors, wholesalers, and retailers. Representatives from the branch offices booked orders from the distributors and wholesalers. Retailers got their requirements from wholesalers, who, in turn, were supplied by distributors. The distributors got their stocks from the branch offices. The branch office "godowns" (warehouses) were supplied directly from the Bhopal plant. The retailers' margin was 15 percent. Wholesalers and distributors each received about 5 percent. Most of the retailers were family or individually owned concerns, although some of UCIL's pesticides were sold at retail through government agricultural sales offices.

THE LEGAL BATTLE

After the Bhopal tragedy UCC and UCIL executives were charged with manslaughter and other crimes. UCC Chairman Anderson, along with the head of UCIL, was arrested and briefly detained by Indian officials when he went to India shortly after the incident. Seven UCIL employees were also arrested.[22] UCC investigators were barred from the plant at first, given only limited access to records and reports and, for over a year, prohibited from interviewing employees.[23]

Anderson said, "The name of the game is not to nail me to the wall but to provide for the victims of the disaster." He volunteered UCC to help provide funding for a hospital to treat the Bhopal victims. The company contributed $1 million to a victims' relief fund. It and UCIL set aside $20 million for relief payments. Though Anderson said the offer was unconditional, the Indian government spurned it.

UCIL offered to build a new plant, one that would use nontoxic inputs, on the Bhopal site. One proposal was for a nonhazardous formulation plant to be constructed by UCIL and operated by the state government. Alternatively, UCIL suggested a battery factory it would own and operate. Both ideas were turned down by the Indian government.

A number of U.S. and Indian lawyers rushed to sign up gas victims and their relatives as clients. On December 7, 1984, the first of some 145 "class action" lawsuits was filed in the United States on behalf of the victims of the disaster. For example, famed attorney Melvin Belli brought suit for $15 billion. In March 1985, India enacted the Bhopal Gas Leak Disaster Act, giving the Indian government the exclusive right to represent the victims. The Attorney General of India was authorized to sue Union Carbide in an American court. A Minneapolis law firm that specialized in product liability cases was retained to represent India. In February 1985, a judicial panel in the United States ordered all the lawsuits related to Bhopal consolidated in a single court—that of Judge John F. Keenan in Manhattan. The Attorney General of India asserted that compensation had to be in accordance with American standards and continued to press the lawsuit while engaging in out-of-court negotiations with Union Carbide.

In his statement before Judge Keenan, he argued:

> Key management personnel of multinationals exercise a closely held power which is neither restricted by national boundaries nor effectively controlled by international law. The complex corporate structure of the multinational, with networks of subsidiaries and divisions, makes it exceedingly difficult or even impossible to pinpoint responsibility for the damage caused by the enterprise to discrete corporate units or individuals. Persons harmed by the acts of a multinational corporation are not in a position to isolate which unit of the enterprise caused the harm, yet it is evident that the multinational enterprise that caused the harm is liable for such harm.

---

[22]Ashok S. Kalelkar (Arthur D. Little, Inc.), "Investigation of Large-Magnitude Incidents: Bhopal As a Case Study" (Paper for presentation at The Institution of Chemical Engineers Conference on Preventing Major Chemical Accidents, London, May 1988), 7.

[23]Ashok S. Kalelkar (Arthur D. Little, Inc.), "Investigation of Large-Magnitude Incidents: Bhopal As a Case Study" (Paper for presentation at The Institution of Chemical Engineers Conference on Preventing Major Chemical Accidents, London, May 1988), 3, 7.

A UCC attorney later remarked, "The government's multinational enterprise theory has never been sustained by any court in the world, and it lacks any legal basis."[24]

The primary focus of the U.S. case was UCC's plea of *forum non-conveniens*— that India, not the United States, was the appropriate place for any trial because most of the documents, litigants, evidence, and witnesses were in India. UCC had reasons in addition to convenience and cost to prefer the Indian forum. Although both the Indian and the U.S. legal systems were based on English common law, punitive damages were almost unheard of in Indian courts, and compensatory damage awards were generally much lower than in the United States. For example, an appeals court in India was soon to estimate the following scale of compensation for Bhopal victims should the matter go to final judgment there:

Death or total permanent disability	Rs. 200,000
Partial permanent disability	Rs. 100,000
Temporary partial disability	Rs. 50,000[25]

As UCC struggled to recover from the disaster and restore its public image, two events thrust the company back to the forefront of international news coverage. First, in June 1985 hundreds of persons were affected by California watermelons grown on soil to which the Union Carbide pesticide Temik had been applied (improperly applied, according to the company). Second, in August a leak of the chemical intermediate aldecarb oxime at the company's Institute, West Virginia, plant, the only U.S. facility to make MIC, sent 135 people to hospitals. West Virginia Governor Arch Moore publicly criticized Union Carbide's handling of the incident, and Anderson admitted the company had waited too long to warn residents.

In May 1986 Judge Keenan ruled the case should be tried in India.[26] The decision would be affirmed by an appeals court in early 1987.[27] In September 1986 consideration of the suit resumed in the Court of the District Judge in Bhopal. UCC attorneys denounced the central and state governments in India for their alleged liability for the disaster. The company's answer denied every charge leveled against UCC. It claimed the factory was run by UCIL and pointed out that no U.S. citizen had been employed there for two years before the disaster. UCC also stated that sabotage was responsible for the disaster and alleged that there was a conspiracy among UCIL employees and a separate conspiracy among government investigators to conceal evidence after the incident.[28] The Indian government expressed outrage at Union Carbide's position and set its damage claim at $3.1 billion.

The hearings continued concurrently with out-of-court negotiations. As 1987 drew to an end, there were rumors of a settlement. Union Carbide offered $500 million in payments over time (then present value, about $350 million). Each dependent of the 2600 Union Carbide said were killed in the incident was to

[24]Robert A. Butler to author, 26 May 1989, 10.

[25]Union Carbide Corporation v. Union of India, Order in Gas Claim No. 1113/86, Civil Revision 26/88 (High Court of Madhya Pradesh, 4 April 1989), 98.

[26]In Re Union Carbide Corp. Gas Plant Disaster, 634 F.Supp. 842 (S.D.N.Y. 1986, as amended 10 June 1986).

[27]In Re Union Carbide Corp. Gas Plant Disaster, 809 F.2d 195 (2nd Cir. 1987).

[28]Robert A. Butler to author, 19 July 1989, 10.

receive $2000 a year for ten years. The chronically ill would get $1000 annually for the same period. And those slightly injured would be given a single payment of $500. The Indian government offered to settle for $615 million in cash. When news of a possible settlement leaked out, there was a furious public outcry in India. Former Indian Supreme Court Chief Justice P. N. Bhagwati demanded that any settlement include an admission of guilt by Union Carbide.

As the settlement talks appeared to break down in December 1987, Judge M. V. Deo ordered UCC to pay $270 million in interim compensation to the gas victims.[29] Union Carbide filed an appeal of the order, calling the idea of interim damages—before a defendant was found to owe anything at all—"unprecedented." The company continued to assert that it was confident of proving that the disaster was the result of sabotage and that it could not be held accountable in any case for the acts or omissions of UCIL, in which it claimed to only own stock. Judge Deo's decision was upheld by the High Court of Madhya Pradesh on April 4, 1988, although the interim award was reduced to about $190 million.[30] Both India and UCC appealed to the Supreme Court of India. Comments from Union Carbide management concerning the disaster are provided in Appendix 1.

THE SETTLEMENT

On Tuesday, February 14, 1989, company lawyers were presenting arguments before the Supreme Court, when Chief Justice R. S. Pathak interrupted the proceeding. He then issued an order that UCC pay $470 million by March 31 "in full and final settlement of all claims, rights and liabilities related to and arising out of the Bhopal gas disaster." Acceptance of the order had reportedly been unanimously approved by the UCC directors in a telephone poll hours earlier. The order applied to all "criminal and civil proceedings" related to the Bhopal tragedy and thus purported to be a complete settlement of the case. UCC and UCIL paid their agreed-upon shares of the settlement—$425 million and $45 million, respectively—on February 24, 1989. The Indian Supreme Court was to oversee distribution of the funds.

UCC had previously set aside $250 million for damages and the company's insurance coverage was estimated at another $200 million. So paying the settlement would only result in an estimated $0.50 per share charge against 1988 earnings of $1.59 per share. UCC stock rose $2 a share on Tuesday and another $1.38 Wednesday, to close at $32.50, more than double the price (corrected for the three-for-one split) before the Bhopal tragedy. UCC was immediately touted as a prime takeover candidate, with an expected purchase price of about $50 a share, or $7 billion.

There was evidence some knew of the approaching settlement. A week before it was ordered, UCC stock jumped $2 a share on volume totaling over 8 percent of all outstanding shares. That was the highest volume for any NYSE stock in five months. UCC said it had no knowledge of any purported leak.

[29]Union of India v. Union Carbide Corporation, Gas Claim Case No. 1113 of 1986 (Court of the District Judge, Bhopal, India, 17 December 1987).

[30]Union Carbide Corporation v. Union of India, Regular Civil Suit No. 1113 (High Court of Madhya Pradesh, Bhopal, India, 4 April 1988).

It was uncertain how and when the settlement money would be distributed to victims—or even how much of it would be. Bruce A. Finzen, one of the Indian government's U.S. lawyers, said, "Even at the rate of one hour per claim, you are talking about years of court time." The Indian government had already paid some survivors $800 or so for each immediate family member who perished. Medical care and certain other benefits had also been furnished by the government. But there were about 500,000 claims for relief, and only about 100,000 persons had been in the disaster area.[31]

There were immediate objections in India to the amount of damages and the nature of the settlement. But an editorial in *The Times of India* took a self-critical view:

> The government has been caught in a trap of its own making. It wanted as many applications for relief as possible to support its case for a bigger settlement. . . . I feel that many decent citizens were suddenly overcome by avarice. . . . It will be a very difficult task now to eliminate wrong claims. . . . In the first few days of the tragedy the whole world sympathised with us. Carbide was prepared to do anything. . . . Aid was offered by several countries. . . . But at that time we thought it would hurt our national pride to take the help. (The Armenian earthquake, has, however, set a new pattern of international help now.) . . . We preferred to arrest the Carbide chairman. . . . The terrible suffering of the victims and their families has been subordinated, even made to appear irrelevant, by all the begging and browbeating. All the bravery shown by those who struggled with the cloud's effect on the first day has been forgotten. . . . Now all that remains is to stand like vultures at the kill. The effect of all the propaganda war against the Union Carbide will be apparent in the coming years when we find that all foreigners, even the Russians, will look at any contract with India with suspicion, and press for safeguards so that the liability of subsidiaries is not transferred to them.[32]

UCC chief Kennedy called the settlement "a fair resolution of all issues." And UCC attorney Bud Holman said the negotiations were like "walking up a winding staircase in total darkness," adding, "It's nice to be in the light." In its 1989 proxy statement, UCC reported it was continuing to spend $7–$8 million a year on "Bhopal-related litigation."

[31]K. F. Rustamji, "Coming to Terms with Bhopal," *The Times of India*, March 8, 1989.
[32]K. F. Rustamji, "Coming to Terms with Bhopal," *The Times of India*, March 8, 1989.

APPENDIX 1: EXCERPTS FROM INTERVIEWS

■ ── ■

Gas victims and government officials in the Bhopal area were questioned in early 1987 concerning the gas incident. Upon reading excerpts from the questions and interviewee comments, a UCC attorney wrote they "are designed to inflame emotions, not inform the mind, and are of questionable value in an educational forum." He continued:

> Such inflammatory rhetoric simply permits the participants to facilely blame companies such as Union Carbide without evidence and without a trial, rather than forcing the participants to confront the fundamental ethical issues facing host countries and companies which, of necessity, use toxic substances in their manufacturing processes.[*]

The abbreviated questions and responses are presented below.

Description of the Incident?

A very thick layer of smoke caused uncontrollable tears, copious coughing, sneezing, vomiting. We ran to save our lives. We saw people in large numbers running here and there in great confusion, crushing each other, not bothering about anyone else.

I felt chilled and soon could not see.

I felt my eyes burning, like smoke coming from burning chilies. I was gasping for a breath of fresh air. I saw my neighbors in the same condition. A thin smoky layer was visible but its source was not known. Soon I was coughing and water was coming from my eyes and I fell unconscious.

At first I did not know what was happening because all my systems were affected. I was vomiting. My stomach was dislocated. My muscles were loose. Everyone was gasping for breath, running without any direction to find a safe place. Some of them demanded death as if it was readily available at a grocery shop.

Aftereffects?

I still do not know how bad it will get. It has become difficult to tolerate anything that is going wrong. I cannot remember like before.

I have become weak in body and mind. My memory has been affected badly. Carrying even small loads and fast walking has become a dream to me. I feel like an asthmatic patient.

The effect has subsided. But the resistance of the body is still down. My body has become allergic to muddy areas. The cough remains permanent and breathlessness occurs sometime.

[*]Robert A. Butler to author, 19 July 1989, 11.

Asthmatic, decreased vision, awfully unpredictable and irritable temper—future unknown, uncertain.

Loss in appetite, loss in weight, breathing trouble, uneasiness, poor eyesight, and weak memory power.

I cannot walk quickly and cannot run.

Assistance Provided?

A mere Rs. 1500 has been provided as compensation and that is only to those whose income is below Rs. 500 a year. So we have not got any assistance so far from anyone.

Symptomatic treatment is being given without knowing the cause and the disease. This should stop.

None.

After three days I was treated at the hospital with antibiotics. But there was no definite diagnosis or treatment.

So far, nil. The policies made by the local government are unbelievable. They pay by economic and social status.

For us railway officers and our families nobody has done anything.

What Should Be Done?

The M.P. [Madhya Pradesh, the state where Bhopal is located] government with the cooperation of the government of India and aided by Union Carbide or the American government should start a fully equipped hospital basically concerned with lungs and eyes. Provision of work, housing, and education should be made.

Government should give proper treatment to the gas affected. They should rehabilitate those who lost their earner. They should stop a recurrence.

Next of kin of the deceased should be given sufficient money by UCIL. All affected people should be given suitable jobs by government. Proper treatment should be given by government out of fines imposed on Union Carbide because they have failed to give a safe design of the project and neglected all safety measures in the factory.

The affected people should be provided with good food to recoup their body. All over the world the Madhya Pradesh government has received donations for this so it must be utilized properly.

Nothing can be done now since everything is over.

Government should arrange to shift the factory to somewhere away from the town area.

The society at large, the government, and above all UCIL itself should have honorably taken to itself to soothe the sufferers. Their needs for the balance of their life span should be given gratis to them.

The government of India should pay compensation as applicable throughout the world. We are Indian nationals and all our interests are to be protected by the elected government.

What Is Likely to Be Done?

I am quite in the dark and disappointed.

It appears no one is serious to do much.

Considering the indifferent attitude of the Indian government, we are forced to compromise with our miserable lives. If anything concrete is done, it will be done only by UCIL.

Well, I wonder if anything is in store, the way it has fallen out.

Victims will be compensated and plants like this will be moved to remote places by government.

I am confident the government of India will pay compensation to all real sufferers.

Nothing.

Mostly nonaffected persons and unemployed illiterate people, who chase the surveyors, get compensated.

Message for U.S. Business School Students?

Press your government not to allow multinationals like Union Carbide to operate anywhere in the world since they play with the life of people to enrich themselves.

More was expected and much better from the advanced elite in the community of nations. There is nothing but delay, tossing it from one door to another and from one country to another. It is a disgrace of the basest order to have left it to an indefinite body to compensate the sufferers, even if it was an additional burden. How can the most advanced society tolerate it?

The advanced nation like America while making any investment in developing countries should themselves ensure that all safety precautions are taken—before installing their factories. When they have already made this mistake at Bhopal, they should pressure their government and the management of Union Carbide to pay compensation without hesitation.

There is no question of talking to any other country. There is nothing to say but to blame the local administration for not arranging in a proper, methodic way in this modern world.

Multinational companies are playing with the lives of people and their property for the self-interest of earning money at any cost and by any means.

Note: All statements excerpted in this appendix were made by gas victims and government officials in the Bhopal area.

COMPANY INDEX

SUBJECT INDEX

Note: headings in bold type refer to cases.

INSTRUCTIONS FOR USING CASE ANALYST

Strategic and Financial Analysis Software to Accompany

Strategic Management: Text and Cases

Prepared by Marshall Schminke and James Anderson of Creighton University

---

CASE ANALYST is an easy-to-use interactive spreadsheet template that helps you better understand and interpret the financial information from 27 cases in this text. It consists of five parts:

1) A guide to generating your case analysis.

2) A financial growth and ratio template that allows you to calculate and analyze the key growth statistics and financial ratios of the firm.

3) A graphics component that allows you to visually inspect multiple ratios over time.

4) A "what if" component that lets you make projections about the future of the firm and assess the impact of these projections.

5) A printing option that allows you to generate hard copy output of these analyses.

HARDWARE AND SOFTWARE REQUIREMENTS

CASE ANALYST will operate on any IBM PC or PC-compatible computer with at least 512K of memory and DOS 2.1 or higher. It requires that you have access to Lotus 1-2-3, Version 2.01 or higher.

Before you attempt to use CASE ANALYST, take a few minutes to familiarize yourself with the computer on which you will be working, as well as with the Lotus 1-2-3 package. CASE ANALYST is very user-friendly, but it always helps to know a little bit about the tools you will be using. Many systems include tutorial software or documentation to help.

Before you begin, you should make backup copies of the CASE ANALYST disks, and use these backups when performing your analyses; store the originals for safe keeping.

You should be sure to save your working files on a separate disk under a new name, to prevent accidentally copying over the original files.

CONTENTS OF THE DISKS

The single 3.5" disk contains financial information for all 27 cases. The cases are divided between the two 5.25" floppy disks as follows:

CASE NO.	CASE NAME	FILE NAME
(Disk 1)		
1	Spec's Music, Inc. (A)	SPECSA
2	Spec's Music, Inc. (B)	SPECSB
3	Kaepa Athletic Shoes, Inc.	KAEPA
4	Northern Telecom, Inc.	NORTHERN
6	Pier 1 Imports, Inc.	PIER
7	KLLM Transport Services, Inc.	KLLM
8	United Federal Savings and Loan	SAVINGS
9	American Airlines	LINES
10	Chaparral Steel Company	CHAP
11	Northrop Corporation	NORTHROP
12	United Airlines, Inc.	UNITED
13	Carmike Cinemas, Inc.	CARMIKE
14	Cineplex Odeon Corporation	CINEPLEX
16	Club Med, Inc.	CLUBMED
(Disk 2)		
17	General Dynamics	GENERAL
18	Browning-Ferris Industries, Inc.	BROWNING
19	Babbitt Brothers Trading Company	BABBITT
20	McMaster Group	MCMASTER
21	Liz Claiborne, Inc.	LIZ
22	Sears, Roebuck and Company	SEARS
23	KNP Paper N.V.	KNP
25	ISM Engineering	ISM
26	Caterpillar, Inc.	CAT
27	Citicorp	CITICORP
28	Crystal Lawn Service	CRYSTAL
29	Harry's Pizza, Spirits	HARRYS
31	Shades of Black, Inc.	SHADES

HOW TO USE CASE ANALYST

CASE ANALYST files behave just like any other Lotus 1-2-3 worksheet files. They contain much of the financial information you see in the cases in the text (balance sheets and income statements). All of this data has been entered for you, and the package calculates a wide variety of financial ratios and growth statistics for you.

This section guides you through loading the worksheets, whether you have a floppy disk system or a hard drive system.

For a single or dual floppy disk system:

1)   Insert your DOS disk in Drive A (usually the top drive of the two) and turn on the computer.

2)   At the A> prompt, remove the DOS disk and insert your Lotus 1-2-3 system disk into Drive A.

3)   Type: 123

4)   Press the [return] or [enter] key, depending on the type of computer on which you are working. (The Lotus spreadsheet will appear on the screen.)

5)   Remove the Lotus system disk and insert the CASE ANALYST disk that contains the case you wish to analyze into Drive A.

6)   Type: /FR (AUTO123.WK1 should be highlighted at this point. If it is not, press the space bar until it is highlighted.)

7)   Press the [return] or [enter] key, and the main menu will appear. From this point, follow the instructions on the screen.

8)   You are now ready to use the CASE ANALYST software. Take a few minutes to browse the template and you will be analyzing in no time!

For a hard drive system:

1)   Be sure the Lotus 1-2-3 system program is installed on your hard drive. If it is not, consult your Lotus installation manual for instructions.

2)   The first time you use CASE ANALYST, you will need to create a subdirectory on your hard drive to store the files. The next steps create this subdirectory, named ANALYST.

3)   Turn on the computer. At the C:\> prompt:

4)   Type: MD C:\ANALYST

5)   Press the [return] or [enter] key. Copy the CASE ANALYST files from the single 3.5" disk or both 5.25" disks to your hard drive, using standard DOS commands, as follows:

6)   Type: COPY A:*.* C:\ANALYST

7)   Press the [return] or [enter] key. If you are using the 5.25" disks, repeat step 6) with the second CASE ANALYST disk.

8)   Run the Lotus system program. When Lotus is loaded:

9)   Type /FD C:\ANALYST\

10)   Press the [return] or [enter] key.

11)   Type: /FR

12)   AUTO123.WK1 should be highlighted at this point. If it is not, press the space bar until it is highlighted.

13)   Press the [return] or [enter] key, and the main menu will appear. From this point, follow the instructions on the screen.

14)   You are now ready to use the CASE ANALYST software. Take a few minutes to browse the template and you will be analyzing in no time!